D1712950

INDEX TO THE 1800 CENSUS
OF PENNSYLVANIA

INDEX TO THE
1800 CENSUS OF
PENNSYLVANIA

Compiled by
JEANNE ROBEY FELLDIN
& GLORIA KAY VANDIVER INMAN

GENEALOGICAL PUBLISHING CO., INC.
Baltimore 1984

HOW TO USE THIS BOOK

This index was transcribed from microfilm copies of the original handwritten census schedules, which are especially difficult to read. Writing skills and styles differ from those in use today. Ink, the kind of paper used, even the microfilming technique affect legibility.

Illiteracy was widespread in 1800. Frequently the census enumerator, himself poorly educated, was forced to guess at spellings. One page, written by one man, may have three or four different spellings of the same name. Therefore, the researcher must try all conceivable spellings when searching for an ancestor. In the case of two equally possible interpretations, names in this index are either cross-referenced or entered both ways. There are possibly 800-900 of these double or cross-referenced entries.

A dash (–) indicates one (or more) illegible letters. Completely illegible names are shown as "——, ——," followed by the county and page number. These entries will be found at the end of the alphabetical listing, many of them being from the counties of Beaver, Franklin, and Mifflin.

Also at the end of the listing: entries in which the first one or more letters are illegible (e.g. *–ollins, John*), plus entries which give no surnames. Many free blacks will be found in the latter category.

The marshal, or census taker, was allowed only a few months in which to complete his enumeration. Can you imagine how many families must have been missed in early, migrant America; how many families were entered twice, or three times, as they travelled from county to county?

Page numbering presented another problem in this particular census. "Although more than one set of numbers often appears on the schedules, the system of numbering, whether stamped or written . . . is generally that which (1) runs consecutively from the beginning to the end of the volume, and (2) appears to be consistent with the numbering for other volumes for the state. Where a schedule begins on a page not numbered, an 'A' number (36A, for example) has been used for identification. . . ."[1]

---

[1]National Archives Microcopy No. 33

29518

The above system is used in this index, unnumbered pages being assigned an 'A' number and, in one or two cases, where two unnumbered pages occur consecutively, a 'B' number. There are, however, a few exceptions:

1) Roll 36 presented a real problem. Not only are parts of Beaver and Bucks Counties impossible to read, but there is no set of numbers running consecutively throughout the roll. We have elected to use the numbers 1 through 161A for the counties of Beaver, Bedford, and Bucks, then another set of numbers for Butler, and a third set for Chester. Therefore, Roll 36 pages are numbered:

      1-161A   Beaver, Bedford, and Bucks Counties
      315-368   Butler County
      699-911   Chester County

2) Berks County (Roll 35) omits nine pages, skipping from page 190 to page 200.

3) Roll 37 begins with "Centre and Mifflin." Centre County is sandwiched in the middle of Mifflin County on pages 18A to 24 inclusive. Parts of Mifflin are so unclear they are more guesswork than actuality.

4) Pages 354 to 360 inclusive are skipped in the Westmoreland County enumeration (Roll 41).

5) The City of Philadelphia (Roll 43) follows the numbers produced by a numbering machine. There are several pages out of place, the numbers suddenly skipping forward about five digits, then going backwards until the correct page number is reached again.

In addition to these research impediments, we have the ever-present possibility of human error, both then and now. Although this index has been checked and re-checked, we are fully aware that errors have undoubtedly infiltrated the work. We hope the researcher will be understanding of the difficulties involved.

The 1800 census records the following data: Name of head of family; Place of residence; Number of males and females under 10 years of age, 10 and under 16, 16 and under 26, 26 and under 45, 45 and upward; Number of all other free persons in household (including persons of color but excluding Indians who were not taxed); Number of slaves in the household.

In this particular census, several religious communities, schools, jails, etc. were enumerated. In Northampton County were the following: a Boarding School with 86 residents (see *Jacob Van Vleek*); two Single Bretherens' Houses with 14 and 25 (see *John Fred. Stadiger* and *Christian Winck–er?*); the Widow's House with 30 (see *Barbara Munster*); two Single Sisters' Houses with 71 and 36 (see *Margaret Motz* and *Elizabeth Hopson*); a School with 39 (see *Rev. Chas. G. Reichell*); 26 Christians (see *Paul Micksch*); and "Gnadenthal" with 26 (see *John Schnall*). In West Town, Chester County, was an "Institution" with 219 persons. Lancaster County listed 4 Prisoners; 86 residents in the Poorhouse (see *Melchoir Mellinger*); 70 in the Sister House; 20 in the Brother House; "Furnace Hills" with 17; and 6 Ministers.

Counties have been abbreviated as follows:

Adams	ADA	Lancaster	LAN
Allegheny	ALL	Luzerne	LUZ
Armstrong	ARM	Lycoming	LYC
Beaver	BEV	Mercer	MER
Berks	BER	Mifflin	MIF
Bedford	BFD	Montgomery	MNT
Bucks	BUC	Northampton	NOH
Butler	BUT	Northumberland	NOU
Centre	CEN	Philadelphia	PHI
Chester	CHE	(excluding Philadelphia City but including Germantown)	
Crawford	CRA	City of Philadelphia	PHA
Cumberland	CUM	Somerset	SOM
Dauphin	DAU	Venango	VEN
Delaware	DEL	Warren	WAR
Erie	ERI	Washington	WAS
Fayette	FAY	Wayne	WAY
Franklin	FRA	Westmoreland	WST
Greene	GRN	York	YOR
Huntingdon	HNT		

Photocopies of specific pages of census records are provided for a fee by the Correspondence Branch (NNCC), National Archives (GSA), Washington, D.C. 20408. No form is now required. Use of GSA Request form 7029 has been discontinued.

As Val D. Greenwood points out in his *Researcher's Guide to American Genealogy*, there is a built-in "error factor" in the original census. We would like to add that there is a built-in *human* error factor in *any index*. Please be aware of both these deficiencies when shopping for ancestors.

Your ancestor may have been in Pennsylvania in 1800 but, for one or many reasons, may not be listed in this index. There are 99,172 entries; we sincerely hope *your* ancestor is among them.

JEANNE ROBEY FELLDIN &
GLORIA KAY VANDIVER INMAN

Stagecoach, Texas
7 April 1984

INDEX TO THE 1800 CENSUS
OF PENNSYLVANIA

Name	Loc	Pg
ADAMS, Isaac	BER	190
Isaac	LAN	192
Jacob	BFD	48
Jacob	GRN	62
Jacob	ALL	104
Jacob Esqr.	ADA	31
James	BFD	48
James	MNT	69
James	BFD	70
James	ALL	79
James	HNT	151
James	NOU	197
James	YOR	197
James	FAY	234
James	WST	305
James Rev.	GRN	92
James	MIF	14A
Jas.	CUM	45
Jas.	CUM	50
Jas.	BUT	358
Jas. Jr.	CUM	50
Jedediah	LUZ	388
Jessee	HNT	161
Jno.	CUM	49
John	PHI	28
John	WAS	48
John	WAS	60
John	PHI 105&PHI	61
John	ALL	66
John	BFD	70
John	WAS	77
John	NOU	103
John	PHI	118
John	HNT	120
John	SOM	133
John	PHI	137
John	BUC	139
John	HNT	151
John	DEL	169
John	NOU	170
John	FAY	219
John	FRA	317
John	BUT	325
John	BUT	359
John	CHE	825
John	CHE	860
John	CHE	892
John Jnr.	BUC	139
John Junr.	WAS	26
John Senr.	WAS	26
John	PHI	81A
Jonathan	MIF	16
Jonathan	DEL	169
Joseph	PHI	1
Joseph	WAS	6
Joseph	HNT	151
Joseph	NOU	197
Magdalena	ADA	31
Magdaline	PHI	127
Martha	PHA	37
Martin	WAS	18
Martin	CUM	151
Mary	MIF	3
Mary	CUM	44
Mary	PHI	97
Mathew	YOR	198
Mathew	YOR	206
Mathew Jr.	YOR	206
Matthew	FAY	230
Mattw.	CUM	147
Michal	ALL	50
Moses	PHI	11A
Mrs.	NOU	153
Nace	ADA	23
Nicholas	BER	172
Obadiah	WAS	36
ADAMS, Paul	NOU	142
Peter	PHI	11
Peter	MNT	40
Peter	PHA	107
Pricilla	MNT	66
Richard	DEL	183
Richard	LAN	192
Richd.	CEN	22
Richd.	PHI	66
Robe-?	ARM	126
Robert	GRN	66
Robert	BFD	70
Robert	ALL	117
Robert	FAY	234
Robert	WST	305
Robert Jr.	BFD	70
Robert Juner	FAY	234
Robt.	CUM	51
Robt.	PHI	80
Saml.	BUC	162
Samuel	ADA	3
Samuel	PHI	7
Samuel	BEV	18
Samuel	GRN	67
Samuel	FAY	230
Samuel	BUC	92A
Solomon	BFD	70
Solomon	FAY	234
St.? Lawrence	PHA	17
Thomas	WAS	18
Thomas	CUM	120
Thomas	FAY	225
Thomas	FRA	299
Thomas Junr.	WAS	18
Thos.	CUM	51
Thos.	CUM	52
Thos.	FRA	301
Thos. Senr.	CUM	49
Weldon	DEL	189
William	CEN	22
William	BFD	61
William	WST	146
William	HNT	162
William	NOU	170
William	NOU	170
William	LAN	192
William	YOR	197
William	YOR	199
William	CHE	742
William	CEN	18A
Wm.	CUM 44 & CUM	48
Wm.	PHA	90
Wm.	PHI	118
ADAMS?, -----	MIF	9A
ADAMSON, James	GRN	86
John	MNT	49
Thomas	GRN	98
ADAMSTON, Eliza.	CUM	147
ADBERT, John	WAS	78
ADCATCH, Wm. Esqr.	PHI	112
ADDAMS, William	VEN	167
ADDERMAN, Elisha	LYC	11
ADDINGTON, Stephen	PHA	93
ADDIS, Eber	BUC	107A
Enoch	BUC	137
Ephraim	BUC	154
Isaac	BUC	107A
John	BUC	137
John	PHI	81A
Jonathen	FAY	207
Josiah	BUC	86
Nehemiah	BUC	154
Richd.	PHI	67
ADDLEBERGER, Philip	HNT	131
ADDLEBERGER, Philip	HNT	131
ADDLEMAN, John	GRN	98
Philip	GRN	98
William	HNT	130
Wm.	CHE	774
ADDLEMAN?, John	HNT	130
ADDLMAN, John	CHE	775
Joseph	CHE	775
ADEAR, James	LAN	127
ADEL, John	PHI	118A
ADEMSON, William	NOU	191
ADGATE, Daniel	PHA	41
John	PHI	106A
ADINGER, Abraham	FAY	254
ADIS, Amos	MNT	42
ADISON, Alexd. Esqr.	ALL	55
ADJUTANT, Edward	LUZ	330
ADKISON, John	NOU	108
ADLE, Mathias	PHI	147
ADLER?, David	MNT	98
ADLEY, Conrad	BFD	70
ADLLEY?, David	MNT	98
ADLUM, Josh.	LYC	10
ADMISTINE, Saml.	CHE	714
ADMISTON, John	FRA	300
ADOLPH, John	PHI	94A
ADY, Elisabeth	WAS	118
AELE, Henry	NOU	148
AFFLICK, Charles	DEL	165
Owen	CHE	898
William	DEL	177
AFFRY, John	WAS	41
AFLICK, William	DEL	188
AFREE?, John Baptist	PHI	135
AFRICA, Jacob	HNT	156
Michael	HNT	154
AFTON, John	PHA	45
AGAIN, Thos.	PHA	85
AGAMS, Sol.	VEN	168
AGE, David	WAS	118
Frederick	WAS	118
George	WAS	118
AGER, Widw.	PHI	83
George	WST	232
John	HNT	127
AGERT, George	PHI	83
AGES, Thankful	BUT	324
AGEY, John	ADA	6
AGIN, James	PHI	130
AGINS, Isaac	CHE	814
AGNEW, Widow	PHI	9
David	ADA	6
James	ADA	3
James	BFD	37
James Junr.	ADA	4
John	ADA	6
John	WAS	54
John	YOR	159
John Esq.	ADA	3
Margaret	PHA	26
Mary	ADA	3
Mattw.	CUM	75
Samuel Junr.	WAS	18
Samuel Senr.	WAS	18
William	ADA	25
AGUSTINE, Baltzer	SOM	136
AHNER, John	NOH	49A
AHRY, Jacob	NOH	72A
AICHHOLLT, Gottleib	DAU	38A
AIKELY?, David (Crossed out)	PHA	26

2

3

ALEXANDER,
Ezekiel	CHE	856
Francis	MIF	3
George	WAS	54
George	PHI	96A
Henry Esqr.	WAS	36
Hugh	BFD	40
Hugh	LAN	175
Hugh	MIF	6A
Hugh	MIF	14A
Hugh	MIF	16A
Isaac	WAS	36
Issabella	BFD	40
Jacob	SOM	145
James	MIF	3
James	WAS	15
James	CEN	20
James	WAS	87
James	PHA	90
James	NOU	97
James	SOM	156
James	WST	159
James	LAN	166
James	YOR	203
James	LAN	240
James	FAY	249
James	FRA	323
James	MIF	14A
James	MIF	16A
James A.	PHA	23
Jane	YOR	201
Jas.	LYC	22
Jas.	WST	305
Jno.	CUM	105
Jno.	MIF	16A
John	MIF	3
John	WAS	18
John	WAS	33
John	NOH	41
John	PHA	54
John	WAS	54
John	PHI	56
John	BFD	61
John	PHA	112
John	NOU	115
John	HNT	153
John	LAN	156
John	SOM	156
John	FRA	292
John	FRA	319
John	BUT	321
John	LUZ	327
John	MER	433
John	CHE	870
John	MIF	11A
John	MIF	14A
Jonathan	MIF	14A
Jos.	WST	364
Jos.	MIF	1A
Joseph	MIF	3
Joseph	CEN	22
Joseph	WAS	36
Joseph	BER	229
Joseph	FAY	249
Joseph Esqr.	WAS	33
Josepht	MER	433
Martha	ERI	59
Petre	LAN	154
Polly	MIF	14A
Robert	ADA	16
Robert	WAS	33
Robert	BFD	40
Robert	LAN	157
Robert	CHE	870
Robt.	YOR	199
Robt.	CHE	818

ALEXANDER, Robt.	MIF	14A
Robt.	PHI	76A
Roger	FAY	261
Saml.	WST	340
Saml.	WST	340
Samuel	FAY	249
Samuel	BUC	92A
See Alexd.	ALL	93
Soloman	PHI	89A
Solomon	LAN	207
Thomas	MIF	3
Thomas	ERI	58A
Thos.	CUM	97
Thos.	YOR	199
Widow	BFD	61
William	MIF	3
William	BFD	40
William	WAS	115
William	LAN	127
William	PHI	142
William	HNT	150
William	YOR	154
William	WST	167
William	LAN	176
Wm.	CEN	22
Wm.	CUM	97
Wm.	FRA	323
Wm.	CHE	837
Wm. W.	MIF	14A
ALEXD., Thomas	ALL	93
ALEXON, James	ADA	8
ALEXR., James	MER	432
Joseph	MER	432
William	MER	432
ALEY, John	NOU	191
ALFICE, Henry	NOU	134
ALFORD, John	CHE	707
John	CHE	722
ALFRED, James	CHE	769
ALGAR, Ezra	LUZ	412
ALGEIR, Sebastn.	BER	241
ALGIER, Joseph	LAN	53
ALGIRE, John	BFD	56
ALGO, John	NOU	115
ALGOE, Thomas	LAN	230
ALGOUSE?, John	PHA	116
ALHISER?, Andw.	PHI	116
ALHISTER, Wm.	PHI	97
ALHMON, William	YOR	217
ALIMAN, Jacob	ARM	125
Nicholas	ARM	125
ALINDON, Arthur	CHE	761
ALISSON, George	MER	433
ALJO?, Thomas	ALL	99
Wilm.	ALL	105
ALKINS, Thomas A.	LUZ	320
ALL, John	NOU	197
Samuel	NOU	98
Samuel	NOU	197
William	NOU	197
ALLABACH, Daniel	LAN	268
ALLABACK, John	MNT	126
ALLAN, Saml.	PHI	99A
ALLAN?, Philip	YOR	176
ALLANDER, Alexr.	CEN	22
ALLASON, David	MIF	6A
Elijah	FAY	225
ALLAWAY, Isariah	YOR	202
Stephen	YOR	202
ALLAYS, John	CHE	857
ALLBRIGHT, Barnet	YOR	186
George	YOR	169
George	YOR	197
Henry	YOR	182
Jacob	YOR	186
Leonard	WST	248

ALLBRIGHT,
Lorence	YOR	168
Michael	YOR	172
Michael Jr.	YOR	196
ALLBUTT, Peter	CUM	53
ALLCHIN, George	PHA	16
ALLEBAC-?,		
Michael	MNT	80
ALLEBACH, Abraham		
(John Crossed		
Out)	NOH	66
John	NOH	66
ALLEBACK,		
Catherine	MNT	67
Christian	MNT	126
ALLEMAN, Henry	DAU	45A
John	DAU	14
John	DAU	18A
Leonard	DAU	40A
Martin	DAU	16A
Mathias	NOH	72A
Nicols.	DAU	15
Stophel	DAU	15
ALLEN, Mrs.	PHI	49
Widow	PHI	10
Widow	PHI	30
Aaron	DEL	180
Acquillah	PHA	63
Adam	SOM	133
Amanuel	NOU	115
Annanias	BEV	5
Charles	ERI	57
Charles	PHA	96
Daniel	BEV	5
Daniel	LUZ	386
Daniel	LUZ	410
Daniel Jr.	LUZ	410
David	PHI	19
David	MNT	66
David	WST	305
David	LUZ	369
David	LUZ	410
E. John	MNT	80
Ebenezer D.	LUZ	338
Edwd.	PHI	113
Eli	FAY	263
Elias	LUZ	323
Elizabeth	PHA	11
Elizabeth	BFD	40
Ephraim	CHE	725
Ezekiel	HNT	131
George	BEV	5
George	FAY	254
George	LAN	311
Hubbard	LUZ	347
Isaac	CRA	11
Isaac	LYC	21
Isaac	WAS	77
Isaac	GRN	98
Isaac	LUZ	410
Israel	BUC	88A
Jacob	WAS	61
Jacob	NOH	81A
James	DAU	10
James	WAS	77
James	SOM	126
James	HNT	131
James	HNT	144
James	LAN	152
James	YOR	198
James	FAY	207
James	FAY	252
James	WST	284
James	BUC	160A
Jeremiah	LUZ	325
Jesse	LUZ	424

ALLEN, John	WAS	15	ALLENBACH,			ALLISON, George	ALL	84
John	PHA	16	Nicholas	YOR	184	Hugh	WAS	18
John	LYC	23	ALLENBACK, David	MNT	127	Isaac	NOU	108
John	PHI	63	ALLENDER, James	CEN	20	James	WAS	6
John	MNT	66	James	CEN	22	James	WAS	18
John	WAS	77	ALLENDERFER,			James	BFD	70
John	WAS	87	Philip	BER	211	James	WAS	73
John	PHA	91	ALLENTON, John	CRA	16	James	WAS	87
John	WAS	96	John	FAY	261	James	WST	146
John	HNT	122	Thomas	LUZ	332	James	NOU	161
John	CUM	135	ALLENWOOD,			James	FAY	212
John	VEN	167	Benjamen	FAY	254	James	CHE	706
John	WST	269	Benjn.	FAY	252	James	CHE	846
John	BUT	350	Jeremia	FAY	252	James Esqr.	WAS	115
John Esqr.	FAY	207	ALLER, James	BFD	40	Jane	WAS	18
John	MIF	24A	Philip	HNT	126	John	WAS	11
John	PHI	76A	ALLES, Thomas	FAY	207	John	WAS	97
Joseph	CRA	14	ALLESON, George	BER	137	John	LAN	128
Joseph	CEN	20	ALLET, Charles	PHI	111	John	WST	146
Joseph	WAS	77	ALLETON, Amos	NOU	155	John	NOU	161
Joseph	PHA	95	Job	NOU	155	John	DEL	191
Joseph	PHA	96	Stephen	NOU	126	John	FAY	207
Joseph Jr.	DAU	22	ALLEWALT, Barnet	ADA	34	John	FAY	212
Joseph Sr.	DAU	22	ALLEXANDER, David	ALL	112	John	DAU	17A
Joseph	BUC	88A	Ewd.	FRA	289	Jos.	YOR	199
Joshua	PHA	57	Hugh Esqr.	ALL	57	Joseph	FRA	274
Joshua	WAS	77	James	BEV	20	Martin	YOR	189
Josiah	WAS	87	John	BEV	17	Matthew	LYC	24
Josiah	FAY	201	John	ALL	83	Nathaniel	WAY	137
Lewis	PHI	11	Joseph	ALL	104	Rebecca	LAN	126
Margeret	FAY	252	Robt.	FRA	319	Richard	MIF	3
Martha	WAS	26	Wm.	FRA	319	Richard	NOU	161
Mary	PHA	115	ALLEY, John	GRN	68	Robert	MIF	3
Michael	BUC	84	Susanna	LAN	110	Robert	BFD	70
Moses	WAS	65	William	WAS	65	Robert	WST	146
Nathan	MIF	3	ALLFORD, James	GRN	74	Robert	BUT	333
Nathan	PHA	117	Martha	BEV	19	Robert	CHE	751
Nathaniel	PHA	59	ALLHOUSE,			Robert	CHE	902
Nathaniel	LUZ	407	Frederick	NOU	161	Robert	FRA	274
Nichs.	BER	280	ALLIBONE, Thos.	PHA	69	Robt.	CHE	819
Olliver	BEV	14	Wm.	PHI	105A	Samuel	WAS	65
Patr.	FRA	300	ALLIBOUGH, George	CHE	896	Samuel	GRN	86
Phillip	CUM	25	ALLICOM, John	PHA	94	Tate	WST	146
Rebecca	DAU	22	ALLICUM, William	PHI	129	Thomas	WST	146
Richard	PHA	117	ALLIMUS?,			Thos.	YOR	205
Robert	PHI	27	Frederick	MNT	40	Thos.	CHE	825
Robt.	CUM	29	ALLIN, Ebenezer	CHE	801	William	WAS	97
Robt.	YOR	202	Joseph	NOU	197	William	DEL	159
Samuel	PHI	11	Obediah	NOU	191	William	YOR	195
Samuel	PHA	34	Samuel	MER	433	William	ERI	56A
Samuel	LUZ	343	ALLINDER, John	HNT	145	William	ERI	57A
Samuel	BUC	88A	ALLINGHAM,			Wilm.	ALL	67
Sarah	MNT	107	William	WAS	73	Wilm.	ALL	84
Stephen	LUZ	410	ALLINGTON, John	LYC	12	Wm.	FRA	295
Stephen	ERI	55A	ALLIS, Arthur	FAY	254	Wm. Senr.	MIF	14A
Thos.	PHA	79	John	MER	432	ALLISONS, James	ALL	119
Thos.	PHA	105	ALLISIN, David	ALL	91	ALLISTON, Robert	PHA	121
Thos.	YOR	202	ALLISON, Aaron	CHE	818	ALLMAN, Durst	NOH	70A
Weilliam	DAU	22	Abner	GRN	86	Jacob	NOU	120
William	WAS	77	Achibald	NOU	173	Peter	NOU	120
William	WAS	88	Andrew	BFD	70	ALLOCK, Wm.	PHI	85
William	PHA	106	Andrew	WST	146	ALLOM, George	BUC	82A
William	NOU	115	Andw.	WST	340	Jacob	BUC	81A
William	HNT	125	Burgis	PHI	138	Jacob	BUC	90A
William	HNT	154	Charles	WAS	73	John	BUC	82A
William	CHE	767	Charles	WAS	73	Michael	BUC	100A
William	ERI	59A	Charles	FRA	315	Philip	BUC	90A
William	NOH	86A	David	ALL	91	ALLOM?, John	ALL	104
William	BUC	88A	Elijah	WAS	36	ALLON, Aaron	ALL	80
Wm.	PHA	44	Elizabeth	FRA	298	David	ALL	78
Wm.	CUM	134	Erasmus	WAS	65	George	ALL	61
Wm.	FRA	286	Erasmus	WAS	73	Jacob	GRN	67
Wm.	CHE	825	Erasmus	WAS	73	James	ALL	52
ALLENBACH, Conrad	BER	148	Francis	ADA	26	James	ALL	112
Jacob	BER	166	Francis	CHE	764	John	ALL	69
John N.	BER	147	Gaven	WAS	11	John	NOU	155

5

ALLON, Robert	NOU	155	ALTHOUSE, John	SOM	126	AMES, Ephraim	LUZ	324
Saml.	PHI	109	John	BER	148	Jabez	WAS	65
ALLONS?, John	ALL	104	John	BER	217	Nathan	LUZ	375
ALLOWAY, Jonathan	CHE	857	Joseph	NOH	62	Saml.	PHI	121
Marina	MNT	137	ALTICK, Danl.	CUM	150	Thomas	PHA	95
Mashelemia	PHI	141	ALTIMUS, John	PHI	124	William	LUZ	375
Wm.	CHE	787	Nicholas	NOH	35	AMEY, George
ALLPAGE, Matthias	NOU	126	ALTMAN, Casper	WST	208	Junr.	BUC	81A
ALLRIGHT, Adam	BER	173	David	WST	208	George	BUC	81A
Christian	BER	173	Fredrick	ARM	127	Philip	BUC	81A
John	BER	173	George	BEV	18	AMHEISER,
ALLSON, Hugh	LAN	130	Georoge	WST	147	Christian	NOH	68A
James	YOR	191	John	WST	208	AMICK, Philip	WAS	1
ALLSPACH, John	NOH	77	John	WST	208	AMILL, Dam	LUZ	357
ALLSPOUGH, Henry	BEV	23	Michl.	WST	284	AMILONG, Christ.	WST	187
ALLSWORTH, Esther	LUZ	367	Peter	ARM	126	AMMA, John	BER	247
ALLUM, Thomas	WAS	73	Philip	WST	147	AMMAN, George	BEV	19
William	WAS	118	Thomas	WST	208	Jacob	BEV	19
ALLWINE, Lawrence	PHA	8	Willim.	WST	284	AMMERMAN, Albert	NOU	170
ALLWOOD, Henry	NOU	161	ALTON, Benjamin	GRN	91	Edward	NOH	64
John	LYC	7	David	YOR	169	AMMON, George	BER	161
ALLWORTH, Andrew	WST	321	Erasmus	FAY	212	George	WST	187
ALMANDINGER,			John	FAY	212	AMNUN, Barnabas	LAN	168
Jacob	PHA	59	John	PHI	67A	AMOLE, Christian	CHE	894
ALMOND, Ebenezer	WAS	78	ALTSHOUSE, Benjn.	BUC	148A	AMON, Conrad	WAS	41
Edwd.	PHI	99A	ALTWELL, John	WST	146	George	WAS	41
John	WAS	78	ALVERT, Abraham	LAN	3	Jacob	WAS	41
Thomas	WAS	78	Philip	LAN	16	AMONS, Isaac	SOM	151
William	WAS	78	ALWAINE, Philip	MIF	3	John	SOM	151
ALMONDS, Thomas	CHE	844	ALWAN?, Conrad	DAU	26A	AMOR, Thomas	WAS	51
ALMOSE, Andw.	WST	364	ALWEIN, John	BER	148	AMOS, John	BFD	54
ALORN, Joseph	PHI	23	ALWEIN?, Conrad	DAU	26A	John	PHI	122
ALRICKS, James	MIF	12	ALWIM?, Conrad	DAU	26A	Walter	MNT	137
ALSDORF, Chris.	LAN	84	ALWINE, Peter	PHI	98	AMPEN, Joseph	PHI	38
ALSHOUSE,			ALWORK, Timothy	ALL	107	AMPSPACHER,
Catharine	NOH	36A	ALY, Sarah	LAN	299	George	YOR	192
Conrad	NOH	79A	AMAGHOST,			Michael	YOR	192
Henry	WST	208	Nicholas	NOU	181	AMRINE, Frederick	BFD	70
John	MNT	125	AMAH, Conrad	MNT	130	Henry	BFD	56
ALSOM, Thos.	PHI	82	AMAN, George	MNT	109	Henry Jr.	BFD	56
ALSOP, John	PHI	71	AMBER, Jacob	MNT	47	AMSBURY, Luther	LUZ	392
ALSPACH, David	BER	284	John	MNT	47	AMSHACKER,
George	CUM	94	John	MNT	47	Michael	YOR	194
George	BER	221	AMBERS, Ann	HNT	130	AMSPACHER, Conrad	YOR	190
Henry	BER	156	AMBERSON, James	BUT	340	AMWEG, Catharine	LAN	251
Henry	BER	158	John	FAY	225	Jacob	LAN	207
Henry	BER	224	Wilm.	ALL	61	AMY, Peter	HNT	151
Jacob	BER	158	AMBLER, Edward	MNT	87	AN----?, Henry	FRA	289
Jacob	BER	224	John	MNT	87	ANAKONY, Widow	WST	232
Michl.	BER	284	Joseph	MNT	87	ANDALL, Anthony	PHA	74
Peter	BER	155	Joseph Junr.	MNT	87	ANDENREIDT, Lewis	BER	217
Philip	BER	277	AMBROSE, Emmery	GRN	91	ANDERON, Enoch	CUM	52
ALSPAGH, Phillip	CUM	82	Frederick	WST	232	ANDERS, Abram	MNT	113
Richd.	CUM	88	Henry	WST	167	John	MNT	47
ALSPAUGH, Henry	CUM	23	John	WST	232	Robert	MNT	66
ALSPOUGH, George	FAY	212	Lewis	PHA	114	ANDERSON, James	NOU	201
ALSTAT, John	DAU	32	AMBROSEY, Jacob	BFD	41	Mr?/ Wm?	PHI	136
ALSWORTH, Benja.	WST	208	AMBROSIER, John	HNT	164	Mrs.	PHI	48
ALT, Adam	YOR	182	AMBROSY, John	BFD	40	Widow	PHI	11
Philip	YOR	192	Matthias	BFD	40	-----	MIF	9A
Philip	YOR	194	Matthias	BFD	40	Abraham	WAS	18
ALTEMORE, Adam	WST	284	AMBRUSE, Levy	PHI	91	Adam	WST	364
ALTEMUS, Adam	WST	284	AMBRUSTER, Widw.	PHI	107	Alen	BUT	316
David	PHI	135	Nichs.	PHI	96	Alexander	PHA	26
James	PHI	94	AMEN, Anthony	YOR	204	Alexander	LAN	48
ALTER, Abm.	BER	241	AMEND, Mary	LAN	106	Alexander	WAS	73
Carnns	NOU	97	AMENT, Adam	LAN	106	Alexander	FAY	263
David	CUM	116	Anthony	YOR	205	Alexander Junr.	WAS	54
Jacob Jr.	CUM	116	Frederick	YOR	167	Alexander Senr.	WAS	54
John	ARM	126	Lorentz	LAN	311	Alexander	MNT	105
Joseph	NOU	97	Richd.	YOR	191	Alexr.	MER	433
Margaret	SOM	141	AMERICA, Cato	PHA	54	Alexr.	CHE	802
ALTERS, Jacob			AMERMAN, Henry	ADA	19	Amos	PHA	117
Senr.	CUM	103	AMES, Andrew	LUZ	380	Andrew	NOH	77
ALTHAUSS, Jost	NOH	55	Elisha	WAS	1	Andrew	WAS	97
ALTHOUSE, George	BER	148	Elisha	WAY	140	Andrew	HNT	123

ANDERSON, Andrew	HNT	142	ANDERSON, Jas.	CUM	50	ANDERSON, Samuel	NOU 126
Andrew	NOU	155	Jas.	CUM	128	Samuel	HNT 163
Ann	PHA	48	Jesse	BUC	107	Sarah	FAY 238
Benjamin	BEV	23	Jesse	NOU	186	Tho.	MIF 6A
Benjamin	WAS	54	Jno.	FRA	299	Thomas	PHI 25
Benjn.	CUM	70	John	PHI	15	Thomas	BFD 35
Charles Ba	GRN	91	John	MIF	18	Thomas	GRN 91
Charles Junr	GRN	86	John	WAS	18	Thomas	WST 146
Charles Senr.	GRN	86	John	WAS	33	Thomas	WST 340
Christn.	PHA	63	John	ERI	57	Thomas	
Daniel	BUC	98A	John	GRN	68	(Mulatto)	WAS 18
David	PHA	61	John	BFD	70	Thos.	BUC 80
David	BFD	70	John	WAS	73	Thos.	MIF 4A
David	WST	321	John	GRN	91	Valuntn.	MNT 127
David Senr.	BFD	79	John	CUM	92	Widow	MIF 4A
David	BUC	98A	John	GRN	93	Widow	MIF 6A
Eleacum	BUT	342	John	PHA	102	William	WAS 48
Elias	BUC	154	John	ALL	107	William	WAS 54
Elizabeth	DEL	178	John	PHA	109	William	BFD 61
Elizabeth	CHE	753	John	ALL	114	William	WAS 65
Elizabeth	MIF	6A	John	HNT	117	William	MNT 89
Evan	CUM	31	John	LAN	126	William	HNT 117
Ezekiel	WST	305	John	SOM	156	William	NOU 126
Frances	ALL	120	John	LAN	166	William	DEL 161
Fredk.	CUM	41	John	WST	167	William	NOU 181
Garbin?	NOU	201	John	LAN	172	William	BER 200
George	WAS	18	John	YOR	202	William	MER 432
George	BUC	104	John	YOR	212	William	MER 433
George	SOM	126	John	WST	269	William	BUC 88A
Gilbert	LAN	168	John	WST	284	Willm.	WST 305
Graham	CUM	70	John	FRA	288	Wilm.	ALL 49
Henery	MER	432	John	BUT	317	Wilm.	ALL 56
Hugh	WAS	97	John	BUT	318	Wm.	BEV 19
Hugh	WST	248	John	WST	321	Wm.	PHA 88
Isaac	ALL	101	John	LUZ	339	Wm.	PHI 98
Isaac	CHE	857	John	WST	340	Wm.	YOR 198
Israel	BUC	86	John	WST	364	Wm.	YOR 203
Issabella	CHE	784	John	MER	433	Wm.	WST 305
Jacob	WAS	1	John	MER	433	Wm.	CHE 821
Jacob	NOU	134	John Revd.	WAS	54	Wm. Senr.	CUM 48
Jacob	WST	248	John?	BEV	23	Wm.	MIF 16A
James	CRA	6	Jonathan	MIF	6A	Wm., Jr.	WST 305
James	LAN	8	Jos.	BUT	333	Zekiel	PHI 66
James	BEV	23	Joseph	CRA	9	Zephaniah	CUM 146
James	PHI	23	Joseph	CUM	94	Oshua	WAS 97
James	WAS	36	Joshua	BUC	86	ANDERSONS, Robt.	CUM 62
James	WAS	54	Joshua	WST	340	ANDES, Rhynhart	ALL 62
James	LAN	55	Joshua	BUC	98A	ANDIG, William	MNT 89
James	ERI	59	Margt.	CUM	62	ANDOVER,	
James	PHI	72	Mary	FRA	321	Christopher	WAS 87
James	WAS	73	Mathew	WAS	6	ANDRAES,	
James	GRN	86	Michael	WST	340	Magdalena	LAN 192
James	GRN	98	Nancy	FAY	212	ANDRE', Francis	PHI 125
James	PHI	117	Oliver	FRA	290	ANDRE, Adam	NOH 72A
James	LAN	128	Peter	LUZ	333	Gottlieb Jr.	NOH 62
James	BUC	143	Quinton	CHE	867	John	CEN 20
James	YOR	156	Rachel	GRN	91	Jonathan	NOH 62
James	NOU	161	Richard	GRN	86	Leonard	NOH 72A
James	HNT	164	Robert	BEV	14	Malcolm	MIF 14A
James	DEL	177	Robert	ALL	61	Michael	NOH 72A
James	YOR	195	Robert	BFD	70	Phillip	WST 208
James	YOR	195	Robert	ALL	98	ANDREAS, Abraham	NOH 31A
James	YOR	204	Robert	WAS	115	Christopher	NOH 58
James	YOR	214	Robert	ALL	119	Friederick	NOH 46A
James	YOR	214	Robert	LAN	166	Jacob	NOH 75
James	YOR	217	Robert	LAN	174	Martin	NOH 44
James	FRA	321	Robert	CHE	812	Nicholas	NOH 62
James	WST	321	Robt.	CEN	22	Nicholas Junr.	NOH 62
James	WST	377	Robt.	PHI	30	Peter	NOH 75
James	MER	433	Robt.	CUM	78	William	NOH 44
James Jr.	BFD	70	Robt.	CHE	722	ANDREE, Wm.	CUM 109
James Senr.	BFD	70	Robt.	CHE	844	ANDRES, Jacob	PHI 78
James Third	BFD	70	Saml.	CEN	20	Michael	FAY 212
James	BUC	98A	Saml. V.	PHA	17A	Philip	DAU 9
James	BUC	107A	Samuel	WAS	73	ANDRESS, Isaac	ALL 95
James	BUC	145A	Samuel	ARM	124	ANDREW, Abm.	LYC 27

ANDREW, Arthur	CHE	747	ANDREWS, Widow	LAN	167	ANSPACH, Adam	BER 265
Benjam.	MNT	114	ANDRIES, Daniel	LAN	160	George	LAN 19
Daniel	BER	247	ANDROS, Silas F.	LUZ	395	Jacob	BER 265
David	WAS	15	ANDROUS, Lewis	PHI	102A	John	BER 265
Elisabeth	WAS	18	ANES, John	PHI	142	John	BER 265
Fransis	PHI	123	ANEWALD,			ANSTINE, George	YOR 196
George	WAS	65	Valentine	NOH	29	ANSTRY, Andw.	PHI 37
Godlieb	NOH	49A	ANEWALT, Peter	NOH	29	ANT, Jacob	BFD 42
Hugh	DAU	34A	ANGELMEIER, John	NOH	49A	ANTER, Widow	PHI 41
Isaac	LAN	234	ANGELMEYER, Henry	NOH	46A	ANTES, Frederick	NOU 170
Jacob	DAU	19	Jacob	NOH	64	Henry	NOU 170
James	WAS	60	ANGEW, John	CUM	76	Henry Senr.	LYC 27
John	WAS	15	ANGLE, Jacob	LAN	9	ANTHONY, Conrad	NOH 35
John	NOH	35	Jacob	FRA	292	Danl.	CUM 32
John	LAN	125	John	LAN	9	Fredk.	PHI 79
John	PHI	127	John	NOU	113	George	WST 187
John	YOR	198	John	FRA	292	George	NOU 191
John	BUT	336	John	MER	433	Jacob	PHI 71
John Sen.	FRA	283	Martha Widow	LAN	6	Jacob	WST 146
Joseph	LAN	138	Nicholas	NOU	113	Jacob	NOH 46A
Joseph	WST	340	ANGLEBRIGHT,			Jacob	PHI 70A
Lemuel	WAS	61	Peter	BFD	42	Jacob	PHI 78A
Moses	WAS	84	ANGLEMOIR, John	BUC	139	John	PHI 92
Nancy	ADA	24	ANGONY, Jacob			John	YOR 182
Nathan	WAS	18	Jnr.	BUC	90A	John	NOH 49A
Peter	LAN	110	Widow	BUC	90A	Joseph	BUC 88A
Peter	BER	207	ANGST, Daniel	BER	263	Joseph L.	PHA 11
Robert	BEV	11	Daniel Jr.	BER	263	Ludowick	HNT 126
Robert	WAS	60	John	DAU	36A	Ludowick	HNT 127
Robt.	PHI	41	Peter	DAU	36A	Ludwig	NOH 49A
Robt.	YOR	197	ANGSTADT, Abm.	BER	256	Michl.	PHI 78A
Robt.	FRA	280	George	BER	256	Nicholas	ADA 16
Samuel	WAS	61	Jacob	BER	256	Nicholas	ADA 39
Samuel	NOU	179	Peter	BER	256	Peter	NOH 49A
William	WAS	15	Peter	BER	256	Philip	LAN 45
William	PHI	91	ANGUE, John	PHA	34	Philip	NOH 88A
William	BUT	318	ANGUISH, Jacob	CHE	821	Phillip	NOU 98
Zacharia	LAN	57	ANKENEY,			Phillip	ARM 123
ANDREWS, Widow	WST	305	Christian	SOM	126	ANTIBUS, Amos	WST 284
Abraham	MNT	118	David	SOM	126	ANTIS, Henry	
Alexr.	CHE	754	David	SOM	142	Junr.	LYC 27
Danl.	PHI	44	George	SOM	133	ANTLE, John	GRN 91
David	LUZ	409	Peter	SOM	126	John Junr.	GRN 91
David	PHI	82A	ANKRAM, Joseph	GRN	62	ANTREM, Caleb	FAY 230
Eliakim	LUZ	336	Martha	GRN	62	ANTRICAN, Thomas	DEL 165
Geo.	CUM	29	Richard	GRN	62	ANTRIM, John	BER 137
George	MNT	118	ANKRIM, Archibald	LAN	162	APEE?, John	
Hugh	CRA	8	James	LAN	240	Baptist	PHI 135
Hugh	CRA	12	Jas.	LAN	168	APELGAIT, James	ALL 73
Hugh	BUC	83	Saml.	CHE	871	APKER, Henry	PHA 62
Humphrey	YOR	201	ANKRIN, Widow	LAN	163	APLAND?, Robert	BER 204
Jacob	PHA	107	ANNADOWN, Thos.	PHA	5	APLEY, Ann	CUM 65
Jacob	CHE	793	ANNAN, Robert	PHA	100	APMEYER, Michael	YOR 188
Jacob	NOH	46A	ANNAWALD, John	SOM	132	APP, Christian	LAN 42
James	DEL	167	ANNER, Thomas	NOU	161	Frederick	NOH 49A
James	PHI	77A	ANNERS, Thos. S.	PHA	86	Matthias	NOU 134
Jeremiah	MIF	4A	ANNESBY, Thomas	PHA	113	Widow	LAN 41
Jno.	WAR	1A	ANNIS, William	WAY	138	APPEL, Andrew	NOH 46A
John	LAN	52	ANOLD, James	FAY	225	Christian	LAN 39
John	LAN	55	ANROADE, John	FRA	294	John	NOH 79A
John	PHA	82	ANROLD, Oliver	LUZ	423	Martin	NOH 79A
John	PHA	104	ANSBEY, George	PHA	106	APPELGAIT, Aaron	ALL 76
John	LAN	167	ANSCRAUGH,			Bengamin	ALL 78
Joseph	CRA	5	Michael	NOU	103	Bengamin	ALL 78
Joseph	LAN	167	ANSEL, Michael	SOM	142	Dannel	ALL 77
Ludwich	FRA	316	Peter	SOM	142	Izea	ALL 77
Mary	DAU	3A	ANSELM, John	YOR	182	Jarrit	ALL 78
Matthias	BFD	70	ANSHIUTS, Philip	WST	232	Robert	ALL 78
Paul	BFD	70	ANSHUTS, George	HNT	131	Wilm.	ALL 77
Peter	PHA	94	ANSLEY, John	WAY	140	APPENZELLER,	
Robert	CRA	12	John Jr.	WAY	140	Jacob	BUC 158A
Robert	CHE	755	Joseph	WAY	140	APPLE, Andrew	NOU 179
Robert Junr.	CRA	12	Robert	PHA	89	Christopher	NOU 179
Robt.	FRA	327	Simeon	WAY	140	Henry	NOU 134
Robt.	WAR	1A	ANSON, John	PHI	114A	Henry	NOU 179
Timothy	PHA	89	ANSPACH, Adam	BER	265	Henry	BER 262

8

APPLE, Henry	BER	263
Henry	PHI	68A
Henry	BUC	81A
Henry	PHI	92A
Jacob	PHA	52
Jacob	BUC	81A
John	PHA	88
John	BER	262
Paul	BUC	147
Peter	NOU	134
Samuel	MNT	67
Valentine	PHI	114
APPLEBACH, George	BUC	81A
Joseph	BUC	147
APPLEBACK, Daniel	BUC	81A
Henry	BUC	147
Ludwk.	BUC	80
APPLEBY, John	HNT	141
Thos.	PHI	66A
APPLEGATE, John	NOU	108
John	NOU	173
Obadiah	BEV	25
William	NOH	86A
Willm.	PHI	72A
APPLEMAN, Conrad	BFD	70
Henry	YOR	179
Jacob	WAS	61
Matthias	NOU	142
Peter	NOU	142
APPLETON,		
Christn.	PHI	78
Samuel	BUC	98A
APPLEY, Leonard	ADA	39
APPMEYER, Michael	YOR	189
APT, Adam	PHI	82A
David	PHI	91A
George	PHI	82A
Michl.	PHI	85
AR--BALD?,		
Richard	WAS	6
ARANDT, Jacob	LAN	18
ARBAGAUST, John	NOU	134
ARBEGAST, Michael	NOH	49A
ARBEGUST, Geo.	PHI	64
ARBER, Joseph	LYC	22
ARBUCKEL, Joseph	ALL	86
ARBUCKL, John	MER	432
ARBUCKLE, Adam	LAN	155
Daniel	MNT	43
James	MIF	4A
James	MIF	4A
John	WAS	41
John	MIF	4A
Joseph	BEV	20
Samuel	BEV	20
William	ERI	58A
Wm.	MIF	4A
ARBUTHNOT, Saml.	WST	147
ARBUTTON, James	WAS	48
ARCHART, Michael	PHA	110
ARCHBOLD, Adam	WST	167
Barthw.	PHI	15
Patrick	WST	232
Thomas	WST	232
ARCHEE?, John	PHI	133
ARCHER, David	PHA	52
Elizabeth	GRN	68
Francis	WAS	18
Jacob	GRN	67
James	LYC	27
John	WAS	61
Joseph	GRN	62
Martha	PHA	18
Moses	CHE	901
Samuel	PHA	30
ARCHIBALD, Wm.	PHA	62

ARCHIBALD, Wm.	FRA	279
ARDERY, John	FRA	322
ARDIS, John	PHI	148
ARDLEY, Caleb	WAS	6
Robt. A.	PHA	85
ARDLY, John	NOU	126
ARDON, Benga.	PHI	34
ARDRY, George	CEN	22
James	CEN	22
ARDZ, Michl.	BER	285
Philip	BER	285
AREHART, George	BFD	48
AREMAN?, (See		
Auman)	FAY	254
ARENHURST, Oliver	WAS	108
ARENS, Henry	BER	245
Jacob	BER	255
Jacob	DAU	29A
John	BER	255
ARFORD, Dewalt	CUM	57
ARGO, Alexander	GRN	74
William	FAY	225
ARGREE?, David	MNT	77
ARGUE?, David	MNT	77
ARICK, Jacob	WAS	96
Leonard	WAS	96
Mich.	PHI	97A
ARIMAN, Henry	MNT	61
ARKFORD, Saml.	PHI	4
ARLEY, William	LAN	225
ARMAT, Thomas	PHI	130
ARMATT, Thos. W.	PHA	82
ARMBREISTER, J		
Ohn	YOR	157
ARMBRISTER,		
Mathias	BER	184
Peter	BER	184
ARMBRUSTER, Henry	PHA	66
Mathias	PHA	67
Peter	PHA	62
ARMBUSTER?, See		
Armbrister	BER	184
ARMEGAST, George	BER	148
ARMEL, Daniel	WST	305
Jacob	WST	305
John	WST	305
ARMENT, Catharine	DEL	159
ARMER, Adam	ALL	55
Hamelton	CRA	9
John	LAN	124
Patrick	HNT	160
Thomas	NOU	161
ARMETROUT, John	BER	204
ARMINGER, Joseph	CHE	879
ARMITAGE, Amos	NOU	108
Benjamin	HNT	131
Caleb	HNT	160
Enock	MNT	49
George	PHA	63
George	YOR	155
James	HNT	131
James	BUC	144A
John	HNT	118
John	HNT	131
John	BUC	144A
ARMOR, James	CHE	776
John	CUM	97
John	NOU	191
Phhebe	CUM	91
Samuel	DEL	165
Samuel Farmer	DEL	165
Thomas	ADA	16
Wm.	CUM	97
ARMOTT, Yost	YOR	163
ARMOUR, Mathw.	PHI	110
ARMS, George	MNT	103

ARMS, Samuel	YOR	199
Thomas	SOM	142
ARMSBACK, Michael	NOU	98
ARMSBUCVK,		
Michael	NOU	98
ARMSEY?, (See		
Ormsey)	FRA	300
ARMSTRON, Gabrial	FAY	263
ARMSTRONG, Widow	YOR	202
Abraham	GRN	86
Abraham Junr.	GRN	86
Adam	ARM	125
Alexr.	FAY	207
Alexr.	WST	284
Andrew	WAS	18
Andrew	ALL	71
Andrew	WAS	96
Andrew	WAS	108
Andrew	BUC	90A
Andw.	CUM	54
Andw.	CUM	72
Andw.	NOU	170
Andw.	WST	340
Archibald	WAS	26
Archibauld	ALL	103
Benjamin	WAS	96
Chrisr.	PHI	43
Davd.	BUT	350
David	WST	167
David	LAN	245
Elijah	PHI	89A
Erwin	DEL	162
George	NOU	126
George	LAN	153
George	WST	208
George	WST	248
Herman	LAN	248
Hugh	BFD	40
Isaac	ADA	7
Isaiah	CHE	888
James	LYC	28
James	WAS	48
James	ALL	80
James	CUM	99
James	CUM	106
James	ARM	122
James	SOM	132
James	WST	147
James	HNT	150
James	YOR	156
James	WST	159
James	NOU	170
James	LAN	285
James	LUZ	362
James	MER	432
James	BUC	81A
Jane	BFD	55
Jane	GRN	93
Jas.	CUM	40
Jas.	CUM	61
Jno.	CUM	50
John	LYC	24
John	CUM	55
John	ALL	65
John	WAS	73
John	ALL	80
John	GRN	86
John	PHA	93
John	WAS	96
John	MNT	103
John	SOM	132
John	HNT	142
John	HNT	158
John	NOU	161
John	NOU	197
John	LAN	242

9

Name	Loc	Pg	Name	Loc	Pg	Name	Loc	Pg
ARMSTRONG, John	CHE	725	ARNEY, Michael	NOU	98	ARNOTT, Henry	NOH	77
John	CHE	779	ARNHOLD, Adam	NOU	134	Henry Dr.	YOR	195
John	CHE	801	Casper	NOU	181	John	NOH	36A
John	CHE	847	George	NOU	181	ARNSPERGER, Henry	CUM	58
John	DAU	10A	John	NOU	191	ARNT, John	LAN	253
John	BUC	90A	Phillip	NOU	181	ARON, Michael C.	PHA	16
Joseph	CRA	15	ARNOLD, Abraham	GRN	98	Obed.	BUC	96
Joseph	MNT	69	Abraham	LUZ	329	ARON?, Fried.?		
Joseph	WST	208	Abriham	YOR	179	Georoge	WST	269
Joseph	FRA	276	Adam	NOH	41	ARONFITER, Mary	PHA	67
Joseph	FRA	276	Andrew	FAY	207	ARONFRIED?,		
Joseph	BER	285	Ase	FAY	207	George	WST	269
Joseph	LUZ	362	Barbara	BER	241	ARREL?, John	WAS	87
Limy?	LUZ	324	Benjaman	FAY	225	ARRENTRUN,		
Margaret	HNT	151	Daniel	FAY	230	Francis	PHA	60
Margt.	CUM	55	David	FAY	230	ARRISON, Jephta	NOH	66
Martin	YOR	198	David	LUZ	379	John	PHI	82
Mary	PHI	98	David	LUZ	382	ARRMINTAGE,		
Quintin	ADA	7	Elizabeth	GRN	98	Shewbert	CHE	729
Quintin	WST	321	Frederick	NOH	79A	ARSHAL, Thomas	NOU	159
Reubin	LAN	16	Geo.	CUM	51	ARSSTRONG?,		
Robert	WAS	26	George	SOM	147	Pearse	PHI	68
Robert	LAN	125	George	YOR	208	ART, James	PHA	121
Robert	WST	248	George	LUZ	380	Lewis	PHI	111
Robert	DAU	10A	George P.	YOR	212	William	PHI	8
Robt.	CUM	28	Henrey	FAY	207	ARTENS, Thomas	LAN	113
Robt.	FRA	278	Henry	ADA	23	ARTER, Abraham	NOU	103
Robt.	WST	305	Henry	CUM	37	Andrew	PHI	122
Robt.	CHE	755	Henry	BFD	42	Andw.	PHI	116
Robt.	CHE	881	Henry	NOH	64	Edward	LAN	248
Sabra	WAS	41	Herman	DAU	29A	James	WAS	97
Saml.	BUC	90A	Herman.	DAU	26	Jane	LAN	248
Samuel	WST	248	Jacob	WAS	36	John	NOU	103
Simon	MNT	77	Jacob	NOH	41	John	NOH	68A
Thomas	WAS	96	Jacob	NOH	84A	ARTES, Isaac	FAY	201
Thomas	ALL	97	Jesse	FAY	207	John	FAY	254
Thomas	WST	321	John	WAS	15	ARTHER, Robt.	VEN	169
Thomas	BUC	158A	John	DAU	26	ARTHERHOLT,		
Thos.	CUM	36	John	ADA	29	Christian	BUC	90A
Thos.	CUM	113	John	NOH	41	Christn.	BUC	104A
Thos.	FRA	301	John	WAS	118	Daniel	BUC	90A
Thos.	FRA	327	John	YOR	199	David	BUC	90A
Thos.	CHE	845	John	YOR	201	Frederik	BUC	90A
William	CRA	4	John Jr.	YOR	197	ARTHUR, Guian	NOU	161
William	LAN	44	John	MIF	6A	Jno.	WAR	1A
William	WAS	65	John	MIF	14A	John	PHI	90
William	HNT	166	John B.	ADA	35	John	CUM	107
William	NOU	173	Jonathan	WAY	143	Mr./ Mrs.	LAN	124
William	NOU	191	Jonathen	FAY	225	William	WAS	18
William	CHE	776	Joseph	WAS	78	William	WAS	65
Wilm.	ALL	54	Levi	FAY	225	William	FAY	207
Wilm.	ALL	62	Martin	NOH	41	Wm.	WAR	1A
Wilm.	ALL	77	Michael	YOR	201	ARTHURS, George	CHE	748
Wm.	FRA	296	Nicholas	MIF	12A	Hugh	HNT	133
Wm. Esq.	MIF	16A	Peter	BFD	48	James	CHE	736
Wm.	MIF	26A	Peter	MNT	77	John	BFD	70
ARNAT, Jacob	NOH	86A	Peter	BER	172	John	WST	146
ARNDT, Jacob	DAU	25	Peter	BER	237	Joseph	CHE	821
John	ADA	11	Richard	FAY	207	Richd.	MIF	16A
Peter	ADA	13	Robert	BUC	80	Robert	CHE	752
ARNEL, John	PHI	21	Samuel	ALL	100	Wm.	CHE	825
Thomas	PHI	15	Samuel	SOM	151	ARTILLIA, Francis	BER	281
Thomas	PHI	23	Samuel Jr.	YOR	179	ARTIS, Seazer	PHA	53
ARNER, George	NOH	62	Samuel Sr.	YOR	179	ARTMAN, Andrew	PHI	123
Henry Sr.	WST	208	Stephen	LUZ	348	Christian	YOR	166
Jacob	NOH	39	Stephen	LUZ	402	George	BUC	102
Jacob	YOR	206	William	GRN	94	Jacob	YOR	166
John	NOH	42A	William	BER	215	John	NOH	41
John	NOH	49A	William	FAY	225	ARTZ, Cornelius	BER	150
William	NOH	75	William	LUZ	417	Jacob	BER	265
ARNET, Bertle	HNT	128	William	CHE	760	John	DAU	51A
Daniel	FAY	242	ARNOLD?, -----	MIF	9A	ARTZ?, Chr.	DAU	38
John	LAN	128	ARNOLL, Thomas	MER	432	ARUST, George	PHI	86A
Samuel	WAS	11	ARNOLT, Frantz	BER	187	ARVECOST, John	WAS	36
ARNETT, Barnet	NOH	70A	Philip	BER	187	Joseph	WAS	36
Jacob Jr.	NOH	36A	ARNOTT, Henry	NOH	35	ARVOSH, Nicholas	LAN	93

Name	Loc	Pg	Name	Loc	Pg	Name	Loc	Pg
ARY, John	FAY	225	ASHMEAD, Peter	PHA	87	ASTLE, William	GRN	94
ASBEL, Benjeman	FAY	201	William	PHI	133	ASTON, George	HNT	129
Benjeman Jr.	FAY	201	ASHMEADE, Samuel	MNT	117	John	NOH	41
Robert	FAY	201	ASHSTEN, Josep	ALL	117	Joseph	LAN	311
ASH--?, William	CEN	18A	ASHTENFELTER,			Owen	HNT	129
ASH, Widow	PHI	6	Peter	YOR	210	Owin	FRA	271
Widow	PHI	88	ASHTON, Widow	PHI	105	Saml.	CEN	18A
Abigail	DEL	167	Widow	PHI	72A	Thomas	NOH	41
Abraham	BFD	58	Benjamin	NOU	108	William	MNT	72
Cilvester	ALL	106	David	PHI	106	ATCHESON, David		
Henry	BFD	42	George	PHA	29	Jun.	WAS	88
Jacob	PHA	10	George	PHI	75	David Sen.	WAS	87
Jacob	DAU	39	George	NOU	108	Humphrey Jun.	WAS	88
James	PHA	19	Isaac	PHA	71	Humphrey Senr.	WAS	88
Jason	HNT	163	Isaac	PHI	154	John	CEN	22
John	DEL	167	James	PHI	17	John	WAS	88
John	LAN	216	Jesse?			Mathew	WAS	87
Joseph	MIF	3	(Erased?)	PHI	151	Mathew R.	WAS	87
Joseph	CHE	775	John	PHA	34	Thos.	YOR	213
Matthew	DEL	169	John	PHI	69	ATCHISON, Jacob	CUM	118
Michl.	PHI	107A	Joseph	PHI	156	James	CUM	118
Samuel	DEL	167	Joseph	DAU	34A	Jno.	CUM	108
Samuel	CHE	706	Joseph	BUC	92A	Mathew	WAS	15
Thomas	PHA	5	Martin	NOU	108	William	WAS	15
Widow	CHE	893	Peter	BUC	147	William	ADA	36
William	PHA	116	Rebecca	PHA	71	ATCOCK, John	YOR	210
Wm.	CHE	776	Robert	BUC	147	ATHERTON, Asahel	LUZ	381
ASHB-?, Joshua	CHE	704	Silas	PHI	133	Asahel Jr.	LUZ	381
ASHBAUCH, Simeon	WAS	6	Stephen	WAY	135	Cornelius	LUZ	370
ASHBAUGH, Fredk.	YOR	194	Thomas	PHI	154	Eleazer	LUZ	370
Henry	ADA	19	Thos.	PHI	104	Elisha	LUZ	333
John	ADA	10	Thos.	YOR	216	Henry	SOM	133
ASHBEY, Joseph	HNT	130	William	PHI	154	Henry	BUC	160A
ASHBOCH, Andrew	ADA	27	Wm.	PHI	114A	James	LUZ	334
Thomas	ADA	30	ASHWAY, Nicholas	FRA	315	John	LUZ	370
ASHBOUGH, Adam	WST	187	ASKAM, William	LUZ	322	Moses	LUZ	340
George	WST	187	ASKEUE, John	DEL	164	Thomas	SOM	133
Martin	WST	187	ASKEW, Benjn.	CUM	148	William	LUZ	381
Valentine	WST	377	John	WAS	36	ATHORIS,		
ASHBRIDGE, Ann	PHA	18	ASKIN, Alexr.	CUM	147	Frederick	NOU	161
Elizabeth	MNT	34	ASKINS, David	FAY	261	ATHURTON, Thos.	CUM	146
Jane	PHA	43	Samuel	FAY	261	ATKESON, Matthew	MIF	24A
Joseph	PHA	98	Thomas	CEN	18A	Ralph	FAY	254
Thos.	PHI	76A	ASKIT, Robert	PHI	147	Thomas	SOM	156
ASHBURN, William	BUC	149	ASMAN, John	BER	285	Wm.	CUM	27
ASHBURNER, John	PHA	4	ASMEAD, Jacob	PHI	92	ATKIN, John	WAS	15
ASHBY, Wm.	PHA	30	ASMITH, John	PHA	77	John	MIF	4A
ASHCRAFT, Daniel	FAY	219	ASPENSTREET,			ATKINS, James	CHE	772
Ichabud	FAY	219	Daniel	LAN	231	Philip	PHI	6
Nimrod	FAY	219	ASPER, Widow	YOR	211	William	CHE	813
ASHCRAFT?, (No			Abraham	YOR	211	William Jr.	CHE	813
Given Name)	BEV	27	Fredk.	YOR	211	ATKINSON,		
ASHCROFT, Mary	HNT	123	George	YOR	177	Alexander	BEV	6
ASHDON, George	NOU	155	George	YOR	211	John	WAS	108
ASHELMAN, John	HNT	152	Henry	CUM	35	John	MNT	141
ASHENFELTER,			Jacob	YOR	211	John	BUC	151
Joseph	MNT	85	Philip	YOR	177	John	CHE	729
ASHENHURST, Ralph	CUM	143	ASPEY, George	NOU	145	Saml.	PHI	77
ASHER, Anthony	BFD	56	John	NOU	197	Stephen	BFD	69
Anthony	GRN	68	ASPIN, Robert	PHI	29	Thomas	BUC	107
Geo.	PHI	118A	ASPY, Hugh	FAY	249	William	WAS	108
John	FAY	219	Jacob	WST	284	William	BUC	151
Luke	BFD	56	William	FAY	249	Zekel	PHI	145
Wm.	PHI	117A	William	BUC	98A	ATKISON, Thomas	HNT	118
ASHETON, Isaac	PHI	152	ASSA, George	NOH	33	Thomas	FAY	254
Jacob	PHI	154	William	NOH	33	ATLAN?, Philip	YOR	176
ASHEY?, George	NOU	145	ASSEYER, Anthony	NOH	77	ATLAND?, Philip	YOR	176
ASHFELLOW,			ASSHTON, Geo.	DAU	38	ATLEE, Samuel J./		
Ludwick	CHE	819	ASSIER, H. Smith	WST	208	I.?	LAN	305
ASHFORD, William	DEL	161	ASSIMINGER, John	GRN	62	William P.	LAN	35
ASHKETTLE, John	FRA	290	AST-S?, Thomas	CEN	18A	Wm. R.	MNT	69
ASHMAN, George			ASTEL, Thoms	FAY	207	ATLIN, Valentine	NOU	179
Esqr.	HNT	139	ASTEN, Samuel	FAY	197	ATMORE, Anne	PHA	23
Godfrey	PHA	40	ASTENS, Thomas	DAU	10	Isaac	PHA	55
ASHMEAD, James	PHI	133	ASTLE, Daniel	GRN	94	Thos.	PHA	92
John	PHA	80	Silas	GRN	94	ATSEL, Peter	LUZ	411

ATSTAT, Adam	YOR	205	AUSTIN, Isaac	PHA	37	B-----?, -----	MIF	9A
Henry	YOR	206	Isaac	ERI	55A	-----	MIF	9A
ATTBERGER, John	PHA	44	James	ERI	59	-----	MIF	9A
ATTEN, Adrian	NOH	66	Johannah	PHA	47	-----	MIF	9A
Derrick	NOH	64	Jonathan	MNT	67	John	ADA	21
Henry	NOH	64	Joshua	LUZ	355	Joseph	LAN	258
ATTERD, Ann	LAN	314	Moses	VEN	167	M----?	NOU	203
ATTLAND, Andw.	YOR	179	Nicholas	BUC	86	B----?, Joseph	ADA	19
Peter	YOR	178	Susannah	MNT	34	B---I-L?, Samuel?	GRN	62
Peter	YOR	180	Thos.	PHA	67	B---MESS?, Jacob	BFD	71
Philip	YOR	178	Willm.	PHI	1	B--YD?, Mrs.	LYC	19
ATTMORE, John	DEL	167	AUSTINE, John	PHI	118A	B-NFORD?, -----	MIF	9A
Jonathan	DEL	185	AUSWELL, Fredk.	CUM	107	B-TZER?, William	NOU	127
ATTWATER,			AUT, John	LUZ	384	BA-SON?, John	PHI	57
Benjamin	LUZ	367	AUTEN, John	NOU	115	BAALMER, John	LAN	257
ATUS, Fortin	PHI	116	AUTHERTON, Caleb	CUM	147	BAATSWAIN, James	CHE	771
ATWELL, Jno.	BUT	361	AUTOR, Rheulof	WAS	6	BABB, Anthony	NOH	44A
John	BUT	359	AVERY, Cyrus	LUZ	377	George	BER	136
John	BUT	360	AVY, George	HNT	161	George Jr.	BER	135
Robt.	BUT	360	AWART, John	WAS	118	John	BER	136
AUCHTNER, Henry	LAN	258	AWL, Sarah	DAU	15A	John	CHE	826
AUCKER, Jacob	ADA	25	Van John	CEN	24	Mathias	BER	235
AUD, Joseph	MIF	6A	AX, Conrad	PHI	137	Richard	PHA	44
AUDLER, Christn.	PHA	51	Frederick	PHI	127	Sampson	CHE	848
AUENBAGH, George	YOR	216	Frederick	PHI	133	Widow	LAN	159
AUGHINBOCH,			George	PHI	127	BABBET, Isaac	GRN	109
Anthony	ADA	38	John	PHI	128	Jacob	GRN	109
John	ADA	37	Peter	PHI	127	Samuel	GRN	109
AUGSTADT, Adam	BER	210	William	CHE	896	BABBING, Hannah	PHA	116
Joseph	BER	210	Willm.	PHI	126	BABCOCK, Benjamin	LUZ	391
AUGUST, Philip	HNT	132	AXER, Christopher	LAN	57	Nathan	LUZ	409
AUGUSTIN, Samuel	GRN	74	George	LAN	77	Nathl.	PHI	42
AUGUSTINE,			AXFORD, Saml.	PHA	84	BABE, Geoge	PHI	21
Frederic	SOM	145	AXTELL, Daniel	MER	433	Richard	PHA	102
George	PHI	83A	Linkin	MER	433	BABELDAY, Widow	PHI	93
Peter	SOM	145	Luther	WAS	60	BABLE, Conrad	NOH	84A
AUKER, Casper	CUM	31	Thomas	WAS	60	BABLITZ, Michael	ADA	33
Henry	YOR	210	Thomas	MER	432	BABS, John	FAY	255
AUKERMAN, Abraham	WAY	143	AXTER, Jacob	NOH	55	BACAN, Ezekial	NOU	98
AULD, David	CUM	143	AXTILL, Eliab	MER	432	Jeremiah	NOU	98
Jacob	MNT	105	AXTILLTOTTLE,			BACANON, Gilbert	ALL	99
James	CHE	757	Isaac	MER	432	BACAS, James	VEN	168
Moses	WST	232	AXTON, Jeremia	FAY	242	BACH, John	PHI	71
Robert	ALL	61	Jeremiah	GRN	79	BACHART,		
Wm.	CUM	114	Robert	WAS	18	Zacharics	BER	224
AULDHOOF, Henry	ADA	30	AYARS, James	NOU	191	BACHELOR, Casper	PHI	66
AULENBACH, Andw.	BER	241	AYCRE?, Hamilton	PHA	53	BACHERT, Jacob	NOH	75
John	BER	265	AYER?, Rudy	DAU	52	Jacob	NOH	58A
AULLS, Barbara	LAN	127	AYERS, David	NOH	66	Nicholas	NOH	75
Philip	LAN	127	Isaac	WAS	61	Solomon Junr.	NOH	75
AULT, Adam	LAN	227	John	NOH	77	Solomonon	NOH	75
Daniel	MER	433	Joseph	WAS	48	BACHERT?, John		
Frederick Junr.	WAS	108	Moses	NOH	66	Geo.	BER	156
Frederick Senr.	WAS	108	William	GRN	74	BACHESTER, John	PHI	92A
Jacob	WAS	65	AYERS?, Hamilton	PHA	53	BACHMAN, Abraham	LAN	4
Matthias	LAN	248	AYLES, Amos	WAS	77	Abraham Esqr.	NOH	36A
Michael	WAS	108	William	WAS	77	Abraham Esqr.	NOH	79A
Peter	WAS	108	AYRES, Alexander	FAY	242	Adam	NOH	44
AULTMAN, Peter	WAS	88	Daniel	LUZ	339	Ann	LAN	70
AUMAN, Abel	FAY	254	Daniel	LUZ	344	Chrisn.	DAU	40
Henry	BER	137	Elisabeth	WAS	54	Christian	LAN	182
Peter	BER	265	Elizabeth	LUZ	339	Conrad	BER	255
AUMENT, Henry	LAN	219	Ezekial	FAY	219	Conrad Jr.	BER	255
AUNER, Peter	PHA	86	John	DAU	10	Conrad	NOH	49A
AUQUERMAN, Philip	WST	305	John	FAY	219	Daniel	NOH	52A
AURANDT /			John	FAY	238	David	NOH	79A
AURANDS?,			John	CHE	910	Fried	NOH	49A
Peter	BER	241	Moses	FAY	219	George	NOH	47
AURANT, Daniel	NOU	97	Robert Revd.	FAY	238	Henry (Crossed		
AURVE?, Ludwick	NOU	145	Samuel	MNT	64	Out)	BUC	148A
AUSBERN, James	HNT	119	Samuel	LUZ	338	Henry	BUC	147
Joseph	PHI	69	Thomas	FAY	234	Henry	BER	259
AUSPACH, George	BER	266	William	LUZ	343	Henry	NOH	46A
AUSTIN, David	LUZ	410	York	PHA	106	Jacob	NOH	29
Edmond	LUZ	366	AZARD, Rodes	LUZ	399	Jacob	NOH	51
Francis	PHI	1				Jacob	NOH	75

BACHMAN, Jacob	NOH	79A	BADY, David	NOU	191	BAILEY, John	MNT	42
Johannes	LAN	273	Wilm.	ALL	91	John	WAS	84
Johannes	LAN	274	BAEHERT?, John			John	BUC	86
John	NOH	33	Geo.	BER	156	John	YOR	194
John	NOH	51	BAER, Jacob	NOH	29	John	YOR	203
John	LAN	73	John	NOH	75	John	YOR	213
John	LAN	74	Martin	NOH	52A	John	CHE	747
John	LAN	187	BAGA---?, -----?			John	CHE	753
John	NOH	46A	J----?	BUC	81A	John	CHE	768
John	NOH	49A	BAGE, Mrs.	NOU	186	John	CHE	908
John	NOH	79A	BAGENSTORE, John	BER	148	Joseph	CHE	700B
Joseph	LAN	66	BAGER, Robert	NOU	191	Joseph	BUC	84A
Lorentz	NOH	85	BAGERS, James	NOU	156	Joshua	LUZ	404
Lowrence Jr.	NOH	52A	BAGGS, Andrew	LAN	152	Joshua	CHE	738
Lowrence	NOH	52A	James	DEL	161	Joshua	CHE	839
Nicholas	NOH	51	James	DEL	162	Justice	LUZ	427
Nicholas	NOH	84A	James	CHE	901	Mary	BFD	42
Paul	NOH	85	John	DEL	162	Nathan	LYC	22
Paul	NOH	52A	Joseph	BEV	14	Nathan	CHE	739
Paul	NOH	58A	William	DEL	164	Nathaniel	CHE	738
Peter	NOH	33	BAGLEY,			Nehemiah	LUZ	404
Peter	LAN	187	Cornelious	PHI	59	Peter	BER	187
Philip	YOR	191	James	LUZ	367	Phebe	BUC	88
Samuel	BUC	156A	Jesse	LUZ	367	Robert	CHE	786
BACHTEL, Peter	NOH	89	John	BFD	54	Samuel	CHE	770
BACK, Fredk.	PHA	55	John	BFD	55	Thomas	LAN	6
BACKAS, Cathrin	FAY	219	William	BFD	54	Thomas	ADA	33
BACKENSTOES, John	NOU	170	BAGNELL, Benjamin	PHA	117	Thomas	WAS	78
BACKENSTOSE,			BAGO, Cesar	WAY	137	Widow	LAN	43
Henry	DAU	52A	BAGS, John	PHI	70A	William	ADA	24
Jacob	LAN	44	John	PHI	83A	William	WAS	84
Jacob	LAN	46	William	LAN	125	William	MNT	104
Jacob	DAU	52A	BAGUN, Joseph	LAN	217	William	BUC	92A
BACKER, Christian	NOH	66	BAHARN, Patrick	WST	187	William	BUC	95A
Frederick	NOU	186	BAHL, Nicholas	NOH	42A	Wm.	LYC	13
John	NOU	134	Philip	NOH	79A	Wm.	CUM	145
Peter	NOU	134	BAHMAN, Conrad	CEN	22	Wm.	CUM	151
Philip	NOH	49A	BAHN, Adam	YOR	167	Wm.	CHE	742
BACKES, Daniel	NOH	85	BAIL, David	BEV	25	Wm.	CHE	902
BACKHAMOR, Martin	WAS	108	George	BEV	25	BAILIFF, Daniel	DEL	160
BACKHOUSE, James	BUC	80	George	DEL	159	Wm.	CHE	804
Mary	BUC	80	John	DEL	160	BAILISS, Elias	FAY	238
BACKIS, Daniel	NOU	201	John	DEL	191	BAILLEY, John	HNT	137
James	NOU	201	BAILER, Jacob	CUM	134	William	HNT	128
BACKMAN, Henry	BUC	148	BAILESS, Thomas	CHE	805	BAILLY, John	HNT	144
Philip	LAN	135	BAILETT?, Elias	MNT	105	Richard	HNT	144
BACKUS, Godfey	PHI	141	BAILEY, Aaron	CHE	742	William	HNT	144
BACON, David	PHA	13	Alexander	WAS	84	BAILS, George	BEV	20
Henry	BER	217	Asa	ERI	59A	Jeremiah	PHI	99A
Isaac	PHA	67	Benjn.	CHE	872	John	BEV	28
Job	PHA	18	Charles	YOR	215	John	BUT	345
Joseph	PHI	68A	Daniel	LYC	22	Thomas	HNT	138
Thomas	ALL	103	Daniel	SOM	133	BAILY, Widow	PHI	5
BACUS, John	PHI	92A	Daniel	YOR	193	Bailer	GRN	78
BADDERS, George	YOR	202	Daniel	LUZ	409	Eli	GRN	99
BADDISON, Joseph	LUZ	418	Daniel M---?	LYC	6	Elisha	MIF	16A
BADDOLETTE, John	GRN	80	Danl. Senr.	LYC	6	Jesse	FAY	219
BADE, David	DAU	43	David	CHE	753	Mrs.	NOU	120
BADER, Adam	NOH	55	Edward	YOR	168	Stephen	GRN	80
Daniel	NOH	47	Elias	FAY	252	William	GRN	74
Frederick	NOH	47	Elisha	CHE	742	William	PHI	153
George	DAU	51	Elizabeth	CHE	838	BAIN?, Nathaniel	PHA	121
George	BER	256	Francis	LAN	123	BAIR, John	DAU	17A
Henry	NOH	47	Gency/ Geney?	LAN	217	Michael	MIF	4A
Henry	BER	286	George	YOR	194	Michl.	MIF	4A
Margaret	BER	220	Isaac	CHE	739	BAIRD, Absalom		
Mathias	BER	229	Isaac	CHE	741	Esqr.	WAS	115
Peter	NOH	58A	Isaac	CHE	770	Amos	ERI	56A
Peter	BUC	158A	Jacob	YOR	190	Benjn.	LYC	18
BADGER, Friend	LUZ	390	Jacob	YOR	194	Charles	WST	340
Giles	ERI	58A	James	WAS	84	Edward	ERI	56A
BADLER, Sarah	MNT	130	James	LAN	170	Hester	WST	341
BADMAN, John	MNT	61	James	MER	435	James	LYC	26
Joseph	MNT	98	Jehu	CUM	151	James	ERI	58
BADORFF, Adam	BER	261	Jesse	CHE	740	James	WST	340
BADSTON, Cathrine	PHA	93	Joel	CHE	750	John	ADA	4

13

BAIRD, John	YOR 196	BAKER, Elizabeth	BUC 92A	BAKER, John	PHA 104		
John	ERI 56A	Fanny	FAY 197	John	CUM 111		
Joseph	CRA 8	Frederick	LAN 133	John	PHA 124		
Joseph	CRA 13	Frederick	CHE 785	John	NOU 134		
Moses	WST 340	Fredk.	YOR 191	John	BER 173		
Robert	HNT 165	Gabriel	YOR 198	John	DEL 175		
Robert	FAY 225	Gabriel	YOR 200	John	YOR 180		
Samuel	MNT 80	George	PHI 1	John	YOR 181		
Samuel	MNT 85	George	BEV 26	John	YOR 182		
Samuel	MNT 98	George	ADA 34	John	YOR 184		
Thomas	BEV 4	George	ADA 35	John	YOR 211		
William	DAU 22	George	WAS 36	John	BER 276		
William	WST 340	George	BFD 56	John	BER 277		
William	WST 340	George	MNT 69	John	FRA 303		
William	ERI 55A	George	MNT 119	John	FRA 305		
William	ERI 56A	George	HNT 137	John	FRA 307		
Wm.	LYC 18	George	CHE 771	John	CHE 831		
Wm.	CUM 146	George Jun.	BEV 26	John	CEN 18A		
Zebulon	LYC 18	George	BUC 92A	John	PHI 78A		
BAIRD?, Mrs.	LYC 19	George A.	PHA 27	John	PHI 85A		
BAIRFIELD, George	ALL 117	Gideon	LUZ 339	John L.	LUZ 334		
John	LYC 19	Godfrey	PHA 42	John N.	BER 277		
Stephen	LYC 19	Godfrey	BER 235	Jonathan	SOM 153		
Wm.	LYC 19	Hannah	PHA 31	Joseph	CRA 11		
BAISH, Martin	PHA 30	Henry	DAU 20	Joseph	CRA 13		
BAITY, David	MER 435	Henry	CUM 33	Joseph	DEL 172		
Hugh	FAY 249	Henry	NOU 99	Joseph	DEL 175		
Thomas	FAY 242	Henry	PHI 105	Joseph	CHE 739		
William	WAS 11	Henry	MNT 127	Joseph	CHE 848		
BAKE, Harman	PHA 113	Henry	SOM 136	Joseph Jun.	DEL 172		
Israel	PHI 18	Henry	SOM 153	Joshua	CHE 752		
Jacob	NOU 99	Henry	BER 174	Levi	CHE 741		
John Junr.	YOR 179	Henry	DEL 175	Lewis	PHI 73		
John Sr.	YOR 179	Henry	YOR 189	Ludwig	SOM 141		
Michael	DAU 40	Henry	BER 278	Margaret	PHA 5		
BAKEN, Barbara	FAY 225	Henry	FRA 307	Martin	LAN 21		
BAKENSTOGE, Geo.	DAU 24A	Isaac	BER 274	Mary	PHA 14		
BAKENSTOSE, Jacob	DAU 35	Jacob	PHI 2	Mary	PHI 84		
BAKEOVEN, John	PHI 87	Jacob	ADA 5	Mary	PHA 100		
BAKER, Widow	PHI 21	Jacob	LYC 14	Mary	SOM 147		
Widow	PHI 69	Jacob	PHI 38	Mathias	DAU 22		
Aaron	WAS 36	Jacob	MNT 53	Matthias	YOR 216		
Aaron	DEL 175	Jacob	PHI 64	Matthias	YOR 217		
Aaron	CHE 739	Jacob	PHA 79	Melchar	FAY 219		
Aaron	CHE 763	Jacob	PHI 80	Michael	DAU 22		
Aaron Junr.	WAS 36	Jacob	NOU 97	Michael	BEV 26		
Abraham	BER 136	Jacob	PHI 122	Michael	SOM 126		
Adam	PHI 146	Jacob	SOM 126	Michael	FAY 243		
Adam	WST 209	Jacob	BER 136	Michael	PHI 96A		
Adam	WST 209	Jacob	SOM 136	Nathan	WAS 36		
Andrew	ERI 57	Jacob	SOM 156	Nathan	CHE 739		
Andrew	SOM 133	Jacob	YOR 190	Nathan	BUC 160A		
Andrew	SOM 153	Jacob	BER 209	Nathan L.	LUZ 378		
Anthony	BEV 27	Jacob	PHI 89A	Nehemiah	DEL 172		
August	BER 155	James	BEV 25	Nehemiah	DEL 172		
Benjamin	MNT 80	James	BUT 321	Nehemiah	DEL 190		
Catharine	YOR 165	James	BUT 347	Nicholas	FAY 219		
Christn.	PHI 111	James	CHE 739	Nicholas	FAY 255		
Christopher	ADA 13	Jeremiah	FRA 322	Nicholas Jur.	FAY 219		
Christopher	FRA 320	John	ADA 5	Nicholas Senr.	FAY 219		
Conrad	MNT 106	John	LYC 14	Peter	ADA 30		
Conrod	PHI 87	John	BEV 26	Peter	CUM 41		
Conrod	PHI 78A	John	NOH 33	Peter	BFD 49		
Conrod	PHI 88A	John	ADA 35	Peter	PHA 61		
Daivd	SOM 156	John	BFD 36	Peter	SOM 137		
Daniel	ADA 11	John	ADA 38	Peter	YOR 179		
Daniel	BEV 26	John	PHA 42	Peter	YOR 192		
Daniel	PHI 30	John	PHA 43	Peter	FAY 225		
Daniel	ADA 34	John	BFD 54	Peter	FAY 242		
Daniel	MNT 80	John	PHA 62	Peter	PHI 87A		
Daniel	NOU 97	John	MNT 66	Philip	DAU 27		
Daniel	NOU 134	John	WAS 78	Philip	SOM 137		
David	BFD 61	John	MNT 80	Philip	YOR 215		
Edward	DEL 172	John	CUM 83	Philip Jr.	YOR 215		
Elisha	BFD 58	John	PHI 87	Phillip	FAY 212		
Elisha	CHE 739	John (Far.)	MNT 80	Revd.	LAN 46		

14

Name	Co.	Pg.	Name	Co.	Pg.	Name	Co.	Pg.
BAKER, Richard	BFD	56	BALDWIN, John	PHI	86A	BALLIOT, John	LUZ	358
Richard	MNT	56	Johnston	CHE	761	Stephen	LUZ	358
Richard	DEL	172	Jonathan	GRN	109	BALLOW, James	FRA	320
Richard	CHE	759	Jonathan	WAR	1A	BALLZEL?, Jacob	GRN	66
Robert	BEV	18	Joseph	BUC	84	BALM, Daniel	CHE	725
Robert	ALL	49	Joseph	CHE	758	Widow	DAU	46A
Robert	LUZ	368	Josiah	PHA	4	William	DAU	31
Saml.	PHI	114A	Jude	LUZ	343	William	DAU	43A
Samuel	PHA	14	Mary	CHE	900	BALMER, Daniel	LAN	20
Samuel	ADA	30	Nathan	CHE	741	Jacob	LAN	18
Samuel	LUZ	399	Thomas	ADA	14	Jacob	LAN	190
Samuel	ERI	58A	Thos.	CHE	773	Jacob	LAN	207
Sarah	PHA	29	Thos.	CHE	774	Michael	LAN	18
Sarah	SOM	126	Thos. Jnr.	CHE	773	BALORT, Jacob	MNT	137
Stephen	PHI	27	Tibbalds	LUZ	343	BALSBAUGH, George	DAU	22
Susannah	PHI	107	William	DEL	155	BALSER, Catharine	PHA	76
Thomas	PHA	106	Wm.	CHE	740	Henry	BER	136
Thomas	HNT	133	Wm.	CHE	786	Henry	BER	217
Thomas	CHE	741	Worthall	CHE	849	Henry	BER	277
Valentine	BER	137	BALDY,			BALSINGER, George	FAY	212
Wentel	NOU	127	Christopher	NOU	127	BALSLEY, Henry	ADA	17
Widow	LAN	20	BALENTINE, Wm.	YOR	198	John	DAU	3A
Widow	MIF	12A	BALES, Abraham	YOR	208	Jos.	YOR	177
William	NOU	99	Caleb	ADA	41	BALT, Fredk.	PHI	84A
William	NOU	103	Isaac	ADA	43	Henry	PHI	84A
William	PHI	130	Jacob	ADA	28	BALTEN, Thos.	CHE	825
William	SOM	133	John	ADA	37	BALTER, Benj.	PHI	116
William	SOM	156	John	PHI	97A	BALTEZLY, Jacob	FAY	197
William	DEL	172	Moses	ADA	43	Jacob Junr.	FAY	197
William	BER	277	Soloman	ADA	43	BALTHAZER, Peter	NOH	52A
William	BER	277	BALES?, Moses	ADA	38	BALTON?, (See		
William	BER	278	BALEY, Christn.	PHI	50	Batton)	HNT	131
William	LUZ	339	George	FRA	302	William	LAN	300
Willm.	DAU	22	Isaac	MNT	47	BALTY?, See Batty	BER	210
Willm.	PHI	92A	Jacob	PHI	1099	BALTZGROVE,		
Wm.	BEV	18	John	MNT	38	George	BER	258
Wm.	CUM	75	Richard	PHA	95	BALUE, Daniel	HNT	144
Wm.	CUM	84	Sally Mrs.	PHI	67A	BALY, Gravener	CRA	10
Wm.	PHI	84	BALF, Widow	WST	364	John	NOU	162
Wm.	VEN	168	BALL, Abraham	BUC	158	Robert	CRA	9
BAKER?, (See			Calib	MER	433	Robt.	PHI	77A
Baken)	FAY	225	Christopher	BFD	56	Wilm.	ALL	59
BAKERLEY, Henry	SOM	136	Conrad	PHI	83	BAM, Susanna	LAN	279
BAKHORN, Joseph	FAY	219	Daniel	BFD	56	BAM?, Jacob	LAN	264
BALANTINE, James	WAS	19	Davis	GRN	99	BAMAN, James	VEN	169
BALD, William	NOH	72A	Ezekial	FAY	242	BAMBA, Casper	BER	226
BALDAUFF, Casper	NOH	52A	Henry	BFD	56	BAMBERGER,		
BALDENON,			Henry	WAY	140	Charles	BER	265
Mordecai	CHE	710	John	DEL	169	Christian	LAN	190
BALDERSON, John	BUC	92A	John	FAY	225	Jacob	LAN	134
John	BUC	144A	Joseph	PHA	60	Jacob	DAU	12A
BALDERSTON,			Joseph	LAN	241	John	DAU	27
Timothy	BUC	151	Nathan	PHA	24	Joseph	DAU	27
BALDERSTONE,			Nathan Jn.	BUC	156A	BAMBRIDGE,		
Jonathan	BUC	103	Nathan	BUC	156A	William	PHA	98
BALDRIDGE, Joseph	WST	306	Thomas	WAS	36	BAMBUGER?, Widw.	PHI	79
Robt.	WST	286	Thomas	HNT	125	BAMFIELD, John	PHA	72
BALDRIGE, Michael	LAN	157	Wm.	PHA	24	BAMFORD, Enogh	PHI	154
BALDWIN, Amos	WAS	48	Wm.	CHE	759	BAMGARTNER, Saml.	LAN	250
Amos	LUZ	343	Wm. Esqr.	PHI	88A	BAMGERTNER, John	LAN	250
Caleb	CHE	772	BALLAME, Joseph	BUC	151	BAMMIS, John	PHA	100
Caleb	CHE	899	BALLARD, John	LUZ	406	BANBRIDGE, David	PHI	119
George	DEL	158	Joseph	LUZ	406	BANCHER?, See		
Gideon	LUZ	398	Nathan	LUZ	405	Baucher	BER	277
Gideon	LUZ	410	Nathaniel	LUZ	406	BANDER?, Peter	ADA	35
Hadley	CHE	773	Stephen	LUZ	406	BANDINE, Saml.	PHI	74
Hester	PHA	40	Thomas	LUZ	406	BANDON, Jno.	CUM	85
Isaac	LUZ	428	BALLENGER,			BANE, Elias	NOH	72A
Jared	LUZ	343	Rudolph	FAY	242	Isaac Esqr.	WAS	1
John	ADA	14	BALLIET, Jacob	NOH	70A	Isaac Junr.	WAS	1
John	BUC	83	John	NOH	88A	James	WAS	1
John	SOM	137	Joseph Junr.	NOH	44	James	NOH	64
John	DEL	157	Joseph Senr.	NOH	44	James	YOR	216
John	CHE	848	Leonard	NOH	75	Jesse	WAS	1
John	CHE	884	Stephen Esqr.	NOH	88A	John	WAS	1
John	CHE	902	BALLIOT, Jacob	LUZ	358	John	WAS	61

Name	Loc	Pg	Name	Loc	Pg	Name	Loc	Pg
BARKER, James	GRN	84	BARNDT, Frederick	MNT	89	BARNETT, Fredk.	CUM	28
James	PHA	100	Henry	MNT	89	George	SOM	145
Jerramia	ALL	51	John	MNT	89	James	DAU	22
Jessy	ALL	52	BARNEARD, Jacob	FRA	284	Jno.	CUM	130
John	PHA	61	Peter	FRA	284	John	DAU	22
John	BUT	316	BARNEILLE,			John	DEL	161
Jonathen	ERI	58A	Timothy	HNT	123	John	CHE	810
Joseph	ALL	63	BARNEL?, (See			Mary	CHE	740
Peter	PHA	98	Barnet)	BFD	36	Matthias	CHE	710
Richard	PHI	2	BARNER, Adam	CUM	33	Moses	DAU	22
Samuel	ERI	57	BARNERT, John	FAY	255	Richard	CHE	769
Sarah	PHI	5	BARNES, Adnw.	PHA	42	Richard	CHE	769
Widow	CHE	821	Caleb	BFD	49	Robert	DEL	189
BARKHIMER,			Cesar	PHA	110	Robt.	WST	208
Elizabeth	BFD	71	David	DAU	7	Thomas	CUM	36
Jacob	BFD	71	David	PHI	146	Thos.	DAU	22
John	BFD	71	David	FAY	200	Timothy	BUT	355
Michael	BFD	71	Dawson	BFD	49	BARNEY, Benjamin	LUZ	344
BARKINS, Thomas	LAN	92	Elija	FAY	242	Charles	LUZ	344
BARKIS, John	BFD	54	Ephraim	FAY	242	Henry	LUZ	344
BARKLEY, Andrew	LAN	167	Floro	PHA	119	John	BFD	42
Benjamin	BER	232	Henry	MIF	12A	Johnathan	LYC	11
Elizabeth M.	PHA	112	Isaac	CHE	864	Nathan	LUZ	330
Francis	FRA	326	Isaac	CHE	877	Phillip	WST	209
John	BER	163	Jerry	WAY	139	BARNHART, Abraham	WAS	108
John	FRA	326	Jesse	MNT	115	Christn.	MNT	56
John	MIF	6A	Jesse	FAY	254	George	BFD	42
Joseph	MER	434	John	WAS	36	Jacob	SOM	156
Robt.	FRA	320	John	PHA	51	Jacob	BUT	335
William	LAN	166	John	WAY	139	Jno.	CUM	63
William Jnr.	LAN	170	John	FAY	219	John	CUM	62
BARKLOW, Barnet	CUM	142	John	FAY	242	John	YOR	171
BARKLY, John	FAY	264	John	CHE	872	John	FAY	200
Wm.	MIF	6A	John Jr.	WAY	139	Peter	SOM	156
BARKOL, Henry	FRA	306	Joshua	FAY	242	Peter	FRA	324
BARKS, James	LAN	237	Patrick	PHA	114	Peter Sen.	SOM	156
BARKSHIRE, Anson	BFD	56	Robert (Crossed			Philip	LYC	27
William	BFD	59	Out)	LAN	150	BARNHEART, Henry	NOU	113
BARKSTRACER,			Robert	CHE	872	BARNHEETER, John	DAU	13
George	HNT	119	Saml.	PHA	82	BARNHERT, Ludwick	PHI	125
George	HNT	136	Stephen	LUZ	325	BARNHILL, David	CUM	59
Henry	HNT	119	Thomas	MNT	49	Henry	MIF	16A
Henry	HNT	136	Thomas	FAY	242	Hugh	FAY	230
BARKSTRESSER,			Thoms.	BUT	356	John	MNT	37
Adam	FRA	303	Wm.	PHA	106	John	BUC	98A
BARLEN, Enoch	NOU	99	BARNET, Abner	BFD	36	Joseph	ERI	60
BARLET, Christn.	BER	142	Abner	HNT	137	Robt.	PHA	22
John	BER	272	Andrew	NOH	86A	Samuel	WAS	18
Margaret	BER	239	Bever?	MNT	44	Samuel	WAS	88
Paul	BER	217	Charles	HNT	156	Sarah	PHA	19
BARLETZ, William	LAN	77	David	FAY	230	William	YOR	174
BARLEYMAN,			Ephraim	WAS	88	Wm.	MIF	14A
Christian	MNT	72	Henry	BUC	80	BARNHISEL, Adam	CUM	43
BARLIP, John	FRA	312	Henry	NOH	36A	Henry	CUM	43
BARLISS?, John	FRA	312	Isaac	YOR	219	Jno.	CUM	39
BARLIT, Elias			Jacob	BUC	149	Martin	CUM	43
(Fred Crossed			Jacob	FAY	240	Saml.	CUM	43
Out)	NOH	75	Jacob	BUC	90A	BARNHOLT, (Blank)	MNT	34
BARLOT, Conrad	FRA	279	Jacob	BUC	156A	John	PHI	116A
BARLOW, Aaron	DEL	165	John	PHI	34	BARNHOLTZ, George	MNT	93
John	MNT	72	John	WAS	108	BARNHOUSE,		
John	HNT	123	John	WST	340	Christian	SOM	147
John	DEL	157	John	NOH	36A	John	SOM	142
BARLY, James	PHI	108A	Joseph	FRA	271	William	SOM	133
BARMER, Henry	LAN	173	Luke	BFD	69	BARNIS, John	PHI	86
BARN, Lisbet	NOU	114	Mary	BUC	149	BARNIT, Andrew	PHI	125
BARN?, Jacob	LAN	264	Peter	BUC	149	John	ALL	83
BARNARD, Ignatius	WAS	119	Saml.	MIF	4A	Joseph	ALL	84
BARNDOLLAR,			Saml.	MIF	6A	BARNITZ, Barbara	YOR	155
Daniel	BFD	48	William	GRN	68	George	YOR	156
Danl.	PHI	73A	William	WST	148	Jacob Esqr.	YOR	155
Michael	BFD	48	William	NOH	36A	John	YOR	156
BARNDOLLER,			Wilm.	ALL	82	Michael	LAN	43
Christopher	PHI	141	BARNETT, Abm.	PHI	68A	BARNITZ?, Daniel	YOR	181
BARNDOTTER,			David	FAY	219	BARNS, Widow	PHI	16
Fredk.	PHA	45	Ezekiel	GRN	111	Andrew	WST	269

BARNS, Baker	MNT	34	BARR, James	FRA	318	BARRICK, Jacob	LAN	4
Baltzer	YOR	170	James Judge	ARM	124	Phillip	CHE	773
Bengamin	ALL	64	Jno.	WAR	1A	William	HNT	127
Charles	YOR	206	John	WAS	6	BARRICKMAN, John	PHI	118
Edmond	MNT	49	John	WAS	66	BARRICKSTRESER,		
Elizabeth	MNT	49	John	CUM	107	Jacob	CUM	53
Henry	FRA	297	John	WST	159	BARRICKSTRESSER,		
Hugh	LAN	160	John	WST	159	Jno.	CUM	53
Isaac	BEV	21	John	NOU	162	BARRIER?, George	BEV	12
Isaac	CHE	766	John	BER	166	BARRIGER, David	BFD	61
Isaac	BUC	92A	John	DEL	173	BARRING, Mr.	PHA	102
James	PHI	16	John	LAN	222	BARRINGER,		
James	MNT	130	John	WST	284	Laurence	BFD	67
James	LAN	161	John	FRA	294	Martin	NOU	103
Job	GRN	67	John	FRA	313	BARRINGTON, Ann	PHA	16
John	PHI	6	John	FRA	314	Henry	CHE	832
John	WAS	11	John	BUT	343	Jonathan	PHI	135
John	BEV	13	John	MIF	24A	Richard	PHI	22
John	NOH	62	Joseph	CHE	833	BARRIS, Wm.	PHI	70A
John	CUM	93	Martin	LAN	221	BARRIT, Danl.	PHI	80A
John	ALL	117	Martin	LAN	243	BARRITT, Tobias	PHI	49
John	BUC	153	Martin	LAN	244	BARRON, George	BUC	147
John	WST	306	Michael	LAN	208	Jacob	BUC	147
Joseph	PHI	113A	Paul	BER	136	John	CEN	22
Joshua	GRN	106	Robert	DAU	3	Philip	PHI	70A
Kittian	LAN	107	Robert	CEN	22	Wiillm.	BUT	367
Lenard	FAY	201	Robert	PHI	60	William	WST	167
Leven	FAY	201	Robert	WAS	66	Willm.	BUT	327
Peter	BEV	15	Robert	WST	148	Willm.	BUT	365
Robert	MNT	64	Robert	HNT	159	Willm.	BUT	367
Robert	LAN	157	Robert	WST	341	BARRONET, John J.	PHA	73
Samuel	MNT	64	Robert	MIF	24A	BARROW, Mary	PHI	150
Stephen	MNT	64	Robt.	CUM	135	BARRY, James	PHA	101
Thomas	BEV	28	Rudolph	CHE	834	James	MNT	104
Thomas	BUC	92A	Saml.	WST	159	Joseph B.	PHA	91
Timothy	CHE	730	Samuel	WAS	118	Thos.	LYC	12
William	BUC	153	Samuel	ARM	126	BARSON, Isaac	BUC	147
William	YOR	169	Samuel	LAN	234	BARSTICKER, Mary	PHA	71
William	YOR	173	Sarah	CHE	839	BART, Stephen	LAN	268
William	FAY	201	Thomas	WAS	51	Tener	PHI	14
William	BER	209	Thomas	WST	148	BARTEL, Philip	PHI	140
William	WST	209	Thomas	BUC	154	BARTELL, Martin	PHA	23
William	WST	306	Thomas	WST	233	BARTELOW, Bernerd	LYC	14
Wm.	PHI	80	William	HNT	159	Cornels.	LYC	14
BARNS?, Thomas	BUC	84	William	WST	341	BARTEN, Eli	FAY	212
BARNSLEY,			Wm.	CUM	149	Joseph	FAY	212
Elizabeth	BUC	103	BARRACK, Nichls.	CUM	46	William	FAY	230
William	BUC	103	BARRACKMAN, Jas.	MIF	12A	BARTER, Andw.	DAU	45
BARNT, John	BUC	158A	Michal	ALL	71	Cepio	PHI	28
BARNUM, David	LUZ	390	BARRACKS, William	HNT	119	BARTH, Thos.	PHI	77A
Philo	ERI	56	BARRALL, Jacob	BER	165	BARTHEW,		
BARNWEL, Mathew	ALL	56	Jacob	BER	256	Thisleap?/		
BARNWELL, Henry	MNT	106	Michael	BER	245	Thisleass	PHI	68
BARONE, George	SOM	126	BARRAT, James	NOU	156	BARTHOLD, Fredck.	NOH	37
John	SOM	126	Richd.	CUM	88	John	NOH	62
Philip	SOM	126	BARREL, Saml.	PHI	82	BARTHOLEMEUX,		
BARR, Abraham	LAN	243	BARRELL, Jacob	CUM	46	Barney	LAN	61
Adam	BUC	88	BARREN, Thomas	VEN	168	BARTHOLEMEW,		
Adam	BER	204	BARRET, James	LYC	17	Conrad	LAN	97
Christian	LAN	243	James	CEN	20	Daniel	YOR	198
David	CEN	22	John	LYC	21	John	LAN	55
Elizabat	LYC	28	John	CHE	765	Matthew	LAN	249
Gabriel	HNT	159	Maria	BER	236	BARTHOLOME, Adam	DAU	34A
George	LAN	14	Widow	LAN	218	Wendel	DAU	35
Henry	PHA	56	Wilm.	ALL	53	BARTHOLOMEW, Adam	BUC	156A
Isaac	LYC	28	BARRETT, Widow	PHI	45	Benjamin	BUC	82A
Jacob	BER	166	Francis	PHI	38	Benjn.	CHE	733
Jacob	LAN	216	Henry	CHE	903	Benjn.	BUC	81A
Jacob	BER	233	Jeremiah	MNT	34	Chas.	PHA	29
Jacob	LAN	245	John	PHI	11	Henry	NOH	64
Jacob	LAN	276	John	MNT	133	Henry Jr.	NOH	29
Jacob Junr.	LAN	243	Robert	PHA	88	Henry Sr.	NOH	29
Jacob Senr.	LAN	243	Thomas	CHE	861	Jacob	BUC	100A
James	ADA	27	William	MNT	65	Jno.	CHE	734
James	WAS	27	William	CHE	866	John	PHA	10
James	ARM	124	BARRICK, Andrew	LAN	4	John	PHA	41

BARTHOLOMEW, John	GRN	68
John	PHI	124
John	NOH	88A
Jos	FRA	275
Lewis	NOH	29
Michl.	BER	235
Peter	NOH	29
Peter	CUM	88
Sarah	DEL	161
Valentine	BFD	49
Widow	CHE	892
Wm.	CHE	893
BARTHOLOMEY,		
Henry	LAN	221
BARTHURST?,		
Laurence	MIF	18A
BARTHUST, John	CHE	724
BARTIN, A. Kimber	NOU	191
Silas? (Crossed		
Out)	BUC	86
BARTION, James	WAY	148
BARTLE, Abraham	MNT	94
Daniel	PHI	140
Elick	BUC	144
George	LAN	61
Georoge	PHI	141
Henry	PHI	116
Peter	MNT	137
Rudolph	PHI	141
Samuel	MNT	94
Seman	PHI	114
BARTLELICK,		
George	VEN	170
BARTLEMAY, John	LAN	108
BARTLESEN, Abner	PHA	7
BARTLESON, Bartle	NOH	41
Bartle	DEL	183
Henry	PHA	41
James	MNT	115
Peter	MNT	115
BARTLET, John	PHI	155
BARTLETT,		
Ebenezer	LUZ	383
Isaac	FAY	213
John	FAY	238
Lemuel	LYC	12
Thomas	PHI	11
Thomas	FAY	219
BARTLEY, George	BEV	17
George	WAS	51
Mary	DAU	4
Robert	LAN	130
Robt.	CUM	91
Saml.	PHI	4
Thomas	BEV	6
BARTLEY?, William	PHA	116
BARTLING, Conrad	PHA	77
BARTLOW, John	FRA	309
BARTLY, Abraham	BER	222
James	PHI	92
John	BER	229
Margaret	BER	229
Richard	NOU	116
BARTNER, John	YOR	196
Ludk.	YOR	190
Peter	YOR	190
BARTO, Jacob	BER	256
William	YOR	162
BARTO?, Christian	MNT	61
BARTOLET, John	BER	229
BARTON, Abner	DEL	161
Adam	SOM	160
B.	PHI	8
Benjn. T.	PHA	80
David R.	LAN	30
Eden	DEL	161

BARTON, Edward	WAS	6
Elijah	BFD	48
George	BFD	55
James	WAY	143
James	DEL	161
John	WAS	19
John	NOU	127
John	LAN	182
Joseph	BUC	154
Joseph	CHE	723
Matthias	LAN	42
Samuel Jr.	MIF	4A
Samuel Senr.	MIF	4A
Silas	BUC	88
Thomas	LAN	47
Thomas	FAY	219
Thomas	BUC	84A
Thos.	BEV	10
William	GRN	87
William Esq.	LAN	30
BARTOW, Sarah	PHA	40
BARTRAAM, James	PHI	63
BARTRAM, Benjamin	DEL	167
Isaac Cenr.	PHA	19
Jane	BUC	103
John	PHI	64
John	DEL	169
Lewes	CUM	36
Moses	PHA	30
Thos.	PHA	35
Wm.	BER	212
BARTRAN, James	NOH	77A
BARTS, John	PHI	6
BARTY, Thomas	FAY	255
BARY, Peter	LAN	193
BASBIN?, Stephen	PHI	94A
BASCK, Chas. C.	PHI	21
BASE, Henry	MNT	137
Jacob	NOU	134
Valuntine	MNT	137
BASEHOUR, John	YOR	163
BASEY, Benj.	YOR	203
BASH, Jacob	BUT	336
John	WST	364
Martin	WST	305
Martin	WST	364
Valuntine	MNT	115
BASHFIEL,		
Fredrick	PHA	13
BASHINGTON,		
Richd.	PHI	133
BASHINS, Michael	CUM	28
BASINS, Thos.	NOU	162
BASKENS, William	DAU	10A
BASKET, Jos.	PHI	103
BASKINS, George	GRN	112
BASLER, Adam	DAU	38
John	LAN	186
Joseph	PHI	97A
Simon	DAU	38
BASLEY, John	BUC	92A
Jonathan	DAU	4
BASOR, Reedy	CUM	31
BASS, James	DAU	45
John	PHI	8
Mathw.	DAU	45A
Robert Doctr.	PHA	11
Wm.	PHA	119
BASSERMAN, John	ADA	38
Phillip	CUM	34
BASSEY, Henry		
Doct.	SOM	141
BASSLER, Henry	DAU	50
John	LAN	102
John	NOH	88A
Ulrich	NOH	55

BASSLER, Widow	NOH	72A
BASSON?, John	PHI	57
BAST, Dewalt	BER	210
John	BER	225
BASTAIN, George	PHI	52
BASTEN, Daniel	NOU	143
Elisha	NOU	143
BASTER, George	NOU	134
BASTIAN, Casper	BER	166
Dewald	LAN	245
Fredk.	DAU	52
Joseph	PHA	83
Michael	NOH	58
Michael Jnr.	NOH	58
BASTINS, John	NOU	162
BASTLER, Jacob	CHE	818
BASTO?, Christian	MNT	61
BASTON,		
Christopher	NOU	116
BATCHELLORS, Two	CHE	889
BATCHELOR, George	FAY	240
Isaac	PHA	99
Wm.	PHA	84
BATELOW, Wm.	LYC	14
BATEMAN, Abram	CHE	890
James	YOR	164
John	SOM	126
John	BUC	162
Thomas	HNT	129
William	YOR	217
Wm.	CHE	897
BATES, Widw.	PHI	91A
Austin	DEL	188
Benj.	PHI	103
Chrisr.	PHI	43
Frederick	BFD	47
Gershom	CHE	703
Huldah	LUZ	378
John	PHI	90A
Richard	DEL	159
Sarah	MNT	87
Solomon	LUZ	368
Stephen	LUZ	408
Thomas	MNT	87
Thos.	PHI	113A
William	LAN	85
BATES?, Martin	ADA	37
BATESON, Henry	HNT	133
BATH, Archibald	LUZ	349
BATHEL, John	WST	147
BATHER, John	DAU	10A
BATHERS, John	LAN	170
BATHWEL,		
Alexander	FAY	242
BATLER, Danl.	PHI	8
Danl.	PHI	82A
Noble	CHE	813
BATMAN, Henry	HNT	129
John	HNT	129
BATNER, John	LAN	259
Peter	LAN	258
BATON, Geo.	PHI	39
BATRICK, William	BER	190
BATSON, Thomas	PHA	96
BATT, Ansella	PHA	120
James	PHI	14
John	NOH	36A
Michael	MNT	80
Michael	MNT	85
Peter	NOH	37
Walter	CHE	799
BATTAN, John	LYC	8
John Junr.	LYC	8
BATTEICHER, Adam	BER	265
Conrad	BER	265
Jacob	BER	265

BATTEICHER, John	BER 265	BAUGHMAN, Peter	YOR 213	BAVER, Adam	LYC 15
Samuel	BER 265	Widow	LAN 247	BAVINGTON, John	PHI 149
BATTEMSTONE,		BAUGHT, Adam	BUT 327	BAVINSTINE, John	PHI 136
Christn.	DAU 20	BAUGMAN, Michael	LAN 307	BAWKER, John	PHI 104
BATTEN, Enoch	CHE 821	BAULDIN, John	ALL 89	BAWLEY, Nicholas	BFD 68
Henry	NOU 156	BAULT, John	LYC 23	BAWMAN, Isaac	MNT 98
James	CHE 828	BAULT?, John	LYC 27	John	LAN 269
Jas. Esqr.	CHE 821	BAUM, Abm.	LAN 259	BAX, Nicholas	NOH 83A
John	WAS 78	Daniel	DAU 19A	BAXTER, David	ADA 15
Mary	CHE 819	Danl.	BER 161	Elizabeth	MNT 34
BATTES, Elijah	PHA 13	Frederick	MIF 1	Francis	PHA 114
BATTIN, Marshall	CHE 758	Frederick	CRA 5	George	YOR 195
BATTO, Daniel	HNT 161	Henry	BUC 147	James	WAS 42
BATTON, John	PHI 28	Jacob	HNT 123	James	WAS 42
John	HNT 164	Jacob	YOR 183	James	LAN 246
Thomas	LAN 123	Jacob	FRA 289	Jas.	CUM 45
Thomas	FAY 243	Jacob	WST 341	Jno.	CUM 53
BATTON?, Samuel	HNT 131	John	CRA 5	John	MNT 37
BATTORFF, Banjn.	BER 151	John	HNT 123	John	LAN 61
Christn.	BER 152	John	BER 172	John	PHA 111
Christopher	BER 153	John	MIF 16A	John	WST 187
Henry	BER 153	John C.	BER 179	John	YOR 217
Hermanus	BER 265	Jonas	BER 136	John	LAN 244
John	BER 153	Joseph	DAU 18A	Margaret	PHA 109
Michl.	BER 151	Michael	BUC 156A	Peter	MNT 56
Michl.	BER 154	Michal	ALL 113	Philip	ADA 17
Rosena	BER 152	Peter	NOU 127	Richard	WAS 42
BATTS, Christian	FAY 225	Peter	YOR 183	Robert	NOU 191
George	FAY 225	Peter	WST 209	Robert	WST 249
John	FAY 225	Peter	MIF 16A	Samuel	WAS 42
BATTY, Jacob	BER 210	Philip	WAS 33	William	PHI 4
BATY, James	ALL 58	Philip	LAN 259	William	WST 187
James	ALL 100	Philip	BUC 104A	William	WST 188
Samuel	ALL 114	Samuel	NOU 126	William	YOR 217
Wilm.	ALL 68	BAUMAN, Abm.	BER 175	William	LAN 239
BATZ, Benedict	BER 256	Bernhart	NOH 83A	BAXTOR, Daniel	GRN 99
Daniel	BER 166	Chris.	LAN 84	John	GRN 99
Eve	BER 187	Christian	LAN 192	BAY, ----	PHI 17
John	DAU 51A	Daniel	LAN 192	Benjamin	WAS 27
BAUCHER,		Jacob	LAN 192	George	PHA 75
Christian	NOH 84A	Jno. Dicter	NOH 83A	Thomas	WAS 27
Peter	BER 277	John	DAU 41	Thomas	WAS 88
BAUCHMAN, Andrew	HNT 132	John	LAN 192	BAYARD, Adam	PHA 66
Christopher	HNT 132	Jost	NOH 83A	John	WAY 143
BAUDER, George	LAN 67	BAUMGARDNER,		BAYE, John	LAN 82
BAUDLER, Abm.	BUC 148A	Henry	BUT 329	BAYER, Jacob	MNT 69
BAUDRY, John	MIF 6	John	BFD 71	Jacob	NOU 182
BAUDWELL, Simon	ALL 78	Leonard	YOR 158	Jacob	LAN 215
BAUER, Albrecht	BER 190	BAUMGARNER, Jacob	ARM 126	Jacob Junr.	MNT 55
Gotlieb	NOH 55	Jacob	ARM 126	John	BER 135
Henry	NOH 55	BAUMGARTNER,		John	LAN 208
Michael	NOH 81A	Henry	YOR 194	Nicholas	BER 136
Peter	LAN 192	Jacob	YOR 194	Nicholas	LAN 194
BAUERMAN, Michael	NOH 84A	Jacob	YOR 218	William	BER 283
BAUFIT?, Jacob	BEV 25	Jno.	DAU 24A	BAYHAM, Robert	WAY 140
BAUGH, Widw.	PHI 102	Jno.	DAU 36A	BAYLEN, Justice	WAY 143
BAUGHER,		Leonard	YOR 154	BAYLES, Thomas	HNT 163
Frederick	ADA 33	Ph.	DAU 35	BAYLETS, Lawrence	CHE 858
George	ADA 33	BAURD?, John	DAU 40A	BAYLEY (CROSSED	
Michael	CRA 10	BAURENMASTER,		OUT), Amos	BUC 92A
Samuel	ADA 34	Andrew	LAN 82	BAYLEY, Amos	BUC 160A
BAUGHMAN, Abraham	WAS 108	BAUSER, John	SOM 136	Daniel	WAY 143
Adam	WAS 108	Peter	SOM 136	Deborah	BUC 92A
Christian	ADA 16	BAUSH, Abm.	PHA 35	Edward	BUC 92A
Christian	SOM 151	Henry	NOH 52A	Edward	BUC 98A
Christian	LAN 292	BAUSHER, Philip	BER 129	James	PHA 46
Christian I.	SOM 151	Whilliam	BER 129	James Capt.	PHA 124
Christopher	YOR 211	BAUSHMAN, John		Jane	PHA 102
David	SOM 151	Sr.	DAU 16	John	LAN 7
Francis	YOR 184	BAUSMAN, Andrew	LAN 103	John	BUC 100
Fredrick	ADA 30	Conrad	BER 223	John	BUC 149
George	LAN 248	John	LAN 30	Joseph	WAY 143
Jas. Sr.	CUM 48	William	LAN 35	Peter	NOU 120
John	DAU 18	BAUTCHER, Henry	BER 277	Samuel	BUC 98A
John	WAS 66	Jacob	BER 277	Thomas Jun.	LAN 6
John	YOR 213	BAUTER, Hannah	LAN 102	BAYLOR, Anthony	BER 175

20

BAYLOR, John	PHI	26	BEALOR, Bernard	BER	149	BEANS, Andrew	MER	433
BAYLY, George	NOU	120	John	BER	150	Aron	BUC	86
Robert	ALL	78	Mark	BER	150	Benjn.	BUC	98A
BAYMILLER, George	YOR	161	BEALS, Benjamin	HNT	116	David	BUC	86
Michael	YOR	204	William	MIF	16A	David	MER	433
BAYNE, Robert	PHA	72	BEALTY, Paul	NOU	103	Evan	BUC	137
BAYNTON, Peter	LAN	53	BEALY, Jno.	MIF	9A	Evan	BUC	153
BAYS, John	SOM	142	Nahan	ALL	69	Hugh	MER	433
Thomas	SOM	142	Nathan	MNT	130	Isaac	MNT	66
William	WAS	97	Wm.	MIF	9A	James	BUC	137
BAYS?, Robert	BER	209	BEAM, Adam	MNT	48	James	WST	209
BAYSON?, John	PHI	57	Christ	LAN	267	James	MER	433
BAYTY, John	FAY	255	Christian	GRN	94	Jesse	BUC	153
BAZAER, Robt.	PHI	119A	Christian	FRA	284	Jonathan	BUC	86
BEA, John	DAU	39A	Christopher	SOM	126	Joseph	BUC	144A
BEABOUT, Beaden	WAS	1	Elizabeth	PHI	79A	Mahlon	BUC	144A
Benjamin	WAS	26	George	BFD	42	Moses	BUC	86
Moses	WAS	11	Godleib	PHA	56	Nathan	BUC	153
Peter	WAS	11	Henry	SOM	156	Robert	MER	433
BEACH, Adam	NOH	46A	Jacob	SOM	126	Samuel	MER	433
Henry	NOU	98	Jacob	LAN	226	Thomas	BUC	153
John	NOU	99	Jacob	FRA	321	Thomas	MER	433
Nathan	LUZ	355	Jacob	CHE	721	William	BUC	86
Theran	LUZ	404	Jacob Jr.	DAU	40A	William	BUC	137
BEACHE, Richard	BUC	88A	John	LAN	166	William	MER	433
BEACHEM, Francis	BUC	92A	John	LAN	268	BEANY, Jacob	DAU	34
BEACHER, Thomas	LYC	10	John	FRA	284	BEAR, Abraham	LAN	193
BEACHEY, Abraham	LAN	219	John	LAN	289	Abraham	LAN	240
BEACHTLE, Daniel	MNT	56	Lewis	LYC	17	Abraham	LAN	242
George	MNT	56	M. Widow	LAN	6	Abrm.	DAU	19A
Isaac	MNT	56	Michael	LAN	268	Adam	ADA	11
John	MNT	133	Peter	BER	161	Adam	NOU	134
BEACKLEY, Daniel	PHA	72	Peter	LAN	268	Adam	WST	269
BEACON, Danl.	WST	209	Rudolph	DAU	40A	Andrew	LAN	174
BEADER, Henry	DAU	5	Samuel	BEV	19	Benjamin	LAN	186
BEADSWORTH,			BEAME, Abraham	NOH	29	Benjamin	LAN	314
Joseph	ALL	79	Isaac	MNT	42	Bernhart	BER	229
BEADY, Jacob	LUZ	415	BEAMEN, Michael	ADA	16	Catharine	CUM	117
BEAGER, James	LAN	236	BEAMER, Adnw.	PHI	63	Christian	LAN	303
BEAGLE, John	CUM	98	Andrew	PHA	65	Christn.	DAU	19
Wm. Senr.	CUM	98	John	CUM	146	Christopher	BEV	11
BEAHER, Samuel	ADA	29	John	WST	249	Daniel	YOR	191
William	ADA	29	William	WAS	26	David	LAN	80
BEAK, Elizabeth	CHE	903	BEAMESDERFER,			David	WST	209
BEAKAM, John	ADA	16	John Junr.	LAN	96	George	LAN	80
BEAKBILL,			BEAMONT, Hannah	PHA	94	George	LAN	80
Christopher	FRA	280	BEAN, Abraham	BUC	159	George	LAN	97
BEAKER, Henry	FRA	317	Abraham	BUC	158A	George	YOR	185
Peter	NOU	145	Andrew	FAY	230	George	WST	210
Saml.	FRA	322	Benj.	MNT	112	Henry	ADA	30
BEAKLEY, Mr.	PHA	79	Christn.	DAU	19A	Henry	NOU	103
BEAKNER, Adam	FRA	305	Daniel	BER	247	Henry	BER	150
BEAL, Benjn.	FAY	230	Elias	GRN	111	Henry	YOR	170
Isaac	FAY	243	Enoch	MNT	44	Henry	WST	210
Jacob	FAY	230	Enoch	GRN	87	Henry	LAN	307
John	BUC	86	George	FRA	298	Isaac	ADA	28
Joseph	BUC	86	Henry	MNT	80	Jacob	ADA	29
Ludwig	DAU	19A	Henry	MNT	127	Jacob	CUM	38
Pennal	PHA	83	Henry Junr.	MNT	127	Jacob	CUM	131
Philip	CEN	20	Jacob	DAU	50A	Jacob	LAN	159
William	DAU	46	Jacob	BUC	158A	Jacob	YOR	185
BEALE, Abner	MIF	4A	James	MNT	80	Jacob	WST	210
David	MIF	4A	Jesse	MNT	69	James	WST	321
John	MIF	4A	Jesse	GRN	111	John	DAU	4
John	MIF	6A	John	DAU	45	John	ADA	26
Peter	MIF	6A	John	FRA	304	John	CUM	26
Tho. Esq.	MIF	6A	Mordcai	GRN	111	John	BFD	61
William	MIF	6A	Moses	GRN	79	John	LAN	75
BEALER, George	DAU	43	Oliver	LAN	217	John	LAN	145
Peter	BUC	100A	Paul	NOU	120	John	BER	150
BEALL, Colmore?	WAS	36	Stephen	MNT	34	John	HNT	153
Reasin	WAS	78	William	GRN	67	John	LAN	159
Thomas	WAS	36	William	SOM	133	John	YOR	166
Zephaniah Esqr.	WAS	36	BEANET, Anthony	NOH	75	John	YOR	185
Zephaniah Junr.	WAS	36	BEANEY, Jacob	FAY	219	John	FRA	323
BEALON, Anthony	ALL	53	BEANS, Alexander	MER	433	Joseph	FRA	316

BEAR, Margaret	WST 270	BEASORE, Peter	FRA 315	BEATY, Thomas	WST 340
Margaret	LAN 304	BEATEA, George	PHA 94	Walter	FRA 272
Maria	LAN 303	BEATES, Christian	BFD 42	William	PHI 36
Martin	BFD 56	Sarah	PHA 67	William	ADA 37
Martin	LAN 97	BEATEY, Mary	PHA 105	William	ERI 57
Martin	LAN 159	Samuel	PHA 92	William	DEL 186
Martin	LAN 160	BEATHEL, George	MNT 98	William	FAY 264
Martin	LAN 170	George Junr.	MNT 103	William	LAN 299
Martin	LAN 307	BEATONS?, Saml.	BER 161	William	MIF 24A
Michael	ADA 13	BEATS, Andw.	YOR 187	BEAUMAN, Joseph	BUC 103
Michael	BFD 36	Christopher	FRA 279	BEAUMONT, John	BUC 151
Michael	LAN 38	Conrad	FRA 279	Ricd.	WST 284
Michael	BFD 56	Edward	YOR 160	William	DEL 179
Michl.	CUM 64	Urban	FRA 279	BEAUTZ, William	YOR 209
Michl.	FRA 323	BEATTEY, Robt.	CUM 29	BEAUVAIS, Peter	PHA 96
Nicholas	ADA 11	BEATTY, David	FRA 319	BEAVANS, Joseph	PHA 17A
Nicholas	BFD 56	Edward	HNT 149	BEAVARD, Robert	BEV 11
Peter	NOU 103	Elizabeth	PHA 108	BEAVENOUR,
Rudolph	DAU 22	Gawin	DAU 2A	Anthony	YOR 177
Saml.	CUM 32	Henry	FRA 292	BEAVER, Anthony	HNT 126
Saml.	CUM 103	James	CUM 124	Devault	CHE 829
Saml.	WST 209	John	ARM 125	Dewald	BER 225
Widow	LAN 80	John	HNT 149	Dewald Jr.	BER 225
William	YOR 210	John	FRA 299	George	FRA 280
BEARA, Christian	FRA 284	John	FRA 300	George	CHE 831
BEARBOWER, Casper	YOR 209	John	WST 321	Jacob	NOU 191
BEARD, Widow	PHI 40	John	WST 364	Jacob	BER 229
Adam	BER 247	Joseph	CUM 137	Jacob	FRA 306
Alexander	PHA 111	Roboert	WST 209	John	BER 225
Alexr.	WST 364	Robt.	WST 286	John Jr.	BER 225
Amos	BER 247	Samuel	PHI 46	Michael	NOU 134
Casper	PHA 75	Samuel	HNT 134	Nicholas	FRA 305
David	LAN 153	Thomas	BEV 18	BEAVERLIN, James	WST 269
Elijah	BER 247	William	ARM 127	BEAVERS, Jane	BEV 23
Francis	BUC 154	William	HNT 162	John	BEV 22
George	CEN 22	Wm.	CUM 22	BEAVINS, Wilder	MNT 56
Henry	BER 161	Wm.	CUM 121	BEAVR, John	LYC 16
Hugh	MIF 1	Wm.	FRA 300	BEBERSON, Conrad	YOR 206
James	NOH 66	Wm. Esqr.	CUM 28	BEBIGHISER, John	BUC 90A
James	NOU 156	BEATY, Abraham	NOU 126	BEBOUT, Ebinezer	FAY 254
James Jr.	NOH 66	Abram	CHE 726	BEBY, William	PHI 22
Jerry?	PHI 30	Alexander	ERI 57	BECACUN?, Thos.	FRA 299
John	BEV 11	Benjn.	ADA 38	BECAL, George	NOU 162
John	SOM 145	Catherine	FRA 275	BECHEL, Charles	BFD 49
John	LAN 168	Ebenezer	BUT 364	BECHEN, Jacob	YOR 178
John	WST 209	Hugh	ERI 57	BECHER, Jacob	DAU 32A
John	FAY 242	Hugh	NOU 127	Philip	LAN 91
John Esqr.	WST 305	James	NOU 99	BECHETL, Jacob	BFD 36
John	MIF 14A	James	WAS 118	BECHEY, George	NOH 29
John	MIF 24A	James	DEL 162	BECHT, John	LAN 107
Mathew	PHA 73	James	DEL 181	BECHTEL, Abraham	BER 207
Nichs.	PHI 93A	James	DEL 181	Abraham Jr.	BER 207
Robert	FAY 235	James	YOR 201	Christian	BER 172
Robert	LAN 311	John	CRA 4	Daniel	NOH 88A
Thomas	NOH 66	John	WAS 19	David	NOH 29
Wm.	MIF 14A	John	WAS 27	Enry	BER 179
BEARDLY?, Robt.	PHI 81A	John	WAS 88	Frederick	BER 190
BEARDNEFF, George	DAU 30A	John	NOU 127	Isaac	BER 166
BEARE, Michael	GRN 75	John	YOR 157	Jacob	NOH 39
BEAREY, Christian	CHE 890	John	MIF 14A	Jacob	PHA 48
Widow	CHE 897	John	MIF 24A	Jacob	BER 166
BEARINER, David	LAN 67	Joseph	WAS 88	Jacob	BER 179
BEARRER, Diedk.	DAU 41A	Margaret	CHE 815	Jacob	BER 179
BEARS, Mary	PHA 6	Mary	BFD 35	Jacob	BER 182
BEARY, Jacob	CHE 896	Mrs.	NOU 126	John	MNT 62
BEASER, John	CUM 32	Patrick	LAN 88	John	BER 179
BEASHORE, David	FRA 296	Patrick	FRA 273	John	BER 229
John	FRA 297	Reading	BUC 92A	Martin	BER 207
BEASON, Henrey	FAY 255	Robert	BUC 151	Peter	BER 179
Henry	CUM 63	Robert	CHE 816	Peter Jr.	BER 179
Jacob	FAY 255	Robt.	VEN 169	Samuel	YOR 184
Jacob Jun.	FAY 252	Saml.	LYC 25	BECHTLE, Jacob	MNT 133
Jesse	FAY 252	Saml.	CHE 821	John	BER 162
William	FAY 201	Susannah	CHE 817	BECHTLER, (No
BEASOR, George	FRA 316	Thomas	WAS 27	Given Name)	LAN 182
BEASORE, Avam	FRA 315	Thomas	DEL 161	BECHTOL, John	LAN 193

BECHTOL, Joseph	LAN	271	BECKET, Humphrey	BFD	68	BEEM?, Ferdr.	FRA	321
BECHTOLD, Abm.	BER	284	Humphry	BFD	55	BEEMAN, George	BFD	61
Fredk.	BER	175	James	WAS	6	Moses	BFD	68
Jacob	BER	284	John	FRA	288	William	BFD	61
BECK, Adam	PHA	73	Samuel	FAY	263	BEEN, Abraham	ALL	85
Andrew	NOH	89	Wm.	FRA	288	Abraham	DAU	26A
Andw.	DAU	34	BECKING,			Adam	MNT	113
Cathrine	PHA	99	Frederick	MNT	137	Conrad	MNT	113
Chris. H.	NOH	69A	BECKLEY, Danl.	PHI	69	John	DAU	16
Christopher	ALL	60	Danl.	BER	256	John	ALL	113
Conrad	BER	135	BECKLY, Adam	BUC	148A	John (Bla.)	MNT	113
Daniel	PHI	126	George	DAU	29	John (Shoe.)	MNT	113
Elizh.	PHA	39	Isaac	PHI	66A	BEEN?, (See Bun)	NOU	191
Frederick	NOH	29	Jacob	PHI	90A	Jacob	MNT	113
Geo.	CUM	38	BECKS, John	LYC	19	William	MNT	69
George	LAN	65	Peter	LAN	192	BEER, Abraham	NOH	62
George	PHA	90	BECKTEL, Abraham	MNT	72	Adam	NOH	85
George	PHA	120	BECKUM, John	LAN	190	Adam (See Beer,		
George Jr.	YOR	160	BECKWITH,			Widow)	NOH	49A
George Senr.	YOR	160	Archibald	SOM	137	Amos (See Beer,		
George	NOH	58A	David	BFD	43	Widow)	NOH	49A
George	NOH	70A	Henry	MER	435	David	LUZ	355
Henry	PHA	35	Sirus	MER	435	Enoch	NOH	49A
Henry	LAN	64	BECOUEN?, George	FRA	299	Henry	LAN	174
Henry	NOH	70A	BECOVEN?, Allen	FRA	319	Isaac	NOH	83A
Henry	PHI	71A	John	FRA	319	Jesse	NOH	49A
Isaah	PHI	68A	BECTAL, George	PHI	95	John	BEV	11
Jacob	PHA	31	BEDDOLT, Maths.	BER	284	John	NOH	83A
Jacob	NOH	64	BEDDY, Widw.	PHI	105A	Jonathan	NOH	83A
Jacob	PHI	103	BEDFORD, Gunning	PHA	122	Joshua	BEV	12
Jacob	SOM	137	Jacob	LUZ	338	Martin	LAN	172
Jacob	BER	190	John	PHA	7	Peter	LAN	39
Jacob	YOR	194	Nathaniel	ALL	53	Peter	LAN	43
John	PHA	16	Thos.	PHA	28	Rachel	MIF	6A
John	LAN	66	Thos.	PHI	105A	Robert	BEV	27
John	LAN	94	BEDKIN, Widw.	PHI	114A	Saml.	CEN	20
John	PHI	110	BEDWELL, Thos.	PHA	65	Thomas	NOH	64
John	PHI	126	BEE, Elizabeth	PHA	87	Widow Of Adam	NOH	49A
John	SOM	137	Jonathan	PHI	64	Widow Of Amos	NOH	49A
John	BER	187	BEEATES, Thos.	CUM	82	William	NOH	49A
John	YOR	194	BEEBE, Clark	LUZ	320	Wilm.	ALL	111
John	BER	282	Eliphalet	ERI	55A	BEERBOWER, Harman	CHE	788
John	DAU	16A	Lemuel	LUZ	322	Henry	YOR	209
John Martin	LAN	48	Timothy	LUZ	320	Philip	YOR	176
Michael	DEL	155	BEEBOUT, Samuel	WAS	66	BEERY, Nicholas	GRN	79
Michael	DEL	156	BEEBY, Wm.	PHA	56	BEESLY, John	PHI	133
Nathaniel	LAN	44	BEECH, Charles	WAS	97	BEESY, Jacob	BUC	158A
Paul	PHA	17A	BEECHAM, James	WAS	48	BEET?, Henry	FRA	313
Peter	LAN	66	BEECHER, John	ADA	20	BEETLE?, (See		
Philip Jr.	DAU	51	BEECHOLD, Borrick	CHE	908	Butle)	DEL	175
Philip Sr.	DAU	51	BEECHTEL, Adam	CHE	726	BEGER, William	LAN	140
Phillip	CUM	128	BEECKLEY, John	SOM	136	BEGG, Frederick	NOU	182
Saml.	CEN	18A	BEED?, Thomas	ALL	102	BEGGS, Alexr.	CEN	22
Thony	MIF	6A	BEEDLER?, Thomas	MNT	130	David	MNT	65
Widow	NOH	70A	BEEGE?, Michael	LAN	98	BEHEL, John	HNT	121
Wm. W.	PHI	46	BEEHER?, (See			Martin	HNT	121
BECK?, George	YOR	180	Becher)	LAN	91	BEHEY?, Peter		
BECKEERN?, Widow	LAN	281	BEEK?, (See			Esqr.	NOH	62
BECKEL, Rudy	DAU	41	Beck?)	YOR	180	BEHLE, David	BER	129
BECKER, Andrew	LAN	316	BEEKER, Henry	NOH	35	Frantz	BER	129
Christn.	DAU	27	Nicholas	NOH	49A	Frederick	BER	129
Conrad	DAU	8	BEEKERN?, Widow	LAN	281	Martin	BER	129
D. Jacob	NOH	58	BEEL, Nicholas	SOM	151	BEHLER, Catharine	YOR	165
Daniel	LAN	192	Philip	SOM	151	Christn.	BER	283
Frederick	LAN	207	BEELER, Anthony	BER	178	John	YOR	161
Godlib	NOH	58A	Catherine	WAS	42	John	YOR	188
Henry	LAN	271	Dieter	LAN	254	John	YOR	217
Henry	LAN	313	Elizab.	DAU	21A	BEHLY, Abraham	BER	277
Jackob	DAU	8A	Frantz	DAU	43	Abraham	NOH	52A
Jacob	DAU	51	Joseph	WAS	73	BEHM, Abm.	BER	256
Jacob	LAN	178	Mary	WAS	73	Adam	BER	150
John	LAN	192	BEELL, Widow	PHI	114	Elizabeth	BER	247
Martin	LAN	193	BEELOR, Frederick	MNT	98	Jacob	LAN	22
Peter	LAN	267	BEELY, Fredrik	DAU	43	Margaret	YOR	154
Peter Jur.	LAN	267	BEEM, Abraham	LAN	172	Michael	LAN	145
William	NOH	47	Mary	HNT	122	Peter	BER	247

BEHM, Rudy	LAN 145	BELL, Widow	YOR 209	BELL, John	HNT 157
BEHMER, Henry	BER 150	(Ink Smear)	HNT 125	John	LAN 160
Valentine	BER 150	(No Given Name)	LAN 148	John	VEN 169
BEHNEY, John	DAU 50A	Aaron	BEV 5	John	FAY 219
John	DAU 51A	Aaron	GRN 99	John	WST 233
Melchor	DAU 48	Alexander	WAS 51	John	FRA 313
BEHR, Jacob	NOH 44	Alexander	HNT 160	John	WST 340
Peter	NOH 44	Andrew	WAS 48	John	WST 341
BEHTEL, Abm.	BUC 147	Andrew	WAS 118	John	BUT 363
John	BUC 147	Andrew Esqr.	HNT 149	John	WST 364
Philip	DAU 7	Andw.	CUM 135	John Junr.	HNT 157
Widow	BUC 147	Anisimus	GRN 99	John	DAU 13A
BEHUNA, John	PHA 87	Arther	LYC 25	Jonathan	BER 137
BEIBER, John	BER 256	Arthur	HNT 157	Joseph	LAN 14
BEIDELMAN, David	NOH 66	Arthur	NOU 186	Joseph	WAS 15
Elias	NOH 29	Arthur	MIF 24A	Joseph	BFD 36
Elias	NOH 79A	Benjamin	GRN 99	Joseph	CHE 884
Valentine	NOH 29	Cathr. Widow	LAN 15	Lewis	BUC 161A
BEIDLER, George	NOH 39	Charles	WAS 15	Mary	GRN 98
Henry	NOH 70A	Christn.	PHI 88A	Mary	DEL 169
John	BER 207	David	BFD 49	Nathaniel	GRN 99
John	BER 247	David	CUM 54	Paterson	LAN 166
BEIDLER?, Peter	BER 172	David	YOR 209	Peter	PHI 45
BEIGHLEY, Jacob	SOM 136	Ebenezer	YOR 208	Reese	CHE 855
Jacob	BUT 329	Edwerd	DEL 188	Reuben	LYC 13
Joseph	SOM 136	Elisha	LUZ 383	Richard	LAN 119
Michael	SOM 136	Elizh.	FRA 316	Richard	FAY 242
BEIGHLY, Conrad	WST 248	Ephraim	BEV 15	Richd.	PHI 87
Henry	BUT 346	Esau	BEV 5	Robert	WAS 6
Jno.	BUT 346	George	WAS 78	Robert	DAU 34
Peter	BUT 347	George	NOU 174	Robert	WAS 73
BEIGHT, Emanuel	MIF 3	George	NOU 186	Robert	ALL 107
Frederick	MIF 3	George	WST 364	Robert	GRN 109
BEIGLER, John A.	BER 260	Hamilton	WAS 6	Robert	WST 232
BEIGNOR, Peter	ADA 36	Hannah	DEL 169	Robert	WST 286
BEILER, Peter	CRA 18	Hugh	BEV 26	Robert	WST 306
BEINDER, Peter	ADA 35	Hugh	FAY 207	Robert	LAN 147A
BEINHAIT?, Ulrich	YOR 187	Isaac	BEV 15	Robt.	CUM 55
BEINHART, Yost	YOR 175	Isaiah	PHI 122	Saml.	CUM 42
BEIR, John	LAN 173	Issabella	CUM 92	Saml.	BER 235
BEIRLY, Henry	BER 241	Jacob	WAS 97	Saml.	BUT 354
BEISHER, Philip	NOH 37	James	BEV 6	Saml.	MIF 9A
BEISLY, George	BER 252	James	WAS 6	Samuel	DAU 22
Michael	NOH 77A	James	ADA 19	Samuel	PHI 27
BEISSEL,		James	CUM 27	Samuel	FAY 235
Frederick	NOH 81A	James	CUM 42	Samuel	FAY 261
Peter	NOH 70A	James	CUM 54	Samuel	CHE 880
BEISSERT,		James	ALL 59	Simeon	BEV 18
Christn.	NOH 69A	James	CUM 62	Stephen	LYC 15
BEITZEL, John	FRA 297	James	CUM 83	Thomas	WAS 15
Jonathan	YOR 175	James	GRN 99	Thomas	CEN 20
Jonathan Jr.	YOR 175	James	ALL 107	Thomas	HNT 145
Lorence	YOR 175	Jame	DAU 0	Thomas	WST 148
BEIVER, Abm.	BER 256	James	PHI 122	Thomas	HNT 157
BEKER, Fredrik	DAU 10	James	HNT 157	Thomas	FAY 234
George	DAU 31	James	BER 236	Thomas	MER 435
George	DAU 31	James	BUT 344	Thomas Capt.	PHA 95
John	DAU 31	James	CHE 864	Thos.	DAU 18
BEKET, Joseph		James	MIF 4A	Walter	CUM 135
Esqr.	ALL 77	Jno. Senr.	CEN 21A	William	PHA 14
BEKIL?, Jacob	MIF 6A	John	DAU 10	William	WAS 15
BEKTEL, Abm.	BUC 148A	John	BEV 18	William	PHI 22
BEKTEL?, (See		John	CUM 27	William	GRN 99
Behtell)	BUC 147	John	WAS 48	William	LAN 108
BELANCHE, Samuel		John	WAS 88	William	WST 248
B.	PHA 14	John	ALL 90	William	WST 341
BELCHER, John	LUZ 385	John	CUM 93	William	MER 435
BELER, George	NOU 103	John	GRN 99	William	MER 436
George	LAN 250	John	CUM 100	William Esq.	MIF 6A
BELETEA, John	PHA 94	Joh	DAU 0	William	ERI 55A
BELEW, Nathanl.	PHI 152	John	ALL 120	Wm.	BEV 23
Rebecca	PHI 153	John	SOM 126	Wm.	PHA 74
BELFERT, Abraham	NOH 83A	John	HNT 130	Wm.	PHA 81
BELICK, Anthony	NOU 162	John	HNT 134	Wm. (Samuel	
BELKNAP, Jonathen	ERI 58	John	HNT 149	Crossed Out)	BER 235
BELL, Widow	PHI 88	John	HNT 149	Wm.	CUM 113

BELL, Wm.	CUM 114	
Wm.	PHA 118	
Wm.	CUM 128	
Zachariah	CHE 872	
BELL?, Catherine	BER 211	
George	ARM 122	
BELLAS, Thomas	LUZ 388	
BELLES, Henry	DAU 7	
Hugh	NOU 142	
Peter	DAU 7	
William	DAU 7	
BELLET, Baltzer	YOR 168	
John	YOR 168	
BELLETOR, Joseph	FAY 263	
BELLIG, Magdelena	BER 187	
Regina	BER 187	
BELLING,		
Gottfried	NOH 69A	
BELLINGER, Fredr.	FRA 305	
George	FRA 305	
Jacob	PHA 63	
Michael	ADA 16	
BELLIS, George	NOU 146	
BELLISFELT,		
Conrad	NOH 41	
David	NOH 41	
George	NOH 41	
Henry	NOH 41	
Jacob	NOH 41	
John	NOH 35	
William	NOH 41	
William	NOH 41	
BELLMAN, Conrad	BER 137	
Dewalt	BER 277	
George	BER 265	
George Jr.	BER 265	
Susanna	BER 265	
BELLOS, Cornelius	LUZ 345	
BELLOWS, Robert	HNT 133	
BELLS, Henry	BFD 49	
Philip	PHI 1	
BELLWOOD, John	ALL 112	
BELMAN, George	BER 236	
Peter	BER 283	
BELONEY, William	FAY 249	
BELOW, John	PHI 96A	
BELSHOVER, Jacob	ALL 99	
BELSTERLING,		
Jacob	PHI 91A	
BELT, John	WAS 42	
BELTNER, Jacob	CUM 57	
BELTZ, Andrew	BFD 53	
Christian	NOU 99	
Christopher	NOU 120	
Jacob	MNT 89	
John	YOR 181	
John	NOH 83A	
Leonard	NOH 83A	
Michael	NOH 75	
BELTZ?, (See		
Bettz?)	WAS 66	
BELTZER, Adam	FRA 316	
Jacob	YOR 194	
BELTZHOOVER,		
Conrad	YOR 176	
Michael	YOR 173	
BELTZNER,		
Elizabeth	YOR 158	
BELY, Peter	BER 283	
BELYFELT, Chuster	NOU 97	
BELZER, G.		
Ludwick	MNT 125	
BEMAN, Ebenezer	LUZ 400	
Nathan	LUZ 396	
Timothy	LUZ 398	
BEMER, Adam	NOU 173	

BEMER?, Willm.	PHI 75	
BEMOND, Joseph	PHI 2	
Joseph (Crossed		
Out)	PHI 2	
BEMONT, Benjamin	CHE 700	
BEMOUNT, Joseph	CHE 702	
Thomas	CHE 700	
Thomas	CHE 700B	
Wilm.	ALL 93	
BEN, (Black)	CHE 705	
BENADE, Benedict	NOH 69A	
BENAGE, George	NOU 197	
George	NOU 197	
John	NOU 197	
Simon	NOU 197	
BENATUM, Peter	LAN 178	
BENCE, John	LAN 301	
Peter	LAN 267	
BENCHOOF, Paul	SOM 156	
BENCK, Samuel	LAN 92	
BENCSEN?, (See		
Benusen)	LAN 72	
BENDEN, James	CHE 731	
BENDER, Abraham	YOR 190	
Christian	NOH 72A	
Conrad	ADA 16	
Conrad	NOH 72A	
Enrst	LAN 43	
George	LAN 17	
George	LAN 103	
George	SOM 136	
Godfry	PHI 120A	
Henry	ADA 16	
Henry	HNT 128	
Henry	SOM 133	
Henry	LAN 147	
Jacob	PHI 77	
Jacob	PHI 87	
Jacob	LAN 258	
Jacob	LAN 264	
Jacob	BER 272	
Jacob Junr.	NOH 72A	
Jacob	NOH 72A	
John	LAN 17	
John	MNT 60	
John	PHI 98	
John Esqr.	ADA 16	
Jos.	PHI 101A	
Leonard	LAN 38	
Lewis	PHI 105A	
Martin	NOH 72A	
Melchior	NOH 86A	
Michael	ADA 17	
Michael	ADA 35	
Michael	LAN 43	
Old	DAU 36	
Peter	NOH 72A	
Val.	BER 151	
William	LAN 16	
Willm.	PHI 72	
BENDERMAN?, Wm. &		
Jr.	MNT 137	
BENEDICK, Abraham	FRA 307	
George	YOR 175	
Jacob	FRA 307	
John	FRA 307	
Leonard	LAN 46	
BENEDICT, George	LUZ 363	
John	LUZ 363	
Philip	LAN 277	
BENEDUM, Geo.	CUM 102	
BENEKE, George	PHA 44	
BENELL, James	SOM 153	
BENER, Adam	DAU 6A	
John	DAU 12A	
Joseph	DAU 3A	

BENER, Nicolaus	DAU 6	
BENESS, Christian	FAY 240	
BENESTER, James	FAY 254	
BENETUM?, John	BER 190	
BENEZET, Ann	BUC 88A	
Samuel	BUC 88A	
BENFIELD, Jacob	NOH 88A	
John	NOH 44	
Samuel	NOH 88A	
BENFORD, George	NOU 134	
George	NOU 134	
Samuel	SOM 126	
BENGER, Thomas	PHI 134	
Timothy	PHI 105A	
BENGLER, Peter	NOU 143	
BENHAM, Ezekia	ALL 74	
BENHEIMER, John	NOU 134	
BENINGHOVE, Jacob		
Cenr.	PHA 17A	
Jacob Junr.	PHA 20	
Philip	BER 129	
BENIT, Benjamen	NOU 162	
Benjamin	CRA 4	
BENIZETT, Anthy.	MNT 34	
BENJAMIN, Isaac	LUZ 339	
Taft	CHE 795	
Wm.	LYC 7	
BENJAMINS,		
Richard	LUZ 415	
BENKES, Henry	MNT 97	
BENKIS, Peter	MNT 60	
Peter	MNT 94	
BENKOOF, Christ.	FRA 304	
BENKUS, George	NOH 52A	
BENLY, Hannah	PHI 106	
BENN, Henry	CEN 20	
Henry	CEN 22	
BENNEN, John	PHI 120A	
BENNER, Abraham	MNT 125	
Abraham	BUC 81A	
Abram	CHE 793	
Christian	ADA 10	
Christian	MNT 47	
Christian	MNT 124	
Christian	PHI 126	
Christian	NOU 127	
Christian	CHE 891	
Christian	CHE 898	
Conrad	BUC 160	
Daniel	CHE 895	
Daniel	BUC 158A	
Geo.	PHI 76A	
George	BFD 71	
George	PHI 149	
George	BUC 81A	
Hannah	PHA 88	
Hanry	BUC 158A	
Henry	CEN 20	
Henry	PHI 149	
Henry	FRA 304	
Henry	CHE 751	
Henry	CHE 794	
Henry	CHE 890	
Henry Jn.	BUC 158A	
Isaac	PHI 126	
Jacob	PHA 41	
Jacob	BFD 71	
Jacob	MNT 110	
Jacob	BUC 160	
Jacob	NOU 162	
Jacob	CHE 726	
Jacob	BUC 158A	
John	CEN 20	
John	PHA 56	
John	BFD 68	
John	MNT 89	

BENNER, John	PHI	149	BENNET, Titus	PHA	39	BENSINGER, Jacob	BER	157
John	CHE	908	Wilber	LUZ	321	BENSLEY, Israel	WAY	148
John	BUC	158A	William	BFD	49	William	WAY	148
John	BUC	158A	William	BUC	137	BENSON, Adam	PHI	115
Ludwick	MNT	126	William	LUZ	348	Benj.	YOR	193
Ludwick	BUC	158A	Wilm.	ALL	51	Flalwood	HNT	119
Matths.	PHI	53A	BENNETT, Abel	PHI	88	Flalwood	HNT	136
Peter	MNT	67	Archd.	PHI	54	Isaac	ERI	60A
Peter	PHI	53A	Benjn.	CUM	34	James	ARM	125
Peter	PHI	74A	Enoch	CHE	866	James	YOR	190
Peter	NOH	79A	Gersham	WST	284	James	FRA	323
Philip	CEN	22	Isaac	WST	286	Thos.	FRA	279
Sebastian	MNT	126	Isaac	CHE	706	Wilm.	ALL	60
BENNER?, Charles	DAU	29A	Jacob	DEL	157	BENT, Andw.	YOR	188
BENNET, Widow	PHI	76	Jacob	CHE	811	Michael	YOR	162
Aaron	BUC	137	James	DEL	161	BENTER, Andrew	BER	147
Aaron	LUZ	418	James	WST	187	Benjamin	DAU	28A
Abigal	PHA	111	James	CHE	706	George	BER	148
Abm.	CUM	123	James	CHE	809	George	BER	148
Abraham	BUC	144A	John	PHA	80	Jacob	DAU	51A
Amos	LUZ	404	Jos.	YOR	219	John	BER	269
Amos	LUZ	415	Joseph	BFD	48	Michael	LAN	283
Andrew	LUZ	336	Martha	LUZ	338	William	BER	147
Anthy.	PHI	106	Robert	PHI	55	Zach.	NOH	68A
Arthur	BUC	162	Silas	CHE	808	BENTLEY, Alice	CHE	771
Benajah	LUZ	393	Thomas	DAU	4	Benjamin	MER	435
Charles	LUZ	319	Thomas	PHI	30	Davis	MER	435
Danl.	PHI	83A	Thomas	DEL	191	George	WAS	108
Elias	CUM	85	Thos.	CUM	24	Henry	DEL	158
Elisha	LUZ	348	William	PHI	14	Jane	WAS	66
George	BUC	149	William	WST	167	Jesse	CHE	750
George	LUZ	385	William	CHE	700B	Joseph	WAS	66
Henry	LAN	47	Wm.	CHE	766	Joshua	MER	436
Henry	BFD	61	BENNETT?, (See			William	LUZ	427
Henry	LUZ	346	Bonnett)	BFD	71	Wm.	CUM	147
Henry	BUC	144A	BENNETTE, Widow	PHI	85	BENTLY, Abel	ALL	89
Isaac	BUC	86	BENNIGHOFF,			Jeffery	MER	435
Isaac	BUC	137	Frederick	NOH	85	Mary	WST	321
Isaac	SOM	137	John	NOH	52A	Ohn	PHI	86
Isaac	BUC	143	Philip	NOH	52A	Sashbezzar?	WAS	108
Isaac	LUZ	346	Valentine	NOH	52A	Sebastian	LAN	89
Ishmael	LUZ	328	BENNINGER,			BENTSLEY, John	LUZ	426
Ishmael Jr.	LUZ	365	Catherine	LAN	313	BENTY, Wm.	PHI	86
Jacob	PHA	121	Henry	ADA	24	BENTZ, Andw.	YOR	189
Jacob	FAY	212	Jacob	NOH	49A	Fredk.	YOR	181
Jacob	LUZ	345	John	WST	167	George	YOR	157
Jacob	BUC	88A	Ulrich	NOH	44	George	YOR	170
James	LYC	21	Widow	NOH	83A	Henry	YOR	155
James	MIF	6A	BENNINGHOVE,			Jacob	LAN	192
John	LYC	20	Fredrick	DEL	182	John	YOR	205
John	BFD	54	BENNINGTON, John	WAS	54	Nicholas	YOR	189
John	BUC	100	BENNIS, Thomas	PHA	117	Peter	YOR	174
John	LAN	102	BENNIT, Abraham	ALL	82	Peter	LAN	192
John	BUC	104	Benjamin	MER	434	BENTZLEY, Casper	YOR	179
John	BUC	137	John	MER	433	BENUSEN, John	LAN	72
John	BUC	137	Leven	ALL	59	BENWARD, Daniel	NOH	66
John	BUC	146	Peter	ALL	62	Isaac	NOH	66
John	LUZ	388	Samuel	ALL	85	BEOCK, Jacob	CUM	22
John	LUZ	415	William	MER	434	BEOHM, Daniel	PHA	31
John	LUZ	417	Wilm.	ALL	102	BEOM, David	LAN	180
John Jn.	BUC	137	BENNY, John	ALL	107	BER---?, Lewis	WAR	1A
Joseph	WAS	61	Peter	BER	272	BERCAW, Abraham	ADA	21
Joseph	BUC	94	BENS, Christn.	BER	148	George	ADA	21
Joseph Jr.	BFD	49	BENSCOTER,			George Jun.	ADA	19
Joshua	LUZ	341	Anthony	LUZ	363	Peter	ADA	26
Mathias	BUC	137	John	LUZ	350	BERCKENSTOCK,		
Moses	LUZ	375	Solomon	LUZ	366	John	NOH	55
Oliver	LUZ	346	BENSEL, Engle	PHI	130	BERCKERMER,		
Robert	BFD	49	George	PHI	125	George	MNT	115
Robert	LUZ	321	BENSELL, Jonathan	PHI	106A	BERDINE, Samuel	BUC	151
Rufus	LUZ	328	BENSINGER, Ann	BER	172	BERE, George	NOU	143
Samuel	PHA	103	Daniel	BER	155	BERELY, Michl.	FRA	298
Sarah	PHA	95	Frederick	BER	157	BERENCE, Henry	LAN	27
Simon	PHI	153	George	BER	157	BEREY, James	ERI	56
Simon	FAY	212	Henry	FRA	294	BERFIELD,		
Stephen	WAY	140	Jacob	BER	157	Benjamin	CRA	13

BERFUSON,			BERKEY, John	SOM	156	BERNHARD, Samuel	LAN	313
Ebenezer	CHE	846	John	DAU	15A	BERNHART, Charles	BER	211
BERG, Christian	LAN	290	Joseph	SOM	156	Christopher	BER	261
David	LAN	312	Joseph	SOM	156	Fredk.	BER	214
Dietrich	NOH	66	Samuel	SOM	126	Herman	DAU	44A
Jacob	LAN	103	Samuel	SOM	156	Jacob	BER	211
BERGEN, George	BUC	83A	Susanna	SOM	126	John	BER	245
Isaac	MNT	125	BERKHEIMER,			John	DAU	46A
BERGENTROFF?, Wm.	DAU	40A	(Blank)	MNT	89	Joseph	LAN	21
BERGENTROST?, Wm.	DAU	40A	Henry	YOR	179	Samuel	BER	245
BERGER, Adam	DAU	5A	Valentine	YOR	179	Wendel	BER	136
Andrew	NOU	134	BERKHEISER,			BERNHEISEL,		
Boston	NOU	134	Christopher	NOU	120	Samuel	BER	276
Catherine	BER	281	George	BER	221	BERNHISEL, John	BER	190
Christian	NOH	66	BERKHOLDER,			BERNINGER, Maths.	BER	175
Christian	NOU	126	Ulrich	LAN	269	BERNOWS?, Abm.	MIF	16A
Conrad	NOU	203	BERKHUSER,			BERNT, Philip	BUC	158A
Conrad	BER	223	Magdalena	BER	221	BEROT, Michael	LAN	138
Conrad	LUZ	362	BERKIPINE?,			BERR-TT?, Jacob	MNT	133
David	NOH	58	Maths.	PHI	89A	BERRETT, Wm.	PHA	28
Fredk.	BER	205	BERKISER, Jacob	CHE	718	BERREY, James	HNT	143
George	BER	154	BERKLEY, David	LAN	247	John	HNT	143
George	YOR	190	Hugh	GRN	87	BERRY, Agnes	HNT	127
George	YOR	218	Jacob	SOM	126	Alexr. (See		
George	BER	263	Jacob	YOR	204	Berry, Widow)	NOH	35
Henry	BER	220	John	SOM	136	Benjamin	GRN	98
Henry	BER	221	Nelly	FRA	291	Betty	WAS	119
Herber/ Herbes?	BER	265	BERKLIE, Philip	WST	284	Charles	CHE	699
Isaac	BER	207	BERKMAN, Baltzer	LAN	228	Conrad	DAU	41
Jacob	WST	209	Jacob	SOM	133	Daniel	NOU	161
John	NOH	62	Jacob Sen.	SOM	133	David	WAS	78
John	BER	148	John	LAN	227	George	HNT	164
Joseph	NOU	134	BERKSHIRE,			Henry	DAU	40A
Michael	LAN	35	William	GRN	86	Irael	YOR	215
Peter	BER	154	BERKY, John	BUC	160A	Jacob	NOU	179
Philip	NOH	58	Peter	BUC	160A	James	SOM	145
Phillip	NOU	127	BERLAUGHER,			James	NOU	161
Tobias	BER	265	George	SOM	147	James	WST	249
William	BER	261	BERLEY, Anthony	NOU	179	Jas.	CUM	73
Wm.	CUM	52	Nicholas	NOU	179	John	WAS	19
BERGERT, Jacob	YOR	217	BERLIN, Abraham	NOH	49A	John	WAS	42
BERGESS?, Cadet?	PHA	31	Frederick	ADA	35	John	NOH	47
BERGEY, John	MNT	89	Jacob	WST	187	John	LAN	130
BERGHOLTER, Henry	LAN	207	Jacob, Jr.	WST	365	John	NOU	135
BERGIE, John	NOH	29	Jacob, Senr.	WST	365	John	LUZ	371
BERGIN, Isaac			Nicholas	ADA	36	John	MIF	4A
Junr.	MNT	125	Thomas	LAN	23	Joseph	NOU	156
John	MNT	125	BERLING, Fredrick			Mark	GRN	67
BERGNER, Jacob	LAN	207	Jr.	ADA	34	Mary	PHI	51
BERGSTRASER, John	BUC	149	George	ADA	34	Micheal	WST	210
BERGY, Abraham	MNT	72	Isaac	ADA	33	Peter	DAU	41
Abrm. Junr.	MNT	72	Michael	YOR	186	Peter	NOU	179
Henry	BUC	96	BERLIT, Jacob	NOU	186	Peter L.	PHA	113
Jacob	MNT	121	BERLOCK, John	LAN	193	Phillip	NOU	135
Jacob	BUC	158A	BERLUE, Peter	NOU	170	Robert	NOH	41
BERIGHER, Henry	LAN	218	BERMINGER, Jacob	MNT	98	Samuel	WAS	78
BERINGER, George	BUC	158A	BERMORE, George	GRN	75	Thomas	WST	306
Widow	LAN	292	BERN, John	CHE	910	Thomas	CHE	745
BERK, John	BER	129	BERNANOSSE, C.	PHA	42	Walter Senr.	NOH	41
John	BER	187	BERNARD, James	DEL	161	Widow Of Alexr.	NOH	35
BERKELBA, Henry	PHI	94	Jeremie	CHE	740	William	WAS	78
BERKENBINE, John	BER	235	John	PHA	84	William	GRN	99
BERKENHOUSER,			Joseph	CHE	774	William	CHE	813
Mary	LAN	81	Martin	PHA	114	William Jr.	CHE	899
BERKENPILE, Jacob	SOM	137	BERND, Nicholas	SOM	136	Wm.	PHA	64
BERKENSTOCK,			Peter	SOM	141	BERRY?, John		
Abraham	NOH	79A	BERNDOLLER, John	PHI	138	Esqr.	PHI	89A
BERKENTUSEN,			BERNDT, Daniel	BER	217	BERRYHILE, Samuel	DAU	3
Elizabeth	LAN	175	Frederick	BER	256	BERRYHILL, Andrew	DAU	2
BERKERHISER,			Stephen	BER	217	Mathilda	DAU	11A
George	LAN	229	BERNER, Michael	NOH	85	Wm.	FRA	301
BERKEY, Adam	SOM	126	BERNERD, William	NOU	127	BERRYHILL?, Wm.	LYC	17
Daniel	SOM	126	BERNET, Robert	FAY	208	BERRYMAN, Jacob	PHA	6
Jacob	SOM	126	BERNETHY,			Joseph	PHA	64
Jacob	SOM	156	Charrels	ALL	75	BERSELY?, See		
Jacob	SOM	156	BERNEY, James	YOR	212	Busely	NOU	145

27

BERSON, Philip	NOH	64	BEST, Thomas	PHI	7	BETZ, Solomon	NOU	127
BERST, John	DAU	20	Thomas	NOU	143	William	NOU	143
BERSTLER, John	BER	180	Thomas	CHE	861	BETZ?, (See		
BERTE, John	PHA	5	Valentine	NOU	162	Butz?)	NOU	127
BERTHOFF?, Peter	ERI	60A	Widow	NOH	49A	BEUNER?, Charles	DAU	29A
BERTI?, Christn.			William	WST	209	BEUTEL, Frederick	NOH	31A
Jr.	BER	285	BEST?, William	MIF	16A	John	NOH	69A
BERTLEY, Robert	LAN	232	BESTE, Christn.			BEUTELMAN,		
BERTLY, John	ALL	87	Jr.	BER	285	Abraham	NOH	55
BERTNER, John	DAU	17A	BESTER, Peter	LAN	140	Daniel	NOH	47
BERTO, Henry	BER	258	BESTLY, Henry	NOU	120	Leonard	NOH	33
Isaac	BER	229	BESTON, Nathaniel	GRN	106	BEVAN, Benjamin	DEL	173
Isaac	BER	256	BETAGH, Margaret	PHA	86	Benjamin	DEL	178
John	BER	229	BETEA, Ann	PHA	123	Davis Esqr.	DEL	161
BERTO?, Henry	BER	178	BETEL, Steven	FAY	208	John	FRA	286
BERTON, Jonthn.	CHE	753	BETEM?, George	BER	137	Mordecai	DEL	177
BERTRAN, Daivd			BETEREY?, Joseph	LYC	12	BEVANS, Eliza.	PHA	7
Dr.	PHI	75	BETERN?, George	BER	137	BEVARD, William	WAS	11
BERTS?, Henry	BER	178	BETEY, Peter	PHI	69	BEVENS, Elizh.	FRA	300
BERTSCH,			BETHEL, Samuel	LAN	300	Jeseph	LYC	11
Christian	NOH	49A	Wm.	PHA	41	John Sr.	FRA	304
BERULL?, Thomas	MIF	4A	BETHELL, Robert	PHA	46	Robt.	CUM	25
BERVER-?, John	LAN	300	BETHTLE, Rosena	BER	175	BEVER, George	NOU	161
BERY, Jacob	ALL	64	BETIECOVER, John	LAN	193	Jacob	MIF	4A
BESBY, Stephen	PHI	19	BETIN?, Thos.	LYC	18	BEVESES, Jonathan	FRA	294
BESHAR, Jacob	BER	151	BETLER, Benjamin	NOU	103	BEVINGTON,		
BESHEAR, George	BER	283	BETNER, Butz	LAN	146	Charles	WAS	88
BESHON, Baltzer	LAN	173	John	CUM	134	John	WAS	88
BESHOR, Benjm.	BER	285	BETS, Paul	DAU	37	Thomas	BEV	14
Peter	BER	284	Samuel	DAU	31A	BEVINS, Alexd.	FRA	321
BESHORE, Adam	DAU	39A	BETSON, Nathaniel	GRN	99	John	FAY	230
Benjn.	DAU	50	William	PHI	11	Wilder	LAN	163
Henry	DAU	25A	BETTER, Valentine	CUM	46	BEVINS?, Anthony	FRA	281
Jno. Jr.	DAU	48A	BETTERLY, Thomas	NOU	153	BEVINTON, Henry	FAY	255
Jno. Sr.	DAU	50	BETTERMAN, Henry	LAN	246	BEWER, Danil	NOU	143
Jno. Sr.	DAU	48A	BETTERSON?,			John	NOU	143
John Jr.	DAU	50A	Catherine	PHI	66A	BEWLEY, Isaac	MNT	48
Peter	DAU	50A	BETTERTON, Wm.	PHA	27	John	MNT	39
Widow	DAU	51	BETTING, Joseph	NOU	126	John	MNT	104
BESINGER, Michael	FAY	240	BETTIS, Jacob	FRA	304	BEXLER, Joseph	LAN	283
BESONET, Charles	BUC	83	BETTLE, Ephraim	PHI	105	BEY, Christianna	PHA	56
BESOR, Daniel	FRA	302	Samuel	PHA	10	Elizh. Widow	LAN	13
John	FRA	302	William	PHI	14	John	MIF	12A
BESORE, (No Given			BETTLEON, Ph.	DAU	44	BEYDLER, George	LAN	187
Name)	DAU	18A	BETTLIN, Isaac	DAU	47A	John	LAN	188
Fredrik	DAU	16A	BETTON, Samuel	PHI	129	Michael	LAN	190
BESS, George	ADA	28	BETTS, Andrew	FAY	225	BEYER, Andrew	NOH	55
BESSALIVE, Frans.	PHI	54	Conrad	FAY	240	Christian	NOU	135
BESSER, Jacob	NOU	170	Isaac	BUC	144A	Daniel	BFD	61
BESSET, Ezekiel	LUZ	366	Jesse	PHI	138	Frederick	NOH	33
BESSLY, Christn.	BER	285	John	BUC	84	Frederick	NOH	83A
BEST, (No Given			John	BUC	86	George	YOR	188
Name) (Negro)	ADA	29	Samuel	BUC	144A	George	YOR	216
Alexander	BUT	320	Sims	BUC	83	George	NOH	83A
Catherine	WAS	54	Stephen	BUC	144A	Henry	BFD	61
Christian	NOH	86A	Zachariah	BUC	151	Henry	YOR	184
Conrad	NOH	70A	BETTSHOVER, Geo.	CUM	73	Henry	BER	286
Edward	WAS	11	BETTY, James	CUM	122	Henry	NOH	88A
Henry	WST	209	John	NOH	35	Jacob	YOR	170
Jacob	NOH	62	BETTZ?, Carlton	WAS	66	Jacob	NOH	70A
Jacob	NOH	70A	John	WAS	66	John	NOH	47
James	WAS	27	John	WAS	66	John	LAN	144
James	WST	232	BETZ, Adam	HNT	163	John	BER	282
Jeremiah	NOH	62	Anthony	BER	162	John	BUT	324
John	WAS	54	Caspar	DAU	25A	Michael	NOH	70A
John	ALL	102	Charles	BER	129	Peter	BFD	61
John	NOH	70A	David	BER	136	Tobias	YOR	181
John	NOH	86A	George	LAN	146	BEYERS, Abraham	PHA	112
Michael	NOH	44	George	HNT	163	Abraham	YOR	209
Nicholas	ARM	122	Hann?	DAU	49A	Ben.	YOR	184
Nicholas	NOU	146	Henry	BER	234	Elizabeth	YOR	189
Nicholas	NOH	86A	John	LYC	13	Henry	YOR	184
Peter	NOH	33	John	MNT	56	Henry Jr.	YOR	184
Robert	BUT	320	John	NOU	127	John	YOR	164
Robert	CHE	845	Jonathan	YOR	204	John	YOR	184
Samuel	WAS	54	Peter	NOU	99	John	YOR	214

28

BEYERS, John Jr.	YOR	194
Jonathan	DAU	22
Peter	LAN	42
William	YOR	214
BEYHTEL, George	DAU	7
BEYL, Abraham	NOH	46A
Henry	NOH	29
John	NOH	46A
BEYMER, Juliana	SOM	126
BEYSEL, Peter	NOH	29
BEYSON?, John	PHI	57
BEZUIEA?, Joseph	PHA	114
BIAS?, Widow	MIF	9A
BIBEL, Widow	PHI	31
BIBELHEIMER,		
Conrad	NOH	75
BIBLE, John	DAU	32
BICE, Abraham	BER	247
Jos.	CUM	44
BICHER, John	LAN	92
Peter	LAN	193
BICHLER?, John	LAN	250
BICHTEL, Detrick	BER	180
BICK, George	BER	187
BICKARD, Conrad	MNT	94
BICKEL, Henry	NOH	42A
Jacob	FAY	252
John Jr.	DAU	49
John Sr.	DAU	49
Peter	DAU	41
BICKENS, James	LAN	194
BICKER, Nicholas	NOH	33
BICKERSTAFF,		
Henry	HNT	141
Matthew	HNT	141
BICKERTON, Widow	PHI	15
Benja.	PHI	14
George	PHA	86
Hugh	PHI	34
Jas.	PHI	45
Robert	PHI	32
BICKETS, William	HNT	158
BICKHAM, Caleb	PHI	13
George	PHA	86
Isabelah	PHA	58
Widow	LAN	40
BICKHUND, John	BER	247
BICKIN, William	NOH	83A
BICKING, John	CHE	821
Joseph	MNT	98
BICKINGS, Richard	PHI	140
BICKIRY, David	MNT	140
Fredk. Junr.	MNT	140
BICKLE, Anthony	BER	190
Daniel	MNT	98
Henry	MNT	98
Jacob	DAU	11
Jacob	MNT	98
John	MNT	98
Tobias	BER	190
BICKLEY, George	PHI	137
George	BER	233
Henry	BER	235
BICKMAN?, Wm.	PHI	103A
BICKNEL, Peter	PHA	34
BICKSLER, Joseph	WST	284
BICKY, Francis	LAN	45
BIDDENBENDER,		
Jacob	LUZ	360
BIDDENBINDER,		
Jacob Jr.	LUZ	359
BIDDIS, John	WAY	143
Samuel	PHI	131
BIDDLE, Abner	WAS	42
Andrew	HNT	127
Charles	PHA	79

BIDDLE, Clement	PHA	7
Fredk.	PHI	60
Israel	NOU	156
John	PHA	80
John	PHA	86
Joseph	WAS	42
Marks J. / I.?	BER	235
Owen	PHA	113
Thomas	ADA	28
Wm. M.	PHA	74
Wm. M.	PHA	107
BIDDLEMAN, Edwd.	CUM	55
BIDELER,		
Christian	BUC	100A
Henry	BUC	156A
John Jn.	BUC	156A
John	BUC	156A
Peter	ADA	20
BIDELL, Ruth	MIF	9A
BIDELMAN, Abram	CUM	151
BIDER, Jacob	CUM	22
BIDERMAN, Danl.	PHI	87A
Jacob	PHI	87A
BIDGOOD,		
Elizabeth	BUC	83
Richard	BUC	84
BIDLACK, Benjamin	LUZ	341
John	LUZ	341
Philemon	LUZ	341
BIDLE, Robert	LYC	25
BIDLEMAN, Abraham	BUC	80
Elias	CUM	149
Jacob	BUC	139
Jacob	BUC	100A
John	BUC	139
Leonard	BUC	148A
BIDLER, Jacob	FRA	275
Richd.	PHA	64
BIDNER, Cath.	BER	147
BIEBELHEIMER,		
George	NOH	75
BIEBER, Abraham	NOH	81A
Christian	NOH	89
Conrad	NOH	81A
George	NOH	81A
John	NOH	47
John	NOH	42A
John	NOH	81A
Peter	NOH	29
BIEGEL, Christian	NOH	66
BIEGLER, Henry	BER	260
John	BER	260
John	BER	260
Magdalena	BER	260
BIEHL, Abraham	BER	225
Christian	BER	225
George	BER	225
Peter	BER	225
BIEHLER?, John	LAN	250
BIER, Rachel	MIF	6A
BIERBOWER, Jno.	CUM	36
BIERS, Henry	WST	232
Micheal	WST	232
BIERY, John	NOH	81A
Widow	NOH	81A
BIEST, Jacob	LAN	14
BIF-Y?, Jacob	BUC	82A
BIGALOW, Lewis	LYC	10
Oliver	LUZ	336
BIGAM, Joseph	DAU	36A
BIGARS, Dinis	NOU	162
Mrs.	NOU	143
BIGART, Margit	ALL	80
Samuel	ALL	104
BIGBEE, Ely	CHE	753
BIGFORD, William	FAY	264

BIGGARDS, Thomas	WAS	84
BIGGARS, James	FAY	207
Robert	NOU	143
Robert	NOU	156
BIGGART, Andr.	FRA	285
James	FRA	285
Thomas	DEL	166
BIGGS, Andrew	WST	249
Benjamin	BUT	323
James	ALL	101
John	ALL	83
Joseph	SOM	142
Josh.	FRA	285
Robt.	CUM	82
Thomas	PHA	9
Thomas	SOM	142
William	GRN	68
William	WAS	73
William	WST	248
BIGGSBEE,		
Ebenezer	LUZ	413
BIGHAM, Bryan	ADA	24
Hugh	ADA	4
Hugh	FAY	225
James	LAN	164
Jean Widow	HNT	140
John	ADA	6
John	HNT	153
John	FRA	310
Mary	ADA	25
Robert	ADA	8
Robert	WAS	54
Robert	ALL	103
Saml.	FRA	319
Thomas	ADA	6
Thomas	ADA	6
William	LAN	162
William Jr.	ADA	6
William Sen.	ADA	6
BIGHLER, John	DAU	12A
BIGHLIN, Jos.	YOR	176
BIGLER, George	BER	256
George M.	BER	222
Martin	BER	278
BIGLEY, Joseph	FAY	207
Phi.llip	PHA	75
William	HNT	135
BIGONOY, Joseph	PHI	140
BIGONY, John	PHI	141
Rancis?	MNT	56
BIGWOOD, James	PHI	103A
BILBENS, Elizh.	FRA	299
BILBY, Richard	WAS	1
BILCHEIMER,		
Christian	NOH	62
BILDERBACK,		
Thomas	WAS	51
BILDHAUSE, Jacob	NOH	55
BILE, Barney	PHA	117
BILER, David	WAS	1
BILES, Charles	ERI	59A
Cornelius	BUC	92A
Henry	WAY	148
Longhorn	BUC	143
Thos. K.	BUC	98A
William	ERI	59A
William	BUC	92A
BILEY, Abener	CHE	767
BILGER, Henry	MNT	127
Ludwick	MNT	126
BILL, William G.	PHI	24
BILLARD, Fredk.	DAU	21
BILLARS, Matthias	NOU	113
BILLE, John	GRN	80
BILLER, George	BFD	35
BILLET, Gotleib	YOR	168

BILLET, Kraft	YOR	168	BINSEL?, John	ARM	122	BISHOP, William	LUZ	370
BILLEW, Widow	CUM	76	BINTER, John	LAN	172	BISHOR, Daniel	LAN	178
BILLGER, George	MNT	92	BIOREN, John	PHA	6	BISHUPBERGER,		
BILLHEIMER,			BIRCH, James	PHI	137	Jacob	PHI	97A
Dieter	NOH	75	Thos. L. Revd.	WAS	115	BISIL, Philip	BFD	71
BILLIG, John	NOH	89	BIRCHALL, Caleb	PHA	19	BISLAND, Wm.	MIF	16A
BILLINGER, Saml.	PHI	73A	John	DEL	161	BISLING, Pot---?	MNT	47
BILLINGS, Cain	LUZ	361	BIRCHARD, Jabez	LUZ	391	BISPHAM, Joseph	PHA	24
Eli	LUZ	398	BIRCHART, William	NOH	64	Samuel	PHA	24
Increase	LUZ	378	BIRCHFIELD, James	CRA	8	BISPING, Peter	MNT	115
Joseph	LUZ	378	BIRD, Andrew	WAS	66	BISS, Samuel	LYC	6
Rannsley	LUZ	361	George	CHE	712	BISSEL, Daniel	CHE	872
BILLINGSLY, James	WAS	78	James	NOU	108	John	PHI	19
John	WAS	78	James	MIF	9A	BISSELL, John	PHA	11
BILLIS, Peter	WAS	42	Joseph	PHI	56	BISSETT, John	LUZ	334
BILLMAER, Michael	PHI	126	Martin	LAN	245	BISSHIP, Philip	ADA	28
BILLMAN, David	WAS	118	Nathaniel	BEV	25	BITCHELL, Jacob	CUM	116
Henry	NOH	52A	Sevanes	NOU	103	BITING, Ludwig	NOH	55
John	NOH	75	Thomas	PHI	44	BITLER, Daniel	BER	247
BILLMEYER, Andw.			Wm.	PHA	63	John	BER	247
Esqr.	YOR	159	BIRDS, Paul	LYC	7	Michael	BER	247
Elenor	YOR	159	BIRELY, Andrew	WST	248	BITNER, Adam	YOR	171
BILLON, Chas.	PHA	4	Jacob	WST	248	Adam	LAN	293
BILLOW, Peter	YOR	167	Ludwich	FRA	271	Daniel	DAU	9A
BILLOWS, James	PHA	41	Saml.	FRA	283	George	SOM	136
BILLS, Allenson	WST	167	BIRGGS, Widow	BUC	154	Henry	SOM	137
BILMAN, Feley	NOU	97	BIRGH, John	LAN	254	Henry	MIF	6A
Henry	NOU	99	BIRKBY, James	NOH	31A	Jacob	YOR	159
Jacob	NOU	120	BIRKHART?, Conrad	MNT	60	Jno.	CUM	68
Michael	NOU	120	BIS-Y?, Jacob	BUC	82A	John	SOM	136
BILMIER, Andrew	NOU	127	BISBING, Andrew	MNT	49	Philip	SOM	136
BILTON, Abrm.	DAU	47A	Bernard	MNT	92	Wm.	CUM	40
BIMENDERF, George	LAN	141	Henry	MNT	122	BITSON, George	LAN	96
BIMGARD, Philip	PHA	112	Jacob	MNT	92	BITTEL, Andreas	BER	221
BINCKLY, Christan	ALL	74	John	WAY	148	BITTEN, Abel	BUC	98
Henry	ALL	74	John	PHI	105A	Philip	BUC	96
Henry	LAN	207	BISBING?, Barnet	MNT	49	BITTENBENDER,		
Jacob	ALL	74	BISEL, Benjamin	BFD	71	Chr.	NOH	37
John	ALL	74	Jacob	ADA	14	Christian	BER	207
Peter	LAN	207	BISH, Joseph	PHI	127	Conrad	NOH	37
BINDER, Charles	CHE	703	BISHER, Christian	YOR	214	George	NOH	37
John	MNT	98	BISHOP, Adam	CUM	71	John	NOH	41
Ludwick	MNT	98	Anthony	NOH	68A	BITTENGER, George	FRA	281
Peter	MNT	48	David	NOH	31A	BITTER, Arnold	NOH	66
BINES, Robert	WAS	54	Deitrick	ADA	29	BITTES, Henry	NOH	66
Thomas	WAS	54	Elihu	LUZ	414	BITTIG, George	NOH	72A
BING, Peter	LAN	284	Ester	FAY	212	BITTIL, Youst	FRA	275
BINGEMAN,			George	DEL	172	BITTING, Anthony	MNT	60
Frederick	BER	245	Ira	LUZ	389	Daniel	BER	172
BINGENMAN, Paul	LAN	193	Jacob	BFD	42	Henry	BER	241
BINGHAM,			Jacob	CUM	120	Henry	NOH	79A
Archibald	PHA	97	Jacob	NOU	134	John	MNT	56
Augustus	LUZ	423	Jacob	NOH	68A	John	MNT	98
Chester	LUZ	423	James	WAS	54	John	BER	207
Christiana	YOR	183	Jno.	CUM	61	Jos. Junr.	MNT	59
Hezekiah	WAY	140	Job	WAS	119	Joseph	MNT	56
Hezekiah Jr.	WAY	140	John	LAN	5	Joseph	BER	235
Hosea	LUZ	404	John	PHA	102	Ludwick	MNT	59
Hugh	LAN	301	John	NOU	134	Peter	MNT	56
Jabez	WAS	36	John	BER	179	Peter	MNT	59
Wm. Esqr.	PHA	102	John	CHE	903	Philip	MNT	56
BINGLE, Jacob	BER	224	Joseph	DEL	160	BITTING?, Lewis	PHA	58
BINGLEMAN, Fredk.	CHE	893	Joseph	DEL	172	BITTINGER, Joseph	ADA	36
BINGMAN, John	NOU	120	Joseph	DEL	181	Michael	ADA	11
John	BER	234	Margarett	DEL	172	Nicholas	ADA	33
John	BER	239	Mrs.	NOU	170	BITTLE, Abraham	CHE	801
BINKER, Adam	WST	270	Paul	PHI	126	David	DEL	174
BINKLEY, David	LAN	293	Paul	BER	265	Eaverd	GRN	91
Henry	LAN	193	Peter	LAN	19	Fredrick	DEL	173
John	LAN	114	Peter	DAU	14A	Fredrick Jun.	DEL	174
John	BER	169	Stephen	LUZ	362	Isaac	DEL	173
Johnson	LAN	114	Thomas	WAS	36	Jacob	DEL	178
Peter	LAN	193	Thomas	CHE	800	John	CHE	705
Susannah	LAN	114	Thomas Esq.	DEL	181	Joseph	DEL	177
BINKLY, Christian	LAN	188	Widow	LAN	121	Samuel	CHE	800
BINN, Thomas	LAN	284	William	LAN	23	William	DEL	173

BITTNER, Andrew	NOH	51	BLACK, Hugh	WST	270	BLACK, Saml.	YOR	203
BITZ, Henry	NOH	79A	Isaac	LAN	235	Saml.	BUT	358
BITZER, Andrew	LAN	63	Jacob	GRN	79	Samuel	WAS	6
John	LAN	63	Jacob	FAY	230	Samuel	WAS	66
John	LAN	177	Jacob	LAN	232	Samuel	DEL	177
Michael	LAN	63	Jacob	BUC	140A	Soloman	DEL	156
Widow	LAN	83	James	PHA	7	Thomas	VEN	170
BIVEN, Wm.	PHI	117A	James	DAU	9	Thomas	MER	435
BIVERT, Robt.	FRA	291	James	ADA	12	Thomas	ERI	59A
BIXLER, Ab.	DAU	48	James	PHI	14	Thos. Esqr.	YOR	214
Abraham	LAN	272	James	PHI	51	Titus	ADA	4
Christian	NOH	37	James	NOU	97	Widow	MIF	14A
Christn.	BER	283	James	WAS	97	William	PHI	35
Danl.	BER	153	James	NOU	126	William	ERI	59
Danl. Junr.	BER	153	James	SOM	153	William	DEL	173
Jacob	LAN	10	James	VEN	166	William	FAY	197
Jacob	BER	153	James	DEL	181	William	FAY	252
Jacob	LAN	192	James	LAN	240	William	CHE	739
John	YOR	183	James	WST	340	William	BUC	107A
John	YOR	185	James	MER	435	Willm	BUT	356
Joseph	FAY	249	James	MER	435	Wm.	LYC	18
Joseph	DAU	45A	James	CHE	873	Wm.	LYC	25
Joseph	DAU	51A	Jane	MIF	4A	Wm.	CUM	59
Magdalena	YOR	164	Jas.	CUM	34	Wm.	CUM	82
Michael	YOR	164	Jno.	CUM	34	Wm.	CUM	91
Peter	DAU	51	Jno.	CUM	67	Wm.	FRA	319
Peter	BER	153	John	MIF	3	Wm.	MIF	12A
BIXLY, Jacob	MIF	6A	John	CRA	5	Wm.	MIF	14A
BIZEL, Stouphel	FRA	318	John	BEV	7	BLACK?, Bet		
BL--KENDERF,			John	ADA	8	(Mulatto)	WAS	88
Christ.	LAN	135	John	ALL	64	BLACKBIN, Ephraim	CHE	888
BLACK, Aaron	DAU	18	John	ALL	67	BLACKBURN,		
Abraham	LAN	5	John	BFD	71	Anthony	BFD	71
Abraham	BUC	96	John	PHA	85	Anthy	WST	284
Abraham	WAS	108	John	WAS	88	Anthy Jr.	WST	284
Abraham	BUC	82A	John	PHI	93	Dibs	WST	249
Abraham	BUC	90A	John	WAS	108	Findley	WST	249
Abraham	BUC	140A	John	NOU	116	John	ADA	16
Abrm.?	BUC	82A	John	CUM	124	John	BFD	71
Adam	ADA	7	John	BUC	147	John	WST	249
Adam	ADA	13	John	HNT	148	John	FRA	278
Adam	DEL	191	John	WST	188	Joseph	ALL	93
Adan	ALL	69	John	YOR	214	Joseph	WST	232
Andrew	FAY	197	John	FAY	225	Leonard	WST	232
Andrew	BUC	140A	John	FRA	311	Moses	ADA	16
Andw.	LYC	13	John	BUT	360	Moses	ADA	17
Andw.	LYC	15	John	BUT	361	Robt	CHE	732
Andw.	CUM	70	John	CHE	825	Saml.	CUM	146
Ann	ADA	26	John	CHE	872	Thomas	ALL	68
Ann	LAN	151	John Revd.	WST	306	Thomas	BFD	71
Archibald	BUT	332	John B. S.	MIF	4A	Thomas	BFD	71
Benjn.	PHI	26	Jonathan	FAY	201	Thomas	BFD	78
Bob	LAN	231	Joseph (Crossed			William	BFD	71
Christian	HNT	150	Out)	BUC	92A	Zacharia	ALL	117
Daniel	LUZ	346	Joseph	FAY	225	BLACKBURNE?, Wm.	PHA	10
Daniel	BUC	83A	Joseph	LAN	231	BLACKE, Saml.	LYC	25
David	ALL	66	Joseph	LUZ	376	BLACKFAN, Edward	BUC	144A
David	ALL	97	Justace	PHI	118	John	BUC	144A
David	LAN	231	Mary	PHI	112	BLACKFORD, Benjn.	CUM	111
Dorothy	PHI	35	Mathew	NOU	162	Jacob	HNT	125
Ebenezer	PHA	113	Michael	BUC	140A	John	WAS	36
Elias	BUC	104A	Nathn.	PHI	115A	Jos.	YOR	208
Geo.	CUM	47	Patrick	WST	249	Richd.	YOR	208
Geo.	CUM	49	Peter	WAS	6	Samuel	LUZ	320
Geo?	VEN	169	Peter	CUM	121	BLACKHEART,		
George	PHI	7	Peter	DEL	165	Andrew	BFD	48
George	WAS	66	Philip	WAS	108	BLACKHOUSE, Wm.	WST	284
George	FRA	312	Philip Junr.	WAS	108	BLACKISTON, James	FAY	249
George	CHE	754	Robert	WAS	19	Prestley	PHA	98
George	BUC	90A	Robert	PHI	28	BLACKJONES, John	PHI	91A
Henry	ADA	9	Robert	LAN	151	BLACKLEDGE,		
Henry	ADA	18	Robert	HNT	159	Robert	BUC	86
Henry	PHA	109	Robert	FAY	225	Thomas	GRN	62
Henry	WST	159	Robert	CHE	703	Thomas	BUC	146
Henry	YOR	205	Robert	MIF	4A	BLACKLEY, David	WST	148
Henry	BUC	140A	Saml.	CUM	57	William B.	WAS	61

BLACKLIDGE, Enoch	GRN	94	BLAIR, James	BUT	345	BLANCK, George	NOH	79A
Isaac	GRN	94	James	MIF	9A	George A.	NOH	88A
Mary	GRN	94	Jane	GRN	87	Jacob	LAN	192
William	GRN	94	Jas.	CUM	150	John	NOH	88A
BLACKLY, David	NOH	29	John	LYC	8	Michael	LAN	92
BLACKMAN, Eleazer	LUZ	319	John	BFD	71	Michael	LAN	207
Elisha	LUZ	319	John	CUM	117	Nicholas	LAN	193
Elisha	LUZ	328	John	LAN	129	Peter	NOH	62
Moses	PHI	118	John	HNT	155	Widow	NOH	88A
Richard	LUZ	336	John	YOR	209	BLANCK?, Geo. A	MNT	133
BLACKMORE, Dawson	BEV	22	John	BUT	358	BLAND, Edward	BER	274
Isaac	WAY	143	John	CHE	868	Frederick	BER	274
Mary	BEV	15	John	CHE	876	William	BER	274
Nathaniel	BEV	15	John	MIF	4A	BLANDEN, Joseph	LUZ	385
Thomas	BEV	15	Jonathan	MNT	112	BLANDIN, John	BUC	160A
Thomas	ALL	112	Joseph	WST	340	BLANE, George	NOU	162
Willin	WAS	73	Runnel	CUM	121	James	NOU	162
Wm.	BEV	22	Samuel	CRA	5	John	NOU	162
BLACKNEY, James	ARM	127	Samuel	BEV	18	Patrick	NOU	162
John	BFD	48	Samuel	PHA	114	Thomas	NOU	162
Wm.	FRA	305	Samuel	LUZ	388	Thomas	NOU	162
BLACKSHIRE,			Thomas	WST	187	BLANEY, Jacob	FAY	243
Ebenezer	GRN	74	Widow	BUC	154	James	WAS	54
BLACKSON, Peter	DAU	14	William	BFD	71	John	WAS	33
BLACKSTON, Saml.	WST	284	William	PHA	93	BLANFORD, John	PHA	59
BLACKSTONE, John	YOR	203	Wm.	PHA	8	BLANK, Christian	BER	261
BLACKWARE,			Wm.	CUM	97	G. Adam	MNT	93
Christr.	CUM	75	BLAIR?, John	PHA	101	John	LAN	126
BLACKWELL, David	BER	252	BLAIRLINN, John	PHA	89	John	LAN	131
Geo.	CEN	22	BLAKE, Abraham	PHI	155	Michael	BUC	158A
Jacob	PHA	96	Anthony	PHI	142	Peter	BER	261
Robert	PHA	95	Jacob	LUZ	386	BLANKENBILLER,		
BLACKWOOD, Widow	PHI	6	James	FAY	249	Jacob	BER	172
John	BFD	42	John	PHI	154	John	BER	172
Saml.	MNT	65	Nicholas	GRN	79	Simon	BER	172
Wm.	CUM	115	Thomas	FAY	249	BLANKENHORN, John	BUC	104A
BLADEN, Wm.	PHA	54	William	PHI	50	BLANKLEY, George	ADA	16
BLADES, Mary	PHA	94	William	ERI	58	Richard	MNT	140
BLAIN, Alexander	ERI	56A	William	PHI	153	BLANSET, Joseph	SOM	145
James	ARM	125	BLAKELEY, John	PHA	90	Joseph Sen.	SOM	145
Mary	ALL	59	BLAKELY, Ephraim	LUZ	407	BLARE, John	MER	434
Robert	WST	233	BLAKENEY, Gabriel			Samuel	NOU	116
Robt.	YOR	196	Esqr.	WAS	115	BLAS, Dorman	LYC	10
BLAIN?, John	PHA	101	James	WAS	97	BLASECK?, Geo. A.	MNT	133
BLAINE, David	CUM	119	Jos.	BUT	359	BLASER, Jacob	FAY	242
Eliza.	CUM	49	BLAKER, Achillis	BUC	154	Jacob	FAY	242
Ephraim	CUM	86	Jesse	BUC	137	Peter	DAU	11A
James	CUM	99	John	BUC	137	BLASHFORD?, James	ALL	64
James	WAS	108	Paul	BUC	137	BLASKFORD?, James	ALL	64
Jas.	CUM	53	William	BUC	155	BLASSER, Geo.	CUM	22
John	LAN	312	BLAKEY, Joshua			Matthias	YOR	170
Leonard	WAS	108	Jn.	BUC	160A	Nicholas	YOR	170
Robt.	CUM	74	Joshua	BUC	160A	BLAT, Widow	LAN	70
Robt.	CUM	81	Saml.	BUC	162	BLATCHLEY,		
William	WAS	19	Saml.	BUC	160A	Ebenezer	GRN	99
William	WAS	108	William Sr.	BUC	160A	Miller Senr.	GRN	99
BLAINEY, James	CHE	703	William	BUC	92A	BLATNER,		
Samuel	FAY	254	William	BUC	160A	Christian	BER	155
BLAIR, Abijah	HNT	152	BLAKLY, Robert	FAY	263	Michael	BER	277
Abraham	BFD	42	BLAKNY, Edward	WST	321	BLATT, Thomas	LAN	68
Alexander	HNT	143	BLALTCHLEY,			BLATTENBERGER,		
Alexder.	ARM	123	Miller Junr.	GRN	99	Christn.	NOH	70A
Alexdr.	WST	167	BLAME, Joseph	PHA	82	Jacob	NOH	39
Ankel	HNT	156	BLANC, Lewis	PHA	32	Peter	LAN	252
Ann	PHA	93	Wictor	PHA	31	BLAUCH, Christly	DAU	45A
Brice	YOR	210	BLANCH, Joseph	PHA	96	BLAUGH, Henry	DAU	47
Bruce	BFD	56	BLANCHAARD,			BLAUSE, George	YOR	204
Cathrin	ARM	123	Jeremiah Jr.	LUZ	361	BLAYER, Adam	YOR	178
David	WAS	36	BLANCHARD, Andrew	LUZ	349	BLAYNEY, Arthur	PHA	58
David	FAY	230	David	WAS	36	BLAZER, Herman	YOR	211
Francis	BFD	47	David	LUZ	411	BLAZIER, George	WAS	51
Hugh	ALL	114	Jeremiah	LUZ	362	BLEACHER, Henry	DAU	38
Isaiah Doctr.	WAS	115	Samuel	DEL	164	Jacob	DAU	38
James	CRA	7	BLANCHER, Widw.	PHI	109A	BLEAK, John	ADA	38
James	BFD	40	Abner	LYC	11	BLEAKLEY, Francis	WAS	48
James	CUM	85	BLANCK, Christian	LAN	68	Jacob	WAS	48

BLEAKLEY, James	ADA	15	BLOOMFIELD, Elias	PHI	84	BLYTHE, John	WAS	42
James	ADA	16	Thomas	CRA	6	Saml.	FRA	307
BLEAKLY, Barry	LAN	112	BLOONER, Christn.	PHA	70	BOADWELL, Joshua	ALL	77
BLEAM, Christian	CHE	903	BLOSON?, Henry	BER	217	BOAK, John	CUM	38
Christian	CHE	903	BLOSS, Christian	NOH	44A	BOAL, John	HNT	156
John	BUC	156A	Conrad	NOH	83A	John	DAU	44A
BLEANEY, John	LAN	243	Daniel	NOH	75	Robert	DAU	35A
BLEAR, John	VEN	168	George	NOH	44	William	LAN	20
Thomas	LAN	76	George	NOH	75	BOAR, Adam	WST	269
BLEASPE, Widow	DAU	38	Henry	NOH	83A	George	WST	269
BLECHER, Cathne.	DAU	33	BLOTTENBERGER,			George	WST	270
BLECKER, Federick	FRA	274	John	DAU	14	John	WST	270
BLECKLEY, George	WAS	19	BLOUGH, Christian	SOM	156	Nicholas	DAU	34A
BLECKLY, Joseph	ALL	73	Christian Sen.	SOM	156	Peter	WST	269
BLEDON, Boe	ERI	56	David	SOM	137	Wm.	CUM	64
BLEE?, (See Blu?)	WAS	41	Henry	SOM	156	BOARD, George	LAN	252
BLEEK, Moses	BEV	27	Jacob	SOM	137	Patrick	FAY	243
BLEILER, Philip	BER	247	Jacob	SOM	156	BOARDSLY, Silas	LUZ	393
BLEISTINE,			Jacob Sen.	SOM	156	BOARDWELL, Joel	LUZ	409
Abraham	DAU	26A	John	SOM	156	Pyrrhus	LUZ	410
BLENSINGER,			Peter	SOM	156	Silas	LUZ	409
George	YOR	181	BLOUGHER, Jacob	BFD	35	BOART, John	LAN	181
BLESINGER,			BLOWER, Robert	PHI	29	BOAS, John	BER	233
Michael	YOR	168	BLOWN?, Henry	BER	217	BOATE, Owen	LAN	94
BLESSINGER,			BLOWSERT, John	NOU	181	BOATFIELD, T.	PHI	48
George	ADA	35	BLOYD, Margaret	PHI	133	BOATMAN, Barnet	BUC	81A
BLESTLER, Henry	LAN	254	BLOZER, Henry	CUM	104	George	PHI	36
BLESTONE, Peter	WST	269	Peter	CUM	104	BOAZ, Mathias	MNT	44
BLEU, John	NOU	103	BLU?, John	MNT	69	BOB, Andw.	CUM	66
BLEW?, (See Blue)	NOU	142	Thomas	WAS	41	Daniel	DAU	30
BLEYER, John	LAN	234	BLUBAUGH, Simeon	SOM	147	Jacob	CUM	61
BLEYLER, Jacob	NOH	58	BLUE, Conrad	BFD	68	Peter	DAU	16A
BLIAR, David	VEN	168	Cornelis	WST	147	Philip	DAU	16A
BLICKENSTERVER,			Frederick	NOU	142	BOBB, Mrs.	LYC	14
Abrm.	FAY	230	Michael	BFD	48	Abraham	BER	207
BLICKER, Matthias	LAN	136	Michael	NOU	142	Daniel	BER	207
BLIGHT, Peter	PHA	107	Mrs.	NOU	116	Peter	PHA	87
Robert	DEL	188	Peter	NOU	142	BOBBENNRYES,		
BLILER, Michael			William	NOU	143	Fredk.	BER	211
Jn.	BUC	156A	BLUE?, Ephraim	CHE	779	BOBBET, Job	WAS	61
Michael	BUC	102A	BLUEBAUGH, Benj.	ADA	10	BOBBINS, Hannah	PHI	66A
Michael	BUC	156A	BLUEBECKER, Peter	FRA	300	BOBENMYER, Jacob	BER	245
BLISBAN, Eliza	PHA	61	BLUM, Daniel	NOH	51	BOBST, Henry	NOH	51
BLISH, Reuben	LUZ	352	John Jn.	BUC	156A	Michael	NOH	84A
BLISS, Nathaniel	LUZ	323	John	NOH	70A	Peter	BER	207
Susannah	PHI	109A	Widow	NOH	86A	Philip	NOH	85
Thomas	PHI	152	BLUMBOUGH, Henry	CHE	816	BOCANNON,		
BLIT, John	LAN	77	BLUME, Charles	PHA	94	Christian	FRA	273
BLITHE, Robert	DEL	187	George	PHA	23	BOCELLEE, Peter	PHA	54
BLITZ, William	LAN	137	George	PHI	72	BOCHMAN,		
BLOAM, Widw.	PHI	112	BLUMENSCHEIN,			Christian	FAY	208
BLOCHER, Danl.	CUM	32	Catharina	LAN	192	Jacob Jur.	FAY	208
John	LAN	187	BLUMER, Abraham			BOCK, Andreas	NOH	83A
Mathias	CUM	32	Revd.	NOH	89	Anthony	NOH	44
BLOCK, Captn.	PHI	98	George	BER	150	Balser	BER	155
Jacob	BER	175	BLUNDEL, William	FAY	264	Benjamin	LAN	91
John	PHI	117A	BLUNK, Wilm.	ALL	106	Christopher	NOH	83A
BLOCKER, Abraham	YOR	185	BLYGHT, Joseph	PHA	48	Dadan	PHI	49
Frederic	SOM	137	Mary	PHA	23	Jacob	LAN	77
Henry	YOR	183	BLYLER, Henry			Joseph	NOH	88A
Mathias	YOR	185	Jnr.	BUC	100A	Peter	NOH	44
Peter	LAN	250	Henry	BUC	100A	Peter	MNT	54
BLODGET, Saml.	PHA	85	Jacob	BUC	100A	BOCKEL, Frederick	NOH	31A
BLOER?, Robert	PHA	115	John	BUC	100A	Tobias	NOH	31A
BLONDO, Nicholas	PHA	46	BLYMEIER, John	DAU	16	BOCKER, John	LYC	14
BLONDSON, Hark	LAN	316	BLYMEYER, Abraham	YOR	159	BOCKFIELD, Fredk.	CEN	22
BLOOD, John	VEN	165	Andw.	YOR	159	BOCKMAN, John	BER	190
Thomas	PHI	71A	Christian	YOR	195	Susannah	PHI	114A
BLOOM, Christ---?	BUC	82A	Martin	YOR	171	BODAFELT, Philip	YOR	183
Daniel	BFD	36	BLYSTINE, George	DAU	27	BODASWAY?, Windle	MNT	69
George	LUZ	405	BLYTH, David	ADA	1	BODDER, Jacob	BUC	104A
John	PHA	55	BLYTHE, Benjn.	CUM	141	BODE, George	BER	223
John	PHI	141	Benjn. Senr.	CUM	141	BODEL, Abraham	WST	286
Samuel	NOU	99	Henry	WAS	42	BODEMHIMER?,		
William	CEN	20	Hugh	WAS	42	William	ADA	35
BLOOME, Adam	MNT	107	James	WAS	42	BODEN, Agness	FAY	207

Name	Loc	Pg	Name	Loc	Pg	Name	Loc	Pg
BODEN, David	FAY	197	BOHAUP, John	FRA	310	BOLICK, Thomas	MNT	94
David	DAU	13A	BOHEL, John	LAN	78	Valentine	MNT	80
Hugh	CUM	93	BOHEN, Cathre.	DAU	33A	Valentine	MNT	85
BODENHIMER, Jacob	ADA	37	BOHLEN, John	PHA	8	BOLIE, John	WAS	15
BODI, Peter	BER	136	BOHLER, Frantz	NOH	31A	BOLIG, Andrew	BER	155
BODIN, Joseph	ALL	108	Jacob	NOH	44	Michael	BER	160
BODINE, John	ADA	18	Ludwig	NOH	81A	BOLIN, Phillip	ADA	26
John	GRN	68	Peter	NOH	44	BOLINDER, Conrod	CUM	88
John	PHI	154	William Jun.	NOH	31A	BOLINER, Abraham	LAN	192
Widow	ADA	18	William	NOH	31A	David	LAN	192
BODLEY, James	CHE	856	BOHM, Baltus	BER	175	Michael	NOU	173
BODY, John	BER	217	George	BER	256	Rudy	LAN	192
BODYNE, Cornelius	LYC	9	John	LAN	279	BOLINGER, Andw.	YOR	184
BOEHM, Daniel	BER	185	Martin	LAN	279	Peter	CUM	93
BOEHMAN, Jacob	FAY	208	Philip Junr.	NOH	47	Peter	YOR	185
BOENIG, Elizabeth	BER	221	Philip	NOH	46A	BOLITHO, C. & L.	PHA	12
BOGAR, Daniel	NOU	97	BOHN, Jacob	ADA	34	L. C. &	PHA	8
Godfrey	NOU	143	John N.	YOR	165	BOLL, James	CEN	20
Jonathen	NOU	143	Ludwich	YOR	165	BOLL?, Catherine	BER	211
BOGARD, Abraham	NOU	156	Philip	BER	148	BOLLAR, Fredrick	FAY	255
Cornelius	NOU	156	Valentine	YOR	165	BOLLARD, William	LUZ	421
BOGART, Bengamin	ALL	86	Wm.	BER	148	BOLLENBACH,		
Martin	NOU	156	BOICE, De Jos.?	MNT	80	Nicholas	BER	160
BOGDIS?, (See			Frances	FAY	213	BOLLER, Jacob	LAN	251
Vogdis)	CHE	881	John	FAY	243	William	NOH	42A
BOGER, Adam	NOH	85	Joseph	FAY	243	BOLLINER, Peter	LAN	192
Christian	NOH	85	Thomas	FAY	213	BOLLINGER, Abm.	CUM	65
Cornelius	GRN	69	BOID, John	FAY	242	Andw.	YOR	185
John	SOM	136	Vallintine	MER	435	Emanl.	DAU	14
Martin	SOM	137	William	BUC	151	Henry	NOH	29
Matthias	FRA	314	BOIDLER, John	LAN	259	Henry	YOR	185
BOGERT, David	NOH	64	John	CHE	786	Henry	BER	187
Jacob	NOH	81A	BOIL, Daniel	FAY	249	Henry	NOH	69A
John	NOH	81A	Hugh	CRA	12	Jacob	YOR	183
Martin	MNT	121	BOILES, Charles	CHE	728	Jacob	YOR	185
BOGGS, Alexander	LAN	8	John	MNT	80	Jno.	CUM	65
Alexr.	CHE	834	John	MNT	85	Phil.	DAU	20
Andrew Esqr.	WAS	41	BOILING?, Aaron	BEV	10	BOLLMAN, Andrew	PHA	103
Andw.	CEN	22	BOILS, Peter	MNT	104	Jacob	BER	172
David	ALL	91	BOILUE, Head	PHI	29	John	BER	172
Ezechal	ALL	91	BOISEL, Jacob	CHE	755	BOLLOR, John	PHI	106A
Frances	CUM	74	BOISH?, Jacob	PHI	133	BOLMAN, John	DAU	37
Francis	MIF	14A	BOISSIER, John	PHA	13	BOLT, George	YOR	191
James	WAS	88	BOITZ, Henry	BER	175	John	NOU	116
James	HNT	151	BOKEN, Wm.	PHI	91A	Savarin	CRA	6
James	MIF	6A	BOKENRIFE?, Widow	MIF	9A	BOLTIN, Charles	FRA	298
John	PHI	22	BOKER, Aron	PHA	5	Wm.	FRA	279
John	MNT	71	BOLAND, Elizabeth	MNT	87	BOLTON, Aaron	MNT	72
John	MIF	6A	BOLANDER, Adam	NOU	134	David	WAS	42
Joseph	CEN	22	Adam	NOU	134	Enos	CHE	759
Joseph	CHE	835	Frederick	NOU	134	Isaac	CHE	704
Mary	LAN	114	Henry	NOU	134	Isaac & William	BUC	143
Parson	CHE	835	John	NOU	135	John	ADA	36
Rebecca	CHE	723	BOLDEN, Sam	CHE	745	John	MNT	72
Rees	WAS	27	BOLDEY, Anthy.	PHI	31	John	CHE	855
Robert	BUT	341	BOLDIN, Robert	ALL	107	Joseph	PHI	38
Robt.	CEN	22	BOLE, Archibald	SOM	133	Joseph	PHI	137
Walter	PHI	19	Henry	CEN	20	Levi	MNT	72
William	NOH	29	Hugh	WAS	19	Mary	YOR	182
William	CHE	873	James	WST	187	Nathan	MNT	75
Wm.	FRA	313	Robert	WAS	19	William (See		
BOGLE, Alex	ADA	19	Robert	WAS	42	Bolton,		
James	WST	209	Robert	HNT	121	Isaacc)	BUC	143
James	FRA	291	William	CUM	61	William	DEL	177
Jos.	FRA	292	BOLEN, George	ADA	21	BOLTZ, (George		
Ralph	MIF	24A	John	WAS	115	Crossed Out)	MNT	110
William	ADA	21	BOLENDER, Adan	NOU	135	Geo.	DAU	41
BOGNER, Jacob	DAU	10A	BOLER, Fredk.	PHA	42	George	BER	265
BOHANAN, John	MER	434	BOLES, Michael	DAU	10	Jacob	DAU	41
Wm.	MER	434	BOLEY, Anthony	WAS	73	Jacob	BER	190
BOHANNES, Philip	DAU	24A	Laurence	CUM	30	Jno.	MNT	110
BOHANNON, James	DAU	8A	BOLICH, Peter	BER	161	Valentine	BER	265
Wm.	BER	203	BOLICK, Frederick	MNT	97	BOLY, David	CUM	30
BOHANON, Nathanl.	DAU	8A	George	MNT	94	BOMAN, Henry	ALL	67
Robert	DAU	8A	John	MNT	55	John	FRA	323
BOHARD, George	NOU	103	Thomas	MNT	60	BOMBACK, Andw.	CUM	111

BOMBARGER, Benjn.	MIF	26A
BOMBERGER, David	LAN	139
Jacob	LAN	162
John	LAN	36
John	LAN	134
Joseph	LAN	136
Joseph	LAN	139
BOMFILL, Daniel	LAN	183
BOMGARDEN, Jacob	PHA	92
BOMGARTNER, Jacob	YOR	181
BONAGE, John	YOR	219
BONAR, Barnet	WAS	48
Charles	WAS	48
James	WAS	48
James	ALL	81
James	ALL	82
William	WAS	48
William	FAY	201
BONAR?, Wilm.	ALL	82
BOND, Amos	DEL	155
Benj.	YOR	202
Elizabeth	DEL	164
Hugh	BEV	7
Isaac	DEL	173
Jacob	PHA	5
Jesse	NOH	35
Joseph	DEL	173
Joseph	CHE	829
Joshua B.	PHA	85
Levi	BUC	103
Lewick?	PHI	79A
Lewis	NOH	41
Rosanna	DEL	161
Samuel	NOU	116
Samuel	CHE	784
Thomas	BFD	54
Thomas	NOH	86A
Wiliamia	PHA	85
William	HNT	120
BONDER, John	LAN	66
BONE, Eliza.	CUM	90
John	CUM	54
John	ERI	56A
Thos.	YOR	199
BONEBREAK, Adam	FRA	311
Dewald	SOM	126
Henry	SOM	156
Peter	FRA	311
BONEHAM, Americah	WAS	118
Malachy	BEV	26
BONEHAR, Jessy	ALL	105
BONEL, John	ERI	56A
BONER, Barnibas	WST	377
Francis	VEN	166
Henry	LAN	189
James	BUC	86
John	LYC	24
John	YOR	203
John	YOR	214
John	YOR	214
Otley	FRA	296
Thomas	ADA	40
William	GRN	97
BONES, William	CHE	734
BONES?, James	BER	287B
James	BER	287B
Robert	PHI	61A
BONEVILLE, Casper	BER	215
George	BER	215
BONEWITZ, John	BER	204
BONEX, George	ADA	34
BONEY, John	WST	306
Joseph	WST	306
BONG, John	YOR	181
William	YOR	182
BONGARD, Adam	FAY	240
BONHAM, Benjn.	NOH	77A

BONHAM, Jeriah	WAS	11
John	WAS	11
William	NOU	170
BONIFACE, Wilm.	ALL	64
BONIX, Henry	YOR	160
BONNARD?, Mr.	PHA	94
BONNEL, Henry	NOH	77A
BONNELL, Chas.	PHA	47
BONNER, Charrels	ALL	64
Eve	CUM	27
Isaac	CUM	25
John	CUM	55
John	CUM	89
John	BUT	332
John	BUT	345
Matthias	CUM	25
Wilm.	ALL	64
BONNET, John	CUM	61
BONNETT, Isaac	BFD	71
Jacob	BFD	35
John Esqr.	WST	270
BONNEUIL?, Peter	PHA	94
BONNILL, Sarah	MNT	37
BONOBAUGH, Abm.	PHI	107A
BONOPLUS, Eve	SOM	151
BONSAL, Edward	BER	161
Isaac	CHE	815
BONSALL, Abram	CHE	808
Benjamin	DEL	169
Caleb	DEL	188
Enoch	DEL	169
George	DEL	173
Isaac	DEL	171
James	DEL	169
James B.	PHI	64
John	PHA	12
Jonathan	DEL	169
Joseph	DEL	169
Levi	DEL	167
Margarett	DEL	167
Obadiah	CHE	741
Ruth	DEL	169
Samuel	DEL	170
William	DEL	169
BONSLER, John	BER	229
BONTELOEN, George	PHI	110
BONTERAKE, Conrod	FRA	306
BONTZ, Henry	ERI	60A
BONUM, Elam	LUZ	349
Samuel	LUZ	349
BOOCHER, George	FAY	240
Peter	FAY	240
Peter Junier	FAY	240
BOOCHMAN, Phillip	CUM	143
BOOGHER, Adam	YOR	183
BOOHER, Jno.	CUM	146
BOOK, David	LAN	217
George	MER	436
Jacob	PHA	66
John	PHA	64
John	LAN	222
John	MER	436
Michael	LAN	220
Michael	MER	436
BOOKER, Casper	HNT	133
Daniel	HNT	136
Henry	BUC	139
Henry	NOU	174
Jacob	MIF	6A
Martin	LAN	159
Michael	YOR	184
Nicholas	YOR	184
Nicholas Jr.	YOR	184
BOOKHOLDER, (No Given Name)	LAN	139
BOOKS, George	DAU	18A

BOOKS, Jacob	DAU	19A
John	DAU	18A
Max	DAU	19A
BOON, Andrew	PHA	101
Andrew	DEL	167
Benjamin	NOU	146
George	FAY	225
Hezekiah	NOU	108
James	GRN	94
Jeremiah	PHA	98
John	CHE	746
Joseph	DEL	167
Margaret	DEL	167
Moses	BFD	41
Peter	NOU	173
Pompey	PHA	118
Samuel	NOU	145
Samuel	NOU	146
Swen	DEL	186
William	DEL	186
BOONBRACK, Bredr.	FRA	282
Daniel	FRA	282
BOONE, David	BER	137
Garret	PHI	6
George	BER	175
Hugh	BER	137
Joseph	BER	179
Joshua	BER	229
Moses	BER	179
Thomas	BER	137
William	NOU	103
BOORS, Henry	MNT	118
John	MNT	118
John Junr.	MNT	118
Susannah	MNT	118
BOORTE, George	LAN	181
Michael	LAN	181
BOOS, Killian	LAN	52
William	BER	233
BOOSE, Christian	GRN	98
George	LAN	227
Henry	LAN	52
Jacob	SOM	153
Nicholas	MNT	94
BOOSER, Henry	CHE	802
Henry	DAU	21A
Jacob	PHI	144
Richd.	CHE	712
BOOT, Elizabeth	CHE	725
John	LAN	51
BOOTH, Charles	CHE	766
John	DEL	164
Joseph	CHE	769
Thomas	DEL	157
Thomas Senr.	DEL	157
Walter	CHE	712
William	PHI	130
William	HNT	135
BOOTHE, John	WAS	36
Thomas	CHE	849
BOOTS, Henry	YOR	213
Jno.	CUM	69
Nicholas	WAS	66
Wm.	CUM	69
BOOYER, Henry (Crossed Out)	NOH	47
BOOZ, Jacob	BUC	92A
John	BUC	84
John Jnr.	BUC	84
Mary	BUC	84
BOOZE, Andrew	MER	435
Thomas	MER	434
BOOZER, Henry	BUC	88A
BOP?, Barnet	YOR	191
BOPP, Barnet	YOR	188
Ludwig	YOR	194

BOR----?, James	FRA	299	BORTEL, M.	LAN	58	BOTTENFELL,		
BORAEF, Martin	PHA	57	BORTERER?, Danl.	BER	151	George	GRN	99
BORAF, Frederick	LAN	251	BORTERN?, Danl.	BER	151	BOTTINGER, Michl.	PHI	98
BORAGH, John	WST	270	BORTHOLOMY, Thos.	FAY	208	BOTTLE, George	BER	215
BORAND, Abraham	HNT	130	BORTNER, Henry	DAU	5A	BOTTLES, John	FRA	293
BORDELL, John	BFD	56	John	DAU	6	BOTTOMFIELD, Adam	BFD	48
BORDEN, Joseph	PHA	5	BORTNOR, William	DAU	5A	BOTZ, John	BER	232
BORDLEY, John B.	PHA	98	BORTUN?, Danl.	BER	151	BOUCHER, George	MNT	56
BORDLY, Adam	FAY	263	BORTY, Widw.	PHI	101	John	MNT	67
BORDMAN, Seth	ERI	59A	BORTZ, Henry	NOH	58A	Joseph	PHA	34
Simeon	ERI	59A	Jacob	NOH	58A	Ludwic	MNT	56
BORDNER, Henry	NOU	120	Michael	NOH	55	Margaret	MNT	56
Joseph	NOH	88A	Philip	NOH	58	Peter	NOU	186
BORDWELL, Peres,			Philip	NOH	58A	BOUCHIR, Anthony	NOU	186
Junr.	LYC	12	BORTZFIELD, Adam	LAN	300	BOUD?, Joseph	PHI	17
Peres, Senr?.	LYC	12	BORUIM?, Joseph	BUC	146	BOUDE, Thomas	LAN	299
BORE, Burkhart	BER	263	BORUM, John	NOH	70A	BOUDEN, John	PHI	85
Michael	BFD	57	BORVER, John	GRN	69	Thomas	BUC	107A
Michael	BFD	71	BORWIN, James	LAN	315	William	BUC	107A
Michael	NOU	186	BOSE, Fredk.	PHI	111A	BOUDENSTINE,		
BORELAND, John	FRA	297	BOSEN, Henry	CUM	43	Henry	BFD	49
John	WST	364	BOSER, Fredk.	YOR	196	BOUDER, Leonard	LAN	271
Saml.	WST	365	Jacob	YOR	188	BOUDIE, Susan	PHA	46
BORELAND?, Andrew	WAS	73	BOSET, Edwd.	PHI	22	BOUDY, Peter	BEV	21
BORELL, George	NOU	120	BOSH, John Junr.	NOH	47	BOUERS, Michael	LAN	91
BOREMAN, Cornad	FAY	249	John Senr.	NOH	47	BOUGH, Andrew	FAY	255
Dewalt	LAN	109	Jos.	YOR	213	Henry	CHE	830
Jacob	BFD	42	Jos. Jr.	YOR	213	Henry	CHE	833
John	GRN	66	BOSH?, Henry	ARM	122	John	CHE	833
BOREY, James	LAN	299	BOSHER, George	DAU	35A	John	CHE	892
BORGER, Abraham	NOH	88A	BOSHORE, Math	DAU	36	Widow	CHE	831
Henry	NOH	35	BOSIER, Wm.	PHA	73	BOUGHAN?, Eve	ALL	54
Jacob	NOH	35	BOSKIRK, Richard	NOU	191	BOUGHER, Abraham	ALL	60
Jacob	BER	285	BOSLER, Christr.	CUM	26	Abraham	BFD	61
Jacob	NOH	70A	Edward	LAN	301	Bartholomew	BFD	61
John	NOH	89	BOSMAN, William	WAS	54	Christian	ALL	120
John	BER	211	BOSS, Barbary	PHA	26	Henry	CRA	10
Nicholas Jr.	NOH	35	BOSSERMAN,			Henry	HNT	126
Nicholas Sr.	NOH	35	Abraham	ADA	37	John	ALL	62
Peter	BER	282	Michael	ADA	3	Math	DAU	35
BORGERT, Jeremiah	BER	150	BOSSERT, Adam	MNT	53	Matthias	BFD	71
BORGET, Jeremiah	BER	282	Conrad	NOH	49A	Peter	DAU	50
BORGIE, John	NOH	88A	George	BER	155	Peter	ALL	58
BORHART, George	NOU	120	Henry	MNT	61	BOUGHMAN, Geo.	CUM	50
BORIFF,			Jacob	BER	155	Geo.	WST	208
Christopher	NOU	203	Rudolph	BER	155	Henry	WST	248
BORIN, Isaiah	HNT	145	BOSSLER, Daniel	LAN	7	John	WST	208
BORING, Ezekial	YOR	168	Jacob	LAN	12	John	WST	248
BORINM?, Joseph	BUC	146	Jacob Senr.	LAN	7	BOUGHTER, John	DAU	43
BORKERT, Michl.	BER	285	Michael	LAN	12	BOUGHTY,		
BORKY, Joseph	BER	277	BOST, Jacob	PHI	52	Christoper	ALL	74
BORLAN, Lodwick	ALL	61	BOST?, Michael	PHI	2	BOUING?, John	BEV	7
BORLAND, Andrew	HNT	145	BOSTEN, Michael	BEV	7	BOUINGOT, Elias		
Anthony	FRA	288	BOSTICK, John	FAY	255	Esqr.	PHI	89A
Archibald	HNT	145	BOSTIG, John	LAN	306	BOULAND?, Andrew	WAS	73
James	HNT	145	BOSTLER, John	CUM	55	BOULBY, Edwd.	PHI	89
John	HNT	145	BOSTON, Andrew	NOU	134	BOULER, George	WST	377
Martha	HNT	145	Charles	PHA	113	BOULTON, James	BUC	98A
Mathew	ALL	92	Christmas	PHI	76	Moses	BUT	346
Patrick	ALL	108	George	NOU	134	Saml.	PHA	46
William	WST	147	George	WST	306	Willm.	BUT	346
BORMAN, Henry	NOH	35	Jacob	NOU	134	Wm.	PHA	84
BORMMAN?, Henry	MNT	133	Mrs.	NOU	134	BOUM, Jacob	LAN	148
BORNBERGER, Widow	LAN	304	BOSTWICK, Benajah	LUZ	393	BOUND, John	CHE	820
BORNEMAN?, Henry	MNT	133	Dimon	LUZ	393	BOUNDS, Thos.	PHI	73
BORNER, George	WST	210	BOSWELL, Mathew	FRA	326	BOUNSER, Nathl.	FAY	219
BORREL, Jacob	PHI	133	BOSWORTH, David	LUZ	427	BOURE, Ralph		
Phillip	NOU	120	Solomon	LUZ	392	Esqr.	YOR	159
BORRES, Israil	FAY	201	BOTEA, Thomas	PHA	121	BOURE?, James	DAU	36
BORRIS, John	BUT	363	BOTHEL, William	MER	434	BOURKE, Theobald	PHI	19
John	MIF	9A	BOTKIN, Robert	FAY	225	BOURNS, Peter	LAN	300
Peter	MIF	9A	BOTT, Izrael	PHI	27	BOUSE, John	BER	207
Philip	MIF	9A	Molley	NOU	97	BOUSER, Benj.	YOR	194
BORROWS, Thomas	LAN	219	Peter	YOR	161	Daniel	YOR	186
BORSTLER, Jacob	NOH	70A	BOTTEN, Benjn.	FAY	219	David	BFD	71
BORT, Jacob	NOU	134	Valentine	DAU	34	Felty	ARM	124

BOUSER, George	BFD	71	BOWER, Casper	NOU	127	BOWERS, David	LAN	249
Henry	SOM	145	Catherine	MNT	107	Ellis	WAS	61
Jacob	BFD	56	Catherine	BER	276	Geo.	DAU	21
Jacob	BFD	61	Charles	PHI	142	George	BFD	61
John	BFD	71	Christo.	DAU	19	George	PHA	109
John Sen.	SOM	136	Christopher	YOR	164	George	BUT	341
Jos.	YOR	185	Christr.	CUM	52	Henry	CUM	104
Michael	BFD	71	Conrad	BER	186	Jacob	GRN	69
Noah	BFD	71	Conrad	FAY	212	Jacob	PHI	97
BOUSHIER, Daniel	PHI	53A	Daniel	BFD	55	Jacob	LAN	247
BOUSHIERS, Judy	PHI	53	David	YOR	208	Jesse	GRN	98
BOUSLOUGH,			Dietrich	NOH	72A	John	BFD	68
Sebastian	HNT	122	Elizabeth	BER	236	John	NOU	156
BOUSMAN, John	DAU	6A	Elizabeth	LAN	303	John	DEL	160
Nicholas	ALL	97	Frederick	LAN	3	John	DEL	160
BOUSQUET,			Frederick	BER	225	Joseph	LAN	227
Agustine	PHA	100	Frederick	BER	255	Mary	HNT	153
BOUTON, Henry	ERI	59A	George	PHA	78	Matthew	FAY	249
BOUVIER, John			George	CUM	145	Michael	DAU	8
Baptist	PHA	94	George A.	YOR	216	Michael	PHA	29
BOUYER, George	NOU	134	Henry	CUM	35	Michael	PHA	98
BOUZER, Samuel	ADA	33	Henry	LAN	92	Obedia	FAY	263
Samuel	ADA	35	Jacob	NOH	33	Saml.	PHI	82
BOVARD, Chas.	CUM	95	Jacob	BFD	36	Samuel	LAN	216
John	WST	321	Jacob	NOH	66	Timothy	FAY	249
BOVEARD, Jas.	WST	209	Jacob	NOU	127	Widow	MIF	14A
BOVERD, James	NOU	127	Jacob	NOU	173	William	FAY	202
BOVO, Peter	PHA	35	Jacob	YOR	210	Wm.	PHI	89A
BOVURS?, Hiffly	FRA	292	Jacob	BER	225	BOWERSOCK,		
BOWAN, John	YOR	219	Jacob	BER	235	Faidour?	MIF	16A
Thos.	PHA	36	Jacob	LAN	302	George	NOU	135
William	PHA	99	Jno.	CUM	139	Michael	NOU	134
Wm.	PHA	37	John	ADA	25	Paul	NOU	134
BOWAN?, Michal	ALL	83	John	CUM	35	Valentine	NOU	186
BOWAR, Michal	ALL	83	John	ADA	36	BOWES, Charlotte	PHA	103
BOWARS, Thomas	FAY	219	John	WAS	36	BOWIN,		
BOWDEN, Daniel	BUC	145	John	ADA	43	Constantine	MER	435
John	WST	284	John	BFD	56	David Jun.	FRA	292
BOWEL, Jesse	GRN	97	John	MNT	98	John	DAU	36
BOWEN, Aaron	BER	157	John	NOU	197	BOWL, James	BEV	4
Aaron Jr.	BER	157	John Crossed			James	WAS	6
Benjn.	CHE	832	Out)	BFD	60	Samuel	BEV	4
Benjn.	CHE	866	John	BUC	156A	William	CRA	5
Danforth	LYC	3	Jonathen	ADA	42	BOWLAND, Mathew	WAS	19
David	BFD	35	Joseph	BER	235	Robert	WAS	19
David	FRA	292	Ludwig	ADA	5	Robert	WAS	19
David	WST	377	Martin	CUM	82	Robert Jr.	WAS	19
Dia	FRA	292	Michael	ADA	41	William	WAS	19
Elijah	PHI	108A	Michael	ADA	44	BOWLEN, Widow	PHI	97
Enos	PHI	66A	Michael	NOU	120	Jane	FAY	252
Esther	BEV	10	Michael	BER	137	BOWLER, John	PHI	135
Ezekiel	CHE	882	Michael	NOU	153	John	WST	377
George	GRN	87	Michael	BER	187	BOWLES, Thomas		
James	LUZ	417	Michael	BER	256	Junr.	WAS	54
John	BFD	71	Moses	LAN	78	Thomas Senr.	WAS	54
John	CHE	883	Moses	BER	137	BOWLEY, George	CHE	785
John Jr.	CHE	884	Moses Jr.	BER	137	BOWLIN, Peter	SOM	147
Jonathan	BFD	71	Mrs.	NOU	153	BOWLOR, Wilm. O.		
Joseph	LAN	91	Nichls.	CUM	45	Esqr.	ALL	116
Ruben	FAY	212	Nicholas	MNT	80	BOWLS, Andrew	MNT	107
Samuel	BEV	10	Peter	LAN	32	Frances	CEN	22
Samuel	FAY	242	Peter	ADA	44	Robert	MER	435
Stephen	CHE	737	Peter	BER	211	Thos.	CEN	22
Thomas	BFD	54	Philip	NOH	49A	William	CRA	11
Thomas	BFD	71	Phillip	NOU	97	BOWLS?, James	ALL	117
Thomas	GRN	80	Solomon	ADA	43	BOWMAN, Widw.	PHI	92
Thomas Jr.	BFD	71	Thomas	MNT	64	Abraham	BER	166
Widow	LAN	92	Thomas	NOU	143	Adam	NOU	103
BOWER, Widow	YOR	208	Widow	NOH	72A	Ann	DEL	181
Widw.	PHI	84	BOWERMASTER,			Benjamin	GRN	69
Adam	SOM	132	Henry	SOM	151	Benjamin	LAN	110
Adam	BER	187	John	SOM	151	Benjn.	FAY	230
Andrew	LAN	5	BOWERS, Bazel	FAY	219	Benjn.	FAY	242
Andrew	ADA	44	Conrad	FAY	197	Charles	PHI	76
Andrew	PHA	55	David	PHI	33	Christian	DAU	9
Boston	CUM	117	David	WAS	73	Christian	LAN	10

BOWMAN, Christian	NOU	113	BOWMAN, Matthias	FRA	275	BOYD, Benjn.	DAU	44A
Christian	BER	172	Michael	DAU	9	Catharine	CHE	844
Christian	BER	172	Michael	CHE	835	Cyrus	WAS	36
Christn.	NOH	64	Peter	BFD	66	David	WAS	54
Chuster	NOU	153	Peter	BUC	147	Dina	ALL	73
Daniel	LAN	245	Peter	BER	217	Enoch	CHE	750
Danl.	PHI	130	Peter	BER	247	Geo.	BUT	340
David	LAN	2	Peter	FRA	290	George	FAY	238
David	WAS	119	Peter	LAN	312	George	LUZ	419
Ebenezer	LUZ	319	Phillip	FAY	213	George	CHE	845
Elias	FAY	243	Robert	WAS	51	Henry	WST	248
Eliz.	DAU	18A	Robert	MER	433	Hugh	LAN	170
Francis	LAN	223	Robt.	PHI	119A	James	MIF	3
George	DAU	28	Roger	MNT	137	James	LYC	23
George	LAN	118	Saml.	CUM	60	James	ALL	90
George	FAY	243	Samuel	HNT	140	James	ALL	99
Henrey	FAY	213	Samuel	FAY	219	James	BUC	103
Henry	ADA	32	Samuel	LUZ	322	James	PHI	107
Henry	LAN	106	Thomas	FAY	238	James	LAN	125
Henry	YOR	182	Thos.	NOU	153	James	SOM	126
Henry	YOR	185	Wendel	BER	172	James	LAN	131
Henry	YOR	217	Wendel	LAN	220	James	WAY	140
Henry	LAN	235	Widow	DAU	28	James	SOM	147
Henry	CHE	800	Widow	LAN	226	James	NOU	156
Henry Jr.	YOR	185	William	PHI	130	James	NOU	161
Henry	DAU	44A	William	LAN	300	James	LAN	169
Henry	NOH	83A	Acob	LUZ	413	James	YOR	193
Henry	BUC	92A	BOWNELER,			James	FRA	315
Henry	BUC	92A	Frederick	LAN	19	James	BUT	340
Isaac	BER	166	BOWSER, Abraham	WAS	119	James	CHE	713
Isaac	LUZ	322	Daniel	BFD	71	James	CHE	751
Jacob	ADA	25	Jacob	BFD	71	James	CHE	843
Jacob	DAU	44	John	BFD	61	James	CHE	845
Jacob	MNT	98	John Jr.	BFD	61	Jane	CHE	843
Jacob	CUM	103	Philip	BFD	61	Jared	HNT	166
Jacob	NOU	113	BOWSHTACH, Jacob	BER	267	Jas.	CUM	136
Jacob	NOU	120	BOX, James	MNT	47	Jno.	CUM	107
Jacob	PHI	128	BOXTON, Joseph	CHE	846	John	PHI	8
Jacob	SOM	136	BOYAR, Isaac	CHE	892	John	BEV	21
Jacob	BUC	147	John	CHE	865	John	BEV	24
Jacob	NOU	181	Philip	CHE	889	John	PHI	25
Jacob	YOR	190	Widow	CHE	889	John	NOH	66
Jacob Esqr.	FAY	238	Widow	CHE	911	John	NOU	116
Jacob	DAU	47A	BOYAR?, Andrew	CHE	702	John	LAN	125
Jno.	CUM	71	BOYARS, Andrew	CHE	787	John	NOU	162
John	ADA	7	Benjn.	CHE	857	John	LAN	241
John	DAU	32	Isaac	CHE	777	John	WST	248
John	ADA	34	Isaac	CHE	826	John	FRA	318
John	CUM	60	John	CHE	885	John	WST	340
John	NOH	64	Philip	YOR	185	John	WST	341
John	LAN	77	Saml.	CHE	819	John	CHE	749
John	GRN	87	BOYCE, David	WAS	18	John	CHE	750
John	LAN	110	J.	DAU	44A	John	CHE	874
John	WAS	119	James	FAY	201	John Esqr.	YOR	201
John	HNT	120	John	WAS	18	John	ERI	57A
John	BER	150	John	DAU	4A	Joseph	LAN	301
John	BER	166	Joseph	PHA	115	Mary	PHA	99
John	YOR	168	Samuel	PHA	24	Mary	PHA	123
John	YOR	196	William	PHA	8	Mary	DAU	4A
John	FAY	208	BOYD, Widow	PHI	71A	Nich (See Boyd,		
John	LAN	237	-----	BEV	24	Stephen)	LAN	162
John	FAY	238	Abm.	CUM	136	Park	PHA	21
John	LUZ	329	Abraham	PHA	63	Rachel	WST	284
John	MER	433	Adam	DAU	4A	Robert	LYC	4
John	MER	435	Alexander	PHI	108	Robert	BEV	18
Jos.	CUM	28	Alexander	PHI	119	Robert	ALL	99
Jos. Esqr.	NOH	66	Alexander	LAN	241	Robert	WAS	119
Joseph	LAN	108	Alexr.	PHI	29	Robt.	LYC	21
Joseph	NOU	120	Andr.	FRA	301	Robt.	FRA	292
Joseph	MNT	131	Andrew	ALL	92	Rowley	WAS	19
Joseph	BER	247	Andrew	CHE	853	Rowley	WAS	19
Joshua	LUZ	417	Andrew	CHE	866	Samuel	ALL	53
Lewis	CHE	893	Andrew	PHA	17A	Samuel	LAN	161
Margaret	DAU	9A	Archibald	ADA	13	Samuel	NOU	191
Martin	BER	172	Benj.	ADA	13	Samuel	YOR	202
Martin	BER	173	Benjn.	ADA	5	Simon	CUM	98

BOYD, Stephen &		
Nich	LAN	162
Thomas	PHI	9
Thomas	PHA	19
Thomas	CUM	36
Thomas	ALL	95
Thomas	ALL	107
Thomas	WST	147
Thomas	WST	187
Thomas	BER	190
Thomas	WST	305
Thomas	CHE	868
Thos.	YOR	203
Valentine	WAS	66
Wallace	CHE	843
Widow	DAU	46
William	LAN	11
William	ADA	16
William	WAS	54
William	HNT	148
William	NOU	162
William	WST	167
William	FAY	219
William	WST	248
William	CHE	866
William Esq.	LAN	132
William Esqr.	FAY	197
William Jnr.	LAN	134
William	DAU	17A
Wilm.	ALL	69
Wilm.	ALL	107
Wlliam	SOM	156
Wm.	CUM	29
Wm.	CUM	122
BOYDE, John	GRN	87
Matthew	GRN	80
Richard	GRN	99
BOYDSTONE, David	GRN	68
George	GRN	69
BOYER, Abraham	BER	205
Abram	MNT	113
Adam	BER	137
Adam	BER	261
Andrew	MNT	80
Andrew	HNT	116
Andrew	HNT	130
Andrew	BER	159
Anthony	MNT	94
Assemus	BER	262
Balser	BER	172
Barbara	HNT	147
Benjn.	BER	154
Boston	NOU	186
Catherine	MNT	94
Catherine	PHI	131
Charles	BER	184
Christoher	BER	179
Christopher	BER	160
Christopher	BER	182
Conrad	MNT	72
Daniel	BER	179
Daniel	BER	179
Daniel	BER	254
David	HNT	128
David	DAU	30A
Dewalt	BER	241
Elizabeth	BER	205
Francis	LYC	25
Frederick	ADA	32
Frederick	BER	223
Frederick	BER	247
Gabriel	PHI	133
Geo.	BER	243
George	MNT	72
George	MNT	94
George	BER	151

BOYER, George	SOM	153
George	BER	207
George	WST	208
George	BER	223
George	DAU	3A
Gotfriedt	BER	223
Henry	MNT	94
Henry	MNT	133
Henry	BER	157
Henry	BER	179
Henry	BER	233
Henry	BER	235
Henry Junr.	MNT	94
Henry Senr.	MNT	80
Jacob	MNT	54
Jacob	MNT	94
Jacob	PHI	99
Jacob	BER	203
Jacob	BER	223
Jacob	BER	234
Jacob	BER	235
Jacob	BER	255
Jacob Jr.	BER	255
James	PHI	105B
John	DAU	3
John	BUC	80
John	MNT	97
John	MNT	98
John	PHI	142
John	PHI	146
John	YOR	188
John	BER	223
John	BER	235
John	BER	274
John	BER	280
John G.	PHA	120
Jonathan	SOM	151
Joseph	SOM	151
Leonard	BER	172
Martin	BER	233
Michael	PHI	138
Michael	BER	277
Michael	DAU	29A
Nicholaus	DAU	9A
Nichs.	DAU	32
Peter	DAU	3
Peter	MNT	94
Philip	DAU	30
Philip	MNT	72
Philip	MNT	94
Philip	BER	137
Philip	BER	247
Philip	BER	256
Saml.	BER	190
Saml.	BER	282
Saml. Jr.	BER	282
Samuel	BER	137
Samuel	SOM	156
Samuel	DAU	6A
Thomas	BUC	100A
Valentine	BER	136
Valentine	BER	137
Valentine	DAU	40A
Volintine	PHI	110
Widow	DAU	40A
William	MNT	94
BOYERS, Abraham	LAN	108
Andrew	WST	270
Conrod	WST	269
Jacob	SOM	160
James	WAS	74
John	WAS	74
Margt.	WST	209
Nichs.	PHI	117
Peter	WST	269
Widow	DAU	46

BOYES, Nathan	PHA	114
BOYL, Charrels	ALL	60
Hugh	LAN	59
James	PHI	87
John	HNT	151
William	NOU	127
William	NOU	162
Wilm.	ALL	115
BOYLE, Widow	PHI	37
Barnabas	YOR	156
Cornelius	WAS	27
Danl.	CUM	83
Edward	PHA	93
Frances	NOU	99
Hugh	PHA	101
James	LYC	15
James	PHA	47
James	PHA	58
James	PHA	99
John	PHI	37
John	PHI	41
John	PHA	69
John	HNT	131
John	WST	210
John	BUC	140A
Neal	PHA	93
Patric	PHI	33
Philemon	WAS	42
Richard	PHI	50
Roger	PHI	5
BOYLES, Absalom	HNT	121
Benj.	PHI	97A
Charles	WAY	140
Charles,	SOM	156
Daniel	WST	306
George	HNT	120
John	CHE	908
Saml.	CHE	780
William	GRN	75
BOYLS, Con	YOR	159
Hugh	ALL	103
Mathew	ALL	115
Patrick	FAY	201
Thos.	PHI	117
BOYMAN?, (See		
Voyman)	CHE	891
BOYS, Conrod	PHI	117
James	BEV	10
James	NOH	77A
John	BFD	71
John	ALL	101
John	NOH	77A
Ritchard	ALL	105
Wilm.	ALL	119
BOYS?, Robert	BER	209
BOYSE, Archd.	PHI	13
BOYSER, Adam	PHI	111A
BOZE?, Valentine	PHI	84
BOZER, Andrew	PHA	73
Adam	PHI	110
BOZSER, John	PHI	110
BR---?, James	FRA	298
BR--C?, John	BEV	15
BRABANT, Peter	PHA	36
BRABSON, John	LAN	151
Thomas	LAN	151
BRACE, Elijah	LUZ	372
BRACEY, Saml.	WST	209
BRACHER,		
Christian	BER	187
BRACKBILL,		
Benjamin	LAN	228
Henry	LAN	228
Henry	MIF	6A
John	LAN	216
John	LAN	224
BRACKEN, Andr.	FRA	310

BRACKEN, Thomas	WAS	15	BRADLEY, Jeremiah	CHE	745	BRAKENRIDGE, John	FRA	307
Thomas, Jr?	WST	377	John	MER	434	Saml.	FRA	307
William	WAS	15	John	CHE	746	BRAKENRIGE, Jno.	CUM	146
BRACKENBRIDGE,			Manus	HNT	131	BRAKINRIDG,		
Davd.	CHE	711	Samuel	DAU	46A	Andrew	ALL	95
BRACKENRIDGE,			Thomas	HNT	139	Hugh H. Esqr.	ALL	52
Andrew	LAN	112	Thomas	CHE	814	Wilm.	ALL	95
David	MIF	1	Thomas	DAU	15A	BRALIER,		
John Esqr.	WAS	74	Thos.	PHA	11	Christian	SOM	126
Wm.	CHE	712	William	YOR	182	Emanuel	SOM	126
BRACKIN, Conrad	LAN	193	BRADLY, Cornelus	PHI	65	BRAMBLE, Thomas	WAS	42
BRACKLEY, Thomas	VEN	170	Danl.	CEN	22	BRAME, Henry	PHA	77
BRACKON, James	ALL	56	Edward	FAY	219	BRAMEL, Levan	FAY	264
Thomas	ALL	56	John	YOR	158	BRAMER, Conrad	DAU	28A
BRACY, John	WAS	1	John	FAY	212	Lewis	PHI	79
BRADBERRY, Abner	WAS	119	John	FAY	255	BRAMFELDER, Henry	LAN	96
BRADBURN,			John	LAN	287	BRAN, David	DAU	19A
Alexander	LAN	48	Matthew	NOU	161	Martha G.	PHA	80
John	LAN	33	Phillop	ALL	115	BRANAN, Oliver	WAS	66
BRADDOCK, John	WAS	11	Thos.	FRA	285	Wilm.	ALL	75
BRADEN, David	WAS	119	BRADO, Widow	DAU	50	BRAND, Abraham	SOM	133
Edward	WST	341	BRADOCK, Henry	ERI	56	Abrm.	DAU	19A
Ezekiel	WAS	119	BRADSHAW, Charles	YOR	199	Adam	DAU	52
Hugh	CHE	712	David	BUC	86	Anthony	MIF	12A
Isaac	CRA	11	James	BUC	155A	Christian	LAN	24
Jacob	WAS	119	John	WAS	11	Christian	LAN	259
James	WAS	119	John	BUC	86	Christian	DAU	29A
James	MER	434	John (Crossed			Christopher	FRA	313
John	WAS	119	Out)	BUC	140A	Cunrod	SOM	136
John	WST	341	John	LUZ	397	Elizabeth	DAU	18
Mary	WAS	119	Robert	BEV	17	George	LAN	237
Richard	WAS	119	Thomas	BFD	49	Hanah	CUM	140
Samuel	WAS	119	William	BUC	140A	Henry	DAU	26A
William	WST	341	BRADY, Widow	PHI	102	Isaac	DAU	26
BRADENBACH, John	BER	137	Adam	CUM	60	Isaac	SOM	153
BRADEY, Alexr.	PHI	52	Enoch	CUM	94	Jacob	CUM	67
John	NOU	170	Ezekiel	BUT	362	Jacob	DAU	29A
BRADFIELD, Abner	MNT	40	James	WAS	6	John	LAN	3
Abner	BUC	86	James	BEV	21	John	LAN	253
Isaac	MNT	42	James	PHI	54	Mary	SOM	153
Jonathn.	MNT	42	James	ALL	73	Michael	DAU	21A
William	BUC	86	James (See			Philip	DAU	22
Wm.	MNT	40	Brady,			Saml.	DAU	45A
BRADFORD, Abner	ARM	124	Robert)	BUC	154	Samuel	LAN	258
East	CHE	809	James	BUC	103	Simon	LAN	253
Elisabeth	WAS	66	James	WST	377	Widow	LAN	79
James	GRN	68	John	PHI	78	Widow	LAN	284
James	WAS	97	John	NOU	103	BRANDEBERRY,		
Jennet	WAS	97	John	WST	286	Anthoney	SOM	145
John	PHA	8	John	WST	377	Henry	SOM	145
John	GRN	80	Joseph	ALL	73	Saml.	CUM	107
John	HNT	152	Joseph	NOU	99	BRANDEN, John	YOR	215
Peter	SOM	142	Lawrence	PHA	97	Jos.	YOR	168
Robert	GRN	67	Nicholas	ALL	85	BRANDERBERRY,		
Saml.	MNT	80	P. William	NOU	170	Jacob	BEV	5
Samuel F.	PHA	26	Patrick	WAS	97	BRANDON, Charles	DAU	14
Thomas	GRN	62	Peter	PHI	30	Ebenzr.	CUM	74
Thomas	DEL	167	Robert	PHI	20	Eliazer	ADA	40
Thos.	PHA	16	Robert	NOU	170	James	VEN	169
Widow	FAY	202	Robert & James	BUC	154	John	WST	208
William	PHA	34	Saml.	YOR	217	Mary	WST	249
BRADGATE, Charles	BFD	56	Walter	NOU	99	Patrick	CRA	12
BRADIN, Robert	ALL	99	BRAEDING, David	FAY	213	Thomas	ADA	41
BRADIS, Arthur	MNT	130	BRAFFET, James	LUZ	405	BRANDSTATTER,		
John	NOU	146	BRAGBILL, Fredk.	MIF	6A	Henry	NOH	44
BRADLEY, Abraham	LUZ	331	BRAGUNER, Henry	LAN	246	Jacob	NOH	44
Charles	HNT	123	BRAIDING, David	FAY	249	BRANDT, Aime	PHA	35
Charles	PHI	138	Nathl. Esqr.	FAY	225	David	YOR	211
Danl.	DAU	35A	William	FAY	249	David	DAU	44A
Dennis	LAN	22	BRAIL, Lewis	PHI	79A	Fredk.	YOR	177
George	MER	433	BRAIN, Jonathan	GRN	75	John	SOM	136
George	CHE	762	BRAINTON, William	YOR	205	BRANDTHISEIL,		
Gilbert	CHE	865	BRAKE, Leonard	BER	284	Mathias	FRA	290
James	LAN	14	Saml.	PHA	76	BRANEAN, Thos.	YOR	203
James	HNT	157	BRAKENRIDGE,			BRANEN, William	MER	434
James	YOR	197	James	FRA	307	BRANFORD, James	WST	232

BRANG, Bastian	NOH	35	BRATTON, Robt.	FRA	280	BREAM, Daniel	SOM	153
Jacob	NOH	42A	William	YOR	215	Henry	ADA	39
Nicholas	NOH	42A	Wm. Coln.	MIF	24A	Jacob	ADA	39
Peter	LAN	28	Wm.	MIF	9A	John	BER	172
BRANHAM, Ebenezer	PHA	87	Wm.	MIF	24A	BREAMAKER, Fredk.	PHA	60
William	LUZ	349	Wm.	MIF	24A	BREAN, John	FRA	319
BRANING, Patrick	ALL	55	BRATZ, John	CUM	57	BREAN?, John	BUC	86A
BRANIZER, David	CUM	71	Simon	CUM	56	BREARD, William	PHA	115
Jno.	CUM	63	BRAUCHER, Conrod	BER	129	BREARLY, Benjn.		
Jno.	CUM	71	Frederick	BER	129	Junr.	MIF	1
BRANNAN, Isaac	PHI	120	John	NOH	52A	Jno.	CUM	146
Mary	PHA	32	Michael	BER	132	BREAT, Henry	CRA	16
Widow	LAN	241	Peter	BER	129	BREATHER, Adam	NOU	153
BRANNER, George	PHA	55	BRAUN, Adam	LAN	62	BREAU?, John	BUC	86A
BRANNIAN?, Thomas	HNT	159	Adam	BER	261	BRECE, Charles	PHA	115
BRANNIFF, John	SOM	161	Adam Jr.	NOH	70A	Samuel	WAS	61
BRANNON, Benjamin	DEL	169	Adam	NOH	70A	BRECH, James	MNT	80
Francis	LAN	152	Christian	BER	262	BRECHBEAL, John	DAU	34A
Henry Sr.	CUM	28	Christian	NOH	70A	Nicolaus	DAU	28
Henry Sr.	CUM	28	George	BER	261	BRECHBIEL, Jacob	FAY	212
Hugh	WAS	115	John	BER	261	BRECHBIRD?, Henry	DAU	41A
James	FRA	293	John Jr.	BER	261	BRECHT, Jacob	BER	235
John	ALL	93	Martin	LAN	62	Peter	LAN	142
Mary	DEL	181	Peter	LAN	62	BRECKEMI-?, John	VEN	169
Richard?	BEV	6	Samuel	LAN	62	BRECKER, Benjn.	FRA	298
BRANON, Thomas	BEV	5	William	LAN	62	BREDEN, Robert	FAY	263
BRANSON, David	CHE	744	BRAUNEAVIL, John	DAU	26	William	ADA	7
Henry	PHI	102A	BRAUNEWILL,			William	FAY	263
BRANT, Widow	PHI	65	Mathias	DAU	26A	BREDY, Thomas	ADA	36
Adam	MNT	56	BRAUNMILLER,			Thomas	LAN	316
Adam	CUM	72	Ludwig	NOH	49A	BREE-?, Peter	BER	265
Benjamin	MNT	72	BRAUNNELLER,			BREECE, Samuel	LUZ	337
Christn.	MIF	6A	Hannes	LAN	193	BREECHER?, Jacob	YOR	186
Ezara	ALL	77	BRAUNSHUGER, (No			BREEDELEEVRE?,		
George	MNT	72	Given Name)	LAN	149	John V.	LUZ	394
George	ALL	74	BRAUS, Peter	NOU	127	BREEN, John	NOU	161
Jacob	CUM	70	BRAUSHER,			John	YOR	187
Jacob	MIF	6A	Christian	BER	129	BREGHT, Elizabeth	DAU	30A
James	PHI	65	BRAUSS, Adam	NOH	58A	BREHAM, Geo.	MIF	6A
Jno.	CUM	73	George	NOH	58A	Hugh	MIF	3
John	WST	232	BRAVER, John	NOU	181	BREHBILL, John	DAU	34
Ludwick	CUM	72	BRAW?, Henry	BUC	86	BREHEM, George	FRA	297
Martin	CUM	72	BRAWLER, Samuel	BFD	61	BREHM, John	BER	256
Martin Jr.	CUM	72	BRAWLEY, Danl.	CUM	71	BREHOM, John	MIF	3
Philip	MNT	56	James	CRA	8	BREIDENSTINE,		
William	WST	286	BRAWLY, Francis	ERI	57A	Christian	BER	172
BRANTES, John	BER	252	BRAWN, Robert	NOU	114	BREIDINGER, Adam	NOH	72A
BRANTHAFER, Adam	WST	364	BRAWN?, John	FRA	285	Michael	NOH	72A
BRANTINHAM,			Robt.	FRA	285	Peter	NOH	72A
Joseph	PHI	61	BRAWNT, John	LYC	24	BREIGHNER,		
BRANTLINGER,			BRAY, Christopher	MNT	55	Stophel	SOM	151
George	WST	232	Hannah	PHA	23	BREIGNER, Gotlieb	YOR	177
Jacob	MNT	98	Henry	PHA	66	BREINER, George	NOH	58A
Joseph	MNT	103	Sarah	PHA	46	John	BER	136
BRANTON, Ann	ALL	98	BRAYBELL, John	NOU	182	Peter	BER	233
Joseph	LAN	176	BRAYGAN, Danl.	PHI	105B	Widow	NOH	52A
William	LAN	176	BRAYTON, Caleb	LUZ	368	BREINGER, John	BER	172
BRANTRAM, Peter	BER	147	BRAZER, John	YOR	154	BREINIG, George		
BRANWOOD, Sarah	ADA	11	BRAZINGTON, Thos.	PHI	80A	Esqr.	NOH	58
BRASHFORD, Jane	FAY	213	BREACAN, Thomas	MIF	4A	George Jnr.	NOH	58
BRASIER, Amable	PHA	19	BRECKNICK,			Jacob	NOH	58
BRASLASKY, Henry	NOU	134	Michael	NOH	75	Peter	NOH	58
BRASS, Lukins	NOU	156	BREAD, James	PHA	97	BREININGER,		
BRATE, John	WAS	36	BREADEN, James	GRN	108	Michael	BER	220
BRATON, Thos.	PHI	80	Thomas	ADA	10	BREISH, George	NOH	52A
BRATTAN, John	FRA	278	BREADING, James	WAS	108	BREISS, Jacob	BER	205
BRATTEN, Jacob	FAY	263	Robert	WAS	51	BREITENBACH, Jno.	DAU	32A
BRATTON, Adam	CUM	131	Wm.	PHI	53A	Phil.	DAU	38A
Edward	MIF	1	BREADY, Ebenezer	WST	167	BREITENSTEIN,		
George	MIF	24A	Jams	WST	209	Nicholas	LAN	208
James	MIF	24A	John	WST	167	BREITESTEEN,		
Jno. Genl.	MIF	24A	Jos.	CUM	150	Philip	LAN	194
John	CUM	129	Mary	LAN	52	BREKBIEL, Jacob	DAU	29A
Margard	MIF	24A	BREAK, Christian	FRA	315	BRELSFORD, Abm.		
Mary	MIF	24A	Madlin	FRA	315	(Crossed Out)	BUC	85A
Robt.	CUM	129	BREAKER, Fredr.	FRA	307	Abm.	BUC	98A

BRIDENBACH, Paul	YOR	165
BRIDGE, Benjamin	WAS	118
Elizabeth	CRA	5
BRIDGEGAM, John	BER	136
BRIDGENS, Robert	LYC	19
BRIDGES, Jane	BFD	49
Jemima	PHA	100
BRIDGET, John	NOH	77A
BRIDGY, George	MIF	14A
BRIEN, Edward	LAN	237
BRIER, David	FRA	278
BRIERLY, George	WAS	78
BRIETT, Robert	CHE	903
BRIGE, Frederick	NOU	162
BRIGGLE, Jacob	SOM	126
BRIGGS, Amos	BUC	98A
David	CUM	54
George	SOM	133
Isaac	FAY	263
Job	FAY	225
John	BUC	107
John	NOU	113
John	NOU	113
John	FAY	225
John Jnr.	BUC	107
Joseph	BUC	103
Nathl.	FAY	238
Richard	DEL	181
Richard Jun.	DEL	182
Rolf	PHI	81A
Saml.	PHA	80
Saml.	PHI	145
Socton	FAY	225
Thomas	BUC	103
William	FAY	225
William	CHE	841
BRIGHT, David	BER	235
Elkana	GRN	78
Ellis	BUC	147
George	HNT	165
George	NOU	174
Jacob	PHA	48
Jacob	BER	241
James	PHI	103A
John	LAN	97
John	PHI	147
John	BER	235
John	DAU	49A
Mary	PHA	94
Michael	PHA	49
Michael	NOU	182
Michael	BER	235
Robert	DEL	181
Wm.	PHA	82
BRIGHTBILL, Jno.	DAU	51
BRIGHTFACE, Jacob	FRA	294
BRIGMAN, William	FAY	249
BRIGS, Benjamin	HNT	142
Benjamin Junr.	HNT	142
Elizabeth	PHI	91
Francis	PHA	32
Francis	PHI	66A
John	HNT	142
Samuel	HNT	142
Samuel Junr.	HNT	142
BRIKER, Jacob	DAU	20A
Maths.	DAU	20A
BRILE?, Wilm.	ALL	105
BRILHART, Abraham	YOR	192
Chrs.	YOR	191
Jacob	YOR	191
Jos.	YOR	191
Peter	YOR	192
Samuel	YOR	183
BRILINGER, Peter	CUM	118
BRILL, Christopher	BFD	49

BRILL, George	BUC	139
BRILLINGER, John	YOR	164
BRILSFORD, John		
Jr.	BUC	83
John Jun.	BUC	83A
John	BUC	83A
BRIMER, Widow	DAU	39
BRIMHALL, William	LUZ	397
BRIMMER, Christ.	LAN	79
William	WAS	88
BRINARD, John	FAY	219
BRINCKER, Conrad	NOH	79A
George	NOH	79A
BRINDLE, Geo.	CUM	66
George	WST	306
Henry	PHI	52
Henry	DAU	4A
James	BER	250
Jno.	FRA	286
Joseph	SOM	136
Larence	FRA	307
Ludwig	DAU	41
Malechia	FRA	286
Mark	FRA	288
Michael	LAN	32
Philip	DAU	2
Philip	WAS	119
Rosanna	HNT	154
Saml.	FRA	307
BRINE, Nathaniel	FRA	323
BRINEMAN,		
Christopher	WST	248
BRINER, Abraham	PHI	140
Andw.	NOU	186
Fredk.	CUM	48
George	BER	131
Phillip	NOU	186
BRINET, Jacob	WST	232
BRINEY, Adam	WST	208
Gilleon	WST	208
Peter	WST	187
BRINGENER, Michl.	WST	306
BRINGHURST,		
Elizabeth	PHI	131
George	PHA	81
Israel	MNT	80
James	PHA	107
Jesse	PHI	131
Samuel	PHI	131
Sarah	PHI	133
BRINGHURT, James		
Junr.	PHA	95
BRINGLINGER,		
Fredk.	WST	270
BRINGMAN, Henry	ADA	29
BRINGOLF, John	LAN	316
BRINICH, George	BER	259
BRININGER,		
Christophr	BER	277
Fredk.	WST	269
BRINK, Abraham	WAY	140
Benjamin	LUZ	421
George	WAY	143
Hannos?	WAY	143
Isaac	WAY	140
James	LUZ	398
John	WAY	140
John	WAY	143
John	WAY	146
Jonathan	WAY	143
Manuel	WAY	143
Peter	LUZ	350
Thomas	LUZ	398
BRINKENHOFF,		
Daniel	YOR	212
Demul/ Dernul?	YOR	212

BRINKER, Abm.	WST	187
George	WST	306
Henry	WST	305
Jacob	NOH	66
Jacob	WST	187
BRINKERHOOF,		
George	ADA	19
Gilbert	ADA	22
Henry	ADA	22
John	ADA	19
BRINKLEY, Thos.	PHA	52
BRINLEY, Michl.	FRA	314
BRINNEMAN, Jacob	WST	187
BRINNING, George	PHI	97
BRINSON, Hugh	DAU	4A
BRINSTON, Jacob	PHA	121
BRINTAN, James	CHE	709
Joseph	CHE	709
William	CHE	708
BRINTNALL, David	PHA	106
BRINTON, Amos	CHE	810
Caleb	CHE	806
Caleb	CHE	810
Edward	CHE	810
George	CHE	812
John	DEL	190
Jos.	CHE	812
Joseph	WAS	78
Joseph	DEL	157
Joseph Esqr.	DEL	190
Meldon	CHE	810
Moses	LAN	125
Newport	PHI	95
Thomas	DEL	190
William	CHE	810
BRINTON?, John H?	PHA	77
BRION, Jeremiah	BER	162
BRIS, William	LAN	70
BRISBIN, John	MIF	16
John	LAN	177
William	LAN	128
Wm.	CEN	22
BRISBON, Arthur	WST	286
BRISE?, Wilm.	ALL	105
BRISH, James	MER	434
John	PHI	111
Michael	BUC	102A
BRISHE, Adam	BUC	100A
George	BUC	158A
Michael	BUC	102
BRISKEO?, John	FAY	225
BRISKER, Jacob	WST	148
BRISON, Alexr.	BUT	338
Andrew	FAY	255
Archibald	BFD	42
Jacob	FRA	274
James	ALL	97
John	LAN	230
Patrick	WAS	11
Peter	FRA	320
William	LAN	133
BRISPIN, Andrew	CHE	888
BRISTER, James	GRN	99
Thos.	PHI	75A
BRISTERON, Fredk.	WST	286
BRISTOLL, Thos.		
L.	PHA	16
BRISTOR, Ryal?	LUZ	393
BRITAIN, Mrs.	LYC	14
John	CHE	890
Joseph	CHE	724
William	NOU	109
BRITANDOL,		
Mathias	FRA	288
BRITBENDER, Wm.	BER	283
BRITEMAN, Catherine	MNT	98

BRITENMAN, Adam	MNT	56	BROBST, Saml.	NOH	88A	BROOKE, Lewis	MNT	130
Fredk.	MNT	98	Valentine	BER	129	Mathew	MNT	72
Freny	MNT	98	BROBSTON, Joseph	PHA	15	Mathew	MNT	80
BRITENSTINE,			BROCCUS, Thomas	ADA	32	Mathew	BER	274
Leonard	BER	168	BROCK, Capt.	PHI	98	Matthew	MNT	85
BRITER, John	NOU	146	John	BUC	147	Owen	MNT	72
John	NOU	146	Sarah	MNT	34	Thomas	MNT	67
Joseph	NOU	146	Wm.	PHA	71	Thomas	MNT	72
Joseph	NOU	146	BROCKMAN, William	CHE	894	William	DEL	173
William	NOU	146	BROCKS, Daniel	FRA	298	BROOKENS, Wm.	CUM	147
BRITON, James	GRN	75	BROCKWAY, Reed	LUZ	411	BROOKER, Barbara	PHI	129
BRITSON, Hannah	MNT	140	BRODA?, Michael	MNT	71	BROOKES, Boyer	PHA	46
BRITT, Edward	PHI	41	BRODAS, Henry	BUC	146A	Cathrine	PHA	18
John	WAS	78	Thos.	BUC	146A	David	PHA	13
BRITTAN, Jno.	CUM	141	BRODBECK,			Elizabeth	PHA	105
Solomon	CUM	34	Catharine	YOR	186	George	CHE	779
Thos.	FRA	323	BRODER, Lowrence	NOH	81A	John	WAS	78
BRITTLE, Joseph	DEL	170	BRODHEAD, John	WAY	143	BROOKHOUSER, Adam	CRA	11
BRITTON,			Luke	NOH	77A	BROOKOVER, John	GRN	91
Elizabeth	YOR	159	Samuel	NOH	77	BROOKS, Andrew	DAU	27A
Hannah	MNT	142	BRODNAX, Charles	BUC	84	Aron	FAY	243
Jerramiah	BEV	18	Joseph	BUC	84	Benjamen	FAY	254
John	ADA	22	Robert	BUC	84	Benjn.	LYC	19
John	BUC	98	Thomas	BUC	92A	Charly	ALL	114
John	PHI	154	William	BUC	84	David	NOU	108
John	PHI	67A	William Jnr.	BUC	92A	Elisha	ALL	118
Joseph	PHA	36	BRODOCK, Nicholas	HNT	123	George	NOU	191
Joseph	MNT	72	BRODT, Barnet	NOH	64	Isaac	DEL	167
Martin	PHI	122	Conrad	NOH	64	James	DAU	10
Nathaniel	NOH	66	Frederick	NOH	64	James	DEL	170
Powell K.	PHI	3	Samuel	HNT	119	James	CHE	737
Richard	DEL	192	Samuel	HNT	136	James	DAU	2A
Thos. Esqr.	PHI	119A	BRODY, James	ALL	96	John	CRA	14
William	NOH	66	BROEDER, George	NOH	42A	John	PHI	75
Willm.	PHI	13	Henry	NOH	42A	John	BUC	103
Wm.	BER	284	Jacob	NOH	42A	John	GRN	106
BRITTS, Adam	PHI	112A	Maria Widow	NOH	42A	John	DEL	167
John	BFD	48	Philip	NOH	33	John	DEL	169
BRITZ, Adam	YOR	181	BROELBECK,			John	FAY	201
Conrod	CUM	56	Margaret	YOR	185	John	FAY	240
Fredk. Junr.	CUM	58	BROGAN, Charles	FRA	280	John	BUT	344
George	LAN	253	Ellis	CHE	755	John	MER	434
John	LAN	253	John	CHE	712	John Jr.	DAU	2
John	LAN	259	Wm.	CHE	750	John	BUC	160A
John Junr.	LAN	259	BROGDEN, David	BUC	92A	Joseph	CUM	68
Philip	LAN	259	BROKE, Robt.	PHI	109	Joseph	GRN	91
Philip	LAN	264	BROKEN, Ashley	PHI	96	Joseph	NOU	109
Valentine	LAN	21	BROMBAUGH, John	BFD	61	Joseph	HNT	159
BRITZIUS, Adam	LAN	60	BROMBOUCH, Jacob	HNT	116	Joseph	FAY	230
Isaac	LAN	55	BROMBOUGH, George	HNT	128	Joseph	FAY	234
BROADFOOT, John	HNT	120	Jacob	HNT	127	Joseph	FAY	235
John	PHI	117A	John	HNT	126	Julian	ADA	8
BROADHEAD, Garret	NOH	77	John	HNT	128	Mary	CHE	902
Garret	WAY	146	BRON, Adam	DAU	38A	Matthias	LAN	129
Richard	WAY	146	BRONER, Jacob	LAN	133	Mattw.	CUM	70
BROADHURST, Henry	BUC	151	BRONGER, Wm.	PHA	67	Nicholas	YOR	160
BROADLEY, James	PHI	42	BRONNER, Wm.	PHI	117A	Quinton	CRA	14
BROADMAN?,			BRONT, Christn.	PHA	78	Robert	FAY	255
William Junr.			BROOK, Abner	LAN	122	Robert	CHE	797
(Crossed Out)	BUC	84A	James	DAU	26	Robt.	LYC	21
BROADSTONE, Jacob	BFD	68	Rees	MNT	106	Samuel	CRA	11
BROADY, Ann	PHA	26	William	GRN	68	Samuel	NOU	109
BROAHEAD, Daniel			William	SOM	142	Samuel	YOR	158
Esq.	LAN	49	BROOKE, Benjamin	MNT	137	Samuel	YOR	196
BROAMWALL, Enos	CHE	706	David	MNT	77	Thomas	BER	274
BROAS?, Henry	MNT	43	David	MNT	107	Thos.	LYC	21
BROAT, Michael	MNT	120	David	CHE	875	Thos.	PHI	68A
BROBAND, Jacob	LAN	189	George	MNT	72	William	PHA	104
BROBSON, John	DEL	187	James	MNT	137	William	LAN	129
BROBST, Daniel	NOH	89	James	DEL	183	William	BUC	151
Daniel	NOH	88A	Jesse	DEL	183	Wm.	PHA	44
George	BER	235	John	MNT	61	Wm.	CUM	68
Henry	NOH	58A	John	DEL	183	BROOM, Hugh	MER	434
Jacob	BER	225	Jonathan	MNT	72	Isaac	BER	247
John	BER	129	Jonathan	MNT	137	James	LAN	95
Michael	BER	129	Joseph	BER	173	John	MER	434

BROOM, Thomas	BUC	83	BROUMFIELD,		BROWN, Charles	BUC 92A
William	LAN	94	Charls	FAY 219	Charrels	ALL 69
BROOMALL, Daniel	DEL	161	Nathn.	FAY 219	Christian	LAN 187
Daniel	DEL	190	Robt.	FAY 219	Christian	NOU 191
David	DEL	161	Robt. Jur.	FAY 219	Christn.	PHI 54
David	DEL	176	BROUS, Adam	NOU 134	Christopher	FAY 254
Isaac	DEL	165	BROUS?, Henry	MNT 43	Conrad	PHI 134
Jacob	DEL	155	BROUSTER,		Conrad	BER 233
James	DEL	175	Alexandr.	MER 434	Conrad	BER 235
John	DEL	176	Charles	YOR 212	Conrod	FRA 273
Nehemiah	DEL	165	David	ALL 118	Daniel	PHI 22
Thomas	DEL	175	John	ALL 91	Daniel	ADA 38
Thomas	DEL	176	BROW, David	DAU 51A	Daniel	NOH 39
Thomas	DEL	182	BROW?, Henry	MNT 43	Daniel	BUC 85
William	DEL	176	BROWAS, Jacob	PHI 95	Daniel	HNT 160
BROOME, Wm.	PHA	82	BROWBEKER, Peter	FRA 302	Daniel	DEL 164
BROOMER,			BROWDEN, Willm.	BUC 85A	Daniel	BER 265
Christopher	CHE	850	BROWER, Abraham	BER 274	Daniel	LUZ 365
Isaac	CHE	742	Abram	CHE 896	Daniel	LUZ 398
John	CHE	851	Daniel	MNT 80	Danl.	BER 190
John	CHE	902	James	CHE 722	David	PHI 9
BROOMWALL, Thos.	CHE	806	BROWKAW, Abraham	WAS 26	David	GRN 74
BROONER, Peter	ALL	87	BROWN, Widw.	PHI 76	David	ALL 105
Thomas	CHE	803	Abner	GRN 98	David	LAN 106
BROOS, George	BUC	92A	Abner Junr.	GRN 98	David	CUM 151
BROOSE, Jas.	CUM	65	Abra.	PHI 69A	David	LAN 161
BROOX, Aaron	BEV	14	Abraham	BEV 4	David	WST 167
BROSIURS, Abraham	NOU	120	Abraham	BER 207	David	LAN 218
Daniel	NOU	120	Abraham	FAY 254	David	FAY 252
George	NOU	120	Abraham	LUZ 367	David	FRA 297
George	NOU	120	Abram	CHE 713	David	LUZ 363
Jacob	NOU	120	Adam	CUM 119	David	WAR 1A
Jacob	NOU	120	Adam	FAY 254	Ebenazer	GRN 105
Nicholas	NOU	120	Addam	CRA 5	Edward	BFD 69
Nicholas	NOU	120	Adley	CHE 700	Edward	FAY 234
BROSIUS, John	LAN	250	Adley	CHE 884	Eliezer	FAY 263
BROSMAN, John	BER	190	Agnes	DAU 19	Elihu	CHE 886
Peter	LAN	193	Alexander	BFD 36	Eliphalet	LUZ 379
BROSS, Garret	PHA	120	Alexander	DEL 157	Elisha	PHA 106
BROSSE, John	CUM	65	Alexander	FAY 230	Elizabeth	PHA 38
BROSTON, John	PHI	55	Alexd.	ALL 111	Elizenar	NOU 201
BROTHERLINE,			Alexd.	FRA 302	Eneas	LUZ 365
Charles	HNT	156	Alexr.	WST 148	Ephm.	CUM 65
Elizqa	HNT	155	Alexr.	WST 284	Ephraim	PHI 79A
BROTHERS, Jacob	ADA	28	Alexr.	BUT 360	Ezekel	MIF 9A
John	WAS	118	Allen	LUZ 419	Ezekiel	LUZ 366
Joseph	CUM	35	Allexander	BEV 14	Ezekiel	LUZ 393
Matthias	BFD	61	Amos	ERI 59A	Ezra	PHI 78
Stephen	HNT	124	Andrew	ADA 3	Federick	BER 225
BROTHERTON,			Andrew	GRN 94	Fredek	BER 190
Elishia	PHI	94	Andrew	SOM 153	Frederick	ADA 33
James	ALL	60	Andrew	FAY 263	Frederick	BER 255
John	FRA	313	Andw.	PHA 15	Fredk.	PHI 109A
Robert	ERI	59A	Armit	PHA 17	Fredrick	ALL 77
Wm.	FRA	280	Baltzer	BER 220	Geo.	CUM 50
BROTZMAN, Abraham	NOH	86A	Bazel	FAY 234	Geo.	PHI 107
Adam	MNT	72	Benj.	PHI 105	Geo.	FRA 273
Danl.	BER	235	Benjamin	PHA 12	Geo.	BUT 368
David	NOH	77A	Benjamin	GRN 105	George	ADA 35
Frederick	NOH	77A	Benjamin	SOM 126	George	PHA 43
George	NOH	77A	Benjamin	HNT 138	George	PHI 54
Jacob	MNT	72	Benjamin	LAN 149	George	ARM 124
Jacob	NOH	72A	Benjamin	DEL 161	George	YOR 165
Jacob	NOH	77A	Benjamin	WST 248	George	BER 173
Jacob	NOH	86A	Benjamin	LUZ 369	George	DEL 181
John	NOH	37	Benjn.	LYC 18	George	BER 190
John	NOH	77A	Benjn.	CUM 27	George	BUT 315
Nicholas	NOH	77A	Benjn. Esqr.	CHE 861	George	WST 321
Nichs. Jn.	NOH	77A	Bernard	BFD 56	George	LUZ 335
Peter	LAN	35	Booth	CHE 864	George	LUZ 409
Philip	NOH	86A	Calop	ALL 77	George Jnr.	NOH 49A
BROUDEN, Bridget	BUC	83	Cedar	PHA 51	George	NOH 49A
BROUGHLER, Adam	BUC	100A	Charity	CHE 703	George	BUC 155A
Michael	BUC	100A	Charles	DAU 22	Gottlieb	NOH 31A
BROUGHT, Danl.	MIF	12A	Charles	PHA 67	Hance	PHA 46
Wm.	FRA	315	Charles	PHI 121	Harman	LAN 112

BROWN, Mathias	BER 158	BROWN, Samuel	PHA 116	BROWN, William	WST 340
Matthias	NOU 120	Samuel	SOM 126	William	CHE 887
Mattw.	CUM 110	Samuel	FAY 263	William	CHE 888
Melchor	DAU 3	Samuel	MER 435	William Jr.	CUM 95
Michael	NOH 77	Samuel	CHE 888	William M.	
Michael	NOU 120	Sarah	PHA 31	Esqr.	FRA 276
Michael	DEL 187	Sarah	PHA 71	Willm.	BUC 83
Michael	MER 434	Sarah	BUC 83	Willm.	BUT 335
Michl.	CUM 49	Sarah	CUM 148	Willm.	BUT 366
Michl.	PHI 72	Sebastian	YOR 168	Wilm.	ALL 106
Michl. Sr.	CUM 49	Solomon	FAY 200	Wm.	LYC 8
Michl.	DAU 39A	Solomon	MER 435	Wm.	PHA 63
Monas	FAY 254	Steven	FAY 197	Wm.	PHA 67
Moses	HNT 159	Susana	FAY 254	Wm.	PHI 70
Mrs.	NOU 162	Susannah	ADA 29	Wm.	PHA 94
Nathan	BUC 98A	Teany	MNT 69	Wm.	PHI 101
Nathaniel	PHA 9	Thadius	PHA 103	Wm.	PHI 121
Nathaniel	DEL 164	Thomas	CEN 22	Wm.	CUM 133
Nathaniel	DEL 165	Thomas	PHI 28	Wm.	YOR 198
Nathaniel	DEL 167	Thomas	PHI 44	Wm.	CHE 821
Nathaniel	LUZ 389	Thomas	PHA 116	Wm.	CHE 862
Nathen	ERI 59A	Thomas	CUM 119	Wm. Esq.	MIF 14A
Obadiah	LUZ 420	Thomas	HNT 152	Wm. Jr.	WST 209
Oliver	FRA 278	Thomas	PHI 152	Wm. Senr.	CUM 94
Pat	LAN 170	Thomas	NOU 170	Wm.	MIF 9A
Patience	LUZ 419	Thomas	FAY 230	Wm.	PHI 67A
Paul	PHA 26	Thomas	FAY 234	Wm.	PHI 76A
Paul	GRN 99	Thomas	MER 435	Wm.	PHI 90A
Paul	ALL 114	Thomas	CHE 806	Zachariah	FAY 238
Peter	ADA 14	Thomas	CHE 889	BROWN?, George	NOU 134
Peter	CUM 49	Thos.	LYC 8	John	FRA 285
Peter	PHI 82	Thos.	PHA 83	John?	NOU 203
Peter	DEL 164	Thos.	PHA 88	Robt.	FRA 285
Peter	BER 211	Thos.	PHA 94	BROWNBACK, Benjn.	CHE 898
Peter Esqr.	PHI 106A	Thos.	CUM 105	Henry	CHE 794
Philip	DAU 37	Thos.	PHA 105	John	CHE 795
Philip	DAU 46	Thos.	FRA 285	Valley	CHE 891
Philip	PHI 120	Thos.	WST 306	Widow	CHE 788
Philip	BER 265	Thos.	MIF 14A	Widow	CHE 897
Philip	DAU 14A	Thos.	DAU 15A	BROWNE, Isaiah	PHA 122
Rachel	PHA 35	Thos.	PHI 107A	Samuel	PHA 12
Richard	ADA 21	Tristrum	ERI 56A	BROWNELLER, Henry	CUM 122
Richard	PHI 60	Trustrim	ALL 75	Wm.	CUM 117
Richard	FAY 242	Uriah	CHE 866	BROWNER, Jno.	CUM 102
Richard	FAY 243	Vinein	FAY 219	BROWNFIELD, James	WST 269
Richard	MER 435	Widow	LAN 154	Robert	CRA 17
Richard	CHE 747	Widow	LAN 218	BROWNHULTZ,	
Richd.	PHA 74	Widow	NOH 31A	Fransis	PHI 126
Robert	ADA 5	Widow Of Jno.	NOH 29	Fransis Junr.	PHI 126
Robert	WAS 19	Wilks	FAY 234	BROWNLEE, George	MER 433
Robert	WAS 48	William	PHI 15	James	WAS 11
Robert	ERI 58	William	PHI 20	John	WAS 6
Robert	BFD 78	William	DAU 22	John	WAS 6
Robert	LAN 89	William	WAS 26	John	WAS 11
Robert	WST 167	William	PHI 28	John Junr.	WAS 11
Robert	WST 167	William	LAN 34	Thomas	WAS 6
Robert	LUZ 364	William	WAS 48	Thomas	WAS 61
Robert	CHE 836	William	WAS 66	William	WAS 11
Robert Esqr.	NOH 29	William	GRN 86	BROWNSHEE, Thomas	GRN 109
Robt.	CUM 52	William	MNT 107	BROWNSON, Daniel	LUZ 369
Robt.	CUM 99	William	HNT 138	David	LUZ 389
Robt.	YOR 198	William	NOU 153	Isaac	LUZ 392
Robt.	WST 209	William	LAN 166	James	HNT 122
Robt.	WST 284	William	WST 167	Lewis	LUZ 343
Robt.	FRA 309	William	VEN 168	Mary	FRA 287
Robt.	BUT 339	William	NOU 173	Samuel	HNT 122
Rodger	CUM 34	William	BER 179	BROWNSTON, Thos.	FRA 302
Ruth	CHE 766	William	DEL 188	BROY, Conrad	MNT 53
Saml.	LYC 25	William	FAY 201	George	MNT 53
Saml.	BUC 84	William	NOU 201	George	MNT 133
Saml. B.	PHA 47	William	FAY 212	BROYN, Abner	LAN 154
Samuel	MIF 1	William	LAN 218	BRREWER, William	WST 364
Samuel	DAU 22	William	FAY 230	BRUA?, Jacob	LAN 110
Samuel	ADA 39	William	LAN 234	Peter	BER 265
Samuel	MNT 98	William	LAN 247	BRUAX, Benjamin	BFD 46
Samuel	NOU 113	William	BUT 315	BRUBACH, Benjn.	DAU 45A

BRUBACHER,			BRUCHER/			BRUNNER, Casper	LAN 32
Abraham	LAN	175	BRUCKER?,			Daniel	DAU 51A
Abraham	LAN	193	Jacob Jr.	YOR	186	George	YOR 176
Benjamin	LAN	190	BRUCK, Fredck.	NOH	37	Henry	DAU 2A
Christian	LAN	190	Henry	NOH	58A	Isaac	LAN 114
Christian	LAN	190	Mathias	NOH	88A	John	PHI 46
Christian	LAN	208	BRUCKER?, (See			John	LAN 193
Daniel	LAN	192	Breecher?)	YOR	186	Michael	LAN 298
George	LAN	78	BRUCKERT, George	NOH	58	Peter	LAN 28
Isaac	LAN	208	BRUCKHART, Daniel	YOR	166	Peter	LAN 193
Jacob	LAN	189	Henry	YOR	166	Peter	LAN 298
Jacob	LAN	193	BRUCKMAN, Charles	BER	233	Susanna	LAN 298
John	LAN	78	BRUDEN, Bob	LAN	139	Widow	NOH 79A
John	LAN	142	Robert	PHA	67	BRUNOR, Steven	FAY 242
John Jr.	LAN	78	BRUDER, Anthony	MNT	56	BRUNSON, Daniel	DAU 12
John	LAN	147A	Jacob	MNT	56	BRUNSTON?, John	YOR 209
BRUBACKER,			William	MNT	137	BRUNER, Felix	BUC 100A
Abraham	LAN	306	Wm. Junr.	MNT	137	Henry	BUT 348
Abraham	LAN	306	BRUDES, (See			John	BUC 100A
Ann	LAN	306	Bruder)	MNT	137	BRUNNER, George	BER 173
Ann Junr.	LAN	306	BRUEBECKER,			Henry	BFD 56
Christian	LAN	304	Detrick	YOR	190	Ulrich	BER 161
David	LAN	304	BRUGH, Abraham	ADA	19	Ulrich	BER 225
Henry	LAN	305	David	DAU	29A	William	BER 173
Henry	LAN	306	Jacob	ADA	37	BRUNTON?, John	BEV 27
Jacob	LAN	303	Jacob	WST	232	BRUSH, Baptist	CHE 875
Jacob	LAN	306	John	ADA	19	Berrard	GRN 79
Maria	LAN	306	Peter	ADA	34	Daniel	YOR 217
Michael	LAN	76	BRUHAL, Martin	BER	225	Isaac	MIF 16A
BRUBAKER, Abm.	LAN	258	BRUHECKER,			John	MNT 34
Abm.	LAN	259	Abraham	FRA	276	Jonas	LUZ 330
Chrisn.	LAN	259	BRUINFIELD, Jesse	BER	137	Joseph	MER 434
Danl.	DAU	38A	BRUISER, Abram	CHE	793	BRUSHIER, Barrick	FAY 234
David	LAN	288	BRUKER, Joseph	FRA	276	Bazel	FAY 234
Henry	DAU	45A	Peter	FRA	280	Marey	FAY 234
Jacob	LAN	12	BRUKINE, Abm.	LAN	59	Regnel	FAY 234
Jacob	LAN	45	BRUM, Widw.	PHI	72A	BRUSIL, Philip	LAN 44
Jacob	LAN	234	Elias	PHI	14	BRUSTER, Bengamin	
John	LAN	10	BRUMBACH,			T.?	ALL 51
John	DAU	43	Hermanus	BER	229	Henry	PHI 84
John	SOM	137	BRUMBAUGH, Cunrod	SOM	156	Saml.	PHI 84
John	LAN	223	Daniel	SOM	156	Wm. Capt.	PHI 71
John	LAN	259	Jacob	SOM	156	BRUTON, Danl.	PHI 5
Martin	LAN	223	John	FRA	295	Robert	PHI 28
Peter	SOM	137	William	SOM	156	BRUVER, John	NOU 148
Peter	LAN	259	BRUMFIELD,			BRWON, Wm. Sr.	WST 209
BRUBECKER, Conrad	YOR	206	Benjamen	FAY	254	BRY, Vogel	MNT 98
Conrad Jr.	YOR	206	John	PHI	155	BRYAN, Danl.	DAU 45
Daniel	DAU	9	Solomon	BER	137	David	LAN 208
Jacob	DAU	8	Thomas	FAY	254	David	BER 267
Jacob	DAU	8	Wm.	WST	270	Eliza	PHA 59
Joh	DAU	0	BRUMGART, George	LAN	40	Esther	BEV 21
Joseph	DAU	8A	BRUMO, Mr.	PHA	122	Frances	FAY 202
Michael	YOR	206	BRUNCER, John	NOU	203	George Wm.	PHA 89
Widow	LAN	144	BRUNDIDGE, Joseph	LUZ	402	Guy	PHA 71
BRUBEKER, Davd.	DAU	16	BRUNDRIDGE,			H.	DAU 45
Jacob	LAN	182	Joseph Jr.	LUZ	402	James	MNT 71
BRUCE, Benjn.	MIF	24A	BRUNER, Adam	PHI	73	James	LAN 116
Charles	BEV	26	Christiana	WAS	115	James	FRA 320
David	WAS	88	David	MNT	47	James	BUC 81A
Isaac	CHE	884	David	MNT	87	Joel	MNT 67
John	BEV	22	Frederick	MNT	69	Joseph	DAU 3
John	NOH	47	George	PHI	3	Margarett	DEL 175
John	WST	341	Henry	PHI	129	Michael	FAY 201
Joseph	CHE	724	Jacob	ADA	4	Molly	LAN 58
Peter	DAU	2A	Jacob	MNT	87	Samuel	LAN 50
Thomas	MIF	24A	Jacob	SOM	145	Samuel	BUC 147
Widow	LAN	244	Joseph	MNT	93	Thomas	BEV 6
Wm.	CUM	78	Peter	NOU	179	Thos.	PHI 111A
Wm.	CUM	85	Peter	FAY	261	William	WAS 66
BRUCE?, John	BEV	15	BRUNKHART, Adam	YOR	186	William	BUC 147
Paul C.	PHA	112	Martin	YOR	186	William	LUZ 357
BRUCH, George	NOH	39	BRUNKHEART, John	FRA	284	William	BUC 140A
Jno. George	NOH	86A	BRUNNER, Abraham	NOH	47	Wm.	PHI 114
Michael	NOH	64	Abraham	NOH	46A	BRYANS, Denis	DAU 27A
Thomas	NOU	108	Andrew	NOH	46A	BRYANT, Benjn.	PHA 3

BRYANT, Elizabeth	PHA	46	BUCHANAN, John			BUCK, David	BFD	48
Henry	BEV	27	Esqr.	WAS	54	Elizabeth	PHI	77A
John Y.	PHA	93	Mary	WAS	54	Enoch D.	LUZ	389
Margaret	PHA	118	Matthew	CHE	717	Ephraim	ERI	55A
Nicholas	BEV	4	Robert	WAS	42	Frederick	MNT	98
Thos.	PHA	44	Robt.	CUM	23	Fredr.	FRA	302
BRYANT?, John O.	PHA	104	Robt.	CUM	131	Geo.	CUM	132
BRYDE, Charles	LYC	28	Robt.	MIF	16A	George	MNT	103
BRYEAN, John	BEV	21	Ross	WAS	54	George	PHI	129
BRYERKOLTZ, John	ADA	17	Saml.	CHE	716	George	LUZ	325
BRYERLY?, Robert	ALL	84	Walter	WAS	54	George	PHI	109A
BRYFOGEL, George	BER	225	Walter	WAS	97	Henry	MIF	1
BRYMAN, Christian	BER	137	William	WAS	54	Ichabod	LUZ	389
BRYNER, John	CUM	48	Wm.	CUM	88	Jacob	BUC	139
BRYON, John	BER	205	Wm.	YOR	198	James	MNT	85
Mary	CUM	126	Wm.	CHE	716	James	MNT	115
Thomas	BER	283	BUCHANNAN, Arthur	WAY	143	John	DAU	16
BRYON?, Widow	MIF	9A	Christian	FAY	212	John	MNT	114
BRYSON, Isaac	WAS	33	George	WAY	143	John	BUC	149
Jas.	CUM	65	George	FAY	212	John	LUZ	380
John	WAS	33	John	CUM	23	Josuah	MER	434
John	NOU	162	John	LAN	162	Leonard	BUC	147
John	FAY	207	William	LAN	74	Leonard	NOU	156
Saml.	CUM	135	BUCHANNON, Arthur			Lewis	PHI	87A
Samuel	HNT	144	(See			Mary	PHI	91A
Samuel	FAY	207	Buchannon,			Michael Junr.	NOH	52A
William	WAS	33	James)	LAN	164	Michael Sen.	NOH	52A
Wm.	CUM	70	David	WST	321	Michael	DAU	47A
BUATT, Joseph	SOM	126	Dorcas Widow	LAN	15	Nicholas	BUC	139
BUBACH, Gerhard	LAN	190	James & Arthur	LAN	164	Richard	MER	434
BUBB, Conrad	NOU	186	John	FRA	324	Thomas	BFD	61
Jacob	NOU	186	William	BFD	71	Wm.	PHA	118
BUBE, George	NOU	191	BUCHECKER,			BUCK?, (See		
George	NOU	191	Baltzer	NOH	79A	Beock)	CUM	22
BUBING?, Jacob	MNT	42	George	NOH	79A	BUCKAN, Robt.	DAU	45
BUBORY, Daniel	VEN	167	Henry	NOH	79A	Thomas	PHI	23
BUBS, David	NOU	174	Philip Junr.	NOH	79A	BUCKANAN, John	HNT	156
BUCCHANNON,			Philip	NOH	79A	Thos.	CUM	124
George	FRA	323	Widow	NOH	79A	William	LUZ	382
James Ssr.	FRA	289	BUCHER, Abraham	NOH	86A	BUCKANER, John	NOU	156
Jos.	FRA	299	Adam	DAU	34	BUCKANON, James		
Thos.	FRA	299	Andrew	BUC	81A	Jr.	DAU	8A
BUCH, Christian	LAN	187	Benedict	DAU	27A	BUCKER, Widw.	PHI	110
Henry	LAN	142	Chrisn.	LAN	264	Jacob	YOR	181
John	LAN	143	Christian	LAN	147A	Jesse	PHI	91
John	BER	234	George	DAU	11	BUCKERTON, Widow	PHI	18
BUCHAM, Abm.	CEN	20	George	DAU	33	BUCKET, Adam	MIF	14A
BUCHAMER, Jacob	BER	136	George	BER	155	BUCKEUS,		
BUCHANAN,			Henry	NOU	97	Christopher	PHI	133
Alexander	CRA	7	Jacob	LAN	193	Fransis	PHI	125
Alexr.	CHE	714	Jacob	DAU	4A	Peter	PHI	133
Arthur	MIF	1	John	DAU	17	BUCKHAMER,		
Arthur	CUM	91	John	LAN	193	Catherine	MNT	67
Boot (Negro)	WAS	74	John	NOH	86A	BUCKHANAN,		
David	WAS	54	BUCHERT, John	BER	256	Alexander	PHA	106
Elisabeth	WAS	54	BUCHEUS, William	PHI	142	Robert	LAN	158
George	CRA	6	BUCHINGER, Fredk.	DAU	52	BUCKHART, Jacob	BUT	316
George	HNT	117	BUCHLER, George	DAU	32	John	BUT	316
George	HNT	136	BUCHMAN, Andrew	NOH	51	BUCKHEART,		
Hannah	CHE	717	Daniel	NOH	49A	Phillip	NOU	182
Henry	ADA	22	Jacob	NOH	49A	BUCKHOLDER, Adam	FRA	312
James	WAS	19	BUCHMYER, John	DAU	52	Christ.	FRA	282
James	WAS	54	BUCHTER, John	LAN	70	George	NOU	197
James	WAS	88	Mathias	BER	173	Henry	MIF	16A
James	LUZ	380	BUCHWALTER, Henry	LAN	305	Jacob	FRA	310
Jas.	CUM	54	John	BER	166	Jacob	FRA	315
Jno.	CUM	143	BUCHWATER,			Mary	FRA	312
John	WAS	19	Abraham	BER	166	BUCKIAS, John	WAS	119
John	WAS	51	BUCK-OR?, Michl.	FRA	312	BUCKINGHAM, Isaac	WAS	119
John	WAS	51	BUCK, Mrs.	LYC	16	James	WAS	36
John	WAS	54	Andrew	LUZ	379	John	PHA	83
John	WST	147	Benjamin	PHI	147	Thos.	WAS	36
John	HNT	162	Benjamin	LUZ	389	William	WAS	36
John	DEL	189	Christn.	DAU	45A	BUCKLAND, James	PHA	68
John	CHE	715	Daniel	LUZ	389	BUCKLER, Nathan	CHE	869
John	CHE	778	Danl.	LYC	15	BUCKLEY, Widow	PHI	6

BUCKLEY, Aaron	LAN	49	BUDLER?, Peter	BER	172	BULL, Wm.	CUM	37
Calvin	LUZ	410	Thomas	MNT	130	BULLARD, Peter	LUZ	343
Daniel	LAN	134	BUDMAN, George	NOU	142	Ruben	FAY	197
Francis	DAU	39	Isaac	NOU	143	BULLER, William	CHE	821
Henry	CHE	908	Jacob	NOU	142	BULLERSLAND, Syp		
John	BFD	36	BUDWINE, James	PHI	27	For	LAN	265
John	HNT	119	BUEHART?, See			BULLES, Saml.	BER	233
John	LAN	226	Buchart	BER	256	BULLINGER, Peter	BUC	147
Johnston	LYC	19	BUEHER?, Adam	DAU	34	BULLMAN, Abraham	BFD	61
William	PHA	103	BUEHLER, Henry	DAU	32A	John	BFD	61
William	HNT	137	BUELL, Timothy	WST	209	BULLMAN?, Andrew	ARM	124
BUCKLOW, John	NOU	148	BUERNA, Willm.	PHI	37	BULLOCK, Aaron	DEL	159
BUCKLY, Israel	LYC	11	BUFF, John	CHE	792	Isaac	DEL	159
BUCKMAN, Abden	BUC	151	BUFFENMEYER,			John	DEL	157
Abner	BUC	103	David	LAN	99	Joseph	PHI	133
Abner	BUC	98A	Henry	LAN	99	Moses	CUM	93
Abraham	BUC	137	Matthias	LAN	99	Moses	DEL	159
Benjn.	BUC	160A	BUFFENTON, George	DAU	5A	Thomas	DEL	157
David	BUC	103	Thomas	LAN	227	BULOINGE, Madame	PHA	95
David	BUC	98A	BUFFINGTON, Abner	DAU	3	BULTER, John	HNT	138
Isaac	BUC	103	Caleb	DEL	162	BULVINE, William	SOM	126
James	BUC	151	Curtis	CHE	762	BULY, Manshion	PHI	74A
Jesse	BUC	103	Eli	DAU	6	BUM, Jacob	PHI	84A
John	BUC	103	Elizabeth	CHE	758	Mickl.	FRA	312
Jonathan	BUC	98A	Ephraim	CHE	741	BUMBACH, George	LAN	11
Joseph	BUC	103	Isaac	CEN	22	BUMBARGER, Geo.	DAU	36A
Marey	FAY	219	Isaac	CHE	774	John	WAS	6
Phineas	BUC	151	John	WAS	78	BUMBAUGH, Conrad	DAU	4
Saml.	FAY	225	Jonathn.	CHE	803	John	ADA	11
Samuel	BUC	98A	Joseph	CHE	808	BUMBERGER, Abrm.	DAU	17
Thomas	BUC	103	Joshua	CHE	774	John	DAU	13
Thomas	BUC	84A	Joshua	CHE	900	Michl.	DAU	14
William	BUC	103	Levi	DAU	6A	William	PHA	14
BUCKMASTER,			Richd.	CHE	762	BUMBOH, Martin	PHI	91
Joseph	BEV	15	Richd.	CHE	829	BUMERSHINE, Henry	SOM	142
William	BEV	16	Robt.	CHE	761	BUMESDERFER, John		
BUCKS, Abm.	BER	148	Seth	WAS	78	Sen.	LAN	99
John	BER	148	BUFFINTON, Robt.	CHE	742	BUMGANER, Daniel	NOU	116
BUCKS?, Jane?	MIF	9A	BUFFMAN, Adam	ARM	123	BUMGARNER, David	HNT	147
BUCKSOME, Henry	MNT	66	BUFFS?, John	ARM	126	Jesse	WAS	36
BUCKUS, Philip	PHI	90A	BUGAR, John	NOU	134	John	HNT	147
BUCKWALTER,			BUGE, Jacob	NOH	33	John	HNT	147
Abraham	LAN	114	BUGE?, Michael	LAN	98	Michael	HNT	147
Abraham	LAN	116	BUGH, Jacob	BEV	4	Peter	ADA	25
Abraham	LAN	179	Peter	BEV	4	BUMGARTNER, Jacob	ADA	4
David	LAN	116	BUGHER, John	WAS	61	BUN, James	NOU	191
David	LAN	117	BUGHNER, William	NOU	197	William	HNT	139
David	CHE	853	BUGHS, Christian	GRN	69	BUN?, William	MNT	69
Francis	LAN	174	BUGLASS, Mary	PHA	22	BUNCH, Thomas	BER	172
Gerhart	BER	225	BUHAL, Martin	NOU	179	BUNDEN, Dan	LAN	147A
Henry	LAN	116	Peter	NOU	179	BUNDIN, Jacob	NOU	156
Jacob	MNT	80	BUISEY, John	BUC	149	BUNDLE, David	BFD	56
Jacob	CHE	854	BUISY, Jacob	BUC	149	Michael	LAN	50
John	LAN	114	BUJAC, John L.	PHA	97	Moses	VEN	170
John	LAN	116	BUKER, Jacob	PHI	83A	Wm.	FRA	313
John	LAN	183	Peter	LAN	147	BUNDY, John	NOU	120
John	CHE	856	BULA, William	LAN	129	Joseph	FAY	225
Joseph	LAN	112	BULER, Jacob	MNT	103	Josia	FAY	234
Joseph	LAN	117	BULES?, See Bales	ADA	38	William	NOU	120
BUCLEY, Adam	PHI	97A	BULEY, Isaac	MNT	130	BUNER / BUNEL?,		
BUCOM, John	WST	188	Jesse	CHE	834	Wm.	BEV	27
BUD, William	MER	435	BULGER, Laurence	BFD	36	BUNG, Fredk.	YOR	172
William Jr.	MER	435	Thomas	BUC	103	BUNHAIT?, Ulrigh	YOR	187
BUDD, Asa	LUZ	401	BULIGER, Abraham	ALL	97	BUNKER, Abm.	CUM	39
Cunketon	BUT	326	BULKER, John	PHI	14	Daniel	BUC	140A
George Esqr.	PHI	67A	BULL, Elijah	BER	247	John	FAY	208
John	WAS	73	Henry	CUM	37	BUNN, Benjn.	CHE	718
John	LUZ	377	John	NOU	170	Henry	BER	172
Joseph	PHA	24	John	LUZ	414	Herman	BER	137
Wm.	PHA	39	John Esqr.	YOR	175	Jacob	BER	173
BUDDEN, Widow	CHE	831	John	PHI	116A	John	CUM	33
BUDDY, Jacob	PHI	128	John G.	CHE	832	Nicholas	BER	137
John	PHI	128	Roger	DEL	171	Nicholas	FRA	320
Peter	PHI	71	Roger	DEL	189	BUNNELL, Aaron	WAS	119
BUDER, Leond.	CUM	59	Samuel	BER	249	John	LUZ	420
BUDINOTT, Elias	PHA	75	Thomas Esqr.	CHE	903	BUNNER, Elizabeth	PHA	98

Name	Place	Page
BUNNER, Henry	DAU	38
Henry	DAU	35A
Sarah	PHA	98
William	PHI	133
BUNNIL, Benjamin	WAY	148
Gersham	WAY	148
BUNNO, Mr.	PHA	95
BUNOWS?, Abm.	MIF	16A
BUNSON, Wm.	WST	377
BUNSTEIN, Jacob	NOH	33
BUNTEN, Marey	FAY	252
BUNTIN, Amos	PHI	150
Joseph	PHI	153
Watty	LAN	168
BUNTING, Asa	BUC	92A
Daniel	BUC	92A
David	CHE	746
George	BUC	92A
John	PHA	46
John	PHI	108
John	WAY	138
John	BUC	147
John	CHE	746
Joshua	BUC	84
Josiah	DEL	167
Nicholas	PHI	32
Philip	PHA	40
Robt.	CHE	748
Saml.	CHE	746
Samuel	DEL	167
Samuel Jnr.	BUC	92A
Samuel Jun.	DEL	167
Samuel	BUC	92A
Samuel	BUC	160A
William	CHE	748
William	CHE	875
William	BUC	92A
William	BUC	160A
William	BUC	160A
Wm.	CHE	772
BUONS, Edwd.	BUC	161
BUOY, Edward	NOU	116
BUPP, John	NOU	120
Nicholas	NOU	120
BUR, Charles	LAN	59
John	ARM	126
Robt.	FRA	322
Ruben	NOU	113
William	NOU	108
BURBACK, George	BFD	71
BURBRIDGE, Thoms.	BUT	321
BURCALEO?, Mary	PHA	94
BURCH, Charles	BER	234
James	CRA	8
Mathias	PHI	72
BURCHELL, Andw.	PHI	47
BURCHFIELD, Adam	ALL	71
Aquilla Sr.	MIF	12A
Aquilla	MIF	12A
Charles	NOU	182
James?	MIF	12A
Robt.	MIF	12A
Rt.	MIF	12A
Tho.	MIF	12A
Thos.	CUM	96
BURCHHOLDER,		
Felix	DAU	40A
BURCK, Edward	DAU	3
BURCKART, Peter	DAU	26
Peter	DAU	29A
BURCKERDI, Jacob	DAU	4A
BURCKERT, George	LAN	85
BURCKHART, Jacob	ALL	114
BURCKHOLD, Ab.	DAU	40A
BURCKHOLDER, John	ALL	93
BURD, Andw.	CUM	31
BURD, Benjamin	BFD	36
Chas.	PHA	93
David	CUM	45
George Captn.	PHI	95A
Isaac	BER	179
Jacob	LAN	81
Jacob	BER	223
James	ADA	4
John	ALL	78
Joseph	DAU	12A
Matthias	CUM	41
Ralph	ALL	106
Samuel	FAY	249
BURD?, Caleb	PHI	79
BURDEN, George	PHI	20
BURDINE, John	MIF	9A
BURDLEMAN, Elias	NOU	145
BURDOCK, George	PHA	65
BURDRAUFF, John	LAN	250
BURDS, Lewis Mr.	PHI	89A
BURFOT, Robert	ARM	125
BURG, Elizabeth	LAN	58
John	LAN	41
BURGE, Jacob (See		
Burge, Widow)	NOH	33
Jacob	HNT	130
Jonathan	FAY	255
Joseph	HNT	130
Joseph	FAY	234
Widow Of Jacob	NOH	33
William	HNT	130
BURGE?, -----	MIF	9A
BURGEN, Anthony	LAN	138
John	YOR	217
BURGER, Adam	BFD	61
Casper	BUC	81A
Daniel	BER	136
Frederick	NOH	88A
George	MNT	60
Henry	NOH	33
Jacob	YOR	216
John	BFD	49
John	SOM	147
Jost	NOH	58A
Peter	ADA	16
Peter	BER	236
BURGERT, Jacob	YOR	178
Peter Jr.	YOR	184
Peter Sr.	YOR	184
BURGES, George	BUC	140A
John	PHA	40
John	BUC	86
Joseph	BUC	140A
Mary	PHA	11
Sarah	BUC	92A
BURGESS, Amos	BUC	92A
Ann	FAY	263
Archibald	WAS	15
John	CHE	762
John	BUC	92A
Joseph	LUZ	401
Joshua	LUZ	333
Rachel	FAY	212
William	CHE	883
William	BUC	104A
BURGET, George	WAS	88
Jacob	BFD	71
Rosanna	WAS	88
BURGH, Henry	GRN	75
Henry Junr.	GRN	75
William	GRN	75
William	GRN	80
BURGHART, George	DAU	33A
BURGIS, John	MER	435
Lewis	ADA	20
BURGOIES, Francis	PHA	105
BURGOON, Jacob	HNT	123
John	HNT	123
Peter	HNT	123
BURGUNTINE, Peter	CHE	712
BURGUR, Saml.	PHI	105A
BURHART, Herman	DAU	46
BURK, Widw.	PHI	104A
& Hecht	LAN	152
Andw.	PHA	46
Benjn.	PHA	61
Edward	MNT	130
Edward	SOM	161
Edward	PHI	79A
Geo. (See Burk,		
Widow)	NOH	37
Henry	DAU	30A
Hugh	LAN	161
Jacob	BUC	156A
James	PHA	4
James	PHA	112
James	NOU	116
James Senr.	NOH	77
Jane	PHI	153
John	NOH	77
John	PHI	108
John	MNT	130
John	LAN	294
John	CHE	859
John Junr.	MNT	130
John	PHI	90A
John	BUC	156A
Joseph P?	PHA	61
Susannah (A		
Boarding		
House	PHA	37
Thomas	FAY	201
Thos.	PHA	69
Thos.	PHI	97A
Valentine	PHI	25
Widow Of Geo.	NOH	37
Widow Of Henry	NOH	37
William	PHI	33
William	WAS	97
BURKARD, Cathrine	PHI	147
Samuel	PHI	59
BURKART, Conrad	MNT	98
Jacob	BER	235
Tobias	BER	280
BURKE, George	PHI	11A
Henry	WAS	78
James	LAN	15
Thos.	YOR	171
William	PHI	42
BURKENBEEL, James	FAY	243
BURKENSHIER, John	FAY	208
BURKET,		
Christopher	SOM	153
Daniel	PHI	2
David	MNT	56
Fredk.	PHA	42
George	WST	305
Israel	SOM	153
Jacob	PHI	103
Jacob	SOM	151
John	PHA	116
John	SOM	141
John	SOM	151
Josh.	FRA	299
Joshua	ADA	3
Saml.	FRA	305
Sarah	PHA	37
Tobias	MNT	56
BURKHALTER, Peter		
Jnr.	NOH	88A
Peter	NOH	88A
BURKHARD, Andrew	PHA	102

BURTNER, Geo.	CUM 118	BUSH?, (See Burk)	NOH 37	BUTEL, John	NOU 179		
John	ALL 57	John	LYC 16	BUTHALL?, (See			
BURTNETT, Adam	GRN 69	BUSHAR, Charles	BER 235	Vuthall)	CHE 909		
Robt.	CUM 40	BUSHARD, Danl.	PHI 1	BUTLAR, John	ALL 119		
BURTNETT?, Daniel	PHA 72	John	LAN 245	BUTLE, Charles	DEL 175		
BURTON, Anthony	BUC 84	BUSHEL, Wm.	PHI 106A	BUTLER, Widow	PHI 99A		
Anthony Jnr.	BUC 85A	BUSHER, Moses	PHI 13	Widw.	PHI 84A		
John Jnr.	BUC 84	BUSHEY, Christian	ADA 38	Abigail	CHE 765		
Thomas	PHI 99A	John	ADA 38	Abraham	YOR 215		
Wm.	PHI 113	Michael	ADA 12	Benjamin	NOH 66		
BURTS, Thomas	FAY 201	Nicholas	ADA 38	Benjn.	CHE 815		
BURUNS, Thos.	PHI 70	BUSHFIELD, J.	LAN 169	Benjna.	CHE 817		
BURWEL, Benjn.	FAY 219	Samuel	WAS 6	Daniel	BUC 88A		
BURWELL, Isaac	WAS 26	BUSHFILL, Jacob	LAN 292	Jacob	CHE 872		
Joseph	WAS 26	BUSHING, Philip	LAN 111	Jain	ALL 49		
Saml.	FAY 225	BUSHMAN, Abraham	LAN 222	James	LYC 30		
Samuel	FAY 230	Andrew	ADA 8	James	PHA 61		
BURY, David	NOH 88A	BUSHONG, Jacob	DAU 32A	James	CUM 121		
Frederick	NOH 88A	BUSHUNG, John	LAN 117	James	CHE 767		
Henry	NOH 89	BUSHY, Elizabeth	BER 286	James	CHE 815		
Henry Junr.	NOH 89	Jacob	BER 286	James Captn.	PHI 154		
BUSBAY, Widow	PHI 26	John Jr.	BER 286	James	PHI 83A		
BUSBY, Abraham	PHI 136	Michael	BER 286	James?	MNT 131		
Benjn.	PHA 74	BUSKENICK, Moris	NOU 99	John	PHA 32		
John	PHA 67	Thos.	NOU 99	John	LAN 84		
Joseph	MNT 106	Thos. Senr.	NOU 99	John	PHI 95		
Mary	PHI 136	BUSKERDS, John	PHI 27	John	NOU 156		
BUSBYSHELL,		BUSKIRK, Andrew	NOH 35	John	FRA 312		
Chrisn.	PHA 47	Andrew	MNT 67	John	CHE 771		
BUSCH, Andw.	PHA 40	Daniel	NOH 35	John	CHE 803		
John	LAN 207	Isaac	BFD 54	John	CHE 814		
BUSE, Jacob	YOR 179	John Esqr.	NOH 58A	John	CHE 829		
John	YOR 175	John	NOH 79A	Joseph	NOH 37		
Peter	ADA 28	Mahlon	MNT 66	Joseph	NOU 156		
BUSE?, Jacob	MNT 113	Mary	MNT 48	Joshua	CHE 818		
BUSEAR, Barthew	PHI 116A	William	NOH 77A	Lord	LUZ 319		
BUSELY?, John	NOU 145	BUSKLEY, Benjamin	LUZ 368	Mary	ALL 49		
BUSER, Jacob	LAN 79	BUSMAN, Amos	PHI 11	Mary	PHA 113		
BUSERD, Jacob	NOU 197	BUSON, Charles	MNT 112	Michael	PHA 9		
BUSH/ BUCH?,		BUSS, Jacob	NOH 33	Pearce	PHA 75		
Elizabeth	MNT 122	John	NOH 33	Peter	BFD 61		
BUSH, Mrs.	LYC 16	John	NOH 70A	Phebe	LUZ 319		
(See Rush)	LYC 1	Philip	NOH 70A	Richd.	PHI 82A		
Aaron	NOU 179	BUSSE, Andreas	NOH 69A	Saml.	CHE 771		
Barbara	ADA 17	BUSSEL, Fredk.	YOR 179	Samuel	ADA 14		
Benjn.	NOH 77	Thos.	YOR 179	Thomas	NOU 156		
Charles	SOM 126	BUSSENBERGER,		Thomas	FAY 225		
Christian	ADA 15	Peter	SOM 142	William	BFD 61		
Christian	BER 256	BUSSER, John	FRA 307	William	BFD 68		
Conrad	FRA 297	BUSSERD, Melchior		William	FAY 234		
Daniel	WST 208	Jun.	NOH 41	William	LAN 265		
David	PHI 28	Philip	NOH 41	William	MER 434		
George	NOH 77	BUSSERT,		William	CHE 888		
Harman	YOR 216	Christopher	NOH 41	Wm.	CHE 771		
Henry	BFD 71	Melchior	NOH 41	Zebulon	LUZ 318		
Henry	PHI 72	BUSSHEE/		Ames	LAN 258		
Jacob	BER 256	BUSHKEE?,		BUTLER?, Elisha	FRA 319		
James Junr.	NOH 77	Christiana	YOR 209	John	GRN 75		
John	LAN 57	BUSTAL, Silas	PHI 94	BUTNER, Jacob			
John	YOR 162	BUSTEN, Daniel	NOU 162	Junr.	CUM 59		
John	BER 225	BUSTLEMAN, Sandy	MNT 42	Jacob Senr.	CUM 59		
John	BER 274	BUSTY, Paul	PHA 83	Philip	BFD 39		
Joseph	LUZ 357	BUSWELL, Willm.	PHI 97	BUTT, Benjn.	CUM 43		
Laurence	PHI 18	BUSY, Christian	BUC 96	Daniel	ADA 23		
Martin	DAU 41	BUT?, William	MIF 16A	Jacob	SOM 156		
Michael	ADA 17	BUTCHER, Charles	BUC 92A	Julian	ADA 23		
Michael	BER 235	Jacob	LAN 96	William	SOM 156		
Peter	NOH 55	Job	PHA 27	BUTTER, (See			
Peter	CUM 117	John	PHI 129	Butler)	GRN 75		
Rebecca	CUM 111	John	PHI 147	BUTTER?, Elisha	FRA 319		
Simeon	WAY 137	Moses	FRA 327	BUTTERBAUGH, John	HNT 128		
Stephen	BER 239	Nathl.	MNT 37	Joseph	HNT 148		
Thomas	NOH 77	Thomas	LAN 36	Peter	HNT 128		
William	PHI 122	Thos.	YOR 198	Peter	HNT 148		
William	FAY 255	BUTE, George	NOU 97	William	HNT 148		
Wm.	LYC 16	Henry	BFD 69	BUTTERFIELD, John	GRN 98		

BUTTERFIELD, John	FAY	230	BYERLEY, Christn.	PHA	78	C--MOUR?, John	LAN	216
Joseph	LUZ	391	Chronimus	LAN	220	C--TARD?, James?	BEV	7
Rachel	FAY	230	George	LAN	225	C-AH?, Adam	NOU	179
Thomas	FAY	230	BYERLY, Adam	WST	270	CA--?, Danial	WAR	1A
BUTTERNICK, Jos.	MNT	94	Andw.	CUM	150	Dines	WAR	1A
BUTTERWAX, Jacob	MNT	49	Conrad	BFD	56	Jno.	WAR	1A
BUTTLER, Harry	FRA	300	Daniel	BER	235	Jno.	WAR	1A
John	ADA	9	Detrick	PHI	85A	CA-EY?, Paul?	FRA	276
Wm.	FRA	299	Jacob	DAU	22	CAARL, Michael	YOR	180
BUTTOMER, Jac.	WST	209	Michl.	WST	208	CAARLE, George	YOR	183
BUTTON, Elizabeth	PHA	44	Michl.	WST	270	CABE, Elias	BUC	84A
James	WAS	27	BYERS, Abraham	ADA	13	Thos.	BUC	84A
BUTTREY?, Joseph	LYC	12	Andr.	FRA	279	CABELL, George	YOR	219
BUTTS, Thos.	CUM	131	Andrew	FRA	278	Margaret	YOR	219
BUTZ, Abraham	NOH	58	Daniel	LAN	168	CABLE, Abraham	SOM	133
Abraham	BER	137	David	ADA	3	Abraham	FRA	281
Adam	NOH	41	Ebenezer	BEV	6	Abraham Esq.	SOM	141
Adam	NOH	47	Fredr.	FRA	281	Charles	PHI	11
Christian	NOH	37	Fredr.	FRA	282	Christian	SOM	137
Christian	NOH	66	Fredr.	FRA	300	Henry	ALL	115
George	NOH	33	George	ADA	4	Jacob Sen.	SOM	137
George	NOH	86A	George	WST	148	Jonathan	SOM	141
John	NOH	58	Henry	LAN	238	Jonathan	SOM	153
John Junr.	NOH	58	Isaac	ADA	14	Jonathan		
Michael	NOH	39	Isaac	BER	173	(Crossed Out)	SOM	137
Michael	NOH	41	Jacob	CUM	27	Martin	SOM	161
Peter	NOH	35	Jacob	CUM	80	Michael	SOM	156
Peter	NOH	47	Jacob	DEL	161	Solomon	BEV	15
Peter	NOH	88A	Jacob	LAN	165	CABOR?, Widw.	PHI	79A
Saml.	BER	211	Jacob	LAN	238	CACE, Peter	NOU	146
BUTZ?, Abraham	NOU	127	Jacob	CEN	18A	CACK, Josepth	MER	438
BUVAT, John	PHA	74	James	WAS	48	Peter	MER	438
BUXTON, Jacob	WAS	26	James	WST	306	CADARGUE, Thomas		
Jacob	WAS	54	James	DAU	17A	Mr.?	PHA	121
BUYER, Charles	NOU	127	Jno.	CUM	138	CADE, Curvil	PHA	9
John	NOU	191	John	MIF	3	CADERMAN, Michael	NOU	120
BUYERLY, John	BUC	104A	John	WAS	33	CADWALADER, Mrs.	PHA	84
BUYERS, John	NOU	97	John	LAN	132	David	YOR	209
BUZARD, -----	ARM	122	John	FRA	278	James	YOR	209
Jacob	CRA	10	John	FRA	281	CADWALEDER, Jones	FAY	226
Jacob	YOR	187	Jonas	ADA	11	CADWALLADER, Abel	MNT	49
BUZEL, Thomas	FAY	249	Martin	LAN	237	Benjn.	MNT	49
BUZZARD, Abraham	BFD	55	Robert	LAN	132	Cyrus	BUC	33
George	BUC	140A	Ross	MER	434	Edward	MNT	64
Hanry	CHE	885	Samuel	WAS	48	Isaac	CHE	816
Jacob	CHE	859	Samuel	GRN	68	Jacob	BUC	152
John	FRA	280	Samuel	MER	435	Jno.	MNT	49
John	CHE	859	Thomas	WAS	48	John	HNT	156
Michael	BUC	104A	William	MER	434	Joseph	MNT	65
BYALL, James	HNT	138	BYINGTON, David	LYC	7	Joseph Esquire	HNT	132
William	HNT	139	Saml.	FAY	242	Martha	MNT	34
BYAR, Francis	PHA	75	BYLAND, John	WAS	78	Richd.	MNT	38
BYARD, Widow	WST	167	BYLER, Christian	LAN	93	CADWALLEDER, Ase	FAY	226
Andw.	PHA	33	Jacob	LAN	93	Septumas	FAY	226
John	PHI	51	BYMOUNT, Jacob	PHI	115A	CADWALSADER,		
Lenord	ALL	96	BYNE, Robert	PHI	6	Charles	LAN	89
Sevan	ALL	74	BYRAM, John	FAY	208	CADWELL, Samuel	CHE	898
BYARS, Andrew	FAY	202	BYRCH, Wm. Y.	PHA	14	CADY, Abel	LYC	11
Benjeman	FAY	201	BYREAR, Joseph	PHI	95	David	WAY	140
David	FAY	201	BYRELY, Frances	ALL	68	Elisha	LYC	11
Isaac	FAY	201	BYRES, David	LAN	168	John	LYC	12
James	FAY	207	BYRNES, Edmond	PHA	17A	Manaseh	LYC	11
John	ALL	110	John	PHA	106	Peter	LYC	11
John	FAY	207	Redman	PHA	9	Zebulon	LYC	12
John Jun.	ALL	110	BYROAD, John	HNT	122	CAFECHART?, Henry	PHI	145
Thomas	FAY	201	BYRON, Capt.	PHA	43	CAFFEE,		
BYDAN, John	PHA	61	Josua	PHI	68A	Allexander	BUC	152
BYE, Enoch	BUC	144A	BYRSAD, Frederick	LAN	16	Samuel	BUC	145A
Hezekiah	HNT	130	BYSEL, Catharine	PHI	86A	CAFFERT, John	NOU	162
Thomas	BUC	86	BYSH, George	PHA	59	CAFFERTY, James	LAN	77
BYEL, Owen	PHI	38				CAFNER, John	LAN	127
BYER, Abraham	WAS	108	C-----?, John	FRA	319	CAG, Boston	BFD	54
Federick	FRA	298	C----, -----	ALL	50	John	BFD	54
George	NOU	174	Conrod	ARM	122	Peter	BFD	54
Margaret	PHI	85A	C---?, Jermeiah	FRA	299	William	BFD	49
BYER?, (See Ryer)	MIF	8A	C--LLEY?, Jno.	WAR	1A	CAGE, Patrick	LAN	172

CAGERT, John	CHE	873	CALDWELL, James	WAS	54	CALHOON, Wilm.	ALL 84
CAGHEY?, Samuel	BEV	17	James	NOU	163	CALHORN, George	NOU 162
CAHEY, Widow	WAS	15	James	DEL	188	William	NOU 163
Nathaniel	WAS	15	James	WST	341	CALHOUN, (See	
CAHILL, Abraham	WST	342	James	WST	342	Colhoun)	BEV 16
James	WST	341	James	MER	439	George	LUZ 332
John	FRA	311	John	HNT	133	James	WST 148
CAHOON, Ann	PHA	48	John	NOU	143	John	BEV 21
James	ALL	56	John	NOU	156	John	FRA 274
CAHRELL, Daniel	MNT	121	John	DEL	161	John	FRA 305
CAHSMAN, George	ADA	18	John	DEL	188	Saml.	FRA 274
CAILLEBAUX,			John	YOR	197	Samuel	BEV 21
William	PHA	94	John	WST	342	Sarah	BEV 15
CAIN, Daniel	PHI	33	John	MER	437	William	WST 148
Dennis	BUC	93	Joseph	WAS	27	Wm.	BEV 16
Jacob	ALL	110	Joseph	WAS	67	CALICAN, Phillip	NOU 174
John	GRN	87	Joseph	WAS	88	CALIH, William	PHI 26
John	CHE	769	Josepth	MER	437	CALKIN, Darius	LUZ 372
John	CHE	885	Mary	WAS	54	CALKINS, Moses	LUZ 407
Moses	LAN	134	Mary	LAN	161	CALKLEIR, Solomon	YOR 168
Neal	BUC	149	Matthew	MER	437	CALL, Bryan	ADA 9
Paul	WST	307	Nichls.	MIF	24A	Daniel	NOU 116
Robert	MNT	69	Oliver	LAN	149	James	YOR 177
Robert	LAN	112	Rebeka	HNT	166	John	NOU 116
Wm.	CHE	828	Robert	WAS	97	John	CHE 847
CAIN?, Barnhard?	ALL	49	Robert	HNT	153	Peter	LAN 22
CAIRNS, Fredk.	YOR	219	Robert	NOU	162	William	PHI 129
George	WST	233	Robert	HNT	166	CALLAHAN, Benjn.	CHE 798
Godfrey	WST	234	Robert	WST	286	Charles	PHA 120
James	DAU	3A	Robert	MER	437	Hugh	CHE 809
John	WST	234	Saml.	FRA	316	James	FAY 264
Nicholas	WST	234	Saml.	WST	322	Jesse	FAY 264
Peter	WST	234	Samuel	ADA	3	Thomas	BFD 72
William	WST	233	Samuel	WAS	55	William	FAY 264
William Junr.	WST	234	Stephen	ADA	6	CALLAN, Jane	PHI 101B
CAISE, Butler	ALL	78	Thomas	WAS	43	CALLAWAY, Mary	WAS 33
Ruben	ALL	78	Thos.	LYC	4	CALLAY, James	NOU 153
CAISWELL, James	CHE	755	Thos.	LYC	22	CALLDWELL, James	WST 249
CAKE, John	PHI	25	Thos.	NOU	156	Joseph	WST 249
John	BER	233	Timothy	PHA	65	CALLENDAR, Darius	LUZ 351
Joseph	PHA	8	William	ADA	2	CALLENDER,	
CAKINS, Heman	LUZ	373	William	WAS	19	Elizabeth	BUC 104A
CAKLE, Patrick	PHI	33	William	WAS	55	Merriman	PHI 43
CAKLER,			William	WAS	74	CALLEWELL, Robert	LAN 69
Christopher	GRN	111	William	GRN	84	CALLIHAN, Nancy	FAY 261
CALAGHAN, Daniel	PHA	97	William	WAS	88	CALLINAN, John	BUC 84A
Michael	HNT	125	William	NOU	116	CALLON, Hugh	ARM 124
CALAHAN, George	WAS	89	William	HNT	133	Patrick	WST 365
Moses Revd.	WAS	89	William	HNT	161	CALLONDER, Robert	
CALAWAY, James	WAS	98	William	HNT	166	Esq.	ALL 49
CALB, John	MNT	89	William	LUZ	326	CALODY, Margaret	FRA 292
CALDWEL, James	DAU	17	CALE, George	HNT	135	CALOWAY, Ben	LAN 59
CALDWELL, Abraham	WAS	62	Jacob	PHA	16	CALTER, George	PHI 45
Alexander	MER	437	CALENDAR, Philip	LUZ	349	CALTON, Robt.	PHI 99A
Alexd.	ADA	3	CALF, Andrew	BUC	139	CALVAN, Floran	PHI 103A
Andrew	LAN	164	Henry	BUC	149	CALVEN, James	FAY 219
Bratten	LYC	20	CALFERT, (Wo---?)	CEN	22	CALVER, Eliza	PHA 78
Charles	HNT	153	CALFLASH, William	DEL	173	Henrey	FAY 264
Chas.	PHA	98	CALHOON, Adly?	ALL	75	CALVERT, Abraham	DEL 179
David	WAS	7	Alexd.	ALL	89	Jas.	CUM 106
David	WAS	54	Andw.	YOR	169	John	LYC 3
David	PHA	69	David	ALL	84	Robt.	VEN 168
David	HNT	153	Elizabeth	BFD	41	CALVIN,	
David	HNT	161	Hugh	PHA	27	Christiana	WAS 15
David	DEL	188	James	ARM	123	George	GRN 69
David	DEL	189	James	YOR	197	Robert	DEL 186
David	MER	437	Jno.	CUM	41	CALWELL, David	ALL 66
Edward	NOU	157	John	BFD	55	Geo.	PHI 81A
F---?	LYC	20	Mary	ALL	54	Hugh	ALL 70
George	NOU	143	Mathew	ALL	85	James	PHA 54
Henry	BFD	72	Patterson	BFD	55	Noble	PHI 80A
Hugh	LYC	24	Peggy	CUM	54	Robert	ALL 56
Hugh	NOU	143	Robert Esqr.	ALL	72	CALY, Christian	FRA 281
Hugh	DEL	155	Saml.	WST	322	CAM----?, John	FRA 278
Hugh	NOU	157	William	LAN	164	CAMBEL, James	ALL 93
James	WAS	51	William	DAU	17A	CAMBELL, Widw.	PHI 102

CAMBELL, Edward	PHI 114A	CAMMONSON, Jos.	YOR 210	CAMPBELL, Hugh		PHA	36
George	CHE 729	CAMP, Albert	LUZ 393	Hugh		NOH	47
John D.	PHA 27	Edward	FAY 261	Hugh		FRA 274
Patrick	LAN 250	Gerhart	WST 210	Hugh		ERI	56A
Pearse	PHI 102A	Hezekiah	DEL 181	James		CRA	11
Richard	PHI 66	Jain	ALL 62	James		WAS	74
Samuel	PHA 124	James	FAY 261	James		WAS	89
CAMBER, Isaac	FAY 226	Job	LUZ 397	James		PHA 119
CAMBERS, John	ALL 84	John	SOM 151	James		SOM 145
Susana	ALL 51	John D.	WAS 119	James		WST 233
CAMBLE, & Mc Vay	LAN 156	Lewis D.	WAS 2	James		WST 250
Andrew	HNT 142	Stephen	LAN 13	James		FRA 286
Benjamin	NOU 103	Stophel	CUM 111	James		FRA 298
Christy	NOU 116	William	PHA 96	James		FRA 301
Daniel	NOU 103	CAMPBEL, Abel	FAY 255	James		FRA 322
Daniel	LAN 113	Alexander	FAY 213	James		LUZ 329
David	NOU 104	Alexr.	WST 378	James		WST 343
Hugh	HNT 135	Benjeman	FAY 252	James		BUT 365
James	HNT 143	Cleany	LYC 25	James		WST 378
Jean Widow	HNT 140	Edward	LAN 225	James		LUZ 405
Jeremiah	PHI 95	Enas	FAY 220	James Jr.		LUZ 405
John	NOU 103	Moses	DAU 20A	James Sr.		WST 233
John	NOU 103	Saml.	CUM 23	Jas.		CUM 44
John	NOU 103	Samuel	FAY 255	Jas.		CUM 143
John	HNT 139	Thomas	BUC 96	Jas. Senr.		FRA 286
John	CHE 826	Thomas	FAY 243	Jean		ERI 59A
Joseph	HNT 141	William	BUC 93	Jno.		CUM 102
Joseph	MER 436	CAMPBELL, Widow	WST 342	Jno.		CUM 151
Obediah	NOU 103	Adam	CHE 778	Jno.		MIF 6A
Robert	NOU 103	Alexander	PHA 92	Jno.		MIF 24A
Robert	NOU 103	Alexander	ARM 123	Jno. R.		FRA 286
Robert	NOU 103	Alexander	ARM 125	John		WAS 7
Robert	NOU 104	Alexr.	NOH 64	John		WAS 15
Robert	LAN 121	Alexr.	YOR 156	John		PHA 17
Saundy	NOU 103	Alexr.	WST 322	John		WAS 19
Walter	CHE 721	Alexr.	WST 341	John		WAS 27
William	LAN 253	Andrew	SOM 156	John		GRN 84
CAMBLIN, Joseph	WAS 1	Andw.	MNT 81	John		GRN 93
Robert	WAS 1	Andw.	WST 378	John		MNT 107
CAMBPELL, Arthur	WAS 89	Anna	BUT 351	John		ARM 124
CAMBRIDGE,		Anthony	PHI 12	John		SOM 132
Archibald	FRA 307	Archibald	LAN 241	John		WST 149
CAMERON, Alexr.	CHE 888	Benjn.	MNT 93	John		BER 158
Alexr.	MIF 14A	Charles	WAS 19	John		HNT 159
Charles	FRA 303	Charles	WAS 27	John		WST 188
Daniel	YOR 200	Charles	PHA 88	John		YOR 197
Duncan	HNT 134	Charles	WAS 89	John		WST 249
Eliza	PHA 55	Charles	WST 148	John		FRA 307
Hugh	MIF 14A	Charles	FRA 286	John		FRA 316
James	PHA 33	Chas.	PHA 8	John		FRA 321
James	CUM 78	Cornelious	BEV 15	John		FRA 322
John	PHA 105	Daniel	BEV 13	John		FRA 322
John	MNT 106	Danl.	WST 343	John		WST 322
John	WAY 143	David	PHI 46	John		FRA 323
Widow	CUM 82	David	WST 322	John		BUT 358
William	LAN 298	David	FRA 323	John		WST 377
Willm.	CHE 888	David	WST 377	John Esqr.		WAS 74
CAMERSON, Daniel	YOR 198	David	LUZ 405	John Jr.		WST 233
Findley	WST 377	Dugal	GRN 75	John Revd.		YOR 160
CAMFER, David	FRA 274	Duncan	WAS 79	John (M)		YOR 198
CAMMEL, Doncan	ALL 55	Ebenezr.	CUM 145	Joh		CHE 0
Egnew	PHA 67	Edward	PHI 25	John		MIF 9A
John	ALL 93	Edward	WAS 27	John		MIF 11A
Joseph	PHI 122	Eliza	CUM 93	John D.		LAN 17
Richard	LAN 244	Finey	WST 233	Joseph		CUM 41
Robert	ALL 53	Francis	CUM 145	Joseph		PHA 88
Robert	ALL 111	Francis	FRA 285	Joseph		MNT 137
William	BUC 147	Frederick	LYC 8	Josias		WST 307
William	BUC 140A	George	PHA 37	Malcom		CUM 114
Wm.	LYC 11	George	WAS 42	Margret		CUM 73
CAMMELL, Andrew	MNT 85	George	BUC 103	Mathew		BER 250
CAMMENS, Sarah	PHI 26	George	YOR 199	Matthew		HNT 133
CAMMERA, John	SOM 151	George	WST 233	Nathaniel		GRN 80
CAMMERER, John	MNT 123	Griffith	MNT 93	Obadiah		GRN 87
CAMMERON, Wm.	BEV 24	Henry	PHI 133	Othniel		LUZ 423
CAMMILL, Wm.	PHI 69	Henry	WST 322	Parker Esqr.		WAS 115

Name	Loc	No	Name	Loc	No	Name	Loc	No
CAMPBELL, Pat.	FRA	287	CAMPBLE, John	NOU	162	CANDY, Jacob	NOH	37
Patrick	WAS	79	John	NOU	163	CANE, Moses	LAN	133
Patrick	LAN	240	Lawrence	NOU	170	CANE?, Peter	PHA	38
Patrick	WST	249	Mrs.	NOU	156	CANEDAY, Hugh	ALL	75
Patrick	FRA	273	Mrs.	NOU	162	CANFIELD, Moses	CRA	13
Robert	WAS	2	Patrick	PHA	73	CANIDAY, David	ALL	91
Robert	MIF	3	Rebeckah	ADA	20	John	ALL	61
Robert	LAN	53	Robert	ADA	19	CANKEY, John	PHI	9
Robert	BFD	57	Samuel	MER	439	CANN?, (See Carn)	NOU	174
Robert	LAN	151	Thomas	MER	438	CANNADY, Widow	PHI	91
Robert	HNT	155	Thos.	NOU	156	Miles	PHI	67
Robert	LAN	219	William	NOU	170	Thos.	PHI	108
Robt.	CUM	36	Wm.	PHA	79	CANNAMAN, Widow	PHI	68
Robt.	CUM	81	CAMPBLE?, Robert	MER	439	CANNAN, Edwd.	BUT	361
Robt.	CUM	102	CAMPEL, Ephraim	DAU	20A	CANNEL, Joseph	ADA	6
Robt.	FRA	283	Widow	DAU	35A	CANNI---?, David	ALL	91
Robt.	FRA	287	Willm.	DAU	35A	CANNIDAY?, David	ALL	91
Robt. Jr.	WST	233	CAMPER, John	PHA	82	CANNON, Widow	PHI	109A
Robt. Jr.	MIF	14A	John	LAN	291	Ann	FAY	202
Robt. Sr.	WST	233	CAMPFEILD, Sela?	LUZ	407	Chas.	CUM	113
Robt.	MIF	9A	CAMPFER,			Daniel	WAS	27
Rosanna	WAS	109	Elizabeth	LAN	305	David	PHA	97
Saml.	CUM	36	CAMPFIELD,			Dennis	PHI	57
Saml.	WST	159	Northrop	LUZ	393	Henry	HNT	153
Saml.	FRA	288	Oliver	LUZ	418	Hugh	PHI	41
Saml.	BUT	352	Warner	LUZ	366	Hugh	WST	148
Samuel	MNT	61	CAMPHER, Widow	PHI	96	Hugh	WST	342
Samuel	YOR	201	CAMPINROW?,			Jacob	MNT	67
Samuel	LUZ	426	Joseph	PHI	65	James	PHA	24
Sarah	WAS	48	CAMPINSON?,			James	HNT	133
Sarah	PHA	89	Joseph	PHI	65	James	WST	341
Sarah	BER	162	CAMPLE, John			James	WST	343
Sylvanus	LUZ	384	(Crossed Out)	LAN	151	Jas.	BUC	152A
Thomas	CRA	10	John	NOU	192	Jennet	WAS	19
Thomas	WST	233	CAMPLE?, Sarah	PHA	92	John	PHI	46
Thos.	YOR	159	CAMPMAN, Danl.			John	PHA	80
Thos.	WST	188	Junr.	PHI	120	John	GRN	85
Thos.	FRA	286	Danl. Senr.	PHI	120	John	HNT	153
Thos.	FRA	316	CAMPSEY, James	DEL	173	John	FAY	202
Thos. Esqr.	YOR	212	CAMPT, Isaac	MER	439	John	FAY	208
Widow	MIF	18	CAMPTON, John	ALL	114	John	LAN	228
Widow	BUC	139	CAMRIN, Mrs.	NOU	143	John	WST	341
Widow	BUC	150A	Mrs.	NOU	143	Mary	PHI	116
William	WAS	15	Robert	BFD	78	Matthew	FAY	208
William	WAS	27	CAMRON, Allen	ALL	86	Patrick	CHE	851
William	WAS	37	Gilbert	ALL	60	Patrick	CHE	885
William	PHI	49	John	ADA	20	Richard	GRN	100
William	WAS	89	Robert	CRA	11	Robert	CHE	764
William	WAS	98	Wilm.	ALL	60	Saml.	CUM	150
William	MNT	104	CAMSLY, Joh	CHE	0	Thomas	PHA	105
William	PHA	120	CAMSTER, John	PHI	77A	Thomas	MER	438
William	SOM	126	CAN/ CAR?, Widow	LAN	247	William	WAS	19
William	WST	233	CANAAN, William	MER	438	William	MNT	66
William	WST	233	CANADA, David	PHA	73	CANNUM, William	HNT	117
William	FAY	255	CANADAY, Agunish	CHE	715	CANON, James	BEV	4
William	LUZ	384	Ebenezer	CHE	715	CANS?, Valentine	BUC	82A
Willm.	BUT	347	Jesse	CHE	802	CANTING?,		
Wm.	BEV	23	Richard	CHE	802	Lebbitice?	PHA	121
Wm.	PHI	35	Robert	CHE	802	CANTLY, James	BUC	103
Wm.	CUM	39	CANADY, John	PHI	77	CANTON, Edward	ADA	5
Wm.	CUM	50	CANAGHAN, Alexd.	ADA	3	CANWELL, Widow	PHI	95
Wm.	CUM	102	CANAHAN, William	NOU	156	CANYNGHAM, David		
Wm.	WST	148	CANBY, Thomas	BUC	107	H.	PHA	107
Wm.	WST	188	Thos.	PHA	96	CAP, Peter	MNT	131
Wm.	FRA	286	Thos. Junr.	PHA	95	CAPCHART?, Henry	PHI	145
Wm.	FRA	321	Whitson	BUC	103	CAPEHART, Andw.	PHI	102
Wm.	FRA	321	William	BUC	144A	CAPEHAT, Widw.	PHI	105
Wm. Senr.	WST	233	CANCALY, Wm.	PHA	58	CAPEL?, John	PHI	3
Wm.	MIF	14A	CANDERS, Thomas	DEL	190	Willm.	PHI	40
Woods	WST	234	CANDLE, Jacob	ADA	11	CAPLEY, Nicholas	WST	211
CAMPBLE,			Nicholas	ADA	11	CAPON?, Aaron	ERI	58
Alexander	NOU	143	William	BUC	148A	CAPP, Anthony	DAU	31
Alexr.	NOU	198	CANDLER, David	YOR	155	Christo.	DAU	49
Jacob	MER	438	CANDLES, Willm.	BUT	322	Jacob	DAU	50A
James	MER	439	CANDOR, Robert	DAU	20A	John	PHA	79
John	LAN	14	CANDY, Alexander	CHE	830	Peter	SOM	126

CAPPES, Jacob	NOH 66A	CARLE, Jacob	MNT 81	CARN, John	BFD 72
CAPRON, Henry	PHA 11	Richard	WAS 61	John	NOU 114
Laban	LUZ 386	CARLES, John	PHA 78	John	NOU 174
Orlan	LUZ 386	Saml.	PHA 64	Nicholas	NOU 114
CAR/ CAN?, Widow	LAN 247	CARLETON, Richard	PHI 30	Philip	BFD 49
CAR, James	HNT 131	CARLEY, Joseph	FRA 285	Youst	NOU 186
James	HNT 145	CARLI, Joseph	LAN 275	CARN?, John	NOU 174
James Junr.	HNT 145	CARLILE, Amos	BUC 93	CARNAHAM, Robert	NOU 197
John	NOU 104	Daniel	FAY 202	CARNAHAN, Widow	WST 286
Robert	LAN 245	Daniel	BUC 140A	Abram	BUT 354
Thos.	FRA 309	John	BUC 93	Adam	WST 365
CARBAUGH, Danl.	PHI 120A	John	FAY 202	Adam	MER 436
John	PHI 66	John	BUC 140A	Alexr.	WST 233
CARBERRY, Henry	BER 247	Jonan.	BUC 160A	David	NOU 156
CARBIN, Shadrick	YOR 195	Wm.	PHA 54	David	WST 365
CARBMAN,		CARLIN, Widw.	PHI 83	Eliza.	WST 287
Christian	LAN 302	Anthony	WAS 74	Jas.	CUM 125
CARBONE, Danl.	PHI 109A	Daniel	ALL 91	John	WST 286
CARBOUGH, Rebeca	FAY 197	John	FRA 287	Robt.	CUM 135
CARCHIK?, James	LAN 308	Mary	BER 173	William	BUC 155A
CARDOZA, Isaac	NOH 37	Moses	DAU 27A	CARNAN, Charles	PHA 90
CARDPAY?, Herman	PHA 109	CARLING, Jonathan	PHI 116A	CARNE, Elizabeth	LAN 300
CARE, Widow	PHI 20	Patrick	PHA 111	Joseph	LUZ 402
George	MNT 40	CARLISLE, Abm.	PHA 35	William	LUZ 402
Jesse	PHA 65	Andrew	WAS 84	CARNEGY, William	BEV 26
John	PHA 56	Danl.	CUM 80	CARNEL, Geo.	PHI 116
Philip	PHA 27	James	LAN 8	Thos.	CUM 66
CARE?, Peter	PHA 38	John	WAS 84	CARNER, Christian	PHA 120
CAREBEER, David	NOH 77A	John	WST 189	CARNES, Daniel	PHA 6
CAREY, Charles	PHA 112	John	CHE 748	Isaac	BFD 56
Comfort	LUZ 328	John	MIF 24A	James	FAY 226
Elias	BUC 140A	Jonathan	DEL 159	CARNETT, Thos.	PHI 80
Elizabeth	PHA 6	Thomas	LAN 181	CARNEY, Anthony	NOU 192
James	PHA 55	William	WAS 27	Darby	PHI 31
John	FAY 264	Wm.	CHE 748	Hugh	FRA 289
John	LUZ 318	CARLOW, James	FAY 213	James	SOM 145
John	LUZ 369	CARLTON, Anthony	ADA 10	John	WST 210
Lemuel	LUZ 383	Mark	CHE 838	John	WST 378
Samson	BUC 103	Samuel	CHE 838	Lawrence	SOM 145
Samuel	BUC 86	Thomas	CHE 838	Patrick	WST 342
Samuel	LUZ 362	Thomas	CHE 838	Philip	PHA 94
Seth	LUZ 382	CARLY, Jacob	LAN 287	Richard	WST 378
Sylvanus	LUZ 376	Richd.	CEN 22	Thomas	BUC 88
CAREY?, Barnabas	LUZ 364	CARMACK, David	PHA 48	Thomas	LAN 129
CARGEADON, Jas.	CUM 51	David	WAS 119	William	WAS 27
CARGER, Frederick	BFD 61	Jacob	ERI 59	William	FAY 226
George	BFD 62	CARMADAY, John	NOU 162	CARNIDAY?, David	ALL 91
John	BFD 61	CARMAKER, James	LAN 122	CARNIHAN, James	ALL 120
Peter	BFD 61	CARMALT, Caleb	PHA 20	John	ALL 120
CARGILL, David	MIF 12A	Jonathn.	CHE 705	William	CRA 6
John	MIF 12A	CARMAN, George	LAN 259	CARNIS, Peter	NOU 146
CARHART, Widow	PHI 13	Jacob	PHA 120	CARNS, Jacob	SOM 151
CARIDER?, Saml.	PHI 115A	James	PHA 24	John	WST 250
CARIGAN, Jacob	PHA 68	Ruben	CRA 11	John	WST 286
CARIHER?, Michael	FRA 307	CARMEN, John	CHE 789	Joseph	WAS 33
CARIS, Frederick	NOU 201	Michael	PHI 136	Michael	SOM 151
Philip	BUC 147	Michael	PHI 139	Thomas	MIF 16A
CARITHERS, Moses	NOU 116	CARMICHAEL,		William	NOU 192
CARKE?, Michael	GRN 62	Alexr.	NOU 157	CARNS?, Zoph	WAS 43
CARL, Conrod	CUM 38	John	WAS 1	CARNY, James	ALL 61
Elisah	BEV 7	John	WAS 62	Wm.	WST 210
Frederick	NOH 52A	CARMICHAL, John	MER 438	CAROLAS, Francis	FRA 288
George	BER 222	Rebecah	MER 438	CAROLES, Charles	YOR 218
Henry	NOH 52A	Thomas	MER 438	John	HNT 141
Jacob Junr.	NOH 52A	CARMIEL, Jahiel	WAS 55	CAROLL, John	PHA 64
Jacob	NOH 52A	CARMOLD, George	PHI 82A	CAROLUS, John	LAN 55
Michael	NOU 186	CARMON, Benjm.		CARON, Andw.	LYC 8
Nickolas	NOH 58A	(Blackman)	PHI 122	CAROTHER, An	YOR 214
Patrick	PHA 9	James	CEN 20	CAROTHERS,	
Peter	BER 221	CARMONT, John	MIF 9A	Christopher	WAS 66
Stephen	HNT 133	CARMONY, Anthy.	DAU 46A	George	WAS 55
CARLAN, James	FRA 276	Joseph	DAU 43A	James	WAS 98
CARLAND, Daniel	CRA 12	Mar.	DAU 41	James	HNT 143
George	BFD 42	Martin	DAU 28A	James Junr.	HNT 143
CARLE, Casper	BUC 158A	CARN, Adam	NOU 186	Jno.	LYC 21
Henry	MNT 81	James	WST 234	John	HNT 148

CAROTHERS, John	YOR	163
Samuel	HNT	143
William	WAS	55
William	CHE	711
CARPE, Adam	SOM	128
CARPENTER,		
Abraham	LAN	86
Abraham	YOR	167
Abraham Esq.	LAN	231
Andrew	LAN	224
Benj.	YOR	207
Benjamin 2nd	LUZ	337
Benjamin	LUZ	337
Benjn.	PHI	141
Car John	NOU	104
Charles	PHI	141
Christ.	LAN	68
Christ.	LAN	68
Christian Jr.	LAN	62
Christian Snr.	LAN	62
Conard	PHI	129
Cyrel	LUZ	386
Daniel	BUC	93
David	LAN	63
Elisha	LUZ	383
Ezra	LUZ	385
Francis	CHE	758
Frederick	LAN	117
Gabriel	FRA	287
George	LAN	79
George	LAN	248
Gilbert	LUZ	337
Gilbert Jr.	LUZ	337
Hannah	PHI	138
Henry	LAN	78
Henry	LAN	80
Henry	LAN	86
Jacob	PHA	54
Jacob	LAN	62
Jacob	DEL	165
Jacob	YOR	210
Jacob Esq.	LAN	43
James	WST	168
James	LUZ	337
James?	PHI	79
Jas.	CUM	57
Joel	LAN	62
John	ADA	6
John	PHA	34
John	LAN	62
John	GRN	67
John	PHI	81
John	LUZ	385
John	CHE	761
John	BUC	160A
Jos.	CHE	761
Joseph	LYC	9
Joseph	WAS	11
Joshua	LUZ	428
Levy	PHI	137
Lewis D.	PHA	57
Martin	LAN	118
Obadiah	LUZ	385
Obadiah Jr.	LUZ	385
Peter	ADA	3
Peter	LAN	68
Saml.	LYC	23
Samuel	PHI	15
Samuel	PHA	97
Samuel	PHI	99
Samuel	LAN	137
Susana	LAN	118
Thomas	PHI	50
Tobias	PHA	116
Widow	LAN	62
Widow	LAN	83
CARPENTER,		
William	DEL	188
Wm.	WAR	1A
CARPER, Nichos.	CUM	131
CARR, Mr.?/ Wm.?		
Revd.	PHA	102
Widow	PHI	11
Absalom	LUZ	410
Adam	CHE	716
Andrew	NOU	163
Andw.	LYC	18
Archibald	WAS	115
Caleb	WAY	136
Charles	DEL	185
Charles	DEL	185
Charles	FAY	249
Danl.	PHI	64
David	BUC	140A
Elizabeth	FAY	220
Felty	WST	159
Hugh	PHI	93A
Jacob	NOU	163
James	WST	234
James	WST	234
John	PHI	16
John	PHA	42
John	PHA	43
John	PHI	84
John	NOU	143
John	BUC	154
John	WST	210
John M.	PHA	36
Joseph	PHI	15
Joseph	MNT	66
Mary	WST	286
Moses	WAS	42
Patrick	PHA	65
Peter	MNT	49
Robert	PHA	20
Robert	PHI	40
Robert	PHA	120
Robert	BER	274
Samuel	DEL	181
Samuel	WST	378
Thomas	PHI	47
Thomas	MNT	110
Thomas	FAY	219
Thomas	NOH	77A
William	MNT	49
William	PHA	104
William	MNT	111
William	PHA	115
William	LAN	169
William	WST	322
CARRACH, James M.	PHA	27
CARRANS, John	ALL	83
CARREL, Thomas	WAS	43
CARRELL, Edward	PHA	107
Ephraim	FAY	264
Jacob	YOR	156
James	BUC	149
James Jun.	BUC	149
John	PHA	16
John	PHA	39
CARREN, John	WAS	1
CARRENDS?, James	ALL	90
CARRESS, Eliga	ALL	111
CARRETHERS, James	WST	249
CARREY, Nichs.	PHI	98
CARRICK, Henry	BFD	68
James	ADA	6
CARRIDEN, Peter	PHI	106
CARRIE, Enock	MNT	86
CARRIER, Jacob	LAN	285
John	LAN	259
CARRIGAN, Robert	NOU	163
CARRIHAN, Saml.	FRA	280
CARRILL, James	FRA	287
CARRINGER, Martin	MER	437
CARROL, Barnet	BUC	153
Benjamin	BUC	143
Cornelius	BUC	153
Edward	WAS	48
George	GRN	62
Hannah	ALL	80
Herculas	WAS	108
Jacob	BUC	137
James	ALL	109
James	GRN	109
James	ALL	118
John	LYC	6
John	WAS	108
John	ALL	118
Ritchard	ALL	75
Robert	WAS	97
Robert	GRN	109
Thomas	ALL	60
Thos.	CUM	66
Wilm.	ALL	85
CARROLL, James	LUZ	391
John	WAS	79
CARROLUS, George	LAN	16
CARSAN, Hugh	HNT	125
CARSCADAN,		
Charles	LUZ	341
CARSER, Jos.	PHI	119
CARSON, Adam	WST	148
Agunish	CHE	766
Allexander	BEV	24
Andrew	FRA	275
Benjamin	WST	378
Benjamin	BUC	98A
Charles	BUC	98A
Christy	NOU	116
Danl. B.	PHA	40
David	CUM	46
David	FRA	297
David	CHE	816
David	CHE	821
Elisha	CUM	123
Eliza	PHA	71
Eliza.	CUM	137
George	CHE	848
George	CHE	849
Henry	PHI	99
Hugh	CHE	748
Isaac	WAS	6
James	WAS	6
James	CUM	38
James	WAS	55
James	PHA	121
James	LAN	159
James	WST	250
James	BUT	330
Jane	DAU	15A
Jas.	CUM	51
Jemimah	PHA	80
John	WAS	6
John	LYC	7
John	LYC	9
John	ADA	15
John	LYC	17
John	WAS	78
John	LAN	93
John	CUM	123
John	WAY	148
John	NOU	174
John	FRA	316
John	BUT	339
John	DAU	11A
John	DAU	17A
John	ERI	57A

CARSON, Jonathan	PHA	30
Joseph	WAS	42
Joseph	PHA	113
Joseph	WST	342
Margt.	CUM	38
Patrick	WAS	42
Robert	NOU	174
Robert	BUT	326
Robert	WST	341
Robt.	FRA	280
Ruben	PHI	27
Samuel	MIF	3
Samuel	PHI	4
Samuel Junr.	WAS	27
Samuel Senr.	WAS	27
Sarah	FIN	7
Thomas	FRA	309
Thomas Junr.	WAS	42
Thomas Senr.	WAS	42
William	WAS	42
William	LAN	168
William	FAY	255
William	WST	343
William	CHE	874
Wm.	BEV	4
CARSON?, Henry	LYC	21
CARSWELL, Widow	PHI	23
Robert	YOR	195
William	BUT	343
CARSY, John	PHI	80
CART, George	CUM	94
Jacob	CUM	89
Peter	PHI	81A
Wendle	PHI	118A
CARTER, Widow	PHI	16
Amos	DEL	156
Benjn.	FAY	255
Brisillah	MER	439
Casper	PHI	36
Charles	BUC	86
Charles	FAY	255
Daniel	WAS	11
Daniel	PHA	68
Daniel	DEL	162
Danl.	BUT	348
Ebenezer	BUC	86
Edward	DEL	162
Elizabeth	CHE	808
George	PHI	43
George	FRA	279
George	CHE	796
George	CHE	808
Helena	BUC	162
Henry Yates	PHI	133
Jacob	PHA	80
Jacob	CHE	794
James	WAS	1
James	PHI	145
Joel	LAN	155
John	PHI	76
John	HNT	127
Jonas	LUZ	403
Joseph	BUC	93
Joseph	DEL	162
Joseph W.	PHI	21
Margret	CUM	92
Martin	DEL	164
Mary	CHE	808
Morgan	MNT	76
Nicholas	CHE	793
Nicks.	MNT	80
Phillip	FAY	243
Redmant	WAS	20
Robert	WAS	11
Robert	PHI	28
Saml.	PHA	55

CARTER, Samuel	CHE	887
Sharan	PHA	34
Thomas	VEN	169
Uzziel	LUZ	412
William	WAS	1
William	MNT	104
William	GRN	108
William	MNT	140
William	WST	306
William	WST	307
Willm.	PHI	91
Wm.	PHI	67A
CARTERET, Daniel	PHI	23
CARTERET?, Danl.	PHI	21
CARTINGHART,		
Danl.	PHI	22
CARTNER, John	WST	307
CARTNER?, Samuel	MNT	44
CARTNEY, John	PHI	36
William	WST	149
CARTWRIGHT, Abner	BER	250
Cirus	BER	275
CARTY, Benjamin	GRN	80
Peggy	WAS	20
Samuel	WAS	27
Thomas	BEV	6
Thomas	GRN	75
CARUTHERS,		
Anthony	PHA	39
George	LAN	32
John	NOU	170
CARVAN, James	ALL	55
CARVE, John	LAN	125
CARVENDER, Edward	BFD	49
CARVER, Abm.	LAN	259
Abraham	SOM	126
Adam	MNT	53
Benjn.	BUC	140A
Christian	SOM	126
Christian	LAN	259
Christr.	CUM	67
Felix	LAN	259
George	VEN	170
George	FRA	276
Jacob	PHA	26
Jacob	ARM	124
Jacob	LAN	259
Jacob Mack &	FRA	303
Joel	BUC	137
John	LAN	9
John	CUM	65
John	BUC	86
John	BUC	141
John	PHI	145
John	FRA	303
John	FRA	304
John	FRA	311
John	WST	342
John	BUC	144A
Jonathan	WAS	120
Jonathan	LUZ	332
Joseph	BUC	86
Joseph	BUC	86
Joseph	BUC	140A
Mahlon	BUC	146
Mahlon	BUC	146A
Martin	WST	286
Mary	CHE	781
Michal	FRA	272
Samuel	PHA	96
Samuel	LUZ	332
Seneca	FRA	311
Thomas	BUC	86
William	MNT	106
William	BUC	154
William Junr.	BUC	86

CARWELL, Widow	YOR	200
Andrew	LAN	176
CARWFFORD, James	FAY	226
CARWIN, John	MNT	137
CARY, Asa	BUC	103
Dennis	BUC	162
John	NOH	37
Thomas	BUC	144A
CARZETT, Jacob	FRA	320
CASADAY, Phillip	CHE	757
CASADINE, Wm.	PHA	77
CASADY, Samuel	LAN	155
CASAL, John	PHA	120
CASAY, Philip	DAU	24
CASBAUGH, Martin	ADA	11
CASCADAN, Hugh	NOU	116
CASCADEN, John	NOU	116
William	NOU	116
CASE, Aaron	LUZ	408
Absalom	WAY	143
Augustus	GRN	99
Butler	WAS	67
John (A		
Boarding		
House)	PHA	48
Peter	BUC	146A
Phillip	WST	168
Reuben	LUZ	408
Samuel	GRN	99
Thomas	WAS	43
Thomas	LUZ	341
William	LUZ	368
CASEBEARER,		
Jonathan	WAS	98
CASEBEER,		
Christian	SOM	126
Elizabeth	WAY	148
John Junr.	WAS	33
John Senr.	WAS	33
Solomon	SOM	126
CASEDY, Henry	CUM	120
CASELY, Sapron	PHI	44
CASER, John	PHI	47
CASEWELL, Charles	CHE	715
Isaac	CHE	715
James	CHE	715
CASEY, Benjamin	LUZ	330
Daniel	CRA	18
Michl.	PHI	95A
Nathan	PHA	11
CASEY?, Barnabas	LUZ	364
CASGROVE, Henry	MIF	14A
John	DEL	190
CASH, Isaac	LUZ	424
Thos.	PHI	107
William	WAS	7
CASHADAY, Patrick	HNT	121
CASHDOLLER, John	ALL	86
CASHDY, James	WST	188
CASHMAN,		
Christian	ADA	23
Christopher	ADA	19
John	ADA	19
CASHNER, David	BFD	53
George	BFD	55
Martin	NOU	143
CASHWEILER,		
Philip	LAN	90
CASIDAY, Saml.	PHI	89
CASIDY, Andw.	PHI	71A
Francis	YOR	203
CASKADON, Geo.	CUM	48
CASKEY, John	MNT	43
CASKY, John	CEN	22
Saml.	MIF	24A
Walter	WAS	19

CAVAT, John			CELSEY, John	BEV 18	CHAMBERLAIN, Free	WAS	89
(Tanner)	WST	188	CELSY, George	ALL 101	Gershom	CHE	845
CAVE, Elizabeth	PHA	119	John	ALL 103	Isaac	CHE	852
Thomas	PHA	114	Marck	ALL 107	Jacob	BFD	49
CAVELEER, Isaac	FAY	235	CELTER, David	PHI 129	James	LAN	120
CAVEN, Robert	LAN	14	CELVEY, Wm.	CUM 114	Jas.	ADA	38
CAVEN?,			CELY, George	BFD 57	Jno.	ADA	38
Allexander?	BEV	7	CEMER, Widow	PHI 11A	John	DEL	157
CAVENAUGH, Jno.	WST	365	CEMMERA,		John	FRA	300
CAVENDER, Chas.	PHA	35	Alexander	SOM 137	John	CHE	805
John	BUC	103	CENERAL, John	BFD 69	Jos.	CHE	852
CAVENNY, Patrick	WAS	79	CENNY, Dennis	PHA 111	Joshua	CHE	846
CAVENOUGH,			CENTMAN, Lawrence	BUC 104A	Robert	WAS	2
Patrick	FAY	202	CENTWELL, Thomas	BFD 55	Stout	WAS	85
CAVERN, Thomas	WST	377	CEPERLEY, Casper	LAN 239	William	WAS	2
CAVET, Francis	DAU	24A	CEPLER, Andrew	NOU 179	William	DEL	159
James	WST	250	John	NOU 179	Wm.	CHE	846
John	WST	250	CERB, Patrick	CHE 738	Wright	LUZ	385
Patrick	ALL	110	CERCHER?, (See		CHAMBERLIN,		
Thomas	ALL	65	Cereher)	LAN 25	Charles	DAU	4A
CAVIN, John	WST	249	CEREHER, Andrew	LAN 25	Clayton	ADA	4
CAVINER, Joseph	NOU	148	CERES, Jacob	DAU 6	John	DAU	4
CAVNY, Rebecca	LAN	107	CERIGHT, Wm.	CHE 846	Lewis	ADA	14
CAVODE, Garrett	WST	168	CERLACH, (No		Ninian?	ADA	22
CAW, Dewalt	FRA	294	Given Name) A		Squire	CRA	3
Henry	FRA	291	Wever	LAN 307	CHAMBERS, Ann	PHA	77
Jacob	FRA	291	CERNY, John	DAU 47A	Arthur	HNT	156
CAWL, Dimnick	BUT	331	CERRY, Abel	GRN 99	Ben	LYC	12
CAWLY, Thomas	NOH	47	CERSON, David	ALL 103	Benja.	WST	365
CAXADEN?, (See			CERTY, Edwd.	PHI 44	Benjamin	FRA	271
Cascaden)	NOU	116	CERVER, Jacob	DAU 21A	Caleb	CHE	768
CAY, Chirsr?	PHI	1	John	DAU 16A	Calvin	LYC	12
CAYGER, Jacob	CHE	792	CESNER, Nichs		Charles	WST	365
CAYNY, John	FAY	243	Junr.	CUM 105	Edward	FAY	264
CAZIER, Abraham	WAS	115	CESSLAND?, Robert	BER 204	Elijah	CEN	20
CEALEY, Jacob	FRA	280	CESSNA, John	BFD 57	Elijah	WST	148
CEARREY, John	CUM	63	John Jr.	BFD 49	Elisha	LYC	12
CEARY, Neathen	VEN	166	Jonathan	BFD 57	Elisha	WST	148
CEASY, John	LAN	96	William	BFD 57	Ezekiel	FRA	282
Noah	LAN	96	CHACE, Samuel	ADA 24	George	PHA	26
CEATCH, Robt.	CHE	763	CHADRON, Simon	PHA 10	George	FRA	319
CEATON, William	GRN	84	CHAFFEN, David	FAY 226	George	WST	365
CEAVER?, John	MNT	87	CHAFFIN, Aaron	CHE 710	Henry	ADA	23
CEBER?, Jacob			Easter	CHE 712	Isaac	CHE	803
(Crossed Out)	BUC	100A	Evan	CHE 774	James	WAS	2
CECHEM, Wilm.	ALL	76	Jesse	GRN 87	James	BEV	24
CECIL, Charles	PHA	119	Jesse	DEL 156	James	WAS	66
Charles	DEL	166	Jesse	CHE 711	James	WAS	98
CEECK, Thos.	DAU	21	Nathl.	FAY 238	James	WAS	115
CEFFERT, Martin	NOU	162	Robert	CHE 772	James	PHI	130
CEFIRS, Martin	NOU	162	CHAFFINCH, Thomas	CHE 850	James	LAN	245
CEIBEEKS, Cuffy	YOR	211	CHAIMBERS, Thomas	FAY 243	James	WST	365
CEIVERS, John	BEV	11	CHAIMS, Richard	FAY 255	James	MER	439
CEIVERT?, Luke	NOU	127	CHAIN, Martha	CUM 54	James Genl.	FRA	286
CELEY?, (See			Mathew	MNT 69	James	PHI	105B
Coley)	BUC	92A	William	FAY 249	Jas.	WST	212
CELL, Adam	ADA	26	CHAINAI, John	NOU 116	Jas.	BUT	359
Adam	ADA	29	CHAINY, Johnson	NOU 116	John	PHA	18
Isaac	ADA	28	CHALFANT, Jane	WAS 78	John	WAS	55
Jacob	ADA	28	Jonthn.	CHE 753	John	ALL	60
Jacob	FRA	284	Thomas	WAS 78	John	WAS	98
Nicholas	FRA	282	CHALFENT, Chads	FAY 264	John	WAS	98
Peter	ADA	26	Mordicai	FAY 264	John	LAN	246
CELLAR, Henry	DAU	11A	CHALFONT, David	CHE 851	John	FRA	271
CELLARS, David	FRA	282	Henry	CHE 852	John	WST	306
CELLER,			Jacob	CHE 742	John	CHE	768
Elizabeth?	ALL	91	Janh.	CHE 752	John	CHE	839
CELLERS, Jacob	FRA	282	CHALK, John	PHA 33	John	NOH	77A
Joseph Junr.	WAS	55	CHALKER, Samuel	LUZ 390	Joseph	WAS	55
Joseph Senr.	WAS	55	CHALONER, John	MNT 47	Joseph	LAN	59
CELLEY, Samuel	DEL	179	CHAM, Susannah	YOR 200	Joseph	ALL	85
CELLON, Klous	LAN	136	CHAMBER, Thomas	MNT 132	Joseph	FRA	280
CELLORS, George	WAS	11	CHAMBERLAIN,		Margt.	BER	242
CELNOR, John	BUC	90A	Widow	WAS 85	Moses Esqr.	NOH	77A
Widow	BUC	90A	Arthur	WAS 2	Peter	LUZ	353
CELSEY, Isaac	BUC	93	Benj. Chas.?	PHA 19	Richd.	PHA	45

62

CHAMBERS, Robert	PHA	55	CHAPMAN, George	BUC	137	CHASE, George	PHA	112
Robert	HNT	136	George	CHE	885	Sam	DEL	176
Robert	LAN	155	George R.	PHA	6	CHASSON?, Willm.	PHI	46
Robert	DAU	3A	Isaac	BUC	107	CHASTANS, John B.	PHA	8
Robt.	CUM	28	James	FAY	213	CHATFIELD, Lewis	WAS	43
Robt.	CUM	83	James	BUC	156A	CHATHAM, John?	LYC	18
Robt.	FRA	292	Jane	PHA	68	Wm.	LYC	18
Saml.	PHA	96	Jas.	CUM	129	CHATLEY, Francis	BEV	13
Soloman	WST	148	John	WAS	98	CHATMAN, Luke	BEV	18
Solomon	ADA	23	John	BUC	151	CHATTEAUDUN, John	PHA	119
Widow	FRA	302	John	NOU	162	CHAUCEY, William	WAS	55
William	BEV	26	John	VEN	169	CHAWKER, Daniel	LUZ	388
Willm.	PHI	47	Joseph	BEV	19	CHEAR, John	HNT	139
Wm.	CUM	86	Joseph	LUZ	386	CHEASEMAN, Mary	PHI	82
CHAMBERT, Widow	LAN	119	Joseph	LUZ	392	CHEDR?, John	HNT	133
CHAMPERS, Joseph	NOU	192	Joseph Jr.	LUZ	392	CHEEKS, Nathaniel	ERI	55A
Robert	NOU	192	Mary	YOR	201	CHEESE, Edward	WAS	15
CHAMPION, Henry			Mary	YOR	203	CHEESMAN, Elijah	PHI	40
V.	LUZ	400	Mathew	YOR	157	CHELAR, Chrisn.	PHI	1
James	HNT	148	Nathaniel	LUZ	326	CHEMFERLING,		
John	HNT	148	Nicholas	WST	341	Enock	NOU	197
CHAMPIONOUR,			Richard	WAS	19	Frederick	NOU	198
Henry	BFD	69	Robt.	PHI	83A	William	NOU	197
CHANCE, Samuel	WAS	11	Rosewell	WAY	141	William	NOU	198
CHANCELLER, Grace	PHA	58	Saml.	LAN	14	CHENEY, Gilbert	HNT	158
Wm.	PHA	80	Samuel	DEL	158	Jesse	DEL	160
CHANCELLOR, Wm.	PHA	20	Samuel	DEL	160	John	DEL	190
CHANDLER, Widow	PHI	32	Seth	MNT	69	John Doctr.	DEL	161
Abraham	CHE	702	Simeon	WAY	141	Joseph	DEL	190
David	PHI	8	Solomon	BER	252	Joshua	HNT	146
Eliza.	PHA	22	T----?,	WAY	140	Mary	DEL	190
Enoch	FAY	226	Thoams	BEV	19	Samuel	DEL	190
George	FAY	226	Thomas	WAS	89	CHER, Michael	YOR	210
George	CHE	861	Thomas	BUC	98A	CHERNA, Widow	PHI	27
Jonathan	FAY	225	William	GRN	106	CHERRINGTON,		
Swithen	GRN	99	William	WAY	141	Thomas	BER	179
Thomas	CHE	863	William	YOR	177	CHERRY, Abm.	BER	283
William	FAY	235	William	YOR	184	Andrew	HNT	151
Wm.	CHE	863	Wm.	PHA	26	Charles	NOU	127
CHANDLEY, William	WAS	37	Wm.	CUM	108	David	PHA	117
CHANER?, George	PHI	92A	Wm.	CUM	127	George	LAN	240
CHANEY, Abraham	BFD	55	CHAPON?, Willm.	PHI	46	Jacob	HNT	151
Charles	BFD	49	CHAPPEL, Thomas	PHI	151	James	NOU	103
Evan	BFD	61	CHARD, George	PHA	46	James	DEL	157
Gabriel	BFD	61	CHARDON, ,anthony	PHA	6	John	NOU	103
John	BFD	61	CHARIAD, John	NOU	182	John	WST	212
Lewis	BFD	61	CHARIT, Jacob	NOU	135	Joseph	BER	276
Nathan	BFD	49	CHARLES,			Mary	WAS	88
Thomas	BFD	49	Christian	FRA	307	Moses	WAS	88
Wm.	PHA	28	Dewalt	BER	175	Peter	WST	211
Zachariah	BFD	61	Frederick	NOH	62	Ralph	WAS	88
CHANHAN, John	NOU	156	Frederick	BUC	147	Thomas	WAS	88
CHANLER, Allen	CHE	765	Henry	LAN	303	William	CHE	865
CHANNEL, John	LAN	154	Hunter	WST	286	CHESEROUND, Adam	WAS	109
CHANNELL, Jesse	CHE	860	Jacob	PHI	99	CHESNET, James	LAN	19
CHANY, John	ALL	117	James	BEV	6	CHESNEY, Andrew	MER	438
Wilm.	ALL	112	John	BUC	147	Roland	CUM	44
CHAPELL, Isaac	LUZ	413	John	LAN	167	William	MIF	6A
CHAPEN, Nathan	PHA	114	John	LAN	259	CHESNUT, Benjamin	WAS	108
CHAPIN, John	LUZ	353	John	LAN	303	John	NOU	162
John Jr.	LUZ	353	John	LAN	306	Saml.	CUM	143
Samuel	LUZ	350	John	BUC	90A	Thos.	FRA	279
Solomon	LUZ	335	Joseph	PHA	28	CHESNUTWOOD,		
CHAPLEN, John	FAY	252	Joseph	LAN	305	Samuel	BER	274
Thomas	FAY	252	Joseph Junr.	LAN	306	CHESS, David	MER	437
William	FAY	261	CHARLESTON,			James	MER	437
CHAPMAN, Aaron	MIF	6A	Nicholas	CRA	16	John	MER	437
Abraham	PHA	53	Thos.	CHE	713	Thomas	WAS	78
Abraham	BUC	103	CHARLETON, James	WST	168	Wilm.	ALL	90
Adoiso?	LUZ	419	CHARLTON, Benj.	PHI	94A	CHESTER, Charles	PHA	53
Benjn.	BUC	107	Samuel	BFD	36	Jas.	CUM	150
Charles	NOU	109	Samuel	HNT	137	Joseph	WAS	42
Daniel	FAY	219	Thos.	FRA	322	Malinda	PHA	66
Edward	BUC	107	CHARRELS, Isaac	ALL	111	Richard	YOR	180
Francis	WST	148	CHARRITON?, Peggy	FRA	278	Saml.	PHI	73A
George	LYC	28	CHARTER, Walter	MIF	12A	CHESTNOR, James	NOH	35

CHUNN, Joseph			CLAPPER, Henry	BFD 62	CLARK, George Sr.	CUM 142
Esqr.	BUC 83	Henry	HNT 128	George	DAU 10A
CHURCH, Almon	LUZ 343	Herman	HNT 128	Henry	BFD 68
Daniel	LUZ 390	Jacob	HNT 128	Henry	BER 162
Field	WST 250	John	HNT 128	Isaac	MER 436
George	GRN 62	John	HNT 148	Isabella	FRA 273
Henry	GRN 62	Mones	HNT 128	Israel	LAN 120
Jeremiah	PHI 75A	CLAPSADDEL, John	FRA 284	James	ADA 5
Joseph	BUC 86	CLAPSADDLE, David	YOR 181	James	PHA 9
Salvenuss Capt.	PHI 76	Michael	ADA 22	James	BFD 37
Samuel	PHI 43	CLAPSADLE, George	FRA 287	James	ERI 60
Samuel	BUC 83	CLARCK, Aaron	NOU 191	James	BFD 72
Thos. Esqr.	CHE 895	Charles	NOU 197	James	LAN 97
William	LAN 218	Daniel	NOU 191	James	PHI 101
CHURCHMAN, Dinah	CHE 871	Henerey	MER 438	James	ARM 122
Edward	DEL 191	John	NOU 192	James	PHI 136
Mordiac	PHA 103	John	NOU 197	James	HNT 144
CHURN, Michael	WST 342	John	NOU 198	James	HNT 156
CIB, Joseph	LAN 121	Joseph	NOU 192	James	WST 168
CIGER, William	DAU 10A	Samuel	NOU 163	James	WST 234
William	DAU 10A	Walter	NOU 198	James	LAN 242
CILE, Jesse	PHI 130	William	NOU 198	James	WST 249
CILGORE, John	LAN 124	CLARCKNER, John	NOU 192	James	FAY 255
John	LAN 124	CLARE, Frederic	CHE 857	James	WST 270
CILL, George		George	PHA 31	James	FRA 288
Junior	ALL 82	Jacob	MNT 81	James	FRA 291
See Gill	ALL 82	S./ L.? Daniel	NOU 103	James	WST 378
Wilm.	ALL 82	CLARIDGE, Phillip	PHA 51	James	LUZ 390
CILMAN, Bathr.	FRA 311	CLARK, Widow	PHI 11A	James	CHE 718
CIMBAL, Adam	BFD 54	Aaron	LUZ 323	James	CHE 769
CIMES, Chister	NOU 163	Abishai	CHE 741	James	CHE 821
CIMPLE,		Abm.	BUC 107	James	CHE 870
Christopher	NOU 104	Abraham	MER 436	Jas.	CUM 72
CINCH?, John W.	DAU 34	Abram	CHE 762	Jesse	MNT 39
CINNINGHAM,		Adam	NOU 116	Jno.	LYC 27
Robert	ALL 57	Alexander	ADA 20	Jno.	CUM 71
CINSTON, Phillip	CUM 62	Alexander	BER 158	Jno. Senr.	CUM 22
CIPE, Bernhard	PHA 48	Alexr.	CUM 38	Job	FAY 261
CIRFMAN, Jacob	HNT 146	Allexander	BEV 22	John	ADA 5
CIRKPATRICK, Wm.	YOR 199	Andrew	MNT 67	John	BEV 16
CISEEL, Wilm.	ALL 49	Andrew	NOU 143	John	CUM 28
CISEEL?, Thomas	ALL 49	Andrew Jr.	BFD 49	John	CUM 49
CISHLER, Jacob	MIF 3	Andrew Senr.	BFD 49	John	ALL 57
CISNA, Evans	ALL 50	Ann	CUM 51	John	ALL 60
James	CUM 146	Avery	BEV 20	John	ALL 72
Theophilis	ALL 50	Barney	LUZ 415	John	BUC 93
CISNEY, Margaret	FRA 320	Bartley	LAN 239	John	NOU 103
Stephen	CUM 51	Ben	LYC 28	John	NOU 109
CIST, Chas.	PHA 31	Ben	DAU 35	John	NOU 116
CITON, John	ALL 105	Benjamin	PHA 112	John	NOU 116
CIVET, Henry	NOU 162	Benjamin	LUZ 423	John	NOU 121
CLACK, Charles	NOU 156	Benjeman	FAY 252	John	HNT 146
CLACKNER,		Benjn.	PHA 16	John	NOU 179
Frederick	WAS 66	Benjn.	CUM 61	John	WST 188
Fredrick	DAU 5	Benjn.	BUC 86	John	FAY 202
CLAEDER, Jacob	NOH 42A	Benjn.	FAY 238	John	YOR 203
CLAG, Samuel	MER 436	Benjn.	BUC 87A	John	YOR 219
Thomas	MER 436	Brice	LAN 3	John	FAY 225
CLAINS, Henrey	FAY 225	Charles	WST 366	John	FAY 230
CLAIR, Abraham	MNT 115	Charles	BUC 98A	John	LAN 240
John	BFD 35	Daniel	PHI 32	John	FAY 249
Thomas	FAY 243	Daniel	BFD 72	John	FRA 299
Thomas	FAY 255	David	BEV 11	John	FRA 302
CLAMPFFER, Adam	PHA 34	David	BEV 18	John	FRA 314
CLAN, Chrisn.	PHI 40	David	ALL 60	John	FRA 318
CLANE, Captain	CHE 835	David	PHI 145	John	LUZ 361
Hannah	CHE 835	Elias	FAY 219	John	LUZ 405
CLANSEE, Lawrence	CRA 2	Elija	FAY 238	John	CHE 762
CLAPEIR, Le	PHA 97	Elijah	LUZ 379	John	YOR 154
CLAPHAMSON, Saml.	PHI 61A	Eneas	CUM 148	John Esqr.	
CLAPPEN, Ludowick	HNT 128	Frank	LYC 27	John Jnr.	CHE 763
CLAPPER,		Geo.	CUM 101	John	NOH 66A
Christina	HNT 128	Geo.	CUM 139	John	PHI 94A
Daniel	HNT 128	George	PHI 52	Jos.	PHI 104
George	HNT 128	George	NOU 127	Joseph	ALL 69
George	FAY 243	George	FRA 297	Joseph	PHA 81
				Joseph	ARM 127

CLARK, Joseph	BUC 151	CLARK, William	NOU 103	CLARLKE?, Mark	PHA 91
Joseph	LAN 236	William	HNT 125	CLARRY, John	LUZ 377
Joshua	FAY 264	William	NOU 162	CLASIER, Henry	PHA 57
Ludlow	FAY 243	William	YOR 167	CLASK, Saml.	FAY 243
Margaret	BFD 72	William	LAN 168	CLASS, Geo.	CUM 25
Margit	ALL 95	William	WST 211	Michael	NOH 66A
Mark	BEV 8	William	FAY 230	Thomas	BER 250
Mary	CUM 50	William	FAY 255	CLATON, Jacob	NOU 156
Mathew	PHA 100	William	LUZ 370	James,	FRA 310
Mathew	YOR 201	William	WST 377	CLATYON,	
Matthew	FAY 255	William	CHE 762	Elizabeth	PHA 116
Nathan	BFD 35	William	CHE 811	CLAUDIUS, Martin	BUC 141A
Nathen	FAY 264	William	ERI 56A	CLAUDY, Martin	CUM 125
Nelly	DAU 11A	Wm.	LYC 28	Martin	CUM 152
Noah	SOM 153	Wm.	PHI 29	Wm.	CUM 140
Peter	LUZ 342	Wm.	CUM 72	CLAUGES, John	PHI 60
Philemon	LUZ 361	Wm.	CUM 80	CLAUGUS?, Daniel	PHA 51
Rhoda	BEV 18	Wm.	PHI 82A	CLAUSE, Adam	LAN 2
Ritchard	ALL 53	Wolter	ALL 62	George	CUM 29
Ritchard	ALL 119	CLARKE, Aaron	WAS 11	CLAUSEN, Philip	BER 144
Robert	BEV 18	Andrew	WAS 27	CLAUSER, Edward	BER 259
Robert	NOU 116	Ann	GRN 105	Peter	BER 185
Robert	NOU 156	Benjamin	WAS 6	Philip A.	BER 148
Robert	LUZ 373	Bethuel	WAS 1	CLAUSON, Conrad	BUC 149
Robert	CHE 863	Calvin	WAS 1	John	BUC 141
Robert	DAU 46A	Daniel	GRN 91	CLAUSS, Abm.	NOH 47
Robt.	CUM 23	Daniel	WAS 97	Daniel	NOH 33
Robt.	CUM 51	David	WAS 11	Henry	NOH 33
Robt.	CUM 141	Ephram	PHA 17	John	NOH 58A
Robt.	VEN 165	Ezekiel	WAS 1	Philip	NOH 33
Saml.	LYC 28	George	WAS 33	Widow	NOH 52A
Saml.	PHI 45	George	DEL 171	CLAUZER, Michael	YOR 204
Saml.	PHA 80	Henry	PHA 4	CLAVENGER, Isaiah	GRN 87
Saml.	CHE 749	Hezekiah	WAS 61	CLAWR, Frederick	
Samuel	ADA 35	Jabez	WAS 61	(Henry-	
Samuel	BFD 49	Jacob	PHA 99	Crossed Out)	BFD 62
Samuel	LAN 69	James	GRN 100	CLAWSON, Andrew	WAS 120
Samuel	SOM 132	James	SOM 128	Cornelius	WST 168
Samuel	SOM 153	John	WAS 6	Isaac	BUC 142
Samuel	YOR 156	John	PHA 27	John	GRN 99
Samuel	LUZ 423	John	WAS 36	Silas	GRN 99
Samuel Esqr.	ARM 127	John	WAS 36	Stout	BUC 142A
Samuel	BUC 100A	John	PHA 38	William	BUC 144A
Sarah	PHI 50	John	WAS 84	CLAXON, William	DEL 160
Sarah	PHA 76	John	GRN 87	CLAXTON, John	PHA 33
Silas	WST 286	John	WAS 97	Mary	PHI 114
Susannah	PHA 76	John	GRN 100	CLAY, Alexander	PHI 56
Susannah	PHA 77	John	PHA 100	Alexr.	PHI 54
Tench?	SOM 142	John	WAS 115	Curtis	PHA 29
Thomas	BEV 18	John	WAS 11	David	NOU 192
Thomas	BFD 49	Joseph	PHA 33	Frederick	NOU 120
Thomas	BUC 93	Joseph	GRN 109	Jacob Junr.	YOR 181
Thomas	HNT 146	Joseph	WAS 51	Jno.	CUM 101
Thomas	BER 162	Joshua	WAS 48	Mary	PHA 114
Thomas	LAN 165	Mathew	WAS 36	Mathias	CUM 101
Thomas	LAN 240	Robert	WAS 66	Slaitor	MNT 81
Thomas	CHE 759	Robert	WAS 1	Slaitor	MNT 86
Thoms.	BUT 363	Samuel	GRN 100	CLAYFIELD, John	MNT 56
Thos.	LYC 27	Samuel	PHA 100	CLAYLON, Thomas	NOU 109
Thos.	LYC 28	Samuel Esqr.	WAS 115	CLAYPOLE, Joseph	PHA 16
Thos.	DAU 33	Thomas	WAS 19	Joseph Senr?	PHA 16
Thos.	CUM 88	William	WAS 33	CLAYPOOL, Joseph	PHI 70
Thos.	CUM 127	William	WAS 66	CLAYR, Godfrey	LUZ 335
Thos.	CUM 127	William	WAS 74	CLAYTON, Widow	PHI 46
Thos.	FRA 291	William	WAS 84	Aaron	CHE 763
Uriah Senr.	LYC 28	William	GRN 99	Charles	PHA 72
Uriah, Junr.	LYC 28	William	PHA 99	John	MIF 3
Walter	FAY 219	William	DEL 171	John	MNT 34
Walter	DAU 44A	William Esqr.	WAS 19	John	CHE 761
Widow	ALL 63	CLARKE?, Michael	GRN 62	Jonathan	MNT 64
Widow	LAN 130	CLARKNER, John	NOU 192	Jonathan Jnr.	BUC 143
Wiliam	LYC 9	CLARKSON, Jacob	PHA 96	Joseph (Jnr.-	
William	DAU 10	James Revd.	YOR 198	Crossed Out)	BUC 143
William	BFD 72	Joseph	LAN 129	Joseph	HNT 157
William	PHA 91	Levinus	BUC 89A	Joseph	DEL 165
William	BUC 93	CLARLEN, John	WST 270	Joseph	FRA 307

66

CLAYTON, Joseph		
Jnr.	BUC	143
Joshua	DEL	175
Joshua	CHE	762
Mary	PHA	74
Powell	DEL	157
Samuel	PHI	40
Samuel	CHE	764
Thomas	PHA	107
Wm.	CHE	761
CLEAR, Jonathn.	PHI	120
Peter	CHE	821
CLEARY, Dennis	FRA	313
CLEAVE, Thos.	PHA	92
CLEAVENGER,		
Squire	PHA	34
CLEAVER, Daniel	NOU	156
David	NOU	109
Ellis	MNT	44
Isaac	MNT	40
Isaac	NOU	109
Jesse	PHI	97
Jesse	PHI	81A
John	NOU	109
John	NOU	109
John	MNT	130
Joseph	NOU	109
Joseph Junr.	MNT	131
Nathan	MNT	87
Peter	MNT	93
Peter	MNT	131
William	MNT	104
CLEAVES, Francis	PHI	15
CLEEK, John	MIF	3
CLEER, John	MNT	34
CLEIMER, John	LAN	86
CLELAND, Arthur	NOU	179
James	NOU	179
Mrs.	NOU	170
Wilm.	ALL	53
CLELDENON, Andw.	WST	287
CLELLAN, James	CHE	719
CLELLAND, Hugh	DAU	47A
John	ERI	58A
CLEM, David	PHI	2
CLEMAN, Nicholas	WST	159
CLEMANCE, George	CHE	719
CLEMANS, Mrs.	NOU	156
CLEMANT, John	PHI	65
CLEMEL, Abraham	MNT	87
CLEMENCE, George	BER	261
John	PHI	77A
Peter	BER	261
Peter	BER	263
CLEMENDS, Patrick	CHE	911
CLEMENS, Abraham	MNT	121
Alexander	WAS	51
Jarrett	MNT	121
John	MNT	47
John	ERI	59
John	MNT	121
John	PHI	154
John	NOH	72A
Ketura	PHI	128
Phil	LUZ	388
CLEMENT, Mary	PHA	5
Richard	ERI	55A
CLEMENTS, Abm.	BER	233
Alexr.	YOR	200
Edward	PHA	13
James	WST	306
Joseph	PHA	104
Nicholas	BER	215
William	WST	270
CLEMER, Henry	MNT	67
CLEMINE, Peter	NOU	135
CLEMMANS, Job	PHA	63
Volentine	PHA	57
CLEMMENS,		
Christian	BUC	154
Jacob	BUC	104A
CLEMMER, Abraham	BUC	158A
Abram	MNT	126
Christian	BUC	158A
Jacob	MNT	113
Jacob	FAY	243
Jacob	BUC	158A
Jasper	FAY	243
CLEMMINS, John	FAY	264
CLEMMON, Cutlin	PHI	71
P.	LAN	59
CLEMONS, Abraham	WAS	7
Adam	WAS	33
Benjn.	CUM	105
Jacob	CHE	792
Jacob	CHE	796
John	WAS	108
Joseph	WAS	97
Joseph	WAS	108
Nicholas	WAS	120
William	WAS	7
CLEMPSON, Thos.	CEN	22
CLEMSON, Jas.	CHE	775
Thomas	HNT	130
Thomas	LAN	133
CLENDENIN, Andrew	LAN	265
CLENDENING, Adam	CHE	873
Adam	CHE	874
Alexander	WAS	108
Alexr.	CHE	843
Isabella	CHE	874
James	WAS	85
James	CHE	886
John	LAN	131
CLENDENNAN, James	LAN	59
CLENDENNEN, Jno.	CUM	59
Samuel	LAN	28
CLENDENNIN, Adam	NOH	29
Jas.	CUM	96
CLENDENNING,		
James	LAN	175
Robt.	CHE	768
Thos.	CHE	748
CLENDENNON, Adam	LAN	60
CLENDINEN, Jas.	BUT	316
CLENDINING,		
Alexd.	FRA	284
Andrew	WAS	85
CLENDINNON, Isaac	GRN	75
CLENTON, Charles	GRN	80
John	FAY	255
CLEPOLE, George	ARM	126
James	ARM	126
Joseph	ARM	126
CLERK, Abram	CHE	714
Robt.	CUM	47
Thomas	FRA	282
CLESTER,		
Christiana	SOM	147
CLETON, Alexd.	FRA	322
CLEVELAND,		
Ephraim	LUZ	406
CLEVENGER,		
Abraham	BFD	47
William	BFD	47
CLEVER, Barney	CUM	144
Henry	WST	270
Isaac	BER	137
John	DAU	19
John	YOR	209
Peter	BER	173
Peter	YOR	209
CLEVER, Philip	PHI	110
CLEVER?, John	BER	137
CLEVIDENCE, John	ALL	114
CLEVINGER, Aaron	BFD	42
Abraham	BFD	42
CLEW, Wm.	PHA	74
CLEWELL, Francil	NOH	72A
CLICK, Conrad	DAU	39
CLICOR, Valentine	ADA	43
CLIFFARD, George	FAY	249
CLIFFORD, Widow	WST	168
Anna	PHA	78
Charles	WST	168
Hugh	BUT	363
Hugh	BUT	364
John	BEV	27
John	PHA	83
Joseph	WST	168
Thomas	WST	168
Thos.	PHA	76
CLIFFTON, Benj.	PHI	68
CLIFT, Benja.	PHI	155
Edward	PHI	155
John	BUC	84A
Jonathan	PHI	155
CLIFTON, Francis	PHA	79
Jehu	PHA	70
William	PHI	15
CLIGE, John	WST	148
CLILAN, John	LAN	92
CLIM, George	BUC	100A
CLIMBINGHAWK,		
Henry	HNT	132
CLIMER, Isaac	NOU	135
Mary	PHI	99
CLIMSON, James		
Esq.	LAN	126
John	LAN	129
CLIMSTE, Martin	BER	232
CLINE, Abm.	PHI	115A
Abraham	PHA	65
Abraham	NOU	151
Abraham	NOU	151
Adam	PHI	53
Adam	SOM	126
Ann	BFD	42
Barbara	WST	210
Barney	WST	210
Bernheart	NOU	135
Christopher	BFD	55
Christopher	NOU	186
Christopher	NOU	186
Conrad	MNT	44
Conrad	MNT	130
Conrad	YOR	175
Daniel	FAY	238
Daniel	BUC	100A
Elizabeth	DEL	183
Elizabeth	DEL	185
George	ADA	29
George	MNT	44
George	PHI	95
George	FRA	309
George	PHI	98
Harman	NOU	146
Harman	NOU	146
Harman	NOU	151
Henry	BFD	47
Henry	YOR	204
Henry Jr.	YOR	192
Henry Sr.	YOR	192
Herman	YOR	219
Jacob	PHI	13
Jacob	NOU	134
Jacob	FAY	252
Jacob	LAN	260

CNAUSE?,		COBLE, Jacob	DAU 45A	COCHRAN, Thos.	PHA 116
Christian	BER 225	Michael	LAN 16	William	ADA 5
CNEP, John	NOU 192	COBLER, Adam	BFD 78	William	ERI 60
CNIPE, Jacob	NOU 135	COBLIN, Jacob	MIF 3	William	WAS 109
CNIPLY, William	NOU 182	Jacob	MIF 3	William	ARM 123
COACH, James	LAN 112	COBOUGH, Frederic	HNT 122	William	WST 189
COACT, Henry	DAU 43	COBOURN, Jacob	DEL 166	William	FAY 264
COADER, Conrod		Joseph	DEL 166	William	WST 342
Jr.	WST 287	Nathaniel	PHA 120	Wm.	WST 148
COADER?, Henry	NOU 114	COBOURNE, Aaron	DEL 162	COCHRANE,	
COAGH, Phillip	CUM 67	Caleb	DEL 162	Alexander	PHA 97
COAH?, Adam	NOU 179	John	PHA 25	COCHREN, Alexd.	ALL 105
COAL, John	LAN 221	Joseph	DEL 164	Allexander	BEV 10
COALSTON, Edwd.	MNT 77	Joseph Jun.	DEL 167	David	ALL 65
COALTER, James	FRA 322	Thomas	DEL 164	George	ALL 51
Margaret	FRA 322	COBURN, Ann	PHA 90	George	ALL 56
COAN, Adam	SOM 156	Parley	LUZ 417	James	DAU 17
John	SOM 156	COBY, Robert	PHA 51	John	DAU 10
Peter	SOM 156	COCH, Bengamin	ALL 95	John	ALL 74
COAPLEY, John	FRA 323	Henry	ALL 118	John	ALL 75
COARD, George	MER 438	Joseph	ADA 30	Ritchard	ALL 115
COARNEY, James	LAN 52	Joseph	ALL 95	Robert	ALL 83
COASER, John	ADA 17	Nethan	ALL 95	Samuel	DAU 10
COASLAIN, John	PHA 105	Nethan Junior	ALL 95	Samuel	ALL 82
COAST, Hugh	BUT 356	Phillop	ALL 95	Samuel	ALL 92
COAT, Jacob		COCHAREN, John		Wilm.	ALL 86
Jeriod	PHI 119	Captn.	PHI 119A	Wilm.	ALL 105
COATES, Abner	BUT 342	COCHENAWER,		COCHRON, Andrew	FAY 202
Daniel	PHA 43	Daniel	FAY 249	Joseph	BEV 11
John	MNT 71	Henry	FAY 197	Joseph	BEV 14
Josiah	PHA 19	COCHER, Geo.	BUT 351	Joseph	FAY 249
Moses	CHE 901	COCHLEN, Richard	FAY 230	Margret	FAY 202
Phillis	PHA 53	COCHMAN, James	ADA 2	Samuel	FAY 249
Rachel	MNT 104	COCHRAM, Samuel	WST 322	Thomas	FAY 202
Samuel	PHA 7	COCHRAN, (No		COCHTERPHER,	
Samuel	DEL 168	Given Name)	DAU 46	Phillip	CUM 48
Samuel	CHE 899	Alex.	MIF 14A	COCK, John	ALL 72
Septemus	MNT 104	Alexander	BUT 343	John	FAY 226
Thos.	PHA 42	Alexr.	BUT 343	John	PHI 82A
Widow	CHE 854	David	CHE 873	William	FAY 226
Wm.	PHA 8	David	MIF 14A	COCK?, See Coch	ALL 95
COATNEY, David	FRA 300	George	CHE 700	COCKEMSPEIR,	
COATS, Widow	PHI 17	Isaac	DEL 177	Martin	PHI 2
Widow	PHI 35	Isaac	DEL 188	COCKENORE, David	HNT 127
Widow	PHI 66	James	CRA 14	COCKER, Christn.	PHI 52
Abraham	PHI 88	James	ERI 56	COCKINS, Vincent	CUM 94
Isaac	PHI 88	James	WAS 109	COCKLEY, David	CUM 109
Isaac	CHE 901	James	LAN 260	Jacob	CUM 71
Jacob	PHI 90A	James	WST 307	COCKLY, John	CUM 71
John	PHI 18	James	CHE 872	Peter	CUM 64
John	PHI 84	James	MIF 14A	COCKRAN, John	PHA 88
John	BUC 86	Jno.	LYC 29	COCKS, Josepth	MER 439
John	PHI 71A	John	CRA 18	COCKSPARER,	
John H.	CHE 853	John	ERI 60	Martin	PHI 2
Sarah	LYC 28	John	NOU 162	CODER, Conrod	WST 287
William	PHI 28	John	DEL 173	Frederick	NOU 153
William	CHE 762	John	WST 286	George	HNT 158
Wm. Esqr.	PHI 77	John	WST 322	George	MIF 6A
COB, Daniel	PHI 25	John	WST 342	Jacob	MIF 6A
COBACH, Abrm. Sr.	DAU 19A	Joseph	PHI 57	Simon	NOU 146
Abrm.	DAU 19A	Linsey, Old	DAU 46	Simon	MIF 6A
Abrm.	DAU 19A	Moses	FRA 288	CODERMAN, George	NOU 192
COBB, Asa	LUZ 369	Patk.	CUM 150	George	WST 211
David	LAN 6	Richd.	CUM 24	COE, Benjamin	ALL 119
Ezekiel	LUZ 365	Robert	PHI 31	James	NOH 64
John	LAN 6	Roboert	PHA 29	Josep	ALL 119
Joseph	LUZ 369	Robt.	BUT 358	Joseph	WAS 61
Sarah	FAY 235	Robt.	BUT 363	Joshua	WAS 61
COBBERT, William	CHE 851	Robt.	WST 365	Moses	WAS 74
COBEAN, Alexander	ADA 9	Robt.	CHE 873	Newman	WAY 141
James	ADA 8	Saml.	WST 342	Peter	WAS 27
Samuel	ADA 13	Saml.	CHE 813	Philip	GRN 109
Samuel Jun.	ADA 8	Saml.	CHE 873	COESON, Abenr.?	CEN 22
William	ADA 8	Samuel	WAS 74	COFFEE, George	PHI 11A
COBLE, Christian	NOU 121	Samuel Esq.	LAN 53	Joseph	CHE 718
Frederick	NOU 121	Thomas Esq.	ADA 14	Joseph	CHE 821

COFFEE, Michael	HNT	130	COHENOUR, Daniel	SOM	157	COLE, Joshua	WST	322
Thos.	CUM	144	Joseph	SOM	151	Leonard	WAY	143
William	CHE	718	Mary	HNT	128	Michael	BUC	139
COFFEY, Wm.	DAU	20	Peter	SOM	157	Michale	ADA	37
COFFIELD, Alexr.	WST	168	COHO, John	BFD	61	Phillip	NOU	127
Arthur	BEV	10	COHONE, James	LAN	92	Samuel	LUZ	414
COFFIN, Arther	ALL	56	COHOR, Adam	NOU	174	Samuel	CEN	18A
Elonar	BUC	96A	COHRAN, Charles	NOU	116	Simon	WAS	66
Jacob	MNT	34	Delany	BER	267	Simon Peter	WAY	135
Robt.	PHI	67	Thomas	MNT	137	Solomon	LUZ	414
William	PHA	118	COHUN?, John	BER	184	Thomas	WAS	51
COFFING, William			COIGAR, Jacob	FAY	255	Thomas	HNT	146
Junr.	WAS	36	COIL, James	LAN	60	Tonas	WAS	33
William Senr.	WAS	36	James	PHI	118A	Tunis	NOH	33
COFFMAN, Abrm.	CHE	737	Roger	CRA	12	Widow	BUC	140
Casper	DEL	159	COIN?, (See Corn)	LAN	28	William	PHI	4
Christian	BFD	48	COINE, Edward	WAS	51	William	WAS	33
Christian	FRA	305	COINER, Geo.	CUM	26	William	NOU	116
Christn.	CUM	56	COITE, Thomas	CHE	839	William	LUZ	424
Christopher	DEL	155	COKE, Mrs.	NOU	174	COLEBURN, Robert	SOM	142
Chrstn.	CHE	733	COKES, Felix	PHI	89A	Robert Jun.	SOM	142
Daniel	MIF	3	William	LAN	311	COLEFIELD, Wm.	PHI	117
David	CHE	734	COL, Ezekial	NOU	151	COLEMAN, Aaron	WAS	1
Fredr.	FRA	305	COLAR, John	MNT	130	Adam	ADA	28
George	WAS	27	COLB, Jacob	NOH	64	Bash	LAN	252
George	BFD	72	John	BUC	139	Benjn.	NOH	33
George	HNT	139	John N.	YOR	191	Burkart	BER	175
George	DEL	155	COLBERS, David	LAN	308	Catharine	PHA	57
Henry	CHE	859	COLBERT, Isaac	GRN	69	Charity	PHA	65
Jacob	CUM	31	Jobe	CRA	15	Charles	BUC	90
Jacob	BFD	49	John	MNT	137	Charles	BUC	88A
Jacob	CHE	735	Robert	GRN	94	Christopher	WAS	98
Jacob	CHE	883	Secel	PHI	2	Elija	FAY	226
John	CUM	150	Thomas	PHA	12	Ephraim	GRN	94
John	CHE	860	COLBETEER?, Adam	NOU	127	Esther	WAS	37
Joseph	WAS	78	COLCHER, Peter	CRA	16	George	SOM	137
Joseph	CHE	860	COLD, Black	PHI	89A	Henry	PHA	77
Peter	CUM	33	COLDRAIN, Isaac	FAY	213	Hugh	LYC	28
Phillip	CUM	70	COLDREIN, John	NOU	99	Isreal	PHI	95
Uley	CHE	720	Peter	NOU	99	Jacob	GRN	110
COFFY, George	FRA	303	Robert	NOU	97	Jacob	SOM	151
COFLER, Ludewick	NOU	162	COLDSMITH, Wm.	FRA	315	Jacob	PHI	78A
COFMAN, Abigal	PHI	109	COLDWATER, Adam	PHI	112A	James	HNT	163
George	FRA	305	COLDWELL, John	FAY	243	Jesse	LUZ	345
Henry	FRA	309	Margeret	FAY	243	Jno.	LYC	28
Jacob	PHI	85A	William	FAY	243	Jno., Senr	LYC	28
Jno.	CUM	71	COLE, Abisha	LUZ	414	John	BEV	25
John	NOU	127	Abraham	WAY	143	John	NOH	37
COFROAD, Henry			Barnet	WAS	33	John	PHI	46
Junr.	LAN	134	Benjamin	LUZ	419	John	PHA	64
Henry Senr.	LAN	134	Christian	LAN	110	John	SOM	137
COGA, James	WAS	78	Conrad	MNT	75	John	FAY	261
COGAN, John	BFD	55	Conrad	BUC	139	John	WST	286
COGGINS, James	CHE	704	Daniel	WAS	2	John	MER	437
Judge	MNT	81	Daniel	FAY	255	Jonathan	LUZ	344
Thomas	MNT	81	Edwd.	BUT	360	Jonathan	NOH	86A
COGGSWEL, Wilm.	ALL	78	Elias	PHI	110	Jos.	YOR	208
COGHAN, John	CUM	131	Elisha	LUZ	414	Joseph	PHA	9
COGHRIN, Francis	MER	436	Elizabeth	FAY	252	Joseph	FAY	220
Francis	MER	436	Frederick	FRA	288	Joseph Jur.	FAY	220
COGLEY, James	ARM	125	George	ADA	37	Leonard	WAS	61
James	ARM	125	George	NOH	62	Nathaniel	MER	437
Joseph	DAU	11A	George	BUC	139	Nathaniel Sr.	WAS	1
Robert	ARM	125	George	BUC	140A	Nicholas	PHA	42
COGON, Wilm.	ALL	53	Gideon	WAY	143	Nicholas	SOM	137
COGSWELL, Edward	LUZ	396	Harmonas	WAS	27	Obed.	LYC	13
COH, John	DAU	6	Henry	NOH	29	Philip	BFD	37
John	DAU	24A	Henry	MNT	75	Philip	PHI	72
COHAN, Chas.	CUM	102	Isaac	WAS	42	Phineas	WAY	141
COHEEN, John	CEN	22	Jacob	BUC	139	Richard	WAS	120
Widow	LAN	93	James	PHA	55	Robert	LAN	260
COHEN, Bell	PHA	11	James	HNT	146	Robert Esq.	LAN	96
Lawrence	PHA	56	James H?	PHA	16	Robt.	CUM	23
COHENDERFFER,			John	MNT	72	Saml.	NOH	33
George	DAU	31	John	BUC	80	Samuel	MER	437
COHENOUR,Christian	SOM	157	John	WST	306	Thomas	WAS	1

COLVER, Jacob	NOH	42A	COMMONS, Elisha	CHE	730	CONKLE, Michl.	CUM	64
COLVILLE, James	WAS	27	John	YOR	201	Michl.	WST	365
COLVIN, James	WAS	85	Owen	PHI	60	CONKLEN, Daniel	FAY	255
John	WAS	43	COMP, Adam	BFD	56	CONKLIN, John	WAS	62
John Senr.	MER	438	Henry	CUM	41	Jonathan	WAY	140
Saml.	BUC	93	COMPASS, Widow	PHI	21	Josia	FAY	252
Stephen	BEV	13	COMPER, Wm.	LAN	288	Samuel	LAN	313
Vincent Junr.	WAS	43	COMPON, Francis	PHA	33	CONLEY, John	BEV	6
Vincent Senr.	WAS	43	COMPOTON, Thos.	PHA	10	Mary An	BEV	0
Wiilliam	YOR	203	COMPTON, Sarah	GRN	80	Nicholas	BEV	23
COLWELL, Agness	CUM	142	COMSTOCK, Abner	LUZ	390	William	CRA	8
Alexr.	CUM	107	Asaph	LUZ	390	William	NOU	162
Hugh	CUM	45	Bethiar	LUZ	390	William	NOU	201
James	FAY	225	Peleg	LUZ	374	CONLOGLE, William	YOR	212
John	LAN	247	Zebulon	LUZ	374	CONLY, Francis	PHI	82A
Joseph Esqr.	BEV	22	COMSTON, Henry	ALL	75	John	ALL	63
Mary	CUM	109	COMTON, Ebenezer	PHI	66A	John	NOU	127
Matthew	FAY	230	CON, Robert	NOU	163	John	NOU	162
Saml.	CUM	94	CONAGO, Joseph	CHE	886	W.	LAN	148
William	PHA	117	CONAH?, David	FRA	273	CONN, George	YOR	160
COLYER, Mary	PHI	50	CONAIN, John	SOM	161	George	YOR	174
COMATH, Agatt	LAN	194	CONARD, Anthony	PHI	124	George	FAY	220
COMATH?,			Jacob	PHI	125	George Snr./		
Catharina	LAN	194	Martin	LYC	15	Jur.?	FAY	220
COMBS, Daniel	VEN	167	Wm. & Sister	FRA	286	Henry	LYC	20
George	PHA	37	CONCHLIN, John	WAY	136	James	LYC	29
Jermon	PHA	15	CONCKEL, Peter	NOH	62	Mary	HNT	143
Jonathan	BUC	140A	CONCLE, George	BEV	16	Samuel	CHE	732
Joseph	FAY	219	Henry	BEV	25	William	FAY	220
William	ADA	13	Lawrence	BEV	13	William	CHE	732
COMCLY, Henry	PHI	138	Michael	BEV	14	William	MIF	4A
COMEGYS,			CONDERY, Daniel	PHI	15	CONNALLY, John	BUT	351
Cornelias	PHA	79	CONDIT, Jonas	WAS	62	Thos.	PHI	105A
COMELY, Isaac	PHI	144	Jonas	WAS	109	CONNARD, Abraham	LAN	113
Jacob	PHI	30	CONDITT, David	MER	437	Dennis	CHE	713
Jacob	ADA	41	Iley	MER	437	Ebenezer	BUC	107
Jacob	PHI	137	CONDO, Peter	PHI	72A	Evrad	CHE	731
Jesse	PHI	136	CONDON, John	BUT	336	Isaac	LAN	111
John	PHI	134	John Senr.	WST	342	John	BUC	154
Joseh	PHI	145	Richd.	WST	342	John	PHI	78A
COMELY?, Nathan	MNT	130	Saml.	PHI	101A	CONNAWAY, Charls	FAY	243
COMES, Patrik	DAU	45	William	FAY	255	John	FAY	261
COMFORT, Andw.	CUM	86	Wm.	PHI	82	Saml.	FAY	220
Christian	HNT	126	CONDREN, James	HNT	120	CONNEL, Alexander	NOU	127
Conrod	FRA	274	CONDY, Jeremiah	PHA	9	Robt.	PHI	87A
David	PHI	144	Jonathan W.	PHA	10	Smith	BFD	55
Ezea Junr.	MNT	110	Thomas	PHI	53A	Susanna	LAN	127
Ezra	MNT	107	CONEDY, David	LYC	11	William	NOU	127
Henry	ADA	42	CONEL, Betsy	PHI	88A	Willm.	BUT	341
Jacob	YOR	173	CONELLY, William	DAU	2A	CONNELE, William	LAN	162
Jacob	LAN	300	CONER, Michael	GRN	69	CONNELL, Eliza	PHA	81
John	MIF	1	CONEWAY, Patrick	WST	250	Ewd.	FRA	320
John	BUC	93	CONEY, Neal	NOU	201	Johardus	PHI	8
John	MNT	109	Patrick	CHE	711	John	DEL	187
John	YOR	211	CONFER?, See			John R.	FAY	197
John Jnr.	BUC	93	Coufer	BER	269	Mathew	FRA	326
Moses	BUC	93	CONFOR, Phillip	NOU	174	Matths.	PHI	53A
Peter	ADA	12	CONGAR, Elias	GRN	106	William	DEL	166
Robert	BUC	151	CONGAWANE, Philip	WST	249	William	FAY	202
Robert	CHE	713	CONGEL, Adam	NOH	44A	William	MIF	4A
Stephen	BUC	93	CONGER, David	WAS	61	Zacharia	FAY	200
Stephen	BUC	160A	CONGERS, Dennis	WAS	74	CONNELLEY, John	PHA	7
COMKE, John	LAN	178	Ishmael	WAS	74	Michael	PHA	111
COMLEY, Esra	PHA	31	Thomas	WAS	15	CONNELLY, Barney	SOM	142
Isaac	PHI	58	CONGGAR, David	FAY	220	James	LUZ	323
John	WAS	51	CONGLETON,			James B.	PHA	66
COMLY, Widw.	PHI	113	William	WAS	55	Jos.	CUM	101
David	PHI	109	CONKEL, George	LAN	159	Mathew	PHA	64
Jacob	PHI	149	Jacob	LAN	160	Thomas	LAN	265
Jonathan	PHI	149	CONKEY, James	PHI	9	Thomas	NOH	66A
Joshua	PHI	149	CONKLE, Baltzer	FRA	279	William	NOH	66A
COMMEL, Alexander	LAN	245	Henry	WAS	119	CONNELY, Adam	MIF	14A
COMMING, Charles	PHI	102A	Jacob	WAS	119	Honor	MIF	14A
James	PHI	95	John	WAS	119	Isaac	CEN	22
COMMINS, John	CHE	849	John	FRA	279	James	LAN	178
Jonathan	LAN	221	John	FRA	280	Jas.	BUT	353

72

CONNELY, Michael	HNT 145		CONNOWAY, Willm.	BUT 352		CONROD, Thos.	PHI 68A
Patk.	MIF 16A		CONOLY, William	CHE 816		CONROE, Thomas	DEL 166
Wm.	CEN 22		CONOVER, Joseph	PHI 33		CONROW, Patty	PHI 93A
CONNER, Abigail	MIF 1		Saml. T. M.d.	PHA 4		CONROY, Peter	FRA 297
Benjamin	WAS 119		CONRAD, Anthoney	FAY 255		CONSAUL?, James	BEV 24
Caleb	DEL 191		Benjamin	MNT 69		CONSER?, George	PHI 78
Charles	BER 274		Catharina	LAN 194		CONSOR, Henry	NOU 174
Charlott	PHA 110		Catherine	BUC 97A		John	NOU 174
Chas.	MIF 6A		Charles	BER 152		John	NOU 191
Conrad	NOU 149		Christena	BER 175		CONWAY, Arthur	DEL 180
Cornelous	ALL 93		Christina	DAU 14		George	CUM 116
David	NOU 197		Christly	DAU 19A		James	FRA 288
Dennis	PHA 88		Christn.	BER 175		John	CHE 854
Edmond	PHA 122		Conrad	DAU 20		Patrick	DEL 182
Edward	MNT 103		D.	DAU 44A		Peter	BER 238
Elizabeth	LAN 36		Dennis	MNT 49		Samuel	SOM 157
Elizabeth	PHI 102A		Dennis	PHA 122		Susannah	CHE 700B
Geo.	CUM 52		Elizabeth	MNT 137		William	YOR 212
Isaac	CRA 9		Ephram	PHA 12		CONWELL, Jehue	FAY 226
James	BFD 36		Frederick	MNT 112		Shephard	FAY 226
James	SOM 142		George	BER 175		Thomas	FAY 226
James	BER 173		George	DAU 27A		William	FAY 226
John	BEV 4		Henry	NOU 99		CONYERS, John	PHA 65
John	BFD 36		Henry	MNT 117		COODER, Henry	BUC 81A
John	BFD 55		Jacob	BUC 86		Jacob	BUC 81A
John	LAN 60		Jacob	WAS 109		Valentine	BUC 100A
John	BFD 69		Jacob	HNT 155		Widow	BUC 100A
John	BUC 83		Jacob	YOR 181		COODMAN, Pheobe	PHA 21
John	ALL 87		Jacob Senr.	NOU 99		COOK, Widow	PHI 52
John	ALL 92		Jacob	DAU 47A		Aaron	LUZ 410
John	MNT 94		Jacob	NOH 66A		Abraham	PHA 31
John	NOU 154		John	MNT 49		Adam	FRA 281
John	DEL 187		John	MNT 49		Alexander	WAS 19
John	BER 207		John	PHA 52		Alexander	PHA 59
John	YOR 214		John	MNT 63		Andw.	YOR 215
John	FAY 243		John	PHA 80		Anthony	HNT 146
John	PHI 98		John	BUC 86		Archb.	PHI 90
Joseph	NOU 149		John	LAN 99		Assa	WST 189
Marcelow	PHA 91		John	NOU 99		Christian	FRA 307
Mary	BFD 55		John	MNT 107		Conrad	NOU 162
Michl.	PHI 99A		John	BER 175		Daniel	FRA 321
Patrick	SOM 142		John Junr.	BUC 86		Daniel	WST 341
Paul	BER 233		Jonathan	MNT 116		David	LAN 8
Thomas	MNT 104		Joseph	PHI 37		Ebenezar	LYC 6
Thomas	ARM 127		Joseph	BER 148		Edward	NOH 29
Thomas	NOU 149		Joshua	DAU 14		Edward	LAN 31
Timothy	ALL 91		M.	DAU 44A		Edward Esqr.	FAY 264
Timothy	MNT 140		Michael	BFD 49		Eliakim	ERI 55A
Wm. Esqr.	BEV 5		Michl.	BER 175		Elias	YOR 210
CONNEWAY, John	BFD 57		Nicholas	NOU 99		Elizabeth	FRA 287
CONNIT, Danniel	ALL 71		Nicols.	DAU 17A		Enion	CHE 811
CONNLING, Ananias	GRN 63		Peter	NOU 99		George	ADA 24
CONNOLLY, Hugh	HNT 121		Peter	MNT 115		George	PHA 35
CONNOLY, Widow	PHI 26		Peter	BER 284		George	FRA 271
Ann	MIF 1		Philip	YOR 209		George	FRA 307
Michael	HNT 148		Samuel	MNT 49		Hannah	MIF 3
Patrick	PHI 32		Samuel	BER 229		Hannah	PHA 94
CONNOR, Widow	PHI 24		Sarah	BFD 49		Henry	YOR 210
Widow	WST 322		Streaper?	MNT 50		Henry	FRA 283
Barny	PHI 46		Widow	LAN 86		Henry	PHI 109A
Chrisr.	PHI 23		William	LUZ 384		Hugh	DEL 157
Christopher	WST 322		Wm.	BUC 86		Isaac	MNT 93
George	CUM 130		CONRALZ?, Leonard	LAN 194		Isaac	YOR 207
Hugh	LUZ 321		CONRATH,			Isaac	CHE 769
James	PHI 14		Christian	LAN 208		Jacob	MNT 34
James	LUZ 368		CONRELISON,			Jacob	YOR 208
James	CHE 771		Margaret	WAS 2		Jacob	FRA 283
John	WAS 88		CONRICK, Michael	FAY 240		James	PHI 4
Robert	HNT 157		CONROD, Charrels	ALL 118		James	WAS 55
Thomas	WAS 78		Cornelius	CHE 836		James	WAS 88
Timothy	WST 342		Ellinor	ALL 49		James	NOU 127
CONNORAN, James	HNT 163		Henry	WAS 79		James	NOU 174
CONNORDE, Thos.	PHI 67		John	PHA 56		Jeremiah	ARM 126
CONNOVER, Daniel	HNT 134		John	WAS 79		Jeremiah	FAY 264
CONNOWAY, Hugh	BUT 350		John	WST 287		Jesse	MNT 106
Timothy	MER 436		Joseph	CHE 833		Jesse	YOR 212

Name	Loc	Name	Loc	Name	Loc
COOK, Jno.	CUM 63	COOKER, Matthe.	PHI 5	COOPER, Widow	WST 322
John	CRA 9	COOKLEN, William	BUC 90	Abraham	BUC 91
John	CRA 14	COOKLER, Mark	PHI 2	Abraham	BUC 82A
John	WAS 19	COOKLIN, William	BUC 88A	Adam	CUM 79
John	CUM 52	COOKSEN, Michl.	CUM 149	Adam	DAU 7A
John	PHA 59	COOKSHEET,		Agnatious	PHI 99A
John	BFD 61	Richard	DEL 165	Alexr.	YOR 201
John	ALL 86	COOKSON, Benjamin	MIF 1	Amos	BUC 137
John	WAS 88	Charles	ADA 17	Benjn.	PHA 44
John	PHI 98	Chas.	MIF 12A	Calvent	CHE 761
John	NOU 116	Daniel	YOR 209	Calvent	CHE 843
John	PHA 119	Danl.	MIF 9A	Calvin	LAN 120
John	PHI 125	Isaac	YOR 209	Catharine	PHA 72
John	NOU 127	Joseph	ADA 9	Charles	CHE 717
John	PHI 130	Joseph	MIF 12A	Chas.	CUM 98
John	FAY 213	Martha	HNT 136	Conrad	PHI 72
John	FAY 230	Thos.	MIF 24A	Cornelius	NOU 146
John	FRA 307	COOKSON?, Wm.	MIF 9A	Daniel	PHA 116
John	CHE 763	COOL, Frederick	WAS 51	Daniel	BUC 149
John	CHE 786	John	FAY 202	Daniel	LAN 218
John	PHI 105B	Peter	ALL 97	Daniel	NOH 79A
John	PHI 94A	COOLBACK,		Danl.	DAU 16
John H.	PHI 82	Cornelius	BUC 146	Davenport	WAS 1
Joseph	HNT 125	COOLBAUGH, John	WAY 148	David	WAS 42
Joseph	FRA 300	Moses	LUZ 414	David	CHE 862
Mary	CHE 757	William	WAY 148	David & Francis	YOR 203
Michael	WAS 74	William	LUZ 414	Elizabeth	CHE 745
Michl.	FRA 321	William Jr.	LUZ 414	Elizabeth	CHE 779
Nathan	PHA 28	COOLEY, Jacob	LUZ 332	Ephraim	WAS 61
Nathan	MNT 107	John	WAS 11	Francis	PHI 92
Nica	PHA 91	COOLON, Joseph	BUC 84A	Francis, David	
Ozen	LUZ 391	COOLY, John	FAY 208	&	YOR 203
Peter	PHI 25	Joseph	BEV 27	Frederick	WAS 42
Peter	PHA 66	Richard	FAY 243	Frederick	WAS 67
Peter	FRA 275	COOM, Isaac	CUM 101	Geo.	CUM 138
Peter	FRA 307	COOMBS, David	PHI 32	George	LAN 120
Phillip	FRA 276	COON, Archibauld	ALL 68	George	LUZ 362
Reuben	LYC 10	Baltzer	FRA 282	George	LUZ 427
Richard	LUZ 369	Christopher	PHI 124	George	CHE 874
Robert	WAS 15	Fredr.	FRA 321	Haggai	YOR 215
Robert	PHA 16	Henry	HNT 144	Henry	CUM 124
Saml.	PHI 103	Henry	WST 307	Henry	BUC 137
Samuel	LAN 6	John	MNT 40	Hugh	PHA 19
Stephen	LAN 89	John	PHI 124	Hugh	FRA 284
Stephen	CHE 764	Michal	ALL 68	Jacob	BUC 145A
Susannah	PHA 3	Peter	FRA 301	James	ALL 111
Thomas	FAY 264	Peter	FRA 324	James	PHA 112
Thos.	PHA 69	Saml.	FRA 301	James	LAN 121
Widow	LAN 39	COONEY, Danl.	CUM 51	James	HNT 145
William	WAS 15	Fredk.	CUM 51	James	YOR 166
William	PHI 27	Melcher	CUM 51	James	LAN 177
William	BFD 54	Peter	CUM 150	James	FRA 272
William	BFD 61	COONS, Andw.	MIF 6A	James Junr.	LAN 120
William	NOU 170	George	HNT 121	James	BUC 84A
William	FAY 220	Peter	HNT 121	Jas.	LAN 167
William	CHE 888	Widow	BUC 147	Jeremiah	BUC 151
Wm.	CHE 754	COONTING?,		John	BEV 13
COOK?, Wm.	BEV 28	Sebtitice?/		John	BEV 26
COOKE, Andw.	BUT 359	Lebbitice?	PHA 121	John	PHA 39
David	WAS 11	COONTZ, Abraham	BFD 72	John	WAS 42
George	WAS 27	Adam	BFD 49	John	NOH 47
Isaac	WAS 1	David	BFD 49	John	NOH 47
Jacob	WAS 1	Frederick	BFD 49	John	PHA 59
John	WAS 61	George	CUM 57	John	WAS 79
John	NOU 170	Henry	BFD 71	John	PHA 84
John	BUT 361	Peter	BFD 49	John	WAS 98
Joseph	WST 210	Peter	BFD 55	John	PHA 118
Noah	WAS 1	Samuel	BFD 54	John	LAN 121
Salvanus	BUT 349	COOOOPER, Joseph	ALL 110	John	CUM 126
Stephen	WAS 1	COOP, John	PHI 133	John	BUC 137
Thomas	WST 322	Widow	LAN 5	John	DEL 160
Ziba	WAS 1	COOPE, Abah.	CHE 807	John	YOR 201
COOKER, Jacob	PHI 53A	Jonathan	CHE 807	John	YOR 203
Jacob	PHI 53A	Joseph	CHE 809	John	WST 249
Martin	PHI 43	Nathan	CHE 809	John	BUT 337
Mathias	PHI 54	Samuel	CHE 809	John	CHE 757

COOPER, John			COPE, Conrod		CUM 120	CORBEL, Joseph	MIF	24A
Esqr.	NOH	37	David	BUC 96		CORBELL, Daniel	CEN	20
John	MIF	14A	David	CHE 887		CORBET, Archibald		
John	PHI	73A	Gatlip	PHI 105		(A Boarding		
Jonathen	NOU	153	George	MNT 124		House)	PHA	37
Joseph	BFD	42	George	WST 211		Asaph	LUZ	387
Joseph	LAN	121	Henry	BUC 96		Enlow	PHA	101
Joseph	CHE	804	Isaac	FAY 264		Hannah	CUM	149
Joseph	BUC	84A	Jacob	BUC 96		Rebecca	PHA	46
Josiah	FRA	284	Jacob Jnr.	BUC 96		Robert	LUZ	387
Martha	FAY	208	Jacob	BUC 158A		William	MIF	16A
Martin	ALL	116	John	PHI 77		CORBIN, Abraham	WAS	27
Mary	PHI	70	John	BUC 96		Asahel	HNT	158
Mary	BER	247	John	CUM 120		Micajah	HNT	137
Mathias	BEV	27	John	MNT 124		William	HNT	153
Matthias	DEL	181	John	FAY 264		CORBLEY, John		
Moses	WAS	1	John Junr.	FAY 264		Revd.	GRN	80
Nathaniel	WAS	61	Ludwig	LAN 290		CORBY, David	CHE	848
Rasmus	ALL	93	Nicols.	DAU 16A		James	BUT	366
Robert	MIF	1	Peter	CUM 113		Joseph	ALL	107
Robert	ALL	110	Samuel	MNT 124		CORD, James	YOR	199
Robert	WST	211	Samuel	FAY 264		John	WAS	11
Robert	CHE	848	Thomas P.	PHA 30		John	FAY	202
Robt.	CUM	139	William	PHI 19		CORDARY, Nathl.	FAY	219
Robt.	FRA	299	Wm.	WST 211		CORDNER, John	PHA	85
Saml.	CHE	777	COPEHEAVER, Henry	DAU 39A		CORE, Christian	FAY	213
Saml.	PHI	76A	COPELAND, George	CHE 861		Henrey	FAY	213
Samuel	WAS	27	George	CHE 873		Jaocb	PHA	42
Samuel	ALL	99	Mathias	ADA 8		Marey	FAY	213
Samuel	PHA	112	Philip	LAN 218		COREY, Aaron	WAS	55
Samuel	PHI	137	Richd.	YOR 217		John	BFD	42
Samuel	BUC	149	Samuel	BUT 326		John	FAY	197
Samuel	VEN	170	Thomas	MIF 4A		Joseph	LUZ	357
Samuel	FRA	289	Wm.	PHA 88		Ralph	MNT	71
Stephen	YOR	201	COPELEY, John	CUM 110		CORFAX, Adam	NOU	174
Stephen T.	YOR	201	COPELY, Saml.	FRA 296		CORFIELD, Adam	PHI	138
Thomas	PHI	19	COPENHAVER,			Frederick	NOU	170
Thomas	WAS	19	Benjn.	CUM 146		CORIAH?, David	FRA	273
Thomas	ADA	42	COPENHOVER,			CORISEN?, George	PHI	78
Thomas	NOU	170	Baltzer	HNT 133		CORKER, John	NOU	170
Thomas	BUC	144A	Joseph	HNT 138		CORKRIN, James	PHA	95
Thos.	PHA	70	COPER, John	LAN 121		CORL, Conrad	NOU	120
Thos.	BUC	93	COPERSMITH, Peter	YOR 188		Henry	CHE	903
Truman	LAN	121	COPERTHWAIT, Jes			Jacob	CHE	787
Widow	ADA	24	Esqr.	PHI 68A		John	CHE	782
William	LAN	44	COPIA?, Jacob	PHI 38		John	CHE	795
William	MNT	49	COPLEN, Christn.	MIF 6A		Peter	CHE	817
William	BUC	137	COPP, Daniel	MNT 93		Wm.	CHE	788
William	BUC	149	COPPENHEFFER,			CORLESS, Mathias	PHA	5
William	PHI	154	Michael	YOR 216		CORLOG, Enos	CHE	700
William	WST	159	Simon	YOR 164		CORMAN, Fredk.	PHI	92
William	FAY	226	Simon	YOR 217		Jno.	CUM	80
William	LUZ	342	COPPER,			Joseph	FAY	219
William	CHE	848	Allexander	BEV 4		Joseph	FAY	219
William Jnr.	LAN	41	Danel	FAY 249		Lary	LAN	237
Wm.	PHA	23	James C.	PHA 23		Ludwick	CUM	47
Wm.	PHI	85	Joseph Jun.	FAY 249		Valentine	CUM	81
Wm.	CHE	761	London	PHA 110		CORMARICK, Robt.	PHI	113A
Zebulon	WAS	61	Michael	BEV 4		CORMEN?, Michael		
COORIN?, James	LAN	259	Nathaniel	BEV 4		(Crossed Out		
Patrick	MIF	4A	Ralph	BEV 4		)	PHI	134
COOSER, James	BEV	11	COPPERSMITH,			CORN, David	WAS	74
COOTCHAL, Phillip	CUM	71	Michl.	WST 212		Joseph	LAN	28
COOVARD, Morris	FAY	230	COPPERTHWAITE,			William	WAS	74
COOVER, Andw.	LYC	17	Thos.	PHI 28		CORNAL, John	ALL	102
John	MIF	16A	COPPINGER, John	PHI 15		CORNELIOUS,		
Petr	CUM	72	COPPLINGER,			Jeremiah	ADA	1
Saml.	MIF	16A	Daniel	YOR 184		Wm.	PHI	87A
COOVIN, James	LAN	259	COPPOCK, Abner	DEL 155		CORNELISON, John	WAY	143
COPAS, James	GRN	67	COR--THWAIT?,			William	NOU	143
COPE, Abm.	BUC	96	Edward	HNT 124		CORNELIUS, Widow	YOR	200
Abraham Jnr.	BUC	96	COR, Timothy	ALL 63		Benjamin	HNT	138
Adam	CUM	89	CORAD, John	PHA 23		Daniel	HNT	139
Adam	BUC	98	CORAHAN, Andrew	NOU 143		Henry	LUZ	394
Caleb	LAN	36	William	NOU 143		Isaac	HNT	139
Caleb	FAY	264	CORBED, Michael	CHE 891		Isaac	CHE	868

CORNELIUS, Isaac	MIF	24A	CORREL, George	LAN	67	COSNER, John	PHI	119
Jacob	MIF	24A	George	LAN	69	John	LUZ	332
James	NOU	198	George	NOU	127	Peter	CHE	711
Jesse	YOR	200	John	LAN	67	COSS, Jacob	DAU	21A
Jno.	MIF	24A	Nicholas	NOH	35	COST, Martin	PHA	44
John	HNT	138	CORRELL, Andrew	NOH	64	COSTELO, John	LAN	237
John	NOU	197	Christian	NOH	39	COSTER, Paul	NOU	135
Joshua	HNT	138	Christian	LAN	292	COSTLE, Joseph	MIF	12A
Peter	HNT	135	Christr.	NOH	83A	COSTLY, David	LAN	260
Samuel	HNT	139	David	LAN	302	Joseph	LAN	260
Stephen	NOU	198	George	NOH	39	COSTOLO, Saml.	FRA	319
Stephen	YOR	199	Jacob	BER	129	COTLAR, Chrisr.	PHI	53A
Winnefred	CHE	748	Martin	DAU	52	COTNER, Jacob	LYC	16
CORNELL, Abraham	BUC	137	Paul	BER	129	Jacob	ALL	85
Adrian	BUC	137	Philip	NOH	39	John	LYC	16
Cornelius	BUC	137	CORREN, James	PHI	8	COTREL, Jonathan	CHE	843
Gilliam	BUC	137	William	PHI	51	COTS, Robert	ALL	67
Gilliam	BUC	144	CORRES, Samuel	LAN	308	COTSON, Nathn.	PHI	111A
John	BUC	137	CORRIER, Richd.	PHA	78	COTT-ELL?, Aber.	ERI	60A
John	BUC	143	CORRIN?, John	MIF	4A	COTT, Jabez	CRA	14
John	PHI	151	Michl.	MIF	4A	COTTEN, James	BEV	26
John Jnr.	BUC	143	Widow	MIF	4A	John	BEV	16
Joseph	MER	436	CORRIPLE,			Wm.	WST	342
Lambert	BUC	137	Christopher	HNT	152	COTTEN?, Joseph	BUC	146
Rem	BUC	137	CORROLL, Daniel	FAY	261	COTTER, Aaron	MIF	6A
William	BFD	49	William	FAY	261	Joseph	MIF	24A
William	FAY	202	CORRY, John	DAU	40	Josiah	FAY	264
CORNELOUS, Marel	ALL	103	CORSBY, William	DEL	171	Thomas	PHI	63
CORNELY, James	PHA	55	CORSEN, Peter	FAY	219	COTTERMAN, Michl.	WST	211
CORNELY?, Nathan	MNT	130	CORSER?, George	PHI	78	COTTLE, William	DEL	192
CORNER, Elizabeth	PHA	93	CORSGROVE, James	PHA	111	COTTMAN, Benjan.	PHI	135
CORNFIELD, Jesse	PHI	116	CORSIN, Daniel	NOU	162	John	PHI	151
CORNHORN, David	NOU	156	CORSON, Cornelius	BUC	137	Joseph	PHI	147
CORNHORSE, Mary			John	BUC	137	COTTNER, Danl.	LYC	15
Widow	LAN	12	Joseph	MNT	77	COTTON, Hugh	WAS	98
CORNHURT, John	PHI	99	Peter (Crossed			James	GRN	69
CORNICK, David	CHE	882	Out)	LYC	9	John	WAS	98
CORNINGTON, John	LYC	12	Richard	MNT	77	John	MNT	105
CORNIS, Jonathan	BUC	142A	Richard	BUC	144A	John	BUC	144A
CORNISH, James	PHA	93	Thomas	MNT	77	Justice	LUZ	397
John	PHI	4	CORST, Craft	FAY	197	William	HNT	138
CORNLEY, Robert	BUC	153	CORSUN, Benjn.	FAY	220	William	MER	439
CORNMAN, Adam	PHA	109	CORTE, John	PHA	43	COTTON?, Eli	ERI	58
Henry	CUM	83	CORTEL, Henry	FRA	305	COTTORY?, James	BEV	26
Jno. Tho.	NOH	32	CORTHORN, John	BUC	146	COTTRINGER, Eliza	PHA	82
William	LAN	38	CORTNEY, Saml.	PHI	101B	COUBERT, John	NOU	198
CORNOG, Daniel	CHE	882	CORTO-?, George	FAY	255	COUBURN, Benjamin	LAN	154
CORNOGG, Abraham	DEL	173	CORTRIGHT,			COUCH, Daniel	MNT	71
John	DEL	173	Abraham	LUZ	355	David	LUZ	420
Thomas	DEL	172	Cornelius	LUZ	323	Edward	MNT	81
Thomas	DEL	183	Elisha	LUZ	355	William	CHE	814
CORNRICH?, Peter	DAU	44	Henry	LUZ	323	COUDING, Peter	PHA	77
CORNSMITS?, Peter	DAU	44B	CORVEL, Christian	GRN	93	COUFER, Valentine	BER	269
CORNWALL, County	BUC	160A	Christian Junr.	GRN	94	COUGH, Chrisn.	DAU	39
CORNWELL, James	GRN	84	Joseph	GRN	93	John	WST	211
William	GRN	80	CORVEN, William	GRN	63	Joseph	CUM	55
COROMONY, John	NOU	191	CORWELL?, John	PHI	142	Peter	MIF	14A
COROTHERS, Alexr.	CUM	83	CORWIN, Stephen	WAS	2	COUGHER, John	CUM	109
Andw.	CUM	59	CORY, John	ALL	85	Michael	SOM	156
Armstrong	CUM	116	Nathan	BEV	13	Peter	ADA	30
Charrels	ALL	66	COSBY, Ann	CHE	715	Philip	SOM	156
Elice	CUM	56	James	HNT	148	COUGHMAN, Andrew	MER	438
Jas.	CUM	118	John	CHE	714	Christopher	CRA	17
Jno.	CUM	98	Thomas	CHE	714	COUGHNOWER,		
Jno. Junr.	CUM	116	COSEADAN?,			Chrisn.	LAN	235
John	CUM	57	William	ARM	124	Joseph	LAN	233
John Senr.	CUM	116	COSEDA-Y?, Wm.	BEV	28	COUGHRAN, Alexr.	FRA	274
Mary	CUM	112	COSELEN?, Barney	PHI	118A	James	FRA	301
Thos.	CUM	54	COSESON, John	YOR	214	James	FRA	301
CORP, Charles	DAU	21A	COSEY, William	PHI	11A	John	FRA	302
CORPENNING, John	SOM	126	COSGROVE, Patrick	FAY	243	John Jnr.	FRA	302
CORR, Peter	NOH	49A	COSGROWE, James	CHE	844	Robt.	FRA	294
CORRAL, Dennis	PHA	86	COSH, Phillip	CUM	101	COUGHRIN,		
CORRAN, Robert	HNT	147	COSHNER, Jacob	FRA	286	Jonathan	MER	437
CORRANTS, James	ALL	76	COSHT, Jacob	CUM	61	COUGHY, Andrew	LAN	170
CORREL, Adam	NOH	35	COSKRY, Mitchel	FRA	303	COUGLAS?, Fredick	LYC	14

COUGLIN, Samuel	MNT 64	COURTER, Peter	LYC 10	COWAN, John	ARM 123
COUHICK, John	LAN 314	COURTER?, John	LYC 8	Joseph	ALL 67
COUIN, Patrick	WST 286	COURTNEY, Dozier	DEL 164	Robert	ALL 67
COUL, Isaac	BFD 42	James	WST 168	Robt.	CUM 100
Matthias	BFD 42	James	WST 168	Samuel	BFD 36
COULB, Peter	CHE 790	John	FAY 255	Thomas	ALL 97
COULSON, Abraham	WAS 97	John	BUT 357	William	ARM 124
Joseph	CHE 887	John	CHE 804	William	LAN 127
Samuel	WAS 1	Mary	PHA 103	Wm.	CUM 145
COULSTON,		Samuel	MNT 141	Wm. Junr.	CUM 148
Cathrine	PHA 110	William	BUT 356	COWARD, Wm.	FRA 319
Eve	MNT 71	COURTWRIGHT, Abm.	NOH 77A	COWDEN, James	DAU 17
Israel	MNT 116	Henry	WAY 146	John	WAS 19
John	MNT 69	Isaac	WAY 146	John	NOU 170
John	MNT 77	James	NOH 77A	Randal	WAS 19
Thomas	MNT 69	John	BEV 5	Robert	CHE 875
William	PHA 121	John	WAY 148	Robt.	CHE 754
COULTER, Widow	WST 211	Joseph	WAY 146	COWDENCE, James	FAY 255
Abigale	BUT 356	Sarah	WAY 146	COWEL, Andrew	GRN 94
Andw.	CUM 68	William	WAY 146	COWELL, Mathias	BUC 144A
Archibald	ADA 20	William	WAY 148	COWEN,	
Henry	WST 211	COUSARD,		Christopher	LUZ 403
James	LAN 244	Valantine	FRA 309	David	CHE 844
James	WST 342	COUSINS, Isaiah	PHI 75	Hugh	FRA 290
Jas.	BUT 356	Thoms.	BUT 344	Isaac	WAS 27
John	CEN 22	COUSTARD, John	FRA 287	James	GRN 69
John	BFD 57	COUSTER, Jacob	FRA 321	James	WST 250
John	WAS 89	COUSTY, Hugh	MNT 127	James	WST 287
John	LAN 247	COUTER?, (See		James	CHE 841
John	CHE 866	Custer)	FRA 296	John	WAS 27
Jonathan Esqr.	BEV 20	COUTNER, Jacob	MIF 3	John	FAY 208
Joseph	PHA 95	Michl.	MIF 3	John	WST 287
Nathaniel	WAS 15	COUTS, Daniel	FRA 309	Jonas	DEL 187
Nathaniel	WAS 97	Michael	GRN 100	Joseph	WST 249
Richard	BFD 57	COUVER?, Jacob	MNT 67	Joseph	CHE 842
Saml.	BUT 356	Peter	MNT 67	Matthias	WST 249
Samuel	WAS 19	COUVERT, Maris	NOU 198	Robert	WST 287
Samuel	WST 149	COUZINS, John	WAS 37	William	DEL 187
Thomas	CRA 11	Wm.	VEN 169	William	DEL 192
Thomas	BFD 57	COVALT, John	ADA 42	Wilm.	ALL 49
Thoms.	BUT 356	Matthias	BFD 42	Wm.	CHE 842
William	BFD 58	COVART, Garrett	MER 439	COWGILL, Jacob	MIF 24A
COULTON, James	PHA 110	Morris	ALL 116	Joseph Esqr.	MIF 1
COULTSTAN, Nathan	PHA 56	COVATT, Chenaniah	WAS 1	COWHACK, Mary	DAU 3
COUMP, Adam	NOU 127	Robert	WAS 1	COWHART, Fredk.	CUM 76
COUNCILMAN, John	BUC 93	COVE, Widow	LAN 259	COWHAWK, Adam	CUM 28
COUNSEL, James	CRA 4	COVELL, Matthew	LUZ 322	John	LYC 28
COUNSELMAN,		Samuel	LUZ 411	COWHEN, Jacob	
Samuel	BUC 160A	COVELY?,		Revd.	PHA 28
COUNTRYMAN,		Bartholomew	BER 207	COWHICK, David	LAN 310
Barbara	SOM 137	COVEN, Eleazer	PHI 119A	Frederick	LAN 310
Henry	WAY 148	COVENTRY, Jacob	HNT 125	COWIN, Daniel	FRA 272
Jacob	SOM 137	John	WAS 89	John	MER 436
Jacob	DAU 39A	COVER, Abraham	FRA 318	COWLEY, Henry	WAS 48
Jno.	PHI 44	Adam	FRA 293	COWMER,	
Michl.	DAU 39A	Andw.	FRA 282	Christiana	SOM 151
COUPER, Geo.	CUM 107	Caspeer	FRA 314	Jacob	SOM 151
COUPER?, See		Henry	FRA 314	COWNOVER, John	ADA 9
Coufer	BER 269	Jacob	LAN 18	John	ADA 25
COUPLAND, Calepd	PHA 64	Jacob	SOM 126	COWPAR, Robert	PHA 25
COURSE, Peter	PHI 75A	Jacob	CHE 797	COWSALT, James	NOU 170
COURSEY, John D.	BUC 154	John	FAY 213	COWSAR, Thomas	FAY 243
John D?	PHA 58	Michael	SOM 126	COWSER, George	PHI 83
COURSEY?, Abm. D.	BUC 155	Tetrick	CUM 72	COWSEY, John	LAN 235
COURSIN, Ben	LYC 9	COVERT, Anthony	LUZ 328	John	LAN 235
Christian	LYC 6	Isaac	NOU 162	Sarah	LAN 301
Derick	LYC 8	John	NOU 162	COX, Widow	PHI 30
Peter	LYC 10	John	NOU 163	Widow	PHI 64
COURSON,		COW, Ann	BFD 41	Abm.	CEN 22
Cornelius	MNT 71	Henry	ADA 5	Agness	ALL 62
John	MNT 65	Ludwick	BFD 62	Amboy	PHA 110
COURT, Frederick	BEV 14	COW?, (See Caw)	FRA 294	Andrew	PHI 65
Henry	CHE 807	COWAN, Catharine	YOR 202	Benajmin	CHE 879
Henry Jr.	CHE 807	Edward	BFD 62	Benjamin	MNT 80
Nicholas	PHA 38	Edward	CHE 844	Benjamin	WAY 143
COURTER, Nathl.	FAY 219	Henry	ALL 101	Benjn.	CHE 812

Name	Loc	No	Name	Loc	No	Name	Loc	No
COX, Casper	YOR	176	COX, Thomas	ALL	108	CRAFORD, James	ALL	70
Charles	BUC	90	Thomas	MNT	109	James	ALL	76
Charles	BUC	88A	Thomas	PHI	131	Jno.	VEN	168
Christopher	GRN	99	Thomas	CHE	908	John	ALL	75
Christopher, Jr.	WAS	119	Tunis	BUC	88	John	ALL	114
Christopher, Senr.	WAS	119	William	WAS	11	John	ALL	118
Church?	MIF	12A	William	ADA	43	John	LAN	166
Conrad	BFD	62	William	LAN	87	John	VEN	166
Cornelius	DAU	11A	William	BUC	93	John	CHE	715
			William	HNT	131	Luke	ALL	59
			William	WAY	140	Martha	CHE	731
Edward	CUM	152	William	NOU	143	Mathew	ALL	57
Elijah	BUC	86	William	FAY	235	Robt.	LYC	26
Esek	PHA	9	William	LAN	301	Thomas	ALL	70
Gabriel	PHI	68A	William	CHE	879	Thomas	ALL	94
Henry	YOR	173	William	CHE	908	Thomas	MER	439
Jacob	PHA	84	William	PHI	11A	William	VEN	168
Jacob	PHI	101	William	MIF	12A	Wm.	VEN	168
Jacob	SOM	133	Wilm.	ALL	113	CRAFT, Abraham	WST	234
Jacob	FAY	225	Wm.	PHA	25	Andrew	ARM	126
Jacob Sen.	SOM	133	Wm.	CUM	68	Ash	BEV	27
James	ADA	9	Wm.	CUM	81	Benjamen	FAY	235
John	PHA	9	Wm.	FRA	283	Bernard	MNT	37
John	PHI	24	COXE, John Redman			David	FAY	235
John	PHI	40	Dr.	PHA	3	David	FRA	280
John	ADA	41	COXX, John	PHA	72	George	BUC	93
John	WAS	54	COY, Jacob	HNT	159	George	WST	211
John	WAS	66	John	HNT	159	George	FAY	235
John	ALL	74	John Junr.	HNT	159	Henry	ADA	30
John	PHA	112	William	HNT	159	Jacob	MNT	37
John	PHA	114	COYL, Daniel	BFD	68	Jacob	PHI	92
John	WAS	119	Henry	PHA	88	Jacob	PHI	93
John	PHI	141	James	LUZ	382	John	MNT	34
John	WST	149	Robert	ALL	91	John	PHA	68
John	NOU	154	COYLE, David	CUM	39	John Junr.	WAS	61
John	NOU	156	Ham--ah?	ARM	124	John Senr.	WAS	61
John	BER	159	John	BUT	332	Laurence Junr.	WAS	61
John	YOR	213	Philip	SOM	156	Laurence Sr.	WAS	61
John	YOR	214	Saml.	WST	365	Mary	BER	222
John	FAY	235	COYLER, Ann	CUM	88	Peter	WST	233
John	BER	250	Peter	BFD	69	Samuel	FAY	226
John D.	PHA	103	COYLES, James	PHA	10	Thomas	WAS	61
Jonas	BUC	93	COYSER, Christian	BFD	36	William	WAS	61
Jonathan	MNT	81	John	BFD	38	Wm.	LYC	15
Joseph	MNT	81	Joh	BFD	0	CRAFTS, John	GRN	80
Joseph	PHA	116	COZAD, Samuel	WAS	61	CRAFTY, William	WST	365
Joseph	DEL	159	COZEDD, Nathaniel	MER	438	CRAGAR, Jacob	NOU	179
Joseph	CHE	879	COZENS, John	DEL	165	CRAGE, Samuel	ALL	54
Joshua	ADA	44	R. William	NOU	170	CRAGER, George	NOU	179
Jospeh	BEV	26	CRAB, George	NOU	120	Peter	NOU	179
Justice	PHI	65	CRABB, William	DAU	12A	CRAGG, Nancy	FAY	226
Laurance	CHE	885	CRABBS, Abraham	WAS	42	CRAGO, Thomas	GRN	87
Martin	FAY	225	Henry	WAS	42	CRAGUR?, Robert	NOU	116
Mary	WAS	55	Jacob	WAS	42	CRAIG, Mrs.	PHI	134
Mary	CHE	827	Philip	WAS	42	Agnes	LAN	48
Michael	GRN	106	CRABS, Jeremiah	ADA	10	Alexander	WAS	11
Michael	FAY	213	CRACK, John	NOH	77A	Alexander	WST	322
Michael	FAY	225	CRACROFF, Joseph	PHI	27	Andw.	WST	342
Mordecai	CHE	802	CRADISKOWSKY,			Archibald	LAN	91
Moses	PHA	92	Fredck.	NOH	58A	Atcheson	HNT	137
Moses	ALL	113	CRADLEBAUGH, John	GRN	69	Bengn.	FRA	321
Moses	WST	250	CRAF, John	LYC	15	Daniel	WAS	7
Paul	PHA	107	CRAFFIAS, Jacob	LYC	3	Daniel	ALL	51
Peter	FAY	225	CRAFFOR, Ephraim	FAY	225	Daniel	BUC	155A
Richard	HNT	130	CRAFFORD, Ann	FAY	202	David	CEN	20
Richard	CHE	879	Elizabeth	FAY	252	David	WAS	33
Robert	ALL	52	George	FAY	264	David	WAS	55
Robert	ALL	113	Hugh	FAY	230	David	MER	436
Saml.	LAN	145	James	FAY	235	David	MIF	14A
Saml.	FRA	278	John	FAY	225	Henry	BEV	23
Saml.	FRA	307	Martha	FAY	264	Henry	WST	250
Samuel	BUC	90	William	FAY	238	Isaac Esqr.	ALL	51
Samuel	NOU	170	CRAFORD, David	MER	439	Jacob	WST	378
Samuel	BER	274	George	ALL	71	Jacob	CHE	837
Tench	LAN	39	George	ALL	73	James	ADA	5
Thomas	BUC	88	James	ALL	63	James	BEV	23

CRAIG, James	WAS	27	CRAIN, Elias	FAY	252	CRATIN, James	ALL	95
James	WAS	48	Even	GRN	69	CRATOR, Jacob	MNT	87
James	WAS	66	Evin	HNT	144	John	PHI	53
James	NOU	156	Ezariah	PHI	95A	John	MNT	72
James	DEL	165	George	GRN	69	CRATTS, John	BUC	96
James	FAY	220	George	CUM	80	John	BUC	140A
James	FAY	255	George	VEN	170	CRATY, Jno.	BUT	338
Jane	WAS	54	John	CUM	32	CRATZER, Benjamin	NOU	135
John	PHA	61	Martha	DAU	22	Jacob	NOU	135
John	WAS	66	Richard	CUM	75	Jacob	NOU	192
John	ALL	82	Richard	CUM	80	Lewis	NOU	135
John	GRN	111	Silas	GRN	99	Mrs.	NOU	191
John	NOU	153	Stephen	GRN	100	Phillip	NOU	135
John	NOU	156	William	LAN	246	CRAUSE, Daniel	MNT	94
John	DEL	162	William	DAU	11A	Jacob	MNT	72
John	DEL	175	CRAINE, James	DAU	36A	Jacob Junr.	MNT	72
John	WST	189	CRAKEN, Wm.	CUM	124	CRAUSE?,		
John	WST	211	CRALL, Abraham	DAU	27	Christian	BER	225
John	FAY	230	Lewis	PHI	130	CRAVAN, John	WST	168
John	WST	307	Samuel	YOR	167	CRAVEN, Giles	BUC	137
John	BUT	336	CRAM, Cornelius	LAN	309	Isaac	BUC	153
John	MER	436	Henry	YOR	172	James	CUM	31
John	CHE	722	CRAME, Frederick	LAN	311	James	WAS	108
John	CHE	722	CRAMER, Abraham	WAY	136	James	BUC	153
John	CHE	837	John	WST	189	John	GRN	80
John Esqr.	NOH	29	Lawrence	BUC	82A	Joseph	GRN	75
John Esqr.	ARM	122	Philip	YOR	192	Joseph	GRN	80
Joseph	FAY	202	CRAMMER, John	LUZ	411	Thomas	WST	148
Joseph	FAY	255	Samuel	LUZ	411	Thomas	BUC	153
Joseph	WST	342	CRAMMOND, William	PHA	91	William	BUC	153
Josuah	CUM	82	CRAMOUR, Adam	LAN	223	William	MIF	16A
Moses	FAY	220	Joseph	LAN	248	William W.	LUZ	344
Mosis	FAY	243	CRAMP, Charles	BER	274	CRAVENS, James	WAS	67
Patrick	WAS	48	Jacob	BER	274	CRAVER?, John	MNT	87
Rebecka	FAY	264	Martin	PHI	87	CRAW, Barbara	FRA	314
Robert	WAS	61	CRANCH, Geo.	PHI	119A	CRAWBERGER,		
Robert	NOU	163	CRANE, Abraham	HNT	150	Leonard	FRA	298
Robt.	PHI	120A	Abrather?	ERI	58	CRAWFFORD, Josia	FAY	226
Rowland	FAY	238	Adam	PHI	21	CRAWFIS, John	HNT	163
Saml.	WST	341	Elihu	ERI	58	Martin	HNT	155
Samuel	CHE	722	George	MIF	6A	Nicholas	HNT	164
Sarah	ALL	98	John	WAS	19	CRAWFOOT, Sela	LUZ	409
Thomas	FAY	202	Joseph	MIF	6A	CRAWFORD, Widw.	PHI	104
Thomas Esqr.	NOH	83A	Miles	ERI	58A	Alexander	PHI	106
Thomas	NOH	86A	Nicholas	CUM	151	Alexander,	WAS	97
Thomas	BUC	155A	Richard	PHI	57	Alexr.	MNT	77
Walter	CHE	837	Roger	PHI	17	Ann	HNT	164
William	WAS	2	Thos.	PHA	110	Benjamin	WAS	66
William	WAS	61	Widow	MIF	6A	Benjamin	LUZ	395
William	FAY	202	CRANE?, George	LYC	26	Bridget	WAS	43
William	FAY	208	CRANER, Agness	ALL	65	Christopher	LAN	54
William	FAY	255	Mary	PHA	56	David	LYC	22
William	MER	436	Samuel (B. Man)	ALL	77	David	PHA	52
William	ERI	60A	CRANK---?, Robert	FRA	302	Dorothy	HNT	126
Wm.	FRA	287	CRANK, Wm.	BEV	27	Edmond	NOU	146
CRAIG?, Wm.	BEV	28	CRANSON, Mathena	PHA	85	Edward Esq.	FRA	271
CRAIGE, Misses	PHA	92	CRANSTON,			Elija	FAY	226
Elizabeth	PHA	104	Alexander	PHA	9	Elijah	NOH	66
James	VEN	168	William	DEL	166	Ewd.	FRA	281
John	PHA	106	CRAP, Anthy.	PHI	74	Felix	PHI	34
John	MER	437	Henry	MNT	94	George	FRA	294
Joseph	PHA	14	Joseph	PHA	106	Henry	BER	285
Mary	PHA	22	CRASS, Cornelius	PHI	53	Hugh	CUM	107
Seth	PHA	18	Daniel	FAY	243	Jacob	NOU	156
William	PHA	99	John	FAY	243	James	WAS	7
CRAIGG, James	SOM	156	John	FAY	243	James	PHI	34
CRAIGHEAD, George			John	DAU	46A	James	BFD	62
Esq	WAS	98	CRASSER, Adam	FAY	197	James	WAS	89
Jno.	CUM	74	Henrey	FAY	197	James	PHA	91
Thomas	WAS	19	CRASSIN, Edward	WST	189	James	WAS	97
Thos. Jr.	CUM	83	CRASTMAN, Charles	FRA	302	James	LAN	117
Thos. Senr.	CUM	83	CRASWELL, Robt.	FRA	311	James	CUM	122
CRAIL, John	BEV	21	CRATCHER, Abraham	FRA	314	James	HNT	151
CRAIMER, Baltzer	FAY	255	CRATE, John	VEN	170	James	NOU	156
CRAIN, Benjn.	CUM	64	CRATER, Jacob	WAY	136	James	FRA	297
Daniel	GRN	100	CRATIN, Ezechal	ALL	66	James	WST	307

CRAWFORD, James	FRA	322	CRAWSER, James	VEN	170	CREIGH, John	CUM	44
James	WST	377	CRAWVAN, Widw.	PHI	86	John	CUM	99
James	MIF	9A	CRAY, Thomas	PHI	8	CREIGHLY, Harmon	WST	234
Jas.	LYC	18	CRAYS, Joseph	HNT	158	CREIGHTON, Andw.	MIF	6A
Jas.	BUT	355	CRAYTON, Edward	NOU	116	Henry	WAS	27
Jas.	BUT	356	John	NOU	116	Richard	WAS	79
Jno.	BUT	355	CRAZER, John	NOU	135	CREINE, Jacob		
John	CRA	7	CREABER, Henry	BUC	100A	(Crossed Out)	LAN	298
John	DAU	22	CREACROFT,			CREINNER, George	LAN	182
John	WAS	84	Charles	WAS	61	CREITLER, Samuel	FAY	213
John	WAS	84	CREAGER, Adam	CUM	67	CRELY, John	PHI	47
John	WAS	84	John	CUM	67	CREM, Jacob	LAN	253
John	WAS	97	CREAGHEAD, James	CUM	99	CREMER, (No Given		
John	BUC	154	Jane	FRA	315	Name)	YOR	157
John	NOU	156	CREAMAR, George	FRA	292	Andrew	YOR	157
John	BER	215	CREAMER, Abraham	NOU	179	Henry	YOR	186
John	FRA	281	Adam	SOM	133	Henry	YOR	187
John	WST	307	Adam	NOU	174	Jacob	YOR	154
John	WST	365	Casper	BFD	57	John	FRA	314
John Jn.	BUC	155A	Christian	FRA	278	CREPPS, Richard	PHI	73A
John Jnr.	BUC	154	Daniel	NOU	174	CREREMER, Francis	PHI	101A
John Jun.	WAS	97	Danl.	NOU	179	CRES-MORE?, Widow	ADA	31
John Sen.	WAS	97	Felty	BUC	96	CRESE, Jno.	CUM	62
John	PHI	77A	Geo.	CUM	51	CRESLER, George	CUM	145
Jos.	CUM	105	Geo.	PHI	88A	CRESMAN, Abraham	HNT	150
Joseph	PHI	143	George	BUC	96	Abraham	BUC	158A
Joseph	DEL	167	Hannah	PHI	85	Frederic	HNT	150
Joseph	LAN	167	Henry	PHA	73	Frederic	HNT	151
Joseph	FAY	226	Henry	BUC	96	Henry	HNT	151
Josiah	WAS	97	Jacob	NOU	179	Jacob	PHI	109
Josiah	FRA	312	John	BFD	68	Mary	PHI	140
Levi	FAY	226	John	BUC	96	Saml.	PHI	80A
Margret	CUM	118	John	NOU	174	CRESMON, George	PHI	122
Mary	MIF	24A	John	NOU	179	CRESS, George	PHI	104
Mathew	WAS	66	John	DAU	5A	Henry	PHA	59
Mathew	WAS	66	Lawrence	BUC	96	Henry	CUM	63
Moses	WST	377	Michael	BFD	57	Henry	PHI	122
Oliver	GRN	87	Michael	NOU	174	Jacob	PHI	123
Paul	DAU	24A	Peter	CUM	142	John	PHA	66
Peter	LUZ	368	Samuel	SOM	133	John	PHI	72
Richard	DAU	22	CREAMMER, Jacob	PHA	118	John	PHI	122
Robert	BEV	18	CREANE, John	PHA	97	Peter	PHA	79
Robert	WST	234	CREATON, Esther	YOR	197	Peter	WST	287
Robert	CHE	898	Robert	YOR	202	William	PHI	124
Robt.	CUM	108	Thomas	WAS	51	CRESSEN, Jeremiah	BUC	93
Robt.	CUM	113	CREBIL, Phillip	FAY	235	CRESSFIELD, Isaac	PHA	121
Robt.	WST	342	Samuel Jur.	FAY	235	CRESSINGER,		
Saml.	PHA	27	CREBILL, Samuel	FAY	235	George	LAN	51
Saml.	DAU	45	CREBS, Adam	CEN	22	CRESSMAN, George	MNT	125
Saml.	PHI	57	Henry	MIF	14	Henry	MNT	72
Sarah	PHA	17A	Henry	MIF	12A	Jacob	MNT	72
Stephn.	BUT	340	John	MIF	12A	Peter	HNT	144
Thomas	WAS	20	CRECK, Elias	DAU	31	Philip	PHI	146
Thomas	WAS	84	CREE, David	HNT	140	Valuntine	MNT	111
Thomas	WAS	89	Elizabeth	GRN	87	CRESSON, Benjn.	PHA	12
Thomas	DEL	167	Robert	GRN	87	Caleb	PHA	68
Thomas	LAN	259	Robt.	CUM	43	James	PHA	79
Thomas	ERI	56A	William	GRN	94	John E.	PHA	13
Thos.	FRA	311	CREECRAFT, Bazel	GRN	98	Richd. C.	PHA	26
Widow	CHE	898	CREEK, Jacob	NOU	186	Sarah	PHA	20
William	ADA	7	John	NOU	186	Sarah	PHA	24
William	WAS	27	Phillip	CUM	35	CREST, George	ADA	12
William	WAS	42	CREEKARD, John	NOU	146	CRESWELL, John	HNT	166
William	WAS	51	CREELY, Micheal	WST	307	Martha	HNT	166
William	BUC	83	Micheal	WST	307	Matthew	HNT	166
William	GRN	87	Nicholas	BUC	160A	Robert	HNT	166
William	MNT	104	CREEMER, Margaret	WAS	115	CRETON, Patrick	WST	250
William	NOU	156	CREENKLETON,			CRETZOR, Widw.	PHI	94
William	WST	159	Saml.	FRA	295	CREUTZ, Adam	BER	129
William	LAN	178	CREER, George	PHA	65	Adam Jr.	BER	129
William	NOU	192	Peter	MNT	64	George	NOH	52A
William	BUC	84A	CREGER, Jacob	PHA	66	Henry	NOH	52A
Wm.	FRA	294	Jacob	FAY	213	Jno. George	NOH	44A
CRAWL, Matthias	CUM	70	John	FAY	230	Simon	NOH	44A
CRAWLE, Abm.	CUM	71	CREGHEAD, Gilston	CUM	75	CREVENDIK, Henry	DAU	8A
Wm.	CUM	85	CREGIHTON, Robt.	MIF	9A	CREVENSTONE, Jacob	BFD	54

CREVENSTONE,			CRISSMAN, William	BFD	72	CROLL, Jacob	YOR	171
William	BFD	62	CRISSPAN, George	HNT	145	John	DAU	14
CREVER, Jacob	CUM	99	CRISSWELL,			Michael	BER	187
John	CUM	99	Eleaner	BFD	36	CROMBIG, Peter	CUM	63
CREVIS, John			CRIST, Casper	PHI	95	CROMER, Francis	BFD	49
(Crossed Out)	PHI	25	Michael	BER	179	John	HNT	128
CREVISTONE,			Phillip	FRA	307	CROMLAUFF, Caleb	FAY	213
Nicholas	SOM	156	CRISTER, Nichs.	CUM	63	CROMLEY, Godfrey	PHA	95
CREWS, Elizabeth	PHA	97	CRISTEY, John	MER	438	Henry	PHA	109
CRIBBIN, John	PHI	33	CRISTIE, David	PHA	99	CROMLINE, Peter	GRN	105
CRIBBS,			CRISTINE, George	PHI	98	CROMWELL, John	PHA	29
Christopher	WST	211	John	PHI	90	John	MNT	111
CRIBS, John	PHI	84	Thos.	PHI	112A	Joseph	WAY	136
CRICK, George	NOU	186	CRISTON, Henry	DAU	13	Robert	HNT	130
CRIDER, Benjamin	LAN	116	CRISTOPHESEMAN,			Thomas	HNT	133
Christian	FRA	279	Delef	ALL	53	CRON, Martin	NOH	52A
Christly	FRA	279	CRISTY, Mrs.	PHI	73A	CRONE, George	YOR	175
Daniel	LAN	226	Archibd.	BUT	323	Henry	YOR	166
Daniel	FAY	264	James	PHI	93A	John	YOR	175
David	FAY	238	Samuel	MER	436	John	YOR	176
George	FRA	279	Valentine	NOU	156	Michael	YOR	206
Henry	FRA	280	CRISWELL, George	CHE	749	Michael	YOR	210
Jacob	PHI	3	Jacob	ADA	37	Philip	YOR	175
Jacob	LAN	117	Joseph	CRA	13	Simon	YOR	176
Jacob	CHE	908	Mary	CHE	747	Simon Senr.	YOR	176
John	LAN	117	Moses	CHE	747	CRONEKER, John	YOR	155
John	LAN	118	Wm.	CHE	872	CRONELIUS,		
John	NOU	179	CRITCHFIELD,			Stephen	CHE	868
John	FRA	279	Benjamin	SOM	151	CRONELL, Philip	LUZ	426
Tobias	LAN	116	Joseph	SOM	151	CRONEMILLER,		
Tobias	LAN	117	Joshua	BFD	57	Martin	DAU	13A
CRIESMAN, Feller	NOU	174	Nathaniel	SOM	151	CRONEY, Thos.	CUM	74
CRIEST, Valentine	NOU	182	CRITENFIELD, John	WAS	55	CRONIN, James	BUC	83A
CRIGAMIRE, Jacob	PHI	91	CRITES, Andrew	WAS	74	CRONINGER,		
CRIGE, Thomas	PHI	23	Jacob	WAS	74	Leonard	MIF	6A
CRIGNER, Joseph	PHI	84A	William	WAS	74	CRONISTER,		
CRILL, John	FRA	301	CRITLE, Harmon	WST	234	Abraham	ADA	38
CRILY, Conrad	CHE	718	CRITMAN, Casper	NOU	109	Conrad	ADA	40
CRIM, Peter	PHA	63	CRITSBERGER, John	PHI	75A	Henry	ADA	38
CRINER, John	PHA	95	CRITZ, Henry	WAS	66	John	ADA	43
CRIPPS, Joseph	CUM	75	Nicholas	WAS	66	John	YOR	211
CRIPS, Jonas	CHE	839	CRIVELAND, Andrew	NOU	146	CRONK, Isaac	BFD	62
Richard	PHI	134	John	NOU	146	CRONKWRIGHT,		
CRISANMAN, Jos.	PHI	95	CRO-ZER, Rebeccah	BEV	10	Henry	WAY	146
CRISEM, John	CHE	895	CROAN, Robert	MIF	4A	Jacob	WAY	141
CRISER, Peter	SOM	151	CROASDALE, Beleze	PHI	144	CRONRAD?,		
CRISEY, Jacob	FRA	301	Benjamin	BUC	143	Elizabeth	BER	184
CRISHER, Adam	NOU	109	Ezra	BUC	143	CRONSOR, Felty	NOU	143
CRISIL, Michael	NOU	143	Jerimiah	BUC	160A	CRONT, Jacob	CHE	904
CRISIN, James	NOU	156	John	BUC	144	CROOK, Conrad	BFD	55
CRISMAN, Adam	MIF	14A	Joseph	BUC	143	Geo.	PHI	117A
Benjamin	HNT	124	Mary	PHI	145	John, Sr.	WST	365
Frederick	LUZ	327	Robert	BUC	160A	Philip	DAU	15A
George	WST	212	CROB, Henry	DAU	8A	Valentine	LAN	259
Michael	NOU	99	CROBAUGH, Fredck.	MIF	24A	CROOKES, Thomas	WAS	119
CRISNER, John	SOM	147	CROBE, Jehu	LAN	65	CROOKHAM, James	HNT	139
CRISON, Widow	PHI	86A	CROCKET, Geo.	CUM	73	CROOKS, Adam	MIF	24A
CRISPIN, Joseph	PHI	153	James	WAS	120	Alexd.	FRA	319
Peter	BUC	153	Jas.	CUM	73	Andrew	WAS	84
Rachel	PHA	20	Thos.	CUM	121	David	NOU	99
Saml.	PHI	84	CROCO, Peter	ALL	96	Henry	WAS	85
Silas	WAS	2	CRODISKOWSKY,			Henry	NOU	99
Silas	PHI	151	Wendel	NOH	51	James	FAY	208
CRISS, Conrad	NOU	203	CROFF, Geo.	CUM	149	James	FRA	303
Elizabeth	WST	307	CROFLEY, James	PHI	96	James	FRA	305
Michael	PHI	144	CROFLY?, Charles	PHI	73A	Robert	WAS	85
CRISSINGER, Andw.	WST	307	CROFT, Robt.	FRA	301	Robt.	FRA	303
CRISSMAN, Abraham	MNT	89	CROGHEAD, Widow	PHI	9	Samuel	FRA	310
Adam	BUC	158A	CROLAY, Matty	PHI	51	Thomas	CHE	764
Christian	BUC	147	CROLL, Widow	YOR	218	Widow	LAN	225
George	BFD	72	Christian	MNT	117	William	WAS	85
Jacob	WST	270	Daniel	MNT	81	William	WST	365
Jacob	BUC	158A	Daniel	MNT	86	CROOKSHANK, Andw.	BUT	333
John	BFD	71	Henry	MNT	81	Joseph	PHA	20
John	BFD	72	Henry	MNT	86	CROOKSHANKS,		
Widow	BUC	158A	Jacob	MNT	89	David	WST	366

CROOKSHANKS, John	WST	365
CROOMLER, Jno.	CUM	68
CROOMLY, Stophill	CUM	68
CROOZER, Jacob	MNT	66
CROP, Casper	CUM	91
CROPH, John	CRA	4
CROROTHERS, Anew.	CUM	121
CROSBEY, Saml.	CUM	118
CROSBIE, Reuben	LUZ	320
CROSBY, Widow	PHI	112
David	CHE	755
James	BFD	57
James	YOR	204
John	CHE	779
John Esqr.	DEL	186
John Jun.	DEL	186
Jonathan	WAY	143
Peirce	DEL	162
Thomas	CHE	911
CROSE, Dewalt	FRA	315
CROSEDILL, Martha	PHA	43
CROSER, Mathias	CUM	23
CROSHER, Susanah	WST	148
CROSIER, Robert	PHA	88
CROSKEY, Robert	WAS	43
CROSLEY, George	BUC	93
James	PHI	49
Samuel	WAS	66
Samuel	DEL	162
CROSLY?, Charles	PHI	73A
CROSON, James	CHE	738
Thomas	CHE	838
CROSS, Allen	HNT	153
Casper	BUC	156A
David	PHA	73
George	PHI	20
Henry	MIF	4A
James	CHE	729
James Esqr.	YOR	204
John	PHA	16
John (Crossed Out)	PHA	15
John	PHI	102A
Joseph	PHI	3
Martha	WAS	51
Mary	SOM	126
Mary	BER	215
Nicholas	FAY	220
Noel	BEV	6
Oliver	ERI	58
Patrick	WST	378
Randle	YOR	204
Samuel	ADA	14
Samuel	CHE	710
Thomas	ADA	14
Thomas	WAS	20
CROSSAN, John	BFD	42
Samuel	BFD	42
CROSSE, Henry Jnr.	BUC	96
CROSSEN, Robt.	FRA	290
CROSSIN, Andr.	FRA	321
CROSSING, Henry	SOM	133
CROSSLEY, Robert	GRN	93
Robert	CHE	810
CROSSLY, Charles	MNT	65
John	FAY	235
CROSSMAN, Henry	PHA	11
CROSURE, Andrew	ALL	50
CROTHERS, John	BUT	349
John	BUT	358
John	BUT	366
Thomas	WST	168
CROTSER, Anthony	HNT	145
CROTTO, Catharine	PHA	80
CROTTS, Abm.	BUC	104A

CROTTS, Christn.	BUC	86
Philip	BUC	140A
CROTZER, Henry	CUM	29
CROUCE?, Andrew	MNT	80
CROUCH, Edward	DAU	14A
John	WAS	66
Robert	WAS	97
CROUL, George	ADA	19
Jacob	PHI	70
John	BEV	6
CROULE, Isaac	CUM	73
CROUMBAUGH, John	FRA	289
CROUS, Christian	NOU	135
CROUSCOOP, Widow	PHI	86
CROUSE, Abram	CHE	715
Andrew	DAU	4A
Frederick	BUC	139
George	FRA	312
Henrey	FAY	240
Henry	MNT	75
Henry	CHE	723
Jacob	CUM	151
John	MNT	75
John	CUM	76
John	CUM	86
John	FRA	323
Michael	PHA	51
Michael	PHA	61
Michael	MNT	94
Michael	BUC	139
Nichs.	CUM	91
Simon	CUM	62
Water	PHI	105
Widow	BUC	139
CROUSELET, Lewis	PHA	27
CROUSHER, John	FAY	220
CROUSS, Leonard	LAN	25
CROUT, Abm.	BUC	104A
Abraham (Crossed Out)	BUC	140A
Barbara	BUC	90A
Chas.	PHA	30
Henry	BUC	90A
John	PHI	133
Widow	BUC	90A
CROUTBOUM, Philip	FAY	252
CROUTHOMEL, Henry	BUC	90A
CROUTS, Jacob	PHI	130
John	PHI	133
CROUTY, Cathrine	PHA	25
CROVEN, Jonathan	CRA	16
CROVER, Jacob	CUM	73
CROW, Abraham	WAS	89
Baltis	MIF	6A
Benjn.	BUC	82A
Christn.	MIF	9A
Elisha	PHI	38
Geo. A.	MIF	9A
George (Crossed Out)	BUC	100A
George	LAN	241
George	CHE	821
George	BUC	156A
Henry	MIF	9A
Jacob	GRN	111
Jacob	MIF	9A
James	WST	341
John	WAS	78
John	WAS	78
John	WST	341
John	CHE	826
Martin	GRN	112
Michael	BFD	49
Michael	GRN	111
Michael	FAY	243
Samuel	PHI	21

CROW, Wm.	CUM	104
CROWEL, Moses	NOH	37
CROWEN, Benj.	PHI	73
Jacob	WAS	33
CROWER, Elizabeth	PHI	130
CROWEY, David	CHE	778
CROWL, John	LAN	55
CROWLE, Henry	YOR	175
Saml.	CUM	127
CROWLES, Alexr.	CHE	868
Alexr. Jr.	CHE	868
John	CHE	868
CROWLEY, Edward	WAS	42
Elizabeth	PHA	5
Jeremiah	CHE	873
Miles	CHE	864
CROWMAN, Conrad	BUC	156A
Michael Jn.	BUC	156A
Michael	BUC	156A
CROWN, David	FRA	316
CROWNER, Jacob	LAN	231
CROWNOBLE, Jacob	NOU	174
Lawrence	NOU	174
CROWNOVER, John	ADA	21
Thomas	HNT	158
CROWS, Fredk.	PHI	80
William	GRN	67
CROWSER, Alexander	FAY	243
John	FAY	243
Marey	FAY	243
Nicholas	FAY	243
CROWSON, John	CHE	875
CROWSOUR, George	WST	210
Henry	WST	211
CROX, Christly	FRA	321
CROXEN, Sarah	DEL	171
CROXFORD, Wm.	PHA	78
CROYL, Adam	BFD	71
Daniel	BFD	72
David	BFD	72
George	BFD	71
John	BFD	71
Joseph	BFD	72
Thomas	BFD	71
Thomas	BFD	72
CROYLE, Philip	SOM	157
CROZAN, Garret	WST	159
CROZER, Issabella	MIF	6A
James	CUM	23
James	DEL	187
John	DEL	188
John	MIF	6A
Rachael	DEL	188
Robert	DEL	178
Samuel	DEL	180
CROZIER, John	BUC	93
Robert	BUC	93
Thomas	BUC	93
William	BUC	93
CRUANT, Widow	PHI	39
CRUCH, Eliza.	PHI	9
CRUEY, Adam	NOU	114
Henry	NOU	114
John	NOU	114
John	NOU	114
Phillip	NOU	114
CRUGAR, John D.	PHI	112
CRUICKSHANK, James	NOH	32
CRUK, Phillip	NOU	120
CRULL, Henry	DAU	27
Jacob	WAS	119
John	BFD	54
John	WAS	61
CRUM, Dorothea	CUM	57

CRUM, Evan	SOM	161	CULBER, Timothy	LUZ	410	CULP, Jacob	PHI	147
Isaac	SOM	161	CULBERSON, Robert	ARM	125	Jeremiah	NOU	153
John	SOM	161	CULBERT, Jonathan	MER	437	John	PHI	140
Nicholas	HNT	146	CULBERTSON, Mrs.	LYC	28	Leonard	MNT	107
Wm.	CUM	58	Alexd.	FRA	312	Mark	MIF	1
CRUMBOCKER, John	ADA	21	Alexd.	FRA	316	Mary	PHI	122
CRUMBOUGH, Conrod	FRA	287	Alexr.	WST	342	Mathias	ADA	10
CRUMBUGH, Fredk.	CUM	63	Andrew	ERI	59A	Michael	CHE	789
CRUME, Frederick	LAN	178	Andw.	CUM	145	Peter	ADA	9
CRUMEIDER?,			Elias	WAS	74	Peter	ADA	26
Martin	CRA	4	James	CHE	725	Peter	NOU	103
CRUMLEY, Francis	NOU	179	James	ERI	59A	Peter	DAU	30A
Henry	WAS	120	Jno.	CUM	53	Peter	NOH	66A
Jacob	PHA	78	Jno.	CHE	821	Simon	CUM	103
CRUMLY, John	ALL	66	Jno.	MIF	24A	Tilman	PHI	147
CRUMMEL, John	LAN	217	John Doctr.	WAS	55	CULPIN, Peter	GRN	79
John	LAN	239	John Esqr.	MIF	1	CULVER, Aaron	LUZ	354
CRUMP, Casper	CUM	42	John	ERI	59A	Amasa	LYC	12
CRUMSON, William	CHE	739	Joseph	WST	341	David	LUZ	375
CRUNKLESTON,			Joseph	WST	342	David	LUZ	381
Josh.	FRA	298	Josh.	FRA	319	George	LUZ	375
CRUNKLUT, Joseph	FRA	295	Margt.	WST	211	Isaiah	WAS	43
CRUP?, John	SOM	151	Robt	CUM	143	John	PHI	104
CRUPAUGH?, Geo.	CUM	46	Robt.	FRA	312	Levi	WAS	43
CRUPE, Casper	ADA	42	Robt.	WST	322	Reuben	LUZ	351
Peter	ADA	42	Robt.	WST	341	Reuben	LUZ	375
Philip	ADA	42	Saml.	CUM	64	Samuel	LUZ	354
CRUSE, George	CUM	93	Saml.	WST	342	Solomon	LUZ	339
John	CEN	20	Saml.	MIF	16A	Timothy	LUZ	421
John	YOR	213	Thos.	WST	342	CULVERT, Cath.	PHI	93A
CRUSER, Mrs.	NOU	162	Widow	CUM	64	CUMBERLAND, John	BUT	352
CRUSINGER, George	NOU	99	William	WAS	19	Thos.	FAY	202
Jacob	NOU	99	William	ERI	59A	Thos.	FAY	202
CRUSON, Wm.	PHI	114	Wm.	PHA	40	William	FAY	202
CRUSWELL, Robert	LAN	221	CULBESON, Francis	VEN	166	CUMINS, Bengaman	ALL	50
William	LAN	219	John	VEN	168	William	PHA	29
CRUT, James	PHI	29	Widow	LAN	131	CUMLER, Henry	DAU	37A
CRUTCHER, John	CHE	780	CULBETSON, Agness	HNT	144	CUMLY, Benjeman	FAY	230
CRUTCHLEY, Edward	NOU	170	CULBRTSON, Saml.	FRA	312	CUMMER, John	SOM	156
CRUTCHLOW, David	WST	188	CULBURTSON, Jos.	FRA	310	CUMMIN--?, Thomas	CHE	700B
Jas.	BUT	338	Wm.	FRA	319	CUMMINGS, James	DEL	176
Willm.	BUT	338	CULIN, Andr.	FRA	321	John	LYC	22
CRUTHERS, Saml.	CHE	726	Geo.	PHI	63	John	PHA	110
CRUZAN, Simon	MNT	43	Isaac	DEL	186	John	DEL	188
CRUZIN,			John	DEL	181	Joseph	LUZ	321
Christopher	MNT	43	John	DEL	187	Michael	PHI	6
Peter	MNT	43	CULL, Hugh	WST	234	Nichs.?	PHI	64
CRY?, Conroad	ALL	96	Jacob	CUM	82	Willm.	PHI	16
CRYDER, David	SOM	128	Jonas	CUM	82	Wm.	PHA	102
David	SOM	147	CULLENS, Pater	FRA	320	CUMMINS,		
Gabriel	SOM	156	CULLER, Widow	LAN	155	Alexander	FAY	240
Isaac	PHA	38	CULLEY, Archibald	LAN	235	Amos	LAN	219
Ubrick?	PHI	2	Isabel	LAN	239	Charles	FRA	316
CRYDLER, Fredk.	CUM	147	James	CUM	111	Chas.	PHA	10
CRYSER, Boston	CUM	88	Thomas	LAN	151	Jacob	WST	365
Jno.	CUM	144	CULLIM, William	FAY	255	James	PHA	6
CU------?, Widow	ADA	23	CULLION, John	CHE	846	James	WAS	120
CU-RY?, -----	LYC	24	CULLONDER, John	ALL	115	James	BUC	154
CUBBIG, George	ALL	93	CULLY, Frances	ALL	91	James	CHE	780
Wilm.	ALL	92	Hannah	PHI	141	James	BUC	98A
CUBBISON, George	MIF	14A	James	LAN	157	Jane	WST	148
John	MIF	14A	Jno.	VEN	166	Jas.	LAN	165
Thomas	MIF	14A	William	YOR	200	Jas.	LAN	167
CUBEN, John	PHI	16	Wilm.	ALL	96	John	DAU	4
CUBERT?, See			CULP, Christopher	ADA	9	John	WST	286
Ceivert	NOU	127	Christopher	ADA	10	John	FRA	307
CUBISON, John	MIF	14A	Christopher	ADA	26	John	FRA	316
CUCKLER, Levinah	SOM	147	Filman	NOU	146	John	WST	342
CUDER, Jacob	NOU	174	George	DAU	30	John	MIF	6A
John	NOU	174	George	MNT	53	John	ERI	55A
CUDINGTON, Benjn.	NOU	151	George	PHI	112	Joseph	WAS	1
CUE?, Christopher	FAY	200	Isaac	NOH	66	Obadiah	BUC	104A
CUFF, Elizabeth	ALL	81	Isaac	BUC	147	Paul	WAS	27
CUFFER, Fredr.	FRA	321	Isaac Junr.	PHI	146	Paul	PHI	38
CUFLER?, Philip	BUC	140	Isaac Senr.	PHI	147	Robert	WAS	55
CUGHEY, Patrick	ALL	104	Jacob	PHI	140	Robert	BUC	104A

CUMMINS, Robert	BUC 154A	CUNNINGHAM,	
Saml.	CHE 760	George	HNT 122
Samuel	WAS 55	George	HNT 122
Thomas	CHE 885	Henry	CUM 79
Thos.	PHA 60	Henry	BUT 322
Thos.	FRA 307	Henry	FRA 326
Willm.	MIF 14A	Hugh	WAS 15
CUMMONS,		Hugh	BEV 17
Alexander	SOM 132	Hugh	WAS 42
Andrew	GRN 62	Hugh	YOR 199
Christian	NOU 151	Hugh	FAY 213
James	NOU 97	James	WAS 11
John	NOU 116	James	WAS 11
John	NOU 127	James	WAS 19
John	NOU 186	James	ARM 125
Thos.	NOU 186	James	FRA 291
CUMP, John	YOR 175	Jas.	CHE 755
Zachariah	YOR 174	Jennet	LAN 48
CUMPTON, David	CRA 4	Jno.	CUM 138
CUNALGAM?, George	PHI 74A	Jno.	FRA 285
CUNDLE, Adam	SOM 126	Jno.	CHE 872
Philip	SOM 151	Jno.	MIF 6A
CUNE, Daniel	PHI 25	Jno.	MIF 24A
CUNEZ, John	PHA 84	John	ALL 59
CUNFER, Jonas	BER 222	John	WAS 89
CUNIHER,		John	ALL 104
Frederick	BFD 40	John	HNT 120
CUNINGHAM, Arther	SOM 151	John	HNT 120
Barnet	FAY 249	John	ARM 125
David	FAY 208	John	DEL 175
David	FAY 243	John	DEL 177
Gustavus	PHA 122	John	FRA 292
James	FAY 202	John	BUT 317
James	FAY 202	John	LUZ 388
James	FAY 226	Jonathan	ALL 116
John	ADA 8	Joseph	MIF 4A
John	NOU 109	Matthw.	BUT 317
John	SOM 142	Moses	FRA 298
Robert	ADA 3	Nathl.	CHE 721
William	FAY 249	Nicholas	ALL 68
William	FAY 264	Robert	WAS 61
CUNITZ, John	PHA 33	Robert	ALL 66
CUNIUS /		Robert	HNT 121
CURRINS?,		Robert	LAN 241
John Jr.	BER 233	Robt.	PHA 67
CUNKLE, John	WST 148	Robt.	YOR 212
John	LAN 233	Robt.	BUT 357
Michl.	FRA 324	Robt.	CHE 872
Phillip	NOU 174	Saml.	BUT 317
William	LAN 244	Saml.	CHE 901
CUNNIGHAM, Robert	ALL 100	Samuel	BEV 17
CUNNING, Henry	WST 159	Thomas	BEV 21
Hugh	LAN 238	Thomas	LAN 240
Robert	BEV 14	Thos.	BUC 98A
Saml.	YOR 203	Vallentine	MER 437
Saml.	WST 286	William	WAS 54
CUNNINGHAM, Widow	YOR 203	William	HNT 123
Adam	CUM 140	Wilm.	ALL 56
Adam	FAY 219	Wm.	BEV 4
Alexander	WAS 115	Wm.	MIF 7
Alexd.	ALL 68	Wm.	WST 287
Allen	CHE 731	Wm.	MIF 9A
Ambrose	WAS 54	Wm.	MIF 14A
Archibald	WAS 11	CUNNINGHAN, James	ALL 82
Archible	BEV 17	CUNNINGS, John	WST 148
Benj.	YOR 202	CUNNNINGHAM,	
Benjamin	BEV 4	Robt.	FRA 301
Charles	HNT 157	CUNNY, Thomas	LAN 152
David	WST 234	CUNROD, Peter	SOM 147
David	CHE 872	CUNS, J. Gebhart	NOH 32
Ellinor	ALL 87	CUNSE, Philip	BUC 100A
Elonor	CUM 39	CUNTRAMAN,	
Francis	GRN 91	Christian	FAY 226
Fredk. L.		CUNTZ, Bartte,	SOM 157
Doctr.	WAS 115	Christian	SOM 157
Geo.	BUT 317	George	SOM 157

CUPP, Frederick	BER 274		
Ludwig	SOM 153		
William	CHE 905		
CUPPLES, James	MIF 16A		
CUPPOCK, Samuel	LAN 152		
CUPS, Adam	NOU 162		
CURADE, Daniel	LAN 21		
CURBY, Dennis	WST 188		
CURDICK, John			
(Negro)	WAS 85		
CURDY, John	MNT 137		
CURELL, Peter	PHI 6		
CURGEE, Thomas	PHI 13		
CURHUN, Corns.	PHI 13		
CURL, Daniel			
(Boarding			
House)	PHA 9		
Wm.	PHA 48		
CURLESS, Widow	PHI 12		
CURLEY, George	FRA 301		
William	LAN 234		
CURLIS, Matths.	PHI 40		
CURLY, Barnard	CUM 92		
CURRAN, Widow	PHI 44		
William	WAS 43		
CURRANTS, Timothy	CHE 867		
CURRAY, James	NOU 143		
Matthew	NOU 162		
CURREL, Daniel	CHE 833		
CURREN, Nathaniel	PHA 41		
William	WAS 7		
CURRETHERS, Hugh	LAN 125		
CURREY, George	WST 234		
George	CHE 750		
James	DAU 21		
John	WST 365		
Thomas	WST 168		
Thos.	DAU 21A		
William	WST 233		
CURRIE, Enock	MNT 81		
John, Esqr.	NOH 47		
Mary	PHA 96		
William	PHA 95		
CURRIN, William	MIF 9A		
Wm.	PHA 90		
CURRINGTON, Wm.	PHI 73		
CURRRY, Robert	CHE 730		
CURRUTHERS,			
Charles	FRA 298		
CURRY, David	FAY 220		
David	CHE 728		
George	FAY 255		
George Snr.	CHE 728		
Hugh	LAN 18		
Isaac	BUT 324		
James	CRA 12		
James	ADA 17		
James	ALL 60		
James	PHA 88		
James	WST 159		
James	FAY 252		
James	CHE 717		
John	BFD 47		
John	ALL 63		
John	ALL 114		
John	FAY 202		
John	CHE 814		
John G.	CEN 22		
Joseph	FAY 255		
Joshua	FAY 226		
Matthew	CHE 717		
Moses	ALL 65		
Mrs.	NOU 143		
Nail	CHE 803		
Peter	BER 262		
Rachel	CHE 866		

CURRY, Robert	CRA	12	CUSTARD, Jacob	FRA	315	DAAABADIE, John	PHA	103
Robert	WAS	19	John	BEV	7	DABBS, Anger	WAS	79
Robert	ALL	66	John	MER	437	Charles	WAS	79
Robert	ALL	79	John Snr.	FRA	315	DABE?, Michl.	PHI	103A
Robert	VEN	166	Jonathan	BER	137	DABESE, John	PHI	53
Robert	FAY	202	Jonathan Jr.	BER	137	DABRU, Jacob	MNT	65
Robert	CHE	730	Noe	BEV	7	DABZELL, Jane	PHA	93
Ruben	FAY	226	Richard	CRA	4	Wm.	PHA	93
Saml.	FAY	243	Richard	CRA	9	DACOS, James	PHI	52
Samuel	ADA	8	Richard	MER	437	DAFFEY, Christian	LAN	225
Samuel	WST	250	Samuel	WAS	27	DAGE, Andrew	WAS	120
Samuel	BUC	104A	Wm.	LYC	19	John	WAS	120
Thomas	PHI	23	CUSTER, Arnold	BUC	156A	Matthias	WAS	120
William	WAS	2	Elias	FRA	296	Michael	WAS	120
William	HNT	144	Henry	MNT	114	DAGER, Catherine	MNT	130
William	FAY	230	Jacob	MNT	114	Jacob	MNT	109
William	LUZ	421	John	MNT	114	Jacob	MNT	109
Wilm.	ALL	69	John Junr.	MNT	114	John	MNT	107
Wm.	LYC	21	Joseph	BUC	156A	Ludwick	MNT	107
Wm.	FRA	323	Peter	MNT	127	Martin	WAS	120
CURSWELL, John	WST	148	CUSTER?, Elias	NOU	146	Peter	MNT	44
CURTAIN, Hannah	PHA	37	CUSTERD, Abraham	ERI	57A	Philip	BER	247
CURTES, Japtha	FAY	243	Nicholas	ERI	56A	DAGEY, Widow	YOR	194
Robert	FAY	238	CUSTOR, Thos.	FRA	293	DAGGS, James	WAS	98
CURTIN, John	FRA	298	CUTCHELLER, John	CHE	724	DAGLY, (No Given		
CURTIS, Asa	PHA	26	CUTCHES, Hannah	PHA	54	Name)	DAU	27A
Asa	LUZ	388	CUTHBERT, Anthony	PHA	101	DAGNIA, William	MNT	66
Benjamin	BFD	42	John	CHE	883	DAGON, Jacob	CUM	114
Clement	FAY	226	Thomas	BER	209	DAGUE, William	NOU	157
Ely H.	PHA	22	Thos.	PHI	43	DAIKALY, George	PHI	26
Frank	LAN	56	CUTHBORT,			DAIKATY, Jas.	PHI	43
Henry	WAY	138	Elizabeth	PHI	66A	DAIL, William	NOU	116
James	BFD	42	CUTHBURT, Samuel	PHA	121	DAILE, Henry	NOU	192
John	PHI	21	CUTHER, George	NOH	42A	DAILEY, Charles	WAS	67
Joseph	PHA	109	CUTLER, David	BUC	93	Dennis	WAS	109
Marmedke	VEN	169	Robert	CHE	798	Edward	BFD	72
Sarah	PHA	65	CUTRIGHT, John	LUZ	324	Isaac	WAS	67
CURTRIGHT,			CUTSHAL, George	FRA	304	John	LAN	221
Abraham	NOU	146	CUTSHALL, Isaac	BFD	57	Nathan Junr.	WAS	67
CURTS, Henry	PHA	68	CUTSHAW, Amos	ADA	3	Nathan Senr.	WAS	67
Stephen	MIF	3	George	ADA	3	Philip	WAS	67
CURTURE, Henry	BFD	62	CUTSHULS, Samuel	ADA	2	Samuel	WAS	67
CURTZ, Frederic	HNT	156	CUTSOLE, John	BFD	60	DAILS, John	PHI	59
George	DAU	9A	CUTT, Thos.	FRA	299	DAILY, David	LUZ	371
George	NOH	42A	CUTTER, Samuel	NOU	151	Jeremiah	MIF	1
Jacob	MIF	24A	CUTTING, Andrew	LAN	124	John	MIF	9
John	CHE	865	CUTTLE, Peter D.	BUC	151	John	LAN	82
Joseph	CHE	733	CUTTS, Ludwick	CUM	31	Joseph	LUZ	374
Low	SOM	156	CUTWALT, George	PHI	62	Michl.	FAY	256
Thos.	LYC	26	CUVERT, John	NOU	201	Susanah	MIF	7
Wm.	PHI	120	CYANSINGER?,			Vincent	GRN	111
CURWIN, George	PHI	31	Abraham	FRA	295	DAIN, John	HNT	116
CUSARD, David	PHA	60	CYDER?, George	YOR	171	DAIR, George	CUM	59
CUSENGER, John	YOR	219	CYKER, William	PHI	29	DAISY, Alexander	HNT	150
CUSHING, Caleb	PHI	18	CYMER, Christian	GRN	84	DAITH, George	FAY	226
CUSHMAN, Isaac	FAY	261	CYPHER, Abm.	CUM	32	Randolph	FAY	226
Mosis	FAY	261	Adam	NOU	146	DAKE, Mathw.	PHI	113A
CUSHUN, John	ADA	24	Joseph	NOU	146	DAKIN, John	LUZ	426
CUSICK, Ann	PHA	77	CYPHERS, Peter	GRN	67	John	LUZ	427
CUSLER?, Philip	BUC	140	CYPHERT, William	BUC	147	DALBY, Aaron	WAS	37
CUSOR, John	NOU	174				DALE, Benjamin	DEL	173
John	NOU	174	D COURSEY, Abm.	BUC	155	Cornelius	CEN	20
CUSSICK?, John	MIF	9A	John	BUC	154	Felix	CEN	22A
CUST, John	WST	210	D CUTTLE?, Peter	BUC	150A	Henry	CEN	22
CUSTARD, Anne	DAU	21	D-----SS?, Thomas	ADA	7	Jacob	MIF	12A
Arnold	BEV	7	D----G?, Peter	MNT	54	John	FAY	220
Benjamin	BER	137	D----T?, John	NOU	192	Peter	CUM	49
Benjamin	BER	179	D---MAN, Martin	ARM	122	Samuel	NOU	128
Benjn.	CHE	792	D---Y?, Jesse	LYC	12	Wm.	LYC	6
Conrad	BUC	139	D--M----?, Jacob	NOU	114	DALEY, Himy	DEL	158
Daniel	DAU	10	D-ENNON?, William	BFD	72	John	WAY	148
Frederic	SOM	157	D-ERISTRY?,			DALHOUSEN, Henry	CUM	130
George	WAS	37	Alexander	MER	440	DALIUS, Frederick	NOH	75
George	FAY	219	D-N--?, Will---?	MER	440	DALL, Christian	MNT	49
George	NOH	52A	D. LITTLEFORD,			DALLAS, Alexander		
Jacob	WAS	43	John	MER	439	T.	PHA	83

DALLASON,			DANIEL, Samuel	CRA	7	DARLINGTON, Amos	CHE	703
Alexander	GRN	63	Samuel	MNT	72	Edward	CHE	810
James	GRN	63	Samuel	HNT	150	George	CHE	706
William	GRN	63	DANIELS, Daniel	BFD	47	Hannah	YOR	197
DALLE, Christn.	CEN	22	John	CRA	15	Jesse	DEL	175
DALLINGER, Widow	YOR	211	John	PHA	62	Jno.	CUM	34
DALLMAN, Stephen	NOH	55	John	GRN	69	Job	CHE	806
DALRYMPLE, Hugh	HNT	151	John S.r.	GRN	69	John	CHE	821
DALTON, Edward	PHI	138	Kinsly	BFD	57	Joseph	CHE	719
James	BFD	72	Reuben	BFD	50	Meridith	CUM	34
DALY?, -----	MIF	10	DANILSON, John	NOU	143	Thomas	CHE	805
Roswell?	MIF	10	DANING,			William	HNT	150
DAMAYER,			Theophilus	LAN	281	DARN, Joseph	NOU	157
Christian	LAN	208	DANKENMYER?,			DARNAL, Edward	NOU	157
DAMBACH, John	LAN	258	Fredk.	BER	205	DARNO, Mr?	PHA	114
Joseph	LAN	257	DANKLE, George	BER	211	DARON, George	YOR	173
DAMBAUGH, Adam	LAN	294	DANL, Titus	LYC	29	DARR, Henry	SOM	128
DAMBOLD, Adam	LAN	214	DANLEY, Lewis	PHI	61	Jacob	PHA	69
DAMER, Daniel	MNT	72	Owen	PHI	61	John	PHI	111
DAMERSON, Fredk.	CUM	112	DANNANHOVER, Geo.	CHE	775	John	BER	137
DAMM, Willis	LAN	306	DANNATT,			DARRA?, (See		
DAMOND, John	BER	245	Christian	MNT	92	Darva?)	LAN	78
DAMPMAN, Adam	CHE	904	DANNEL, Andrew	LAN	246	DARRACH, James	PHA	20
DAMSTER, Alexd.	ALL	63	DANNELS, Benjamin	SOM	151	Mary	DEL	177
DANA, Anderson	LUZ	319	DANNER, Abraham	NOH	62	DARRAGH, John	WAS	67
Azeil	LUZ	319	Abraham	YOR	157	DARRAH, Archibald	MNT	69
DANAHOVER, Peter	CHE	908	Abraham	BER	256	George	BFD	37
DANAKER, Chrn.	PHA	42	Adam	NOH	62	Jas.	BUC	153
DANCE, Gilbert	MNT	44	Adam	LAN	194	John	BFD	37
John	BUC	153	Barnet	NOH	62	Mary	PHA	20
DANCKE, Ann Mary	NOH	70	Casper	YOR	175	Robert	BUC	90A
DANCKEL,			Christian	YOR	215	Samuel	MNT	106
Christian	NOH	58A	Henry	YOR	183	Thomas	BUC	90A
David	NOH	58A	Henry	LAN	208	William	BUC	96
Jacob	NOH	58A	Jacob	NOH	62	William	BUC	104A
Widow	NOH	58A	Jacob	NOH	62	DARRAIGH, John	ALL	54
DANDSDILL, George	BFD	37	Jacob	BER	211	DARRIS, James	YOR	202
Richard	BFD	37	Jacob	NOH	58A	DART, Samuel	LUZ	420
DANE, Caleb	LAN	65	Jonathan	YOR	185	DARTH?, (See		
John	NOU	163	Leonard	NOH	85	Daith)	FAY	226
Samuel	CHE	875	Melchior	NOH	62	DARVA, Widow	LAN	78
Thomas	BUT	362	Michael	NOH	62	DASEY, Madam	PHA	120
DANEHAUER,			Michael	LAN	63	DASHER, Alexr.	DAU	43A
Christian	BER	247	Peter	YOR	175	Caspar	DAU	43A
DANEHE, George	BEV	13	Philip	YOR	175	Henry	CHE	791
DANEL, Mary	YOR	203	Samuel	YOR	183	John	PHI	106
Wm.	YOR	203	Tobias	YOR	219	Peter	FRA	312
DANELS, David	FAY	261	DANNIAL, Jesse	FAY	256	DASSAUX, P. F.	MNT	109
Ebinezer	FAY	261	DANY, Peter	NOH	55	DATES, Monseur	PHA	100
DANENHOUR, George	PHI	131	Philip	NOH	55	DATESMAN, John	NOH	64
DANENHOWER,			DANYALS, John	WST	235	DATON, Nancy	LUZ	397
Charles	PHI	133	DAPORTAIL, Lewis	MNT	104	William	WAY	141
DANFELTZER, Peter	CHE	817	DARBARROW, Isaac			DATZ, Henry	MNT	34
DANFIELD, Conrad	CHE	786	Sen.	ADA	27	DAUB, Conrad	DAU	29A
DANGER, Andrew	LAN	275	DARBEE, Sarah	PHI	109A	Dillman	DAU	26
DANIEL, Mr.	PHI	101B	DARBERRY, Isaac	ADA	26	Joseph	LAN	61
Abraham	NOH	71	DARBISHIER,			DAUBENSPECK,		
Adam	BER	232	Thomas	FAY	231	Jacob	NOH	75
Aron	PHI	88	DARBY, George	PHI	153	DAUBER, Abraham	NOH	52A
Daniel O.	BUC	150	John	DEL	180	DAUBERT, Henry	NOH	55
David	CHE	798	John	FRA	275	Michael	BER	254
Edward	BFD	49	Moses	LUZ	349	DAUBINSPECK,		
Godfrey	BER	190	DARCH, Mrs.	NOU	99	Lewis	LUZ	360
Henry	NOU	121	DARCUS, Aneagroe	FAY	226	Philip	LUZ	360
Jacob	BER	154	DARE, John	YOR	181	DAUGHERTY, Alexd.	FRA	302
James	PHI	117	Peter	NOU	163	Andw.	WST	235
John	CRA	7	DARIEL, Henry	PHI	25	Charles	WAR	1A
John	PHI	47	DARKEBY, Roger	PHI	29	Cornelius	FRA	301
John	PHA	77	DARLIN, John	NOU	127	Daniel	BUT	323
John	MNT	113	John	CHE	842	Dinnis	ALL	50
John	FAY	222	DARLING, David	NOU	157	Edward	BEV	10
John	CHE	873	Garret	NOH	64	Ewd.	FRA	287
John	CHE	874	Garret	NOU	157	Geo.	BUT	334
Joseph	NOH	42A	George	CHE	723	James	ALL	118
Peter	NOH	29A	Nathan	CHE	726	James	FRA	310
Phineas	PHA	24	DARLINGTON, Abm.	CHE	812	James	WST	323

DAVIS, Isaac	WAS	37	DAVIS, John	FAY 202	DAVIS, Moses	WAS	33
Isaac	LAN	61	John	FAY 208	Moses	NOH	37
Isaac	MNT	64	John	YOR 209	Moses	NOU	154
Isaac	LAN	72	John	WST 212	Moses	YOR	173
Isaac	MNT	106	John	FAY 226	Nathan	ARM	125
Isaac	WAS	120	John	FAY 256	Nathan	DEL	179
Isaac	DEL	183	John	FRA 278	Nathaniel	SOM	145
Isaac	MER	440	John	FRA 288	Nathaniel	LAN	230
Isaac	CHE	705	John	FRA 288	Nathaniel	CHE	776
Isaac	CHE	723	John	FRA 292	Nathaniel	CHE	800
Isaiah	MNT	72	John	FRA 294	Nathaniel	PHI	94A
Israel	MNT	137	John	WST 308	Nathl.	PHI	7
Israel	CHE	832	John	FRA 310	Nathl.	PHI	91A
Izaker	MNT	49	John	FRA 316	Neal	NOU	201
J---?	CHE	854	John	WST 323	Nicholas	WAS	28
J.	LAN	92	John	WST 378	Nicholas	NOH	49A
Jacob	LAN	68	John	CHE 717	None	PHI	103
Jacob	NOH	75	John	CHE 744	Owen	PHI	96
James	MIF	7	John	CHE 822	Patrick	CRA	3
James	CRA	10	John	CHE 826	Patrick	CRA	17
James	BEV	22	John	CHE 828	Phillip	NOU	163
James	WAS	55	John	CHE 830	Phillip	FAY	243
James	CUM	76	John	MIF 14A	Phillip	WST	287
James	LAN	91	John	NOH 72A	Phillip	FRA	291
James	CUM	95	John	BUC 104A	Philmore	WAS	27
James	PHI	104	Jonas	BEV 27	Rachael	PHI	95
James	HNT	119	Jonathan	MNT 106	Rebecca	FRA	292
James	FAY	213	Jonathan	FAY 202	Reuben	BER	277
James	FAY	220	Jonathan	MER 440	Rice	PHA	100
James	WST	287	Joseph	ADA 17	Richard	FAY	226
James	BUT	341	Joseph	CEN 20	Robert	BEV	22
James	BUT	343	Joseph	ALL 54	Robert	PHI	40
James	CHE	724	Joseph	BFD 55	Roger	CHE	853
James	CHE	901	Joseph	PHA 63	Rowland	CHE	817
Jane	DEL	162	Joseph	GRN 69	Saml.	MIF	15
Jason	CHE	740	Joseph	CUM 77	Saml.	MIF	12A
Jerman	CHE	843	Joseph	MNT 132	Sampson	PHA	67
Jesse	MNT	69	Joseph	NOU 149	Sampson	CHE	876
Jesse	DEL	173	Joseph	DEL 157	Samuel	WAS	28
Jesse	DEL	175	Joseph	DEL 173	Samuel	WAS	48
Jesse	CHE	902	Joseph	DEL 179	Samuel	ALL	62
Jno.	CUM	73	Joseph	FAY 226	Samuel	ALL	64
Joel	CHE	821	Joseph	FAY 231	Samuel	BUC	107
John	CRA	4	Joseph	FRA 299	Samuel	NOU	109
John	MIF	7	Joseph	LUZ 319	Samuel	PHA	122
John	PHI	8	Joshua	NOH 75	Samuel	DEL	170
John	LYC	21	Joshua	WAS 79	Samuel	DEL	174
John	BEV	22	Joshua	WAS 109	Samuel	DEL	185
John	PHA	27	Joshua	WAS 109	Samuel	FAY	243
John	BFD	37	Joshua	NOU 127	Samuel	FAY	264
John	LAN	44	Joshua	NOU 149	Samuel B.	DAU	4A
John	MNT	44	Joshua	NOU 149	Sarah	PHA	64
John	WAS	51	Joshua	CHE 723	Shedrick	FAY	240
John	BFD	54	Josiah	DEL 157	Stephen	PHI	27
John	PHI	62	Josiah	WST 168	Stephen	MNT	77
John	MNT	69	Levy	NOU 143	Susanhah	YOR	217
John	PHA	74	Lewis	DEL 173	Theophilis	CHE	854
John	MNT	77	Llewellen	CHE 855	Thomas	BEV	19
John	LAN	79	Llewellen	CHE 855	Thomas	LAN	28
John	GRN	80	Llewellin	CHE 859	Thomas	MNT	49
John	BUC	104	Marey	FAY 255	Thomas	MNT	67
John	MNT	112	Mary	BFD 50	Thomas	LAN	69
John	MNT	115	Mary	HNT 117	Thomas	WAS	98
John	ARM	123	Mary	HNT 136	Thomas	MNT	108
John	ARM	126	Mary	PHI 147	Thomas	MNT	110
John	LAN	126	Mary	FRA 309	Thomas	PHI	134
John	PHI	131	Mary	CHE 821	Thomas	PHI	135
John	MNT	141	Mems	FAY 226	Thomas	NOU	143
John	HNT	143	Meshach	FAY 220	Thomas	NOU	151
John	HNT	144	Meshack	FAY 252	Thomas	DEL	183
John	WST	149	Methusalem	CHE 723	Thomas	YOR	213
John	HNT	152	Michael	NOU 127	Thomas	BER	277
John	BER	163	Miles	CHE 817	Thomas	CHE	796
John	NOU	163	Mordecai	MNT 118	Thomas	CHE	798
John	YOR	176	Mordecai	MNT 137	Thomas	CHE	833
John	NOU	198	Mordecai	CHE 800	Thomas	CHE	841

DAVIS, Thomas		DAVISON, Robert	MIF 1	DAY, Philip	BER 137
Thomas	CHE 889	Robt.	CHE 730	Robert	LUZ 373
Thos.	CHE 893	Samuel	FAY 265	Samuel	YOR 165
Thos.	PHI 111	Thomas	NOU 116	Sylvanus	ADA 43
Thos.	CHE 818	Thomas	NOU 116	William	YOR 212
Timothy	BUC 98A	Thomas	FAY 249	DAYLEY, Edmond	BFD 42
Walter	SOM 161	William	NOU 116	John	ALL 95
Widow	LAN 247	William	NOU 116	John Capt.	PHA 48
Widow	ADA 19	William	NOU 116	DAYLONG, Isaac	NOU 149
William	CUM 62	William	VEN 170	John	NOU 97
William	CRA 10	DAVLIN, Danl.	WST 344	DAYLY, Elias	NOH 64
William	BFD 50	William	WST 149	DAYRL?, Mathw.	PHI 118A
William	WAS 51	DAVY, Elijah	CUM 110	DAYS, Wm.	PHA 75
William	BFD 62	John	PHI 41	DAYTON, Jane	PHA 121
William	BUC 86	Lewis	PHI 21	DDAVIS, Isaac	PHI 62
William	BUC 88	Wm.	PHA 105	DE -ALMOURS?,	
William	BUC 93	DAWEN, Owan	NOU 146	Charles	PHA 100
William	LAN 95	DAWES, Abija	PHA 107	DE ARMAND, James	HNT 129
William	LAN 145	Adrian	NOH 77A	James	HNT 166
William	WST 149	Deborah	PHA 7	John	HNT 159
William	SOM 161	Jonathan	PHA 79	William	HNT 159
William	DEL 162	Rumforod	PHA 17A	DE BARTHOLT,	
William	NOU 163	DAWNHOVEN, John	FRA 291	David	PHA 99
William	DEL 169	DAWS, Jeremiah	CHE 866	DE BEELEN, Baren	YOR 162
William	FAY 200	DAWSON, Benjamin	BEV 22	DE BENNERVILLE,	
William	FAY 203	Bennoni Seigr.	BEV 22	Geo.	PHI 146
William	FAY 208	Benoni	BEV 15	DE BENNEVILLE,	
William	FAY 231	Daniel	PHA 68	Danl.	PHI 146
William	LUZ 328	Elias	PHA 70	DE BOFONTANE,	
William	CHE 811	George	CUM 95	Jno.	PHI 148
William	CHE 818	George B.	PHA 98	DE BOICE?, Jos.	MNT 80
William	CHE 822	Jacob	CHE 888	DE CHARMES, Sarah	PHA 18
William	CHE 829	John	PHA 53	DE FRESNE, Docr.	LAN 46
William	CHE 851	John Capt.	PHA 47	DE GRUSHA, P. J./	
Willm.	CHE 818	John	BUC 151A	I.?	NOU 171
Wilm.	ALL 51	Meachal	BEV 15	DE HART, George	NOH 78
Wilm.	ALL 62	Robert	WAS 20	DE HASPERT?,	
Wilm.	ALL 64	Robert	PHA 36	Joseph	PHI 122
Wilm.	ALL 108	Robert	LAN 45	DE HASS, John	PHA 106
Wm.	PHA 52	Thomas	BEV 22	DE HAVEN, Samuel	MNT 49
Wm.	PHA 62	Thomas	PHI 95A	DE LAVUE?, John	PHI 13
Wm.	VEN 170	William	PHA 12	DE NICE, Jane	PHI 155
Wm.	FRA 314	William	GRN 69	DE PUI, Levi	LUZ 328
Wm.	FRA 316	William	CHE 705	DE SILVER, Thomas	PHA 103
Wm.	WST 343	Wm.	PHA 14	DE VILLIA, Pettit	PHA 114
Wm.	CHE 737	Wm.	CUM 91	DE WEES, David	MNT 81
Wm. Captn.	PHI 109A	Wm.	PHI 82A	Lewis	PHI 20
Wm.	PHI 66A	DAWTHET, William	WST 149	DE---?, Andr.	FRA 296
Zechariah	DEL 183	DAY, Widow	PHI 37	DEA, John	BER 178
DAVIS?, Joseph	MIF 10	Abraham	DAU 47	DEAGE, Peter	LAN 125
DAVISDON, Geo.	CUM 118	Agustus	PHA 8	DEAL, Widw.	PHI 110
John	CHE 802	Amos	WAS 62	Abraham	DAU 39A
DAVISON, --rah?	BUC 142	Andw.	PHI 86	Andrew	MNT 127
Archabald	CRA 5	Benj.	PHI 84	Andw.	PHI 119A
Charles	CHE 728	Benjamin	WAS 62	Catharine	PHI 93A
Chas.	PHI 11A	Benjamin	YOR 158	Christn.	CUM 41
Fleming	NOU 116	Benjamin	BUC 140A	Christn.	PHI 115
Francies	VEN 170	Cathrine	PHI 85	Daniel	MNT 77
George	FRA 275	Daniel	WAS 62	Danl.	PHI 84
Hugh	HNT 140	Danniel	ALL 119	Elizabeth	ADA 43
James	PHI 68	Edward	ALL 50	Francis	PHI 119
James	NOU 163	Ezechal	ALL 119	Frederick	ADA 15
James	VEN 170	George Jun.	WAS 89	Geo.	CUM 22
James	NOU 192	George Sen.	WAS 89	George	BFD 50
James	FRA 293	Jacob	ALL 90	George	CUM 76
Jerimia	FAY 213	Jacob	YOR 218	Helphrey	SOM 157
Jno. Senr.	CUM 118	James	DEL 175	Henry	BFD 49
John	NOU 198	John	PHA 51	Jacob	ADA 25
John	WST 250	John	CUM 92	Jacob	PHI 84
John	FRA 320	John	BER 137	Jacob	PHI 136
John	BUT 329	John	YOR 213	Jacob	CHE 843
John	MIF 16A	John	CHE 757	Jacob	BUC 100A
John	NOH 66A	Jos.	BUC 107A	Jacob	BUC 156A
Joseph	FRA 293	Joseph	WAS 115	John	PHI 131
Martha	LUZ 365	Mathew	YOR 193	John	FRA 292
Mrs.	NOU 163	Moses	GRN 110	John	CHE 726
Phineas	HNT 130	Nicholas	WST 344		

DEAL, John	PHI 91A	DEARDORFF, John	YOR 211	DECKER, Isaac	WAY 146		
John	PHI 111A	John	YOR 213	Isaac	LUZ 320		
John	BUC 156A	DEARE, Thomas	LAN 302	Jacob	WAY 146		
Leonard	ADA 10	DEARM, Widow	ADA 36	Jacob	FRA 274		
Michael	CUM 129	DEARMAN, Hugh	FAY 220	James	LUZ 358		
Michael	BUC 156A	John	LAN 89	James	LUZ 378		
Paul	BFD 62	DEARMENT, William	CRA 9	Jeremiah	LUZ 427		
Peter	CUM 22	DEARMIN, Samuel	ALL 65	Johannes	WAY 146		
Peter	ADA 43	DEARMON, Joseph	PHI 154	John	CEN 20		
Peter	PHI 84	DEARMOND, Joseph	DAU 43A	John	LUZ 358		
Peter	PHI 131	Richd.	DAU 22	Levi	WAY 146		
Philip	BFD 50	DEARS, David	LAN 229	Levi	LUZ 378		
Richd.	PHA 83	DEARY, Andrew	LAN 133	Lewis	BFD 62		
Saml.	PHI 120	Francis	BUT 343	Manuel	WAY 146		
Samuel	BFD 50	DEAS, John	CHE 789	Martin	MNT 61		
Solomon	BFD 50	DEAS?, Thos.	YOR 192	Mary	YOR 159		
William	PHI 123	DEATH, Widow	PHI 83A	Mathias	MNT 60		
DEALBY, Dennis	BEV 5	DEATZ, John	NOH 66A	Michael	MNT 56		
DEALING, Widow	NOH 70	DEAVES, Abraham	PHI 125	Moses	PHI 75A		
DEAM, Boston	LAN 125	Jacob	MNT 107	Nicholas	HNT 161		
DEAM?, Catherine	MNT 117	Samuel	PHI 125	Peter	LUZ 362		
DEAMAN, Thomas	NOU 163	DEBBALEER?, John	PHA 60	Philip	YOR 160		
DEAMWOOD, (No		DEBELION, Francis	CHE 719	Rheubin	WAY 138		
Given Name)	DAU 46	DEBLER, Mrs.	NOU 104	Salmon	LUZ 429		
DEAN, Widow	PHA 86	Nicholas	BER 211	Samuel	WAY 146		
Aaron	LUZ 335	DEBOICE, John	MNT 66	Samuel Jr.	WAY 146		
Alexander	PHA 121	DEBOLD, Abraham	FAY 213	Solomon	WAY 138		
Alexander	HNT 154	David	FAY 213	DECKERST, Sarah	CEN 20		
Ann (Aged 60,		George	FAY 213	DECKERT, Henry	BER 220		
Dau/o Hannah)	DEL 161	Michael	FAY 213	Jacob	BER 152		
Benjamin	WAS 55	DEBOLT, George	GRN 80	DECKEY, Thomas	LAN 131		
Conrod	PHI 81A	Nicholas	GRN 80	DECLERY, Peter	ALL 55		
Daniel	MNT 65	DEBON, M.	LAN 47	DECOMB, Phillip	BEV 22		
Dennis	WST 323	DEBRAY, Peter	PHA 90	DECORMES, John	PHA 109		
Ezra	LUZ 381	DEBREE, John	PHA 113	DECORSY, Dinis	ALL 77		
George	MNT 62	DEBRITH, Robt.	PHI 33	Peter	ALL 85		
Hannah (Aged		DEBRY, Jacob	BER 136	DECOSTER, Joseph			
111 Yrs)	DEL 161	John	BER 136	Capt.	PHI 72		
Henry	LAN 132	DEBURG, Michael	LAN 27	DECOURSE, Mariah	PHA 55		
Jacob	HNT 147	DECALO, Henry	PHI 130	DEDECKER, Charles	PHI 90		
Jacob	BUC 83A	DECAMBA?, Monseur	PHA 7	DEDIER, Peter	PHI 123		
Jesse	BUC 87A	DECAMP, Moses	WAS 62	Peter	PHI 128		
John	HNT 116	DECARHOOF,		DEDIGH, Widow	YOR 182		
John	HNT 149	Ferdenand	BFD 62	DEDWEILER, John	LAN 208		
John	FRA 279	DECATER, Capt.	PHA 100	DEEBLES,			
John	BUC 89A	DECH, Jacob	NOH 71	Frederick	LAN 75		
John	BUC 160A	John	NOH 71	DEEDS, Jacob	WST 212		
Jonathan	HNT 147	Michael	NOH 71	John	WST 271		
Joseph	PHI 84	DECHTMEYER,		John Junr.	WST 271		
Joseph	WST 149	Ludwig	LAN 59	Thomas	MNT 81		
Joseph	BUC 98A	DECK, Frederick	BER 265	DEEKER, Daniel	WST 168		
Robert	HNT 162	George	NOH 33A	Ebenezer	WST 169		
Saml.	CUM 44	Jacob	NOH 29	DEEL, Dewal	PHI 94		
Saml.	CUM 110	John	CUM 41	John	BER 261		
Samuel	BUC 140A	John N.	BER 154	Stephen	BER 261		
William	CRA 6	DECK?, (See Dech)	NOH 71	DEEL?, John	BER 286		
William	MIF 25	DECKART, David	DAU 10A	DEELER, Conrad	BER 179		
William	MNT 64	DECKER, Abraham	WAY 146	DEELNECK?,			
Zachariah	HNT 147	Andrew	LUZ 345	Matthias	YOR 181		
DEANE?, Catherine	MNT 117	Barbara	YOR 188	DEEM, George	FAY 226		
DEANS, Ebenezer	GRN 67	Benjamin	WAY 146	John	WAS 43		
DEANY, Michl.	CUM 121	Benjamin	LUZ 374	Lewis	FAY 226		
DEARBORN, John	WST 235	Benjamin	NOH 77A	Mark	WAS 79		
DEARDOFF, David	FRA 297	Brewer	WAS 12	DEEM?, William	BER 233		
DEARDORF, Anthony	ADA 38	Charity	WAY 144	DEEMER, Andw.	WST 212		
Anthy.	MIF 12A	Christn.	CUM 93	Fredrick	WST 159		
Daniel	ADA 35	Ebenzr.	CUM 107	Fredrick	WST 159		
Daniel	ADA 40	Elias	WAY 146	George	CHE 793		
Daniel	ADA 43	Elias	LUZ 348	DEEMMER, Adam	ALL 109		
Elizabeth	ADA 42	Elisha	WAY 146	John	ALL 109		
Isaac	ADA 44	Elisha	LUZ 357	DEEMS, George			
Jacob	ADA 40	Elisha	LUZ 358	(Negro)	WAS 115		
Peter	ADA 38	Frederick	ADA 32	DEEN, Allexander	BEV 25		
DEARDORFF, Andw.	YOR 176	Henry	ADA 33	John	FAY 220		
Anthony	YOR 211	Henry	HNT 116	Joseph	NOU 157		
Henry	YOR 212	Henry	LUZ 425	Margaret.	DAU 19		

DEENAH, Phillip	NOU 174	DEHAVEN, Isaac	MNT 104	DEITOR, Conrad	YOR 170
DEEP, Thos.	PHI 107A	Jacob	PHI 110	DEITRICH,	
DEER, John	ALL 115	Jacob	MNT 123	Christian	LAN 92
Stephen	BER 259	Jarrett	MNT 121	Conrad	BER 211
DEERDUFF, Isaac	CUM 110	Jesse	PHI 141	Henry	LAN 274
DEERINGER,		John	MNT 127	Henry Senr.	LAN 112
Danniel	ALL 66	John	DEL 184	Lorentz	LAN 57
DEERMAN, Henry	CUM 117	John	FRA 317	Michael	LAN 28
DEERMONT, Henry	FRA 279	Jonathan	PHA 54	Michael	BER 187
DEERWEGHTER, (No		Joseph	PHI 61A	Nicholas	BER 286
Given Name)	DAU 37	Nathan	MNT 106	Widow	LAN 59
Fredk.	DAU 37	Rachael	BER 274	DEITRICK, Baltzer	ADA 16
DEERY, George	CHE 793	Samuel	MNT 137	Jacob	ADA 21
DEES, Frederick	BER 172	William	SOM 151	Joseph	ADA 21
DEEST, Chris.	LAN 91	DEHEAVEN, Abrahan	ALL 108	Martin	ADA 39
DEETER, Catharine	YOR 179	Edward	LAN 91	Michael	ADA 39
Jacob	BER 229	DEHEVAN, Peter	NOU 109	Nicholas	ADA 17
Jacob	DAU 6A	DEHEVEN, John	YOR 194	DEITRIN,	
John	SOM 137	DEHL, Catharine	YOR 160	Christopher	MNT 89
John	BER 285	Charles	YOR 194	DEITZ, Conrad	YOR 166
John	DAU 6A	Daniel	YOR 188	Daniel	PHI 41
Martin	BER 285	Daniel	YOR 190	Fredk.	PHI 39
DEETH, Isaac	WAS 120	David	YOR 182	George Jr.	YOR 166
DEETS, Andrew	WAS 33	George	YOR 188	George Sr.	YOR 166
Christian	WAS 33	John	PHA 46	Henry Junr.	MNT 89
Ernest	ERI 58	Nicholas	PHA 114	Jacob	YOR 166
Henry	BER 172	DEHOFF, Abraham	YOR 155	DEKINS, Jesse	BFD 54
DEETZ, Earnst	SOM 137	Christian	YOR 190	DEKOVER, Henry	LAN 286
Fredk.	PHI 116	Christian	YOR 191	DEL, Samuel	ALL 51
Jacob	SOM 137	George	YOR 190	Wilm.	ALL 51
John	SOM 141	George P.	YOR 190	DELACOAR?, James	MNT 81
John	SOM 148	Mathias	LAN 304	DELAGRUE, Peter	NOH 77A
Yoast	SOM 137	Peter	YOR 188	DELANCY, Nathan	BUC 143
DEEVEN, Edmond	ERI 60	Peter	YOR 190	DELANEY, Eliza.	PHI 26
DEFERT, John	NOU 163	DEHR, Henry	YOR 174	Francis	CUM 48
DEFFENBAUGH,		DEHUFF, Abraham	LAN 42	Francis	BUC 98A
Andrew	LAN 216	Henry	LAN 39	John	CUM 97
DEFIANCE?,		John	WAS 115	John	FAY 202
Abraham	WAR 1A	DEIBERT, Adam	NOH 89	John	FAY 220
DEFIELD, Peter	PHI 39	Henry	PHI 126	Jonathan	BUC 153
DEFINTAFER, Jacob	NOU 143	John	NOH 89	William	MER 440
DEFORD, John	FAY 256	Michael	NOH 89	Wm. & Mc Clure	BUC 93
John Jun.	FAY 256	Michael	BER 223	DELANO, Elisha	LUZ 364
DEFORE, John	PHI 114A	Michael Junr.	NOH 51	DELANY, Abigail	CUM 127
DEFOSE?, Widow	PHI 72A	William	BER 220	Danl.	WST 344
DEFRANCE, Hawkins	LYC 17	DEIBLER, Abm.	DAU 33	Dennis	GRN 69
James	CRA 6	Anthy.	DAU 33	Joseph	PHI 138
John	WAS 89	Daniel	DAU 5A	Mrs.	DEL 180
DEFRANCE?,		Mathias	DAU 5A	William	WAS 37
Abraham	WAR 1A	DEICHMAN, John	NOH 29A	William	MNT 65
DEFRANE, Peter	CHE 894	DEICKIS?, Godfrey	PHI 71A	William	GRN 69
DEFREDERRICK,		DEIGMAN, John	NOH 89	DELAP, Widow	PHI 3
Philip	CHE 853	DEIHL, David	PHI 57	John	ADA 40
DEFREHN, George	NOH 75	George	BER 190	Mary	PHI 54
Jacob	NOH 75	Henry	BER 237	William	ADA 40
DEFT, Daniel	YOR 173	Jacob	YOR 170	DELAPLAIN, Yetta	BER 184
DEGLER, Jacob	BER 265	Michl.	BER 237	DELASY, Stephen	BFD 67
John	BER 148	Peter Jr.	YOR 170	DELAWAR, J. P.	MNT 75
DEGNER, Peter	MNT 88	Peter Sr.	YOR 170	DELAWAR?, James	MNT 81
DEGON, Ludwig	DAU 14A	DEILMAN, Anthony	BER 223	DELBOS, Peter	PHA 34
DEGROFF, Abraham	ADA 27	John	BER 223	DELBOW, Franck	LAN 311
Margaret	ADA 21	DEILY, Philip	NOH 72A	DELEEL, George	ALL 79
DEHAAS, Philip	PHI 152	William	NOH 35	DELENY, Phillip	FAY 235
DEHANEN, William	WST 250	DEIM, Andrew	YOR 172	DELFE?, Conrad	BER 211
DEHART, Cornelius	BER 275	DEIMER, James	BER 233	DELHORN, George	FAY 226
Elizabeth	BER 140	John	NOU 97	DELILLE, John	WAS 115
Jacob	PHA 68	DEIMLING,		DELINGOR, Fredr.	CHE 892
John	BER 137	Friederich	NOH 58A	DELION, Abigal	PHA 40
John Jur.	BER 137	DEININGER, Adam	DAU 44A	DELL, George	BER 156
DEHAVEN, Abraham	NOH 78	Michl.	DAU 44A	Henry	HNT 147
Abraham	YOR 179	DEISERT, Michael	ADA 29	James	MIF 12
David	MNT 115	DEISHER, Daniel	BER 207	John	PHA 118
Harman	LAN 93	DEISSINGER,		DELL?, Mathias	PHI 141
Hugh	PHA 72	George	DAU 30A	DELLAM, Saml.	PHA 69
Hugh	DEL 183	Jno.	DAU 30A	DELLEBAUGH,	
Isaac	PHI 93	DEITDER, Adam	NOH 49A	Valentine	SOM 157

DELLER, Lawrence	YOR 211	DEN?, Andrew	BER 209	DENNY, Peter	ALL 61
DELLINGER,		DENAS, Peter	FRA 282	Thoms.	BUT 323
Barbara	FAY 213	DENCKLER,		Walter	WAS 20
Henry	YOR 205	Christian H.	PHA 29	Widow	CUM 62
John	LAN 283	DENEEN, Joseph	BFD 42	Widow	CUM 77
DELLOW, Michael	YOR 177	DENEHAM, James	PHA 74	William	WAS 28
Nicholas	YOR 177	DENET, Captn.	PHI 74	William	CHE 815
Widow	LAN 55	DENEY, Jonas	PHI 96A	Wm.	CUM 74
DELONEY, Francis	BUC 152	DENGER, Fredk.	BER 285	DENNY?, John	DAU 22
DELONG, Andrew	NOH 72A	George	BER 283	DENSMORE, Henry	YOR 203
Christian	NOH 51	DENGES, John	NOU 127	James	WAS 11
David	BER 211	DENGLER, John	DAU 31A	John	WAS 12
David	CEN 18A	DENHART, Henry	NOH 68A	DENSTINE, Michael	NOU 182
Frederick	NOH 75	DENIBARKER?,		DENTINGER, Widow	LAN 225
John	NOH 75	Jacob	DEL 164	DENTLER,
John	BER 279	DENICK, Zechariah	DEL 166	Christina	DAU 10A
John Jn.	NOH 77A	DENIGH, Luis		Jacob	NOU 171
John	NOH 77A	Esqr.	FRA 273	Solomon	DAU 10A
Moses	BER 256	DENIGHT, Davis		DENTON, Jacob	PHI 71
Peter	BER 211	Captn.	PHI 103	DENTZ, Philip	BUC 102
Peter	BER 256	DENIS--N?, James	MER 441	DENTZEL, John	DAU 2
Sarah	WST 212	DENIS, Levy	NOU 109	Peter	DAU 14
Widow & Son	NOH 52A	Michael	CRA 4	DENZER, George	WAS 120
DELOT, John	BUC 90	DENISON, James	YOR 209	John	WAS 120
John	BUC 88A	Nathan	LUZ 335	DEPEW, Jacob	NOU 99
DELP, Abraham	MNT 125	DENISTON, Andrew	MER 441	DEPING, Henry	NOU 192
George	BUC 96	George	MER 440	DEPOLLY, Peter	PHI 15
George	LUZ 361	John	WST 343	DEPPEN, Christn.	BER 215
Isaac	MNT 121	Johnston	MER 440	David	BER 190
John	LUZ 358	DENIUS, John	BER 210	John	BER 190
Valentine	BER 255	DENLIGER, Mary	LAN 110	Joseph	BER 190
DELP?, Conrad	BER 211	DENLINGER, Abrham	LAN 111	DEPPER, John	NOH 83A
DELPH, Frederick	YOR 165	Chris.	LAN 112	DEPPY, Peter	BER 263
Peter	YOR 164	Jacob	LAN 110	DEPUE, Aaron	NOH 77A
DELPHEA, Madam	PHA 96	DENNEL, John	ARM 123	Abraham	NOH 66A
DELT, Valentine	NOU 163	DENNER, (No Given		Benjn.	NOH 66A
DELZEL, Wm.	CUM 47	Name)	LAN 142	Cornelius	NOH 77A
DEMENIL, Francis	LUZ 394	DENNEY, John	BEV 4	Daniel Esqr.	WAS 43
DEMER, Lewis	PHI 14	John	PHI 119A	Daniel Junr.	WAS 43
DEMER?, Andw.	PHI 92	DENNICK, John	FAY 197	Isaac	YOR 216
DEMICK?, John	MNT 133	DENNIN, Robert	PHA 112	Jonathan	NOH 78
DEMIG, Adam	BUC 147	Samuel	NOU 198	Joseph	WAS 43
Adam	BUC 156A	DENNING, John	WAS 12	Nicholas	WAS 43
DEMIL?, Benjamin	BEV 11	William	WAS 33	Nicholas	NOH 77A
DEMILLER, Ester	LAN 11	DENNIS, Amos	BUC 156A	Samuel	NOH 37
DEMIN?, Peter	BUC 144	Anthony	BER 178	DEPUEY?, Daniel	PHA 13
DEMMENE, George	LAN 208	Henry	WAS 62	DER, Conrad	DAU 21
DEMMY?, John	DAU 22	Jacob	MNT 66	George	DAU 20A
DEMOCK, Asa	LUZ 365	James	FRA 323	DERBOROUGH, Danl.	CHE 734
David	LUZ 363	John	PHA 66	Hugh	CHE 734
Davis	LUZ 363	John	HNT 132	Hugh	CHE 814
DEMOND, Sarah	CHE 876	John	LAN 185	DERBORY, John	FRA 274
DEMOR, Jacob	FRA 286	John	FAY 235	DERBRO, William	LAN 208
DEMORE, David	ADA 23	Joseph	PHI 77	DERBY, Hugh	WST 287
DEMOREE, Garret	ADA 22	Josiah	BUC 81A	DERBYSHIRE,
DEMOREE?, David	ADA 19	Mary	FRA 315	Alexand.	BUC 98A
DEMOTT, Richard	NOU 157	Michael	WAS 7	DERCHMER, Jacob	NOU 192
DEMOW?, Jacob	FRA 327	Philip	BUC 151	DERCK, Philip	LAN 66
DEMPSTER, James	PHA 63	Robt.	PHI 108	DERHAM, John	CHE 752
DEMSEY, Geo.	CUM 90	William	NOH 68A	Miller	DEL 156
John	CHE 831	DENNISON, Joseph	ADA 18	DERICK, Adam	NOU 192
Mrs.	NOU 128	DENNISTON, Andrew	WAS 109	George	PHI 67
Richard	WST 378	Archd.	WST 343	John	PHI 115
Timothy	CUM 118	DENNY, Allundo	PHA 74	John	WAY 148
William	WAS 7	Daniel	PHA 78	John	PHI 115A
DEMUTDH, Godlieb	NOH 72A	David	CHE 724	Nimrod	CUM 55
DEMUTH, Christian	NOH 72A	David Revd.	FRA 271	DERIN, John	NOU 104
Christopher	LAN 37	Ebinezer	ALL 51	DERINBAKER,
David	NOH 64	James	GRN 75	Frederick	NOU 157
Henry	YOR 167	James	CHE 727	DERING,
John	LAN 37	Jane	PHA 32	Christopher	NOU 171
John	YOR 219	John	GRN 100	DERINGER, Henry	NOH 37
John	NOH 72A	John	CHE 703	DERIS, Jonathen	NOU 146
Joseph	NOH 62	John	PHI 99A	DERISBOUGH?, John	NOU 192
Joseph	NOH 70	Nancy	CUM 98	DERK, Adam	NOH 58A
Joseph	NOH 71	Peter	CEN 22	Jacob	NOH 58A

DEVORE, Moses	BFD 57	DEYLY, Daniel	NOH 81A	DICK, William	CRA 3
Moses	ALL 77	Frederick	NOH 71	William	DAU 8
DEVORES, John	WAS 7	George	NOH 81A	William	BUT 339
DEVOSS, Barbara	WST 287	DEYSHER, David	BER 255	DICKARD, Susannah	PHI 133
DEVOUR, James	FRA 322	Jacob	BER 225	DICKASON, John	ALL 108
Josh.	FRA 323	Jacob Jr.	BER 255	DICKENSHIT, Widow	NOH 55
DEVOWE, John	VEN 166	Peter	BER 225	DICKENSON,	
DEW, Joseph	WAS 37	DHIL, Henry	NOU 121	Barrick	WAS 11
DEWALD, Henry	PHI 118A	John	NOU 121	James	LAN 126
DEWALT, Christian	NOH 33A	Michael	NOU 121	John	PHI 61
Fredk.	YOR 185	Phillip	NOU 121	Joseph	LAN 126
George	BER 281	DIALOUGH, John	PHA 80	Mary	LAN 126
Henry	BER 217	DIAMOND, Cornelia	DEL 192	Philp.	PHA 83
Henry	BER 221	Daniel	SOM 161	Richard	WAS 11
Jno.	CUM 130	Dominick	HNT 158	DICKENSON?, Jno.	WAR 1A
John	NOH 33A	Henry	BER 247	DICKERS, Adam	BFD 42
Moats	FAY 213	Michael	HNT 119	DICKERSON,	
P---?	MNT 72	Patrick	HNT 127	Benjamin	MNT 103
Peter	FRA 310	DIAS, Thomas	WST 378	Henry	WAS 62
Philip	YOR 181	DIBBEN, George	DAU 34	Joseph	WAS 62
Valentine	YOR 185	DIBBIN, Widow	DAU 36	Joshua	WAS 62
DEWALTIN, Widow	LAN 279	DIBBINS, Henry	BUC 93	Lydia	WAS 62
Widow	LAN 281	DIBBON, Widow	DAU 52A	Ruth	WAS 62
DEWART, William	NOU 97	DIBERT, Charles	BFD 72	DICKERT, Jacob	LAN 32
DEWAULD, Michl.	FRA 306	Frederick	BFD 72	John	BUC 100A
DEWEES, Agnes	MNT 109	John	BFD 72	DICKES, Eli	YOR 198
Charles	PHI 146	Michael	BFD 72	DICKEY, Widow	WST 323
George W.	PHA 9	DIBLON, Frederick	LAN 131	Ann	CUM 84
Jacob	MNT 109	DIBOW, Abm.	CUM 130	Archibald	ADA 9
John	MNT 77	DIBY, Widow	NOH 49A	Benjn.	CHE 754
John	PHI 146	DICASON, James	CRA 7	Charles	MNT 117
Jonathn.	PHI 122	James	CRA 10	David	SOM 142
Paul	LAN 50	Joseph	CRA 8	George	SOM 148
Saml.	BER 237	DICASON?, George	CRA 5	George	NOU 198
Samuel	PHI 129	DICE, Adam	PHA 62	James	CRA 16
Sarah	BER 246	Christian	CHE 832	James	WAS 33
Thos.	BUC 156A	Henry	DAU 10	James	CHE 730
Waters	CHE 830	Henry	PHI 78A	James	CHE 757
William	PHA 21	John	WAS 109	Jas.	CUM 59
William	MNT 109	John Jr.	FRA 315	Jas. Junr.	FRA 287
William 2nd	MNT 110	Michl.	FRA 315	Jno.	CUM 151
Wm.	PHA 8	DICHENSON,		John	WAS 33
Wm.	PHA 29	Richard	NOU 121	John	BFD 37
DEWEESE,		DICHL, Jacob	NOH 72A	John	BUT 352
Cornelius	CHE 882	Sim. Jacob	NOH 72A	John	CHE 747
DEWEL, John Junr.	GRN 84	DICK, Widow	PHI 7	John	CHE 887
John Senr.	GRN 84	Christian Jun.	ADA 34	Moses	WST 323
DEWERS, Henry	MNT 92	Christian Senr.	ADA 36	Nathl.	MIF 7
DEWERST?, John	NOU 192	Daniel	PHA 17A	Robert	CHE 730
DEWESE, Cornelius	CHE 776	Frederick	BER 153	Robt.	WST 212
DEWEY, Adam	CUM 132	Fredk.	PHI 39	Saml.	CHE 871
Conrod	CUM 85	Hartman	YOR 159	Samuel	WAS 33
Jacob	CUM 73	Henrey	FAY 231	Thomas	WST 323
Martin	CUM 85	Hermon	BFD 62	Thos.	DAU 12A
Peter	CUM 108	Jacob	CEN 20	William	WST 271
DEWIT, Danl.	LYC 25	Jacob	PHI 83	Willm.	DAU 12
Danl.	CUM 59	Jacob	BER 237	Wm.	CHE 754
Isaac	NOU 104	James	LAN 98	DICKHOUTS, John	
Joseph	WAS 2	James	LAN 236	Danl.	PHI 130
Paul	LYC 21	James	MER 440	DICKINGS, John	LAN 92
Paul	NOU 121	John	PHI 54	DICKINS, Amos	BFD 57
DEWITT, Abraham	LUZ 405	John	ALL 102	Asbury	PHA 23
Cornelius Jr.	WAY 143	John	BER 204	Edward	PHI 67
Isaac	LUZ 406	John	FRA 283	John	BFD 57
Jacob	WAY 143	John	FRA 315	John	BFD 57
John	WAY 148	John N.	BER 151	Jonathan	BFD 60
John	FAY 244	Maria	BER 236	DICKINSKIT, David	MNT 55
Joshua	WAY 143	Nicholas	BER 233	DICKINSON,	
Ludwig	WAY 143	Peter	PHA 8	Abraham	PHA 112
Paul	LUZ 407	Philip	PHA 17A	Anne	BUT 356
Peter	PHI 67	Phillip	PHA 84	Daniel	PHA 13
Peter	FAY 197	Richard	CRA 16	David	PHI 78
Rivere/ Rinere?	WAY 143	Robt.	FRA 320	Eli	PHI 73A
William	LUZ 408	Tho. B. Esqr.	NOH 37	Isaac	BER 247
DEWS, Jesse	LYC 24	Thomas	ADA 1	Israel	PHI 140
DEY, Jacob	BER 256	Valentine	DEL 166	Jerman	DEL 184

DICKINSON, Jesse	PHI	77
Jesse	LUZ	375
Jesse	PHI	73A
John	DEL	173
John	PHI	71A
Jonathan	PHI	147
Joseph	DEL	181
Joseph	BER	274
Josiah	PHI	80A
Nathaniel	BER	247
Saml.	BUT	333
William	HNT	132
William	DEL	173
DICKIS, Francis	BFD	37
Fredk.	PHI	86A
Peter	PHI	83A
DICKISON, Eli	FAY	202
Joshua	FAY	202
Lester	ERI	56
Levy	FAY	203
Morgan	GRN	95
Thomas	FAY	202
DICKMAN, John	DAU	30A
DICKS, Adam	ADA	37
Fredrick	DEL	180
James	DEL	181
Job	DEL	175
John	WAS	51
Joseph	DEL	180
Mary	PHA	93
Peter	ADA	34
Peter	CHE	878
Roger	DEL	180
Ruth	YOR	177
Ruth	YOR	178
DICKSAN, Wm.	FRA	276
DICKSON, Widow	WAS	20
Ambrose	LUZ	379
Andrew	BFD	62
Andw.	CUM	74
Barney	CUM	100
David	CUM	123
David	LUZ	378
Elizabeth	PHA	16
Elizabeth	BER	209
Enoch	CHE	836
George	CUM	35
George	PHA	46
George	FRA	327
Hannah	LUZ	378
Henry	WAS	74
James	ADA	20
James	WAS	89
James	DEL	188
James	LUZ	325
James	WST	343
John	WAS	20
John	ADA	21
John	CUM	30
John	GRN	69
John	PHA	92
John	CUM	111
John	NOU	157
John	HNT	165
Joseph	ADA	40
Joseph	GRN	63
Joseph	WST	343
Martial	LUZ	378
Mrs.	NOU	201
Nathaniel	LUZ	379
Patrick	NOU	163
Saml.	FRA	317
Samuel	ADA	18
William	LAN	30
William	NOU	143
William	LUZ	324

DICKY, Adam	FAY	202
Adam Captn.	PHI	95A
James	WAS	98
James Snr.	FRA	287
John	HNT	157
Moses	LYC	25
Moses	HNT	160
Rachel	YOR	217
William	YOR	192
DICUS, Wm.	PHA	54
DIDEY, Peter	SOM	153
DIDMAN, Henry	WST	250
DIDO, Franck	NOU	186
DIEBER, Michael	BER	159
DIECK?, (See		
Derck)	LAN	66
DIEDRICH, John	NOH	72A
DIEDRIK, Phil.	DAU	36
DIEFENBACH, Peter	BER	265
DIEFFENDORFFER,		
Godfried	NOH	58A
Henry	NOH	58A
Jacob	NOH	58A
John	NOH	68A
Philip	NOH	58A
DIEHL, Abraham	YOR	184
Adam	NOH	58A
Charles	YOR	193
Daniel	NOH	81A
Jacob	NOH	58A
John	DAU	22
John	NOH	81A
Michael	NOH	55
Nicholas	DEL	192
Nicholas	BER	266
DIEHLMAN, John	BER	159
DIEKERT, John	WST	378
DIEL, Conrad	NOH	62
Daniel	BUC	81A
Frederick	BUC	156A
George	NOH	62
George	BUC	81A
Isaac	BUC	81A
Maria	LAN	194
Martin	NOH	75
Peter	BUC	81A
Philip	NOH	35A
Samuel	LAN	208
William	BUC	81A
DIELL, Michael	LAN	208
DIELMAN, George	BER	160
DIEMER, Henry	NOH	86A
Jacob	BUC	80
Jacob	NOH	86A
Simon	LAN	208
Soloman	BUC	80
DIENEAS, Jacob	DAU	29
Nicols.	DAU	29
Philip	DAU	29
DIENER, Henry	BER	184
John	BER	184
DIER, Walter	PHI	55
DIES, Richard	WST	378
DIETER, Elias	NOH	77A
Frantz	BER	221
George	NOH	77A
Jacob	NOH	33A
John Junr.	NOH	62
John Senr.	NOH	62
William	NOH	62
William	NOH	49A
DIETRICH, Conrad	NOH	62
Frederick	NOH	72A
Henry	LAN	274
DIETS, Conrad	DAU	6
Samuel	LAN	280

DIETTERICH,		
Bastian	NOH	72A
Casper	NOH	89
Elias	NOH	37
Elias	NOH	64
Frederick	NOH	64
Jacob	NOH	64
DIETY, John	DAU	8
DIETZ, Daniel	PHA	43
Henry	MNT	89
John	NOH	72A
Nicholas	NOH	55
Nicholas	NOH	86A
Peter	PHA	32
DIFFEBAUGH,		
Benjn.	DAU	40
DIFFENBACH, Henry	LAN	106
Jno. A.	BER	151
John J. / I.?	BER	151
DIFFENBAUGH,		
George	LAN	114
John	LAN	114
DIFFENDAFFER,		
Alexr.	CHE	892
Henry	CHE	892
Philip	CHE	892
DIFFENDAL,		
Abraham	ADA	25
John	ADA	26
DIFFENDALL, Saml.	ADA	27
DIFFENDERFER,		
Daniel	LAN	33
David	LAN	77
George	LAN	34
Jacob	LAN	78
John	LAN	74
John	LAN	78
Saml.	LAN	74
Susana	LAN	79
DIFFENDORFER,		
Philip	LAN	37
DIFFERT, Wannah	PHA	62
DIFFY?, John	ALL	88
DIGGONS, John	HNT	148
William	HNT	127
DILCAM, Henry	BER	175
Philip	BER	207
DILCART, John	PHI	104
DILCKEY, John	LAN	217
DILDEN, Jacob	NOU	157
DILDIN, Daniel	NOU	157
Ralph	CRA	17
DILDINE, Daniel	NOU	157
Henry	NOH	64
Henry	NOU	151
John	NOU	146
Mrs.	NOU	151
Widow	NOH	64
DILEPLINE, Joseph	PHI	98
DILGERT, Jacob	NOH	55
Joseph	NOH	62
DILL, Adam	BFD	72
Elizabeth	BFD	72
Frederick	BFD	72
Frederick	BUC	158A
George	YOR	211
Henry	BFD	72
Hugh	PHA	115
Jacob	LAN	67
Mary	WAS	98
Mathew	MNT	113
Mathew	YOR	213
Matthew	WST	378
Michael	CRA	8
Michael	DAU	3A
Michl.	CUM	58

DILL, Peter	PHI	51	DILMAN, Christian	MNT	93	DIRDORF, Abraham	LAN	70
Peter	PHA	66	Christopher	YOR	182	Jacob	LAN	147
Prescilla	YOR	183	Conrad	CEN	20	DIRE, William	PHI	130
Solomon	PHA	94	Jacob	PHI	102	DIREN?, Edward	NOU	157
William	MIF	11A	DILP, John	NOU	135	DIRICH, Henry	LAN	184
Willm.	PHI	61A	DILTZ, John	BFD	68	Philip	LAN	184
DILL?, Mathias	PHI	141	John Jr.	BFD	62	DIRNN?,		
DILLAN, Ann	FRA	284	John Senr.	BFD	62	Christopher	NOU	163
John	MIF	7	William	BFD	62	DISAUQUE, Lewis	PHA	6
Wm.	CHE	735	DILWORTH, Ann	PHA	102	DISBER, Robert	PHI	10
DILLE, David	WAS	62	Caleb	CHE	810	DISBERRY, Thos.	PHA	55
Ichabod	WAS	62	Caleb	CHE	812	DISCAMP, John	PHA	86
Isaac	WAS	62	George	BEV	12	DISCRAY, Thomas	PHI	50
Israel	WAS	62	Jacob	PHI	146	DISE, Christian	CHE	833
Lewis	WAS	62	James	PHA	22	George	YOR	206
Price	WAS	62	James	PHA	74	John	YOR	206
DILLEN, James	CEN	22	James	CHE	736	John	FRA	314
John	WST	235	James	CHE	810	DISEL?, Michael	NOU	174
Jonathan	BUC	80	John	BEV	12	DISEMAN, Henry	YOR	207
Patk.	CUM	144	John	CHE	803	DISHER, David	PHI	44
DILLENGER, Jacob	WST	287	Joseph	BEV	12	DISHONG,		
DILLER, Abram	CUM	116	Joseph	PHA	81	Christian	BFD	43
Adam	LAN	75	Joseph	CHE	878	David	DAU	32A
Benjn.	CUM	86	Lydia	CHE	809	Frederick	BFD	42
David	CUM	78	Nicholas	PHI	146	Henry	BFD	43
Elizabeth	LAN	69	Richard	PHA	22	Peter	BFD	37
Francis	CUM	116	Samuel	ALL	117	DISING?, Peter		
George	LAN	75	Sarah	PHA	106	Junr.	MNT	54
Isaac	LAN	75	Wm.	CHE	811	Peter,	MNT	54
John	ALL	60	DIMAND, Daniel	FAY	220	DISINGER, Jacob	MIF	9A
John	LAN	89	DIMEY?, Lalrrance	VEN	165	John	LAN	70
Margt.	CUM	94	DIMILLER, John	LAN	12	Nichls.	CUM	53
Martin	CUM	86	DIMIT, Henry	ALL	59	DISLER, John	BER	233
Peter	LAN	34	DIMN?,			DISMARY, Widow	PHI	74
Peter	LAN	70	Christopher	NOU	163	DISMIER,		
Peter	CUM	116	DIMNER, John	BER	277	Christian	NOU	203
Widow	LAN	69	DIMON, Jonathan	LUZ	389	DISMIRE, Lewis	NOU	203
DILLIN, Joab	FAY	235	DIMOND, Barnabas	CHE	877	DISMONT, Benjn.	MNT	81
DILLINDER, George	GRN	75	DIMSEY, Dennis	CHE	860	Daniel	MNT	81
DILLINGAR, Gaspar	HNT	128	DINCKY, Jacob	NOH	89	Daniel	MNT	85
DILLINGER,			DINE, John	FRA	311	John	MNT	81
Augustus	GRN	79	DINE?, James	MNT	91	DISOHANG, William	LAN	194
Henry	YOR	167	DINEN?, Edward	NOU	157	DISSLER, David	LAN	194
Jacob	NOH	55	DINGEE, Charles	DEL	164	Jacob	LAN	194
Jacob	YOR	205	Jacob	CHE	851	DITCH, Abraham	HNT	127
John	NOH	55	DINGES, John	DEL	173	David	FAY	213
John	YOR	167	DINGLER/			Susanna	FRA	304
John Junr.	NOH	55	DINGLES?,			DITE, John	MNT	137
Jos.	YOR	167	Jacob	MNT	56	DITLOW, Abm.	BUC	147
Matthias	LAN	294	DINGLER,			Abraham	BUC	102A
Michael	YOR	167	Catherine	MNT	98	Abram	CHE	893
DILLINGHAM,			George	MNT	98	David	NOH	55
Simeon (A			Henry	BER	137	David	CHE	891
Boarding			Jacob	NOH	44A	John	CHE	893
House)	PHA	37	John	CHE	725	DITONE, Jacob	WST	212
DILLIOW, Jacob	MNT	34	DINGMAN, Andrew	WAY	146	DITSWORTH, Isaac	CUM	111
DILLON, Abraham	WAY	135	Daniel	WAY	146	DITTANNYE,		
Alexr.	PHI	28	James	NOH	77A	Francis	LUZ	394
And.	FRA	287	DINIG?, Peter	MNT	54	DITTERLINE,		
Edward	WAS	7	DINISTON, Wilm.	ALL	93	William	HNT	158
John	WAS	7	DINKLE, Peter	YOR	155	DITTESTINE, Henry	BUC	100A
Mathew	BEV	19	Peter	FRA	274	DITTIKER?,		
Peter	GRN	63	DINMAN, Jacob	BUC	140A	Frederick	MNT	60
Robert	WAS	7	DINNER, Peter	LAN	208	DITTO, Joseph	ADA	33
DILLOW, Charles	ADA	18	DINNIS, George	DAU	46	DITTOW, Abraham	BUC	100A
Peter	ADA	18	DINSIE, Adam	DAU	38	John	BUC	100A
DILLS, David	NOH	77A	DINSMAN, John	LAN	3	DITTWILER,		
George	WST	212	DINSMORE, Adam	VEN	169	Elizabeth	FRA	284
Henry	NOH	64	Henry	HNT	145	Jacob	FRA	293
DILLWORTH,			Robert	ALL	65	John	FRA	289
Charles	CHE	700B	DINWEEHTER,			DITTWILLER, Jacob		
DILLY, Adam	LUZ	330	Joseph	BER	269	Snr.	FRA	289
Jonathan	LUZ	327	DINWIDY, Wilm.	ALL	77	DITWILER, Henry	FRA	316
Richard	LUZ	327	DIPNER, John	SOM	148	Jacob	HNT	116
DILLYER, Simon	LAN	94	DIPPLE, Daniel	CRA	17	John	LAN	4
DILMAN, Anthony	BER	145	DIPWING, Henry	PHI	1	DITWILLER, Jacob	FRA	289

Name	Co.	Pg.	Name	Co.	Pg.	Name	Co.	Pg.
DITZ, John	DAU	40A	DOAGE, Mrs.	NOU	157	DODDS, Andrew	WAS	109
DITZLER, Jacob	BER	265	DOAN, Amos	BUC	151	Andrew	HNT	164
Thomas	BER	265	Benjamin	BUC	151	James	CUM	123
DIVANPORT, John	FRA	310	Danl.	LYC	21	John	ADA	7
DIVEL, Jacob	WST	189	Ebenezer	BUC	144A	Jos. Esqr.	CUM	73
DIVELEY, George	SOM	141	Eleazer	BUC	140A	Thomas	WST	366
Martin	SOM	141	Elijah	LUZ	357	Widow	ADA	39
DIVELLIES?, Jacob	FRA	321	Henry	BER	284	William	BUT	339
DIVELLUS, John	FRA	320	Jesse	BUC	146	DODENDORFF, John	NOH	37
DIVELY, Frederic	SOM	142	Jesse	BUC	151	DODGE, John	PHA	68
Jacob	BFD	62	Joel	BUC	151	Oliver	LUZ	395
DIVEN, Jacob	WAS	109	John	LYC	6	Thomas	LUZ	397
Joseph	CEN	22	John	BUC	144A	William	LUZ	395
Leonard	WAS	109	Jonas	NOH	64	DODLY, John	LAN	299
DIVER, William	FRA	308	Joseph	BUC	146	DODSON, Elizabeth	LUZ	352
DIVERS, John	ALL	73	Mahlon	BUC	151	James	LUZ	357
DIVERT, Frederic	SOM	157	Mahlon	BUC	144A	John	BFD	62
DIVIN, John	DAU	10A	Samuel	BUC	151	John	LUZ	352
DIVINGER, Killian	YOR	154	Samuel	BUC	88A	Joseph	BFD	62
DIVINNEY, Neal	CHE	737	DOARAN, Henry	YOR	168	Joseph	FAY	264
DIVINS, John	SOM	128	DOBANAY, Cathrine	PHA	29	Joseph	LUZ	348
Mary	FRA	287	DOBB?, William	BUC	93	Joseph	LUZ	358
DIVIT, Cornels.	DAU	45	DOBBELAIRE, Wm.	PHI	69A	Michael	BFD	62
John	ALL	67	DOBBIN, Alex			Michael Jr.	BFD	62
DIVON, Jas.	CUM	40	Revd.	ADA	8	Thomas	BFD	62
DIX, Benjamin	WAY	136	Daniel	ALL	105	Thomas	LUZ	351
Elijah	WAY	136	Hugh	WAS	20	Thomas	LUZ	352
George	FAY	226	DOBBINS, Anthony	YOR	182	Widow	NOH	75
DIXE?, James	MNT	91	James	WAS	55	William	HNT	123
DIXEN, Wm.	PHA	51	John	BEV	10	William	SOM	161
DIXON, George	WAS	55	John	GRN	69	William	FAY	202
George	PHA	75	John	YOR	156	DOE, Widow	PHI	19
George	WST	149	John	LUZ	405	DOEY, Emanuel	DAU	22
Henry	MIF	25	John	CHE	779	DOFF, Stephen	LYC	11
Henry	PHI	108	Leonard	BEV	4	DOFFERT, Jacob	NOH	35A
James	DAU	22	Robert	BEV	11	DOGAN, Michl.	PHI	81A
James	HNT	132	Thos.	PHA	17	DOGHERTY, Edward	HNT	135
James	FAY	213	William	LUZ	405	Hugh	HNT	143
John	PHA	8	DOBBS, Henry	MNT	117	John	HNT	136
John	WAS	120	Tho. Senr.	MIF	4A	William	HNT	134
John	FAY	264	Thomas	MIF	4A	DOGNESS, Mary	LAN	51
John	NOH	86A	DOBENS, James	PHI	18	DOHERTY, Jas.	LAN	169
Joseph	FAY	213	DOBIN, Thomas	ALL	55	John	VEN	165
Margaret	FRA	279	DOBINS, Robert	NOU	192	DOHNER, Henry	DAU	28
Martin	FAY	213	DOBLE?, William	BUC	93	Jacob	DAU	27A
Patrick	PHA	94	DOBLES, George	LAN	49	Joseph	DAU	25
Robt.	YOR	202	DOBSON, George	PHA	11	DOIL, John	CRA	9
Saml.	WST	149	Samuel	PHA	25	DOILE, Barthow.	PHA	84
Samuel	HNT	132	Samuel	PHA	110	DOINMYER?, Peter	BER	187
Samuel	BUC	143	Thomas	NOU	121	DOKE, Patrick	CUM	50
Stafford	FAY	213	Thos.	PHA	15	Robert	LAN	14
Stafford Jur.	FAY	213	William	NOU	121	Robert	WAS	98
Stevan	ALL	59	DOBSTER, Geo.	BUT	366	Saml.	FRA	327
Thomas	MIF	25	DOBSTON, Geo.	BUT	349	William	WAS	98
Thomas	BUC	80	DOCK, Robert	BEV	24	DOLAN, Michael	LAN	10
Thos.	YOR	196	DOCKENBACH, John	MNT	61	DOLBY, Abel	BUC	156A
William	BUC	139	DOCKERT, Charles	LAN	266A	Abm.	PHA	29
William	FAY	231	DOCKEY, Anthony	NOU	121	Abram	CHE	904
William	FAY	231	DOCKS, Adam	LAN	208	Daniel	PHA	101
William	WST	323	DOCTOR, Felty	LYC	13	Joseph	PHA	29
William Junr.	FAY	231	Fredrick	LYC	15	Mary	PHA	101
DIXON?, -----	ARM	123	George	LYC	15	Thos.	CHE	817
DIXSEY, Charles	PHI	107	Gotfriet	LYC	14	DOLCHESS, Sandess	CUM	76
Isaiah	PHI	110	Leonard	LYC	25	DOLEMAN, Samuel	FAY	235
DIXSON, George	ALL	102	DODD, Daniel	WAS	2	DOLEN, William	VEN	169
Henry	WAS	79	James	FRA	293	DOLIN, John	DEL	176
James	CHE	836	Mary	WAS	115	DOLL, Conrad	YOR	178
Joseph	NOH	55	Rufus	MER	439	Daniel	YOR	186
Joshua	WAS	79	Thiall	MER	439	Daniel	YOR	187
Sarah	ALL	113	Thomas	PHI	138	Henry	YOR	188
Wilm.	ALL	117	Thos.	WST	212	Jacob	YOR	156
DIXSON?, Jacob	ALL	114	Wm.	PHA	109	John	ADA	15
DIZER, James	DEL	175	DODDRIGE, Philip	WAS	55	John	LAN	46
DIZLER, Caspar	DAU	52A	DODDS, Widow	PHI	24	John	YOR	177
DOAGAN, Mich	BUT	331	Widow	WST	308	John Jr.	YOR	177
Thomas	BUT	331	Andrew	GRN	66	Joseph	DAU	4

DOLL, Martin	YOR 206	DONALDSON, John	ARM 124	DONNEL, Alexr.	NOU 202
DOLLAHAN, John	LAN 130	Jos.	YOR 155	Henry	LYC 3
DOLLAT, Charles	PHI 29	Richard	WAS 20	Robert	LAN 51
DOLLEN, James	WAS 11	Robert	NOU 143	DONNELL, Jonathan	MER 441
DOLLERICH, Jacob	BER 259	Thos.	CUM 55	Rosannah	PHA 46
DOLLET, Adam	LAN 59	William	ADA 34	DONNELLY, George	SOM 137
DOLLINGER, Geo.	DAU 49A	William	WAS 89	Henry	CUM 74
John	BER 260	William	NOU 143	James	GRN 75
Peter	BER 207	Wm.	CUM 113	John	ADA 24
DOLLON, James	MNT 62	DONALDSON?, Eloy/		John	HNT 152
DOLMAN, John	YOR 157	Elcy?	ADA 34	Wm.	CUM 109
DOLPH, Charles	LUZ 367	DONALLY, Cathanne	PHA 77	DONNELSON, John	ERI 56A
Jonathan	LUZ 370	John	WAS 48	Widdow	FAY 231
Moses	WAY 139	John Junr.	WAS 48	Wilm.	ALL 82
Moses	LUZ 368	John Senr.	WAS 48	DONNELY, Widow	PHI 14
Simon	LUZ 375	William	WAS 48	Feliz	GRN 87
DOLTON, John	NOH 72A	DONALSON, Andrew	HNT 153	Thomas	HNT 148
DOM, Philip	LAN 136	DONALY, Arthur	FRA 309	DONNER, Christian	LAN 254
DOMAN, Barbara	CHE 727	DONAT, Jacob	BER 129	DONNIER, James	DAU 45
Jacob	YOR 183	Peter	NOH 52A	DONNLEY, Hugh	WST 287
John	DEL 192	DONAUGHTY,		DONOGHY, Ann	WAS 28
DOMAS, John	BER 187	Patrick	LAN 97	DONOHOE, John	HNT 136
DOMBACH, Anthony	LAN 194	DONAVAN, Richard	YOR 157	DONOLDSON,	
DOME, Benedick	YOR 172	DONAWAN,		Richard	BFD 55
Christian	YOR 172	Catharine	PHI 91A	DONOUGHY, John	FAY 220
DOMER, Michael		DONCAN, James	ALL 88	DONOVEN, Jeremiah	FRA 273
/S/	SOM 148	James	ALL 112	DONSEATH, Andrew	ALL 54
Michael Sen.	SOM 148	John	ALL 64	David	ALL 65
DOMINECK, Martha	PHA 91	Mardit	ALL 60	DONSETH, Thomas	ALL 77
DOMINICK, Chas.	PHA 45	DONDAS, William	ERI 56A	DONSHE, Margit	ALL 112
John	PHA 92	DONDORE, Henry	YOR 173	DONSHEE, Thomas	ALL 88
DOMLINSON, John	BER 277	DONE, Benjamin	NOU 154	DOOD, David	FAY 248
DOMON?, John	WAS 51	Danl. (Crossed		DOODS, James	WST 307
DOMOUTET, J./ I.?	PHA 6	Out)	LYC 20	DOOGAN, Widow	WST 323
DONAGHUE, Paul	HNT 164	Israel	CHE 751	John	WST 366
DONAGHY, James	WST 343	Nathan	NOU 109	Richd.	PHI 108A
Wm.	WST 343	Sarah	ALL 65	DOOLING, John	LAN 223
DONAHAVER, Abrm.	MNT 44	DONEGAN, Thos.	PHI 36	DOOLITTLE,	
Henry	MNT 44	DONEGHY, Joseph	WAS 7	Benjamin	LUZ 387
DONAHEN, Peter	DAU 9	William	WAS 98	Luther	LUZ 427
DONAHEY, James	FRA 300	DONEHE, George	BEV 13	DOOLON, Frances	FAY 226
DONAHOE, Humphry	PHA 80	DONEHOE, James	BFD 50	DOOLY, Joseph	FRA 312
DONAKER, Widw.	PHI 111A	DONEHOWER, George	PHI 59	DOOME, George	SOM 128
DONAL, James	YOR 177	DONELLY, Henry	CUM 84	DOOMY, Hugh	BFD 48
DONALD, Widow	WST 343	James	ADA 24	DOOTY, William	VEN 167
Condon	WST 344	DONELY, Alexr.	BUT 365	DOOVES, David	CUM 66
Francis	CUM 132	David	DAU 13	DOPHINE,	
James	WST 149	Fransis	PHI 131	Catharine	DAU 30A
John	WAS 15	Mary	MIF 7	DORAN, Adam	YOR 168
Saml.	WST 343	DONER, John	DAU 28A	Jacob	YOR 168
Thomas	CUM 132	DONEY, Isaac	FAY 226	Michael	PHA 15
Wm.	CUM 129	DONIBE?, James	ALL 65	DORATH, Harman	CUM 42
DONALDSON, Wm.	PHI 18	DONIFAN, John	ALL 98	DORBIT, Nicholas	NOU 97
Aaron	PHI 18	DONIGHE, John	WAS 37	DORBYR, John	PHI 106A
Aaron	BFD 62	DONIKER, Adam	CHE 883	DORCOUGH, Benjn.	FAY 256
Alexander	HNT 156	DONILE?, James	ALL 65	DORCY, Sarah	DEL 169
Andrew	WAS 15	DONLAN, Andrew	ALL 116	DOREL, Jeremiah	CRA 11
Andw.	CUM 112	DONLAP, John	LAN 174	DOREMAN, John	FAY 202
Chas.	CUM 52	DONLEY, John	WST 149	DORENSLY, Widow	LAN 91
David	WAS 67	John	FRA 327	DOREWARD?, Jacob	MNT 112
Ebenezer	WAS 20	DONLY, Francis	PHA 62	DORFILE, Godfry	PHI 131
Elizh.	PHA 67	Hugh	WST 366	DORITY, John	NOU 116
Isaac	WAS 89	James	NOU 198	DORLAND, John	HNT 155
Jacob	WAS 55	John	ALL 52	DORLER?, Jacob	PHA 29
James	WAS 20	John	PHA 53	DORMANT, Henry	CHE 889
James	WAS 85	DONNAHEO, Thos.	PHA 47	DORMEIER, Martin	NOH 51
James	NOU 143	DONNALDSON, Isaac	PHA 30	DORMEYER, Peter	NOH 58A
James	NOU 143	John	LAN 49	DORNAN, James	WAS 89
James	WST 168	DONNALL, Isaac	MER 441	DORNBACH, John	BER 157
James	CHE 821	DONNALLY, David	CHE 718	DORNBAUGH, John	YOR 185
Jane	WAS 67	John	BUC 104A	DORNBLISER, Paul	NOH 71
Jno.	CUM 59	Thomas	CHE 777	DORNER, Jacob	NOH 89
John	WAS 67	DONNALSON, Hugh	MER 440	DORNICK, Eliza.	PHA 19
John	PHA 81	Marey	MER 440	DORNLINSON, John	BER 277
John	WAS 85	DONNE, Nathan	DEL 188	DORNMYER, John	BER 225
John	NOU 116	DONNEL, Alexd.	ALL 74	Michael	BER 263

DORNMYER?, Peter	BER 187	DOTTY, Jesse	WST 343	DOUGHERTY,			
DORNON?, John	WAS 51	John	GRN 105	Manassah?	WAS 98		
DORNY, Adam	NOH 89	Jonathan	WST 343	Michael	LAN 87		
Henry	NOH 89	Nathl.	WST 343	Michael	FAY 264		
Peter	NOH 89	William	WST 344	Mordicea	CUM 35		
Peter Junr.	NOH 89	DOTY, Anthony	WAS 2	Neal	WST 168		
DORON, Daniel	CHE 775	Danl.	WST 343	Neal	LAN 232		
DORR, Charles	NOH 79A	Edward	BFD 37	Patk.	MIF 16A		
Henry	NOH 85	Edward	BFD 47	Patrick	ARM 126		
John Captn.	NOH 85	Saml.	WST 343	Peter	LYC 28		
John Senr.	NOH 85	Thomas	ALL 111	Philip	CHE 753		
Michael	NOH 55	Timothy	MIF 25	Richard	PHA 112		
DORRANCE,		DOTZ, Adam	MNT 48	Roger	WAS 20		
Benjamin	LUZ 333	DOUB, Henry	MNT 89	Thos.	CHE 781		
John	LUZ 333	Henry	DAU 52A	William	BFD 62		
DORRON, Henry	GRN 69	Jacob	MNT 89	William	WAS 67		
Joseph	GRN 69	DOUBERMAN, John	NOU 135	William	BUC 143		
DORROUGH, Charles	FAY 249	Peter	NOU 135	William	LUZ 411		
DORROW, John	LUZ 390	Phillip	NOU 135	Willm.	PHI 5		
DORSERMON?, Widw.	PHI 82	DOUBERT, John	BER 190	Wm.	MIF 25		
DORSEY, Benedict	PHA 11	DOUD, John	PHA 117	Wm.	BEV 27		
Darling	GRN 87	DOUDEN, Jonan.	PHI 11A	Wm.	CUM 128		
Greenberry	HNT 163	DOUDES, Timothy	CHE 863	Wm.	WST 212		
John	PHA 18	DOUDLE, Michael	YOR 154	DOUGHETY, Abel	CEN 19A		
Joseph	WAS 37	DOUDS, Andw.	CUM 110	DOUGHTERMAN,			
Joshua	PHA 36	DOUGAL, James	FRA 324	Christr.	CUM 142		
Nathan	PHA 106	DOUGALL, John	HNT 126	DOUGHTERTY,			
William	SOM 153	DOUGAN, James	WST 235	George	PHA 107		
DORSH, Widow	LAN 46	Wm.	LYC 21	John	PHA 100		
DORSHEIMER, Widow	NOH 35	DOUGHERTY,		DOUGHTON, Saml.	CHE 719		
DORSON, James	WAS 109	Barnabas	LAN 242	DOUGHTY, Danl.	PHI 74A		
John	WAS 37	Barnabas	CHE 900	James	PHI 11		
Mathew	WAS 109	Barnett	CHE 711	Patrick	LAN 119		
Sarah	FAY 220	Charles	LAN 78	Stephen	BER 211		
William	PHI 148	Charles	LAN 111	DOUGLAS, Albert	BUC 153		
William	FAY 235	Charles	LAN 216	Alexr.	DAU 10		
William	FAY 264	Daniel	LYC 19	Andw.	BUT 366		
DORUM, Benjamin	NOH 89	Daniel	PHA 83	David	HNT 150		
DORUS, Elizabeth	PHA 111	Daniel	FAY 238	James	LAN 285		
DORVAL, John	PHA 53	Danl.	DAU 3	Jno. Junr.	CUM 54		
DORWART, Danl.	BER 187	Danl.	CUM 151	John	BEV 27		
DOSH, Frederick	LAN 295	Danl.	PHI 105B	John	CUM 54		
Philip	BUC 158A	David	BUC 154A	John	HNT 123		
DOSHER, Elizabeth	FRA 272	Dennis	CHE 845	John	WST 168		
DOSSER, Thomas	PHI 37	Edward	DEL 160	John	YOR 215		
DOSSING, Andrew	MER 440	Edward	BER 179	Joseph	MIF 4A		
Ralf	MER 440	Edwd.	MIF 25	Michael	WAS 109		
DOSSON, Jacob	MER 440	Geo.	CUM 78	Patrick	WAS 15		
DOTERER, Mathias	BER 184	George	NOU 104	Price	CHE 798		
DOTHWAIT, William	PHI 137	George	LAN 216	Robt.	FRA 323		
DOTSON, John	HNT 129	Henry	LYC 21	Robt.	MIF 4A		
Richard	HNT 144	Henry	LYC 30	William	NOU 192		
DOTT---S?,		Henry	LAN 221	Wm.	BEV 23		
Christopher	MNT 54	Hugh	LAN 154	Wm.	CUM 101		
DOTTEN, John	PHI 49	James	CUM 23	Wm.	MIF 4A		
DOTTEREE, Danl.	BER 175	James	PHI 32	DOUGLASS, Andw.	WST 235		
DOTTERER,		James	WAS 67	Ephram	FAY 252		
Christian	MNT 127	James	BFD 72	Francis	PHA 70		
Conrad	NOH 35	James	WAS 115	Geo.	CUM 43		
Henry	BUC 147	James	FAY 238	Geo.	CUM 52		
John	MNT 94	James	FAY 264	George	BER 139		
John	BER 256	Jan	DAU 0	James	YOR 198		
Michael	MNT 94	Jas. Jun.	FAY 238	James	WST 307		
Phiip	NOH 79A	Jeremiah	CHE 911	James	BUT 327		
Solomon	NOH 35	John	PHA 11	Jas.	CUM 65		
DOTTERRER, Abram	MNT 112	John	LYC 23	Jas.	CUM 67		
Abreck	MNT 97	John	CUM 36	John	GRN 80		
Bernard	MNT 56	John	WAS 67	John	CUM 82		
Michael	MNT 72	John	PHA 83	John	PHA 95		
DOTTEVNS?,		John (Crossed		John	CUM 99		
Christopher	MNT 54	Out)	BUC 98A	John	LAN 155		
DOTTEVRES?,		John	PHA 112	John	LAN 238		
Christopher	MNT 54	John	CHE 740	John Junr.	PHI 41		
DOTTIORIS?,		John	PHI 112A	John	DAU 46A		
Christopher	MNT 54	Joseph	LAN 289	Margaret	ADA 8		
DOTTS, Philip	PHI 153			Robert	PHA 21		

DOUGLASS, Saml.	WST	149	DOWNARD, William	FAY	252	DOYLE, Matthew	CHE	861
Saml.	BUT	327	DOWNER, Abraham	LAN	111	Matthew	CHE	865
Samuel	FAY	213	David	LAN	111	Richard	HNT	136
Sarah	BUT	320	Henry	LAN	116	Robert	ADA	33
Thomas	BFD	37	John	LAN	116	William	DEL	175
Thomas	FAY	243	Joseph	WAS	15	DOYLY, Charles	NOH	77A
Thomas F.	ADA	8	Joseph	FAY	264	DRACK, Samuel	ALL	115
Timothy	GRN	80	DOWNES, Henry	BFD	42	DRAGOE, Fredrick	FAY	244
William	YOR	197	John	BFD	41	Peter	FAY	244
Wm.	PHA	28	Michael	BFD	37	DRAI--LE?, Geo.	PHI	39
Wm.	CUM	41	DOWNEY, Archibeld	FAY	208	DRAIN, Alexandr.	PHI	105B
DOUGLE, Jacob	YOR	154	Charles	DAU	43	DRAINE, Frances	MER	439
DOUGLUSS, James	ADA	7	James	FRA	304	DRAISCH, Adam	LAN	208
DOUNSLY?, (See			John	WST	149	DRAKE, Andrew	MNT	88
Dorensly)	LAN	91	John	DAU	2A	Asahel	LUZ	338
DOURAS?, Henry	BER	162	Samuel	FAY	208	Benjamin	NOU	146
DOURGH, Ephraim	NOU	198	Samuel	FRA	295	Benjamin	LUZ	321
DOUROUGH, Thomas	LAN	162	William	WST	235	Charles	BEV	21
DOUT, Roger	LAN	240	William	CHE	833	Cornelius	NOU	104
DOUTCHEE, Alexr.	PHA	87	DOWNHOVER, Jacob	CHE	897	David	SOM	142
DOUTHERT, Joseph	CUM	136	DOWNING, Alexr.	YOR	199	David	NOU	163
DOUTHET?, Joseph	BEV	17	Daniel	LUZ	319	Dennis	WAS	62
DOUTRICH, Jacob	BER	203	Daniel Jr.	LUZ	325	Edward	BEV	27
John	BER	136	David	LUZ	412	George	LAN	152
DOUTTON, Samuel	LAN	132	David	CHE	826	Henry	WAS	12
DOUTY, George	NOU	163	Dvid	CHE	898	Henry	ERI	59A
James	HNT	119	Francis	PHA	82	Jacob	LYC	28
James	NOU	163	Hunt	CHE	898	Jacob	WAS	67
Mrs.	NOU	143	Jacob	PHA	82	Jacob	NOU	104
Mrs.	NOU	163	James	YOR	200	Jacob	LUZ	372
Nathaniel	FAY	235	James	CHE	899	Jacob Jr.	LUZ	400
DOVE, John	PHI	78	Joel	LUZ	401	James	LUZ	415
DOVER, Abraham	NOU	186	John	HNT	146	Jesse	WAY	138
Andw.	PHI	90A	John	HNT	162	Jesse	LUZ	407
Fredk.	PHI	118A	John	LAN	168	John	MNT	87
John	PHI	90A	Joseph (F.)	CHE	899	John	NOU	146
DOVERMON?, Widw.	PHI	82	Joseph	CHE	899	John	NOU	163
DOVIENS?, John	FRA	290	Reuben	LUZ	321	John Junr.	MNT	88
DOW, George	PHI	23	Richard	HNT	116	Joseph	NOU	149
DOWD, Isaac	LUZ	383	Richard	CHE	898	Joseph	NOH	77A
DOWDALL, Joseph	WAS	120	Richard J.?	CHE	899	Josia	FAY	220
Michael	WAS	120	Saml.	CHE	774	Levi	MNT	112
DOWDERMAN, Jacob	PHA	32	Samuel	LAN	244	Levi	NOH	77A
DOWDLE, John	PHI	98	Thomas	HNT	129	Lewis	GRN	80
John	CHE	761	Thomas	CHE	813	Mary	GRN	80
Wm.	CHE	761	Thomas	CHE	898	Moses	WST	250
DOWDS, John	BEV	27	Thos. R.	CHE	898	Oliver	SOM	142
DOWELL, Alexander	DEL	177	William	LAN	166	Oliver	NOU	163
Nero (A Negro)	BEV	27	DOWNS, Widow	PHI	20	Oliver	NOH	86A
DOWENHOUER, John	LAN	298	Widow	PHI	22	Robert	BUC	160A
DOWENT, Philip	BUC	102	Earl	PHI	77	Samauel	NOH	41
DOWER, Robert	CRA	9	Henry	YOR	193	Samuel	MIF	25
DOWERS, Conrad	YOR	208	Jeremia	FAY	235	Samuel	NOU	146
Edward	PHA	105	Jesse	YOR	193	Sidney	WAY	136
John	PHA	106	Saml.	YOR	193	Thomas	NOU	163
DOWING, Jas.	LAN	168	Thomas	DEL	174	Widow	NOH	77A
Richard	CHE	898	Thomas	FAY	235	William	BFD	60
DOWLEN, Jacob	CHE	826	Thomas	FAY	265	William	NOH	77A
DOWLER, George	WAS	79	William	MIF	3	Zeph.	NOU	146
Margaret	WAS	67	DOWNY, James	WAS	43	DRAPER, Amos	LUZ	344
Richd.	MIF	7	DOWTHERD, Ezekia	ALL	78	John	WAS	62
Thomas	WAS	79	DOWTHET, Nathl.	WST	159	Nathan	LUZ	324
DOWLIN, Jeremie	CHE	880	DOWTY, ---?	VEN	167	DRAPIER, Jonathan	PHA	118
John	CHE	816	DOWVERMAN, Andrew	CHE	898	DRAPPER, Henry	GRN	108
Michael	WAS	98	DOYL, George	NOU	157	DRASBACH, Henry	NOU	127
DOWLING, David	MNT	49	Thomas	MER	439	DRAUB, Jacob	BER	283
Jno.	DAU	41A	DOYLE, David	LAN	34	DRAUD, Eve	LAN	194
John	DEL	178	Dennis	PHA	99	DRAVENSTAT,		
Paul	MNT	49	Dennis	HNT	131	Frederick	LAN	15
DOWLY, Frances	LAN	28	Edward	WAY	135	John	LAN	11
DOWN, Mathew	MNT	104	Felix	FRA	322	DRAWBAUGH, Wm.	CUM	67
DOWNAR, Jonathn.	FAY	256	Henry	CUM	107	DRAWYER, Andrew	LAN	54
DOWNARD, Jacob	FAY	220	John	PHA	108	DRAXELL, Adam	NOH	89
James	FAY	220	Jonathan	HNT	134	Daniel	NOH	89
Jonathen	FAY	252	Jonathan	BUC	104A	Danl. (See		
Thos.	FAY	220	Mary	FRA	322	Draxell, Peter NOH		89

DRAXELL, Jacob	NOH	89	DRIBELBIS,			DRUMBORE, Andrew	BUC 158A
John	NOH	89	Catherine	BER	223	Jacob	BUC 158A
Lowrence	NOH	89	DRIBLEBIS,			DRUMHELLER, Danl.	BER 175
Peter	NOH	89	Abraham	BER	255	Dewald	NOH 86A
Peter (Near			Abraham Jr.	BER	255	George	BER 165
Boltich?)	NOH	89	Daniel	BER	255	George	NOH 86A
Peter (Son Of			Jacob	BER	255	John	BER 184
Danl.)	NOH	89	DRIBREAD,			John	BER 185
Peter Junr.	NOH	89	Matthias	YOR	197	Nicholas	BER 184
DRAYDON, James	WAS	98	DRIES, John	BER	283	Philip	NOH 86A
DRAYK, Stephen	NOU	149	DRIESBACH, Henry	BUC	158A	DRUMMER, John (A	
DRAYRINGER, John	WAS	33	Jacob	BUC	158A	Negrow)	BEV 15
DREAH, William	YOR	168	DRIFFIELD, John	PHI	134	DRUMMON, Jas.	CUM 137
DREER, Widow	PHI	73	DRIMER, Anthony	YOR	210	DRUMMOND,	
Adam	BER	179	DRIMING, Wilm.	ALL	66	Alexander	HNT 166
Jacob	BER	179	DRINKER, Daniel	PHI	3	George	WST 343
DREES, Jacob	BER	253	Henry	PHA	35	James	WAS 67
John	BER	253	Henry	BUC	93	John	WST 343
Leonard	BER	225	Henry Junr.	PHA	24	DRUNBACH, Jacob	YOR 170
DREHER, George	NOH	41	John	PHA	103	DRUREY, Michael	SOM 133
DREIGHLER,			Joseph	PHA	21	DRURY, Elfred	PHI 105A
Dorothea	YOR	169	Joseph	PHA	89	John	WAS 43
DREIN, George	BER	212	Mary	PHA	21	John	MNT 97
DREISBACH, Adam	NOH	37	DRINKHOUSE, Jacob	MNT	56	Stephen	HNT 156
Adam	NOH	49A	DRIPPS, John	GRN	63	DRY, George	BER 256
George	NOH	75	DRIPS, James	CEN	20	Paul	BER 259
Henry	NOH	75	Thomas	WST	235	DRYBROUGH, Alexd.	FRA 279
Henry	NOH	49A	DRISCHOL, Charles	LAN	194	DRYER, Andrew	PHA 80
John	NOH	62	DRISKLE, Charles	ADA	31	DU VALL, Jeramiah	BFD 62
John (Tanner)	NOH	49A	James	ADA	23	DUANE, Thomas	LUZ 322
John Jr.	NOH	49A	DRISS, Cunrod	SOM	153	Wm.	PHA 74
Joseph	NOH	62	DRISSEL, John	BUC	100A	DUARD, Henrey	FAY 249
Jost	NOH	75	Olery / Olcry?	BUC	100A	DUBANKS, James	WST 168
Jost	NOH	83A	DRITT, Jospeh	DAU	4	DUBARREY, John	PHA 11
Michael	NOH	49A	DRIVER, Casper	FAY	240	DUBB, Daniel	YOR 184
Peter	NOH	49A	James	YOR	208	DUBBING, Justice	PHA 85
Peter	NOH	72A	John	SOM	141	DUBBS, Daniel	NOH 55
Simon	NOH	75	John	FAY	197	Frederick	BFD 37
DREISBACK, Jacob	NOH	29	John (Crossed			Leonard	DAU 2A
Peter	NOH	33A	Out)	SOM	137	Michael	PHA 79
Simon	NOH	29	Michael	YOR	166	Oswald	YOR 186
DREISCH, Adam	LAN	194	DRIVOW?, Anthony	ALL	49	DUBE?, Michl.	PHI 103A
Michael	LAN	194	DROLLINGER, Henry	BUC	158A	DUBENDORFF,	
DREMMER, John	YOR	180	DROLLY, John	DAU	3	Fredk.	DAU 6A
William	YOR	180	DRONE, John	LUZ	425	DUBERRY, James	MNT 141
DRENEN, Mercer	FRA	288	DRORBAUGH, Jacob	YOR	217	DUBLER, Frederick	LAN 208
DRENING, David	BEV	16	DROSTLE, George	LAN	208	DUBLICAN, William	WST 159
DRENKLE, John	BER	237	DROWINER, Casper			DUBOIS, Abm.	PHA 22
DRENNIN, Mary	ALL	79	(See			Henry	BUC 137
DRENNING, Thomas	ALL	80	Crowiner,			Uriah	BUC 92
DRENNON, David	YOR	167	Elish.)	LAN	208	Widow	BUC 137
Joseph	CHE	869	DROWMAN, Alexd.	ALL	109	DUBOSQ?, Henry	PHA 113
DRENON, James	CHE	869	DROWN, Sollomon	FAY	256	DUBREE, Joseph	PHA 4
DRESBAUGH, Simon	YOR	169	DROWNINER, Elish.			Rebecca	MNT 64
DRESH, Andreas	NOH	75	& Casper	LAN	208	DUBS, John	DAU 16
Dewalt	NOH	75	DROZ, Humbert	PHA	25	Martin	PHA 78
DRESHER, Abraham	MNT	118	DRUCHER, Martin	YOR	178	DUBUE?, John	LAN 119
George	MNT	130	DRUCK, George	YOR	168	DUCAS, Philip	BFD 62
DRESLER, Adam	MIF	12A	DRUCKENBROD,			DUCATE, John	BUC 89
George	YOR	177	Matthias	LAN	208	Josiah	BUC 90
Jacob	BER	283	DRUKER, Peter	FRA	301	DUCATS, Josiah	BUC 138A
DRESS, George	BER	211	DRUM, Charles	NOU	135	DUCE, Simon	PHA 19
Jacob	NOH	75	Conrod	PHI	115	DUCHEE, John	PHI 17
Jacob	BER	220	George	NOU	114	DUCHMAN, George	LAN 82
John Geo.	BER	220	George	BER	129	Jacob	LAN 111
Michael	BER	211	George Jr.	BER	129	Widow	LAN 84
DRESSLER, Andrew	NOH	85	Henry	NOH	75	DUCK, Geo.	CUM 122
David	BER	187	Jacob	WST	366	Henry	PHI 84A
Jacob	BER	256	Joseph	NOH	62	John	NOU 135
Peter	BER	187	Joseph	DEL	190	Phillip	CUM 125
DREVENSTAT,			Peter	BER	129	Wm.	CUM 127
Stufel	LAN	13	Philip	BER	186	DUCK?, (See	
DREVISH, Wm.	CUM	95	Phillip	WST	366	Derck)	LAN 66
DREWITZ, Jacob	BER	245	Simeon	WST	212	DUCKIS?, Godfry	PHI 71A
DREXLER, John	YOR	188	Widow	NOH	62	DUCOMB, Vincent	PHA 5
DREYDON, Samuel	FRA	271	DRUMBAUER, Henry	NOH	89	DUDEN, Daniel	YOR 181

DUDER, Abraham	NOU	151	DUFFY, W.	PHI	15	DUM, Agnes	BER 236
Philli	NOU	0	DUG--?, Wm.	FRA	295	Nichs.	CUM 102
DUDLE, John	PHI	14	DUGAL, James	NOU	163	Pilda	NOU 186
DUDLY, John	YOR	187	DUGAN, Charles	YOR	169	Thomas	BER 254
DUEL?, Michael	NOU	174	Dennis	WST	287	DUM?, John	ALL 64
DUER, James	BUC	98A	Dennis	BUT	334	Michael	BER 136
John	BUC	98A	James	NOU	146	DUMARASS, Alexr.	WST 378
Joseph	BUC	151	James	FAY	213	DUMARS, Alexander	MER 440
Joseph	BUC	140A	James	CHE	904	Chr./ Chs?	WST 169
Joseph	BUC	144A	John	WAS	37	James	MER 440
William	BUC	152	John	FAY	197	Thomas	MER 440
DUERAM?, John	MER	439	John	CHE	878	Timothy	MER 440
DUESING, John	NOU	135	Joseph	PHA	11	DUMAS, John F.	PHA 47
DUEY, Adam	PHA	17	Robert	NOU	127	DUMBAR?/ DUMBAS?,	
Fredrik	DAU	36A	DUGEE, Mr.	PHA	39	Robert	WAS 89
Jacob	DEL	169	Samuel	PHA	122	DUMHART, Godfried	LAN 136
DUFF, Allexander	BEV	12	DUGGAN, Hugh	FAY	249	DUMM, Caspr	BER 255
Cornelius	BER	163	John	FAY	202	DUMMA, Jacob	CUM 82
David	BEV	12	Robert	FAY	202	DUMOTET, John	PHA 96
David	ALL	117	Robert Jun.	FAY	202	DUMPHY, George	ADA 8
Frances	FAY	197	DUGLAS, Alexd.	ALL	95	DUN, Alexander	CRA 5
James	WAS	85	Andw.	MIF	9A	Daniel	MIF 7
James	ALL	117	Ezabela	ALL	81	Jacob	ALL 74
James	WST	250	Francis	NOU	192	James	CRA 11
John	ALL	58	George	BUC	93	James	HNT 148
John	WST	366	James	ALL	61	James	FAY 213
John Senr.	WST	189	John	ALL	94	James Junr.	CRA 12
Robert	ALL	65	Robert	ALL	94	John	ALL 87
Sarah	BEV	12	Thomas	ALL	95	Justice	CRA 8
Wilm.	ALL	65	Thos.	FRA	295	Margeret	FAY 208
DUFFE, Thos.	PHI	95A	DUGLASS, Andw.	PHI	109A	Patrick	CRA 5
DUFFEE, John	ARM	124	Eliza	PHA	58	Peter	HNT 150
DUFFERD,			Joshua	FAY	202	Thomas	FAY 208
Frederick	NOH	39	DUGLES, William	CRA	18	DUN?, Hugh	ALL 117
DUFFERT, George	NOH	33A	DUGLIS, James	ALL	91	DUNACRES, John	PHI 110
DUFFEY, Daniel	NOU	121	DUHER?, Peter	LYC	23	DUNAGNESS, John	NOU 128
James	ERI	58	DUIGAN, William	CHE	903	DUNAHOO, Charles	FRA 286
James	BUC	81	DUKE, Jacob	ALL	99	DUNAHOUR,	
Jno.	CUM	147	Patrick	PHI	119	Elizabeth	BUC 96
John	CUM	63	Philip	PHI	120A	DUNAN, Nancy	PHI 93A
John	CUM	89	DUKENEER, Saml.	PHI	83	DUNBAR, Alexr.	MNT 81
Percifor	CHE	902	DUKENSLIT, John	MNT	122	David	DEL 171
DUFFIELD, (See			DUKEY, John	WAS	28	George	PHA 100
Walton &			DULBARTUS,			James	WAS 28
Duffield)	BUC	153A	Christn.	PHI	107A	James	WAS 85
Abraham	PHI	137	DULEM, John	PHI	30	James	WAS 89
David	FRA	291	DULEN, Joshua	FAY	208	Jas.	CUM 115
Edward	PHI	150	DULEY, Mr.	PHA	63	Jno.	CUM 128
George Esq.	LAN	217	DULHUGH, Joseph	PHI	19	Jno. Junr.	CUM 45
Jacob	PHI	153	DULIBAN, John	LAN	188	Jno. Senr.	CUM 45
Jas.	FRA	292	DULIN, John	WAS	55	John	ALL 62
Jno.	CUM	50	DULL, Casper	MIF	25	John	CUM 115
John	PHA	17	Christian Junr.	MNT	44	John	DEL 170
John	ADA	39	Christian	NOH	72A	John Jun.	ALL 62
John	BUC	88A	Christina	MNT	44	Martha	MNT 49
Patk.	CUM	47	Christn.	CUM	62	Robert	DAU 19A
Richd.	MNT	117	Christn.	MNT	81	Wm.	CUM 96
Saml. Doct.	FRA	291	Daniel	WAS	43	Wm.	CUM 115
Samuel M.d.	PHA	8	Elizabeth	MNT	77	DUNBARE, Alexr.	NOU 163
Susanna	FRA	292	Frederick	MNT	77	DUNBARR, Alexr.	WST 287
Thomas	PHI	151	Isaac	LUZ	403	Charles	CHE 876
William	BFD	37	John	NOH	41	George	DAU 19
William	LAN	217	John	SOM	133	Joseph	CHE 826
Wm.	VEN	169	John	CHE	862	Peter	PHA 39
Wm.	FRA	292	John Sen.	SOM	133	Saml.	BUT 329
DUFFMAN, Frederic	HNT	129	Joseph	FRA	305	DUNCAMP, Francis	PHI 105
DUFFY, Aaron	WAY	141	Leonard	DAU	44	DUNCAN, Alexd.	FRA 285
Charles	BUT	323	Peter	BFD	72	Andrew	WAS 20
Charrly	ALL	105	Stophel	FRA	307	Andw.	WST 271
Frances	FAY	244	Valentine	BER	255	Andw.	WST 287
James	ALL	116	Valentine	BUC	148A	Andw. Esqr.	YOR 195
John	NOU	116	DULLEBAHN, Henry	LAN	62	Arnold	CUM 152
Laurence	LYC	17	DULMAN, Widow	PHI	114	Benjn.	DAU 17
Michael	PHI	50	DULRAL?, Jeremiah	PHI	79A	Benjn.	CUM 28
Michael	FAY	244	DULTY, John	FRA	313	David	CUM 142
Philip	BUT	362	DUM, Aandrew	ALL	69	David	WST 343

DUNCAN, Henry	WAS 20	DUNGAN, James	FAY 235	DUNLAP, Andrew	FAY 226
James	DAU 5	Jeremiah	BUC 137	Andrew	BUC 140A
James	ADA 9	Jeremiah	BUC 155	Ann	CHE 875
James	WAS 67	Jeremiah	BUC 104A	Archibald	HNT 144
James	WAS 74	Jesse	PHI 153	Daniel	LAN 73
James	CUM 97	Jesse	BUC 138A	Daniel	CHE 777
James	CUM 114	John	BUC 154	Henry	PHA 59
James	HNT 160	John Jnr.	BUC 104A	Isaac	BUC 87A
James	NOU 174	John	BUC 104A	James	PHI 55
James	YOR 202	Jonathan	PHI 135	James	WAS 55
James	FRA 285	Joseph	BUC 137	James	BFD 72
James	WST 307	Joseph	FAY 265	James	LAN 128
Jane	DAU 15A	Joshua	BUC 137	James	LAN 142
Jas.	CUM 49	Joshua	BUC 154	James	YOR 191
John	BEV 23	Levy	BEV 24	James	CHE 873
John	WAS 43	Mahlon	MNT 61	James Esq.	CEN 22
John	WAS 89	Rachel	MNT 76	James M.d.	PHA 4
John	CUM 137	Robert	BEV 22	James Revd.	FAY 202
John	MIF 4A	Robert	MNT 38	James	BUC 87A
Joseph	CUM 151	Saml.	PHI 152	Jas.	BUT 346
Joseph	SOM 157	Thomas	PHI 130	Jerome	CHE 867
Judith	PHA 26	Thomas	BUC 137	Jno.	LYC 21
Margaret	CHE 870	Thos.	PHA 70	John	LYC 4
Mary	PHA 66	Thos.	BUC 138A	John	PHI 10
Mathew	PHA 83	Widow	BUC 104A	John	CEN 20
Mathew	FRA 311	DUNGIN, Jushia	FRA 302	John	LYC 23
Pheobe	PHA 25	DUNGUN, Esau	BEV 24	John	WAS 48
Primus	PHI 91	DUNHAM, Asa	NOU 143	John	WAS 74
Robert	PHA 7	David	GRN 75	John	LAN 82
Robert	LAN 182	Elizabeth	FAY 244	John	PHA 83
Robt.	YOR 202	Gidian	FAY 220	John	WAS 85
Robt.	WST 307	Jeerimia	FAY 220	John	LAN 124
Saml.	CUM 97	Jenias	FAY 226	John	BUC 144
Saml.	BUT 340	Joseph	FAY 220	John	BUC 154
Samuel	SOM 157	Matthias	NOU 171	John	NOU 157
Stephen	LYC 17	Mordica	FAY 220	John	LAN 230
Thomas	CUM 97	Moris	FAY 220	John	WST 366
Thomas	WST 159	Peter	PHI 4	John	MER 440
Thos.	PHA 14	DUNING, John	WST 250	John	BUC 140A
Thos.	FRA 281	Jonathan	PHA 17	Moses	BUC 104A
Thos.	DAU 24A	DUNINGER, Jacob	NOU 187	Moses	BUC 104A
Widow	DAU 45A	DUNKEBERGER,		Rachel	FAY 213
William	WAS 55	Abram	BER 136	Richard	LAN 284
William	DAU 21A	DUNKELBERGER,		Robert	PHA 92
William	BUC 88A	Clement	BER 277	Robert	WST 159
Wm.	PHA 70	DUNKER, Robert	PHI 36	Robert	LAN 229
Wm.	CUM 119	DUNKERLY, Luke	PHI 102	Samuel	FAY 202
Wm.	CUM 131	Mary	PHI 102	Thomas	BEV 17
DUNCKEL, Peter	LAN 276	DUNKIL, Michl.	FRA 323	Thomas	WAS 48
DUNCLE, Jacob	NOU 127	DUNKILL, Jacob	FRA 276	Thoms.	BUT 358
Peter	NOU 128	Jacob	FRA 320	Thos.	WST 271
DUNCLEBARGER,		DUNKIN, Alexander	FAY 197	Thos.	WST 307
Christopher	NOU 121	Henry	PHA 34	Thos.	WST 343
Frederick	NOU 121	James	PHI 23	Widow	LAN 159
John	NOU 121	DUNKLE, Cynad?	BER 246	William	WAS 15
Phillip	NOU 121	Henry	FRA 323	William	NOU 128
DUNCLEBERGER,		Jacob	BER 187	William	HNT 152
Christopher	NOU 121	Jacob	BER 217	Wm.	WST 343
DUNDAS, Thomas	BER 233	John	BER 217	DUNLAP?, -----	MIF 10
DUNDORE, Jacob	BER 148	John	BER 277	DUNLARY, John	PHI 30
Jacob	BER 265	John	FRA 312	DUNLAVY, Anthy.?	MIF 25
John	BER 148	John	DAU 9A	John	CHE 730
DUNEGARE, John	PHA 70	Killian	BER 277	DUNLEVY, Anthony	WAS 43
DUNEN, Ann	PHI 32	Peter	BER 187	Darby	ALL 104
DUNGAN, Amos	BUC 153	Peter	BER 217	Joseph	FAY 213
Benjamin	PHI 153	Sebastian	LAN 260	Morris	FAY 264
Cath.?	MNT 81	DUNKLEBERGEN,		William	FAY 264
Cornelius	BUC 107	Peter	LYC 13	DUNLOP, Andw.	
David	BUC 93	DUNKLEBERGER,		Deqr.	FRA 276
David	BUC 137	Peter	LYC 16	Danl.	CUM 89
Elias	BUC 137	DUNKOUP, Adam	BER 233	James	FRA 287
Garret	BUC 137	DUNLAP, Widow	PHI 14	James	FRA 313
Garrett	MNT 34	Adam	FAY 202	James	ERI 55A
Garrett?	MNT 42	Alexander	WAS 85	Jno.	CUM 70
James	BUC 137	Alexr.	CEN 20	John	CEN 22
James	PHI 151	Alexr.	BUT 359	Joseph	FRA 287

DUNLOP, Thomas	MIF	16A	DUNSMORE, William	FAY	213	DUSBA, William	NOU 182
Wm.	CUM	120	DUNT, Jacob	NOU	97	DUSENBERRY,	
DUNLY, Ephraim	FRA	317	DUNTON, Jacob.	PHA	41	George	NOH 66A
DUNMIRE, Jacob	FRA	283	DUNWICK, Wm.			DUSHAM, George	BER 207
DUNMYER, Jacob	NOU	174	(Note Says			DUSHANE, Andrew	ADA 20
Nicholas	NOU	174	Error)	PHI	31	DUSINGER, John	LAN 187
DUNN, Captn.	PHA	61	DUNWODY, Geo.	VEN	169	DUSKEY, John	DAU 31A
Widow	PHI	113	DUNWOODY, David	FRA	289	DUSMAN, Henry	WAS 2
Alice	DEL	183	David Jun.	ADA	7	DUSS?, Jacob	DAU 35A
Allen	WST	250	David Sen.	ADA	7	DUST, Joseph	WAS 11
Andrew	ADA	9	Elizabeth	ADA	19	DUSTON, Michl.	PHI 104A
Andrew	FAY	264	Hugh	ADA	9	DUTCHER, Abraham	LUZ 326
Andw.	CUM	83	James	FAY	261	Wm.	LYC 22
Ase	FAY	256	James	CHE	726	DUTCHMAN, Francis	PHI 119A
Daniel	PHA	16	James	CHE	885	DUTEL, Jacob	MNT 120
Danl.	LYC	20	John	PHA	77	DUTH, Christian	NOH 81A
David	DEL	178	John	PHA	88	DUTILK?, Stephen	PHA 96
Ewd.	FRA	319	Jos.	FRA	289	DUTILL?, John	PHI 97
Fredk.	CUM	44	DUON, Henry	PHA	40	DUTON, Israel	PHI 109
George	DEL	183	DUPENXEAU?, Peter			DUTOT?, Anthony	NOH 77A
Henry	FRA	298	L.	PHA	103	DUTT, George	LAN 147
Isaac	GRN	100	DUPESING, Madam	PHA	96	George	BUC 148
Jacob	DEL	181	DUPLESSE, Peter	PHA	19	DUTTIS, Asahel	LUZ 421
James	LYC	19	DUPS?, Jacob	DAU	35A	DUTTON, Elizabeth	DEL 166
James	MNT	49	DUPUY, John F.	LUZ	322	Francis	WAS 37
James	NOH	29A	DUQUIN, Peter	PHA	45	John	DEL 165
John	PHI	7	DURAIN, Widow	PHI	76	Jonathan	DEL 164
John	LYC	19	DURANEY, Widow	PHI	29	Jonathan	DEL 175
John	DEL	163	DURANG, John	PHI	56	Rachael	DEL 164
John	LUZ	359	DURANGE, Jacob	PHA	96	Richard	DEL 155
John	WST	366	DURANT, Widow	PHI	25	Richard	DEL 164
John	PHI	101B	Edward	PHA	95	Silas	PHA 112
Joseph	PHI	65	DURAT, John	BUC	90	Thomas	DEL 155
Josh.	FRA	321	John	CHE	710	DUTTWEILER, Jno.	DAU 41A
Luther	LUZ	400	DURBEN, Nicholas	FAY	202	DUTWEILER, David	DAU 20A
Oliver	ERI	55A	DURBIN, Thomas	WAS	79	Michl.	DAU 18A
Patrick	PHA	54	Thomas	SOM	161	DUVAL, James T./	
Rich.	MIF	13A	DURBORROW, Thos.	CUM	142	S.?	PHA 31
Robert	DAU	47	DURBY, Hugh	PHI	7	Morin	PHA 11
Robert	LUZ	355	DURCH, Adam	LAN	64	DUVALL, Alexander	WAS 79
Robt.	FRA	293	DURFAR, George	PHA	74	DUVOLL, Elisha	PHA 99
Samuel	GRN	100	DURGLES?, Jacob	MNT	56	DUVY, John	PHI 27
William	PHI	30	DURHAM, Edward	NOH	64	DUY, George	PHI 133
William	FAY	264	Richard	CRA	16	Jacob	PHI 131
William	FAY	264	DURK, Jacob	BUC	93	John K.	PHI 123
Wm. Junr.	LYC	18	Jacob Jnr.	BUC	93	DUZENBERY, John	FAY 244
Wm. Senr.	LYC	19	DURLIN, Joseph	BFD	42	DWIRE, Isaac	SOM 142
DUNN?, John	ALL	64	Mary	BFD	42	Shaffat Esq.	SOM 148
DUNNAFIN, Widow	LAN	253	DURN, Joseph	HNT	145	Thomas	WAS 79
DUNNAM, Jas.	CUM	50	DURN?, Michael	BER	136	DYAL, George	FAY 197
DUNNAVA, James	PHI	109A	DURNALL, Thomas	PHA	120	DYAR, Thomas	CEN 20
DUNNAVAN, Robt	FRA	318	DURNBACH, John	LAN	208	DYE, Andres Junr.	GRN 69
DUNNBALL, James	NOU	163	DURNBLESER, John	NOH	72A	Andrew Senr.	GRN 69
DUNNEGER, Joseph	SOM	161	DURNELL, John	DEL	169	Daniel	WAS 11
DUNNETT, George	MNT	132	DURNING, Charles	SOM	142	Enoch	WAS 11
DUNNIM, Finnis	MER	440	DURNY, Michael	PHI	4	Ezeikel	WST 250
Finnis Jur.	MER	440	DURNYON, John	BUT	334	James	GRN 69
DUNNING, Ezekiel	ERI	55A	DURR, Nicholas	PHA	68	John	GRN 94
Jacob	PHI	43	DURRIAN, Philip	NOH	71	DYER, Benjamin	NOU 109
James	SOM	128	DURRON, Darby	MER	440	Charles	PHI 135
Thos.	CUM	82	Michal	MER	440	Charles	BUC 140A
Wilm.	ALL	53	DURST, Abraham	DAU	43	Edwd.	BUC 137
Wm.	CUM	121	Casper	SOM	148	Edwd. Jnr.	BUC 137
Wm.	YOR	201	Henry	SOM	148	Emanl.	LAN 253
DUNNION, Elisha	FAY	231	Jacob	SOM	148	Henry	NOU 109
Samuel	FAY	197	John	SOM	148	James	MNT 64
DUNNOVAN, John	FRA	318	Peter	DAU	32	James	PHI 134
DUNON, John	DEL	182	Peter	DAU	32	John	PHI 149
DUNPHY, James	PHA	78	Zachariah	MIF	9A	John	BUC 140A
DUNSEATH, Robt.	WST	323	DURSTINE, Abm.	BUC	96	Joseph	MNT 64
DUNSHEE, William	GRN	111	George	BUC	158A	Joseph	PHI 134
William	LUZ	345	Isaac	BUC	158A	Joseph	NOH 66A
DUNSMORE, Andw.	YOR	201	DURWALD, Martin	LAN	54	Joshua	NOU 109
Henry	FAY	264	DURWARD, Jonas	LAN	54	Thomas	BUC 140A
John	YOR	201	DUSALT, John	BER	222	Wm.	PHA 72
Robt.	WST	189	DUSAR, Florimand	PHA	89	DYERMINT, John	FRA 306

DYERMOND, John	FRA 298	EAKIN, George	LAN 155	EARNEST, Baltis	MNT 40
DYESHER, Jacob	BER 255	James	MIF 7	Conrod	CUM 45
DYKE, Peter	WST 168	Joseph	WAS 89	David	DAU 19
DYSART, Joseph	MIF 25	EAKINS, George	CHE 830	George	BFD 79
DYSERT, Benjn.	CUM 136	Wm.	CUM 109	Jacob	PHA 16
Widow	CUM 136	EAKNESS, Andrew	NOU 175	Jacob	PHA 102
		EAKS, John	BEV 18	Jno.	CUM 48
E-----T?, Henry	PHI 96A	EAL, Alexander	MNT 133	John	DAU 18
E----, James?	MIF 10	EALER, Abraham	NOH 29A	John	BFD 72
E----?,		Fredk.	PHI 33	John	CUM 77
Elizabeth?	MIF 10	Peter	NOH 29A	John	CUM 103
E----KEN?, George	CHE 745	EALEY, John	PHA 54	John	CUM 116
E---?, Dennis	MNT 43	Joseph	LAN 148	Stophel	DAU 19
George	FRA 293	EALY, Jacob	CUM 59	Willm.	DAU 18
E---TH?, Jacob	NOU 114	John	FRA 281	EARNEY, Conrad	DAU 17
EABACH, Charles	BER 184	Phillip	CUM 101	EARNSFELT, John	PHI 102
William	BER 184	EALY?, Andw.	YOR 208	EARNST, Daniel	SOM 151
EABAUCH, Wm.	DAU 30	EAMOLD, John	CHE 911	EARNSTS, Susannah	PHI 128
EABY, Abraham	LAN 180	EANICH, See		EARRICH,	
Daniel	LAN 174	Earrich	BER 266	Christian	BER 266
David	LAN 176	EANS, George	NOU 175	EARRONTS, John	CUM 61
Isaac	LAN 176	EAPERT, Michl.	WST 212	EARS, Jacob	LAN 134
Jacob	LAN 178	EARBURK, Adam	DAU 34	EARTHMAN, Andrew	BUC 96
John	LAN 172	EARCLIP, Andrew	CHE 714	Joseph	BUC 96
Peter	LAN 130	EARES, Willm.	PHI 45	EASHER, Fredk.	PHI 41
Peter	LAN 176	EARGOOD, Bernard	NOU 104	EASLEY, Andrew	ARM 124
EACHUS, Abner	CHE 879	John	NOU 104	Gasper	ARM 124
Benjn.	CHE 797	EARHART, Anthony	WST 308	Samuel	ARM 123
Evan	DEL 182	Cathrine	PHA 113	EASLY, Ferdinand	WST 308
Phineas	DEL 191	George	FRA 312	EASON, Jno.	LYC 28
Thos.	CHE 775	Henry	BUC 147A	Robert	LYC 28
Virgil	DEL 176	John	ADA 38	EAST, Abraham	BER 166
William	CHE 701	John	CHE 754	Daniel	BER 184
EACKMAN, Jno.	CUM 123	Peter	FRA 312	Michl.	BER 237
EACKUS, Pares	CHE 723	Peter	BUC 147A	Samuel	BER 166
EACLS?, Stephen	LAN 154	EARHEART, Michl.	WST 213	EASTBURN, Aaron	BUC 144A
EACLY, Abraham	PHA 71	EARICH, Michael	BER 186	Amos	BUC 86
EADER, Joseph	WAS 120	EARKHART, Michl.	WST 212	Benjn.	CHE 765
EADINGER, Melihor	BUC 147	EARL, Abraham	PHI 67A	Benjn.	BUC 137A
EAGAN, Dominick	LAN 15	Benj. Capt.	PHI 68	John	MNT 104
William	BUC 103	Benjamin	LUZ 380	John	BUC 151
EAGANS, Jno.	WAR 1A	Caleb	PHI 17	Joseph	BUC 144A
Wm.	WAR 1A	Clayton	PHA 76	Margaret	MNT 106
EAGARY, John	CHE 834	David	FRA 307	Moses	BUC 144A
EAGEL, John	BUC 90A	David	PHI 67A	Robert	BUC 144A
EAGELTON, William	LAN 133	Isaac	DEL 171	Samuel	MNT 107
EAGEN, James	LAN 14	James	LUZ 354	Thomas	CHE 763
EAGER, Capt.	DEL 192	EARLE, Edward	WAS 43	EASTER, Jacob	SOM 148
Edward	NOU 151	Edward	WAS 43	Stophel	CUM 122
James	PHI 37	Isaac	DEL 171	EASTERHOOT, John	PHI 92A
James	NOU 151	James	WAS 43	EASTERLINE, John	BUC 147
John	FRA 295	James	PHA 96	EASTERLY, Geo.	PHI 90A
Peggy	MIF 1	John	WAS 43	George	NOU 109
Robert	BEV 16	Martha	PHA 100	EASTIS, John	PHI 67A
EAGEY, Abraham	FRA 285	EARLEY, Edward	CHE 762	EASTMAN, Aaron	ERI 56A
EAGLE, Adam	LAN 131	Henry	CHE 872	EASTNICK, John	DEL 157
Christie	FRA 310	Hugh	SOM 153	EASTON, Abraham	HNT 116
Henry	BER 139	William	LAN 225	George	HNT 138
Henry	BUC 147	EARLEY?, See		Isaac	HNT 116
Herny	BER 173	Easley	ARM 124	Saml.	PHA 64
Philip	BER 173	EARLOCKER, Michl.	ADA 44	EATER, Christn.	FRA 311
EAGLESON, John	DEL 156	EARLY, Widow	PHI 97A	William	NOU 157
William	MER 441	Abraham	NOU 128	EATON, David	LAN 145
EAGLEY, Caspar	DAU 5	Christn.	DAU 22A	David	YOR 203
EAGON, Barnet	GRN 94	George	PHI 103	David	CHE 750
James	GRN 94	Jacob	DAU 12A	Edward	BUC 153
Solomon	GRN 63	John	DAU 47	Elizabeth	HNT 160
EAGY, Adam Jun.	ADA 19	John	NOU 128	Isaac	FRA 280
EAKEN, Samuel	MIF 1	John	FRA 281	James	BEV 23
EAKENS, James	BEV 5	John	CHE 762	James	WAS 109
James	BEV 14	Robt.	CUM 139	James	WST 344
John	BEV 5	Thomas	DAU 46A	John	BEV 23
John Junr.	BEV 14	William	WAS 20	John	WAS 109
John Seignr.	BEV 14	William	WAS 98	John	YOR 158
Samuel	BEV 14	William Junr.	WAS 20	Jonathan	BUC 155
EAKIN, Alexander	LAN 153	Wm. Esq.	CEN 20	Jonathan	PHI 81A

EATON, Jos.	CUM	53	EBERT, George	FAY	252	ECKARD, Christian	FAY	240
Joseph	HNT	160	Henry	NOH	89	Conrod	CUM	81
Joseph	FRA	280	Jacob	ADA	23	Jacob	CUM	81
Nathaniel	PHA	30	Martin	YOR	161	ECKART, David	ADA	6
Saml.	WST	344	Peter	NOH	89	George	PHI	152
Thos.	BUC	104A	Peter	NOH	52A	Henry	ADA	6
EATTEN?, See			Philip	YOR	161	John	ADA	28
Cotten?	BEV	16	Philip	NOH	52A	John Senr.	ADA	28
EAVAN, William	LAN	93	Rosina Widow	NOH	32	Jonas	DAU	39A
EAVANS, Hugh	LAN	95	Tobias	NOH	52A	Philip	PHI	152
Isaac	LAN	89	EBERTH, Cathrine	PHA	42	ECKEBERGER, Adam	HNT	154
James Junr.	LAN	95	EBERTS, Adam	NOH	52A	ECKEL, Jacob	NOH	41
James Senr.	LAN	95	George	NOH	73	ECKELBERGER,		
John	LAN	93	EBEY, Abram	CUM	89	George	LAN	31
John	LAN	93	John	DAU	5	ECKELS, Andrew	WST	251
John	LAN	101	EBICKE, Jacob			Charls	WST	251
Joshua	LAN	95	Christian	NOH	71	Saml.	CHE	757
Lot	LAN	94	EBIE, Joseph	LAN	195	Samuel	WST	251
Widow	LAN	93	EBITS, Joseph	LAN	173	ECKENBERGER,		
William	LAN	92	EBLESON, John	CHE	851	Lawrence	MNT	72
EAVANSON, George	DEL	190	EBLING, Henry	BER	136	ECKENROAD,		
Joseph	DEL	159	Henry	BER	172	Christian	LAN	11
Joseph	DEL	190	Jacob	BER	265	ECKENRODE, Henry	ADA	24
EAVEN, Robert	LAN	148	Paul	BER	136	Henry	ADA	34
EAVENS, Widow	LAN	79	Philipini	BER	136	John	ADA	23
William	MER	441	William	BER	255	ECKER, Henry	CHE	895
EAVERNS, James	LAN	233	EBORN, John	BER	274	Jacob	CHE	894
EAVERS, Phillip	CUM	64	EBRECHT, Jacob	DAU	33	Jacob	NOH	49A
EBACK, John	YOR	196	EBRIGHT, John	LAN	106	Peter	NOH	49A
EBBA, Emmenel?	PHI	77A	Phillip	CUM	100	ECKERMAN, Jacob &		
EBBERT, John	DAU	2	EBY, Abraham	LAN	111	John	NOH	66A
EBBY, Peter	FRA	301	Abraham	LAN	144	John & Jacob	NOH	66A
EBEN, Thomas	PHI	18	Andrew	LAN	174	ECKERS, John	ERI	58A
EBENREUTER,			Andrew	FAY	311	ECKERT, Abraham	LAN	12
George	NOH	42A	Christ.	FRA	311	Abraham	NOH	64
Margaret	NOH	33A	Christian	LAN	144	Adam	BFD	72
EBENS, Joshua	PHI	66	Christian	LAN	171	Baltzer	NOH	86A
EBERHARD, Fred.	NOH	49A	Christian	YOR	194	Charles	BUC	104A
EBERHART, (No			Christly	DAU	14A	Elizabeth	BER	190
Given Name)	CEN	22A	David	FRA	311	George	BUC	80
Catharine	YOR	190	George	DAU	27	George	BER	237
George	NOH	89	George	FRA	311	George Junr.	LAN	229
John	NOH	80	Henry	DAU	26A	George Senr.	LAN	230
Michael	NOH	42A	Jacob	LAN	140	Jacob	LAN	178
EBERLE, Charles	PHA	81	Jacob	LAN	186	John	BER	143
EBERLEIN, John	LAN	300	Jacob	LAN	292	John	BER	190
EBERLEY, Joh	LAN	0	Jacob	DAU	26A	John	BER	217
EBERLIE, Jacob	LAN	195	John	LAN	144	John	NOH	68A
Jacob Big	LAN	194	John	YOR	192	John	NOH	86A
Michael	LAN	194	John	FAY	244	John	BUC	104A
Peter	LAN	195	John	LAN	147B	Jonas	LAN	56
EBERLY, Abraham	LAN	209	Jos.	FRA	310	Leonard	BUC	158A
Abraham	LAN	233	M.	LAN	148	Peter	LAN	176
David	LAN	209	Michael	LAN	306	Peter	YOR	181
Henry	LAN	98	Sam	LAN	147B	Peter	BER	215
Henry	LAN	209	Saml.	FRA	311	Philip	DAU	29
Henry	LAN	233	Samuel	LAN	181	Philip	BER	237
John	LAN	24	Widow	LAN	74	Solomon	BER	255
John	LAN	306	ECHBACK, Abraham	MNT	98	Valentine	BER	255
EBERMAN, Godleib	LAN	43	ECHERT, Nichola	BER	190	William	NOH	68A
Jacob	LAN	32	ECHHOLD?, Michael	MNT	137	ECKFELT, Adam	PHA	51
John	LAN	32	ECHLER, Jacob	BER	260	Jacob	PHA	81
John	LAN	42	ECHO, Saml.	CHE	849	ECKHARDT, Geo.	PHI	33
Philip	LAN	34	Wm.	CHE	902	ECKHART, Adam	NOH	83A
EBERS, Mathew	ALL	67	ECHOLTZ,			Elizabeth	NOH	68A
EBERSOLE, Anna,			Frederick	ADA	17	John	PHI	2
Widow	LAN	6	ECHTENACH, Andrew	LAN	224	John	WST	308
Ben	LAN	5	Jacob	LAN	217	Ludwich	FRA	295
Jacob	LAN	12	ECK, Cathrine	PHA	102	William	NOH	83A
Jacob	LAN	19	John	LYC	10	ECKINS?, John	ARM	127
Martin	LAN	12	John	MNT	89	ECKLE, Daniel	FRA	279
EBERT, Adam	MIF	1	John	BER	211	John	BER	153
Adam	NOH	47	John	BER	256	ECKLEBERGER,		
Conrod	PHI	113	Joseph	BER	211	Conrad	FRA	293
Elizabeth	YOR	162	Peter	BER	211	Daniel	FRA	293
George	BER	220	Tores?	BER	207	Godfry	FRA	293

ECKLEBERGER,			EDGAR, Hugh	YOR 201	EDWARDS, Isaac			
Jacob	CUM	60	James	PHI 59	Jnr.	BUC	137A
ECKLES, Francis	CUM	97	James Esq.	WAS 89	Isaac	BUC	137A
Jas.	CUM	40	John	WAS 15	Isachar	DEL	175
Nathl.	CUM	108	John Esqr.	WST 271	Jacob	PHA	17
Saml.	CUM	29	Jos.	YOR 197	James	PHA	101
ECKLESON, Robert	WAS	20	Joseph	BEV 20	James	DEL	188
Samuel	WAS	20	Mary	YOR 201	Jas.	PHA	48
ECKLEY, Frederick	LUZ	416	Samuel	YOR 201	Jesse	PHI	136
ECKLY, John	CEN	22A	Wm.	PHI 117	Jesse	BUC	137A
ECKMAN, Daniel	LAN	224	EDGATE, Elias	FAY 265	John	PHI	16
Jacob	LAN	224	EDGE, David	LAN 312	John	PHI	30
Jacob	FAY	249	John	CHE 899	John	PHI	31
John	LAN	109	Philip	LAN 312	John	MNT	81
Martin	LAN	224	EDGEDON, John	PHI 118A	John	ALL	98
Martin	LAN	244	EDGER, Owen	PHI 112A	John	PHI	111
Peter	LAN	224	EDGINGTON, Jesse	WAS 98	John	ALL	117
Widow	LAN	37	EDGLIFF?, Thomas	GRN 86	John	MNT	118
ECKOPS, Isaac	PHI	155	EDIE, James	YOR 195	John	NOU	146
Jacob	PHI	155	John	YOR 154	John	LAN	154
Michael	PHI	155	Samuel Esqr.	ADA 10	John	LAN	209
ECKROAD, Adam	NOU	117	William	WAS 98	John	FRA	284
ECKROT, Christn.			William	YOR 195	John	CHE	730
& Son	NOH	52A	EDINGEN, Martin	PHI 17	John	CHE	740
George	NOH	52A	EDINGER, Abm.	BUC 80	John Esqr.	DEL	190
ECKSTINE, David	DAU	18A	Abm. Jnr.	BUC 80	John	BUC	100A
Fredk.	PHA	81	Fredk.	BER 175	John	BUC	137A
ECKY, John	PHI	142	George	NOH 86A	Jonathn.	PHI	75
ECO, Joseph	CHE	770	Peter	NOH 86A	Joseph	BFD	62
ECOPS, David	MNT	107	Wm.	BUC 80	Joseph	BFD	62
ECROYD, James	LYC	7	EDIR, Levy	LYC 7	Joseph	PHA	95
ECTOR, John	CHE	737	Mathis.	LYC 7	Joshua	PHA	76
EDAIR, Wilm.	ALL	79	EDMAN, Robt.	FRA 286	Joshua	CHE	738
EDAM, Peter	DAU	25	EDMISON, Andrew	ALL 119	Margt.	MNT	81
EDAMS, Gayn	BUC	137A	John	ALL 68	Mary	PHI	115
Hugh	BUC	137A	EDMISTON, James	MIF 7	Michael	YOR	160
James	BUC	137A	Jas.	CUM 39	Moses	CHE	822
EDDELMON, George	PHI	122	John	HNT 125	Nathan	BUC	101
EDDEY, Caleb	GRN	110	Joseph Esqr.	MIF 1	Nathan	MNT	104
EDDIE, George	PHA	94	Robt.	CUM 45	Ralph	PHA	89
EDDLEMON, Jacob	PHI	122	Saml.	MIF 1	Robert	MNT	49
EDDOWS, Ralp	PHI	155	EDMOND, Francis		Robert	HNT	146
EDDS, John	MNT	82	Captn.	PHI 106A	Samuel	BUC	98A
EDDY, Abner	LUZ	388	John	DAU 39	Thomas	DEL	191
Assa	LUZ	388	Thomas	SOM 157	Thos.	LYC	15
Charles	PHA	76	EDMONDS, Daniel	NOH 75	Thos.	CHE	740
George	NOH	42A	George	SOM 157	Thos. Stevens	LAN	14
John	WAS	2	John	NOH 73	William	PHI	16
Joseph	WAS	2	EDMUNDSON, John	YOR 208	William	NOU	146
EDEBURN?, Jacob	CUM	81	John	YOR 210	William	PHI	152
EDEBWIN?, (See			Jos.	YOR 214	William	BUC	153
Edeburn?)	CUM	81	Thos.	YOR 207	William	DEL	180
EDEL, Sebastian	NOH	51	EDOVILLE,		William Jn.	BUC	160
EDELBLUT, Jacob	CUM	84	(Frenchman)	DEL 187	William Jnr.	BUC	100A
EDELMAN, Adam	NOH	47	Charles	DEL 186	William	BUC	100A
Conrad	NOH	39	EDSALL, Nathaniel	LUZ 410	Wm.	PHI	116A
George	NOH	47	EDSON, Sarah	LUZ 322	EFFERS, Fredk.	DAU	18A
George	NOH	62A	EDWARD, Widow	PHI 99	EFFINGER, Agnes	DEL	178
John	PHA	61	Evan	PHA 66	Malachi	CHE	759
John	NOH	42A	Robt.	PHI 104	Rachael	DEL	186
John	NOH	62A	William	WST 189	EFLELIN, Daniel	NOU	202
Valentine	BFD	37	EDWARDS, Widow	PHI1099	EFLIN, Samuel	BUC	153
EDELMANN, Adam	DAU	2A	Abner	DEL 188	EGAR, Widow	YOR	203
EDELY, Michael	BUC	158A	Alice	DEL 189	EGBERT, Job	ALL	78
EDENBURG, Jacob	PHA	29	Amos	SOM 157	John	MNT	107
EDENFIELD,			Azariah	WAS 55	Lawrence	MNT	77
William	FAY	220	Benjamin	BFD 62	Nicholas	NOU	192
EDENTON, Jonathan	HNT	125	Charles	HNT 137	Sarah	MNT	109
Robert	HNT	125	David	BER 161	Wilm.	ALL	78
Samuel	HNT	125	David	SOM 161	EGBIRD?, (See		
EDER, John	BER	285	Edward	MNT 40	Eglurd)	NOU	143A
EDERBURG, Peter	PHI	44	Edwd.	PHA 89	EGE, Adam	BER	237
EDES, Andrew	BER	265	Elizabeth	PHA 100	Henry	BER	237
EDGAR, Adam	WAS	89	Enoch	PHI 134	Margt.	BER	239
David	BUC	84A	Griffeth	PHA 20	Michl.	CUM	84
Hugh	WAS	89	Isaac	DEL 175	Peter	CUM	108

EGE?, George	BER	267	EHRNZELLER?,			EISENBERY, Peter	PHA	60
EGEE, John	PHI	150	Jacob	BER	287B	EISENHART, Andrew	NOH	58A
EGELBERGER,			EHRO, Daniel	NOH	75	George	WAS	67
George	LAN	140	Michael	NOH	75	George	YOR	163
John	LAN	260	EHRS, Daniel	BER	272	Jacob	YOR	175
EGELER, Jacob	NOU	187	EICHARD, Jacob	NOU	182	John	NOH	58A
EGENBONE, John	DAU	2A	EICHBAUM, Wilm.	ALL	56	Samuel	NOH	58A
EGENRODE, Simon	DAU	20A	EICHELBER, George	LAN	136	EISENHAUER,		
EGENROTE, Henry	LAN	19	EICHELBERGER,			Christopher	BER	173
EGENROTH, Widow	LAN	24	Adam	YOR	184	EISENHOUER, Jacob	BER	245
EGES, Jerema.	PHI	29	Daniel	YOR	155	John	BER	245
EGGAR, Thos.	PHA	72	Deonard	YOR	214	EISENHOUR,		
EGGERT, Christian	NOH	32	Frederick	YOR	162	Leonard	YOR	198
EGGINS, Pattrick	FAY	203	John	MNT	55	EISENHOURER,		
EGLE, John	DAU	4A	John	YOR	155	Martin	BER	187
Valentine	DAU	5	John	YOR	211	EISENHUT, Bernard	BER	159
EGLER, Jerome	NOU	163	Ludwig	ADA	24	George	BER	132
EGLESTON, Joseph	PHA	22	Magdalena	YOR	183	EISENNAGEL, Henry	FAY	214
EGLETON, John	HNT	140	Michael	YOR	183	EISIG, Andrew	LAN	209
EGLEY, John	MIF	12A	Samuel	YOR	183	EIST, John	BER	256
Susanna	DAU	14A	Thomas	YOR	162	EIVIS, Andrew	NOU	149
William	MIF	12A	EICHENGER, John	YOR	174	John	NOU	149
EGLURD, James	NOU	143A	EICHHOLTZ, George	LAN	42	Thomas	NOU	149
John	NOU	143A	Leonard	LAN	36	William	NOU	149
EGMAN, Isaac	FAY	203	EICHLER, Godleib	LAN	135	EKENBERGER, Jacob	BFD	57
EGNER, Henry	BER	211	EICHLINE, Charles	BUC	80	EKENROAD, Henry	LAN	7
Peter	NOU	163	John	BUC	147	EKEROUT,		
EGNEW, Archibald	CHE	862	EICHMAN, Peter	NOH	37	Chrystian	NOU	114
Daniel	HNT	150	EICHOLTZ, George	YOR	175	EKERS, Conrad	BFD	62
Robert	BEV	27	Matthias	YOR	175	EKERT, John	PHA	109
Thomas	CHE	865	Peter	YOR	175	EKIN, Benjamin	WST	251
EGOLF, Henry	CUM	76	Philip	YOR	176	Robert	WST	251
Joseph	CUM	121	EICKLEBERGER,			EKINGS, David	ALL	90
Michl.	CUM	93	John	SOM	148	George	ALL	90
EGOLFF, Jacob	BER	256	EIDENMILLER,			John	ALL	99
Michael	BER	173	Jacob	MNT	55	John	ALL	106
EGULPH, Henry	MNT	57	EIERLAND, John	NOH	75	John	ALL	114
EGY, Anthony	BFD	72	EIFLAND, Peter	NOU	149	EKINGS?, Robert	ALL	70
EH-----N?, John	LAN	3	EIGELBERGER,			EKIS, Jas./ Jos.?	LAN	170
EHINGER, John	DAU	11A	Martin	LAN	209	EKKLES, Arthur	BEV	10
EHLENBAUM,			EIGENER, Henry	NOU	135	EKLE, Nicholas	BER	261
Frederick	BER	272	EIGER, John	NOU	149	ELAP, Michael	LAN	132
EHLER, Chrisian	LAN	59	EIGHENGER, Peter	ARM	126	ELBERSON, Widow	PHI	36
Daniel	LAN	60	EIGMIRE, Andrew	NOU	121	ELBERT, Richd.	PHA	60
Michael	DAU	50	EIGNER, Daniel	NOH	80	ELBERT?, John	MIF	10
EHRENFELT, Fredk.	BER	204	Henry	NOH	80	ELBURN, John	BFD	50
EHRENHARD, Jacob	NOH	55A	Mathias	NOH	55	ELCOCK, Mary	DEL	164
EHRENHART, Jacob	NOH	82	Mathias	NOH	80	ELCORN, George	WST	366
EHRENZELLER,			Mathias	NOH	80	John	WST	366
Catharine	PHA	68	Peter	NOH	80	ELDER, Widow	YOR	199
EHRERMAN, John	LAN	51	EIGR, William	NOU	151	Abraham	HNT	130
EHRET, George	NOH	42A	EILBERT, Jonathan	MNT	64	Andrew	PHA	98
Jacob	NOH	71	EILENBERGER,			Ann	FRA	284
EHRHART, Widow	YOR	192	Andrew	NOH	64	David	DAU	4
Christian	LAN	260	Christian	WAY	148	David	WAS	85
Jacob	YOR	194	Christn.	NOH	64	David	WAS	85
Jacob	YOR	206	Frederick	NOH	64A	David	HNT	144
John	YOR	192	EILER, Anthony	BER	238	David	FRA	322
John	NOH	42A	Christopher	NOU	192	David & Nesbit,		
Michael	YOR	186	Christopher	BER	237	John	WST	162
Philip	YOR	208	Frederick	YOR	182	G. William	SOM	132
William	YOR	193	John	YOR	184	George	BFD	57
EHRIG, George	NOH	71	Justina	BER	148	Hanah	FRA	326
EHRIGHT, Isaac	MER	441	Philippina	BER	148	James	WST	160
EHRISMAN, Abraham	LAN	101	EIMAN, Christian	LAN	281	James	YOR	197
Christian	LAN	66	EINGLE, George	NOU	135	James	FRA	322
Daniel	LAN	57	EINLEY?, James	BEV	23	James	BUT	357
George	LAN	284	EINSBY, George	ADA	5	John	ADA	33
Jacob	LAN	101	EIP, Matthias Jr.	YOR	165	John	WAS	55
Widow	LAN	101	Matthias Sr.	YOR	165	John	WAS	89
EHRMAN, Casper	LAN	45	Peter	YOR	165	John	PHA	109
Christian	LAN	146	EIPE, Jacob	YOR	207	John	WST	149
George	YOR	192	EIRICH, Geo.	BER	190	John	NOU	192
John	YOR	192	Geo. Jr.	BER	190	John	FRA	322
Peter	LAN	147	EISEHOWER,			John	FRA	322
EHRNZELLER, Jacob	BER	287B	Benjamin	DAU	9	John	FRA	323

ELDER, John	WST 378	ELIOTT, John	CRA 17	ELLIOT, William	FAY 265		
John Jr.	BFD 58	ELISON, --nd-.?	PHI 79	Wm.	CUM 38		
John	DAU 41A	ELKIN, Angle	PHA 75	Wm.	FRA 289		
Josepth	MER 441	ELKINGTON, Asa	PHA 33	ELLIOTT, Absalom	WAS 120		
Josh.	FRA 323	ELKINS, Mary	DEL 162	Andrew	ERI 56		
Joshua	DAU 4A	ELKINS?, John	ARM 127	Benjamin	DEL 167		
Lorence	YOR 192	ELKS, Henry	BUC 152A	Charles	WAS 89		
Mathew	FRA 323	ELLCOCK, Richard	YOR 210	Elias?	BEV 21		
Michael	DAU 14	ELLDER?, -----	BEV 8	Ellinnor	ALL 56		
Robert	DAU 15	ELLEBERGER, John	DAU 39	George	ALL 109		
Robert	NOU 128	ELLEBUDE, Chas.	CUM 107	George	ERI 58A		
Robert	WST 160	ELLEGAM, Geo.	PHI 18	Isaac	WAS 48		
Robert	WST 344	ELLENDER, Joseph	NOH 80	Israel Esqr.	DEL 167		
Robt.	FRA 323	ELLEOT, Alexr.	YOR 217	James	CRA 13		
Robt.	FRA 323	ELLER, Frederick	WST 235	James	WAS 55		
Samuel	DAU 2	John	HNT 147	James	ALL 109		
Samuel	ARM 123	John	HNT 153	James	DEL 183		
Samuel, Esqr.	WST 378	Ludowick	HNT 147	John	MIF 1		
Thomas	DAU 5	ELLES, Amus	FAY 226	John	PHA 8		
Thomas	WAS 28	ELLET, Robt.	YOR 212	John	WAS 28		
Thomas	NOU 192	Samuel	LAN 236	John	ALL 85		
Thos.	PHA 38	ELLEY, John	WAS 7	John			
Walter	BFD 62	Michael	WAS 7	(Shoemaker)	MIF 1		
William	WST 169	ELLICK, Christn./		John	ALL 101		
ELDERSON, James	WST 235	Christr.?	NOH 86A	John	MNT 104		
ELDERTON, James	WST 235	John	NOH 47	John	SOM 145		
ELDLER, Robert	DAU 16A	Leonard	DAU 31	John	BUT 366		
ELDRID, Edward	LYC 7	ELLICOTT, Andrew	PHA 79	John	MER 441		
ELDRIDGE, Enos	DEL 167	Thomas (Crossed		Joseph	WAS 109		
F.	PHI 47	Out)	BUC 142	Joseph	LUZ 396		
John	LYC 3	ELLIN, Rebecca	LAN 194	Mary	MIF 1		
Joseph	CHE 705	ELLINGBERGER,		Rebecca	MIF 3		
Saml.	PHA 18	John	DAU 38A	Robert	MIF 25		
Willm.	CHE 819	ELLINGER, Caspar	DAU 27A	Robert	MNT 137		
ELDUFF, Joseph M.	CHE 718	ELLIOT, -----	DAU 2A	Robert	VEN 168		
ELEBERGER, Widow	YOR 165	Alexr.	CUM 131	Robert	BUT 326		
Christian	YOR 166	Ann	CUM 95	Samuel	PHA 9		
Jacob Jr.	DAU 41A	Archd.	FRA 326	Samuel	ALL 78		
Jacob	DAU 41A	Bengn.	FRA 301	Samuel	WAS 89		
Jno.	DAU 41A	Benjamin	HNT 154	Simon	WAS 89		
Ulrich	YOR 166	Chas.	CUM 41	West	ALL 99		
ELEELE?, Wm.	CHE 788	David	CUM 76	William	PHA 95		
ELEN, William	LAN 237	Edward	FAY 235	William	BUT 317		
ELENBERGER, Chr.	DAU 44A	Felex	FAY 235	William	MER 441		
ELENBERGER?,		James	CUM 79	William	MER 441		
George	MNT 62	James	CUM 113	William	CHE 822		
ELES, Thomas	NOU 109	James	HNT 154	William Jun.	DEL 162		
ELESEBERGER?,		James	CHE 849	Willm.	PHI 36		
George	MNT 62	Jas.	CUM 38	Wilm.	ALL 64		
ELET, George	NOU 192	Jas.	CUM 88	Wm.	PHA 80		
ELEY, (See Eby)	FRA 311	Jas.	CUM 93	Wm.	PHA 82		
John	DAU 33	Johana	FRA 326	Wm.	BUT 367		
Mary	CUM 146	John	CUM 27	ELLIS, Alexander	HNT 162		
Stophel	DAU 15	John	CUM 96	Amos	MNT 115		
ELEY?, (See Eby)	FRA 310	John	WST 169	Amos	DEL 171		
ELFERY, John	DEL 180	John	WST 189	Amos	DEL 174		
ELFREY, Jacob	PHA 78	John	FAY 203	Bridget	DEL 183		
John	CUM 127	John	YOR 213	Charles	PHI 45		
ELGENFRITZ, John	YOR 161	John	FAY 235	David	PHA 94		
ELGER, Henry	YOR 210	John	CHE 751	Elisha	CHE 717		
ELGIN, Daniel	WST 149	John Junr.	FAY 203	Elnathan	LUZ 402		
James	ARM 126	John	DAU 19A	Francis	CUM 28		
James	WST 160	Johnston	FRA 286	George	ADA 20		
ELHOTT, Thos.	PHI 114	Joseph	CUM 72	Griffith	CHE 835		
ELIAS, George	YOR 199	Marcus	FAY 261	Hezekiah	WAS 43		
George	YOR 199	Moses	CHE 751	Isaac	DEL 171		
John	FAY 222	Peter	GRN 90	Isaac	DEL 173		
Mary	YOR 200	Peter	GRN 91	Jacob	CHE 789		
ELIEN, Frances	BER 176	Robt.	CUM 38	James	PHI 23		
John	BER 176	Robt.	CHE 751	James Junr.	WAS 43		
ELIGH, George	LAN 123	Simon	BER 160	James Senr.	WAS 43		
ELIN, Widow	LAN 92	Sophea	FRA 274	Jesse	DEL 173		
ELINBAUGH, Henry	BFD 69	Susanna	FRA 291	John	BUC 86		
ELINE, Joseph	BER 139	Thomas	FAY 203	John	NOU 163		
ELINGER, George	DAU 33	Thos.	CUM 41	John	DEL 166		
Jacob	DAU 47	William	GRN 110	John	WST 235		

ELLIS, John	CHE	856	ELY, George	LAN	79	EMLEY?, James	BEV	23
Jonathan	DEL	173	George Junr.	NOU	104	EMLIN, George	PHI	134
Joseph	NOU	157	George Senr.	NOU	104	EMLY, John	ALL	77
Judith	MNT	46	George	BUC	144A	EMMEL, Henry	BFD	37
Lazarus	LUZ	402	Hugh	PHI	71	EMMENHISER, John	CEN	22A
Nicholas	FRA	290	Hugh	BUC	144A	EMMERICK, Sirac	PHI	137
Robert	BEV	21	Isaac	BER	237	EMMERT, Mary	SOM	128
Roland	BUC	86	Jacob	BER	187	EMMERY, Jacob	BFD	43
Rowland	PHA	39	Jacob	LUZ	321	John	BFD	43
Stephen	NOU	157	Jacob	BUC	107A	Lewis	PHI	103A
Thomas	PHI	54	Jesse	BUC	146	Thomas	WAS	55
Thomas	BFD	70	John	BUC	86	EMMINS, Lewis	FAY	208
Thomas	NOU	163	John	BUC	144A	EMMIT, Barbara	YOR	161
Thomas	LUZ	402	Joseph	BUC	144A	John	ALL	115
Thomas	LUZ	425	Joshua Jnr.	BUC	144A	Saml.	WST	213
William	MNT	115	Joshua	BUC	144A	EMMONDS, Thos.	LYC	3
Willliam	NOU	202	Peter & Abraham	FRA	305	EMONY, Isaac	CUM	62
Wm.	LYC	10	Samuel	BER	225	EMOREY, John	PHA	77
ELLISON, Mary	CEN	20	Sarah	DEL	180	EMORY, Conrad	FAY	244
ELLISSON, Samuel	ALL	110	Wm.	BUC	86	EMPFIELD, George	BFD	62
ELLMAKER, Anthony	LAN	80	EMAN, Alexander	NOU	146	EMPTY, Jno.	BUT	332
Isaac	LAN	77	Levy	NOU	146	EMPUGH, Phillip	FRA	289
Jacob	CUM	23	EMBER, Joseph	BFD	62	EMRICH, (No Given		
Leonard	LAN	125	EMBERSON, John	PHA	45	Name)	DAU	38
Nathl.	LAN	80	EMBIGH, Bernard	DAU	25	Adam	BER	262
Widow	LAN	125	Jacob	DAU	32	Adam	BER	267
ELLMAN, Frederick	LAN	117	Stophel	DAU	25	Andrew	SOM	151
ELLOT, Mrs.	NOU	171	EMBREY, Elizabeth	CHE	784	Henry	BER	153
Thomas	NOU	117	George	CHE	783	Herman	BER	256
ELLSON, Andw.	VEN	168	George	CHE	785	Jacob	BER	256
ELLSWORTH, Henry	LUZ	395	Jas.	CHE	761	Jacob	BER	262
James	LUZ	398	Jas. Sr.	CHE	761	Jacob	NOH	64A
William	LUZ	395	John	CHE	782	John	BER	154
ELMER/ ELMES?,			Philip	CHE	782	John	BER	223
George	MNT	81	Philip	CHE	783	John	NOH	64A
ELMORE, Fredk.	PHI	97	Samuel	CHE	884	John Ad. / Od.?	BER	222
Peter	FRA	300	EMELONG, Chr.	WST	213	Joseph	NOH	64A
ELMSLIE,			EMER--?, Luswich	FRA	304	Leond.	BER	154
Alexander	PHA	15	EMERICK, Baltis	PHA	84	Michael	BER	223
ELPHENSTON,			Geo.	CUM	43	Philip	NOH	64
Thomas	PHI	150	George	PHA	46	Philip	BER	135
ELPRETH, Rachel	PHA	34	John	PHI	103A	Wm.	BER	154
ELRICK, George	BFD	57	EMERY, Jacob	PHI	99	EMRICK, Andrew	NOU	121
ELROD, Wilm.	ALL	81	John	FRA	324	Andrew	NOU	121
ELSE, Jacob	BER	207	Lawrence	BUC	154	Gasher	NOU	175
John	BER	207	Lewis	PHA	36	Jacob	NOU	121
ELSER, George	YOR	182	Mary	YOR	217	John	MNT	97
John	LAN	194	Peter	BUC	82A	Michael	NOU	121
Peter	LAN	147A	Wm.	PHI	91A	Michael	NOU	121
ELSON, Henry	CRA	6	EMES, Benj.	YOR	199	Nicholas	NOU	174
Peter	CRA	8	John	BER	251	Peter	MNT	66
Tunes	CRA	8	Valentine	BER	173	William	NOU	121
ELSROD, Peter	CUM	149	William	BER	140	EMRIK, George	DAU	12
ELSTON, Ephraim	GRN	100	Worsley	PHA	56	EMRY, Christopher	NOU	174
John	GRN	100	EMHOFF, Henry	FRA	285	Jacob	NOU	128
ELSWORTH, Daniel	PHA	116	EMICH, John	BFD	72	Jacob	NOU	192
Jas.	BUT	355	Michael	BFD	72	John	MNT	75
ELTON, Joseph	PHA	68	EMIG, Charles	YOR	188	John	MNT	82
Robert	MIF	25	EMIGH, George	YOR	178	John	NOU	117
Robert	MIF	4A	George	YOR	189	John	NOU	192
ELURD, John	NOU	143A	John	YOR	161	John	NOU	192
ELURT, William	FRA	288	John	YOR	189	Joseph	NOU	192
ELWOOD, James	FRA	298	John	YOR	191	Peter	NOU	149
Robert	FAY	231	Michael	YOR	188	William	NOU	192
Wm.	WST	366	Valentine	YOR	161	William	NOU	192
ELY, Aaron	BER	259	EMILY, Wilm.	ALL	120	EMS, Henry	PHI	112A
Abner	BUC	86	EMINGER, Andw.	CUM	63	EMY, John	LAN	138
Abner	BUC	146	Conrod	CUM	63	ENCK, Jacob	ADA	32
Abraham & Peter	FRA	305	EMISON, Stephen	WAY	140	ENDICH, Michael	FAY	240
Adam	LAN	71	EMIT, Anna	ARM	125	ENDLER, Jacob	YOR	155
Amos	BUC	144A	John	NOU	143A	ENDLICH, Michael		
Arthur	CHE	864	Samuel	NOU	143A	Jun.	FAY	240
Ashur	BUC	146	EMLEN, Ann	PHA	85	ENDSLEY, Thomas	ALL	111
Calab	NOU	104	George	PHA	102	ENDSLOW, Thomas	BEV	27
Danl.	BER	237	Warder	PHA	76	Wm.	CUM	41
David	BER	280	EMLET, Michael	ADA	31	ENEFER, James	PHA	79

Name	Loc	Pg
ENEKE, Lewis	NOH	75
ENGARIM, Arthur	FRA	286
ENGEL, Chn.	NOH	37
Conrad	LAN	3
Frederick	LAN	85
George	LAN	148
George	LAN	251
George	NOH	64A
Henry	NOH	73
Jacob	NOH	73
Sarah Widow	NOH	73
ENGELBERT,		
Leonard	PHA	17A
ENGELHART, John	LAN	90
ENGELMAN, Adam	NOH	55A
Andrew Jr.	NOH	55A
Andrew	NOH	55A
Daniel	PHA	62
Peter	NOH	55A
Solomon	NOH	80
ENGELSWORTH,		
Andrew	NOU	128
ENGHART, Charles	PHI	155
Jacob	MNT	131
Mary	MNT	130
Nicholas	MNT	110
Philip	MNT	132
William	MNT	132
ENGLAND, David	WAS	79
Israil	FAY	265
John	BFD	50
Joseph	GRN	110
Moses	DAU	22
Nun	HNT	129
Robert	GRN	110
Samuel Esqr.	WAS	48
Sarah	CHE	742
William	DAU	13
William	LAN	179
William	CHE	758
ENGLE, Barbara	PHI	127
Benj.	PHI	77A
Benjamin	PHI	147
Charles	PHI	129
Christian	NOH	80
Clemmence	SOM	148
Edward	DEL	162
Elias	DEL	176
Francis	PHA	42
George	MIF	1
George Esqr.	PHI	71
Goerge Junr.	NOH	64A
Henry	MNT	98
Henry	BER	209
Isaac	DEL	180
Jacob	MNT	69
Jacob	MNT	98
Jacob	BUC	143
Jacob	PHI	146
Jacob	BER	277
Jacob	DAU	20A
John	LAN	67
John	MNT	98
John	NOU	121
John	NOU	121
John	PHI	128
John Henry	BER	166
Joseph	PHI	146
Joseph	DEL	162
Joseph	PHI	70A
Peter	LAN	25
Thomas	BUC	83A
ENGLEHART, Geo.	BER	161
Henry	PHI	53A
Jacob	BER	215
ENGLEHAUBT, John	BER	129
ENGLEMAN, Mary	VEN	165
ENGLEMOOR, Peter	YOR	157
ENGLER, Casper	NOH	73
George	NOH	62A
Jacob	NOH	73
John George	NOH	62A
Leonard	NOH	73
ENGLES, James	PHI	36
John	PHI	44
ENGLIN?, George	WAY	139
ENGLIS, George	HNT	136
John	MNT	43
ENGLISH, Andrew	BEV	4
Andrew	FAY	220
David	CUM	35
David	WST	323
James	BEV	21
John	WAS	79
John	DEL	162
John	CHE	890
John	PHI	102A
Samuel	ALL	108
Thomas	BEV	20
Thos.	PHI	114
William	ADA	39
Wm.	CUM	24
ENIES, Robert	WST	271
ENIS, James		
(Jesse		
Crossed Out)	MIF	7
John	NOU	163
ENIX, Brice	FAY	231
John	FAY	231
ENK, Jacob	YOR	179
ENLOWS, Abraham	WAS	48
Elliott	WAS	48
Luke	WAS	48
ENNALEY?, Saml.	LYC	18
ENNESLEY, George	LUZ	346
ENNIS, Joshua	HNT	156
Robert	BUC	88A
ENNIS?, Robert		
(Crossed Out)	BUC	90
ENNSLEY?, Saml.	LYC	18
ENOCH, David	WAS	120
Henry	WAS	37
ENOCHS, Jonathan	PHI	153
ENOCK, Joseph	MNT	66
ENOCO, Obadiah	LYC	12
ENOK, George	LAN	140
John	LAN	140
ENOS, Widow	PHI	22
Widow	PHI	68A
George	SOM	133
James	PHI	96A
John	SOM	133
ENOX, Thomas	DEL	165
ENRICK, Valantine	MNT	72
ENSEMENGEL, Jacob	FAY	244
ENSLEY, James	FRA	314
John	FRA	314
Solomon	WAS	37
ENSLO, Abner·	MIF	4A
ENSLOW,		
Christopher	BFD	50
George Jr.	BFD	50
ENSMINGER,		
Christr.	CUM	66
Danl.	DAU	41A
Henry	CUM	57
Henry	FRA	295
Jacob	CUM	133
Jonathn.	DAU	41A
Mary	YOR	165
Michl.	DAU	3
Michl.	DAU	3
ENSMINGER, Peter	DAU	41A
Samuel	LAN	250
ENSWORTH, Jacob	ERI	57A
John	PHI	17
Lars?	DAU	35
Peggy	DAU	36A
ENTE, John	BER	256
ENTERLY, John	DAU	7A
Michael	DAU	7A
ENTERS, John	DAU	29
ENTRES,		
Christopher	FRA	297
Nicholas	YOR	180
ENTRICKEN, George	CHE	760
ENTRIKEN, Caleb	CHE	805
James	HNT	119
James	CHE	776
Saml.	CHE	805
Samuel	CHE	704
ENTY, Mathias	BER	185
Philip	BER	185
Tobias	MNT	110
ENYART, William	HNT	116
ENZLIN?, George	WAY	139
EOK, Joseph	NOU	154
EPHOT, Michael	NOU	179
EPINGTON, Jos.	YOR	168
EPLER, Christly	DAU	20A
David	DAU	16A
George	BER	150
Jacob	BER	148
Jacob	BER	148
Jacob	BER	148
John	NOU	135
John	BER	142
John	BER	148
Peter Senr.	BER	148
Philip	BER	148
EPLEY, Willm.	DAU	21A
EPLIE, Andw.	PHA	29
EPLING, John	PHI	113A
EPPELY, Henry	YOR	217
Jacob	YOR	188
John	YOR	218
EPPLE, Henry	NOH	29A
John	NOU	97
EPPLE?, Peter	YOR	187
EPPLER, John A.	BER	142
Peter	BER	148
EPPLEY, Jacob	YOR	156
EPPLY, Henry	YOR	162
Jacob	YOR	154
Martin	NOU	97
Peter	YOR	183
EPPRIGHT, Jacob	DAU	4A
EPRIGHT, Henry	DEL	171
Jacob	DEL	171
Jacob	DEL	173
John	DEL	178
ERACH, Peter	WAS	67
ERB, Casper	MNT	60
Christ	LAN	147B
Christian	LAN	147A
Daniel	LAN	141
Daniel	LAN	144
David	ADA	35
Frederick	BUC	100A
Henry	MNT	60
Henry 2nd	MNT	61
Jacob	MNT	54
Jacob	LAN	142
Jacob	LAN	195
Jacob	FRA	284
Jacob	NOH	62A
John	MNT	60
John	LAN	141

Name	Loc	Name	Loc	Name	Loc
ERB, John	LAN 144	ERNST, Nicholas	BER 255	ESHENBACH, David	BUC 158A
John	YOR 172	Paul	BER 209	John	BER 166
John	LAN 147A	ERNY, John	BER 207	Widow	NOH 47
Lewis	NOH 73	EROC, Joseph	NOU 154	ESHENBACK, John	NOH 47
Low.	NOH 37	ERP, Philip	DAU 30	ESHENOWER, Caspar	DAU 14A
Michael	NOH 37	Robert	PHI 151	Christn.	DAU 14
Michael	LAN 106	ERRET, John	WST 213	ESHLEMAN,	
Peter	MNT 60	ERRETTE, George	PHA 104	Christian	LAN 258
Peter	LAN 144	ERRIGER, Fredk.	PHI 108A	Henry	LAN 289
Urristead	FRA 284	ERRINGER, Widw.	PHI 108	Isaac	LAN 258
ERBEN, John	LAN 209	ERRIS, Elizabeth	LAN 94	Jacob	LAN 139
Margaret	PHI 137	ERRIT, Christian	WST 212	Jacob	LAN 258
ERCHHOLZ, John	LAN 34	ERSHUN, Widow	LAN 254	Jacob Junr.	LAN 230
ERD, Widow	NOH 32	ERSKINE, Thomas	GRN 91	Jacob Senr.	LAN 226
ERDMAN, Jacob	NOH 80	Thos.	CUM 148	Jacob Senr.	LAN 258
John	NOH 80	William	WAS 115	John	LAN 11
ERDMANN, Chas	PHA 8	ERTMAN, Abraham	BER 282	John	LAN 226
EREART, Phillip	NOU 163	George	BER 282	John	LAN 258
EREMAN, Wm.	PHA 40	ERUPAUGH?, Geo.	CUM 46	John	LAN 290
ERFORD, Henry	LAN 287	ERVIN, Hugh	PHA 69	Martin	LAN 233
Jacob	LAN 310	John	PHA 76	Martin Sr.	LAN 233
John	LAN 310	ERWIN, David	WAS 12	Samuel	LAN 236
Widow	LAN 310	James	SOM 148	ESHLIMAN, Abraham	FRA 305
ERGOOD, Jacob	BER 274	Jared	MER 441	ESICK, Jacob	FRA 281
ERGOT, Sebastian	BER 247	John	PHI 38	ESIG, Simon	CUM 119
ERHARD, George	LAN 86	John	MNT 46	ESINGTON, Joseph	FAY 208
M.	LAN 55	John	MNT 67	ESIS?, Dennis	MNT 43
ERHART, Jacob	LAN 260	John	MNT 137	ESLENPIFER, Jacob	PHA 74
ERICH, George	NOH 82	John	CHE 737	ESLICK, Alexander	WAY 144
John	SOM 137	Joseph	BUC 149	ESLIN, Nicholas	PHA 85
Peter	SOM 137	Robert	PHI 41	ESPENSHEDE,	
ERICK, John	YOR 170	Robert	MER 441	Valentn.	DAU 15
ERIE?, Dennis	MNT 43	Robt.	PHA 84	ESPEY, Rachel	CUM 103
ERINS, David	PHI 1	Widow	NOH 37	Thos.	CUM 105
ERION, Jacob	YOR 160	William	BUC 149	Wm.	PHA 75
ERIS, Chandly	NOU 157	William	MER 441	Wm.	CUM 105
ERIS?, Dennis	MNT 43	ERY?, Conroad	ALL 96	ESPIE, Christian	WST 213
ERISMAN, Daniel	DAU 13A	ESAL, John	PHI 54	George	LUZ 329
ERLENHEISEN,		ESBIN, John	PHI 39	ESPY, George	FAY 265
Peter	YOR 206	ESBURN, Jonathn.	PHI 25	Jacob	WST 288
ERLEWINE, John	GRN 111	ESBY, David	DEL 175	Jane	BFD 35
ERLING, Mary	PHA 109	ESCHBAM, Ab.	LAN 148	Joseph	DAU 16A
ERLY, James	FRA 271	ESCHELMAN, John	LAN 277	Josiah Esq.	SOM 132
ERMAN, George	LAN 45	ESH, Christian	NOH 62A	ESS, William	PHI 17
ERMEL, Isaac	BER 172	Henry	NOH 62A	ESSECK, Basler	CHE 790
ERMOLT, Mary	DAU 16A	Michael Jr.		George	CHE 792
Peter	DAU 16A	(Henry		ESSELMAN, John	CUM 24
ERNEST, Baltis	MNT 130	Crossed Out)	NOH 62A	ESSENGER, Peter	CUM 41
Henry	WST 212	Michael	NOH 62A	ESSER, George	BER 210
Henry	PHI 75A	Nicholas	NOH 35A	Jacob	BER 210
Martin	BER 151	ESHBACH,		ESSERY, Joseph	DEL 179
ERNHART, Jacob	MNT 107	Christian	BER 207	ESSEX, Dick	DEL 191
ERNIG, Christian	HNT 151	George	NOH 82	Henry	CHE 817
Christian	HNT 151	Henry	BER 207	Richard	DEL 160
Christian	HNT 151	John	NOH 47	Rudolph	CHE 724
Peter	HNT 151	John	LAN 102	ESSICK, Adam	ADA 20
ERNOLD, George	YOR 168	John Jr.	NOH 47	George	ADA 41
ERNOT, Adam	LAN 147A	Michael	LAN 103	ESTBOWRNE, Joseph	PHA 43
ERNSMINGER,		ESHBACK, Anthony	NOH 80	ESTEP, John	HNT 119
George	YOR 214	Peter	BER 207	ESTER, Adam	PHA 94
ERNST, Abm.	BER 256	ESHELMAN, Abraham	LAN 268	Adam	FAY 214
Christian	NOH 75	Benedict	LAN 279	Conrad	FAY 220
Conrad	NOH 70	Benedict	LAN 281	George	FAY 214
Conrad	BER 258	Christian	LAN 268	Jacob	FAY 214
Dichus	BER 229	Christian Jun.	LAN 268	John	FAY 214
Frederick	BER 129	Christn.	DAU 20	Marcus	FAY 214
Henry	LAN 53	David	BER 172	ESTERDAY, David	PHI 20
Henry	BER 187	Henry	DAU 45A	Jacob	FAY 214
Ignatius	YOR 177	Jacob	NOH 80	ESTERLEIN, Daniel	NOH 32
Jacob	CUM 39	Jacob	BUC 147	ESTERLIN,	
John	YOR 161	John	DAU 47	Christo.	DAU 41A
John	YOR 183	John	NOH 80	Frederick	NOU 135
John	BER 190	Martin	BER 172	ESTERLINE,	
John	BER 229	Peter	DAU 20	Elizath.	MNT 97
John	BER 256	Peter	BER 172	Peter	MNT 60
Michael	NOH 47	ESHENBACH, Andw.	NOH 83A	ESTERLY, Daniel	BER 179

ESTERLY, Jacob	BER 282	EVANS, Amos	MNT 112	EVANS, Jeremiah	CHE 904
ESTHERLEY, George	PHA 81	Andrew	GRN 105	Jesse	MIF 7
ESTIL, John	MNT 65	Ann	GRN 81	Jesse	BER 280
ESTILL, Briton	PHA 31	Ann	DEL 173	Jesse	MIF 16A
John	LUZ 337	Ann	LAN 301	Job	DEL 170
Joseph	CHE 710	Benjamin	DEL 182	Joel	LAN 149
ESTIP, James	HNT 147	Cadwalader	PHA 72	John	PHA 6
Nathaniel	HNT 146	Cadwallader	BFD 50	John	NOH 41
Robert	WAS 74	Cadwallader	WAS 79	John	MNT 44
William	HNT 119	Cadwallador	DEL 179	John	WAS 48
William	HNT 147	Caleb	LAN 221	John	PHA 55
ESTON, John	LAN 260	Charles	PHA 79	John	MNT 67
ESTTERT, John	YOR 213	Charles	BER 237	John	GRN 75
ESWORTHY, Nathan	DEL 156	Charles	LAN 301	John	GRN 95
ETCHBERGER, Peter	BER 265	Daniel	CHE 817	John	BUC 96
ETCHHELL, Wm.	CHE 774	Daniel Esq.	CHE 815	John	MNT 118
ETERSBURN, Peter	WAS 67	David	ALL 49	John	BER 137
ETHER, Henry	FRA 283	David	PHA 71	John	HNT 139
ETINMILLER,		David	PHA 123	John	WST 149
Michael	MNT 55	David	MNT 141	John	SOM 157
ETISINPARIOR?,		David	LAN 160	John	BER 161
Devault	ALL 74	David	DEL 183	John	DEL 178
ETKINS, William	GRN 78	David	BER 274	John	LAN 300
ETMAN, Henry	CHE 785	David Junr.	WAS 2	John	LUZ 357
ETON, George	ALL 111	David Senr.	WAS 2	John	BUT 363
James	PHI 41	David	PHI 103A	John	CHE 704
Joseph	MNT 127	David	BUC 104A	John	CHE 790
Ritchard	ALL 109	Edward	PHI 8	John	CHE 797
Thomas	ALL 111	Edward	DEL 173	John	CHE 800
Wm.	PHI 88A	Edward	DEL 177	John	CHE 819
ETRESS, John	PHA 56	Eli	CHE 908	John	CHE 878
Wm.	PHA 56	Elisha	MNT 81	John Junr.	MNT 44
ETRIS, James	PHI 34	Elisha	CHE 904	John	NOH 64A
ETSLEMAN, Henry	MNT 60	Elizabeth	PHA 13	John B.	PHA 95
ETSLER, George	ADA 31	Elizabeth	PHI 136	John B.	PHA 106
ETSWILER, Fredrik	DAU 6	Elizabeth	DEL 183	Jonatha	PHA 123
ETTENEIER, Mary	DAU 5	Elizabeth	CEN 22A	Jonathan	MNT 71
ETTER, Abraham	LAN 12	Ellis	BFD 62	Jonathan	DEL 170
Christian	YOR 189	Enoch	BUC 143	Jonathan	CHE 832
George	PHA 80	Enos	CHE 795	Joseph	WAS 2
John	LAN 10	Evan	BFD 50	Joseph	DAU 19
John	YOR 193	Evan	MNT 87	Joseph	PHA 62
John	DAU 22A	Evan (See		Joseph	BUC 143
ETTINGER, Abraham	MNT 89	Evans, Widow)	NOH 29A	Joseph	BUT 318
Abraham	DAU 8A	Evan	DEL 170	Joseph	CHE 784
Adam	YOR 176	Evan	DEL 179	Joseph	CHE 820
John	BUC 93	Evan	CHE 815	Joseph	CHE 896
John Junr.	BUC 93A	Evan Esqr.	CHE 817	Joseph	CHE 904
Manuel	NOH 85	Even	GRN 100	Levi	CHE 820
Philip	DAU 8A	Ezekiel	CHE 820	Lewis	SOM 161
ETTLEY, David	DAU 13A	Fthames?	CHE 787	Margaret	PHA 39
ETTLY, Philip	DAU 13A	George	GRN 80	Margaret	WST 149
ETTON, Isaac	FAY 226	George	SOM 132	Mark	LAN 113
ETTOR, Saml.	CUM 76	Griffeth	PHA 39	Mark	HNT 161
ETTWEIN, John		Henry	BUT 340	Martin	BER 284
Rev.	NOH 32	Hugh	SOM 161	Mary	BUC 96
Regina Widow	NOH 32	Hugh	CHE 730	Michael	YOR 205
ETWINE, Widw.	PHI 107	Isaac	LAN 114	Nathan	LAN 124
ETZEL, Andrew	BER 172	Isaac	LAN 235	Nathan	BER 163
ETZLER, Andrew	BER 159	Isaac	BUT 347	Nathan	DEL 183
Andw.	YOR 180	Isaiah	PHA 66	Oliver	PHA 74
ETZWILER, George	NOU 135	Isaiah	PHA 117	Owen	MNT 73
EUCK, Jacob	LAN 194	J./ I.? John	SOM 161	Owen	MNT 81
EUING, John	CRA 18	Jacob	PHI 43	Owen	MNT 117
EULERY, Fredk.	PHI 52	Jacob	MNT 69	Peter	PHA 57
EUST, Obediah	NOU 143A	James	ALL 71	Peter	MNT 87
EUSTOR, James	PHI 28	James	MNT 72	Peter	PHA 106
EVAN, John	PHI 154	James	MNT 81	Peter	MNT 137
Thomas	PHA 117	James	BUC 143	Philip	BER 172
EVANS, Abel	PHI 69	James	LAN 143	Randal	CHE 833
Abner	PHI 59	James	NOU 154	Richard	BUC 143
Abner	DEL 170	James	SOM 161	Robt.	PHA 68
Abraham	WAS 2	James	CHE 790	Roland	CHE 878
Adna	MNT 72	James Junr.	MNT 72	Samuel	MNT 72
Amos	BFD 62	James	BUC 104A	Samuel	MNT 117
Amos	MNT 72	Jenkin	BUC 104A	Samuel	WAS 120

EVANS, Samuel	LAN 121	EVERHART,			EVERLY, Jacob	DAU	13
Samuel	LAN 124	Adulphs.	FAY	244	Jacob	PHI	77
Samuel	MNT 137	Anthony	PHI	69A	Jno.	CUM	61
Samuel	DEL 155	Benjn.	CHE	795	John	CHE	816
Samuel Junr.	MNT 73	Christn.	CEN	22A	Leonard	WAS	43
Sarah	MNT 44	Conrad	NOH	55	Nicholas	FAY	214
Sarah	PHA 70	Elizabeth	WAS	12	Peter	FRA	281
Septimus	CHE 801	Frederick	NOH	78	Wm.	CUM	31
Susannah	MNT 137	Fredrick	ARM	122	EVERMAN, Benjn.	CUM	111
Thomas	MNT 44	George	HNT	127	Jacob	PHI	142
Thomas	LAN 111	Henry	NOH	55	John	PHI	119
Thomas	MNT 111	Henry	WAS	109	EVERRARD, Thos.	PHI	74A
Thomas	PHA 114	Jacob	MNT	47	EVERS?, (See		
Thomas	BER 252	James	CHE	795	Overs?)	CUM	59
Thomas	LUZ 364	John	WAS	12	EVERSOHL, Abrm.	DAU	15A
Thomas	CHE 777	John	HNT	127	EVERSOL, Jacob	CUM	86
Thomas	CHE 793	John	MNT	130	John	FRA	282
Thomas	CHE 797	John	BER	175	Peter Jr.	DAU	22A
Thomas	CHE 797	John	BER	281	Peter	DAU	22A
Thomas	CHE 820	John	FRA	295	EVERSOLE,		
Thomas	CEN 22A	John	BUC	100A	Christian	LAN	10
Thomas	BUC 88A	Joseph	NOH	55A	John	LAN	10
Thos.	CUM 115	Josepth	MER	441	Peter	DAU	24
Thos.	YOR 214	Mathias	BER	184	EVERSON, Barnet	FAY	231
Thos.	FRA 285	Michael	YOR	184	EVERSOUL, Widow	LAN	257
Walter	MNT 87	Peter	CEN	22A	EVERST, Abel	MIF	15
Walter	WST 212	Philip	WAS	28	EVERT, Godlip	FRA	326
Widow	LAN 156	Philip	NOH	55	John	ADA	42
Widow Of Evan	NOH 29A	Saml.	CEN	22A	Michl.	WST	212
Wilder	LAN 210	Torob?	ARM	122	Phillip	FRA	319
William	LAN 113	Widow	CHE	795	EVERY, Fredk.	PHI	26
William	LAN 124	EVERHEART,			EVEY, Henry	CUM	89
William	LAN 128	Bernard	NOU	187	John	HNT	144
William	LAN 130	Chr.	WST	189	Moses	CUM	89
William	WST 149	Frederick	NOU	187	EVIGE, Adam	NOU	135
William	DEL 162	Frederick	NOU	187	EVIL, Christian	SOM	141
William	BER 163	John	NOU	187	EVIN?, Johnathan	LYC	25
William	DEL 181	Michl.	FRA	285	EVINGER, Thomas	PHI	134
William	DEL 185	EVERINGEM, James	GRN	93	EVINS, Abner	CRA	13
William	LUZ 342	EVERIT, Godfrey	WST	308	Evin	FAY	220
William	CHE 822	Joseph	BFD	72	Frederick	NOU	135
William	CHE 883	Joseph	WST	308	John	MIF	3
Wm.	CUM 51	Peter	WST	213	John	FAY	220
EVANSON, Aaron	CHE 805	EVERITT,			John	FRA	290
George	CHE 812	Alexander	NOH	66A	Nathen	NOU	192
Seth	CHE 703	Conrad	NOH	44A	EVINSEY, Dewel	PHI	84A
EVE, Adam	MNT 104	Ephenetas	NOH	64A	EVNAS, Morgan	LAN	123
Daniel	CHE 859	Garret	NOH	66A	EVY, John	LAN	250
EVEANS, David	CEN 22A	Henry	NOH	35A	EWALT, Jacob	CUM	152
Sarah	ALL 119	Jacob	NOH	35A	Jno.	CUM	35
EVELING, Valentn.	DAU 16	John Senr.	NOH	44A	John	BFD	50
EVEN?, Even -?	PHI 90A	John	NOH	35A	Ludwig	LAN	57
EVENER, Conrad	NOH 75	John	NOH	44A	Richard	BFD	72
Lowrence	NOH 75	Lowrence	NOH	44A	Samuel Esqr.	ALL	57
EVENS, Andrew	WAR 1A	Michael	NOH	44A	EWARD, John	LAN	69
Benjeman	FAY 197	Peter	NOH	52A	EWART, Archibald	GRN	92
James	NOU 109	Samuel Esqr.	NOH	52A	James	WAS	109
Jesse	FAY 244	Thomas	NOH	52A	James	BUT	357
John	FAY 197	Thos.	NOH	82	EWE, Danl.	CUM	100
R. Evens	NOU 97	EVERLEIGH, Henry	CUM	64	EWEING, John	CHE	867
EVERALL, Nicholas	HNT 165	EVERLEY, Adam	PHA	15	EWEN, William	ERI	55A
EVERBERT, Jonas	WST 235	Adam	GRN	75	EWERS, Robert	BUC	155
EVERCROMEY, John	ALL 110	Henry	SOM	145	EWIG, John	DAU	8A
EVERD, Daniel	NOH 75	Jacob	PHA	86	EWIN, Emus	ALL	100
EVERET, Adam	BFD 42	John	PHA	86	Jain	ALL	101
Aron	BUC 160A	Michael	LAN	165	Joseph	NOU	128
Isaac	ADA 43	EVERLIN, Henry	PHI	95A	Moses	ALL	106
Jacob	BUC 160A	Sigmon	BER	190	Samuel	ALL	100
EVERETT, Elisha	NOH 64	EVERLY, Widw.	PHI	102A	Samuel Senr.	ALL	100
John	NOH 52A	Christ.	FRA	301	Thomas	CHE	711
EVERHARD,		Christian	BER	275	EWING, Adam	WST	212
Frederick	BUC 139	Christn.	BER	190	Alexander	HNT	144
Widow	NOH 37	Danl.	BER	190	Alexander	LAN	153
EVERHARDT, John	PHI 39	George	DAU	32A	Alexander	WST	235
John	PHI 44	Henry	HNT	118	Alexander	MER	441
EVERHART, Adam	WAS 98	Henry Junr.	HNT	118	Alexd.	ALL	107

EWING, Alexr.	WST 213	EYAMS, Richard	GRN 109	FACK, William	ARM 123
Alexr. Junr.	YOR 202	EYCK, Arthur	LUZ 325	FACKENTHALL,	
Alexr. Junr.	YOR 204	EYDEL, Conard	PHI 126	Henry	BUC 147A
Alexr. Sr.	YOR 204	EYER, John	DAU 25	Michael	BUC 80
Allexander	BEV 21	John	NOH 64A	FACKLER, Adam	DAU 3A
Archibald	NOU 174	Martin	NOH 64A	George	DAU 16
Cathne.	PHI 11	EYERES, John	PHI 65	John	DAU 16A
David	PHA 82	EYERLY, Jacob	NOH 70	Vendle	DAU 16
David	FAY 252	Widow Of Jacob	NOH 70	FADDES, John	CHE 751
Isaac	ADA 21	EYERMAN, Mathias	NOH 37	Robert	CHE 848
James	WAS 28	EYERS, Jesue	PHI 88	FADDIS, Abiah	CHE 769
James	WST 149	Jonathan	LAN 229	John	CHE 759
James	YOR 166	Lidia	PHI 88	FADE, John	LUZ 349
James	YOR 202	Saml.	PHA 57	FADELEY, Peter	SOM 148
James Esqr.	ALL 107	EYHART, Alexr.	PHI 16	FADLER, Stephen	NOU 193
James Junr.	BEV 26	EYLER, Andw.	CUM 105	FADLEY, Adam	SOM 148
James S.	PHA 70	Jacob	CUM 87	FADNEY, Michl.	CUM 23
James Segnr.	BEV 26	EYLER?/ EYLES?,		FAEGER, George	DAU 40A
John	ADA 10	James	PHI 134	John	DAU 4
John	WAS 67	EYOND, Jacob	NOU 187	FAGAN, Alexander	WAS 90
John	PHA 69	Peter	NOU 187	Asaph	HNT 158
John	CUM 114	EYRE, Caleb	DEL 164	Harman	HNT 129
John	HNT 158	Frederick	CHE 788	Peter	HNT 139
John	WST 160	Isaac, Esqr.	DEL 162	FAGART, Archibald	PHA 75
John	NOU 174	John	DEL 164	FAGELEY, George	MNT 98
John	WST 235	Jonas Esqr.	DEL 162	John	MNT 57
John	CHE 868	Nathan	PHA 26	Jonathan	MNT 57
John	CHE 910	Nathaniel	DEL 158	Yost	MNT 54
John Sen.	ADA 24	William	DEL 157	FAGEN?, Joseph	
Joshua	NOU 128	EYRES, Abijah	PHI 83A	M.?	CHE 851
Mary	PHA 89	Charles	MNT 66	FAGET, George	NOU 193
Mathew	FRA 326	David	MNT 82	FAGHINDER, David	ALL 118
Matthew	CHE 748	George	PHI 88A	FAGIN, George	LAN 109
Nathaniel	FAY 213	John	PHI 96A	Thomas	BFD 69
Robert	ADA 24	Manuel Esqr.	PHI 88	FAGUNDIS, John	CHE 751
Robert	WST 160	EYSHAWER,		FAGY, George	LAN 122
Robert	FAY 213	Christian	MNT 103	FAHLER, Leonard	BER 237
Robert	WST 235	EYSTER, Adam	YOR 163	FAHNASTOCK,	
Samuel	ALL 111	Conrad	YOR 163	Deitrich	LAN 195
Samuel	HNT 163	Elias	YOR 163	Peter	LAN 195
Samuel	HNT 166	George Jr.	YOR 161	FAHNER, John	BEV 10
Samuel	CHE 748	George Senr.	YOR 161	FAHNESTOCK,	
Samuel, Junr	HNT 166	Peter	MIF 5	Boreas?	ADA 33
Thomas	PHA 15	Peter	YOR 178	Conrad	DAU 4
Thomas	CRA 16	Widow	ADA 31	George	ADA 34
Thomas	MIF 25	EYWALT, Henry	DAU 30	Henry	DAU 4
Thomas	LAN 96	EZE, George	BER 267	Jacob	ADA 33
Thomas	HNT 166			Obed	DAU 2A
Thomas Esqr.	ADA 12	F----?, Enos?	LYC 25	Saml.	ADA 34
Thomas, Junr.	HNT 166	James	BEV 16	Samuel	LAN 41
Thos.	CHE 749	William?	MIF 10	William	YOR 208
Widow	LAN 155	F---?, John	BEV 11	FAHNMAN, Jacob	YOR 183
William	ADA 11	F-ISTER?, Godfrey	LYC 16	FAHNSTOCK, Chas.	CHE 735
William	PHA 121	FA--DAYS?, Geo	PHI 112A	FAHS, Henry	YOR 172
William	LAN 153	FAAS, Philip	NOH 71	Jacob	YOR 156
William	HNT 157	FABER, Adam	DAU 35	Jacob Jr.	YOR 157
William	WST 189	Jacob	DAU 34	John	YOR 162
William	CHE 748	Jacob	DAU 48A	Jos.	YOR 160
William Esquire	FAY 226	John	BER 179	FAIKS, Charles	FAY 240
Willm.	PHI 31	Margaret	DAU 48A	FAIL, Philip	ADA 16
Wilm.	ALL 107	Michael	DAU 26A	Valentine	ADA 16
Wilm.	ALL 111	Philip	DAU 48A	FAILOR, John	HNT 149
Wm.	CUM 115	FABION, Casper	BUC 80	FAILS, Alexr.	WST 344
Wm.	DAU 15A	Casper Jnr.	BUC 80	Thomas	WST 366
EWING?, See Owing	BEV 16	George	BUC 80	FAILURE, Andw.	CUM 134
EWINS, Hugh	WST 378	Henry	BUC 147A	Christian	CUM 129
EWIS, John	NOU 157	Michael	BUC 147	Facob	CUM 134
Joseph	NOU 157	FABLE, Anthy.	PHI 118	Leonard	CUM 129
EWORTS, John	CHE 788	Geo.	PHI 118	FAINES?, William	PHI 65
EXLER, Samuel	DAU 44	George	PHI 70	FAIR, Jacob	NOH 47
EXLEY, John	PHA 41	FABOR, Abraham	LUZ 412	Jacob	BER 161
EXLINE, Adam	BFD 50	FACELTON?, John	BEV 8	John	BER 161
Henry	BFD 50	FACEY, John	PHA 94	John	BUT 333
John	BFD 50	FACHT, Peter	DAU 34	Michl.	BUT 333
EXPORT, Widow	PHI 41	FACK, James	ARM 123	Philip	BER 247
EXTINE, Jacob	PHA 38	John	ARM 123	FAIRBEARN, John	PHA 88

FAIRBER?, John	PHI	45	FANSLER, Peter	DAU	43A	FARRELL, Thos.	PHA	93
FAIRCHILD,			Philip	DAU	29A	FARRENCE?, John	PHI	137
Abraham	LUZ	347	FANSTOCK, Casper	CHE	733	FARRENTON,		
Elizabeth	FAY	244	FANTZER?,			Abraham	FAY	235
Ephraim	LUZ	393	Christn.	DAU	29A	FARRER, Jesse	PHI	18
John	LUZ	347	FANY, Patrick	LAN	96	FARRIER, Hugh		
Steven	FAY	197	FARA, Thomas	YOR	216	(Crossed Out)	WST	379
FAIRLAMB,			FARALEY, Owen	PHI	97	John	MNT	107
Fredrick	DEL	175	FARAN, Mrs.	LYC	25	Neal	CHE	810
John	DEL	179	FARE, Francis	SOM	133	Thomas	WST	379
Nicholas Esqr.	DEL	162	John	FAY	256	William	WST	379
Robert	DEL	177	John	WST	344	FARRILL, Wm.	FRA	287
FAIRMAN, James	CEN	18A	Peter	WST	150	FARRINGER, Henry	MNT	110
FAIRWEATHER,			FARECHILD, Calob	NOU	128	Jacob	LAN	103
Edward	NOU	171	FAREE, John	ALL	60	John	MNT	107
FAISTER, Alexd.	ALL	62	FARES, John	PHI	20	FARRIS, Ichiel?	LUZ	407
FAITH, Abraham	SOM	128	FARES?, William	PHI	65	Robert	FAY	244
Jacob	SOM	157	FAREY?, Herman			FARRO, James	YOR	210
James	LAN	171	Jnr.	NOH	62A	FARRON, Robert	PHI	56
Thomas	SOM	157	Herman Senr.	NOH	62A	FARROW, Samuel	WAS	85
FALCK, Daniel	NOH	85	FARGURSON, David	ALL	120	FARTBINDER, Wm.	LYC	22
George	NOH	85	FARIDY, John	PHI	84A	FARTEGH, John	MIF	15
George	NOH	51A	FARIES, Joseph	NOU	198	FARTZINGER, Jacob	NOH	29A
FALCKENBACH,			FARING, Widow	PHI	97	FARVER, Adam	BFD	54
Peter	YOR	217	FARIS, James	BUC	86A	FARWEL, Edward	LYC	19
FALCONER, Abraham	WAS	109	John	DEL	169	FASEY?, (See		
Elisabeth	WAS	109	Josiah	BUC	93A	Farey?)	NOH	62A
Nathaniel	PHA	45	Moses	HNT	157	FASHOLD,		
Samuel	WAS	109	Thos.	PHI	101	Valentine	NOH	89A
William	PHI	18	FARLEE, Geo.	DAU	35	FASHOLT, Caspar	NOH	89A
FALER, James	PHI	45	FARLEY, Andrew	WAS	49	FASNACH, Adam	LAN	85
John	DAU	39	Andrew	GRN	111	John	LAN	64
FALK, Abel	FAY	261	Benjamin	GRN	112	Martin	LAN	64
FALKENBACH, Andw.	YOR	217	Calab	NOU	104	Widow	LAN	64
FALKENSTINE,			Caleb	NOU	109	FASNAGHT, Conrad	DAU	25
Jacob	YOR	91	Calob	NOU	198	FASSET, Josiah	LUZ	401
FALKLER, George	YOR	163	John	NOU	128	FASSNACHTD,		
Gotleib	YOR	163	Minard	NOU	143A	Conrad	LAN	209
FALKNER, Abram	CHE	860	FARLING, Jacob	DAU	18	FASSNACHTT, John	LAN	209
FALL, Daniel	BER	222	FARLOW, Isaac	LAN	114	FASSNAUGHT, John	DAU	49A
Elizabeth	BER	155	FARLY, Widw.	PHI	81A	FAST, Adam	GRN	75
James	CHE	711	John	NOU	202	Christian	GRN	75
John	LAN	213	FARMER, Edward	MNT	49	Frances	FAY	214
John Deter	BER	222	Ellis	BFD	57	Francis	MNT	110
Jost	BER	222	Gregory	LAN	242	Jacob	GRN	75
FALLAUR, John	ALL	117	Jane	WAS	33	Nicholas	FAY	214
FALLER, James	FRA	316	John	BFD	57	FASTER, Casper	CUM	79
FALLERTON?, Wm.	MNT	141	John	BFD	60	Jerimia	FAY	256
FALLIDAY, Solomon	LUZ	413	Lewis	PHA	86	Joseph	FAY	256
FALLIS, John	FAY	256	Lot	CHE	829	FASY, Jno.	DAU	38A
FALLON, Daniel	WST	379	Robert A.	BER	273	FATE, Frederick	BFD	57
John	WST	169	Willm.	PHI	123	John	BFD	57
FALLOW, James	YOR	199	FARNE, Jacob	BER	217	Martain	WST	379
FALLS, Henry	CEN	20	FARNER, John	PHI	29	FATE?, Abraham	PHI	96A
James	NOU	157	FARNEY, John	DAU	47A	FATHER, David	LAN	63
Moore	CHE	732	FARNSWORTH, John	NOU	104	FATHERBY, John	BUC	146
FALMSON, Nathl.	PHI	32	Robt.	NOU	104	FATSBATRICK, Mary	PHI	102
FALSTER, David	FAY	208	FARNWALT, Peter	NOU	109	FATZINGER, Henry	NOH	43
FALSTICK, John	NOH	62A	FARNWORTH,			Valentine	NOH	68A
FAMOUS, John	MNT	106	Jonathan	NOU	104	FAUBER, Margaret	FRA	271
William	MNT	106	FARON, Widw.	PHI	88A	FAUCET, Henry	CHE	745
FAMY, Madam	PHI	78A	FAROW, James	NOU	104	John	CHE	745
FANASTOCK, Benjn.	MIF	7	FARQUHAR, Thomas	WAS	37	Robt.	CUM	99
FANCE, Chritn.	PHI	96A	FARR, Abraham	DEL	172	FAUCETT, George	CHE	745
FANCHARD, William	LUZ	379	Jacob	LAN	309	FAUCKENROTH,		
FANCKHAUSER,			Joseph	CHE	865	George	YOR	187
Peter Jur.	LAN	271	Wm.	LYC	14	FAUGHNER, James	BEV	21
FANCKHAUSERN,			Wm.	PHA	97	FAULK, George	YOR	185
Widow	LAN	271	FARRA, Atkinson	MNT	69	FAULKLER, George	MIF	16A
FANESTOCK, Danl.	CUM	36	FARRAN, Edward	CHE	715	FAULKNER, Daniel	NOU	164
FANHORN?, William	BEV	23	John	WST	150	Henry	WAS	44
FANNIN, Anthony	PHA	110	Mary	PHA	99	Jacob	NOU	157
FANSE, Jacob	PHI	136	FARRAR, Andrew	WAS	90	James	HNT	141
FANSLER, Fredrik	DAU	27	FARREL, John	HNT	139	John	BFD	63
John	PHA	53	FARRELL, Widow	PHI	10	John	HNT	132
John	DAU	29A	John	PHA	97	John	NOU	164

FAULKNER, Robert	LUZ	363	FEASTER, David			FEGUSON, Henry	WAS	99
Samuel	HNT	141	Jnr.	BUC	137A	FEHAVO, Widow	PHI	109
FAULKS, Wilm.	ALL	65	David	BUC	137A	FEHL, Frederick	LAN	282
FAULOR?, Patrick	PHI	65	Henry	BUC	143	George	LAN	278
FAULTER?, Thomas	BEV	22	Henry	BUC	153	Jacob	LAN	281
FAULTON?, John	BEV	8	Henry Jnr.	BUC	143	FEHLER, Adam	NOH	78
FAUNCE, Widw.	PHI	79A	Henry	BUC	137A	FEHMAN, George	DAU	47A
Christn.	PHI	87A	John	BUC	137A	FEHR, Henry	BER	147
Geo.	PHI	85A	FEASTOR, Daniel	SOM	157	John	NOH	39
Henry	PHI	95	FEATERLY, Henry	BUC	91A	FEICH, Christian	LAN	139
Henry	PHI	79A	John	BUC	91A	FEIGHLY, Martin	YOR	192
Jacob	PHI	79A	FEATHER, Chrisr.	WST	271	FEIGHTNER, Martin	SOM	137
Jacob	PHI	87A	Isaac	MNT	62	FEIGLE, Melchoir	BER	148
Lawrance	PHI	89	Jacob	SOM	142	Peter	BER	169
Rebecca	PHI	87A	Peter	BER	237	FEIGLEY, Abraham	WAS	67
FAUNCE?, John	PHI	90A	Peter Jr.	BER	237	Jacob	WAS	67
FAUNER, John	PHI	5	Samuel	MNT	62	FEIGLS?, (See		
FAUNTT, William	LAN	97	Stephen	WST	271	Teigls)	LYC	16
FAUST, Adam	BER	187	FEATHERBY, Joseph	BUC	87A	FEILD, John	LAN	153
Anthony	BER	135	Thos.	BUC	142	FEILER, John	HNT	138
Anthony	BER	144	FEATHERBY?, (See			FEINSTERMAKER,		
Baltzer	YOR	193	Featherley)	BUC	152A	John	BER	211
Catherine	BER	148	FEATHERHOFF,			FEIRSTEIN, George	LAN	195
George	NOH	43	Fredk.	DAU	17	Jacob	LAN	195
George	BER	187	FEATHERLEY,			John	LAN	195
George	FRA	307	George	BUC	152A	FEIS, Tobias	BER	233
Henry	YOR	163	FEATHERMAN,			FEISER, Barnabas	YOR	175
Henry	BER	202	Hermon	BFD	63	George	DAU	17A
Jacob	BER	144	FEATHERS,			Michael	YOR	175
Jacob	BER	158	Cornelius	WAS	43	FEISTRANAUER,		
John	BER	142	Stephen	WAS	43	John	LAN	195
John	BER	156	FEAZEL, Laurence	WAS	52	FEIT, Ben.	LAN	101
John	BER	187	FEBLE, Frederick	NOH	73	Henry	BER	284
Ludwig	BER	144	FEDLER, Jacob	NOU	175	John	BER	144
Michael	NOH	29A	FEDROW, Andrew	SOM	148	FELAN?, James	PHI	5
Peter	BER	155	FEDTER, Jacob	NOU	121	FELCHER,		
Peter	BER	202	FEE, Andw.	WST	379	Archibauld	ALL	92
Peter	BER	202	John	HNT	160	FELCKER, George	NOH	78
Philip	BER	155	Robert	PHI	38	Stoffel	NOH	78
Philip	BER	187	William	PHI	15	FELDEBERGER,		
Philip	BER	203	FEEAND?, Martin	BER	245	Frederick	LAN	304
Philip Jr.	BER	155	FEEBECKER, Eliza	PHA	78	FELDER, David	PHI	39
Sebastian	BER	129	FEELY, James	LAN	307	FELE, James	PHA	48
FAUSTER, James	ALL	84	William	HNT	119	FELEMING, Samuel	ALL	116
Major	FAY	203	FEERER, Peter	DAU	48	FELIN/ FELIX?,		
FAUTS, Henry	FRA	291	FEES, Peter	BER	257	Nichl.	BER	237
FAUTTER /			Samuel	DAU	25	FELIX, John	ADA	33
FAUTLER?,			FEESE, James	LAN	36	Martin	BER	239
Thomas	BEV	22	FEESER, Nicholas	ADA	27	Peter	BER	239
FAWCET, John	WAS	15	FEESSER, Peter	DAU	50A	FELKER, Dorothe	YOR	165
FAWKES, George	DEL	169	FEESTER?, (See			George	PHA	66
John	DEL	179	Fuster)	LAN	129	John	YOR	214
Joseph	DEL	180	FEET, Peter	NOU	143A	John	DAU	51A
Nathan	DEL	180	FEG, Jacob	BER	202	Joseph	HNT	160
Richard	DEL	179	FEGAN, James	FRA	323	FELKIN, Craft	PHI	95A
FAWN, John	FRA	321	John	CUM	90	FELL, Amos	LUZ	362
FAWNER, Jacob	BFD	43	FEGE, Peter	DAU	52	Asa Junr.	BUC	86A
FAY, James	LAN	96	FEGELEY, Christn.	BER	213	David	BUC	86A
William	FRA	304	Christn. Jr.	BER	213	Edward	DEL	188
FAYETT, Mary	PHA	113	Henry	BER	213	George	BUC	141
FC FITEN, James	NOU	118	Peter	MNT	99	George	MER	441
FEAGER, Caleb	HNT	124	Philip	BER	213	Heney	NOH	66A
Conrad	BER	179	FEGELY, Andrew	BER	255	Israil	FAY	252
Elizabeth	HNT	124	Bernard	BER	173	Israil Jun.	FAY	252
FEALOR, Daniel	HNT	124	Christian	BER	217	Jesse	LUZ	321
George	HNT	124	Conrad	BER	164	John	BUC	142
FEALS, Thomas	ARM	124	David	NOH	59	John	CHE	731
FEAR, Jos.	FRA	319	George	BER	255	John Junr.	CHE	731
Samuel	MIF	7	Henry	BER	213	Jonas	BUC	86A
FEARER, Christian	NOU	135	John	BER	276	Jonathan	PHA	21
Joseph	NOU	135	Nicholas	BER	166	Jonathan	BUC	154
FEARESS, Isabella	CUM	98	Peter	NOH	59	Jonathan Jur.	BUC	86A
FEARIS, Edwd.	PHA	70	FEGER, Christn.	DAU	29	Jonathan	BUC	86A
FEARMAN, Thomas	HNT	141	Godf.	LAN	135	Jonathan	BUC	146A
William	HNT	141	FEGLEY, Jonas	BEV	26	Joseph	BUC	151
FEARON, Joseph	PHA	3	Zakariah	BEV	27	Joseph	BUC	104A

FELL, Joseph BUC 154A
Nelen FAY 252
Richard PHA 18
Samuel BUC 86A
Seneca BUC 86A
Thomas CHE 710
Thomas BUC 86A
Thomas BUC 86A
Watson BUC 144A
William MER 441
William CHE 887
FELLENGER, Peter NOH 41
FELLENZER, John
Junr. NOH 41
John Senr. NOH 41
FELLER, Andrew NOH 75A
John NOH 75A
FELLOWS, Abiel LUZ 353
Ephraim LUZ 350
Jonathan LUZ 353
Obel LUZ 349
FELMAN, (Blank) MNT 89
Jacob MNT 61
John Jne. BUC 159
FELNULIN, Mosis NOU 163
FELP, Samuel BUC 87A
FELT, Mathias MNT 116
FELTEBERGER, John FRA 278
John FRA 278
FELTEN, Christn. PHI 118
Godfry PHI 118
Philip PHI 118
FELTENBERRY,
Michl. FRA 278
FELTER, Adam NOU 135
Jacob NOU 135
Phillip NOU 135
FELTER?, (See
Fetter) CUM 93
FELTERS, H. J./
I.? Revd. NOH 37A
FELTHOFF,
Christian NOH 89A
FELTON, Henry LUZ 382
John LUZ 404
Thomas MER 442
FELTY, Deitrick ADA 33
Earnest PHI 124
Fredrik DAU 2
Henry YOR 181
Henry BER 260
Jacob MNT 38
John DAU 16
John ADA 18
John YOR 184
Joseph PHI 124
Peter DAU 17
Sebastn. DAU 50
Ulrik DAU 49A
FEMINGTON, John PHA 83
FENDERSLICE, John CHE 858
FENDY, Ferdinand PHI 129
FENEFRAUGH,
Stephen FRA 315
FENEX, Taylor FAY 221
FENNAL, Henry LAN 314
FENNATEE?, James BEV 12
FENNEL,
Christopher NOH 62A
Conrad NOH 62A
Frederick Jnr. NOH 62A
Frederick NOH 62A
Wm. PHA 12
FENNER, Barnet NOH 41
Casper NOH 33A
Felix NOH 73

FENNER, Godfrey CUM 111
Henry PHA 102
John HNT 146
John NOH 66A
William NOU 146
FENNING, John BUC 138
FENNY, Andrew ALL 84
James ALL 79
Robert ALL 79
Wilm. ALL 79
FENSHTERMAKER,
Devalt ADA 14
FENSLER, Fredk. DAU 41A
Jacob DAU 41A
Philip DAU 41A
FENSTERMACHER,
Abraham NOH 85
Christn. NOH 29A
Frederick LAN 245
George NOH 75A
Jac. NOH 89A
Jacob NOH 51A
John NOH 51A
Michael NOH 53
Philip NOH 44A
Philip NOH 51A
William NOH 44A
FENSTERMAKER,
Christn. BER 211
Danl. BER 211
Jacob BER 211
FENSTERMASHER,
John NOH 50
FENTON, Ann PHI 68A
Eleazer BUC 86
Ephraim MNT 40
John WAS 43
John PHA 44
Joseph WAS 43
Joseph BUC 137A
Patrick BUC 86A
Randle BUC 86A
Thomas BUC 143
Thos. PHA 35
Thos. BUC 86A
Warren LUZ 427
William WAS 43
FENWICK?, Godfry PHI 105A
FER--?, John MIF 6
FERA, Samuel HNT 130
FERAS, William WAS 12
FERBER, Conrad NOH 44A
Jacob NOH 44A
Peter NOH 44A
FERDER, Ludewick NOU 114
FERDINO-?,
Justice ADA 25
FEREING?, Philip PHI 95A
FEREW, Alexander WAS 79
FERGASON, Saml. PHI 70
FERGAY?, Francis LYC 19
FERGESON, Mathew FRA 280
FERGUS, Hugh ADA 10
FERGUSON, Allen ADA 1
Andrew WAS 28
Andw. CUM 59
Andw. PHI 101
Benjamin BFD 50
Benjn. PHA 33
Catharine ADA 11
David DAU 22A
Ebenezer PHI 47
Elizabeth CHE 778
Esther DAU 11A
Frans. PHI 33
George GRN 112

FERGUSON, Henry ADA 23
Hugh ADA 1
Hugh PHA 21
Hugh BFD 50
Hugh Sen. ADA 1
James BEV 16
James WAS 67
James WST 150
James WST 160
James WST 323
James WST 344
James WST 344
James CEN 22A
James BUC 140A
John BFD 50
John PHA 75
John WAS 90
John HNT 151
John LAN 261
John WST 323
John WST 344
John DAU 24A
Joseph BFD 50
Joseph CUM 148
Mary WAS 109
Richard ADA 5
Robert WAS 55
Robert GRN 68
Robert WAS 109
Robt. PHI 46
Robt. PHA 75
Samuel WAS 109
Samuel WST 150
Thos. PHA 37
Thos. CUM 126
Thos. YOR 214
Widow ADA 14
Widow MIF 12A
Will'm. Junr. WAS 109
William ADA 6
William WAS 90
William WAS 109
William WST 150
William LUZ 422
Wm. CUM 121
Wm. CUM 127
FERGUY?, Francis LYC 19
FERIES, Barney PHI 62
FERIG?, Elizabeth BER 215
FERIN, John CRA 7
FERMAN, Isreal PHI 73A
Samuel NOU 187
FERMATEE?, James BEV 12
FERNELL, Peter MER 442
FERNER, Daniel
Junr. SOM 128
Daniel Sen. SOM 128
Henry DAU 50
Valentine BFD 68
FERNEY, Abraham LAN 87
Lewis PHA 8
FERNSLER, Peter DAU 46A
FERQUY?, Francis LYC 19
FERRAL, Margret ERI 59A
Thomas BEV 25
FERRCE, Andw. YOR 167
Joseph PHA 40
FERREE, Abraham LAN 231
Daniel LAN 110
David LAN 220
Elisha LAN 229
Emanuel LAN 175
Ephraim LAN 218
Isaac LAN 231
Isaac Junr. LAN 231
Israel LAN 226

FERREE, Jacob	LAN 110	FETERMAN, James	CRA 14	FEW, Benjamin	CHE 883
Joel	LAN 179	FETERONEN, John	CUM 24	Eli	DEL 156
Joel	LAN 231	FETHER, Joseph	DAU 18A	Isaac	CHE 902
John	LAN 228	FETHERHOFF,		Richard	CHE 744
John Senr.	LAN 217	Baltzer	DAU 48	FEWCET, Joseph	ALL 105
Laughlin	LAN 10	Balzer	DAU 51	FEWEL, Daniel	BFD 54
Peter	ADA 39	George	FRA 281	FEY, Abraham	BER 220
Richard	LAN 231	FETHERS, Casper	MNT 64	George	HNT 119
Samuel	LAN 246	FETICK, John	NOU 157	George	BER 286
William	LAN 35	FETLER, Jacob	HNT 125	Joseph	HNT 119
FERREL, Elisabeth	SOM 141	FETMAN, John	BUC 159	FEYER, Peter	YOR 169
James	BEV 24	FETSER, Isaac	MIF 16A	FIBBS, John	FAY 227
John	WAS 2	FETTER, Barbara	NOH 68A	William	WAS 15
John	BEV 27	Christn.	PHI 117A	FICHDHORN, Jacob	LAN 195
Michael	FAY 203	Daniel	HNT 124	FICHTHORN, Andw.	BER 237
FERRELL, Edwards	WAS 62	Frederick	NOH 51A	Andw.	BER 244
John	WAS 62	George	CHE 735	Michl.	BER 237
John	CHE 826	Henry	BFD 73	FICK, John	BER 136
Patrick	CHE 776	Henry	NOH 82	John	NOU 187
Ruth	CHE 761	J.	LAN 147	Peter	BER 136
FERREN, Bernerd	NOU 164	Jacob	BFD 72	FICKEL, William	ADA 43
FERRENCE,		Jacob	CUM 93	FICKES, Abraham	ADA 19
Nicholas	SOM 128	Jacob	DAU 3A	Abraham	ADA 41
FERRER, Anthony	MIF 1	John	BFD 73	Jacob	ADA 41
FERREY, O Manus	NOU 171	John	NOH 82	John	ADA 34
FERRILL, John	BUC 84A	John	LAN 251	John	ADA 40
Joseph	WAS 55	John Junr.	NOH 82	Martin	YOR 162
FERRIN, John	BUT 361	John	NOH 75A	Valentine	ADA 19
FERRINGER, Geo	BES.284	Luke	BFD 43	Valentine	ADA 41
FERRIOR, Andrew	FAY 249	Marcus	NOH 32	Valentine	ADA 42
James	MIF 5	Peter	NOH 59	FICKIS, Isaac	BFD 73
FERRIS, Daniel	VEN 168	Peter	BFD 72	FIDAL, John	NOU 157
John	FAY 252	Philip	BER 225	FIDLER, Andw.	BER 190
Samuel	LUZ 369	Varley	NOU 154	Conrad	ADA 40
William	YOR 196	FETTERHOF,		Elizabeth	BER 215
FERRISON, John	SOM 141	Mathias	ADA 24	Henry	BER 202
FERRON, Patrick	BUT 335	Mathias	ADA 24	Henry	BER 202
FERRY, Silas	LUZ 353	FETTERHOFF, Jacob	DAU 50A	Jacob	ADA 40
FERRY?, See Terry	LUZ 395	Michael	YOR 189	John	FAY 197
FERST, George	LYC 24	FETTERHOLFF,		John	BER 203
FERSTER,		Peter	BER 277	Ludwig	BER 215
Christian	NOU 121	Philip	BER 277	Nathan	BFD 43
FERSYTH, John	FRA 320	FETTERING, George	BER 172	Peter	ADA 40
FERTICK, Abram	CHE 791	Michael	BER 169	FIDNER, Lewis	PHI 88A
Adam	CHE 791	FETTERMAN,		FIDWILER?, (See	
John	CHE 791	Cassimire	NOH 62A	Tidwiler)	CHE 725
John Jr.	CHE 791	George	BER 225	FIE, Conrad	BFD 63
Peter	CHE 794	John	NOH 85	Jacob	BFD 63
FERTIG, Peter	DAU 11	Philip	NOH 55A	FIELD, Benjn.	PHI 145
FERTNEY,		Widow	CUM 24	Christiana	PHA 90
Christian	YOR 212	FETTERO, John	YOR 217	Jacob	BFD 43
FERY, John	BER 173	Jos.	YOR 217	John	PHA 73
Martin	LAN 66	Jos. Jr.	YOR 217	Joseph	PHI 134
FESIG, Conrad	BER 237	Michael	YOR 217	Nathan	PHA 26
Dewalt	DAU 49A	Philip	YOR 217	Nathan	DEL 178
George	DAU 50	Philip Jr.	YOR 217	Peter	PHI 112
Philip	LAN 28	FETTERS, Andrew	MNT 50	Peter	PHI 53A
Philip J. / I.?	BER 242	George	MNT 64	Polly	PHI 1
William	BER 237	George	HNT 124	Robert	NOU 109
FESLER, Henry	GRN 66	James	PHI 85A	Rudolph	PHI 2
John	CUM 22	Michal	MER 442	Stephen	PHI 91
Nicholas	CUM 32	Peter	HNT 121	Steven	LYC 29
Peter	CUM 60	FETTEY, Geo.	CUM 52	Thos.	PHI 87A
FESS?, John	MNT 137	FETTSGERALD,		William	PHA 95
FESSENGER, Saml.	PHI 66	Daniel	FAY 221	William	BUC 100
FESSLER, George	BER 203	FETTY, Henry	PHI 126	FIELDER, Jacob	PHI 81
Henry	BER 205	FETZER, Jacob	YOR 191	FIELDING, John	BFD 37
Jacob	DAU 12	John	MNT 118	FIELDING?, Robt.	PHA 76
Michael	BER 262	FEUGELY, Conrad	MNT 99	FIELDS, Asa	NOH 78
FESSMIRE, John	PHI 138	FEUL, Philip	ADA 1	David	BFD 37
FESTER, Henry	YOR 208	FEVEING?, Philip	PHI 95A	Grace	LUZ 379
FESTOON, Richd.	PHI 3	FEVENER?, Adam	MNT 82	James	FAY 221
FETERER, Stephen	DAU 49A	Frederick	MNT 82	John	CUM 112
FETERHOFF,		FEVERIGHT,		John	LUZ 379
Frederick	NOU 187	Stouple	FRA 282	Joseph	GRN 81
FETERMAN, George	CRA 6	FEW, Abner	CHE 804	Joseph	GRN 93

119

FIELDS, Nicholas	YOR	181
Samuel	LUZ	379
Seth	LUZ	379
Walter	BUC	80
William	YOR	162
FIES?, Henry	BER	136
FIESS, Peter	BER	129
FIETY, Peter	FRA	298
FIFE, James	ALL	94
John	ALL	93
John Senior	ALL	94
Margit	ALL	93
Wilm.	ALL	93
Wilm. Senior	ALL	94
FIFHER, John	ALL	54
FIFS, Geo.	PHI	118A
FIGHT, Arnel	LAN	246
Jacob	CUM	133
John	BFD	50
FIGHTNER, Henry	WST	213
FIGNER, Abm.	WST	213
John	ADA	14
FIGUIERES,		
Francis	PHA	119
FIKE, Christian	SOM	148
Isaac	SOM	148
Jacob	SOM	148
FILBERRY, Abraham	LUZ	344
Henry	LUZ	331
FILBERT, Henry	BER	144
Peter	BER	237
Philip	BER	202
Saml.	BER	144
Samuel	BER	229
Thomas	BER	204
FILBS, Henry	BER	148
Jacob	BER	148
FILBY, John	YOR	154
FILE, John	DAU	3
John	DAU	50
John	DAU	9A
FILES, Roger	BUC	143
FILEY, Jacob	YOR	214
FILHOUS, John	ALL	90
FILLABAM, David	LAN	171
FILLY, Ambrose	LUZ	359
John Junr.	YOR	212
John Senr.	YOR	212
Roger	BUT	346
FILMAN, Abm.	MNT	61
Frederic	CHE	891
Frederick	NOH	41
Jacob	MNT	73
Philip	MNT	57
FILMLY, Jacob	NOU	136
FILSAN, Dauisan	FRA	276
FILSON, George	CHE	776
James	CUM	113
John	CHE	717
Joseph	CHE	717
Joseph	CHE	751
Joseph	CHE	781
Margaret	CHE	779
Mary	CUM	113
Robt.	FRA	299
FIMPLE, John	DEL	191
Michael	DEL	178
FIN, Casel	CHE	844
George	BER	237
Lawrence	BER	237
FINCH, Isaac	LUZ	375
John	PHA	15
Joseph	CHE	766
FINCHEL, John	BER	270
FINCHER, John	BER	169
Jonathen	NOU	152
FINCK, Abraham	NOH	80
Benedict	NOH	80
Christian	NOH	53
Christian	NOH	59
Daniel	NOH	53
Henry	NOH	51A
Jacob	NOH	55A
Jacob	NOH	83A
John	NOH	53
Peter	NOH	82
Philip	NOH	82
FINCKEL, Widow	DAU	49
FINCKENBINE,		
Frederick	CHE	783
FINDALL, Thomas		
D.	DEL	185
FINDLAY, Samuel	SOM	148
FINDLEY,		
Alexander	GRN	100
Andw. Esqr.	WST	288
Archibald	WST	344
David	WST	308
George	WST	379
Hugh	FAY	252
James	GRN	75
James	FRA	312
Jno.	FRA	310
John	HNT	129
John	YOR	199
John	FRA	288
John	WST	288
John	WST	308
John	WST	379
Joseph	WST	288
Martha	YOR	198
Robert	FAY	226
Samuel	WST	169
William	SOM	148
William	FRA	288
Wm. Esqr.	WST	308
FINDLY, Ebenezer	FAY	235
James Esqr.	FAY	256
Samuel	FAY	208
FINEBROUGH,		
Michl.	FRA	279
FINEFROCK, Geo.	CUM	42
John	YOR	164
FINEGAN, James	PHA	35
FINERTY, James	FRA	326
FINES?, William	PHI	65
FINEY, James	NOU	157
John	PHA	14
John	FRA	289
Joseph	CHE	732
Lazarus	NOU	198
FINFROCK, Henry	LAN	87
Michael	LAN	234
Nathaniel	LAN	52
FINGLE, Maths.	BER	162
FINIFROCK, Andrew	ADA	28
FINK, Casper	WAS	98
Chrs.	YOR	215
Conrad	BER	255
Ferdinand	YOR	164
George	YOR	176
George	LUZ	351
Henry	ADA	32
Henry	YOR	164
Jacob	WAS	37
Jacob	PHA	80
Jacob	WST	190
Jacob	BER	206
John	LYC	22
John	ADA	30
John	WAS	98
John	BER	175
FINK, John	BER	210
John	YOR	218
Mary	ALL	103
Michael	HNT	126
Michael	SOM	161
Peter	BER	207
Rachel	PHI	79A
Valentine	BER	206
FINKBON, Jacob	BER	255
FINKLE, John	LAN	260
FINLAW, Michl.	DAU	22A
FINLAY, Archibald	HNT	145
Joseph	HNT	135
Patrick	HNT	163
FINLEY, Alexr.	CEN	20
Archibd.	ADA	3
David	ARM	127
Eleoner	ADA	3
Isabella	DAU	22A
James	LAN	45
James	PHA	71
James	BUT	327
James	BUC	104A
John	LAN	3
John	LAN	7
John	BFD	35
John	BFD	63
John	HNT	135
John	YOR	200
John Esqr.	ARM	127
Margaret	ADA	1
Matthias	LUZ	417
Moses	LAN	2
Richard	WAS	52
Richd.	DAU	22A
Robert	WAS	20
Robert	WAS	33
Saml.	BUT	328
Samuel	CHE	758
William	YOR	200
William Junr.	YOR	200
FINLY, Daniel	ERI	60A
David	ALL	80
John Esqr.	ALL	87
John	BUC	144A
FINN, Hannah	LUZ	379
John	LUZ	379
Solomon	LUZ	365
FINNACKE, Adam	CUM	44
FINNER?, Peter	PHA	33
FINNEY, Charles	PHA	105
James	FAY	265
John	MIF	6
John	DAU	18
John	WAS	79
John	FAY	197
John	CHE	713
John	DAU	22A
Margeret	FAY	197
Mary	DAU	36A
Robert	CRA	5
Robert	NOU	117
Robert	NOU	198
Robert	CHE	732
Saml.	DAU	22A
Walter	CHE	731
William	CHE	732
FINNICUM?,		
William	WAS	56
FINNIMEN?,		
William	WAS	56
FINNY, James	FAY	265
James	FAY	265
Robert	FAY	265
Saml.	YOR	203
FINSTERMAKER,		
Joseph	BER	212

FINSTERMAKER,		FISHER, Christley	LAN 132	FISHER, James	PHA 33
Joseph	BER 211	Christn.	DAU 29	James	CUM 79
FINTON, Benjamin	HNT 129	Christn.	BER 202	James Senr.	CUM 79
James	CUM 23	Conrad	ADA 11	Jessy	ALL 113
Saml.	CUM 132	Daniel	DAU 15	Jno.	DAU 36
FIPE, Jos.	PHI 108	Daniel	NOH 55A	John	WAS 2
FIPPS, Henry	YOR 206	Danl.	BER 202	John	LYC 10
FIPS, Samuel	WST 169	David	PHA 55	John	DAU 15
FIREOCKER, Henry	PHI 108A	David	YOR 217	John	LAN 19
FIREOVERT, Jno.	CUM 79	David	DAU 29A	John	MNT 34
FIRESTONE,		Earnst	SOM 128	John	BFD 43
Mathias	BEV 12	Elias	PHI 66A	John	PHI 47
FIRMAN, Aaron	NOU 99	Elisha	PHA 27	John	LAN 50
Daniel	NOU 104	Elizabeth	BER 144	John	MNT 53
Elijah	NOU 179	Elizabeth	CHE 775	John	PHA 55
Isaac	NOU 104	Ernst	BER 156	John	PHA 62
John	NOU 109	Francis	CHE 834	John	MNT 67
William	NOU 104	Frederic	SOM 133	John	ALL 69
FIRNASTER?,		Frederick	MNT 67	John	PHI 80
Eliza.	PHA 116	Frederick	BER 172	John	PHA 87
FIRREN?, Christer	NOU 157	Frederick	BER 202	John	MNT 93
FIRRER?, Christer	NOU 157	Frederick	BER 277	John	PHA 99
FIRST, George	NOU 121	Fredk.	PHI 90	John	NOU 121
Jacob	FAY 221	Fredk.	PHI 105	John	SOM 128
FIRSTER, Leonard	NOU 121	Fredk.	YOR 181	John	HNT 131
FIRTH, John	PHA 29	Fredr.	FRA 306	John	BER 136
Preston	PHI 109	George	DAU 2	John	NOU 136
Wm.	CHE 862	George	WAS 12	John	BER 139
FIRTING, Casper	LAN 79	George	MNT 34	John	BER 140
FISAPLE?, George	MNT 137	George	LAN 44	John	HNT 151
FISCHER, George	LAN 189	George	PHI 77	John	DEL 167
FISEL, Michael	YOR 177	George	BER 133	John	BER 169
FISH, Benjn.	CUM 86	George	MNT 141	John	BER 175
Christian	BFD 67	George	NOU 198	John	NOU 175
David	NOH 78	George	NOU 198	John	NOU 175
Jabez	LUZ 318	George	BER 222	John	YOR 185
Nathan	BUT 324	George	FAY 240	John	YOR 190
Robt.	NOH 78	George	WST 288	John	BER 202
Widow	NOH 78	George	CHE 759	John	BER 203
FISHAN, Stoffel	LAN 307	George	NOH 89A	John	LAN 209
FISHBACH, Yost	BER 190	Hance	FAY 261	John	BER 223
FISHBAUGH, Mrs.	CUM 95	Henry	DAU 5	John	FRA 306
FISHBURN, Conrad		Henry	ADA 29	John	CHE 772
(Crossed Out)	FRA 308	Henry	NOU 104	John Jr.	YOR 158
Conrod	FRA 309	Henry	PHA 109	John Junr.	MNT 64
Fredr.	FRA 309	Henry	MNT 130	John Junr.	MNT 110
Peter	CUM 115	Henry	BER 136	John Junr.	NOH 55A
Philip	DAU 19A	Henry	BER 139	John Senr.	YOR 158
FISHER, Widow	PHI 5	Henry	BER 144	John	NOH 55A
Widow	MNT 133	Henry	SOM 160	John	NOH 66A
Widw.	PHI 119	Henry	YOR 168	John	PHI 116A
Abel	WST 236	Henry	NOU 193	John	NOU 143A
Abraham	MNT 130	Henry	BER 202	John	NOU 143A
Abraham	YOR 174	Henry	BER 213	John	BUC 158A
Adam	PHI 58	Henry	WST 271	John H.	PHI 89A
Adam	NOU 136	Henry	BER 282	Jonathan	MNT 37
Adam	BER 213	Henry	DAU 50A	Joseph	NOU 109
Adam	WST 271	Isaac	BER 133	Joseph	CHE 819
Adam	WST 271	Isaac	PHI 154	Joseph	BUC 147A
Adam	LAN 308	Israel	CHE 901	Jospeh	ALL 113
Andrew	MNT 109	Jacob	WAS 7	Leonard	NOH 89
Anthony	NOH 55A	Jacob	LYC 10	Leonard	BER 152
Archd.	PHI 19	Jacob	DAU 15	Leond.	CUM 62
Benjamin	WAS 15	Jacob	DAU 15	Levi	MNT 38
Benjamin	BFD 62	Jacob	BFD 43	Lewis	MNT 109
Benjamin	NOU 109	Jacob	CUM 60	Lorence	YOR 168
Benjamin	PHI 128	Jacob	BFD 73	Lowrence	NOH 35A
Benjan.	PHI 134	Jacob	PHA 87	Ludwick	BFD 40
Casper	YOR 171	Jacob	WAS 90	Ludwig	SOM 128
Catherine	MNT 109	Jacob	MNT 137	Ludwig	BER 190
Christian	BFD 40	Jacob	PHI 147	Malachi	MNT 38
Christian	MNT 93	Jacob	BER 184	Male	NOU 193
Christian	NOU 136	Jacob	FRA 296	Malichar Junr,	MNT 34
Christian	SOM 141	Jacob	LUZ 330	Margarit	MNT 99
Christian	BER 236	Jacob	DAU 50A	Martin	PHA 68
Christian	BER 270	Jacob	NOH 55A	Martin	SOM 137

FISHER, Martin	NOU 175	FISHER, William	WST 271	FITSGARALD,			
Mary	PHA 16	Wilm.	ALL 59	Edward	ALL 59		
Mathew	ALL 101	Wilm.	ALL 59	FITTER, John	LAN 138		
Mathias	BER 147	Wilm.	ALL 119	John	LAN 230		
Mathias	WST 236	Wm.	CEN 22A	FITTSMORRIS,			
Michael	NOU 117	Wm.	PHI 109A	James	FAY 244		
Michael	PHI 123	Zachariah	MIF 9	John	FAY 244		
Michael	BER 136	FISHER?, John	ALL 54	FITZ GERALD,			
Michael	HNT 151	FISHT,		William	NOU 97		
Michael	HNT 151	Christopher	YOR 171	FITZ RANDOLPH,			
Michael	BER 202	George	YOR 171	James Junr.	GRN 95		
Michael	BER 205	FISHWATER, David	NOU 202	James Senr.	GRN 95		
Michael	BER 223	Joseph	NOH 35A	John	NOH 37A		
Michael	BER 225	FISK, John	PHI 20	FITZ WILLIAMS,			
Michael	BER 229	Peter	MIF 25	William	WAS 12		
Michl.	BER 213	FISKEY, Abraham	WST 308	FITZ, Fredk.	YOR 206		
Michl.	DAU 48A	Charles	WST 308	Henary	FAY 208		
Miers	PHA 107	FISLE, Henry		Samuel	GRN 92		
Mrs.	NOU 117	(Sadler)	YOR 177	Samuel	GRN 92		
Nicholas	PHA 30	FISLER, David	LAN 174	FITZCHARLES,			
Nicholas	BER 136	Jacob	CHE 898	David	LAN 51		
Nicholas	BER 186	Widow	LAN 62	FITZEIMMEN, John	YOR 169		
Paul	NOU 193	FISS, Widow	PHI 34	FITZER, Andw.	CEN 22A		
Peter	DAU 32	Henry	PHI 113A	John	MNT 110		
Peter	NOU 109	John	PHA 77	Peter	GRN 100		
Peter	NOU 135	Joseph	PHA 63	FITZERALD, Thomas	MNT 122		
Peter	BER 136	FISSEL, Daniel	YOR 195	FITZGARALD, Agnes			
Peter	LAN 178	Henry	ADA 39	(Mol. Woman)	ALL 49		
Peter	NOU 193	Philip	ADA 39	FITZGERALD, Debby	FRA 283		
Peter	BER 202	Philip	ADA 42	Deborah	FRA 281		
Peter	BER 202	FISSELL, Henry		James	PHA 12		
Peter	BER 245	Jr.	YOR 179	James	HNT 158		
Philip	DAU 15	Michael	YOR 211	Jno.	CUM 51		
Philip	PHI 133	Michael Sr.	YOR 178	John	MNT 114		
Philip	BER 202	FISSLE, Henry	YOR 187	John	DEL 171		
Philip	BER 202	John	YOR 170	Peter	MNT 69		
Philip	BER 202	John	YOR 186	Robert	PHA 101		
Philip Jr.	BER 202	John Jr.	YOR 186	William	MNT 82		
Philip	DAU 32A	Michael	YOR 170	FITZGERRALD,			
Phillip	CUM 132	Michael Jr.	YOR 177	Daniel	ARM 126		
Phillip	FAY 249	FISTER, Felix	WAS 120	FITZIMMONS,			
Phillip	CHE 819	George	BER 210	Philip	LAN 99		
Saml.	PHA 28	Henry	WAS 120	FITZIMONS, Thos.	PHA 83		
Saml.	PHA 70	Henry	BER 281	FITZINGER, John	BUC 104A		
Saml.	YOR 217	Jacob	WAS 120	FITZJAROL, Thos.	YOR 202		
Saml. W.	PHA 33	John	PHI 52	FITZPATRICK,			
Samuel	CRA 14	John	WAS 120	Widow	PHI 15		
Samuel	WAS 55	John	BER 135	Daniel	CHE 700		
Samuel	PHA 107	Thomas	BER 237	Owen	LAN 305		
Samuel	FAY 231	FISTLE, Conrad	YOR 180	Wm.	CUM 46		
Simon	GRN 67	Henry	YOR 174	FITZRANDOLPH,			
Stophel	LAN 28	John	YOR 174	Isaac	PHA 15		
Thomas	ADA 30	Michael Sr.	YOR 180	FITZS, Danl.	PHI 119		
Thomas	CUM 61	Philip	YOR 180	FITZSIMMINS,			
Thomas	PHA 104	FISTLER, Cathrine	PHA 45	James	NOU 171		
Thomas	WST 236	FIT, John	LAN 147B	FITZSIMMONS,			
Thomas	MER 442	FITCH, Gideon	LUZ 372	Caleb	CHE 905		
Thomas Senr.	MER 442	John	ALL 79	Caleb	CHE 905		
Thomas (Tavr.?)	WST 236	John	WAS 99	George	WAS 79		
Thos.	CUM 59	John	BER 232	Henry	HNT 143		
Thos.	PHA 60	John	LUZ 371	James	FRA 275		
Thos. Jr.	CUM 55	Joseph	ALL 79	Patrick	HNT 141		
Thos.	PHI 120A	Mary	LUZ 387	FITZSIMONS, Geo.	CHE 796		
Tobias	BER 184	Petateak	LUZ 331	Robt.	NOU 164		
Tobias	FRA 289	Samuel	WAS 99	FITZSISE?, John	NOU 149		
Valentine	BER 173	William	WAS 99	FITZWATER, Hannah	MNT 130		
Valentine	YOR 184	FITE, Andrew		John	MNT 132		
Wendel	DAU 52	Junr.	PHI 140	Joseph	BUC 143		
Wendlle	MNT 125	Andrew Snr.	PHI 140	Mathew	MNT 130		
Widow	NOH 59	George	PHI 125	Wm.	MNT 118		
William	MNT 89	George	DAU 7A	FITZWILLIAMS,			
William	MNT 109	Jacob	SOM 128	John	CHE 724		
William	NOU 128	Jacob	SOM 161	FIX, Catherine	BER 238		
William	PHI 149	John	PHI 88A	Henry	GRN 100		
William	BER 169	FITHEROFF, Peter	NOU 121	FIZASSLE?, George	MNT 137		
William	BER 202	FITHIAN, Israel	PHI 13	FLACK, James	WST 169		
William	NOU 202						

122

FLACK, John	WAS	7
John	WST	169
John	BUC	86A
Joseph	BUC	86A
Robert	WST	169
Robert	BUC	104A
Samuel	BUC	154
FLAGG, Jonathan	PHI	13
FLAGGERTY,		
William	DAU	22A
FLAGLER,		
Volentine	PHA	80
FLAM, Mathias	DAU	10A
FLAMMER, John	BER	211
FLAN?, Christn.	PHI	112
FLANAGAN, Andw.	MIF	25
James	PHA	53
Timothy	CUM	106
FLANAGEN, John	PHA	69
FLANEY, Jacob	PHI	149
FLANIGAM, Andrew	FAY	261
FLANIGAN, John	NOU	164
Thomas	LAN	50
Thos.	CHE	741
Wm.	CHE	769
FLANIGEN, William	CHE	700
FLANNAGAN, Steven	PHI	6
FLANNIGAN, James	LAN	166
FLANNIS, Benj.	PHI	92
FLASHER, John	DAU	22A
FLAT, Andw.	LYC	8
FLATCHER, David	WST	236
David	WST	236
John	FRA	272
John A?	ALL	71
FLATTERY, Barnerd	NOU	109
FLAUCH, Casper-	FAY	261
FLAUER, Jacob	DAU	26A
FLAUGH, Sarah	PHA	49
FLAVAHAN, Sarah	PHA	14
FLAVER, Jacob	DAU	28
FLAVERS, John	PHI	12
FLAXBERG, Lewis	PHA	78
FLAYD, William	CHE	728
FLEAK, John	FRA	284
Phillip	FRA	284
FLEAMING, Andw.	VEN	166
FLEASER, Jno.	DAU	44
FLECK, Adam	MNT	44
Daniel	ADA	40
David	YOR	174
Fredk.	CUM	42
George	PHA	72
George	HNT	151
George Junr.	HNT	151
Jacob	ADA	41
Jacob	BUT	323
John	CUM	40
John	MNT	70
Peter	ADA	21
Peter	ADA	32
Peter	ADA	42
Peter	HNT	150
Valentine	ADA	40
FLEEGER, Henry	WST	236
John	WST	213
Peter	WST	213
FLEEHART, James	FAY	214
FLEEK, Frederick	WST	236
FLEESON, Thomas	PHI	141
FLEETLINE, John	PHA	28
FLEGE, Valentine	CEN	22A
FLEGER, George	YOR	188
Margaret	YOR	159
FLEGHER, Christy	BUT	324
FLEIGER, Barnet	YOR	171

FLEIGER, Fredk.	YOR	211
John	YOR	159
FLEISCHER, Henry	LAN	209
FLEISHER, Andrew	BER	202
FLEKENER, John	FRA	319
Saml.	FRA	320
FLEKINGER, John	DAU	12
Michael	DAU	12
FLEKMER, Christn.	DAU	10A
FLEMING, Andrew	CHE	755
Archd.	CUM	146
Benjamin	LUZ	330
Daniel	WST	251
George	ALL	76
Henry	MIF	3
Henry	HNT	157
Hugh	ALL	115
Isaac	NOU	99
James	MIF	3
James	MIF	15
James	ALL	60
James	HNT	141
James	HNT	157
Jeremiah	WAY	146
Jno.	CUM	22
John	MIF	5
John	MIF	15
John	LYC	25
John	WST	160
John	CHE	708
John	CHE	842
John	CHE	901
John Jr.	CHE	842
Jos.	CUM	73
Joseph	MIF	3
Joseph	CHE	841
Mary	PHI	108
Michael	PHI	2
Mrs.	NOU	109
Rebecca	CHE	902
Robert	ALL	58
Robert	NOU	99
Robert	ARM	123
Robert	HNT	141
Robert	FAY	249
Robt.	CUM	106
Saml.	CHE	871
Sarah	FAY	249
Thomas	BUT	326
Thomas	CHE	883
Widow	CEN	24
Widow	CEN	22A
William	ADA	20
Wilm.	ALL	115
Wm.	MIF	5
Wm.	LYC	9
FLEMINGS, Abner	BUC	93A
FLEMINS, David	ERI	59
FLEMMAN, James	PHI	73A
FLEMMIN, George	FRA	311
James	FAY	256
Joseph H.	PHI	11
Mathew	FRA	286
FLEMMING,		
Alexander	WAS	43
Andrew	FAY	203
Cezar	DEL	191
Charles	WAS	43
Chas.	PHA	48
David	WAS	120
James	ADA	18
James	WAS	52
James	WST	213
Jas.	CUM	81
Jno.	CUM	81
John	WAS	79

FLEMMING, John	FAY	256
Peter	WAS	2
Robt.	WST	213
Robt.	DAU	22A
Samuel Esqr.	WAS	52
Wm.	MIF	3
Wm.	WST	213
FLEMMONS, William	LAN	93
FLENEGAN, James	YOR	198
FLENNIKEN,		
William	WAS	85
FLENNIKIN, Elias	GRN	87
James	GRN	87
John	GRN	87
John Junr.	GRN	92
FLENOR, John	BFD	63
FLENTHAM, Wm.	PHA	44
FLERINGER, John	CHE	775
FLESHER, Geo.	CUM	44
Jno.	CUM	47
FLESHMAN, Anthony	ADA	23
Martin	YOR	194
Philip	ADA	22
FLESHOCKER,		
George	MNT	50
FLESON, Thos.	PHI	67A
FLETCHER, Benjn.	BUT	351
Charles	ADA	9
David	WST	308
Henry	HNT	129
Henry	CEN	18A
Hugh	CRA	16
Jacob	BFD	35
Jacob	BFD	50
James	BFD	37
John	ADA	13
John	PHA	66
John	SOM	141
John Sr.	ADA	13
Philip	BFD	54
Philliip	FAY	231
Richd.	PHA	45
Robert	MNT	34
Robt.	CHE	755
Simon	ALL	83
Thomas	MNT	34
Thomas	ALL	58
William	HNT	164
Wilm.	ALL	65
Wm.	PHA	54
FLEURY, Peter	ERI	58A
FLEW, William	PHI	141
FLEXER, Jeremiah	NOH	75A
John Junr.	NOH	89A
John	NOH	89A
Philip &		
Fathr.?	NOH	80
FLEY, Adam	NOH	35A
FLICH, Henry	CEN	22A
FLICK, Adam	SOM	128
Betsey	PHI	86
Casper	NOH	62A
Daniel	SOM	148
George	SOM	128
Henry	LAN	135
Jacob	SOM	128
Ludwig	SOM	133
Martin	NOH	35A
Paul	NOH	62A
Philip	NOH	29A
William	LAN	47
William	FAY	214
FLICKEINER,		
Catharine &		
Christel	LAN	196

FLICKEINER,		FLOREY, John	LAN 260	FOCHT, George	BER 229
Joseph	LAN 196	John	LAN 260	Jacob	BER 206
FLICKENGER, Peter	CUM 37	Stophel	LAN 260	John	BER 175
Samuel	YOR 184	FLORRINGTON, John	PHI 9	John	BER 277
FLICKER, Peter	YOR 181	FLORY, Abraham	YOR 167	John Geo.	BER 277
FLICKIENER, John	LAN 196	Isaac	YOR 167	Peter	BER 277
FLICKINER, Henry	LAN 209	Jacob	YOR 167	FOCHT?, James	BEV 21
Jacob	LAN 195	John	NOH 47	FOCKLER, George	SOM 128
FLICKINGER,		John	NOH 86A	George	HNT 154
Christian	BER 184	Michael	NOH 55A	FODEL?, James	BEV 21
Christopher	CRA 14	FLOTZBESTER?,		FOEHT?, See Focht	BER 272
George	NOH 89A	Fredk. Henry	PHA 4	FOERING, John	PHA 43
Jacob	SOM 133	FLOUDER, Widow	PHI 56	FOGAL, George	FAY 227
Jacob	SOM 151	FLOUGH, Matthias	CUM 53	Jacob	FAY 235
Jacob Jr.	NOH 89A	FLOUGHER, Jacob	FRA 296	FOGEL, Abraham	NOH 71
Jacob	NOH 89A	FLOUNDERS, Edward	DEL 188	Abraham	NOH 33A
Joseph	BFD 37	FLOWARS, David	YOR 201	Andrew	DAU 49
FLICKINGSTAFF,		FLOWER, John	DAU 39A	Andrew	NOH 71
John	BFD 69	Richard	DEL 162	Frederich Junr.	NOH 33A
FLICKWIRE, Mary	PHA 15	Richard	CHE 764	Frederick	NOH 33A
FLIED?, Widow	PHI 23	FLOWERS, Widw.	PHI 77A	Jacob	LAN 226
FLIGER, John	WST 236	Aaron	GRN 81	John	NOH 59
FLIMER, Jacob	CEN 23A	David	GRN 81	John	NOH 71
FLIN, Richd.		David	YOR 203	John Junr.	NOH 59
Capt.	PHI 74A	Geroge	PHA 61	John Junr.	NOH 71
Thomas	HNT 126	Henry	BFD 37	Leonard	NOH 71
Thos.	PHA 32	Jacob	WST 288	FOGEL?, Matths	PHI 40
FLINCHBACH, Adam	YOR 172	James	WAS 12	FOGELESONG, Jacob	CUM 140
Frederick	YOR 206	James Sr.	BUC 160A	FOGELMAN, Conrd.	NOH 50
John	YOR 172	James	BUC 160A	FOGELSANGER, John	FRA 309
FLINCHBACK,		Jeremiah	PHI 112A	FOGELSINGER,	
Martin	YOR 196	John	BFD 41	Michl.	CUM 141
FLINDER, John	FRA 276	John	YOR 203	Michl. Sr.	CUM 142
John	FRA 276	Joseph	BFD 41	FOGG, Daniel	DEL 163
FLING, David	CHE 806	Rachel	GRN 84	Daniel	DEL 164
Edward	PHA 45	Thomas	GRN 81	FOGHT, George	DAU 38A
John	PHA 10	Thos.	PHA 47	FOGLE, Frederic	CHE 885
Wm.	PHA 48	Zephon	LUZ 419	William Doct.	SOM 141
FLINGNER, Peter	NOU 128	FLOYD, Aaron	CHE 738	FOGLEMAN, Jacob	NOU 164
FLINN, James	GRN 70	James	DAU 12	Michael	NOU 164
John	PHI 20	William	PHI 50	FOGLESENG,	
Luke	LAN 31	FLUBACHER, Jacob	LAN 47	Christian	YOR 207
Patrick	DEL 156	FLUCK, Casper	BFD 62	FOGLESONG, Philip	YOR 208
Simeon	LAN 11	Joseph	BER 286	FOHLER, George	NOH 71
Thomas	WST 379	Ritchard	ALL 82	FOIL, David	PHI 131
Wm.	PHA 36	FLUDD, Ann	FAY 265	Stephan	PHI 126
FLINN?, Christn	PHI 112	Henry	SOM 128	FOILER, Oris	CRA 4
FLINT, Asa	LUZ 375	William	FAY 235	FOIZBY?,	
Edward	MNT 121	FLUELLEN, James	YOR 187	Johnathan	LYC 7
Edward	MNT 123	FLUGER, John	ADA 35	FOKARD, George	MNT 50
John	PHA 75	FLUKE, Adam	BUC 96	FOLCK, George	NOH 75A
Joseph	LAN 14	Casper	BUC 158A	Joseph	NOH 59
Michael	PHI 65	Christian	BUC 96	Valentine	NOH 68A
Michael	YOR 207	Elizabeth	BUC 156A	Widow	NOH 44A
FLINTHAM, John	PHI 106A	Frederick	BUC 96	FOLER, Alexr.	PHI 18
FLITERAFT,		Jacob	BUC 81A	FOLEY, Bartle	DEL 192
Francis	PHA 52	Jacob	BUC 156A	Margaret	HNT 156
FLOID, John	FAY 244	John	BUC 147	Thomas	BFD 43
FLON?, Christn.	PHI 112	John	BUC 90A	FOLGAT, James	DAU 44
FLONE?, Isaac	MNT 106	Ludwick	BUC 156A	FOLGEMER, Jacob	YOR 187
FLONY, Francis	PHI 78A	Philip	BUC 156A	FOLGLEMAN, Conrad	NOU 164
FLOOD, Margaret	FRA 304	Widow	BUC 157	FOLIN, William	CHE 845
Wm.	PHI 78A	FLUMMERY, John	DEL 188	FOLK, Casper	FRA 303
FLOORE, Fetty	ADA 13	FLURY, Henry	CUM 35	Daniel	FRA 290
Leonard	ADA 13	FLUSHART?, T.	PHI 22	George	LAN 59
Valentine	ADA 9	FLY, Frederick	BUC 92	George	LAN 308
FLORA, Catherine	DAU 12A	John	BUC 92	Henry	BER 213
Henry	SOM 148	FLYBACK, Widw.	PHI 79A	Jacob	BER 213
John	YOR 169	FO-?, Rudolph	LUZ 412	John	BER 229
Joseph	SOM 148	FOAL, David	ADA 17	Stephen	ADA 43
Mary	SOM 148	Jacob	ADA 17	FOLKENER, Wm.	PHA 28
FLORE, Valentine	YOR 175	FOCHT, Andrew	BER 272	FOLKES, Edward	NOU 105
FLORENCE, Peter	LUZ 417	Charles	BER 139	FOLKIN, Thomas	NOU 175
FLOREY, Abraham	SOM 148	Christian	BER 270	FOLKNER, Samuel	NOU 128
David	LAN 261	Daniel	YOR 206	FOLKRODE, George	PHI 135
Henry	LAN 260	George	BER 139	George P.	PHI 135

FOLKRODE, Jacob	PHI	135	FORBUS?, Robt.	FRA	276	FORE, Valentine	FRA	303
FOLKS, John	YOR	159	FORCE, Benjn.	BUC	98A	FOREACRE, William	SOM	162
FOLLER, Casper	PHI	125	Edward	BUC	98A	William Sen.	SOM	161
FOLLET, Ezra	LUZ	386	John	MNT	86	FOREACRES,		
George	LUZ	386	John	BUC	160A	William	BFD	63
Warren	LUZ	385	Jonathan	BUC	160A	FOREDICE, William	FAY	214
FOLLETT, Robert	LUZ	385	Peter	PHA	22	FOREMAN,		
FOLLIARD, Michal	ERI	55A	Thomas	CHE	819	Alexander	BUC	104A
FOLLMER, Jacob	DAU	32A	William	BUC	98A	Andr.	FRA	323
Mich.	DAU	35A	FORCYTHE, Abraham	FAY	256	Charles	WST	323
FOLLY, Barney	MIF	12A	FORD, Alexander	WST	308	Daniel	FRA	305
L.	PHI	24	Barny	FRA	320	Daniel	FRA	306
FOLMER, John	DAU	35	Benjn.	CHE	741	Ezekiel	LAN	35
John	NOH	66A	Charles	FAY	238	Fredr.	FRA	306
Jost	NOH	66A	Charles	CHE	713	Fredr.	FRA	306
FOLNER, John	BUC	159	Christopher	CRA	16	George	MER	442
FOLS, Christian	LAN	189	Christr.	MIF	5	James	WAS	20
FOLTZ, Adam	LAN	54	Eliza	PHA	65	James Junr.	WAS	20
Andrew	LAN	48	Elizabeth	PHI	112	John	LAN	16
Andrew	NOH	64A	Hannah	PHA	12	John	SOM	137
Bard.	LAN	11	Jacob	BFD	37	John	CHE	902
Frederick	BER	202	Jacob	PHA	54	Peter	SOM	153
Fredr.	FRA	315	Jacob	FRA	320	Peter	FRA	322
George	LAN	72	Jacob	FRA	320	Robert	LYC	29
George	BER	190	James	MNT	125	Saml	WST	160
Henry	LAN	137	James	CHE	733	Widow	DAU	46A
Jacob	LAN	68	Jas.	PHI	79	William	NOU	149
Peter	LAN	53	Jenny (Negro)	WAS	79	FOREMAN?, David	WST	236
FOLWELL, Jacob	PHA	31	John	PHI	10	FOREPAUGH, Fredk.	PHA	43
John	PHA	25	John	PHI	15	FORESEE, Peter	DAU	14
John	BUC	143	John	BFD	69	FORESMAN, Saml.	NOU	202
Joseph	MNT	64	John	DEL	157	Wm.	LYC	29
Nathan	PHA	21	John	LUZ	397	FOREST, Arin? P.	PHI	80
Richard	PHA	26	John	CHE	771	Daniel	NOU	164
Thomas	BUC	143	John D.	PHA	117	John	HNT	165
William	PHA	21	Michl.	FRA	290	Thomas	HNT	165
William	BUC	143	Morgan	FAY	265	FORESTER, James	CHE	818
FOLZ, Francis	DAU	29A	Moses Esqr.	BEV	20	FORG---?, -----	MIF	10
FONDELET, John	MNT	113	Philip Docr.	DEL	166	FORGE, Cordorus?	YOR	168
FONDERAU, Adam	LAN	294	Robert	FAY	214	FORGESON, John	NOU	164
FONFER, Arens	PHI	3	Simon	BFD	62	FORGEY, John	HNT	149
FONKINNEN, Michl.	MIF	1	Standish	PHI	70A	Samuel	HNT	149
FONPOLE?, Susanna	HNT	145	Thomas	WAS	55	FORGISON, Alex.	LAN	157
FONT, David	BUC	144A	Thomas	NOU	171	James	FAY	256
FOOF, John	CUM	42	William	PHI	12	John	MER	441
FOOL, Simeon	PHA	78	William	DEL	157	Thomas	FAY	197
FOON?, George	FRA	286	William	DEL	163	FORGIT, Charrels	ALL	54
FOOPS, Henry	DAU	33	William	DEL	166	FORGOSSON, James	ALL	118
FOOR, Michael	BUC	139	William	CHE	882	Samuel	ALL	83
FOORMAN, Adam	DAU	30A	William Sen.	DEL	166	FORGUS, Thomas	WAS	20
Jacob	DAU	8A	FORDE, Hugh	CUM	107	FORGUSON, Fargus	ALL	61
FOOS, Felty	CHE	781	FORDENBACH,			John	ALL	110
Frederick	CHE	784	Philip	DAU	10	FORGUSSON, Wilm.	ALL	87
Mathias	PHI	147	FORDHAM, Benjn.	PHA	47	FORGY, Robt.	MIF	25
Wm.	CUM	41	John	PHI	88	FORHAND, Samuel	PHI	51
FOOSE, Daniel	BER	139	FORDICE, Isaac	FAY	227	FORIGLEY?,		
John	BER	186	James	FAY	214	Johnathan	LYC	7
FOOT, Fredk.	BER	162	FORDIN,			FORING, Saml.	PHI	105A
FOOTE, Mary	PHA	16	Christopher	GRN	67	FORK, Joseph	DAU	45A
FOQUET, Lewis	PHA	64	FORDNEY, Casper	LAN	30	FORKER, Adam	FAY	226
FOR---E?, John	FRA	321	Jacob	LAN	39	Adam	BUC	93A
FORBAS, Wilm.	ALL	112	Jacob Junr.	LAN	55	John	BUT	331
FORBES, Alexander	WAS	33	Widow	LAN	39	Patrick	WAS	43
Andrew	CHE	826	FORDSMAN, Alexr.	NOU	164	FORLING, William	PHI	19
Arthur	PHI	7	George	NOU	164	FORLOW, John	LAN	268
James	MIF	1	Joseph	NOU	164	FORMAN, Abram	MNT	140
John	WAS	49	FORDYCE, Jacob	GRN	81	Frederick	BER	248
John	CUM	115	John	GRN	70	Thomas	ALL	83
John	CHE	826	Samuel	WAS	62	FORMWALD, John	LAN	67
Joseph	PHA	122	Samuel	GRN	70	FORNEY, Adam	YOR	180
Nathan	LUZ	350	Samuel	GRN	81	Christn.	DAU	46A
Robert	WAS	20	FORE, David	BFD	62	Christn.	DAU	47A
William	MIF	7	George	BFD	54	Jacob	CUM	64
Wm.	BEV	4	Henry	FRA	304	Jacob	LAN	86
FORBS, Mary	PHI	131	John	BFD	54	Jacob	SOM	148
FORBUS, George	CHE	822	Michael	HNT	128	John	DAU	3

INDEX TO THE 1800 CENSUS OF PENNSYLVANIA

Name	Co.	Pg.	Name	Co.	Pg.	Name	Co.	Pg.
FORNEY, John	LAN	87	FORSTER, Mary	BFD	62	FOSTER, John	PHI	150
Joseph	SOM	148	Richard	BFD	63	John	LAN	231
Mark	YOR	182	Robert	ERI	59	John	FAY	244
Peter	DAU	7	Robert	NOU	193	John	WST	323
Peter	DAU	41	Thomas	NOU	193	John	WST	366
Peter	LAN	110	William	NOU	193	John	BUC	87A
Peter	SOM	148	William	CEN	22A	John	PHI	101A
Samuel	YOR	181	FORSYTH, David	PHI	37	John	PHI	118A
FORNSHELT,			Isaac	YOR	182	Jonn.	CUM	149
William	YOR	155	John Esqr.	YOR	154	Joseph	BUC	88A
FORNY, Adam			Robert	MIF	1	Josiah	CUM	109
(Farmer)	YOR	185	Wm.	FRA	291	Mary	PHI	126
Christian	YOR	185	FORSYTHE, Charles	WAS	49	Miles	PHI	151
Henry	YOR	168	Eli	FAY	265	Moses	GRN	106
FORQUERE, Isaiah	FAY	265	Gabriel	SOM	132	Peter	BUC	88A
Robert	FAY	265	James	WST	213	Philip	PHI	88A
Robert	FAY	265	Jesse	FAY	265	Richard	GRN	87
Samuel	FAY	265	John	CHE	744	Robert	PHI	37
William	FAY	265	William	FAY	265	Robert	WST	323
FORRER, John			FORT, Marmaduke	BUC	89A	Robt.	VEN	167
Junr.	LAN	109	FORTENDER, Lewis	LUZ	388	Rufus	LUZ	404
John Senr.	LAN	109	FORTER?, Abraham	LUZ	403	Samuel	ALL	85
Martin	LAN	109	FORTESCUE, Widow	PHI	24	Samuel B.	CRA	11
FORREST, Henry D.	PHA	72	FORTH, Joseph	PHI	98	Silas	PHI	24
John	ALL	63	FORTNAR, James	PHI	51	Stricland	PHI	152
Lawrence	PHA	9	FORTNER, John	GRN	69	Thomas	GRN	87
Thomas	PHI	129	John	CUM	114	Thomas	CUM	99
Thos.	PHA	72	FORTNEY,			Thomas	ARM	125
William	PHI	38	Christian	YOR	214	Thomas	CUM	148
William	PHI	144	David	DAU	32	Thomas	HNT	166
William	DEL	180	David	YOR	213	Thomas	CHE	701
FORRESTER, Wm.	PHA	46	Henry	DAU	38	Thomas	BUC	93A
Wm.	BUT	342	Michael	FRA	275	Thos.	FRA	305
FORREY, John	LAN	303	FORTNY, George	FAY	265	Walter	PHI	15
John Junr.	LAN	303	John	FRA	279	William	CRA	12
FORRINER, Martin	BER	285	FORTNY?, Michael	FAY	265	William	PHI	151
FORRISON, John	SOM	137	FORTUNE, Nichs.	PHI	108	William	FRA	283
FORRISTER, Lewis	BFD	62	Walter	PHI	115	Willm. A.	PHI	15
FORRY, Christian	LAN	274	FORWARD, Jacob	LYC	16	Wm.	BEV	7
Jacob	YOR	158	FOSBENNER, Jacob	BUC	158A	FOSTER?, (See		
Widow	LAN	274	John	BUC	158A	Faster)	CUM	79
FORSCYTHE, John	BFD	37	FOSE, Abm.	LAN	260	Abraham	LUZ	403
FORSET, Arther	PHI	111	FOSEY, Henry	NOU	146	FOSTIUS, Andrew	CHE	793
FORSHEE,			John	NOU	146	FOTID, Solomon	HNT	153
Catharine	SOM	145	FOSLER?, George	CUM	78	FOTRELL, Stephen	PHI	7
John	SOM	145	FOSSELMAN, Philip	NOH	53	FOTTEL, Mary	PHI	131
Thomas	GRN	106	FOSSET, Thomas	PHA	22	FOUCK?, Abraham	SOM	148
FORSITH, James	ALL	87	Thomas	FAY	214	FOUGHT, Fredk.	CUM	81
James	ALL	100	FOSTER, Widow	WST	323	Jacob	CUM	78
John	ALL	69	Aaaron	YOR	203	John	CUM	82
Robt.	PHI	85A	Abiel	LUZ	404	John	NOU	128
Thomas	FAY	249	Alexander	WST	323	Leond.	CUM	142
FORSITHE, James	BUC	104A	Alexr. Junr.	WST	323	Mathias	DAU	40
Samuel	FAY	203	Amos	PHI	151	Michael	NOU	128
FORSMAN, Hugh			Aron	WST	379	FOUGRAY, Rene	PHA	98
Esqr.	NOH	64A	Chambers	CRA	3	FOULK, Aqullia	LYC	15
Robert	NOH	64A	Fredk.	PHI	90	Cadwalr.	PHI	70
William	NOH	64A	George	PHA	65	Caleb	PHA	76
FORST, Adam	YOR	174	George	WST	251	Caspar	PHA	40
Jacob	NOU	149	George	CHE	732	Christn.	BER	213
John	YOR	210	George	BUC	86A	Fredk.	PHA	56
John	BUC	87A	Hugh/ Nugh?	MER	441	George	SOM	148
Joseph	NOU	149	James	BEV	7	James	ERI	56
Martin	YOR	210	James	WAS	99	John Jr.	BER	213
William	NOU	149	James	YOR	188	Judah	LYC	13
FORSTER, Andrew	NOU	164	James	WST	288	Ludwig	BER	256
Andw.	DAU	45A	James	MER	441	Peter	BFD	63
Benjamin	MNT	34	Jane	WAS	20	Peter	BER	213
Catherine	DAU	3	Jas.	CUM	112	Peter	BER	259
David	DAU	45	John	BEV	6	FOULKE, Ashur	BUC	141
George	MNT	34	John	ADA	13	Benjamin	BUC	156A
James	NOU	193	John	CRA	14	Cadwallader	BUC	156A
James	CEN	22A	John	DAU	28	Caleb	MNT	44
Jas.	LYC	24	John	WAS	28	Christn.	DAU	49
John	DAU	16A	John	GRN	87	Edward	BUC	156A
John	CEN	22A	John	HNT	144	Elizabeth	PHA	24

FOULKE, Evan	BUC 156A	FOWLAR, Thomas	FAY 256	FOX, George		NOH 68A
Everard	BUC 156A	FOWLER, Widow	WST 213	George		PHI 71A
George	DEL 181	Abel	BUC 159	George		PHI 79A
Hugh	MNT 44	Abraham	BUC 93A	George		BUC 150A
Hugh	BUC 157	Adam	BUC 96	Henry		MNT 82
Israel	BUC 156A	Alexd. Esqr.	ALL 61	Henry		SOM 137
Issachar	BUC 157	Archibald	BUT 367	Henry		WST 288
Jane	BUC 156A	Benjamin	NOU 154	Henry		FRA 323
Jesse	MNT 44	Daniel	NOU 146	Jacob		ADA 7
Jesse	BUC 156A	David	NOU 154	Jacob		MNT 73
John	BUC 156A	David	CHE 755	Jacob (The		
Levi _? Wm &		Eseal	NOU 146	Great?)		MNT 73
Z?	MNT 44	George	VEN 165	Jacob		BUC 149
Mary	CUM 46	James	BEV 17	Jacob		HNT 164
Peter	CUM 29	James	FAY 238	Jacob		BER 206
Phillip	CUM 29	John	LAN 13	Jacob		CHE 785
Widow	CUM 74	John	BEV 17	Jacob		DAU 42A
William	DAU 11	John	PHI 104	James		PHA 23
FOULKS, George	BEV 12	John	ALL 114	James		PHI 32
James	PHI 92A	John	WAS 120	James		MIF 16A
William	BEV 14	John	FRA 327	James		DAU 18A
FOULLIET, Wilm.	ALL 55	Jonathan	LUZ 411	John		ADA 32
FOULTIS, Mary	PHA 91	Jonathan Jr.	LUZ 411	John		PHI 34
FOULTON, Henry	DAU 4	Joseph	WAS 37	John		ADA 37
Richd.	DAU 12	Michael	PHI 7	John		PHI 37
FOULTS, Jacob	NOU 136	Morris	CUM 34	John		MNT 99
FOURE, Christian	NOU 182	Morris	PHI 58	John		NOU 104
FOURPAUGH, George	PHI 71A	Patrick	WAS 55	John		NOU 121
FOUSE, Nicholas	HNT 127	Robert	BEV 17	John		CUM 128
FOUSHER, Barbara	FAY 203	Robert	MER 441	John		NOU 146
John	FAY 203	Roger	LUZ 426	John		DEL 172
FOUST, Adam	SOM 137	Thos.	PHI 68	John		BER 244
Anthony	NOU 143A	Wm.	CUM 24	John		WST 288
Christian	NOU 136	Wm.	FRA 279	John		DAU 38A
David	NOU 104	Wm.	CHE 754	John		PHI 76A
George	LAN 38	FOWLES, Edward	DEL 174	John		PHI 118A
Henry	MNT 89	John	DEL 174	John		PHA 40
Henry	MNT 94	Mary	CHE 749	Joseph		GRN 70
Henry	SOM 137	FOWZER, John	PHI 106	Joseph		NOH 66A
Henry	NOU 193	FOX, Widow	PHI 23	Joseph		DEL 172
Jacob	CUM 100	Abraham	SOM 128	Joshua		PHA 20
John	MNT 57	Abraham	BUC 149	Justian		PHI 133
John	NOU 143A	Adam	BFD 37	Justis		WST 150
Michael	PHA 77	Adam	BER 184	Laurence		ADA 38
Nicholas	MNT 94	Adam	BER 273	Margaret		PHA 16
Nicholas	SOM 137	Adam	PHI 120A	Martha		CHE 787
Peter	MNT 60	Andw.	BER 237	Matthias		PHA 41
Phillip	FRA 318	Anthony	MNT 99	Michael		PHA 75
FOUT, Catherine	MNT 73	Anthy.	DAU 35A	Michael		SOM 137
Jacob	PHA 62	Barnet	BUC 149	Michl.		PHI 108A
Ludwick	MNT 99	Benjn.	CHE 757	Nicholas		BER 273
William	WAS 52	Charles	DAU 48	Nicholas Junr.		NOH 33A
FOUTCH, James	FAY 221	Charles	WAS 115	Nicholas		NOH 33A
FOUTNER?,		Christian	PHA 51	Nicholas		NOH 68A
Catharina	ADA 37	Christian	BER 217	Peter		GRN 70
FOUTS, David	ADA 11	Christn.	BER 237	Peter		SOM 128
Jacob	LAN 218	Christn.	BER 244	Peter		NOU 146
Martin	LAN 218	Conrad	NOU 114	Peter		SOM 157
Michael	LAN 218	Conrad	NOH 33A	Peter		DAU 16A
Widow	LAN 222	Daniel	LUZ 412	Peter		NOH 33A
FOUTTS, Christn.	PHI 85A	David	NOU 146	Philip		LUZ 415
FOUTZ, Doctor	LAN 28	David	BER 237	Phillip		NOU 143A
FOW, Henry	PHI 83	David	BER 244	Samuel		DAU 15
Jacob	PHI 83	Elizabeth	PHA 18	Samuel		DEL 190
Wm.	PHI 83A	Emanuel	PHI 123	Simon		HNT 152
FOW?, Widow	PHI 110	Francis	DAU 24	Susan		HNT 159
FOWL, Martha	CUM 35	Francis	NOH 82	Syroc		PHI 135
FOWLAR, Caleb	FAY 221	Fredk.	PHI 118	Thomas		LUZ 416
Jacob	FAY 235	George	PHI 82	Wm.		PHA 66
John	FAY 235	George	PHI 85	FOX?, John		BER 237
John	FAY 238	George	PHA 88	FOXALL, Henry		PHI 117
John	FAY 244	George	PHI 135	FOXE, Benjamin		DEL 162
John	FAY 256	George	HNT 159	Jacob		WST 271
Jonas	FAY 238	George	YOR 185	Peter Junr.		WST 213
Joseph	FAY 235	George	DEL 191	Peter Senr.		WST 213
Thomas	FAY 208	George	YOR 206	FOXX, Samuel		PHA 90

FOY, Widow	PHI 36	FRANCIS, Danl.	WST 366	FRANKENFIELD,			
Frederick	LAN 266A	David	PHI 90	Adam	BUC 90A		
Mary	PHI 153	Henry	PHI 115	Henry	BUC 149		
Michael	PHA 14	James	PHI 86	Henry	BUC 147A		
William	PHI 24	John	PHI 76	John	NOH 73		
William	HNT 131	John	PHI 78	Lawrence	BUC 139A		
FOY?, Wilson	PHA 39	John	PHA 85	Leonard	NOH 80		
FOZONE, Mary	PHI 142	John	PHI 96	Leonard	NOH 33A		
FRACE, Henry	NOH 37A	John	WST 288	Michael	BUC 90A		
FRACIS, Jacob	PHA 116	John	CHE 854	Philip	NOH 33A		
Thos.	PHA 102	Joseph	PHI 37	FRANKFORD, John	PHI 11		
FRACK, Jacob	NOH 29A	Joseph	SOM 128	FRANKFORT, Widow	LAN 56		
John	NOH 43	Mary	PHA 40	FRANKFORTER,			
FRAETZ, Jacob	LAN 143	Michael	PHA 121	Philip	LAN 312		
FRAGAL, Nicks.	PHI 76	Michael	NOU 182	FRANKHOUSEN,			
FRAGO, Jacob	BUC 87A	Philip	DEL 170	Michael	BER 150		
William	BUC 87A	Robert	BEV 8	FRANKLEBURY,			
FRAILEY, John	WST 213	Robert	CHE 888	Sarah	PHA 47		
Peter	BER 235	Samuel	SOM 145	FRANKLIN, Arnold	LUZ 422		
FRAIM, David	FAY 244	Tenoh	PHI 101	Christn.	PHA 73		
James	LAN 120	Thomas	PHA 110	Eliza	PHA 68		
James	FAY 226	Thomas	CHE 893	Jehiel	LUZ 413		
John	FAY 214	William	MNT 34	John	WAS 79		
Thomas	FAY 214	William	FAY 203	John	LUZ 396		
William	FAY 214	Wm.	PHA 72	John	LUZ 425		
FRAINER, James	CHE 747	Wm.	PHI 76A	Lemuel	PHI 31		
FRAIZER, Joseph	FAY 256	FRANCISCUS, John	LAN 58	Mary	BER 204		
Roderick	CRA 4	FRANCK, George	NOH 80	Saml. R.	PHA 87		
FRAIZIER, Wm.	DAU 45A	George	LAN 180	Samuel	DAU 11		
FRAKES, Joseph	GRN 69	John	LAN 143	Samuel	LUZ 352		
Robert	GRN 70	Mary	YOR 160	Solomon	LUZ 413		
FRALE, Edwd.	PHI 41	Michael	LAN 189	Thomas	MER 442		
FRALEY, Widow	PHI 95A	FRANGH?, (See		Walter	PHA 7		
Jacob	BUC 139	Fraugh)		Wm.	PHA 110		
FRALY, Henry	PHI 131	FRANK, Abm.	BUC 81	FRANKS, Abraham	FAY 244		
John	PHI 131	Andrew	CUM 63	George	FAY 214		
Rudolph	PHI 131	Cunrod	LAN 225	Henrey	FAY 214		
FRAMBO, Henry	PHI 88A	Daniel	SOM 128	Isaac	PHA 39		
FRAME, Henry	CHE 894	Danl.	LAN 45	Jacob	CUM 89		
Isaac	DEL 172	Danl.	CUM 24	Jacob	NOU 171		
John	DEL 177	Danl. Jr.	CUM 96	Jacob	FAY 214		
Joseph	CHE 745	David	CUM 22	Jacob	FAY 221		
Moses	SOM 157	George	DAU 8	John	FAY 214		
Robert	DEL 157	George	PHA 65	Michael	FAY 214		
Thomas	CRA 16	George	WAS 99	Michael	FAY 214		
Thomas	DEL 158	Henry	PHI 105	Michael	CHE 789		
Thomas	CHE 714	Henry	CUM 24	FRANKSBERGER,			
Thomas Jun.	CHE 714	Jacob	BER 219	Conrad	MNT 60		
William	WST 323	Jacob	DAU 41A	FRANSIS, Barnit	PHI 125		
William	CHE 711	Jacob	DAU 19	Charles	PHI 127		
FRAMPTON, Arther	ALL 113	Jacob	CUM 24	FRANSISCUS,			
John	CEN 20	Jacob	LAN 107	Christopher	LAN 47		
John	MIF 16A	Jacob	BER 233	Widow	LAN 59		
Nat.	CEN 20	Jacob	PHI 105A	FRANTS, Mary	LAN 117		
Widow	MIF 18	John	DAU 8	FRANTZ, Abraham	YOR 165		
Wm.	MIF 16A	John	ALL 117	Adam	YOR 204		
FRAN, Nathan	PHI 31	John A.	BUC 158A	Christian	LAN 187		
FRANCE, Henry	WST 308	Johnb	YOR 209	Christn.	BER 153		
Jacob	WST 213	Laurence	PHA 114	Christopher	NOU 128		
John	BFD 50	Leonard	PHI 128	Christopher	BER 286		
John	BFD 54	Peter	PHI 130	David	LAN 195		
John	PHA 67	Peter	CUM 57	George	BUC 96		
Joseph	BFD 53	Peter	BUC 158A	George	NOH 89A		
Michl.	WST 213	Peter	BUC 158A	Henry	NOH 59		
Nicholas	WST 308	Widow	BUC 159	Henry	NOH 35A		
Philip	BUC 149	Widow	LAN 225	Jacob	NOH 89		
FRANCE?, John	PHI 90A	Widow	DAU 51A	Jacob	BUC 97		
FRANCES, Elihugh	ALL 70	FRANKE, George	PHA 27	Jacob	NOU 128		
James	FAY 200	Jacob	PHA 110	Jacob	NOU 135		
John	MIF 7	FRANKEBERGER,		Jacob	YOR 206		
John	ALL 55	Geo.	CUM 63	Jacob	NOH 35A		
Thomas	MNT 85	Jacob	YOR 182	Jacob	NOH 83A		
FRANCIS, Arnold	MNT 82	FRANKENBERGER,		John	BUC 96		
Bo-----?,	FRA 278	Conrad	YOR 212	John	LAN 143		
Cavet	DAU 24A	Geo.	CUM 62	John	NOU 128		
Charles	PHA 73	FRANKENFIELD,		Lewis	NOU 128		
		Adam	BUC 147	Mathias	BER 267		

128

FRANTZ, Nicholas	BUC	96	FREBEL, Daniel	NOH	73	FREED, Henry	
Paul	BUC	96	FREBLE, George	NOH	35A	Junr.	MNT 69
Peter	NOH	59	Moses	NOH	35A	Jacob	PHI 122
Peter	NOH	35A	FREBO?, Francis	PHA	26	John	PHI 122
Peter	NOH	83A	FREBREGER, Jacob	PHI	73	John	MNT 127
Philip	NOH	35A	FREBY, John	BER	209	Margaret	PHI 122
FRANZ, William	DAU	5A	FRECKELTON, Robt.	DAU	22A	FREEDENBERG,	
FRASE, Michael	NOH	39	FREDEBORNE,			Isaac	PHA 14
FRASER, Benjamin	BFD	72	Catharine	LAN	300	FREEDLEY, Henry	MNT 69
John	BFD	62	FREDEGLE, Ann	BFD	50	FREEDWAY, Daniel	ALL 86
John	BFD	63	FREDERICK,			FREEL, John	MIF 16A
Matthe.	PHI	6	Abraham	LAN	10	FREELAND, Aaron	GRN 81
Peter	BER	212	Abraham	YOR	213	Benjamin	GRN 75
William	BFD	73	Adam	FRA	303	Benjeman	FAY 214
FRASHER, John	ALL	103	Andrew	PHA	81	James	WAS 79
FRASKER, Danl.	NOU	143A	Benjamin	MNT	89	Mary	CUM 92
FRATZ, Abm. &			Casper	BER	132	Robert	WAY 139
Isaac	BUC	149	Christian	NOH	41	Susannah	GRN 81
Abraham	BUC	90A	Daniel	WAS	120	FREEMAN, Abrm.	BUC 162
Abraham	BUC	104A	George	MNT	89	Alexander	CRA 15
Anthony	BUC	142A	George	NOU	128	Benjiman	FAY 261
Christian	BUC	149	Henry	BER	227	Benjn.	PHI 53A
Isaac (See			Jacob	WAS	37	Caspar	DAU 48A
Fratz, Abm.)	BUC	149	Jacob	NOU	136	Casper	BER 148
John	BUC	154	Jacob	FRA	307	David	ADA 23
John	BUC	155	John	BFD	57	David	LUZ 355
Joseph	BUC	141	John	NOH	78	Edman	FAY 208
Joseph	BUC	81A	John	BUC	159	Edman Jur.	FAY 208
Mark	BUC	149	John	BER	206	Edward	NOH 47
Mark	BUC	104A	John	WST	213	Francis	PHI 91A
FRAUENFELDER,			John	FRA	283	Isaac	NOH 47
Adam	BER	277	John Esqr.	LAN	18	Isacher	CHE 826
FRAUGER, Henrey	FAY	208	Joseph	BUC	160	Jacob	WST 169
FRAUGH, Adam	BUC	91A	Lawrence	NOU	157	Jacob	DEL 188
Peter	BUC	81	Michael	MNT	98	Jacob Senr.	NOH 44A
FRAUST, Philip	NOH	29A	Michael	BUC	159	Jacob	NOH 44A
FRAYLEY, Fredrick	PHA	19	Michael	NOH	29A	James	CRA 5
John	PHI	60	Nichls.	MIF	5	John	FAY 208
John U.	PHA	41	Peter	LAN	19	John	YOR 217
FRAZE, Henry	WAS	44	Peter	NOH	41	John	LUZ 341
FRAZER, Alexr.	CUM	69	Peter	NOH	78	Joseph	PHI 61A
Andw.	YOR	197	FREDERITZE, John	BER	210	Lend.	DAU 48A
Danniel	ALL	64	FREDK., Fredk.	BER	175	Michal	ALL 62
Frances	FAY	227	Jacob	PHI	86	Nathaniel	YOR 217
Fredk.	YOR	190	FREDKSON, Fredk.			Peter	GRN 68
Hugh	LYC	19	A.	PHI	107	Phillip	WST 236
James	MIF	16A	FREDLY, John	FAY	197	Robert	FAY 221
John	PHA	60	FREDRICK, Abm.	PHI	103	Robt.	DAU 2A
John	CUM	88	George	LYC	9	Samuel	BUC 93A
John	LAN	240	George	WST	150	Thomas	GRN 94
Ludk.	YOR	190	Joseph	WST	344	Thoms.	BUT 341
Mary W.	DEL	190	FREDRIGAL, John	BFD	63	Thoms.	BUT 350
Nalbro	PHA	107	FREDRIK, Herman	DAU	5	Tristram B.	PHA 86
Paul	CUM	26	John	DAU	12A	William	NOH 73
Paul	HNT	120	FREE, Abraham	DEL	179	William	ARM 125
Percival	CUM	28	Benj.	PHI	72A	Wilm.	ALL 99
Peter	CUM	79	Conrad	YOR	193	FREEMEN, Abel	CHE 826
Peter Senr.	YOR	156	Hanah	ALL	51	FREENAN?, Hannah	CHE 726
Razor	WST	150	Henry	CUM	65	FREEOUF, Frederic	
Rory	CUM	30	Henry	CUM	67	Revd.	PHA 31
Sophia	YOR	214	Jacob	ADA	4	FREER, Frances	ALL 55
William	CHE	837	Jacob	ALL	89	FREES, Catherine	PHI 128
FRAZEY, Ananiah	WAS	2	Jesse	YOR	219	George	ADA 28
FRAZIER,			Joel	ALL	87	George	NOH 47
Alexander	WAS	20	John	CUM	94	John	NOU 114
Andrew	WAS	49	John	DEL	173	John	NOU 117
Andw.	PHI	78A	John	DEL	174	John	BER 248
Daniel	WAS	37	John	DEL	179	Martin	PHI 127
Edward	WAS	20	Peter	YOR	194	Simion	MNT 109
George	LUZ	329	Samuel	DEL	173	Simon	NOH 78
Jesse	LUZ	372	Thomas	ALL	49	FREETS, Paul	CEN 18A
John	WAY	146	FREEBORN, Agness	CHE	757	FREETZ, Jacob	FRA 287
Thomas	WAS	67	FREEBURN, John	DAU	9A	FREEZE, Joel	LYC 24
Willm.	PHI	37	FREEBURNE, Hil	DAU	9A	FREEZER?, (See	
Wm.?	BEV	23	FREED, Abraham	YOR	165	Fruzer)	LAN 219
FREADA, Chris.	LAN	80	Henry	MNT	69	FREGER, Jacob	WST 288

Name	Loc	Pg
FREHN, Michael	BER	278
Peter	BER	175
FREID, Adam	BER	223
Henry	YOR	168
Jacob	ADA	11
Peter	ADA	31
Peter	MNT	55
FREID?, Christian		
Jun.	ADA	23
Christian Sen.	ADA	23
FREIDAG, Eberhart	NOH	32
FREIEL?,		
Christian		
Jun.	ADA	23
Christian Sen.	ADA	23
FREIL, Patrick	PHA	104
FREIS, Daniel	MNT	112
John	NOU	146
Samuel	MNT	113
Simon	YOR	167
Simon	YOR	177
Solomon	MNT	133
FREISINGER,		
Susannah	YOR	216
FREIST, Samuel	YOR	167
FREIT, Abraham	FRA	278
Jacob	FRA	278
Jno.	FRA	278
John	ADA	25
FREITZ, Jacob	BER	206
FREIVLEY,		
Christopher	LAN	164
FREIZE, Christian	CHE	865
FREKE, Agustine	PHA	11
FREKER, Andr.	FRA	314
FRELEIGH, Geo.	CUM	79
Geo. Senr.	CUM	79
Jacob	YOR	217
FRELICK, Abrm.	DAU	7A
John	DAU	7A
FRELINGSHOUSE, C.		
Peter	DAU	49A
FRELY, Jacob	FRA	291
Jacob	FRA	291
John	FRA	291
FREMAN, Randolph	CRA	5
FREMER, Parson	DAU	17A
FRENCH, Aaron	WAS	62
Aaron	BUT	359
Aaron Junr.	GRN	106
Aaron Senr.	GRN	106
Alexander	WAS	52
Alexander	FAY	221
Andrew	PHI	146
Chas.	PHA	32
Daniel	BFD	50
David	DEL	186
Enoch	FAY	231
George	HNT	139
James	BFD	50
John	WAS	121
John	HNT	143
John	WST	251
Jotham	LUZ	387
Mary	WST	150
Samuel	FRA	323
Thomas	FAY	226
Wilm.	ALL	99
Wm.	BEV	6
Wm.	PHA	103
FRENCHMAN,		
Edoville	DEL	187
FRENEBRAUGH,		
Peter	FRA	286
FRENER, (No Given		
Name)	DAU	35A
FRENICK, Allein/		
Albin?	FRA	301
FRENO, Paul	PHA	108
FRENSH, Joseph	ALL	98
FRENTZLER,		
Frederick	LAN	196
FRESH?, Nathaniel	NOU	157
FRESHCORN,		
Leonard	CHE	725
FRESHER, Conrad	BER	212
George	LAN	139
Lawrence	BER	212
FRESHMOOD, Daniel	PHA	57
FRESHWATER,		
Willm.	FAY	249
FRESINGER,		
Ludwick	YOR	217
FRESTON, Robert	PHI	39
FRETLOW, L.	PHI	6
FRETTS, Christian	FAY	249
FRETTWELL?,		
William	DEL	169
FRETWELL, John	PHA	85
FRETZ, Abraham		
Jnr.	BUC	90A
Abraham	NOH	55A
Christian	BUC	139
Christian	BUC	90A
Daniel	BUC	90A
Henry Jnr.	BUC	90A
Henry	BUC	90A
John	BUC	96
Martin	BUC	96
Menassa	BUC	96
William	BUC	90A
FREVY, John F.	PHI	41
FREW, Allexander	BEV	4
Archibald	YOR	202
Charles	CRA	13
James	BEV	4
James	ALL	107
John	CRA	12
John	ALL	90
Thomas	CRA	7
FREY, Abraham	BER	184
Adam	BER	175
Anthony	YOR	170
Barnet	YOR	204
Christian	BER	140
Christopher	BER	256
Conrad	DAU	21
Conrad	YOR	164
Conrad	BER	225
Conrad	LAN	290
Conrad	NOH	33A
Danl.	BER	213
David	NOH	53
Frantz	BER	129
Frederick	NOH	71
Frederick	LUZ	364
George	YOR	166
George	YOR	206
George	BER	239
George	BER	247
George	DAU	13A
Godfrey	YOR	174
Henry	BER	129
Henry	BER	175
Henry	LAN	190
Henry	YOR	194
Jacob	LAN	42
Jacob	LAN	143
Jacob	YOR	166
Jacob	BER	175
Jacob	LAN	195
Jacob	LAN	290
FREY, John	LAN	41
John	YOR	192
John	LAN	195
John	YOR	206
John	LAN	290
John Jr.	YOR	192
John & Peter	NOH	44A
John	NOH	89A
Jonathen	MIF	12A
Leonard	NOH	51A
Martin	NOH	73
Martin	YOR	158
Mary	YOR	170
Michael	NOH	51A
Moses	BER	129
Peter	LAN	195
Peter	YOR	204
Peter	LAN	289
Peter & John	NOH	44A
Philip	NOH	39
Philip	BER	139
Samuel	MIF	12A
Tobias	YOR	176
Tobias Jr.	YOR	176
William	NOH	85
FREYBERG, John	PHA	72
FREYDAY, John	LAN	85
FREYER, Abram	BUT	330
George	LAN	5
Peter	BUT	321
FREYMAN, Stoffel	NOH	89
FREYMAYER, John	LAN	196
FREYMER, John	LAN	142
FREYMYER,		
Elizabeth	BER	236
FREYS, Peter	NOH	51A
FRIAN, Jacob	PHI	5
FRIAR, Abraham	LUZ	381
FRICH, Jacob	MIF	3
FRICK, Abraham	LAN	98
Abraham	LAN	186
Christian	LAN	186
Christian	LAN	187
David	LAN	311
Frederick	LAN	43
George	WST	288
Henry	MNT	113
Henry Junr.	MNT	113
Jacob	PHI	99
John	MNT	67
John	BUC	101
John	NOU	154
John	NOU	171
John	LAN	185
John	LAN	186
John	CHE	896
Michl.	PHI	102
Peter	MNT	67
Phillip	NOU	171
FRICKER, Andrew	HNT	140
Eve	BER	237
Joseph	PHI	96
Martin	CHE	794
FRICKEY, Fredk.	PHI	96
FRICLE, Charles	PHA	57
FRIDAY, Christian	LAN	311
Jacob	LAN	315
Mathias	LAN	314
Solome	LAN	298
FRIDER, Philip	LAN	138
FRIDERICH, John	LAN	195
FRIDLE, Jacob	FRA	282
FRIDLEY, Andr.	FRA	306
George	CRA	4
John	FRA	305
Ludwick	CUM	31

FRIDLEY, Martin DAU 18A
Peter DAU 18A
Uly FRA 306
FRIDLY, Jacob FAY 240
FRIDOCH, Michael PHI 48
FRIECE, Peter NOU 182
FRIED, Henry MNT 119
Henry BUC 160
Henry BUC 156A
Jacob MNT 126
John BEV 7
John MNT 126
John BUC 158A
Joseph MNT 124
Saml. NOH 55A
William WST 308
FRIEDERICH,
Daniel NOH 43
John NOH 44A
FRIEDLEIN, Conrad BER 285
FRIEDLINE, George SOM 157
Ludwig SOM 128
Peter SOM 128
FRIEL, Cornelius BER 158
FRIEND, Andrew FAY 261
Christopher WAS 121
George WAS 109
George SOM 133
Joseph BFD 50
Nicholas BFD 43
Philip WAS 121
Samuel SOM 133
Tobias WAS 121
FRIER, Conrad MNT 57
James ALL 68
Lenord ALL 105
FRIES, Daniel BER 157
George MNT 107
George Junr. MNT 107
Jacob CUM 58
Jacob BUC 101
John PHA 11
John BUC 101
John BER 136
John BUC 158
John LUZ 358
Michael LAN 195
Michael LUZ 361
Peter NOU 99
FRIES?, Henry BER 136
FRIESE, Jacob PHA 43
FRIESS, Barned NOH 51A
FRIEST, Peter LAN 79
FRIGER, John LAN 142
FRIGLER, Jacob BUC 148A
FRIHOPPER, John PHI 152
FRILING, Casper BUC 139
Casper BUC 149
John BUC 149
FRINK?, John LUZ 400
FRIPPLER, John PHI 101A
FRIRE?, Leonard HNT 131
FRIS, Jacob LAN 74
FRISBY, Calvin ERI 60
Levi LUZ 416
FRISKIRK, Thomas NOU 193
FRISTER?, Godfrey LYC 16
FRITCH, Jacob BER 171
John BER 213
FRITCHLEY,
Godfrey DAU 17
FRITCHMAN, John ALL 58
Michel WST 251
FRITLEY, Jacob DAU 3A
John DAU 11A
FRITS, George DAU 9A

FRITS, Michl. FRA 309
Peter PHA 65
FRITSCHMAN, Elias NOH 33A
FRITSPATERICK,
Barbara PHI 104
FRITZ, Widow PHI 11A
Adam NOH 75A
Andrew MNT 37
Andrew NOH 75A
Balser BER 150
Baltzer YOR 166
Baltzer NOH 51A
Daniel LAN 261
David LAN 261
Dennis? LAN 260
Frederick MNT 73
Frederick BER 248
George NOH 85
George NOH 75A
Hanner NOH 73
Henry BUC 101
Henry LUZ 347
Henry NOH 64A
Jacob LAN 260
Jacob FRA 320
Jacob CHE 786
Jacob Junr. NOH 75A
Jacob NOH 75A
John LYC 6
John CUM 25
John DAU 29
John NOH 73
John MNT 99
John PHA 114
John BER 169
John BER 169
John YOR 169
John BER 173
Joseph BER 213
Ludwig LAN 118
Martin MNT 99
Martin BER 173
Martin LAN 260
Melchior BER 277
Nicholas LAN 273
Peter MNT 99
Peter PHA 117
Philip MNT 137
Philip YOR 168
Phillip PHA 60
Valentine SOM 137
Valentine LAN 188
William SOM 137
FRITZINGER,
Benjm. BER 282
Ernst BER 132
Jacob NOH 44A
John NOH 44A
FRITZMAN, Miss LAN 58
FRITZPATRICK,
Edward PHI 117A
FRIX, Henry WST 366
FRIZE?, Henry CRA 14
FROCK, Henry NOU 128
Jacob NOU 193
Jacob CHE 794
FROGELSINGER,
David CUM 140
FROGMORTON,
Daniel GRN 63
FROLEG, Christ-. LAN 252
FROLICH, John LAN 282
FROM, Frederick BER 148
John BER 148
FROMBERGER, Jane BUC 83
John PHI 130

FRONCH, James DAU 22A
FRONFELDT, Jacob MNT 86
FRONKEIZER, Jacob SOM 157
FRONT?, (See
Trout) PHI 117
FRONTZ, Nichs. DAU 41A
FROST, David Jr. BUC 146A
James FAY 231
James FAY 235
John BUC 146A
Reley FAY 244
William FAY 231
William FAY 235
William FAY 244
FROUGH, Adam WST 190
Daniel WAS 55
Henry NOU 154
FROUP, Paul YOR 211
FROUT, David LAN 228
FROVERT, John PHA 81
FROW, Rosina DAU 9
FROWSER, Widow PHI 46
FROY, David LAN 260
FRUICE, William NOU 154
FRUMMIN, Benjn. PHA 60
FRUNCK, Isaac NOH 29A
Samuel NOH 29A
FRUS?, (See
Frees) NOU 114
John NOU 117
FRUTCH, John NOH 71
FRUTCHE,
Frederick NOH 64A
Mathias NOH 66A
Peter NOH 64A
William NOH 64A
FRUTE, Robert NOU 198
FRUZER, Barnard LAN 219
FRY, Abm. BUC 140A
Abraham WAS 44
Abraham WAS 44
Abraham BFD 57
Abraham NOU 187
Adam CUM 38
Andrew MNT 92
Andrew WAS 109
Andrew BUC 147
Christn. CUM 151
Daniel BFD 57
Daniel WAS 110
Daniel FRA 304
David WAS 109
David NOU 136
Ellis PHA 66
Ephram FRA 272
Gabriel MIF 13A
George PHI 91
George MNT 118
George PHI 126
George SOM 157
George NOU 187
George FRA 308
George MER 441
George NOH 29A
Henry CEN 24
Henry PHA 47
Henry BFD 63
Henry MNT 118
Henry DEL 178
Henry LAN 271
Henry FRA 283
Henry PHA 34
Jacob ALL 74
Jacob NOU 104
Jacob MNT 118
Jacob PHI 130

Name	Code	Pg	Name	Code	Pg	Name	Code	Pg
FRY, Jacob	MNT	133	FRYHOFFER, Wolery	PHI	133	FULLERTON,		
Jacob	CUM	151	FRYMIRE, Henry	FRA	279	Humphry	FRA	300
Jacob	BUC	153	FRYMYER, Daniel	BER	261	Jno	CUM	43
Jacob	NOU	187	Danl.	BER	152	Robt.	PHI	88
Jacob	NOU	187	William	BER	169	Tho.	LYC	25
Jacob	NOU	193	FUCH, John	LAN	99	Thomas	WAS	28
Jacob	WST	288	FUCHS, Henry	DAU	47A	Valeria	PHA	28
Jesse	MIF	7	Jacob	DAU	26	William	WAS	7
John	CUM	28	Jacob	BER	284	William	WST	251
John	MNT	34	Peter	NOH	80	Wm.	CHE	835
John	BFD	57	Philip	BER	144	FULLINBY, John	PHI	80A
John	MNT	73	FUCKS, Dores	BER	245	FULLSTON, Isaac	LAN	237
John	MNT	82	Ernst	BER	245	FULLUM, Mary	SOM	148
John	WAS	110	George	BER	262	FULMAN, Casper	PHI	76A
John	PHI	130	Henry	BER	181	Fredk.	PHI	93
John	PHI	133	John	BER	153	FULMER, Adam	NOU	163
John	NOU	136	Mathias	BER	150	Daniel Jnr.	BUC	90A
John	WST	236	Michael	BER	270	Daniel	BUC	90A
John	BER	237	Peter	BER	169	Frederick	NOU	202
John	BER	237	FUG, Henry	PHI	23	George	MNT	130
John	LAN	271	John	BUC	159	George	NOU	163
John	FRA	275	FUGATE, Edward	GRN	70	George	NOU	164
John	FRA	311	FUGET, John	HNT	129	George	NOU	164
John	WST	323	FUHR, John Junr.	NOH	75A	George	BUC	81A
John Senr.	NOU	136	John Senr.	NOH	75A	Henry	NOU	163
Jonathan	BFD	72	FUHRER, Frederick	NOH	33A	Henry	NOU	164
Joseph	BER	239	Valentine	NOH	32	Jacob	MNT	34
Joseph	CHE	733	FUHRMAN, Conrad	LAN	138	Jacob	PHI	103
Joseph	CHE	794	Henry	LAN	138	Jacob	BUC	147
Joseph Jr.	BUC	147A	Jacob	YOR	184	Jacob	BUC	149
Joseph	BUC	147A	Jacob	YOR	186	Jacob	NOU	163
Lodwick	ALL	60	Jacob	BER	281	Jacob	NOU	143A
Martin	WST	288	Jacob Jr.	YOR	186	John	NOU	163
Matthias	NOU	187	John	LAN	257	John	PHI	117A
Michael	PHA	70	John	LAN	266A	John	BUC	147A
Michael	MNT	75	Michael	YOR	186	Yost	BUC	81A
Michal	MER	442	Pete	LAN	0	FULMORE, Jacob	BFD	72
Micheal	WST	236	Valentine	YOR	186	Jacob	MNT	111
Micheal	WST	308	FUIRBER?, John	PHI	45	John	LAN	159
Paul	MNT	73	FULERTON, Wm.	YOR	198	FULP, Michael	BER	173
Peter	MNT	73	FULETON, Henry	NOU	164	FULSE, Michael	PHI	148
Peter	FRA	309	William	NOU	164	FULTEN, John Sr.	YOR	212
Philip	MNT	107	FULIM, Benjamin			FULTENBERGER,		
Rachel	PHI	133	(Mulatto)	WAS	85	Christn.	LAN	282
Saml.	MIF	7	FULK, Widw.	PHI	107A	FULTERINGTON,		
Samuel	ADA	7	Henry	PHI	112	Alexander	LAN	241
Samuel	WAS	44	Martin	HNT	136	FULTERTON, Jno.	FRA	299
Soloman	BUC	147A	FULKESON, Jacob	LUZ	322	FULTIN, Hugh	YOR	200
Solomon	PHI	122	FULKS, Daniel	BUC	83	Thomas	CHE	728
Widow	LAN	269	Joseph	FAY	235	FULTMAN, Christ.	FRA	293
Widow	LAN	270	FULLAR, Daniel	FAY	208	FULTON, Abraham	WST	344
William	MNT	87	FULLENDER, Aron	PHI	85	Alexander	NOH	47
FRY?, -----	MIF	10	FULLER, Adam	ADA	24	Alexander	HNT	121
James?	MIF	10	Benajah	LUZ	343	Alexr.	CHE	711
John?	MIF	10	Benjamin	LUZ	350	Andrew	WAS	90
FRYAR, David	CHE	743	Daniel	LUZ	351	Benjamin	WAS	55
Isaac	MNT	106	Eli	WAY	144	Benjn.	CUM	26
FRYBAGER, John	NOU	175	Elizabeth	BER	236	David	YOR	196
FRYBEARG, John	PHI	115	Ira	WAY	144	David	CEN	22A
FRYBERGER, Andw.	MIF	7	James	CHE	740	Francis	CUM	114
FRYE, Martin	ADA	20	Jehiel	LUZ	372	Henry	NOU	157
Michael	ADA	26	Johiel	WAY	144	Hugh	SOM	133
Peter	FAY	226	John	PHI	15	Hugh	WST	150
FRYER, Barnt	MNT	62	John	LUZ	418	Hugh	YOR	199
Bernard	MNT	121	Joshua	LUZ	343	Jame	WAS	33
Christian	MNT	60	Reuben	LUZ	418	James	MNT	64
George	BFD	55	William	CHE	742	James	ARM	125
George	PHI	90	William	CHE	797	James	SOM	133
Henry	MNT	57	Wm.	CHE	841	James	HNT	161
Henry Senr.	MNT	60	FULLERTON, Widow	PHI	17	James	YOR	199
Jacob	MNT	98	Alexander	PHA	16	James	LAN	221
John	PHI	107A	Alexr.	CUM	122	James	WST	251
Joseph	MNT	60	Clarke	WAS	7	James	FAY	261
Philip	MNT	57	David	FRA	300	James	BUT	325
Philip	MNT	60	Esther	PHA	33	James	WST	344
Thos.	LYC	20	Henry	WAS	90	James	CHE	866

FULTON, James	CEN	18A	FUNDERSMITH, John	LAN 216	FURMAN, William	GRN	75
Jesse	YOR	213	John	LAN 219	FURNACE, Cornwall	DAU	27A
Jno.	CUM	106	Valentine	LAN 217	John	DEL	158
Jno.	CUM	112	FUNDERWHILE,		Thomas	DEL	157
John	LAN	50	Jacob	PHI 78A	FURNBECK, Wm.	LYC	13
John	WAS	52	FUNDERWISE, John	CHE 858	FURNEY, Andrew	ADA	27
John	MNT	69	FUNK, Adam	BFD 41	Francis	DAU	13
John	GRN	100	Adam	BUT 366	Henry	ADA	27
John	WAS	120	Ann	HNT 131	Jacob	DAU	13
John	FAY	235	Benedick	YOR 157	John	ADA	25
John	FRA	306	Christo.	WST 288	John	ADA	27
John	CHE	713	Christopher	NOU 175	FURNEY?, Henry	WAS	43
John	CHE	775	David	BUC 140A	FURNIS, George	PHA	57
John	CHE	866	Elijah	CHE 857	FURNMYER, Daniel	NOU	175
Joseph	ALL	76	George	BFD 35	Peter	NOU	175
Peter	CEN	18A	George	BUC 102	FURNY, Jacob	FRA	310
Robert	WST	251	George	YOR 174	FURREY, George	DAU	51A
Robert	WST	288	Henry	CUM 26	Henry	WST	308
Samuel	WAS	90	Henry	HNT 136	Jacob	FAY	203
Samuel	ALL	112	Henry	PHI 88A	John	SOM	157
Samuel	YOR	199	Henry	BUC 147A	Joseph	LAN	54
Samuel	FAY	265	Jacob	MNT 40	FURRIM, John	PHI	55
Thomas	CRA	15	Jacob	BUC 148	FURROW, John	NOU	109
Thomas	CHE	846	Jacob	YOR 158	FURRY, Daniel	LAN	5
William	HNT	144	John	MNT 67	Daniel	YOR	165
William	LAN	150	John	BUC 96	Daniel	DAU	27A
William	WST	150	John	MNT 127	David	CHE	729
William	CEN	18A	John	BUC 147	John	LAN	4
Wilm.	ALL	97	John	FRA 303	John	YOR	181
Wm.	CUM	123	John	CHE 794	Joseph	NOU	164
FULTON?, (See			John	BUC 90A	William	LAN	96
Tulton)	FRA	304	Joseph	PHI 82A	FURRY?, (See		
James	CRA	13	Martin	BFD 37	Finey)	CHE	732
James	PHI	21	Martin	BUC 96	(See Turry)	LAN	12
FULTS, John	LAN	173	Martin	HNT 131	FURTNEY, Henry	GRN	75
FULTZ, Frederic	CHE	885	Martin	YOR 160	FURY, Eliza.	CUM	94
Jacob	BUC	147A	Samuel	MNT 42	John	CUM	76
John	BUC	147A	Widow	BUC 147A	Leonard	FRA	316
FULWEILER, Barnet	NOH	53	FUNK?, John	LUZ 400	Menathis	PHI	28
Daniel	NOH	53	FUNKHAUSER, Peter	LAN 271	Robert	WAS	110
Ferdinand	NOH	53	FUNKHOUSER, Jacob	BEV 7	FUSH?, Nathaniel	NOU	157
John	YOR	210	FUNKKIRKHOUSE?,		FUSHEY, Andrew	NOU	143A
John	BER	237	Ephraim	BEV 27	FUSINGER, John	YOR	163
John Jr.	BER	237	FUNKLE, George	LAN 242	FUSSEL, Barthw.	CHE	794
Michael	YOR	210	FUNKS, John	CUM 23	FUSSELL, William	CHE	789
FULWELLER, Mary	CUM	42	FUNLADA, Nicholas	NOU 175	FUSSELMAN, Danl.	CUM	46
FULWOOD, Chr.	WST	288	FUNSON, William	LUZ 344	George	BER	130
FUNCK, Andrew	MNT	40	FUNSTER, William	NOH 71	Jno.	CUM	53
Francis	DAU	9	FUNSTON, James	NOH 66A	FUSSER, Thomas		
George	LAN	91	Jesse	NOU 117	(B. Man)	ALL	72
Henry	LAN	274	John	NOU 157	FUST, William	PHI	41
Henry	LAN	295	FUR, Elizah.	PHI 53A	FUSTER, David	PHI	38
Jacob	WST	271	FURD, Henry	LAN 195	Thos.	FRA	313
Jacob	LAN	295	FURGASON, James	BUT 335	Widow	LAN	129
Jacob	NOH	55A	Willm.	BUT 336	FUT?, Peter	NOU	143A
John	DAU	21	Willm.	BUT 352	FUTER, William	PHI	32
John	DAU	43	FURGESON, Archbd.	MIF 25	FUTHY, Saml.	CHE	873
John	LAN	196	George	LAN 133	Samuel	WAS	28
John	LAN	216	John	LAN 245	FUTLY, Daniel	FAY	227
John	LAN	295	Robt.	CHE 759	FUTTWELL?,		
Martin	LAN	295	Samuel	LAN 218	William	DEL	169
Martin	DAU	25A	FURGISON, Andrew	LAN 167	FUTZ, Phillip	NOU	152
Michael	LAN	12	James	LAN 162	FYAN, John	PHI	77
Michael	LAN	82	Samuel	PHA 117	FYGART, Ann	HNT	155
Peter	DAU	11A	FURGUSON, Thomas	CEN 22A	FYSCK, Jacob	SOM	157
Philip	LAN	143	FURINGTON, Putnam	LAN 97	John	SOM	157
Rudy	LAN	283	FURLONG, James	BUC 157	FYSEL, Andrew	PHA	79
Samuel	LAN	209	John	PHI 99	FYYZER, Joseph	ARM	127
Samuel	LAN	295	Wm.	FRA 290			
Sophia	LAN	195	FURMAN, Adam	CUM 65	G----?, -----	MIF	10
Widow	LAN	40	Edman	NOU 114	-----	FRA	297
Widow	LAN	295	Francis	LAN 188	G--ER?, Guien?	BEV	20
Widow	NOH	55A	Henry	MNT 124	G--SS?, Philip	MIF	10
William	MIF	5	Henry	BUC 147A	G--THER?, Widow	PHI	79
FUNDAY, Andw.	PHI	36	John	PHI 93A	G--TINE?, John	MIF	10
FUNDERSAHL, Henry	LAN	214	Richard	GRN 75	G-R--N?, Thomas	FRA	284

Name	Loc	Pg
GA---Y?, Wm.	FRA	315
GA--AM, Wilm	ALL	53
GABBY, James	WAS	12
John	YOR	200
William	WAS	20
GABE, Martin	BER	182
GABEL, Abraham	FRA	301
Peter	PHI	79
Phillip	ALL	115
GABLE, Adam	NOU	122
Conrod	FRA	322
Daniel	LAN	286
Danl.	BER	163
Eve	LAN	170
Henry	CUM	99
Henry	BER	166
Jacob	LAN	37
Jacob	BER	161
John	BER	166
John	PHI	79A
Lewis	BER	203
Peter	BUC	159
Philip	MNT	89
Richd.	FRA	301
Valentine	LAN	62
Vanentine	YOR	197
Widow	BUC	160
GABREL, Jonathn.	FAY	244
GABRELL, Philip	YOR	157
GABRIEL, Gordon	WST	272
Jacob	BER	162
John	BER	162
GACKENBACH,		
Charles Jr.	NOH	85
John	BER	277
GAD, Ignatius	HNT	134
Robert	PHI	37
Thos.	BUC	93A
William	HNT	134
GADDES, James	FAY	256
John	FAY	256
Robt.	FAY	256
Thomas	FAY	256
William	FAY	256
GADGEBY, Neal	FRA	275
GAERMAN, John	DAU	10A
GAFEY?, Jemima	DEL	163
GAFF, George	FRA	298
Hugh	FRA	295
James	WST	214
Sarah	FRA	303
Thomas	PHI	18
GAGEBY, James	WST	169
GAGHEN, Francis	LAN	244
John	LAN	244
GAGLIN, Bastian	LAN	197
Dietrick	LAN	196
John	LAN	197
GAHAGEM, Thomas	WST	236
GAHEEN, Lehna	LAN	91
GAHUM, Edward	NOU	110
GAILBREATH, James	FRA	273
GAILEY, Alexr.	CUM	28
Charles	CHE	908
James	MER	443
John	MER	443
GAILY, James	WAS	74
GAIREY, John	WST	160
GALA--CA?, James	CRA	10
GALACHER,		
Isabella	CHE	779
GALAGHER, James	ADA	3
Philip	LAN	286
GALAGON, Thos.	BER	163
GALAHER, Hugh	ADA	11
GALASPEY, Mark	MER	443
GALASPIE, Charles	NOU	198
John	NOU	117
GALBRAITH, Alexr.	YOR	202
Alice	WAS	99
Archibald	HNT	148
Eliza	BUT	333
Ephraim	HNT	125
James	HNT	125
James	WST	169
James Junr.	HNT	125
John	WAS	99
John	HNT	125
Joseph	ARM	124
Margaret	WAS	28
Patrick	HNT	135
Peter	DEL	188
Robert	ARM	124
Robert	HNT	136
Samuel	HNT	125
W?	PHI	24
William	WAS	99
William	HNT	125
GALBREATH, Alexr.	CUM	94
Andw.	CUM	54
Barham	LAN	7
Barbara	MIF	26A
Geo	CUM	136
Hannah	CEN	20
James	CUM	94
James	MER	442
John	CUM	108
Robt.	CUM	27
Saml.	CUM	108
Saml.	CUM	122
Saml.	LAN	7
Samuel	CUM	27
Wm.	CUM	103
Wm.	ALL	120
GALBRETH, Doncan	ALL	120
Elspy	ALL	120
Hugh	ALL	120
James	ALL	118
John	ALL	59
Robert Esqr.	ALL	103
Samuel	LUZ	320
GALE, Anna	HNT	159
David	BUC	84A
Isaac	LUZ	327
Israel	PHI	67
John	FAY	203
John	PHA	54
Joseph	CRA	12
GALEN?, Joel	CEN	22A
GALES, George	NOU	136
Michael	WAS	121
GALHAMPTON, John	WAS	121
Thos. Junr.	WAS	121
Thos. Senr.	PHI	133
GALIGAR, James	LAN	115
GALL, Henry	LAN	42
John	PHI	52
William	LYC	17
GALLA----, Wm.	LAN	41
GALLACHER, James	PHA	94
GALLAGER, Chas.		
GALLAGHER,		
Abraham	YOR	204
Charles	HNT	141
Edwd.	WST	367
Geoe.	PHI	33
George	HNT	159
James	PHA	16
James	WAS	68
James	WST	345
John	LAN	13
John	WAS	28
John	YOR	199
GALLAGHER,		
Michael	WAS	20
Michael	LAN	231
Patrick	PHI	50
Thomas	HNT	159
Widow	LAN	40
William	MIF	1
Willm.	PHI	26
Wm.	PHI	29
GALLAHAN, Jeremh.	BUT	349
GALLAHER,		
Catharine	MIF	7
Daniel	SOM	157
Francis	LAN	31
Francis	FRA	311
Hugh	CEN	22A
John	BUT	334
John	BUC	88A
Lewis	BEV	8
Michael	ADA	22
Michael	ADA	36
Patrick	ADA	36
Peter	BUT	334
Richd.	MIF	25
Thomas	MIF	7
GALLAHOE, Francis	CUM	34
GALLAKER, Wm.	PHI	95
GALLASPEE, Hugh	BUT	331
GALLASPIE, David	FRA	316
John	BUT	331
William	NOU	128
GALLASPY, James	LAN	130
GALLAWAY, Robert	FAY	231
GALLBRAITH, John	WST	236
Joseph	WST	236
GALLENTINE, John	FAY	256
GALLET, Francis	PHA	80
GALLETIN, Albert	FAY	244
GALLEY, Jacob	DEL	187
Joseph	PHA	44
GALLIAN, Gilburt	FRA	291
GALLIHER, John	BFD	37
Thomas	ERI	56A
GALLILEM, Wm.	CHE	872
GALLIPON, Widow	PHI	37
GALLISPIE, Margt.	FRA	311
GALLOGHER, Hugh	WST	379
GALLOP, William		
Jr.	LUZ	375
GALLOWAY, Enoch	WAS	37
Henry	GRN	100
James	WST	288
Jas.	CUM	93
John	ADA	9
John	FAY	208
John	WST	288
Joseph	PHI	29
Joseph	HNT	135
Robert	NOH	66A
Samuel	ERI	59A
Sarah	ADA	10
William	GRN	100
William	GRN	108
William	FAY	209
Wm.	CHE	777
GALLUP, Hallet	LUZ	334
William	LUZ	334
GALOCK, Godfried	DAU	26A
GALSEY, Peter	LAN	246
GALT, Adam	LAN	123
Alexander	LAN	125
Jacob	LAN	134
James	LAN	69
James	LAN	124
James	LAN	124
GALVEN, Jeremiah	CRA	17

Name	Loc	Pg
GALWICK, Peter	FRA	278
GALY, James	ALL	111
GAM, John	FRA	303
GAMBEL, Wilm.	ALL	95
GAMBELL, Adam	CUM	114
GAMBER, Widow	PHI	95
Fredk.	CUM	38
Jno.	CUM	38
Valentine	CUM	39
Wm.	CUM	43
GAMBLE, Aaron	HNT	161
Agness	MIF	1
Andrew	CHE	732
Elizabeth	HNT	161
Elizh.	FRA	321
Hambleton	CHE	846
Hugh	CHE	877
James	LYC	25
James	PHI	47
James	PHA	113
James	WST	150
James	CHE	699
John	LYC	17
John	PHI	18
John	LAN	226
John	BER	232
Joseph	SOM	148
Josiah	WAS	68
Mary	PHA	68
Moses	WST	150
Patrick	DEL	159
Peter	CHE	828
Robt.	FRA	285
Saml.	FRA	321
Samuel	BUC	98
Samuel	BUC	105
Solomon	WAS	67
Thomas	WAS	90
William	WAS	15
William	BFD	40
William	GRN	70
William	LUZ	399
GAMGER?, George	BER	223
GAMMELL, William	YOR	197
GAMMILL, Robert	YOR	195
Sarah	YOR	202
GAN?, (See Yan)	LAN	90
GANBY, Robert	MNT	54
GANCHER?, (See Gaucher)	BER	220
GANDLER, Neal	PHA	111
GANERTHAM?, James	BFD	69
GANGER, George	BER	223
John	BER	223
GANGES, Josep	ALL	119
GANGEWARE, Jacob	NOH	47A
GANGWEHR, Abraham	NOH	68A
Andw.	NOH	68A
Daniel	NOH	80
David	NOH	80
George	NOH	89A
Henry	NOH	80
Jacob	NOH	68A
Math.	NOH	68A
GANINE, William	LAN	170
GANN, Casper	NOU	128
GANNER?, Ephrim	MIF	9
GANNOW, Nicholas	FAY	221
GANO, Jacob	HNT	131
GANS, Benjaman	FAY	244
George	DAU	32
George	FAY	244
John	FAY	244
Joseph	FAY	244
GANSALUS, Richd.	CEN	18A
GANSER, George	DAU	14
GANSERT?, Jacob	BER	142
GANSEY, John	CUM	32
GANSINGER?, Abraham	FRA	295
GANSON, Francis	CHE	704
GANSY, Benjn.	LYC	27
GANT, Jacob	FAY	265
GANTZ, Andrew	WAS	121
Baltzer	LAN	97
George	ADA	9
George	BER	135
George	YOR	190
George	LAN	261
Jacob	FRA	291
John	WAS	121
John	SOM	153
John	BER	240
GANTZEL, Adam	NOH	59
GANTZER, Gabriel	BER	133
GAOLE, John	LAN	261
GAPEN, Eli	GRN	76
John	GRN	76
Stephen	GRN	75
William	GRN	75
Zachariah	GRN	76
GARAGAN, Thomas	HNT	153
GARAUD, Jacob	PHA	6
GARAVINE, Francis	CHE	731
GARBER, Andw.	YOR	167.
Benedict	MNT	82
Charles	MNT	82
Christian	LAN	308
Christian	LAN	308
Conrad	MNT	99
David	DAU	37
Jacob	MNT	82
Jacob	BER	147
John	MNT	94
John	YOR	184
GARBERICK, Fredk.	YOR	190
George	YOR	190
Michael	YOR	190
Michael	YOR	192
Peter	YOR	190
GARBERIK, Phil.	DAU	34A
GARBOCH, John	LAN	40
GARBREK, Adam	DAU	35
GARBS, Thomas	VEN	167
GARD, Ephraim	FAY	214
Jacob	FAY	221
Jerimia	FAY	256
Levi	FAY	256
Noah	FAY	221
Timothy	FAY	261
GARDEN, John	PHI	86
John	PHI	112
Samuel	NOU	109
GARDENER, Daniel	WAS	121
Francis	WAS	67
George	CHE	797
James	GRN	88
James	GRN	92
John	WAS	28
GARDETTE, James	PHA	4
GARDING, Jonathan	BER	175
GARDNER, Adam	WAS	2
Adam	DAU	10
Andrew	CHE	835
Andw.	MIF	7
Archibald	DEL	169
Aron	PHA	60
Aron	PHA	84
Arthur	WAS	44
Bart	DAU	35A
Basilla	PHA	37
Benjn.	PHA	110
GARDNER, Cuff	PHA	60
David	WST	271
Francis	FRA	302
Francis	CHE	901
Geo.	DAU	35A
George	WAS	2
George	MIF	17
George	PHA	45
George	SOM	151
George	SOM	157
George	WST	169
George	BER	235
George Jr.	BER	235
George	MIF	16A
Hester	PHA	103
Jacob	PHI	133
Jacob	YOR	154
Jacob	WST	288
Jacob	PHI	106A
James	MIF	5
James	PHI	9
James	PHA	113
James	LUZ	335
Jesse	LUZ	361
Jesse	LUZ	368
Jno. Junr.	CUM	48
Jno. Senr.	CUM	52
John	WAS	2
John	LYC	11
John	MNT	44
John	PHA	44
John	DEL	186
John	FAY	214
John	FRA	290
John	WST	309
John	LUZ	374
John	CEN	18A
John	PHI	71A
Joseph	HNT	166
Maria	PHI	38
Martin	DAU	34A
Michael	HNT	127
Mona	LAN	50
Nathaniel D.	DEL	188
Peter	BFD	57
Peter	LUZ	426
Rebecca	PHA	10
Richard	LUZ	374
Robert	MIF	3
Stephen	LYC	11
Stephen	LUZ	323
Thomas	LUZ	375
Volentine	PHI	116
William Doc	DEL	167
Wm.	PHA	44
Wm.	CUM	73
GAREN, Clatworthy	BER	162
GAREY, Cornelius	BFD	57
GARGATY?, Richd.	FRA	321
GARIGUES, Saml., Esqr.	PHI	68A
GARING, Michl.	PHI	86A
GARIS, Frederick	BUC	90A
John	BUC	149
Nicholas	BUC	91
GARISON, Benjamin	NOU	99
Jared	DAU	13A
GARLACH, George	LAN	51
GARLAND, Widw.	PHI	114
Ebenezer S.	DEL	192
Geo.	CUM	39
George	BFD	43
GARLEFTS, John	SOM	145
GARLET, Joseph	PHA	52
GARLETTS, Henry	SOM	148
GARLEY, Hugh	PHI	12

GARLEY, James	FRA	273	GARRETT, Jonathan	CHE	705	GARVES, Benjn.	BUT	344
GARLICK, Barbary	PHA	56	Joseph	CHE	702	GARVES?, Richd.	BUT	360
Stephen	BFD	50	Josiah	CHE	702	GARVEY, Widow	WST	367
GARLIN, James	CHE	877	Levi	CHE	881	GARWOOD, Charity	GRN	81
Jno.	CUM	42	Levy	PHA	107	Isaac	GRN	95
GARLINGER, Widow	PHI	86	Mathew	FAY	261	James	PHI	14
GARLITZ,			Nathan Jun.	DEL	170	Jesse	FAY	227
Christopher	YOR	183	Oborne	DEL	170	Joseph	CRA	15
GARLOCK, Henry	LAN	40	Saml.	CHE	878	Joseph Junr.	PHA	63
GARMAN, Conrad	DAU	39A	Samuel	DEL	170	Medien?	VEN	166
George	LAN	64	Samuel	CHE	702	Obed	CRA	16
Jacob	CEN	20	Thomas	DEL	170	Samuel	CRA	10
John	PHI	133	Thomas	CHE	735	Samuel	CRA	13
Peter	NOU	182	William	DEL	170	Stacy	GRN	81
GARMER?, Ephrim	MIF	9	William	DEL	181	William	PHI	7
GARMON, Henry	DAU	39	Wm.	CHE	878	William	GRN	81
Michael	DAU	39	GARRIGAN, Widow	PHI	81A	GARY, Mathias	MNT	89
GARN, Jacob	FAY	244	GARRIGUES, Widow	PHI	85A	Phebe	CHE	699
John	SOM	153	Widw.	PHI	102	William	WAS	85
GARNER, Adam	GRN	81	Abm.	PHA	38	GASGO, Elizabeth	CHE	735
Andw.	MIF	25	Benjn. F.	PHA	104	GASKEL, Caleb	FAY	265
Careswell	CHE	733	Edward	DEL	192	Samuel	FAY	265
Frederick	LAN	196	GARRIGUS, Edwd.	PHA	68	GASKET, D. Lisle	MNT	103
George	MNT	118	Saml.	PHA	55	GASKILL, Ebenezer	PHA	75
Henry	MIF	15	Wm.	PHA	68	GASKIN, Daniel	NOU	171
James	PHA	64	GARRIS?, Joseph	LUZ	425	Hugh	LYC	29
James	GRN	95	GARRISON,			Patrick	WST	309
John	ALL	63	Cornilius	LUZ	328	Thomas	NOU	171
John	HNT	116	Ephraim	GRN	100	GASKINS, Edward	FAY	221
John	BUC	156	Frederick	GRN	76	Larry	LYC	22
John	LAN	244	George	GRN	76	Samuel	FAY	221
Martin	MIF	15	George	GRN	81	GASNEL, Joshua	HNT	146
Peter	FAY	250	Jacob	GRN	76	GASNER, John	LAN	109
Robert	HNT	134	Jonathan	GRN	74	GASS, George	PHA	5
Samuel	BUC	105	Jonathan	GRN	76	George	NOU	104
William	HNT	132	Leonard	GRN	76	Martin	NOU	104
GAROM, Saml.	PHI	109	Leonard Junr.	GRN	76	Peter	LAN	274
GARR, George	NOH	89A	GARRISSON, Thos.	PHI	149	Peter	LAN	275
GARRELL, Edward	FAY	265	GARRIT, Saml.	PHI	62	Wm.	FRA	281
GARREN, James	CHE	876	GARRITSON, John	BFD	73	GASSART, Adam	DAU	38A
William	PHA	118	GARRITT, James	PHI	105A	John	DAU	34A
GARRET, Andrew	WAS	56	GARROW, Patrick	LAN	245	GASSER, Christn.	DAU	33A
James	WAS	7	GARRUN, James	FRA	294	John	DAU	33A
Jane	CUM	35	GARSON, Saml.	FRA	283	GASSERT, Geo.	BER	152
John	WAS	56	GARST, David	LAN	2	Widow	DAU	52
Michel	WST	251	Peter	DAU	52	GASSKILL, Peter	DEL	184
Morton	PHI	62	GARSTER, Jacob	SOM	132	GASSLER, Henry	BER	252
William	WAS	28	GARTEN, Jacob	DAU	27A	GAST, Mathias	DAU	38
GARRETSON, Aaron	BFD	73	GARTLAND, John	PHA	36	GASTEN, Joseph	NOU	164
Cornelius	YOR	163	GARTLEY, John	PHA	27	GASTINE, Amos	BUC	96
Jacob	YOR	216	GARTLY, George	ALL	65	GASTON, James	WAS	15
John	ADA	44	GARTNER, Adam	ADA	43	James	WAS	74
Jos.	YOR	216	George	ADA	28	James	WAS	90
William	WAS	79	John	ADA	38	John	WAS	74
GARRETT, Aaron	CHE	881	Marks	YOR	172	John	WST	251
Abner	CHE	879	Martin	YOR	167	Samuel	WAS	68
Abraham	DEL	189	Michael	YOR	156	William	WAS	74
Alexander	LAN	156	Peter	YOR	210	William	NOH	64A
Amos	CHE	881	Philip	YOR	167	GATCHELL, David	CHE	869
Andw.	YOR	183	Valentine	LAN	240	Harman	CHE	869
Andw.	PHI	119A	William	ADA	41	GATEIR, Rene	PHA	79
Benjamin	CHE	702	GARUS, Christer	NOU	164	GATER, Edward	WAS	33
Christopher	MNT	57	GARVAN, David	MER	443	Prince	PHA	111
David	DEL	175	John	MER	443	GATES, Benjamin	WST	169
David	CHE	881	GARVEN, Benjn.	BUT	340	John	GRN	81
Elisha	CHE	877	James	WAS	28	Martin	WAS	44
George	CHE	701	James	PHI	31	Martin	YOR	212
George	CHE	886	GARVER, Abraham	MIF	3	GATLIFF, Samuel	PHA	91
Gideon	CHE	818	Adam	CHE	890	GATTES, Henrey	FAY	231
Isaac	CHE	881	Chris.	LAN	87	James	FAY	214
Jehu	DEL	179	Isaac	MIF	3	GATTIS, Joseph	HNT	133
Jesse	CHE	878	Jacob	LAN	173	GATZ, Fredk.	PHI	103
Jesse Jr.	CHE	878	Jacob	LAN	180	Nathl.	PHI	11A
John	PHI	1	John	CRA	2	GAUATON, John	CEN	22A
John	PHI	63	John	MNT	107	GAUCHER, Gotfrey	BER	220
Jonas	DEL	180	Peter	LAN	182	John	BER	270

GAUFF, Philip	NOH	47
GAUGE, Edward	PHI	147
GAUGER, Danl.	BER	175
Nicholas	BER	270
GAUGHLER,		
Nicholas	NOU	136
GAUL, Adam	PHI	65
Fredk.	PHI	102
Henry	BER	169
John	CUM	43
John	BER	169
Matthias	LAN	78
GAULCHER, James	HNT	117
GAULLINGS,		
Michael	NOU	128
GAULT, Adam	WAS	74
Adam	WAS	74
James	WAS	74
John	WAS	74
John	WAS	74
Soloman	FRA	275
GAUMER, Adam	NOH	59
Dietter Jun.	NOH	59
Friederick	NOH	59
Henry	NOH	59
Jacob	NOH	59
Jno. Dieter	NOH	59
Mathias	NOH	59
GAUN, Jacob	PHI	84
John	PHI	84
GAUS, Charles	FAY	227
Enoch	FAY	227
Solomon	FAY	227
GAUSE, William	CHE	848
GAUT, Andrew	WAS	99
David	WAS	20
James	WAS	20
John	WAS	56
John	WST	272
Mathew Esqr.	FAY	250
Samuel	FAY	214
William	WAS	20
GAUTHOP, Jane	CHE	766
GAUTHROP, Thos.	CHE	766
GAUTIER, Andrew	PHA	73
GAUVEL, George	ADA	30
GAVEN, Widow	PHI	75
GAVIN, William	ADA	9
GAW, Chamber	PHA	38
Gilbert	PHA	34
Job	PHI	136
William	WAS	68
GAWLEY, Phillip	FAY	250
GAWN, Thomas	BUC	107
GAY, Hugh	CHE	870
Thomas	WAY	144
GAYE, Peter	WST	236
GAYLOR, Eleazar	LUZ	400
GAYLORD, Ambrose	LUZ	400
Charles E.	LUZ	352
Justice	LUZ	396
Justus Senr.	LUZ	400
GAYMAN, Abraham	BUC	102
Abrm.	DAU	14
Christian	BUC	96
Daniel	WAS	121
Jacob	BUC	147A
GAYMON, Christian	BUC	141
GAYNS?, Valentine	BUC	159
GAYRIS?,		
Valentine	BUC	159
GAZZAM?, Wilm.	ALL	53
GE----ESS?,		
Josepth	MER	442
GEALLY, John	BEV	12
Wm.	BEV	12

GEARHART, Jacob	BFD	47
Jno.	CEN	22A
GEARHEART, George	NOU	104
Henry	NOU	175
Jacob	NOU	104
Jacob	NOU	104
John	NOU	104
John	NOU	175
John	NOU	187
John	NOU	187
Michael	NOU	182
Peter	NOU	114
Tunis	NOU	143A
William	NOU	104
William	NOU	171
GEARHOUSE, George	PHI	98
GEARY, Allexd.	ALL	101
Jacob	MNT	133
William	MNT	77
GEARY?, John	MNT	134
GEBEL, Christian	NOH	59
George	BER	135
Henry	LAN	185
John	NOH	82
John	LAN	189
Peter	LAN	186
William	LAN	185
GEBGAHART, Henry	BER	158
GEBHART, Abraham	NOH	59
Adam	BER	263
Adam	BER	274
Cathn.	BER	151
Daniel	NOH	59
George	BER	130
George	BER	262
George	BER	270
George Sr.	BER	270
Henry	BER	262
Jacob	LAN	21
Jacob	BER	270
Jacob	BER	274
John	NOH	47
John	BER	162
John	BER	266
John	BER	270
John	BER	270
John	NOH	35A
John P.	BER	151
Leonhard	NOH	75A
Nicols.	DAU	48A
Peter	BER	270
Peter	BER	270
Valentine	BER	270
GEBLER, Godfrey	PHA	5
Mathias	PHA	31
Peter	LAN	209
GECK, Adam	LAN	185
GEDDES, Jas.	CUM	100
Jno.	CUM	100
John	CUM	128
GEDDIS, George	BUC	141
Henry	BUC	141
John	BUC	141
Wm.	PHA	89
GEDMACHER, Henry	LAN	314
GEE, Wm.	FRA	314
GEEBLER, David	DAU	38A
GEEDY, John	LAN	311
GEER, Chrles	LUZ	387
Martin	ALL	52
Mary	SOM	132
Peter	CUM	104
William	MNT	99
GEERHART, Peter	CUM	45
GEERING, Joseph	FAY	244
GEESE, Christian	YOR	192

GEESE, Conrod	CUM	133
GEESEY, Henry	LAN	307
John	LAN	307
GEESY, Catharine	YOR	160
Conrad	YOR	172
Conrad Jr.	YOR	171
Conrad Senr.	YOR	172
John	YOR	172
GEETING, Henry	SOM	138
John	SOM	137
GEETINGER, Martin	SOM	137
GEETS, John	PHI	2
GEETY, Martin	LAN	61
GEETZ, John	LAN	307
GEFFERESS,		
William	MER	443
GEFFREYS, Jas.	PHA	92
GEGREY?, Peter	SOM	133
GEHER, David	CRA	13
Jacob	CRA	15
John	CRA	14
GEHFER, (No Given		
Name)	LAN	144
GEHMAN, Daniel	LAN	270
Isaac	BER	257
Jacob	BER	206
John	BUC	159
John	BER	206
John Jr.	BER	206
Samuel	BUC	159
GEHMAN?, Abram	MNT	134
GEHO, Jacob	NOH	59
Mathias	NOH	55A
GEHR, Andw.	YOR	217
Andw. Sr.	YOR	218
Balser	BER	225
David	YOR	206
George	LAN	197
Philip	BER	210
GEHRET, George	BER	133
Henry	BER	135
John	BER	133
John Jr.	BER	133
Valentine	BER	133
GEHRHARD,		
Frederick	LAN	197
GEHRMAN, Adam	DAU	28
GEHRY, George	BER	176
Martin	BER	206
Michael	BER	206
GEIB, George	ADA	35
Henry	LAN	144
Henry	YOR	167
John	DAU	27
John	LAN	144
Michael	YOR	189
GEIDNER, Ludwig	NOH	55A
GEIER, Maria	LAN	197
GEIGER, Bernard	DAU	5
Charles	MNT	57
Christian	BER	133
Christopher	BER	248
Detrich	BER	166
Elijah	BER	251
George	MNT	54
Henry	BER	151
Jacob	BER	273
Jacob	DAU	29A
Jacob	NOH	44A
John	BER	179
Leonard	NOH	47
Martin	PHI	96
Paul	BER	248
Peter	BER	134
Peter	BER	267
Philip	BER	166

Name	Loc	Pg	Name	Loc	Pg	Name	Loc	Pg
GEIGER, Widow	NOH	68A	GENER, Thomas	WST	236	GEORGE, Rachell	CUM	89
GEIGLEY, George	FRA	311	GENGER?, John	BER	282	Rebecca	PHI	61
GEIS, Henry	BER	184	GENINGS, Charles	NOU	110	Richard	PHI	23
Michl.	BER	144	GENNINGS,			Robert	WAS	20
GEISE, Peter	YOR	177	Jonathen	NOU	110	Robert	ALL	70
Peter	NOH	47A	GENSEL, George	BER	144	Robt.	CUM	90
GEISELMAN, Fredk.	YOR	193	GENSEMER, George	LAN	196	Samuel	GRN	100
Fredk.	YOR	193	George Junr.	LAN	196	Samuel	WST	309
George	YOR	193	GENSIL, Matthias	NOU	187	Simon Jun.	NOH	51A
Jacob	YOR	208	GENSINGER, John	DAU	9A	Simon Senr.	NOH	51A
John	YOR	164	GENTER, John	YOR	215	Stophel	NOH	43
Michael	YOR	193	GENTHER, August	PHA	43	Stouffle	FRA	282
Michael	YOR	193	Charles Jr?	PHI	97A	Thomas	PHI	62
GEISLER, Joseph	BER	270	Charles	PHI	97A	Widow	NOH	71
GEISMAN, George	BER	270	GENTO, Joseph	PHA	29	William	PHI	136
William	BER	270	GENTZ, Jacob	PHI	118	William	WST	190
GEISONOR, John	YOR	182	GENTZLER, George	YOR	189	William	LUZ	322
GEISS, Jno. Peter	NOH	59	Hannah	YOR	160	William	CHE	810
John	LAN	109	Philip	YOR	189	William	NOH	51A
GEISSEL, Jacob	NOH	50	GEOGES?, Widow	BUC	154	Wilm.	ALL	112
GEISSINGER,			GEORGE, Abraham	BER	206	Wm.	PHA	72
Abraham	NOH	80	Achine	LAN	209	Wm?	PHI	57
Abraham Jnr.	NOH	80	Adam	WST	214	Yost	BER	187
Daniel	NOH	47A	Adam Jur.	FRA	282	GEORGES, Abram	MNT	127
George	NOH	82	Adam Senr.	FRA	282	Evin	CHE	798
Isaac	NOH	80	Alexander	WAS	44	GEOSS, Michael	DAU	21A
Jacob	NOH	82	Ann?	PHI	57	GEPFORD, John	LAN	25
John	NOH	80	Bedford	CHE	753	GEPHART, John	MNT	44
Philip	NOH	80	Carman	LAN	259	John	SOM	133
Samuel	NOH	80	Catharine	PHI	107A	Martin	FRA	301
GEIST, August	DAU	28A	Cather	ADA	10	GERAHAN, Peter	HNT	117
George	BER	187	Charles	PHA	95	GERARD, Samuel	BEV	25
Val.	BER	213	Charles	FRA	307	Stephen	PHA	27
Widow	BUC	139	Conrad	NOH	71	Thomas	BEV	25
GEISTEVISE?,			Conrod	WST	236	GERAUD, Maria	PHA	45
George	NOU	136	David	CUM	83	GERBER, Henry	NOH	75A
GEISWEIT,			David	MNT	104	Jacob	LAN	49
Everhart	BER	255	David	CUM	129	John	NOH	53
GEITNER, George	LAN	135	David	HNT	161	John	BER	169
GELASPIE, William	NOU	149	David	WST	324	John	LAN	196
GELASPY, John	LAN	89	Edward	PHA	95	Peter	LAN	196
GELBAUGH,			Edward	PHI	61A	Philip	NOH	29A
Frederick	LAN	15	Frederick	BUC	149	GERBERICHT, John	YOR	194
GELEY, Peter	PHA	86	George	MNT	50	GERCHWIN, John	BER	142
GELLER, George	BFD	73	George	NOH	51A	GERCHWIND, Danl.	BER	144
GELLESPEY, Geo.	CUM	104	Henry	DAU	49	John	BER	144
Jane	CUM	104	Henry	NOH	53	GERDEL, Margaret	LAN	314
Nathl.	CUM	132	Henry	NOH	71	GERDON, Perthenia	LUZ	364
Robt.	CUM	132	Henry	BER	187	GERE, John	LAN	171
GELSINGER, John	BER	169	Henry	WST	214	GEREHART, Jacob	DAU	30A
GELSMAN?, Abram	MNT	134	Henry	NOH	55A	Maths.	BER	213
GELTIS, Paul	NOU	117	Henry	NOH	62A	Maths. Jr.	BER	213
GELTNETT, Casper	NOU	182	Jacob	CUM	134	Peter	BER	202
GELURCHS,			Jacob	BUC	149	GEREHEART,		
Nicholas	YOR	159	Jacob	BER	187	Christian	FRA	293
GELVEX, Federick	FRA	296	Jacob	FRA	307	GERET, Barbara	BER	214
GELVIN, James	WST	345	James	WST	345	GEREY, John	FAY	240
GELWICH, Andrew	FRA	272	James	MER	442	Thomas	NOU	171
Daniel	FRA	280	John	GRN	81	GERGE, Samuel	NOU	193
Daniel	FRA	280	John	SOM	157	GERGES, (Blank)	MNT	121
GELWICKS, Daniel	FRA	283	John	HNT	160	Conrad	MNT	121
Frederick	YOR	183	John	BER	248	GERGES?, Widow	BUC	154
George	ADA	31	John	DAU	32A	GERGIS, Abraham	MNT	125
GELWIN, Jeremiah	FRA	315	John	NOH	51A	GERHARD, Conrad	PHA	42
GEMAN, Daniel	LAN	209	John	NOH	89A	Gottfried	NOH	37A
John	LAN	196	Joseph	PHI	61A	John	LAN	196
GEMISON, Duke	MER	443	Lowrence	NOH	51A	John Junr.	LAN	196
Robert	MER	443	Martin	CUM	65	GERHARDT, Conrad	DAU	28A
GEMMEL, William	LAN	251	Martin	CUM	100	GERHART, Abm.	BUC	159
GEMMILL,			Martin Senr.	CUM	105	Abraham	BUC	96A
Eilzabeth	YOR	197	Matthew	WST	344	Adam	BER	217
Jane	YOR	195	Matthew	WST	345	Daniel	MNT	99
GEMPSHORN, Adam	YOR	181	Nathal.	WST	214	Daniel	BER	135
GEMSINGER, John	LAN	44	Nicholas	NOH	83A	Daniel	BUC	154
GENBLE, Henry	BER	260	Peter	NOH	51A	Daniel	BER	206
GENCLER, George	YOR	208	Philip	NOH	43	Frederick	BER	270

GERHART, George	DAU	37	GERRON, Robert	NOH	66A	GETZ, Philip	LAN 209
Isaac	MNT	89	GERRY, John	FAY	265	GEUBERTSON,	
Jacob	MNT	117	GERTEN, William	FAY	214	Reuben	DAU 3A
Jacob	MNT	124	GERTIN, Isaac	NOU	157	GEUGER?, John	BER 282
Jacob	BER	217	Jacob	NOU	157	GEUSS, Henry	GRN 110
Jacob Junr.	MNT	124	John	NOU	157	GEUST, William	DEL 157
Jacob	NOH	55A	Michael	NOU	157	GEVEL, Casper	BER 169
Jacob	NOH	55A	William	NOU	157	GEWINNER,	
John	ADA	9	William	NOU	157	Frederick	NOH 37A
John	MNT	124	GERVER, Jacob	BER	139	GEYER, Widow	PHI 65
John	BER	170	GERVIN, Robert	LAN	225	Andw.	YOR 205
Mathias	MNT	134	GERVIS, Joseph	WST	272	Conrad	MNT 134
Nicholas	MNT	117	GERWICK, Henrey	FAY	221	John	MNT 134
Peter	MNT	99	GERY, John	FAY	235	John	LAN 137
Peter	MNT	113	Martha	FRA	290	GEYGER, Andw.	YOR 206
Peter	CHE	796	GESELL,			Henry	MNT 99
Philip	NOH	35A	Christopher	LAN	196	Jacob	MNT 99
GERHEART, Phillip	NOU	122	William	LAN	142	Paul	YOR 206
GERHERT, Widow	MNT	124	GESHACT, Conrad	MNT	44	GEYREY, Gillian	SOM 128
GERHOUSER, John	YOR	174	GESHART, Isaac	MNT	125	GEYREY?, Peter	SOM 133
GERHRIS, Peter	BER	206	GESHOUR, John	BER	135	GHAHAM, William	CHE 902
GERICH, John	BER	217	GESS, Abraham	DEL	158	GHANT, Joseph	CUM 35
Philip	LAN	270	Henry	WAS	67	GHEEN, Hugh	CHE 721
GERINGER, Jno			James	WAS	68	John	CHE 701
(See			Jonathan	SOM	138	Joseph	CHE 701
Geringer,			Liddy	CUM	91	Thomas	CHE 701
Widow)	NOH	33A	GESSLER, Adam	ADA	30	GHEEN?, Soloman	CHE 752
John	NOH	85	Henry	ADA	17	GHOST, George	LAN 226
Peter	NOH	85	GETCHELL, Saml.	CHE	872	Philip	LAN 224
Widow Of Jno.	NOH	33A	GETES, Martin	DAU	24	Simon	LAN 248
GERIS, Jacob	BER	206	GETHER, Martin	PHA	55	GHOUNLY, Thos.	MIF 9
GERLING, Michael	NOH	75A	GETMAN, Christian	BUC	159	GIBB, Allexander	BEV 27
GERMAN, Abraham	PHA	55	George	BUC	101	David	WST 272
Adam	LAN	64	John	BUC	101	Hugh	BUT 318
Adam	NOH	44A	William	BUC	101	Robert	WST 272
Conrad	NOH	44A	GETS, Charles	NOU	104	GIBBENS, George	YOR 203
David	NOH	37A	Martin	DAU	9A	GIBBENY,	
George	LAN	22	GETSENDONER,			Alexander	MIF 3
George	LAN	68	Christn./			James	YOR 199
Jacob	LAN	66	Christr.?	FAY	221	GIBBIN, James	BEV 14
Jeremiah	CHE	817	GETTEY, James	FRA	302	GIBBINS, James	BEV 16
John	LAN	72	GETTHEN, Wm.	PHA	8	James	GRN 70
John	BER	215	GETTIES, Polly	FRA	326	John	BFD 63
John	BER	260	GETTIG,			John	GRN 70
Leomard	LAN	81	Christopher	NOU	99	GIBBLE, Abram	LAN 253
Leonard	LAN	66	Chuster	NOU	97	GIBBONS, Francis	PHA 119
Leonard Jnr.	LAN	66	Frederick	NOU	136	Jacob	DEL 167
Ludwig	LAN	64	Henry	NOU	97	James	LAN 113
Mrs.	NOU	121	Mrs.	NOU	97	James	CHE 809
Philip	NOH	44A	Mrs.	NOU	97	James	CHE 809
Richd.	PHI	89A	GETTING, William	WST	237	James Esq.	CHE 753
GERMANTON, Conrad	NOH	73	GETTINGER,			Jesse	DAU 13A
GERNAN, Benjamin	LAN	83	Fredrick	ERI	55A	John	LAN 52
GERNAND,			John	PHI	123	John	CUM 97
Christian	BER	169	GETTIS, Robert	HNT	164	John	NOU 136
George	BER	169	William	WAS	99	John	DEL 163
John	BER	169	GETTLE, Henry	BER	281	John	NOU 164
GERNANDT, John	BER	217	GETTS, Adam	YOR	165	John	CHE 826
GERNANT?, Henry	BER	187	John	YOR	179	Joseph	DEL 189
GERNER, Jacob	LAN	197	GETTY, David	MNT	82	Joseph	CHE 820
GERNET, Christian	NOH	82	Isabella	ADA	8	Margery	DEL 188
George	NOH	82	James	ADA	8	Philip	CHE 780
Jacob	BER	186	John	FRA	302	Saml.	NOU 171
John	NOH	82	Joseph	FAY	214	Samuel	LAN 113
GERNON, Richd.	PHA	79	GETTZ, Jacob	PHI	98	Thomas	CHE 806
GERNON?,			GETZ, Conrad	NOH	35A	William	NOU 171
Bartholomew	LUZ	428	George	LAN	311	William	LAN 181
GERRARD, Justice	GRN	81	George	NOH	35A	Wm.	CHE 806
GERRART,			Jacob	PHI	125	GIBBONY, Barney	WST 251
Christian	DAU	30	Jacob	LAN	307	GIBBS, Abraham	LAN 40
Fredrik	DAU	30	Jacob Senr.	LAN	316	Adin	BUC 93A
GERRET, Jacob	BER	255	John	LAN	41	Benjn.	PHA 33
John	BER	153	Leonard	LAN	196	Gilbert	CHE 779
Michael	BER	246	Nicholas	BER	169	Jacob	PHA 122
GERREY, Richard	ARM	124	Nichs.	DAU	35	Joel	PHA 25
GERRINGER, Andrew	BER	130	Peter	LAN	53	John	PHI 84

Name	Ref		Name	Ref		Name	Ref
GIBBS, John	CUM 140		GIBSON, James	CHE 703		GIETING, Henry	BER 144
Josiah W.	PHA 89		James	CHE 715		GIFF--?, Alexr.	MIF 6
Peter	PHA 121		James Junr.	YOR 195		GIFFAD, Polly	LUZ 369
Russell	LUZ 417		Jas.	BUT 353		GIFFEE, James	WST 251
Samuel	BUC 88A		John	BFD 37		GIFFEN, Andrew	WAS 15
Thos.	PHI 77A		John	CUM 106		Stephen	ADA 19
GIBBY, Daniel	SOM 162		John	ARM 122		GIFFENS, Widow	PHI 5
GIBEN, Robert	LAN 179		John	WST 150		GIFFERESS, James	MER 443
GIBENNY, Jno.	CUM 71		John	WST 190		GIFFESON, Willm.	PHI 29
GIBENS, Brabson	MER 443		John	FAY 197		GIFFIN, George	NOH 85
GIBESON, Mary	PHA 30		John	FAY 203		John	MNT 132
Zekel	PHA 23		John	FAY 208		John	WST 271
GIBFORD, Henry	LAN 21		John	FAY 231		Robert	ALL 53
Jacob	LAN 24		John	BUT 354		Stephen	WST 272
GIBIN, Andrew	LAN 189		John	MER 442		GIFFNY, Edwd.	WST 289
GIBINY, Hugh	DAU 28		John	CHE 732		GIFFORD, Isaac	HNT 142
GIBLE, Jno.			John	NOU 143A		Joseph	HNT 142
Single &	DAU 38		John			William	HNT 142
GIBLER, Henry	LAN 209		Joseph	BER 206		GIFFORT, James	PHI 67A
Henry Jun.	LAN 209		Joshua	FAY 200		GIFT, Adam	BFD 37
Jacob Sen.	SOM 137		Levy	BUT 354		Frederick	NOH 53
John	SOM 138		Mary	BFD 37		George	FRA 282
GIBLET, Henry	LAN 147B		Moses	NOU 164		Jacob	BER 187
GIBS, James	PHI 76A		Nancy	FRA 275		Peter	NOH 53
GIBSINER, Philip	LAN 196		Nathaniel	FAY 197		GIFTY?, George	BEV 26
GIBSON, Adam	NOU 198		Patrick	WAS 85		GIGER, Charles	PHA 58
Alexander	ARM 122		Rachel	VEN 167		Jacob	PHI 122
Alexander	NOU 143A		Robert	WAS 52		John	SOM 151
Alexd.	ALL 99		Robert	ALL 57		GILAND, Patrick	CRA 11
Ambrose	WAS 37		Robert	BFD 73		GILASPY, Francis	CHE 725
Andrew	CRA 6		Robert	CHE 875		George	PHA 89
Andrew	WAS 20		Saml.	PHI 64		GILBERT, Abner	WST 251
Andrew	WAS 28		Samuel	WST 150		Adam	MNT 99
Andrew	CHE 872		Samuel	FAY 209		Adam	BER 173
Ann	CUM 90		Samuel	MER 442		Adam	BER 278
Benjamin	PHA 112		St. Clair	BUT 325		Andw.	YOR 205
Charles	WST 150		Thomas	FAY 200		Ann	PHA 39
Charles	WST 345		Thomas	FAY 209		Anthony	PHI 133
Charles	MER 442		Thomas	LUZ 417		Barnabas	FRA 288
David	DEL 178		Thomas	CHE 872		Benjamin	BUC 153
David	FAY 209		Thos.	PHI 76		Benjamin	WST 251
David	LAN 241		Widow	FRA 318		Bernard	MNT 99
David	NOH 47A		William	WAS 2		Caleb	PHI 145
Edward	FAY 208		William	PHI 24		Catharina	ADA 27
Edwd.	PHA 82		William	ADA 26		Conrad	BER 155
Elizabeth	BUC 141		William	WAS 44		Conrod	PHI 79A
Esther	WAS 99		William	WAS 68		David	MNT 60
Francis	WST 345		William	LAN 150		David	PHA 79
George	PHI 73		William	NOU 157		David	PHA 86
George	HNT 122		William	FAY 231		Eber	MNT 66
George	WST 309		William	WST 288		Eleazor	YOR 193
George	CHE 715		Wilm.	ALL 57		Fredrick	PHA 9
Gideon	ARM 125		Wm.	FRA 280		Fredrik	DAU 33A
Henry	BEV 16		Wm.	WST 288		Geo.	CUM 139
Henry	BER 206		GICE, Rachel	PHI 85A		George	ADA 16
Hugh	CRA 6		GICKER, Daniel	BER 270		George	PHA 73
Hugh	ALL 88		Henry	BER 144		George	MNT 99
Isaac	ALL 68		Henry Jr.	BER 144		George	NOU 110
Isaac	CHE 717		Michael	BER 248		George	BER 166
Isaac	CHE 720		GICSEY, Henry			George	BER 286
Israel	BUT 348		Revd.	SOM 141		Godfrey	
Jacob Esqr.	YOR 201		GIDDINGS,			Henry	ADA 22
James	CRA 3		Nathaniel	LUZ 363		Henry	DAU 33
James	BFD 37		GIDEON, George	PHA 44		Henry	MNT 57
James	PHI 51		Jacob	PHA 70		Henry	BER 166
James	WAS 52		GIDIAN, Henry	PHI 111A		Henry	DAU 38A
James	WAS 68		Jacob	PHI 116		Henry, Junr.	MNT 57
James	PHA 103		GIE, Samuel	CHE 714		Jacob	PHA 9
James	ARM 124		GIERING, Andrew	NOH 82		Jacob	ADA 12
James	BUC 141		Andrew Junr.	NOH 82		Jacob	ADA 22
James	WST 190		John	NOH 82		Jacob	MNT 93
James	FAY 227		GIESEMANN, Henry	DAU 28		Jacob	MNT 99
James	LAN 246		GIESS, David	LAN 144		Jacob	MNT 107
James	FRA 294		GIEST, Andrew	NOU 122		Jacob	CUM 139
James	FRA 297		Conrad	NOU 136		Jacob	NOU 147
James	WST 345		John	NOU 136		Jacob	NOH 75A
			GIESY, John	LAN 186		James	PHA 20

GILBERT, James	DAU 43	GILKY, Mary	CHE 717
John	PHA 57	GILL, Aices	NOU 128
John	MNT 99	David	PHA 61
John	PHI 153	Ebinezer	ALL 66
John	BER 173	Edward	DEL 173
John	YOR 205	Elisabeth	WAS 56
John	WST 214	Georg	NOU 187
John	FRA 300	George	ALL 82
John	CHE 780	George	DEL 163
Joseph	PHI 76A	James	ALL 69
Joshua	PHI 145	John`	ALL 70
Leonard	ADA 21	John	HNT 150
Maria	BER 175	John	DEL 163
Mary	PHA 46	John	BUC 88A
Mathias	PHI 137	John	BUC 90A
Michael	GRN 64	Joseph H.	PHI 16
Peter	PHI 112	Matthew	BUC 104A
Peter	BER 155	Neel	ALL 66
Peter	HNT 157	See Cill	ALL 82
Philip	ADA 25	Stephen	NOU 122
Philip	NOH 75A	William	CRA 10
Robert	PHA 13	William	PHI 54
Robert	LAN 89	William	WAS 56
Samuel	BER 166	William	NOU 187
Samuel	LUZ 395	Wilm.	ALL 65
Samuel	DAU 48A	GILLAM, Isaac	NOH 78
Samuel	BUC 86A	Jeremiah	BUC 84A
Stephen	GRN 81	Simon	BUC 160A
Stephen	BUC 152A	GILLAN, John	PHA 78
Thomas	GRN 92	John	MIF 16A
Thomas	PHI 137	GILLAND, James	ALL 104
Thomas	BUC 86A	John	BEV 24
Widow	BUC 154	Joseph	NOU 97
William	BUC 143	Patrick	CRA 11
GILBRAITH, Joseph	NOU 164	Wilm.	ALL 104
GILBREATH, John	ADA 15	GILLARD, John	LAN 54
Robert	ADA 22	GILLASPY, Samuel	ALL 54
William	ADA 22	William	FAY 256
GILBY, William	PHI 6	GILLEGER,	
GILCASON, James	ALL 92	Christian	PHA 36
GILCHREAST, John	WAS 56	GILLELAN, David	WST 345
GILCHRIST, Chas.	PHA 11	Mathew	FRA 279
James	WAS 28	GILLELAND, Davd.	BUT 348
John	DAU 3	David	HNT 165
John	DAU 17	David, Junr	HNT 165
Peter	DEL 173	Henrey	FAY 209
Robt.	CUM 49	Hugh	BUT 341
GILCREAST,		James	BUT 325
William	WAS 56	John	HNT 143
GILCREIST, James	ADA 12	John	FAY 214
GILCREST, John	FAY 203	Mary	WAS 79
Margret	FAY 203	Matthew	HNT 165
Mattw. Esqr.	FAY 203	Richd.?	MIF 10
GILDERSLEAVE,		Thoms.	BUT 349
Samuel	MER 442	GILLEN, Ames	FRA 280
GILDS, John	BFD 41	GILLEND, Thos.	CHE 791
GILEGAN, George	PHA 11	GILLESPEY,	
GILES, John	CHE 893	Clements	CUM 29
Thomas	LUZ 387	GILLESPIE, Allen	WAS 62
Thomas	NOU 143A	Andrew	WAS 20
Wm.	PHI 76A	Charles	FRA 289
GILFILINY?, James	ALL 50	David	FAY 244
GILFILLIN, Alexd.	ALL 93	Elisabeth	WAS 56
James	MER 443	Henry	GRN 88
GILFRY, Matthw.	PHI 19	James	WAS 56
GILGAR, Adam	NOU 104	John	MIF 1
GILGOR, Thos.	YOR 203	John	WST 169
GILGORE, Jesse	CUM 122	John	FAY 244
Robt.	CUM 122	Neal	WAS 37
Wm.	CUM 122	Neal	WAS 79
GILGREEST, Thomas	ADA 11	Thomas	WAS 56
GILKESON, Allen	WAS 90	Wm.	LYC 21
GILKEY, Charles	MER 443	Wm.	WST 367
Charrels	ALL 70	GILLESPY, John	HNT 166
GILKISON, Andrew	MNT 130	Wm. (Crossed	
GILKSON, Wilm. H.	ALL 87	Out)	LYC 20

GILLET, Aaron	LYC 10
Grishom	LUZ 407
Wilkes	LUZ 407
GILLFILLIN, Jas.	CUM 31
Thomas	ALL 96
GILLIAMS, Lewis	PHA 25
GILLILAND, Hugh	CRA 14
John	MER 443
Philip	BFD 43
Samuel	ADA 15
Sarah	BUT 349
Thomas	MNT 38
William	ADA 20
GILLIMER, Wm.	FRA 309
GILLING, John	PHA 92
John	PHI 80A
William	PHI 21
GILLINGER,	
Michael	DAU 42
GILLINGHAM,	
Benjn.	BUC 144A
George	PHA 55
James	PHA 20
James	PHA 36
Jas.	PHI 39
John Jnr.	BUC 86A
John	BUC 86A
Joseph	BUC 98A
Moses	PHI 137
Samuel	BUC 86A
Thomas	PHI 136
Thomas Capt?	PHI 137
Yeamens	PHI 136
GILLINGLAND,	
Isaac	NOU 143A
GILLION, Daniel	WAS 37
Joseph	NOU 193
GILLIS, John	WAS 68
John	MER 443
Thomas	MER 443
GILLISON, John	WST 345
GILLISPIE, Daniel	WAS 20
GILLMAN, Daniel	LAN 14
Jacob	NOU 198
Samuel	FAY 252
GILLON, John	PHA 9
GILLPY, Willm	PHI 18
GILLS, Robt.	PHA 81
GILLUM, John	DAU 3
Thomas	BFD 50
GILLY, William	WAS 90
GILMAN, Henerey	MER 443
John ---.?	FRA 313
Thomas	NOU 164
GILMER, Ephraim	CHE 727
George	PHA 12
GILMOE, John	BEV 23
GILMOR, John	YOR 207
GILMORE, Andw.	PHI 111A
Brice	VEN 170
David	ADA 37
David	ALL 76
David	WAS 90
Henry	ADA 37
Hugh	BUT 359
Isaac	LAN 53
Isaac	FAY 197
James	WAS 12
James	ALL 104
James	WST 169
James	BUC 93A
Jno.	CUM 129
John	ALL 76
John	ALL 85
John	LAN 168
John	MER 442

GILMORE, John	CEN	22A	GINGRIGH, Michael	DAU	27	GIZEL, Leonard	ADA	31
Jos.	BUT	359	Widow	DAU	27	GLA---A?, Jessee	CRA	13
Joseph	BEV	5	GINGRIK, David	DAU	20A	GLADDEN, William	WAS	15
Mathew	ALL	90	Joseph	DAU	20A	Wm.	YOR	199
Moses	DAU	2	GINKIN, Widw.	PHI	112A	GLADEN, Joseph	PHI	95A
Nancy	PHI	61	GINN, Kain	MNT	57	Wm.	CUM	44
Perry	NOH	41	GINNEY, Thomas	MER	443	GLADFELTY, Adam	SOM	148
Rhodum	WAS	80	GINNIS, Willm.	PHI	32	Solomon	SOM	148
Robert	MER	442	GINRICH, Emanuel	LAN	11	GLADING, James	PHA	102
Robert	CHE	908	Henry	LAN	184	Rebecca	PHA	101
Saml.	MIF	13A	Jno. Sr.	DAU	41A	GLADNEY, Joseph	CHE	751
Samuel	WAS	56	John	DAU	40A	GLADSTONE, Wm.	CUM	149
Samuel	DEL	188	GINRIGH, Christn.	DAU	40A	GLAHS, George	NOU	136
Thomas	WAS	90	John	DAU	41	GLAINN, Anthony	LAN	281
Thomas	LUZ	359	John	DAU	40A	GLAMCO?, Jessee	CRA	13
Thos.	FRA	317	GINTER, Anthony	LAN	31	GLANCEA?, Jessee	CRA	13
Wilm.	ALL	64	Christian	BFD	73	GLANCEY, Gesse	YOR	215
GILMORE?, -----	MIF	10	John	PHA	40	John	CHE	719
John	MER	442	Jonathan	YOR	216	Jos.	YOR	216
GILPHIN, Lydya	PHA	106	Peter	BFD	57	Owen	CHE	717
GILPIN, Gideon	DEL	157	Peter	DAU	28A	GLANS, John	BER	282
Isaac G.	DEL	158	Philip	NOH	75A	Yost	BER	282
John B.	PHI	155	GIPE, Jacob	ADA	20	GLANSEY, Wm.	BUT	345
Thomas	HNT	129	GIPPEL, Jacob	LAN	148	GLAS, Henry	DAU	8A
Thos.	PHA	47	John	LAN	145	GLASBRENER, John	DAU	16
GILSINGER, Acob	LAN	209	GIPPLE, Abm.	LAN	263	GLASBRENNER,		
GILSON, Gideon	LUZ	396	Chrisn.	LAN	263	Anstat	DAU	26A
John	CRA	12	Henry	LAN	254	George	DAU	26A
John	LUZ	396	Joseph	LAN	254	John	DAU	19
Moses	ALL	105	GIRAUD, Alexander	PHA	24	GLASBY, Widow	PHI	23
Richd.	CUM	55	GIRD, Christly	HNT	161	GLASEL, Christian	NOU	136
Robert	WST	345	GIRDON, John	LUZ	359	GLASGO, Hugh	LAN	156
Samuel	LUZ	396	GIREY?, Jacob	BUC	139	James	MIF	16A
Thomas	MIF	7	GIRFFITH, Powel	FAY	244	John	HNT	125
Thomas	ALL	105	GIRL, John	FRA	305	GLASGOE, Samuel	FAY	250
William	BFD	63	GIRLING, Wm.	CUM	96	GLASGOW, Hugh		
William	WST	345	GIRST, George	LAN	80	Esqr.	YOR	201
GIMBLE, Conrad	YOR	208	GIRT?, John	ARM	122	Jacob	CHE	749
GIMBLING, George	YOR	175	GIRTLEY, Jacob	CHE	805	Saml.	CHE	750
GIMEL?, Michael	DAU	40A	GIRTON, James	BUC	151	William	BER	181
GIMMERLING,			GIRTY, Thoms.	BUT	348	GLASMYER, George	BER	139
George	NOU	136	GIRVEN, James	PHA	85	Jacob	BER	181
Jacob	NOU	136	GIRY?, David	BUC	82A	GLASS, Adam	WAS	90
Jacob	NOU	136	GISBER, Andrew	FAY	256	Adam	FRA	308
Phillip	NOU	136	GISCH, Abraham	LAN	4	Andrew	ALL	98
GIMOR, James	PHI	46	Jacob	LAN	4	Andrew	BER	248
GIN, John	PHI	29	John	LAN	4	Daniel	YOR	210
GINDER, Daniel	BER	230	GISE, Adam	ADA	15	David	WST	190
Danl.	BER	257	Baltzer	LAN	99	Frederic	SOM	151
Frederick	BER	258	John	YOR	205	George	HNT	135
Jacob	LAN	21	Wm.	PHA	59	George Junr.	HNT	135
Jacob	BER	175	GISEL, John	PHI	127	George	NOH	29A
John	PHA	63	GISEY?, Jacob	BUC	139	Henry	BER	248
GINDLESBERGER,			GISH, John	NOU	121	Jacob	ADA	5
Albright	SOM	153	GISS, George	NOH	82	Jacob	HNT	123
Barbara	SOM	153	Philip	NOH	82	James	WAS	7
GINEY/ GINCY?,			GIST, Joseph	LAN	119	James	MIF	15
Robt	FRA	296	GIST?, John	ARM	122	James	WAS	37
GINGER, John	BER	217	GISTEWHITE, Sarah	DAU	14A	Jane	WAS	90
Ludwick	CUM	56	GITER, John	NOU	182	John	BEV	13
GINGERICH, David	LAN	21	GITHEY, Anthy.	PHI	1	John	WAS	90
GINGERICK, David	LAN	147B	GITING, Abraham	ALL	115	John	ALL	98
Michael	YOR	164	GITNER, John	FRA	300	John	LAN	113
GINGINER, Michael	NOH	55A	GITT, Peter	YOR	184	John	HNT	154
GINGINGER,			GITZ, Adrthee?	NOU	128	John	LAN	223
Christian	NOH	68A	GIVEN, George	CHE	884	John	BER	255
GINGLE, John	BER	224	James	CUM	80	John	YOR	203
GINGLES, Andrew	NOU	158	James	CUM	96	Mark	DAU	38
John	NOU	158	John	PHI	121	Martin	ADA	13
Mrs.	NOU	158	Mathew	YOR	159	Mathias	DAU	38A
William	NOU	158	GIVENER, Charles	MER	443	Peter	WAS	7
William	NOU	158	GIVENS, John	WAS	74	Robert	WAS	37
William	NOU	158	GIVENS?, Stephen?	MIF	10	Samuel	ALL	98
GINGRICH, George	LAN	139	GIVIN, David	ALL	93	Thomas	BER	247
Henry	DAU	25A	William	FAY	265	William	DAU	2A
GINGRIGH, John	DAU	28A	GIVINS, Solomon	FAY	240	GLASS?, See Grass	BER	248

GLASSBRENNER,			GLENTWORTH, James	PHA	8	GODSHALK,		
Margaret	YOR	158	Plunket F.	PHA	76	Godshalk	MNT	94
Peter	DAU	26A	GLESS, Abraham	NOH	89A	Godshalk	MNT	119
GLASSCOE, Nathl.	PHI	65	Christian	BER	184	Godshalk	MNT	121
Thomas	DEL	192	Jacob	BER	232	Harman	BUC	141
GLASSER, Jacob	LAN	83	Leonard	LAN	73	Jacob	BUC	91
Jacob	BER	225	Peter	LAN	66	Jacob	MNT	121
Jacob Junr.	LAN	83	GLESSNER, Henry			Jacob	MNT	125
Peter	BER	255	Junr.	SOM	141	John Jn.	BUC	105
GLASSFORD, Alexr.	MIF	7	Henry Sen.	SOM	138	Poll	PHI	41
Geo.	MIF	7	Jacob	SOM	141	Samuel	BUC	154
Geo. Jr.	MIF	7	Jacob	SOM	153	William	BUC	105
Ruben	WST	379	John	SOM	141	William	MNT	118
Saml.	MIF	7	John	YOR	159	GODSHALKE, Fredk.	PHI	18
Thos.	MIF	25	Peter	SOM	138	GODSHALL, Barbara	LAN	311
GLASSGOE, James	GRN	70	GLICK, Peter	BER	270	GODVEEN, Matthias	LAN	270
John	GRN	70	GLINGMAN, Peter	BER	130	GODWALT, Henry	MNT	82
John Junr.	GRN	70	GLONINGER, George	DAU	25A	GODWIN, Conrad	MNT	140
GLATFELTER,			John	DAU	25	Joseph	WAR	1A
Casper	YOR	193	Peter	DAU	32	GOE, Henry B.	FAY	265
Henry	YOR	192	Philip	LAN	47	William Junr.	FAY	265
GLATIN, Daniel	LAN	279	GLOSON, John	CRA	7	William, Senr.	FAY	265
GLATON, Daniel	LAN	280	GLOSS, Juliana	SOM	137	GOE?, Samuel	BEV	21
GLATT, Jacob	BER	276	GLOSSER, Daniel	BER	225	GOERING, Jacob		
GLATZ, George	LAN	36	GLOUSE, Christn.	PHI	89A	Revd.	YOR	158
GLAUGHLIN, Alexr.	PHI	41	Jacob	PHI	74A	GOEROUST, Wm.	PHA	107
GLAZIER, Daniel	HNT	154	GLOUSER, David	PHI	95A	GOETZ, Henry	DAU	44
Henry	PHI	102	GLOVER, Archibald	WAS	33	GOFORTH, William	BUC	88A
Joseph	HNT	132	Hugh	WAS	7	GOGIN, Lewis	NOU	193
GLEAVIS, James	NOU	109	James	BUT	343	GOGLEY, David	LAN	209
GLEN, Danl.	PHI	83A	John	NOU	193	William	LAN	82
Hugh	HNT	143	Joseph	MNT	71	GOHEAN, Charles	BUC	160A
James	PHI	136	Nehemiah	GRN	73	GOHEEN, Hugh	LAN	94
James	HNT	145	Samuel	GRN	70	Samuel	LAN	68
James	HNT	157	William	PHI	64	GOHN, Philip	YOR	205
James	FRA	298	William	HNT	152	Philip	YOR	205
Jesse	ARM	122	Wm.	CUM	29	GOLD, Mrs.	LYC	15
John	ALL	97	GLUCK, George	NOH	89A	Aexd.	ALL	100
John	HNT	145	Ludwig	LAN	275	Ben	LYC	15
John	NOU	158	GLUNT, Adam	BFD	41	David	NOH	32
John Junr.	HNT	145	Andrew	BFD	40	David	ERI	58
John	PHI	87A	GNERT, James	CHE	904	George	NOH	73
Jos.	YOR	199	John	CHE	904	James	CHE	888
Jos.	YOR	200	Thomas	CHE	904	Jos.	PHI	79
Robert	HNT	145	GOAKLER, John	MNT	59	Joseph	BUT	319
William	CRA	18	GOARDER, James	LAN	247	Mary	HNT	124
GLEN?, Gabriel	ALL	92	GOBEL, Joseph	FAY	209	Richard	DAU	17A
GLENEN, William	YOR	200	GOBIN, Mrs.	NOU	97	Stephen	LYC	16
GLENN, Alexr.	CUM	114	GOBLE, Abraham	NOU	121	Stophel	CUM	91
And.	FRA	285	Casper	NOU	121	Widow	NOH	70
Captn.	DEL	169	Ebenezer Esqr.	WAS	62	GOLDDEN, Jeffrey	PHI	91
David	CUM	120	Jacob	NOU	121	GOLDE, Daniel	ARM	126
Elizabeth	CUM	114	John	NOU	121	John	ARM	126
James	MIF	5	Widow	LAN	44	GOLDEN, John	FAY	227
James	WAS	90	GOBRIGHT, Chrs.			Stephen	FAY	227
James	LAN	98	Revd.	YOR	182	GOLDIN, John	FRA	288
James	VEN	170	Daniel	YOR	182	Wm.	WST	272
James	WST	251	GOCHLEY, David	YOR	205	GOLDINSMITH?,		
James	WST	345	GODDARD, George	PHI	70A	John	WAS	121
James	MER	442	Luther	LUZ	407	GOLDMAN, Christn.	DAU	29
James	CHE	822	GODDART, Anson	ERI	59A	Jacob	DAU	33
Jane	CUM	119	GODEN, Peter	LUZ	409	Jacob	DAU	39A
John	MIF	5	GODFREY, John	WST	169	GOLDON, Mattw.	CUM	113
John	WAS	15	John W.	PHA	85	GOLDRINGER,		
John	WAS	56	Robert	HNT	159	Anthy.	WST	367
John	WAS	90	William	YOR	214	GOLDSMITH, Thos.	PHI	96
John	CUM	135	GODLINK, John	ALL	71	GOLDY, David	MNT	69
Joseph	PHA	92	GODLSON, William	PHI	146	Jacob	MNT	69
Robert	DEL	175	GODSCHALK, John	BUC	104A	John	LYC	7
Robert	DEL	177	GODSHAL, Andrew	NOU	136	GOLIHER, Edinezer	ALL	85
Thos.	CUM	114	Michael	NOU	198	GOLLAGER, John	PHA	118
William	WAS	85	Peter	NOU	136	GOLLARD, Lemuel	LYC	12
William	FAY	197	GODSHALK,			GOLLENTINE, John	ADA	20
William	MER	442	Catherine	MNT	118	GOLLIDY, Abraham	FRA	297
William	CHE	757	Fredrick	PHI	134	GOLLIHER, Wm.	CHE	723
GLENSER, John	BER	169	Garrett	MNT	118	GOLLMAN, Widow	MNT	133

GOLLMAN, (John		GOOD, John	LAN 92
Crossed Out)	MNT 133	John	SOM 128
GOLLOUGHER, Adam	FAY 250	John	LAN 238
Anthony	FAY 250	John	LAN 267
James	FAY 203	John	LAN 279
James	FAY 256	John	CHE 733
John	FAY 250	John S. Of	
Neal	FAY 250	Jacob	LAN 267
Patrick	FAY 221	Jonathan	BUC 105
Thomas	FAY 235	Jonathan	BUC 93A
GOLTNER?, (See		Jos.	PHI 77A
Gottner)	NOH 75A	Joseph	LAN 269
GOLWICKS,		Martin	LAN 269
Fredrick	ADA 38	Michael	LAN 75
GOMBAY, George	NOU 136	Patrick	WAS 115
GOMELEY, Elizh.		Peter	LAN 67
Widow	LAN 16	Peter	CUM 108
GOMERY?, Isaac	MNT 111	Peter	CUM 118
GOMINGER?, John	PHI 126	Peter	LAN 267
GONDER, George	LAN 196	Peter	LAN 268
Widow	LAN 234	Peter	FRA 289
GONER, Jacob	NOU 97	Samuel	LAN 269
GONGLEWARE,		Samuel	LAN 285
Joseph	BEV 5	Samuel	DAU 15A
GONKLER, Michael	MNT 94	Sarah	CHE 728
GONNER, Saml.	LAN 141	Thomas	PHA 119
GONSALIS,		Thomas	CHE 710
Benjamin	WAY 144	Widow	LAN 267
Samuel	WAY 148	Widow	LAN 284
GONSAUL, Bengamin	ALL 108	Widow	LAN 307
Samuel	ALL 108	GOODANEW, Dennis	PHA 89
GONSERD, (No		GOODARD, William	GRN 75
Given Name)	NOU 193	GOODEN, Abraham	GRN 106
GONTER, Peter	LAN 30	Daniel	FAY 244
Widow	LAN 45	David	SOM 142
GONTREY, Widow	LAN 288	James	GRN 67
GOOD, Abraham	SOM 128	Moses	SOM 142
Abraham	LAN 267	Saml.	FAY 227
Adam	NOU 136	Smith	SOM 142
Anna, Widow	LAN 10	GOODERMAN, John	WST 169
Benjn.	FRA 287	GOODETTLE, George	CHE 848
Bolswar	ALL 117	GOODFELLOW, David	LYC 19
Catharine	LAN 68	Wm.	PHA 5
Chris.	LAN 86	GOODFELLY, David	LYC 24
Christ	LAN 267	Thos.	LYC 24
Christ	LAN 268	GOODHART,	
Christian	LAN 10	Frederick	BER 179
Christian	SOM 157	John	BER 235
Christian	LAN 261	William	BER 133
Christopher	CHE 804	GOODHEART, Henry	NOU 97
Edward	BUC 141	Henry	LAN 107
Edwd.	CUM 29	GOODIN, Abraham	LUZ 376
Francis	CHE 767	John	FAY 244
George	NOU 136	Joseph	FAY 244
George	NOU 136	GOODING, Daniel	NOU 152
George	NOH 64A	Jacob	WAR 1A
Henry	LAN 72	GOODKNECHT,	
Henry	BUC 139	Christn.	PHI 125
Henry	LAN 268	GOODLANDER, Chris	NOU 198
Henry	LAN 310	Henry	WST 213
Jacob	LAN 76	Jacob	CUM 42
Jacob	LAN 85	Marclis	NOU 198
Jacob	PHI 126	GOODLING, Henry	WST 214
Jacob	SOM 128	Peter	YOR 191
Jacob	SOM 138	GOODMAN, Andw.	DAU 34A
Jacob	SOM 153	Catherine	BER 270
Jacob	SOM 157	Charles	BUC 149
Jacob	YOR 207	Charles	CHE 724
Jacob	LAN 267	Elizabeth	MNT 138
Jacob	LAN 279	Geo.	DAU 31A
Jacob	CHE 875	George	NOU 128
Jacob	DAU 14A	Henry	BER 270
James	CHE 725	Henry Jr.	BER 270
Jesse	CHE 711	Jacob	BER 230
John	LAN 10	Jacob	WST 251
John	ADA 11	Jacob	LAN 293

GOODMAN, John	BER 179
John	WST 251
John	BER 252
John Jr.	PHI 109
John	DAU 2A
John	PHI 113A
John Wm.	BER 266
Jos.	PHI 116A
Peter	PHI 125
Peter	LAN 227
Peter	BER 235
Saml.	PHI 107
Simon	DAU 18
Simon	BER 269
Thos.	PHI 45
George	BER 154
GOODNOUGH,	
Margaret	BER 173
GOODS, Joseph	FAY 256
William	FAY 197
GOODSELL, Lloyd	LUZ 392
GOODURN, Seth	YOR 175
GOODWEIG, Jacob	MNT 71
GOODWIN, Mrs.	LYC 27
Benjamin	NOH 64A
Edward	LUZ 386
Elijah	LUZ 351
Elisha	CHE 743
George	CHE 735
Jacob	WAY 141
John	PHA 25
John	MNT 39
John	DEL 166
John	DEL 179
John	CHE 798
Jonathan	PHA 71
Joseph	PHI 127
Joseph	WAY 140
Richard	CHE 705
Thomas	DEL 155
William	MNT 39
GOODYEAR, George	YOR 157
Matthias	MIF 1
GOOF, Samuel	PHI 11A
GOOFHEAD, Phillip	FRA 282
GOOK, Abraham	DAU 25
GOOLD, Jonathen	NOU 109
Joseph	NOU 109
GOOLDING, John	LAN 71
GOOLDY, Jacob	PHA 67
GOOSEHORN, George	HNT 143
George Junr.	HNT 143
Jacob	HNT 143
Jacob Junr.	HNT 142
Leonard	HNT 143
GOOSH, Philip	LAN 81
Stofel	LAN 81
GOOSHOM, Nicholas	MIF 5
GOOSHORN, George	ALL 96
GOOSMAN, (No	
Given Name)	LAN 143
GOOSS, Widow	LAN 42
GORBY, Eli	GRN 110
Job	GRN 110
Thomas	GRN 110
GORDAEL, Lewis	PHA 97
GORDAN, David	BEV 24
James	BFD 73
John	BEV 6
Joseph	FAY 214
Samuel	FAY 214
Sarah	FAY 214
GORDE, Joseph	CUM 115
GORDEN, Alexd.	FRA 299
Archd.	FRA 287
Charles	PHI 77A

GORDEN, David	BUC	149	GORDON, Robt.	CEN	22A	GOSKET, Isaac	LAN	75
Elijah	PHI	152	Samuel	MNT	82	GOSLIN, Elizabeth	BUC	160A
George	FAY	221	Samuel	WAS	121	Ellizabeth	BUC	84
Hans	FRA	303	Samuel	LUZ	396	Levi	BUC	84
Hans	FRA	303	Thomas	WAS	2	Wm.	PHI	103
John	VEN	170	Thomas	WAS	7	GOSLINE, Jacob	BUC	83
Jos	PHI	80	Thomas	WAS	12	John	BUC	83
Josiah	PHA	22	Thomas	WAS	15	Richard	BUC	83
Margaret	BUC	103	Thomas	BFD	50	GOSLING, Jacob	PHI	94
Mary	FRA	297	Thomas	BER	248	GOSNER, George	PHA	35
Robert	MNT	87	Thomas	NOU	143A	Henry	PHI	43
Robt.	FRA	288	William	MIF	17	Jos.	PHI	104A
Thomas	BUC	149	William	NOH	59	GOSS, Christian	NOU	179
Thomas	VEN	167	William	GRN	70	Christian	NOU	179
William	LAN	55	William	WAS	121	George	NOU	128
Wm.	FRA	285	William	NOU	202	Honical	NOU	179
GORDIN, John	ALL	99	Willis	NOU	182	Jacob	DAU	30
John	CHE	819	GORE, Daniel	LUZ	323	John	LUZ	351
Widow	LAN	279	John	DEL	171	Joseph	PHI	33
Widow	LAN	281	John	FAY	231	Martin	YOR	205
Wilm.	ALL	109	John	LUZ	333	Matthias	NOU	128
GORDMAN,			Samuel	LUZ	419	Nathaniel	LUZ	351
Catharine	YOR	159	GORE?, Obadiah	LUZ	421	Philip	LUZ	350
GORDNER,			Samuel	BEV	21	GOSSAGE, Benjamin	WAS	56
Christian	LAN	67	GORELAND, Nathl.	CUM	51	Nathan	HNT	161
Peter	BER	276	GORELEY, Robert	WAS	33	GOSSER, John	FRA	303
GORDON, Widow	WST	324	GORELY, James	CUM	127	Philip	PHI	87
Adam	PHA	39	John	CUM	113	GOSSLER, Andw.	BER	240
Adams	GRN	70	Saml.	CUM	120	John	ADA	37
Alexander	BFD	40	Thomas	ADA	6	John Sen.	ADA	37
Alexander	WAS	49	GORGAR, Joseph	PHI	126	Joh	BER	0
Archd.	WST	367	GORGAS, Benjamin	LAN	196	Philip	YOR	155
Betsy	WAS	115	Benjn.	PHI	125	GOSTHALL, Thomas	BER	156
Charles	BEV	22	Jacob	PHI	127	GOSTHERD,		
Charles	BFD	50	John	PHI	126	Frederick	LAN	197
David	BEV	25	John	PHI	141	GOSTNER, Rebecca	PHA	86
David	WAS	85	Joseph	LAN	196	GOTES, Henry	CEN	22A
Eliza.	PHA	121	Juliana	LAN	210	GOTHER, Michael	NOH	83A
Francis	YOR	197	Maria	LAN	196	GOTHOP, Richad	BFD	41
George	WAS	12	Solomon	LAN	196	William	BFD	41
George	BFD	73	GORGEOUS, Jacob	LAN	71	GOTSHAL, John	PHI	91
George	MNT	88	GORGUS, George	PHI	74A	GOTSHALL, Michael	BER	173
Henry	PHI	32	GORMAN, Archd.	WST	324	Michl.	CUM	53
Hester	PHA	116	Daniel	WAS	79	GOTT, John	MNT	141
James	WAS	20	Daniel	WST	324	William	MNT	71
James	WST	150	Dennis	HNT	150	GOTTE?, Thomas	VEN	165
James	YOR	195	Edward	PHA	37	GOTTNER, Geo. J./		
James	YOR	201	Enoch	CHE	878	I.	NOH	75A
James	BUT	329	Henry	DEL	175	George	NOH	75A
James	LUZ	394	Henry	DEL	176	GOTTSCHALL,		
James Jr.	BFD	73	James	DEL	182	William	LAN	209
Jno.	CUM	30	Michael	BFD	63	GOTTSHALK, Thomas	NOH	75A
John	DAU	17	Patrick	PHI	43	GOTWALT, Andw.	YOR	166
John	WAS	28	GORMLEY, Hugh	CUM	35	George	YOR	154
John	DAU	39	James	MER	442	GOUDGE, Richd.	FRA	321
John	BFD	43	Jno.	CUM	103	GOUDY, Agnes	ADA	13
John	ERI	57	GORMLY, James	ALL	49	John	FRA	290
John	GRN	64	John	ALL	51	Wm.	WST	214
John	NOU	182	Willm.	ALL	50	Wm.	WST	288
John	YOR	195	GORMON, Cornelius	NOU	97	GOUGH, Jesse	PHI	133
John	BER	248	Henry	NOU	182	Richard	LUZ	412
John	LUZ	394	GORNER, Cornelius	LYC	19	GOUGHER, William	NOU	164
John	NOU	143A	Elizh. Widow	LAN	13	GOUGLER, George	NOU	182
Jos.	YOR	204	Philip	LAN	15	GOUKLER?, John	MNT	59
Mattw.	WST	367	GORNERY, Joseph	BUC	138	GOUL, John	PHI	63
Moses	BFD	43	GORNERY?, Isaac	MNT	111	Volentine	PHA	64
Moses Senr.	BFD	43	Samuel	MNT	50	GOULD, Daniel	LUZ	362
Mrs.	NOU	198	GORNINGER?, John	PHI	126	Elijah	LUZ	362
Patrick	WST	345	GORSUCH, Elisha	HNT	139	Isaac	LUZ	362
Peter	PHI	16	GORTON, Casper	LAN	172	Jacob	LUZ	340
Phillip	NOU	136	GOSCHEND, Isaac	LAN	209	John	LUZ	362
Rebecca	PHA	118	GOSCHERD, Berned	LAN	215	Peter	LUZ	340
Robert	BFD	50	GOSHET, Deitrich	LAN	99	Thos.	YOR	215
Robert	PHA	117	Isaac	LAN	92	GOULDEN, Charles	YOR	187
Robert	WST	150	GOSHOW, Henry	LAN	287	John	DEL	187
Robert	YOR	199	GOSIN, Jacob	BER	235	Joseph	DEL	163

GOURLEY, John	WST	214	GRAFF, Abraham	LAN	86	GRAHAM, Hugh	DAU	22A
Saml.	WST	324	Abraham	BER	217	Isiah	CUM	117
GOURLY, Samuel	MNT	64	Abraham	LAN	294	Jack	FRA	298
GOUST, Jacob	NOU	193	Andrew Esq.	LAN	101	James	BEV	7
GOUTCHER, Thos.	PHI	60	Benjamin	LAN	222	James	BEV	10
GOVERNATER,			Chris.	LAN	86	James	CRA	14
Lorena	YOR	182	Christian	LAN	73	James	BFD	37
GOVET, Elioner	PHA	12	George	LAN	41	James	WAS	56
Wiliam	PHA	12	George	LAN	43	James	GRN	81
GOW, William	PHI	16	George	HNT	153	James	CUM	117
GOWDY, Edward	ALL	54	George	NOH	68A	James	LAN	121
James	ALL	63	George	NOH	89A	James	LAN	121
James	FAY	250	Henry	PHA	11	James	NOU	128
John	FAY	203	Jacob	LAN	74	James	HNT	161
Robert	DAU	11	Jacob	HNT	119	James	YOR	203
Robert	WAS	33	Jacob	BER	217	James	WST	379
Robert	ALL	83	Jacob	LAN	226	James	CHE	720
Samuel	CRA	14	Jacob	LAN	243	James	PHI	53A
William	WAS	33	James	MIF	25	Jarred	CUM	117
GOWEN, John	CHE	905	John	PHA	79	Jas.	CUM	65
GOWER, George	NOH	41	John	LAN	86	John	MIF	16
George	NOH	35A	John	LAN	86	John	PHA	28
John	NOH	35A	John	LAN	86	John	WAS	28
Ludwig	NOH	35A	John	BER	184	John	WAS	33
Michl.	LYC	14	John	LAN	233	John	BFD	35
GOY, Frederick	NOU	182	John	LAN	233	John	BFD	40
GOYER, George	ADA	9	Joseph	LAN	233	John	ALL	99
George	ADA	10	Marck	LAN	86	John	WAS	110
Henry	ADA	5	Paul	BER	270	John	ARM	124
John	ADA	4	Robert	PHA	117	John	PHI	153
John	ADA	5	Solomon	NOH	89A	John	DEL	171
GR---ER?, John	FRA	314	Sophia	PHA	28	John	FRA	287
GRA-HWOHL,			Valentine	NOH	68A	John Senr.	BFD	73
Theobald	NOH	33A	Widow	LAN	46	John (Crossed		
GRA-N?, Christian	FRA	276	Widow	LAN	73	Out)	WST	379
GRAA, John	PHI	6	GRAFF?, Frederick	BER	170	Joseph	FRA	278
GRABEL, George	DAU	44	GRAFFIUS, Abraham	YOR	156	Joseph	WST	379
GRABER, Adam	YOR	183	GRAFFLEY,			Mary	MNT	57
Andrew	MNT	133	Christian	MNT	92	Mary	VEN	168
Andrew Junr.	MNT	133	GRAFFORD, Thomas	LAN	265	Mary	CHE	719
David	NOH	29A	GRAFFT, George	DAU	19	Michael	WAS	85
Gabriel	YOR	185	GRAFLEY, George	PHI	124	Michael	CHE	717
George	NOH	50	GRAFT, Jacob	SOM	132	Michal	ALL	79
John	NOH	55A	John	ADA	20	Moses	BFD	43
Ludwick	MNT	133	Philip	ADA	20	Nancy	WAS	56
Mathias	NOH	50	GRAGG, James	FAY	252	Peter	CHE	828
GRABY, John	PHI	97	John	FAY	238	Richd.	WST	169
GRACCY, John	DEL	173	William	FAY	238	Robert	CRA	14
GRACE, Widow	PHI	106A	GRAGORY, Jacob	NOU	164	Robert	ADA	20
Aaron	PHA	53	GRAGUE?, Robert	NOU	116	Robert	WAS	33
George	PHI	155	GRAHAM, Widow	PHI	72	Robert	ALL	107
Henry	PHI	118A	Abraham	ALL	105	Robert	HNT	164
Jacob	PHA	80	Alex.	WST	379	Robert	WST	214
Jacob	BUC	92	Alexander	CHE	804	Robt.	WST	214
Jacob	PHI	106	Alexdr	VEN	167	Robt.	FRA	280
James	PHI	52	Alexr.	PHI	29	Samuel	ALL	102
John	MER	442	Ann	PHA	72	Sarah	MIF	7
Philip	PHI	119	Arthur	CUM	102	Sarah	CUM	98
Sarah	PHI	73	Benjn.	CUM	81	Thomas	ADA	17
GRACENEY, David	NOU	193	Daniel	CHE	804	Thomas	WAS	28
GRACY, John	BFD	57	David	PHI	22	Thomas	YOR	197
William	WAS	99	David	BFD	40	Thomas	MER	442
GRACY?, John	MNT	134	Edwd.	PHA	56	Thoms.	MIF	16A
GRADON, Barnet	GRN	111	Frances	PHA	79	Thos.	CUM	141
Edward	GRN	111	Francis	CEN	18A	William	BFD	55
GRADY, Elisha	BFD	73	Geo.	CUM	58	William	GRN	75
Jacob	LAN	287	George	GRN	63	William	LAN	133
Thomas	PHI	34	George	PHI	151	William	HNT	159
William	HNT	161	George	SOM	160	William	WST	271
GRAEFF, Christian	YOR	178	George (Erased)	SOM	157	William	WST	379
George	LAN	35	Gilbert	MIF	25	William	MER	442
Henry	YOR	179	Gilbert	ALL	84	William Esqr.	DEL	163
Jacob Esqr.	LAN	40	Henry	DEL	180	Wilm.	ALL	52
John	LAN	35	Henry Esqr.	WAS	28	Wilm.	ALL	86
Mary	SOM	138	Hugh	BEV	16	Wm.	CUM	37
GRAFF, Abraham	LAN	73	Hugh	PHI	32	Wm.	CUM	74

146

GRAHAM, Wm.	VEN	167	GRANTHAM, Peter	PHI	28	GRAY, Hugh	WST	190
Wm.	WST	379	GRANTHSON,			Isaac	BFD	43
Wm.	CHE	754	Charles	PHI	20	James	MIF	7
Wm. Esqr.	MIF	7	GRANVEL, Wm	PHI	47	James	LAN	103
GRAHAM?, (See			GRASEY, Robert	NOU	193	James	BUC	105
Ghaham)	CHE	902	GRASMIRE, Adam	MIF	25	James	ALL	120
GRAHAMS, Anges	BUT	348	GRASS, Andrew	YOR	163	James	HNT	124
Daniel	BUT	349	George	BER	248	James	HNT	149
Danl.	BUT	347	GRASSER, Chrn. &			Jno. & Robt.	DAU	15
Danl.	BUT	347	Jacob	DAU	34	Joel	YOR	156
George	FAY	256	Jacob & Chrn.	DAU	34	John	MIF	5
John	MIF	25	GRASSLEY, George	NOH	75A	John	MIF	5
Malcam	BUT	347	GRASWEID, John	LAN	209	John	MIF	7
Robt.	BUT	328	GRATE, John	BER	206	John	PHA	93
Saml.	BUT	355	John	BER	211	John	ALL	109
GRAHAN, John	MER	443	Nicholas	YOR	182	John	GRN	111
Marey	MER	442	GRATER, John	MNT	127	John	CUM	120
GRAHEMS, Patrick	BUT	321	GRATHWOHL, John			John	HNT	122
GRAHMS, Matthw.	BUT	340	Junr.	NOH	71	John	PHI	138
Robert	LAN	169	Valentine	NOH	71	John	HNT	144
GRAIFF, Danl.	BER	240	GRATHWOHN, John			John	WST	150
Jacob	BER	144	Senr.	NOH	71	John	NOU	198
John	BER	142	GRATTS?, Michael	PHA	83	John	YOR	213
Sebastian	BER	144	GRATZ, John	YOR	209	John	FAY	256
Wm.	BER	240	Philip	NOH	85	John	FAY	256
Wm. Jr.	BER	240	GRAUFF, Danl.	BER	215	John	FAY	265
GRAINTREE?, Jacob	LUZ	413	GRAUM, Fredk.	LAN	7	John	CHE	749
GRAIVNER, Georg	ALL	63	GRAUSE, George	BER	284	John	CEN	22A
GRALL, Adam	LAN	197	GRAVATT, John	MER	443	John	NOU	143A
Christian	DAU	16A	GRAVEL, John	DEL	184	Jonathan	FAY	256
Henry	DAU	37A	Mathias	PHA	71	Joseph	PHA	70
John	DAU	16	GRAVELL, John R.	PHA	30	Joseph (Crossed		
GRAM, George	ADA	35	GRAVENSTINE,			Out)	LAN	151
GRAMER, Christn.	PHI	93A	George	PHI	128	Joseph	NOU	157
Helfred	YOR	190	Henry	PHI	127	Mary	PHA	34
GRAMES, Andrew	BER	221	John	PHA	11	Mary	ALL	68
Andrew Jr.	BER	221	Peter	PHA	84	Matthew	ERI	60
GRAMLICH,			Saml.	PHA	32	Mrs.	NOU	198
Christian	NOH	75A	GRAVEOR, John	LAN	126	Nathan	PHA	67
Paul	NOH	85	GRAVES, John	BFD	43	Neal	WST	288
GRANAHAN, John	MER	443	John Esqr.	CHE	699	Peter	LAN	59
GRANDUM, John	PHA	79	Joseph	BFD	43	Peter	PHI	118
GRANDY, Joseph	LYC	14	Samuel?	BFD	43	Peter Jr.	CEN	22A
GRANGEE, John	CHE	885	GRAVEY, Fredk.	PHA	41	Peter	CEN	22A
GRANIS, Eanos	WST	214	GRAVIN, Thomas	WST	190	Rachel	MIF	7
GRANLIN, Maria	LAN	250	GRAWOZS?, Peter	ERI	55A	Richard	LAN	30
GRANT, Alexr.	MIF	15	GRAY, Abm.	BUC	146	Richd.	PHA	65
Alexr.	PHI	11A	Alexander	WAS	33	Robert	MIF	7
Benjamin	ERI	59	Alexr.	CUM	91	Robert	BEV	23
Charles	BUC	85	Allexander	BEV	23	Robert	PHI	59
David	CRA	3	Anthony	CHE	807	Robert	NOU	97
George	WAS	44	Archibald	NOU	117	Robert	NOU	128
Henry	CHE	911	Cathrine	CUM	96	Robert	CHE	762
Hugh	PHI	55	Cela	PHA	118	Robt. & Jno.	DAU	15
Hugh	ALL	98	Charles	BER	163	Saml.	CUM	28
Jacob	MNT	106	Daniel	FAY	221	Saml.	LAN	91
James	ALL	55	David	MIF	5	Saml.	PHI	109A
James	GRN	100	David	BFD	55	Samuel	ALL	58
Jeremiah	WAS	44	David	PHA	57	Samuel	CHE	810
John	PHA	17	David	GRN	111	Thomas	ADA	36
John	PHA	32	David	CHE	804	Thomas	WAS	99
John	WAS	44	David	CHE	804	Thomas	PHA	104
John	BER	139	Edward	NOU	117	Thomas	HNT	164
John	CHE	731	Elijah	CHE	807	Thomas	BUT	341
John	CHE	801	Elizabeth	DAU	15	Thomas	MIF	16A
Jonathan	BEV	16	Enoch	CHE	756	Thos.	PHA	111
Jonathan	DEL	171	Enoch	CHE	864	Thos.	YOR	209
Jonathan	DEL	189	George	NOH	71	Widow	MIF	5
Josiah	LUZ	416	George	WAS	99	William	BFD	50
Noah	FAY	265	George	MNT	130	William	PHI	54
Peter	BEV	6	George	LAN	156	William	NOU	97
Thomas	NOU	99	George	HNT	164	William	GRN	111
William	PHI	127	George	NOU	193	William	PHA	114
Willm.	PHI	94	George	CHE	807	William	HNT	161
Wm.	PHI	107A	George	CHE	884	William	HNT	164
GRANTABAUGH, Jacob	PHI	90A	George	PHI	76A	William	NOU	198
			Henry	NOU	193			

GRAY, Wilm.	ALL	53	GREEN, Daniel	YOR	158	GREEN, Richard	SOM	145
Wm.	PHA	8	Daniel	DEL	159	Robert	PHA	114
GRAYBEAL, Peter	DAU	41	David	PHI	21	Robert	DEL	172
GRAYBELL,			David	ALL	75	Robert	NOU	143A
Christian	NOU	182	Ebinezer	FAY	200	Robt.	CHE	761
Jacob	NOU	182	Elioner	PHA	120	Samuel	ARM	125
John	NOU	182	Elisha	HNT	166	Sarah	DAU	10A
GRAYBILL,			Elisha	CHE	700	Stephen	PHI	102
Christian	LAN	276	Elisha	DAU	13A	Thomas	ADA	18
John	WAS	44	Emmor	DEL	159	Thomas	HNT	139
John	LAN	160	Enock	PHA	20	Thomas	SOM	145
GRAYBLE, Jacob	YOR	158	George	ADA	25	Thomas	HNT	165
John	YOR	163	George	BUC	99	Thomas	LUZ	409
Joseph	ADA	13	George	HNT	139	Thos.	PHI	80A
Michael	YOR	158	George	HNT	159	Timothy	WST	214
Michael	YOR	163	George	DEL	172	Timothy	LUZ	325
Samuel	ADA	13	George	NOU	187	Timothy	DAU	22A
GRAYDON,			George	FRA	301	Widow	BUC	157
Alexander	WAS	80	Henrey	FAY	231	Widow	MIF	12A
Alexander	DAU	4A	Henry	LUZ	403	Willard	LUZ	323
William	DAU	3A	Isaac	HNT	158	William	CRA	6
GRAYER, Neal	PHI	26	Isaiah	NOH	35A	William	PHA	14
GRAYHAM, John	FRA	319	Israel	BER	281	William	ARM	123
GRAYSON, Robt.	CUM	88	Jacob	PHI	133	GREEN?, Mrs.	LYC	15
Wm.	CUM	55	James	ARM	125	David	MIF	10
GRAZER, William			James	VEN	165	Joseph	WAR	1A
Rush.	PHA	32	James	FAY	265	Sarah	BEV	28
GREABON, John	NOU	175	Jesse	DEL	158	See Grun	BUC	83
GREADY, John	FRA	285	Jesse	PHI	81A	GREENAMYER, Jacob	ADA	17
GREAHAM, James	VEN	168	Jno.	CUM	103	GREENAWALD,		
GREAN, Joseph	LAN	247	John	PHI	16	Abraham	LAN	293
GREAR, James	PHI	146	John	ADA	17	Jacob	LAN	94
GREARY, Jacob			John	PHI	33	GREENAWALT, Mary	WST	150
Junr.	MNT	133	John	PHI	47	GREENE, George	GRN	81
Peter	MNT	133	John	PHA	51	John	WAS	80
GREASY, Fredk.	PHI	2	John	BUC	84	Joseph	WAS	110
GREATHOUSE,			John	PHA	96	Widow	CUM	61
Harman	FAY	261	John	ARM	125	William	WAS	62
GREAUD, Despaign	PHA	75	John	BUC	157	Wm.	PHA	100
GREAVES, David	WAS	79	John	HNT	158	GREENEWALD,		
GREBEL, Jacob	PHI	33	John	FAY	235	Abraham	NOH	85
GREBER, (No Given			John	FRA	302	John	DAU	28
Name)	LAN	210	John	BUT	357	GREENEWALT,		
George Senr.	NOH	62A	John	LUZ	408	Abraham	YOR	160
Peter	NOH	62A	John	CHE	787	Benjn.	DAU	52A
GREBILL, -----	LAN	2	John	CHE	828	Christopher	YOR	163
Abraham	LAN	62	John	CHE	843	Frederick	YOR	163
Ann	LAN	3	John	NOH	37A	Henry	FRA	273
Isaac	LAN	75	John	NOU	143A	Jacob	ADA	28
Jacob	LAN	73	Jonathan	CHE	779	Jacob	WST	251
Jacob	LAN	284	Jos. Junr.	NOH	35A	Jacob	DAU	18A
John	LAN	73	Josep	BUC	98A	Martin	ADA	29
Michael	LAN	98	Joseph	PHI	133	Nicholas		
Saml.	LAN	75	Joseph	NOU	136	(Crossed Out)	FRA	308
Samuel	LAN	75	Joseph	DEL	157	Nicholas	FRA	310
Widow	LAN	62	Joseph	NOU	175	Phil.	DAU	32
GREBLE, George	PHA	74	Joseph	DEL	191	Phil.	DAU	32A
Wm.	PHA	74	Joseph	CEN	22A	GREENFIELD, Amos	CHE	740
GREBS, Henry	BER	186	Joseph	NOH	35A	Evan	CHE	861
GRECY?, Joseph	WAR	1A	Joseph	BUC	93A	Jas.	CHE	770
GREDER, John	NOH	80	Lemuel Revd.	PHA	6	Richard	FRA	272
GREEGG, Isaac	CHE	836	Lucuss	PHA	49	Stephen	CHE	861
GREEK, William	LUZ	390	Marey	FAY	235	William	WAS	121
GREEN, Abel	DEL	190	Mary	CUM	46	William	FAY	214
Adam	PHA	117	Mary	PHA	122	GREENHOES?,		
Alice/ Alec?	BUC	84	Mary	DEL	159	Michael	NOU	128
Andrew	FAY	240	Mary	PHI	87A	GREENLAND, Moses	HNT	147
Aquila	HNT	166	Michael	PHI	3	Nathaniel	HNT	147
Ashbel Revd.	PHA	44	Michael	PHI	45	GREENLEAF, Jacob	LAN	129
Asop	PHI	83A	Mrs.	NOU	179	James	NOH	68A
Benjn.	BUC	157	Nathaniel	ALL	73	Martin	LAN	129
Benjn.	NOH	37A	Nehemiah	WAS	33	GREENLEE, James	HNT	159
Charles	HNT	161	Patrick	LAN	39	John	CRA	7
Charles	CHE	749	Peter	PHI	28	John	WAS	110
Christr.	CUM	152	Peter	PHI	79	Marey	FAY	244
Daniel	ARM	123	Peter	PHI	69A	Robert	LYC	23

GREENLEE, Robert	ALL	110	GREGG, Daniel	WAS	80	GREIDER, Tobias	DAU	28
Thomas	ALL	110	George	GRN	87	GREILING, Adam	NOH	59
William	GRN	112	George	CHE	840	GREIMM, Philip	YOR	172
GREENLEY, John	LAN	295	Henry	WAS	80	GREIN, Charles	BEV	14
GREENLY, James	LAN	286	Henry Esqr.	WAS	80	GREINER, Daniel	BER	169
Robt.	VEN	170	Herman	CHE	707	George	PHI	147
GREENOW, John	WAS	68	Isaac	CHE	865	John	LAN	144
GREENTREE,			Isaac Jr.	CHE	865	Martin	LAN	144
Alexander	FAY	214	Israel	FAY	227	Philip	BER	223
GREENWALD,			John	CUM	78	GREIR, Christina	CUM	61
Elizabeth	BER	247	John	VEN	166	James	CUM	106
George	BER	130	John Junr.	WAS	80	James	CHE	779
John	BER	130	John Senr.	WAS	80	Jno.	CUM	69
Joseph	BER	130	Levi	GRN	88	John	CHE	734
GREENWALT, Henry	MNT	115	Mahlon	BUC	160A	Matthew	CHE	822
Jacob	BER	187	Margaret	WAS	80	Saml.	CUM	95
Maths.	DAU	32A	Michael	CHE	836	Thomas	CUM	106
GREENWAY, Joseph	PHA	45	Nimrod	FAY	227	Thos.	CUM	49
GREENWOLT, John	FRA	306	Richard	GRN	87	GREISEMER, Felix	NOH	68A
GREENWOOD, John	CUM	90	Roger	WAS	80	GREITER, John	DAU	25A
John	ERI	59A	Saml.	CEN	18A	Michael	DAU	25A
Rebecca	PHI	80A	Samuel	WST	190	GREKER?, George	MNT	134
Sarah	PHA	68	Thomas Dr.	FAY	200	GREMER, Andrew	LAN	52
Thomas	DAU	10	Thos. Esqrere	FAY	227	Michael	LAN	31
GREENZWEIG, David	NOH	83A	Widow	NOH	29A	GREMLY, Soloman	MNT	127
Godfrey	NOH	35A	William	WAS	80	Solomon Junr.	MNT	127
Henry	NOH	35A	William	GRN	88	GREMUS?,		
Jonathan	NOH	83A	William	WST	150	Sebastian	BER	169
Tobias	NOH	83A	William	BUC	151	GRENEWALT,		
GREER, Alexd.	ALL	70	William	LUZ	338	Christian	MNT	130
Dixon	ADA	8	GREGGORY, Benona	BUC	139	GRENNOUGH,		
George	FRA	287	GREGOR, Abram	CUM	85	William	FAY	265
Hanah	ALL	81	George	MNT	77	GRENOW, Thomas	FAY	203
Isaac	ALL	81	George	MNT	115	GRENWAY?, Abigal	PHA	26
Jacob	PHI	110	Jacob	YOR	219	GREPE?, William	DAU	20
James	LAN	163	John	YOR	219	GREPS, Thamas	CHE	790
John	CRA	6	Margaritta	MNT	111	GRESH, George	BER	173
John	ALL	81	GREGORY, Asahel	LUZ	384	GRESS, Mathias		
John	PHI	115	Eliza.	CUM	71	Esqr.	NOH	33A
John	YOR	155	Jas.	CUM	72	GRESSING, Ludwig	SOM	151
Joseph	DEL	181	John	BFD	43	GRESSLER, John	YOR	158
Margaret	HNT	144	John	PHA	97	GRETHOUSE, Wm.	MIF	12A
Michl.	FRA	308	John	DEL	184	GREVEN, John	PHI	34
Nathh. Revnd.	CHE	821	John	DEL	184	GREVENGER?, Henry	LAN	285
Nichs.	PHI	115A	John	DEL	184	Henry	LAN	285
Thomas	WAS	85	John	BER	206	GREVES, Jesse	FAY	252
Thomas	ERI	56A	Joshua	HNT	133	GREVIS, Samuel B.	ERI	57
Thos.	FRA	311	Mark	FRA	276	GREWER, Henry	FRA	308
William	WAS	20	Patrick	GRN	106	GREY, Caleb	DEL	155
Willm.	PHI	97	Samuel	GRN	106	GRHAM, Margit	ALL	50
GREERE?, Ernst	BER	235	GREHAM, James	FRA	273	GRI-N, Jonathan	BER	225
GREESE, Detrich	BER	215	John	FAY	197	GRIBBON, James	PHA	53
GREESE?, Ernst	BER	235	John	FAY	209	Patrick	PHA	119
GREESEMER?, See			Joseph	FAY	256	GRIBEN, James	CHE	775
Grusemer	BER	229	Robert	CEN	20	GRIBIER, George ·	PHA	81
GREESINGER, Aron	SOM	138	Robert	FAY	238	GRICE, Isaac	PHI	6
Catherin	FRA	274	Thomas	FAY	244	Joseph	PHI	82
Peter	SOM	138	GREHAMS, John	FAY	203	GRIDER, Daniel	BER	173
GREESMER?,			Richard	FAY	244	Frederick	LAN	266A
Leonard	BER	206	Thomas	FAY	203	Maichael	LAN	261
GREEVES, Thomas	PHA	4	GREHIMS, Saml.	MIF	20	GRIDLEY, Daniel	LUZ	321
GREEVS, Enes	FAY	227	GREIDER, Abraham	LAN	101	GRIEER?, Guien?	BEV	20
GREFF, Jacob	DAU	7	Christn.	DAU	28A	GRIEFT, Adam	NOU	187
GREFFITH,			George	DAU	28	Anthony	NOU	187
Ebenazer Esq.	SOM	148	Jacob	DAU	28	Jeremiah	NOU	187
Rachel	SOM	148	Jacob	LAN	277	GRIENER, Andrew	BER	169
GREG, Aron	PHI	75A	Jacob	LAN	310	GRIER, Alexr.	NOU	164
Isaac	ALL	57	Jacob	DAU	28A	Andrew	NOU	164
John	DAU	21	John	DAU	27	Henrey	FAY	231
GREGAMY, Henry	PHA	61	John	DAU	28	Humphrey	NOU	164
GREGERY, Mary	PHA	22	John	LAN	298	Jennet	YOR	155
GREGG, Amos	BUC	83	Martin	DAU	28	John	BUC	154
Andrew	WAS	80	Martin	LAN	309	John	FAY	231
Andrew	NOU	171	Michael	LAN	277	John	CHE	822
Andrew	LUZ	421	Peter	DAU	28	Joseph	BUC	96
Andw.	CEN	20	Tobias	DAU	28	Joseph	CHE	822

GRIER, Matthew	BUC	141	GRIFFITH, George	LAN	133	GRIGOR, Widow	PHI	5
Nathan	CHE	826	Griffith	CHE	904	GRIGORY, Wm.	PHI	81A
Patrick	WST	190	Howel	MNT	88	GRIGRIG, John	PHI	22
Robt.	FRA	280	Howell	BUC	142A	GRIGS, V?.	LYC	11
Saml. E.	LYC	3	Isaac	BFD	73	GRILL, Jacob	LAN	209
Thomas	FAY	209	Isaac	LAN	119	John	BER	259
William	WST	309	Isaac	YOR	195	GRIM, Widow	PHI	97
Wm. Esqr.	LYC	21	Isaac	PHI	109A	Charles	YOR	175
GRIESEMER, Widow	NOH	55A	Jacob	WAS	79	Henry	LAN	77
GRIESOR, Anthony	BUC	139	Jacob	CHE	857	Henry	BER	225
GRIESSEMER,			Jacob	PHI	82A	Jacob	HNT	143
Abraham	NOH	89A	James	ADA	17	John	DEL	177
GRIEVS, James	ALL	86	James	ADA	29	John Jun.	DEL	177
GRIFFEE, John	WST	251	James	YOR	195	Val.	BER	144
GRIFFEN, Moses	PHA	98	Jedadiah	CHE	855	Widow	CHE	894
Patrick	BUC	83	Jesse	BFD	73	GRIM?, Mrs.	LYC	15
Peter	PHA	93	Jesse	BER	248	George	ADA	34
William	PHI	16	Jesse	CHE	895	John	DAU	2A
GRIFFETH, Benjn.	PHA	22	John	WAS	12	GRIMER, James	NOU	147
Cadwallader	PHA	110	John	BFD	73	GRIMES, Widow	PHI	21
Elizabeth	PHA	32	John	BUC	88	Widow	PHI	95A
Hannah	PHA	7	John	WAS	90	Archibald	WAS	110
Jonathn.	FAY	221	John	PHI	114	Archibald	BUC	151
Levi	FAY	261	John	HNT	155	Edwd.	BUT	350
Mary	PHA	115	John	DEL	156	Elison	FAY	265
Thomas	FAY	200	John	BUC	157	Forcke/ Foroke?	LAN	179
Thos.	DAU	22A	John	YOR	201	Francis	FRA	317
GRIFFETHS,			John	BER	248	Galem	PHI	37
Elizabeth	PHA	4	John	CHE	830	Hugh	FRA	291
Saml. P. M.D.	PHA	8	John	CHE	860	Hugh	DAU	34A
GRIFFEY, Joseph	LAN	244	John	BUC	86A	James	HNT	145
GRIFFIN, Charles	FAY	244	Jonathan	BUC	157	James	HNT	152
Daniel	BUC	84	Jos.	YOR	177	James	YOR	202
Edward	HNT	163	Jos.	YOR	208	James	FAY	265
Even	LAN	269	Joseph	PHI	15	James	FRA	317
Henry	WST	309	Joseph	MNT	44	James	CEN	22A
Isaac Esqr.	FAY	244	Joseph	DEL	156	James	NOH	37A
Joshua	LUZ	365	Joseph	DEL	173	John	PHI	7
Josiah	CUM	147	Joseph	CHE	799	John	PHI	8
Patrick	WST	272	Joshua	WAS	44	John	CRA	17
Robert	WAS	44	Lewis	DEL	174	John	WAS	34
Samuel	LUZ	408	Nathan	YOR	214	John	PHA	63
Samuel Jr.	LUZ	408	Richard	PHI	61	John	PHA	73
Seth Capt.	PHI	67A	Robert	PHI	11	John	WST	344
William	CRA	11	Robert	ERI	60	John	CHE	862
William	FAY	244	Sam. R.	PHI	134	John	CHE	865
GRIFFIS, Abner	LUZ	391	Saml.	PHI	152	John	CEN	22A
GRIFFIT, Wilm.	ALL	108	Samuel	BER	248	Joseph	NOH	78
GRIFFITH, Mr.	PHA	79	Samuel Jr.	PHI	151	Patrick	PHI	142
Widow	YOR	210	Thomas	BFD	73	Patrick	NOU	175
Abel	BFD	63	Thomas	BFD	73	Philip	PHA	38
Abijah	WST	272	Thomas	WAS	99	Robert	LAN	229
Abner	CHE	878	Thomas	DEL	155	Robt.	MIF	10
Abraham	PHI	152	Thomas	SOM	162	Samuel	LAN	16
Abraham	YOR	209	Thomas	CHE	847	Samuel	VEN	170
Abraham	CHE	814	Thomas	CHE	883	Thomas	FAY	261
Amos	BUC	105	Thos.	BUC	155A	Widow	DAU	47
Amos	YOR	207	William	WAS	62	William	WAS	34
Benjn.	CHE	721	William	BFD	73	William	WAS	44
Christopher	LAN	126	William	DEL	155	William	WST	237
Dan	CHE	904	William	SOM	162	Wm.	VEN	167
Daniel	SOM	162	William	YOR	180	GRIMLER, Hannah	LAN	50
David	BFD	37	Williams	MNT	111	GRIMM, Henry	NOH	59
David	WAS	99	Wm.	WST	289	Jacob	YOR	192
David	MNT	112	Wm.	CHE	753	Jacob Junr.	NOH	59
David	CHE	712	GRIFFITH?, David	MIF	10	Jacob Senr.	NOH	59
David	CHE	895	GRIFFITHS, Amos	MNT	44	Peter	NOH	59
David Jr.	CHE	895	Hannah	PHI	52	Peter		
David	BUC	137A	GRIFFY, John	BUT	327	(Storekeeper)	NOH	59
Elisha	BUC	105	Richard	PHI	141	Philip	NOH	68A
Enoch	CHE	864	GRIFFY?, (See			GRIMSON, Saml.	DAU	21
Evan	BFD	63	Guffy)	BUT	322	GRIN, Jacob	NOU	187
Evan	PHI	106A	GRIFHILL?, Daniel	BEV	14	GRINAH, Martin	FRA	285
Ezekiel	CHE	743	GRIFITH, Griffy?	PHI	72A	GRIND?, Michael	DAU	40A
Frances	FAY	238	GRIGAMIRE, George	PHI	96A	GRINDEL, Jacob	FAY	240
George	PHI	39	GRIGERS, George	PHI	19	GRINDING, James	BER	233

GRINDLE, Henry	SOM 128	GROFF, Henry	BUC 159	GROSS, Jacob	NOU 128
John	SOM 128	Jacob	MNT 89	Jacob	LAN 316
GRINER, Fredrick	PHA 27	Jacob	MNT 97	Jacob	NOH 33A
John	PHA 60	Jacob	BER 163	Jesse	WST 214
Martin	LAN 261	Jacob	BUC 147A	John	ADA 12
Philip	BER 139	John	MNT 82	John	ADA 13
Philip	DAU 14A	John	MNT 94	John	MNT 97
Widow	LAN 253	John	LAN 146	John	SOM 133
GRININGER, Jacob	NOU 122	John	BUC 159	John	YOR 174
GRINNES?,		John	CHE 898	John	NOU 187
Sebastian	BER 169	Joseph	MNT 89	John	LAN 312
GRINOPP, Widow	PHI 66A	Joseph	MNT 94	John	NOH 47A
GRIPE, Daniel	HNT 122	Michael	BER 181	Lewis	LAN 87
Jacob	HNT 122	Michale	BER 135	M.	LAN 147B
John	HNT 122	Peter	BER 163	Martin (Crossed	
Joseph	HNT 122	GROG, Jacob	DAU 28A	Out)	LAN 261
GRIPE?, William	DAU 20	GROGAN, Patrick	GRN 70	Martin	LAN 313
GRIPS, Christian	NOU 175	GROGEN, William	PHI 153	Mathias	LAN 312
Jacob	NOU 175	GROGG, Barth	PHI 101B	Mathias	NOH 47A
GRISE, George	HNT 123	David	PHI 101B	Mathias	NOH 86A
GRISENHEIMER,		George	PHI 118	Michael	LAN 4
Fredk.	MNT 57	GROH, George A.	BER 281	Michael	LAN 27
GRISHILL?, Daniel	BEV 14	Jacob	NOH 47	Michael	YOR 173
GRISINGER,		John	DAU 51	Peter (See	
Stephen	LAN 313	Peter	DAU 52	Gross, Widow)	NOH 29A
GRISLER, George	BUC 80	GROLL, John	NOU 99	Peter	YOR 173
Philip	BUC 139	GRONER, Jacob	NOH 41	Peter	NOU 187
GRISMER, John	MNT 134	John	SOM 153	Peter	WST 214
GRISON, James	CEN 22A	GROOM, John	BUC 151	Peter	LAN 313
Thomas	CEN 22A	Thomas Jn.	BUC 143	Peter	NOH 89A
GRISSELL, Edward	DEL 155	William	BUC 143	Philip	ADA 42
Edward	DEL 165	GROP, George	YOR 209	Philip	NOH 82
Elisha	DEL 176	GROPE, Mathias	DAU 29A	Philip	LAN 312
Thomas	WAS 79	GROSCOP, Samuel	NOU 187	Philip	NOH 39A
GRIST, Abraham	ADA 6	GROSCUP, Paul	BER 257	Samuel	MNT 127
Conrad	MNT 97	GROSE, Fredk.	PHA 77	Samuel	YOR 164
Conrad	FAY 227	George	DAU 13	Ulicrh	PHA 105
Daniel	ADA 44	George	CHE 852	Wendle	YOR 175
David	ADA 42	Henry	NOU 136	Widow	BUC 141
Edward	LAN 155	Henry	DAU 10A	Widow Of Chn.	NOH 47A
George	LUZ 403	Jacob	DAU 11	Widow Of Jacob	NOH 47
Isaac	ADA 42	John	DAU 11	Widow Of Petr.	NOH 29A
Isaac	FAY 208	Michl.	DAU 14	GROSSART, Adam	YOR 179
Jacob	ADA 42	William	BER 139	GROSSCOSS, John	ADA 36
John	ADA 44	GROSH, John	LAN 135	GROSSCROSS,	
John	YOR 208	Samuel	LAN 135	Alexander	BEV 13
John	YOR 213	GROSMAN, Nicholas	NOU 175	Daniel	BEV 16
John	LUZ 402	GROSS, Abm.	CEN 22A	Jacob	CUM 110
Joseph	ADA 44	Abraham	LAN 196	John	BEV 14
Joseph Junr.	ADA 41	Abraham	NOH 29A	GROSSCUP, Jacob	MNT 92
Mathias	MNT 94	Andrew	LAN 16	GROSSLEY, William	NOH 53
Thos.	YOR 213	C.	LAN 253	GROSSMAN, Benjn.	ADA 4
William	FAY 209	Chn. (See		Jacob	LAN 143
William	YOR 209	Gross, Widow)	NOH 47A	GROTZ, Jacob	
William Jur.	FAY 209	Christian	LAN 310	Junr.	NOH 37A
Willin	ADA 44	Christian	BUC 147A	John	NOH 39A
GRISTOCK, William	MNT 85	Conrad	LAN 16	GROUL, George	BER 244
GRISTWEID, Martin	LAN 197	Danforth	LUZ 403	Jacob	BER 244
GRISWOLD,		Daniel	YOR 173	Jacob Jr.	BER 244
Johnathan	LYC 12	Daniel	BER 225	John	BER 244
GRO, Ludwick	YOR 182	Daniel	LAN 312	Saml.	BER 244
GROCE, John	MIF 1	David	LAN 196	GROUND, Nicholas	CHE 789
GROCEMAN,		David	BER 225	Peter	CHE 789
Lawrence	CEN 20	Elizabeth	NOH 29A	GROUP, Phillip	CUM 111
GRODON, Andrew	CHE 725	Frederich	BER 157	GROUS, David	DAU 32A
GROE, Michael	NOU 182	Frederick	NOH 47A	John	PHI 31
GROEST, Thomas	CHE 887	George	YOR 207	Joseph	DAU 33A
GROF, Jacob	DAU 29	George	LAN 147B	GROUSE, Jacob	CUM 133
GROFE, Joseph	PHI 111	George	NOH 66A	Phillip	CUM 140
GROFF, Abraham	MNT 94	Henry	LAN 25	GROVE, Ab.	DAU 46A
Balzer	PHI 1099	Henry	ADA 37	Abm.	CUM 48
Frederick	LAN 102	Henry	NOU 187	Abm.	LAN 261
George	MNT 57	Henry	NOU 187	Abraham	FRA 312
George	BER 151	Henry	NOH 68A	Adam	NOU 117
George	BER 151	Isaac	NOH 39A	Andrew	DAU 37
Henry	MNT 89	Jacob	LAN 53	Andrew	NOU 97

GROVE, Barnet	WAS	33	GROVES, Widw.	PHI	92	GRUBE, George	YOR	215
Christian	LAN	6	Alexander	PHA	121	Peter Jnr.	BUC	80
Christian	LAN	22	Christn.	PHA	76	GRUBENSEE, George	DAU	33A
Christian	ADA	35	Danl.	PHI	104	GRUBER, Adam	BER	202
Christopher	FRA	276	George	LAN	229	Albrecht	BER	270
Christr.	CUM	25	Henry	PHA	43	Christn.	DAU	41A
Danl.	CUM	26	Isaac	BFD	68	Elizabeth	NOU	121
David	CUM	48	James	BUC	93A	George	DEL	167
David	LAN	111	Jesse	PHI	105B	George	BER	202
David	BUC	154	Peter	PHI	92	Henry	BER	202
Francis	LAN	21	Peter	BUC	93A	Jacob	NOH	29A
Francis	YOR	186	Samuel	YOR	215	John	BER	202
Francis	LAN	261	Wendle	BEV	19	Philip	BER	206
George	LAN	114	GROW, Chrisn.	LAN	8	Simon	BER	187
George	NOU	128	Frederick	MNT	138	Solomon	NOH	50
George	YOR	194	George	MNT	138	Willm.	NOH	47A
Henry	CUM	32	John	YOR	193	GRUBOCK, Jacob	CUM	51
Henry	WST	272	Michl.	CUM	22	GRUBUM?, William	NOU	175
Henry Senr.	LAN	9	GROWDEN, Joseph	MNT	132	GRUCKAMILLER,		
Isaac	ADA	34	GROWL, John	PHI	70	Jacob	LAN	251
Isaac	LAN	261	GRUB/ GRUBL?,			GRUFF?, Frederick	BER	170
Jacob	DAU	19	Jacob	LAN	185	GRUGER, Christian	NOU	99
Jacob	CUM	48	GRUB, Abraham	HNT	116	GRULL, Christn.	PHI	69
Jacob	NOU	187	Andrew	ALL	115	GRUM, Widow	PHI	99A
Jacob	YOR	198	Christian	LAN	187	Elizabeth	LAN	273
Jacob	WST	236	Coon	ALL	115	Ludwig	BER	144
Jean	NOH	47	Frederick	NOH	39A	William	PHA	30
John	LAN	8	Fredric	PHI	146	GRUMBACH, George	NOU	182
John	BFD	54	George	ALL	116	GRUMBLE, Godfrey	PHI	1
John	MNT	82	George	NOH	86A	Philip	PHI	1
John	MNT	85	Henry	LAN	116	GRUMLAFE, George	LAN	209
John	NOU	136	Jacob	ALL	60	GRUMLING,		
John	HNT	148	Jacob	ALL	115	Christian	YOR	168
John	HNT	152	Jacob	NOU	143A	George	YOR	206
John	YOR	206	John	ALL	57	GRUMMOW, Abram	FAY	235
John	FAY	214	John	YOR	179	GRUN, Ebenezer	BUC	83
John	WST	236	John	NOH	39A	Joseph	BUC	83
John	WST	309	Mary	DEL	163	Luke	WST	190
John	FRA	314	Philip	NOH	35A	GRUN?, (See		
John	FRA	315	Phillop	ALL	115	Green)	BUC	84
Jonas	DAU	17A	GRUBAUGH, Michl.	CUM	48	(See Green)	NOU	143A
Joseph	BEV	19	GRUBB, Abraham	MNT	57	GRUNDACKER, Geo.	DAU	18A
Joseph	NOU	175	Abram	CHE	895	GRUNDAN, Samuel	WAR	1A
Martin	LAN	115	Abram	CHE	906	GRUNEMEYER,		
Martin	FRA	315	Andrew	WAS	68	Edward	NOH	62A
Michael	NOU	128	Benjamin	ERI	56	GRUSEMER, Jacob	BER	229
Michael	SOM	153	Christian	FRA	302	John	BER	229
Michael	YOR	178	Christina	BER	210	Peter	BER	229
Michael	YOR	190	Christn.	PHI	88A	GRUSMER?, Leonard	BER	206
Peter	DAU	5	Conrod	CHE	727	GRUSS, Casper	LAN	143
Peter	LYC	18	Conrod	CHE	892	GRUVER, Isaac	BUC	157
Peter	DAU	51	Daniel	CHE	895	Peter	FRA	317
Peter	PHI	118	David	CHE	894	Soloman	BUC	157
Peter	CHE	833	David	CHE	895	GRUVERT, Powel	NOU	114
Philip	LYC	23	George	MNT	57	GRYDER, Jacob	LAN	164
Philip	YOR	163	George	YOR	219	Martin	LAN	150
Phillip	CUM	92	Henry	MNT	130	GUAAN, James	FAY	265
Samuel	NOU	175	Henry	LAN	261	James Jur.	FAY	265
Thos.	YOR	197	Henry B.	LAN	142	GUARD, Thomas	CHE	864
Widow	DAU	27	Israel	LAN	24	GUBB, John	NOU	136
GROVENOR, Isaiah	LUZ	409	Jacob	CHE	771	GUBBINS, John	LAN	122
GROVER, Christian	NOU	136	Jacob	CHE	891	GUBY, Peter	CHE	729
Daniel	WAS	99	John	ERI	56	GUCHES, John	YOR	156
David	LAN	115	John	CHE	896	GUCKERLE, Peter	LAN	258
George	PHA	109	John	DAU	46A	GUDERMAN, Michael	MNT	55
John	PHI	4	Joseph	FRA	287	GUDGION, Benjamen	FAY	214
John	BUC	147A	Joseph	FRA	288	GUDHARD, Jacob	LAN	197
Michael	PHI	152	Nathl.	CHE	879	GUDON?, Perthenia	LUZ	364
Nicholas	BUC	140	Peter	YOR	215	GUEN, M.	LAN	286
Peter Jr.	BUC	147A	Peter	LUZ	342	GUEST, Amelia	PHA	13
Peter	BUC	147A	Thomas	LAN	150	Daniel	CHE	881
Philip	BUC	149	Widow	CHE	891	George	PHA	105
Robt.	CHE	834	GRUBBIN, George	BUC	144A	John	PHA	76
Timothy	FAY	203	GRUBE, Bernhard			John	CHE	745
Wm.	PHI	59	Adam	NOH	32	Leonard	WAS	68
GROVES, Widow	PHI	104	George	BUC	80	GUFFY, James	BUT	322

GUGER, George	LAN 55	GUMBER, Conrad	NOH 39A	GUST, Morijah	CHE 794
GUGESS, Herman	YOR 156	GUMERY?, Levina	FAY 231	GUSTIN, Eliphalet	LUZ 422
GUIAR?, -ichael	ARM 124	GUMMORE, Barney	WAS 99	James	MIF 7
GUIER, Adam	PHA 73	GUMMY, John	PHI 106	Jeremiah	GRN 81
Andw.	PHA 39	John	PHI 106	GUSTINE, Lemuel	CUM 97
Andw.	PHA 40	GUMP, Fredrick	GRN 70	GUSTUS, Ceaser	PHI 102A
Eliza	PHA 80	GUMPF,		GUTATH, Michael	LAN 253
John	PHA 81	Christopher	LAN 32	GUTDIEDER,	
John	PHA 120	Deitrich	LAN 58	Frederick	LAN 253
GUIGER, Casper	PHA 16	Michael	LAN 58	GUTE, Abraham	LAN 172
James	PHA 65	GUMPORT, Abm.	PHI 70	GUTEKUNST, Adam	NOH 68A
Mrs.	NOU 97	GUMRER, Abm.	BER 187	GUTH, Adam Junr.	NOH 89A
Valentine	NOU 97	GUNANT?, Henry	BER 187	Adam	NOH 89A
GUILAR, Alexander	FAY 209	GUNCKEL, John	LAN 196	Daniel Jr.	NOH 89A
GUILDER, Philip	PHI 67A	GUNDACKER, John	LAN 36	Daniel Junr.	NOH 55A
GUILDFORD, George	MIF 7	Michael	LAN 37	Daniel Senr.	NOH 55A
GUILDNER,		GUNDAY, Peter	MER 443	Daniel	NOH 89A
Christian	NOU 136	GUNDER, George	ADA 20	George	NOH 55A
GUILE, Abraham	BUC 86A	Martin	SOM 153	Jacob	LAN 26
GUILER, Samuel	CHE 700	GUNDERMAN, Jacob	DAU 29A	Jacob	NOH 71
GUILEY, John	CHE 721	GUNDLEN, Isaac	FAY 228	Jacob	BER 144
GUILKY, Benjamin	MNT 107	GUNDRUM, George	BER 151	Jacob	BER 240
GUILMER, William	CHE 810	Martin	BER 152	Jacob	LAN 281
GUILTNER, Andrew	NOH 44A	GUNDY, Benjamin	BER 270	Jacob	NOH 89A
GUIN, Ann	PHA 23	Christian	NOU 128	John	LAN 273
Daniel	VEN 166	David	SOM 145	John	LAN 281
Daniel	FAY 250	John	LAN 66	Lowrence Junr.	NOH 89A
James	FAY 203	Joseph	SOM 148	Lowrence	NOH 89A
GUIN?, George	ADA 34	Mary	DAU 2A	Peter	LAN 98
GUINDER, John	YOR 165	Mrs.	NOU 128	Peter	BER 139
GUINDER?, George	YOR 166	Peter	YOR 186	Peter	YOR 164
GUINEA, Joseph	WAS 99	GUNESON, William	PHI 16	Peter Junr.	NOH 89A
GUINESS?, Rebecca		GUNGLE, Jacob	NOU 182	Peter	NOH 89A
M.?	CUM 145	GUNING, Charles	WST 345	Widow	NOH 89A
GUINEVAN, John	FRA 322	GUNING?, Thomas	NOU 164	GUTHEL, Daniel	FAY 227
GUININGER, Jacob	PHI 109A	GUNKLE, Baltzer	YOR 176	GUTHENKUNST, John	NOH 59
GUINN, Azariah	LUZ 325	George	CHE 798	GUTHERIE, William	FRA 290
John	BEV 19	Jacob	YOR 176	GUTHMAN, John	BER 240
John	CHE 884	Michael	CHE 735	Saml.	BER 240
John	DAU 2A	Wm.	CHE 857	GUTHREY, James	ARM 126
Thomas	BEV 19	GUNN, Alexander	WAS 49	James	ARM 127
GUINNOP?, (See		James	MNT 40	GUTHRIE, Adam	CHE 822
Guinnoss)	FAY 238	John	BFD 63	Alexr.	WST 345
GUINNOSS, George	FAY 238	John	BUT 343	George	HNT 120
GUINTER, Nicholas	ADA 31	William	WAS 49	James	WAS 20
GUIR?, Jacob	LAN 138	GUNNEL, Jonathan	BFD 42	James	WST 160
GUIRE, Catharine	FRA 326	GUNNING, Chas.	WST 344	James	WST 214
GUIRE?, (See		Joseph	WST 345	John	CRA 5
Guise)	LAN 123	GUNNYAN, Jospeh	WST 345	John	BEV 23
GUISE, Edwd.	PHA 88	GUNSALIS, Emanuel	WAS 85	John	FRA 310
John	LAN 123	GUNTER, Michl.	FRA 304	John	WST 345
GUISENHEIMER,		GUNTRUM, Jno. Jr.	DAU 41A	John	WST 367
Henry Reved.	CHE 781	Jno.	DAU 41A	John	CHE 822
Widow	CHE 895	GUNY, Mary	PHI 50	John	CHE 842
GUISER, John	LAN 235	GURGES, Samues	YOR 156	John Junr.	BEV 26
GUISTE, Jacob	WAS 44	GURL, James Junr.	BEV 14	John Seignr.	BEV 26
GUKER?, George	MNT 134	James Seignr.	BEV 14	Robert	WAS 20
GUKES, Henry	MNT 55	GURLEY, Willm.	PHI 16	Robt.	CUM 96
GULBERSON, Thomas	NOU 97	GURLING, Abram.	PHI 7	Tho.	LYC 15
GULDIN, Daniel	BER 166	GURMES, Robert	LAN 121	William	WAS 110
John	BER 166	GURN?, Jane	BEV 21	William	WST 309
John	BER 232	GURNEY, Francis		William	WST 345
GULDIN?, Daniel	BER 229	Esqr.	PHA 98	William	WST 367
Daniel Jr.	BER 229	GURR, George	NOH 59	William	CHE 822
Jacob	BER 229	Jacob	NOH 82	William	CHE 822
GULICKS, Samuel	BUC 149	Lorentz	NOH 59	GUTJAHN,	
GULL, Jacob	SOM 141	GURRAL, Robt.	CUM 37	Christian	LAN 142
GULLESKEY, Henry	LAN 51	GURRILL, John	CUM 131	Ludwig	LAN 138
GULLIFORD,		GUSE, Nicholas	NOH 85	GUTLENDELSIN,	
William	MER 443	GUSHA, Isaiah	BER 152	Widow	LAN 251
GULMAN, George	DAU 6	GUSHWA, Jacob	SOM 133	GUTLIN, George	PHI 53A
John	DAU 6	GUSINGER, Adam	LAN 248	GUTRIDGE,	
GULP, Craft	CUM 101	GUSS, Charles	BER 280	Nathaniel	WAY 139
GUM, Michael	NOH 66A	Samuel	CHE 789	GUTRY, David	ALL 49
GUM?, Jane	BEV 21	GUSSY, Franz	DAU 26	Robert	ALL 95
GUMBER, Christian	WST 272	GUST, Michael	PHI 52		

153

GUTSHALL, Fredk.	CUM 49	HAAS, Conrad	NOH 43	HACKMAN, Henry	LAN 278
GUTTERTON, Wilson	PHI 35	Daniel	NOH 59	Henry	LAN 280
GUTTRY, Robert	VEN 169	Daniel	BER 135	Jacob	CUM 115
GUTZ, Peter	LAN 19	Daniel Junr.	MNT 73	Jacob	LAN 147A
GUY, Absolom	LYC 15	Daniel	NOH 59A	Melchor	LAN 273
Edward	HNT 162	Frederick	MNT 92	Philip	WST 367
Henry	WAS 15	George	NOH 30	Phillip	CUM 130
John	WAS 33	George	YOR 182	Susan	CUM 148
Jonathan	MNT 44	George	BER 252	HACKNEY, Aron	FAY 227
Richard	PHA 93	George	BER 252	Aron	MER 445
Robert	LYC 15	George	NOH 30	Jehue	MER 445
Samuel	BUC 84A	Henry	NOH 59A	Joseph	CRA 2
Thomas	CUM 83	Henry (Capt.)	NOH 51A	Josepth	MER 445
Thos.	BUC 84A	Henry	MNT 45	HACKS, David	DAU 40
GUYANT, David	BUC 84A	Jacob	NOH 47A	HACOKE, Peter	LAN 24
Grace	BUC 84A	Jacob	MNT 73	HAD, George	LUZ 405
Jacob	BUC 84A	John	NOH 59A	HADDEN, John	CUM 110
GUYER, Casper	PHI 123	John	BER 144	Joseph	FAY 221
George	LAN 137	Lawrence	BER 144	Samuel	ADA 21
John	PHA 71	Nicholas	BER 144	Thos. Esqr.	FAY 252
Wm.	PHA 81	Nicholas Jr.	BER 254	HADDLE, Samuel	BUC 102
GUYGER?, George	PHA 99	Peter	NOH 59A	HADE, Mathias	BER 226
GUYN, Arthur	LYC 15	Peter	BER 142	HADESTY, James	BER 219
GUYNN, George	CHE 888	HAAS?, Abraham	LAN 307	HADFEG, Andrew	PHA 71
GUYRE, Jacob	PHI 123	HAASS, Margaret	NOH 59	HADFEG?, Andrw.	PHA 92
Nicholas	PHI 123	HAASS?, Jacob	LAN 134	HADLY?, Samuel	BUC 162
GUYSINGER, Philip	MNT 53	HABACKER, Charles	LAN 287	HADRICH, Nicholas	BER 273
GWIN, Daniel	PHA 64	HABAKER, Christ.	LAN 139	HAEBEL, Henry	LAN 198
John	HNT 125	HABECKER, Daniel		HAEFER, Lewis	NOU 129
William	ADA 9	HABENSTEIN,		HAEFET, Robert	NOU 165
William	WST 160	Frederick	NOH 75A	HAEGER, Jacob	DAU 24
GWINNERS, Michl.	PHI 112A	HABERACKER,		HAENBAUGH, Peter	NOU 183
GWYNE, Joseph	GRN 88	Dewah?	BER 133	HAERKEY?, George	LAN 78
GWYNN, Andrew		Margaret	BER 133	HAFER, Jacob	CRA 15
Revd.	WAS 110	HABERMAN, Jacob	NOH 75A	HAFF, James	NOU 182
Patrick	HNT 155	HABERSEY, Abraham	NOU 188	Stephen	NOH 78
GY, Wilm.	ALL 109	Michael	NOU 188	HAFFECHER?, John	YOR 186
Wilm. Junior	ALL 109	Phillip	NOU 188	Michael	YOR 186
GYDER?, (See		HABERSTICK,		HAFFEEKER?, (See	
Cyder?)	YOR 171	Matthias	LAN 35	Haffecher)	YOR 186
GYGER, George	DEL 185	Rudolf	LAN 68	HAFFEL, George	LAN 197
Henry	MNT 61	Wm.	LAN 33	HAFFERD, John	BUC 91
Jacob	DEL 185	HABERSTROK,		HAFFLIE, John	LAN 210
Jesse	DEL 183	Josias?/		HAFFLIN, Joseph	LAN 197
John	DEL 184	Jonas?	MNT 37	HAFFNER, Andrew	NOH 41A
Windle	WST 309	HABETHON, John	PHI 27	Conrad	BER 188
GYLINGER, Henry	MNT 77	HABLE, Fredk.	WST 215	HAFLER, John	BUC 81A
		HABOULT, Joseph	PHI 42	HAFLINE, John	PHA 55
H----?, Asa	PHA 123	HACK--Y?, George	MER 444	HAFT, Christian	BUC 82A
George	FRA 316	HACK, Henry	DAU 38A	HAGA, Adam	HNT 152
H--ATE?, Jonathan	BEV 24	Jno.	CUM 151	Daniel	MNT 108
H--WAY?, Isaac	NOU 154	Mich.	DAU 38A	Godfrey	PHA 42
HA-----?, Wm.	LYC 22	HACK?, Jacob	FRA 275	Jacob	HNT 140
HA--WORTH,		HACKASON, Robt.	FRA 297	John	MNT 107
William	MNT 67	HACKATEEN?,		Patrick	PHI 74A
HAACK, Michael	LAN 198	Christn.	CUM 44	William	MNT 138
HAACKS, Christian	LAN 198	HACKENDORN, John	HNT 156	HAGAMAN, Aaron	LYC 23
HAAFF, Jacob	NOH 59	HACKER, Andr.	FRA 282	James	LYC 3
HAAG, Christian	BER 144	Frederick	LAN 197	HAGAN, Abraham	HNT 154
HAAK, Anthony	BER 222	HACKERT, Andw.	FAY 227	Caward	ADA 18
Christian	BER 170	HACKET, Eliza.	CUM 43	David	HNT 150
Daniel	BER 170	Henry	MIF 7A	James	PHI 29
Henry	BER 270	James	CRA 9	John	HNT 164
Jacob	BER 170	James	CUM 43	John	HNT 165
Jacob	BER 225	John	PHI 66	Simon	HNT 163
Jacob	BER 270	Robt.	CUM 43	HAGAN?, (See	
John	BER 135	William	NOH 66A	Hgan)	MIF 17
John	BER 257	HACKETT, Ann	CHE 816	Henry	CHE 852
John	BER 270	James	BUC 146	HAGANEY, John H.	PHA 86
Nicholas	BER 144	John	CHE 718	HAGAR, Black	CHE 763
HAARS, Danl.	BER 144	HACKEY, James	CHE 819	Jacob	FAY 252
HAAS, Adam	YOR 191	HACKHOUSE, &		Nicholas	GRN 66
Christn.	BER 239	Serrill	BUC 83	HAGARTY, John	HNT 160
Christopher	LAN 45	HACKLEY, Henry	DAU 38A	Patrick	WST 346
Conrad	PHA 32	HACKMAN, Abram	LAN 252	William	HNT 160
Conrad	LAN 43	Christian	NOH 87	William	FAY 257
		David	LAN 140		

HAMILTON, Wm.	PHI	57	HAMMOND, Nicholas	PHA	55	HANCOOK, Benjamin	BFD	74
Wm.	WST	289	Phillip	PHA	61	HAND, Edward	LAN	115
HAMILTON?, See			Reuben	WAS	38	Isaac	WAS	99
Hamiltn	ALL	58	Robert	WAS	21	John	BFD	73
HAMINGER, John	CHE	720	Timothy	WAS	122	John Capt.	PHI	74A
HAMLEN, John	WAS	90	William	WAS	91	Margaret	PHA	18
HAMLER, Daniel	NOU	193	HAMNOND, David	NOU	164	Mary	DEL	188
HAMLIN, Isaac	MIF	7A	HAMON, John	PHI	71A	Mathew	PHA	52
Joseph	PHI	95A	HAMOR, Thomas	DEL	172	Nicholas	PHA	59
Ruben	MIF	7	HAMOTT, James	CRA	12	William	BFD	73
Thos.	MIF	7	HAMPHER, Joseph	PHA	109	HANDBEST, John	PHI	63
HAMLIT, Godfry	PHI	106A	HAMPSHIER, John	ALL	51	HANDCOCK, John	CRA	9
HAMM, Andrew	NOH	53	HAMPSHIRE, Barny	FRA	312	HANDLE, Casper	BFD	44
Baltzer	YOR	173	Jno.	PHI	44	Dennis	WST	309
Christian	YOR	175	HAMPSON, Robert	HNT	160	HANDLEY, William	WAS	38
Daniel	NOH	53	HAMPSTON, Thomas	GRN	70	Willm.	PHI	105B
HAMMA, Peter	BER	260	HAMPTON, Benjamin	DEL	173	HANDLIMAN, Henry	LAN	45
Phliip	BER	260	Benjn.	BUC	107	HANDLIN, Dennis	HNT	141
HAMMAN, George	NOH	55A	Daniel	WAS	44	James	WST	170
Jacob	NOH	89A	James	LYC	9	William	WST	170
Philip	NOH	84	John	BUC	107	HANDLINE,		
HAMMEL, Henry	NOU	137	John	BUC	161	Alexander	SOM	158
John	NOH	90	John	DEL	184	Cornelius	SOM	129
John	SOM	143	John	CHE	830	HANDLY, Wm.		
Philip	NOH	90	John	CHE	833	(Crossed Out)	PHI	105A
Robert	BFD	37	Jonathan	WAS	62	HANDSCHU, Ludwig	NOH	71
Thomas	SOM	142	Jonathan	CHE	714	HANDSHEW, John	NOH	43
HAMMELL, Andrew	FAY	265	Jos.	CHE	831	HANDSPACH, George		
James	PHA	94	Joseph	CHE	830	Jr.	FRA	315
HAMMELTON, John	FAY	203	Moses	BEV	12	HANDWERCK,		
HAMMER, Daniel	CHE	793	Oliver	BUC	145	Frederick	NOH	75A
Frederick	YOR	168	Samuel	PHI	30	Jacob Junr.	NOH	45
Fredk.	YOR	205	Thomas	CHE	830	Jacob Senr.	NOH	45
Geo.	CUM	44	Thomas	DAU	27A	John	NOH	45
Henry	YOR	205	Wm.	PHA	98	Peter Senr.	NOH	45
Jacob	HNT	146	Oseph	NOU	110	Peter, Junr.	NOH	45
James	MNT	87	HAMSBEGER, George	YOR	216	HANE, Daniel	LAN	65
John	MNT	109	HAMSHER, Adam	NOH	50	David	WST	290
John	NOU	171	Daniel	NOH	50	HANEE, Thomas	DEL	156
Lewis (Crossed			Daniel	NOH	80	HANES, Anthy.	PHI	82A
Out)	BUC	155A	HAMSHER?, Adam	MNT	113	Benjamin	BEV	6
Michael	BFD	73	HAMSON, James	HNT	161	Casper W.	PHI	128
Tobias	BFD	74	Samuel	ERI	57	Daniel	BEV	15
HAMMERLEY, Eve	LAN	217	HAMSTEIN, George	LAN	257	Mary	BUC	162A
HAMMERS,			HAMTADEN, Jacob	LAN	309	Michl.	PHI	88A
Catherine	PHI	130	HAMWALT?, (See			Peter	PHI	129
John	GRN	108	Haniwalt?)	MIF	25	Samue	ALL	110
Jonas	ADA	7	HAMWOOD, Jno.	CUM	78	HANEVAULT, Henry	HNT	119
HAMMERSTONE,			HAN, William	NOU	100	Henry	HNT	136
Andrew	BUC	139	HANAGAN, Oliver	FRA	316	HANEVERS?, Jacob	DAU	33
HAMMET, Wm.	PHA	63	HANAH, John	ALL	51	HANEY, Abraham	FAY	215
HAMMIL, John	BEV	11	John	NOU	171	Alexander	HNT	131
Patrick	ALL	61	Patrick	LAN	163	Anthony	BUC	81A
HAMMILL, Henry	MNT	85	Thomas	ALL	99	Edward	HNT	130
Jacob	MNT	123	Wilm.	ALL	99	Jacob	BUC	81A
HAMMILTON, John	BEV	4	HANAN?, Samuel	BUC	86A	James	PHI	128
Richd.	PHI	87A	HANBY, Benjamin	DEL	157	James	HNT	165
Thomas	BEV	14	HANCE, Isaac	DEL	187	John	BUC	149
Thomas	BEV	17	James	CHE	883	John	FAY	215
HAMMITT, Daniel	FAY	227	John	MNT	108	John	BUC	106A
Jacob	CUM	42	Joseph	CHE	806	Joseph	BUC	149
HAMMON, Widw.	PHI	113	Thomas	CHE	875	Michael	PHI	55
Archbold	PHI	75A	HANCE?, (See			Michael	BUC	149
Jacob	FRA	323	Hanee)	DEL	156	Patrick	BFD	51
John	WST	252	HANCK, George	PHI	147	Simon	BUC	149
Nathan	BFD	73	HANCKEL, Henry	DAU	49	William	FAY	215
Peter	FAY	236	HANCOCK, Cutlope	ARM	127	HANG, Aaron	CHE	826
William	CRA	8	Isaac	LUZ	392	HANGER, John	PHA	58
William	BEV	24	James	BFD	73	HANICH?, Jacob	FRA	308
Wm.	BEV	24	Joel	BFD	74	HANICK, Jacob	LAN	129
HAMMOND, David	WAS	21	John	BFD	73	HANILMAN, George	NOU	100
George	NOU	164	John	LAN	288	HANING, Adam	BFD	54
Jas.	NOU	202	Jonathan	LUZ	319	John	NOU	164
John	WAS	21	Richd.	PHI	5	HANIWALT?,		
John	PHI	53	Ritchard	ALL	53	Christy	MIF	25
Joseph	NOU	165	William	PHA	97	Geo. & Jno.	MIF	25

HANIWALT?, Jno. &		
Geo.	MIF	25
HANK, Christian	PHI	131
Lewis	PHI	86
HANKEY, John	NOH	50
HANKINGS, Emins?	ALL	86
HANKINS, Caleb	BFD	38
Isaac	WAS	122
Rodey	FAY	256
Timothey	FAY	200
HANKLE, Peter	WST	310
HANKS, Jacob	ADA	19
John	GRN	95
John	DEL	164
William	BFD	50
HANLAN, James	PHA	13
HANLEN, John	FAY	215
HANLEY, Thomas	LAN	125
Thomas	CHE	750
HANLIE, Christian	LAN	210
John	LAN	210
HANLIN, Ann	ALL	50
Casper	LAN	198
Jane	WAS	56
John	ALL	90
Michael	LAN	198
Moses	BUT	331
William	BUT	331
HANLINE, Tobias	FRA	304
HANLON, William	WAS	28
William	WAS	28
HANLY, John	PHI	114
HANMER, (See		
Hanner)	MNT	110
George	LAN	142
HANMERSLEY, John	FRA	283
HANN?, Christian	LUZ	355
HANNA, Widow	WST	237
Adam	WAS	16
David	LYC	19
Ezkeel	CUM	139
Hugh	WAS	68
Isaac	NOU	128
James	WAS	16
James	WAS	100
James	BUC	103
James	HNT	139
John	MIF	1
John	WAS	116
John	WST	214
John	FAY	266
John	WST	289
John A.	DAU	4
Johnth.	LYC	19
Robt.	CUM	50
Saml.	CUM	136
Samuel	WAS	21
William	HNT	139
William	WST	170
Wm.	CUM	103
HANNA?, James	LYC	19
HANNAGAN, William	HNT	156
HANNAH, Widow	PHI	45
Abenzaer	VEN	170
Abigail	CHE	752
Allexander	BEV	19
Andrew	NOU	176
Anthony	FAY	245
Benjamin	WAY	149
David	ALL	64
Edward	PHA	117
Edward	LAN	168
Francis	GRN	82
James	GRN	82
James	ARM	123
James	ARM	125

HANNAH, James	SOM	134
James	FAY	227
James	FAY	236
James & John	LAN	153
Jane	BEV	17
John (See		
Hannah,		
James)	LAN	153
John	HNT	149
John	YOR	213
John	WST	290
Patrik	CRA	17
Robert	ARM	127
Robert	WAY	149
Robert	FAY	221
Robert	WST	252
Samuel	NOU	171
Thomas	BEV	18
Thomas	WAS	56
Thomas	ARM	123
William	NOU	202
Wilm.	ALL	93
Wm.	LYC	26
HANNAN, Matthew	GRN	76
Thomas	GRN	79
HANNAS, John	NOU	158
Mrs.	NOU	164
HANNER, Abraham	BER	210
HANNER?, Amos	MNT	110
John Junr.	MNT	110
HANNIS, John	LUZ	321
HANNON, William	FAY	203
HANNON?, James	LYC	19
James	CHE	719
HANNOT, James	YOR	208
HANNOW?, James	CHE	719
HANNS, Christian	NOU	114
HANNUM, Ann	DEL	158
George	DEL	159
James	CHE	743
James Esqr.	CHE	741
Peter	DEL	158
Robert	DEL	158
Saml.	CHE	838
Samuel	DEL	160
William	DEL	159
HANNY, Andrew	PHI	56
Andrew	LAN	168
HANS, John	YOR	176
John	LAN	147B
John	DAU	17A
HANSBAUGH, John	CEN	20A
HANSBERGER, Abram	MNT	67
Abrm.	MNT	94
Jacob	MNT	67
Jacob	DAU	21A
HANSBERRY, Daniel		
(Negro)	WAS	116
HANSBURY, Jacob	MNT	138
HANSE, Conrad	PHA	90
Joseph	LUZ	356
HANSE?, Christian	LUZ	355
HANSEL, Francis	SOM	158
George	PHI	61
Jacob	PHA	60
Michael	WAS	121
William	DEL	167
HANSELL, Andrew	PHI	63
Barnet	PHA	79
Frederic	SOM	134
Peter	PHI	63
Rachael	PHI	64
Saml.	PHA	109
HANSELMAN, Andrew	ADA	11
Dietrich	NOH	53
George	NOH	85A

HANSELMAN, John	NOH	53
HANSEY, Frederick	BFD	54
HANSHAW, James	FAY	257
Nicholas	FAY	256
HANSIL, Christ.	FRA	300
HANSLIFF, Michael	SOM	149
HANSMAN, John	PHA	60
John Junr.	PHA	60
HANSON, John	BUC	105
HANSPACH, George		
Snr.	FRA	315
HANSPAUGH, Jacob	SOM	154
HANSS, Jacob	NOH	53
Jacob	NOH	75A
Leonard	NOH	85A
HANSY, Benjamin	MNT	44
HANT?, Elias	MNT	115
HANTCH, Nathaniel	LAN	50
HANTHORN, George	CHE	745
James	FAY	257
John	FAY	257
Marey	FAY	257
Nathen	FAY	257
HANTWERT, Susanna	BER	173
HANTZ, Andw.	YOR	174
Jacob	ADA	35
Jacob	YOR	193
HANVICK, John	BUC	157
HANY, Andrew	DAU	45A
Edward	BER	240
John	PHI	120A
Patrick	ALL	64
Steward	ALL	61
HANYCOCK, Mary	PHA	78
HAPENNY, Mark	BUC	89
HAPKUS, Alexr.	PHI	34
HAPNER, Henry	BER	279
HAPP, Gasper	VEN	165
HAPPEL, Adam	NOH	35A
Casper	NOH	73A
Henry	NOH	73
Jacob	NOH	84
Jacob	NOH	35A
HAPPER, Jacob	NOH	75A
John	WAS	68
Michael	NOH	75A
Samuel	CHE	838
HAPPERSETT, Jacob	DEL	176
Jacob	CHE	722
John	DEL	156
John	DEL	165
HAPPLE, Geo.	CUM	66
John	DAU	5A
HAR, Christian /		
Pequea	LAN	108
HARA, Charrels	ALL	81
Wilm.	ALL	81
HARAN?, (See		
Horon)	FRA	310
HARB, Catherine	BER	184
HARBENDY,		
Thaddeus	LUZ	421
HARBERSON,		
Benjamin	PHA	20
John	FAY	203
HARBERT, Eliza	PHA	71
HARBISON, Benj.	PHI	106A
Hugh	WST	238
Jas.	BUT	316
John	WST	160
John	CEN	22A
Wm.	BUT	316
HARBIT, Dannel	ALL	93
Moses	ALL	64
HARBOLT, Adam	BFD	74
Machael	YOR	211

HARBONE, Danl.	PHI	98	HARDA, Joseph	PHI	93	HARDY, James	BUT	365
HARBOR, Samuel	GRN	95	HARDABAH, Daniel	NOU	100	John	MIF	7
Thomas	GRN	95	HARDEN, Cato	FAY	245	John	FAY	203
HARBOUR, Isaac	PHA	67	Dennis	DAU	7A	John	NOH	35A
HARBRIGE, Edward	WST	151	George	SOM	151	Joseph	PHA	11
HARBUCKLE,			George	FAY	244	Randols	ALL	116
William	FRA	309	Hector	FAY	244	Saml.	LYC	28
HARBY, John	PHI	78A	Isaac	SOM	152	William	SOM	152
HARCULES, James	DAU	13	Joshua	DEL	156	William	FAY	203
HARCULOR, Mary	YOR	206	Savel	SOM	152	Wm.	MIF	7A
HARD, Jacob	FAY	250	Thomas	SOM	152	HARDZOCK, George	FAY	245
Wm. (Schoolmaster)	MIF	7A	Thomas	CHE	720	Margret	FAY	245
			William	DEL	156	HARE, Mrs.	LYC	19
			HARDENBERGH,			Abm.	CUM	66
			Peter	LUZ	375	Abraham	LAN	106
			HARDER, William	LUZ	369	Abraham	LAN	108
			HARDESTY, Francis	FAY	265	Adam	LAN	107
			Henrey	FAY	265	Benjamin	MNT	50
NOTE:			HARDGROVE,			Christian	LAN	108
			William	WAS	37	Christian		
Although the remainder of			HARDIN, James	BFD	37	Miller	LAN	108
this column is blank, no			John	BFD	63	Daniel	FAY	203
names have been omitted.			John	FAY	245	Danl.	CUM	69
			Thomas	ALL	83	David	LAN	107
			William	BFD	63	Edward	FAY	245
			William	CHE	878	Francis	LAN	118
			Wm.	PHA	67	Jacob	LAN	108
			HARDING, Abraham	BUC	143	John	LAN	108
			Amos	LUZ	383	John	SOM	157
			David	LUZ	375	John	LAN	262
			Elisha	LUZ	381	John	CHE	745
			Henry (See			John Doctr.	WAS	68
			Harding,			John Miller	LAN	109
			Thos.)	BUC	143	Joseph	CEN	22B
			Henry	BUC	137A	Martin	LAN	108
			Isaac	BUC	143	Mathew	MNT	50
			Isaiah	DEL	181	Robert	PHA	85
			Israel	LUZ	381	Widow	LAN	107
			Jacob	BUC	143	William	HNT	123
			John	DEL	166	HAREBAUGH, George	BFD	73
			John	LUZ	380	George	BFD	73
			Jonathan	BUC	143	HARELIFF, Joseph	PHI	91A
			Jonathan	LUZ	417	HARES, Mary	PHI	42
			Joseph	BUC	143	HARFF, John	BER	240
			Joshua	DEL	181	Nichl.	BER	240
			Luke	LUZ	384	HARFORD, Caleb	CHE	849
			Micajah	LUZ	376	Charles	FAY	236
			Michael	LAN	197	John	PHI	33
			Stephen	LUZ	375	HARGBROD,		
			Stephen	LUZ	384	Christn.	LAN	253
			Thomas	LUZ	376	HARGER, Jacob	ALL	90
			Thos. & Henry	BUC	143	Peter	ALL	86
			William	PHA	114	HARGET, John	BFD	50
			William	LUZ	381	HARGNET, Jacob	WST	237
			HARDINGER, Andrew	BFD	58	HARGRAVE, John	FRA	298
			Conrad	BFD	57	HARHOLD,		
			George	BFD	57	Christopher	WST	151
			HARDISTY, Frances			John	WST	151
			Jur.	FAY	209	HARIET, Andrew	ALL	104
			Francis	WAS	49	David	ALL	105
			Henry	WAS	122	Ephram	ALL	104
			Richard	WAS	49	George	ALL	104
			Robert	WAS	3	HARING, Hannakle	MNT	55
			HARDLY, Henry	NOU	136	Henry	BUC	147A
			HARDMAN, Daniel	BFD	57	John	BUC	81A
			David	BFD	57	Philip	BUC	81A
			Philip	LAN	197	HARINGTON, Aaron	LYC	15
			HARDON, George	PHI	34	HARISON, George	NOU	97A
			HARDOY, William	HNT	127	James	NOU	165
			HARDS, Alexr.	PHI	33	John	NOU	97A
			HARDY, Ann	PHA	97	HARISS, Peter	BUC	105
			David	PHA	122	HARITY, Hugh	NOU	164
			David	MIF	7A	HARKENS, William	PHA	15
			Elias	FAY	250	HARKER, Jesse	MNT	64
			Hugh	MIF	7A	John	PHI	153
			James	PHI	69	Joseph	PHI	76

HARKER, Mathew	FRA	300	HARMAN, David	DAU	49	HARNISH, Michael	LAN	273
HARKERSHEIMER,			Frederick	YOR	209	Michael	LAN	275
Jno.	PHI	30	George	ADA	34	Samuel	YOR	184
HARKESSEIMER,			George	ADA	42	Samuel Sr.	YOR	184
Saml.	PHI	8	George	PHA	60	HARNISHT, John	LAN	273
HARKIN, John	CRA	9	George	PHI	91A	HARNIST, David	LAN	282
John	PHI	73A	Jacob	PHA	45	Jacob	LAN	279
Neal	PHI	73A	Jacob	WAY	149	HARNITSH, Jacob	LAN	280
Owen	FAY	203	Jacob	YOR	176	HARNLIN,		
William	LUZ	386	Jacob	BUC	146A	Christian	LAN	198
HARKINGS, Daniel	ALL	103	James	MNT	40	HARNLY, Christn.	LAN	262
HARKINS, Daniel	PHI	49	John	ADA	4	HARO, Widw.	PHI	105A
Daniel	CHE	776	John	ADA	33	Christn.	PHI	105A
John	PHI	42	John	DAU	48	HARP, Daniel	CHE	856
John	LAN	275	John	PHA	59	HARPEL, John	PHI	117
Patrick	NOU	171	John	LAN	87	HARPER, Adam	NOU	175
Thomas	CHE	780	John	LAN	114	Cornelius	FRA	316
HARKLEY, James	BUT	362	John	LAN	117	Daniel	MER	444
HARKNESS, John	CUM	93	John	PHI	135	Davd.	BUT	328
Wm.	CUM	65	John	NOU	136	Davd.	BUT	353
HARKNROAD, John	FRA	283	John	NOU	137	David	CRA	4
HARLACHER, Ann	LAN	198	John	NOU	188	Ebenzr.	CUM	102
Samuel	LAN	197	John	NOU	188	Elisha	HNT	156
HARLAIN, Jas.	LAN	157	John	NOU	188	George	MNT	38
HARLAN, Alexr.	CHE	740	John Jun.	ADA	33	George Junr.	MNT	38
Enoch	CHE	741	Jonathan	BUC	161	George K.	FRA	271
Ezekiel	CHE	741	Joseph	PHA	116	Henry	NOU	180
Joshua	PHA	89	Martin	CUM	59	Jacob	ADA	7
Liles	CHE	740	Nancy	FAY	252	Jacob	PHI	136
Thomas	CRA	9	Peter	NOU	188	James	MIF	1
HARLAND, Isaac	PHI	17	Phillip	WST	237	James	PHI	27
John	PHA	6	Rudolph	FRA	300	James	WAS	49
Samuel	ADA	14	Saml.	CHE	780	James	HNT	156
HARLDECKER, Peter	YOR	211	Samuel	WAS	44	James	DEL	191
HARLEN, Caleb	CHE	838	William	PHI	10	James	FAY	251
Caleb / Cabeb?	CHE	772	HARMANCE, John	LUZ	362	Jas.	CUM	132
Henrey	FAY	227	HARMAR, General	PHI	2	Jno. Senr.	CUM	114
Israel	LAN	154	HARMER, Widow	PHI	72A	John	CRA	3
James	CHE	750	(See Hanner)	MNT	110	John	WAS	16
Jesse	CHE	753	Catherine	PHI	69A	John	PHA	108
Joel	CHE	772	HARMER?/ HARMES?,			John	HNT	143
Jonathn.	FAY	238	Chacley	PHI	154	John	FRA	327
Joseph	CHE	838	HARMIN, Chrisley	CUM	54	John	CHE	809
Joshua	CHE	838	Martin	CUM	54	John Junr.	CUM	114
Joshua	CHE	838	HARMON, John	PHI	67	John	DAU	35A
Saml.	CHE	839	John	FRA	272	John	PHI	67A
Stephen	CHE	760	John	FRA	275	John	PHI	83A
Thomas	CHE	837	Peter	WST	216	Joseph	FAY	214
HARLEY, Chas.	MIF	17	HARMONY, Daniel	DEL	164	Joseph	CHE	736
Rudolph	CHE	890	John	FRA	282	Lacky	CHE	849
Rudolph	CHE	904	John	FRA	324	Margt.	CUM	27
HARLIN, Geo.	CUM	71	Peter	FRA	282	Mary	PHA	46
George	CHE	852	Phillip	NOU	128	Mary	PHA	66
James	MIF	25	Wm.	FRA	282	Mary	PHA	17A
Jonathan	MER	446	HARMOR, Jos.	PHI	116	Mathew	WAS	7
Joseph	LAN	150	HARN?, Henry	ALL	67	Nathan	PHI	138
Solomon	CHE	874	HARNAR, Henrey	FAY	245	Robert	ADA	8
HARLMAN, Conrod	CHE	895	HARNEL?, John	ARM	126	Robert	WAS	16
Jacob	CHE	895	HARNER, (See			Robert	WAS	21
John	CHE	894	Hanner)	MNT	110	Robert	WAS	21
HARLOW, Godfrey	NOU	180	Abram	CHE	822	Robert	MNT	85
Stephen	FRA	318	Christian	MNT	130	Samuel	MNT	42
HARLY, Widw.	PHI	92	Henry	MNT	110	Samuel	GRN	91
Daniel	FAY	245	Jacob	MNT	132	Samuel	NOU	117
Henry	MNT	114	John	MNT	108	Samuel	YOR	196
Rudolph	MNT	121	John	CHE	845	Thomas	PHA	106
Samuel	MNT	121	Michael	DAU	52A	Thomas	DEL	171
HARM, James	PHA	89	Thomas	CHE	844	Thos.	PHA	87
HARMAN, Revd.	MNT	61	HARNES, Michael	CHE	908	William	MIF	18
Andw.	WST	237	HARNESS, Tobias	HNT	149	William	NOU	136
Christ.	LAN	87	HARNETT, Anna	SOM	146	William	BUC	93A
Christian	FAY	257	HARNETTE, Samuel	BEV	12	Wm.	CUM	132
Christn.	CUM	36	HARNIGAN, John	BUC	94	Wm.	CHE	780
Conrad	LUZ	356	HARNISCH, Jacob	LAN	198	HARPLE, Conrad	BUC	91
Daniel	ADA	35	Jacob	LAN	198	Jacob	MNT	60
Daniel	DAU	49	HARNISH, David	LAN	274	John	MNT	82

HARPLE, John	CHE	904	HARRIS, Jesse	CHE	871	HARRISON, John	BER	273
Ludwick	MNT	82	Jessey	NOU	149	Joshua	DEL	176
Philip	BUC	91	John	WAS	3	Moses	WAS	110
Philip	BUC	140	John	BFD	44	Peter	FAY	221
HARPST, John	CUM	90	John	PHA	54	Richard	FAY	221
HARPSTER, Fredrk.	DAU	50	John	BUC	105	Richard	FAY	261
HARPSTER?,			John	YOR	158	Richard	BER	273
Christopher	HNT	145	John	LAN	224	Robert	FAY	215
HARPUR, Edwd.	PHA	61	John	CHE	879	Saml.	FAY	221
HARR, Eliza	PHA	71	John	MIF	7A	Stephen	LUZ	352
Isaiah	ADA	15	Jonathan	LUZ	426	Stephen Jr.	LUZ	352
John	MNT	47	Joseph	WAS	3	Thomas	FAY	261
HARR?, Robt.	PHI	70A	Joseph	ALL	55	Thos.	PHA	4
HARRAH?, (See			Joseph	FAY	257	Thos.	YOR	213
Hannah)	LAN	163	Joshua	CHE	880	William	FAY	221
HARRAN, Martin	BFD	63	Laird	NOU	128	William	FAY	221
HARRET, Elias	CUM	66	Margaret	FAY	266	William	LUZ	351
John	BFD	63	Margaret	CHE	737	Wm.	PHI	68
HARRETT, Robt.	LYC	27	Parker	PHI	74A	HARRISS, Charles	PHA	14
HARREY, Jesse	CHE	902	Peter	CUM	49	Elizabeth	PHA	26
John	SOM	160	Peter	PHA	109	James	PHA	103
Jonathan	SOM	146	Peter	LUZ	376	John	PHA	43
HARRIDER, Andrew	SOM	146	Peter	NOH	47A	Thomas	PHA	120
HARRIER, Andrew	BFD	58	Prudence	BEV	8	HARRISSON,		
HARRIGAR, George	HNT	150	Richd.	YOR	216	Ambross	PHA	109
John	HNT	150	Richd.	FRA	286	Francis	PHA	22
HARRIMAN, David	WAS	56	Robert	DAU	5	John	PHA	13
George	WAS	56	Robert	GRN	101	Mary	PHA	113
Simpkin	WAS	56	Robert	PHA	102	Mathias	PHA	113
HARRIN, Frances	FAY	204	Rowland	FRA	286	William	PHA	123
Michael	LUZ	360	Saml.	CUM	27	HARROD, John	GRN	101
HARRIN?, (See			Samuel	LYC	6	Levi	GRN	101
Horrin)	FRA	322	Siles	FAY	227	Levi Junr.	GRN	105
HARRING, John	PHA	94	Stephen	GRN	100	HARROLD, Danl.	WST	216
HARRINGTON, Danl.	CHE	716	Stephen	YOR	183	Joseph	BUC	86A
Nathl.	WST	368	Thomas	GRN	100	Samuel Junr.	BUC	86A
Saml.	LAN	89	Thomas	LAN	229	Samuel	BUC	86A
Thoms	LAN	266A	Thomas	LAN	238	HARRON, James	NOU	154
HARRINSON, Isaac	MNT	107	Thomas	LUZ	401	HARROW, Daniel	BUC	105
HARRIOLD,			Thomas	MIF	7A	John	PHI	40
Nathaniel	CRA	18	Thomas	MIF	7A	Michael	PHI	146
Sidney	CRA	18	Thos.	YOR	167	HARROW?, Samuel		
HARRIS, Abraham	BFD	50	Widow	MIF	10	M.?	CHE	876
Abraham	GRN	100	William	LYC	6	HARRY, Benj.	YOR	154
Alexander	NOU	110	William	WAS	44	Daniel	BER	260
Amos	BER	137	William	WAY	146	Daniel	FAY	266
Amos	PHI	75A	William	NOU	149	Evan	DAU	41
B.	LYC	12	William	LAN	152	George	PHA	55
Barnet	WAS	52	William	LUZ	332	George	GRN	95
Benjeman	FAY	240	William	LUZ	356	Hannah	PHA	7
Benjn.	CHE	893	Wm.	CUM	54	Henry	DAU	29
Charles	LUZ	332	Wm.	WST	215	Jesse	CHE	738
Conrod	PHI	79	Wm.	FRA	321	John	MNT	108
Daniel	WAS	80	Wm.	CHE	736	John	PHA	111
Elijah	LUZ	322	HARRISON, Abraham	PHI	134	Stephen	CHE	739
Elisha	YOR	219	Andw.	DAU	17A	Thomas	CHE	707
Elisha	CHE	888	Bazil	WAS	110	Thomas	CHE	810
Elizabeth	LAN	49	Charles	HNT	164	HARS, John	PHI	28
Elizabeth	BER	273	Charles	FAY	197	HARSCHBARGER,		
Elizabeth	FRA	286	Elizabeth	DEL	163	David	LAN	210
Emas	NOU	100	F.	PHI	14	HARSCHBERGER,		
Ephraian	FRA	319	George	PHA	89	John	LAN	198
George	WAS	52	George	BUC	142	HARSH, Andrew	BEV	26
George	ALL	108	Isaac	DAU	36	Henry	BER	215
George	YOR	216	James	ALL	70	Jacob	MNT	110
George	FAY	227	James	BUC	83	Jacob	HNT	139
George	FRA	278	James	FAY	198	Leonard	YOR	206
George	DAU	3A	James	CEN	18A	William	BEV	23
Isaac	NOH	47A	Jarius	LUZ	352	HARSHE, George	WAS	62
Jacob	MIF	3	Jemima	BER	273	Henry	WAS	68
Jacob	FAY	265	Job	PHI	78A	Henry	WAS	121
James	VEN	168	John	BEV	22	Henry Junr.	WAS	121
James	YOR	219	John	PHI	69	Henry Senr.	WAS	121
James	LAN	233	John	PHI	153	James	WAS	21
James Esq.	CEN	22A	John	NOU	171	Lewis	WAS	122
James	NOU	143A	John	FAY	203	Philip	WAS	121

HARSHE, Simon	WAS	121	HART, William	NOU	110	HARTLY, Johnathan	LYC	7
William	WAS	21	William	BUC	154	HARTMAN, Abraham	NOH	30
HARSHIE, Jacob			Wilm.	ALL	62	Adam	WAS	37
(See Harshie,			Wm. Doct.	BUC	153	Adam	NOH	87
Jno.)	LAN	197	HART?, John	ALL	67	Andrew	ADA	42
Jno. & Jacob	LAN	197	Thomas	BFD	73	Charles	FRA	298
HARST?, Elias	MNT	115	HARTE, John	LAN	175	Christian	NOH	30
HART, Adam	LAN	56	Margaret	GRN	86	Christian	NOH	43
Andrew	MNT	109	Margaret	GRN	91	Christian	LAN	118
Benjamin	BFD	37	HARTE?, John	WST	309	Daniel	NOH	29A
Benjamin	LAN	236	HARTENSTEIN,			Elisabeth	WAS	38
Bernard	CHE	911	Jacob	BER	273	Francis	YOR	197
Daniel	YOR	192	Peter	BER	273	Frantz	NOH	80
David	ADA	3	HARTEPER, William	WAS	21	Frantz	BER	236
David	CHE	908	HARTER, Christian	NOU	176	Frederick	MNT	61
Edward	ADA	43	Jacob	NOU	176	Frederick	BUC	141
Elijah	ADA	4	Jacob	FRA	303	Fredk.	YOR	197
Eloner	BER	244	John	NOU	175	George	YOR	157
Felix	FRA	278	Martin	LUZ	359	George	NOU	158
Gaspar	HNT	118	HARTFORD, Agness	BEV	6	George	BER	183
Geo.	PHI	119	Elias	WAY	141	George	FRA	303
George	DAU	12	James	BEV	24	George	NOH	73A
Hannah	CHE	850	Mathew	WAS	90	Henry	LAN	114
Hugh	DEL	171	Mathew	FAY	198	Henry	BER	133
Hugh	MIF	7A	Robert	WAY	141	Henry	WST	170
Jacob	BFD	43	Samuel	WAY	141	Henry	LAN	225
Jacob	YOR	196	Wm.	BEV	24	Henry	FRA	310
James	ALL	90	HARTGOOD, Henry	WAS	37	Henry	CHE	795
James (Edward			HARTING,			Henry	NOH	51A
Crossed Out)	PHI	101A	Christian	BER	150	Henry	NOH	75A
John	ADA	11	John	LAN	198	Herman	NOH	59A
John	PHA	13	Nicholas	BER	150	Jacob	CUM	51
John	BEV	28	Peter	BER	277	Jacob	NOH	80
John	BFD	43	HARTINGER, George	NOU	114	Jacob	LAN	110
John	PHA	55	John	NOH	53	Jacob	BER	133
John	NOH	59	HARTINSTON, John	PHI	117A	Jacob	BER	181
John	BFD	63	HARTLE, Abraham	NOU	188	Jacob	BER	244
John	MNT	77	Frederick	BFD	63	Jacob	FRA	294
John	PHI	101	Jacob	BFD	69	Jacob	NOH	44A
John	PHA	109	Michl.	FRA	309	Jacob	NOH	85A
John	NOU	165	HARTLERODE, John	BFD	51	Jacob	NOH	89A
John	YOR	218	HARTLEY, Anthony	BUC	145	John	ADA	43
John	LAN	236	Benjamin	WAS	80	John	NOH	43
John	WST	324	Benjn.	BUC	144A	John	MNT	77
John	CHE	911	Charles	YOR	155	John	BER	133
Jonathn.	PHI	111	Christopher	PHI	136	John	YOR	170
Jos.	PHI	106	Geoe.	PHI	73	John	BER	184
Joseph	BUC	153	George	PHI	152	John	CHE	892
Josiah	BUC	155	Henry	PHI	152	John Jr.	BER	135
Josiah	BUC	143A	James	PHA	35	John	NOH	51A
Ludwig	SOM	128	James	WAS	80	John	NOH	85A
Margaret	FRA	278	James	WAS	91	John	NOU	143A
Matthias	NOU	158	James	WST	346	Josh?	BER	185
Michael	FAY	198	John	PHA	43	Ludwig	ADA	19
Michael	NOH	37A	John	PHA	94	Mathews	BUC	159
Mitche	BEV	28	John	GRN	105	Matthew	CHE	786
Naptila	PHA	41	Joseph	BUC	144A	Michael	ARM	126
Nathaniel	BFD	43	Malon	GRN	88	Michael	BER	135
Nathl.	CHE	837	Margaret	LAN	50	Michael	BER	160
Nicholas	PHA	91	Mark	LUZ	383	Michl.	MNT	124
Richard	FAY	266	Michael	PHI	155	Nicols.	DAU	15
Rodger	ADA	1	Peter	WAS	38	Peter	CUM	39
Rodger	ADA	3	Robert	WST	346	Peter	PHA	45
Samuel	PHA	114	Robert	DAU	27A	Peter (See		
Silas	BUC	153	Roger	BUC	145	Hartman,		
Simons	PHI	109A	Thomas	BUC	86A	Widow)	NOH	47A
Soloman	BUC	153	Thomas	BUC	93A	Peter	ARM	126
Thos.	BUC	99	Thos. Esqr.	YOR	155	Peter	CHE	782
Valentine	LAN	239	William	GRN	101	Peter	NOH	51A
Widow	MIF	5	William	BUC	144A	Philip	MNT	57
Widow	MIF	12A	HARTLINE, Jacob	CUM	151	Philip	LAN	262
William	MIF	5	Leonard	HNT	145	Philip	NOH	47A
William	BFD	43	Leond.	BER	176	Phillip	NOU	149
William	BFD	63	Michael	WAY	136	Samuel	LAN	295
William	MNT	65	HARTLY, Widw.	PHI	104	Thomas	NOH	39A
William	PHA	102	Henry	PHI	58	Tividrick	LAN	267

HARTMAN,			HARVAY, Joshua	CHE 709	HASING, Jane	FRA 271
Valentine	BER 133	HARVERY, Elonor	BUC 107	Jeramia	ALL 111
Widow	ADA 12	HARVEY, Abner	CHE 881	HASINGBAUGH,
Widow	LAN 111	Abraham	BUC 151A	Henry	NOU 193
Widow	NOH 59A	Absalom	CHE 709	HASINGER, Abraham	NOU 188
Widow Of Petr.	NOH 47A	Amos	CHE 708	Catharine	NOU 136
HARTMANN, Mathias	PHA 38	Amos Jnr.	CHE 709	Jacob	NOU 188
HARTNESS,		Amos Sen.	CHE 709	Jacob	NOU 188
Charrels	ALL 67	Andw.	CUM 103	John	NOU 188
John	WST 191	Eli	DEL 158	HASKIEL, Benjamin	HNT 131
HARTNETT, Thos.	PHA 52	Evan	CHE 769	George	HNT 131
HARTRANFT,		George	MER 445	HASKIEL?,
Leonard	BER 166	Henry	BUC 151	Fredric?	HNT 130
William	BER 183	Isaac	BER 167	HASKINS, Thos.	PHA 39
HARTRANOFF, Jno.	PHI 44	Isaac	CHE 761	William	WST 170
HARTSHAN, Thomas	BEV 12	James	WAS 49	HASKINS?, John	LAN 275
HARTSHORN, George	ALL 82	James	FRA 326	HASLER, John	BFD 43
George	ALL 82	Jane	HNT 145	HASLET, Andw.	MIF 3
Paterson	PHA 80	Jno.	CUM 35	James	MIF 3
HARTSHORNE, Jacob	DEL 158	Job	WAS 28	John	LYC 23
HARTSHOUF,		Job	BER 169	John	WST 151
Zachariah	LUZ 332	John	BUC 153	Joseph	MIF 3
HARTSICKER,		John	DEL 191	Peter	MNT 99
Andrew	ADA 27	John	FRA 319	Peter	YOR 209
HARTSLER, Chrisn.	LAN 261	Joseph	BUC 152	Robert	CUM 136
John	LAN 261	Joseph	BUC 161	Robert	WST 151
HARTSMAN, James	FRA 311	Joseph	WST 324	Robert	WST 151
HARTSOCK, Isaac	HNT 116	Joseph	BUC 86A	Robt.	CUM 91
John	BFD 58	Josiah	WST 310	Wilm.	ALL 120
John	HNT 150	Mathias	BUC 151	Wm.	PHA 100
Jonathan	HNT 145	Patrick	BUT 325	HASLETT, James	FAY 245
HARTSOOK, Conrad	CEN 22B	Peter	PHA 120	Mary	PHI 131
HARTSORN, Benjn.	CEN 22A	Peter	CHE 707	Robert	WAS 116
HARTUNG, Chrisn.	NOH 75A	Robert	HNT 135	HASLEY, Leonard	WST 191
Elizabeth	PHA 19	Rosanna	LUZ 344	HASLING, Edward	PHI 1
HARTWELL, Oliver	ALL 120	Samuel	PHA 25	HASNER, Michl.	BER 286
Redd.	PHI 74	Samuel	MNT 43	HASON, Jonn.	CUM 83
HARTWICK,		Samuel	BUC 104	Patk.	CUM 141
Frederick	YOR 157	Samuel	BUC 161	HASPLE, Philip	BUC 149A
HARTY, Christian	NOU 110	Stephin	LYC 3	HASS, Abraham	NOU 137
Err	NOU 110	Thomas	LUZ 351	David	LAN 277
Peter	NOU 110	Titus	FRA 323	Elizabeth	PHI 127
HARTZ,		William	BFD 63	Feldy	NOU 137
Christophel	LAN 314	William	SOM 152	Fred.	PHI 94A
David	BER 248	William	FAY 204	Fredk.	PHI 102A
Ludwig	DAU 12	William	BUC 151A	Henry	PHI 94
Maria	LAN 299	Wm.	CUM 103	Henry	NOU 137
Peter	BER 248	Wm.	FRA 326	Henry Senr.	NOU 137
HARTZEL, Adam	WST 310	Wm.	CHE 708	Henry	PHI 66A
George Junr.	ADA 15	HARVOUT, Joseph	CHE 819	Jacob	LAN 24
Henry	SOM 145	HARVY, Alexander	NOU 117	Jacob	PHI 124
Henry	BUC 157	Benjn.	MIF 12	John	NOU 100
Henry Jnr.	BUC 96A	Geo.	PHI 36	John	NOU 122
Jacob	BUC 102	Joab	MIF 10	John	YOR 163
Jacob	BER 281	John	PHI 10	John	YOR 173
Jacob	WST 310	William	NOU 117	John	LAN 277
Jacob Esq.	SOM 142	HARWARD,		John	LAN 278
John	SOM 143	Christopher	MNT 55	William	NOU 137
John	BUC 160	HARWICK, Andw.	YOR 195	HASSELLACH, Henry	LAN 44
Leonard	ADA 15	Samuel	BUC 101	HASSEN, Barney	CEN 21A
Melchor	SOM 142	William	YOR 182	HASSER, Benjamin	LAN 106
Nicholas	SOM 142	HARWOOD, Robt.	PHA 15	HASSINGER, Jacob	PHA 81
HARTZELL, Adam	WST 273	HASBAGER, Samuel	CHE 874	HASSLER, Abraham	YOR 190
Adam	WST 273	Samuel	CHE 874	Casper	LAN 198
John	WST 273	HASEL, Charles	PHI 92	Christian	YOR 189
Jonas Esqr.	NOH 71	HASELET, John	WST 237	Fredk.	BER 142
HARTZLER,		Robert	WST 170	Fredk. Jr.	BER 142
Christian	LAN 93	William	NOU 158	Michael	YOR 196
David	MIF 3	HASELTON,		Stephen	LAN 215
Jacob	MIF 3	Hamilton	CUM 124	HASSLIR, Michael	LAN 210
John	MIF 3	Hugh	CUM 120	HASSON, John	MIF 17
HARTZLER?,		HASER, David	NOU 158	HASTING, Christ.	LAN 270
Abraham	YOR 205	HASFORD, Widw.	PHI 74	HASTINGS,
HARTZOG, Nicholas	LAN 198	HASHBAGER, Jacob	CHE 873	Alexander	WAS 116
HARTZWICK, Jno.	CEN 22B	John	CHE 873	Enoch	LAN 14
HARUM, Thos.	PHI 111A	HASHNESS, Saml.	PHI 130	Eno ch	CEN 20A

HAWKES, William	PHA	7	HAY, Thomas	BFD	73	HAYS, Job	CHE 849
HAWKINS, Absalom	WAS	38	Valentine	BFD	63	John	MIF	10
Charles	FRA	273	William	FRA	279	John	LYC	15
Henry	PHA	95	HAYBERGER, George	ERI	58	John	WAS	16
Henry	WST	215	HAYCOCK, John	CHE	728	John	WAS	21
Isaac	MNT	64	Jonathen	NOU	110	John	LYC	22
Jesse	MNT	64	Josiah	NOH	35A	John	ALL	91
John	PHA	6	HAYDDOCK, Robert	PHA	13	John	ALL	96
John	PHA	85	HAYDON, Benjamin	LUZ	387	John	CUM	114
Philip	WAS	49	John	LUZ	425	John	CUM	126
Robert	YOR	202	Wm.	PHA	5	John	HNT	148
Thomas	WAS	38	HAYERMAN, Abrahm	SOM	157	John	VEN	169
Thomas	MNT	93	HAYES, Widow	WST	324	John	VEN	170
Thomas	LAN	218	Abraham	WST	237	John	YOR	203
Thomas	FRA	296	Benajah	LUZ	424	John	LAN	262
William	WAS	56	David	BEV	20	John Junr.	YOR	203
William	BFD	58	Elizn.	PHA	54	John Junr.	LAN	262
William	DEL	163	George	ADA	18	John, Jun.	LYC	6
William	CHE	894	James	PHA	104	Joseph	WAS	80
HAWKLEY, Richd.	WST	368	James	WST	215	Joseph	CUM	94
HAWKS, Mrs.	LYC	28	James	CHE	746	Mordecai	CHE	772
Johathan	LUZ	387	James	CHE	757	Moses	CUM	22
John	WST	151	Jas. & Pat.	LAN	261	Moses	WAS	90
Mrs.	NOU	136	John	NOU	129	Nathan	CHE	740
HAWKSWERTH,			John	NOU	165	Nathan	CHE	849
Elizth.	MNT	67	John Mason	LAN	156	Patrick	DAU	44
HAWKSWORTH, Ester	MNT	67	John	PHI	61A	Pliney	LUZ	357
Israel	MNT	67	Micheal	WST	237	Reobert	ALL	91
Peter	MNT	67	Oliver	LUZ	403	Robert	DAU	46
HAWKWORTH, Peter			Oliver	LUZ	420	Robert	ALL	83
Junr.	MNT	67	Pat. (See			Robert	NOH	29A
HAWLEY, Benjn.	CHE	808	Hayes, Jas.)	LAN	261	Saml.	CUM	120
Caleb	CHE	808	Patrick	PHA	95	Samuel	WAS	21
Daniel	LUZ	415	Richard	DEL	171	Samuel	WST	309
John	LUZ	387	Robert	NOU	158	Samuel Jun.	ADA	18
John	LUZ	390	Robt.	BUT	340	Samuel Sen.	ADA	18
Joseph	CHE	814	Saml.	FRA	324	Sarah	WAS	80
Robert	CHE	758	Samuel	PHA	103	Solomon	CHE	773
William	CHE	743	William	NOU	117	Thomas	WAS	90
William	CHE	899	HAYHERST, James	FAY	261	William	DAU	45
HAWMAN, Henry	BFD	37	HAYHURS, Bazaleel	NOU	110	William	WAS	63
HAWORTH, John	PHA	107	HAYHURST, John	BUC	151	William	WAS	122
HAWRTORN, Adam	CUM	124	John	BUC	137A	William	VEN	169
HAWSER, Abram	MNT	108	Joseph	BUC	161	William	WST	368
HAWTHORN, David	WAS	74	HAYLANDER, Jacob	PHA	42	William Esqr.	WAS	21
Elizabeth	PHA	3	HAYLEY, John	DEL	169	Wilm.	ALL	94
Jas.	CUM	125	HAYLON, Isaac	MNT	38	Wm.	FRA	284
John	WAS	68	HAYMAKER,			HAYWARD, John	PHA	13
Thos.	PHA	103	Frederick	CRA	2	HAYWOOD, Jonathan	LAN	55
William	WAS	7	Henrey	FAY	231	HAYWORTH, George	DEL	173
HAY, Adam	NOH	37A	Saml.	FRA	312	John	DEL	174
Daniel	BFD	63	HAYMAN, Wm.	CHE	704	Mahlon	DEL	178
David	WAS	28	HAYNES, John	DAU	10A	Stephanus	DEL	181
David	DAU	46	John	DAU	12A	HAZARD, Comfat	LUZ	362
Edwd.	PHI	26	Maximilian	CUM	40	Ebenezer	PHA	70
Francis	SOM	138	HAYS, Abiah	WAS	80	George	FRA	291
George	YOR	155	Abraham	ALL	83	Hap	PHA	44
George	BER	205	Abraham Jun.	ALL	83	HAZART, Jno.	FRA	287
George	BER	266	Addis	PHI	116A	HAZE, Jos.	LYC	25
Jacob Esqr.	YOR	155	Andrew	LAN	221	HAZELGASER?,		
James	YOR	197	Aron	PHA	26	Jacob	WST	171
John	PHA	40	David	WAS	63	HAZELOTT, James	YOR	197
John	PHI	44	Edward	MIF	12A	HAZELTON, John	PHI	133
John	ERI	56	Francis	ALL	83	John	WST	237
John	NOH	87	George	BUT	316	HAZEN, James	WAS	75
John Esqr.	YOR	155	Henry	CUM	116	John	WAS	75
John D.	ERI	55A	Isaac	PHI	60	William	LUZ	367
Melchior	NOH	39A	Isaac	CHE	771	HAZLE, William	HNT	161
Michael	BFD	63	Jacob	ALL	83	HAZLEBAKER,		
Michael Jr.	BFD	63	James	ADA	18	Elisabeth	WAS	80
Peter Esqr.	NOH	87	James	BEV	25	HAZLEHURST, Isaac	PHA	36
Philip	BER	159	James	LYC	25	HAZLET, Alen	HNT	131
Sieon	SOM	138	James	FAY	236	Isaac	WAS	21
Simon	BFD	63	James	DAU	11A	Robert	DAU	21
Thomas	WAS	21	James	NOH	29A	William	BFD	73
Thomas	PHI	55	Jesse	YOR	219	HAZLETT, Andrew	SOM	149

HECKMAN, Jacob	MNT	62	HEFFNER, Anthony	BER	257	HEIDSMAN, William	NOH	73
John	YOR	187	Anthony Jur.	BER	257	HEIFER, William	YOR	177
John	NOH	47A	Danl.	BER	257	HEIGE?, George	MNT	68
Ulrich	NOH	29A	George	BER	188	HEIGEL, William	CUM	94
HECKOWELDER,			Henry	BER	255	HEIGERT, John	DAU	18
Christian	NOH	55A	Jacob	BER	257	HEIGEY, Henry	DAU	12A
HECKS, Gilbert	NOU	110	HEFFRON, Hugh	ERI	60A	HEIGLE, Jacob	CUM	22
HECOCK, Nathaniel	LUZ	416	HEFFT, William	NOH	78	HEIKERT,		
HEDDINGS, James	NOU	171	HEFLICH, John	DAU	2A	Christley	DAU	18A
HEDDINS, Wm.	CEN	22B	HEFMAN, Michael	YOR	218	HEIL, Adam	SOM	138
HEDDLESTON,			HEFNER, Christian	YOR	191	George	NOH	59
Robert	BFD	37	George	FRA	305	George	BER	282
HEDDLSON, Robt.	CHE	760	Jacob	BER	257	John	NOH	53
HEDGE, Absalom	WAS	122	HEFNER?, John	BER	226	Martin	NOU	122
Jacob	GRN	101	HEFOHNER?,			HEILER, Jacob	SOM	134
Jester	WAS	122	Sebastian	LAN	107	John	PHA	32
HEDINGS, William	NOU	114	HEFSER, Frederick	BER	158	John	SOM	141
William	NOU	117	HEFT, Casper	PHI	129	HEILIG, George	MNT	134
HEDLESTON, Jas.	CUM	51	Christopher	YOR	219	John	PHA	48
HEDLEY, Benjamin	GRN	106	Daniel	BUC	147A	Peter	MNT	134
Ephraim	GRN	70	George	PHI	94	HEILIGH, John	MNT	82
Joseph	GRN	107	George	BUC	81A	HEILMAN, Adam	DAU	25A
Samuel	GRN	106	Henry	BUC	157	Adam	DAU	41A
HEDLY, Jos.	PHI	105B	Henry	BUC	82A	Ansteat	DAU	29A
HEDMAN, Wm.	PHA	83	Jacob	LAN	308	George	NOH	53
HEDRICK, Abraham	BUC	101	John	CUM	106	Jacob Jun.	NOH	51A
Jacob	BUC	159	John	CUM	112	Jacob Senr.	NOH	51A
John	BUC	149A	John	PHI	129	Jno.	DAU	41A
Peter	CRA	7	Philip	BUC	147A	John Jr.	DAU	41A
Peter	BUC	101	William	BUC	81A	Michael	YOR	189
Peter	NOU	175	HEFTON, Edward			Peter	YOR	174
HEDRIK, Peter	DAU	43A	Esqr.	PHI	61	Tobias	NOH	51A
HEDSELL, Stephen	LUZ	333	HEGAR, Marey	FAY	245	HEIM, Charles	YOR	180
HEDSILL, Edward	LUZ	376	HEGAS, George			Christian	YOR	180
John	LUZ	376	(B.S.)	YOR	212	Jacob	BER	159
HEEL?, (See Hub)	LAN	165	HEGE, Peter	LAN	258	John	BER	155
(See Hul)	NOU	187	HEGEMAN, John	PHI	124	Leonard	BER	221
HEEPNER, Jacob	ALL	109	HEGETSWILE, Geo.	DAU	50	Mathias	BER	221
HEERS, Elisabeth	WAS	56	HEGGARTY, Thoms.	BUT	332	Paul	BER	155
HEESLEY, Michael	LAN	38	HEGGISWELER,			Paul Jr.	BER	155
HEESON?,			Jacob	ALL	61	Peter	BER	155
Archibald	YOR	195	HEGINS, William	LAN	245	William	YOR	180
HEFCHNER, (See			HEGLEY, Abraham	FRA	323	William	YOR	184
Hefohner?)	LAN	107	HEGNER, Christn.	PHI	119	HEIMBACH,		
HEFELFINGER,			John	PHI	91	Christian	BER	276
Peter	DAU	16	John	PHI	119	David Jr.	NOH	56
HEFF, Jacob	BER	240	Mary	PHI	119	David	NOH	55A
HEFFELFINGER,			HEGNEY, John	LAN	222	Henry	NOH	50
Henry	NOH	89A	HEHN, Adam	BER	202	Henry	BER	257
Jacob	CHE	797	Danl.	BER	202	Jacob	NOH	53
John	NOH	50	David	BER	202	John	BER	248
John	NOH	90	Frederick	BER	202	HEIME, Adam	NOU	122
HEFFELINGER, John	DAU	38A	Frederick Jr.	BER	202	George	NOU	122
HEFFELLRAUGER,			George	BER	202	John	NOU	122
(No Given			John	BER	144	William	NOU	122
Name)	BUC	102A	John	BER	202	HEIMER, Adam	NOH	73A
HEFFELY,			John Ad?	BER	203	Charles	NOH	73
Christopher	BER	277	Joseph	BER	202	Henry	YOR	179
George	BER	203	Peter	BER	156	Jacob	PHI	36
John	BER	181	Peter	BER	202	Yost	YOR	179
HEFFER, Garloch	LAN	71	Philip	BER	144	HEIMERLINE?,		
Julina	BER	232	HEHNS, George	BER	217	Peter	BER	284
Martin	PHI	87	HEIBLE, John	YOR	172	HEIMES, Benjn.	DAU	18A
HEFFERMAN, Jno.	PHI	45	HEIBLY, Michael	YOR	168	HEIN, Henry	BER	139
HEFFLEFINGER,			HEIBNER, Abraham	MNT	69	John	BER	130
Christian	MNT	73	Baltzer	MNT	113	John	BER	232
Fredk.	CUM	136	Christopher	MNT	69	Nicholas	PHI	147
Jno.	CUM	136	John	MNT	69	William	BER	283
Martin	CUM	136	HEIDEKAM, Wm.	BER	240	HEINBACH, Henry	BER	206
Phillip	CUM	136	HEIDELBACH, Jacob	YOR	162	HEINBACK?,		
Thos.	CUM	136	John	YOR	165	Francis	PHI	102A
HEFFLEY, Charles	HNT	166	HEIDELBAUGH,			HEINDLE, Adam	YOR	171
John	BFD	37	Henry	ADA	33	George	YOR	195
HEFFLINGER, Wm.	WST	346	HEIDEMAN, Nicols.	DAU	18	Lorence	YOR	195
HEFFMAN, George	LAN	68	HEIDLER, John	YOR	178	HEINE?, Mathias	NOU	122
HEFFNER, Anthony	BER	226	John Jr.	YOR	178	HEINEHO/ HEINEKD?,	YOR	171
						Michael		

HEINEKEN, T. H. C.	PHA	14
HEINELBERGER, John	BER	270
HEINEMAN, John	BER	210
Yost	LAN	313
HEINER, Margaret	BER	240
Rudolph	LAN	313
HEINES, John	SOM	162
HEINEY, Isaac	LAN	102
John	DAU	5
John	YOR	172
HEINITSH, Charles	LAN	37
HEINLEIN, George	NOH	78
James	NOH	87
Lowrence	NOH	78
HEINLY, George	BER	188
Jacob	BER	276
John	NOH	59A
HEINMAN, Peter	BER	130
HEINNICKE, Christian	LAN	198
HEINOLD, Charles	PHI	107
HEINS, Elizabeth	YOR	170
John	BER	254
John	LAN	313
HEINTZ, Frederick	NOH	59A
George	NOH	59
Jacob	NOH	59A
Jacob	NOH	59A
Michael	NOH	82
Peter	NOH	59A
William Junr.	NOH	59A
William	NOH	59A
HEINY, Christian	NOH	55A
George	NOH	55A
John	NOH	30
HEIR?, Charles	YOR	219
HEIRING, Nicholas	MNT	89
HEIRS, James	WST	309
William	MER	445
HEISE, Jacob	YOR	193
Wendle	YOR	193
HEISEN, Henry	CHE	703
HEISER, Andrew	MNT	128
Fredk.	BER	142
Henry	BER	157
John Od.?	BER	222
Ulrich	BER	157
HEISEY, Michael	DAU	27A
Peter	DAU	40A
HEISINGER, John	LAN	286
HEISLER, Jacob	MNT	45
Jacob Junr.	MNT	45
HEISS, Christley	LAN	132
Clara	PHA	71
Deitrich	LAN	35
Deitrich	LAN	56
Jacob	NOH	36A
Johh	LAN	161
John	LAN	39
John	BFD	44
John	DAU	4A
HEIST, Adam	BER	257
Catharine	NOH	87
Frederick	MNT	134
Geo.	BER	240
George	MNT	134
George Junr.	MNT	134
Hannah	BER	210
Henry	MNT	53
Henry	MNT	134
Henry	BER	210
Henry Junr.	MNT	53
John	MNT	134
Melchoir	BER	257

HEIST, Nicholas	BER	230
Solomon	NOU	193
HEISTAND, Abraham	NOH	55A
Henry	LAN	296
HEISTE, George	MNT	45
HEISTER, Gabrial	BER	144
John	BER	144
John	CHE	896
Joseph	BER	240
Wm.	BER	144
HEISTON, Isaac	SOM	145
Malan	CHE	710
HEISY, Danl.	DAU	40
Henry	DAU	28A
HEITELBAUGH, Jacob	LAN	226
HEITER, Geo.	CUM	119
John	BER	257
HEITER?, Benjamin	BER	206
HEITMAN, Mathias	DAU	3A
HEITSHER, Philip	LAN	79
HEITZ, Christopher	LAN	210
HEIZER, John	MNT	99
HELAN, Mercus	WAS	100
HELBERN, Amos	NOU	110
Thomas	NOU	110
HELBOURN?, Thomas	MNT	73
HELD, John	NOH	59A
HELDEBRANT, John	BER	186
HELDER, Henry	BER	267
Jacob	BER	200
HELDIN, Widow	LAN	254
HELDON, James	YOR	193
HELEBRAND, Conrad	NOU	149
HELER, Catharine	PHA	83
HELEY, John	WAS	12
HELF, George	WAS	122
HELFENSTINE, Catherine	PHI	126
Saml.	PHA	27
HELFFRICH, George	NOH	89A
Henry	NOH	90
Jno. Henry Revd.	NOH	85A
John	NOH	90
Michael	NOH	90
HELFRISH, George	NOH	44A
HELIARD, Thomas	FAY	215
HELICK, Wm.	NOH	71A
HELIG, Thos.	YOR	159
HELINGER, Adam	LAN	141
HELL, George	BER	219
Henry	YOR	189
Jacob	SOM	138
Jacob	BER	245
HELLAR, Henry	DAU	38
HELLEBRAND, Andrew	NOH	62A
William	NOH	62A
HELLEKIS, Edward	NOU	165
HELLEM, Adam	SOM	154
George	SOM	153
Henry	SOM	154
Mary	BFD	54
HELLEMS, Francis	ADA	27
HELLEN, Joseph	LAN	182
HELLEND, Martin	CHE	755
HELLER, Abraham	NOH	73
Adam	DAU	7
Adam	CUM	112
Andrew	NOH	47A
Barnet	BUC	157
Casper	CUM	112
Christopher	BUC	106A
D. John	NOU	105

HELLER, Daniel	NOH	82
Daniel	MNT	92
David	NOH	47A
Dieter	NOH	47A
Fred.?/ T---?	BER	240
George	NOU	105
George	CUM	112
Isaac	DAU	7
Jacob	NOH	73
Job	NOH	47A
John	NOH	50
John	LAN	117
John	BUC	159
John	NOH	41A
Joseph	NOH	39A
Ludwig	NOH	47A
Mathew (Crossed Out)	NOH	42
Michael (Potter)	NOH	47A
Michael Jr.	NOH	47A
Michael Sr.	NOH	47A
Michael (--1?)	NOH	47A
Simon	NOH	80
Simon	NOH	41A
Simon	NOH	73A
Widdow	CUM	60
William	GRN	95
HELLERMAN, George	PHI	146
John	PHI	112
John	PHI	96A
HELLFORD, Christ-.	CEN	19A
HELLIGASS, John	NOH	47A
HELLINGER, Andrew	PHI	155
Martin	PHI	151
HELLINGS, Benjn.	PHA	89
Flincher	BUC	83A
Hannah	BUC	143
John	BUC	143
John Jn.	BUC	162
John	BUC	93A
John	BUC	137A
John	BUC	160A
Jonathan	BUC	143
Robert	PHI	141
Saml.	BUC	160A
Tunis	BUC	160A
HELLM, Conrad	DAU	34A
HELLMAN, Christian	NOH	30
Daniel	FRA	307
George	FRA	307
HELLSON, Peter	YOR	213
HELM, Adam	PHI	104A
Carl	NOH	53
Christn.	PHA	81
Eliza	PHA	68
Elizabeth	PHA	32
Enos	DEL	171
Frederick	BFD	73
George	LAN	223
George W.	PHA	94
Jacob	BFD	73
Jacob	CUM	143
Jacob	LAN	224
John	BFD	73
John	LAN	223
Mary	PHA	58
HELMAN, Barbara	YOR	182
Michael	YOR	182
Peter	LAN	40
Peter	YOR	191
Widow	LAN	140
HELMBOLD, George	PHA	18
Henry	MNT	138

INDEX TO THE 1800 CENSUS OF PENNSYLVANIA

Name	Loc	Pg	Name	Loc	Pg	Name	Loc	Pg
HELMES, Aaron	DEL	187	HEMPERLY, Martin	DAU	13	HENDERSON,		
Israel	DEL	168	Michael	DAU	12A	Elizabeth	MIF	10
Job	DEL	168	HEMPHILL, Adley	BFD	73	Elizh.	CHE	764
HELMICK, Adam	FAY	244	Adm.	BUT	332	Frederick	WAS	16
Klous	DAU	8A	Andrew	WAS	44	George	WAS	7
Nicholas	FAY	245	Ann	DEL	190	George	WAS	16
HELMIGH, Peter	SOM	146	Edward	WAS	44	George	LAN	179
HELMINICK, Wm.	CUM	23	Henry	MIF	5	H.	LYC	10
HELMRICK,			James	WAS	75	Hugh	ALL	71
Frederick	BFD	35	James	HNT	133	Hugh	YOR	206
HELMS, Aaron	DEL	187	Jas.	CUM	138	James	LYC	7
Enos	DEL	189	Jas.	BUT	332	James	MIF	7
Oliver	LUZ	336	Jas.	CHE	705	James	PHI	35
Rebecca	FRA	296	Jno.	BUT	332	James	LAN	76
HELMUTE, John	DAU	34A	Joh	FAY	0	James	GRN	88
HELMUTH, J.?/ I.?			Jos.	CUM	67	James	LAN	126
Henry	PHA	84	Joseph	BEV	20	James	WST	160
John K.	PHA	106	Moses Esqr.	NOH	43	James	DEL	165
HELPER, Jacob	WST	289	Robert	BFD	73	James	BER	204
HELSE, Jacob	PHI	112	Samuel	LAN	218	James	FRA	308
HELSEL, John	BFD	73	Thomas	WAS	7	James	FRA	312
Tobias	SOM	158	Thomas	WAS	12	James	CHE	701
HELSIL, Henry	BFD	63	Widow	MIF	5	James	CHE	703
HELSLEIGH, Jacob	NOU	183	HEMPHREY,			James Junr.	WAS	16
Matthias	NOU	183	Benjamin	LAN	249	James Senr.	WAS	16
HELT, Henry	PHI	144	HEMPLE, Chrisn.	PHI	70	James. C.	GRN	92
Henry	LAN	262	Saml.	PHI	111	Jane	PHA	120
John	PHI	135	HEMPSHIRE, David	LAN	169	Jas.	CUM	138
John	PHI	149	HEMPSTED, Joshua	FAY	236	John	MIF	7
John	BER	240	HEMPT, Casmer	BUC	147A	John	MIF	10
Lewis	BER	240	HEMROD, Aaron	ERI	59	John	MIF	10
Peter	PHI	103	Andrew	NOU	164	John	ADA	32
HELT?, Daniel	PHA	52	HENCH, George	CUM	37	John	BFD	38
George	WAS	12	Jacob	MIF	7	John	PHA	44
John	WAS	7	Jno.	CUM	40	John	WAS	56
HELTER?, Benjamin	BER	206	HENCHIN, John	ADA	4	John	WAS	91
HELTEY?, (See			HENCHING,			John	MNT	94
Hettey)	NOU	143A	Barbarah	FRA	300	John	LAN	107
HELTINGER, Henry	BER	153	HENCKY, Jacob	NOH	84	John	HNT	155
HELTON, James	PHI	155	HENDDRICKS,			John	WST	272
John	PHI	146	Stephen	ADA	15	John	FRA	305
Jonathn.	PHI	94	HENDEL, Jacob	CUM	95	John	MER	444
William	FAY	221	M. Elizabeth	PHA	42	John	CHE	704
HELTZEL, Nicholas	YOR	171	HENDELONG,			John	CHE	766
HELTZHEIMER,			Christian	NOH	66A	John	CHE	868
Peter	YOR	214	HENDERSHOT,			John Junr.	LAN	107
HELVESTON, John	PHI	153	Casper	WAS	3	Jonathan	WAS	56
Nicholas	PHI	153	David	NOU	143A	Jonathan	HNT	154
HELWIG, Adam	BER	213	Isaac	NOU	158	Josa. R. Dr.	FRA	313
Andrew	BER	158	Jacob	NOU	149	Joseph	WAS	34
Fredk.	BER	213	Jacob	NOU	158	Joseph	PHA	65
HELZER?, William	ADA	8	John	BFD	43	Joseph	HNT	155
HEMBERGER, Balser	BER	169	John	LUZ	326	Joseph	NOU	158
HEMBLE, Widw.	PHI	115A	Michael	NOU	158	Joseph	WST	191
Wm.	PHA	26	William	NOU	158	Joseph Revd.	WST	151
HEMBOTT, Jacob	NOH	47A	Wm.	CUM	31	Margt.	CUM	148
Widow	NOH	37A	HENDERSON, Adm.	WST	216	Martha	PHA	13
HEME?, Francis	YOR	181	Agness	CHE	722	Mary	WAS	21
HEMICH, John Jr.	BER	169	Alexr.	MNT	104	Mary	CUM	50
HEMICK, John	BER	169	Alexr.	WST	171	Mary	PHA	102
HEMINGER?,			Andrew	HNT	154	Mathew	ALL	80
Frederick	BER	150	Andrew Junr.	WAS	7	Matthew	LAN	126
HEMLER, Christian	HNT	162	Andrew Senr.	WAS	7	Mattw.	CUM	85
Henry	ADA	31	Archibald	LAN	133	Misses	PHA	25
HEMMBRIGHT,			Arthur	BUC	147A	Richard	NOU	117
Philip	MNT	73	Barton	LAN	126	Robert	BEV	24
HEMMELRICK, Peter	NOU	136	Benjn.	CUM	78	Robert	BFD	38
HEMMING, Eliza.	CUM	87	Charles	WAS	56	Robert	ALL	56
HEMMINGER, Andrew	SOM	128	Chas.	LYC	17	Robert	PHA	98
Frederic	SOM	134	Chas.	WST	170	Robert	HNT	130
George	SOM	128	Chas. Sr.?	WST	170	Robert	WST	151
HEMOUR, Moses	LAN	219	Daniel	ERI	59	Robert	FAY	245
Solomon	LAN	248	David	LAN	15	Robert	MER	444
HEMPEH, Fredrick	DAU	32	David	CUM	152	Robert	CHE	766
HEMPERLY, Anthony	DAU	47A	Eliza	PHA	75	Robt.	CHE	747
Geo.	DAU	44	Eliza.	CUM	146	Saml.	PHI	82

HENDERSON, Saml.	WST	151	HENDRICKS, Widow	ADA	15	HENORE, John	CHE	718
Saml.	WST	171	Wm.	MNT	35	HENREY, James	GRN	108
Saml.	FAY	221	HENDRICKSON,			James	FAY	203
Samuel	BFD	58	Abraham	NOU	117	John	FAY	203
Samuel	MNT	104	Daniel	MER	445	John	FAY	251
Samuel	BUC	153	Isaac	DEL	188	Peter	FAY	257
Samuel	FAY	203	John	BFD	58	Steven	FAY	240
Sarah	MIF	15	Joseph	PHA	46	William	FAY	203
Tho.	MIF	7	Justice	DEL	171	William	FAY	209
Thomas	WAS	7	Thomas	DEL	156	HENRICH, Peter	LAN	294
Thomas	WAS	56	HENDRIX, Adam	YOR	193	HENRICKEL, Jacob	PHA	51
Thomas	LAN	126	Isaac	YOR	192	HENRICKS, Andrew	SOM	149
Thomas	CHE	701	HENDRIXSON,			Henry	NOU	193
Thomas	CHE	728	Cornelious			Jacob	NOU	183
Thos.	CUM	55	Jun.	BEV	4	John	NOU	137
Thos.	CHE	748	Cornelius	BEV	4	John	SOM	149
Thos. Capt.	PHA	96	Thomas	BEV	4	HENRY, Widw.	PHI	91
William	WAS	21	HENDRSON, Henry	CHE	781	Abm.	CUM	52
William	WAS	91	HENE, Henry	DAU	6	Abm.	CUM	130
William	MNT	104	HENEKY?, Henery	YOR	169	Abm.	NOH	68A
William	SOM	158	HENER, John	BER	156	Abraham	LAN	37
William	MER	444	HENEREY, George	MER	444	Abraham	LAN	176
Wilm.	ALL	97	Jeremiah	MER	444	Adam	MIF	10
Wm.	MIF	1	HENERITZI, Henry	NOH	45	Adam	MNT	53
Wm.	BEV	6	HENERY, John	FRA	313	Adam	CUM	72
Wm.	MIF	7	HENERY?, Henery	YOR	169	Alexander	PHA	81
Wm.	MIF	10	HENES, Mosis	FAY	221	Andw.	PHA	32
Wm.	WST	170	HENEY, Christn.	CEN	21A	Barbara	DAU	41A
Wm.	WST	310	HENGER, Moderca/			Benjamin	LAN	35
Wm.	CHE	722	Mocliner?	MNT	94	Benjamin	NOU	158
Wm. (Crossed			HENGIN, George	MNT	124	Black	BUC	146A
Out)	LYC	9	Jacob	MNT	124	Casper	PHI	105
Wm.	PHI	68A	Jacob Junr.	MNT	124	Christian	NOH	53
HENDIRSON,			Jacob Junr.	MNT	126	Christian	NOU	114
William	NOU	198	HENGST, Michael	YOR	171	Christian	BER	156
HENDLE, Mrs.	DAU	40	Michael	YOR	205	Christian	YOR	190
HENDORFF, Andw.	YOR	169	HENIBERGER, John	FRA	274	Christian	YOR	190
HENDRICK, John	CUM	83	HENIG, Andrew	BER	266	Christian	WST	216
Susanah	CUM	145	Jacob	YOR	190	Christian	BER	257
HENDRICKS, Abm.	WST	170	John	YOR	190	Christn.	PHI	93
Abraham	MNT	118	Peter	YOR	190	Conrad	BER	144
Abraham	NOH	55A	HENING, Frederick	CEN	20A	Conrad	BER	240
Benjamin	NOU	136	George	DAU	33A	Conrad	CHE	784
Benjamin	BUC	96A	John	ALL	107	Daniel	YOR	213
Daniel	WST	170	Michael	DAU	6	David	MNT	131
Daniel	WST	170	HENINGEN, Leonard	NOU	100	David	WST	151
Danl. Jr.	WST	171	HENINGER,			David	WST	237
Geo.	MNT	123	Frederick	BER	130	Ebinezer	ALL	80
George Junr.	MNT	121	George	NOU	122	Edward	WST	252
Henry	BFD	69	George	BER	130	Elizabeth	ADA	34
Henry	MNT	128	John	BER	130	Elizabeth	BFD	35
Jacob	MNT	73	HENKEY, Ben Junr.	LAN	101	Francis	WAS	56
Jacob	BUC	98	HENKLE, Anthony	YOR	186	Francis	WAS	75
Jacob	MNT	123	John	YOR	181	Francis	HNT	122
James	PHA	120	HENKSON, Thos.	YOR	205	Frederick	NOU	175
Jas.	CUM	144	HENLOCK, Jonathan	LUZ	348	Fredk.	WST	215
John	PHI	7	HENLY, Peter	MNT	99	Gawin	DAU	11A
John	BFD	50	HENN, Jacob	PHI	133	George	ADA	33
John	MNT	73	John	NOH	82	George	NOH	82
John	CUM	75	Michael	NOH	82	George	BER	147
John	MNT	110	HENNEBERGER,			George	YOR	194
John	MNT	118	Peter	LAN	24	George	WST	310
Joseph	MIF	10	HENNEEN, Benjm.	PHA	92	Godfrey	PHI	135
Joseph	MNT	118	HENNERY, Adam	MIF	10	Hugh	PHA	71
Leonarad	MNT	39	HENNEY, Charles	WAS	90	Hugh	CHE	735
Leonard	MNT	117	HENNICK, Adam	NOU	175	Jacob	PHI	124
Leonard	MNT	121	HENNICKS, John	LAN	80	Jacob	YOR	188
Leond. Junr.	MNT	118	HENNING, Danl.	DAU	41A	Jacob	YOR	191
Magdelen	MNT	67	Jacob	DAU	5	Jacob	BER	257
Mary	MNT	119	Math.	DAU	35A	Jacob Jr.	YOR	190
Moses	WAS	80	HENNINGER, George	NOH	90	Jacob Jr.	YOR	191
Paul	MNT	118	Jacob	NOH	90	Jacob Sr.	YOR	190
Peter	BFD	38	HENNOLD, George	PHA	37	James	BEV	14
Peter	MNT	73	HENNY, Charles			James	WAS	34
Samuel	NOU	136	Esqr.	CHE	809	James	LAN	38
Thomas	WST	170	James	PHI	39	James	ALL	103

Name	Loc	Pg	Name	Loc	Pg	Name	Loc	Pg
HENRY, James	ARM	126	HENRY, William	WST	368	HERALD, George	NOU	182
James	HNT	166	William Esqr.	NOH	70	HERB-T?, Conrad	BER	176
James	WST	191	Wm.	BEV	5	HERB, Abm.	BER	176
James	LAN	247	Wm.	BEV	20	Abraham	BER	166
James	CHE	747	Wm.	CUM	39	Abraham	BER	206
James Jr.	CHE	747	Wm.	YOR	198	Danl.	BER	257
Jesse	BUC	93A	Wm.	BUC	93A	Frederick	BER	206
Jno. Junr.	CUM	88	HENRY?, Philip	BER	279	John	BER	185
John	MIF	3	HENS, Amos	LAN	186	Jonathan	NOH	51A
John	LAN	13	Andrew	MNT	125	Solomon	BER	206
John	LAN	21	Christian	YOR	193	HERBACH,		
John	WAS	49	Margaret	PHA	42	Elizabeth	YOR	169
John	NOH	50	HENSEL, Casper	YOR	185	George	YOR	158
John	CUM	90	HENSELL, William	LAN	46	George	BER	246
John	ALL	91	HENSELLER,			John Esqr.	YOR	169
John	ALL	92	Michael	PHA	109	Yost	YOR	163
John	MNT	106	Michael	PHA	109	HERBAUGH, Casper	SOM	133
John	MNT	111	Wm.	PHA	109	Jacob	SOM	133
John	ARM	127	HENSELMAN, John	LAN	250	John	SOM	134
John	BER	130	HENSHAW, John	BUT	326	John	FRA	305
John	CUM	130	HENSHING, Henry	FRA	306	HERBEIN, Abraham	BER	230
John	PHI	137	HENSINGER,			Daniel	BER	230
John	WAY	146	Christian	BER	132	David	BER	139
John	HNT	158	HENSMAN, Adam	PHA	75	Isaac	BER	230
John	VEN	165	HENSON, Jacob	ALL	102	John	BER	254
John	BER	166	Thomas	HNT	152	Peter	BER	230
John	YOR	194	HENSTIN, John	MNT	73	HERBER, Henry	BER	187
John	WST	346	HENSYL, Conrad	LAN	271	Philip	NOH	85
John	LUZ	361	HENTERLITER,			HERBERT, Arther	ADA	19
John	CHE	835	Jacob	BER	225	Lawrence	PHA	82
John	NOH	44A	Margaret	BER	186	HERBINE, Peter	BER	144
John	PHI	103A	HENTON, James	ERI	57	HERBISON, David	CHE	727
John. Jos.	DAU	4A	Robert	BER	181	John	WST	238
Joseph	NOH	90	HENTZEL, Jacob	YOR	205	Mathew	BEV	17
Michael	YOR	190	Philip	YOR	205	HERBISON?, John	ARM	122
Nicholas	YOR	178	HENUSEY, John	YOR	173	HERBOLT, Michael	YOR	218
P.	DAU	44A	Philip	YOR	173	Wm.	YOR	174
Patrick	CHE	748	HENVIS?, Ashman	PHI	61	HERBST, Andw.	BER	257
Peter	PHA	29	HENVIST, Robert	DEL	163	George	MNT	62
Peter	PHI	93	HENWOOD, Elisha	WAS	28	George	BER	213
Peter	CUM	130	HENY, John	PHI	10	Henry	NOH	47A
Peter	BUC	159	William	HNT	153	HERBSTER,		
Peter	BER	257	HEORBACH, Frances	FAY	197	Frederick	BER	130
Peters	WST	215	Henrey	FAY	197	HERCH, John	ADA	33
Phillip	NOU	175	Jacob	FAY	252	HERCHIE, Andrew	ADA	41
Richard	LAN	241	John	FAY	197	HERCKETE, James	LAN	178
Robert	CRA	15	HEORBACK, Jacob	FAY	198	HERCLEROAD?,		
Robert	CRA	17	HEORBAUGH, Jacob	FAY	256	Henry Jr.	DAU	47A
Robert	WAS	21	HEPBOURN, Sarah	PHI	150	John	DAU	47A
Robert	WAS	75	HEPBURN, James	NOU	171	HERCUSHIMER,		
Robert	WAS	99	John	LYC	27	George	PHI	126
Robert	WAS	100	Samuel	NOU	164	HERD, John	LAN	122
Robert	WST	324	Wm. Esqr.	LYC	3	Stephen	LAN	120
Robert	WST	346	HEPEENHEIMER,			HERDLY, John	MNT	113
Robert Junr.	WST	324	Jacob	BER	174	HERE, Christian	FAY	250
Robert	DAU	21A	HEPENSTULL, Geo.	CUM	141	HEREDEN, Jacob	YOR	182
Robert	NOH	75A	HEPLER,			HERENTON, Jesse	WAY	149
Samuel	DAU	12	Christopher	BER	283	HERGASHIMER,		
Samuel	HNT	165	George	MNT	82	Christopher	PHI	128
Samuel	LAN	248	George	NOH	90	HERGELROTH,		
Stewart	WST	160	Gilum	PHI	107A	Lorentz	LAN	147A
Thomas	MIF	10	John	BER	283	HERGERSHEIMER?,		
Thomas	BUC	141	HEPLER?, Henry	LUZ	357	William	PHI	125
Thos.	PHA	81	HEPLERING, John	ADA	26	HERGUSHIMER,		
Thos.	NOH	75A	HEPLING, Christn.	DAU	41A	Anthony	PHI	130
Wendle	YOR	178	HEPPENHEIMER,			Joseph	PHI	127
Widow	LAN	36	George	BER	173	HERHOFF, John	BER	260
William	PHA	3	Henry	BER	174	HERIN, Edward	PHI	114
William	MIF	10	William	BER	173	HERING, Conrad	HNT	119
William	CRA	16	HEPPERT, Geo.	DAU	31A	George	HNT	119
William	MIF	16	HEPPICK, John	DAU	14	Henry	YOR	176
William	LAN	21	HEPPIGH,			Henry	NOU	180
William	WAS	28	Christoph	DAU	14	Henry	YOR	186
William	BFD	35	HEPPINHEIMER,			Ludwig	NOH	56
William	LAN	154	David	LAN	65	Michael	NOH	73
William	WST	252	HEPPLE, William	YOR	213	Philip	YOR	176

HERINGTON, Jame/			HERR, Abraham	LAN 283	HERRON, David	ALL	67
Janie?	CRA	4	Abraham	LAN 283	David	CUM	87
Jonathn.	PHI	116	Abraham	LAN 292	James	BEV	16
HERINTAGE, Henry	DAU	9A	Abrham	LAN 233	James	ALL	71
HERISE?, John	LAN	218	Christian	LAN 21	John	PHI	3
HERITAGE, John	PHI	152	Christian	LAN 101	John	NOU	164
William	PHI	140	Christian	LAN 102	John Esqr.	ALL	69
HERKES, Jonathan	PHI	124	Christian	LAN 283	Robert	BEV	17
HERKINS, John	PHA	110	Christian	LAN 283	HERRY, Edward	DAU	28A
HERKIS, Michael	LAN	45	Christian	LAN 288	HERS, Jonathan	LAN	266A
HERLIN, Thomas	NOU	136	Christian	LAN 292	HERSCH, Frederick		
HERMAN, Adam	DAU	7	Christian	LAN 295	Jr.	NOH	85
Catharine	YOR	161	Christian	LAN 295	Jacob	NOH	45
Conrad	NOH	30	David (See		HERSEY, John	LUZ	392
Conrad	NOH	50	Herr, Jacob)	BUC 159	HERSH, Benj.	YOR	159
Conrad	BER	159	David	LAN 224	Christian	YOR	165
David	DAU	5A	David	LAN 243	Fredck. Senr.	NOH	85A
Frederick	NOH	71	David	LAN 294	George	LAN	245
Frederick	NOH	73	Emanuel	LAN 102	George	CHE	783
George	NOH	50	Emanuel	LAN 216	Jacob	LAN	243
George	BER	135	Henry	DAU 16	John	LAN	111
George	DAU	5A	Henry	LAN 224	Samuel	CHE	783
Henry	LAN	222	Henry	LAN 234	HERSHBARGER, John	BFD	50
Jacob	DAU	7	Isaac	LAN 234	HERSHBERGER, Ab.	DAU	34
Jacob	BER	210	Jacob & David	BUC 159	Christian	SOM	149
Jacob	BER	226	John	LAN 21	Christn.	BER	144
Jacob	DAU	5A	John	YOR 167	Chrn.	DAU	41A
John	DAU	7	John	LAN 220	Danl.	DAU	43A
John	BER	130	John	LAN 243	John	SOM	149
John	SOM	145	John	LAN 283	John Sen.	SOM	149
John	NOH	75A	John	LAN 296	Joseph	SOM	149
Lorentz	NOH	50	John	LAN 296	Peter	SOM	149
Philip	LAN	281	John Esq.	LAN 216	Widow	LAN	65
Philip	NOH	75A	John Miller	LAN 220	HERSHELMAN,		
Susannah	YOR	158	Martin Junr.	LAN 220	George	FAY	240
HERMANY, Abraham	NOH	90	Martin Senr.	LAN 220	HERSHEW, Joseph	CUM	108
George	NOH	53	Rudy	LAN 288	HERSHEY, Abraham	LAN	290
Isaac	NOH	90	Samuel	LAN 224	Abraham	LAN	292
Jacob	BER	226	Tobias	LAN 231	Andrew	LAN	8
Philip	NOH	53	HERRALD, Simon	NOU 183	Andrew Jnr.	LAN	8
HERMEL, Killian	BER	188	HERRAN, James	FRA 308	Chrisn.	LAN	8
HERMEN, Conrad	BEV	16	John	FRA 308	Isaac	DAU	47
HERMES, Widow	PHI	87A	Wm.	FRA 308	Isaac	DAU	44A
HERMILTON, Nathan	NOU	193	HERREN, Gashan	NOU 158	Jacob	LAN	133
HERMIN, Henry	YOR	177	Michael	DAU 10A	Jacob	LAN	296
HERMINGWAY, Asa	ERI	56A	HERRH, Henry	LAN 226	John	LAN	5
HERMISTEAD,			HERRIN, James G.	VEN 165	John	NOU	182
Cathrine	PHA	11	John	BFD 51	John	LAN	294
HERMSTEAD, Martin	PHA	44	John	WST 238	John	DAU	21A
HERN, Elias	FRA	306	John	WST 346	John	LAN	292
HERNARD, Elija	MIF	7	Laurence	WST 310	Joseph	LAN	8
HERNER, Andrew	BER	217	Thomas	ARM 123	Mary	DAU	44A
Daniel	BER	181	Thomas	WST 309	Peter	LAN	8
Henry	BER	133	HERRING,		Widow	LAN	302
Jacob	BER	139	Frederick	BER 280	HERSHIE,		
John	BER	158	George	BER 188	Christian	ADA	9
Nicholas	BER	181	Hannah	PHA 119	HERSHING, John	YOR	178
HERNEST, Jacob	BFD	55	Henry	BER 156	HERSHINGER,		
HERNISER, Jacob	PHA	78	John	LAN 168	Andrew	YOR	157
HERNISH,			John	BER 188	Jacob	YOR	204
Christian	YOR	161	John G.	BER 188	John	YOR	204
Christian	YOR	172	Ludwig	BER 156	HERSHISER, Lewis	BFD	51
Martin	YOR	172	Peter	DAU 49	HERSHMAN, Jacob	FAY	197
HERNLY, Christian	LAN	313	HERRINGTON, Aaron	LYC 15	John	DAU	20
Isaac	LAN	17	Constant	ERI 58	Wm.	FRA	304
HEROFF, Lewis	DAU	18A	Daniel	ERI 60	HERSHNER, Conrad	BER	135
HEROLD, Frederick	NOU	183	Eldad	ERI 58A	HERSHY, Andrew	LAN	115
HERON, Andrew	WAS	7	Henry	PHI 70A	Andw.	YOR	178
Charles	WAS	21	Israel	ERI 58A	Benjamin	LAN	147
James	WAS	90	Jonathen	ERI 58	Benjamin	LAN	304
James	WAS	100	Matthew	ERI 58A	Christian	LAN	17
Thomas	WAS	75	Seth	ERI 58	Christian	LAN	147
HEROUF, Jacob	FRA	309	HERRIOTT, John	LYC 14	Christian	YOR	174
HERPSER, Jacob	NOU	187	Joseph	LYC 14	Christian	YOR	178
John	NOU	188	HERRLING, John	LAN 65	Christian	YOR	178
HERPST, Henry	YOR	171	HERROLD, Peter	WST 216	Christian	LAN	184
					Christian	LAN	189

HERSHY, Christian		
Jr.	YOR	184
Henry	LAN	262
Jacob	LAN	2
Jacob	YOR	178
John	YOR	184
John	LAN	185
Jos.	YOR	178
Peter	YOR	178
HERSPER, George	NOU	187
HERST, Benjamin	NOU	175
David	NOU	175
Frederick	NOU	152
Geo.	FRA	273
Samuel	NOU	175
William	HNT	158
HERSTER, Daniel	NOH	37A
John	NOH	37A
HERSTINE, John	FAY	250
HERTER, Andrew	NOU	122
Charles	LAN	252
Elias	NOH	47A
Jacob	NOU	122
John	NOU	122
Matthias	NOU	122
Michael	NOH	45
Michael	LAN	74
HERTLEIN,		
Laurence	BER	184
HERTLINE, Joel	BER	176
HERTMAN, William	NOU	110
HERTONG, Wm.	PHI	113
HERTSKEY, John	LAN	113
HERTY, Andrew	NOU	110
HERTZ, Andrew	NOH	71
Conrad	BER	169
Daniel	DAU	2A
Henry	BER	135
Jacob	NOH	69
John	DAU	20A
John Geo.	BER	246
Peter	NOH	68A
HERTZEL, George	MNT	89
Henry	BUC	159
John & Paul	BUC	159
Paul (See		
Hertzel,		
John)	BUC	159
Paul	BUC	159
Philip	BUC	159
Ulrick	MNT	89
HERTZELL,		
Christian	NOH	87
Christn.	NOH	37A
Fredk.	CUM	111
George	NOH	71
George Jnr.	NOH	33A
George Junr.	NOH	43
George Senr.	NOH	43
George	NOH	33A
Henry	NOH	82
Henry	NOH	64A
Isaac Esqr.	NOH	71
Jacob	NOH	80
Jacob	NOH	87
John	NOH	71
John	NOH	78
John	NOH	87
Jonas Junr.	NOH	71
Peter	NOH	55A
HERTZLE, Danl.	BER	144
HERTZLER, Barbara	LAN	314
Christian	LAN	298
Christian	LAN	314
Christn.	BER	203
Jacob	LAN	93
HERTZLER, John	LAN	314
HERTZOG, Andw.	PHA	17
George	BER	213
Jacob	BER	176
Peter	PHA	44
Theobald	NOH	89A
HERVEY, John	MNT	40
William Junr.	WAS	56
William Senr.	WAS	56
HERVEY?, Wm.	BEV	19
HERWAGGON, Peter	BUC	93A
HERWICH, Jacob	YOR	156
HERWICK, Jacob	BUC	81A
HERWIG, Michael	NOH	47A
HERZOG, Widow	PHI	28
HESAMAN, Robert	WST	252
HESERMAN?, John	WST	252
HESETER, James	PHI	19
HESEY, Christian	FRA	307
Daniel	LAN	2
HESHAN, Thos.	PHI	119
HESHISAN, Mariah	PHA	65
HESIL, Bernard	NOU	180
HESKY, Martin	CUM	122
HESLEP, Thomas	CHE	841
HESLER, Henry	PHA	109
Jacob	MNT	50
HESLET, Lesley	FRA	319
HESLETT, Jane	CHE	873
HESLY, Henry	WST	215
HESNER?, John	BER	226
HESON, Jacob	CUM	111
HESS, Widow	PHI	97
Widw.	PHI	110
Abm. (See Hess,		
John)	LAN	153
Abraham	BFD	43
Abraham	LAN	106
Abraham	SOM	128
Abraham	LAN	149
Abraham	LUZ	361
Andrew	PHI	133
August	HNT	119
Casper	BER	240
Christian	LAN	106
Christian	PHI	133
Christian	LAN	275
Christian	LAN	276
Christian	NOH	64A
Christley	LAN	167
Conrad	NOH	30
Conrad	HNT	119
Conrad	BUC	147A
David	NOH	30
David	MNT	96
Elizabeth	LAN	118
Elizabeth	YOR	194
Frederick	NOH	87
George	PHI	95
George	LAN	236
George	DAU	32A
George	NOH	47A
George	BUC	147A
Geroge	NOU	175
Henry	ADA	42
Henry	SOM	153
Henry	BER	176
Henry	LAN	273
Henry	DAU	35A
Henry	NOH	62A
Jacob	BFD	43
Jacob	NOH	73
Jacob	WST	151
Jacob	BER	176
Jacob	WST	238
Jeremiah	NOH	73
HESS, Jeremiah	BER	279
Jno.	CUM	52
Jno.	CUM	137
John	BFD	43
John	DAU	49
John	NOH	73
John	LAN	138
John	SOM	138
John	YOR	157
John	LAN	274
John	LAN	275
John	LAN	280
John Dr.	LAN	220
John Junr.	NOH	64A
John & Abm.	LAN	153
John	NOH	64A
Mathias	DAU	36
Mathiw	DAU	35
Michael	YOR	171
Michael	LAN	275
Michael	LAN	277
Nicholas	NOH	64A
Nicholas	BUC	147A
Peter	SOM	128
Peter	HNT	137
Peter	FAY	231
Peter	NOH	47A
Peter	PHI	103A
Philip	LAN	12
Philip	NOH	53
Philip	LAN	292
Philip	BUC	147A
Samuel	LAN	11
Thomas	MNT	117
Tobias	BER	285
Widow	LAN	139
William	BFD	43
Wm.	PHI	90
HESSEL, Barry	PHI	101
HESSER, Elizabeth	PHI	126
Frederick	BER	158
George	PHI	126
John	FAY	214
Leonard	PHI	126
Peter	FAY	214
Wm.	PHI	82
HESSINGER, Peter	BER	276
HESSLER, Philip	BER	176
HESSLER?, Henry	LUZ	357
See Hepler	BER	283
HEST, Conrad	NOU	152
George	NOU	152
John	NOU	152
William	NOU	152
HEST?, Fredr.	FRA	314
HESTAND, Abraham	YOR	188
HESTER, Widw.	PHI	105A
Fredk.	CUM	30
John	GRN	76
Philip	GRN	76
William	DAU	33
HESTING, Daniel	ALL	105
HESTON, Abner	WAS	37
Abraham	PHI	61
Abrm.	DAU	19A
David	BUC	144A
Eber	WAS	37
Henry	LAN	236
Isaac	PHI	59
Jacob	BUC	107
Jarrett	MNT	87
Jesse	BUC	151
John	WAS	37
John	MNT	87
John	BUC	151
Jonathan	BUC	86A

HESTON, Phineas	GRN 81	HEWIT, Nicholas	HNT 164	HIBBS, John	BUC 84A
Robt.	FRA 319	Peter	WAS 3	John	BUC 137A
Samuel	BUC 151A	Philip	WAS 12	Jonathan	CHE 699
William	GRN 76	HEWITT, Ephraim	FAY 231	Jonathn.	BUC 160A
Zebulon Senr.	WAS 37	Isaac	LUZ 362	Lamb	BUC 151A
HESTON?, Levi	MNT 45	John	HNT 153	Mahlon	BUC 93A
HESTS, Matthew	NOU 175	John	FAY 245	Mary	BUC 160A
Michael	NOU 175	Wm.	PHA 98	Phineas	BUC 152A
HESTY, James	WAS 37	Wm.	CHE 757	Stephen	BUC 85
HETBARN, John	NOU 149	HEWLING, Nancy	PHI 103A	William	GRN 82
HETELY, Banser?	NOU 175	HEWRY?, (See		HIBERD, Calvin	LUZ 327
George	NOU 175	Henry)	BEV 26	Ebenezer	LUZ 327
HETER, John	NOU 187	HEWS, Isaac	FAY 221	HIBERGER, George	PHI 75
John	NOU 187	HEWSON, William	BUC 84A	HIBS, James	NOU 110
HETERICK,		HEXON, John	NOU 193	Jason	NOU 110
Christian	YOR 188	HEYBERGER,		Laicy	FAY 236
John	YOR 185	Christian	NOH 82	HICHCOCK, Godfry	WST 346
HETH, Andrew	BFD 43	HEYBOURNE, George	DEL 158	HICK, John	HNT 152
HETHENEY, Henry	CHE 904	HEYDE, William	LUZ 328	Joseph	PHI 97A
HETHERHOLFF,		HEYDEGER, Hugh	PHA 111	William	FAY 227
Jacob	BER 129	HEYDLE, Sarah	PHA 31	HICK?, Philip	WST 252
HETHERINGTON,		HEYDON, James	BFD 35	HICKAMS, Richd.	PHI 119A
David	LYC 28	HEYDRECK, Baltzer	MNT 93	HICKATHORN,
George	PHA 111	HEYDRICK, Abraham	MNT 92	George	WAS 52
HETHERLING, Jacob	BER 252	HEYER, George	BER 133	HICKEL, Andrew	NOU 198
HETHEROCK,		Jacob	BER 133	HICKENAL, David	CUM 70
Charles	MNT 38	Ludewick	LAN 267	HICKENBOTTEM,
HETICH, Geo.	FRA 273	Ludwig	LAN 68	Charles	FAY 227
John	FRA 273	HEYL, Conrad	BER 206	George	FAY 231
HETINGER, Jacob	NOU 175	Daniel	BER 206	John	FAY 231
HETON, Robert	PHI 123	Daniel	NOH 75A	HICKENEL, Abm.	CUM 71
HETON?, Joseph	PHI 97	Feldi?	LAN 258	HICKENLUPER,
HETRICK, Geo.	CUM 78	George	PHA 87	Andw.	WST 310
Henry	BER 144	George	LAN 97	HICKENOW, Phillip	CUM 70
John	CUM 78	John	LAN 98	HICKEY, James	MIF 26A
Nicholas	NOU 122	John	NOH 39A	William	FAY 245
Nicholas	NOU 122	Philip	PHA 31	HICKINBAUGH,
Peter	NOU 122	HEYLEY, Edward	PHI 58	Jacob	GRN 95
HETT?, John	WAS 7	Edward	NOU 193	HICKINLIEBER,
HETTEBECK, Henry	DAU 44	HEYLY, James	PHA 88	George	ADA 15
HETTENBAUGH, John	DAU 5	HEYMAN, Joseph	BER 213	HICKLIN, Jacob	BFD 51
HETTERICK, Jacob	YOR 193	HEYN, Philip	BER 226	HICKLING,
HETTEY, George	NOU 143A	HEYNEMAN,		Ebenezer Esq.	SOM 162
HETTINGER, Peter	BER 267	Fredrick	PHA 19	HICKLROAD?, John	FRA 283
Peter	BER 272	John	PHA 37	HICKMAN, Abraham	WAS 44
HETZ, Ben	LAN 38	HEYNMAN, John	PHA 41	Benj.	PHI 114A
HETZELBERGER,		HEYSENGER, Mathw.	PHA 115	Benjn.	CHE 743
Elizabeth	LAN 299	HGAN, Margt.	MIF 17	Charles	FAY 215
Mary	LAN 51	HIB-?, Charles	BUC 82A	Francis	CHE 744
HETZER, Adam	YOR 173	HIBAUGH, Henry	CUM 73	Hannah	CHE 837
HETZLE, Peter	BER 151	HIBBENS, Thomas	FAY 252	Henry	FRA 284
HEVEN, Steven	FAY 236	HIBBERD, Amos	CHE 879	Hermonius	FAY 266
HEVENDER, Abm.	BUC 91	Ann	DEL 171	Jacob	BFD 51
Jacob	BUC 91	Benjn.	CHE 878	James	LAN 114
HEVENER, John	BUC 149A	Caleb	CHE 878	James	DEL 191
HEVENOR, Belvi	LYC 18	Godfrey	CHE 808	John	CHE 762
HEVERLIN, Mrs.	NOU 97A	Hezekiah	DEL 170	Michl.	FRA 280
HEVERLING, John	BER 153	Jacob	DEL 176	Moses	CHE 804
HEVLICK, Michael	NOU 147	John	DEL 170	Peter	CHE 860
HEWEL, Conrad	LAN 273	Joseph		Robert	GRN 70
HEWER, John	NOU 193	(Carpenter)	DEL 171	Selby	PHA 103
HEWES, James	PHI 17	Joseph	DEL 190	Solomon	FAY 231
John	PHI 59	Joseph Jun.	DEL 170	Thos.	CHE 812
Owen	MNT 118	Josiah	CHE 734	HICKMEN, Joseph	CHE 837
Thos.	PHA 73	Owen	CHE 733	HICKOCK, Henerey	MER 445
HEWET, William	FAY 215	Widow	CHE 883	HICKS, Abraham	HNT 152
HEWEY, Catherine	WST 290	Wm.	CHE 878	Ann	CUM 39
John	WST 290	HIBBINS, James	DEL 173	Aron	CUM 39
HEWEY?, Wm.	BEV 19	HIBBITS, John	FAY 257	Christian	ADA 41
HEWING, Thomas	NOU 187	HIBBS, Alexr.	PHI 145	Daniel	ADA 7
HEWIT, George	ADA 17	Benjn.	BUC 137A	Edward	CRA 11
Henry	WAS 12	Britewell M.	PHA 105	Edward	CHE 701
Jacob	WAS 122	Jacob	GRN 74	Gazzim	VEN 165
Joseph	ADA 14	Jacob	GRN 88	George	BUC 90
Joseph	BFD 73	Jacob	BUC 84A	George	BUC 157
Lewis	WAS 12	John	BUC 161	Isaac	BUC 103

Name	Ref		Name	Ref		Name	Ref
HICKS, Isaac	HNT 152		HIGGINS, Aaron	NOU 171		HILDEBRAN, Andrew	HNT 124
Jacb.?	CEN 22B		Charles	PHA 86		Saml.	CEN 22A
Jacob	SOM 128		Christiana	SOM 160		HILDEBRAND,	
Jesse	BUC 157		Francis	PHA 110		Abraham	SOM 157
John	VEN 165		John	PHI 64		Abraham Sen.	SOM 157
John	FRA 293		John	PHA 116		Adam	LAN 65
John	LUZ 419		Price	PHI 7		Casper	YOR 193
Joseph	BUC 151		HIGGS, Mahlon	MNT 66		Catharine	LAN 310
Joses	VEN 165		HIGH, Daniel	CHE 854		George	LAN 79
Levi	VEN 165		David	BUC 96		George	MER 443
Levy	VEN 165		David	CHE 904		Jacob	ADA 36
Mahlon	BUC 88A		George	PHI 3		Jacob	YOR 194
Nicholas	PHA 44		George	CHE 789		John	ADA 37
Samuel	LUZ 357		Henly	BER 166		Levi	BER 140
Sylvenes	PHA 117		Isaac	BER 217		Martin	LAN 305
Thos.	CEN 22B		Jacob	BUC 96		Michael	BER 226
William	MNT 92		Jacob	BER 217		Richd.	LAN 81
William	CHE 901		Jacob	CHE 736		HILDEBRANDT,	
William Jn.	BUC 157		Jacob	CHE 815		Felix	YOR 192
Wm.	PHA 58		Jacob	CHE 853		John	YOR 192
HICKSON, Benj.	ADA 7		Jacob	CHE 855		John	YOR 192
James	WAS 99		Jacob	CHE 904		HILDEN, E.	LAN 148
John	YOR 156		John	BER 217		HILE, Widw.	PHI 105B
Joseph	WST 289		John	CHE 890		Frederick	BER 248
Timothy	BFD 55		John	BUC 96A		Henry	BER 250
HICKSTON, Robert	WAS 21		Philip	BUC 91		John	DAU 49
HICKY, Timothy	YOR 201		Philip	BER 206		Jonathan	WST 215
HICMAN, Adams	ALL 105		Samuel	BER 137		Peter	BER 248
Peter	ALL 105		HIGHBERGER, John	WST 252		Phillip	BER 248
HIDE, George	PHA 85		HIGHET, Joseph	LAN 4		Walter	SOM 138
George	LAN 101		HIGHFEILD, John	CHE 699		HILE?, (See Hill)	FRA 276
John	CUM 66		HIGHLAND, Jno.	CUM 144		William	NOH 73
John	PHA 75		Wm.	CUM 144		HILEMAN, Martin	SOM 146
HIDENRICK,			HIGHLANDS, James	WAS 56		HILEMANN, Geo.	DAU 50
Susannah	NOU 110		John	FAY 200		HILEN, John	ADA 10
HIDER, Henry	BUC 93A		Thomas	MIF 7A		HILES,	
John	PHA 54		Thos. (Crossed			Christopher	FAY 244
HIDLER, Henry	NOU 147		Out)	MIF 9		Conrad	FAY 197
HIDON, John	PHA 61		William	FAY 250		Frederick	WST 309
HIDRICK, Christn.	PHI 123		HIGHLY, Henry	CHE 856		Jonathan	WST 310
HIEBNER,			HIGHMAN?, Philip	ADA 8		HILEY, Casper	PHI 28
Christopr.	MNT 114		HIGHMILLER, Widow	LAN 254		HILGARD, Francis	MNT 113
Frederick	MNT 53		HIGHNAGLE,			HILGERT, Abraham	NOH 39A
HIEDER, Jacob	BER 245		Valentine.	DAU 34		George	NOH 64A
HIEGE?, George	MNT 68		HIGHT, Christn.	PHA 76		Isaac	NOH 64A
HIEMAN, Peter	NOU 176		James	HNT 158		John	NOH 64A
HIENLY, John	NOU 129		John	CHE 846		Peter	NOH 64A
HIER, Daniel	BER 170		Jonthn.	PHI 74A		HILHOUSE, John	NOU 129
HIESTAND, Jacob	NOH 55A		Nicholas	LAN 10		HILL, Widow	PHI 30
John	NOH 55A		HIGHTS, Jacob	CRA 11		Widow	PHI 87
HIESTANT, Peter	LAN 17		HIGUS, Lorence	YOR 213		Widow	WST 345
HIESTER, Daniel	BER 270		HIKAS, Catharine	ADA 42		---ick	LYC 17
Henry	NOU 183		HIKER?, Eleanor	PHI 54		Abraham	BUC 105
John	BER 170		HIKES, Andw.	CUM 117		Adam	MER 444
HIETER, Adam	BER 166		HILAND, John	NOU 128		Alexd.	FRA 281
Adam	BER 184		Joseph	HNT 146		Ann	PHA 9
Jacob	BER 183		HILANDS, Martha	ALL 115		Archabald	CRA 8
HIF--ER?, Peter	ERI 60A		Mathew	FRA 311		Arthur	HNT 150
HIFELD, Wilm.	ALL 116		HILBERT, Abm.	BER 257		Assa	WST 170
HIFFNER, Jacob	HNT 153		Baltzer	ADA 30		Benj.	PHI 102
John	LAN 67		Bernard	BER 228		Charles	PHI 89
Valentine	HNT 153		Danl.	BER 176		Constant	WAS 52
HIFNER, Christian	LAN 107		Fredk.	BER 257		Daniel	BEV 19
HIGAMIN, John	NOU 183		George	BER 257		Daniel	WST 289
HIGAS, George	YOR 213		John	BER 257		Edwd.	WST 289
Jacob	ADA 42		John Jr.	BER 257		Elizabeth	PHA 29
Jacob	YOR 213		Michl.	MNT 60		Francis	WST 289
HIGBY, Bengamin	ALL 96		Michl. Junr.	MNT 61		Frederick	LAN 42
Joseph	ALL 95		HILBORN, Benjn.	PHA 67		Frederick	BFD 56
Obidia	ALL 95		Joseph	PHA 82		Frederick	NOU 154
Stevan	ALL 95		HILBURN, Samuel	NOU 110		Frederick	BER 225
HIGES, Valentine	YOR 208		Samuel	NOU 110		Frederick	NOH 89A
HIGGANS, Joseph	BFD 43		HILCAP, Peter	DAU 34A		Gasper (Crossed	
Joseph	BFD 43		HILDEBEDLER, John	MNT 82		Out?)	WST 379
HIGGASON, Jos.	PHI 77A		HILDEBIDDLE, Adam	MNT 89		George	MIF 1
HIGGINS, Widw.	PHI 111		John	MNT 94		George	BER 170

HILL, George	WST 290	HILL, Mary	WAS 21	HILLEDOLER?,	
George Revd.	WST 170	Mary	WAS 34	Philip	PHA 118
George	NOH 89A	Mary	PHA 35	HILLEGAS, George	
Godleib	LAN 42	Mary	PHA 93	(B.smith)	BUC 101
Henry	CUM 137	Mathew	FAY 229	George Sen.	BUC 101
Henry	NOU 165	Moses	PHI 66	Michael	PHA 36
Henry	BUC 93A	Peter (See		Michael	NOH 56
Henry	BUC 137A	Hill, Thomas)	LAN 150	HILLEN, Elias	LAN 180
Hugh	MER 444	Peter	DEL 186	Jacob	LAN 182
Isaac	BEV 8	Peter	FAY 209	John	LAN 183
Isaac	BEV 18	Peter	WST 368	HILLENBRAND,	
Isaac	BUC 141	Reece	GRN 95	Conrad	LAN 171
Jacob	PHI 87	Reuben	ERI 58A	HILLER, George	DAU 49A
Jacob	BER 135	Richard	BUC 141	John	LAN 181
Jacob	BER 139	Richard	WST 346	Samuel	LAN 181
Jacob	BER 170	Richard	MER 444	Widow	LAN 262
Jacob	BER 225	Robert	WAS 16	HILLEY, Wm. -.	CHE 847
Jacob	BER 255	Robert	PHI 30	HILLIARD, John W.	
Jacob	WST 368	Robert	BFD 73	Esqr.	WAS 21
Jacob	NOH 55A	Robert	PHA 76	HILLIGAS, Widow?	MNT 134
James	CRA 17	Robert	WAS 80	Adam	MNT 134
James	PHI 43	Robert	GRN 107	Conrad	MNT 134
James	WAS 68	Robert	GRN 108	Conrad	FAY 215
James	PHA 92	Robert	WST 368	Frederick	MNT 134
James	GRN 100	Robt.	PHA 66	George	MNT 134
James	WAS 121	Samuel	DAU 2	Jacob	MNT 134
James	ARM 122	Samuel	PHA 23	Jacob	FAY 215
James	YOR 198	Samuel	GRN 64	John	MNT 134
James	WST 289	Samuel	ARM 126	Michael	MNT 134
James, Esqr.	WST 368	Samuel	HNT 150	Peter	MNT 53
Job?/Joseph?	LYC 13	Samuel	BER 170	Peter	MNT 134
Johannah	PHA 34	Samuel	FAY 209	HILLING, Andrew	PHA 56
John	ADA 4	Shedrick	FAY 198	HILLINGS, Jacob	BUC 162A
John	CRA 6	Stephen	WAS 121	Thomas	BUC 137A
John	LYC 7	Stephen	WAS 121	William	MNT 109
John	BEV 18	Stephen	WAS 121	HILLIOT, Jacob	LUZ 360
John	WAS 37	Susanna	SOM 138	HILLIS, David	CHE 896
John	BFD 43	Thomas	WAS 16	John	CHE 867
John	PHI 44	Thomas	MNT 40	Mathew	WAS 91
John	MNT 60	Thomas	MNT 43	Robert	CHE 867
John	GRN 64	Thomas	WAS 49	William	WAS 38
John	PHA 97	Thomas	BUC 105	William	WST 272
John	WAS 110	Thomas	ALL 112	William	CHE 887
John	CUM 116	Thomas	PHI 145	William	DAU 24A
John	WAS 121	Thomas	BUC 146	HILLMAN, Benjamin	LUZ 337
John	BER 169	Thomas	DEL 157	George	FRA 282
John	DEL 176	Thomas Jnr.	BUC 86A	James	ALL 118
John	BER 181	Thomas & Peter	LAN 150	John	BUC 147A
John	NOU 183	Thos.	YOR 212	John T.	PHA 34
John	WST 191	Widow	LAN 44	Joseph	LUZ 334
John	NOU 198	William	CRA 16	HILLS, Furnace	LAN 149
John	BER 230	William	PHI 64	John	PHA 84
John	FAY 231	William	ARM 127	William	ADA 1
John	FAY 245	William	BUC 141	HILLS?, Michael	MNT 106
John	FRA 276	William	LAN 152	HILMAN, Cornelius	PHA 101
John	FRA 318	William	BER 169	HILPOT, Barnet	BUC 149
John	WST 368	William	WST 170	George	BUC 149
John	CHE 703	William	DEL 188	John	BUC 149
John (Crossed		William	DEL 188	HILSHER, Henry	LAN 303
Out)	LYC 6	William	FAY 209	HILT, Joseph	ADA 24
John	DAU 22A	William	FAY 245	HILTEBIDLE, Jacob	BUC 101
John	PHI 71A	William	BUC 86A	HILTEBRAND, Jacob	CRA 18
John	NOU 97A	Wm.	CUM 25	HILTENBEIDEL,	
John, Capt.	WST 368	Wm.	WST 368	Jacob	LAN 198
Jonathan	BEV 18	Wm. Berry	LYC 17	HILTENBRAND,	
Jonathen	FAY 209	HILL?, William	NOH 73	George	LAN 215
Jonothan	CRA 16	HILLAMAN, David	CHE 847	HILTNER, John	MNT 109
Jos.	PHI 104	HILLARMAN?, Jacob	MNT 40	Michael	MNT 107
Joseph	LYC 13	HILLBORN, Amos	BUC 104	William	MNT 107
Joseph	WAS 37	John	LUZ 390	HILTON, Mathias	FRA 288
Joseph	FAY 209	Robert	BUC 103	Nat	CHE 847
Joseph	WST 345	Thomas	BUC 103	William	DAU 10
Joseph	CHE 763	HILLBURN, Amos	PHI 144	HILTS?, Michael	MNT 106
Joseph Esqr.	WAS 121	Peter Revd.	WST 310	HILTZIMER, Thos.	PHA 84
Joseph	BUC 93A	HILLE, Nichs.	PHI 85A	HILY, Jacob	PHI 45
Lawrance	PHI 85	HILLEBRUSH,	ADA 31	HILYARD, Guy	BUT 356
		No given name)			

HILYARD, James	ALL	52	HINDMAN, John	CHE	887	HINKSON, John	YOR	205
Vollontine	ALL	98	Saml.	PHI	32	Thomas Esqr.	DEL	180
HILYER, Barnet	BUC	87A	Samuel	WAS	3	HINMAN, John	LUZ	414
HIM, Nicholas	WST	238	Thomas	ARM	124	Wheeler	LUZ	409
HIMBBRIGHT?, John	PHI	122	Thomas	WST	160	HINNA, Henry	LAN	197
HIMBELWRIGHT,			HINDS, Bartlett	LUZ	391	HINNEY, James	PHI	45
Wilm.	ALL	58	Benjamin	WAS	38	HINNON, Jas.	WST	289
HIMBERLEY?,			Benjamin	WAS	63	HINROY?, George	LUZ	358
Walliston	BEV	22	Elizabeth	DEL	169	HINS, Samuel	LAN	171
HIME, John	PHI	96A	John	WAS	68	Samuel	LAN	172
William	NOU	122	Michael	HNT	149	HINSHAW?, Andrew	BEV	24
HIMELREICH,			Moses	WAS	80	HINSON, Wm.	BEV	10
William	BER	230	Peter	ALL	119	HINT, Geo.	PHI	117A
HIMELRIGHT,			Stephen	MIF	16	HINTERLITER,		
Charles	PHI	128	HINE, Andrew	NOU	100	Fredk.	BER	188
HIMER, John	PHA	51	Daniel	ALL	78	Maths.	BER	213
HIMES, Widw.	PHI	79A	HINEBACK, Widow	PHI	84	HINTERSHIT, Jacob	BER	135
Benj.	YOR	208	Jacob	PHI	95A	HINTERSHITZ,		
Casper	CHE	794	HINEBAUGH, George	SOM	145	Conrad	BER	168
Catharine C.	CHE	787	Peter	ERI	59A	George	BER	133
Fredk.	PHI	79	HINEMAN, Adam	NOU	97A	HINTON, Barbary	PHA	119
John	FRA	321	James	FAY	203	Wm.	CEN	22B
Paul	MIF	13A	John	ALL	88	HIPERT, Jacob	DAU	31A
Peter	NOU	180	John	WAS	99	HIPGE, Jacob	NOH	35A
Philip	YOR	208	John	BUT	342	HIPP, Godlib	NOH	37A
Thomas	CHE	721	HINER, Robert	WST	252	HIPPLE, Conrod	CHE	904
William	ADA	37	Samuel	BEV	13	Frederick	LAN	7
Wm. Junr.	PHI	86	HINES, Isaac	BUC	105	Henry	CHE	785
HIMMELBERGER,			Jacob	BEV	13	Henry	CHE	788
David	BER	144	Jacob	NOU	97A	Jacob	CHE	782
George	BER	144	John	BUC	105	John	BFD	63
Jacob	BER	144	John	LAN	150	John	CHE	785
HIMMELWRIGHT,			Matthew	CHE	737	John Esqr.	YOR	210
Joseph	BUC	157	Patrick	BUC	81A	Joseph	LAN	116
Samuel	DEL	169	Peter	PHA	88	Lawrance	CHE	885
HIMOY?, George	LUZ	358	Peter	WST	238	HIPSH, Andrew	SOM	129
HIN, Benjamin	LAN	217	Robert	NOU	117	HIPSHER, Fredrik	DAU	11A
HINAMAN, George	PHI	108	William	BUC	105	Jacob	YOR	216
HINBARG, Michael	NOU	143A	Willm. Senr.	PHI	86	HIPSHIRE, Mattw.	CUM	28
Phillip	NOU	143A	HINEY, Wendel	DAU	44A	HIRSCHY,		
HINCH, Ludwig	ADA	14	HINGST, Wm.	CUM	112	Christian	LAN	147B
HINCKEL, (No			HINISH, Henry	BFD	63	Joseph	LAN	147B
Given Name)	DAU	46	HINKEL, John	LAN	300	HIRSH, Frederick	LAN	102
Michael	NOH	33A	Samuel	LAN	229	Henry	BER	215
Michael	NOH	47A	HINKLE, Abraham	BER	277	Joseph	LAN	243
Philip	NOH	75A	Adam	BUC	157	HIRSHY, Abraham	LAN	313
HINCKLE, Mrs.	LYC	7	Adam	PHI	111A	Andrew	LAN	308
John	FRA	293	Caspar	DAU	17A	Christian	LAN	288
HINCKSMAN,			Casper	LAN	115	Jacob	LAN	147B
Chrisn.	PHA	44	Casper	PHI	128	HIRST, Jonathan	FRA	311
HINCLE, Anthy.	PHI	98	Casper	BUC	141	HIRTE, John	LAN	176
Conrad	PHI	98	Charls.	PHI	116	Martin	LUZ	357
Conrad	PHI	70A	Fredrick	ADA	43	HIRTTER, John	WAS	116
Henry	PHI	116A	Gasper	FRA	304	HISBENHEIMER,		
John	PHI	116A	George	BER	276	David	LAN	198
John M. Dr.	PHI	96	Henry	PHI	122	HISE, Daniel	WST	252
Peter	PHI	111A	John	PHI	116	George	WST	380
HINCLINE, George	BUC	80	John	PHI	124	Henry	WST	379
HIND, Simeon	WST	367	John	BUC	157	Michael	LAN	182
HINDBAUGH, Conrod	WST	290	John	PHI	111A	William	WST	380
HINDLE, Adam	YOR	206	Jonathan	LAN	72	HISER, Jacob	MIF	25
Christopher	YOR	206	Jos.	YOR	205	Michael	BUC	159
David	CHE	852	Jos.	PHI	108A	HISERT, Henry	LAN	178
Jacob	YOR	206	Leonard	BUC	157	HISEY, Jacob	LAN	23
John	YOR	206	Michael	BER	220	Jacob	FRA	307
Michael	YOR	206	Peter	PHI	124	Peter	LAN	12
HINDMAN, Widw.	WST	368	Philip	BUC	141	HISKEY, Michael	NOH	59A
Andw.	WST	367	Widow	LAN	72	HISKINS, John	FRA	275
Chr.	WST	273	William	LAN	311	HISLER, Jacob	NOH	41A
David	CHE	763	HINKLE?, Jacob	CHE	890	Peter	PHI	125
James	ALL	85	Jacob	CHE	890	HISONG, John	BFD	63
James	ARM	124	HINKLEMAN, Peter	LAN	252	John	BFD	63
James	FRA	280	HINKNER, Philip	PHI	116	HISS, William	WST	191
John	WAS	68	HINKSON, George	DEL	181	HISSIM, John	WST	272
John	WST	160	James	DEL	180	Thomas	WST	310
John	BUT	351	John	DEL	182	HISSINGER, Henry	DAU	38

HISSNER, Adam	LAN	210	HOALSTAIN, Jacob	FRA	283	HOCKMAN, Henr	DAU	39
HIST?, Henry	FRA	284	HOAN, Stophel	CUM	127	Henry	BUC	96A
HISTAND, Abram	MNT	134	HOAP, Anthony	MNT	132	Jacob Jnr.	BUC	91
Elizabeth	LAN	314	HOAR, Benjamin	LAN	122	Jacob	BUC	90A
Jacob	LAN	315	Isaac	LAN	119	Ulrick	BUC	91
Jacob Senr.	LAN	315	John	LAN	133	HOCOLY, Fredk.	PHI	104A
John	LAN	309	Jonathan	LAN	132	HOCOMILLER, Jacob	PHI	69A
HISTANS, Peter	LAN	285	Joseph	LAN	126	HODDESPOLE,		
HISTANT, Johns	YOR	165	HOASTER, Conrad	LAN	11	Frederick	GRN	101
HISTEL, Irwin	NOU	143A	HOB, Peter	BFD	63	HODDGS, Joseph	NOU	158
HITCHCOCK, Danl.	PHI	8	HOBART, Hannah	PHA	4	HODGDEN, Saml.	PHA	79
Joseph	LUZ	318	Robert E.	MNT	57	HODGE, Andrew	PHA	82
Mary	LUZ	322	HOBBS, Hanson	WAS	91	Hannah	PHA	20
Randal	WAS	99	Samuel	HNT	158	Isaac	CUM	45
HITCHEN, Richard	ADA	32	Solomon	GRN	81	Sarah	LUZ	341
HITCHINS, Charles	BUC	155	HOBSON, John	PHA	118	William	ADA	38
HITCHISON, Robt.	CHE	728	Moses	MNT	73	William	HNT	138
HITCHLER?, Geo.	PHI	18A	HOBSTON, Joseph	WST	252	William	WST	324
HITE, Charles	MIF	7A	HOCH, Abraham	BER	230	William	MER	445
Christopher	BFD	73	Abraham	BER	257	Wm.	PHI	82A
Cunrod	SOM	154	Daniel	BER	226	HODGEHY, Daniel	FRA	299
David	CEN	22B	Daniel	BER	230	HODGESHINS, James	FRA	285
HITHERLY, George	HNT	137	David	BER	255	HODGSON, Abel	CHE	870
HITLER, Christian	LAN	182	George	ADA	14	Thomas	PHA	17A
HITNER, Daniel	MNT	107	George	LAN	139	HODLEY, Mobell	CHE	862
George	MNT	77	John	BER	230	HODSON, Saml.	PHI	138
HITSMILLER,			John	BER	245	HOE, George	FRA	289
George	ADA	32	Joseph	BER	257	George Senr.	FRA	289
John	ADA	32	Philip	BER	255	HOEFFER, Jacob	LAN	39
Martin	ADA	32	Samuel	BER	230	HOEMAN, Michael	SOM	158
HITT?, George	WAS	12	HOCHSTEDLER, John	BER	270	HOEPKER, James/		
HITTADEL, George	NOU	100	Joseph	BER	202	Johanes?	DAU	45A
HITTEL, George	NOH	30	HOCHSTETLER,			HOESTATLER,		
Nicholas	NOH	55A	Henry	BER	203	Daniel	GRN	70
Peter	NOH	55A	HOCHSTETTER,			Samuel	GRN	70
Peter	NOH	55A	Chrisn.	LAN	8	HOET, John	BER	133
Widow	NOH	69	John	LAN	147	HOETH, Chas.	PHA	36
HITTENBRAND,			HOCHTELIN,			HOEVER, Jno.	DAU	38A
Peter	LAN	171	Abraham	ADA	22	HOEY, John	WAS	110
HITTER, George	NOH	75A	Hesekiah	ADA	22	Thomas	WAS	37
HITTLE, Adam	MNT	134	Hesekiah Sen.	ADA	22	HOFF, Adam	YOR	188
Adam	BER	262	Wm.	ADA	27	Amos	LUZ	347
Barthow.	CUM	48	HOCK, Andrew	FRA	275	Andrew	LAN	304
David	NOU	147	David	BER	254	Benj.	LYC	27
Frederick	NOU	110	George	DAU	28	Charles	MNT	73
Michael	NOU	147	Melchior	NOH	30	Charles	MNT	127
Nicholas	BER	262	Peter	FAY	257	Daniel	YOR	214
Nicholas Jr.	BER	262	HOCKAEYE, Saml.	PHI	95A	David	NOH	78
Philip	PHI	74A	HOCKENBERG,			Edmond	LYC	6
HITWOL, Jacob	LAN	84	Caspar	HNT	142	George	LAN	41
HITZEL, Peter	BER	263	HOCKENBERRY,			George	PHA	76
HITZLER, Widow	LAN	98	-----	FRA	322	Henry	YOR	178
HIVELY, Jacob	YOR	157	Henry	FRA	322	Hermina	DAU	18A
Sophia	YOR	160	James	FRA	322	Isaiah	NOH	78
HIVINER, Jacob	BUC	142	John	FRA	322	Jacob	YOR	165
HIX, Conrad	BER	281	Peter	FRA	322	Jacob	PHI	114A
George	DAU	43	Phillip	FRA	322	John	LYC	23
George	BER	142	Wm.	FRA	322	John	LYC	28
Henry	BER	203	HOCKENBERY, Henry	HNT	141	John	LAN	34
John	BER	203	HOCKER, Adam	DAU	19A	John	YOR	216
HIXAM, John	NOU	104	George	MNT	108	John	BER	240
HIXMAN, Joseph	BER	213	Jno.	CUM	60	John	NOH	33A
HIXON, Abner	NOU	105	John	DAU	19	Jonathan	YOR	201
David	NOU	193	Leonard	PHI	72	Margaret	PHA	69
Isaiah	BFD	43	Martin	DAU	47	Michael	MNT	97
HIXSON, James	NOU	117	Martin	MNT	109	Michael	BER	139
HIYSER, John	MNT	127	Martin 2nd	MNT	109	Peter	YOR	215
HNEER?, Henry	CHE	791	Stophel	DAU	12	Saml.	YOR	186
HO-----?, Elias	MIF	10	HOCKIN, Wm.	PHI	69A	Wm.	LYC	28
HOAFMAN, Isaac	LAN	249	HOCKINS, Joshua	GRN	73	HOFFA?, Henry	BER	240
HOAK, Jacob	MNT	94	HOCKLEY, Elioner	PHA	41	John	DAU	49A
HOAKE, Adam Senr.	CUM	109	Sarah	MNT	103	HOFFENDER, Richd.	PHI	11A
Conrad	LAN	223	Thos.	PHA	75	HOFFER, Abraham	BER	181
Henry	LAN	218	HOCKMAN,			Christian	LAN	144
Jacob	LAN	219	Christian	BUC	92	Isaac	CUM	93
Jacob	LAN	226	Daniel	DAU	15	Melcher	CUM	78

Name	Loc	Page
HOFFER, Philip	BER	215
HOFFERT, George	DAU	20A
John	BER	169
John	LAN	312
John	DAU	20A
Joseph	BUC	159
Joseph	LAN	181
Ulrich	BER	169
HOFFHEINS, Jacob	LAN	115
HOFFMAN, Widow	PHI	88A
Adam	MIF	10
Adam	MNT	113
Andrew	MNT	99
Andw. Junr.	MNT	99
Anthony	BER	157
Baltis	LAN	198
Baltzer	MNT	45
Barthold	NOH	89A
Benjamin	CHE	884
Casper	PHI	87
Casper	BER	232
Chris.	LAN	90
Chrisn.	LAN	261
Christian	ADA	31
Christian	DAU	6A
Conrad	BUC	139
Conrad	LAN	217
Corneluis	BER	157
Daniel	ADA	20
Daniel	MNT	45
Daniel	MNT	134
David	PHI	125
David	YOR	211
David	BER	273
Detreik	FRA	292
Frances	BUC	89A
Frederick	LAN	284
Geo.	CUM	22
George	LAN	90
George	BER	277
George	FRA	312
George	CHE	884
George	DAU	5A
George	NOH	41A
George	NOH	75A
Godfreid	LAN	79
Henry	NOH	90
Henry	MNT	99
Henry	CHE	906
Henry	NOH	44A
Jacob	LAN	19
Jacob	DAU	31
Jacob	PHA	57
Jacob	PHI	59
Jacob	MNT	69
Jacob	NOH	90
Jacob	BER	156
Jacob	BER	230
Jacob	LAN	262
Jacob	BER	276
Jacob	LAN	301
Jacob	CHE	703
Jacob	DAU	41A
James	PHI	89
John	PHI	1
John	CUM	22
John	PHI	26
John	LAN	90
John	MNT	99
John	BUC	139
John	BUC	157
John	BER	161
John	CHE	783
John Junr.	NOH	90
John	DAU	5A
John	DAU	6A
HOFFMAN, John	DAU	6A
John	PHI	88A
John	NOH	89A
Libs	LAN	210
Ludwig	NOH	30
Marc	NOH	75A
Michael	NOH	30
Michael	BER	221
Michael	LAN	298
Michael	LUZ	345
Michael	NOH	44A
Michl.	DAU	51A
Nicholas	MNT	112
Nicolaus	DAU	6A
Peter	NOH	45
Peter	NOH	90
Philip	MNT	138
Philip	YOR	166
Philip	YOR	216
Philip	LAN	284
Philip Jr.	YOR	166
Philip	NOH	62A
Philip	NOH	64A
Phillip	CUM	33
Samuel	LAN	197
Sebastian	PHI	89
Valentine	LAN	54
Volentine	PHA	60
Widow	CUM	23
Widow	BUC	139
William	MNT	45
William	BUC	139
William	NOH	44A
Wolfgate	PHA	60
HOFFMEISTER, Henry	BER	181
HOFFMEYER, Henry Revd.	NOH	47A
HOFFMNA, George	NOH	89A
Peter Sr.	NOH	89A
HOFFNER, George	PHI	3
George	DEL	169
George, Junr.	PHI	2
Henry	PHA	74
Jacob	PHI	10
Jacob	FRA	289
Lucy	PHA	119
Rebecca	PHA	39
Sophia	PHA	57
HOFFSTICKLER, Henry	DEL	171
HOPHEINS, Sebastian	YOR	174
HOFMAN, (No Given Name)	LAN	147B
Adam	YOR	188
Adam	YOR	212
Charles	YOR	176
Chris.	DAU	36
Conrad	DAU	29
Danl.	BER	154
Fredk.	DAU	29
Fredk.	YOR	174
George	PHI	87
George	BER	206
George	BER	248
Godfry	PHI	124
Henry	ADA	19
Henry	BER	142
Henry	BER	259
Jacob	DAU	19
Jacob	PHI	141
Jacob	YOR	175
John	BER	185
John	YOR	219
John Jr.	YOR	219
HOFMAN, John	DAU	20A
Ludwig	BER	170
Martin	ADA	27
Michael	YOR	183
Michael	BER	206
Michael	BER	248
Michael	BER	257
Michael	LAN	261
Nicholas	YOR	174
Nicholas	YOR	175
Philip	YOR	175
Valentine	BER	273
William	PHI	127
HOFNAGLE, Jacob	BER	246
HOG, James	ALL	53
Mary	ALL	55
Thomas	ALL	110
HOGAN, David	PHA	4
James	DEL	164
James	BUT	353
John	MIF	25
Joseph	PHI	147
Michael	DEL	163
HOGAN?, (See Hgan)	MIF	17
HOGARTH, John	PHA	118
HOGE, Christian	FRA	282
David	CUM	63
David	WAS	116
Ebenezer	NOU	165
Geo.	CUM	72
George	GRN	100
James	CUM	74
James	MER	445
Jas.	CUM	54
John	CUM	54
John	NOU	165
John	YOR	214
John	FAY	236
John Esquire	WAS	12
Jonathan Jr.	CUM	63
Michl.	CUM	61
Robert	WAS	68
Saml.	CUM	49
Solomon	GRN	64
Thomas	GRN	64
Thomas	WST	214
William Esqr.	WAS	12
HOGE?, George	FAY	227
HOGELIN, Henerey	MER	445
HOGENBERGER, George	LAN	10
HOGENDOBLER, John	LAN	286
HOGENSCHILT, John	NOH	41A
HOGENTOBLER, Ann	LAN	311
Isaac	LAN	315
John	LAN	315
Susanna	LAN	315
HOGG, George	PHI	22
James	CHE	750
James	CHE	859
James	MIF	7A
John	BEV	21
John	WAS	21
Letitia	MIF	7A
Robert	CHE	859
Robt.	CHE	749
William	FAY	238
HOGGAT, Samuel	PHI	21
HOGGINS, Merrit	BUC	93A
HOGHLANDER, George	DAU	47A
HOGINIRE, Cunrod	SOM	129
HOGLAND, Amos	LYC	9
Daniel	BUC	143
Derrick Jn.	BUC	143A

HOGLAND, Derrick	BUC	143A	HOLDIMAN, John	HNT	145	HOLLEBECK, Geo.	CUM	47
John	MNT	64	HOLDINBRENT,			HOLLEBUSH,		
Joseph	LYC	9	Michal	ALL	96	Christian	BER	230
HOGLEN, Samuel	NOU	164	HOLDREN, Joseph	WAS	3	John	MNT	75
William	NOU	165	HOLDRIDGE, Dudley	LUZ	388	Peter	BER	230
HOGMIRE, Samuel	BFD	43	HOLDRY, John	BER	169	HOLLECK, Charles	PHA	66
HOGSHEAD, John	WAS	20	John Jr.	BER	169	HOLLEM, Abraham	HNT	127
HOGUE, Jacob	NOU	198	HOLDSHIP, George	ALL	49	HOLLEN, John	FAY	256
Samuel	NOU	187	HOLDTS, John	YOR	208	William	WST	151
HOHENSHILD,			HOLE, Abm.	PHI	101	HOLLENBACH,		
George	NOH	73	Henry	CUM	103	Conrad	BER	277
HOHL, Aphrean	LAN	138	HOLEM, George	CHE	781	George	NOH	51A
Peter	LAN	147A	HOLEMAN, Eli	VEN	165	Henry	BER	279
HOIL, Henry	LAN	237	Richard	PHA	118	Nicholas	BER	160
HOKE, Andrew	YOR	163	HOLEMES, Joseph	WAS	21	Peter	BER	188
Casper	YOR	178	HOLESISON, Jacob	NOU	117	HOLLENBACK, John	LUZ	322
Conrad	ADA	8	HOLESWORTH,			Matthias	LUZ	321
Conrad	YOR	181	Samuel	ADA	20	HOLLER, Catherine	BER	222
Frederick	YOR	165	HOLGATE,			David	LUZ	371
Fredk.	YOR	175	Cornelius	PHI	142	Francis	YOR	164
Fredk.	YOR	210	Jacob	PHI	124	Geo.	CUM	46
Henry	ADA	10	William	PHI	124	Henry	BFD	50
Jacob	YOR	161	William	MNT	138	Jesse	NOU	176
John	YOR	178	HOLIDA, Eliza	PHA	61	Jno.	CUM	40
Martin	LAN	111	HOLIDAY, James	WAS	7	Joseph	LAN	23
Peter	YOR	161	John	WAS	68	Philip	BER	220
Peter Jr.	YOR	161	HOLINGER,			Valentine	BFD	50
Phillip	FRA	278	Christn.	DAU	20	HOLLIDAY, Hugh	LAN	160
Rudy	DAU	7	George	LAN	14	John	HNT	120
HOKER, Jacob	FRA	291	HOLINGSHEAD,			John	FRA	271
HOLABACK, Henry	NOU	137	Anthony	NOU	193	John	FRA	321
HOLBEIN,			HOLINGSWORTH,			Mary	HNT	120
Christian	NOH	53	John	LYC	9	Robt.	CUM	52
Christian	NOH	51A	HOLL, Abraham	YOR	218	Samuel	ERI	58
Jacob Jn.	NOH	53	Christian	LAN	74	Sarah	HNT	120
Jacob Senr.	NOH	53	Henry	LAN	85	Thos.	FRA	319
Peter	NOH	53	Jacob	LAN	85	William	HNT	121
HOLBERE, John	CUM	78	James	PHI	28	HOLLINBACK,		
HOLBERT, John	YOR	200	John	ADA	32	Henery	MER	444
HOLBIG, Frederick	NOH	51A	John	YOR	168	Matthias	MER	444
Peter	NOH	53	John	LAN	210	HOLLINGER,		
HOLBY, Dewald	NOH	85	John	LAN	220	Christopher	ADA	11
John	PHI	147	Melchior	BER	169	Christr.	CUM	79
Lowrence	NOH	85	Michael	YOR	188	Daniel	LAN	146
William	PHI	147	Nicholas	ADA	36	Jacob	YOR	211
HOLCOM, Widow	CEN	22A	Peter Junr.	LAN	217	Jacob	FRA	299
HOLCOMB, Eli	LUZ	424	Peter Senr.	LAN	217	John	BER	252
Hugh	LUZ	409	Saml.	LAN	74	Nathaniel	FRA	305
John	BUC	145	Wendle	LAN	78	Phillip	FRA	305
Jonah	LUZ	408	HOLLABUSH, Adam	MNT	94	Thomas	LAN	145
Jonathan	LUZ	423	Henry	MNT	73	Tobias	FRA	305
Samuel	BUC	151A	Henry	MNT	94	Valentine	ADA	37
Trueman	LUZ	410	Peter	MNT	94	HOLLINGSHEAD,		
HOLCROFT, John	WAS	68	HOLLADAY, Francis	WST	345	James	BFD	47
HOLCUM, Eli	PHI	93A	HOLLAN, John	FRA	284	Lucy	PHA	22
HOLDEN, Jeremh.	PHI	19	HOLLAND, Mr.	PHA	52	HOLLINGSWORTH,		
John	GRN	111	Ann	PHA	26	Abner	CHE	836
Richard	WAS	121	Barny	FRA	291	David	HNT	129
HOLDENHOUSE,			Benj.	MNT	141	David Junr.	HNT	129
Henry	HNT	128	Jonathn.	FAY	257	Isaac	CHE	836
HOLDER, Charles	WST	367	Jos.	YOR	198	Israel	HNT	129
George	NOH	90	Lilly	DEL	169	Jehu	PHA	101
John	BER	184	Mary	YOR	162	Joseph	MIF	5
John	YOR	205	Nathaniel	PHA	6	Levy	DAU	47
John	BER	247	Othey	FAY	257	Levy	PHA	106
HOLDERMAN, Abram	CHE	859	Peter	BER	232	Nathl.	CHE	704
Christian	BUC	105	Robert	MNT	106	Wm.	CHE	838
Christn.	CHE	892	HOLLAR, Matthew	NOU	176	HOLLINGWORTH,		
Christopher	CHE	796	HOLLAS, William	MNT	131	James	PHI	94A
Danl.	CHE	892	HOLLDEMAN, John	BER	285	Robert	CHE	707
Jacob	CHE	894	HOLLEBACH, Geo.	BER	285	HOLLINSHEAD,		
Jacob	CHE	905	John G.	BER	147	James Esqr.	NOH	78
John	BUC	105	Killian	BER	187	HOLLIS, James	CHE	749
Joseph	BUC	155A	HOLLEBACK, John			Joseph	CHE	828
Nichs.	CHE	789	N.	BER	147	Thomas	LUZ	411
Samuel	BER	273	Nicholas	BER	188	Thomas	CHE	750

HOLLIS, Widow	CHE	826	HOLMAN, John	CHE	777	HOLSOR, George	FRA	291
William	HNT	121	John	CHE	782	HOLSSRUNER?, Paul	WAS	122
HOLLISTER, John	LUZ	363	Michael	CHE	908	HOLSTEIN, Mathias	MNT	104
Stephen	LUZ	333	Philip	CHE	791	Samuel	MNT	104
HOLLMAN, George	PHI	116A	Stephen	CHE	785	HOLSTINE, George	DAU	37A
Henry	MNT	127	Widow	LAN	28	HOLSTON, Benjamin	DEL	172
Isaac	MNT	82	HOLME, Jacques	PHI	155	John	DEL	172
John	MNT	82	John	PHI	152	Joseph	DEL	173
HOLLMANZ?,			John Junr.	PHI	155	Mathias	PHI	58
Ferdinand	MNT	115	Thomas	PHI	152	Matthias	DEL	168
HOLLOBACH, Peter	LAN	101	HOLMES, Abram	CUM	93	Michael	BUC	158
HOLLOBAUGH,			Abram	LUZ	372	Peter	PHI	64
Christopher	ADA	36	Adam	NOU	176	HOLSY, Andrew	ERI	60A
Martin	ADA	36	Andrew	WAS	68	HOLT, Evan	CEN	20A
Wm.	ADA	22	Andw.	CUM	85	George	PHA	19
HOLLOBOCH,			Andw. Senr.	CUM	84	Jesse	MNT	50
Christopher	ADA	23	Cornelius	NOU	171	John	FAY	245
HOLLOBOCK,			Danl.	CUM	83	John	CEN	22A
Nichls.	CUM	42	Enoch	LUZ	365	Levi	MNT	67
HOLLOCK, Michael	PHA	68	Esther	CHE	755	Mordecai	MNT	50
Philips	PHA	99	Frances	WAS	100	Robert	PHI	47
HOLLODAY, William	LAN	129	George	CUM	135	Robert Junr.	CUM	108
HOLLOWAY, Isaac	MER	444	George	CUM	136	Robt.	CUM	107
John	MER	444	Hannah	PHA	5	Sarah	MNT	50
William	BFD	74	Henry	WAS	49	Willm.	MIF	17
HOLLOWBUSH, Peter	PHI	103	Hugh	CUM	126	HOLTAIN, Matthias	LAN	210
Yost	PHA	38	James	WAS	90	HOLTAN, John	ALL	70
HOLLOWDAY, James	FAY	203	Jas.	CUM	62	HOLTEMAN, John	DAU	51A
Nichs.	PHI	111	Jno.	CUM	99	HOLTENSTINE,		
HOLLOWELL,			John	PHA	62	Samuel	BER	169
Anthony	MNT	43	John	WAS	100	HOLTER, David	LAN	262
Benj., Junr	MNT	35	John	PHI	117	HOLTIDAY, Saml.	MIF	25
Benjamin	MNT	35	John	MER	445	HOLTON, David	PHA	103
Benjamin	MNT	69	John	CHE	755	Thos.	CHE	746
Caleb	MNT	35	Jonathen	NOU	193	HOLTRIE, George	LAN	210
Daniel	MNT	40	Joseph Jr.	CUM	135	HOLTRIN, Peter	LAN	210
Ephraim	PHI	114	Joseph Senr.	CUM	135	HOLTS, Jno.	CUM	57
George	MNT	37	Joshua	PHI	34	HOLTSHETER, Peter	DAU	31A
Hester	PHA	117	Richard	DEL	186	HOLTZ, George	DAU	40
Jesse	MNT	35	Robert	WAS	90	Henry	BFD	37
Jesse	MNT	64	Robert	DEL	192	Jacob	BFD	73
John	MNT	35	Robert	NOU	193	Jacob	YOR	184
John	MNT	50	Seth	LUZ	384	Michael	CUM	135
John	PHA	105	Thomas	WAS	52	Michael	YOR	176
John	CHE	731	Thomas	NOU	164	HOLTZAPLE, Mary		
Jos.	PHI	114	William	PHI	39	Widow	LAN	3
Joseph	MNT	64	William	WAS	49	HOLTZAPPLE,		
Marhta	MNT	35	William	WAS	90	Barnet	YOR	163
Mathew	MNT	35	Wm.	CUM	84	HOLTZINGER,		
Mathw. Junr.	MNT	42	Wm.	PHA	86	Conrad	LAN	63
Nathan	MNT	35	Zalmon	LUZ	383	George	LAN	286
Peter	MNT	38	HOLMON, Michal	ALL	69	John	YOR	168
Samuel	MNT	130	HOLMS, Isaac	ADA	14	William	YOR	167
Thomas	MNT	50	James	MIF	17	HOLTZMAN,		
Thos.	MNT	77	Thomas	ADA	14	Gotfried	BER	272
Wm.	MNT	34	Zalmon	LUZ	384	Henry	BER	153
Wm.	PHI	104	HOLMSBERCE?,			Jacob	BER	279
Wm.	PHI	108	Willm.	PHI	153	Peter	BER	270
Wm.	MNT	111	HOLONES, William			HOLTZWORTH, Adam	LAN	56
HOLLOWPETER, Jno.	CUM	36	(Negro)	WAS	21	HOLVERSTAT, Jacob	HNT	128
HOLLWELL, Jesse	MNT	132	HOLSAPLE, Adam	CUM	115	HOLVERSTOT,		
John	MNT	130	HOLSAPPLE, Henry	NOU	183	George	PHA	29
HOLLY, Dennis	FRA	295	HOLSBACH, Henry	DAU	36	HOLWAY, Henry	FRA	313
Ludwick	CUM	61	HOLSECAMP, Garret	PHI	22	HOLZ, George	DAU	22A
HOLMAM, John	ALL	117	HOLSER, Jacob	WST	310	HOLZBERGER, Andw.	DAU	43
HOLMAN, Adam	HNT	164	HOLSHIP, Thos.	FRA	313	HOMAN, Abraham	PHA	61
Conrad	CHE	785	HOLSHOE, George	NOH	75A	Henry	BER	240
Conrod	CHE	793	HOLSHUE, George	BER	176	John	BER	240
Frederick	CHE	784	HOLSINGER, George	BFD	63	John	BER	248
Henry	MNT	44	Jacob	ADA	14	Joseph	PHI	53A
Henry	MNT	126	Jacob	YOR	208	Saml.	BER	240
Issabella	CEN	20	Jacob	FRA	307	HOMAND, Josiah	PHI	65
Jacob	MNT	104	John	BFD	63	HOMBERG, Ann	PHA	40
John	MIF	10	Wm.	WST	215	HOMBERGER, Jacob	LAN	197
John	MNT	77	HOLSMAN, George	DAU	7A	HOME?, Michl	FRA	290
John	ALL	116	HOLSMANN, John	DAU	37A	HOMEN, Ebezr.	FAY	227

HOMEN, Fredrick	FAY 227	HOOD, Jno.	WAR 1A	HOOPENGARDENER,		
HOMER, Barbara	YOR 199	John	PHI 13	John	WAS 75
James	LAN 247	John	PHI 30	HOOPENGARDNER,	
John	LUZ 388	John	PHA 58	George	BFD 44
HOMER?, John	LAN 262	John	WAS 80	HOOPER, Benjamin	BFD 43
HOMERCOM, Henry	LAN 305	John	BUC 159	Isaac	WAS 99
HOMES, James	ALL 58	John	CHE 754	John	BFD 44
John	FRA 278	John P.	PHA 48	John	ALL 110
Obidia	ALL 102	Joseph	DEL 179	John	FAY 203
Thomas	ALL 59	Moses	LYC 29	Paul	LAN 141
Thomas	WST 310	Robert	BEV 21	Phillop	ALL 110
Thomas	WST 345	Saml.	MIF 25	Sarah	HNT 138
Thomas	WST 346	Saml.	CHE 746	Thomas	HNT 139
HOMILLER, Mary	MNT 47	Thomas	PHI 9	Thomas	DEL 169
HOMISH, (No Given		Thomas	PHA 101	Thomas	FAY 198
Name)	LAN 145	William	WST 237	HOOPERT, Daniel	ADA 22
HOMLER, Andrew	BFD 44	HOODRICK, Rebecca	LUZ 370	HOOPES, Abiah	CHE 808
HOMMANN, John	PHA 74	HOOEY, William	MER 446	Abner	CHE 700
HOMMINGER, Tacy	PHA 111	HOOF, John	DAU 8A	Abraham	CHE 701
HOMPSTON, John	CRA 2	John	BUC 149A	Amos	CHE 701
HOMRICK?, Henry	BUC 147A	HOOFAIRE, Michael	MNT 115	Benjn.	CHE 704
HOMSHAR?, Peter	MNT 89	HOOFBAUGH, George	MIF 5	Caleb	CHE 838
HON, Andrew	NOU 183	HOOFF, John	DEL 186	Daniel	CHE 767
Michael	NOU 183	Samuel	DEL 187	David	CHE 861
HONCEMAN, Andw.	NOU 176	HOOFFMAN, Joseph	CHE 705	Elisha?	CHE 705
HONE, Adam	PHI 103	HOOFMAN, Daniel	HNT 131	Emor	CHE 709
John	HNT 160	Henry	WST 289	Enos	CHE 837
HONEBOUGH,		John	MNT 94	Ezekiel	CHE 743
Valintine	WST 252	Lewas	ALL 89	Ezra	CHE 743
HONECKER, Heny	BER 254	Peter	HNT 152	George	CHE 702
HONEL, Mc Mu-in?	DAU 13A	HOOFNAGEL, Adolph	PHI 128	George	CHE 758
HONEY, Catharine	PHA 72	Geoege	LAN 40	Henry	CHE 700
George	PHA 40	HOOFNAGLE, Danl.	DAU 22A	Isacher	CHE 849
HONEYCOMB, Mr.	PHA 78	Jacob	DAU 22A	Israel	CHE 704
HONG, Andrew	PHI 142	John	ADA 27	Jabez	CHE 700B
Valentine	PHI 143	Peter	LAN 54	Jacob	CHE 743
HONNAGIM?, Andr.	FRA 279	Peter	LAN 61	Jesse	CHE 702
HONNAKER, Jacob	PHI 53A	HOOG, Jacob	NOH 33A	John	CHE 700
HONNALL, Jacob	MER 444	John	NOH 73A	John	CHE 861
HONNINGS, John	NOH 85A	HOOH, Adam	LAN 198	John	CHE 900
HONSBERGER,		HOOK, Anthony	LAN 37	Jonathan	CHE 861
George	BER 174	Conrad	FRA 303	Joseph	CHE 705
HONSHOLD, Sarah	PHI 71	Henry	BEV 23	Joseph	CHE 816
HOOBER, Abraham	LAN 109	James	GRN 101	Joshua	CHE 808
Abraham	LAN 109	James Junr.	GRN 66	Moses	CHE 707
Abraham	LAN 218	John	ADA 5	Nathan	CHE 865
Andrew	DAU 27	John	PHI 28	Stephen	CHE 703
Christian	LAN 238	John	PHI 155	Thomas	CHE 700B
Christian	LAN 239	John	PHI 104A	William	CHE 762
Christian	LAN 243	Mathew	BEV 22	William	CHE 769
Christian	LAN 308	Michael	LAN 28	HOOPFIELD,	
Henry	LAN 115	Samuel	FAY 231	Charles	PHA 59
Henry	LAN 223	HOOKE, John	BER 273	HOOPINGARDNER,	
Henry	LAN 235	Matthias	HNT 118	Casper	BFD 73
Jacob	DAU 27	HOOKER, Jacob	BUC 147A	HOOPLICK, Conrad	FRA 282
Jacob	LAN 218	HOOKEY, Widow	PHI 96	HOOPPER, Robert	WST 252
Jacob	LAN 224	HOOKS, Thomas	ARM 124	HOOPS, Abner	DEL 190
Jacob Senr.	LAN 235	HOOKS?, James	YOR 210	Abraham	DEL 172
John	LAN 234	HOOKY, Widw.	PHI 92	Amasa	DEL 180
John	LAN 235	Anthy.	PHI 96	Amos	DEL 192
John	LAN 235	HOOLEY, John	HNT 160	Daniel	DEL 172
Martin	LAN 235	HOOLY, Chresly	MIF 15	Isaac	DEL 175
Martin	LAN 236	John	MIF 15	Israel	PHA 72
Peter	LAN 239	HOOMAN, Fredk.	DAU 49	Joshua	DEL 190
Widow	LAN 235	HOON, Felty	CUM 117	Seth	DEL 173
HOOBER?, Jacob	CHE 893	Garret	PHI 95A	HOOPS?, James	YOR 210
HOOBLER, Adam	CUM 49	Henry	DAU 11	HOOT, Jacob	MNT 119
Catharine	CUM 49	John	SOM 132	Peter	MNT 44
Jacob	CUM 49	HOONLY, Phillip	CUM 81	HOOVEN, Francis	MNT 69
Jno.	CUM 50	HOOP, Adam	ALL 69	HOOVER, Widow	PHI 8
Michl.	CUM 49	George	BFD 44	(Martin)	CEN 22B
HOOBOUGHER, Jacob	HNT 150	George	BFD 44	Abraham	DAU 20
HOOD, Alexd.	FRA 278	Henry	MIF 12A	Abraham	HNT 147
Edward	PHA 111	Thomas	ALL 96	Abraham	DAU 3A
George	PHI 16	HOOPE, Adam	WST 272	Adam	HNT 127
James	WAS 80	James	WST 252	Andrew	FAY 215

Name	Loc
HOOVER, Andrew	DAU 33A
Casper	SOM 138
Christian	HNT 127
Christly	FRA 284
Christn.	DAU 20
Christn.	CUM 43
Christn.	DAU 15A
Christn.	DAU 18A
Christopher	HNT 132
Christr.	CUM 142
Crisly	MIF 16
Daniel	HNT 122
Daniel	FRA 284
Emanuel	WAS 44
Emanuel	LUZ 356
Felix	LUZ 330
Frederic	SOM 138
George	ADA 15
George	SOM 138
George	YOR 175
George	FAY 256
George	FAY 261
George	DAU 41A
Henerey	MER 445
Henrey	FAY 261
Henry	MIF 10
Henry	ADA 13
Henry	ADA 26
Henry	WAS 44
Henry	CUM 104
Henry	MNT 104
Henry	YOR 178
Henry	FRA 316
Henry	LUZ 346
Henry	MIF 12A
Jacob	WAS 21
Jacob	BFD 63
Jacob	PHI 104
Jacob	HNT 118
Jacob	HNT 128
Jacob	CUM 152
Jacob (Crossed Out)	SOM 129
Jacob	CEN 22A
Jno.	CUM 66
John	DAU 10
John	DAU 11
John	LAN 17
John	DAU 20
John	DAU 31
John	PHA 38
John	YOR 175
John	YOR 194
John	FAY 256
John	FRA 279
John	FRA 315
John	LUZ 356
John	CEN 22B
John	DAU 20A
John	DAU 33A
Joseph	FAY 215
Marey	FAY 215
Martin	FRA 287
Michael	LAN 3
Michael	DAU 40
Michael	SOM 138
Michael	DAU 32A
Michael	DAU 44
Michl.	CEN 18A
Michl.	BFD 63
Peter	FRA 279
Peter	FRA 289
Peter Sr.	WST 215
Peter, Jr.	WST 215
Philip	BFD 38
Phillip	FRA 310
HOOVER, Susanna	DAU 3
Widdow	FAY 251
HOOVER?, Jacob	CHE 893
HOOVERES, Andrew	DAU 6A
Andrew, Daniel & Jacob In Same H.h.	DAU 6A
Daniel	DAU 6A
Jacob	DAU 6A
HOPE, Adam	CHE 873
Conrad	NOU 122
Godfry	PHI 129
Hannah	CHE 842
James	BEV 5
Phillip	NOU 105
Phillip	NOU 122
Richd.	MIF 15
Robt.	MIF 17
Thomas	CHE 842
Thos.	PHA 30
Tobias	CHE 722
William	CRA 4
HOPELL, George	FRA 300
HOPER, Cornelius	NOU 100
Paul	NOU 100
HOPHES, George	MER 445
HOPKINS,	
Alexander	WAS 80
Alexander	DEL 182
Calab	NOU 158
Elisha B.	MNT 40
Eward	ALL 88
George	FAY 240
Hezekiah	PHI 153
Isaac	LUZ 353
Jacob (Molato Man)	ALL 71
James	LAN 35
James	HNT 125
James	LUZ 354
John	PHA 4
John	WAS 110
John	WST 151
John Esqr.	LAN 128
Johns	PHA 14
Joseph	FAY 240
Marey	FAY 197
Marey	FAY 266
Matthew	DEL 156
Matthew	WST 324
Nathaniel	ERI 57A
Patrick	PHI 51
Rebecca	PHA 76
Richard	PHA 16
Richd.	FRA 298
Robert	PHA 112
Stephen	LUZ 426
Thomas	WAS 80
Thomas	PHA 120
Timothy	LUZ 354
William	PHA 7
Wm.	PHI 81
HOPKINSON, Joseph	PHA 90
HOPP, Andrew	BER 254
George	BER 254
HOPPER, Isaac T.	PHA 98
Jacob	NOH 51A
James	CHE 721
Levy	PHA 9
William	NOU 100
HOPPLE, Geo.	PHI 94
George	PHA 74
Jacob	MNT 87
Joseph	MNT 85
HOPPLES, David	YOR 214
HOPS, Saml.	PHI 73A
HOPSON, Elizabeth	CHE 864
Elizabeth Warden Of The Single Sisters House	NOH 70
Francis	CHE 864
HOPSTAT, Peter	YOR 218
HOPTON, Edward	CHE 769
Joseph	CHE 852
HOPWOOD, Mosis	FAY 257
HORACE, Adam	CUM 60
HORCH, Philip	LAN 116
HORD, James	YOR 214
HORDER, William	PHI 150
HORE, David	NOU 110
HOREBAUGH, Henry	WST 215
HOREBAUGH?, Peter	WST 214
HORF, George	DAU 31A
HORGES, (No Given Name)	LAN 143
HORIT, Michael	DAU 10
HORLACHER, Daniel	NOH 82
George	NOH 80
John	NOH 80
Michael	NOH 82
HORLACKER, Peter	MNT 134
HORLOCKER, George	BUC 101
HORMACK, August	HNT 147
HORMEL, Henry	WAS 38
Jacob	WAS 38
HORN, Abraham	FRA 313
Abraham	NOH 37A
Adam	WST 252
Andrew	NOU 110
Bostian	BUC 158
Bostian	BUC 81A
Carter Henry	SOM 151
Christian	WAS 7
Christian	NOH 45
Christian	LAN 57
Christiana	PHA 120
Christopher	WAS 122
Daniel	BUC 157
Ewd.	FRA 322
Frederick	ADA 27
Frederick	BER 130
Geo. Henry	NOH 75A
George	ADA 19
George	NOH 45
Hartman	WAS 7
Henry	NOH 59A
Jacob	NOH 45
Jacob	PHA 58
John	WAS 2
John	LAN 52
John	WAS 122
John	WST 151
John	YOR 190
John	FAY 245
John	FRA 305
John Junr.	NOH 68A
John	NOH 68A
Martin	WAS 7
Michaeal	YOR 204
Samuel	NOU 154
Sebastian Jn.	BUC 157
Stephen	NOU 117
Stephen	BUC 157
Stephen Jn.	BUC 157
Valentine	BFD 58
HORN?, Henry	BER 202
John	BER 202
HORNAR, Isaac	FAY 245
James	FAY 227
John	FAY 221
William	FAY 227

HORNBACK, Daniel	NOU 100	HORNISH, Jacob	LAN 115
HORNBECK, Jacob	WAY 146	HORNNER?, Elias	MIF 11
Tobias	WAY 144	HORNNIG, Lewis	MNT 82
HORNBECKER,		HORNRICK, Henry	BUC 147A
Philip	FRA 282	HORNUNG, Conrad	DAU 3
HORNBEKER, Daniel	DAU 14A	Philip	DAU 5
HORNBERGER,		Stephen	DAU 4A
Conrad	BER 150	HORON, James	FRA 310
David	BER 170	HORP, Henry	NOU 122
George	BER 248	HORREL, James	MIF 7A
John	ADA 24	John	MIF 7A
Stephen	LAN 304	HORRELL, Christr.	MIF 7
HORNCAKE,		Clement	MIF 7A
Jeremiah	PHA 61	HORRIN, Patr.	FRA 322
HORNE, Edward	DEL 167	HORSE, Christ.	FRA 312
George	MNT 138	Israel	FRA 309
Isaac	PHI 140	Michael	LAN 122
John	MNT 138	Michael	LAN 130
John	DEL 167	HORSFIELD, Joseph	
Thomas	DEL 167	Esqr.	NOH 32
William		William	NOH 32
(Miller)	DEL 169	HORSHAVER,	
William	MNT 141	William	LAN 269
William	DEL 167	HORSMAN, Ebenezer	BFD 74
HORNE?,		John	BFD 74
Chirsttan?	BUC 148A	HORST, Abrm.	DAU 21
Michl.	FRA 290	Jacob	CUM 57
HORNECKER, Joseph	NOH 71A	John	LAN 7
HORNED, Jonathan	LUZ 330	Michael	LAN 261
HORNER, Abm.	LAN 262	Peter	DAU 27A
Abraham	SOM 138	HORSTMAN, Anthony	WAS 37
Abraham	NOH 51A	HORTAN, Wm.	LYC 22
Adam	SOM 128	HORTENSTEIN, John	BER 173
Alexr.	ADA 26	HORTER, Georoge	PHI 141
Andw.	DAU 22A	HORTER?, Jacob	
Benjn. Cenr.	PHA 24	Junr.	PHI 127
Benjn. Junr.	PHA 19	Jacob Senr.	PHI 127
Christian	SOM 157	HORTIN, Samuel	BFD 63
Daniel	SOM 157	HORTMAN, Phillip	WST 214
Daniel	SOM 158	Willm.	WST 214
David	ADA 26	HORTON, Charles	WAS 37
David Jun.	ADA 7	Daniel	GRN 70
Ephran	ALL 103	Foster	LUZ 380
Frederic	SOM 158	Jesse	MNT 138
George	DAU 17	John	DEL 184
George	WST 252	John	LUZ 395
George	NOH 55A	Nathan	DEL 185
Hugh	NOH 30	Samuel	LUZ 322
Jacob	SOM 158	Thomas	DEL 185
Jacob Esqr.	NOH 51A	Thoms.	BUT 326
James	ADA 24	Thos.	PHA 34
James	ALL 63	HORVARD, Duncan	GRN 76
John	BUC 153	Silvy	GRN 79
John	SOM 158	HOSABAUGH, Nichs.	WST 214
Joseph	NOH 30	HOSACK, David	WST 310
Phillip	PHA 78	George	WAS 49
Robert	ADA 25	John	WAS 121
Robert	WAS 75	Michael	WAS 121
Solomon	SOM 158	HOSAR, Wm.	FRA 274
Thomas	NOH 34	HOSBROUGH, John	WST 252
William	ADA 26	HOSE, Detrich	YOR 171
HORNER?, Jacob	PHI 79A	Henry	NOU 188
James	LAN 247	HOSECK, John	CRA 13
John	LAN 262	Thomas	CRA 13
HORNET, Charles	LUZ 394	HOSEY, Isaac	PHI 17
David	GRN 95	Mattw.	MIF 15
HORNETTER,		HOSHALL, Henry	HNT 135
Bernard	BER 173	HOSHAUR, Peter	BER 169
Peter	MNT 99	HOSHOUR, Widow	YOR 185
Valentine	BER 166	HOSICK, Henry	ADA 12
HORNIG, Christian	NOH 32	HOSIER, Henry	PHA 117
HORNING,		HOSINGLI-GER,	
Christopher	ALL 87	Gorg.	FRA 300
Jacob	MNT 128	HOSKINS, Eleanor	DEL 164
John	NOH 62A	Eleonor	DEL 164
Michael	MNT 82	Francis	PHI 107

HOSKINS, John	CHE 880
Joseph	DEL 184
Richd.	CHE 826
Thos.	PHA 71
William	DEL 163
HOSLACKER,	
Christn.	MNT 134
George	MNT 134
HOSLER, Michael	LAN 262
HOSMAN, Adam	PHI 85A
Charity	PHI 50
HOSNER, Michael	MNT 132
HOSNOCK, Jesse	PHI 92
HOSS, Daniel	LAN 316
Lewis	PHA 57
HOSTALTER, Henry	SOM 148
HOSTATLER, David	SOM 148
John Sen.	SOM 148
HOSTATTER, Daniel	SOM 149
Jacob Esqr.	YOR 181
Joseph	SOM 154
HOSTEDER, Henry	LAN 188
HOSTER, John	DAU 31
HOSTETLER,	
Nicholas	FAY 215
HOSTETLER?,	
Christian	ADA 15
HOSTETTER,	
Abraham	LAN 295
Abraham	LAN 295
Abram	LAN 253
Benj.	LAN 294
Christian	ADA 40
Christian	LAN 143
Jacob	LAN 103
Jacob	LAN 148
Jacob	YOR 212
Jno.	DAU 40A
John	LAN 296
Michael	DAU 37
HOSTETTER?,	
Christian	ADA 15
HOSTLER, George	ADA 20
Jacob	ALL 79
Jacob	FRA 316
John	FRA 316
HOSTLER?, Mary	FRA 285
HOSTOTLER, Jacob	SOM 148
Jacob	SOM 149
John	SOM 148
Jonathan	SOM 148
Joseph	SOM 149
Peter	SOM 149
HOSTUTER, Widow	WST 215
Joseph	WST 214
HOSWER, Adam	PHI 133
HOTCHKISS,	
Abigail	LUZ 321
HOTH, Charles	NOH 80
HOTSON, John B.	PHI 4
HOTSTED, John T.	WAS 56
HOTTENDORF, Henry	YOR 162
HOTTENSTEIN,	
Barbara	LAN 302
David	BER 226
David Jr.	BER 226
Docr.	LAN 32
John	LAN 312
Philip	LAN 302
Solomon	BER 226
HOTTENSTINE,	
Henry	BER 217
HOTTON, Daniel	CRA 2
Mary	PHI 147
Thomas	CRA 11
HOTZ,	DAU 36A
(No given name)	

HOTZ, George	NOH	53	HOUSE, Widow	YOR	182	HOUSHOLDER, John	ALL	50
Jacob	DAU	10	Alexander	PHI	115	HOUSICKLE,		
John	LAN	31	Amos	CHE	706	Frederick	YOR	171
John	DAU	20A	Conrod	CHE	897	HOUSEKEEPER, John	LAN	270
Michael	NOH	45	Francis	CHE	888	Mathias	BUC	96A
HOUCH, Andrew	BER	139	George	YOR	180	HOUSLEY, Levi	FRA	306
Conrad	BER	215	George	BER	240	HOUSMAN, Charles	FAY	215
John	BER	184	George	CHE	749	Christan	CHE	799
John	BER	185	Jacob	CHE	894	Elizabeth	BER	239
John Jr.	BER	183	James	BER	206	Frederick	CHE	831
Justis	LAN	65	Jefery	PHI	117	Michael	CHE	831
Oliver	BUC	151A	John	YOR	217	HOUST, Christn.	CUM	91
Peter	BER	209	Michl.	FRA	297	Emanuel	LAN	312
HOUCK, Fredk.	PHA	63	Peter	PHI	99	Henrey	FAY	266
John	PHA	55	Richd.	PHI	82	Henry	CUM	79
John	LAN	80	Samuel	GRN	101	John	YOR	212
HOUDER, David	LAN	127	Samuel	CHE	887	HOUSTER,		
HOUDESHELD, Jacob	YOR	209	Thomas	WAS	80	Christian	NOU	137
HOUER, John Geo.	BER	186	HOUSE?, John	LAN	218	HOUSTON, Daniel	FRA	283
HOUGH, Benjamin	WAS	44	HOUSEHOLDER,			John	PHA	73
Benjamin	BUC	154	Henry	YOR	195	Wm.	FRA	276
David	WST	290	Jacob	YOR	171	HOUSWERT, Jacob	NOU	182
Elisabeth	WAS	44	Jacob	YOR	195	HOUSWORT, Jacob	BUC	149A
Frederick	YOR	173	John	WST	309	Soloman	BUC	149A
George Jr.	YOR	173	John	WST	324	Widow	BUC	149A
Henry	BUC	99	HOUSEKEEPER,			HOUT, Jacob	WST	273
Jacob	WST	289	Philip	CHE	702	HOUTER, Jacob	FRA	301
Jacob	LUZ	394	Philip	CHE	882	HOUTON, Joseph	BUC	103
Jacob Sr.	WST	290	HOUSEL, Jacob	NOU	193	HOUTZ, Anthoy.	CUM	87
John	BUC	99	John	NOU	105	Balser	BER	260
John	BUC	151	John	NOU	117	Christn.	DAU	51
John	BUC	153	Joshua	NOU	193	Henry	DAU	51
John	WST	289	Ludwich	YOR	170	Jacob	DAU	34
John Jn.	BUC	154	Martin	NOU	193	John	DAU	51
Joseph	BUC	154	Mrs.	NOU	164	Wendle	BER	152
Joseph Jn.	BUC	154	Phillip	NOU	164	Widow	DAU	51
Matthias	CUM	144	William	NOU	117	HOUVER, Abraham	MER	446
Paul	WST	289	HOUSEMAN, John	BER	228	HOVATTER, Chrn.	DAU	40A
Richard	BUC	145	Mary	YOR	160	HOVER, Abraham	DAU	20
Richard	BUC	154	Peter	CRA	9	Anthy.	PHI	102A
Silas	MNT	87	HOUSER, Abrm.	DAU	22A	Christian	ARM	126
Simeon	SOM	128	Christian	LAN	112	Daniel	DAU	15A
Thomas	PHA	98	Danl.	DAU	15A	George	ARM	126
Thomas	BUC	154	Danl.	DAU	22A	Jacob	DAU	14A
HOUGHENBERG,			George	LAN	58	John	WAY	146
Jeremiah	MIF	5	George	WAY	149	John	MER	446
HOUGHENBERRY, Jno.	CUM	.47	Jacob	BFD	63	Jonathan	ALL	50
HOUGHEY, Francis	MER	444	Jacob	BUC	98	Ludwig	WAY	146
HOUGHLINE, John	NOH	78	Jacob	ARM	126	Michal	MER	446
HOUGHT, Henry	CHE	791	Jacob	NOU	188	Solomon	WAY	146
Jacob	FAY	245	Jacob	YOR	189	HOVERTON, George	FRA	304
HOUGHY, Jacob	MNT	126	Jacob	CEN	22B	HOVEY, Simeon	WST	215
HOUGMATER,			Jacob	DAU	22A	HOVLER, Goodlib	MER	444
Charles	NOU	182	Jacob	PHI	86A	HOVNER?, Jacob	PHI	79A
HOUK, John	ALL	76	Jacob	PHI	97A	HOVY, Josiah	LYC	10
William	LUZ	415	Jno.	CUM	128	Josiah	LYC	12
HOUKE, Adam Junr.	CUM	109	John	CUM	130	Simeons	LYC	12
George	CUM	58	John	YOR	168	HOVY?, Jesse	LYC	12
Jno.	CUM	56	John	NOU	182	HOW, Widw	PHI	101B
Michael	HNT	146	John	WST	215	Abraham	HNT	156
Philip	DAU	22A	Ludwich	FRA	315	Ann	ALL	70
William Junr.	HNT	146	Martin	BFD	63	Archibald	WAS	110
HOUP, Henry	MNT	130	Martin	CUM	67	Daniel	ALL	119
Phillip	NOU	122	Peter	DAU	30A	Jacob	MIF	12
Samuel	MNT	50	Simon	BFD	55	John	PHA	66
HOUP?, Jacob	MNT	130	HOUSERS, Martin	LAN	179	John	PHI	101A
HOUPT, Henry	BUC	80	HOUSEWERT, Jacob	NOU	137	Levi	LAN	226
Henry	CHE	909	HOUSEWOOD, Jacob	NOU	137	Walter	ERI	59
John	BUC	147A	HOUSEWORTH, John	NOU	97A	HOWAL, John	YOR	202
Valentine Jr.	SOM	132	HOUSHNEET,			HOWAR, Henry	DAU	34
Valentine Sen.	SOM	132	Frederick	BER	276	HOWARD, Capt.	PHA	98
HOUR, Adam	YOR	188	HOUSHOLDER,			Abraham	GRN	78
HOUR?, Henry	BER	202	Fredrick	ALL	68	Abraham	FAY	203
John	BER	202	George	HNT	152	Adam	YOR	189
HOURL, Walter	MNT	44	George	HNT	154	Anthony	YOR	201
HOURNICK?, John	LYC	15	Jacob	HNT	118	Ariel	LUZ	344

HOWARD, Benjn.	FAY 221	HOWELL, Joseph	WST 170	HUBBARD, Ansell	LUZ 389
Cornelius	GRN 76	Lot	WAS 21	Elizth.	PHI 58
David	SOM 129	Mary	PHA 44	Sarah	PHI 58
David	FAY 203	Peter	BUC 93A	HUBBART, David	WAY 144
Edward	MIF 10	Reading	PHA 68	HUBBERT,	
Edwd.	CUM 93	Reding	PHI 122	Christain	PHI 99A
Frederick	NOU 165	Reese	CHE 833	HUBBLE, Christr.	CUM 108
Gordon	GRN 70	Richd.	CHE 839	George W.	WAY 135
Horton	WAS 38	Saml.	PHI 134	Henry	HNT 139
Hugh	WST 252	Saml. Junr.	PHI 134	Hezekiah	LUZ 329
Jacob	YOR 201	Saml. E.	PHA 82	HUBBORD, Widw.	PHI 120A
James	GRN 82	Samuel Cenr.	PHA 6	John	PHI 95
James	DEL 172	Spencer	NOH 37A	HUBBORN, Chrisn.	PHI 99A
John	PHA 48	Thomas	CHE 744	HUBBS, Charles	PHI 126
John	PHI 75	Timothy	BUC 151	Elijah	WAS 49
John	GRN 76	William	DEL 166	Isaac	WAS 49
John	PHI 104	HOWER, Andrew	NOH 62A	Isaiah	MNT 35
John	WST 252	Benjamen	FAY 214	Joseph	WAS 49
John N.	LUZ 335	Fredk.	DAU 48	Joseph	MNT 88
Jos.	MIF 25	Henry	YOR 190	HUBER, Widow	PHI 60
Joseph	WAS 7	Jacob	NOH 43	Abraham	LAN 139
Lawrence	DEL 170	Jacob	YOR 197	Abraham	LAN 139
Lewis	PHA 7	John	NOH 30	Abraham	LAN 278
Nicholas	FAY 203	Jonathan	NOH 43	Adam	YOR 174
Peter	PHA 105	Michael	NOU 110	Adam	BER 203
Peter	YOR 201	Nicholas	NOH 30	Balzer	BER 190
Samuel	ALL 101	Rachel	NOH 43	Bar. W.?	NOH 47A
Thomas	PHA 13	Wendel	NOH 43	Barbara	DAU 48
Thomas	WAS 34	Widow	DAU 48	Charles	NOH 59
Thomas	WST 252	HOWERD, Thomas	NOU 198	Christian	BUC 101
William	DEL 159	HOWERDER, George	LAN 139	Christian	YOR 161
Wm.	PHI 66	HOWERTER, Adam	NOU 122	Conrad	YOR 176
HOWART, Fredr.	FRA 306	Adam	NOU 122	Conrad	NOH 68A
HOWCRAFT, Thos.	PHI 104A	Henry	BER 213	Elizabeth	NOH 87
HOWDESHER, Jacob	YOR 210	HOWET, James	LAN 156	Frantz	BER 202
HOWDON, Andrew	WAS 122	HOWEY, Bowdoin	WAY 147	Frederick	ADA 34
HOWE, Henry	CUM 138	John	LUZ 329	Fredk.	CUM 130
James	WAS 28	HOWGAN, John	CUM 32	Fredrik	DAU 49
John	ADA 41	HOWIE, David	ADA 4	George	NOH 32
John	LUZ 366	David	ADA 5	George	LAN 54
John	LUZ 367	William	ADA 5	George	MNT 99
Katherine	CUM 92	HOWK, Frederic	CHE 905	George (Conrad	
Maness	CUM 123	HOWLEY, Joseph	CHE 763	Crossed Out)	LAN 51
Maness	CUM 139	HOWLING, Patrick	PHA 48	Harvy	MNT 45
Seth	LUZ 366	HOWMAN, George	NOU 180	Henry	NOH 87
Stophell	CUM 141	John	BFD 47	Henry	BUC 102
William	WAS 80	Peter	NOU 122	Henry	LAN 270
William	YOR 216	Philip	DAU 7	Henry Junr.	NOH 33A
William	CHE 816	Phillip	NOU 176	Henry	NOH 33A
William	BUC 88A	HOWREY, Jacob	LAN 232	Isaac	CUM 24
Wm.	CUM 24	HOWRY, John	LAN 220	Jacob	LAN 61
HOWEL, Andrew	ALL 80	HOWSER,		Jacob	LAN 76
Daniel	MNT 67	Christopher	FAY 198	Jacob	PHI 85
Jeremiah	ADA 37	John	PHA 112	Jacob	MNT 99
John	NOU 187	HOWTON, Mathew	PHA 112	Jacob	BUC 101
John	FRA 303	HOX, Jacob	ALL 118	Jacob	SOM 132
Joseph	HNT 158	HOY, Albert	BER 270	Jacob	YOR 161
Leveling?	ALL 79	Bernard	BER 270	Jacob	LAN 198
Lewellon	ALL 80	John	PHA 115	Jacob	FRA 306
Liveling?	ALL 79	Samuel	WST 191	Jacob Sen.	SOM 141
Phillip	ALL 80	HOYATT, Charles	SOM 143	Jacob	NOH 47A
HOWELL, Abraham	PHI 66	John	SOM 143	Jacob	NOH 55A
Arthur	PHA 10	HOYER, George	DAU 4A	John	DAU 4
David	BUC 151	Henry	DAU 7	John	NOH 59
Eseck	NOH 37A	HOYL, Conrad	BER 206	John	LAN 72
Ezekiel	PHA 79	HOYLE, Christina	HNT 149	John	LAN 74
Ezekiel	CHE 853	Jacob	SOM 138	John	BUC 101
George	HNT 139	HOYLES?, Edward	PHI 118	John	SOM 141
George	PHI 107A	HOYNY, Michael	NOH 62A	John	SOM 145
Hannah	PHA 57	HOYT, Caleb	LUZ 354	John	YOR 164
Hannah	PHA 70	Daniel	LUZ 334	John	FRA 306
Henry	NOH 68A	Thomas	BEV 15	John Esquire	LAN 298
Isaac	WAS 38	HSIL, Jacob	NOU 180	Jos.	YOR 218
Jacob	HNT 135	HUB, William Esq.	LAN 165	Joseph	LAN 76
James	MNT 117	HUB?, See Herb	BER 206	Joseph	BER 203
Joseph	BUC 151	HUBARR, Isaac	PHA 92	Joseph	LAN 303

HUBER, Lawre. PHI 7
Margaret MNT 99
Martin LAN 74
Martin YOR 167
Matthias LAN 55
Michael NOH 43
Michael LAN 51
Michael MNT 99
Michael DAU 28A
Michael NOH 33A
Nicholas PHI 123
Peter LAN 147
Philip YOR 164
Valentine BUC 102
Widow LAN 41
William SOM 141
William YOR 164
HUBERD, Casper LAN 190
HUBERT, Henry LAN 44
Henry BER 260
Henry Jr. BER 260
Jacob LAN 42
Jacob FRA 289
John LAN 306
Mary YOR 184
HUBLER, Abraham NOH 43
Abraham NOH 66A
Adam NOU 175
Frederick MNT 73
Jacob NOU 175
Jacob BER 260
Jacob Jr. BER 260
Jacob NOH 62A
John NOU 129
John NOU 175
HUBLEY, Adm. (See
Hubley, Hen.) LAN 261
Bernard LAN 30
Bernard NOU 171
Fredrik DAU 32
Hen. & Adm. LAN 261
Jacob BER 240
John YOR 158
John Esq. LAN 36
Michael YOR 165
Michael Esq. LAN 33
Widow LAN 28
HUBLY, Frederick YOR 163
HUBNER, Abraham NOH 32
HUCHESON, James NOU 154
John NOU 165
Joseph NOU 165
William NOU 154
HUCHI NSON, Wm. BER 162
HUCKELBURY, Jacob CRA 10
HUCKLE, Wm. PHA 9
HUCKLEBERRY,
George ARM 125
Mury WST 160
HUDDELL, Joseph PHI 11
Joseph PHI 13
HUDDERS, John CHE 866
Nathl. CHE 866
HUDDLE, Benja. PHI 21
HUDDLESON, Henry MNT 69
Isaac MNT 71
HUDDLESTON, Jacob BUC 161
Jacob CHE 750
Thomas BUC 161
William BUC 161
HUDEN, James NOU 158
HUDLEY, Jacob CHE 862
HUDNER, Widow PHI 21
HUDNER?, John PHA 109
HUDNOT, Isaac BUC 104
HUDSON, Widow PHI 42

HUDSON, George HNT 143
John WAS 56
John BUC 104
John HNT 127
John HNT 143
Joseph BUT 349
Richard HNT 127
Susanna HNT 127
William GRN 81
William NOU 129
William HNT 143
HUERING?, Peter MNT 89
HUESTON, Dirkson MER 445
James MER 445
HUET, John Jr. BER 181
Philip BER 248
HUETT, Henry BER 181
Jacob BER 169
John BER 181
Mary BER 169
HUEY, Abraham DAU 12
Adam CEN 22B
Edward WAS 75
John WAS 75
Joseph WST 368
Robert WAS 75
Robt. CEN 22A
Samuel Doc. ADA 10
Wm. BEV 4
HUFF, (Blank) LYC 26
Abraham SOM 143
Benjn. WST 346
Daniel WAS 91
Elisha BFD 50
Frederick BER 206
Frederick BER 206
Godfrid BFD 63
Jacob SOM 132
Jacob PHI 116A
Jessee SOM 146
John MNT 40
John PHI 116
John WAY 149
John LUZ 328
John PHI 98
Jonathan LAN 162
Jonathan Jr. MIF 7
Joseph NOU 198
Phillip WST 237
Richard FAY 221
Samuel BER 206
Stephen Junr. NOH 78
Thomas SOM 146
Thomas Sen. SOM 146
HUFFEMAN, Willian NOU 165
HUFFERD, John BUC 96A
HUFFERT, George LAN 20
Lawrence BUC 159
Martin BUC 91
Martin BUC 149A
HUFFIRT, Joseph LAN 23
HUFFMAN, (Blank) LYC 15
Abraham NOU 105
Adam BFD 78
Adam WST 310
Christian LAN 17
Daniel NOU 97A
David WAS 110
Dorothy WAS 110
Gasper ALL 75
George GRN 88
George SOM 154
George NOU 183
George NOU 198
George Sen. SOM 153
George, Junr. GRN 88

HUFFMAN, Jacob LAN 26
Jacob WAS 110
Jacob SOM 158
Jacob NOU 187
Jacob WST 309
Jacob WST 310
Jacob WAR 1A
John WAS 110
John SOM 138
John NOU 154
John NOU 198
John WST 309
Jonathan WAS 110
Lidia FAY 252
Michael NOU 198
Michl. WST 309
Peter NOU 188
Philip NOU 114
Philip SOM 154
William NOU 171
Wm. CUM 98
HUFFNAGLE, Cathr. WST 214
HUFFORAS, Widow WST 238
HUFFORD, Abraham MIF 1
Christopher WAS 122
Nicholas CHE 862
Simon PHA 53
HUFFSTATER, Adam CUM 42
HUFFSTATTER,
James BEV 19
HUFFTY, Jacob GRN 95
HUFMAN, Henry FRA 274
John FAY 215
Peter NOU 117
Peter NOU 147
Phillip NOU 154
HUFSMITH, Adam NOH 35A
HUFSTATER, Jacob CUM 101
HUFTY, David MNT 35
Jacob BUC 143A
Jane PHA 51
John PHA 54
John BUC 153
John BUC 143A
Joseph PHI 154
Simon PHI 154
HUGBANK, James WST 171
HUGG, Jacob PHI 84
HUGGANS, Jacob ALL 116
HUGGERT,
Elisabeth WAS 99
HUGGINS, Edward
(Mulatto) WAS 116
Jacob CUM 32
William WAS 80
HUGGONS, William GRN 81
HUGGS, Benga. PHI 39
HUGH, Isaac MNT 48
Jonathan MIF 7
Peter WST 289
HUGHEN, John MER 444
HUGHES, Ann CUM 89
Benjamin MNT 138
Caleb PHA 43
Cathrine PHA 31
Charles DEL 155
Edward NOU 110
Edward DEL 155
Edward DEL 173
Edward BER 273
Elias WST 367
Elizabeth BER 163
Ellis NOU 110
Esther DEL 165
Esther DEL 190
Evan BER 279

HUGHES, Ewd.	FRA 287	HUGHS, Daniel	YOR 160	HULL, Jacob	PHA 65˙
Felix Junr.	GRN 91	Edward	LAN 305	James	NOU 100
Fr.	LYC 27	John	BEV 13	Joel	LUZ 388
Griffith	DEL 185	John	PHI 150	John	WAS 44
Henry	PHI 79A	John	YOR 204	John	WAS 44
Hugh	NOU 105	John	YOR 205	John	WAS 85
Isaac	MNT 47	John	CHE 774	John	YOR 210
Isaac	BER 217	John	BUC 86A	John	MER 445
Isaac	WST 346	Joseph	PHI 137	Nicholas	SOM 129
Isaac	WST 346	Mark	CHE 765	Peter	PHA 55
Isaiah	NOU 110	Mary	CHE 779	Peter	FRA 301
James	GRN 88	Matthew	BUC 141	Phillip	CUM 127
James	WAS 99	Matthew	BUC 149A	Samuel	BFD 73
James	NOU 110	Patk.	CEN 18A	Solomon	WAS 52
James B. S.	GRN 88	Patrick	LAN 303	Solomon	WAS 62
James	DAU 18A	Richard	FRA 275	Thomas	NOU 129
Jeremiah	NOU 110	Thoams	BEV 13	Thomas	NOU 129
Job	NOU 110	Thomas	CHE 860	Thomas	CHE 842
John	WAS 3	Thomas Rev.	BEV 19	William	NOU 164
John	LYC 20	Thomas	ERI 55A	HULLEHER, Thomas	NOU 164
John	PHA 24	Walter	SOM 129	HULLEY, David	SOM 157
John	WAS 44	William	LAN 49	HULME, John	BUC 161
John	MNT 45	HUGHY, James	FAY 221	Saml.	BUC 161
John	PHI 73	William	MNT 42	William	BUC 161
John	GRN 95	HUGS, Edwd.	PHI 45	HULOX, John	NOU 143A
John	CUM 97	HUGUENIN, Charles		Mine	NOU 143A
John	MNT 104	F.	PHA 81	HULS, Ezekia	ALL 96
John	NOU 110	HUGUS, Jacob	WST 215	Henry	ALL 95
John	HNT 158	John	WST 310	Henry	ALL 120
John	BER 244	Michael	SOM 132	Hery Senior	ALL 95
John	CHE 911	HUHN, Daniel	PHA 54	John	ALL 67
Joseph	BFD 74	John	FAY 245	Ritchard	ALL 95
Levi	NOU 110	John Jun.	FAY 245	HULSAPPLE, Adam	NOU 183
Levy	PHI 82	HUKIS?, (See		HULTON/ HUTTON?	
Lewis	MNT 128	Herkis?)	LAN 45	Simeon	YOR 209
Michael	NOU 110	HUKLIN, Ebenezer	MNT 39	HULTS, Abraham	WST 368
Moses	DEL 155	HUKMAN, John	LAN 233	HULTZ, John	YOR 209
Moses	DEL 157	HUL, Daniel	NOU 187	Willm.	BUT 323
Nathaniel	GRN 64	David	ALL 60	HULY, John	PHI 50
Patr.	FRA 322	HULER, Christian	LAN 187	HUM, Christian	WST 215
Richard	GRN 64	Fredk.	CUM 95	Conrod	WST 215
Richd.	FRA 279	HULET, Lewis	NOU 129	Henry	WST 367
Robert	WAS 21	William	ARM 122	HUMBERGER, Henry	FRA 313
Roland	NOU 110	HULEY?, -oyd?	ARM 124	Henry	FRA 318
Samuel	NOU 110	Eares?	PHI 23	Peter	FRA 318
Samuel	DEL 155	HULFORD, John	FAY 215	HUMBERT, Adam	BFD 40
Samuel	BER 181	HULICK, Isaac	ADA 26	Frederic	SOM 154
Thomas	WAS 38	Wendle	ADA 26	Frederick	BFD 38
Thomas	GRN 95	HULIG, Adam	MNT 92	George	SOM 134
Thomas	NOU 110	HULIN, Samuel	ALL 119	Jacob	BER 210
Thomas	BER 181	HULING, John	CRA 8	HUMBLE, Chr.	WST 215
Thomas	BER 219	Marcus	LYC 21	Christley	LAN 132
Thomas	NOU 143A	Marcus?	VEN 165	Henry	FRA 300
Uriah	BFD 50	Myer	NOU 154	Widow	LAN 87
Uriah	NOU 110	HULINGS, John	LYC 28	HUMBS, William	FRA 274
William	WAS 28	Thos.	LYC 28	HUME, James	GRN 76
William	NOU 110	Wm.	LYC 21	John	DAU 22A
William	DEL 157	HULKLBAUGH, John	LAN 246	Joseph	CUM 132
William	DEL 159	HULL, Abraham	FRA 321	William	FRA 275
Wm.	WST 346	Andrew	WAS 121	HUMEL, Adam	BER 220
HUGHET, John	ALL 84	Anor	ERI 59	Andrew	BER 276
HUGHEY, Ephram	ALL 91	Bengamin	ALL 85	Chrisn.	DAU 18A
John	ALL 66	Benjamin	SOM 129	David	BER 253
John	ALL 83	Benjeman	FAY 240	Frederick	NOU 104
John	ALL 115	Besherrey	MER 445	Fredk.	DAU 19
Jonas	FAY 221	Daniel	MER 445	Fredk.	BER 186
Robert	FAY 197	Elijah	MER 445	George	NOU 105
Robert Jun.	FAY 197	Elizabeth	HNT 133	Jacob	BER 156
Wilm.	ALL 94	Francis	NOU 136	Jacob	BER 220
Wilm.	ALL 108	George	BFD 44	Jacob	BER 279
Wm.	CHE 745	George	WAS 44	John	DAU 21
HUGHINBERG, John	NOU 137	Gersham	WAS 91	John	NOU 128
HUGHISON, John	NOU 198	Henry	ADA 38	John	BER 130
Thomas	NOU 198	Henry	WAS 44	John	NOU 154
HUGHMAN, Francis	CHE 876	Henry	CUM 104	John	DAU 19A
HUGHS, Amos	BUC 86A	Isaac	FAY 245	Martin	BER 186

HUMEL, Mary	DAU	19	HUN, Nicholas	LAN 184	HUNT, Jos.	PHI 66A
Michael	BER	220	HUNDEBERGER,		Joseph	LYC 23
Peter	BER	188	Math.	MNT 111	Joseph	BFD 43
Simon	BER	220	HUNE, Philip	MER 444	Joseph	BUC 143
Valentn.	DAU	18A	HUNES?, (See		Joseph D.	LUZ 385
HUMER, Jacob	LAN	46	Himes)	MIF 13A	Joshua	GRN 81
Jacob	LAN	185	HUNESKER?, John	MNT 113	Joshua	FAY 197
Peter	LAN	262	HUNGIN, Jacob	MNT 126	Joshua	CHE 743
HUMERY, Mrs.	LYC	17	HUNKLE, Adam	CUM 35	Martha	CRA 12
HUMES, Archabald	CRA	8	HUNN, John	PHI 11	Mrs.	NOU 143A
Charles	YOR	198	HUNNAWELL, John	LUZ 338	Rachel	PHA 47
Jas.	CUM	59	HUNNEL, David	CRA 8	Richd.	PHA 86
John	CUM	74	John	GRN 64	Robert	WAS 38
John	CUM	83	HUNSAKER, Henry	MNT 127	Robert	BER 160
John	PHI	83	Isaac	MNT 127	Robert	FAY 227
John	NOU	164	Jacob Jnr.	BUC 96A	Roger	FAY 245
John	WST	191	Jacob	BUC 96A	Samuel	GRN 81
Michael	LAN	157	John	MNT 127	Samuel	LUZ 380
Robert	CRA	6	Valuntn.	MNT 128	Samuel	CHE 899
Samuel	LAN	31	HUNSBERGER,		Thos.	PHA 35
Thos.	CUM	84	Christ.	MNT 126	Waltar	LUZ 428
Willm.	BUT	348	Christian	BER 274	William	NOU 100
HUMES?, (See			Christn. Junr.	MNT 124	William	FAY 203
Humys)	CHE	730	Christn. Junr.	MNT 124	William	FAY 227
HUMMEL, Adam	NOH	71A	Christn.		William	LUZ 343
David	LAN	48	(Taylor)	MNT 124	Wilm.	ALL 71
Elias	NOH	71A	Christn.		Wm.	PHA 25
Frederick	NOU	136	(Weaver)	MNT 124	HUNT?, Jacob	LUZ 318
Georges	NOU	137	Frederick	MNT 124	Thomas	BFD 73
Jacob	NOU	136	Isaac	MNT 128	HUNTER, Widow	PHI 2
John	CHE	908	Jacob	BER 273	Widow	PHI 30
Mathias	NOH	43	John	MNT 124	Aaron	ERI 58A
HUMMELL, Fredk.	YOR	216	Ulrich	NOH 66A	Alex	ADA 27
HUMMER, Abraham	LAN	139	Wm.	MNT 132	Alexander	WAS 28
Daniel	YOR	171	HUNSBERRY,		Alexander	NOU 99
Jacob	LAN	180	Christian	BUC 101	Alexander	ARM 122
William	MNT	130	Owen	NOH 66A	Alexander	SOM 158
HUMMOND, Elisha	YOR	214	HUNSBERY, Abraham	BUC 96	Alexander	FAY 203
HUMMONT, John	YOR	190	HUNSBURY, Isaac	BUC 97A	Alexandr.	WST 237
HUMPARD, Jacob	ALL	97	HUNSELMAN, George	NOU 104	Alexr.	WST 273
Michal	ALL	91	HUNSHBERGER, John	BER 206	Andrew	ARM 126
HUMPFRIES,			HUNSICKER, Casper	NOH 44A	Andrew	BUC 161
William	BER	250	Henry	NOH 44A	Andrew Junr.	DEL 157
HUMPHEYS, Thomas	LAN	169	John Junr.	NOH 44A	Andw.	CEN 22B
HUMPHREY, Charles	DEL	168	John Senr.	NOH 44A	Ann	PHA 118
David	MNT	141	Joseph	NOH 44A	Benjn.	BUC 104
Eliz.	MNT	141	Nicholas	FAY 221	Charles	SOM 157
Jacob	CHE	750	Peter	NOH 53	Charles	BUT 332
John	DEL	167	HUNSMAN, James	WAS 110	Davd.	WST 290
John	CHE	840	Jonathan	BUC 141	David	BEV 11
Thomas	MNT	115	William	WAS 110	David	MNT 104
Thomas	MNT	138	HUNSON, Andw.	PHI 4	David	HNT 134
HUMPHREYS, Abel	PHA	104	HUNSPERGER, Widow	LAN 73	David	HNT 153
Ann	DEL	167	HUNT, Abraham	ALL 92	David	NOU 165
Catherine	PHA	116	Alexd.	FRA 313	David	WST 272
Charles	PHA	99	Benjn.	CHE 760	Edward Esqr.	DEL 179
Daniel	PHA	99	Daniel	BUC 107	Eliza.	CUM 90
Edward	NOH	29A	Daniel	NOU 147	Ephraim	BEV 5
James	PHA	11	Edward	ADA 18	Frederick	BER 230
James	PHI	88	Eli	CHE 745	George	ALL 69
James	PHA	103	Ester	FAY 236	George	PHA 104
James	PHI	103	George	ALL 99	George	DEL 172
John	NOU	171	George	NOU 143A	George	DEL 179
Josha	PHI	19	Grivel	PHI 25	George	CHE 716
Mary	PHA	5	Hannah	FAY 256	George	DEL 180
Rebecca	DEL	167	Jacob	FAY 203	Hiram	CHE 814
Richd.	PHA	81	James	PHA 57	Hugh	BUC 162
Richd.	MNT	138	James	PHI 65	Jacob	BER 139
Thos.	PHA	76	Jeremiah	PHI 90A	James	CUM 22
HUMPHRIES, Edward	BUC	149A	Jesse	PHI 15	James	CUM 77
HUMPHRY, Richd.	MIF	25	Jesse	LYC 23	James	PHA 89
Wm.	MIF	25	John	BUC 88	James	PHI 108
HUMPHRYS, David	FRA	291	John	NOU 117	James	HNT 145
HUMRICH, Chris.	LAN	36	John	DEL 167	James	WST 151
HUMYS, William	CHE	730	John	FAY 245	James	DEL 184
HUN, John	LAN	184	Jonathan	NOH 29A	James	WST 272

HUNTER, James	WST	310	HUNTER, William	WST	346	HURST, Henry	MNT	46
James	CHE	839	William	MER	446	Henry	YOR	218
James Jr.	WST	309	Wiliam	CHE	800	Jacob	LAN	75
Jno.	CUM	50	Wm.	BEV	5	Jacob Junr.	LAN	7
Jno.	WST	289	Wm.	PHA	89	Jacob Senr.	LAN	7
Jno. Senr.	CUM	77	Wm.	CUM	108	James	WST	272
John	WAS	7	Wm.	CUM	131	John	LAN	177
John	CRA	11	Wm.	CUM	143	John	FRA	295
John	PHI	11	Wm.	WST	289	John Carpr.	LAN	9
John	ADA	12	Wm.	FRA	302	John	CEN	20A
John	WAS	16	Wm.	FRA	318	Jonathan H.	PHA	75
John	MIF	25	Wm. Esqr.	CHE	718	Joseph	LAN	70
John	BFD	38	HUNTERMAN, Willm.	MNT	43	Joseph	LAN	89
John	MNT	39	HUNTINGTON, Abner	GRN	111	Joseph	LAN	177
John	WAS	56	Abraham	NOU	117	Nathaniel	WST	272
John	ALL	67	Issachar	GRN	111	Philip	MNT	45
John	BFD	68	Nathl.	FRA	319	Rebecah	ERI	56
John	CUM	78	Silas	GRN	111	Saml.	PHA	66
John	CUM	116	HUNTSMAN, James	WAS	68	HURT, Conrad	MNT	134
John	HNT	125	Jesse	WAS	68	Jacob	YOR	218
John	BER	139	John	WAS	68	Mary	ALL	76
John	DEL	156	HUNTWORK, John	CHE	725	HURTER, Valentine	DAU	3A
John	DEL	179	HUNTZBERRY, Isaac	PHI	126	HURTMAN, Adam	CUM	111
John	YOR	213	HUNTZICKER,			Henry	CUM	111
John	BER	230	Christn.	DAU	52	HURTS, Catharine	FRA	306
John	WST	237	Saml.	DAU	50A	John	PHI	112A
John	WST	272	HUNTZINGER,			HURTZ, Abram	CHE	820
John Junr.	HNT	125	George	BER	159	Jacob	PHA	36
John	ERI	56A	Jacob	BER	155	Peter	PHI	40
John W.	LYC	3	HUNTZMAN,			HURY, Jacob	LAN	96
Joseph	WAS	12	Hezekiah	PHI	125	HUSARD, Abraham	FRA	301
Joseph	CUM	22	James	WAS	121	HUSBAND, Isaac	SOM	129
Joseph	ADA	25	HUNZICKER,			John	LAN	217
Joseph	CUM	126	Christn.	DAU	52A	HUSBANDS, Wm.	WST	290
Joseph	BUC	143A	HUOIT?, Mrs.	NOU	97A	HUSE, Henry	MIF	15
Magdalena	BER	139	HUPP, Everard	WAS	38	HUSE?, Henry	MIF	16
Margaret	BEV	16	HUPPAGH, John	YOR	209	HUSEL, Peter	NOU	129
Martha	CUM	53	HUPPAUGH, Conrad	YOR	210	HUSER, Gudr	51	0
Mary	CUM	115	HUPSCHMAN, Jacob	LAN	210	HUSH, Christopher	NOU	99
Michal	ALL	61	John	LAN	210	HUSHER, George	SOM	145
Michal	ALL	91	HURD, Wilm.	ALL	98	HUSICKER,		
Nicholas	BER	257	HURDER, John	LAN	16	Nicholas	FAY	244
Noble	BUT	331	HURDMAN, Wilm.	ALL	103	HUSINGER, Bernerd	NOU	114
Patrick	BUC	103	HURLAKER, Peter	NOU	165	George	NOU	114
Peter	NOU	110	HURLBERT, Abigail	LUZ	331	HUSK, David	FRA	275
Philip	LUZ	337	Naphtali	LUZ	320	Elizabeth	LAN	111
Polland	WST	346	HURLBUTT, Jacob	LUZ	358	George	WST	215
Robert	WAS	16	HURLEY, Cornelius	GRN	107	HUSLEPAUGH,		
Robert	PHI	138	Daniel	NOU	97A	Haunus	DEL	161
Robert	HNT	154	Jeremiah	HNT	123	HUSONG, George	FRA	301
Robert	WST	324	John	PHA	46	Jacob	WAS	2
Robt.	MIF	17	Thomas	PHA	5	HUSPSCHMAN,		
Robt.	CUM	49	Thomas	GRN	107	Wendel	LAN	197
Robt.	PHI	115	Thos.	PHI	81	HUSS, Jacob	CHE	889
Robt.	WST	289	William	GRN	106	HUSSAM, Peter	BER	170
Robt.	CEN	22B	Zachariah	GRN	106	HUSSELTON, Jacob	BFD	38
Saml.	WST	237	HURLICHER,			HUSSER?, George	PHI	115
Samuel	ADA	25	Benjamin	YOR	207	HUSSEY, Amos	YOR	210
Samuel	NOU	128	HURLY, Hannah	ALL	98	Jedediah	YOR	208
Samuel	DEL	157	John	PHI	22	HUSTED, Henry	WAY	141
Samuel	DEL	185	HURN, Fredk.	YOR	155	Robert	FAY	245
Sarah	PHA	79	HURNBACK, John	PHI	129	HUSTEN, Allen	BFD	55
Thomas	WST	237	HURON, Lawrence	PHA	38	Andrew	BFD	58
Thomas	WST	238	HURROW, Matthias	LAN	236	Edward	BFD	58
Thomas	CEN	18A	HURRY, Arthur	FAY	204	Robert	BFD	58
Thomas	CEN	18A	Saml.	PHA	89	Sarah	FAY	209
Thos.	BUC	162	HURST, Abarham	YOR	218	HUSTEND, David	CHE	783
William	MIF	3	Aniner	ERI	56A	HUSTES?, Francis	NOU	117
William	MIF	5	Charles	PHA	119	HUSTIN, John	ALL	84
William	BFD	37	Christ.	LAN	90	Joseph	ALL	83
William	MNT	38	Christian	LAN	7	HUSTING, John	ALL	86
William	GRN	64	Christn.	LAN	70	HUSTINS, James	DAU	30
William	GRN	82	David	LAN	90	HUSTON, Alexander	WAS	16
William	NOU	158	Elias	MNT	55	Alexander	BFD	58
William	YOR	216	Fredk.	PHA	60	Andw.	CUM	107
William	WST	346	George	ERI	56A	Ann	DEL	164

HYATT, Noah	FAY 256	ICKES, Jacob	YOR 180	IMMEL, Christian	BER 160
HYBERGER, Jacob	PHI 107A	Nicholas	CUM 41	John	FRA 311
HYDE, Geoe.	PHA 45	Peter	ADA 33	Leonard	DAU 39A
Jabez	LUZ 392	Saml.	CUM 45	Michael	PHA 28
John	PHA 48	ICKIS, Henry	BFD 68	Paul	FRA 311
John	WAS 56	John	BFD 74	IMMER, John	PHI 136
Samuel	WAS 56	John Jr.	BFD 74	IMMIL, Jacob	LAN 288
Samuel	GRN 81	IDDINGS, William	NOU 199	IMSON, Benjamin	WAY 147
Thomas	WAS 56	IDDINS, Abigail	CHE 823	IMSWELLER, Peter	YOR 206
Wyllys	LUZ 328	John	CHE 822	INA?, Michael	BER 164
HYDEL, Leonard	PHI 109A	IDEA, Mark U.	PHA 105	INAN?, John	BEV 24
HYDER, John	SOM 142	IDELBERT, William	WST 290	INBRAKE, John	BFD 51
John Sen.	SOM 142	IDEN, George	BUC 157	INCH, John	HNT 145
HYDLE, Geo.	PHI 76A	Randle	BUC 157	INERST, Jacob	YOR 172
HYELL, Ezekia	FAY 261	IDINGS, Isaiah	NOU 199	INFIELD, John	SOM 149
HYER, Waler	PHI 69A	Jonthen	NOU 199	Philip	SOM 149
HYET, John	PHA 46	Thomas	NOU 199	INGARD, Adam	PHI 95
Peter	BEV 16	IDLE, Bernard	BER 232	INGARSOL, Danl.	LYC 11
HYETT, Abednego	FAY 227	Jacob	MNT 106	INGERHAM, Francis	PHA 106
John	FAY 227	John	BER 139	INGERSOL,	
HYETT?, (See		IDOL, Jacob	CHE 834	Artemadorius	LUZ 375
Hyell)	FAY 261	John	YOR 199	INGERSOLD, Jarerd	PHA 85
HYLAND, Samuel	DEL 191	IFFEND, Peter	NOU 143A	INGHAM, Daniel	LUZ 409
HYLANDS, Thos.	LYC 6	IGO, Daniel	HNT 149	John	BER 181
HYLE, George	LAN 262	Joshua	HNT 149	Jonas	LUZ 397
Henry	NOU 100	William	HNT 160	Joseph	LUZ 396
Henry	BUC 138	IHRIE, Conrad	NOH 37A	Widow	BUC 146
Jacob	FRA 284	Peter	NOH 37A	INGHRAM, Arthur	
John	MER 444	IHRIE?, Conrad	LAN 32	Junr.	GRN 64
HYLMUN, Morda.	LYC 3	IKE, Paul	NOU 158	Arthur Senr.	GRN 64
HYMAN, Christian	SOM 151	IKERT, Abm.	WST 273	Elijah	GRN 88
Conrad	HNT 124	Abrm.	WST 273	Merideth	GRN 88
Jacob	LYC 3	John	WST 311	William	GRN 64
Philip	SOM 151	Micheal	WST 273	William	GRN 88
Saml.	PHA 77	Peter	WST 216	INGILHEART,	
HYMER, Adam	PHI 85	IKLEBERRY, Jacob	GRN 71	George	NOU 100
Adam	PHI 93A	John	GRN 71	INGILLHEART,	
Fredk.	PHI 84	Valentine	GRN 71	George	NOU 100
John	PHI 93	ILESTON, John	NOU 143A	INGLE, Haney	CUM 145
HYMES, Andw.	PHI 84	ILGENFRITZ,		Henry	CHE 725
HYMNS, Jacob	DAU 47A	Christian	YOR 154	John	BUC 157
HYNEA, Jacob	PHI 110	Christian	YOR 161	John Junr.	WAS 100
HYNEMON,		Fredk.	YOR 174	John Senr.	WAS 100
Charlotte	PHA 43	George	YOR 154	Silas	NOU 154
HYNER, Fredk.	WST 170	Jacob	YOR 154	INGLER, Casper	LUZ 345
James	VEN 167	Jacob	YOR 155	John	LUZ 345
HYNES, Fredk.	PHI 3	Martin	YOR 164	Joseph	LUZ 345
Henry Andw.	PHA 43	Samuel	YOR 154	INGLES, Benjamin	MNT 106
James	PHI 11A	ILIFF, Benjn.	BUC 149A	Joh	PHI 151
HYOTT, Barney	FAY 245	John	BUC 139	Thomas	PHI 152
HYPLE, Christian	SOM 129	ILLIG, George	LAN 199	INGLIS, Silas	PHI 29
Christian Senr.	SOM 128	George	LAN 210	INGLISH, Charles	BUC 93A
Henry	SOM 129	ILLING,		David	WAS 8
John	SOM 129	Christophr.	LAN 32	George	WAS 8
HYSER, Jacob	FRA 273	IMBE, Peter	PHA 97	William	BUC 153
Rudolp	CUM 101	IMBERT, Felix	PHA 92	INGRAHAM,	
HYSHAM, David	NOH 78	IMBODEN, Adam	DAU 42	Ebenezer	LUZ 392
HYSLER, Peter	PHI 113A	George	DAU 42	James	DAU 3A
Wm.	PHI 71	John	DAU 42	Willm.	DAU 3A
HYSOP, Samuel	HNT 153	Philip	DAU 42	INGRAM, Benjamin	DEL 176
HYSTAND, Jacob	NOH 30	IMBODY, Adam	BER 176	Elisha	CHE 902
John	NOH 29A	Danl.	BER 257	Francis	BUC 88A
HYZER, George	DEL 166	IMEL, John	PHA 55	John	CHE 750
George	DEL 187	IMFELT, Vincence	YOR 158	John	CHE 808
Gideon	DEL 159	IMFIELD, William	YOR 159	Jos.	CUM 142
Gideon	DEL 161	IMGRICH, Joseph	LAN 139	Joseph	CHE 763
		IMHOF, Martin	DAU 29	Lucy	PHA 114
IAHMAN, (See		IMHOFF, Benedict	BER 204	Peter	CHE 759
Lawman)	MNT 1	Jacob	LAN 294	Robert	CHE 761
IAMPS?, John	PHI 95	John	NOU 193	Saml.	CUM 142
IAMS, James	BFD 58	Martin	NOU 194	Thomas	CHE 884
IAMS?, Mary	WAS 122	IMLER, Abraham	HNT 117	William	DEL 156
Thomas	WAS 122	Conrad	BFD 74	William	DEL 157
IBATT?, John	CHE 867	George	BFD 74	William	CHE 885
IBERRY, John	BER 200	Henry	BFD 74	Wm.	CHE 900
ICE, George	BFD 74	Peter	HNT 117	INGRAN, Eleazer	CHE 884

INGRIN, William	HNT 144	IRVIN, Jas.		MIF 25	IRWIN, James	WAS 34
INGRUM, Abel	FAY 252	John		CEN 20A	James	NOH 87
INHUSEN, Jacob	YOR 206	John		BUC 143A	James	HNT 117
INIS, Brice	NOU 165	Nathaniel E.		BUC 155A	James	NOU 117
INK, John	DAU 34A	Robert		FAY 198	James	NOU 117
Peter	NOH 64A	Saml.		CUM 86	James	HNT 121
INKS, Thomas	FAY 261	William		GRN 82	James	NOU 129
INKS?, John	ALL 115	William		MIF 7A	James	HNT 136
INKSKIP, John		IRVINE, Agness		CUM 55	James	HNT 166
Esqr.	PHA 34	Alex		ADA 14	James	LAN 245
INMAN, Edward	LUZ 326	Andrew		ADA 19	James	FRA 295
Elijah	LUZ 326	Andrew		DAU 47	James	CHE 754
Elijah	LUZ 331	Andw.		CUM 63	James	CHE 780
Richard	LUZ 326	Andw.		CUM 142	James Junr.	HNT 121
INNAS, Henry	PHA 69	Henry		WST 290	James Ssr.	FRA 289
INNES, Robert Jr.	NOH 37A	Israel		ADA 6	Jared	HNT 121
INNIS, Alexander	HNT 166	James		CUM 78	Jared	CHE 719
James	PHI 97	James		CUM 106	Jerred	NOU 165
John	PHA 34	James		CUM 124	Jno.	BUT 367
John	ALL 102	James Esqr.		PHA 28	John	CRA 13
Wm.	PHA 49	James (Major)		WST 325	John	LYC 15
INNLY, John	NOU 147	James (Miller)		WST 325	John	WAS 34
INNMAN, Ezechal	ALL 110	Jarred		CUM 49	John	CUM 93
Henry	BEV 17	Jas.		CUM 54	John	HNT 121
INSHOUT?, (See		Jno.		CUM 34	John	NOU 129
Inskout)	NOH 78	Jno.		CUM 40	John	LAN 164
INSIGN, Eliphalet	LUZ 424	John		MIF 1	John	VEN 167
INSKEP, John	PHA 67	John		ADA 3	John	DEL 186
INSKIP, John	MNT 35	John		ALL 49	John	NOU 193
Rebecca	PHA 47	John		CUM 55	John	LAN 237
INSKOUT, Joseph	NOH 78	John		GRN 91	John	WST 290
INSTITUTION, (219		John		GRN 92	John	FRA 298
Persons		Joseph		ARM 122	John	FRA 316
Shown)	CHE 743	Joseph		WST 325	John	WST 368
INTORF, Milchoir	MIF 17	Nathaniel		GRN 88	John	CHE 740
INVITER, Widow	PHI 97	Rebeca		PHA 35	John	CHE 822
IR---, James	FRA 287	Robert		PHA 28	John	CHE 823
IRANAGLE, Thos.	WST 216	Robt.		CUM 40	John	CHE 823
IRAUGH?, Rudolph	BUC 82A	Saml.		CUM 140	John	CHE 868
IRE, George	PHA 63	Samuel		PHA 28	John	CHE 869
IREDELL, John	MNT 50	Sarah		CUM 89	John	CHE 876
Jonathan	MNT 50	William		CUM 55	John Esqr.	WST 253
Robert	MNT 87	William		CUM 97	John & Moses	LAN 164
Seth	NOU 199	Wm.		CUM 50	John	CEN 21A
IRELAND, Alfenco		Wm.		CUM 71	Joseph	LAN 86
C.	PHA 113	IRWIN, Agness		ALL 54	Joseph	NOU 129
David	NOU 165	Alexander		WAS 34	Joseph	FRA 287
Elizabeth	FAY 231	Alexd.		FRA 322	Joseph	CHE 822
John	WAS 100	Alexr.		WST 160	Margaret	WST 290
Reuben	LUZ 369	Alexr.		BUT 366	Mary	LAN 88
Robert	NOU 165	Alexr.		CHE 719	Matthew	NOU 194
Susanna	WAS 100	Andrew		NOU 158	Moses & John	LAN 164
Thomas	CHE 852	Archd.		FRA 289	Mrs.	NOU 117
William	NOU 165	Archibald		ERI 59A	Mrs.	NOU 194
IRELEY?, John	PHA 110	Arther		YOR 218	Nathaniel	CHE 721
IREMAN, Andw.	WST 216	Beigh		WST 160	Nathen	NOU 165
Chr.	WST 216	Catharine		LAN 66	Patrick	YOR 215
Henry	WST 368	Charles		NOU 117	Peter	NOU 202
Michl.	WST 216	Christian		NOU 129	Rebecca	CHE 845
Peter	WST 216	David		ALL 57	Richard	NOU 117
IREY, John	WAS 100	David		WAS 57	Richard	NOU 199
IRIE, Frederick	WAS 21	David		CHE 869	Robert	CRA 4
IRISH, Andrew		Edward		WST 171	Robert	CRA 16
Kerr	CRA 12	Ezekiel		LAN 120	Robert	NOU 171
Job	LUZ 413	Ezekiel		WST 273	Robert	BUT 318
IRONDEL, Robt.	PHI 114A	Frances		WAS 21	Robert Junr.	ERI 59
IRONS, David	WAS 100	Francis		NOU 117	Robert Senr.	ERI 59
Joseph	WAS 12	George		WAS 34	Robt.	BUT 348
Michael	HNT 126	George		YOR 155	Robt.	CHE 868
Sarah	HNT 132	George		YOR 218	Rubin	BUT 356
Soloman	PHA 76	George		CHE 719	Saml.	WST 346
IRVIN, Christr.	MIF 10	George		CHE 775	Saml.	BUT 350
Christr.	MIF 7A	Guyan		CEN 20A	Saml.	CHE 719
George	MIF 10A	Hannah		CHE 845	Samuel	DAU 8
James	MIF 10	Henry		DAU 21A	Samuel	NOU 165
Jas.	LYC 18	James		WAS 21	Samuel	NOU 199

JACKSON, John	PHA	54	JACOB, John	YOR 180	JACOBY, John	YOR	164
John	LAN	96	John	LAN 199	John	NOU	165
John	ARM	127	John Junr.	LAN 199	John	NOH	59A
John	LAN	159	Jonathan	YOR 161	Lawrence	MNT	53
John	HNT	166	Joseph	LAN 199	Leonard	PHA	45
John	LAN	168	Kaller	LAN 211	Michael	NOH	69
John	BER	240	Lorence	YOR 157	Michael	NOH	59A
John	FAY	257	Michael	FRA 303	Nicholas	ADA	28
John	FAY	266	Peter	CUM 41	Peter	BUC	80
John	FRA	283	Philip	YOR 180	Peter	CUM	131
John	CHE	732	Philip	YOR 205	Peter	NOH	66A
John	CHE	765	Samuel	ADA 35	Philip	NOH	80A
John	CHE	848	Witson	LAN 147	Philip	BUC	96A
John	PHI	116A	JACOBS, Widow	MNT 101	Phillip	CUM	134
John Francis	PHA	61	Adam	FAY 238	Wicard	PHI	123
Joseph	WAS	52	Benj.	PHI 69	Widow	BUC	90A
Joseph	WAS	52	Benjn.	CHE 893	JACQUES, William	BFD	43
Joseph	WAS	91	Benjn. Esqr.	CHE 885	JACQUET, Jno.		
Joseph	NOU	110	Catharine	MIF 1	Daniel	NOH	62A
Joseph	PHI	153	Charles	LAN 124	JACSON, George	ALL	103
Joseph	HNT	158	Christn.	PHI 102	JAG, John	NOH	70
Joseph Jr.	PHI	152	Cyrus	LAN 68	JAGAL?, Fredk.	PHI	86
Joseph	BUC	151A	Daniel	WAS 68	JAGER, Conrad		
Josiah	NOU	154	Daniel	BUC 93A	Revd.	NOH	87
Mary	LAN	71	Edia	MIF 7A	John	NOH	45
Mary	PHA	107	Eli	SOM 146	Leonard	NOH	84
Moses	YOR	177	George	PHA 51	Philip	NOH	67
Peter	PHI	115	George	MNT 93	JAKSON, William	WAS	91
Peter	HNT	130	George	CEN 18A	JAMES, Widow	PHI	17
Peter	BUC	162	Henry	DEL 180	Aaron	CHE	743
Philip	WAS	91	Isaac	CHE 820	Abel	BUC	143A
Philip	LUZ	337	Israel	PHA 24	Abiah	BUC	105
Rebecca	PHA	111	James	PHA 74	Balser	PHI	80A
Rebecca	YOR	163	James	DEL 169	Barbara	YOR	157
Richard	WAS	44	John	LAN 72	Benjami	BUC	105
Richd.	WST	171	John	MNT 82	Benjamin	BEV	13
Robert	FAY	232	John	MNT 86	Benjamin	PHI	137
Robert	FAY	257	John	FAY 227	Benjn.	CHE	744
Robert Jur.	FAY	232	John	LUZ 327	Caleb	CHE	743
Robt.	CUM	65	John	CHE 886	Caleb	CHE	908
Saml.	CUM	90	John Junr.	LUZ 327	Caleb Jun.	CHE	743
Saml.	CHE	852	Jonathan	MIF 25A	Cochran	LAN	260
Saml.	PHI	98	Jonathan	ALL 73	David	DEL	184
Saml.	MIF	11A	Joseph	YOR 165	David	YOR	213
Samuel	WAS	21	Michael	PHI 133	David	BER	284
Samuel	BFD	51	Nicholas	LAN 253	Ebinezer (See		
Samuel	GRN	88	Peter	PHI 24	James, Simon)	BUC	105
Samuel	NOU	154	Philip	PHI 43	Edward	LAN	53
Samuel	FAY	266	Richard	PHI 123	Elizabeth	BUC	105
Silas	LUZ	346	Richard	CHE 699	Evan	BUC	105
Thomas	BEV	16	Richard	CHE 855	Evan	SOM	162
Thomas	WAS	52	Samuel	NOH 64A	Evan	CHE	725
Thomas	BER	248	Samuel	LAN 22	Evans	WAS	38
Thomas	BUT	335	Samuel	MNT 128	Ezekial	NOU	111
Thomas	CHE	849	Samuel	LUZ 326	Fredrick	DEL	176
Thomas	CHE	852	Samuel	LAN 266A	Fredrick	DEL	178
William	DAU	9	Thomas	WAS 68	George	BFD	54
William	WAS	21	Thomas	WAS 75	Hugh	BFD	51
William	WAS	52	Thos.	CUM 131	Isaac	WAS	44
William	LUZ	346	William	ADA 37	Isaac	PHI	91
William	LUZ	382	William	MIF 7A	Isaac	CHE	722
Wm.	PHA	83	Willm.	PHI 71A	Isaac	CHE	881
Wm.	CUM	137	JACOBSON, Matts.	PHI 10	James	PHI	12
Wm.	CHE	767	JACOBY, Adam	DAU 27	Jemima	FAY	221
JACKWIT, Nicholas	LAN	187	Benj.	BUC 82	Jesse	MNT	47
JACOB, Christian	NOH	90	Christn.	PHI 124	Jesse	CHE	743
Christopher	YOR	160	Conrad	BER 279	Jesse	BUC	88A
Daniel	ADA	34	Cunrad	NOH 51A	John	ALL	62
Daniel	BFD	38	Elizabeth	PHI 123	John	PHA	81
George	YOR	179	George	NOH 59A	John	DEL	190
George	YOR	206	Henry	BUC 91	John	YOR	218
George Junr.	MIF	7A	Henry	NOH 59A	John	FRA	293
George Senr.	MIF	7A	Henry	NOH 66A	John	FRA	319
Guir?	LAN	138	Jacob	NOH 82	Jonathan	CHE	857
Henry	YOR	179	John	BUC 80	Jos.	CHE	705
John	ADA	35	John	PHI 133	Joseph	DEL	159

196

JENKINS, Mary	HNT	159	JEWEL, Robert	ALL	92	JOHN, David	CHE	705

Name	Co.	Pg.	Name	Co.	Pg.	Name	Co.	Pg.
JENKINS, Mary	HNT	159	JEWEL, Robert	ALL	92	JOHN, David	CHE	705
Moses	ADA	13	Samuel	GRN	64	David	CHE	796
Mrs.	NOU	129	Seth	GRN	109	David	CHE	817
Mrs.	NOU	97A	JEWELL, John	PHA	119	David	CHE	835
Nathaniel	WAS	56	Joseph	VEN	167	David	CHE	858
Nathaniel	LAN	156	Kenneth	PHA	22	Elezaer	YOR	218
Palmer	LUZ	380	William	WAS	44	Enoch	CHE	835
Richard	NOU	129	JEY, James	ALL	98	Evan	CUM	57
Robert	LAN	94	JHNSON, Robert	NOU	158	George	GRN	70
Stephen	PHA	114	JIFFEE?, Betsy	PHI	87A	Gideon	FAY	266
Stephen	LUZ	381	JILLY, Samuel	PHI	93	Griffith	CHE	858
Thomas	LUZ	376	JINGERICH, Danl.	LAN	148	Henry	CUM	57
Thomas	CHE	769	JININGS, David	FAY	232	Isaac	NOU	111
Walter	ADA	13	Jonathen	FAY	232	Isaiah	HNT	129
William	BEV	25	JINKENLINE, Jacob	CHE	793	Jacob	GRN	107
William	MNT	68	JINKENS, Benjn.	CUM	70	Jacob	NOU	111
William	SOM	162	Evan	BFD	47	Jacob	FRA	321
Willy	CHE	737	William	BFD	47	James	HNT	138
Wm.	CHE	908	JINKINS, Benjn.			James	FAY	257
JENKINSON, Isaac	WAS	38	Junr.	CUM	65	James	CHE	796
JENKS, Joseph	BUC	161	Nathaniel			Jane	YOR	215
Thos.	BUC	161	(Crossed Out)	LAN	151	Jehu	FAY	245
William	BUC	161	JINNETH, Edward	FAY	257	Jehu	CHE	712
William	BUC	161	JINNINGS,			Jesse	CHE	815
JENNINGS,			Benjamin	SOM	143	John	ADA	43
Ebenezer	WAS	91	Benjamin	FAY	232	John	GRN	73
Elnathan	LUZ	352	Jacob	FAY	236	Jos.	YOR	218
Henrey	FAY	215	John	BFD	44	Joseph	ADA	14
Henry	GRN	101	Jonathn.	FAY	245	Levi	CHE	833
Hugh	WAS	110	JINWING, John C.	PHI	104A	Melechia	HNT	138
Isaac	WAS	3	JNKS?, John	ALL	115	Mordicai	FAY	266
Isaac	WST	346	JO---THAN?, Wm.	FRA	287	Nathan	CHE	836
Jacob	GRN	88	JO--?, Robt.	FRA	289	Reese Esq.	CHE	781
Jacob	FAY	215	JOABS, James	FAY	209	Reuben	CHE	813
Jacob	BER	244	Samuel	FAY	266	Thomas	SOM	129
James	LYC	12	JOAD, John	PHA	98	Thomas	CHE	832
John	WAS	3	JOB, Ezechal	ALL	78	William	WST	160
John	WAY	147	Nicholas	LAN	37	JOHNES, Bengamin	ALL	81
John Esqr.	PHA	122	Robert	ALL	88	John	ALL	119
Jonathan	WAY	141	JOBES, George	BUC	99	Joshua	ALL	81
Joseph	WAS	3	JOBS, George	GRN	82	Thomas	ALL	99
Nathaniel	GRN	64	Jas.	BUC	138A	Wilm.	ALL	118
Solomon	BER	266	Saml.	FAY	257	JOHNNSTON,		
Widow	MIF	10A	JOBSON, John	MIF	12A	Ccharrles	ALL	82
JENNINS, Jeremia	FAY	266	Joseph	BUC	145	JOHNS, Abraham	LAN	182
JENNY, Elizath	PHI	87A	Joseph	DEL	176	David	MIF	17
Jacob	BUC	103	Saml.	PHI	104A	David	MIF	17
JENSON, George	NOH	53	JOCK, John	PHI	78	Jacob	LAN	173
Mathew	WAY	135	JOCKSON, Benj.	PHI	107A	Jacob	FRA	285
JENTRY, Robt.	PHI	75	Richd. B.	PHI	108	Jacob	LAN	312
JENZER, Jacob	BER	130	JODER, Abraham	NOH	80	Jacob Junr.	LAN	174
JEQUISH, John	FAY	238	Danl.	BER	257	James	FRA	294
JERGER, John	BER	142	David	BER	142	John	LAN	174
Solomon	BER	176	Jacob	BER	161	Jonathan	LAN	312
JERHARN, Madam	PHA	122	Jacob	BER	257	Joseph	ADA	36
JERMAN, John	DEL	179	Jacob	BER	270	Joseph	SOM	158
JERMON, John	PHA	19	Jacob Jur.	BER	257	Nathan	WAS	81
JEROULD, Jabez	LUZ	428	John	NOH	80	Nathan	BUC	161
JERRET, Daniel	NOH	59A	John	BER	142	Richard	WAS	81
Edward	NOH	59A	John	BER	257	Saml.	FRA	316
John	NOH	59A	Peter	BER	176	Samuel Esqr.	ALL	55
JERRETT, Jacob	FRA	276	Saml.	BER	176	Thomas	ALL	58
JERRY, Joseph	BFD	44	JODON, Francis	BUC	155A	Thomas	FRA	273
JERVIS, Chas.	PHA	12	Peter	BUC	156	Willm.	PHI	47
Samuel	MNT	138	JOH, George	BER	147	Wm.	FRA	316
JESRO, George	BER	244	John	BER	276	JOHNS?, Wm.	FRA	315
JESS, Frederic	CHE	905	JOHN, Widow	PHI	7	JOHNSON, Widow	PHI	5
JESSOP, Isaac	PHA	116	Abel	ADA	14	Widow	PHI	12
Jonathan	YOR	156	Abia	NOU	105	Widow	PHI	13
JESTER, Thomas	WAS	69	Abraham	ADA	28	(See Jhnson)	NOU	158
JEVLY?, Joseph	PHI	70A	Adams	PHI	1099	Abner	NOU	105
JEWEL, George	BEV	5	Ashbel	BUC	105	Abner	BUC	84A
Hopewell	FAY	209	Asper	YOR	213	Abraham	WAS	3
John	FAY	209	Colemery	LAN	172	Abraham	BUC	83
Jonathan	GRN	101	Daniel	BUT	349	Abraham	MNT	120
Moses	GRN	101	David	FRA	321	Adam	BER	250

JOHNSON, Adm.	BUT 343	JOHNSON, Jacob	CHE 710	JOHNSON, Lawrence	PHI 153		
Adm.	BUT 343	Jacob	PHI 69A	Lawrence Sr.	PHI 153		
Alexander	WAS 8	Jacob	BUC 137A	Lawrence	BUC 88A		
Alexander	WAS 85	James	MIF 5	Leonard	MNT 71		
Alexander	WAS 91	James	MIF 15	Leven?	PHI 102A		
Alexander	LAN 151	James	WAS 21	Margaret	WAS 29		
Alexander	DEL 169	James	WAS 56	Margaret	PHA 66		
Alexr.	CHE 732	James	PHI 135	Mark	CHE 876		
Alexr.	CEN 20A	James	NOU 158	Martha	BUC 83		
Alexr.	PHI 75A	James	DEL 163	Mary	BUC 107		
Andrew	LAN 170	James	MIF 25A	Mary	WAS 122		
Andw.	MIF 10	James	BUC 93A	Mathew	WAS 21		
Andw.	PHI 28	James	BUC 138A	Mathias	MNT 68		
Anthony	PHI 128	Jane	PHI 103	Michael	DEL 171		
Aquilla	WAS 110	Jas. (Plow?)	MIF 25A	Moses	LUZ 355		
Asahel	LUZ 416	Jas.	CEN 22B	Nancy	PHI 92A		
Barnaby	PHI 32	Jas.	MIF 25A	Nathan	CHE 768		
Benja.	PHI 151	Jas.	PHI 78A	Nathl.	MIF 10		
Benjamin	MNT 114	Jehoiada P.	LUZ 320	Nehemiah	WAS 49		
Benjamin	MNT 127	Jesse	BUC 84A	Nicholas	BER 166		
Benjamin	DEL 166	Job	DAU 47A	Nicholas	LUZ 411		
Benjn.	PHI 51	John	WAS 3	Nicholas	BUC 88A		
Benjn.	BUT 343	John	WAS 8	Peggy	MIF 7A		
Benjn.	PHI 70A	John	MIF 10	Peter	MNT 114		
Benjn.	BUC 86A	John	WAS 21	Peter	PHI 154		
Caleb	WAS 81	John	WAS 21	Peter	LUZ 417		
Caleb	PHI 99	John	WAS 21	Philip	PHI 105		
Caleb	CHE 768	John	BFD 51	Rachel	WAS 56		
Caleb	CHE 849	John	PHA 51	Rebecca	WAS 100		
Casper	BUC 157	John	WAS 56	Rebecca	PHI 153		
Casper Jr/sr?	BUC 157	John	WAS 63	Richard	PHI 29		
Catherine	PHI 122	John	MNT 64	Richard	WAS 85		
Charles	PHI 17	John	MNT 65	Richard	WAS 100		
Charles	MNT 65	John	LAN 66	Richard	LAN 216		
Christopher	CHE 744	John	MNT 68	Richard	LUZ 331		
Christopr.	NOU 194	John	WAS 69	Richard	BUC 84A		
Conrod	PHI 66	John	PHI 75	Robert	WAS 81		
Daniel	WAS 63	John	BUC 83	Robert	NOU 158		
Daniel	BUC 80	John	BUC 103	Robert	DEL 185		
David	WAS 63	John	PHI 127	Robert	NOH 37A		
David	BUC 103	John	MNT 128	Robt.	MIF 10		
David	BUC 154	John	LAN 151	Robt.	PHI 89A		
David	DEL 166	John	PHI 153	Saml.	PHA 53		
David	BER 273	John	BER 156	Saml.	PHI 102A		
David	NOH 51A	John	NOU 158	Saml.	PHI 103A		
Elias	PHI 151	John	LAN 160	Samuel	WAS 8		
Eliza.	PHI 37	John	DEL 164	Samuel	BUC 83		
Esabelly	PHI 67A	John	DEL 169	Samuel	WAS 100		
Esther	MNT 45	John	LAN 177	Samuel	NOU 158		
Evan	PHI 145	John	NOU 183	Samuel	BUC 161		
Evan	BUC 143A	John	LUZ 325	Samuel	WST 380		
Ezekiel	DEL 191	John	LUZ 354	Samuel	CHE 730		
Francis Esqr.	PHI 62	John	LUZ 413	Samuel	BUC 86A		
Frank	LAN 22	John	NOH 66A	Samuel	BUC 88A		
Garret	BUC 151A	John	PHI 84A	Sidney	WAS 81		
George	MIF 1	John	BUC 93A	Solomon	LUZ 322		
Gersham	PHI 117A	John	PHI 101A	Thomas	MIF 5		
Gideon	PHI 153	John	PHI 117A	Thomas	WAS 44		
Henry	MNT 87	Jonathan	BUC 146	Thomas	BFD 51		
Henry	BUC 157	Jonathan	BUC 93A	Thomas	HNT 161		
Henry	NOU 165	Joseph	MNT 39	Thomas	NOU 199		
Henry	NOU 194	Joseph	MNT 40	Thomas	BER 250		
Humphrey	FAY 227	Joseph	PHI 44	Thomas	CHE 810		
Isaac	NOU 149	Joseph	PHA 79	Thomas.	BUT 367		
Isaac	MIF 7A	Joseph	BUC 86	Thos.	MIF 1		
Isaac	PHI 95A	Joseph	MNT 114	Thos.	PHI 77		
Isaac	BUC 143A	Joseph	LAN 121	Thos.	PHI 89A		
Jack	LAN 304	Joseph	MNT 128	Tobias	MNT 57		
Jacob	MNT 47	Joseph	PHI 140	Tobias Junr.	MNT 57		
Jacob	PHI 62	Joseph	BUC 146	Venus	PHI 149		
Jacob	PHI 110	Joseph	PHI 153	Widow	MIF 10		
Jacob	MNT 128	Joseph	DEL 163	Willaim	WAS 91		
Jacob	NOU 147	Joseph	BUC 93A	William	WAS 3		
Jacob	PHI 153	Joseph	BUC 137A	William	WAS 8		
Jacob	NOU 165	Joseph	BUC 151A	William	PHI 14		
Jacob	LUZ 321	Joshua	BFD 44	William	WAS 21		

JOHNSON, William	WAS	21	JOHNSTON, David	GRN	74	JOHNSTON, John		FAY	266
William	WAS	57	David	HNT	130	John		LAN	300
William	MNT	65	David	WST	252	John		WST	310
William	MNT	66	David	WST	311	John		FRA	312
William	NOH	78	David	MER	446	John		FRA	322
William	MNT	82	Edward	WAS	52	John		WST	325
William	WAS	85	Elija	FAY	204	John		WST	368
William	LAN	112	Elizabeth	CUM	50	John		MER	446
William	MNT	114	Elizh.	FRA	313	John		MER	446
William	PHI	134	Ephraim	ADA	14	John		MER	447
William	PHI	135	Ephraim	DAU	45	John		CHE	704
William	LAN	154	Ephraim	FAY	204	John		CHE	724
William	HNT	159	Frances	BEV	10	John Esqr.		ALL	51
William	LAN	159	George	LYC	27	John Esqr.		ALL	63
William	HNT	163	George	BFD	58	John Junr.		GRN	74
William	DEL	176	George (Crossed			John Rev.		HNT	156
William	FAY	245	Out)	FRA	308	John J.		MER	446
William	BER	273	George	FRA	310	Jonathan		PHA	74
William 2nd	MNT	66	George Esq.	SOM	141	Jonathan		GRN	88
William	LUZ	394	Hanah	MER	446	Jonathan		ALL	106
William	LUZ	408	Harah	ALL	106	Jonathan		HNT	145
William	CHE	823	Henry	WST	310	Jos.		CUM	141
Willm.	BUT	338	Henry	CHE	704	Joseph		ALL	62
Willm.	BUT	343	Hugh	ADA	40	Joseph		GRN	76
Willm. B.	PHI	137	Hugh	CUM	94	Joseph		ALL	100
Wm.	PHA	53	Hugh	ALL	109	Joseph		FAY	251
Wm.	PHA	62	Hugh	HNT	143	Joseph		WST	325
Wm.	CHE	722	Hugh	VEN	167	Joseph		CHE	840
Wm.	MIF	11A	Isaac	WAS	28	Joshua		BFD	63
JOHNSTON, Mrs.	LYC	24	Isaac	GRN	76	Joshua		GRN	95
Aaron	DEL	174	Isaac	WAY	137	Natt		ADA	19
Abraham	BEV	12	Jacob	WAS	34	Nicholas		GRN	64
Abraham	YOR	216	James	BEV	10	Peter		LYC	10
Adam	WAS	34	James	BEV	13	Peter		PHI	11A
Adam	CUM	92	James	BEV	13	Richd.		PHA	89
Adam	ALL	104	James	BEV	28	Ritchard		ALL	78
Adan	ALL	71	James	WAS	69	Robert		BEV	10
Alexander	CRA	5	James	HNT	146	Robert		WAS	12
Alexdr.	VEN	170	James	HNT	151	Robert		WAS	12
Alexr.	CUM	115	James	HNT	151	Robert		BEV	13
Alexr.	CUM	121	James	FAY	215	Robert		ALL	66
Alexr.	CUM	144	James	LAN	223	Robert		WAS	69
Alexr.	WST	171	James	WST	238	Robert		GRN	79
Alexr.	WST	216	James	LAN	245	Robert		ALL	94
Alexr.	WST	238	James	WST	252	Robert		ALL	103
Andrew	BEV	13	James	WST	253	Robert		HNT	140
Andrew	BEV	18	James	FRA	299	Robert		VEN	167
Andrew	ADA	22	James	MER	447	Robert		MER	446
Andrew	BEV	28	James	CHE	747	Robert Esqr.		ALL	92
Andrew	ALL	53	James	DAU	22A	Robt.		FRA	302
Andrew	HNT	142	James	DAU	24A	Robt. Doct.		FRA	295
Andrew	DEL	178	Jas.	CUM	53	Saml.		CUM	65
Andrew	BER	209	Jas.	CUM	100	Saml.		CUM	70
Andrew	FAY	215	Jas.	CUM	119	Saml.		CUM	77
Andw.	YOR	155	Jas.	FRA	298	Saml.		CUM	92
Andw.	WST	216	Jesse	WAS	34	Saml.		CUM	110
Anthony	HNT	149	Jesse	FAY	204	Saml.		DAU	19A
Archibauld	ALL	69	Jno.	CUM	61	Samuel		BEV	14
Archibeld	FAY	232	Jno.	CUM	88	Samuel		BEV	20
Arther	ALL	107	Jno.	CUM	140	Samuel		WAS	28
Arthur	CUM	105	Jno. Ssr.	FRA	306	Samuel		HNT	157
Baily	GRN	70	John	WAS	28	Samuel		YOR	167
Barnet	WAS	34	John	ADA	39	Samuel		WST	252
Bengm.	FRA	308	John	GRN	70	Samuel		MER	446
Benj.	YOR	160	John	BFD	74	Samuel		CHE	757
Benjamin	HNT	132	John	PHA	74	Simon		CHE	848
Benjamin	DEL	159	John	GRN	88	Solomon		ALL	78
Catharine	HNT	161	John	ARM	123	Stephen		WAS	28
Cathr.	WST	171	John	ARM	125	Sterlin		ALL	71
Cathr.	WST	171	John	ARM	127	Thomas		ARM	122
Charles	BEV	11	John	HNT	131	Thomas		HNT	143
Charles	MER	446	John	WST	152	Thomas		FAY	215
Cornelius	GRN	70	John	DEL	164	Thomas		WST	325
Daniel	WAS	28	John	NOU	203	Thomas		CHE	738
Daniel	FAY	232	John	WST	238	Thomas		CHE	881
David	DAU	46	John	WST	253	Thos.		CUM	106

JOHNSTON, Thos.	YOR 183	JONES, Benjamin	NOU 194	JONES, Hannah	PHA 96
Thos.	YOR 199	Benjamin	LUZ 375	Hannah	BUC 86A
Thos.	YOR 214	Benjamin Jr.	LUZ 371	Henry	ADA 43
Thos.	FRA 290	Benjamin	MIF 10A	Henry	BUC 99
Thos.	FRA 298	Benjn.	CUM 44	Henry	LAN 108
Thos.	FRA 319	Benjn.	CUM 56	Henry	YOR 185
William	ADA 38	Benjn.	PHA 101	Hetty	CUM 40
William	HNT 147	Benjn.	CHE 717	Hugh	MNT 57
William	YOR 169	Benjn.	CHE 744	Hugh	MNT 87
William	DEL 173	Benjn.	CHE 829	Idea	PHA 77
William	FAY 204	Cadwalider	FAY 215	Isaac	LYC 18
William	LAN 315	Caleb	BER 161	Isaac	CUM 27
William	MER 447	Catharine	PHA 60	Isaac	PHA 48
William Esqr.	WAS 34	Catharine	PHA 66	Isaac	MNT 87
William	DAU 9A	Catharine	YOR 206	Isaac	PHA 98
Wilm.	ALL 58	Cdwalr.	PHI 101A	Isaac	PHA 118
Wilm.	ALL 65	Charles	PHA 119	Isaac	YOR 157
Wilm.	ALL 73	Clement	PHA 117	Isaac	DEL 184
Wilm.	ALL 76	Crocker	LUZ 340	Isaac	CHE 786
Wm.	LYC 15	Daniel	BEV 8	Isaac Jr.	YOR 202
Wm.	LYC 20	Daniel	WST 171	Isaac	MNT 105
Wm.	LYC 27	Daniel Revd.	YOR 213	Isaac	DAU 8A
Wm.	PHA 71	Danl. Jr.	MIF 17	Isaac	PHI 76A
Wm.	CUM 145	Danl. Sr.	MIF 17	Isaac C.	PHA 30
Wm.	VEN 167	David	MNT 39	Isaiah	WAS 12
Wm.	FRA 302	David	PHA 44	Isaiah	BUC 86A
Wm.	WST 346	David	PHI 60	Israel	PHA 85
Zachariah	MER 447	David	HNT 122	Jacob	WAS 38
Zepheniah	GRN 101	David	SOM 134	Jacob	ADA 43
JOHNSTONE, David	WAY 144	David	PHI 150	Jacob	MNT 108
Thomas	SOM 146	David	NOU 154	Jacob	MNT 138
Thomas	SOM 162	David	DEL 156	Jacob	BUT 319
William	SOM 143	David	BER 161	Jacob	LUZ 334
JOICE, Dominick	PHA 98	David	MER 446	James	BEV 7
Walter	BUC 93A	David	CHE 705	James	PHI 60
JOINER?, Zacariah	ERI 60	David	CHE 800	James	BER 140
JOINT, Charles	PHI 69	David	CHE 883	James	MNT 141
JOLLEY, Lukins	NOU 183	David Esq.	CHE 716	James	YOR 158
JOLLY, Widow	PHI 6	David	NOH 39A	James	DEL 179
Charles	WAS 12	Dennis	WAS 38	James	FRA 312
Charles	PHA 59	Diana	PHI 5	James	WST 325
Elisha	WAS 12	Edward	PHI 24	James	NOH 66A
John	FAY 245	Edward	MNT 96	James	PHI 97A
Malachi	WAS 80	Edward	PHA 115	Janathan	CHE 786
Robert	BUC 161	Edward	FAY 198	Janathan	CHE 820
Samuel	VEN 168	Edward	YOR 215	Jehu	ADA 25
Thomas	MER 446	Edward Junr.	YOR 215	Jehu	SOM 134
Thoms.	BUT 356	Edward Revd.	YOR 217	Jehu	DEL 173
William	WAS 68	Edward	DAU 51A	Jehu	CHE 823
JONE, Jeremiah	PHI 116	Edwd.	LYC 7	Jenkin	BUC 96A
JONES, Widow	PHI 18	Eleazer	BUC 142	Jesse	PHI 122
Widow	PHI 24	Elias	YOR 201	Jesse	PHI 149
Widow	PHI 95	Elias	LUZ 324	Jesse	DEL 174
Widw.	PHI 87A	Elisha	GRN 84	Jesse	DEL 174
Abednego	WAS 110	Elizabeth	PHA 6	Jesse	CHE 820
Abel	FAY 245	Elizabeth	PHA 14	Jethrow	FRA 282
Able	BFD 74	Elizth.	PHI 57	John	BEV 4
Abm.	PHI 80A	Eloner	MER 446	John	PHA 5
Abner	CHE 818	Enoch	FRA 279	John	PHA 18
Abraham	PHA 52	Enoch	FRA 316	John	PHI 18
Abraham	NOU 105	Enoch	CHE 831	John	PHA 22
Abram	CHE 833	Enock	MNT 141	John	WAS 29
Absolom	PHA 92	Ephraim	BUC 87A	John	NOH 30
Alpheus	WAY 141	Evan	MNT 45	John	PHA 30
Amos	MNT 40	Evan	MNT 87	John	CUM 32
Amos	MNT 99	Evan	PHA 91	John	CUM 34
Andrew	BFD 51	Evan	CHE 828	John	NOH 34
Ann	MIF 25	Evens	NOU 147	John	MNT 37
Ann	PHA 75	Ezekial	FAY 204	John	PHA 37
Asaph	LUZ 380	Ezekiel	BEV 8	John	WAS 38
Benj.	PHI 82	Ezekiel	CHE 723	John	PHA 41
Benj.	YOR 201	George	ADA 38	John	PHI 42
Benjamin	BFD 74	George	PHI 99	John	MNT 50
Benjamin	PHA 101	Gibson	DEL 170	John	GRN 64
Benjamin	GRN 110	Griffith	CHE 880	John	PHI 72
Benjamin	DEL 191	Griffith	BUC 96A	John	PHI 75

JONES, John	MNT 87	JONES, Lloyd	MNT 138	JONES, Saml.	PHI 155
John	LAN 93	Lloyd Capt.	PHA 100	Saml.	FAY 227
John	PHI 95	Luther	LUZ 378	Samuel	MNT 40
John (S)	CHE 901	Malachia	BUC 141	Samuel	PHA 93
John /A/	SOM 146	Margaret	CHE 720	Samuel	NOU 100
John	NOU 105	Maria	LAN 301	Samuel	PHA 114
John	NOU 105	Martha	PHA 31	Samuel	NOU 117
John	CUM 111	Mary	PHA 17	Samuel	BER 203
John	PHI 111	Mary	PHA 21	Samuel	CHE 786
John	WAS 116	Mary	DEL 177	Samuel	CHE 811
John	PHA 118	Mary	YOR 203	Sarah	CHE 752
John	PHI 128	Mary Widow	NOH 32	Sarah	CHE 868
John	BUC 141	Mathan Jr.	LUZ 371	Saufrau	PHI 98
John	LAN 142	Matthew	DEL 168	Silas	MNT 118
John	SOM 146	Mordecai	MNT 115	Silas	MNT 138
John	NOU 154	Morgan	BFD 74	Soloman	PHI 104A
John	BER 161	Morgan	GRN 76	Stephen	GRN 101
John	DEL 168	Moses	GRN 93	Thara	LAN 24
John	YOR 171	Moses	DEL 191	Thoams	MIF 13A
John	DEL 184	Nancy	LAN 149	Thomas	CUM 37
John	NOU 194	Nathan	PHA 13	Thomas	MNT 40
John	FAY 204	Nathan	CUM 31	Thomas	BFD 74
John	FAY 227	Nathan	PHI 57	Thomas	BUC 101
John	FAY 232	Nathan	PHI 74	Thomas	MNT 141
John	FAY 238	Nathan	PHA 87	Thomas	HNT 152
John	FAY 266	Nathan	LUZ 374	Thomas	DEL 155
John	WST 290	Nathan	CHE 823	Thomas	WST 238
John	LUZ 386	Nathaniel	BUC 96A	Thomas	FAY 240
John	CHE 699	Nathn.	PHI 119	Thomas	FAY 251
John	CHE 796	Nicholas	BER 139	Thomas	CHE 811
John	CHE 865	Olliver	BEV 8	Thomas	PHI 69A
John Esq.	MNT 138	Owen	BUC 101	Thomas	BUC 96A
John (Crossed		Owen	PHA 104	Thos.	CUM 70
Out; Followed		Owen	CHE 798	Thos.	CUM 89
By Priscilla)	MNT 40	Paul	MNT 138	Thos.	PHA 110
John (Gulph)	MNT 137	Paul	YOR 201	Thos.	PHI 118
John	MIF 7A	Peregrine	NOH 37A	Thos.	YOR 207
John	CEN 20A	Peter	MIF 10	Thos.	YOR 209
John	PHI 119A	Peter	LYC 13	Thos. Junr.	BUC 96A
John	BUC 155A	Peter	DAU 44	Thos. Senr.	CUM 69
John B.	PHI 78	Peter	ARM 124	Thos.	PHI 76A
Jonahtan	MNT 112	Peter	HNT 138	Thos. A.	PHI 78
Jonathan	PHA 18	Peter	BER 139	W. Thomas	SOM 162
Jonathan	CUM 26	Peter	NOU 171	William	CRA 4
Jonathan	MNT 40	Peter	CEN 18A	William	WAS 21
Jonathan	MNT 45	Peter	BUC 155A	William	WAS 44
Jonathan	MNT 108	Phebe	LYC 3	William	BFD 54
Jonathan	BER 139	Philip	PHA 5	William	PHI 65
Jonathan	DEL 171	Phillip	PHA 54	William	BFD 74
Jonathan	DEL 189	Phoebe	MNT 50	William	GRN 74
Jonathan	FAY 227	Polly	LUZ 411	William	BUC 99
Jonathan	FRA 294	Pricilla	MNT 40	William	PHA 103
Jonathan	CHE 718	Rebeca	FAY 240	William	WAS 110
Jonathan	BUC 155A	Rebecca	PHA 46	William	PHA 120
Jonathen	NOU 105	Reuben	LUZ 409	William	SOM 134
Jones	NOU 105	Rheuben	WAY 141	William	HNT 138
Joseph	PHA 21	Richard	PHA 18	William	NOU 152
Joseph	CUM 34	Richard	LAN 237	William	PHI 154
Joseph	NOH 34	Richard	FAY 251	William	HNT 159
Joseph	PHA 67	Richard	CHE 798	William	SOM 162
Joseph	LAN 77	Richard	CHE 804	William	HNT 164
Joseph	GRN 92	Robert	PHI 19	William	FAY 236
Joseph	PHI 146	Robert	GRN 82	William	CHE 720
Joseph	CHE 787	Robert	GRN 92	William	CHE 831
Joseph	DAU 21A	Robert	WAS 122	William /M/	SOM 134
Joshua	CUM 90	Robert	SOM 162	William	BUC 93A
Joshua	PHI 154	Robert	YOR 164	William	BUC 96A
Joshua	BUC 143A	Robert	DEL 169	Willm.	PHI 40
Justice	LUZ 371	Robert	DEL 170	Wm.	PHA 14
Levi	BFD 51	Robert	VEN 170	Wm.	BEV 18
Levi	WAS 110	Robert	LAN 284	Wm.	CUM 26
Levi	PHI 133	Robert	LAN 284	Wm.	PHA 67
Levi	HNT 152	Robt.	CUM 44	Wm.	CUM 68
Lewis	GRN 93	Saml.	CUM 26	Wm.	PHA 82
Lewis	LUZ 369	Saml.	PHA 43	Wm.	PHA 85
Lewis	CHE 882	Saml.	LAN 141	Wm.	PHA 89

Name	Loc	Pg
JONES, Wm.	PHI	118
Wm.	CHE	834
Wm.	CHE	866
Wm. Jr.	MIF	25A
Wm.	MIF	25A
Wm.	PHI	117A
JONES?, Samuel	BUC	105
JONGEN?, John	CHE	896
JONNES, Ephram	ALL	90
JONS, Regird	LAN	190
JONSON, John	LAN	188
John	LAN	189
Richd.	PHA	44
JONSTON,		
Alexander	PHA	46
Benjn.	PHA	23
Brian	MER	446
George	CHE	910
Isaac	PHA	48
Isaac	PHA	121
Jacob	PHA	18
John	PHA	97
Josiah	PHA	5
Mary	PHA	37
Mary	PHA	113
Mary	PHA	115
Peter	PHA	92
Robert	PHA	111
Sarah	PHA	122
William	PHA	113
William	CHE	700B
Wm.	PHA	99
JORDAN, Bisban	PHI	83
Christopher	BEV	22
David	MIF	1
David	BFD	43
Francis	WST	346
George	DEL	186
George	DAU	47A
Hugh	CEN	20A
James	BEV	28
John	LYC	20
John	BEV	28
John	LAN	36
John	LAN	56
John	HNT	130
John	BUT	360
Michael	PHI	50
Nicholas	PHI	133
Owen	LAN	40
Robert	WST	152
Saml.	LYC	22
Saml.	PHA	63
Stewart	LAN	127
Thos.	WST	346
Thos.	MIF	12A
Widow	LAN	230
William	ADA	4
JORDAN?, John B.?	BFD	47
JORDE, Adolph	NOH	73A
JORDEN, James	CHE	803
Sarah	PHI	105B
Thomas	CHE	823
JORDINE, See		
Porter,		
Jordine &		
JORDON, Amos	BUC	94A
Charles	CUM	34
Francis	WAS	8
Henry	CUM	34
Hugh	YOR	183
Jacob	CHE	752
James	GRN	64
James	WAS	100
Jno.	CHE	852
John	CUM	30
John	WAS	75
JORDON, John	CHE	752
John Jr.	CHE	752
Joseph	CHE	864
Mark	CUM	53
Martin	LAN	32
Mary	PHA	60
Mrs.	CUM	96
Nailor	PHA	93
Rachel	CHE	747
Samuel	WAS	100
William	WAS	49
William	WAS	100
JORDY, Henry	DAU	25
JORG, Jacob	BER	186
JORGER, John	NOH	87
JORMLY, James	ALL	56
JORSEN, Henry	PHI	33
JORTY, John	DAU	28A
JOSEPH, Bucher	LAN	139
Isaac	WAS	100
John	PHI	78
John	PHA	115
John	YOR	179
John	YOR	215
John	LUZ	342
Noah	BFD	45
JOSIAH, Capt.	PHA	100
James	BUC	88A
JOSLAN, Thomas	LUZ	374
Thomas Jr.	LUZ	374
JOSLIN, Jeremiah	BFD	55
JOST, Abraham	BER	133
Christian	WAS	38
George	LAN	210
Joseph	NOH	82
JOUEDAN?, Robert	ARM	127
JOURDAN, Widow	PHI	10
Robert	SOM	132
Robert (Erased)	SOM	129
JOURDON, Alexr.	PHA	61
JOURNEY, Peter	BUC	99
JOUS, Peter	LAN	210
JOY, John	PHI	47
JOYCE, George	ADA	17
JUA?, Michael	BER	164
JUD, Dannel	ALL	102
JUDGE, George	PHI	95A
Paul	BUC	151A
JUDSON, Amos	ERI	59
JUDY, Chri.	DAU	44A
Jacob	LAN	254
John	NOH	59A
Mathias	SOM	138
JUELL, Richard	FAY	266
William	FAY	266
JUKINS, Henry	CHE	890
JULEY, Balsom	NOU	97A
JULIAN, Isaac	GRN	107
John	GRN	107
Julian	PHA	92
William	PHA	113
JULIN, John	WAS	122
JULIUS, George J.	YOR	174
Peter	YOR	174
JUMPER, Abm.	CUM	130
Conrod	CUM	102
Jacob	CUM	102
Joseph	CUM	102
JUNCKER,		
Frederick	NOH	73A
Simon	NOH	76
JUND, Daniel	NOH	90
George	NOH	90
Jacob	NOH	90
JUNG, Christian	NOH	80
Dewalt	NOH	50
JUNG, Henry	NOH	34
Jacob	LAN	147B
Jacob	NOH	71A
Jacob	NOH	73A
John	BER	203
John	NOH	73A
Peter	BER	188
Samuel	BER	279
JUNGBERG, John	NOH	70
JUNGER, Casper	NOH	90
George	NOH	90
JUNGLING, Andrew	NOH	47A
JUNGMAN, George		
Revd.	NOH	32
Gotlob	BER	244
John	NOH	32
Peter	LAN	136
JUNKEN, Benjn.	CUM	61
JUNKENS, Adam	CUM	41
Joseph	CUM	119
JUNKIN, Benjn.	CUM	38
James	MIF	25A
Margaret	CHE	800
Marst.?	MIF	25A
Saml.	MIF	25A
Wm.	MIF	25
Wm.	MIF	25
JUNKINS, Hugh	WST	380
JUNKS, Thomas	FAY	257
JUNRITE?, John	PHA	66
JUNY, Christian	LAN	141
JURA?, Samuel	DAU	8
JURDAN, Edward	FAY	209
Joseph	FAY	209
JURDIN, James	NOU	117
JURE?, Louis T.		
L.	PHA	32
Peter T.	PHA	32
JUS, Daniel	NOH	59A
JUSHEAU, Martin	PHA	7
JUSTACE, Widow	PHI	66
JUSTICE, Widow	PHI	104A
Chas.	PHA	45
David	FRA	308
Equilla	BFD	64
George	PHI	109
Griffith	BFD	64
Isaac	BEV	27
Jacob	BEV	4
Jesse	BFD	64
John	PHA	10
John	WAS	81
Joseph	WAS	38
Joseph	DEL	192
Nathan	SOM	134
Nicholas	BFD	64
Peter	WST	171
Philip	PHI	113
William	BFD	38
JUSTINCE, Isaac	DEL	171
JUSTIS, James	WAR	1A
JUTT?, Wm.	PHI	79A
JUTY, J.	LAN	148
JUVENAL, Nichs.	PHI	105
K-----?, John	MIF	1
K----N?, Simon	BFD	74
KAARL, Martin	ADA	34
Michael	ADA	32
KABB, Adam	MNT	99
KABLE, John	LAN	292
KABLER, Michael	LAN	185
KACHEL, John	BER	170
John Jr.	BER	170
Leonard	BER	247
Samuel	BER	170

KACHEL, Samuel		KAMP, David Jr.	BER 254	KARMANY, George	DAU 43A
Jr.	BER 170	Fredk.	BER 188	KARMONY, Anthony	DAU 42
KACHLEIN, Andrew	NOH 67	Henry	BER 254	Anthony	DAU 44A
Peter	NOH 39A	Henry	BER 254	KARN, Matthew	NOU 180
KACK?, Aron	MNT 93	Jacob	DAU 47	Matthew	NOU 180
KACKE, George	NOU 111	John	DAU 50	KARNAN, Jno.	CUM 74
KACKLEIN, Jacob	NOH 82	John	BER 279	KARNES, John	FAY 227
KADON, Ann	CUM 149	Martin	BER 130	KARNEY, Joseph	DAU 44
KADOO, James	ALL 88	Mathias	DAU 48	KARNS, Ann	CUM 58
Sarah	ALL 98	KAMPEL, John	DAU 49A	Conrad	FRA 280
KADWALEDER, John	FAY 236	KAMPFER, Jacob	LAN 313	Hannah	WST 253
KAFFERROTH, Jacob	LAN 199	KAMPLER, Abram	MNT 128	Richard	PHI 49
KAFFMAN, Andrew	LAN 287	KAMREN, Math.	LAN 147	Thomas	MIF 17
Ben.	LAN 287	KAMRER, Jacob	LAN 147	William	WST 253
David	LAN 263	KAN--A?, John	WST 217	KARPER, John	DAU 44
Isaac	LAN 287	KANAAN, William	MER 447	KARR, Francis	SOM 143
Isaac	LAN 287	KANADAY, Andrew	NOU 171	Joseph	ADA 8
Jacob	LAN 262	KANADY, Alexr.	NOU 194	Joseph	SOM 158
John	LAN 252	Alexr.	NOU 194	Sarah	ADA 36
John	WST 290	John	NOU 147	KARR?, Jacob	NOU 137
Michael	LAN 252	KANAN, John	NOU 117	Robt.	PHI 70A
Widow	LAN 288	KANDA, John	LAN 263	KARREL, Benjn.	BUC 144
KAGEY, Widow	LAN 275	KANDECKER, Saml.	FRA 286	KARRICK, Jacob	DAU 33
KAGLEY, Jacob	CUM 89	KANE, James	HNT 125	Joseph	PHA 89
KAHAL, Peter	FRA 311	John	PHI 52	KARRIGAN, Jacob	LAN 277
KAHLER, Emanul	BER 244	KANERER, Adam	WST 217	KARRIGO, Daniel	GRN 71
KAHM, Michael	NOH 59A	KANGEN, Ignatius		KARSHNER,	
KAHR, Conrad	LAN 278	(Negro)	WAS 116	Jonathan	BER 262
KAIGHN?, Mary	PHA 21	KANGER, Martin	BER 243	KARSNER, Michael	BFD 74
KAIL?, George	PHI 99	KANIDAY, James	ALL 82	KARSON, Eliz.	BER 244
KAIN, Ann	PHA 23	John	ALL 82	KARST, Nicols.	DAU 23
Anthony	PHA 93	John	ALL 96	KART, Jacob	BER 244
George	NOU 183	Joshua	ALL 70	KARTZ, John	LAN 185
Jno.	CEN 22B	Wilm.	ALL 96	KASEY / KASCY?,	
John	PHA 16	KANN, Eve	YOR 162	Elinor?	BUC 106A
John	WAS 34	Henry	LAN 56	KASEY, Peter	PHI 116A
John	PHA 92	John	LAN 56	KASHERBERIAN,	
John	NOU 194	Peter	LAN 56	John	PHI 1
John	CEN 22B	KANOUSE, Philip	PHI 82A	KASKE, Renatus	NOH 70
Manus	DEL 192	KANSER, Christn.	DAU 29A	KASLER, William	LAN 143
Michael	DEL 192	KANTNER, Adam	BER 244	KASS, Ishmal	MIF 17
Moses	NOH 60	Cathr.	BER 239	KASSEL, Abraham	MNT 68
Peter	PHA 115	George	BER 271	Jacob	YOR 219
Robort	ERI 59	John	BER 223	Yellis	MNT 68
Stephen	WAS 16	John	BER 244	KASSNER, Adam	BER 162
KAIN?, R---?	PHA 5	Nicholas	BER 271	KATBRIDER, Henry	YOR 204
KAINER, Christr.	CUM 32	Peter	BER 242	KATELY, Widw.	PHI 81
KAIRNS, Jacob	WST 347	Simon	BER 205	KATES, Michl.	PHI 61
KAISOR, Frederick	BUC 139	Susanna	BER 223	KATHORN?, Danl.	PHI 78
KAISTER, John	NOU 194	Val.	BER 147	KATLOR?, Conrod	WST 217
John	NOU 194	KANTRICE, Abraham	HNT 135	KATTERMAN, John	BER 271
KAISY, John	PHI 152	KAPINGBERGER,		John	BER 272
KAKE?, Michl	PHI 117	Conrad	WST 191	KATTEW, Aaron	BER 161
KALBACH, Adam	BER 201	KAPP, Ffredrik	DAU 31A	KATTOR?, Conrod	WST 217
Georg	BER 205	George	DAU 30	KATTS, Michael	PHI 107A
Henry	BER 201	George	LAN 136	KATZ, Andrew	MNT 108
Michl.	BER 141	John	DAU 30	Catherine	MNT 108
KALBREATH, Joseph	CUM 108	John	DAU 4A	Henry	MNT 109
KALE?, Raphael	PHA 114	Jos.	YOR 187	KATZEMAN, Anrw.	BER 201
KALER, Henry	NOU 105	Maria	YOR 162	KATZMYER, Ludwig	BER 134
Mathias	BER 251	Martin	LAN 18	KATZS, Catheren	ALL 98
KALKENBINE,		Michael	DAU 2	KAUB, George	NOH 82A
Anthony	BER 252	Michael	DAU 2	KAUCHER, George	BER 203
KALKINS, Oliver	WAY 138	Susannah	YOR 177	Jacob	BER 201
KALLER, Jacob	LAN 211	Widow	LAN 23	KAUFFELT, Michael	YOR 205
John	LAN 200	KAPPES, George	LAN 200	KAUFFMAN, (No	
Leonard	LAN 200	KAPPS, Martin	BER 150	Given Name)	LAN 147B
KALTENSTINE?,		KARCH, John	LAN 40	Abrm.	DAU 42
Ludwick	YOR 186	KARCHER,		Andrew	LAN 187
KALTOR?, Conrod	WST 217	Christian	BER 160	Andrew	LAN 187
KAMERLO, Fredk.	PHI 78A	Daniel	BER 278	Andrew	LAN 291
KAMERON, James	PHA 77	KARHART, John	FRA 299	Christian	LAN 2
KAMMERER,		KARKWOOD, John	NOU 165	Christian	LAN 28
Christian	LAN 98	KARL, George	BER 212	Christian	LAN 291
KAMP, Andrew	BER 188	Jacob	BER 213	Christian	LAN 291
David	BER 254	KARMANY, Adam	YOR 167	Christian	LAN 316

KAUFFMAN, David	NOH	80A	KAYLOR, John	NOU	122	KEARSLEY, Jane	CUM 148
Henry	LAN	12	KAYSMAN,			Valentine	DEL 174
Henry	LAN	102	Frederick	BER	226	KEARSLY, Samuel	DAU 3A
Isaac	LAN	291	KAYTON, John	WAS	22	KEAS, Elizabeth	ADA 10
Isaac	LAN	305	Saml.	CUM	126	Peter	BER 258
Jacob	HNT	160	KEACH, Joseph	LAN	244	KEASBEY, Jesse	PHA 4
Jacob	LAN	189	Nathaniel	CHE	739	KEASLER, Conrad	PHA 23
Jacob	LAN	296	Nathl.	CHE	849	KEASOR, Leonard	BUC 107
Jacob	NOH	47A	Samuel	LAN	243	KEATON, Joohn	SOM 149
John	LAN	12	KEADY, John	WAS	116	Loftus	GRN 71
John	LAN	24	William	WAS	116	KEATS, Mary	PHA 12
John	LAN	283	KEAFER, Frederick	ADA	27	KEBLE, John	PHA 78
John	LAN	291	Henry	ADA	27	KEBLEHOUSE,	
John	LAN	305	Jacob	ADA	29	George	PHI 91A
John	NOH	47A	John	ADA	28	KEBLER, George	CUM 80
Joseph	LAN	289	John Sen.	ADA	27	George	WST 325
Michael	LAN	283	KEAFF, William	LAN	38	Jos.	PHI 106
Michael	LAN	291	KEAFHAUVER,			Widow	LAN 271
Philip	NOH	80A	Conrad	ADA	7	KECHLER, John	DEL 171
Rudolph	NOH	80A	KEAFHAUVER?,			KECHLER?, (See	
Saml.	NOH	47A	Peter	ADA	7	Keehler)	LAN 44
Solomon	LAN	37	KEAGY, Abraham	LAN	238	KECK, Andrew	SOM 158
Widow	LAN	289	John	SOM	149	Andrew	NOH 82A
KAUFFMANN, Widow	NOH	69	Rudolph	LAN	228	Conrad	NOH 85A
KAUFMAN, Abm.	BER	141	KEALER, George	BUC	149A	Cunrod	SOM 158
Adam	BER	141	Mary	BUC	149A	John	NOH 45
Adam	SOM	154	William	BUC	149A	John	NOH 45
Andrew	LAN	308	KEAMER, Adam	WST	191	John	DEL 185
Christian	BER	267	KEAMP, Hercules	HNT	137	John Junr.	NOH 82A
Christiana	YOR	170	KEAN, Barnard	CUM	90	John	NOH 82A
Christn.	DAU	19	Charles	CUM	28	KECKLER, Abraham	ADA 16
Christn.	BER	141	Conrod	CHE	905	Peter	ADA 16
Christn.	BER	142	Dennis	WST	311	KECTER, Jacob	NOH 73A
Christn.	BER	200	Hugh	DEL	180	KEDSON?, James	BEV 17
David	BER	141	James	WST	217	KEE, John	FRA 294
George	BER	141	James	LAN	227	KEEBEL, Christian	LAN 141
Henry	WAS	38	Jas.	LAN	165	KEECH, John	CHE 852
Henry	YOR	205	John	PHA	15	KEEFE, David	BFD 35
Isaac	BER	141	John	BEV	21	KEEFER, Andw.	DAU 23
Isaac	BER	141	John	DAU	42	George	DAU 20
Isaac	LAN	301	John	CUM	121	Jacob	DAU 15
Jacob	BER	141	John	WST	171	Jacob	SOM 138
Jacob	YOR	200	John Junr.	BEV	21	John	FRA 312
Jacob	YOR	215	John Sr.	DAU	4	Joseph	DAU 40A
Jacob	BER	230	Mary	BEV	11	Mathias	DAU 13
Jacob	BER	279	Neal	MIF	17	Peter	CUM 140
Jacob	BER	284	Patrick	PHI	15	Peter	BER 214
John	BER	141	Patrick	WAS	85	Peter	LAN 270
John	BER	141	Philip	HNT	120	KEEFER?, Gasper	WST 253
John	YOR	159	Robert	PHI	17	KEEFFER,	
John	BER	200	Robert	PHI	150	Christian	WAS 116
John	YOR	215	Samuel	WAS	57	KEEHLER, Jacob	LAN 44
John	BER	219	William	WST	325	KEEK, Georoge	WST 217
John	LAN	308	KEANEY, Peter	YOR	190	Henry	WST 216
Jos.	YOR	167	KEANON, Widow	LAN	222	Phillip	WST 216
Joseph	BER	279	KEANY, John	YOR	188	KEEL, Adam	BER 131
Jost	BER	141	KEARHOOF, Henry	HNT	145	Baltis	PHA 65
Mary	YOR	171	KEARL, James	BER	155	George	PHI 133
Michael	LAN	313	KEARMANY, John	DAU	42	George	PHI 142
Peter	BER	230	KEARN, Abraham	LAN	268	Henry	PHA 52
Philip	BER	141	George	LAN	267	John	CUM 28
Solomon	YOR	160	Henry	LAN	270	Peter	PHA 63
Stephen	BER	141	Jacob	CUM	150	Philip	BFD 51
Stephen	BER	141	Michael	HNT	142	KEELER, Ebenezer	PHI 101A
Stephen	BER	141	Peter	LAN	268	Elisha	LUZ 397
Val.	BER	141	Stophel	LAN	269	John	MNT 73
KAUL, John	NOH	59A	Wm.	BUC	82	Martin	DAU 33A
KAUNLET, Peter	LAN	50	KEARNEY, John	LUZ	403	Paul	LUZ 372
KAUP, Christian	BER	157	KEARNLY, John	MNT	62	Rinehart	MNT 73
Peter	BER	157	KEARNS, Francis	BUT	317	William	MNT 73
KAUTZ, Philip	LAN	15	John	CUM	27	KEELEY, Elizth.	CHE 790
KAUTZMAN, Benard	LAN	199	William	BUT	317	Francis	WAS 111
KAVENOCH, Edward	YOR	214	KEARSLEY, Doctr			John	CHE 790
KAY, Daniel	PHI	3	Hospital For			Mathias	PHA 42
William	BFD	64	Asstiant?			Matthias	CHE 815
KAYLOR, George	NOU	122	Weoman	PHA	28	KEELLEY, Conrod	CHE 815

KEELLEY, Conrod		KEESTER, Peter	BUT 340	KEIGH, Peter	HNT 116
Jr.	CHE 815	KEETH?, Benjn.	PHI 35	KEIGHFER, Abram	CHE 793
KEELY, Conrad	MNT 121	KEEVER, Lewis	HNT 118	KEIGHLER,
Henry	BER 174	KEFFER, Abraham	SOM 146	Christn.	PHA 86
Jacob	MNT 73	Adam	SOM 134	KEIGLER, Killian	YOR 177
Jacob	BER 174	Adam	SOM 158	KEIHLER?, Andrew	LAN 190
Jacob Jr.	BER 174	Adam Sen.	SOM 134	KEIHN?, John	BER 244
Nelly	PHA 51	Casper	SOM 141	KEIL, John	LAN 140
KEELY?, Henry	PHI 140	Henry	LAN 33	Peter	NOU 122
KEEM?, George	BER 230	Jacob	SOM 138	KEILER, Widow	PHI 29
KEEMER, John	LAN 70	Jacob	SOM 154	KEILOUGH, Thomas	LAN 153
KEEN, Adam	FAY 266	Jacob Sen.	SOM 141	KEIM, Daniel	BER 279
Andw.	PHI 83A	John	PHA 37	George	BER 244
Ann	PHA 61	John	SOM 146	Henry	BER 176
Anthony	BUC 93A	Joseph	BER 170	Jacob	BER 219
Christn.	BER 204	Michael	SOM 138	John	NOH 34
Isaac	PHI 134	Michael	SOM 146	John	HNT 154
Jacob	PHI 66	Valentine	SOM 141	John	BER 224
Jacob	PHI 73	KEFNER, Bingn.	FRA 304	John	BER 244
James	PHI 85	David	FRA 304	John	BER 257
John	PHI 74	Mary	FRA 304	John	BER 276
John	PHI 82	KEGENISE,		Nicholas	BER 244
John	PHI 134	Christian	ADA 6	Saml.	BER 176
John	BUC 89A	KEGERREIS, Jacob	LAN 199	Valentine	BER 219
John	BUC 93A	Jacob Jnr.	LAN 200	KEIM?, George	BER 230
Joseph	PHA 10	John	LAN 200	KEIME, Martin	NOU 129
Joseph	BUC 161	Michael	LAN 199	KEIMLEY, Leonard	PHA 29
Joseph	BUC 89A	KEGGY, Christian	FRA 304	KEIMLEY?, John	MNT 73
Rachel	PHA 29	KEGHLIDGE,		KEIMLY, John	NOH 80A
Rueben	PHI 137	Anthony	NOH 67	KEIMM, George	NOH 90A
Samuel	PHI 98	KEGLE, Henry	PHI 97	John	NOH 90A
Timothy	ALL 91	KEHART, Adam	CEN 20A	KEIN, Jane	CUM 94
Wm. Jonas	PHA 98	Henry	CEN 20A	KEINE, Conrad	BER 284
KEENAN, John	ALL 84	Mary	CEN 20A	KEINER, Adam	YOR 176
KEENER, George	YOR 197	KEHL, Adam	BER 203	Christian	BER 271
Jacob	LAN 22	Andrew	MNT 82	John	ADA 36
John	LAN 42	Anthony	MNT 134	KEINERT, Michael	NOH 60
Peter	YOR 212	George	BER 153	KEINIGER, Henry	BER 283
KEENTZ, Anthony		John	MNT 60	KEIP, Conrad	YOR 171
Esqr.	NOH 41A	John	BER 153	KEIPE, Peter	DAU 20
Ludwig	NOH 36	Leonard	BER 201	KEIPER, Casper	LAN 200
KEEP, James	ALL 116	Philip	NOH 80A	Conrad	NOH 71A
Michael	YOR 188	Simon	NOH 56	Jacob	NOH 43
KEEPER, Saml.	CHE 751	KEHLER, Daniel	YOR 206	Jacob	LAN 200
KEEPER?, Gasper	WST 253	Godleib	LAN 43	John	NOH 43
KEEPERS, John	FAY 200	Henry	YOR 186	John	NOH 69
KEEPHART, Jacob	LYC 10	Jacob	LAN 42	Ludwig	NOH 43
KEER, Jacob	PHA 66	John	YOR 166	Peter	NOH 69
James	WST 291	John	YOR 180	KEIR, Charles	PHA 91
Matthew	WST 191	John Jr.	YOR 166	David	WST 161
Samuel	WST 380	Michael	LAN 102	Mary	WST 161
Thomas	WST 253	Michael	LAN 292	William	WST 161
KEER?, Peter	MNT 109	Samuel	YOR 166	KEIRITHERS, James	BEV 24
KEERS, Thomas	WST 152	KEHLINE, Abram.	BUC 82	William	BEV 24
KEES, Abraham	WAS 122	John	BUC 159	KEISER, Abraham	MIF 10A
Ephraim	FAY 232	Widow	BUC 82	Abram	LAN 251
Henry	PHI 94	KEHR, Christian	YOR 184	Adam	PHI 44
Jacob	WAS 38	KEHR?, John	YOR 217	Adam	BER 280
Jacob	NOH 50	John	PHI 96A	Andrew	MIF 1
John	NOH 50	KEIBER, John	BER 188	Conrad	NOH 65
John	WAS 122	KEIDER, Jacob	NOH 43	George	MNT 110
John	DEL 163	KEIFE, Dolly	PHA 32	George	BER 271
Mathias	NOH 50	KEIFER, Andw. Sr.	DAU 23	Henry	MIF 13
Nicholas	WAS 122	Christo.	DAU 46A	Henry	MIF 13
Peter	NOH 50	Danl.	BER 257	Henry	MIF 13
William	FAY 232	Dorothea	YOR 156	Henry	BER 226
William	WST 253	Henry	WST 217	Jacob	NOH 60
KEESE, James	CHE 775	Jacob	BER 130	John	BER 201
KEESER?, Gasper	WST 253	KEIFFER, Abraham	FRA 315	John	MIF 10A
KEESEY, Philip	LAN 8	Dewald Snr.	FRA 318	John	NOH 60
KEESEY?, Simon	MNT 69	Frederick	BUT 323	Joseph	BER 213
KEESS, Andrew	LAN 30	Jacob	FRA 313	Michael	NOH 65
George	LAN 34	John	YOR 156	Michael	BER 201
KEESTER,		John	BER 213	Michael	BER 271
Elizabeth	YOR 216	Peter	FRA 315	Peter	MNT 127
George	YOR 216	KEIFR, Philip	BER 176	Peter	NOH 41A

KEISER, Samuel	YOR	171	KELLER, Christian	BER	257	KELLER, Samuel	YOR	215
KEISER?, Mary	MNT	40	Christn.	BUC	82	Sebastian	LAN	263
KEISSINGER, Jacob	NOH	64A	Conrad	MNT	57	Simon	NOH	67
KEIST, Isaac	LAN	172	Conrad	PHA	66	Valentine	BER	226
KEISTER, Henry	NOU	137	Conrad	BER	133	William	NOH	73A
KEITH, Adam	HNT	119	Conrad	BER	258	Yost	MNT	55
Adam	HNT	119	Daniel	WST	347	KELLERMAN, Andw.	YOR	216
Adam Junr.	HNT	119	Danl.	BER	147	Fredk.	LAN	264
Adam (Of			George	PHA	57	KELLESON, George	WAS	8
Michael)	HNT	119	George	LAN	102	KELLEY, Abraham	NOU	188
Baltzer	HNT	119	George	PHI	133	Daniel	PHA	93
Jack	LAN	316	George	SOM	138	Daniel	MER	447
Jacob	HNT	119	George	CUM	142	Hugh	NOU	188
John	PHA	47	George	YOR	190	John	CUM	74
John	HNT	119	George	YOR	216	John	PHA	101
Lewis	HNT	116	George	YOR	219	John	LAN	125
Michael	HNT	119	George	BER	246	John	NOU	188
Wm.	PHA	100	George	LAN	286	John	WST	243
KEIZEL, Jacob	CUM	57	George	DAU	29A	John	MER	447
John	CUM	57	George	NOH	41A	John	CHE	832
KEIZER, (See			Henry	CUM	62	John Junr.	MER	447
Kriser)	MNT	99	Henry	SOM	132	Johnston	LAN	48
KEKART?, (See			Henry	BER	188	Joseph	BFD	58
Kehart)	CEN	20A	Henry	YOR	190	Joseph	BFD	64
KELB, Adam & Jon.	LAN	211	Henry	YOR	193	Lawrence	NOU	188
Jon. (See Kelb,			Henry	YOR	219	Morris	BFD	47
Adam)	LAN	211	Henry Jnr.	BUC	82	Saml.	CUM	40
KELCHNER, Jacob	BER	254	Henry	BUC	149A	Samuel	ARM	125
John	NOH	84	Isaac	PHA	61	Samuel	ARM	125
John	BER	142	Isaac	BER	244	Samuel	MER	447
Michael	NOH	43	Jacob	DAU	46	Simsey?	BEV	8
Peter	BER	254	Jacob	ALL	50	Thomas	PHA	12
Peter	NOH	43A	Jacob	LAN	60	Thomas (Hapdin-		
Stoffel	NOH	90A	Jacob	NOH	87	Crossed Out)	BFD	58
KELCKER, Anthy.	DAU	33	Jacob	WAS	111	Thos.	CUM	82
Henry	DAU	32	Jacob	YOR	186	Wm.	PHA	47
Jacob	DAU	38A	Jacob	BER	188	KELLIAN, Leslen?	LAN	200
KELEHAN, Edward	YOR	200	Jacob	YOR	188	Sebastian	LAN	199
KELER, Leonard	DAU	32A	Jacob	YOR	193	KELLING, Robert	ALL	72
KELEY, Andrew	PHA	63	Jacob	LAN	199	KELLISON, Daniel	WAS	12
KELIPS?,			Jacob Jr.	BER	188	KELLOGG, Eldad	LUZ	425
Christopher	FRA	290	Jacob Junr.	LAN	199	Eliphalett	WAY	137
KELKER, John	DAU	49A	Jacob	DAU	47A	Jonathan	LUZ	346
Rucolph	DAU	33	John	LAN	11	Silas	WAY	137
KELKNER, Henry	NOU	154	John	LAN	55	KELLS, Ralph	WST	311
KELL, Adam	FRA	275	John	BUC	82	KELLY, Widow	PHI	68
James	DAU	51	John	MNT	90	---athan?	BUC	142
Jane	DAU	36	John	LAN	116	Abraham	GRN	93
John	YOR	179	John	HNT	149	Abraham	BUC	85A
John	CHE	739	John	BER	201	Alexander	WST	152
John	CHE	850	John	LAN	264	Alexander	WST	325
KELLAR, Joseph	LAN	11	John	BER	274	Andrew	DAU	12
KELLBRIDGE,			John	LAN	284	Archd.	CUM	80
Francis	PHI	55	Joseph	CUM	34	Archd.	BUT	353
KELLEBERGER, Adam	ADA	30	Joseph	NOH	78	Bartholomew	WAS	16
George	ADA	3	Joseph	WAS	111	Benjamin	NOU	105
Jacob	ADA	3	Leond.	CUM	93	Benjamin	BUC	96A
KELLEHR,			Martin	LAN	98	Charles	CUM	123
Catharine	PHA	90	Martin	SOM	154	Charles	HNT	161
KELLEN, John	YOR	158	Martin	LAN	263	Daniel	LUZ	324
KELLENGER, Philip	FAY	204	Michael	MNT	55	Denis	NOU	117
KELLER, Abraham	BER	133	Michael	HNT	149	Edward	NOU	158
Abraham	YOR	182	Michael	YOR	205	Edward	CHE	832
Abraham	BER	245	Michael	BER	286	Edwd.	MIF	17
Adam	ALL	106	Michl.	DAU	22A	Erasmus	BUC	96A
Adam	PHI	106	Peter	DAU	2	Francis	FRA	319
Andrew	LAN	52	Peter	LAN	26	George	WAS	12
Andrew	BER	206	Peter	BUC	82	George	MIF	17
Andrew	NOH	59A	Peter	WST	311	Henry	LYC	22
Anthony	YOR	206	Peter	CHE	895	Hugh	PHA	90
Anthony	NOH	41A	Peter	NOH	41A	Isaac	CRA	7
Casper	SOM	154	Philip	SOM	154	Jacob	NOH	76
Christ.	WST	380	Philip	NOH	73A	James	WAS	3
Christian	WAS	3	Saml. Jr.	YOR	219	James	DAU	45
Christian	WAS	100	Saml. Junr.	YOR	215	James	WST	152
Christian	YOR	165	Samuel	YOR	204	James	WST	152

KENER, Michl.	PHI	110	KENNEDY, William	CHE	823	KEPLER, Andrew	YOR	170
KENEROD, Jacob	NOU	100	Wm.	CUM	38	Barnet	BUC	141
KENEY, Aaron	NOU	147	Wm.	MIF	10A	Christian	ARM	123
James	NOU	158	KENNEL, John	NOH	90	David	BER	165
KENGLE?, Peter	BER	161	Michael	NOH	90A	George	YOR	189
KENIGMACHER,			Theobald	NOH	90	Jacob	ARM	125
Abraham	LAN	199	KENNELL, John	MER	447	Jacob	YOR	215
KENLEY, Wm.	PHA	90	KENNER, Boston	GRN	82	John	CUM	31
KENLY, Valentine	NOH	60	George	WST	217	John	WAS	91
KENNADY, James	LAN	129	KENNEY, Benjn.	FAY	227	John	MIF	12A
Michael	LAN	125	Danl.	PHA	46	Michael	YOR	189
Thomas	LAN	156	David	NOU	194	Peter	ADA	33
KENNARD, Anthy.	PHI	93A	James	LAN	227	Saml.	LYC	28
Thos.	PHA	73	Patrick	LAN	125	Simon	BER	174
KENNEDAY, Ambrus	BUT	325	Robt.	PHI	47	Tobias	PHI	124
Henry	PHA	82	Thomas	HNT	124	William	MNT	57
James	LAN	128	William	LAN	230	KEPLEY, George	BUC	82A
Jane	BUC	149A	KENNIER, George	FAY	238	Jacob	BUC	157
John	BUT	325	KENNY, Abraham	NOU	158	Michl.	WST	217
Jos.	BUT	360	Alexr.	CHE	858	KEPLEY?, Daniel	ARM	127
Wm.	BUT	325	Daniel	CHE	858	KEPLINER, Jacob	LAN	200
KENNEDY, Andrew	WAS	49	David	GRN	64	KEPLINGER,		
Andw. (Crossed			Elizath.	PHI	151	Leonard	LAN	91
Out)	PHA	15	George	CUM	123	Peter	ADA	32
Archd.	CUM	81	John	HNT	143	Peter	BER	150
David	MIF	17	Margaret	CHE	725	Sam	ADA	10
David	CUM	48	Matthew	MIF	4	KEPLOR, Jacob	CEN	20A
David	WAY	137	Peter	NOU	158	Jacob	CEN	20A
Elizabeth	FRA	319	Robert	MIF	7A	KEPLY, George	WST	216
George	NOH	67	Thomas	HNT	143	Ludwick	WST	216
Gilbert	HNT	143	Thomas	CHE	743	KEPMAN, Peter	NOH	36
Henry	PHI	38	William	CHE	801	KEPNER, Andrw.	BER	244
Hugh	CUM	89	KENNYD, John	LAN	170	Benjamin	BER	157
James	BEV	7	KENOUSE, Jacob	PHI	114A	Benjn. Senr.	MIF	7A
James	BEV	19	KENRY?, Daniel	ARM	123	Bernard	MNT	128
James	CUM	127	KENSEL, Chas.	PHI	110	Bernard	BER	155
James	HNT	152	Christn.	PHI	115A	Bernard Jr.	BER	155
James	FAY	232	John	PHA	72	Jacob	MIF	7A
James	LAN	286	Margaret	PHI	106	John	MNT	73
James	LUZ	361	Michl.	PHI	109A	Saml.	MIF	7A
James	CHE	748	KENSELL, John	PHI	108A	Samuel	MNT	128
James	BUC	151A	KENSINGER, Daniel	LAN	10	Tobias	ADA	33
Jno.	CUM	48	Daniel	BFD	62	KEPNOR, Benjn.	MIF	7A
John	PHI	16	KENSLER, Jno.	CUM	72	John	MIF	7A
John	ADA	17	Michael	YOR	194	KEPORTS, Barbara	LAN	118
John	PHI	27	KENT, Abel	LUZ	384	David	LAN	107
John	DAU	45	Abel Junr.	LUZ	384	David	LAN	114
John	SOM	141	Abel Senr.	LUZ	385	KEPP, John	NOH	90A
John	FRA	294	Absolem	FAY	251	KEPPELE, George		
John	FRA	295	Elisha	LUZ	385	H. Esqr.	WAS	116
John	LUZ	324	George	PHI	134	Valentine	BER	170
John Jr.	LUZ	324	Gideon	LUZ	384	KEPPENHEBER,		
John	MIF	7A	Israel	PHI	134	Tobias	BER	285
John	DAU	45A	John	FAY	251	KEPPER, Fredrick	PHI	151
Joseph	PHI	36	Joseph	WAS	57	KEPPLE, Andw.	WST	369
Joseph	CUM	80	Thomas	GRN	64	John	LAN	39
Joseph	MNT	142	William	YOR	212	Joh	DAU	0
Joseph	FRA	302	KENTZINGER,			Michael	PHA	90
Mathew	BEV	7	Nichs.	NOH	51A	Nichs.	WST	217
Patrick	ERI	58A	KENWORTHY,			Phillip	WST	217
Peter	BEV	14	William	BFD	74	KEPPLER, John	LAN	38
Philip	LYC	8	KENY, Simon	NOU	149	KEPWHITE, George	DAU	32
Richd.	MIF	5	Widow	MIF	7A	KER-EL?, Benjn.	BUC	138A
Robert	WAY	137	KEOGY, Abraham	ADA	31	KER, Widow	PHI	93A
Robert	WST	291	Jacob	ADA	31	Joseph Majr.	PHI	103
Robt.	MNT	77	Jacob	ADA	32	Michl.	PHI	117A
Samuel	BEV	21	KEOMIG, Conrad	LAN	51	KERBACH, Danl.	PHI	147
Sarah	FRA	296	KEPHARD, Jacob	PHI	91A	Michael	PHI	147
Stephen	WST	290	KEPHART, Adam	MNT	73	Peter	ADA	36
Thomas	BEV	4	John	PHI	133	KERBACK, David	MNT	92
Thomas	HNT	124	KEPHEART, Dean	NOU	100	KERBAUGH,		
Thomas	SOM	129	KEPHORT, Mary	PHI	96A	Christian	ADA	11
Thos.	CUM	38	KEPLE, Peter	WST	216	John	ADA	13
Thos.	CUM	128	Stophle	DAU	20A	Martin	ADA	12
William	WAY	149	KEPLER, Abm.	MIF	12A	Martin Jr.	ADA	14
William	LAN	165	Adrew	BFD	55	Nicholas	ADA	13

209

KERBER, Adam	BER	170	KERN, Michl.	CUM	50	KERR, Jacob	DAU	14A
John	YOR	183	Nicholas	NOH	45	James	PHA	4
KERBRIGHT, Joseph	PHA	38	Nicholas	NOH	90	James	WAS	8
Richard	PHA	99	Nicholas (Son			James	ADA	13
KERCHER, Fredk.	BER	213	Of W.)	NOH	45	James	NOH	30
George	BER	212	Nicholas Esqr.	NOH	37A	James	WAS	57
Jacob	YOR	190	Peter	NOH	90	James	ERI	59
John	BER	213	Peter	BUC	159	James	WAS	69
Peter	BER	212	Stophel	NOH	45	James	WAS	75
KERCHNER, Gotleib	BER	181	W. (See Kern,			James	WAS	100
Henry	BER	181	Nicholas)	NOH	45	James	ALL	105
John	BER	133	William	FAY	240	James	HNT	120
John	BER	220	William Junr.	NOH	45	James	YOR	196
KEREKART, Conrad	DAU	25	William Senr.	NOH	45	James	FRA	278
KERES, Jacob	BER	284	Willm.	PHI	61A	James	BUT	315
Philip	BER	284	KERNAHAN, James	WAS	38	Jane	ADA	6
Philip	BER	285	KERNER, John	BER	263	Jane	DEL	183
KERGEMAN, John	LAN	299	KERNES?, (See			Jas.	CUM	86
KERGER, W.	LAN	148	Kemes)	CHE	786	Joh	MNT	103
KERGESLEGER, John	DAU	18A	Daniel	CEN	18A	John	MIF	5
KERISH, Hanagle	CUM	102	KERNEY, David	DEL	182	John	BFD	38
KERIVER?, Adam	WAY	137	James	BFD	47	John	LAN	44
KERK, William	FAY	198	William	BFD	47	John	WAS	49
KERKENDAL, Henry	BEV	8	William	NOH	76	John	WAS	52
Samuel	BEV	5	KERNHIEFER,			John	ERI	58
KERL, Elizabeth	CHE	762	Philip	MNT	128	John	LAN	65
James	WAS	122	KERNS, Andrew	WST	171	John	WAS	85
William	MER	447	Barny	WST	369	John	MNT	103
KERLIN, Daniel	BER	184	Henry	CUM	103	John	ALL	112
George	DEL	163	Jacob	LAN	10	John	HNT	120
John	BER	139	Jacob	LAN	122	John	ARM	123
John	BER	139	Jacob	CHE	823	John	BUC	154
John	BER	275	James	WST	369	John	WST	191
Matthias	DEL	164	John	WST	217	John	FRA	280
Peter	NOU	100	John	DAU	14A	John	BUT	358
Samuel	BER	181	Philip	MNT	78	John	MER	447
William	DEL	163	Simon	CHE	761	John	CEN	20A
KERLING, James (A			Thos.	DAU	16	Jos.	YOR	197
Boarding			Thos.	CHE	699	Joseph	BEV	26
House)	PHA	36	Wm.	BEV	4	Joseph	PHA	69
KERMEL, Lawrence	NOU	129	KERPER, Danl.	BER	244	Joseph	LUZ	359
KERMER, Ludwig	BER	135	Frederick	PHI	124	Manassah	WST	291
Peter	LAN	140	George	PHI	123	Margt.	CUM	37
KERMON, John	PHI	152	Jacob	PHI	123	Mathew	ADA	10
KERN, Adam	BUC	159	Julius	PHI	124	Mathew	WAS	69
Adam	BUC	96A	Valuntine	MNT	92	Mathew	WAS	100
Anthony	CHE	703	KERR, Widw.	PHI	105	Matthew	CUM	37
Anthy.	PHI	80	Adam	BUC	154	Michl.	WST	369
Christian	BUC	96A	Alexr.	MIF	5	Peggy	LUZ	359
Christopher	BER	271	Andrew	CRA	12	Priscilla	WAS	57
Daniel	NOH	90A	Andrew	WAS	49	Robert	WAS	81
Ernst	NOH	78	Andrew	WAS	85	Robert	ALL	95
Frederick	BFD	74	Andrew	HNT	123	Robert	ARM	125
Frederick	BUC	159	Andrew Irish	CRA	12	Samuel	CRA	12
Fredk.	YOR	216	Andw.	CUM	92	Samuel	WAS	16
George	ADA	36	Archibald	WAS	34	Samuel	BFD	38
George	NOH	45	Barcle	HNT	134	Samuel	WAS	69
George Jacob	NOH	90A	Barnabas	ADA	7	Samuel	ALL	97
Henry	LUZ	360	Charrels	ALL	87	Samuel	HNT	123
Henry	NOH	59A	Daniel	WAS	116	Samuel	LUZ	359
Henry	NOH	73A	David	BEV	23	Sarah	BFD	60
James	BER	274	David	BEV	25	Susannah	PHA	32
John	BFD	74	David	BUT	315	Thomas	CRA	5
John Jr.	BFD	74	Eleonor	DAU	36A	Thomas	MIF	5
John Senr.	NOH	45	Frederick	MNT	100	Thomas	WAS	100
Jos.	YOR	156	George	ADA	3	Thomas	HNT	132
Lawrence	LUZ	360	George	MIF	5	Thomas	HNT	155
Leonard Junr.	NOH	73A	George	ADA	10	Thos.	CUM	91
Leonard	NOH	73A	George	PHI	17	Thos.	CUM	141
Lodawick	LUZ	419	George	ERI	59	Waltar	LUZ	359
Ludwick	CUM	49	George	BUC	105	William	MIF	5
Mathias	NOH	56	Hannah	ALL	96	William	MIF	5
Mathias	NOH	56	Henry	BUC	159A	William	WAS	16
Mathias Junr.	NOH	56	Hugh	ARM	122	William	ADA	23
Michael	NOH	70	Hugh	DEL	165	William	WAS	34
Michael	NOH	90	Hugh	MER	447	William	WAS	52

KERR, William	WAS	91	KESSLER, George	NOH	73A	KEYSER, Chas.	PHA	39

KIEL, Hartman	BUC	159	KILLGORE, James	MER	447	KIME, Nicholas	SOM	158
Jacob	NOU	100	Jonathan	ARM	126	Samuel	SOM	158
John	NOU	97A	Patrick	MER	447	William	PHI	133
Ludwig	LAN	136	Wm.	WST	273	KIMERY, John	SOM	152
Peter	BEV	15	Zekiel	ARM	126	KIMES, Emanuel	PHI	56
KIEMER, Sarah	CHE	725	KILLIAN, Abraham	LAN	65	George	LAN	230
KIEN, George	LUZ	361	Andrew	LAN	65	George	CHE	905
KIESEN, Jacob	NOU	149	Jacob	DAU	27	Jos.	BUT	363
KIESER, Jacob	NOU	183	John	DAU	27	KIMLY, George	PHI	23
John	BER	271	John	DAU	28	Lawrence	MIF	13
KIESTER, John	NOU	149	Nicholas	LAN	65	KIMMEL, Abraham	SOM	154
Peter	NOU	149	Philip	LAN	65	Abraham	SOM	158
Phillip	WST	369	KILLINGER, George	PHA	94	David	SOM	154
KIETH, John	BUC	151A	Jacob	FRA	318	Emanuel	LAN	120
William	MNT	105	John	DAU	43A	George	SOM	154
KIETHIGH, Adam	NOU	194	Michl.	CUM	100	George	BER	158
KIFFER, Abraham	BER	261	Peter	DAU	24A	George	SOM	160
Henry	LAN	82	Peter	DAU	43A	Isaac	SOM	154
Jacob	BER	276	KILLINGSHURST,			Jacob	SOM	154
KIGAR, Conrad	NOU	111	Edwd.	PHA	88	Jacob	LAN	199
Daniel	NOU	111	KILLMAR, David	BER	271	Jacob	LAN	211
Michael	NOU	111	Nicholas	BER	271	John Doc.	SOM	141
KIGER, Widow	CHE	830	KILLS, James	PHI	54	Jonas	YOR	211
KIGIN, James	PHA	71	KILLWELL, Wm.	BEV	14	Joseph	NOU	129
KIHCUT, Andrew	NOU	158	KILM?, Robert	PHI	96A	Michael	SOM	158
KILBREADTH, Andw.	PHI	83A	KILMER, Henry	BUC	91	Michael	YOR	211
KILCART, John	NOU	165	Nicholas	BER	267	Peter Esq.	SOM	132
KILCHNER, Jacob	BER	210	Philip	MIF	7A	S----? (Erased)	SOM	158
KILCUST, Robert	NOU	165	KILPATERICK,			Samuel	SOM	161
KILDARE, John	PHI	136	Daniel	BEV	12	Solomon	SOM	158
KILE, Abm.	BUC	86A	KILPATRICK, James	CHE	741	KIMMELL, Jacob	CHE	823
Betsy	PHI	88	John	PHI	55	Saml.	CUM	61
Jas.	CUM	47	Margaret	PHA	5	KIMMERLAIN, Jacob	MIF	25A
John	NOU	152	Robert	LAN	159	KIMMERLANE,		
John	WST	253	KILROW, Thomas	PHI	51	George	HNT	135
Robert	DAU	47	KILWELL, James	BEV	7	KIMMERLING, Jacob	NOU	188
William	LAN	2	Samuel	BEV	7	KIMMING, Charles	WST	152
KILER, John	NOU	152	KILWELL?, George	BEV	15	KIMMONS, Jane	WAS	91
KILES, Caspar	DAU	5	KILY, David	NOU	105	KIMMS, John	ADA	11
Enos	PHI	136	KIMBER, Amer	PHA	98	KIMPTON, David	SOM	162
James	NOU	117	Hannah	PHA	48	KIMSY, -osal?	PHI	49
William	LAN	257	KIMBERLAND, .John	GRN	101	KINBLE, William	CHE	867
KILEY, Thomas	CHE	728	KIMBERLEY?,			KINBORD, Daniel	LAN	273
KILFILLIN,			Walliston	BEV	22	Daniel Jur.	LAN	273
Archibald	CHE	874	KIMBLE, Abel	WAY	141	KINCADE, Samuel	GRN	84
KILGORE, Charles	FRA	320	Adam	NOU	165	KINCAID, Hannah	CHE	841
David	CEN	24	Anthy.	CUM	42	John	WAS	12
Hugh	CUM	39	Benjamin	WAY	141	John	WAS	22
James	FRA	324	Chester	WAY	139	John	PHI	69
Josh.	FRA	319	Daniel	WAY	141	John	WAS	69
Mathew	YOR	198	David	YOR	210	Joseph	CHE	827
Nehemiah	FRA	319	Ephraim	WAY	140	KINCH, Jacob	LAN	307
KILHEFER,			Isaac	WAS	63	KIND, Adam	BER	219
Christian	LAN	313	Isaac	CHE	728	Martin Junr.	NOH	73A
KILHEFFER, Ann	LAN	88	Jacob	ADA	37	Martin	NOH	73A
Jacob	LAN	81	Jacob	WAY	141	KINDALE,		
Jacob	LAN	294	Jacob Jr.	WAY	141	--sebeus?	WAY	141
John	LAN	81	James	PHI	45	KINDALL, Dyer	LUZ	406
KILHINGAR,			John	BUC	90	Ebenezer	LUZ	406
Michael	HNT	125	John	BUC	92	Jerimia Esq.	FAY	215
KILHOFFER,			John	CHE	729	KINDEG, Daniel	LAN	293
Frederick	BER	219	John Jun.	CHE	729	KINDELL, James	FAY	257
Peter	LAN	86	John Junr.	WAS	63	John	FAY	257
KILINGER, Jacob	NOU	176	John Senr.	WAS	63	John Jun.	FAY	257
KILKOWER, Martin	PHI	2	Jonathan	MNT	35	Samuel	FAY	257
KILL, Margaret	CHE	729	Jonathan	BUC	92	Thomas	FAY	257
Sam.	DAU	34A	Nathan	WAS	91	KINDER, George	SOM	134
KILLAM, Ephraim	WAY	141	Peter	LYC	8	Valentine	WAS	38
John	WAY	141	Peter	LYC	8	Valentine	YOR	213
Moses	WAY	141	Thomas	MNT	57	KINDERDINE,		
Silas	WAY	141	Timothy	YOR	208	Benjn.	MNT	50
KILLBROOK, John	ALL	81	Walter	WAY	141	Isaac?	505	50
KILLER, John	PHI	20	William	DEL	170	John	PHI	155
KILLEY, Edward	PHA	46	William	BUC	86A	Jos. Jnr.	MNT	50
KILLGORE, Daniel	WST	273	KIMBO, Richard	CHE	851	Jos. Snr?	MNT	50
David	WST	273	KIME, George	SOM	158	KINDIG, Adam	LAN	273

KITTS, Lawrance	PHI	90A	KLEIN, Lowrence	NOH	82	KLINE, Adam	WST	290
Michael	PHA	14	Lowrence	NOH	85A	Barbara	MNT	68
KITTS?, Abigal	PHA	51	Michael	NOH	56	Christr.	WST	217
Adam	PHI	99	Michael	MNT	134	Conrad	WAY	147
KITWELL?, George	BEV	15	Nicholas	NOH	60	Conrod	CUM	120
KITWILER?, John	PHI	124	Nicholas	NOH	87	David	YOR	209
KITZ MILLER?,			Peter	NOH	82	David	BER	213
Casper	SOM	134	Peter	BER	226	Dedrik	DAU	42
John	SOM	134	Peter	LAN	274	Dewald	PHI	84
KITZ?, Miller			Peter	LAN	279	Frederick	MNT	47
Casper	SOM	134	Peter	LAN	281	Frederick	NOU	122
KITZMILLER,			Peter	LAN	290	George	CUM	98
Benjamin	BER	266	Peter	NOH	85A	George	CUM	145
John	DAU	48	Philip	LAN	30	Georoge	PHI	102A
Martin	ADA	36	Philip	BER	270	Gottlieb	DAU	9
KIZER, Bengamin	ALL	97	Philip	BER	279	Harman	NOU	100
John	ALL	70	Philip	NOH	82A	Henry	MNT	38
KIZOR, Phillip	FRA	315	Susana	LAN	11	Henry	CUM	46
KIZSER, Andr.	FRA	282	Widow	NOH	71A	Henry	BFD	74
KLAHR, Philip	BER	270	KLEINDUSS,			Henry	PHA	78
KLAIR, Frederick	MNT	78	Christopher	LUZ	356	Henry	LAN	218
KLAIR?, John	LAN	310	KLEINFELTER,			Isaac	NOU	100
KLAIS?, John	LAN	310	Albert	DAU	51A	Isaac	NOU	100
KLAPP, Henrich	LAN	200	Martin	DAU	51A	Isaac	MNT	121
John	BER	141	KLEINHANSS,			Jacob	CRA	15
KLAPPER, Michael	YOR	181	Frederick	NOH	87	Jacob	MNT	90
KLARR, Jacob	BER	154	George Jr.	NOH	87	Jacob	NOU	105
KLASSER, George	BER	210	George H.	NOH	87	Jacob	MNT	119
KLASSMYER, Peter	BER	214	KLEINSCHMIT,			Jacob	PHI	135
KLATFELTER, Felix	YOR	189	Andrew	NOH	56	Jacob	BER	142
KLAUSER, David	BER	183	KLEINTOB, Conrad	NOH	36	Jacob	WAY	147
George	BER	183	KLEISE, John	LAN	39	Jacob	BER	151
Henry	BER	133	KLEMAN, Widow	NOH	37A	Jacob	BER	153
KLAY, Aaron	BER	176	KLEMMER, Christ.	NOH	56	Jacob	YOR	186
KLECH, Christn.	BER	141	KLEN, Jacob	LAN	200	Jacob	YOR	187
Jacob	BER	141	KLENEPETER,			Jacob	YOR	209
KLECKNER, Andrew	BER	156	Rudolph	YOR	179	Jacob	BER	213
Anthony	NOH	62A	KLEPFORD, Joseph	LAN	8	Jacob	WST	369
Daniel	NOH	62A	KLEPPER,			Jacob	PHI	104A
John	BER	156	Frederick	YOR	176	John	LAN	15
Nicholas	NOH	82A	Michael	LAN	293	John	BFD	74
KLEH, Jeremiah	BER	271	KLEPPINGER,			John	CUM	81
KLEIN, Abraham	NOH	56	George	NOH	30	John	MNT	114
Abraham	LAN	199	Ludwig	NOH	50	John	BER	142
Adam	BER	213	KLER, Frederick	LAN	315	John	BER	142
Adam	NOH	82A	KLERE, Henry	LAN	315	John	YOR	193
Chn.	NOH	82	KLES, George	BER	286	John	YOR	216
Christian	LAN	272	KLESS, John	BER	158	John	DAU	30A
Daniel	BER	140	KLEWELL,			Joseph	PHI	74
Daniel	LAN	199	Christian	NOH	71A	Joseph	HNT	119
David	BER	180	Daniel	NOH	71A	Joseph	DAU	22A
David	BER	226	Frantz	NOH	71A	Leond.	CUM	32
David	BER	270	George	NOH	71A	Mattas.	CUM	148
Elizabeth	BER	253	Jacob	NOH	34	Michael	LAN	35
Frederick	NOH	84	John	NOH	34	Michael	FAY	215
Gabriel	MNT	121	John	NOH	70	Michael	LAN	314
George	NOH	56	Joseph	NOH	82A	Michael	DAU	7A
George	MNT	134	Nathl.	NOH	71A	Nicholas	MNT	47
George	BER	139	Widow	NOH	70	Nicholas	MNT	92
Henry	NOH	60	Widow	NOH	71A	Nicholas	BER	142
Henry	BER	147	KLICH, Maths.	BER	147	Nichols.	CEN	22B
Henry	LAN	291	KLICK, Abraham	BER	141	Peter	MNT	62
Henry	LAN	313	Daniel	BER	130	Peter	PHI	91
Isaac	NOH	56	Frederick	BER	131	Peter	MNT	111
Jacob	NOH	56	Henry	BER	130	Peter	YOR	166
Jacob	NOH	60	John	DAU	52A	Philip	BER	142
Jacob	BER	137	Peter	NOH	85A	Philip	BER	254
Jacob	BER	139	Philip	NOH	82A	Richard	MNT	90
Jacob	BER	217	KLIEST, Danl.			Werner	BER	142
John	NOH	60	Esqr.	NOH	32	Widow	LAN	253
John	MNT	68	KLINDENST,			William	DAU	9
John	NOH	84	Godfrey	YOR	190	William	YOR	215
John	BER	139	KLINE, Widow	PHI	76	KLINEDINST, Andw.	YOR	189
John	BER	266	Abraham	ADA	40	Christian	YOR	189
Joseph	BER	271	Adam	LAN	15	Elizabeth	YOR	181
Lawrence	BER	232	Adam	ADA	39	KLINEFELTER, Albe	DAU	52

KLINEFELTER,			KNABB, Nicholas	BER	230	KNECHT, Widow	NOH	71A
Jacob	YOR	192	Peter	BER	230	KNEE, George	BFD	65
Jacob	YOR	199	Peter Jr.	BER	230	Jacob	BFD	68
Lorence	YOR	194	KNABLE, Jacob	SOM	134	Philip	BFD	69
Michael	YOR	159	KNAFSKER, Chr.	DAU	44	KNEER?, Henry	CHE	791
KLINEPETER, Adam	YOR	177	Joseph	DAU	46A	KNEISLEY, Michael	LAN	278
Casper	YOR	178	KNAP, Casper	YOR	164	KNEISLY, George	LAN	185
Elizabeth	YOR	192	Mary	YOR	160	Michael	LAN	280
KLINESMITH,			Matthew	LYC	20	KNEISSLY, John	LAN	305
Andrew	GRN	82	KNAPENBARGER,			John Junr.	LAN	305
KLING, Abraham	LAN	77	George	NOU	111	KNEPLER, George	YOR	182
Henry	LAN	251	KNAPP, Daniel W.	LUZ	384	KNEPLY, Conrad	DAU	17
Peter	LAN	172	Edward	LUZ	384	KNEPPER, John	BER	130
KLINGEMAN, Cors.	NOH	76	John	LUZ	410	John	SOM	138
George	SOM	149	Joseph	LUZ	364	Peter	BER	130
John	NOH	53A	Peter	YOR	164	William	SOM	138
Peter	NOH	76	William	LUZ	364	KNEPPLEY, Widow	NOH	80A
KLINGENBERG,			William	LUZ	405	KNEPPLY, Widow Of		
Fredk.	BUC	82	William Jr.	LUZ	364	Math.	NOH	80A
KLINGER, Elex.	BER	244	Zephaniah	LUZ	364	KNERR, Abraham	NOH	85A
George	BER	282	KNAPPENBERGER,			Andreas	NOH	85A
Martin	BER	201	Adam	NOH	60	Andrew	NOH	51A
Peter	DAU	6	Adam	NOH	84	Henry	PHA	83
Philip	DAU	6	Henry	NOH	59A	John	NOH	85A
Philip	DAU	7	Philip	NOH	90	KNERR?, George	MNT	109
Philip	BER	244	KNAPSCHNEIDER,			KNESLY, Anthony		
Philip Jr.	DAU	6	George	NOH	34	Junr.	YOR	208
Pter	BER	249	KNAPT, John	BFD	44	KNETTLE, Henry	CUM	128
KLINGLE, Andw.	PHI	70	KNATCHER, Michael	DAU	3A	KNEW, James	PHI	50
KLINGLER, Peter	BER	272	KNAUP, Jacob	YOR	163	KNGHT, Amos	PHI	144
KLINGMAN, Jacob	BER	156	KNAUS, Abraham	NOU	137	KNIGHT, Abel	BUC	141
Jacob	BER	244	KNAUSE, Henry	BER	181	Abm.	BUC	143A
KLINK, John	SOM	149	KNAUSS, Abraham	NOH	43	Absolem	BUC	143A
KLINKER,			Daniel	NOH	85A	Asa	BUC	88A
Christian	BUC	149A	Frederick	NOH	36	Cornelious	ADA	24
Jacob	BUC	104A	George	NOH	90	Daniel	PHA	70
Widow	BUC	82A	George	NOH	59A	Daniel	PHI	144
KLINKINNY, John	BER	170	Gottfried	NOH	90	Danl. P.	PHI	67
KLISER, Notches	DAU	33	Henry	NOH	80A	David	BUC	137A
KLISER?, Gabriel	MNT	99	Henry	NOH	82A	Elihu	LUZ	409
KLITE, John	YOR	160	John	NOH	43	Evan	BUC	88A
KLIVENSTINE,			John	NOH	37A	Ezekiel	GRN	71
George	BER	250	John	NOH	82A	George H.	BUC	80
KLOCH, George	BER	221	Jonathan	NOH	85A	Hannah	DEL	176
KLOCK, Henry	BER	283	Lewis	NOH	30	Inglish	PHI	144
Jacob	BER	283	Michael	NOH	73A	Isaac	PHA	29
Peter	BER	283	Paul	NOH	30	Israel	BUC	88A
Peter Jr.	BER	283	Philip	NOH	59A	James	SOM	134
KLOCKNER, Philip	NOH	43	KNAVE, Jacob	CUM	55	James	FAY	257
KLOPP, Peter	BER	201	Jacob	HNT	134	John	PHA	69
KLOSE, Daniel	NOH	50	Jacob	FRA	292	John	BUC	80
George	BER	213	Jacob	FRA	324	John	GRN	92
Jacob	BER	131	John	FRA	314	John	GRN	97
Jacob	BER	133	Leonard	FRA	292	John	BUC	100
Melchior	NOH	50	Michl.	FRA	314	John	BUC	137
KLOSS, Daniel	NOH	85A	KNAVELINE, George	BFD	48	John Junr.	ADA	36
George	NOH	76	KNAVES, Henry	LUZ	358	John	BUC	147A
John Junr.	NOH	34	KNEAGEY,			Jonathan Jr.	PHI	144
John Senr.	NOH	34	Christian	SOM	149	Joseph	PHI	144
Valentine	NOH	34	Christian Sen.	SOM	149	Joseph	PHI	144
KLOTZ, Andrew	NOH	90A	John	SOM	149	Joshua	WAY	144
Casper	NOH	51A	KNEAGY, Joel?	DAU	34A	Nicholas	SOM	134
George	NOH	51A	KNEBEL, Jacob	LAN	199	Peter	BUC	80
John	NOH	60	KNEBLE,			Peter	SOM	134
John	BER	176	Christopher	BER	152	Philip	BFD	74
John	NOH	51A	Cristn.	MNT	112	Richard	ADA	36
Ludwig	NOH	82A	Herman	BER	152	Sarah	BUC	88A
Nicholas	NOH	90A	John	BER	142	Thomas	PHI	144
Philip	NOH	69	KNECHLE, Bartel	NOH	80A	Thomas	FAY	257
KLUG, Godfrid	LAN	288	KNECHT, Adam	NOH	71A	William	BUC	153
KLUGH, Charles	LAN	43	George	NOH	87	KNIGHT?, Thos. M.	CHE	735
KLUK, Ludwig	DAU	35A	Jacob	NOH	62A	KNIGHTZ, Phillip	NOU	183
KLUNCK, Henry	FRA	272	John	NOH	69	KNIP?, George	NOU	137
KNAB, Danl.	BER	258	Leonard	NOH	62A	KNIPE, Christian	MNT	45
Peter	YOR	164	Philip	NOH	39A	David	MNT	45
KNABB, John	BER	230	Ulrich	NOH	39A	Joseph	MNT	45

KNISELEY, Jno.	CUM	28
KNISELY, Abraham	YOR	208
Anthony	YOR	209
Christian	YOR	197
George	YOR	212
John	BFD	64
John	BFD	74
John	BFD	75
John	YOR	175
Michael	YOR	213
Samuel	YOR	213
KNISLEY, Jacob	BUC	157
John	BUC	157
Stephen	BUC	157
KNISS, John	NOU	122
KNISS?, George	NOU	137
KNITTILL?, Daniel	NOU	111
KNITTLE, Adam	BER	157
John Geo.	BER	157
Joseph	NOH	76
Michael	BER	254
KNIVER, Adam	WAY	135
KNOB, Valentine	ADA	38
William	WST	238
KNOBLE, John	NOH	87
KNOCH, Conrad	NOH	43
KNOCKSTED, Ludwig	BER	267
KNODLE, John	PHA	78
Mary	PHA	73
KNOGHT, Jonathan	PHI	144
KNOLL, Chrisn.	DAU	42
Francis	YOR	180
Jacob	LAN	27
Jacob	DAU	42
Jacob	BER	266
John	BER	270
KNOLLS, Solomon	GRN	76
KNOOP, Jacob	DAU	12
Philip	DAU	31A
KNOOSS, John	DAU	37
KNOP, Philip	PHI	128
KNOPHOKER, Henry	LAN	14
KNOPP, Christian	LAN	199
KNOPPENBERGER,		
Henry	NOH	56
KNOPSNYDER,		
Cunrod	SOM	134
KNOR, Bernard	PHI	135
Christn.	BER	201
Dewalt	BER	233
Frederick	PHI	129
George	PHI	127
Jacob	PHI	127
Jacob	BER	151
Mathias	PHI	128
KNORR, George	PHA	10
Henry	NOH	73A
Jacob	PHA	19
John	PHA	82
Leonard	NOH	73A
Mathias	PHI	121
KNOTT, Eliza	PHA	64
KNOTTS, Benjamin	GRN	82
James	GRN	82
Nathaniel	GRN	82
William	GRN	76
KNOTZ, Conrad	MNT	99
KNOUF, John	ADA	27
KNOUF?, Peter	BFD	74
KNOUP?, Peter	BFD	74
KNOUR, Adam	BER	181
William	BER	240
KNOUS, Christiana	ADA	17
Jacob	PHI	140
Joseph	PHI	140
KNOUSE, Francis	ADA	11

KNOWER,		
Christopher	CHE	905
Christopher Jr.	CHE	911
John	CHE	905
KNOWLES, Isaac	BUC	143A
James	DEL	186
John	PHI	134
John	DEL	186
John	BUC	151A
Joseph	BUC	151A
Robert	CHE	858
Robert	BUC	151A
Sarah	PHA	8
KNOWLIN, Robert	CHE	713
KNOWLS, Jacob	BUC	152A
KNOX OR NOX,		
Robert	LAN	180
KNOX, Widow	PHI	12
Widw.	PHI	112A
Abner	FRA	288
Andrew	MNT	115
Factor	MIF	5
Francis	PHA	7
Galbreath	CEN	22B
George	ARM	123
Hugh	MNT	138
Hugh	MIF	10A
James	WAS	16
James	ALL	98
James	LAN	175
James	MIF	10A
Jessy	ALL	87
John	LYC	17
John	PHI	35
John	PHI	48
John	FRA	318
Joseph	CUM	94
Joseph	PHA	121
Mathew	WAS	22
Mathew	MNT	117
Robert	ALL	55
Robert	LAN	113
Robert	WST	171
Saml. Doct.	ADA	3
Saml.	PHI	67A
Samuel	ADA	3
Thomas	FRA	276
William	WAS	8
William	WST	238
Wilm.	ALL	58
Wm.	LYC	11
Wm.	PHI	66
Wm.	PHA	90
KNOX?, Robt.?	FRA	312
KNUBLE, Abram	MNT	112
KNUDLER, Jacob	MNT	50
KNULL, Jacob	LAN	22
Ludwick	DEL	173
KNUZLE, John	MNT	71
KNYER, Conrad		
(Crossed Out)	FRA	308
KOAH, John	BER	144
KOAP, Geo.	DAU	42
KOBB?, Frederick	BER	201
KOBER, George	NOH	73A
George Adam	BUC	159
Paul	BUC	159
KOBLE, Abraham	YOR	168
Christian	LAN	4
George	BER	151
John	BER	151
KOBLE?, Frederick	BER	201
KOBLER, Jacob	BER	154
KOCH, Adam	BER	141
Adam Jr.	BER	144
Bastian	BER	165

KOCH, Charles	BER	165
Charles Ludwig	NOH	80A
Christian	BER	155
Christian	BER	221
Christian	BER	222
Danl.	BER	188
George	NOH	30
George	NOH	43
Henry	NOH	60
Henry	BER	221
Henry	NOH	59A
Jacob	ADA	16
Jacob	YOR	176
Jacob	BER	181
Jacob	BER	183
Jacob	NOH	47A
Jacob	NOH	80A
John	NOH	30
John	NOH	34
John	LAN	78
John	BER	150
John	YOR	157
John	BER	165
John	YOR	169
John	YOR	170
John	YOR	171
John	BER	185
John	LAN	254
John	NOH	47A
Ludwig	NOH	47A
Martin	DAU	15A
Mathias	NOH	80A
Michael	YOR	216
Michael	BER	223
Nicholas	NOH	34
Peter	BER	183
Peter	BER	219
Rachael	BER	222
Rochard	YOR	158
William	BER	223
William	NOH	80A
KOCHENAUER,		
Abraham	LAN	276
Jacob	LAN	276
KOCHENOUER,		
Joseph	LAN	313
KOCHENOUR, Jacob	YOR	176
John	YOR	212
Martin	YOR	174
Michael	YOR	174
KOCHENTOERFFER,		
Jno.	DAU	26
KOCHER,		
Chrisstopher	NOH	34
Conrad	NOH	34
George	NOH	34
Henry	NOH	76
Henry	LUZ	359
Henry	NOH	39A
John	NOH	39A
John	NOH	90A
Joshua	NOH	76
Levi	NOH	76
Peter	NOH	52
Peter	NOH	39A
Simon	NOH	52
Thomas	LUZ	359
KOCHLER, Jacob		
Senr.	NOH	56
Peter	NOH	30
KOCK, Adam	BER	244
George	BUC	148A
Peter	BER	267
KOCKERT, Widow	NOH	48
KOCLER?, Jacob	LAN	141
KOCLING?, Anthony	PHI	116

KODER?, Jacob	LAN 141	KON, Conrad	NOU 194	KORN, Daniel	NOH	59A
KOEHLER, John	NOH 39A	Henry	NOU 194	KORNKEPLE, John	BER	154
John	NOH 43A	KONCLE?, Henry	PHI 67A	KORNMAN, George	DAU	26
KOELER, Nicholas	BER 205	KONELL, Daniel	NOU 176	John	LAN	200
KOELING?, Anthony	PHI 116	KONES, Peter	NOU 129	KORP, Adam	BER	176
KOELN?, Frederick	LAN 141	KONEY, Archebald	FAY 204	KORR, Thomas	BER	271
KOEM, Nichs.	DAU 35A	KONIG, Adam	NOH 39A	KORTS, Joseph	WST	217
KOENHOUR, Jos.	YOR 174	Christopher	NOH 34	KORTZ, Adam	BER	271
KOENIG, Daniel	BER 156	David	LAN 37	Christian	LAN	191
Jacob	BER 156	Frederick	NOH 48	Nicholas	NOH	73A
Michael	BER 134	George	LAN 37	KOSER, Christian	BER	188
KOFFEL, Peter	BUC 159	George	NOH 76	Geo.	BER	188
KOFFMAN, Henry	SOM 149	Jacob	NOH 34	John	BER	188
John	ADA 36	Jacob	BER 251	KOSS, John	ERI	57
KOHL, Philip	MNT 96	John	LAN 111	KOSTENBADER,		
Solomon	BER 219	John	NOH 71A	Henry	NOH	73A
KOHLER, Abraham	NOH 56	Mathias	NOH 34	KOSTER, Marken	NOH	76
Adam	YOR 194	Solomon	BER 170	KOSTIKEN, Francis	SOM	146
Baltzer	YOR 166	KONIGMACHER,		KOTZ, David Junr.	NOH	71A
Christn.	NOH 37A	Benjamin	LAN 211	Frederick	NOH	71A
Frederick	NOH 73A	Jacob	LAN 199	KOUCHER, George	PHI	146
Henry	BER 188	KONN, Daniel	YOR 167	KOUKLXOR?, John	PHI	107
Jacob	NOH 90	Henry	YOR 166	KOUSE, John	PHA	117
Jacob	YOR 194	KONRAD, Andrew	BER 170	KOUTZ, Jacob	LAN	57
Jacob Junr.	NOH 56	KONRATH, John	BER 259	Thomas	LAN	57
Jacob Junr.	YOR 194	KOOGLER, Peter	YOR 180	KOWHER, Jacob	PHI	89
John	BER 188	KOOK, Henry	CHE 890	KOWKER, Danl.	PHI	143
Michael	NOH 34	Jacob	MNT 96	KOY, Wm.	CEN	22B
Peter	NOH 60	KOOKEN, Eve	NOH 56	KOYLES?, Edward	PHI	118
Stephen	NOH 43	Henry Esqr.	NOH 80A	KRAAG, John	NOH	90A
Valentine	NOH 87	Peter	NOH 62A	KRABER, Philip	LAN	200
Widow	NOH 56	KOOLER, Michael	YOR 183	KRACH, Conrad	NOH	59A
Widow	NOH 90	KOOLY, John	ADA 39	KRAEMER, Nicholas	NOH	34
KOHLSTOCK,		KOOM, Henry	LAN 263	Timothy	NOH	64A
Christian	HNT 154	KOON, Adam	WST 253	KRAFD, Henry	LAN	184
KOHLY, Martin	NOH 76	David	CEN 20A	KRAFT, Jos.	YOR	158
KOHNS, Jacob	NOU 137	Peter	FAY 266	Peter	PHA	17A
John	NOU 137	Thomas	FAY 266	KRAIN, Daniel	VEN	168
KOHO, Jacob	NOH 36	William	FAY 251	KRAM, Abraham	NOH	48
KOHR, Caspar Sr.	DAU 50A	KOONS, Daniel	NOH 41A	Frederick	YOR	215
John	DAU 50A	Frederick	MNT 73	Jacob (See		
John	DAU 52A	Michael	MNT 96	Kram, Widow)	NOH	48
Mich.	DAU 50A	Philip	YOR 213	John	NOH	48
Michael	DAU 17	KOONTZ, Abram	CUM 33	Peter	NOH	48
Widow	DAU 52A	KOOP, Isaac	NOH 73A	Widow Of Jacob	NOH	48
KOIL, Melchor	BUC 147A	John	NOH 34	KRAMBERGER,		
Patrick	LAN 161	Jonas	CUM 63	Christn.	BER	141
KOKE, Rudy	DAU 6A	KOOPER, Peter	BUC 139	KRAMER, Casper	BUC	91
KOL--?, Fredr.	FRA 300	KOOPRIDER, John	FAY 257	Frederick	NOH	56
KOLB, Abm.	BUC 96A	KOOPSER, Jacob	ADA 31	Henry	BUC	91
Andrew	LAN 71	KOOSER, John	SOM 134	Jacob	BUC	91
Delman	MNT 118	KOOSLER, Noah	BFD 64	Lawrence	BUC	91
George	MNT 134	KOOTZ, Christian	BER 210	KRAMES, Nicholas	NOH	59A
Henry	MNT 128	KOOVER, Geo.	CUM 68	KRAMLING, Adam	BER	168
Isaac	BUC 96A	Geo. Senr.	CUM 67	KRANTZ, George	YOR	157
Jacob	BUC 98	George	CUM 67	KRASSKILL, John	SOM	154
Jacob	MNT 118	Gidion	CUM 68	KRASSLER, Jacob	NOH	62A
Jacob	BUC 96A	Peter	SOM 138	KRATZ, Isaac	MNT	121
John	BUC 96A	Peter Sen.	SOM 138	Martin	ERI	55A
Mathias	MNT 112	KOPENHAVEN, John	NOU 122	Valuntine	MNT	90
Michael	NOH 90	KOPENHAVER, Thos.	DAU 36	KRATZER, Anthony	NOH	65
Michael	BUC 91	KOPER, Michael	LAN 199	Daniel	NOH	90
Peter	MNT 60	KOPLIN, John	MNT 61	Henry	NOH	30
Valentine	ADA 36	John	NOH 87	Henry	NOH	64A
KOLL, Andrew	LAN 88	Mathias	MNT 82	John	DAU	47
KOLLER, Daniel	BER 254	KOPP, Andw.	BER 213	Joseph	LAN	98
John	BER 186	Conrad	NOH 85A	Peter	LAN	145
John	BER 254	KOPPELBERGER,		Philip	NOH	64A
John Jr.	YOR 192	Nicholas	BER 176	Widow	NOH	30
John Sr.	YOR 192	KOPPENHAVER,		KRAUL, Jacob	NOH	59A
KOLP, Adam	LAN 114	Michl.	BER 154	KRAUS, Joseph	LAN	184
Conrad	BER 254	KOPPLEBERGER,		KRAUSE, Andrew	DAU	2A
George	BER 257	Christopher	BER 244	Charles	MNT	128
Helfrich	BER 204	Herny	MNT 55	David	DAU	33A
Jacob	BER 130	KORE, Christn.	DAU 35A	Jacob	LAN	288
KOMER, Philip	GRN 79	KORLET, Abraham	LAN 292	Jeremiah	MNT	134

219

KRAUSE, Leonard	LAN	50	KREIDLER, Daniel	NOH	71A	KREYLEY, Widow	YOR	185		
Mathias	NOH	70	Frederick Sn.	NOH	71A	KRIB, John	DAU	37A		
Michael	BER	133	Frederick	NOH	71A	KRICE, Stephen	ADA	30		
KRAUSER, Adam	BER	244	John	LAN	283	KRICK, Adam	BER	150		
Balser	BER	133	KREIFS, Peter	BER	206	Adam	LAN	200		
KRAUSING, Woidow	YOR	186	KREIG, Jacob	BER	226	Frances	BER	203		
KRAUSS, Andreas	NOH	56	Nicholas	BER	226	Frantz	BER	170		
Andrew	NOH	51A	KREIGBAUM, Adam	BER	272	George	BER	170		
Baltzer	NOH	56	John A	BER	263	Jacob	BER	167		
George Senr.	NOH	52	KREIGER, Jacob	BER	271	John	BER	170		
George	NOH	51A	KREIN, Christn.	BER	282	Peter	BER	170		
John	NOH	45	KREIST--?, John	BER	236	Peter	LAN	211		
John	NOH	56	KRELES, Jacob	FRA	297	Philip	LAN	211		
Leonhard	NOH	32	KREMER, Andw.	YOR	206	Solomon	BER	171		
KRAUSSE, Gottlieb	NOH	32	Baltzer	FAY	245	KRICKBAUM, Conrad	MNT	138		
KRAUTH, John	NOH	71A	Baltzer Jur.	FAY	245	Jno. Geo.	BER	154		
KRAYMER, John	BUC	159	Christian	FAY	245	KRICKORY, Richard	BER	212		
Lawrence	BUC	159	Christopher	BER	188	KRIDER, Henry	LAN	111		
Philip	BUC	159A	Conrad	NOH	34	Henry	LAN	116		
KREAMER, Adam	DAU	43	Daniel	BER	261	Isaac	NOU	137		
John	LAN	284	David	YOR	157	Widow	LAN	307		
Lawrence	BUC	82	David	YOR	160	KRIEBEL, Abraham	NOH	56		
Paul	MNT	46	Fredk.	BER	188	George	NOH	56		
KREBBS, John	WAS	38	Geo.	BER	188	Jacob	NOH	56		
KREBEL, David	LAN	148	George	FAY	245	KRIEBLE, Malchoir	MNT	45		
KREBER, Adam	YOR	154	George	BER	261	KRIFE, John	LAN	85		
John	YOR	156	George	BER	261	KRIG, Philip	LAN	211		
Martin	YOR	155	Godfrey	NOU	122	KRILL, Philip	BER	170		
KREBILL, Jacob	LAN	2	Henry	BER	155	KRIME, John	BER	266		
KREBS, Catherine	MNT	73	Henry	YOR	210	KRIMM, George	NOH	85A		
Fredk.	DAU	14	Henry	BER	261	KRINBACK?,				
Fredk.	DAU	15	Henry	LAN	268	Francis	PHI	102A		
George	PHA	81	Jacob	DAU	23	KRINER, Val	LAN	148		
Henry	ADA	4	Jacob	BER	130	KRING, David	BER	170		
Henry	NOU	122	Jacob	YOR	154	Henry	BER	170		
Jacob	BER	159	John	BER	188	John	BER	170		
Jacob	NOU	188	Martin	DAU	28A	KRINNE?, Henry	LAN	263		
Michael	DAU	32	Mathias	BER	156	KRINVE?, Henry	LAN	263		
KREDE, Andrew	BER	279	Peter	YOR	156	KRISE, Philip	DAU	29A		
Michael	BER	276	Philip	BER	244	KRISER?, Mary	MNT	40		
Nicholas	BER	279	Wentel	LAN	268	KRISMAN, Jacob	BUC	80		
KREDER, Daniel	NOH	56	William	BER	156	KRISSLEY, Killiam	BUC	149A		
John	NOH	73A	William	BER	261	KRIST, Simon	BER	261		
KREE, John	HNT	159	KREMSER, John	NOH	70	KRITENHOUSER,				
KREEG, Charles	NOH	76	KREPPS, Widw.	PHI	104A	John	DAU	47		
KREER?, Andrew	MNT	67	George	YOR	187	KRITZER, Michl.	DAU	40		
KREESS, George	WST	347	KREPS, Henry	MNT	57	KRIZER, Widow	MNT	99		
KREGBOURN, Peter	NOU	129	Peter	ADA	29	KRIZER?, George	MNT	99		
KREGEL-?, Henry	NOH	51A	Peter	YOR	190	KROB, Henry	NOH	90A		
KREGEL, Andreas	NOH	76	Peter Jun.	ADA	30	John	NOH	90		
KREGOR, Henry	YOR	215	Philip	DAU	48	KROFT, Jacob	YOR	204		
KREHL, Michael	DAU	4A	KRES-LER?, Da	52	0	KROH, George	BER	240		
KREIDER, Abraham	NOH	62A	KRESNER, John	BER	154	Henry	BER	271		
Andrew	LAN	136	KRESS, Charles	NOH	78	Jacob	BER	257		
Christian	LAN	103	Michael	NOH	87	Jacob Jur.	BER	258		
Christian	YOR	157	KRESSLER, Philip	NOH	30	Nicholas	BER	201		
Conrad	NOH	30	KRESSLY, Adam	NOH	45	KROHMAN, Rudolph	NOH	30		
Daniel	LAN	238	Barnet	NOH	45	KROLL, Christian	LAN	99		
Jacob	NOH	39A	Jacob	NOH	45	John	YOR	187		
John	DAU	46A	John	NOH	45	Jos.	YOR	208		
Mich	LAN	147	KRESY, Conrad			Nicholas	LAN	32		
Michael	LAN	103	Senr.	NOH	36	KROMBAUGH, Widow	YOR	176		
Michael	LAN	273	Jacob	NOH	36	KROMER, John	NOH	30		
Peter	LAN	136	Philip	NOH	36	Revd.	NOH	82		
Peter Senr.	LAN	136	KRETZINGER,			KRON, Henry	NOH	85A		
Peter A.	LAN	136	George	YOR	161	KRONE, Lorentz	BER	133		
Wm.	PHA	21	KREUTZ, George	NOH	90A	KRONEBACH,				
KREIDER?, (See			KREUTZER, Andrew	BER	271	Nicholas	YOR	174		
Kruder)	LAN	34	Peter	BER	271	KRONER, Andrew	MNT	112		
KREIDLER, Adam	YOR	166	KREWSEN, Jesse	PHI	149	KRONINGER, John	NOH	85A		
Adam	YOR	167	John	PHI	144	KRONTZ, Joseph	BFD	74		
Andreas	NOH	50	KREWSON, Derrick	PHI	155	KROOS, Christian	MNT	42		
Andrew	NOH	43	Garret	BUC	143A	KROSEN, Derrick	BUC	138		
Andrew	NOH	71A	John Jn.	BUC	143A	Derrick	BUC	137A		
Casper	YOR	159	John	BUC	143A	Derrick	BUC	137A		
Daniel Jn.	NOH	71A	Leonard	BUC	143A	Garret	BUC	137A		

KROSEN, Garrit	BUC	138	KUGLER, Charles	PHA	58	KUNCKEL, Adam	NOH	36
Jacob	BUC	137A	Paul	MNT	138	Christian	DAU	4A
John	BUC	137A	KUHERLY, Jacob	YOR	170	David	NOH	53A
John	BUC	137A	KUHL, Fredrick	PHA	45	George Jnr.	NOH	36
KROSIER, John	WST	152	Henry	PHA	59	George Sr.	NOH	36
KROTY, Henry	MNT	96	Peter	YOR	170	Lowrence	NOH	41A
KROUSE, David	MNT	134	Yost	YOR	170	Widow	NOH	56
Elizabeth	BER	239	KUHLER, Henry	LAN	57	KUNCKLE, Eve	DAU	4
John	BER	244	KUHLER?, Andrew	LAN	190	Michl.	DAU	15A
Michael	MNT	96	KUHN, Frederic	HNT	149	KUNCKLER, Widow	NOH	32
Michl.	BER	243	Frederick	LAN	231	KUNCLE, Widow	PHI	70
KROW, Jacob	HNT	143	Fredk. Dr.	LAN	41	Christn.	PHI	73
KROWLE, John Geo.	BER	222	Freney	YOR	201	KUNFER, Peter	BER	262
KRUB, Peter	NOH	87	Henry	ADA	22	KUNK, John	CUM	33
KRUBB, David	MNT	120	Henry	ADA	36	KUNKEL, Andrew	NOH	53A
Isaac	MNT	119	Isaac	NOH	39A	Henry	LAN	244
Isaac Junr.	MNT	119	Jacob	ADA	31	Jacob	NOH	53A
Jacob	MNT	118	Jacob	ADA	36	KUNKLE, Baltzer	YOR	168
KRUBER, Christian	BER	279	Jacob	ADA	38	Bastain	WST	253
Nicholas	NOH	30	Jacob	BER	141	Christian	YOR	168
KRUBLE, Abraham	MNT	118	Jacob	NOH	39A	George	PHA	57
Abram	MNT	121	John	ADA	22	Gotleib	YOR	168
Andrew	MNT	121	John	ADA	31	Jacob	YOR	168
Esther	MNT	123	John	YOR	201	Jacob	BER	260
Jeremiah	MNT	121	John Dr.	LAN	41	John	BFD	64
Mary	MNT	111	John	NOH	37A	John	WST	253
KRUDER, John	LAN	34	Jos.	YOR	193	John	BER	260
KRUG, George	BER	230	Joseph	ADA	22	Magdalena	YOR	157
Jacob	LAN	41	Katharine	YOR	180	Peter	WST	253
Valentine	LAN	44	Michael	BER	206	KUNKLE?, George	BER	130
KRUGER, Nicholas	BUC	139	Michl.	PHI	39	KUNKLEMAN, George	BER	215
KRUM, Christian	NOH	45	Susannah	MNT	93	KUNNER, John	DAU	35A
Francis	ADA	15	KUHN?, John	BER	244	William	LAN	152
Frantz	NOH	45	KUHNER, Daniel	NOH	34	KUNS, Daniel	DAU	6
Henry	DAU	17A	KUHNS, David	BER	258	Daniel	BER	226
John	DAU	30	John	NOH	76	Francis	NOU	100
John			John	WST	217	George	NOU	100
(Shoemaker)	NOH	45	Peter	WST	191	George	LAN	199
John Senr.	NOH	45	Phillip	WST	217	John	LAN	200
Perter	DAU	17A	KUHR?, John	PHI	97	John	BER	206
Peter	ADA	15	KUKER, Mary	PHA	31	KUNSELMAN, John	BER	285
KRUMBEIN, Jacob	DAU	50A	KULB, Abraham	MNT	120	Philip	BER	285
Leonard	LAN	211	Andrew	MNT	128	KUNSER, Andrew	BUC	159
KRUMBINE, Peter	YOR	181	Henry	MNT	128	Henry	MNT	125
Widow	DAU	30A	Jacob	MNT	73	KUNSMAN, Jacob	BER	244
KRUMER, Daniel	MNT	122	Jacob	MNT	90	Wm.	BER	152
KRUMM, Henry	NOH	53A	Jellis	MNT	128	KUNSSMAN, John	NOH	45
KRUMRAIN, Michael	NOH	87	Joseph	MNT	57	KUNTSMAN, Philip	NOH	47A
KRUMREIN, Adam	NOH	87	Mastin	MNT	128	KUNTZ, Abraham	ADA	30
Stephen	NOH	87	Michael	MNT	57	Abraham	ADA	30
KRUR?, Andrew	MNT	67	KULEY?, -oyd?	ARM	124	Abram	MNT	128
KRUTZER, Adam	CUM	60	KULING, Jno.	CUM	91	Andrew	ADA	28
KRYDER, Daniel	HNT	154	John	CUM	89	Conrad	LAN	293
Fredk.	PHI	119A	KULLOUGH, John	LAN	152	David	NOH	52
George	HNT	150	KULP, Abraham	BUC	92	Emanuel	SOM	138
Henry	HNT	151	Andrew	MNT	121	Frances	YOR	157
Israel	HNT	153	Christian	LAN	18	Frederick Esqr.	NOH	50
John	LAN	7	George	MNT	60	George	ADA	30
John	HNT	154	Henry	MNT	121	George	NOH	50
KRYLY, John	LAN	64	Isaac	MNT	45	George	LAN	51
KRYSER, Martin	LYC	13	Jacob	LAN	17	George	NOH	60
KUBER, Samuel	LAN	215	Jacob	BUC	92	George	YOR	206
KUBOUCHES, Isaac	NOU	122	John	BUC	149A	George Senr.	ADA	29
KUBZ, George	BER	258	KULY, Henry	MNT	128	George	DAU	22A
KUCHLY, Jacob	NOH	59A	John	MNT	128	Hanah	SOM	134
KUCK?, Aron	MNT	93	Valuntine	MNT	128	Henry	NOH	60
KUDER, Adam	NOH	71A	KUMBLE, Stepphen	NOU	159	Henry	BER	130
John	NOH	60	KUMLER, Jacob	BER	150	Jacob	LAN	17
KUESER, Andrew	NOU	129	Jacob	BER	150	Jacob	NOH	60
KUFFER, Christian	FRA	313	Jacob	LAN	200	Jacob Esqr.	NOH	50
KUGHN, Adam	PHA	90	KUMMER, Wm.	PHA	41	Jacob	NOH	53A
John	PHA	58	KUMP, William	YOR	165	John	ADA	31
Martin	PHA	56	KUMRER, Isaa	BER	166	John	YOR	157
Michael	GRN	71	Jacob	BER	130	John	LAN	211
Peter	PHA	82	KUNCE, Michael	NOU	111	John	BER	260
KUGLER, Benjamin	MNT	73	John	NOU	111	John	LAN	292

221

KUNTZ, John Geo.	BER	151
Lawrenz	DAU	29
Ludwig	LAN	211
Mary	ADA	29
Mary	LAN	51
Michael	LAN	51
Michael	SOM	138
Michael	YOR	157
Michael	NOH	53A
Peter	DAU	42
Peter	NOH	50
Peter	BER	261
Peter Junr.	NOH	50
Phil.	DAU	35
Philip	NOH	60
Philip	BER	260
William	ADA	10
William	SOM	138
William	YOR	182
KUNTZIGER, Rudy	DAU	52A
KUNTZMAN,		
Christopher	BER	170
David	NOU	122
George	NOH	80A
Henry	BER	170
KURBMAN, Henry	YOR	166
KURFES, Andrew	PHA	82
KURKINDALL,		
Dengamin	ALL	89
KURKINGDAL, Sarah	ALL	87
KURM, Christian	NOH	45
KURR, Anna O.	MNT	117
KURTS, Geo. Mr.	PHI	66
KURTZ, Abraham	BER	170
Abram	CHE	831
Adam	NOH	80A
Andrew	NOH	80A
Barbara	LAN	211
Benjamin	DAU	4
Chrisstian	LAN	92
Christian	LAN	33
Christley	LAN	127
David	LAN	93
George	DAU	33
George	PHI	98
George	SOM	149
George Junr.	PHI	98
Henry	PHI	130
Jacob	LAN	128
Jacob	HNT	138
Jacob	LAN	183
Jacob	LAN	199
Jacob	CHE	831
Jno. Casper	NOH	41A
John	DAU	37
John	SOM	132
John	LAN	189
John Junr.	LAN	127
John Senr.	LAN	128
Jonathan	SOM	141
Lorenz	LAN	55
Martin	YOR	193
Michael	MNT	57
Michael	SOM	138
Michael	YOR	156
Michael	YOR	157
Peter	YOR	155
Peter	CHE	897
Philip	DAU	9
Samuel	LAN	80
Samuel	YOR	213
Valuntine	MNT	73
Widow	DAU	49A
William	LAN	45
KURVIN, Jacob	WST	191
KUSARD, Andrew	HNT	117
KUSER, Michael	BER	165
Polly	SOM	129
KUSEY?, Simon	MNT	69
KUSHLING, Fredk.	LAN	262
KUSLER, John		
Junr.	MNT	75
KUSSOCK, Henry	WST	191
KUST, John	LAN	143
KUSTER, Henry	LAN	13
John	DAU	38
Michael	LAN	15
Tobias	LAN	9
KUSY, Philip	MNT	92
KUTCHELL, Leonard	CHE	724
KUTH?, Benjn.	PHI	36
KUTSCHLER,		
Christopher	NOH	67
KUTZ, Adam	BER	244
Catherine	BER	228
Dewalt	BER	210
Elizabeth	BER	140
George	BER	158
George Ad?	BER	210
Jacob	BER	161
Jacob	BER	226
John	BER	226
John	BER	279
Nicholas	BER	226
Peter	BER	159
Peter	BER	210
Peter	BER	226
Solomon	BER	225
KUYRKINDALL,		
Lewas	ALL	89
KUZER, George	LAN	227
KUZEY, Jacob	MNT	71
KYAR, Frederick	FAY	198
KYDA, John	PHI	94
KYGAR, Charles	FAY	222
KYHER?, Henry	HNT	152
KYLE, Crawford	MIF	15
Douglass	LAN	145
Elizabeth	FRA	274
Henry	MIF	25A
Jacob	FAY	222
John	LYC	3
John	MIF	15
John	FRA	319
Joseph	MIF	15
Laughlin	FRA	322
Mathew	FRA	322
Peter	FRA	282
Robt.	YOR	202
Samuel	HNT	151
Samuel	MER	447
Samuel	CHE	754
Thomas	FAY	266
KYLER, Ann	HNT	147
George	HNT	147
Henry	CUM	144
John	HNT	139
KYLES, James	LYC	22
William	WAS	69
William	MER	447
KYMER, Philip	SOM	138
KYMES, Peter	BUT	361
KYNAN?, John	LYC	11
KYNON, Benjn.	LYC	12
James	LYC	12
KYPER, Adam	BUC	101
George	BUC	101
KYSAKER, Nichs.	CUM	68
KYSELLER, Charles	PHI	105
KYSER, Conrad	CUM	33
Cunrod	SOM	129
Daniel	SOM	129
KYSER, Jacob	SOM	134
John	PHI	95
John	LAN	128
John	SOM	129
John	PHI	101A
Lewis	SOM	129
Michael	LAN	263
Michl.	PHI	73A
Philip	LAN	263
Saml.	PHI	93
KYTELE?, Isaac	LYC	9
KYZER, Jacob	DEL	164
William	DEL	165
L----?, Thomas	HNT	125
Thos.	FRA	321
L---ELY?, Jack	LAN	298
L-SLE-?, George	BEV	10
LA FEVRE, Anthony	LUZ	395
LA MARE, Mathias	PHA	14
LA PORTE,		
Bartholomew	LUZ	395
LA RUE, Casimer	LUZ	394
LA---S?, Adam	MNT	37
LAAGE?, John	FRA	292
LABAR, Abraham	NOH	65
Daniel	NOH	65
George	NOH	65
George		
(Shoemr.)	NOH	65
George	WAY	149
George Junr.	NOH	65
Jacob	NOH	78A
Jno. George	NOH	65
John	NOH	65
Joseph	NOH	65
Peter	NOH	65
Peter	WAY	147
William	NOH	65
LABBEE, Sarah	PHA	39
LABER, George	LAN	211
John	LAN	211
Martin	LAN	201
LABERE, Benj.	PHI	88A
LABETTE, Madam	PHA	116
LABINGOOD, Jacob	NOU	129
Jacob	NOU	183
LABULL, Peter	PHI	94
LABY, Mrs.	PHI	50
LACANS, Joseph	NOU	159
LACAVE, John	PHA	6
LACE, Wm.	PHA	84
LACEY, Isaac	BUC	155
Jesse	BUC	87
John	BUC	107
Joseph	BUC	87
Moses	BUC	149A
LACEY?, Stephen	LYC	12
LACK?, Patrick	PHA	110
LACKERY, Thos.	YOR	217
LACKET, M.	LAN	266A
LACKEY, Alexander	FAY	215
Edward	NOH	37A
Henry	CUM	25
Henry	CUM	38
Hugh	CRA	9
Jacob	NOU	195
James	PHA	74
James	ALL	99
John	NOU	199
John	BER	243
Thomas	LAN	225
LACKINS, Edwd.	CEN	22B
LACKY, John	WAS	3
John	FAY	215
Thomas	WAS	3

LACOMB, John	PHI	30	LAIR, Philip	YOR	171	LAMBERT, Joseph	BER	201
LACOMBE, Peter	PHA	46	LAIRD, Hugh	CUM	69	Lott	FAY	266
LACTEN, Thomas	FAY	266	Hugh	YOR	176	Michael	BUC	80
LACY, Ebenezer	LUZ	399	James	WAS	75	Moses	SOM	154
Isaac	LUZ	399	James	NOU	159	Nichls.	CUM	51
Peter	FAY	266	Jas.	CUM	100	Nicholas	NOH	84
LADD, Ephraim	LUZ	412	John	ADA	13	Noah	BUC	107
Horatio	LUZ	412	John	DAU	21	Peter	PHA	40
LADIG, Peter	NOH	87	John	WST	161	Peter	YOR	176
Peter	BER	286	John	NOU	165	LAMBERTON, Jas.	CUM	79
Peter Junr.	NOH	87	John	YOR	202	Jas.	CUM	98
LADIG?, Jacob	BER	157	Matthew	NOU	199	Simon	CUM	79
LADLEY, Richard	CHE	753	Mattw.	CUM	74	LAMBETH, Cathrine	PHA	43
LADLY, Susanna	LAN	300	Moses	NOU	165	LAMBFARE, Jesse	LUZ	413
LADSHAW, Joseph	CUM	77	Saml.	CUM	69	LAMBORN, Joseph	CEN	22B
Peter	CUM	107	Saml.	CUM	96	Josiah	CEN	22B
LADY, Daniel	FRA	303	Samuel	DAU	3	LAMBOURN, Danl.	CHE	738
LAFABUA, Lewesa	PHA	45	Thomas	NOU	159	David	CHE	769
LAFAVER, Daniel	HNT	138	William	ADA	13	Francis	CHE	768
LAFERTY, Edward	PHA	104	William	DAU	21	George	CHE	706
James	CRA	11	William	NOU	159	Robt.	CHE	839
James	ALL	97	William	NOH	90A	Thos.	CHE	838
James	HNT	121	Zackeriah	WST	161	Wm.	CHE	840
John	YOR	161	LAITEN, Abraham	FAY	266	LAMBRIGHT, John	NOU	129
LAFEY?, Jemima	DEL	163	Peter	FAY	266	LAME, Caleb	PHI	80A
LAFFER, Adam	MER	448	LAK?, Jacob (See			LAMERSON, Zachr.	CUM	112
Chr.	WST	192	Lah)	BUC	159A	LAMESON, Lowrence	NOH	67
John	WST	192	LAKE, Aaron	WAS	69	LAMESTER, William	BER	141
LAFFERTY, Alexr.	NOU	202	Charles	PHA	67	LAMISON,		
Bernard	LAN	128	Daniel	LUZ	323	Cornelius	NOU	100
Edward	NOH	65	David	PHI	104	Jacob	NOU	111
Edward	WAS	69	David	LUZ	401	LAMMERSON, Conrad	ADA	15
Edward	FAY	198	Harmon	PHI	118	LAMMIN, James	CHE	772
Jackson	WAS	75	John	BUC	145	LAMMOTTE, Francis	YOR	182
James	FAY	201	John	PHI	118A	LAMOY, John	MNT	64
James	MER	448	Moses	WAS	69	LAMPAUGH, George	PHI	115
Jesse	CHE	751	Moses	NOU	194	LAMPE, Rudolph	BER	134
John	BFD	74	Robert	PHI	61A	LAMPING, John	ADA	18
Patrick	ALL	63	William	NOU	165	John	ADA	40
Robert	WST	161	LAKELY, Henry	HNT	142	LAMPLEIGH, Daniel	DEL	187
William	WAS	45	LAKY, Francis	MNT	82	LAMPSING, Stophel	BUC	139A
William	BFD	74	LALERBURN?, Widow	PHI	21	LAMSON?, Jacob	LYC	8
Wilm.	ALL	106	LALON, Joseph	BUC	100	LAMY, Edward	CHE	737
LAFFERTY?, Joseph	SOM	146	LALOR, John	PHA	107	Stephen	CHE	800
LAFIT, Johannes	HNT	161	LAM, John	ALL	95	LANBAUGH, Chuster	NOU	152
LAFORD, Thomas	WST	369	LAMAREUX, James	LUZ	339	LANCASTER, David	CHE	739
LAFORGUE, Mr.	PHA	25	LAMARK, James	PHA	81	Israel	BUC	157
LAFRANCE, Peter	LUZ	335	LAMB, Charles	NOH	65	Jacob	PHA	38
LAGAN, James	NOU	159	David	CEN	18A	James	DEL	160
LAGE, Lida	PHI	96	Gad.	LYC	12	John	FAY	209
LAGESS?, Adam	MNT	37	George	FAY	209	John	PHI	114A
LAGIRE?, Adam	MNT	37	George	FAY	240	Moses	BUC	157
LAH, Jacob	BUC	159A	George	FRA	311	Thomas	BUC	94
LAHMAN, Abrm.	MNT	71	James	CEN	22B	Thomas	MNT	108
John	MNT	47	John	CUM	66	Thos.	PHI	103
LAHMAN?, Thomas	MNT	47	John	PHI	131	Thos.	PHI	108
LAHR, Abraham	NOH	87	John	BER	201	LANCE, Abe	BUC	88A
Balser	WAS	123	John	FAY	209	Christian	MIF	4
George	BER	208	John	WST	292	Jacob	PHA	115
Henry	NOH	34	John	CEN	18A	John	MIF	4
Jacob	NOH	73A	Michael	FAY	209	Margaret	PHA	56
LAIDLEY, James	PHA	4	Saml.	CEN	18A	Peter	WAS	75
LAIMAN, Jacob	LAN	277	William	CEN	18A	Saml.	FRA	305
LAIN, Abraham	ALL	61	LAMBACH, Philip	BUC	147A	LANCE?, James	ALL	81
Andw.	VEN	167	LAMBARDO, Philip	PHA	117	LANCESTER, Seneca	CHE	729
Esa	ALL	57	LAMBARTT, Ulrich	LAN	46	LANCETON, Peter	MIF	25A
Hanna	FAY	257	LAMBERSON,			LANCOLN, Benjamen	FAY	257
Henry	WST	292	Laurence	BFD	74	John	FAY	257
Isaac	ALL	58	LAMBERT, Francis	LAN	42	Mordica	FAY	257
Jacob	ALL	57	Geo.	CUM	51	LAND, George	WAS	22
John	BFD	51	George	SOM	154	John	WAY	138
John	BFD	68	Henry	LAN	107	Michael	MNT	87
Laurance	ALL	61	Jacob	SOM	154	LANDA, John	PHI	77
LAINMAN, Jacob	LAN	276	Jacob	BER	167	LANDAN, Wm.	LYC	6
LAIR, George	MNT	111	Jacob Jr.	BER	167	LANDBERGER,		
Philip	MNT	108	John Esq.	SOM	154	Bastian	NOH	76

LANDEL, Widow	PHI	67	LANDIS, John	LAN	118	LANG, John	LAN 147B
LANDEMODE, Jacob	LAN	264	John	MNT	125	Ludwig	BER 271
LANDENBERGER,			John	SOM	138	Robert Revd.	WAS 12
Jacob	PHI	120A	John Jr.	DAU	44A	LANG?, (See Long)	FRA 299
Jno.	PHI	147	John	DAU	15A	John	ALL 84
John	PHI	120A	John	BUC	159A	Peter	LYC 13
LANDER/ LANDES?,			Joseph	BUC	91	LANGABARGER,	
Michael	NOH	80A	Joseph	BUC	141	George	NOU 114
LANDER, Peter	NOH	78A	Philip	CHE	734	LANGDON, Wm.	CHE 713
LANDERBAG?,			Ralph	BUC	91	LANGE, Christian	NOH 32
George	PHI	97A	Saml.	BUC	91	LANGEN, Hugh	WAS 29
LANDERS, David	PHA	83	Samuel	BUC	101	William	WAS 16
Isaac	FAY	236	Solomon	LAN	123	LANGENECKER,	
William	NOH	67	Yellis	MNT	125	Henry	DAU 43A
LANDERS?, John	HNT	121	LANDMESER, George	FAY	245	Joseph	LAN 185
LANDES/ LANDRE?,			Jacob	FAY	245	LANGENTON, Jacob	NOU 183
Michael	NOH	80A	LANDNER, John	PHI	134	LANGESLAGER,	
LANDES, Abraham	YOR	163	LANDON, Laban	LYC	3	Richd.	PHI 111
Abraham	YOR	166	Nathaniel	LUZ	334	LANGFIELD, John	PHA 115
Abraham	FAY	215	Thomas	BEV	19	LANGFORD, Wm.	BEV 25
Abraham	NOH	30A	LANDOW, Henry	CHE	903	LANGHAM, John	BFD 79
Benjamin	LAN	98	LANDR ESS, Henry	CUM	44	William	BFD 64
Benjn.	MIF	13	LANDRIM, Tyrone			LANGHEAD, Thos.	
Jacob	YOR	206	(Black)	MIF	17	Captn.	PHI 105B
John	YOR	206	LANDS, Geo.	CUM	56	LANGINGE, Lewis	PHI 116
Samuel	YOR	168	John	BER	174	LANGIS, George	NOU 165
Samuel	NOH	30A	Thomas	BER	259	William	NOU 165
Stephen	YOR	169	LANDSDOWN, John	ALL	118	LANGLEY, James	WAS 116
LANDESIS, John	NOU	183	LANE, Abner	LUZ	389	Thoms.	BUT 345
LANDING, Laban	LUZ	409	Abraham	WAS	69	LANGLY, John	CRA 5
LANDIS, Abraham	LAN	116	Abraham	HNT	146	LANGS, Jacob	NOU 150
Abraham	LAN	137	Alexander	LUZ	424	LANGSLEY, James	FAY 253
Abraham	LAN	200	David	WAS	8	LANGTHOTH, Thomas	MNT 64
Anne	DAU	21A	David	FAY	198	LANGWELL, Jno.	CUM 124
Benjamin	BUC	91	Edward	PHA	117	Wm.	CHE 733
Benjamin	LAN	116	Edward	CHE	854	LANING, John	DAU 13
Benjamin	LAN	189	Hugh	FRA	278	LANINGBAUGH,	
Christo.	DAU	44	Jacob	DAU	40	Henry	NOU 194
Daniel	BUC	91	Jacob	WAS	69	LANIUS, Barbara	YOR 157
David	LAN	124	Jacob	WAY	149	Christian	YOR 159
David	BUC	161	James G.	PHA	62	Henry	YOR 156
David	LAN	200	Joel	DEL	181	Henry Jr.	YOR 157
Felix	DAU	12	John	PHA	33	Jacob	YOR 195
George	LAN	124	John	PHI	33	Michael	YOR 195
George	BUC	157	John	FAY	245	William	LAN 134
Henry	LAN	17	Margaret	BEV	14	LANKENMYER?,	
Henry	DAU	44	Presly C.	FAY	198	Fredk.	BER 205
Henry	BUC	91	Richard	HNT	137	LANKERT, George	DAU 36A
Henry	LAN	117	Samuel	HNT	161	LANNING, Isaac	LUZ 324
Henry	LAN	117	Samuel	CHE	856	James	PHA 71
Henry	MNT	125	Stephen	LYC	12	LANS, (No Given	
Henry	LAN	138	Thomas	WAS	8	Name)	DAU 9
Henry	SOM	138	Willeby W.	FRA	312	Andrew	DAU 8A
Henry	BUC	157	William	PHA	19	John	NOU 114
Henry	LAN	188	William	BFD	38	LANSINGER, Jacob	PHA 87
Henry	LAN	189	William	DEL	189	LANTEN, James	CRA 7
Henry	LAN	302	LANE?, John	PHA	78	LANTER, Abraham	BER 157
Henry	CHE	905	LANEKER, Peter			Godfrey	BER 157
Henry	BUC	159A	Junr.	LAN	257	LANTERMAN, Peter	WAS 63
Isaac	MNT	125	LANES, Favey	PHI	41	LANTES, Eve	BER 203
Jacob	LAN	17	Mrs.	NOU	165	John	NOH 67
Jacob	DAU	19	Othenial	BER	138	LANTESS, John	NOH 65
Jacob	LAN	106	LANEUS, John	YOR	170	LANTIS, George	BER 165
Jacob	MNT	125	LANG, Anthony	DAU	9A	George Jr.	BER 165
Jacob	MNT	128	Casper	BER	263	Henry	BER 176
Jacob	LAN	200	Charles	PHI	20	Jacob Esqr.	CHE 897
Jacob	LAN	200	David	FAY	227	John	BER 165
Jacob	BUC	96A	George	BER	165	Martin	BER 176
Jacob	BUC	157A	Jacob	NOH	71A	Michael	BER 165
Jaocb	MNT	90	James	FAY	239	Samuel	BER 208
John	MNT	90	Jno.	CUM	136	LANTMAN,	
John	MNT	100	John	PHA	100	Christopher	FAY 262
John	BUC	101	John	PHA	117	LANTSINGER?,	
John	LAN	117	John	NOU	118	Henry	PHA 81
John	LAN	117	John	FRA	301	LANTZ, Andrew	GRN 71
John	LAN	117	John	ALL	84	Andrew	GRN 82

LATTIMER, John	PHA	99	LAUGHEAD, John	FRA	294	LAUTENSLAGER,	
Robert	WAY	147	Joseph	WST	291	Leonard	NOH 56
LATTIMORE, James	WAS	13	William	BFD	44	LAUTERMILCH, John	DAU 25A
William Esqr.	NOH	30A	William	FAY	253	LAUTHER, David	WST 172
William	NOH	30A	LAUGHED, James	CHE	875	James	WST 172
LATTINGER, Henry	MNT	141	LAUGHHEAD, Thomas	MER	448	LAUTHERS, William	WST 172
LATTON, Jonas	YOR	171	Wilm.	ALL	71	LAUTSENHISER?,	
LATTY, Widow	LAN	247	Wilm.	ALL	114	Peter	BEV 12
LATZ, Martin	LAN	200	LAUGHLAGE, Geo.	PHI	111A	LAUVER, Henry	ADA 13
LAUB, Conrad	YOR	158	LAUGHLIN, Adam	NOU	194	LAVEL, John	FAY 227
Henry	BER	188	Alexr.	CUM	135	LAVENA, Monseur	PHA 4
John	BER	170	Allexander	BEV	25	LAVENBARGE,	
John	BER	188	David	MIF	7A	Frederick	NOU 111
John	WST	274	James	BEV	22	LAVENSLAGER,	
John	NOH	30A	James	ERI	58	Jacob	PHA 51
Michael	BER	170	James	ALL	97	LAVER?, Jacob	MIF 13
LAUB?, Jacob	DAU	5A	James	WST	172	LAVERING, Daniel	BFD 44
LAUBACH, Adam	NOH	34	James	CHE	755	Henry	BFD 44
Adam & Rudy	NOH	48	Jno.	CUM	138	John	BFD 44
Adam	NOH	30A	John	BEV	22	LAVERTEY, James	PHA 7
Conrad	NOH	63	John	BEV	22	LAVERTY, Patrick	BUT 336
Conrad	NOH	87	John	WAS	111	Saml.	BER 163
Conrad	NOH	30A	John	ARM	127	LAVERY, Henry	WAS 13
George Junr.	NOH	87	Mary	CUM	128	LAVES?, (See	
George Senr.	NOH	87	Mattw.	MIF	5	Laver?)	MIF 13
George	NOH	43A	Moses	CUM	115	LAW, Abm.	CUM 24
John	NOH	48	Randal	WST	153	Abraham	LAN 70
Leonard	NOH	43A	Robert	BEV	22	Andw.	YOR 177
Michael	NOH	67	Robert	WST	239	Andw.	YOR 189
Peter Junr.	NOH	30A	Robert Jun.	BEV	22	Caleb	YOR 192
Peter Senr.	NOH	30A	Robert Jun.	BEV	22	Charles	MNT 113
Peter	NOH	90A	Robt.	MIF	5	Fredk.	YOR 189
Rudy & Adam	NOH	48	Robt.	CUM	43	George	YOR 178
LAUBACK, Lewis	MIF	11A	Robt.	BEV	22	George	YOR 178
LAUBENSTEIN,			Thomas	MER	448	George	YOR 189
George	NOH	80A	Thos.	MIF	5	Hugh	FAY 251
Peter	NOH	80A	Thos.	CUM	112	Isaac	YOR 193
LAUCH, Andrew	BER	167	William	WAS	102	Isaac	FRA 296
John	BER	167	Wm.	BEV	22	James	ALL 76
John	YOR	177	Wm.	BEV	24	James	ALL 103
Philip	LAN	201	LAUGHMAN,			James	HNT 149
LAUCHENOT, Widow	NOH	45	Christian	YOR	215	James	YOR 193
LAUCHS, Jacob	YOR	164	Daniel	YOR	218	John	WST 326
LAUCK, David	PHA	69	Jacob	YOR	216	John	CHE 908
Michael	YOR	185	LAUGHRIDY, James	ALL	71	John	NOH 60
LAUCKS, Casper	BER	271	LAUGHRY, John	ALL	120	Joseph	HNT 156
Henry	YOR	206	Mary	ALL	52	Mark	FAY 232
Henry	NOH	39A	Willm.	BUT	345	Mathew	YOR 161
John	YOR	206	LAUGHTY, Peter	LAN	57	Michael	YOR 189
Peter	BER	271	LAUGLIN, Atchison	CUM	128	Michael	YOR 189
LAUCKS?, John	YOR	169	Hugh	CUM	135	Peter	YOR 189
LAUDENBACH,			LAUKS?, George	BER	215	Peter	YOR 189
Michael	LAN	55	LAUMAN,			Peter Jr.	YOR 189
LAUDENBERGER,			Christopher	YOR	155	Rachel	HNT 120
Adam	NOH	48	Daniel	YOR	155	Robert	WAS 57
Leonard	NOH	48	Elizh. Widow	LAN	61	Robert	HNT 149
LAUDENSLAGER,			George	ADA	1	Samuel	HNT 148
Adam	NOH	82A	George Jun.	ADA	1	Thomas	HNT 148
Anthony	NOH	48	LAUMBERIN,			Widow	CHE 834
Conrad	NOH	48	Barbara	LAN	250	LAW?, John	LYC 14
George	NOH	60	LAUNCEL, George	YOR	182	LAWALL, Henry	NOH 34
Jacob	NOH	90A	LAUR, Catharine	YOR	186	Michael	NOH 71A
Nicholas	NOH	60	LAURANCE,			LAWCK?, Abner	
Widow	NOH	90A	Christian	LAN	131	Esqr.	BEV 20
LAUDERMILK, (No			Philip	GRN	98	LAWER, George	PHA 64
Given Name)	DAU	31	LAURENCE, Henry	CUM	46	George	NOH 69
LAUFER, Philip	BER	227	Henry	BER	227	George	LAN 289
LAUFFER, Bartel	BUT	348	Jacob	ADA	24	LAWERSWILER,	
Peter	NOH	63	John	GRN	102	Jacob	PHA 31
LAUFFMAN, Phillip	CUM	99	John	FRA	296	LAWFER, Henry	WST 274
LAUG, John	LAN	187	Moretz	ADA	36	LAWHED, John	WAS 81
LAUGHBAUBH, Henry	CHE	820	Moses	LUZ	353	LAWINGSTINE,	
LAUGHBAUGH, John	CHE	782	Samuel	CHE	823	Christn.	BUC 139A
John Jr.	CHE	782	Sarah	WAS	122	LAWLER, Alexd.	PHI 73A
LAUGHEAD, John	WAS	57	LAURENCE?, John	MIF	17	LAWMAN, Absalom	WST 153
John	FAY	257	LAURMAN, Michael	NOU	194	LAWN, Law	NOU 105
						Paul	NOU 123

LAWN, Robt.	BUT	344	LAWYER, Christn.	PHA	57	LEACOCK, Thomas	DEL	169
William	NOU	105	LAY, Cathrine	CUM	145	LEACON, Meredeth	GRN	108
LAWPY, John V.	LAN	164	Christina	CUM	146	LEADER, Christian	NOH	63
LAWR, John	NOU	123	Henry	BUC	82A	Frederick	YOR	197
LAWRA, Lewis	PHI	72A	John	CUM	130	Henry	BFD	51
LAWRANCE, Widow	PHI	105B	Misses	PHA	32	Lewis	YOR	198
John	PHI	102	LAYBOLT, John	CHE	721	LEADIS, Henry	GRN	101
John	LAN	131	LAYCOCK, Jos.	PHI	107A	LEADY, John	ADA	12
John	PHI	115A	Margrt.	CUM	129	LEAFF, William	FAY	246
Wm.	PHI	111A	LAYD, John	NOU	129	LEAG, Robt.	PHI	82A
LAWRECE, Polly	FAY	204	LAYER, John	PHI	2	LEAGLY, Henry	DAU	35
LAWRENCE,			John	PHI	3	LEAH, Henry	NOH	63
Alexander	WAS	57	John	PHA	109	Henry Junr.	NOH	63
Ama	LUZ	350	Melchor	PHA	34	LEAHEA, Michael	PHA	23
Benja.	PHI	137	LAYEY, Susannah	PHA	37	LEAHM, Jospeh	PHA	84
Benjn.	PHA	12	LAYMAN, Abm.	CUM	128	LEAL, William	CHE	811
Charlotte	PHA	10	Danl.	CUM	68	LEALAND, James	BEV	6
Christn.	PHA	54	Geo.	CUM	34	LEAMAN, Benedic	SOM	138
Christn.	PHA	66	Jacob	CUM	100	Christian	SOM	139
Daniel	BUC	161	Jacob	CUM	102	John Jun.	SOM	158
David	PHI	155	Jas.	CUM	127	Joseph	VEN	167
Henry	BEV	7	Jno.	CUM	68	LEAMER, Jacob	SOM	129
Henry	PHA	21	Jno.	CUM	105	LEAMING, John	PHA	103
Henry	DEL	177	John	SOM	158	LEAMON, Jacob	LAN	47
Henry	LUZ	405	Joseph	PHI	140	LEAMON?, -----	WAY	136
Isaac	BEV	7	Peter	MNT	83	LEAN, Thos. C.	FRA	289
Isaac	DEL	166	Saml.	PHI	72A	LEANDAL, Florence	CHE	755
Jacob	PHI	8	LAYMOINE, James	CHE	909	LEANEY, John	CUM	129
Jno.	MIF	25A	LAYPOLE, Widow	BUC	101	LEANHEART, Chr.	WST	311
John	WAS	8	LAYTON, Asher	BFD	44	Peter	WST	311
John	BEV	20	William	WAS	44	Stophel	WST	311
John	PHI	155	LAZARES,			LEANS, William	PHI	8
John	CHE	836	Frederick	NOU	97A	LEANY, Christn.	CUM	50
John	NOH	41A	LAZARUS, Daniel	NOH	43A	Wm.	CUM	107
Joshua	DEL	177	Frederick	NOH	78A	LEAP, Daniel	FRA	307
Lemuel	LUZ	352	George	HNT	137	LEAPER, James	WAS	44
Philip	MNT	142	George	NOH	78A	LEAR, Anthony	BUC	141
Robert	HNT	155	Leonard	NOH	43A	Anthony	BUC	149A
Rufus	LUZ	352	Martin	NOH	43A	Arnold	BUC	149A
Rufus Jr.	LUZ	350	LAZEAR, Jeremiah	GRN	111	Christian	FRA	289
Saml.	NOH	41A	Joseph	GRN	112	Henry	BUC	87
Samuel	BEV	7	Thomas	GRN	111	Henry	BER	139
Susana	BEV	7	LAZER, Peter	WAS	3	Henry	CUM	152
Thomas	MNT	110	LAZERUS, Peter	LAN	39	Henry	FRA	309
Thos.	PHA	27	LAZIER, Anthony	HNT	161	Henry	BUC	159A
William	PHA	106	LAZURE, Abraham	BFD	38	Hoopry/ Hoossy?	BUC	149A
William	BUC	161	John	BFD	58	Jacob	BER	141
Wintel	NOU	97A	John M.	BFD	58	James	PHI	33
Wm.	PHI	67A	Jonathan	BFD	60	John	BER	139
LAWRENS, Joseph	NOU	97A	Joseph	BFD	58	John	BUC	141
LAWRY, Cornelius	CHE	888	Samuel	BFD	60	John	FRA	309
William	LAN	266A	Thomas	BFD	58	John	BUC	149A
LAWS, Betsy	PHI	79A	Thomas Jr.	BFD	58	Peter	LAN	304
LAWSE?, Richard	BUC	88	William	BFD	58	LEAR?, William	PHI	153
LAWSEN, Thos.	PHI	83A	William Jr.	BFD	58	LEARD, Stewart	MIF	7A
LAWSER, Frederick	FRA	275	LBRICK, George	NOU	194	LEARER, Philip	PHI	152
LAWSHA, John	NOU	129	LE BRUCE?, Paul	PHA	112	LEARN, Jacob	NOH	78A
LAWSHET,			LE CAUDIANS?, Mr.	PHA	113	John	NOH	78A
Christian	PHI	131	LE DRUE, Widow	PHI	14	LEARNED,		
Christopher V.	PHI	131	LE FEATE?, Peter	PHA	93	Theophilus	LUZ	323
LAWSON, Mrs.	LYC	29	LE GUA, Mitchel	PHA	119	LEARNER, Andw.	WST	369
James	WST	171	LE ROCH, Ja---?	PHA	113	LEARS, Henry	PHI	72
James	FRA	297	LEA, Widow	PHI	88	LEASE, Daniel	YOR	171
James Sr.	WST	172	Francis Esqr.	CHE	737	George	YOR	171
Jos.	YOR	187	LEACE, Benjn.	CUM	36	John	ADA	37
Joseph	PHA	12	LEACH, Henry	PHA	43	John	ADA	41
Robt.	MIF	18	Jane	PHA	117	John	YOR	213
Sarah	PHA	10	Joseph	CHE	885	Leonard	ADA	37
Sarah	FRA	293	Thos.	PHA	12	Valentine	YOR	178
Thomas	WST	380	William	CHE	762	LEASE?, Samuel	YOR	213
William	CHE	754	LEACOCK, Elisha	WAS	3	LEASEY, Isaac	CUM	47
LAWTHER, Robert	HNT	158	Isaac	WAS	3	Job	CUM	47
LAWTHERS,			John	PHA	85	LEASLEY, Jonathan	MER	448
Alexander	WAS	29	Joseph	WAS	3	LEASOR, Andrew	HNT	124
Gavin	WAS	29	Samuel	WAS	3	John	NOH	90A
LAWVER, John	NOU	188	Samuel	DEL	163	LEASURE, Abm.	WST	347

Name	County	Page
LEWIS, Michl.		
Junr.	CUM	27
Michl. Sr.	CUM	27
Mordecai	DEL	174
Morgan	BER	273
Mrs.	NOU	129
Mrs.	NOU	188
Nancy	PHI	137
Nathan	WAS	122
Nathaniel	LUZ	390
Nehemiah	BER	167
Obed	CHE	900
Paskel	NOU	194
Peter	PHA	112
Peter	BUC	159A
Phinas	CHE	761
Phineas	CHE	733
Richard	BUC	105
Richard	BER	274
Robert	GRN	88
Robert	NOU	165
Robert	NOU	165
Rueban	CUM	84
Ruth	BFD	64
Saml.	PHI	17
Saml.	WST	153
Saml.	BER	162
Samuel	WAS	38
Samuel	WAS	122
Samuel	DEL	172
Samuel	DEL	174
Samuel	BER	223
Samuel	FAY	251
Samuel	LUZ	391
Samuel Junr.	WAS	81
Samuel Senr.	WAS	81
Samuel	BUC	151A
Sarah	PHI	31
Sarah	MNT	87
Snider	FAY	199
Stephen	BEV	25
Stephen	DEL	185
Thomas	BEV	18
Thomas	MNT	45
Thomas	DEL	170
Thomas	FAY	222
Thomas	BER	248
Thomas	BER	251
Thomas	LUZ	396
Walter	GRN	107
Webster	YOR	214
Widow	LAN	84
Widow	LAN	124
William	HNT	127
William	MNT	138
William	BER	251
William	WST	254
William	CHE	722
William	CHE	735
William	CHE	885
William	CHE	902
William	BUC	96A
Wm.	PHA	11
Wm. Attorney	PHA	103
Wm.	PHI	114A
Zachariah	BUC	155A
LEWIS?, John?	BEV	18
LEWKAS, Ephraim	FAY	246
LEWMAN, Noah	FAY	262
LEWTON, Thos.	DAU	36A
LEWTS, Jacob	HNT	136
LEX, Andw.	PHI	111A
Henry	PHI	111A
John	PHI	111
LEY, Andrew	DAU	26
Christian	DAU	39A
LEY, George	BER	188
LEYBURN, Robt.	CUM	97
LEYDIG, John	NOH	37A
LEYDY, Conrad	NOH	67
LEYER, Frederick	LAN	190
LEYMAN, Anthony	YOR	189
LEYMER, Christian	YOR	168
LEYTER, Joseph	DAU	45A
LIABARRIGER,		
George	BFD	58
LIANS, Richd.	FRA	298
LIB, John	BER	284
LIBARRIGER,		
Andrew	BFD	60
Daniel	BFD	35
Frederick	BFD	58
Ludwick	BFD	60
Nicholas	BFD	58
Nicholas Jr.	BFD	58
LIBE, Christian	YOR	196
LIBEGOOD, Jacob	WST	347
LIBENSTINE,		
George	YOR	165
John	YOR	170
LIBERGER, John	SOM	132
LIBERRIGER, Henry	BFD	58
Ludwick	BFD	58
Ludwick Jr.	BFD	58
LIBERT, Jacob	NOU	129
Peter	PHI	126
Peter	NOU	147
William	PHI	126
LIBERTS, John	PHI	128
LIBFRITZ, Geo.	CUM	130
LIBRANT, Michael	PHI	53A
LICE?, Peter	DAU	31A
LICEY, Christian	BUC	96A
Henry	BUC	96A
John	BUC	96A
LICHIMS, William	MER	448
LICHLENWALLER, P.	NOH	60
LICHLER, Michael	NOU	172
LICHT, Abrahm.	DAU	28A
Felix	DAU	28A
Henry	DAU	52
Henry	DAU	25A
Jacob	DAU	28A
John	DAU	25A
Martin	DAU	29
Martin	DAU	28A
LICHTENBERGER,		
George	YOR	163
LICHTENTHALER,		
Jacob	HNT	155
LICHTENWALLNER,		
George	NOH	60
John	NOH	60
LICHTY, Benj.	YOR	211
Conrad	BER	141
Jacob	LAN	103
John	YOR	165
John	YOR	211
Marks	BER	226
Martin	LAN	115
Nicholas	YOR	176
Samuel	LAN	102
LICHTY?, David	BER	186
LICK, John	LAN	278
John	DAU	48A
LICKERT, James	LAN	182
LICTEBARGER,		
Thomas	ALL	117
LIDAY, Paul	NOU	150
LIDDEUS, Anthony	MNT	105
LIDE, Simon	FRA	284
LIDE?, George	FRA	285
LIDEH, Jacob	DAU	30
LIDEWALTER,		
Abraham	ADA	26
LIDEY, Daniel	FRA	316
LIDICK, Jacob	WST	311
Phillip	CUM	23
LIEBENGUTH, Peter	NOH	50A
LIEBREICH, John	LAN	252
Widow	LAN	252
LIED, George	LAN	200
LIEDIE, Phili	MNT	96
LIEDIG, Jacob	MNT	124
LIEPER, Robt.	FRA	279
LIEPLANT?, Adolph	LAN	134
LIES, Henry	BER	258
Peter	BER	134
LIETMAN, George	PHA	29
LIFE, Christian	YOR	168
LIFERT, Widow	CHE	895
LIGET, Patrick	CUM	92
Stephen	CUM	113
LIGGET, Alexr.	YOR	196
James	CUM	69
James	WAS	69
Robert	WAS	69
Robert	WST	380
Sulton	WAS	57
Thomas	ALL	104
William	PHA	115
William	YOR	205
Wm.	YOR	196
Wm. Senr.	YOR	196
LIGGETT, Mary	CHE	905
Thomas	CHE	763
William	CHE	748
LIGGEY, John	LAN	236
LIGGIT, John	WAS	57
John	LAN	167
LIGHT, Daniel	PHI	124
George	PHI	130
Henry	DAU	47A
Jacob	DAU	26A
John	LAN	35
John	FRA	301
John Junr.	DAU	47A
John Senr.	DAU	47A
John	DAU	25A
Martin	DAU	26A
Peter	DAU	13
Peter	DAU	21
Samuel	BFD	69
Varner	YOR	171
LIGHTADER, Jacob	BUC	139
LIGHTBERGER,		
George	ALL	52
LIGHTBOURNE,		
Benja.	WST	292
LIGHTCAP, George	BUC	91
Jacob Jnr.	BUC	149A
Jacob	BUC	149A
Levi	CUM	152
Soloman	BUC	139
Wm.	CUM	133
LIGHTEAP, Saml.	CUM	83
Solomon	CUM	127
LIGHTEBERGER,		
Gilliam	SOM	129
LIGHTEL, Andrew	FAY	209
LIGHTENBERGER,		
Adam	YOR	165
Conrad	YOR	165
LIGHTFOOT, Jacob	BER	219
Jeptha	YOR	215
Saml.	CHE	786
Thomas	BER	219
LIGHTHINTALTER, Matt.	MIF	13

LIGHTLIDER, John	SOM 143	LIMES, John	ALL 52	LINDLEY, Levi	WAS 63
LIGHTLY, Jacob	WST 292	LIMINGTON, Hagar	PHA 95	Naphtali	WAS 63
Jacob Junr.	WST 292	LIMPART, Peter	CUM 31	Timothy	WAS 63
John	WST 274	LIN, Jacob	PHI 140	Ziba	WAS 63
Mark	WST 292	John	CRA 17	LINDNER, John	LAN 302
LIGHTNER, Adam	HNT 164	Philip	BER 188	Thomas	NOH 76
Adam	LAN 173	LINABERY, John	CEN 20A	LINDON, David	LAN 265
Danl. & Michl.	LAN 212	LINABURY, Joseph	LUZ 373	James	CHE 755
Eve	CUM 45	LINAH, Thomas	ADA 7	LINDOWOULD,	
George	YOR 162	LINARD, Adam	ADA 22	Christopher	PHA 35
George Jr.	YOR 154	Yost	ADA 11	LINDSAY, Alexr.	CUM 43
Henry	GRN 64	LINARD?, Peter	ADA 27	Andw.	CUM 131
Isaac	LAN 227	LINCH, Cornetious	FAY 253	Andy	PHI 50
Jacob	FRA 286	George	FAY 209	Benjn.	CUM 97
Joel	LAN 178	James	PHA 41	David	CUM 42
John	MNT 62	James	FAY 266	David	CUM 44
John	LAN 173	John	ALL 115	David	CUM 48
Joseph	FRA 290	John W.	DAU 34	David	HNT 157
Ludwick	CUM 76	Martin	FRA 314	James	DEL 155
Matthias	HNT 157	Patrick	ALL 75	James	CHE 744
Michl. (See		Patrick	CUM 85	John	CUM 41
Lightner,		Robert	FAY 209	John	PHI 63
Danl.)	LAN 212	Wm.	PHA 97	John	DEL 178
William	ADA 29	LINCH?, Cornelius	YOR 201	John Esqr.	DEL 173
William	LAN 173	Cornelius	YOR 203	Joyce	DEL 155
William	LAN 188	Matthias	YOR 202	Robert	CHE 708
LIGHTWOOD, Jacob	BUC 143A	Matthias	YOR 203	Robt.	CUM 102
LIGHTY, John	CUM 78	LINCK?, (See		Sidney	CUM 92
Peter	LAN 6	Linch?)	YOR 201	Thos.	CHE 880
LIGLER, Mark	CUM 94	LINCKART, George	DAU 24	William	HNT 150
LIGTLE, Joseph	LAN 264	LINCOLN, Abraham	BER 181	Wm.	CUM 27
LIHTEY, Jacob	DAU 32	James	BER 181	Wm.	CUM 100
LIKENS, Ann	DEL 171	Joseph	DEL 183	Wm.	PHA 113
Ann	DEL 188	Joseph	DEL 184	LINDSEY,	
David	DEL 166	Moses	DEL 168	Alexander	FAY 229
George	DEL 169	LINCORN, Abram	PHI 64	Alexd.	FRA 309
George	DEL 187	Ann	PHI 64	Doctor	LYC 27
John	BER 251	Jacob	PHI 64	Enon?	BER 243
LIKER, Eliza.	PHI 44	LIND, Conrad	LAN 49	George	BEV 17
LIKES, John	PHI 84A	John	LAN 27	James	BFD 40
Philip	WAS 22	Michael	LAN 53	James	GRN 95
LIKING, Wilm.	ALL 85	Peter Junr.	YOR 162	James	FAY 253
LIKLENS, Jonan.	PHI 2	Peter Sr.	YOR 162	James	FRA 283
LILE, James	WST 291	LINDALL, Benjamin	PHA 119	John	WAS 22
James	CHE 837	LINDCORT, Martin	NOU 111	John	BFD 38
Wilm.	ALL 99	LINDELL, Joseph	PHI 6	John	FAY 222
LILLEY, David	WST 171	LINDEMAN,		John	FAY 246
Ellis	CHE 750	Christian	BER 252	Patrick	WAS 16
Jacob	NOU 166	Conrad	BER 274	Robt.	YOR 198
John	CHE 753	Henry	SOM 138	Samuel	WAS 22
Samuel	CHE 771	Jacob	LAN 281	William	FAY 245
Thomas	CHE 749	Jacob	NOH 30A	LINDSEYBIGLER,	
Walter	CHE 759	Widow	LAN 58	Abm.	MNT 59
LILLY, Andrew	NOH 30A	LINDEMODE, George	NOU 111	LINDSY, Mongo	LYC 25
Henry	PHI 82A	Michael	NOU 111	LINDY, Jacob	LAN 47
Jacob	NOU 165	LINDEMOOD, John	DAU 2A	LINE, Abm.	CUM 105
John	ADA 31	Michael	BER 160	David	LAN 180
John	NOU 144	LINDEMUTH, George	LAN 7	Henry	CUM 57
Joseph	ADA 31	George	LAN 25	Henry	CUM 128
Joseph	BFD 64	Jacob	BER 280	Henry	CUM 128
Leonard	NOH 30A	Martin	LAN 6	Henry	LAN 275
Samuel	ADA 22	Peter	LAN 2	Jacob	LAN 24
Stephen	PHI 83	LINDENER, Henry	LAN 285	Jacob	LAN 183
Thomas	ADA 32	LINDENMEYER,		Jno.	CUM 105
William	ADA 4	Henry	NOH 32	John	DAU 37A
LIMBER, James	PHA 42	LINDERMUTH,		Peter	DAU 38
LIME, Michl.	CUM 104	Jonathan	BER 223	Wm.	CUM 105
Michl. Senr.	CUM 129	LINDERSMITH,		LINEBERGER, Jacob	NOH 50
LIMEBURNER, John	PHI 69A	Yoast	SOM 138	LINENBACK, Jos.	MNT 78
Philip	PHA 44	LINDLEY, Caleb		LINENGER, Jacob	CHE 890
LIMEHOUSE,		Junr.	WAS 63	LINER, Fredk.	BER 284
Anthony	BUC 107A	Caleb Senr.	WAS 63	Jacob	BER 283
Joseph	BUC 104	Demas	WAS 63	LINERS, James	LAN 89
Richd.	PHI 104	Israel	WAS 63	LINES, Conrad	LUZ 329
Thomas	BUC 94	John	WAS 63	Conrad	LUZ 348
LIMERICK, Patrick	WAS 22	Joseph	WAS 63	Jacob	DAU 15A

LINEWEAVER, Peter	DAU	44	LINN, Samuel	DAU	36A	LION, James	WST	254
LINEWEVER, Henry	CHE	777	William	WAS	102	LIONS, John	WAS	123
Peter	DAU	33A	William	WST	172	LIPE, Jos.	YOR	193
LINFELL, George	PHI	97A	Wm.	CUM	40	Peter	CUM	74
LING, Anthoney	SOM	154	Wm.	FRA	317	LIPINCOTT, Joshua	PHA	25
Peter	BFD	74	LINNCON, John	CHE	751	LIPLENG?, Widow	PHI	56
LINGEFELTER,			LINNENSHEET, John	PHI	122	LIPP, Henry	MNT	138
Jacob	ADA	33	LINNER, Widow	PHI	11A	LIPPENCOTT, Allen	BUC	94
Michael	YOR	160	Joseph	PHI	83	LIPPENCUT, James	FAY	198
LINGEFETTER,			LINNET, Allaver	LAN	276	John	WST	291
William	HNT	117	LINNINGSHEAT,			Saml.	FAY	198
LINGERFELT, John	HNT	145	Charles	PHI	79A	Wm.	PHI	70A
LINGERFIELD, John	LAN	248	LINSAY, James	ADA	23	LIPPERT,		
Michael	LAN	248	Joseph	ADA	23	Frederick	BER	210
LINGHORSE, Casper	LAN	18	LINSEN, James	PHI	141	LIPPINCOTT,		
LINGINFELTER,			LINSEY, Wid.	PHI	94	William	PHA	33
George	BFD	64	Jeremiah	MIF	10A	LIPPINCUT,		
LINGINFELTY,			John	PHI	81	William	GRN	79
Christian	BFD	64	John	CHE	771	LIPPLE, Henry	BER	203
Jacob	BFD	64	Nathaniel	BEV	13	LIREW, Isaac	CHE	731
LINGLE, Fredk.	DAU	16	Robt.	PHA	71	Mary	CHE	731
John	BER	263	Susannah	PHI	81	LISCO, James	LAN	181
Nicholas	WST	311	Thomas	MIF	5	John	LAN	181
Simon	DAU	23	William	MER	448	LISCORY?, Morda.	LYC	4
Thomas	DAU	17A	William	CHE	834	LISE, Widow	PHI	47
Thomas	DAU	36A	LINSEYBECKLE,			LISHER, John	PHI	87A
LINHEART, Adam	WST	311	Danl.	WST	218	LISHIA, Henry	PHI	90A
George	WST	347	John	WST	218	LISHMET, Wm.	PHA	103
Micheal	WST	291	LINSEYBIGLER,			LISINGER, George	FRA	276
LININGER, George	YOR	157	Daniel	MNT	58	John	PHI	126
George	YOR	183	Lewis	MNT	57	John	FRA	297
John	WST	218	Paul	MNT	58	LISLE, Alexr.	PHI	154
LININGS?, Richard	NOU	144	LINSY, John	VEN	170	Ann	PHA	70
LININGTON, Widow	PHI	74A	Samuel	VEN	167	Henry	PHA	106
LINK, Adam	ALL	111	LINT, Christian	SOM	129	Isaac	PHI	135
Daniel	ALL	101	Cunrod	SOM	132	James	MIF	7A
David	ALL	101	Cunrod Senr.	SOM	129	John	PHA	18
George	YOR	174	Hendrick	LUZ	416	Peter	ALL	88
George	PHI	79A	Henry	SOM	129	Robert	LAN	244
Henry	PHI	106	John	SOM	129	LISLE?, Charrels	ALL	88
Jacob	YOR	219	John	LUZ	424	James	PHA	84
LINKER, Danl.	PHI	104	LINTH, George	WST	239	LISLI, James	DAU	47A
John	PHI	103	LINTNER,			LISSLENG?, Widow	PHI	168
LINKERT, Philip	DAU	7A	Christian	MIF	10A	LIST, Geo.	CUM	62
Stephen	DAU	7	Conrad	MIF	10A	LISTON, John	SOM	146
LINKY, Richard	HNT	159	Daniel	LAN	296	LITCAP, Jacob	MNT	78
William	HNT	159	Peter	MIF	10A	LITCHERD, Joeph	LYC	15
LINLEY, James	CHE	768	LINTON, Benjn.	BUC	99	LITE, Peter	DAU	50A
LINN, Widow	PHI	89	Daniel	WAS	81	LITECAP, Solomon	PHI	140
Addis	BFD	44	David	LAN	18	LITENER, Peter	DAU	39
Alexander	SOM	132	George	PHI	34	LITER, John	NOU	183
Alexander G.	WAS	22	Hannah	BUC	99	LITEWEILER, John	NOH	85A
Charles	FRA	300	Henry	MNT	142	LITHCOE, Edward	PHA	93
Christian	YOR	155	Hezekiah	CHE	755	LITHER, Jacob	FRA	283
Daniel	WAS	63	Jacob	LAN	73	LITHGOW, John	PHI	116
David	WST	326	John	BUC	103A	LITLE, George	CUM	104
Elisha	BFD	44	Mary	BUC	94	Henry	ADA	30
Elizabeth	PHA	122	Samuel	LAN	71	Henry	PHA	73
Hugh	ADA	8	Samuel	LAN	85	James	WST	254
Hugh	CUM	47	Samuel	BUC	94	John	PHA	79
Hugh	PHI	80	Thomas	CUM	23	John	FRA	278
Jacob	BEV	16	Thos.	BUC	162	Martin	PHI	97A
James	WAS	92	William	BUC	103A	Robert	CRA	11
James	WAS	102	Wm.	PHA	108	Samuel	DEL	163
James	FRA	317	Wm. Jnr.	BUC	103A	Thomas	WST	254
James	LUZ	339	LINTZ, John	NOH	45	LITLE?, Ephrim	MIF	25A
Jno.	CUM	44	LINVEL, Peter	WAS	92	Saml.	MIF	25A
Jno. Junr.	CUM	39	LINVELL, William			LITNER, Jacob	CUM	149
John	ADA	27	Senr.	LAN	129	LITS, John &		
John	PHI	142	LINVILL, Arthur	LAN	133	Matthew	LAN	168
John	SOM	158	Pheby	LAN	130	Matthew (See		
John	PHI	71A	William	LAN	130	Lits, John)	LAN	168
Mathew	FRA	300	William Jnr.	LAN	133	LITSINGER,		
Michl.	PHI	88	LINY, Scot	LAN	59	Leonard	ADA	30
Robert	BUT	323	LINZEY, Walter	BUT	368	Simon	HNT	151
Samuel	ADA	27	LION, David	WAS	3	LITTEL, Emus	ALL	109

237

LOWREY, John	PHI 130	LOXLEY, Mary	PHA 28	LUCHENBAUGH,	
John	LUZ 380	Wm.	DAU 24A	Henry	YOR 183
Joseph	LUZ 334	LOY, Geo.	CUM 39	LUCHNER, Henry	YOR 156
Lawrence	DEL 171	Martin	BFD 64	LUCK, George	NOU 137
Levi	GRN 84	Michl.	CUM 44	Henry	MNT 66
Martin	CHE 779	Nichls.	CUM 44	Jacob	MNT 100
Mary	PHA 100	LOYAL?, John	PHA 93	Margaret	MNT 64
Sarah	FAY 215	LOYD, Danl.	PHI 103	LUCKAS, Philip	BER 285
William	PHA 23	David	PHI 98	LUCKENBACH, Adam	NOH 34
William	DEL 161	Hugh (Crossed		E. Widow	NOH 32
LOWRY, Alexander		Out)	BUC 153	John	NOH 43A
Esq.	LAN 3	James	BUC 147A	LUCKENBEIL, John	NOH 85A
Alexander	ERI 56A	John	LAN 24	LUCKET, Thomas	HNT 132
Andrew	ERI 57A	John	CUM 74	LUCKEY, Andrew	FAY 204
Armstrong	MIF 18	John	NOU 111	LUCKLE, George	YOR 175
Christianna	PHA 57	John	FAY 266	LUCKY, John	LAN 14
Danl.	PHI 78	John	BUC 147A	Samuel	LUZ 397
David	CHE 834	Joseph	FAY 209	LUDENBERG,	
Edward	NOH 65	Joseph	FAY 266	Lawrence	MNT 47
George	ERI 57	Thomas	NOU 147	LUDER, Christian	LAN 211
Godfrey	NOH 90A	Thos.	LYC 9	LUDEWIG, Samuel	DAU 5A
Hugh	NOU 129	William	NOU 111	LUDIA, Martin	PHI 101A
Jacob	NOH 30	LOYD?, Matths.	PHI 39	LUDING, Jacob	NOH 65
Jacob	SOM 141	LOYNS, William	FAY 246	LUDISILL, Ludwick	YOR 189
James	BEV 26	LOZER, Christo.	DAU 39A	LUDLAM, George	PHA 105
James	ALL 86	LOZIER, Chr.		LUDLOFF, Henry	BER 230
James	ALL 89	Senr.	WST 239	LUDLOW, Joseph	WAS 111
James	CUM 124	Christopher	WST 239	LUDOM/ LUDORN?,	
James	MER 448	LUAR, William	PHI 43	John	MNT 138
James	ERI 56A	LUBOLD, Charles	BER 174	LUDOM, Elijah	BUC 99
Jno.	BUT 355	Frederic	CHE 892	Hannah	BUC 138A
John	DAU 13	John	CHE 890	Richard	BUC 137A
John	WAS 22	Samuel	BER 138	William	MNT 35
John	DAU 28	LUCACS, John	FRA 302	William	BUC 137A
John	ERI 57	LUCANBACH, John	YOR 163	LUDWICH, George	FRA 321
John	WAS 57	LUCANS, Charles	FRA 282	LUDWICK, Balster,	CUM 126
John	NOH 65	David	FRA 282	Christn.	PHA 57
John	ALL 86	LUCARD, Samuel	LUZ 422	Conrod	WST 192
John	SOM 141	LUCAS, Adam	YOR 194	George	PHA 109
John	HNT 151	Benedict	CEN 18A	Lorena	YOR 193
John	VEN 168	Charles	MER 448	Peter	CHE 783
Joseph	WST 161	Chas.	CEN 18A	Valentin	CHE 784
Josiah	GRN 88	George	BFD 74	LUDWIG, Abraham	BER 180
Lazarus	HNT 121	George	FRA 313	Adam	BER 251
Lewis	PHI 111A	Isaac	WAS 102	Caspar	DAU 48A
Margaret	CHE 749	Isaiah	LUZ 333	Christn.	DAU 23
Martin	BUC 141	James	GRN 71	Conrad	LAN 126
Mathew	WAS 45	James	PHI 114A	Daniel	BER 139
Michael	SOM 141	Joel	LUZ 343	Daniel	BER 271
Morrow	ERI 56A	John B. C.		Francis	NOH 34
Philip	PHI 111A	Esqr.	ALL 97	George	BER 141
Rachel	MIF 10A	Joseph	CEN 18A	Gottfried	NOH 48
Robert	BEV 26	Patrick	WST 152	Henry	NOH 60
Robert	LAN 81	Philip	FAY 251	Henry	BER 251
Robert	NOU 149	Raptist?	CEN 18A	Jacob	LAN 11
Robert	WST 152	Richard	GRN 82	Jacob	LAN 49
Robert	ERI 56A	Richard	HNT 162	Jacob	BER 167
Samuel	NOU 159	Robert	WST 161	Jacob	CHE 787
Thomas	MNT 104	Samuel	GRN 71	Jacob	NOH 37A
Thomas	PHI 104	Samuel	WST 152	John	BER 170
William	DAU 28	Samuel	LUZ 342	John	BER 181
William	ERI 57	Thomas	WST 152	Michael	BER 139
William	MNT 112	Thoms.	GRN 97	Peter	BER 141
William	WST 152	Thos.	FRA 284	Philip	BER 139
William	NOH 90A	William	GRN 82	LUDY, John	BER 164
Wm.	BEV 10	William	GRN 82	John	BER 165
Wm.	CHE 749	William	WST 274	Michael	LAN 99
LOWS, John	FAY 204	LUCAS?, John?	BEV 18	LUFBERRY, John	PHI 88
LOWSCH, Gabriel	LAN 270	LUCE, David	CRA 15	LUFBOROUGH,	
LOWSER, John	DAU 30A	Jacob	CHE 783	Nathaniel	PHA 10
LOWSLY, Widow	PHI 73A	Shubel	CRA 15	LUFF, Adam	PHI 103A
LOWSTUTTER, Jacob	WAS 45	LUCH, Isaac	MNT 41	LUFFD, John	LAN 201
LOWTHERS, Adam	WAS 91	Jacob	NOH 32	Lehna	LAN 201
LOX?, John	BUC 159A	Jacob	MNT 41	LUGAN, The	
LOXLEY, Benjn.	PHA 99	Jacob	MNT 41	Frenchman	BUC 94
G. Washington	SOM 162	Samuel	MNT 41	LUGAR, Jacob	PHI 81
		Thomas	MNT 131		

LUGAR, John	PHI	80	LUMMIS, Boham	ERI	56A	LUTT?, Widw.	PHI	79
LUGER, Abraham	BER	38	Dyer	ERI	56A	LUTTS, Widw.	PHI	79A
LUGOR, Philip	PHI	99A	Joel	ERI	57	Jacob	BUC	91
LUICE, Edward	CHE	802	Oliver	ERI	56A	John	BUC	91
LUIELSBERGER,			Seth	ERI	56A	LUTY, John	PHI	97A
John	ADA	11	LUNABAUGH, Geo.	PHI	119A	LUTYENS, Godhelp		
LUK-BILL,			LUNAR, Thomas	PHI	3	N.	LUZ	368
Christian	BER	222	LUNARD?, (See			LUTZ , Ichael	DAU	7
LUKE, Christian	YOR	207	Leonard)	LAN	34	LUTZ, Adam	DAU	2
David	YOR	218	LUNBECK, Nicholas	GRN	96	Adam	MNT	115
Hill	CRA	2	LUNDAG, Jacob	DAU	27	Adam	BER	178
James	WST	380	LUNDY, Enos	LYC	8	Adam	LAN	201
John	BFD	44	Ephram	LYC	6	Baltzer	NOH	52
John	NOU	105	John	LYC	8	Barnard	FRA	311
Margaret	WAS	29	Richard	BUC	162A	Benedict	NOH	48
Patrick	PHI	120	Ruben	NOU	150	Bultzer	CUM	82
Thomas	CUM	33	Samuel	LYC	8	Catharine	LAN	309
LUKEHART, Conrad	HNT	150	Wm.	LYC	8	Christian	PHI	146
LUKEN, Abm. Junr.	MIF	10A	LUNE, Philip	CHE	728	Christian	NOH	53A
Abm.	MIF	10A	LUNERD, Charles	PHI	6	Christn.	DAU	39A
Daniel	PHI	150	LUNGREN, John	DEL	155	Christopher	BER	168
Gabriel	MIF	10A	William	DEL	156	Conrad	LUZ	369
LUKENBILL,			LUNHART, George	MNT	131	Conrod	PHI	88
Abraham	BER	221	LUNKINS, Jesse	MNT	35	Daniel	BER	167
Christian	BER	227	LUNN, Elisha	BUC	96A	Frederick	NOH	53A
Henry	BER	221	Joseph	MNT	87	George	MNT	117
Joseph	BER	226	Josiah	BUC	106A	George	YOR	217
LUKENS, -----?	PHI	149	Lewis	BUC	141	George	PHI	75A
Evan	BUC	153	Thomas	BUC	106A	Godfrey	WST	218
Jacob	PHI	129	LUNTON, Wm.	PHI	79	Henry	LAN	14
James	PHI	146	LUPARDUS, Peter	GRN	91	Henry	NOH	63
Levi	DEL	170	LUPE, Anthony	ADA	11	Henry	CUM	115
Robert	MNT	132	Anthony	ADA	16	Henry	BER	141
Robert	BUC	153	Jacob	ADA	16	Henry	BER	157
Thomas	BER	258	LUPFER, Casper	CUM	36	Henry	BER	167
LUKER, Edward	PHI	36	Jacob	CUM	36	Henry	LAN	201
James	PHA	14	Jacob Junr.	CUM	36	Henry	LAN	308
James	PHA	58	LUPOLD, David	BER	174	Henry	CHE	827
LUKINS, Aaron	MNT	50	LUPPER, John	CUM	25	Isaac	DAU	43A
Abner	MNT	131	LURICH, John	PHI	43	Jacob	BFD	38
Abraham	MNT	117	LURMER, Hugh	LAN	249	Jacob	PHA	58
Abram	MNT	111	LUSBY, John	PHI	39	Jacob	NOU	129
Amos	DEL	173	Josiah	PHA	22	Jacob	BER	243
Benjamin	MNT	51	LUSE, Eleazer	GRN	101	Jacob	LUZ	346
Daniel	CHE	753	Joseph	GRN	101	Jacob	LUZ	369
Daniel	CHE	753	Matthias	WAS	3	John	NOU	129
David	MNT	45	Nathaniel	GRN	102	John	LAN	201
David	MNT	78	Samuel	GRN	102	John	LAN	201
Elijah	MNT	131	LUSEL?, John	PHI	19	John	LAN	211
Isaac	MNT	45	LUSH, Philip	PHI	2	John	YOR	218
Jacob	MNT	131	LUSHER, George	PHI	87A	John	LUZ	369
Jesse	MNT	45	Jacob	PHI	3	John	NOH	53A
Job	MNT	88	LUSINGER, Jacob	NOU	199	John	PHI	92A
Joel	MNT	118	LUSK, David	LYC	23	Jonathan	YOR	218
John	MNT	82	John	ALL	101	Margaret	LAN	201
John	MNT	118	John	ALL	107	Margaret	LAN	201
John	MNT	119	John	WST	192	Michael	NOH	48
Jonathan	PHA	11	John	YOR	198	Michael	PHA	55
Jonathan	MNT	51	Patrick	LYC	21	Michael	LUZ	368
Jos. (Mason)	MNT	51	Patrick	YOR	198	Mrs.	NOU	176
Jos. (Tar.)	MNT	51	Robert	CUM	134	Nicholas	LAN	201
Joseph	MNT	51	Robert	WST	192	Nicholas	LAN	308
Joseph	MNT	108	Thos.	YOR	198	Peter	MNT	113
Joseph	MNT	132	Thos.	YOR	200	Peter	BER	201
Levi	MNT	51	Wm.	WST	192	Peter	NOH	53A
Nathan	MNT	51	LUSTER, Cornelius	WAS	57	Phil.	DAU	47A
Peter	MNT	51	LUTE, Nicholas	WST	171	Philip	LAN	303
Peter	MNT	119	LUTER, Charles	BER	183	Stephen	LAN	28
Senica	MNT	51	LUTES, Geo.	CUM	63	Susannah	BER	170
Thomas	MNT	45	LUTHER, Andw.	NOU	199	Widow	NOH	48
William	MNT	35	Conrad	HNT	163	Widow	LAN	295
William	MNT	51	John	MIF	4	Widow Old	LAN	295
LUMAN, Widow	PHI	10	John	DAU	4A	LUTZEY, John	LUZ	345
LUMBARTER, Widow	PHI	111	LUTHEROCK, Henry	MNT	114	LUTZGESELL,		
LUMMAS, William	CHE	906	LUTLEGE, Sophy	FRA	274	Michael	SOM	149
LUMMIS, Abner	ERI	58	LUTMAN, Jacob	LAN	246	LUVETSEN?, Benjn.	PHA	114

LUZADO?, Samuel	PHA	115	LYNN, John	NOU	199	LYONS, Zediah	DEL	163
LYBRAN, Jacob	PHA	77	John	CHE	806	LYSINGER, Charles	MNT	78
LYBRAND,			Joseph	MNT	43	LYSLE, John Junr.	MNT	105
Elizabeth	BER	239	Marey	FAY	236	LYTEL, Frances	FAY	236
LYBRAND?, George	PHA	75	Mary	PHA	9	LYTLE, Alexander	WAS	116
LYBRANT,			Peter	NOH	48	Alexander	WST	312
Christian	PHA	38	Peter	NOH	56	Andrew	LAN	174
Saml.	PHA	72	Peter	NOH	53A	Andrew	LAN	177
LYCAN, George	PHI	81A	Robert	MNT	65	David	ALL	89
Jonathan	PHI	92	William	FAY	236	David	ALL	89
LYDA, Benjamin	WAS	111	William Jur.	FAY	236	Edward	MIF	10A
Frederick	WAS	111	LYNTCH, John	DAU	46	Francis	WST	312
James	WAS	69	LYON, Alexr.	WST	161	James	WAS	57
John	WAS	111	Andrew	PHA	88	James	LAN	128
LYDICK, Caty	DAU	49A	Benjamin	WAS	69	John	ERI	59
Major	DAU	34A	Benjamin	NOU	171	John	DEL	163
LYDIG, Martin	DAU	29A	Christian	LAN	233	John	MIF	7A
LYDOCK, John			Christian	LAN	234	Robert	ALL	89
Senr.	WST	152	David	WAS	44	Samuel	ERI	59
Patrick	WST	152	David	FRA	317	Stewart	ERI	59
LYEL, John	PHI	82A	Eleazer	PHA	26	Thomas	DEL	191
LYGHTLY, George	WST	291	Eleazer	PHI	72	William	WAS	116
LYKENS, Andrew	PHI	154	Francis	DAU	33A	LYTTLE, Robert	MIF	7A
LYLE, Aaron Esqr.	WAS	29	Hector	WAS	92	Widow	LAN	265
Benjamin	MNT	107	Hugh	ALL	110			
James	WAS	75	James	BEV	20	M ---?, Robt.	MIF	10A
John	MNT	71	James	BER	158	M AFFEE, John	CHE	834
John	WAS	91	James	FAY	266	M ALISTER, -----	MIF	10A
John	MNT	106	John	MIF	17	Hugh	MIF	10A
John 2nd	MNT	71	John	ALL	58	M ALLA, Charles	CHE	742
Robert	WAS	75	John	PHA	78	M ALLISTER,		
Robert	WAS	75	John	CUM	84	Winnefred	CHE	870
Robert	WAS	91	John	NOU	159	M BAUGH, William	CHE	801
Walter	PHI	24	John Esqr.	FAY	253	M BRIDE, John	CHE	777
LYLES, Phillis	FAY	253	John	NOU	97A	Saml.	CHE	845
LYMAN, John	NOU	137	Joseph	WAS	52	M C----?, -----	MIF	10A
John	NOU	144	Joseph	NOU	159	M CABE, Edward	CHE	819
Patrick	NOU	176	Joseph	FAY	266	M CACHREN, James	CHE	828
LYMASTER, Andr.	FRA	287	Marey	FAY	253	John	CHE	724
LYN, Adam	HNT	135	Margaret	PHA	97	Patrick	CHE	823
John	WST	380	Mrs.	LAN	41	Robt.	CHE	827
Samuel	HNT	135	Mrs.	NOU	97A	M CAHEY, Robert	CHE	757
LYNAM, John	PHA	105	Nathaniel	ALL	85	Wm.	CHE	757
LYNCH, Daniel	PHI	26	Nathaniel	NOU	123	M CALIP?, (See M		
David	ARM	122	Nichls.	CUM	41	Caliss)	MIF	5
Edwd.	PHA	85	Rachel	PHA	60	M CALISS, Danl.	MIF	5
George	CHE	875	Saml.	CUM	86	John	MIF	5
Hugh	CHE	736	Samuel	BEV	22	M CALL, Jesse	CHE	705
James	ARM	127	Samuel	NOU	137	M CALMONT, Jas.	CHE	720
Jane	CUM	48	Solomon	PHA	40	M CAM?, Hugh	MIF	10A
John	FAY	266	Thomas	NOU	118	M CAMMON, Isaac	MIF	13
Mary	PHI	60	Thomas	LAN	172	M CARAHER, Dennis	CHE	832
Michael	CHE	854	Waltar	LUZ	384	M CARTER, Dunkin	CHE	847
Patk.	CUM	80	William	CUM	99	M CARTNEY, James	MIF	10A
Patrick	ADA	31	William	BER	158	M CARTY, James	CHE	818
Philip	CHE	844	William	WST	171	M CAY?, Andw.	FRA	291
Robt.	CUM	105	William	MIF	7A	M CHARG?, Robert	MIF	17A
Robt.	CUM	123	LYONS, David	DEL	173	M CIEVER, Charles	CHE	803
Thomas	WST	218	George	WAS	8	M CINLY, James	MIF	5
William	WST	218	Isaac	LYC	6	M CLANE, Archd.	CHE	880
LYND, James	PHI	126	James	WAS	8	Samuel	CHE	841
LYNN, Adam	WST	380	James	WST	153	M CLARY, Jacob	CHE	889
Andrew	WST	239	James	WST	311	M CLEAN, Esther	CHE	824
Eleonor	DEL	161	John	WAS	8	M CLEARY, Thos.	MIF	5A
Felix	NOH	48	John	PHI	24	M CLEAVE, George	CHE	802
Geo. Felix	NOH	48	John	PHI	50	M CLELLAN, Henry	CHE	843
Isaac	MNT	126	John	PHI	73	James	CHE	776
Isaac	FAY	236	Joseph	WAS	8	Jno.?	MIF	10A
Isaiah	NOU	199	Mathew	PHA	69	John	CHE	845
Jacob	NOH	45A	Robert	NOU	172	Joseph Esqr.	CHE	699
James	NOU	147	Saml.	WST	161	Robt.	CHE	844
James	HNT	158	Thomas	LAN	49	Saml.	CHE	845
James	WST	381	William	WAS	8	Wm.	CHE	847
John	NOH	48	William	PHI	13	M CLELLAND, James	CHE	757
John	NOH	63	William	WST	291	Jno.	MIF	7A
John	MNT	138	Wm.	WST	369	M CLENNAHIN,	CHE	799
						Robert		

M	CLERY, Wm.	CHE 755	M ELHENNY, Eliza	CHE 828	M NEAL, Catharine	CHE 790
M	CLISS, Patk.	MIF 5	M ELHENY, George	MIF 8	M NEAL?, John	CHE 875
M	CLOSKY, Edward	CHE 745	Margarett	CHE 875	John Jr.	CHE 875
	Edward	CHE 700B	M FAGEN, James	CHE 836	M PYLE, Dennis	CHE 750
M	CLUNE, James	CHE 908	M FAGEN?, Joseph	CHE 851	M REA, Walter	CHE 849
M	CLURE, Benjn.	CHE 816	M FARLEN, Isaac	CHE 901	M SANEY, William	CHE 850
	James	CHE 722	James	CHE 824	M VAUGH, Jeremiah	CHE 784
	James	CHE 727	John	CHE 777	Nathan	CHE 858
	Joseph	CHE 816	John	CHE 780	M VEW, James	CHE 817
	Richard	CHE 842	John	CHE 850	M WHENNEY, Wm.	CHE 886
	Thos.	CHE 775	Samuel	CHE 824	M WILLIAMS, Saml.	CHE 752
	Wm.	MIF 5	Wm.	CHE 824	M WILLIAMS?,
	Wm.	CHE 818	M FERSON, Alexr.	CHE 841	Isaac	CHE 854
M	COLLOUGH, Widow	BUC 155	John	CHE 780	John	MIF 6
M	CON, Thomas	CHE 876	Richd.	CHE 841	Thenny	MIF 6
M	CONALD,		M FIRSON, Wm.	CHE 751	M'ADAMS, Gilbert	WAS 86
	Theopolus	MIF 8	M FLANNUM,		M'AFEE, Gilbert	WAS 23
M	CONNELL, Henry	MIF 13	Richard	CHE 700B	M'AFFEE, David	WAS 17
	Isaac	CHE 836	M GARVEY, James	CHE 844	Henry	WAS 23
	James	MIF 5	M GAUGIN, Joseph	CHE 748	M'ALEER, Samuel	YOR 214
	James	CHE 811	M GILL, James	CHE 806	M'ALLISTER,
	Jno.	MIF 5	John	MIF 17	Archibald	WAS 123
	Richard	CHE 870	M GINNES, Saml.	CHE 747	James	YOR 195
M	CONNOR, John	CHE 882	M GINNESS?,		M'BRATNEY, Robert	WAS 103
M	CONOHY, David	CHE 776	Rebecca	CUM 145	M'BRIDE,
M	CORD, John	CHE 723	M GLAUGHLIN,		Alexander	WAS 53
M	CORKLE,		Benjn.	CHE 772	James	WAS 86
	Archibald	CHE 780	Eleanor	CHE 805	Robert	WAS 57
	George	CHE 752	Peter	CHE 753	Samuel	WAS 23
	James	CHE 760	M GOLERAKE?,		William	WAS 57
	John	CHE 739	Peter	CHE 779	M'BURNEY, James	WAS 103
	Wm.	CHE 867	M GOWIN, James	CHE 910	James Esqr.	WAS 16
M	CORMICK, John	CHE 838	M GROERTY, John	CHE 845	John	WAS 16
	John	CHE 901	M GUEAN, James	CHE 724	M'CAFFERY, John	YOR 215
	Peter	CHE 809	M GUIGAN, John	CHE 756	M'CAHEN, Daniel	WAS 58
	Thomas	CHE 871	M GUIRE, Thomas	CHE 902	M'CALA, Wm.	YOR 198
	William	MIF 8	M HARROW?, Samuel	CHE 876	M'CALL, James	WAS 24
	Wm.	CHE 868	M ILROY, Thos.	PHA 105	James	YOR 197
M	COUCH, Joanna	CHE 705	M ILWANE, Alexr.	MIF 5A	John	WAS 17
M	COY, Alik	CHE 766	M INTIRE, John	CHE 864	John	WAS 23
	George	CHE 734	Matthew	CHE 749	John	WAS 23
	Joseph	MIF 7A	M INTOSH, Alexr.	CHE 745	John	WAS 45
	Mary	CHE 744	M JELLER?, Wm.	CHE 812	Robert	YOR 200
	William	MIF 8	M KEAN, James	CHE 765	Thomas	WAS 23
	William	MIF 10A	M KEE, James	CHE 736	M'CALLA, Joshua	WAS 30
M	CRACKEN, John	MIF 8	John	MIF 8	M'CALLEY, Francis	WAS 30
M	CRAKEN, John	CHE 790	William	CHE 888	M'CALLISTER,
	Thomas	CHE 870	M KENNY, Philip	CHE 812	James	WAS 45
	William	CHE 870	M KENRICK,		M'CALMOND, Jane	YOR 154
M	CROSKY, Widow	CHE 828	Patrick	CHE 869	M'CAMONT, William	WAS 116
M	CRUM, Philip	MIF 8	M KINLEY,		M'CAN, Michael	YOR 165
	William	MIF 8	Elizabeth	CHE 828	M'CANAGHY, Samuel	WAS 58
M	CULLOCH,		George	CHE 827	M'CANCE, George	WAS 93
	Derborough	CHE 810	Samuel	CHE 823	M'CANCLESS, James	YOR 196
	John	CHE 701	M KINN, William	CHE 841	M'CANDLES, James	YOR 160
M	CULLOUGH, John	CHE 747	M KINSEY,		M'CANDLESS,
	Wm.	CHE 747	Rhoderick	CHE 834	Alexander	WAS 86
M	CULLY, Enoch	CHE 801	M KISSEN,		Alexr.	YOR 202
	Thos.	MIF 13	Archibel	CHE 748	George	YOR 199
	William	MIF 8	M KNIGHT, Thos.	CHE 735	Hugh	WAS 86
M	CUNE, John	CHE 885	M LAUGHLIN,		James	WAS 86
M	CUNE?, Michl.?	MIF 10A	Alexr.	CHE 780	John	WAS 112
M	CURDY, Robert	MIF 8	Hugh	CHE 760	Peter	YOR 164
M	CUTERY?, Robt.	FRA 312	Jesse	CHE 845	William	YOR 203
M	DERMOND, John	CHE 798	John	MIF 8	M'CANNAGHY, James	WAS 8
M	DONALD, Alexr.	MIF 5A	John	CHE 872	Samuel	WAS 8
	David	MIF 13	Joseph	CHE 851	M'CANNET, Adam	WAS 24
	Joseph	CHE 885	M LAUGLIN, James	CHE 824	M'CANNIGHY,
	Saml.	CHE 885	M LEAS, Michael	CHE 880	Alexander	WAS 70
	Wm.	CHE 883	M LEES, John	CHE 718	M'CARDEL,
M	DONALL, Benjn.	CHE 868	M MASTERS?, James	CHE 889	Elisabetjh	WAS 70
M	DOWEL, Joseph	CHE 738	M MIN, Jane	MIF 10A	M'CARDLE, Patrick	WAS 45
M	ELAR?, Peggy	CHE 774	M MINN, Thomas	CHE 703	M'CARREL, Thomas	WAS 30
M	ELDUFF, Joseph	CHE 718	M MLELLAND, Robt.	CEN 19A	M'CARTNEY, James	WAS 76
	Saml.	CHE 727	M MULLEN, Wm.	MIF 5A	Robert	WAS 52
M	ELHENEY, George	CHE 895	M MULLIN, John	CHE 910	Thomas	WAS 52

M'CARTY, John	WAS	92	M'COMB, William	WAS	13	M'CULLOCK, James	WAS	58
John	WAS	123	William	WAS	23	Samuel	WAS	4
Nicholas	YOR	144	William	WAS	30	M'CULLOUGH,		
Paul	WAS	123	M'COMBES, Jane	WAS	86	George	WAS	93
Timothy	WAS	93	M'COMBS, John	WAS	103	John Junr.	WAS	123
M'CASKEY, John	YOR	196	Robert	WAS	111	John Senr.	WAS	123
M'CASKY, William	WAS	30	M'CONKY, John	WAS	104	Kennedy	WAS	123
M'CASLIN, George	WAS	52	M'CONNEHE, David	WAS	93	Patrick	WAS	112
M'CAUGHAN, John	WAS	23	M'CONNELL,			M'CULLUM, Abraham	WAS	45
M'CEE, (No Given			Alexander	WAS	17	Samuel	WAS	45
Name)	YOR	200	Alexander	WAS	35	M'CULOUGH, John	YOR	200
M'CELVEY, Wm.	YOR	196	Alexander	WAS	93	M'CUNE, Andrew	WAS	23
M'CENLEY, Stephen	YOR	198	Alexander	WAS	93	James	WAS	13
M'CINLEY, Thos.	YOR	198	George	WAS	58	John	YOR	200
M'CLAIN, William	WAS	86	James	WAS	93	Samuel	WAS	58
M'CLANE, Samuel	WAS	70	John	WAS	52	M'CURDY, Daniel	YOR	212
M'CLARREN, Hugh	WAS	24	John	WAS	58	David	WAS	58
M'CLAY, William	WAS	81	Mathew Esqr.	WAS	17	Elijah Revd.	WAS	93
M'CLEAN,			Samuel	WAS	30	James	WAS	30
Alexander	WAS	50	Thomas	WAS	86	John	WAS	52
Andrew	WAS	92	William	WAS	52	Robert	WAS	23
Andrew	WAS	103	M'COOK, George	WAS	23	M'CURRY, John	WAS	103
Esther	WAS	9	M'COOL, William	WAS	81	M'CURTLE, James	WAS	103
George	WAS	8	M'CORD, James	YOR	203	M'CURTNEY,		
George	YOR	167	Mark	WAS	70	Ephraim	YOR	203
John	WAS	13	M'CORKLE, Maryr	WAS	24	M'DIVIT, John	WAS	50
John Junr.	WAS	103	M'CORMACK, John	WAS	58	M'DONALD, Widow	YOR	196
John Senr.	WAS	103	William	WAS	58	Archibald	WAS	50
William	WAS	34	M'CORMICK, James			Daniel	WAS	50
M'CLEARY, Widow	YOR	200	Junr.	WAS	111	Enos	WAS	70
Andw.	YOR	198	James Senr.	WAS	111	George	WAS	50
Elizabeth	YOR	199	John	WAS	76	Hugh	WAS	23
Henry	YOR	203	John	YOR	210	James	YOR	215
John	YOR	198	John	YOR	214	James	YOR	219
John Sr.	YOR	195	Michael	WAS	76	John	WAS	86
Jonathan	YOR	215	M'COSKY, John	WAS	9	John	YOR	170
William	YOR	202	M'COUGHAN, Jean	YOR	155	John	YOR	192
M'CLEENEY, Martha	WAS	116	M'COY, Alexander	WAS	13	Jos.	YOR	218
M'CLELLAN, David	YOR	197	Augus	WAS	50	Murdock	WAS	50
John	YOR	207	Daniel	WAS	50	Patrick	WAS	53
John Junr.	YOR	207	Daniel	WAS	92	Thomas	WAS	50
William	YOR	196	Hugh	WAS	52	William	WAS	23
M'CLELLAND, James	WAS	58	James	WAS	50	William	WAS	50
Robert	WAS	23	James	WAS	86	M'DONOGH, Henry	WAS	112
Thomas	WAS	23	John	WAS	23	M'DOWAL, William	YOR	197
William	WAS	58	John	WAS	81	William	YOR	199
M'CLENAGAN, Jan	WAS	124	John	YOR	201	M'DOWEL, John	YOR	199
M'CLENECHAN,			John Junr.	YOR	204	M'DOWELL, Widow	WAS	103
William	WAS	4	John Senr.	YOR	204	Archibald	WAS	103
M'CLENEHAN, John	YOR	169	Nathaniel	WAS	86	James	WAS	23
M'CLINTOCK,			Neill	WAS	24	John	WAS	103
Robert	WAS	13	Perry	WAS	8	John Esqr.	WAS	103
William	WAS	58	Perry	WAS	58	John Junr.	WAS	103
M'CLOSKEY, Robert	WAS	23	William Junr.	WAS	50	Joseph	WAS	23
M'CLOSKY, William	WAS	17	William Senr.	WAS	50	Nathaniel	WAS	9
M'CLUNEY, Michael	WAS	58	M'CRACKEN, Andrew	WAS	4	Polly	WAS	93
William	WAS	9	David	WAS	63	William	WAS	103
M'CLURE,			John	WAS	35	M'ELORY, Jonathan	WAS	103
Alexander	WAS	104	Robert	WAS	58	M'ELROY,		
David	YOR	214	M'CREADY,			Alexander	WAS	23
James	WAS	104	Alexander	WAS	93	Charles	WAS	104
James	YOR	214	James	WAS	103	James	WAS	23
Nathaniel	YOR	201	Thomas	WAS	17	John	WAS	23
Nathaniel	YOR	203	M'CREARY, David	WAS	93	John	WAS	103
Robert	WAS	93	George	WAS	34	M'ELWEE, Charles	WAS	70
M'CLURG, John	WAS	92	John	YOR	216	M'ENART, Biddy	WAS	117
John	YOR	199	Thomas	WAS	30	M'FADDEN, Dennis	YOR	215
Robert	WAS	52	Thos.	YOR	207	Hugh	YOR	201
William	WAS	30	William	WAS	103	Terrence	YOR	156
William	YOR	206	M'CREDDY, Robert	WAS	30	M'FADDON, John	WAS	58
M'COLLOM, David	WAS	63	M'CRORY, David	WAS	17	Samuel	WAS	58
John	WAS	63	M'CULLEY, Patrick	WAS	13	M'FALLS, Michael	WAS	58
M'COMAS, Daniel	WAS	45	M'CULLOCH, Samuel	WAS	9	M'FARLAND, Abel	WAS	124
M'COMB, David	WAS	30	Samuel	WAS	9	Daniel	WAS	124
Joseph	WAS	17	William	WAS	70	David	WAS	45
Robert	WAS	30	M'CULLOCK, David	WAS	9	John	WAS	23

MANMILLER, Daniel	BER 232	MANSHAL, Henry	BER 246	MARDES, Thos.	FRA 321		
MANN, Aarod	FRA 305	MANSINGER,		MARDIS, George	BFD 44		
Abel	GRN 102	Ludewick	NOU 114	MARE?, John	ALL 55		
Andrew	BFD 44	MANSON, Charles	PHI 149	MARELEY, Solomon	NOU 97A		
Barnet	BFD 44	John	WAS 13	MARES, Lawrence	NOU 147		
Barnet	BFD 44	John	WAS 22	Lawrence	NOU 166		
Bernard Jnr.	LAN 295	John	ALL 102	Richard	NOU 166		
Bernhard	LAN 294	Mary	WAS 23	Susanna	LAN 282		
Christian	BUC 148	Thos.	PHA 88	MAREWINE, Andrew	PHI 141		
Conrod	FRA 305	MANTEN, James	PHA 99	Philip	PHI 141		
Danl.	PHA 42	MANTIS, George	YOR 195	MARGARET, Peter	BER 138		
David	FRA 307	MANTLE, George	SOM 139	MARGERAM, Thomas	PHI 145		
George	NOH 67	William	YOR 202	MARGOREM, Benjn.	BUC 99		
Henry	BFD 45	MANUELL, Patrick	FAY 253	Israel	BUC 99		
Henry	WAY 149	MANUGH, John	CHE 728	Robert	BUC 99		
Henry	NOH 67A	MANVILL, Ira	LUZ 339	MARGUET?, Conrad	DAU 39		
Isaac	GRN 102	MANWELL, Richard	YOR 200	MARGUT, John	DAU 43A		
Jacob	BFD 44	MANWILL, Nicholas	ALL 90	MARIA, Ann	YOR 205		
Jacob	BFD 48	MANY, Adam	NOH 65	MARICAL, Chuster	NOU 154		
Jacob	BUC 148	John	NOH 65	MARINER, Benjamin	BFD 68		
James	WST 219	John	NOH 67	MARIS, Caleb	CHE 882		
John	WAS 22	Margaratta	PHI 79A	David	DEL 177		
John	BFD 44	MANY?, James	BFD 60	Elizabeth	DEL 177		
John	GRN 77	MAPEL, Aron	FAY 216	George	MNT 45		
John	BUC 80	Robert	FAY 216	Jane	DEL 189		
John	PHI 119	MAPES, William	WAY 147	Jesse	CHE 878		
John	MNT 131	MAPLE, Stephen	GRN 83	John	CHE 860		
John	CHE 742	William	GRN 64	Joseph	DEL 177		
John Jr.	BFD 44	MARACHE, Solomon	PHA 3	Richard Jun.	DEL 177		
John	PHI 118A	MARADY, Thos.	CEN 20A	William	PHI 20		
John	BUC 147A	MARAEL, Adam	CUM 36	MARITN, Paul			
John	BUC 154A	MARAJO, Simon	BUC 88A	Senr.	CUM 134		
Levi Junr.	GRN 102	MARBARGER,		MARJOREM, Edwd.	BUC 99		
Levi Senr.	GRN 105	Christn./		Henry	BUC 99		
Nancy	LUZ 414	Christr.?	NOH 85A	Joseph	BUC 99		
Noah	DEL 188	MARBEL, John	FAY 215	Richd.	BUC 99		
Noah	DEL 190	Nethan	FAY 216	William	BUC 99		
Peter	NOH 67	MARBLE, Eleazar	LUZ 326	MARK, Adam	DAU 35		
Peter	WAY 149	Jeremiah	LAN 48	Adam	DAU 34A		
Philip	WAY 149	Martin	LUZ 338	Bernard	NOU 176		
Philip	BUC 147A	MARBURGER, Daniel	BER 180	Conrad	DAU 32		
Phillip	NOU 194	Simon	BER 222	Geo	DAU 35A		
Samuel	MNT 51	MARC?, John	ALL 55	Henry	DAU 50A		
Samuel	GRN 102	MARCER, James	DAU 9	Jacob	DAU 33A		
Wm.	PHA 9	Michael	DAU 13	John	CHE 796		
Wm.	PHA 69	Samuel	ALL 52	Joseph	HNT 157		
Wm.	CHE 844	MARCH, Charles	FAY 210	Peter	HNT 157		
MANN?, Michael	LUZ 326	David	YOR 213	MARK?, John	CUM 24		
MANNA?, Robt.	BUT 354	Elizabeth	PHI 118A	MARKE, Rudy	NOU 176		
MANNAFIELD, John	PHI 77	Jacob	NOU 137	MARKEE, James	HNT 117		
MANNAN, Peter	FAY 236	Jacob	YOR 174	MARKEL, Jacob	CUM 56		
MANNEN, Barnet	BUC 149A	John	CHE 787	Nicholas	CUM 56		
MANNER, Conrad	MNT 100	Stephen	LUZ 388	MARKER, George	PHI 52		
J.	DAU 45	MARCHAL, John	LAN 159	Godfrey	PHI 43		
MANNIN, Ewd.	FRA 290	Joseph	FRA 280	Jacob	PHI 1		
MANNING, Edward	DEL 161	MARCHANT, Samuel	WAS 92	Jacob	PHI 74		
Patrick	WAS 82	Sarah	WAS 92	John	WAS 39		
Wm.	PHA 93	MARCHBANK, Jas.	CUM 117	Matt.	WST 240		
MANNINGTON,		MARCHEL, James	FAY 251	MARKER?,			
William	WAY 138	Stephen	NOU 199	Frederick	MNT 138		
MANNON, Edmund	GRN 107	MARCK, Christian	LAN 256	MARKES, Henry	SOM 139		
James	GRN 108	Conrad	LAN 146	Nicholas	PHA 117		
Patr.	FRA 279	MARCKER, George	LAN 85	MARKHAM, Daniel	FAY 253		
MANNS, Conrad	NOH 76	MARCKES, James	VEN 167	MARKLAND, John	PHA 60		
Henry	NOH 53A	MARCKLEY, Jacob	NOU 172	Mathew	WAS 13		
Jacob	NOH 53A	MARCKS, David	ALL 111	MARKLE, Conard	PHI 142		
John	NOH 76	Peter	NOH 91	Ephraim	HNT 126		
Philip	NOH 53A	Wilm.	ALL 106	Esther	HNT 126		
MANPECK, Leonard	NOU 189	MARCLE, Jacob	NOU 183	George	NOU 138		
MANS, John	FAY 267	John	NOU 130	George	NOU 188		
Samuel	NOU 172	MARCLEY,		George	YOR 192		
MANSELL, John	PHA 12	Christopher	BFD 64	Jacob	PHI 142		
MANSFIELD, Jacob	PHA 70	Henry	BFD 64	Jacob	YOR 190		
John	PHI 45	MARCY, John	LUZ 383	Jacob	FRA 312		
Joseph	NOH 41A	Zebulon	LUZ 377	John	PHI 127		
William	CHE 836	MARDAY, John	WST 173	MARKLER, Peter	WAS 103		

MARKLET, (Blank)	MNT	123	MARPLE, Nathan	MNT	64	MARSHALL,		
MARKLEY, Abraham	MNT	122	MARPOLE, Edward	PHI	154	Alexander	NOH	78A
Benjn.	MNT	58	Enock	MNT	78	Alexr.	CHE	724
Daniel	CHE	835	MARPOOL, Abm.	PHI	74	Amer	PHA	5
George	PHA	58	MARQUART, Abraham	BER	167	Andrew	WST	255
George	MNT	122	MARQUET?, Conrad	DAU	39	Archd.	WST	162
George	LAN	222	MARQUIS, Abrm.	FAY	246	Archd.	WST	162
Henry	MNT	121	John	WAS	29	Barbary	PHA	115
Isaac	MNT	122	Robert	WAS	92	Benjm.	PHA	96
Isaac	CHE	906	Samuel	WAS	22	Caleb	CHE	774
Jacob	MNT	128	Thomas	WAS	29	Charles	PHA	6
Jacob	LAN	223	Thomas Revd.	WAS	29	Chas. Junr.	PHA	6
Jane	MNT	75	William	WAS	29	Chrisn. Junr.	PHA	42
John	MNT	58	MARR, John	PHA	32	Christopher		
John	MNT	70	MARRELL, Mathias	FAY	267	Cenr.	PHA	12
John	LAN	240	MARREMY, William	FAY	267	David	WAS	8
Martin	LAN	74	MARRICAL, William	WST	254	David	DAU	42
Mathias	SOM	149	MARRICK, Else	CUM	69	David	DEL	166
MARKLLEY, Joseph	SOM	149	MARRINER, Benjn.	PHI	31	David	CHE	762
MARKOE, Abraham	PHA	83	MARRINOE, Michael	PHA	7	Elizth.	PHI	58
MARKS, Widw.	PHI	114	MARRIOT, Daniel	LUZ	395	Gilbert	WAS	8
Adam	MNT	103	Gilbert	LUZ	395	Hannah	PHA	48
Catherine	MNT	100	Hezekiah	LUZ	395	Henry	ADA	20
Conrad	BUC	101	MARRIOTT,			Hugh	GRN	110
Daniel	ADA	26	Devenport	PHA	22	Hugh	PHI	98
Fredrick	DEL	174	MARRITT, Abram	FAY	228	Humphrey	CHE	758
George	MNT	58	MARROW, John	DEL	160	Isaac	CHE	762
George	NOH	67A	Nicholas	DEL	160	Jacob	BER	205
Henry	PHI	114	Peter	LAN	114	Jacob	CHE	761
Isaac	PHA	39	Richard	DEL	161	James	ADA	5
Jacob	CUM	34	MARSBACK,			James	WAS	8
Jacob	YOR	172	Charrels	ALL	52	James	WAS	92
James	PHI	80	MARSDAL, Jonathan	WAS	81	James	HNT	143
John	WAS	16	MARSDEN, James	ADA	24	James	DEL	159
John	HNT	152	Mathew	ADA	24	James	WST	162
John	YOR	178	MARSDON, Jonathn	MIF	25A	James	DEL	166
John	YOR	178	MARSH, Adam	ARM	127	James	YOR	192
John	PHI	105B	David	YOR	218	James	WST	312
John	PHI	71A	James	CHE	741	James	CHE	742
Nathaniel	NOH	67A	John	HNT	159	James	CHE	819
Nicholas	ADA	12	John	YOR	209	Jno. Jr.	CUM	34
Peter	ADA	12	Jos.	YOR	218	John	WAS	29
Peter	SOM	135	Joseph	PHI	19	John	WAS	29
Philip	PHI	96	Joseph	PHI	20	John	ADA	34
Robt.	PHI	97A	Wilm.	ALL	87	John	CUM	37
Sevell	YOR	178	MARSHAL, Abraham	NOU	159	John	WAS	49
MARKS?, Conrad	BER	167	Andw.	LYC	20	John	PHA	115
MARKWARD,			Conrad	BER	167	John	PHI	154
Mordecai	DEL	177	Detrich	BER	167	John	WST	162
MARLATT, George	WAS	70	Francis	NOU	166	John	DEL	166
MARLER, Benjamin	NOU	144	Hugh	BEV	19	John	DEL	168
MARLEY, Charles	CHE	882	Hugh	ALL	65	John	DEL	190
Richd. T.	PHA	80	James	LAN	44	John	WST	220
Thos.	PHA	96	James	FAY	222	John	CHE	759
Wm.	PHA	84	John	BEV	11	John	CHE	836
MARLIN, James	PHA	111	John	ALL	55	Jos.	CUM	34
John	CUM	35	John	ALL	109	Joseph	PHA	9
Robt.	YOR	200	John	CUM	133	Joseph	ADA	33
Thomas	LAN	310	John	BUC	138	Joseph	PHI	154
William	YOR	199	John	BER	142	Joseph	DEL	166
MARLING, Peter	NOU	111	John	BER	145	Joshua	CHE	759
Phillip	NOU	111	Joseph	BEV	12	Josiah	LUZ	419
MARLOW, Joseph	DEL	163	Martin	BUC	149A	Lloyd	LUZ	351
MARLY, Henry	CRA	6	Nathl.	WST	275	Michael	CRA	14
John	FAY	251	Peter	LYC	6	Michael	ADA	24
Wm.	PHI	116	Robt.	FRA	298	Michl.	CUM	34
MARM?, John	PHI	115A	Robt.	WST	312	Moses	WAS	39
Michael	LUZ	326	Samuel	ALL	75	Moses	BUC	105
MARN, Geo.	BER	237	Samuel	ALL	91	Moses	CHE	759
MARNBAUR?, George	WAS	45	William	NOU	159	Nathan	PHI	152
MARO, Mr.	PHA	95	William	BUC	149A	Nicholas	ADA	36
MARPIS, Jacob	MNT	41	Wilm.	ALL	101	Robert	WAS	29
MARPLE, Abel	MNT	64	Wm.	CUM	133	Robert	HNT	140
Benjn.	CHE	718	Wm.	WST	369	Saml.	MIF	2
Jacob	BUC	153A	MARSHALL, Abram	CHE	760	Saml.	WST	162
Joseph	MNT	39	Alexander	PHA	54	Saml.	CHE	759

MARTIN, John	NOU 199	MARTIN, Robert	FAY 236	MARTS, Jonathen	NOU 118
John	YOR 200	Robt.	PHA 76	Peter	NOU 118
John	LAN 202	Robt.	FRA 290	Peter	FRA 285
John	LAN 221	Robt.	MIF 25A	MARTZ, Daniel	
John	BER 232	Robt. C.	PHA 87	Junr.	MNT 74
John	FAY 233	Roger	NOU 118	David	NOU 101
John	FAY 240	Saml.	CEN 23	George	NOH 76
John	BER 272	Saml.	CUM 24	Henry &	
John	FRA 272	Saml.	CUM 66	Reinhart	NOH 91
John	FRA 293	Samuel	WAS 75	Isaac	NOU 138
John	WST 349	Samuel	LAN 166	Jacob	NOU 101
John	BUT 353	Samuel	YOR 196	John	BER 227
John	CHE 795	Samuel	FAY 204	Michael	MNT 74
John Junr.	LAN 97	Samuel	FAY 205	Nicholas	NOU 138
John Senr.	BFD 64	Samuel	LAN 272	Peter	NOU 138
John Senr.	GRN 102	Samuel Revd.	YOR 201	Philip	BER 227
John	DAU 10A	Sarah	BUC 94	Phillip	NOU 138
John	BUC 103A	Sarah	BUC 84A	Reinhart &	
John B.	PHI 73	Silas	MIF 8	Henry	NOH 91
Jonan.	CUM 50	Simon	YOR 185	Thomas	LAN 85
Jonathan	GRN 89	Stephen	LAN 36	MARUN?, Paul	BER 167
Jonathan	DEL 176	Stockman	FAY 199	MARUSEIN, Jacob	NOH 36
Joseph	LAN 10	Thomas	DAU 15	MARVEL, Joseph	PHI 31
Joseph	LAN 69	Thomas	BUC 94	MARVEN, William	LAN 80
Joseph	PHA 120	Thomas	LAN 180	MARVEROE,	
Joseph	DEL 164	Thomas	CHE 709	Nicholas	PHA 96
Joseph	DEL 182	Thomas	CHE 763	MARVIN, Elisha	ERI 57
Joseph	FRA 288	Thoms.	BUT 324	Enock	ERI 57
Joseph	LAN 307	Thos.	CUM 57	James	LUZ 373
Joseph	CHE 759	Thos.	PHA 94	Lebius? K.	ERI 56
Joseph	CHE 760	Thos.	CUM 128	Matthew	LUZ 332
Joshua	CUM 112	Thos.	CUM 151	Samuel	LUZ 373
Jost	LAN 99	Thos.	YOR 216	Zere/ Zese?	LUZ 349
Lettice	WAS 92	Uriah	FAY 258	MARX, Daniel	LAN 215
Lewis	GRN 102	Warwick	CHE 759	Peter	BER 178
Lewis	PHI 121	Widdow	FAY 222	William	BER 253
M./ W.?	LYC 25	Widow	NOH 67	MASBURGER, Daniel	BER 222
Manan	WAS 49	William	MIF 8	MASCO, David	LUZ 373
Martin	LAN 63	William	LAN 50	MASDEN, Wm.	MIF 25A
Martin	FRA 296	William	LAN 52	MASDON, John	CEN 18A
Martin Senr.	LAN 84	William	WAS 117	MASE, Benjamin	PHI 91
Mary	BFD 45	William	YOR 160	Daniel	LAN 179
Mathew	FRA 290	William	FAY 246	Joseph	CHE 852
Mathias	ADA 33	William	FAY 267	MASEY, Richd.	PHI 113
Matthew	HNT 141	William	FRA 287	MASH, Christian	WST 370
Max	DAU 10A	William	FRA 292	Daniel	ERI 57
Michael	PHI 131	William	WST 292	Elias	FAY 232
Michael	LAN 132	William	BUT 323	Elizabeth	FAY 236
Michal	ALL 80	Windle	FRA 308	Enoch	FAY 232
Micheal	BUC 157A	Wm.	BEV 4	Ephraim	WAY 147
Nathaniel	FRA 302	Wm.	BEV 13	Gravenor	CHE 759
Nathl.	FAY 222	Wm.	PHA 75	Henry	CHE 846
Nicholas	MNT 114	Wm. (Weaver)	MIF 8	Hugh	WAR 1A
Nicholas	FRA 292	Wm. M.d.	PHA 43	James	CHE 847
Patrick	DAU 4	Zephaniah	WAS 123	Mulford	WAR 1A
Patrick	GRN 64	MARTIN?, Jacob?	MIF 10A	Simon	BUT 333
Paul	BFD 75	Wm.	MIF 10A	Volintine	WST 370
Paul Jr.	CUM 134	MARTINDALE, Amos	BUC 151A	William	MIF 25A
Peter	ADA 42	Isaac	BUC 103A	MASHMAN, Jno.	CHE 770
Peter	LAN 84	Jonathan	BUC 103A	MASHOLDER, Jacob	PHI 97
Peter	SOM 139	Joseph	BUC 151A	John	SOM 139
Peter	BER 165	Miles	BUC 151A	MASIGS, Jacob	LAN 275
Peter	YOR 165	Strickland	BUC 99	MASINA, Lyon	NOU 176
Peter	YOR 196	Thos.	BUC 107	MASNER, Anthony	DAU 27
Peter	LAN 201	Wm.	BUC 103A	Jacob	PHI 78A
Phillip	CUM 134	MARTINEY, John	SOM 132	MASON, Widw.	PHI 109A
Ralph	LUZ 414	MARTINO, Sarah	PHA 38	Alexander	NOH 67
Richard	MNT 41	MARTINS, Ebenezer	FRA 285	Andrew	BUC 154A
Richard	BUC 90	MARTINUS,		Benjamin	LAN 155
Richard	BUC 162	Cornelius	SOM 152	Christopher	PHI 126
Robert	CEN 19	MARTLAND, Robt.	YOR 208	David	CRA 11
Robert	WAS 57	MARTON, Chrisoper	ALL 113	Elizabeth	PHA 27
Robert	WAS 57	Hugh	BUT 365	Elizabeth	PHI 125
Robert	HNT 149	John	ALL 119	Francis	PHA 85
Robert	DEL 184	Jonathan	ALL 104	Frank	LAN 91
Robert	NOU 202	Mary	BUT 366	George	CRA 11

MASON, Hampton	PHI	34	MASTERS, Joseph	PHA	22	MATHEWS, James	BUC	86A
Isaac	PHA	41	Joseph	GRN	107	John	PHA	33
Isaac	CUM	137	Warner	GRN	84	John	PHA	72
Jacob	BFD	44	Widow	LAN	253	John	FAY	258
Jacob	CEN	20A	Widow	LAN	254	John	FRA	296
James	CRA	14	Wm.	PHA	5	Joseph	SOM	139
James	CUM	150	Wm.	LYC	23	Joseph	BUC	87A
James	VEN	169	MASTERS?, James			Lucy	PHA	21
John	BFD	44	M.?	CHE	889	Lydia	PHA	104
John	WAS	81	MASTERSOL, C.			Mary	PHA	53
John	PHI	98	Alexander	GRN	88	Paul	WAS	75
John	ALL	117	MASTERSON, Geo.	PHI	118	Robert	WAS	75
John	WAY	140	Heny	FAY	258	Samuel	BUC	88
John	CHE	813	Richard	FAY	246	Samuel	SOM	159
John	PHI	93A	MASTIN, Eleanor	WAS	104	William	ADA	5
Jonathan	ARM	126	MASTMAN, James	WAS	22	William	BEV	15
Joseph	CRA	5	MASTON?, William	HNT	166	William	WST	172
Josiah	BUC	146	MASUSON, Francis	LUZ	416	MATHEWSON,		
Luther	LUZ	362	MATCHENOR, John	PHI	145	Christopher	WAS	16
Michael	LAN	161	MATE, Elizabeth	YOR	167	James	WAS	16
Peter	MNT	92	MATEER, Jas.			Robert Jr.	WAS	16
Robert	PHA	98	Junr.	CUM	68	Robert Sr.	WAS	16
Robert	CHE	874	Jas. Senr.	CUM	68	Thomas	BFD	35
Saml.	PHI	61	Rosanna	CUM	68	MATHEY, Fredrik	DAU	31A
Samuel	BFD	44	Wm.	CUM	68	MATHIAS, Widow	WST	218
Samuel	BUC	105A	MATER, Jno.	CUM	58	Abel	BUC	97
Simon	HNT	120	Michl.	CUM	61	Able	PHI	66A
Tanton	PHI	107	MATERLINCK,			Daniel	WST	292
Thomas	BER	131	Balsor	NOU	183	Danl.	WST	313
Thomas	FRA	298	MATERNES, David	LAN	137	Jacob	BER	183
Thos.	PHI	107A	MATERNUS, Henry	BER	147	John		
William	GRN	102	MATES, James	BEV	21	(Carpenterr)	BUC	97
William	YOR	156	Thomas	BEV	23	John (Joiner)	BUC	97
Wm.	PHA	25	MATETOR, Widow	NOH	70	John (Sadler)	BUC	97
Wm.	PHA	84	MATH?, John	BUC	157A	John	LAN	111
MASONCOOP, John	ALL	55	MATHAN, Thomas	NOU	150	John	WST	239
MASONER, Jacob	CUM	111	MATHER, Isaac	MNT	108	John	WST	240
MASS, Cumfort	FRA	291	John	BUC	155A	John	FAY	251
MASSE, John	NOH	87A	Michael	MNT	70	John Junr.	BUC	97
MASSER, Abraham	BER	134	Richd.	PHA	52	Peter	YOR	163
Peter	LAN	267	Robert	DEL	184	Philip	BER	183
MASSES, Matthew	LAN	244	Samuel	NOU	194	Thomas	BUC	97
MASSEX, Cuff	DEL	175	MATHERS, David	WAS	8	Thomas	BUC	96A
MASSEY, Chas.	PHA	17A	James	PHA	64	MATHIEFF, William	HNT	116
Daniel	CHE	881	John	WAS	16	Zach?	HNT	116
George	CHE	880	John	CHE	901	MATHIOT, John	LAN	301
George	CHE	885	John	PHI	107A	MATHISSON, Neal	PHA	101
James	CHE	877	Joseph	CUM	106	MATICK, Robert	DAU	29
John	PHA	101	Peter	PHA	43	MATLACK, Benjamin	CHE	701
Joseph	CHE	800	Robt.	CUM	135	Caleb	PHI	152
Levi	CHE	880	Saml.	CUM	120	George	CHE	701
Mordecai	HNT	144	Thomas	MER	454	Jesse	CHE	701
Thomas	LUZ	365	Thos.	LYC	18	Jonathan	CHE	705
Wm.	PHA	12	William	MER	454	Jonathan Jr.	CHE	702
Wm.	PHA	77	Wm.	CUM	133	Josiah	PHI	151
MASSICK, James	PHI	67A	MATHERY, Michl.	BER	243	Nathan	CHE	879
MAST, Christn.	BER	162	MATHES, Benj.	MNT	41	MATLER, Phillip	NOU	167
Frederick	NOH	48	Charly	ALL	107	MATLIN, Patrick	NOU	194
Jacob	NOH	48	James	ALL	95	MATLOCK, Amos	DEL	192
Jacob	BER	147	Thomas	MNT	41	George	DEL	184
Jacob Jr.	BER	161	MATHEW, John			Josiah	PHA	81
John	BER	145	(Crossed Out)	BUC	97	Mary	PHA	71
John	BER	161	Joseph	BUC	105A	Nathan	PHA	77
MASTER, Gasham	NOU	150	Thomas	BUC	105A	Sarah	PHA	104
Movits/			MATHEWS, Abram	FAY	251	Simeon	DEL	184
Moreits?	FRA	297	Anna	BUC	151A	Timothy	LAN	49
MASTERMAN, Mary	PHI	91	Benjn.	PHA	8	MATOCKS, Edward	MER	452
MASTERS, Anthony	HNT	130	Charles	PHA	116	Jacob	CRA	15
Bastian	FRA	298	Edward	PHI	105	Joseph	CRA	15
Clement	BFD	60	Elizabeth	FRA	280	Richard	CRA	15
George	ALL	67	Frances	FAY	258	MATOX, Peter	CRA	14
George	MNT	119	George	BEV	15	MATRABER, Susan	DAU	38
Gideon	WAS	123	George	SOM	139	MATRAN, Andw.	PHI	70
Henry	GRN	83	Hannah	YOR	154	MATRIX, Joseph	MNT	78
James	CRA	11	Jacob	SOM	139	MATS, Widow	PHI	41
Jesse	BFD	59	James	PHA	8	Jacob	WST	294

MATSINGER, Adam	PHI	63	MATTHIAS, William	NOU	159	MAUS, Frederick	BUC	157A
Geo.	PHI	63	MATTHORN, George	HNT	144	James	NOU	166
Michl.	PHI	63	Jacob	HNT	144	Mrs.	NOU	166
MATSON, Aaron	DEL	155	MATTHULL?, George			MAUSE, Nancy	PHI	66A
George	DEL	159	Esqr.	FAY	201	MAUSER, Michael	MNT	103
Jacob	CHE	877	MATTINGER, Ludwig	NOH	56A	MAUSTEN, James	FAY	267
Levi	DEL	155	Michael Jr.	NOH	56A	Peter Jur.	FAY	267
Peter	PHI	19	Michael	NOH	56A	Peter Ser.	FAY	267
Uriah	WST	154	MATTIS, Christian	MNT	75	William	FAY	267
Uriah	WST	349	Henry	BUC	101	MAVIS, Andrew	WAS	9
MATSON?, Jacob	PHI	57	Henry	LUZ	360	Henry	WAS	57
MATT, Catharine	LAN	202	Jacob	MNT	78	MAWER, Thos.	PHA	63
MATTENTY, Mathias	PHA	35	Jacob (Far?)	MNT	78	MAWHORTER, Wm.	WST	172
MATTER, Adam	LAN	79	Peter	MNT	111	MAWRER, John	NOU	138
George	LAN	27	Robert	MIF	4	MAXAMMER, Adam	PHI	108
George	DAU	41	William	PHI	52	MAXEL, David	ALL	69
Henry	YOR	187	MATTIS?, Casper	NOH	38	MAXFIELD, Frances	FAY	215
Jacob	CUM	61	MATTISON, Joseph	BUC	161	James	BFD	47
James	YOR	218	Morris	BUC	85A	James	CHE	839
John	DAU	41	MATTOCK, Henry	MIF	7A	John	ERI	59A
Mary	LAN	78	William L.	PHA	92	Robert	DEL	158
MATTERN, George	NOH	60	MATTOM, John	LAN	177	Robert	DEL	165
Henry	NOH	60A	MATTORF, Conrad	ADA	41	Samuel	MNT	51
John	NOH	60A	MATTS, Jacob	YOR	196	Stephen	ERI	58A
Peter	BER	272	MATTS?, John	BUC	157A	Wm.	PHI	85
MATTEWS, Charles	PHI	80	MATTSON, Aaron	DEL	172	MAXHAMER, Wm.	FRA	312
MATTHESON, Thos.	PHI	35	Peter	MNT	104	MAXINELL, John	PHI	119
MATTHEW, Abel	BUC	105	MATUR, John	CRA	15	MAXTON, George	LAN	300
Benjamin	BUC	105A	MATURN, John	BER	227	George	CHE	777
Edward	BUC	105A	Peter	BER	227	James	CHE	899
George Junr.	HNT	130	MATZ, George	BER	160	John	CHE	771
Jas.	CUM	39	John	FRA	283	William	CHE	899
MATTHEWS, Abram	LAN	252	MAUDY?, Christian	BER	174	MAXVEL, Steven	FAY	210
Adam	CUM	92	John	BER	185	MAXWELL, Adam	ARM	123
Duncan	MER	449	MAUER, Philip	BER	251	Archabald	CRA	5
Ezekiel	WST	162	MAUFET, Amry	CUM	55	Archibald	PHA	113
Fredk.	WST	239	John	CUM	113	David	CHE	831
James	PHI	32	MAUFFET, Wm.	CUM	130	Eliza	PHA	85
James	CUM	121	MAUGEL, Daniel	BUC	159A	Hannah	FRA	288
James	WST	161	George	BUC	159A	Hugh	PHA	109
James	WST	371	Thomas	BUC	159A	Jacob	LAN	180
Jiles	FAY	210	MAUGER, Henry	BER	174	James	WAS	23
John	LAN	30	Mrs.	NOU	138	James	CUM	28
John	ARM	122	MAUGHIN, William	CHE	869	James	WAS	29
John	WST	162	MAUGHLIN, Wm.	YOR	198	James Sr.	FRA	288
John	DEL	170	MAUGICE, Andrew	CHE	712	Jas	WST	173
John	WST	348	MAUGLE, Adam	BFD	64	Jas.	CUM	53
John	WST	371	MAUK, Ephraim	LUZ	398	Jno.	CUM	136
Joseph (Crossed			MAUL, Benjamin	DEL	184	John	MIF	4
Out)	BUC	146	Casper	BER	231	John	ADA	39
Joseph	BUC	145	Conrad	YOR	184	John	YOR	159
Richard	HNT	130	Daniel	DEL	184	John	LAN	181
Samuel	NOU	150	Jacob	DEL	184	John	WST	219
Sarah	PHI	35	John	PHA	22	John	LUZ	393
Thomas	HNT	133	John	PHI	102	John	CHE	831
Thomas	BUT	319	Joshua	DEL	185	John	DAU	3A
Uriah	BUC	142	Peter	LAN	278	Jonathen	FAY	209
William	WST	193	Philip	YOR	184	Joseph	WAS	29
William	CHE	860	MAULSBURY, Aron	BUC	87	Patr.	FRA	286
Wm.	MIF	17	MAULSBY, Samuel	MNT	108	Philip	WAS	123
Wm.	PHI	58	MAURER, Abm.	MNT	58	Robert	WAS	29
MATTHEWS?, -----	MIF	10A	Abraham	BER	219	Robert	ADA	39
MATTHEWSON,			Daniel	BER	219	Robert	HNT	161
Elisha	LUZ	382	Frederick	BER	219	Robert	LAN	163
Elisha	LUZ	425	George	NOH	85A	Robert	BUT	319
Joseph	PHI	22	Jacob	BER	180	Robt.	CUM	111
MATTHIAS, Barnit	PHI	127	Jacob Jr.	BER	180	Samuel	MNT	88
David	NOU	144	John	BER	216	Stephen	DEL	179
Henry	YOR	215	Martin	LAN	146	Susanna	LAN	183
Jacob	LAN	76	Michael	NOH	76	William	DEL	166
Jacob	NOU	138	Peter	NOH	34	William	DEL	171
Joseph	LAN	99	Peter	BER	138	Wm.	CUM	95
Joseph	PHI	155	Peter	LAN	190	Wm.	CUM	143
Philip	BFD	38	Peter	NOH	85A	Wm.	WST	312
Philip	BFD	41	Philip	NOH	91	MAY, Adam	PHA	75
Thomas	NOU	144	MAURER?, Paul	BER	167	Alexander	WAS	16

MAY, Barbara	YOR 173	MAYER, John	MNT 128	MC AFEE, John	FRA 286
Barhart	PHI 111A	John	NOU 138	John	MIF 7A
Cuff	CHE 773	John	NOU 138	Joseph	DEL 172
David	YOR 181	John	NOU 183	Michael	HNT 119
George	BFD 51	John	NOU 188	William	NOU 111
George	PHA 111	John	NOU 188	MC AFFEE, Daniel	FRA 286
George	SOM 154	John	NOU 188	David	NOU 166
George	NOU 166	Michael	LAN 63	Mark	FRA 285
Henry	BFD 55	Michael	LAN 73	Thos.	FRA 285
Jacob	ADA 21	Michael	LAN 87	MC AGRATH, Michl.	PHI 109
Jacob	BFD 55	Michael	NOU 138	MC ALESTER, James	GRN 92
Jacob	MNT 117	Michael	NOU 189	MC ALILISTER,	
Jacob	LAN 234	Nicholas	NOU 188	John	PHA 63
Jacob	LAN 315	Phillip	NOU 138	MC ALISTER,	
James	WAS 13	Rudy	LAN 86	Archd.	WST 313
James	BER 234	Samuel	LAN 73	Chas.	PHA 123
John	WAS 13	Samuel	MNT 90	Danl.	WST 312
John	WAS 16	Widow	LAN 90	Danl. (A	
John	WAS 34	William	NOU 138	Boarding	
John	BFD 51	MAYER?, See Mager	ALL 51	House)	PHA 37
John	DEL 170	MAYES, Lancelot	BEV 24	Hugh	MIF 13
John	YOR 211	MAYFIELD, Kitty	PHA 121	John	PHA 104
John (Labourer)	YOR 173	MAYHORN, Benjamin	WAS 81	MC ALLEN, John	FRA 320
John A.	BFD 75	MAYHUE, Richard	NOU 167	MC ALLESTER,	
Joseph	LAN 315	Richard	NOU 167	Alexr.	PHA 61
Lewis	PHA 56	MAYINIM, Jonathen	NOU 111	MC ALLISTER,	
Michael	BEV 19	MAYLAND, Saml.	PHA 56	Andw.	CUM 121
Michael	BFD 53	MAYO, John	DEL 159	Archibald	LAN 219
Nicholas	FAY 236	MAYOR, Widow	PHI 99	Archibd.	DAU 11A
Patrick	WAS 13	MAYS, Andrew	MIF 17A	Archid.	FRA 298
Peter	MNT 138	Charles	WAS 34	Daniel	LAN 230
Philip	LAN 165	Charles	WAS 49	Gresham	LAN 22
Robert Esqr.	CHE 889	Charles	FAY 210	Hugh	BUC 139A
Samuel	WAS 16	David	FRA 285	J./ I.?	DAU 45
Sarah	MNT 103	Samuel	WST 254	James	ADA 27
Thomas	CEN 20A	Thomas	WAS 49	Jesse	ADA 27
MAYBERRY, Isarael	LAN 77	MAYSNER,		John	FRA 296
John	MER 452	Christian	LAN 267	John	CHE 774
Johnathan	FRA 279	Christian Senr.	LAN 267	Mary	PHA 20
Richard	LUZ 323	Philip	LAN 267	Saml.	PHI 31
MAYBIN, John	PHA 44	MAZAMER, Ann		MC ALPIN, Andw.	PHA 28
MAYBONE, Wm.	WST 381	Maria	YOR 185	James	PHA 10
MAYBURY, Rebecca	MNT 100	John	YOR 185	MC ALROY, Hugh	BUT 332
Richard	BER 252	MAZAURE, James	PHA 15	MC AMEE, John	SOM 143
Sylvanus	CUM 84	MAZE, George	PHI 77A	MC ANALLA, John	WST 275
Thomas	BER 138	John	PHI 80A	MC ANCAR, Wm.	PHA 73
Willoubgby?	MNT 53	Wm.	LYC 22	MC ANEAR, John	FRA 300
MAYCUMBER, Zenus	BUC 137A	MAZILTON, Wm.	PHI 113A	MC ANEE, John	BFD 69
MAYER, Abraham	LAN 90	MC CLELLAND,		MC ANELLY, Henry	CUM 114
Adam	NOU 194	James	HNT 144	MC ANINEH, John	ARM 125
Charles	NOU 138	MC (UNFINISHED),		MC ANINEH?,	
Chris.	LAN 63	James	LAN 69	D----?	ARM 123
Christian	LAN 75	MC ----?, Daniel	BEV 27	MC ANNA, Henry	WST 313
Christian	LAN 88	Jno.	WAR 1A	MC ANNELL, John	MNT 106
Christian	MNT 90	Wm.	WAR 1A	MC ANOLTY,	
Christian	NOU 138	MC ----T?, Robert	BEV 13	Richard	WST 255
Christian	NOU 189	MC ---E?,		MC ANULTY, Hugh	FRA 274
Christopher	NOU 138	Cornelius	NOU 202	John	FRA 299
David	NOU 130	MC ---SSARTY?,		Mary	FRA 322
Frederick	NOU 138	Thomas	BEV 21	Robt.	FRA 297
George	NOU 130	MC ---SY?, David		MC ANURLAND,	
George	NOU 138	Senr.	ADA 14	James	HNT 142
Henry	NOU 188	MC ---Y?, Daniel	WAR 1A	MC ARTHUR, Danl.	PHA 108
Jacob	MNT 35	MC --DOL?, Robert	HNT 150	MC AULEY, James	PHA 69
Jacob	MNT 90	MC --INNY?, -----	LYC 27	MC AUTHUR,	
Jacob	MNT 100	MC --LEIGH?,		William	CRA 14
Jacob	NOU 138	Wilm.	MER 450	MC AVOY, Margret	CUM 127
Jacob	NOU 138	MC ADAMS, David	ALL 111	MC AZGAR, Jonas	LAN 40
Jacob	NOU 138	John	LYC 6	MC BARRON, Michl.	PHI 71A
Jacob	NOU 138	John	FAY 267	MC BATE, John	NOU 176
Jacob	NOU 188	Robt.	PHA 84	MC BATH, Robert	NOU 176
Jacob	LAN 255	William	NOU 97A	MC BATT?, (See Mc	
Jacob	LAN 272	MC ADDAMS, David	BUC 146	Bate)	NOU 176
Jacob	LAN 277	MC ADDEN, James	CHE 745	MC BAY, Archibald	HNT 134
John	LAN 64	MC AFEE, Archabd.	FRA 274	Joseph	DAU 23
John	LAN 75	Jacob	PHI 47	William	MNT 71

MC CARTHER,			MC CASTLAND,			MC CLAIN, David	ALL 67
William	SOM	143	Maxwell	LAN	103	Dunkin	FAY 210
MC CARTLIN,			MC CASTLES,			Elia	HNT 146
Tarrence	DAU	18	Thomas	ADA	8	Enus	ALL 94
MC CARTMY, Wm.	FRA	323	MC CAUGHAN, James	MIF	8	Hugh	CUM 123
MC CARTNEY,			Jno.	MIF	7A	James	FAY 258
Catharne	LAN	9	MC CAUL, James	ALL	74	John	HNT 139
Daniel	BFD	55	John	ALL	104	John	HNT 151
Daniel	HNT	157	Robt.	BUT	326	John	HNT 152
Dugald	HNT	125	MC CAULAY, James	HNT	134	John	FAY 210
Elizabeth	WST	154	James	HNT	150	John Rd.	ALL 100
George	HNT	158	John	HNT	166	Joseph	WST 239
Henry	NOU	202	Robert	HNT	165	Mordecai	HNT 150
James	HNT	165	MC CAULEY, Henry	PHI	35	Paul	WST 219
Jos.	WST	381	MC CAULLEY, Saml.	WST	326	Robert	FAY 215
Laughlin	NOU	172	MC CAULY, Adwy?	PHI	28	Robert	WST 239
Margaret	LAN	168	MC CAUN, Robt.	WST	369	Roger	HNT 147
Patk.	CUM	91	MC CAUSLAND,			Saml.	FAY 258
Patrick	HNT	131	----?	LYC	9	Thomas	MER 449
Richard	PHI	127	Andw.	BUT	330	William	HNT 137
Robert	HNT	144	George	LAN	177	William	MER 454
Saml.	WST	154	James	BUT	320	Wm.	WST 240
Sarah	PHA	34	Thomas	LAN	177	Wm.	FAY 258
Wm.	WST	276	Thomas	LAN	178	MC CLAIR, William	FRA 290
MC CARTNY, Alexr.	WST	220	William	LAN	177	MC CLAMMONS, Hugh	BUT 352
James	ALL	99	William	LAN	178	MC CLAN, James	CHE 708
Robert	ALL	88	Wm.	LYC	10	Joseph	CHE 729
MC CARTY, Widow	PHI	22	MC CAWIN, Dennis	FRA	276	MC CLANAHAN,	
Andw.	MIF	16	MC CAWN, William	CHE	715	George	MNT 138
Benjn.	LYC	15	MC CAY, &			John	NOU 189
Callehen	ALL	118	Kerrigan	LAN	152	MC CLANE, Alexr.	CHE 723
Caty	BUC	149A	Alexander	MER	453	Anthony	PHA 74
Daniel	PHI	52	Allexander	BEV	21	Daniel	LAN 298
Denis	FAY	210	Danl.	PHI	46	John	SOM 146
George	BEV	25	George	NOU	166	Joseph	PHI 146
Henry	MIF	25A	James	BEV	18	Willm.	PHI 23
Isaac	PHI	79	James	FRA	289	MC CLAREN, Hugh	WST 327
Isaiah	LAN	131	James	FRA	307	MC CLAREY, Thos.	FAY 246
Jerah.	CUM	54	John	BEV	16	MC CLARIN, Archd.	PHI 51
Jerh.	CUM	84	Katharine	BEV	16	John	LAN 61
Jno.	VEN	168	Neal	CRA	15	MC CLARMAN, John	VEN 169
John	WAY	144	Patrick	BEV	14	MC CLARNAN, James	VEN 169
John	LAN	299	Thomas	BEV	13	Thos.	VEN 169
John	BUC	81A	Widow	FRA	310	MC CLARRIN, Wm.	FRA 291
John	BUC	149A	MC CE-?, James	BEV	18	MC CLARWIN, James	ALL 52
Michael	GRN	83	MC CEG, Patrick	ALL	76	MC CLASKEY,	
Michl.	FRA	282	MC CEHN, Benjn.	MIF	25A	Michael	DEL 188
Nicholas Jnr.	BUC	82A	MC CELVY, Wm.	LYC	15	Michl.	WST 192
Nicholas	BUC	81A	MC CERN, Barney	PHA	102	MC CLASKY, Mrs.	LYC 19
Nicholas	BUC	139A	MC CHALASTER,			Edwd.	PHI 37
Philip	WAY	144	Wilm.	ALL	71	Manes	WST 192
Silas	LYC	13	MC CHEMEY,			MC CLASPE,	
Thos.	BUC	81A	William	DAU	5	William	LAN 300
Thos.	BUC	82A	MC CHESNEY, James	LAN	133	MC CLATCHEY,	
William	WAY	144	Margaret	LAN	134	Charles	ARM 123
William	DEL	177	MC CHIRGH, James	WST	254	James	ARM 123
Wm.	LYC	15	MC CHOLASTER,			James	ARM 123
Wm.	VEN	168	Allexander	BEV	22	MC CLATERIN, John	LAN 93
MC CARVEL, John	NOU	130	MC CHOLLASTER,			MC CLAUGHLIN,	
MC CARVERY, James	DAU	10	John	ALL	82	Hugh	NOU 130
MC CARY, Wm.	CHE	707	MC CHUGIN, Archd.	WST	381	MC CLAVER, John	MIF 25A
MC CASEY, Daniel	BEV	22	MC CIBBIN, James	BEV	12	MC CLAY, Charles	FRA 318
MC CASHLAN,			MC CIM, Wilm.	ALL	105	Henry	BER 285
Samuel	BFD	53	MC CIMLEY, Bill	FRA	313	John	FRA 317
Samuel	BFD	75	MC CINEY, Susanna	LAN	311	Moses	FRA 311
Samuel Jr.	BFD	75	MC CINSTREY,			Samuel	NOU 130
MC CASHLEN,			Robert	GRN	91	Wm.	PHA 52
Thomas	ADA	17	MC CLAIN,			MC CLEAF, Robert	ADA 2
MC CASHLIN,			Alexander	FAY	210	Robert	ADA 2
Abigal	FRA	288	Alexander	FAY	253	Robert	ADA 17
Alexd.	FRA	287	Andrew	WST	239	MC CLEALAND,	
MC CASHLON, John	ALL	114	Andw.	CUM	147	Robert	LAN 126
MC CASKEY, James	WST	221	Archd.	CUM	150	MC CLEAN, Andw.	WST 349
John	BEV	13	Azariah	HNT	139	Benjamin	DEL 191
MC CASLIN, James	CUM	133	Charles	FAY	236	Charles	WST 349
MC CASTER, Dancan	MIF	25A	Danl.	PHI	72A		

MC CLEAN, Hector	PHI	42	
James	ADA	34	
James	WST	162	
John	BFD	45	
John	WST	162	
Kenith	DEL	171	
Mary	WST	255	
Samuel	MNT	51	
William	MNT	51	
William	MNT	62	
William Esq.	ADA	5	
MC CLEAREY, John	SOM	154	
MC CLEARY, Danl.	WST	162	
Elizabeth	ADA	14	
Henry	WST	348	
James	ADA	1	
James	ADA	2	
John	LAN	69	
John	WST	173	
Joseph	ADA	2	
Thomas	BUT	319	
MC CLEAS, Mausa?	HNT	135	
MC CLEBLAND,			
Thos.	CUM	137	
MC CLEERY, Alexr.	DAU	20A	
Alexr.	DAU	45A	
Alexr.	DAU	47A	
Hugh	DAU	3A	
John	DAU	9	
MC CLEES, Edward	BER	163	
James	DEL	168	
MC CLEKAR, Daniel	DAU	10A	
George	DAU	10A	
Jacob	DAU	10A	
Martin	DAU	10A	
Thos.	DAU	10A	
MC CLELAN,			
Anthony	NOU	166	
MC CLELAND,			
Andrew	GRN	83	
Andrew	GRN	89	
Asa	GRN	66	
Carry	GRN	102	
Elizabeth	CRA	6	
James	GRN	89	
John	GRN	89	
John	GRN	91	
John Senr.	GRN	92	
John	DAU	36A	
Robert	GRN	83	
William	GRN	89	
William	NOU	130	
MC CLELIN, Thomas	MER	453	
MC CLELLAN, Hugh	WST	370	
Hugh Esqr.	MIF	4	
Jacob	ADA	2	
Jacob	ADA	6	
James	LAN	57	
Jenett	YOR	154	
Joel	DEL	170	
John	ADA	19	
John	PHI	138	
Mary	ADA	9	
Michael	ADA	2	
Robert	DEL	170	
Robert	BER	208	
Robert	CHE	824	
Thos.	WST	347	
Thos.	CEN	22B	
William	ADA	5	
William	ADA	9	
MC CLELLAND,			
David	BFD	59	
David	HNT	130	
George	MIF	2	
George	FRA	313	

MC CLELLAND,			
George	WST	313	
Hans	WAS	23	
James	WAS	23	
James	FRA	287	
James	WST	327	
Jno.	FRA	289	
Jno.	FRA	300	
Jno. Doct.	FRA	296	
John	HNT	122	
John	HNT	132	
John	WST	220	
Robt.	MIF	2	
Robt.	FRA	300	
Samuel	LAN	14	
Samuel	FRA	275	
Thos.	FRA	317	
William	HNT	130	
William Junr.	HNT	130	
Wm.	CUM	48	
Wm.	FRA	288	
Wm.	FRA	300	
Wm.	FRA	323	
Wm. Sr.	FRA	289	
MC CLELLANT,			
David	CUM	26	
MC CLELLEN, John	WST	292	
Robt.	WST	276	
MC CLELLIN, John	MER	451	
Megy	MER	453	
Robert	MER	451	
MC CLELON, James	NOU	130	
MC CLEMMENTS, Wm.	WST	154	
MC CLEMONS,			
Samuel	HNT	136	
MC CLEN, James	DAU	8	
MC CLENAGAN,			
Blair	PHA	89	
MC CLENAGHAN,			
Henry	HNT	158	
John	WST	154	
Patrick	HNT	3	
Robt.	WST	154	
MC CLENAHAN,			
Elijah	CHE	713	
Michael	PHA	58	
MC CLENEHAN,			
Charles	MIF	4	
MC CLENNAN,			
Samuel	LAN	166	
MC CLENNON, James	BEV	27	
MC CLENTOCK,			
Joseph	NOU	166	
MC CLENTOE, Mrs.	NOU	166	
MC CLEREY,			
Benjiman	FAY	204	
John	FAY	215	
MC CLERIN,			
William	MNT	132	
MC CLERR, Saml.	PHI	71A	
MC CLERRAN, James	WST	348	
Matthew	WST	348	
MC CLERY, James	MIF	25A	
Joseph	NOU	130	
Mrs.	NOU	130	
Mrs.	NOU	130	
Thomas	NOU	176	
MC CLESTER,			
Dannel	ALL	111	
Mrs.	NOU	199	
MC CLEW, Charles	BUT	333	
MC CLIMONS, James	HNT	143	
MC CLINBY, Hugh	PHI	14	
MC CLINE, James			
Sr.	MIF	15A	
MC CLINTIC, Alexd.	ALL	66	

MC CLINTIC,			
Andrew	ALL	66	
Joseph	ALL	66	
Thomas	BEV	23	
MC CLINTICK,			
Francis	VEN	166	
Hambleton	VEN	166	
James	BER	250	
John	ALL	54	
Mary	FRA	273	
Michael	BFD	64	
MC CLINTIG, Wm.	CHE	732	
MC CLINTOCH, Jno.	FRA	309	
MC CLINTOCK,			
Alexander	SOM	146	
Alexr.	WST	294	
Henry	WST	292	
Hugh	CUM	53	
James	CUM	29	
Jno.	CUM	29	
John	CUM	79	
John	WST	292	
Jos.	CUM	48	
Robert	MNT	103	
Robert	SOM	146	
Robt.	CUM	60	
Sarah	MNT	58	
Thomas	ERI	58	
Widow	CUM	132	
William	SOM	146	
William	MER	449	
Wm.	CUM	53	
Wm.	WST	292	
MC CLISH, Isaac	BFD	59	
MC CLISTER,			
Archbd.	MIF	17A	
Collin	DEL	178	
Jams.	MIF	15	
MC CLIVE, James	DEL	156	
MC CLONG, Wm.	PHI	77A	
MC CLOSKEY,			
Banney	LAN	45	
Henry	DAU	10	
Patrick	LAN	27	
Patrick	CHE	745	
MC CLOSKY, James	HNT	124	
John	FAY	267	
Joseph	LYC	25	
Robt.	WST	348	
Thomas	LAN	89	
Wm.	CEN	20A	
MC CLOUD,			
Alexander	LAN	53	
John	PHI	5	
John	WST	381	
Malcom	PHA	59	
MC CLOWDON, Myles	PHA	47	
MC CLOY, Charles	FRA	317	
David	FRA	318	
John Sr.	FRA	318	
Robert	LAN	169	
Wm.	FRA	319	
MC CLUE, Saml.	WST	275	
MC CLUER, Andrew	MER	452	
Robert	MER	452	
MC CLUES,			
Alexander	MER	450	
MC CLUIN, John	PHI	128	
MC CLULEY,			
Archibald	LAN	236	
MC CLUN, Sarah	CUM	43	
William	CUM	43	
MC CLUNEY, Martha	PHA	21	
MC CLUNG, Charles	NOU	166	
Ezekiel	LAN	241	
John	LAN	131	

MC CLUNG?, See Mc			MC CLUTCHON, Jas.	WST	370	MC CONAGHY, Jas.	WST	174
Clurg?	ALL	53	MC CMILLIN,			MC CONAHUE,		
MC CLUON, James	NOU	147	Daniel	FAY	210	Francis	VEN	167
MC CLURE, (See			MC COCCLE?,			MC CONAKY, Robert	CRA	18
Delaney, Wm.)	BUC	93	Edward	PHI	93A	MC CONAUGHE,		
Abdiel	BUT	339	MC COCHANY, David	CRA	14	Robert	ARM	122
Alex.	ALL	75	MC COCKELL, Jas.			MC CONAUGHY,		
Alexander	LAN	121	R.	PHI	23	Robert	ARM	123
Alice	PHA	101	MC COEL, Catahne.	DAU	33	Samuel	ADA	15
Andrew	MNT	78	MC COLDEN,			Widow	ADA	7
Andrew	LUZ	331	Margaret	PHA	69	MC CONEGHEY, Geo.	CUM	144
Andw.	BUT	339	MC COLGAN, John	CRA	10	Jas.	CUM	34
Arther	LAN	58	John	HNT	162	Robt.	CUM	141
Arthur	LAN	38	MC COLGATE, Asaph	HNT	134	MC CONEGHY, Jas.	CUM	141
Charles	CUM	74	MC COLL?, -----	ALL	88	MC CONEHEA,		
Charles	FAY	198	MC COLLAM, Jas.	BUT	339	Daniel	HNT	136
Finley	NOU	159	John	BUT	339	MC CONIHE, John	ALL	106
Frances	ALL	83	MC COLLASTER,			MC CONKEY, Henry	MIF	4
Francis	CEN	18A	David	BEV	21	James	MIF	4
Geore	PHA	4	MC COLLATE,			Robt.	WST	173
James	CEN	19	Alexr.	DAU	44A	MC CONKY, Hugh	LAN	149
James	CEN	23	MC COLLAUGH,			William	FAY	210
James	DAU	23	Andrew	ALL	72	MC CONNAKY, John	PHI	31
James	PHI	146	Robert	ALL	86	MC CONNAL, Danl.	BUT	363
James	CEN	18A	MC COLLE, William	MER	452	Thomas	ALL	120
Jane	ADA	7	MC COLLEM,			MC CONNALL,		
Jas.	CUM	137	Ephraim	NOU	159	George	FAY	227
Jas.	DAU	24A	Thomas	CUM	35	MC CONNALLY,		
Jinny	DAU	12A	MC COLLIN, John	PHA	123	Thomas	LAN	302
John	CRA	4	MC COLLISTER,			MC CONNAMY, Neal	PHI	69A
John	LAN	12	Archibald	NOU	118	MC CONNEHE, John	BEV	18
John	CRA	13	MC COLLOM, John	WAS	3	MC CONNEL, Adam	ALL	78
John	ADA	18	John	PHA	98	Daniel	LAN	169
John	CEN	19	MC COLLOUGH,			Forbes	CHE	715
John	ALL	77	Frances	ALL	112	George	ADA	4
John	GRN	77	John	ALL	70	George	ALL	93
John	ALL	83	John	LAN	164	Hugh	LAN	169
John	LAN	118	John	FAY	216	Hugh	LAN	288
John	HNT	166	John	WST	294	James	BEV	14
John	LAN	246	Joseph	ALL	71	James	HNT	144
John	WST	255	Robert	ALL	112	James	FRA	286
John	WST	274	Robert	PHA	113	John	BEV	14
John	WST	275	Samuel	PHA	113	John	CUM	120
Jonathan	CEN	19	Wilm.	ALL	112	John	LAN	165
Mathew	CRA	13	Wilm.	ALL	112	Joseph	ALL	79
Miles	WST	292	MC COLLOUH,			Joseph	WST	369
Rebecca	FRA	313	Joseph	ALL	50	Mattw.	CUM	62
Ritchard	ALL	75	MC COLLUM, Jno.	CUM	125	Robert	ALL	79
Robt.	DAU	15A	Mary	CUM	58	Robert	SOM	134
Rowan	NOU	199	MC COLLY, Robert	LAN	88	Robert	BER	215
Saml.	CUM	150	William	FAY	205	Robert Ju.	ALL	79
Samuel	DEL	177	MC COLM, James	VEN	166	Samuel	ALL	79
Thomas	LAN	247	Jas.	BUT	316	Samuel	LAN	167
Thos.	LYC	26	John	VEN	166	Widow	LAN	124
Widow	LAN	54	MC COLOUGH,			Wilm.	ALL	80
William	PHI	48	George	LAN	227	Wilm.	ALL	111
William	LAN	121	Jacob	NOU	130	MC CONNELL,		
William	WST	154	James	ARM	124	Alexander	HNT	155
William	DEL	184	Peter	DEL	158	Alexd.	FRA	296
William	LAN	247	MC COMB, Allen	WST	162	Alexr.	FAY	216
Wilm.	ALL	75	Benjamin	PHA	119	Arthur	PHI	37
Wilm. Esqr.	ALL	73	George	WAS	23	Daniel	BFD	38
Wilson	CUM	38	George	NOU	152	Daniel Senr.	BFD	39
Wm.	DAU	23	James	WST	154	Danl.	CUM	55
MC CLURG, David	MER	450	Jeremeah	PHA	109	David	WST	348
John	MER	450	Malcomb	WST	348	Dennis	MER	454
Joseph	MER	450	MC COMBS, Alexd.	ALL	56	Elizabeth	CEN	20A
Mark	MER	450	John	FRA	318	Geo.	CUM	52
William	MER	450	Lawrence	PHA	39	Henry	HNT	121
MC CLURG?, Joseph	ALL	53	William	MER	454	Hugh	PHI	46
MC CLURKIN, Hugh	ALL	56	Wm.	FAY	258	James	PHI	27
MC CLUSKEY, John	PHA	110	MC COMMON, Hugh	CUM	91	James	PHI	36
John	FAY	210	James	MER	454	James	HNT	121
MC CLUTCHEY,			MC COMON, Robert	ALL	67	James	HNT	152
Widow	WST	347	Robert	NOU	159	James	FRA	315
MC CLUTCHON, Davi	WST	255	MC CON, Harrison	FAY	239	James	CHE	719

MC CONNELL, John	HNT	155	MC CORMAC, Thos.	NOU	202	MC COUN, Andrew	LAN	124
John	FRA	315	Wm.	NOU	166	Laurance	WST	312
John	WST	371	MC CORMACK, James	NOU	118	MC COURLAND?,		
John	WST	371	James	FAY	210	David		
Mathew	PHA	83	James	FAY	237	(Crossed Out)	LYC	9
Richard	WST	348	Patrick	WST	381	MC COURTY, Jas.	FRA	286
Robt.	FRA	315	Sarah	FAY	205	MC COWAN, Hugh	PHA	63
Robt.	FRA	326	William	FAY	198	James	BEV	11
Thos.	FRA	313	Willm.	FAY	236	Wm.	CUM	90
William	HNT	155	MC CORMEL, Jane	DAU	11A	MC COWEL, John	ALL	111
William	MER	454	MC CORMES,			MC COWEN, James	GRN	102
Wm.	PHI	25	William	NOU	166	John	GRN	102
Wm.	PHI	60	MC CORMIC, Hugh	ALL	109	Joseph	CEN	23
Wm.	CUM	147	James	BEV	21	Joseph	CEN	23
Wm.	WST	371	James	ALL	109	Walker	CUM	43
MC CONNICHE,			John	NOU	159	MC COWIN, Andrew	FAY	204
Thomas	BEV	26	Patrick	ALL	111	MC COWN, James	LAN	125
MC CONNILS, James	CHE	770	Samuel	ALL	50	James	WST	239
MC CONNINS,			MC CORMICK, Adam	CUM	139	Michael	BFD	65
Robert	LAN	168	Alexander	HNT	141	Nathan	BUC	152A
MC CONOUGHY,			Alexander	HNT	166	William	LAN	31
David	FRA	326	Charles	DAU	13A	MC COY, Alexander	HNT	148
John	LAN	73	Edward	HNT	138	Alexd.	FRA	287
MC CONWAY, Mackey	PHA	100	Eliza.	CUM	139	Alexr.	CUM	27
MC COOING, Robert	BUC	93	Esther	WST	294	Archd.	CUM	134
MC COOK,			Francis	ADA	1	Archd.	CUM	144
Alexander	PHA	92	Geo.	CEN	23	Barney	DEL	165
John	CUM	117	Geo. Jr.	CEN	23	Bernard	DEL	167
MC COOL, George	ARM	126	George	DAU	14	Charles	BUT	359
Samuel	MNT	108	Henry	DAU	23	Chas.	CUM	38
MC COON, William	FAY	204	Henry	PHI	56	Daniel	ARM	127
MC CORCHEL,			Hugh	CUM	76	Daniel	WST	154
Joseph	LAN	265	Hugh	LAN	180	Daniel	WST	172
MC CORCLE,			James	PHI	31	Danl.	BER	234
William	ADA	38	James	PHA	77	Elisha	CUM	36
MC CORD, Abner	LAN	246	James	CUM	98	Ephraim	LUZ	338
Barnard	ALL	52	James	ARM	122	George	GRN	96
Isaac	FAY	198	James	HNT	134	Hugh	GRN	68
James	CUM	43	Jas.	CEN	23	Hugh	ALL	100
James	CUM	48	Jas.	CUM	54	Hugh	HNT	123
John	LAN	15	Jas.	FRA	281	Isabela	PHA	12
John	CEN	23	Jno.	LYC	25	James	ALL	108
John	DAU	23	John	PHI	54	James	FAY	258
John	LUZ	377	John	WST	192	James	FAY	258
Joseph	NOU	172	Joseph	CUM	131	James	FRA	290
Joseph	ERI	56A	Joseph	DEL	188	John	CUM	27
Richard	LAN	169	Joseph	WST	192	John	BFD	58
Robert	DAU	10	Lowrey	MER	452	John	CUM	94
Robert	MER	450	Michl.	WST	292	John	ALL	106
Saml.	DAU	23	Robert	HNT	166	John	HNT	123
Saml.	CUM	49	Robt.	CUM	125	John	HNT	163
Saml.	WST	218	Saml.	CEN	23	John	WST	255
Samuel	ALL	50	Saml.	CUM	131	John	FAY	258
Thomas	DAU	12A	Susanna	BER	275	John	FRA	287
Thomas	MIF	17A	Thos.	DAU	17	John	LUZ	396
William	DEL	169	Thos.	CUM	49	John	MIF	15A
Wilm.	ALL	98	Thos.	CUM	131	John	MIF	26A
Wm.	CUM	48	Widow	CUM	76	Joseph	WST	275
MC CORDAL, John	HNT	140	William	NOH	65	Liddia	FAY	258
MC CORDY, Daniel	FAY	228	Wm.	DAU	23	Margaret	PHA	23
Thos.	NOU	202	Wm.	CUM	54	Markem	PHI	8
MC CORKLE,			MC CORMICK?,			Matthew	FAY	210
Archibald			Robt.	WST	349	Neal	MIF	5A
Jnr.	BUC	103	MC CORMIK, Isabel	DAU	24A	Rachell	CUM	26
John	BUC	103	John	DAU	23	Robert	CRA	15
Robert	PHI	136	MC CORNEL, John	DAU	33A	Robert	DEL	159
Robert	PHI	139	MC CORTNY,			Robert	DEL	161
Wm.	WST	220	Alexander	FAY	239	Saml.	BUT	361
MC CORKLY,			John	FAY	246	Sarah	BUC	103
Archibald	BUC	103	MC COSH, Samuel	ALL	94	Sarah	PHA	120
MC CORLEY, James	NOU	202	MC COSKRY, Saml.			Thomas	ALL	106
MC CORMAC, James	NOU	180	A.	CUM	99	Thomas	WST	275
John	NOU	166	MC COUGHLIN, John	FAY	205	Thomas	MER	449
Mrs.	NOU	172	MC COULLOCH, John	WST	218	Thomas	MER	452
Mrs.	NOU	176	MC COULOUGH,			William	MNT	132
Seth	NOU	202	George	LAN	150	William	FAY	210

MC DOWELL, Wm.	FRA	299	MC ELROY, James	ALL	65	MC FADDEN, Daniel	LAN	177
Wm. Junr.	FRA	285	James	LAN	74	Hugh	LAN	232
MC DOWL, John	FAY	262	James	LAN	84	James	FRA	312
Samuel	FAY	205	James	HNT	159	Jno.	MIF	8
MC DUFF, John	WST	192	James	WST	173	Jno.	MIF	17A
MC DUFFEE, Daniel	LUZ	427	James	BUC	139A	John	FRA	319
MC DUFFY,			John	BUC	89	Neal	FAY	222
Archibald	PHA	62	John	GRN	92	MC FADDIAN, Sarah	HNT	156
MC DUGALD, Jno.	PHI	46	John	CUM	124	MC FADDIEN, Wm.	MIF	15A
MC DULL, Georg	PHA	108	Mathew	BEV	14	MC FADDIN, Denis	FAY	204
MC DUNNEL,			Thos.	BUC	149A	Denis	FAY	204
William	LAN	236	William	GRN	96	Dennis	LAN	46
MC DURMENT, Paul	BUT	336	Wilm.	ALL	65	James	CEN	21
MC DURMUT, Dunkin	MNT	41	MC ELVAIN, Ann	CHE	778	John	DAU	25
MC EDOO, James	ALL	100	Jno.	BFD	64	John	WST	292
MC EFEE, Patrick	FAY	267	William	BFD	68	John	WST	294
William	FAY	267	MC ELVANNON, Jas.	MIF	13	Magey	DAU	16
MC EFERTY, Arthur	NOU	155	MC ELVEY,			Michl.	FAY	204
MC ELDUFF, Eliza	WST	192	Barnibas	ALL	95	Neal	FAY	204
John	WST	192	MC ELWAIN, Andrew	WST	327	Patrick	DAU	36A
MC ELERY, Samuel	DAU	9	Andw.	CUM	135	MC FADDION, John	BFD	44
MC ELFISH, Bazil	FAY	267	John	ALL	54	MC FADDISON, Hugh	BFD	38
Eli	FAY	267	Moses	WST	327	MC FADEN, Susan	PHA	24
Henrey	FAY	267	Robt.	WST	219	Thos.	CUM	95
Nathen	FAY	267	Robt.	WST	221	MC FADGIN, Neal	DEL	171
Richard	FAY	267	Wm.	WST	173	MC FADIAN, Andrew	CRA	6
Richard	FAY	267	Wm.	WST	219	John	CRA	8
Zadock	FAY	267	MC ELWAINE,			John Another	CRA	8
MC ELHANEY,			Alexander	LAN	82	John Jnr.	CRA	8
William	BUC	83	Ester	LAN	214	William	CRA	4
MC ELHANY, James	BFD	64	Geoe.	PHI	37	MC FADIN, James	FAY	251
James	ALL	116	George	LAN	128	Jas.	WST	219
James	FRA	322	George	LAN	129	Joseph	LYC	24
John	DAU	18	James	LAN	108	MC FADION, Thomas	LAN	57
John	BFD	64	John	LAN	75	MC FAHER, John	NOU	159
John	ALL	101	Jos.	CUM	133	MC FALL, Alexr.	PHI	28
John	ALL	101	Robert	LAN	228	Henry	LAN	237
Joseph	ALL	100	MC ELWAN, Thos.	PHA	88	John	BUC	145
Saml.	CUM	134	MC ELWE, Roger	BER	236	John	BUC	148
Thomas	ALL	84	MC ELWEE, Jas.	CUM	107	Peter	PHA	54
Thomas	ALL	89	Thos.	CUM	92	Rosannah	PHA	70
Thos.	DAU	23	MC ELY,			MC FALLS, James	NOU	159
Wilm.	ALL	86	Cornelious	ALL	56	MC FANN, Aaron	LAN	236
Wm.	FRA	322	MC ENELLY,			Nathaniel	LAN	236
MC ELHEANY,			Patrick	BUT	360	MC FARLAN,		
George	BEV	21	MC ENTIRE,			William	BER	250
Hugh	CUM	134	(Blank)	DAU	44A	MC FARLAND,		
Robert	BEV	21	Alexr.	DAU	21	Andrew	ALL	89
Widow	CUM	134	Andrew	ALL	56	Daniel	FRA	310
MC ELHENEY,			Danl.	MIF	15	Daniel Junr.	WAS	3
Eloner	WST	221	Darby	NOU	118	James	ADA	38
MC ELHENY, Alexr.	FRA	274	Hugh	ALL	59	James	FRA	290
John	ALL	87	John	MIF	5A	Jas.	MIF	15
Joseph	MIF	25A	Joseph	NOU	111	John	PHA	62
Thomas	ERI	60	Patrick	HNT	163	John	MNT	70
Wilm.	ALL	87	William	BUC	149A	John	HNT	142
MC ELHERAN, John	ALL	106	MC EROY?, See Mc			John	FAY	246
MC ELHINNY, James	HNT	155	Croy?	ALL	60	John	FRA	276
William	HNT	165	MC EWEN, Francis	CUM	36	Joseph	LUZ	428
MC ELKERR, John	FRA	323	James	DAU	23	Patrick	YOR	173
MC ELKINY, M.	LYC	24	James	DAU	35	Robert	ALL	61
MC ELRATH, Robert	LYC	3	John	DAU	23	Robert	ALL	74
MC ELREAVY, John	CUM	88	Joseph	CUM	47	Robert	DEL	187
MC ELREE, William	DEL	191	Robert	PHI	137	Robt.	FRA	287
MC ELROY,			MC EWIN, Henry	PHI	27	Robt.	FRA	323
Alexander	HNT	141	John	PHA	110	Saml.	WST	312
Alexander	ERI	59A	Thomas	ALL	103	Thomas	GRN	83
Alexr.	BUC	139A	Thos.	PHA	4	Thomas	WST	240
Archibald	BUC	83	MC EWING, Matthw.	BUT	340	Thomas	WST	312
Daniel	LAN	131	MC EWNE, Henry			William	GRN	83
Daniel	DEL	174	Sr.	CEN	19	William	WST	154
George	FRA	311	MC FADAN, Mrs.	LYC	18	William	FAY	232
Hannah	PHA	120	John	ALL	106	Wm. Esqr.	WAS	3
Henry	LAN	237	Saml.	LYC	18	MC FARLANE,		
Hugh	ADA	15	MC FADDAN, John	FRA	279	Alexr.	PHI	155
Issabel	LAN	74	Wm.	LYC	17	Jas.	CUM	116

MC FARLANE, Jas.	CUM 132	MC GAFFOCK,		MC GEE, John	BEV 28		
Jno.	CUM 131	Benjamin	HNT 166	John	NOU 118		
John	PHI 5	MC GAHAN, Anthy.	CUM 62	John	FRA 324		
John	HNT 139	Johnb	PHA 93	John	BUT 334		
Margaret	CUM 103	MC GAHAN?, Thomas	ERI 60A	Patrick	CRA 12		
Patk.	PHI 45	MC GALIN, Andrew	LAN 215	Robert	FAY 236		
Robert	MIF 4	MC GANCKER, James	LAN 246	Wm.	BEV 28		
Robert	HNT 154	MC GARBY, Hannah	MNT 117	Wm.	PHI 73A		
Robt.	CUM 116	MC GARGEN, James	PHI 136	Wm.	PHI 113A		
Robt.	CUM 126	MC GARGLE, -----		MC GEEHEN, Brice?	BEV 10		
Wm.	CUM 123	Widow	MNT 41	MC GEHAN, Samuel	HNT 135		
MC FARLEN, Jennet	LAN 165	Jacob	MNT 41	MC GELL, Robert	FAY 210		
MC FARLIN, Agnis	MER 453	Jas. Junr.	MNT 38	William	BUC 83		
Alexander	BUC 149A	Jonathan	MNT 37	MC GEONIGLE,			
Andw.	PHA 41	MC GARGUE, John	PHI 137	Senr.	CEN 20A		
Francis	MER 453	Joseph	PHI 155	MC GERR, Nathl.	LAN 13		
James	LAN 126	MC GARGY,		MC GEW?, Wm.	LYC 24		
James	LAN 127	Benjamin	PHI 146	MC GHEE, Patrick	WST 154		
John	LAN 126	Joseph	PHI 147	MC GIBBEN, Hugh	BEV 5		
John	MER 453	MC GARL, Hugh	VEN 165	MC GIGIN, John	FAY 232		
John Jnr.	LAN 126	MC GARROUGH,		MC GIL---?, James	FRA 315		
Margaret	PHA 117	Joseph	FAY 267	MC GILL--IS?, Wm	PHI 117		
William	LAN 124	MC GARVEY,		MC GILL, Widow	PHI 28		
William	FAY 253	Connell	DEL 188	Widow	PHI 34		
Wm.	FRA 303	Samuel	PHA 93	Authen	CRA 6		
MC FARLING, Robt.	PHI 99A	MC GARVY, John	PHI 5	Esther	GRN 83		
Wm.	PHI 80A	Nanthony	ALL 112	Henry	PHA 110		
MC FARON, Mary	PHI 96A	MC GARY, Peter	BFD 40	Hugh	FAY 210		
MC FARQUER, Colon		MC GASGLE, Allen	MNT 35	John	DAU 43		
Revd.	LAN 13	Isaac	MNT 36	John	PHI 50		
MC FARREN, Andrew	HNT 136	John	MNT 36	Margaret			
Matthew	BFD 58	MC GASLEY, John	MNT 55	(Boarding			
William	NOH 67	MC GATHOM?,		House)	PHA 9		
William Jr.	NOH 67	Joseph	ERI 60A	Margit	ALL 85		
MC FARSON,		MC GATRON?,		Margit	ALL 101		
Alexander	LAN 125	Joseph	ERI 60A	Patrick	CRA 7		
Edward	FAY 262	Thomas	ERI 60A	Robert	ALL 66		
Pat.	WST 240	MC GAUEN, John	NOH 65	Samuel	GRN 86		
MC FARTH, Manus	LAN 263	John Junr.	NOH 65	Stephen	PHA 68		
MC FATE, Robert	WST 220	MC GAUER, John	HNT 131	William	MNT 63		
MC FATORS, John	PHI 65	MC GAUGHEY, Danl.	WST 221	MC GILLIH,			
MC FATUSK, Heckla	DAU 47	Saml.	CUM 48	Patrick	PHI 5		
MC FAUL, Jas.	CUM 39	William	BFD 55	MC GIMSY, Joseph	ADA 5		
MC FEARSON,		MC GAUGHY, John	WST 349	MC GIN?, Thomas	ALL 89		
Daniel	PHA 113	Thos.	WST 348	MC GINIS, James	NOU 199		
MC FEE, Widow	PHI 4	MC GAUGY, John	PHA 101	MC GINLAY, James	HNT 165		
MC FEELY,		MC GAURIN, Edwd.	CUM 96	MC GINLEY,			
Barnabas	HNT 166	MC GAUROUGH,		Cornelius	DEL 187		
John	CUM 77	Robert	FAY 267	Jacob	ARM 124		
MC FEGIN?, Capt?	PHI 1	MC GAVARD, Hugh	FAY 210	John	PHI 44		
MC FELLAMY,		MC GAVEN, Michl.	PHI 54	John	FRA 294		
Patrick	PHA 87	MC GAW, James	BEV 6	John	BUT 334		
MC FENNEL, David	LAN 292	James	PHI 71A	Michl.	FRA 298		
MC FERCY?, John	VEN 167	John	MNT 142	Neal	LAN 96		
MC FERREN, Andrew	HNT 117	John	WST 240	Neal	DEL 190		
John	NOU 172	Patr.	FRA 323	Willm.	PHI 50		
Jos.	BUT 350	MC GEARY, Jno.	CUM 66	Wm.	FRA 301		
Joseph	ALL 114	Michl.	CUM 34	MC GINLEY?,			
MC FERRIN, Henry	FRA 281	Patrick	CUM 34	Colem?	ARM 122		
Jacob	FRA 283	Wm.	WST 370	MC GINLY,			
Jno.	FRA 305	Wm.	WST 370	Cornelius	DEL 171		
Thos. Revd.	FRA 291	Wm.	WST 371	David	FRA 302		
MC FERRON, Joseph	ALL 84	MC GEAUGHLIN,		John	VEN 166		
MC FERSON, Jas.	LAN 162	Francis	NOU 111	Neal	DEL 171		
MC FETERS, James	HNT 143	MC GEE, Alexr.	CUM 152	Neal	DEL 188		
MC FETTERS,		Andrew	HNT 162	MC GINNES,			
Michael	MER 453	Anthony	PHI 38	Charles	BUT 342		
Patrick	FAY 205	Bernard	NOU 159	Daniel	NOH 30A		
MC FIELD, Widow	PHI 35	Charles	HNT 141	Francis	WST 370		
James	ALL 119	Gabriel	PHI 5	Jesse	NOH 30A		
John	PHI 39	Henry	NOU 118	John	WST 370		
MC FIRE, Jean	LAN 165	James	PHA 104	Philip	PHA 99		
John	LAN 162	James	NOU 130	Robt.	BUT 325		
MC FLASKY, James	PHI 45	James	BUT 345	Saml.	WST 239		
MC FORD, Widow	PHI 21	James	CEN 18A	MC GINNESS, James			
MC FREDERICK,	LAN 22	John	MIF 4	Jr.	CUM 24		
James							

MC GINNESS, James			MC GLOUGHLIN,			MC GREW,		
Senr.	CUM	23	Robt. Jur.	FAY	205	Archabald	WST	255
John	CUM	95	William	FAY	267	Archd.	CUM	70
MC GINNIGLE, Wm.	MNT	71	MC GLOWEN,			Archibald	ADA	15
MC GINNIS, Andrew	LAN	169	Patrick	PHI	112	Archibald	ADA	42
Andrew	LAN	242	MC GLUE, Luke	PHA	102	Findley	WST	255
James	HNT	161	MC GLUMPY, John	GRN	102	James	WST	254
James	LAN	169	MC GO--?, Maskel	MNT	54	James	WST	254
James Junr.	HNT	161	MC GOFFEN, Joseph	PHA	16	James	BUT	339
John	GRN	102	MC GOGNY, John	ALL	84	John	ADA	42
John	HNT	159	MC GOLDRICK,			John	FAY	253
Mathew	SOM	143	James	ALL	119	John	FAY	258
Neal	PHI	26	MC GOLLEN,			Joseph	WST	255
Paul	HNT	120	Francis	LAN	163	Nathan	ADA	39
Robert	LAN	169	MC GOMERY, Mary	CUM	88	Peter	ADA	39
William	ADA	40	MC GONAGLE,			Phillip	FAY	210
William	LAN	158	Archibald	DEL	192	Simon	WST	254
William	HNT	159	Jas.	CEN	23	William	ADA	20
Wm.	CEN	20A	MC GONEGHY, David	CUM	122	William	ADA	42
MC GINNISS,			MC GONIGAL,			William	WST	254
Arthur	PHA	110	George	ALL	49	William	WST	256
MC GINSTY, Robt.	FRA	309	MC GONIGLE, Thos.	CEN	20A	Wm.	WST	254
MC GIR?, Thomas	ALL	89	MC GOOGIN, Hugh	BUC	155A	Wm.	WST	254
MC GITTEGEN?,			MC GOOGY, Daniel	BUC	95	MC GRIFF,		
Charles	BEV	10	MC GOOHIN, John	BUC	85A	Elizabeth	WST	381
MC GIVER, Wm.	PHI	68	MC GORGON, Thomas	ADA	6	MC GRIGER, Mary	ALL	103
MC GIVILLEN,			MC GORMAN, James	PHI	14	Mathew	ALL	100
Garret	CEN	23	MC GORN, Patrick	PHA	28	Wilm.	ALL	103
MC GLADE, J./ I.?	DAU	45	MC GOUCH, Edwd.	PHI	26	MC GRIGGER, John	ALL	60
MC GLASAN, John	FRA	297	MC GOUGH, Arthur	HNT	123	MC GRIGOR, John	PHI	37
MC GLASKEY,			MC GOUGHLIN,			MC GROTE, Edward	PHA	111
Daniel	PHI	51	Willm.	FAY	210	MC GUCKIN,		
MC GLASSIN, Saml.	PHI	26	MC GOWAN, Andw.	BUT	342	Patrick	DEL	176
MC GLATHENY,			David	CUM	84	MC GUFFIN,		
Mordica	PHA	18	John	BUT	322	Ebinezer	ALL	51
MC GLATHEREY,			John	BUT	322	George	WST	292
James	PHA	17	Owen	PHA	120	Robert	WST	292
MC GLATHERY,			Samuel	HNT	121	Robert	WST	292
Widow	PHI	38	MC GOWEN, Daniel	DEL	172	MC GUIER, Roger	WST	276
Isaac	MNT	115	Patrick	ERI	60A	MC GUIN, Hugh	FAY	205
MC GLATTENY,			Thos.	PHI	92A	MC GUINLY,		
Sarah	MNT	118	Wm.	PHI	81	Charles	NOU	172
MC GLATTURY,			MC GOWIN, Adam	FAY	251	MC GUIRE, Archd.	WST	172
William	MNT	70	John	BER	273	Bernard	WST	348
MC GLAUGHLIN,			Nathaniel	BER	275	Bridget	HNT	163
Andw.	NOU	199	MC GOWN, Charrels	ALL	84	Catharine	FRA	326
Buryman	BUT	341	John	ALL	87	Charrels	ALL	62
Chas.	WST	326	John	ALL	104	Cornelius	HNT	123
Danl.	CUM	133	Samuel	ALL	83	Daniel	FRA	289
Danl.	MNT	142	Samuel	ALL	104	Francis	PHI	38
Danl.	WST	153	MC GRA, George	PHA	32	George	WST	349
Danl.	WST	154	MC GRADY, Alexr.	NOU	199	Hugh	MNT	42
James	PHA	93	Gavin	BUC	154A	Hugh	HNT	163
James	PHA	104	John	BUC	154A	James	BEV	6
James	NOU	199	Sarah	PHI	115A	James	HNT	123
James	BUT	323	MC GRAFF, Michael	PHA	88	James	SOM	162
Jno.	CUM	41	MC GRAHAM, Geo	PHI	81A	James	WST	275
Patrick	BUT	336	Robt.	PHI	43	John	GRN	89
Thomas	ARM	127	MC GRAND, Hugh	LAN	48	John	FAY	210
William	ARM	123	MC GRANDLES, John	WST	256	John	WST	349
Willm.	BUT	362	MC GRATH, Jno.	FRA	286	Luke	HNT	123
Wm.	NOU	200	MC GRAW, Francis	HNT	144	Michael	PHA	111
MC GLAUGLIN, Mrs.	NOU	199	Francis	HNT	163	Michael	HNT	163
Patk.	CUM	90	MC GREADY,			Michael	FAY	253
MC GLENNY, Neal	FAY	233	William	CRA	6	Nicholas	BFD	64
MC GLIMMING,			MC GREEGER, James	MIF	4	Peter	HNT	123
Geoe.	PHI	37	MC GREGGOR,			Philip	LAN	120
MC GLOCHLIN,			Duncan	BEV	7	Rachel	HNT	123
James	ADA	13	MC GREGOR, Alexr.	BFD	75	Richard	HNT	123
MC GLOGIN,			John	BFD	75	Richard	FAY	267
Patrick	NOU	166	John	WST	348	Ross	ADA	4
MC GLOUGHLEN,			MC GREGORY,			Saml.	WST	193
Robt.	FAY	205	William	LUZ	349	Thos.	LYC	28
MC GLOUGHLIN,			William	NOH	78A	Thos.	WST	220
John	FAY	205	MC GREW, Alexr.	WST	255	Widow	LAN	48
Robt.	FAY	258	Alexr. Sen.	ADA	39	MC GUMERY, Charles	FAY	205

MC GUMERY, Jesse	FAY 201	MC INNIS,		MC KEAN, Jane	LUZ 405
Oliver	FAY 251	Cornelon	PHI 28	John	BEV 10
William	FAY 204	MC INTAG, Hugh	CUM 111	John	WST 193
MC GUNEGAL, James	FAY 228	MC INTIER,		Mathew	DAU 8A
MC GUNIGLE,		Alexander	LAN 33	Robert	MIF 4
Charles	ARM 123	Hugh	LAN 58	Robt.	FRA 274
MC GUNNES, George	PHI 49	MC INTINE, James	CRA 13	Thomas	FRA 272
MC GUNNY, Hugh	LAN 177	MC INTIRE, Widow	PHI 93A	Thos.	PHI 68
MC GURK, Stephn.	CUM 152	Alexr.	WST 153	Wm.	WST 370
MC HAFFEE, Domeck	LAN 152	Daniel	GRN 102	MC KEANE, John	
MC HAFFY, Wilm.	ALL 62	David	WST 349	Jr.	WST 193
MC HARG, Peter	WST 172	George	WST 381	MC KEARN, Widow	PHI 26
Wm.	BEV 26	Henry	CUM 107	James	PHA 73
MC HART, William	BER 160	Hugh	WST 154	MC KEARY,	
MC HEE, James	MER 451	James	PHA 61	Alexander	LAN 229
MC HEIL, Hector	NOH 65	James	WST 348	MC KEE, Adam	CEN 22B
MC HELVY, James	MIF 4	Jno.	CUM 121	Alexander	LAN 125
MC HENRY,		Jno.	CUM 126	Alexander	ERI 55A
Benjamin	NOU 152	John	BFD 75	Alexr.	WST 219
Charles	PHI 95A	John	PHI 86A	Andrew	ARM 123
Daniel	NOU 152	Joseph	WST 240	Andw.	MIF 17A
Dannel	ALL 52	Mary	PHA 74	Archibald	FAY 267
Francis	FRA 296	Robert	ADA 21	Benjn.	FRA 318
Isaac	WST 153	Robt.	PHI 98	Danl. Sr.	CUM 45
James	WST 153	Robt.	CUM 139	Danl. Senr.	CUM 45
John	ALL 101	Robt. Senr.	CUM 137	David	CUM 120
John	WST 275	Saml.	WST 240	David	WST 371
Joseph	GRN 107	Sarah	CUM 74	George	ALL 100
Malcom	WST 292	William	ERI 58	George	NOU 167
Ritchard	ALL 94	William	LAN 164	George	FRA 319
Robert	ALL 76	William	WST 254	Hugh	FRA 295
Thomas	NOU 152	Wm.	BEV 18	Hugh	WST 326
William	ERI 60	Wm.	CUM 139	Hugh	MER 451
Wilm.	ALL 94	MC INTOSH, Andrew	BEV 7	Hugh Senr.	WST 326
Wm.	BUC 91	David	VEN 166	Hugh	MIF 15A
MC HIRE, William	LAN 161	Jas.	CEN 22B	Isabella	DAU 20A
MC HIRTER, Hugh	NOU 118	MC INTYRE,		James	ALL 59
MC HOLLAND, Hugh	PHI 150	Alexander	HNT 145	James	ALL 106
MC HOLLEN, John	PHI 25	James	HNT 122	James	ALL 108
MC HOSE, Saml.	NOH 48	MC JENNET, John	CEN 20A	James	HNT 140
William	NOH 48	MC JILTON,		James	WST 154
MC HURLEY, Mrs.	NOU 199	Benjamin	DEL 171	James	FRA 318
MC IL-ONE?, Hugh	PHI 49	MC JUNCKINGS,		James	WST 327
MC ILHANEY, Wm.	PHA 21	Wilm.	ALL 67	James	MER 452
MC ILHENY, James	NOH 67	MC JUNKINS, David	BUT 325	Jas.	CUM 51
Thomas	NOH 67A	MC KAIN, Joseph		Jno.	CUM 52
MC ILHINNY, James	ADA 25	B.	PHA 36	Jno.	CUM 137
Robert	ADA 21	Margaret	PHA 111	Jno. Senr.	CUM 52
Robert	ADA 29	Robert	PHA 49	John	LAN 62
Samuel	ADA 26	Robert	WST 254	John	NOH 65
MC ILHOOSE,		Thos. Hon.	PHA 92	John	ALL 71
George	MNT 93	MC KAKEY, Mathew	BEV 25	John	GRN 72
MC ILLHENY, Robt.	WST 347	MC KALL, Daniel	DAU 29	John	GRN 84
MC ILLHOSE, Thos.	WST 153	MC KANE, James	NOU 166	John	FRA 295
MC ILNNY?,		John	NOU 166	John	FRA 318
Rodrick	ALL 52	MC KANN, Daniel	ADA 9	John	MIF 15A
MC ILROY, John	HNT 140	MC KANNEL, John	PHI 51	John	CEN 18A
Thomas	MIF 4	MC KASKEY, John	WST 221	John	MIF 25A
MC ILVAINE,		MC KASKY, John	WST 275	Joseph	ARM 127
Ferguson	PHA 122	MC KAY, Alexr.	PHI 20	Martha	WST 219
Isaac	DEL 186	Daniel	NOU 172	Patrick	ERI 55A
James	DEL 186	Neal	NOU 172	Robert	ALL 96
Jeremiah	DEL 186	Susannah	PHA 92	Robert	NOU 159
John	PHA 99	Thos.	PHA 78	Robert	NOU 167
John	DEL 186	William	NOU 172	Robert	WST 220
MC ILWAIN, Andrew	ADA 22	Wm.	PHI 47	Robert	FAY 222
Andrew	ADA 33	MC KEAG, Hugh	DAU 43	Robert	LAN 286
Jno.	MIF 25A	MC KEAGS, Patrick	LAN 178	Robert	LAN 311
Joh	ADA 0	MC KEAL,		Robt.	CUM 52
Moses	ADA 27	Catharine	CHE 740	Samuel	LAN 120
Rebecah	ADA 23	MC KEAN, Alexd.	FRA 281	Samuel	WST 221
Robert	WST 256	Andrew	LAN 160	Susana	ALL 72
MC INDAFFER, Geo.	WST 220	Culbertson	FRA 272	Thomas	ADA 2
MC INELTY, James	NOU 166	George	BEV 12	Thomas	HNT 159
MC INLY, Tarrance	NOU 167	James	WST 292	Thomas	FAY 267
MC INNES, Dunkin	PHA 4	James	LUZ 406		

MC MASTER, James	FRA 292	MC MONAGLE, Hugh	VEN 170	MC MULLIN, Saml.	BUT 361
Jas. Jr.	WST 275	Mary	PHA 96	MC MULLON,
William	FAY 198	MC MONEYGHE, John	PHA 116	Danniel	ALL 67
MC MASTERS,		MC MULLAN,		James	GRN 77
Andrew	ALL 119	Charrels	ALL 95	MC MUN, Alexd.	ALL 63
James	BUC 151A	Danl.	WST 154	Dannel	ALL 63
John	MNT 38	Elizabeth	ALL 94	Joseph	ALL 107
John	ALL 65	James	ALL 50	MC MURDIE, John	FRA 290
Wm.	WST 348	James	ALL 83	MC MURDY, Robert	ADA 12
MC MATH, Daniel	ALL 81	James	ALL 88	MC MURRAY, Alexr.	WST 239
John	WST 219	John	ALL 72	Elizabeth	GRN 102
Samuel	HNT 142	Laurence	HNT 123	John	GRN 102
MC MAUGHIN, John	DAU 15A	Patrick	HNT 121	Joseph	NOU 166
MC MAUL, John	ALL 62	Patrick	HNT 150	Thos.	CUM 94
MC MEAN, Jno.	CUM 70	Peter	HNT 150	MC MURRIN,
Robert	BEV 13	Samuel	HNT 141	Francis	FRA 283
Wm.	CUM 69	Thomas	ALL 88	MC MURRY, Jas.	LYC 27
MC MEANS,		Thomas	ALL 107	Joseph	FRA 276
Archibald	ARM 127	Thomas	HNT 150	Wm.	CUM 62
Joseph	BUT 315	Wilm.	ALL 71	MC MURTNEY,
Wm.	LYC 21	MC MULLEN, Widow	PHI 5	Joseph	CRA 12
MC MENEANY, Patk.	CEN 23	Alexr.	PHI 144	MC MURTREY?, (See
MC MENNY, Rubin	FAY 233	Alexr.	FAY 210	Mc Murtney)	CRA 12
MC MICAL, Samuel	ALL 94	Daniel	LUZ 346	MC MURTRIE, David	HNT 154
MC MICEL, Isaac	ALL 107	Duncan	DEL 155	James	HNT 155
John	ALL 107	Geo.	CUM 48	MC MUTON, George	ALL 87
MC MICHAEL,		George	CUM 140	MC MUTREE, Wm.	PHA 113
Archid.	BER 162	Hugh	FRA 322	MC NACHTINE,
Christian	BUT 328	James	PHI 133	Cornelia	PHA 58
Danl.	PHI 46	James	FAY 210	MC NAGHTON, James	LAN 56
John	CRA 14	James	FRA 321	MC NAIL, Daniel	CHE 764
Robert	BUT 328	Jas.	WST 240	MC NAIR, Alex	ADA 2
Robt.	BUT 329	Jas.	BUC 141A	Ann	ALL 64
Thomas	CRA 17	John	MIF 4	Archibald	LAN 242
William	NOU 150	John	PHI 14	David	ERI 56
MC MICHAEN,		John	NOU 118	Dunning	ALL 63
Joseph	CRA 17	John	WST 349	James	BUC 151A
MC MICHAEN?, (See		John	LUZ 376	John	NOH 30A
Michaen?)	CRA 17	Mary	MIF 2	John	BUC 143A
MC MICHAL, James	FRA 294	Mary	FRA 321	Robert	ERI 55A
MC MICHALE, John	BER 161	Micl.	LAN 279	Sam	ADA 2
MC MICHEAL, Anne	WST 294	Robert	FAY 239	Saml.	NOH 30A
MC MICHL.,		Robt.	PHI 47	Samuel	MNT 51
William	BER 161	Robt.	FRA 326	Thos.	DAU 23
MC MICKEN, Andw.		Robt.	MIF 7A	Thos.	CUM 114
& Chas.	BUC 154A	Rose	PHA 116	William	ERI 60
Chas. (See Mc		Samuel	ADA 12	MC NAMARA, Jas.	CUM 37
Micken,		Thos.	NOH 48	John	HNT 155
Andw.)	BUC 154A	William Jr.	ADA 4	Richard	LUZ 384
Cormick	BUC 99	William Jr.	ADA 4	MC NATEN,
James	LYC 26	Willm.	PHI 14	Alexander	BER 248
MC MICLE, David	MER 453	Willm.	PHI 25	MC NATTON, Alexr.	CEN 23
MC MILLEN, John	WST 349	Wm.	CEN 23	MC NAUGHT, Edwd.	MIF 15
Marey	FAY 253	Wm.	PHA 77	Hugh	WAS 23
Robert	PHI 27	MC MULLIN, Alexr.	CHE 839	John	MIF 17A
Robert	WST 349	Charles	CHE 827	MC NAUGHTON, Jno.	CUM 43
Thomas	HNT 132	Daniel	HNT 142	Patk.	CUM 27
Wm.	CUM 127	Daniel	DAU 27A	MC NAUL, James	ALL 111
MC MILLIN, ------	MER 448	Eneas	HNT 135	MC NEAL, Widow	PHI 15
Daniel	MER 455	Geo.	CHE 819	Alexr.	CHE 757
Stewart	LAN 240	James	HNT 141	Andrew	CHE 757
MC MILLUS, Jane	LAN 239	James	SOM 143	Archbd.	MIF 25A
MC MIN, Hugh	LAN 121	James	FRA 296	Benjn.	CEN 19
MC MINN, Andrew	BUC 103A	James Sen.	SOM 143	Daniel	MNT 43
James	CHE 743	Jas.	CHE 813	Danl.	PHI 15
James	BUC 154A	John	NOU 118	Danl.	CUM 66
Robert	ALL 112	John	HNT 141	Issabella	CUM 95
Saml.	CHE 830	John	HNT 142	James	CUM 48
Saml.	CHE 835	John	SOM 143	James	HNT 142
MC MISTERY, Hugh	NOU 138	John	FRA 287	James	WST 162
MC MITCHENOR,		John	CHE 728	John	LYC 25
Price	PHI 147	Michl.	MIF 25A	John	MNT 106
MC MOLLIN,		Mrs.	NOU 118	John	PHA 116
Michael	LAN 281	Mrs.	NOU 155	John	LAN 127
MC MONAGH, Wm.	MIF 15A	Mrs.	NOU 180	Pat.	FRA 285
MC MONAGLE, Daniel	HNT 159	Robert	PHI 15	Robert	NOU 118

269

MC NEAL, Saml.	NOH	30A	MC NUTT, Jos.	FRA	281	MC ROY, John	LAN 164
Sarah	SOM	143	Matthew	WST	348	MC ROYDS, Mrs.	NOU 199
William	HNT	125	MC NUTTY, Michael	LAN	126	MC S----Y?,	
William	CHE	738	MC OLEVY, William	HNT	159	Barnabas	ADA 3
Zaughby	LAN	131	MC PA-TERAGE?,			MC SALOCK?,	
MC NEALY, George	DEL	172	George	MER	453	Alexr.	PHI 29
MC NEAR, Robert	WST	172	MC PAID, David	PHI	49	MC SHAIN, Robt.	FAY 246
William	MIF	17	MC PAKE, Ewd.	FRA	319	MC SHANE,	
MC NEEL, John	ALL	80	MC PEACK, James	PHA	54	Barnabas	PHA 19
Laughlin	MIF	15	MC PEAK, Daniel	FAY	262	Margeret	PHA 93
MC NEELAN, Wilm.	ALL	84	Sarah	ADA	7	MC SHERRY, Cady	FAY 239
MC NEELY,			MC PEEK, John	FAY	198	James	ADA 27
Charrels	ALL	93	Wm.	PHA	4	John	ADA 24
David	MNT	112	MC PHAIL, John	PHA	98	Widow	ADA 24
James	GRN	77	MC PHAN, David	WST	292	William	ADA 2
Robert	GRN	83	MC PHARSON, John	NOU	176	William	ADA 6
MC NEELY?, Widow	LAN	246	MC PHEARSON, John	PHA	3	MC SPARRAN, James	LAN 150
MC NEER, David	SOM	146	MC PHERRIN, John			MC SPARRIN, Jos.	CEN 20A
James	SOM	146	Revd.	WST	348	MC SPARRON,	
Robert	SOM	146	Saml.	WST	349	Willm.	PHI 69A
Samuel	SOM	146	Wm.	WST	348	MC SPERIN, Duncan	BUT 364
MC NEES, Jas.	BUT	364	MC PHERSON, Widow	PHI	18	MC SURLY, James	FRA 296
Willm.	BUT	364	Alexr.	PHI	43	MC SWADY, Dennis	DEL 178
MC NEIL, Hyram	MNT	63	Hugh	PHI	16	MC TAGUE, Patrick	NOU 118
James	MNT	64	James	HNT	134	MC TATE, John	WST 220
James	BUC	146	John	PHI	24	MC TEER, James	MIF 4
William	NOU	166	John	HNT	122	MC TOWN, James	FAY 198
MC NEILL,			John	NOU	130	MC UNLY, John	LAN 309
Archibald	HNT	164	John	DEL	192	MC VAEY, Patrick	NOU 166
James	LUZ	359	Joseph	HNT	145	MC VAIN, Patrick	LAN 161
MC NELEY, Andw.	PHA	40	Nathaniel	NOU	189	MC VAUGH, Aquilla	MNT 138
MC NELL, John	MIF	15	Thomas	HNT	145	Benjamin	MNT 87
Robert	VEN	167	William Esq.	ADA	7	Charles	MNT 88
MC NEWART, Geoe.	PHI	55	Wm.	PHA	83	Jacob	MNT 67
MC NICKLE, Alexr.	CUM	132	Wm.	CUM	90	Joseph	MNT 132
Arthur	HNT	134	Wm.	CUM	28	William	PHI 142
MC NIDLY,			MC QUAD, Wm.			MC VAY, & Camble	LAN 156
Cornelious	PHI	114	MC QUADE, Patrick	WST	327	Daniel	LAN 156
MC NIELD,			Patrick	WST	371	Enoch	MIF 25A
Jonathan	CHE	772	MC QUE, Daniel	WST	327	George	NOU 118
MC NIER, George	PHI	51	MC QUEAS, John	CRA	10	Isaac	GRN 107
MC NIGHT, Alexr.	WST	153	MC QUIGGY, Robt.	MIF	25A	James Junr.	GRN 107
Arthur	MIF	13	MC QUILKIN, Jas.	WST	327	James Senr.	GRN 107
Dennis	SOM	143	MC QUILLAN,			William	GRN 107
James	ALL	103	Edward	LUZ	413	MC VEAR, Thomas	PHI 49
James	NOU	166	MC QUILLER, John	SOM	154	MC VEAS, Matts.	PHI 29
John	ALL	57	MC QUILLIN, Abrm.	PHI	50	MC VEE, Solomon	LAN 309
John	ALL	70	MC QUIN, David	NOU	166	MC VEY, Hugh	WST 154
John	ALL	80	James	NOU	97A	Patrick	WST 370
Joseph	ALL	96	Robt.	CUM	104	MC VICAR, Duncan	HNT 158
Thomas?	ALL	79	MC QUINN, Anthony	LAN	13	MC VICKER, Alexr.	BFD 74
MC NIKLE, Alexdr.	VEN	165	MC QUIRE, Jas.	CUM	56	David	BFD 74
MC NINCH, Patrick	NOU	159	Wm.	CUM	53	Duncan	BFD 74
Samuel	NOU	118	MC QUISTON, James	WST	348	Joseph	BFD 75
MC NIT, Barny	DAU	23	John	BEV	7	William	NOU 159
MC NITT, Joseph	BEV	10	John	WST	219	MC VINES, Widow	PHI 21
Robt.	MIF	15A	John	BUT	319	MC VINIA, Owen	MNT 54
Saml.	MIF	15A	Robt.	WST	348	MC VITEY, Ewd.	FRA 324
Wm.	MIF	15	Wm.	WST	348	John	FRA 324
MC NODEY, John	LAN	306	MC QUITZ, William	LAN	93	MC WALLISTER,	
MC NOLDY, Samuel	MNT	135	MC QUOWN, David	WST	348	John	MNT 62
MC NORRING, M.	PHI	10	James	BUC	155A	MC WAUGH, Revd.	CUM 62
MC NORTHEY, Elias	FAY	253	William	BUC	154A	MC WAYNE, Widow	PHI 112
MC NORTON, John	ALL	62	MC QUWAN, Robt.	FRA	290	MC WHARTER,	
Wilm.	ALL	116	MC RAE?, Andw.	PHI	93A	Thomas Esqr.	NOH 69
MC NULTY, James	ALL	87	MC RIGHT, Charles	BUT	355	MC WILLER, James	SOM 129
Peter	SOM	158	MC RINEHART?,			MC WILLIAMS,	
MC NULY?, Widow	LAN	246	Geo.	BER	189	Alexander	FAY 232
MC NUT, Benjamin	LAN	156	MC ROBERTS, James	ALL	84	Alexr.	CEN 23
James	HNT	131	James	ALL	86	Geo.	WST 193
John	BFD	51	James	FRA	300	George	PHI 81
William	WST	153	John	ALL	84	George	MER 454
Wilm.	ALL	110	Robt.	DAU	17A	Henry	HNT 145
MC NUTT, Francis	ADA	15	Wm.	DAU	17A	Hugh	LAN 91
John	HNT	155	MC RORY, Saml.	MIF	15	James	MIF 2
John	LAN	164	MC ROY, James	PHI	98	James	NOU 166
			John	PHI	97		

MC WILLIAMS,			MEANS, Thoms.	BUT 349	MECKLIN, Joseph	BUC 141A		
James	YOR	185	William	WST 255	Samuel Jr.	PHI 131		
James	WST	193	William	LUZ 413	MECKLINE, Jacob	MNT 60		
James	NOU	199	Wm.	FRA 317	Philip	MNT 60		
James	MER	453	MEAR?, James	FRA 290	MECORMACK, Hugh	FAY 258		
Jas.	FRA	281	MEARNS, John	PHA 83	MECS?, Daniel	BUC 148		
Jas.	MIF	15A	Robt. & Mary	BUC 154A	MEDARY?, Jacob	MNT 88		
John	ADA	13	Robt. & Wm.	BUC 154A	MEDCALF, Edward	WAS 29		
John	NOU	118	Wm. (See		Vachel	WAS 29		
John	FAY	216	Mearns,		Vachel Senr.	WAS 30		
John	FRA	318	Robt.)	BUC 154A	MEDD, John	CRA 5		
Mrs.	NOU	144	MEARS, Alexd.	FRA 279	MEDDARD, Jacob	FAY 253		
Robert	NOU	118	Benjamin	PHA 117	MEDDAUGH, C.			
Samuel	HNT	144	Benjamin	HNT 124	Henry	WAY 144		
Samuel	FAY	216	Fredk.	BER 243	Cornelius	WAY 144		
Thomas	ALL	60	James	HNT 124	MEDDICK, George	PHA 88		
William	NOU	166	James	LUZ 344	MEDDIS, Gidion	FAY 236		
William	WST	193	John	NOU 111	MEDEITH, Benjamin	PHI 114		
MC WINGLE, John	VEN	170	John	WST 292	MEDER, John	DAU 17		
MC WORTER, John	NOU	138	Joseph	HNT 124	MEDILL, Hugh	ALL 79		
MC---RRAN, John	ALL	89	Samuel	NOU 111	MEDLEY, William	WAS 86		
MC, (Also See			William	NOU 111	MEDOCK, John	MIF 8		
Muc)	MER	450	MEARSE, David	NOU 199	MEDOWEL, David	MER 452		
MCCLURE, James	ADA	7	Lawrence	NOU 199	MEE, Elizabeth	BER 273		
Jennet	ADA	12	MEAS., George	DAU 35A	John	CHE 891		
MCCULLOUGH, Sarah	DAU	2	MEAS, Daniel	BER 132	Thomas	CHE 894		
MCDONNALD, Marey	FAY	215	MEASE, Barney	DAU 51A	MEED?, Nathan	FRA 274		
MCFERRAN, Ann	ADA	1	George	DAU 34	MEEK, Bazil	WAS 123		
MCLOY, George	MIF	8	Henry	DAU 51	James	FRA 275		
Patrick	FAY	222	James	PHA 80	John Junr.	WAS 123		
MCVAY, John	MIF	25A	John	PHA 7	John Senr.	WAS 123		
ME ELHOSE, Robert	LUZ	424	John	DAU 51	Mathew	CHE 870		
MEAD, Darius	WAR	1A	Ph.	DAU 36	Nicholas	LAN 108		
David Esqr.	CRA	2	MEASHY, Jacob	LAN 256	Philip	LAN 108		
Ezekiel	WAY	135	John	LAN 255	Samuel	SOM 134		
George	PHA	73	John Senr.	LAN 256	William	WAS 123		
James	PHI	17	MEASKY, John	LAN 266A	William	WAS 123		
John	PHA	62	MEASON, George	BEV 16	MEEK?, Jacob	DAU 2		
Joseph	WAR	1A	George	FAY 216	MEEKER, Amos	LUZ 349		
Robert	PHI	3	Isaac Esqr.	FAY 251	Arron	LUZ 349		
MEADDOCK, Mosses	WAR	1A	John	FAY 216	Forrest	WAS 123		
MEADE, Richard W.	PHA	118	John	FAY 228	Grove	WAS 123		
MEAGOR, Edy	ALL	78	John Esqr.	FAY 198	Isaac	WAS 45		
MEAL, Jno.	CUM	107	John Jur.	FAY 216	Jacob	LUZ 349		
MEALBANK, Samuel	PHA	105	Martin	FAY 216	Jeremiah	LUZ 391		
MEALEY, George	CHE	778	Martin Jur.	FAY 216	Samuel	PHI 34		
MEALMAN, Adam	FRA	327	Phillip	FAY 216	Timothy	LUZ 349		
MEALY, Philip	GRN	72	Thomas	WST 326	MEEKES, Valentine	NOH 36		
MEAN, Elisha	NOH	65	MEAST, Henry	BER 176	MEEKLY, Henry	YOR 186		
John	BEV	18	MEATER, Phillip	FAY 241	MEEKS, Adam	WAS 112		
MEANICH, Leonard	FRA	276	MEBANE?/ MEBUNI?,		David	FRA 292		
MEANOM, Michael	CRA	12	Ann	PHA 5	Elisha	GRN 107		
MEANOR, Saml.	WST	371	MEBRINE?, Mary	YOR 199	John	GRN 109		
William	FRA	320	MEC MILLIN, John	MER 452	Peter	WAS 69		
MEANS, Andrew	DEL	158	Thomas	MER 452	Samuel	WAS 69		
Benjamin	WAS	102	MECALF, Ezekiah	BEV 24	William	WAS 76		
Catharine	YOR	158	MECARTNEY, Robert	MER 452	MEEKS?, (See			
Daniel	BFD	51	MECASKI, James	LAN 172	Micks)	FRA 292		
David	WST	255	MECELBURY,		MEELLY, John	ALL 106		
Hugh	HNT	148	Charles	PHI 72	MEELUNG, Marty	LAN 177		
Hugh	MER	454	MECHLEHENEY, John	MER 449	MEEM, John	NOH 45A		
Isaac	WST	255	MECHLIN, Saml.	PHA 59	MEENACHAN, Andrew	LAN 3		
James	MIF	8	Samuel	PHI 133	MEENAN, Darby	HNT 164		
James	CUM	152	MECHLING, John	NOH 56A	MEENER, Isaac	ALL 109		
James	WST	255	MECK, David	HNT 145	Isaac	ALL 109		
James	WST	327	George	HNT 145	Samuel	ALL 109		
John	CUM	152	Robert	HNT 145	Samuel	ALL 110		
John	WST	240	William	HNT 145	MEENES?, Joseph	ALL 110		
John	FRA	308	MECK?, (See Meek)	LAN 108	MEENS, Adam	ALL 117		
Marshall	FRA	308	Henry	DAU 8	Allon	ALL 110		
Martha	FRA	321	Jacob	DAU 2	Andrew	ALL 114		
Patrick	WAS	112	MECKEL, Ludwig	NOH 60	John	ALL 81		
Robert	MIF	17	Ludwig Junr.	NOH 60A	Martha	ALL 88		
Robert	BUT	349	MECKES, Jacob	NOH 74	Samuel	ALL 105		
Saml.	CEN	19	MECKLE, George	YOR 191	MEER?, John	PHA 79		
Samuel	BFD	35	MECKLEREVY, James	MER 450	MEES?, Daniel	BUC 148		

271

MEES?, Jacob	NOU	194	MEISHE, John	LAN	307	MELLON, John	WST	313
MEESE, Balser	SOM	154	MEISSON, Joseph	PHA	14	Samuel	WAS	9
Christian	BFD	58	MEISSOUNNIER,			MELLOT, John	FAY	240
John	BFD	58	John Bt.	PHA	29	Theodore	FAY	240
MEESER, Philip	PHA	34	MEISTER, Peter	NOH	50A	MELLSON, John	PHA	114
MEETCH, John	DAU	8	MEITZER, Conrad	LAN	212	MELNOR, Saml.	PHI	63
MEETKERKE, Wm.			MEITZLER, Conrad	NOH	60A	MELON, John	DAU	8A
Esqr.	WAS	116	Henry	NOH	60	MELONE, Andrew	ADA	11
MEETS, John	PHI	6	MEIXSELL, Chr.	NOH	38	Daniel	ADA	37
MEEVEY?, Eli	LAN	223	Jacob	NOH	36	Edward	BUC	153A
MEEX, Joshua	ALL	109	Jacob	NOH	38	Eleanor	WAS	102
MEFFARD, William	FAY	201	John	NOH	36	James	CHE	702
MEFFORD, John	DAU	2A	Michael	NOH	36	John	BUC	87
MEGAIN, Timothy	FAY	210	Philip	NOH	36	John $	WAS	102
MEGARVEY, Francis	MER	454	MEKAN, William	LAN	286	John	YOR	211
MEGEE, John	MER	452	MEKER, Samuel	PHA	15	Margaret	ADA	4
MEGEEHAN, James	MER	451	MEKESELL, John	HNT	117	Michael	ADA	13
MEGGS, Richard	MNT	104	MEKUM?, (See			Thos.	FRA	327
MEGIL?, James	DAU	16A	Mehum?)	YOR	181	William	ADA	11
MEGILL, Patr.	FRA	327	MELBAN, James	LAN	59	William	ADA	21
Thomas	MER	450	MELBECK, John	PHA	4	William	ADA	24
MEGINS, John	MIF	8	MELCHOR, Israel	YOR	173	MELONEY, William	BUC	141
MEGINTY, Patrick	DAU	20	Michael	BUC	149A	William	FAY	210
MEGLOGHLIN, Henry	MER	449	MELCKS, Jacob	ALL	90	MELONY, John	LAN	60
Jack	MER	449	MELDERAM, Henry	LAN	302	Samuel	ALL	111
Manasa?	MER	454	MELDREM, Robert	FAY	201	MELOT, John	LAN	290
MEGLOGLIN, John	MER	449	MELDRUM, Garret	BUC	144A	MELOW, Adam	LAN	222
MEGNO, Andw.	PHA	42	Robt.	PHI	104	MELOY, John	MIF	8
MEGRANAHAN, John	MER	449	MELEY, Abraham	FAY	228	John	GRN	98
MEGREW, Jonathn.	DAU	7	Phillip	FAY	228	John	LAN	226
MEHAFFEY, Andrew	FAY	201	MELHORN, Andrew	ADA	31	Wm.	FRA	304
Andrew	LAN	217	Andw.	YOR	173	MELROW, James	FAY	222
James?	ARM	122	Casper	ADA	36	MELTICK, Andrew	NOU	147
Jane	FAY	201	David	ADA	31	MELTON, Hugh	WST	219
John	LYC	23	Michael	YOR	165	William	FAY	236
Robert	LYC	22	MELICH, John	SOM	143	MELTZ, Widow	PHI	112A
Stephen	ARM	122	MELINGER, Jacob	DAU	25	MELTZHEIMER, F.		
Thos.	LYC	23	MELKER, John	PHI	94	A. Revd.	YOR	182
MEHAFFY, Hugh	LAN	216	MELL, Adam	CUM	102	MELVIN, John	CHE	712
John	LAN	275	Charles	BER	205	Richard	MER	449
Robert	LAN	216	John	CUM	116	MEMBOUR, Mary	WAS	45
Samuel	LAN	235	Wm.	CUM	145	MENCER, Jacob	DAU	42
MEHARG?, Robert	MIF	17A	MELLAR?, See			MENCH, Abraham	BER	177
MEHL, Martin	PHI	133	Millar	BEV	16	John	BUC	148
MEHLER, Jacob	LAN	62	MELLCKER, Michl.	DAU	7	Nicholas	BER	176
MEHLEY, Jacob	BFD	75	MELLENER, John			Peter	BUC	148
MEHLING, John	LAN	43	Young	LAN	212	MENDENALL, Isaac	FAY	232
MEHOLE, William	LAN	179	MELLENGER,			Joseph	FAY	232
MEHS, Jacob	NOH	76	William	WST	239	MENDENHALL, Aaron	CHE	823
MEHUM?, Christian	YOR	181	MELLENS, Samuel	BER	134	Benjamin	DEL	159
MEIER, Daniel	LAN	212	MELLES, John	LAN	232	David	CHE	824
Jacob	LAN	212	MELLIG, Danl.	LAN	143	James	DEL	160
Michael	LAN	274	MELLIN, James	CHE	729	James	CHE	823
MEIERS, Adam	NOH	67A	Thomas	CHE	814	John	DEL	172
Isaac	NOH	67A	MELLINER, Anthony	LAN	202	John	CHE	900
John	NOH	67A	Isaac	LAN	212	Joshua	CHE	828
MEIK, Jacob	DAU	2	Jacob	LAN	212	Moses	CHE	900
MEIKER, Jacob	YOR	158	John	LAN	212	Noah	CHE	707
MEIL, John	SOM	130	Martin	LAN	212	Philip	DEL	159
MEILEY, Jacob	DAU	48	William	LAN	212	Thomas	GRN	93
John	DAU	52	MELLINGER,			Thomas	DEL	179
Martin	DAU	49A	Benedict	LAN	309	MENDINGHALL,		
Saml. Jr.	DAU	33A	David	LAN	286	Abner	NOU	111
Widow	DAU	28A	Jacob	ADA	13	Adam	PHA	95
MEILY, Philip	DAU	27A	Jacob	LAN	86	Caleb	CHE	707
MEIMAN, Jacob	MNT	74	John	LAN	289	Isaac	CHE	707
MEINERT, Widow	NOH	60A	Jos. (See			Isaac	CHE	707
MEINTZER,			Mellinger,			Moses	CHE	708
Frederick	LAN	202	Saml.)	LAN	202	Stephen	NOU	101
John	LAN	202	Martin	LAN	114	Thomas	CHE	707
MEIRIK, Samuel	DAU	13A	Matty	LAN	114	MENEFIN, Samuel	NOU	144
MEISENHELDER,			Melchior			MENEHART, Jacob	FAY	246
David	YOR	175	Overseer Of			MENER, John	ALL	109
Stophel	LAN	21	The Poorhouse	LAN	101	MENERT, Frederick	LAN	280
MEISER, Henry	NOU	183	Saml. & Jos.	LAN	202	Jacob	LAN	280
Phillip	NOU	183	MELLON, James	WST	153	MENESS, Elizabeth	ALL	94

MENEY, William		MERADITH, Ann	PHA 100	MERHURTLE, John	PHA 65
(Crossed Out)	LAN 151	MERANS, Mary (See		MERICH, William	LAN 185
MENG, Melchor	PHI 130	Mearns,		MERIDETH, Joseph	PHA 55
MENGAS, Adam	SOM 154	Robt.)	BUC 154A	Samuel	PHA 87
Jacob	SOM 154	MERCAM, Abm.	NOH 36	Walter	PHA 67
John	SOM 139	Jacob	NOH 84	Wm.	PHA 86
MENGEL, George	LAN 271	MERCER, Boyd		MERIMAN, Fredrick	ALL 112
MENGES, Ann	YOR 205	Revd.	WAS 112	John	ALL 112
Henry	BER 161	Daniel	CHE 850	Ritchard	ALL 112
Jacob	YOR 179	David	CRA 8	Ruth	ALL 112
John	YOR 179	David	CHE 744	MERINER, James	NOU 130
Peter	YOR 163	George	PHA 111	MERING, Henry	LAN 81
MENGLE, Adam	BER 159	James	WAS 22	MERIT, Henry	PHI 88A
Frederick	BER 254	Jesse	CHE 702	J./ I.?	DAU 45
Mary	BER 219	Jesse	CHE 744	Robt.	FRA 306
MENGLE?, Peter	BER 161	John	WAS 22	MERK, Peter	BER 176
MENHALL, Fransis	PHI 129	Joseph	PHA 39	MERKER, Andrew	PHA 64
MENIAM, George	CRA 7	Joseph	WAS 39	MERKEY, Andrew	BER 176
Henry	NOU 123	Joseph	CHE 807	David	BER 151
Nicholas	NOU 123	Mordecai	CHE 807	Jacob	YOR 171
MENIC, Samuel	PHI 141	Moses	GRN 89	John	BER 152
MENICH, George	BER 189	Nathl.	CHE 880	MERKL, William	BER 254
Henry	FRA 300	Richard	DEL 190	MERKLE, Barbara	LAN 79
John	LAN 221	Robert	PHA 111	Casper	BER 254
Peter	BER 153	Thomas	WAS 92	Daniel	BER 254
MENICK, Geo.	DAU 16	Thomas	CHE 812	Dewald	DAU 13
George	DAU 7	Thomas	CHE 850	George	BER 167
George	NOU 176	William	WAS 103	George	BER 254
Joseph	BUC 83	William	CHE 807	Henry	YOR 190
Joseph	PHA 103	Wm.	BEV 13	Jacob	PHI 137
Vendel	DAU 19A	Wm.	CHE 846	Jacob	PHI 138
MENIHEW, Joseph	DEL 166	MERCHAND, David	WST 220	Jacob	BER 155
MENINGER, George	BER 183	Fredk.	WST 218	John	LAN 103
Joseph	BUC 157A	MERCKEL, Abraham	NOH 60A	Michael	BER 220
Samuel	BUC 148A	Daniel	LAN 202	Peter	MNT 132
Yost	BER 183	George	LAN 201	MERKLEWAY, Philip	PHI 137
MENIUM, George	WST 218	MERCKLE,		MERKLEY, Jacob	YOR 194
MENNERS, John	LAN 212	Christopher	NOH 60A	Joh	CRA 0
MENNERT,		Jacob	YOR 194	MERKY, John	YOR 193
Frederick	LAN 278	MERCKLEY, Godfrey	NOH 30A	John	BER 264
Jacob	LAN 278	MERCLE, Christn.	BER 243	MERNER, Henry	HNT 126
MENOCH, Nancy	WAS 9	Danl.	BER 189	MERNS, John	MIF 15
MENOUGHU, John	WST 173	Jacob	BER 189	MERO, Fredr.	FRA 303
MENSCH, Abraham	NOH 69	Jacob Jr.	BER 189	MERR, John	ALL 116
Abraham	NOH 30A	John	BER 214	MERRIATTA, Jacob	FAY 240
Adam	NOH 91	MERCUS, Samuel	WAS 52	MERRICK (CROSSED	
Christian	NOH 65	MERCY, Ceasar	BEV 5	OUT), Joseph	BUC 83
MENSER, Christo.	DAU 42A	MEREADY, Elijah	YOR 216	MERRICK, Daniel	WAS 102
MENSH, Christian	NOH 56A	MEREDITH, Danl.	CHE 885	Enos	BUC 151A
John	NOH 56A	David	PHI 130	George	BUC 83
MENSINGER, Joseph	FAY 246	David	HNT 150	Isaac	WAS 102
MENSKER, Ludwig	DAU 10	David	CHE 737	Jason	BUC 83
MENSNIGER, Wido	DAU 42	George	CHE 886	Joseph	BUC 94
MENSON, David	FRA 304	Hugh Docr.	BUC 105A	Joseph Jnr.	BUC 94
Joseph	FRA 305	James	CHE 818	Joshua	PHI 7
MENSOR, Saml.	FRA 305	James	CHE 895	Marmaduke	PHI 20
MENSORE, Able	FRA 310	James	BUC 154A	Robert	PHI 7
MENTEER, Joseph	FAY 205	Jesse	MIF 13	Robert	BUC 83
MENTEETH, James	FAY 267	John	BUC 105	Robert	BUC 151A
MENTEITH, Daniel	ADA 20	John	DEL 161	Samuel	PHA 21
Stewart	ADA 23	John	CHE 799	Samuel	BUC 151A
MENTHORN, John	FAY 222	John	CHE 819	MERRICLE, Abm.	WST 294
MENTOTH, James	ALL 79	John	CHE 884	Casper	WST 292
MENTSOR,		John	BUC 154A	Peter	BFD 51
Christopher	HNT 144	Joseph	DEL 172	MERRIHEW, James	DEL 167
George	HNT 131	Joseph	CHE 886	MERRIL, Richard	NOH 38
MENTZ, Elizabeth	PHA 31	Morgan	BUC 154A	MERRILLS, Isaac	LUZ 363
MENTZER,		Richard	CHE 708	MERRILS, Adrian	LUZ 363
Frederick	LAN 294	Samon	CHE 895	MERRIMAN, Benjn.	FAY 246
George	LAN 141	Simon	BUC 154A	Marey	FAY 215
George T?	PHI 96	Thomas	ADA 5	Samuel	ALL 113
Jacob	LAN 85	Thomas	PHI 143	William	FAY 253
Widow	LAN 85	William	HNT 150	MERRIMY, William	FAY 239
MEOLLEM, John	LAN 82	MEREIDTH, William	BUC 141A	MERRION, Joseph	DEL 168
MEPPES, Frederich	NOH 63	MERES, Daniel	CRA 6	MERRIOT, Sarah	BUC 83
MER, Jonathan	BER 243	MERGAN, Michl.	FAY 251	MERRIT, Bija/Bijn?	FAY 209

MERRIT, Daniel	WAS	57	MESSERLY, Abraham	YOR	175	METZER, George	NOU	130
Mathew	WAS	57	Peter	YOR	175	Henry	SOM	143
MERRITT, John	PHI	10	MESSERSMITH,			Jacob	NOU	194
MERRYMAN, Elijah	HNT	130	Andw.	DAU	9	John	NOU	130
Philip	YOR	211	Danl.	BER	234	METZGAR, Adam	LAN	38
MERSCH, Abraham	NOH	41A	Geo.	ADA	44	George	YOR	165
MERSER, George	LAN	130	George	LAN	27	John	BFD	64
John	FAY	215	Leonard	BER	134	John	BFD	65
MERSH, Adam	NOH	63	Nicholas	YOR	188	Marcus	SOM	129
Casper	NOH	63	MESSIMER, Benj.	MNT	58	Peter	NOU	123
David	NOH	60A	Casimer	MNT	58	Widow	LAN	41
George	NOH	50A	Frederick	MNT	58	Widow	LAN	66
John	NOH	63	George	MNT	61	William	YOR	165
John	NOH	60A	Henry	MNT	58	METZGER, Abraham	NOH	74
Widow	NOH	63	Jacob	MNT	58	Andrew	NOH	39A
MERSHAL, William	DAU	30A	MESSINA,			Caspar	NOH	41A
MERSHIMER, Sebs.	BER	161	Zachariah	NOU	130	Christian	NOH	56A
MERSHON, John	ERI	58	MESSINGER,			Frederick	LAN	276
Peter	ERI	58	Abraham	WAS	45	George	MNT	68
MERSICK, Joseph	BUC	161	G. (Ee			George Junr.	MNT	68
MERTEL, Chrn.	DAU	45A	Messinger,			Jacob	LAN	276
MERTZ, Abraham	BER	209	John)	NOH	39A	Jacob	DAU	20A
Conrad	BER	284	George	NOH	39A	Jacob	NOH	56A
Conrad	NOH	60A	Jacob	NOH	39A	John	LAN	43
George H.	NOH	91	John (Son Of			John	LAN	273
Henry	BER	223	G.)	NOH	39A	John	DAU	13A
Henry	NOH	30A	John Esqr.	NOH	39A	Jonas	NOH	65
Jacob	SOM	152	Michael Jr.	NOH	39A	Widow	NOH	78A
Jacob	BER	258	Michael	NOH	39A	METZKER, Philip	LAN	39
John	BER	214	Philip	NOH	39A	METZLER, Abraham	LAN	93
Leonard	PHI	128	MESSMORE, John	FAY	216	Christian	LAN	190
Philip	NOH	45A	John	FAY	232	Henry	SOM	129
William	SOM	152	MESSNER, John	DAU	7A	Peter	SOM	130
William	BER	254	Michl.	CUM	40	MEURAGH, Mr.	PHA	84
William	NOH	45A	Michl.	CUM	130	MEVEY, Dengamin	ALL	102
MERUCK, Robert	PHI	20	MESTER, S.	LAN	147	Wilm.	ALL	102
MERVINE, George	PHI	27	MESURSMITH, Henry	FRA	274	MEVIS, John	FRA	321
MERWEIR,			METCALFE, Daniel	LUZ	392	MEWELEVY?, Wm.	NOU	176
Christina	BER	251	METED, John	HNT	150	MEWHOLMN, James	LAN	161
MERYER?, John	PHI	79	METEER, Alexd.	FRA	309	Samuel	LAN	161
MESE, George	DAU	37A	John	MER	452	MEY--?, Daniel	NOH	60A
Jacob	DAU	37A	METHANDS, Absolem	FAY	246	MEY?, Daniel	NOH	60A
John	YOR	164	METLEN, Patrick	CHE	823	MEYEL?, James	DAU	16A
Nicolaus	DAU	31	Thos.	CHE	827	MEYER, Abraham	DAU	29
MESER, Amos	WST	381	Wm.	CHE	827	Abraham	BFD	41
Joseph	WST	381	METLER, George	BER	159	Abraham	LAN	53
MESHEY, Jacob	LAN	7	William	BUC	145A	Abraham		
MESINER, Adam	NOU	194	METLIN, Samuel	CHE	823	(Tanner)	LAN	18
MESON, Josia	FAY	258	METLIRS?,			Abraham	LAN	142
MESS, Christian			Alexander	BUC	105	Abraham	NOH	80A
Jr.?	LAN	137	METONIA, Abram	FAY	236	Adam	NOH	74
Isaac	ADA	43	METS, Henry	LAN	226	Andrew	NOH	76
MESSABAUGH,			METSLER, Martin	LAN	138	Andrew	NOH	50A
George	SOM	158	METTLEMAN, Andw.	MIF	15	Andrew	NOH	53A
MESSEA, John	PHA	109	Jno.	MIF	15	Andw.	YOR	191
MESSED, Solomon	CHE	852	METTLER, Henry	DAU	47	Benjamin	DAU	3
MESSEMER, Henry	BUC	157A	METZ, Abm.	LAN	264	Casper	NOH	43A
John	MNT	58	Chrisn.	LAN	264	Charles	NOH	45A
MESSENGER,			Henry	BER	203	Chris.	LAN	33
William	YOR	213	Henry Jr.	BER	203	Christian	LAN	190
MESSENHIMER,			Jacob	MNT	70	Christian	YOR	195
Conrad	BFD	75	Jacob	MNT	119	Christian	LAN	201
MESSENKOP, Adam	LAN	35	Jacob	BER	154	Christian	YOR	204
John	LAN	37	Jacob Junr.	BER	154	Christopher	LAN	98
Philip	LAN	36	Jacob Ser.	BER	227	Chrst. S.	YOR	205
MESSENRY, John	YOR	205	John	MNT	69	Conrad	NOH	63
MESSER, Daniel	NOU	176	Joseph	BER	280	Conrad	LAN	146
George	LAN	50	Lewis	HNT	118	Conrad	YOR	191
Jacob	NOU	176	Peter	BER	219	Conrad	YOR	206
James Esq.	LAN	229	Peter	DAU	5A	Conrad	NOH	56A
Lawrence	BUC	140	Samuel	MNT	119	Daniel	NOH	60
Margaret	LAN	299	Sebastian	DAU	5A	Daniel (Son Of		
Peter	PHA	69	Valentine	NOH	74	Heichs.)	NOH	60
Phillip	NOU	176	METZBE, John	LAN	252	Daniel	YOR	165
Wm.	CUM	79	METZEL, George	YOR	159	David	NOH	91
MESSER?, Conrad	MNT	38	METZER, Daniel	NOU	130	David	LAN	188

Name	Loc	Pg
MEYER, David	LAN	189
Elias	YOR	169
Frederick	BER	279
Fredk.	YOR	176
Fredk.	YOR	189
Fredk.	YOR	191
George	LAN	52
George	YOR	170
George	YOR	178
George	BER	272
George	LAN	298
George Sr.	YOR	218
George	NOH	78A
George	NOH	90A
Godlip	PHA	47
Heichs. (See Meyer, Daniel)	NOH	60
Henry	LAN	16
Henry	LAN	20
Henry	LAN	25
Henry	YOR	197
Henry	NOH	56A
Isaac	MNT	125
Jacob	LAN	23
Jacob	LAN	38
Jacob	LAN	49
Jacob	NOH	60
Jacob	MNT	135
Jacob	LAN	146
Jacob	LAN	186
Jacob	LAN	189
Jacob	YOR	192
Jacob	YOR	204
Jacob	YOR	217
Jacob Junr.	LYC	19
Jacob Senr.	LAN	146
Jacob	DAU	36A
Jacob	NOH	50A
Jacob	NOH	56A
Jacob	NOH	90A
John	LAN	8
John	LAN	16
John	NOH	36
John	NOH	38
John	LAN	57
John	NOH	60
John	NOH	69
John	YOR	154
John	YOR	169
John	YOR	172
John	LAN	174
John	YOR	180
John	LAN	189
John	YOR	191
John	LAN	201
John	YOR	207
John	LAN	243
John	NOH	43A
Leonard	NOH	60
Lewis	NOH	41A
Martin	LAN	4
Martin	NOH	74
Martin	NOH	91
Martin	YOR	169
Martin	LAN	187
Martin	LAN	191
Martin	YOR	218
Martin	DAU	27A
Matthias	YOR	179
Matthias	YOR	186
Meter	YOR	217
Michael	YOR	196
Michael	LAN	212
Michael	NOH	30A
Michl.	DAU	23
MEYER, Nicholas	NOH	85A
Nicholas	NOH	90A
Peter	NOH	74
Peter	YOR	167
Peter	YOR	189
Peter	YOR	208
Peter	YOR	216
Peter Jr.	YOR	170
Peter	NOH	53A
Peter	NOH	67A
Peter	NOH	80A
Peter	NOH	90A
Philip	YOR	158
Philip	YOR	180
Philip	LAN	304
Philip	NOH	41A
Philip	NOH	85A
Samuel	NOH	80A
Simon	YOR	207
Simon	NOH	45A
Solomon	YOR	161
Thomas	LAN	59
Tobias	YOR	157
Valentine	NOH	43A
Widow	NOH	73A
William	NOH	36
William	NOH	53A
William	NOH	80A
MEYERS, Abraham	YOR	164
Andrew	MNT	138
Barbara	BFD	40
David	YOR	212
Francis	ADA	25
Frederick	ADA	43
George	YOR	213
Henry	BFD	40
Henry	PHA	42
Henry	YOR	170
Henry	LAN	219
John	PHA	30
John	NOH	65
John	PHI	135
John	YOR	209
John	YOR	216
Martin	ADA	6
Nicholas	ADA	38
Peter	PHA	34
Samuel	YOR	164
MEYSTER, John	LAN	184
MEZ, John	DAU	20
MG GINLEY, James	FAY	204
MI---?, Daniel	FRA	301
MIARS, George	MER	449
Jacob	FAY	216
Jacob	MER	450
MIASWANGER, Abraham	BFD	65
MICAM, Jacob	NOU	101
John	NOU	101
Joseph	NOU	101
MICCOE, Robert	DEL	180
MICH, Miller	LAN	141
MICHAEL, Andrew	HNT	143
Balmer	LAN	141
Bieber	NOH	29
Christ. S.	NOH	70
Christn.	CUM	31
Christn.	BER	205
Frederick	LAN	255
Fredk.	BER	203
Geo. Junr.	MNT	96
George	MNT	96
George	WAY	149
George	NOU	203
George Jr.	WAY	149
George	BUC	139A
MICHAEL, Henry	DAU	17
Henry	LAN	85
Henry	YOR	162
Isaac	NOU	147
Jacob	DAU	11
Jacob	CUM	31
Jacob	DAU	43
Jacob	LAN	137
Jacob	DAU	51A
John	LAN	30
John	LAN	52
John	NOH	63
John	NOU	106
John	NOU	106
John	WAY	149
John	WST	154
John	YOR	158
John	NOU	180
John	YOR	182
John	NOH	71A
Lilly	NOH	30A
Martin	CUM	32
Mosis	LAN	23
Mrs.	NOU	137
Nicholas	YOR	176
Nicholas	NOH	41A
Peter	NOH	74
Peter	HNT	122
Peter	WAY	149
Peter	DAU	11A
Peter	DAU	16A
Philip	BER	210
Philip	NOH	71A
Rueben	GRN	83
Ulrich	NOH	91
Wendle	YOR	159
Widow	LAN	28
William	LAN	44
William	GRN	77
William	YOR	183
William	BER	201
Wm.	CEN	20A
MICHAEN?, William	CRA	17
MICHAL, George	WST	381
Henry	CEN	20A
MICHEL, Widow	PHI	71
John	PHI	84
John	NOU	188
John	PHI	67A
Wm.	PHI	120
MICHENOR, Arnold	CHE	763
Thomas	MNT	63
Willm.	MNT	63
MICHLER, David	NOH	73A
Nathl. Esqr.	NOH	73A
MICHNER, John	MNT	35
MICHOL, Silas	MIF	5
MICHSCH, Christian	NOH	70
MICK, Andrew	NOU	189
Henry	NOU	189
Philip	DAU	27A
MICKESAL, Andw.	CUM	123
MICKEY, David	CUM	122
James	CUM	122
Lewis	BUC	158
Robert	WST	239
Robt.	CUM	122
William	WST	239
MICKFLING, Daniel	LAN	177
MICKLE, William	MIF	10A
MICKLEY, Daniel	ADA	13
Danl.	WST	220
MICKLY, Peter	BUC	91
MICKS, David	FRA	292
MICKSCH, Nathaniel	NOH	70

MICKSCH, Paul,		
Stewart Of		
Christians -		
Brunn	NOH	71A
MICMICHAEL, James	PHI	88A
MICOMER, John	MNT	96
MIDCALF, Jas.	LAN	154
Moses	LAN	153
MIDDAGH, Daniel	PHA	89
Garret	NOH	67
Peter	NOH	67
MIDDELSATH, Moses	ALL	104
MIDDLECALF, Jacob	ADA	13
Leonard	ADA	32
MIDDLECUT, James	NOH	78A
MIDDLESATH, Henry	ALL	104
MIDDLETON, Widw.	PHI	105B
Aaaron	PHI	19
Andw.	CUM	129
Jacob	LAN	230
James	MNT	35
James	MNT	41
John	LAN	130
John	DEL	165
Joseph (Crossed		
Out Followed		
By James)	MNT	41
Thomas	DEL	167
Walter	PHI	46
Wm.	CEN	23
Wm.	FRA	320
MIDDOCK, Derick	SOM	158
Ephraim	SOM	158
MIDEEF?, Thos.	CHE	867
MIDES, John	LAN	215
MIDEY?, Thos.	CHE	867
MIDHOUR, Andrew	ADA	24
MIDLETON, Cabriel	PHI	114A
MIERCKEN, Henry	PHI	38
Peter	PHI	38
MIERS, Fredk.	PHI	3
Jacob	BFD	64
Laurence	PHI	19
Martin	BFD	64
Nicholas	MIF	13
Sarah	FAY	201
MIESSER,		
Christian	LAN	222
MIETY, George	LAN	61
MIFFLIN, John F.	PHA	98
Jonathan	LAN	299
MIFFLON?, Thomas	PHA	98
MIFLIN, Bengn.	PHA	76
Samuel	PHA	83
MIGHT, John	WAS	81
MIGHTER, Peter	NOU	184
MIHAND, George	NOU	183
George	NOU	183
Jacob	NOU	183
Jacob	NOU	183
MIHTELL?, Wm	LYC	8
MIKEY, Matthias	LAN	138
MILAN, Jacob	PHA	58
Joseph	PHI	105A
MILAND, Geoe.	PHI	45
Richd.	YOR	218
MILB?, Jacob	BFD	79
MILBEY, Robt.	CUM	54
MILBINE, John	PHA	91
MILBURN, John	GRN	77
MILCHSACH, Philip	WAS	116
MILCHSACK, Widow	LAN	44
MILDEBERGER,		
Jacob	SOM	159
MILDREDGE,		
Stephen	FRA	327

MILDY, Carl	BER	211
MILECHSACK,		
George	LAN	57
MILEISEN, John	LAN	250
MILEM, Willm.	DAU	12A
MILES, Ebenezer	NOU	180
Enos	CHE	820
Evan	CEN	23
George	LAN	108
George	CHE	773
Gideon	CHE	743
Griffith	BUC	137A
Jacob	PHI	154
Jacob	BER	239
James	CEN	23
James	PHA	104
James	NOU	180
John	CHE	875
John	PHI	99A
Jos.	YOR	203
Joseph	PHI	155
Mordacia	YOR	170
Mrs.	NOU	180
Nathaniel	CHE	897
Richd. Esq.	CEN	23
Robt.	WAR	1A
Saml. (Bigg)	CEN	23
Saml. (Little)	CEN	23
Saml.	PHI	144
Samuel	MNT	42
Samuel	NOU	180
Samuel	CHE	769
Sarah	PHA	61
Thomas	PHA	92
Thomas	PHI	155
Thomas	LUZ	401
Thomas	ERI	57A
Thomas.	BUT	363
William	CEN	23
William	ERI	60
MILES?, Mc Clure?	WST	292
MILEY, Abraham	YOR	209
Fredk.	PHA	87
Henrey	FAY	228
Henry	DAU	28
Henry	DAU	51
Jacob	CHE	893
John	ADA	38
John	MNT	142
Martin	YOR	166
Samuel	DAU	33A
MILFORD, John	PHI	78A
Sippy	PHI	133
MILFRED, James	CHE	894
MILHEIM,		
Christian	YOR	187
John	NOH	63
MILHOFF, Philip	YOR	204
Samuel	MNT	96
MILHOUSE, Casper	PHI	93A
John	SOM	129
John	MIF	7A
Peter	SOM	129
MILICK, David	NOU	101
MILIGAN, James	YOR	202
MILIGON, James	ALL	60
MILL, Abraham	BUC	139A
George	PHI	97A
Henry	BUC	82A
Isaac	BUC	139A
John	NOH	67
Sam. Jr.	DAU	38
MILLA-?, Samuel	YOR	218
MILLAJAN, Tho.	CEN	20A
MILLAR, Abraham	SOM	154
Andrew	SOM	154

MILLAR, Andrew	FAY	222
Andrew	FAY	258
Barney	SOM	154
Chas.	BEV	16
Daniel	FAY	205
David	FAY	222
Edward	PHI	52
George	SOM	146
Godfrey	CHE	842
Henrey	FAY	198
Henrey Jur.	FAY	198
Henry	FAY	241
Hugh	BEV	25
Jacob	MIF	17
Jacob	BEV	27
Jacob /Γ/	SOM	149
Jacob	SOM	149
James	BEV	25
James	BEV	26
James	FAY	205
James	FAY	205
James	FAY	205
James	CHE	861
James Jur.	FAY	205
John	SOM	149
John	SOM	154
John	SOM	158
John	FAY	210
John	FAY	215
John	FAY	216
John	FAY	222
John	FAY	229
John	FAY	237
John	FAY	258
John	FAY	258
John	CHE	861
John Jr.	CHE	862
John (Amity)	WAS	4
Jonathan	SOM	149
Jonathen	FAY	253
Joseph	BEV	19
Joseph	SOM	154
Levi	FAY	228
Ludwich	FAY	241
Ludwick	FAY	216
Marey	FAY	233
Martin	MIF	13
Michael	PHI	52
Michael /A/	SOM	149
Michael	SOM	149
Nicholas	FAY	215
Nicholas	FAY	228
Peter	BEV	7
Peter	SOM	158
Peter	FAY	267
Robert	BEV	26
Saml.	FAY	228
Samuel	FAY	228
Sollomon	FAY	216
Thomas	MIF	15
Thomas	FAY	228
William	SOM	154
William	FAY	204
William	FAY	227
William	FAY	246
Wm.	CHE	861
Wm.	CHE	865
MILLARD, Benjamin	NOU	111
Benjn.	CHE	716
Jonathen	NOU	111
Joseph	NOU	155
Solomon	LUZ	383
Thomas	NOU	111
Thomas	NOU	155
Thomas	CHE	727
Thos.	PHI	77A

MILLEDGE,			MILLER, Andrew	ADA	19	MILLER, Christn.	PHA	62
Humphrey	LUZ	348	Andrew	LAN	53	Christn.	PHI	108
James	LUZ	348	Andrew	NOH	74	Christn.	BER	236
MILLEGAN, James	WST	275	Andrew	PHA	77	Christopher	LAN	72
Jane	ADA	12	Andrew	PHA	96	Christopher	MNT	75
Jno.	CUM	44	Andrew (Full			Christopher	HNT	149
Ribert	WAS	102	Name Crossed			Christopher	WST	162
Saml.	CUM	44	Out)	NOH	60A	Christopher	LAN	202
Thomas	WAS	22	Andrew	WAS	111	Christopher	FRA	301
MILLEISEN, Jacob	DAU	15A	Andrew	YOR	164	Christopher	LUZ	368
MILLEN, Elizah	FRA	291	Andrew	LAN	233	Chrs.	YOR	184
Joseph	ARM	124	Andrew	LAN	235	Chuster	NOU	97A
MILLEN?, Robt.	PHI	102	Andrew	LAN	256	Conrad	ADA	40
MILLEND, Joseph	CHE	906	Andrew Jn.	NOH	53A	Conrad	DAU	51
MILLENDER, Philip	WST	294	Andrew	NOH	53A	Conrad	NOU	130
MILLENGER,			Andw.	CUM	59	Conrad	BER	131
Catherine	WAS	69	Andw.	CUM	68	Conrad	BER	131
MILLER, Widow	PHI	22	Andw.	PHI	120	Conrad	YOR	173
Widow	WAS	57	Andw.	YOR	183	Conrad	YOR	195
Widow	PHI	85	Andw.	YOR	187	Conrad	YOR	217
Widw.	PHI	107A	Andw.	YOR	191	Conrad	LAN	226
Abel	BUC	97	Andw.	YOR	216	Conrad	NOH	80A
Abm.	MIF	17	Ann	BER	264	Conrad	NOH	82A
Abm.	CUM	68	Anthony	MNT	68	Conrod	LYC	29
Abraham	WAS	4	Anthony	WAS	70	Conrod	CHE	790
Abraham	WAS	4	Anthony	BER	134	Conrod	CHE	890
Abraham	LAN	21	Arthur	BUC	83	Conrod	PHI	84A
Abraham	NOH	91	Augustine	NOU	105	Cristian	FRA	273
Abraham	BUC	97	Barbara	FRA	283	Cronimus	LAN	223
Abraham	HNT	127	Barbary	PHA	56	Daniel	DAU	8
Abraham	SOM	132	Bastian	NOH	91	Daniel	CRA	13
Abraham	SOM	139	Benjamin	LAN	8	Daniel	DAU	26
Abraham	NOU	154	Benjamin	NOH	48	Daniel	ADA	29
Abraham	YOR	158	Benjamin	GRN	107	Daniel	BFD	58
Abraham	NOU	176	Benjamin	LAN	110	Daniel	GRN	96
Abraham	BER	219	Benjamin	NOU	130	Daniel	BUC	101
Abraham	LAN	238	Benjamin	BER	264	Daniel	MNT	114
Abraham	LAN	277	Benjamin	BER	273	Daniel	HNT	124
Abraham	LAN	283	Benjamin	CHE	699	Daniel	SOM	139
Abraham Sr.	MIF	4	Black	PHI	93	Daniel	YOR	171
Abraham Sr.	MIF	4	Boston	NOU	194	Daniel	LAN	175
Abraham	NOH	87A	Caleb	CHE	837	Daniel	NOU	176
Abrham	YOR	197	Casper	NOH	80A	Daniel	FRA	301
Adam	DAU	3	Cath.	DAU	31	Daniel	DAU	8A
Adam	DAU	8	Catharine	YOR	192	Daniel	NOH	30A
Adam	ADA	10	Catherine	BER	150	Daniel	DAU	46A
Adam	ADA	13	Catherine	BER	208	Daniel	BUC	83A
Adam	DAU	41	Cathn.	PHI	92A	Daniel	NOH	90A
Adam	WAS	52	Ch. H.	NOH	70	Daniel	PHI	96A
Adam	MNT	53	Charles	NOH	74	Danl.	DAU	39
Adam	BUC	101	Charles	BUC	97	Danl.	CUM	56
Adam	NOU	101	Charles	NOH	45A	Danl.	PHI	106A
Adam	PHA	101	Charles	PHI	109A	David	CUM	31
Adam	PHI	141	Chris.	DAU	48	David	DAU	39
Adam	PHI	142	Christepher	VEN	165	David	DAU	48
Adam	YOR	166	Christian	NOH	63	David	NOH	63
Adam	NOU	180	Christian	BUC	101	David	PHA	93
Adam	YOR	187	Christian	NOU	114	David	GRN	98
Adam	WST	218	Christian	NOU	114	David	LAN	109
Adam	LAN	250	Christian	NOU	118	David	ALL	117
Adam	LUZ	383	Christian	MNT	128	David	LAN	171
Adam	CHE	782	Christian	SOM	139	David	NOU	176
Adam	CHE	889	Christian	PHI	140	David	LAN	306
Adam Esq.	SOM	141	Christian	SOM	154	David	CHE	837
Adam Junr.	LAN	171	Christian	SOM	158	David	MIF	17A
Adam Snr.	LAN	171	Christian	SOM	159	David	PHI	109A
Adam	NOH	53A	Christian	HNT	166	Dorothea	CUM	148
Adam	NOH	90A	Christian	BER	167	Dorothea	YOR	185
Alexander	MNT	43	Christian	YOR	183	Earhart	CUM	73
Alexander	NOU	111	Christian	YOR	192	Edward	BER	287B
Alexander	PHA	117	Christian	BER	264	Edward	BER	287B
Alexander J.?	PHA	107	Christian	BER	274	Eli	CUM	71
Alexd.	ALL	94	Christian	LAN	305	Elias	BFD	75
Alexr.	NOH	67	Christian	FRA	306	Elija	PHA	101
Andreas	BER	222	Christian	NOH	41A	Elijah	MIF	17A
Andrew	ADA	11	Christian	NOH	53A	Eliza.	CUM	143

MILLER, Elizabeth	DAU	12	MILLER, George	BER	183	MILLER, Henry		
Elizabeth	MNT	45	George	NOU	189	Esqr.	YOR	155
Elizabeth	PHA	93	George	BER	214	Henry Esqr.	YOR	188
Elizabeth	BER	219	George	YOR	215	Henry Junr.	NOH	76
Enoch	MNT	68	George	LAN	216	Henry Junr.	NOH	30A
Ernst	LAN	63	George	LAN	216	Henry & Geo.	DAU	30
Ezecal	ALL	119	George	BER	219	Henry	PHI	105B
Felix	BFD	64	George	YOR	219	Henry	DAU	14A
Felix	HNT	152	George	LAN	227	Henry	DAU	51A
Felty	DAU	38	George	BER	262	Henry	NOH	56A
Francis	BFD	38	George	BER	279	Henry	NOH	60A
Francis	NOH	67	George	BER	281	Henry	NOH	67A
Fredck.	NOH	41A	George	LAN	292	Henry	BUC	139A
Frederic	HNT	119	George	FRA	306	Herman	YOR	193
Frederic	HNT	139	George	LUZ	381	Hester A.	PHA	12
Frederic	HNT	143	George	CHE	788	Heyronimus	LAN	120
Frederic	HNT	154	George	CHE	856	Hugh	CUM	36
Frederick	WAS	34	George Jr.	YOR	170	Hugh	PHA	111
Frederick	NOH	36	George	DAU	17A	Hugh	CHE	717
Frederick	NOH	56	George	NOH	45A	Hy?	YOR	211
Frederick	NOH	67	George	NOH	78A	Isaac	WAS	22
Frederick	MNT	108	George	NOH	80A	Isaac	WAS	52
Frederick	MNT	110	George	BUC	139A	Isaac	WAS	102
Frederick	NOU	138	Gerret	LYC	12	Isaac	WAS	123
Frederick	YOR	194	Gideon	MER	455	Isaac	WAS	123
Frederick	BER	209	Godfreid	LAN	70	Isaac	WST	219
Frederick	BER	263	Godfrey	NOH	48	Isaac	BER	279
Frederick	BER	276	Godfrey	YOR	194	Isaac	FRA	296
Frederick	NOH	56A	Henry	LAN	8	Isaac	FRA	317
Frederick	NOH	60A	Henry	PHA	30	Isaac	CHE	708
Frederik	DAU	31	Henry	DAU	35	Jacob	MIF	4
Fredk.	YOR	192	Henry	ADA	43	Jacob	ADA	11
Fredrik	DAU	37	Henry	MNT	47	Jacob	NOH	34
Freny	CUM	144	Henry	DAU	50	Jacob	WAS	34
Friederich	LAN	275	Henry	CUM	54	Jacob	WAS	34
Geo.	CUM	122	Henry	BFD	55	Jacob	ADA	35
Geo.	BUT	353	Henry	LAN	63	Jacob	LAN	35
Geo. & Henry	DAU	30	Henry	NOH	63	Jacob	DAU	37
Geo.	PHI	120A	Henry	NOH	63	Jacob	DAU	42
Geo. H.	NOH	87A	Henry	CUM	72	Jacob	BFD	44
George	DAU	13	Henry	NOH	76	Jacob	CUM	46
George	LAN	13	Henry	GRN	77	Jacob	NOH	48
George	DAU	23	Henry	MNT	91	Jacob	WAS	52
George	WAS	29	Henry	ALL	96	Jacob	CUM	56
George	DAU	31	Henry	MNT	97	Jacob	BFD	59
George	LAN	34	Henry	MNT	97	Jacob	BFD	59
George	LAN	44	Henry	PHA	101	Jacob	NOH	60
George	BFD	60	Henry	PHI	103	Jacob	PHA	60
George	ALL	69	Henry	PHI	111	Jacob	CUM	62
George	GRN	73	Henry	HNT	135	Jacob	NOH	63
George	NOH	74	Henry	SOM	139	Jacob	BFD	64
George	NOH	74	Henry	SOM	149	Jacob	CUM	64
George	WAS	92	Henry	BUC	153	Jacob	NOH	67
George	LAN	96	Henry	HNT	155	Jacob	NOH	74
George	BUC	101	Henry	NOU	166	Jacob	NOH	76
George	NOU	114	Henry	YOR	176	Jacob	PHA	77
George	NOU	114	Henry	YOR	186	Jacob	BFD	78
George	NOU	123	Henry	YOR	193	Jacob	PHI	83
George	NOU	130	Henry	YOR	195	Jacob	PHI	89
George	SOM	130	Henry	LAN	201	Jacob	NOH	91
George	BER	131	Henry	BER	203	Jacob	MNT	92
George	BER	131	Henry	BER	205	Jacob	ALL	96
George	MNT	135	Henry	YOR	214	Jacob	ALL	103
George	LAN	136	Henry	YOR	216	Jacob	PHI	103
George	NOU	137	Henry	LAN	221	Jacob	LAN	129
George	NOU	138	Henry	BER	243	Jacob	BER	131
George	BER	152	Henry	WST	275	Jacob	PHI	133
George	BER	160	Henry	WST	276	Jacob	SOM	134
George	HNT	161	Henry	LAN	278	Jacob	MNT	135
George	BER	162	Henry	BER	280	Jacob	NOU	138
George	YOR	164	Henry	LAN	280	Jacob	SOM	143
George	YOR	170	Henry	BER	286	Jacob	BER	145
George	LAN	171	Henry	FRA	303	Jacob	PHI	146
George	WST	173	Henry	LAN	308	Jacob	BER	154
George	YOR	174	Henry	FRA	313	Jacob	BER	159
George	DEL	182	Henry	CHE	792	Jacob	BER	159

Name	Location	Name	Location	Name	Location
MILLER, Jacob	YOR 162	MILLER, Jno. Jr.	DAU 42	MILLER, John	HNT 136
Jacob	YOR 164	Jno. Dieter	NOH 80A	John	NOU 138
Jacob	YOR 175	Joel	PHA 37	John	SOM 139
Jacob	NOU 176	Joh	WAS 45	John	BER 140
Jacob	BER 178	John	WAS 4	John	HNT 140
Jacob	YOR 183	John	WAS 4	John	SOM 143
Jacob	YOR 184	John	ADA 12	John	BER 145
Jacob	LAN 190	John	MIF 15	John	HNT 145
Jacob	BER 201	John	DAU 16	John	HNT 145
Jacob	BER 202	John	WAS 16	John	HNT 155
Jacob	LAN 212	John	WAS 16	John	BER 156
Jacob	BER 214	John	PHI 19	John	BUC 161
Jacob	LAN 216	John	WAS 22	John	YOR 161
Jacob	YOR 216	John	CEN 23	John	HNT 166
Jacob	BER 219	John	ADA 26	John	VEN 166
Jacob	BER 220	John	ADA 27	John	BER 167
Jacob	WST 220	John	PHI 31	John	YOR 168
Jacob	BER 223	John	WAS 34	John	VEN 169
Jacob	BER 223	John	CUM 36	John	BER 174
Jacob	LAN 231	John	PHA 36	John	DEL 175
Jacob	WST 240	John	CUM 38	John	YOR 175
Jacob	BER 246	John	PHA 39	John	YOR 180
Jacob	BER 246	John	BFD 41	John	YOR 182
Jacob	BER 251	John	DAU 42	John	YOR 184
Jacob	BER 279	John	BFD 44	John	YOR 186
Jacob	LAN 293	John	WAS 45	John	YOR 188
Jacob	FRA 301	John	PHI 46	John	YOR 188
Jacob	LAN 306	John	LAN 50	John	YOR 195
Jacob	FRA 311	John	WAS 52	John	YOR 198
Jacob	FRA 314	John	PHA 53	John	LAN 202
Jacob	LAN 315	John	ALL 56	John	BER 205
Jacob	LUZ 403	John	LAN 57	John	BER 208
Jacob	CHE 720	John	WAS 57	John	YOR 212
Jacob	CHE 727	John	PHI 59	John	YOR 215
Jacob	CHE 788	John	WAS 63	John	WST 220
Jacob	CHE 901	John	NOH 65	John	LAN 223
Jacob Jr.	CEN 24	John	PHA 66	John	LAN 225
Jacob Junr.	MNT 93	John	LAN 67	John	LAN 227
Jacob Junr.	LAN 217	John	MNT 69	John	LAN 228
Jacob	DAU 16A	John	CUM 72	John	BER 231
Jacob	DAU 18A	John	NOH 74	John	FAY 236
Jacob	DAU 30A	John	BFD 75	John	WST 240
Jacob	DAU 37A	John	BFD 75	John	BER 243
Jacob	NOH 56A	John	LAN 80	John	BER 251
Jacob	BUC 105A	John	BUC 82	John	BER 262
Jacob	PHI 113A	John	PHA 83	John	BER 262
James	PHA 19	John	CUM 86	John	BER 262
James	LAN 21	John	BUC 87	John	BER 271
James	WAS 22	John	MNT 88	John	LAN 271
James	PHA 24	John	BUC 89	John	BER 276
James	WAS 39	John	NOH 91	John	LAN 276
James	PHI 58	John	PHI 95	John	FRA 286
James	ALL 61	John	CUM 97	John	FRA 288
James	GRN 64	John (At Knittles)		John	FRA 301
James	ALL 88	John (Mason)	NOH 76	John	FRA 303
James	WAS 92	John (Shoemr.)	NOH 69	John	FRA 308
James	WAS 102	John (Taylor)	NOH 69	John	LAN 315
James	LAN 120	John	NOH 69	John	LUZ 329
James	ARM 127	John	NOU 105	John	BUT 354
James	HNT 132	John	CUM 106	John	LUZ 368
James	WST 161	John	PHA 108	John	MER 449
James	NOU 167	John	ALL 109	John	CHE 714
James	YOR 183	John	ALL 109	John	CHE 751
James	FRA 289	John	LAN 109	John	CHE 770
James	FRA 327	John	PHA 112	John	CHE 789
James	MER 449	John	WAS 123	John	CHE 795
James	CHE 845	John	ARM 124	John Esq.	LAN 32
James	NOH 67A	John	PHI 124	John Jnur.	PHA 98
Jas.	CUM 51	John	ARM 127	John Jr.	BER 262
Jereh.	CUM 96	John	HNT 128	John Junr.	NOH 63
Jeremiah	SOM 129	John	NOU 130	John Junr.	PHI 135
Jesse	ADA 11	John	BER 134	John Junr.	YOR 215
Jesse	YOR 218	John	SOM 134	John Senr.	NOH 63
Jesse	CHE 876	John	HNT 135	Joh	BER 0
Jessee	FRA 308	John	LAN 135	John	CEN 22B
Jno.	CUM 54	John	PHI 135	John	DAU 5A

MILLER, John			MILLER, Martin	BER 176	MILLER, Nicholas	MNT 58
John	DAU	18A	Martin	NOU 176	Nicholas	LAN 67
John	DAU	26A	Martin	YOR 187	Nicholas	NOU 118
John	DAU	28A	Martin	LAN 235	Nicholas	NOU 118
John	NOH	39A	Martin	PHI 79A	Nicholas	MNT 135
John	NOH	41A	Mary	DAU 14	Nicholas	SOM 139
John	NOH	45A	Mary	PHI 45	Nicholas	BER 149
John	NOH	53A	Mary	MNT 83	Nicholas	BER 167
John	NOH	60A	Mary	CUM 148	Nicholas	NOH 45A
John	BUC	87A	Mary	DEL 174	Nicholas	NOH 60A
John	NOH	87A	Mary	DAU 17A	Nicholas	NOU 97A
John	BUC	105A	Mary	BUC 153A	Nichs.	WST 219
John F.P	PHI	102	Mary	WAS 39	Nichs.	WST 220
John Geo.	BER	220	Mason	NOH 63	Nicolaus	DAU 37
John Jacob	BER	266	Mathias	BER 205	Odele	DAU 34A
John T.	LUZ	348	Mathias	NOH 56A	Peter	WAS 34
Jonathan	PHA	85	Mathias	HNT 158	Peter	BFD 38
Jonathan	DEL	174	Matthew	WST 370	Peter	LAN 38
Jonathan	BER	266	Matthew	PHI 20	Peter	NOH 38
Jonathan	CHE	838	Matthias	NOU 114	Peter	PHI 53
Jonathan	DAU	6A	Matthias	YOR 192	Peter	MNT 58
Jonthan	BER	275	Matthias	LAN 216	Peter	CUM 62
Jos.	YOR	196	Matthias	LAN 273	Peter	PHA 65
Joseph	WAS	63	Matthias	CUM 85	Peter	PHI 72
Joseph	GRN	64	Mattw.	CUM 71	Peter	MNT 73
Joseph	WAS	75	Meeker/ Mecher?	CUM 71	Peter	NOH 74
Joseph	WAS	82	Mich.	DAU 31	Peter	BFD 75
Joseph	WAS	103	Michael	WAS 4	Peter	BFD 75
Joseph	PHI	125	Michael	ADA 7	Peter	NOH 91
Joseph	PHI	130	Michael	PHA 21	Peter	
Joseph	NOU	138	Michael	DAU 31	(Clockmakr)	NOH 53A
Joseph	SOM	139	Michael	DAU 39	Peter	PHI 102
Joseph	HNT	149	Michael	BFD 45	Peter	LAN 137
Joseph	NOU	159	Michael	BFD 45	Peter	SOM 139
Joseph	LAN	176	Michael	NOH 76	Peter	WAY 144
Joseph	NOU	189	Michael	NOH 91	Peter	BER 156
Joseph	NOU	194	Michael	PHA 117	Peter	YOR 172
Joseph	LAN	234	Michael	SOM 139	Peter	LAN 175
Joseph	WST	275	Michael	LAN 142	Peter	WST 220
Joseph	CHE	699	Michael	HNT 150	Peter	BER 234
Joseph	CHE	827	Michael	BER 154	Peter	LAN 238
Joseph	CHE	862	Michael	YOR 157	Peter	BER 243
Joseph	BUC	153A	Michael	YOR 165	Peter	BER 243
Joseph T.	PHA	76	Michael	YOR 186	Peter	WST 255
Jost	NOH	45A	Michael	YOR 187	Peter	LAN 268
Laurence	PHI	142	Michael	YOR 191	Peter	FRA 300
Lawrence	MNT	83	Michael	YOR 191	Peter	FRA 309
Lazarus	DAU	31	Michael	YOR 194	Peter	FRA 312
Leonard	MNT	135	Michael	BER 201	Peter	FRA 321
Leonard	LAN	146	Michael	BER 204	Peter	CHE 720
Leonard	BER	154	Michael	YOR 206	Peter	CHE 792
Leonard	YOR	179	Michael	BER 220	Peter Revd.	NOH 53A
Leonard	NOH	45A	Michael	BER 221	Peter	NOH 43A
Leonard	NOH	90A	Michael	BER 267	Peter	NOH 53A
Leond. Junr.	BER	154	Michael	BER 272	Peter	BUC 139A
Levi	ADA	43	Michael	CHE 723	Peter	PHI 3
Lewis	ADA	23	Michael Junr.	NOH 76	Philip	ADA 28
Ludwick	BFD	53	Michael	DAU 29A	Philip	ADA 43
Ludwick	MNT	73	Michael	DAU 37A	Philip	WAS 45
Ludwick	CUM	136	Michael	NOH 56A	Philip	PHI 83
Ludwick	YOR	160	Michal	ALL 97	Philip	WAS 102
Ludwig	ADA	28	Michl.	CUM 96	Philip	PHI 124
Ludwig	SOM	134	Michl.	CUM 141	Philip	NOU 137
Magdalene	SOM	139	Michl.	CUM 147	Philip	BER 156
Magdelena	BER	142	Michl.	WST 220	Philip	YOR 157
Magdelena	LAN	298	Michl.	BER 243	Philip	DEL 176
Magnus	PHA	106	Michl.	FRA 304	Philip	BER 180
Manus	BER	266	Michl.	DAU 24A	Philip	DEL 181
Margaret	ADA	28	Michl.	DAU 33A	Philip	YOR 186
Margaret	PHA	70	Mordecai	BER 273	Philip	YOR 199
Margaret	BER	220	Mrs.	NOU 130	Philip	LAN 212
Margaret	FRA	309	Nathan	MNT 107	Philip	BER 234
Margaret	LUZ	427	Nicholas	ADA 15	Philip	LAN 242
Martin	LAN	38	Nicholas	ADA 26	Philip	BER 245
Martin	CUM	61	Nicholas	ADA 30	Philip	LAN 268
Martin	BFD	69	Nicholas	ADA 39	Philip	LAN 268
Martin	MNT	138	Nicholas	MNT 56		

Name	Code	Name	Code	Name	Code
MILLER, Philip	LAN 284	MILLER, Thomas		MILLESON, Caleb	WAS 81
Philip	CHE 790	Thomas	WAS 102	Jacob	CHE 720
Philip	CHE 797	Thomas	NOU 114	James	WAS 81
Philip	CHE 893	Thomas	ARM 125	Jesse	CHE 704
Philip (M.)	YOR 157	Thomas	HNT 146	Jonathan	CHE 701
Philip	MIF 17A	Thomas P.	ERI 56	Richd.	CHE 760
Philip	BUC 105A	Thos.	CUM 67	MILLHIM, Michael	NOU 159
Phillip	CUM 35	Thos.	YOR 216	MILLHOUSE, Amos	CHE 709
Phillip	BFD 38	Thos.	YOR 218	Nicholas	BER 224
Phillip	PHA 64	Thos. Jr.	YOR 218	Paskell	CHE 851
Phillip	NOU 114	Thos.	PHI 104A	Saml.	FAY 253
Phillip	CUM 129	Thos?	PHI 74A	Wm.	CHE 817
Phillip	NOU 172	Titus	WST 313	MILLICK, Henry	NOU 147
Phillip	NOU 97A	Tobias	DEL 185	Peter	NOU 147
Phillop	ALL 81	Tobias	LAN 288	MILLICKLE, James	WAS 23
Polly	PHI 94	Tobias	LAN 266A	MILLIDGES,	
Reonhard	LAN 141	Ulrich	LAN 273	Humphrey	LUZ 347
Reuben	CHE 901	Valentine	DAU 37	MILLIGAN, Widow	PHI 33
Reubin	LAN 166	Valentine	BFD 59	Andrew	ARM 125
Richard	WAS 22	Valentine	NOH 67	David	CUM 29
Richard	BUT 318	Valentine	NOU 100	Edward	MIF 8
Richard	LUZ 405	Valentine	YOR 174	Edward	HNT 122
Right	PHA 73	Valentine	NOU 176	James	WAS 4
Robert	ALL 68	Valentine	CHE 892	James	WAS 4
Robert	BFD 75	Walter	NOH 74	James	MIF 8
Robert	WAS 86	Widow	NOH 69	James	ADA 40
Robert	ALL 111	Widow	LAN 79	James	PHA 83
Robert	WST 154	Widow	GRN 96	James	WAS 86
Robert	WST 162	Widow	BUC 148	James	MNT 87
Robert	NOU 166	Widow	LAN 233	John	MIF 8
Robert	LAN 170	Widow	LAN 239	John	WST 254
Robert	DEL 176	William	ADA 4	Saml.	MIF 8
Robert	LAN 263	William	DAU 8	Saml.	MIF 15
Robert	CHE 763	William	WAS 34	William	CRA 5
Robert	CHE 813	William	WAS 57	William	LAN 160
Robert Esqr.	CHE 901	William	LAN 79	William	LAN 160
Robert	NOH 67A	William	GRN 89	William	YOR 199
Robert	NOH 87A	William	CUM 99	MILLIGEN, William	NOU 166
Robt.	MIF 5	William	WAS 123	MILLIGIN, David	CHE 721
Robt.	CUM 99	William	HNT 132	James	CHE 721
Robt.	YOR 202	William	BUC 146	MILLIGON, Margit	ALL 79
Robt.	YOR 216	William	NOU 147	MILLIKIN,	
Robt.	WST 326	William	HNT 154	Margaret	GRN 102
Rudolph	LAN 123	William	YOR 171	Robert	PHA 13
Rudy	DAU 42	William	BER 177	William	GRN 110
Rudy	LAN 202	William	YOR 216	MILLIN, Ab.	LAN 148
Sam.	LAN 147B	William	YOR 218	MILLING, Matthew	NOU 167
Saml.	CUM 67	William	FRA 308	MILLINGER,	
Saml.	BER 234	William	LUZ 326	Christ.	LAN 286
Saml.	FRA 295	William	LUZ 343	David	YOR 167
Saml.	CHE 903	William	LUZ 364	MILLION, Isaiah	CHE 728
Saml.	MIF 15A	William	CHE 744	MILLIORN, Anthony	WST 153
Samuel	WAS 16	William	CHE 845	MILLIRON,	
Samuel	WAS 22	William Jr.	YOR 171	Barnabas	HNT 126
Samuel	WAS 22	William	NOH 71A	John	WST 219
Samuel	DAU 39	Wilm.	ALL 66	Nicholas	BUT 346
Samuel	WAS 92	Wilm.	ALL 113	Philip	WST 381
Samuel	MNT 120	Wm.	LYC 24	MILLIRONS, Jacob	ARM 122
Samuel	VEN 169	Wm.	PHA 26	MILLIS, Abraham	NOU 147
Samuel	NOU 199	Wm.	CUM 27	MILLISON, William	WAS 45
Samuel	YOR 215	Wm.	CUM 56	MILLMAN, John	BFD 78
Samuel	LAN 230	Wm.	PHA 65	MILLOW?, Peter	YOR 170
Samuel	LAN 301	Wm.	CUM 118	MILLROY, Jno.	BUT 368
Samuel	LUZ 363	Wm.	FRA 306	MILLS, Widow	PHI 21
Samuel	LUZ 363	Wm.	PHI 118A	Widow	PHI 97A
Samuel	BUC 157A	Yost	DAU 9A	Alexander	WAS 52
Sarah	FRA 284	Zachariah	LAN 258	Benjamin	LAN 264
Sebastian	MNT 41	Ohn	LAN 108	David	FAY 258
Sebastian	PHI 140	MILLER?, Kitz		Edmond	PHI 109
Sebastian	BER 167	John	SOM 134	Fredk.	PHI 72A
Siles	BUT 321	Robt.	PHI 102	George	FAY 222
Simon	PHI 41	MILLERS, Jacob	DAU 8A	Henry	WAS 81
Simon	BER 266	MILLERY?, See		Jacob	CUM 26
Solomon	MNT 35	Millvey	NOU 155	Jacob	DEL 182
Susana	WST 255	MILLES, Henry	FRA 318	James	PHA 67
Thomas	WAS 92	Lawrence	NOU 144	James	YOR 215

MITCHEL, Henry	BUC 161	MITCHELL, George	CUM 24	MITCHENOR,		
Hugh	ALL 79	George	WAS 24	Mashich	BUC 87	
Jacob	PHA 121	George	YOR 201	Mashich Jnr.	BUC 87	
Jain	ALL 80	George	CHE 740	Mordecai	CHE 769	
James	SOM 146	George	BUC 85A	William	BUC 141A	
James	SOM 158	Hans	WAS 49	Wm.	BUC 87	
James	FAY 251	Henry	PHA 98	MITCHIM, Francis	CHE 804	
James	LAN 309	Henry	CHE 867	John	CHE 911	
James	FRA 316	Hugh	HNT 153	MITCHLER, Frances	BUC 84	
James	BUT 357	Hugh	WST 292	MITEN, Henry	CUM 64	
John	LYC 4	Isaac	WAS 49	MITER, Saml.	CUM 66	
John	ALL 76	Jacob	MNT 92	MITGLER, Casper	MNT 120	
John	WST 154	James	WAS 13	MITH, John	ALL 113	
John	NOU 176	James	CUM 23	MITHART,		
John	MER 450	James	PHA 29	Frederick	NOH 52	
John	MER 454	James	WAS 57	MITLAR?, Peter	BEV 7	
John Esq.	SOM 146	James	WAS 81	MITLING?, Mary	PHI 106	
John (Bonds		James	CUM 93	MITMAN, Phillip	PHA 37	
Place)	PHI 129	James	PHA 116	MITTARY, Wm.		
John	BUC 137A	James	BUT 317	(Negro)	WAS 39	
Jos.	YOR 201	James Esqr.	WAS 75	MITTEN, Jas.	CUM 46	
Joseph	ALL 115	Jesse	WAS 29	Job	CHE 736	
Joseph	WST 162	Jno.	CUM 129	John	HNT 166	
Joseph	FRA 278	Jno. Senr.	CUM 132	William	HNT 166	
Lewis	SOM 143	Jno.	MIF 25A	MITTENBERGER,		
Mary	YOR 199	John	MIF 15	Nicholas	NOH 50A	
Mary	FRA 298	John	CEN 19	MITTERFIELD?,		
Mathew	ALL 75	John	MNT 75	William	ALL 73	
Mathew	ALL 75	John	WAS 112	MITTEY, Jacob	FRA 304	
Olliver	BEV 16	John	WAS 116	MITTMAN, Conrad	BUC 91	
Pearson	BUC 161	John	CUM 136	MITTS, David	FAY 204	
Richard	BUC 99	John	CHE 740	MITZEL, Jacob	YOR 194	
Richard	BUC 161	John	CHE 870	John	YOR 193	
Richard Jn.	BUC 161	Joseph	MNT 63	MITZER, Joseph	PHI 81A	
Robert	BEV 6	Mathew	WAS 57	MITZLER, George	WST 292	
Robert	PHI 137	Nathaniel	WAS 8	MIXEL, Andrew	BFD 64	
Robert	WST 162	Reuben	LUZ 420	MIXELL, George	SOM 143	
Robert	LAN 225	Richd.	LYC 11	Martin	SOM 162	
Robt.	FRA 315	Robert	LYC 11	MIXON, Old	PHA 71	
Saml.	BUC 161	Robt.	MIF 15	MIXSELL, John	NOH 87A	
Samuel	ADA 17	Ross	CUM 83	MIXWELL, Andrew	SOM 162	
Samuel	FAY 267	Saml.	CUM 132	MIZNER, John	NOU 130	
Shadrach	GRN 64	Saml.	CUM 149	MOAH?, Conrad	MNT 74	
Thomas	GRN 66	Saml.	WST 294	MOAN, Joab	CUM 69	
Thomas	ALL 109	Saml.	CEN 19A	MOAS, George	DAU 50A	
Thomas	SOM 146	Samuel	PHI 52	MOATS, George	NOU 138	
Thomas	MER 451	Samuel	HNT 159	John	NOU 176	
Thos.	DAU 42	Thomas	HNT 123	Michael	NOU 176	
Walter	BUC 161	Thomas	WST 292	MOBEL, Henry Esq.	ALL 102	
William	BUC 145	Thos.	LYC 11	MOBLEY, Denton	HNT 126	
Wilm.	ALL 77	William	WAS 45	Samuel	HNT 126	
Wm.	LYC 18	William	WAS 49	William	HNT 126	
Wm.	FRA 312	William	CHE 867	MOCK, Widow	PHI 78	
MITCHELL, Widow	WAS 17	William	CHE 908	David	BFD 75	
Widow	PHI 47	Wm.	MIF 15	Elizabeth	PHI 123	
-----	MIF 10A	Wm.	MIF 17	Fredk.	PHI 98	
Abel	PHI 47	MITCHELL?, Saml.	PHA 54	George	BFD 65	
Abm.	PHA 48	William?	MIF 10A	George	MNT 100	
Alexander	PHA 37	MITCHELTREE, Jas.	MIF 13	George Jr.	BFD 65	
Alexr.	CHE 843	Jas.	MIF 13	Henry	CHE 893	
Andrew	WAS 69	MITCHEM, John	CHE 786	Henry Jr.	DAU 30A	
Andw.	CUM 120	MITCHENER, John	CHE 710	Henry Sr.	DAU 30A	
Charles	WST 292	Robert	CHE 710	Jacob	BFD 75	
Charlotte	PHA 114	MITCHENON, Israel	CHE 863	Jacob	BFD 75	
Chas.	PHA 109	MITCHENOR,		Jacob	BFD 75	
Davd.	CEN 19	Barrick	CHE 769	Jacob	BER 232	
David	CEN 19	David	BUC 145	Jacob	BER 273	
David	CUM 35	George	BUC 141A	Jacob	BER 275	
Ebenezr.	CUM 107	George	BUC 142A	John	BFD 75	
Edward	YOR 201	George Jn.	BUC 141A	John	BFD 75	
Ensign	LUZ 407	Harman	BUC 142	John	CHE 789	
Florens	PHI 4	Isaac	BUC 141A	Paul	BFD 75	
Francis	PHA 111	Isaiah	BUC 87	Peter	BFD 75	
Francis	PHA 116	John	BUC 141A	Peter	CHE 795	
Geo.	MIF 25A	Joseph	CHE 764	Peter Jr.	BFD 75	
George	PHI 19	Malon	CHE 766	MOCKBEE, Reuben	HNT 137	

MOCKEL, Benjamin	LAN	272	MOLER, Widw.	PHI	103A	MONTGOMERY,	
MOCKER, John	CHE	795	Charles	NOU	97A	Alexr.	DAU 27
MOCKINHAUPT,			Gasper,	WAS	92	Andw.	PHI 21
Philip	NOH	91	MOLHOLLEN, James	LAN	245	Archd.	CUM 22
MOCKLE, Val.	BER	145	MOLIER, Henry	PHI	43	Benja.	WST 371
MOCWELL, Martin	LAN	173	MOLL, Anthony	LAN	80	Charles	HNT 144
Martin	LAN	174	Christopher	NOU	200	Daniel	NOU 144
MODDERW?, M. John	WAS	57	Frederick	LAN	75	Danl.	NOU 172
MODDERWILL?, John	WAS	57	Frederick	NOH	50A	David	DAU 18
MODE, Andrew	BUC	161	Gerhard	LAN	80	David	GRN 102
John	PHI	33	Henry	NOH	56A	David	LAN 150
Joseph	BUC	162	John	NOH	69	David	NOU 166
William	BUC	161	John	BER	208	David	LAN 236
Wm.	CHE	750	Michael	MNT	135	Dorcas	PHA 94
MODERWEL, John	LAN	33	Michael	BER	219	George	LYC 11
MODERWELL, John	LAN	55	Michael	BER	281	Henry	LAN 179
MODNELL, Adam	LAN	159	MOLLEM, William	LAN	140	Hugh	BEV 26
MOFATT, Joseph	BEV	25	MOLLER, Henry	DAU	4	Hugh	WAS 92
MOFFACER, Widow	CHE	894	John	WAS	45	Hugh	NOU 166
MOFFATT, David	PHI	5	MOLLESTON, Reuben	LUZ	378	Hugh S.	CRA 16
James	PHI	23	MOLLIN, James	PHA	110	James	WAS 22
James	PHI	27	MOLLINEAUZ, Wm.	LYC	7	James	WAS 92
MOFFET, William	HNT	161	MOLLIPS, Peter	FAY	246	James	LAN 107
MOFFETT, James	PHI	36	MOLONE, Sussannah	YOR	211	James	NOU 118
James	WAS	81	MONAHAN, Elizah.	PHA	83	James	PHA 122
William	WAS	81	MONBOUR, Philip	BUC	101	James	WST 292
MOGAR, John	CHE	717	MONBOUR?, George	WAS	45	James	MER 451
MOGLE, Caspar	HNT	149	MONDAS, Gasper	HNT	140	James Esq.	WST 312
MOHLER, Jacob	LAN	202	MONDAY, John	CHE	831	Jas	CHE 754
Jacob Junr.	LAN	202	Tarrenc?	BUC	146A	Jas.	CUM 92
John	LAN	202	MONDEBAUGH, Jacob	LAN	294	Jas.	CUM 127
John Junr.	LAN	202	Wm.	LAN	294	Jno.	LYC 18
John? Y.?	LAN	202	MONDITH, John	MNT	78	Jno.	CUM 107
MOHN, Daniel	BER	150	MONELL?, James	HNT	163	John	PHA 62
Henry	BER	149	MONETT?, James	HNT	163	John	WAS 81
John	BER	254	MONEY, Frederick	LAN	299	John	GRN 89
John	NOH	87A	Henry	PHI	97A	John	WAS 92
Ludwig	BER	150	Patk.	CEN	22B	John	CUM 99
Peter	BER	150	William	GRN	71	John	WAS 102
Peter	BER	231	William	LAN	155	John	NOU 144
MOHORVERT, Robert	GRN	110	MONFORT, Peter	ADA	26	John	HNT 148
MOHR, Christopher	NOH	56A	MONG, John	SOM	130	John	NOU 167
Frederick Jr.	NOH	80A	MONGOMERY, Widw.	PHI	76A	John	LAN 222
Frederick	NOH	80A	Cloe	PHA	118	John	WST 312
Henry	NOH	60A	William	PHA	95	John	MER 451
Henry	NOH	80A	MONICH, Abraham	NOH	43A	Joseph	PHI 112
Henry	NOH	80A	Peter Junr.	NOH	43A	Josh.	CHE 754
Herman	NOH	60A	Peter	NOH	43A	Martha	MER 451
Jacob Junr.	NOH	56A	MONINGER, John	WAS	4	Mary	PHA 30
Jacob	NOH	56A	MONK, George	PHA	47	Mrs.	NOU 166
Jacob	NOH	60A	MONMEY, George	WST	292	Richard	LAN 225
John	NOH	69	Jacob	WST	292	Robert	WAS 22
John	NOH	60A	MONMINE, George	WST	292	Robert	GRN 71
John	NOH	60A	MONOHAN, Geo.	CHE	704	Robert	GRN 83
Michael	LAN	147B	MONRACK, Peter	NOU	144	Robert	PHA 118
Peter	NOH	74	MONRO, Samuel	BUC	94	Robt.	NOU 150
Widow	NOH	32A	Solmon	ALL	75	Robt.	NOU 166
William	NOH	56A	MONROE, John	CUM	35	Saml.	FRA 309
MOHRHART, John	NOH	76	John	BER	162	William	GRN 88
MOHRING, Widow	NOH	70	MONS, Nicholas	NOU	100	William	WAS 102
MOHRY, Gotthart	NOH	80A	MONSE, John	NOU	105	William	NOU 144
Jacob	NOH	65	MONTABACH, Henry	LAN	286	William	NOU 144
Peter	NOH	80A	MONTAGE, Henry	WAS	34	William	NOU 166
William	NOH	80A	MONTAINE, Wm.	PHA	47	William	MER 449
MOIRES?, Danl.	BER	234	MONTANYE, Andrew	LUZ	375	Willm. Sr.	WAS 39
MOKE, Samuel	WAS	16	Isaac	LUZ	331	Wm.	PHA 6
MOKEL, Adam	NOU	180	Isaac	LUZ	332	Wm.	LYC 18
MOLANBERRY,			John	LUZ	332	Wm.	MIF 18
Francis	PHI	119	Joseph	LUZ	332	Wm.	LAN 33
MOLAND, Jacob	BFD	54	MONTE----?, Saml.			Wm.	PHA 79
Wilm.	ALL	98	(Crossed Out)	FRA	308	Wm.	CUM 134
MOLD, Robert	MNT	141	MONTEER, William	LAN	244	Wm.	FRA 287
MOLE, George	BER	209	MONTEETH, Alexr.	FAY	246	Wm.	WST 313
John	BER	209	MONTGAR, Saml.	WST	313	Wm.	MER 449
MOLEN, (No Given			MONTGOMERY,			Wm. Junr.	WAS 39
Name)	LAN	149	Alexander	HNT	165	MONTGOMERY?, ----	LYC 24

MONTGOMRY, John	ALL	58
Joseph	ALL	81
Nathaniel	ALL	63
MONTIAR, Alexdr.	VEN	169
MONTIER, Joseph	MNT	43
MONTIETH,		
Benjamin	PHA	121
MONTMOLIN, Fredk.	PHI	106
MONTONDON, Henry	LAN	30
MONTOOTH, Adly	ALL	97
John	MER	451
MONTROW, Thos.	WST	220
MONVILLE, Andrew	LUZ	413
MOOCHER,		
Christian	LAN	3
MOOD, Andrew	BUC	91A
Anthony	PHI	127
John	PHI	87
John	BUC	82A
John	BUC	150A
Philip	BUC	91
Thomas	BFD	44
William	BEV	25
MOODT, Frederick	BER	266
MOODY,		
Christopher	YOR	214
David	WAS	29
James	WAS	29
James	NOU	166
James	FAY	198
Jemima	FAY	201
Jonathan	FAY	201
Nathaniel	LUZ	416
Peter	WAS	13
Robert	DAU	23
Robert	NOH	67
Robt.	YOR	209
Samuel	WAS	45
Samuel	NOU	100
William	NOU	166
MOOKE, Christian	SOM	129
MOON, Abraham	NOU	105
David	PHA	5
Hamilton	CEN	19
Henry	ALL	115
Isaac	BUC	94
Isaac	MNT	105
Jacob	MNT	140
James	BUC	99
James	SOM	143
James	FAY	267
John	LYC	8
John (Sad.?)	MNT	38
John	ALL	115
Michael	NOU	105
Moses	BUC	161
Saml.	PHA	90
Samuel	BUC	94
Thomas	CHE	819
William	BUC	94
MOON?, Abel	CEN	20A
MOONEY, Abraham	DAU	12
Abraham	SOM	132
Dennis	DEL	160
Esther	WAS	75
Gasper	GRN	83
George Junr.	LAN	119
George Senr.	LAN	119
James	LAN	222
Joseph	LAN	221
Patr.	FRA	304
Rachel	FAY	210
Sarah	DAU	3
MOONY, John	FRA	317
Thomas	PHA	93
Wm.	PHA	9

MOOORE, John	BEV	10
MOOR, Andrew	FAY	262
Ann	FAY	262
Charles	PHI	140
Christian	YOR	166
David	FAY	262
David	FRA	278
Elisha	YOR	167
Elizabeth	ALL	82
Ephraim	FAY	239
Garrit	ALL	62
George	ALL	118
George	FAY	236
George	FRA	276
Heak	FRA	299
Jacob	YOR	211
James	ALL	73
James	DEL	181
James	YOR	193
James	FAY	216
James	FAY	267
James	FRA	284
James	FRA	297
James	FRA	307
James	FRA	312
James Senr.	WST	327
Jeremiah	YOR	167
Jno. Senr.	CUM	28
John	CEN	23
John	ALL	90
John	YOR	166
John	FAY	210
John	FAY	216
John	FAY	236
John	FAY	241
John	FRA	284
John	FRA	323
John	WST	326
John Capt.	FAY	236
John Esqr.	WST	327
Jos.	FRA	322
Joseph	ALL	73
Joseph	FRA	276
Josia	FAY	222
Michael	LAN	256
Peter	YOR	163
Philip	YOR	219
Phillip	FAY	236
Rachel	FAY	232
Robert	FAY	233
Robert Esqr.	FAY	253
Robt.	CEN	22B
Saml.	FRA	278
Saml.	FRA	299
Saml.	FRA	323
Samuel	YOR	182
Samuel	FAY	262
Stephn.	CUM	91
Thomas	ALL	103
Thomas	FAY	262
Thomas	FAY	267
Thomas	WST	327
William	FAY	222
William	WST	327
William Junr.	WST	327
Wilm.	ALL	75
Wm.	CUM	96
MOORE, Widw.	PHI	104A
Aaron	WAS	102
Aaron	BUT	338
Abm.	PHI	46
Abner	DEL	179
Abraham	ADA	43
Abraham	BFD	75
Abraham	NOU	106
Abraham	WST	313

MOORE, Adam	DAU	30
Adam	LAN	241
Adam	CHE	850
Alexander	WAS	57
Alexander	BUC	104
Alexander	NOU	106
Alexander	WAS	111
Alexander	HNT	152
Alexr.	PHA	90
Amos	GRN	77
Amos	GRN	89
Andrew	WAS	8
Andrew	BEV	11
Andrew	WAS	57
Andrew	WAS	57
Andrew	PHA	63
Andrew	WAS	111
Andrew	LAN	119
Andrew	LAN	299
Andrew Senr.	LAN	119
Andw.	CUM	61
Andw.	BUT	320
Anthony	GRN	71
Anthony	NOU	166
Archbd.	MIF	25A
Augustine	WAS	52
Benjn.	DAU	33
Caleb	LUZ	384
Charles	WAS	16
Charles	MNT	87
Charles	DEL	160
Christian	BER	251
Christian	CHE	886
Christopher	HNT	132
Conrad	BER	251
Daniel	GRN	89
Daniel	WAS	116
Daniel	HNT	122
Daniel	SOM	129
Daniel	SOM	134
Daniel	NOU	199
Daniel	LUZ	424
David	ADA	9
David	GRN	67
David	NOH	67
David	GRN	96
David	HNT	122
David	LAN	298
David	CHE	714
David	CHE	765
David	CHE	765
Edward	BUC	141A
Elijah	WAS	29
Elijah	HNT	129
Elilsabeth	WAS	52
Elisha	DEL	184
Elizabeth	MNT	132
Enoch	CHE	850
Ezekiel	GRN	92
Fanny	WAS	81
Frances	PHI	10
Frederick	LAN	226
Geo. Dr.	LAN	41
George	MIF	8
George	LAN	36
George	ERI	56
George	MNT	96
George	HNT	140
George	HNT	152
George	BER	251
George	BUT	350
Ghener	CHE	845
Gilbert	WST	312
Hannah	DEL	166
Hannah	CHE	771
Hanry	BER	251

MOORE, Henry	GRN	68	MOORE, John	GRN	89	MOORE, Robert	WAS	29
Henry	GRN	89	John	WAS	92	Robert	BFD	51
Henry	GRN	105	John	WAS	92	Robert	WAS	86
Henry	HNT	139	John	GRN	96	Robert	GRN	92
Henry	HNT	150	John	GRN	102	Robert	LAN	119
Henry	NOU	194	John	WAS	102	Robert	LAN	155
Henry	CHE	710	John	WAS	102	Robert	HNT	158
Henry Doct.	WAS	13	John	MNT	104	Robert	WST	240
Hugh	GRN	102	John	CUM	109	Robert	WST	255
Hugh	HNT	125	John	PHA	109	Robert	LUZ	372
Hugh	HNT	155	John	LAN	119	Robert	CHE	726
Isaac	HNT	129	John	PHA	119	Robert Junr.	LAN	119
Isaac	LAN	165	John	ARM	124	Robt.	CUM	77
J. Joshua Esq.	SOM	162	John	SOM	134	Robt.	WST	371
Jacob	PHI	41	John	NOU	144	Rudo.	DAU	45
Jacob	MNT	78	John	DEL	167	Saml. (See		
Jacob	BER	183	John	WST	173	Moore, Widow)	NOH	38
Jacob	BER	219	John	WST	173	Saml.	PHI	102A
Jacob	LAN	233	John	NOU	194	Samuel	BEV	14
Jacob	BER	251	John	NOU	199	Samuel	WAS	29
James	CRA	2	John	YOR	218	Samuel	NOU	105
James	BEV	6	John	FAY	227	Samuel	NOU	111
James	PHI	26	John	LAN	236	Samuel	WAS	124
James	PHA	32	John	BER	237	Samuel	NOU	159
James	ADA	41	John	BER	251	Samuel	LAN	225
James	WAS	57	John	BUT	360	Sarah	PHA	80
James	WAS	57	John	LUZ	362	Sarah	CHE	703
James	LAN	82	John	WST	370	Seth	LAN	145
James	WAS	92	John	CHE	757	Stephen	PHI	60
James	WAS	92	John	CHE	845	Thomas	ADA	14
James	WAS	102	John	CHE	868	Thomas	BEV	23
James	CUM	108	John	CHE	869	Thomas	BEV	28
James	LAN	119	John	CHE	909	Thomas	WAS	92
James	LAN	121	John Junr.	CUM	29	Thomas	PHA	94
James	HNT	122	John Junr.	GRN	71	Thomas	GRN	102
James	PHA	122	John Senr.	GRN	71	Thomas	WAS	103
James	ARM	126	John	MIF	25A	Thomas	MNT	104
James	ARM	126	Jonathan	GRN	102	Thomas	HNT	129
James	HNT	129	Jonathan	ARM	124	Thomas	HNT	129
James	HNT	151	Jonathen	NOU	147	Thomas	CUM	151
James	NOU	159	Joseph	BEV	14	Thomas	LAN	155
James	LAN	165	Joseph	PHA	14	Thomas	DEL	179
James	LAN	172	Joseph	PHA	60	Thomas	DEL	184
James	NOU	180	Joseph	BFD	75	Thomas	CHE	864
James	NOU	194	Joseph	HNT	122	Thomas Revd.	WAS	4
James	FAY	246	Joseph	HNT	130	Tim	MNT	66
James	BUT	321	Joseph	HNT	151	Trestan	CHE	741
James	CHE	721	Joseph	DEL	190	Widow	MIF	15
James Esq.	CHE	723	Joseph	NOU	199	Widow	LAN	103
James	CEN	20A	Joseph	CHE	768	Widow	LAN	119
James	ERI	57A	Joseph	CHE	771	Widow Of Saml.	NOH	38
Jane	ADA	9	Levy	WST	172	William	CRA	2
Jane	CHE	846	Ludowick	HNT	119	William	PHA	3
Jane	CHE	888	Lydia	HNT	130	William	WAS	22
Jas.	CUM	150	Mary	WAS	16	William	DAU	32
Jean	NOH	67A	Mary	PHI	51	William	WAS	57
Jephtha	GRN	89	Mary	ARM	125	William	GRN	89
Jesse	DEL	174	Mary	DEL	167	William	WAS	92
John	LYC	3	Michael	DAU	31	William	HNT	153
John	DAU	8	Michael	LAN	98	William	WST	154
John	CEN	19	Mordecai	MNT	87	William	DEL	165
John	BEV	23	Mordecai	MNT	104	William	DEL	170
John	WAS	29	Mordecai	DEL	184	William	LAN	175
John	MNT	35	Moris	MIF	17A	William	NOU	202
John	DAU	37	Nathan	DEL	184	William	BER	234
John	BFD	51	Patrick	WAS	116	William	LAN	247
John	WAS	52	Peter	DAU	30	William	LAN	249
John	PHI	55	Peter	PHA	117	William	BUT	334
John	WAS	57	Philip	GRN	77	William	LUZ	354
John	WAS	57	Philip	DEL	177	William	LUZ	360
John	PHA	60	Phineas	GRN	92	William	CHE	723
John	PHI	60	Ralph	CUM	90	William	CHE	807
John	MNT	66	Reese	BER	251	William	CHE	824
John	WAS	69	Richard	WAS	92	William	CHE	842
John	PHA	72	Richard	MNT	104	William	CHE	900
John	WAS	75	Robert	WAS	8	Wm.	LYC	24

MOROON, William	PHI	55	MORRIS, Jennet	YOR	207	MORRISON,	
MORRAW, &			Jesse	WAS	39	Alexander	WAS 57
Hamilton	LAN	157	John	MNT	48	Alexander	LAN 167
MORRE, James	CHE	846	John	WAS	49	Alexander	FAY 204
MORREHEAD,			John	PHA	60	Alexander	FAY 232
Michael	ARM	127	John	GRN	72	Alexander	FAY 267
MORREL, Lewes	CUM	28	John	GRN	96	Alexandr.	FAY 262
MORRELL, James	PHA	91	John	DEL	177	Alexr.	PHI 20
John	PHA	24	John	LAN	237	Alexr.	CHE 729
John	HNT	158	John Dr.	YOR	155	Alexr.	CHE 872
Robert	HNT	158	John Senr.	YOR	155	Alexr.	CHE 899
MORRET, Peter	ADA	12	John	PHI	95A	Andr.	FRA 294
MORREY, Jacob	CHE	892	John	BUC	139A	Benjn.	CHE 743
MORRILL, Robert	PHA	114	John	BUC	157A	Daniel	LAN 162
MORRINOR, T.	PHI	11A	John I./ J.?	FAY	253	Daniel	FRA 283
MORRIS, Widow	PHI	4	Jonathan	MNT	38	Danl.	WST 349
Widw.	PHI	105B	Jonathan	GRN	71	David (Mulatto)	WAS 117
Abel	BUC	105A	Jonathan	GRN	83	Ephraim	CHE 729
Absolem	FAY	246	Jonathan	DEL	163	Fitch	VEN 166
Adam	ADA	29	Jonathan	DEL	177	Francis	WAS 86
Alce	PHA	10	Jonathan	BUT	361	George	WAS 86
Amos	GRN	71	Jonathan M.c.	GRN	72	Hannah	BUC 158
Anthony	PHA	86	Jonathan Senr.	GRN	71	Henry	WAS 70
Anthony	MNT	108	Joseph	WAS	63	Hugh	PHI 29
Anthony	CHE	812	Joseph	PHA	72	Hugh	HNT 157
Asa	GRN	92	Joseph	GRN	83	James	WAS 22
Benj.	YOR	191	Joseph	PHA	98	James	WAS 22
Benjn.	BUC	84	Joseph	BER	242	James	DAU 45
Benjn.	BUC	97	Joshua	MNT	36	James	ALL 54
Benjn.	BER	243	L.	PHI	7	James	GRN 83
Cadwalr.	BUC	91	Levi	GRN	83	James	DEL 156
Casper W.	PHA	76	Levi	FAY	222	James	LAN 164
Catherine	MNT	47	Lewis	WAS	49	James	FRA 318
Charles	YOR	208	Luke	PHI	44	James	CHE 711
Daniel	LYC	7	Mason	BUC	98	James	CHE 729
David	WAS	4	Moris	FAY	258	James	CHE 887
David	PHI	64	Morris	MNT	47	Jane	GRN 105
David	WAS	116	Morris	CHE	799	Jas.	CUM 53
David	DEL	184	Morris Junr.	BUC	105A	Jas.	CUM 139
David	CHE	858	Morris	BUC	105A	Jas. Junr.	CUM 49
Eliam	CHE	780	Nicholas	BER	251	Jas. Junr.	CUM 87
Elias	BUC	105A	Parker	FAY	267	Jas. Senr.	CUM 87
Eliza	PHA	65	Patrick	FAY	204	Jerima.	WAR 1A
Elizabeth	MNT	115	Peter	DEL	192	Jno.	CUM 51
Elizabeth	DEL	177	Philip	PHI	63	John	LAN 7
Elizabeth	DEL	189	Reed	MNT	115	John	WAS 22
Elizabeth Jun.	DEL	177	Robert	PHA	89	John	PHI 25
Evan (See			Robert	GRN	93	John	WAS 29
Morris,			Robert	PHI	146	John	ALL 68
Saml.)	CHE	765	Saml.	LYC	13	John	WAS 70
George	ALL	82	Saml.	PHI	64	John	LAN 94
George	GRN	83	Saml. & Evan	CHE	765	John	ALL 114
George	FAY	253	Samuel Cenr.	PHA	6	John	HNT 156
Henry	MNT	35	Sarah	BER	243	John	WST 220
Hezekial	NOU	159	Solomon	GRN	89	John	FAY 251
Hugh	SOM	143	Susannah	PHA	74	John	FRA 280
Innes	BER	251	Thomas	GRN	72	John	FRA 294
Isaac	WAS	39	Thomas	PHA	101	John	WST 312
Isaac	PHA	67	Thomas	BER	232	John	FRA 318
Isaac	MNT	71	Thomas	CHE	886	John	CHE 843
Isaac	BUC	97	Thomas	BUC	105A	John	CHE 887
Isaac	YOR	203	Thos.	PHA	31	John	BUC 157A
Isaac	BER	251	Thos.	BUC	105A	Joseph	ADA 11
Isaac	NOH	67A	William	BFD	45	Joseph	MIF 16
Isaac	BUC	141A	William	BFD	45	Joseph	DEL 156
Israel	BFD	51	William	HNT	145	Joseph	DEL 157
Issachar	BUC	107	William	DEL	169	Joseph	DEL 158
Issachar Jn.	BUC	107	William	FAY	246	Joseph	WST 312
Jacob	WAS	4	William	LAN	293	Joseph	CHE 729
Jacob	MNT	139	William	CHE	779	Joseph Esqr.	FAY 232
James	GRN	73	William	BUC	141A	Joshua	YOR 176
James	PHA	93	Wm.	BER	243	Martha	YOR 198
James	BER	180	MORRIS?, -----	ADA	25	Mary	PHA 18
James	CHE	799	Danl.	BER	234	Mary	BFD 51
James	BUC	105A	MORRISIN, Duncan	YOR	197	Matt.	WST 312
James C.	PHA	8	MORRISON, Abraham	SOM	132	Michael	YOR 195

```
MORRISON,                       MORROW, Samuel    WST 292   MORTON, John       GRN 105
    Mordicai      BUT 346           Susan         BUT 348       John           PHA 107
    Nancy         FAY 262           Thomas        BEV   4       John           PHI 130
    Noble         CUM  53           Thomas        HNT 142       John           PHI 146
    Robert        ADA  11           Thomas        DEL 191       John           DEL 160
    Robert        GRN  83           William       ADA   6       John           CHE 778
    Robert        FAY 198           William       BFD  38       Jonas          DEL 169
    Robert        LAN 225           William       WAS 123       Joseph         WAS 111
    Robt.         CUM  79           William       HNT 141       Mark           CHE 725
    Robt.         CUM 137           William       SOM 146       Martin         DEL 164
    Robt.         WST 274           William       FAY 246       Michale        BUC 145
    Saml.         YOR 203           William       WST 292       Moses          WAS  81
    Saml.         CHE 729           Willm.        BUT 366       P---?          ALL  81
    Samuel        SOM 135           Wilm.         ALL  56       Thomas         PHI   8
    Samuel        LAN 167           Wm.           CUM  40       Thomas         BFD  44
    Samuel        WST 327           Wm.           YOR 196       Thomas         ALL  80
    Samuel        NOH 30A           Wm.           WST 292       Thomas         NOU 130
    Thomas        WAS  29       MORROWM, Gorvin   FRA 318       William        WAS  81
    Thos.         WST 218       MORRY, William    ADA  28       William        BUC  94
    Thos.         CHE 817       MORS, Patrick     NOU 194       William        CHE 847
    Widdow        FAY 236       MORSE, Amos       LUZ 384       Wm.            BEV   8
    William       BEV  22           Anna          LUZ 340   MORTYOE, John      LAN 220
    William       WAS  75       MORSIN, Thos.     LYC  24   MOSE, Christn.     PHI 111A
    William       YOR 198       MORSTELLER,                     John Jr.       YOR 154
    William       YOR 210           Frederic      CHE 785   MOSE?, Amos        LUZ 383
    William       FAY 216           Frederic      CHE 890   MOSER, Adam        ADA  38
    William       MER 453       MORSTLER,                       Andrew         NOH 87A
    Wm.           LYC  17           Benjamin      BFD  60       Burkhard Jun.  NOH 53A
    Wm.           CUM  68       MORSTOLLER, Jacob SOM 139       Burkhart Senr. NOH 53A
MORRISON?, James  WAR  1A       MORSTTER?, (See                 Christian      MNT 112
MORRISS, Anthony  PHA  92           Morstler)     BFD  60       Daniel         WAS 124
    Isaac W.      PHA 105       MORT?, Joseph     PHI  68       Daniel         YOR 172
    Israel W.     PHA 106       MORTA, Patrick    ALL  69       Daniel         LAN 278
    Sarah         PHA 102       MORTEN, George    FRA 272       Daniel         LAN 278
MORRISSON, Arter  ALL  96       MORTENGER, George BEV  20       Daniel         LAN 280
    James         ALL 110       MORTER, Jacob     CUM  78       David          NOH 53A
    James         PHA 121           John          FRA 281       Francis Mrs.   PHI  69A
    Wilm.         ALL  85       MORTERIBNER,                     George         NOH  38
    Wilm.         ALL 110           Peter         PHI  85       George         MNT  46
MORRISTON, Peter  PHA  54       MORTIMER, John    BER 252       George         NOH  60A
MORROW, Abraham   CUM  36           John          MER 453       Henry          LAN 175
    Abraham       PHA  85           William       MER 453       Jacob          ADA  36
    Adam          ARM 125       MORTIMORE, James  BFD  51       Jacob          YOR 172
    Alexr.        WST 370           John          BUT 351       Jacob          NOH  53A
    Andw.         MIF   8       MORTIN?,                        Jacob          NOH  73A
    Benjamin      WAS  45           Alexander     PHI 138       Jacob          NOH  87A
    Charles       BEV   4       MORTLAND, Alexr.  MIF  25A      John           NOH  52
    Charles       WAS 111           Hugh          YOR 210       John           NOH  63
    Chas.         MIF   8       MORTO, Abraham    NOU 183       John           YOR 172
    David         ALL  86       MORTON, Widow     PHI  10       John           LAN 180
    David         CUM 135           Widow         PHI  11       John           BER 215
    Francis       WAS  57           Widow         PHI  22       John           LAN 278
    Henry         ALL  63           Aaron Esqr.   DEL 186       John Jr.       LAN 278
    Hugh          CHE 844           Ann           DEL 186       John Junr.     NOH  91
    James         ALL  93           Daniel        DEL 188       John Senr.     NOH  91
    James         WAS 123           David         WAS  13       Martin         PHI 104A
    John          ADA   3           Edwd.         CUM  61       Michael (Big)  NOH  52
    John          WAS   8           Erasmus       DEL 162       Michael        BER 160
    John          CEN  23           George        PHI  22       Michael        NOU 176
    John          PHA  62           George        ALL  89       Michael Junr.  NOH  52
    John          WAS 111           George        PHA 107       Michael Senr.  NOH  52
    John          CUM 134           Hugh          BUC  94       Michael        NOH  53A
    John          WST 292           Hugh          CHE 718       Paul           NOH  74
    John          BUT 322           Isaac         PHI   4       Peter          NOH  48
    John          FRA 322           Isaac         PHI  13       Samuel         BEV  13
    John          BUT 353           Isaac         DEL 186       Samuel         YOR 169
    Lenard        ALL 102           Israel        DEL 187       Smauel         YOR 195
    Mathew        WAS  13           James         ALL  73       Tobias         NOH  34
    Paul          WST 220           James         HNT 141       Tobias         NOH  52
    Rebekah       HNT 151           James         CHE 717       Valentine      FAY 222
    Richd.        FRA 322           James         CHE 869       Widow          NOH  39A
    Richd.        FRA 323           Jane          HNT 141   MOSES, Abm.        PHI  70
    Ritchard      ALL 115           Jeptha        NOU 130       Adam           CHE 781
    Robert        LAN 170           Jesse         ADA  17       Henry          PHA  64
    Saml.         CUM 133           John          BEV   8       Henry          PHI  77A
    Samuel        FAY 246           John          WAS  53       Jacob          BFD  75
```

MOSES, Jacob	CHE 791	MOTT, Ebenezer		MOUSKENOUGH,			
Jacob	CHE 906	Jr.	LUZ 374	George	ADA 19		
John	BFD 75	Edward	NOH 38	Peter	ADA 19		
John	CHE 781	John	BUC 94	MOUSMAN, John	ALL 61		
Sophia	PHA 98	Wm.	PHA 8	MOUT, Widow	WAS 104		
MOSEY, Christian	LAN 310	MOTT?, Adam	FRA 276	MOUTEL, George	PHA 78		
Jacob	SOM 154	MOTTEE, Abram	CHE 726	MOVEN, Matthew	CHE 891		
William	ADA 41	MOTTS, Henry	GRN 91	MOWAN, James	CUM 66		
MOSHER, Abraham	FAY 222	Simon	FRA 307	MOWAR, Leonard	FRA 292		
Susanna	WAS 39	MOTZ, John	BER 159	MOWDY, John	HNT 146		
MOSIER, Joshua	LUZ 414	Lawrence	BER 167	MOWEN, Francis	BFD 64		
Theophilus	LUZ 414	Margaret,		MOWER, Andrew	NOU 114		
MOSLICK, Godlieb	LAN 135	Warden Of The		Christ.	CUM 66		
MOSNER, John	PHI 10	Single		George	MNT 135		
MOSS, Carthus?	CHE 864	Sister's		George	LAN 232		
Elija	FAY 222	House	NOH 32A	Henry	CUM 41		
Geoe. W.	PHI 23	Michael	BER 183	Henry	NOU 106		
George	PHI 141	MOTZ?, Adam	FRA 276	Jacob	PHI 118A		
James	WAS 76	MOUDY, Matthias	YOR 212	John	NOU 101		
James	NOH 30A	MOUGHAN, John	FAY 209	John	PHI 120		
John	PHA 19	MOUH?, Conrad	MNT 74	John	MNT 135		
John	PHI 76	MOUL, Conrad	YOR 184	John	FRA 286		
John	WAS 76	Conrad	YOR 185	Michael	BFD 53		
John	FAY 216	Philip	YOR 184	Michael	HNT 139		
John	FAY 233	MOULDER/		Peter	MNT 135		
Joseph	FAY 216	MOULDES?,		Peter	CHE 894		
Joseph	LUZ 351	John	DEL 163	MOWERER, Philip	PHI 60		
Peter	CUM 42	MOULDER, John		MOWIN, Daniel	FRA 302		
Phillip	NOU 144	Revd.	YOR 160	John	FRA 301		
Samuel	BFD 51	Margaret	DEL 162	Peter	FRA 297		
Samuel	BFD 51	Wm.	PHA 46	Stephen	FRA 292		
Solomon	LUZ 420	MOULFAIR, Michl.	DAU 42	Wm.	FRA 283		
William	MIF 13	MOULFER, John	DAU 23	MOWRA, Isaac	CHE 791		
William	FAY 233	MOUN, John	CHE 905	MOWRER, Adam	LAN 243		
MOSSENET, Henry	FRA 298	MOUN?, Peter	PHA 73	Andrew	BFD 75		
MOSSER, Abraham	YOR 207	MOUNCH, John	NOU 188	Baltzer	LAN 108		
Adam	LAN 202	MOUNT, James	CRA 6	Baltzer	LAN 239		
Christn.	BER 176	MOUNTAIM, Hugh	FRA 323	Christian	NOU 188		
George	LAN 212	MOUNTAIN, John	SOM 146	Daniel	NOU 123		
Henry	BER 273	Joseph	SOM 146	Daniel	LAN 217		
John	BER 145	MOUNTS, -----	ARM 123	Henry	NOU 188		
John	BER 150	Caleb	FAY 198	Henry	LAN 243		
John	BER 174	John	WAS 102	Jacob	CHE 891		
John	CHE 891	John	ARM 123	John	NOU 123		
Michael	YOR 172	Joshua	FAY 198	John	NOU 123		
Michael	BER 209	Matthias	WAS 8	John	PHI 136		
Nicholas	BER 150	Rachel	FAY 198	Michael	NOU 188		
Peter	BER 174	Richard	WAS 102	Peter	NOU 123		
Robert	PHI 7	MOUNTZ, Christian	BER 267	MOWRY, Nicholas	FRA 288		
MOSSEY?, (See		George Jr.	BER 205	MOWSER, Samuel	BFD 75		
Missey)	BER 145	John	BER 205	MOY, Christian	MNT 90		
MOSSLEY, Ann	PHA 121	John	BER 267	John	MIF 8		
MOSSMAN, James	FAY 210	Joseph	BER 205	MOYAN, Ludwick	BFD 65		
MOST, Christian	SOM 150	Lazarus	BER 203	MOYAR, Christn.	CHE 896		
George	BUC 149A	MOUREN, Michael	NOU 189	MOYARS, George	CHE 756		
Jacob	BUC 91	MOURER, Anderew	ADA 34	Jacob	CHE 878		
Jacob	LAN 131	Andrew	NOU 138	MOYE, John	MNT 55		
Jacob	SOM 150	Cunrod	SOM 143	MOYER, Widow	MNT 126		
John	BUC 149A	George	DAU 40	A.	DAU 45		
Joseph	SOM 150	Jacob	NOU 138	Abm.	BUC 147A		
MOSTALLER, John	SOM 159	Jacob	CHE 796	Abraham	MNT 68		
MOSTELLER,		John	ADA 17	Abraham	BUC 97		
Valentine	BUC 148	John	ADA 21	Abraham	MNT 119		
MOSTOLLER,		John	LAN 312	Abraham	BER 167		
Frederic	SOM 130	John	CHE 789	Abraham	BER 208		
MOT, Ezacaria?	ALL 97	John	BUC 139A	Abraham	BER 215		
MOTE, Isaac	CHE 801	Michael	SOM 158	Adam	BER 236		
John	CHE 811	Michl.	DAU 34	Anthony	NOU 101		
MOTHEREL, John	WAS 102	Peter	CHE 783	Anthony	NOU 101		
MOTHERSPACK, John	HNT 128	Philip	SOM 139	Benj.	DAU 41		
MOTLEE?, (See		Rudolph	PHI 136	Benjamin	MNT 100		
Mottee)	CHE 726	MOUSE, John	ADA 23	Casper	HNT 119		
MOTLEY, Mary	PHA 45	John	ADA 30	Casper	PHI 131		
MOTS, George	LAN 174	MOUSER, Daniel	NOU 189	Casper	BER 251		
Peter	NOU 147	Jacob	BER 189	Christian	BFD 59		
MOTT, Ebenezer	LUZ 374	Nusess?	NOU 144	Christian	SOM 139		

MOYER, Christian	BER 208	MOYER, John	SOM 152	MOYS, Widow	PHI	9
Christian	BER 209	John	BER 165	MOZE, John Senr.	YOR	160
Christn. Jr.	DAU 48A	John	BER 167	MTHALOMUS?, Jacob	LAN	171
Chrn.	DAU 40A	John	BER 180	MUBERY, William	YOR	202
Conrad	BER 165	John	BER 261	MUC CULEIGH,		
Cunrod	SOM 154	John	BUC 106A	Francis	MER	451
Daniel	BER 219	John J. / I.?	BER 154	MUC CULLEIG,		
Daniel	BER 221	Jonathan	BER 167	Robert	MER	451
Daniel	BER 264	Joseph	BUC 97	MUC CULLEIGH,		
Daniel Jr.	BER 221	Julina	BER 223	Charles	MER	451
Danl.	BER 204	Leonard	BER 157	MUC ENULTY, Calib	MER	452
David	MNT 93	Leonrd	BER 245	James	MER	452
David	BER 167	Lewis	DAU 18A	John	MER	452
Felty	LAN 110	Mar	DAU 38	MUC FARLIN,		
Frederick	BER 167	Maria	BER 221	William	MER	451
Fredk.	DAU 52	Martin	DAU 41	MUC KLEREVY, John	MER	451
Fredrik	DAU 9	Martin	BER 251	MUC KLEWAIN, John	MER	452
George	DAU 14	Mattis	MNT 83	MUC MILLIN,		
George	MNT 53	Michael	MNT 76	Isabil	MER	449
George	MNT 74	Michael	MNT 83	James	MER	451
George	BER 145	Michael	BUC 97	Wilm.	MER	450
George	SOM 149	Michael	SOM 139	MUCH, Jeremh.	PHI	19
George	BER 177	Michael	BER 167	MUCHLER, Andrew	NOU	105
George	BER 219	Michael	BER 272	MUCHMER, Andreas	BER	221
George Jr.	BER 145	Michael	BER 272	MUCK, Widow	PHI	19
George Sen.	SOM 149	Michael	DAU 42A	Widow	PHI	27
George, Jur.	BER 176	Nicholas	BER 227	George	NOU	188
Henry	DAU 37	Nicholas	BER 264	Jacob	NOU	130
Henry	DAU 41	Peter	BUC 148	Phillip	PHA	73
Henry	MNT 74	Peter	BER 154	MUCKELROY, John	FAY	198
Henry	MNT 86	Peter	BER 221	Thomas	FAY	210
Henry	BUC 97	Peter	BER 251	MUCKLER, Samuel	NOU	111
Henry	PHI 128	Peter	CHE 783	MUCKLEWANE, Jas.	PHI	146
Henry	BER 153	Peter	DAU 49A	MUCKLEWANY, John	FRA	299
Henry	BER 157	Philip	BER 154	MUCKLY, Christian	NOH	91
Henry	BER 159	Philip	BER 227	Jacob Junr.	NOH	90A
Henry	BER 167	Philip	BER 264	Jacob	NOH	90A
Henry	NOU 180	Philip	BER 273	Peter	NOH	90A
Henry	BER 222	Philip Jr.	BER 264	MUD?, Nathan	FRA	274
Henry	BER 264	Rachael	BER 234	MUDROE, Samuel	NOU	183
Henry	BER 264	Rudolph	SOM 149	MUDY, Peter F.	PHI	19
Henry	DAU 40A	Samuel	BUC 97	MUFFLE, John	WST	370
Henry	DAU 43A	Samuel	MNT 114	MUFFLEY, John	NOH	84
Hester	PHA 34	Samuel	MNT 124	Peter	NOH	84
Isaac	MNT 100	Samuel	BER 250	MUFFLY, Christian	NOH	67A
Jacob	DAU 35	Samuel Jnr.	BUC 97	Henry	NOH	30A
Jacob	MNT 68	Simon	LUZ 359	Peter Junr.	NOH	30A
Jacob	LAN 106	Sophia	BER 251	Peter	NOH	30A
Jacob	MNT 121	Valentine	BER 205	MUFLEY, Joseph	BUC	157A
Jacob	BUC 148	William	NOU 123	MUFLY, John	ARM	126
Jacob	BER 160	William	BUC 148	MUG, John	PHI	2
Jacob	BER 177	William	BER 156	MUGALL, John	PHA	87
Jacob	BER 183	MOYERS, Adam	CUM 144	MUHLENBERG,		
Jacob	BER 210	Christian	BUC 148	Frederick A.	LAN	27
Jacob	BER 215	Christian	BUC 157A	Henry	LAN	46
Jacob	BER 263	Eliza	PHA 76	Peter	MNT	83
Jacob	CHE 783	Geo.	CUM 106	MUING, George	LAN	51
Jacob Jr.	BER 160	Geo.	CUM 144	MUIR, Sarah	FAY	210
Jacob	DAU 43A	George	BUC 101	MUKEN, John	WST	221
Jacob	BUC 147A	George	WST 219	MULBREITH, Robert	NOU	118
Jno.	DAU 33	Henry	BUC 148	MULBURY, Peter	CHE	712
John	DAU 37	Isaac	BUC 141	MULEGAN, John	ARM	123
John	DAU 39	Jacob	BUC 91	MULENBERG, Henry		
John	DAU 40	Jacob	BUC 82A	W.	PHA	77
John	DAU 42	John	BUC 91	MULFORD, Abraham	WAY	144
John	DAU 51	John	WST 218	James	PHI	38
John	DAU 52	John	WST 292	MULHALL, Thos.	CUM	70
John	BUC 82	John	BUC 105A	MULHALLON, John		
John	MNT 83	John	BUC 141A	Esqr.	NOH	38
John (Crossed Out)	BUC 97	Joseph	BUC 105A	MULHARIN, Edward	ALL	103
John	NOU 101	Saml.	BUC 148	MULHERON, Joheph	BER	251
John	CUM 131	William	BUC 148	MULHOLLA, Roger	ALL	52
John	PHI 140	MOYES, James	PHA 122	MULHOLLAN, Joseph	MIF	10A
John	CUM 147	MOYLAN, Gaspar	PHA 107	MULHOLLAND,		
John	BER 150	Stephen	PHA 3	George	MIF	2
		MOYNIHAN, Maurice	PHA 65	MULHOLLEN, Thos.	CUM	120

MULIGIN,			
Alexander	NOU 144		
MULINBERGER,			
Michael	PHI 124		
MULL, Anthony	NOU 138		
Christopher	NOU 167		
George	FAY 267		
Henry	WAS 23		
Henry	SOM 152		
Martin	BUC 94		
MULLAN, Barnherd	LAN 128		
John	LAN 51		
MULLEN, Arthur	CHE 887		
Barney	PHA 113		
Catharine	CUM 60		
George	DEL 178		
James	CUM 123		
James	LUZ 347		
James Jr.	LUZ 347		
Jane	PHA 97		
Jas.	CUM 141		
John	PHA 82		
John	WAS 92		
John	DEL 173		
John	DEL 191		
Stephen	LAN 115		
Thomas	WAS 45		
Thomas	LUZ 346		
Thos. J.	YOR 212		
Wm.	CEN 24		
MULLER, Joseph	CHE 766		
Lorans	PHI 50		
MULLESON, Lewis	LUZ 378		
MULLIGAN, Widow	PHI 27		
MULLIN, Charles	NOU 101		
Charles	CHE 730		
Francis	WST 313		
George	DEL 177		
Hugh	ARM 127		
James	BEV 13		
James	PHI 82A		
Michl.	MIF 25A		
Nicholas	FAY 267		
Patrick	MIF 17A		
Patrick	PHI 81A		
William	MNT 51		
MULLIN?, Daniel			
M.	YOR 207		
MULLOCK, Edwd.	PHA 86		
MULLON, Alexander	GRN 96		
MULLOW?, Peter	YOR 170		
MULRAY, Matts.	CUM 69		
MULTINBERGER,			
Wid.	PHI 102A		
MULTZ, Geo.	CUM 60		
MULVANY, Philip	MNT 106		
MULVETS, Henry	BFD 38		
MULVEY, Charles	PHA 119		
MUMA, Fredk.	DAU 21A		
John	DAU 20		
John	YOR 181		
John	DAU 14A		
Leonard	LAN 64		
Peter	LAN 309		
Philip	LAN 314		
MUMAR, Frederick	LAN 2		
MUMART, Richard	YOR 179		
MUMAT?, -----	LAN 3		
MUMAUGH?, John	DAU 42		
MUMBAUER, John	NOH 56A		
MUMBOUR, Conrad	BUC 82		
George	BUC 101		
Henry	BUC 101		
MUME, John	NOU 189		
John	NOH 85A		
MUMFORD, Jerah.	WAY 137		

MUMFORD,			
Margarett	DEL 162		
Nathan	LUZ 332		
Wm.	PHA 57		
MUMMA, Jacob	LAN 212		
MUMMERT, John	ADA 34		
Saml.	ADA 34		
MUMMERT?, Mathias	ADA 35		
MUMMY,			
Christopher	WAS 57		
Jacob	NOH 50A		
MUMOE?, Jacob	FAY 198		
MUMONA, John	NOU 138		
MUMPER, Michael	YOR 212		
MUN---AND?, James	FRA 313		
MUNCH, John	NOH 34		
MUNCY, Detrick	PHA 53		
Levi	WAS 57		
MUNDLE, Abner	GRN 83		
Ann	CHE 876		
Eli	GRN 83		
James	GRN 83		
James Junr.	GRN 83		
MUNDORF, David	ADA 41		
John	ADA 40		
John	ADA 42		
MUNDORFF, Peter	YOR 158		
MUNDY, Benjamin	NOU 105		
MUNERSHER, John	PHA 73		
MUNFORT, John	ADA 20		
MUNG, Adam	HNT 131		
MUNGAN, Denis	FAY 258		
MUNGLE, Adam	BER 223		
MUNHOLLAN, Hugh	HNT 148		
William	HNT 148		
MUNIG, Peter			
(Crossed Out)	NOH 30A		
MUNING, David	LAN 292		
MUNINGER, Jacob	LAN 290		
John	LAN 290		
MUNKS, John	CHE 758		
Wm.	CEN 20A		
MUNN, John Junr.	WAS 69		
John Senr.	WAS 69		
Zadock	FAY 205		
MUNNELL, John	WAS 102		
William	MER 454		
MUNNON, Cornelius	GRN 84		
MUNNS, Thomas	PHA 17A		
MUNRO, Alexander	WAS 50		
Andrew	WAS 22		
Andrew Esqr.	WAS 22		
George	WAS 22		
MUNROE, George	ARM 126		
Jehu	FAY 229		
John	PHA 63		
Mehitable	LUZ 352		
MUNSCHAUER, Henry	LAN 212		
MUNSEY, James	WAS 29		
MUNSHOWER, Jacob	CHE 793		
Jacob	CHE 889		
John	CHE 893		
Michael	CHE 785		
Robt.	CHE 908		
MUNSON, Almon	LUZ 389		
Wilmot	LUZ 332		
MUNSTER, Barbara,			
Warden Of The			
Widow's House	NOH 32A		
MUNT, Janathan	CHE 745		
MUNTEETH,			
Issabella	BEV 21		
John	FRA 327		
MUNTGOMRY, John	ALL 87		
MUNTOOTH, Henry	BUT 342		
MUNTORF, Henry	ADA 43		

MUNTORF, Jacob	ADA 5		
John	ADA 40		
MUNTZ, John	LYC 9		
Peter	LYC 9		
MUNY, James	PHI 55		
Thomas	PHI 55		
MUNY?, James	BFD 60		
MUNYAN, Thomas	BUC 94		
MURCH, David	LUZ 428		
MURCLOCK, John	PHI 84		
MURDOCH, Alexr.	CHE 726		
Elizabeth	PHA 35		
John	PHA 5		
William	WAS 76		
MURDOCK, Adam	WAS 92		
David	WAS 22		
James	DAU 30A		
Jas.	MIF 25A		
John	WAS 17		
John	WAS 103		
John	ALL 105		
John	WST 240		
John	CHE 779		
Joseph	CHE 756		
Josh.	CHE 780		
Mary	CUM 58		
Mathew	ALL 105		
Robert	ALL 105		
Robt.	WST 349		
Robt.	WST 381		
Samuel	WAS 22		
Thomas	HNT 133		
Wm.	PHA 39		
Wm.	PHA 60		
MURFFEY, Widow	PHI 68		
MURGATROYD, Saml.	PHA 84		
Thos.	PHA 84		
MURIN, John	PHI 36		
MURKEL, James	PHI 30		
MURPHEY, Adam	MER 452		
Barney	BUC 103A		
Christian	LAN 236		
Daniel	PHA 86		
John	CRA 11		
John	DAU 19		
John	PHA 27		
John	SOM 158		
Michael	BFD 58		
Moses	FRA 288		
Phebe	DAU 3		
Robt.	PHA 29		
Samuel	ARM 122		
Thomas	PHA 101		
Thomas	CHE 902		
MURPHIN, Willm.	PHI 75A		
MURPHIN?, Isaac	BUC 105		
MURPHY, Andr.	FRA 317		
Andw.	CUM 87		
Archy	FAY 258		
Asa	GRN 96		
Benjn.	FAY 210		
Cornelius	WAS 92		
Daniel	ADA 8		
Daniel	PHA 63		
Edwd.	CUM 121		
Elisha	HNT 163		
Hazael	CHE 789		
Henrey	FAY 267		
Henry	BUT 350		
Hugh	ALL 75		
Isaac	FAY 239		
Jacob	FAY 205		
James	CUM 25		
Jane	FAY 210		
Jesse	CRA 10		
John	MIF 15		

MURPHY, John	ADA	21	MURRAY, Patrick	NOU	166	MUSGEMIING /	
John	WAS	22	Patt.	WST	219	MUSGENUNG,	
John	CUM	25	Richd.	CUM	50	Jacob	BER 279
John	PHA	62	Robt.	LYC	26	MUSGENUNG, David	NOH 91
John	BUC	94	Thomas	PHA	99	MUSGENUS, Sophia	YOR 194
John	DEL	160	Thomas	NOU	118	MUSGRAVE, Aaron	PHI 23
John	VEN	165	Thomas	CUM	130	Aron Junr.	PHA 96
John	BER	167	Thos.	CUM	47	James	PHA 13
John	WST	172	William	DAU	2	Joseph	CHE 846
John	YOR	198	William	DAU	11	MUSHART, Widow	PHI 95
John	FAY	233	William	PHA	96	MUSHETT, Thomas	PHI 11
John	LUZ	419	William	NOU	118	MUSHGAN, Aaron	NOU 150
John	CHE	765	William	HNT	161	MUSHKIN?, Isaac	BUC 105
Joseph	FAY	216	William	HNT	165	MUSHLITY, Jacob	NOH 50A
Lackey	MIF	10A	Wm.	LYC	3	MUSHLITZ OR	
Maria	BER	239	Wm.	LYC	25	MUSICK, David	NOH 91
Mary	ALL	53	Wm.	CUM	53	MUSHLITZ, Widow	NOH 80A
Nancy	FAY	253	Wm. Senr.	LYC	6	MUSHRUSH, George	ALL 97
Owen	PHI	14	MURRER, Willm.	PHI	40	Jacob	WAS 112
Patk.	MIF	5	MURREY, Jacob	SOM	158	MUSHRUSH?,	
Phillip	CUM	118	Jacob	CHE	906	Michael	CRA 4
Robert	PHI	12	John	CHE	906	MUSI, Monseur	PHA 97
Robert	FAY	267	MURRIARTY, Hugh	FRA	287	MUSICK OR	
Samuel	PHI	39	MURRIN, Barny	FRA	278	MUSHLITZ,	
Samuel	ALL	59	Hugh	BUT	357	David	NOH 91
Segal	PHI	92A	James	CHE	728	MUSICK, Widow	NOH 91
Thomas	WAS	8	MURRITZ, David	HNT	156	MUSIGS?, Jacob	LAN 275
Thomas	MNT	62	MURROW, Albert	NOU	118	MUSKETNUSS, Adam	LAN 52
Thomas	HNT	143	James	CHE	843	Peter	LAN 52
Timothy	ALL	49	John	SOM	130	MUSLEMAN, Jacob	NOU 138
Widow	MIF	5A	MURRY, Andrew	ADA	9	MUSSARD, Amus	FAY 246
William	WST	172	Barnabas	NOU	167	MUSSELM, Abraham	LAN 136
William	YOR	172	Charles	BEV	26	MUSSELMAN,	
Wm.	BEV	16	Charles	FAY	205	Christian	LAN 189
Wm. Junr.	CUM	26	Charles	FAY	232	Christian	NOH 56A
Wm. Senr.	CUM	25	Daniel	WAS	22	Christn.	LAN 288
MURPY, John	FAY	240	Danil	FAY	262	David	LAN 314
MURRAL, Mary	CUM	146	David	ALL	115	David	NOH 71A
MURRAN, Jno.	CUM	126	Elizabeth	CRA	7	Geo.	CUM 116
MURRAT, Nichs.	CUM	137	Francis	YOR	199	Henry	BUC 97
MURRAY, Abner	LUZ	428	Hugh	PHI	48	Henry	LAN 274
Alexr.	CUM	53	Jacob	DEL	191	Henry	LAN 307
Andw.	CUM	96	James	YOR	156	Henry	LAN 307
Ann	CUM	49	James	NOH	78A	Jacob	BUC 101
Archebald	WAY	142	John	ALL	88	Jacob	CUM 116
Charles	LAN	13	John	FRA	296	Jacob	LAN 136
Charles	PHI	26	John	WST	379	Jacob	LAN 304
Charles	PHA	116	John (Added			John Jun.	ADA 43
Charles	LAN	128	Referrence)	WST	381	John	NOH 30A
Daniel	LAN	80	Joseph	ALL	94	Joseph	CUM 70
Daniel	HNT	121	Margrt.	ALL	51	Matthias	LAN 269
Ephraim	NOU	166	Mathew	BEV	8	Michael	NOH 74
Francis	BUC	103A	Neal	BUT	333	Peter	YOR 208
George	NOU	114	Neill	WAS	69	Peter	LAN 307
Halbert	CUM	53	Peter	ALL	51	Peter	NOH 56A
Henry	NOU	166	Phillop	ALL	52	Samuel	BUC 91
James	DAU	11	Robert	FAY	233	Samuel	BUC 101
James	PHI	71	Stephen	MNT	51	MUSSER, Benjamin	LAN 283
James	NOU	166	Thomas	ALL	59	Christian	LAN 298
James	WST	369	Thomas	NOU	118	Christopher	WAS 103
Jas.	CUM	50	Thomas	FRA	275	Devault	ALL 74
Jer. Esqr	WST	192	MURRY?, George	LAN	154	George	WAS 103
Joel	LUZ	427	MURSTELLER,			Henry	LAN 269
John	NOU	118	Catherine	BER	208	Henry	LAN 289
John	PHA	118	MURTO, James	PHI	107	Henry	LAN 298
John	LAN	119	MURTZ, David	NOU	97A	Henry	LAN 309
John	HNT	124	MURY, John	FRA	274	Jacob	CUM 29
John	LAN	129	MUSCH, Jno. (See			Jacob	LAN 111
John	NOU	167	Musch, Widow)	NOH	38	Jacob	LAN 223
John	WST	219	Widow Of Jno.	NOH	38	Jacob	LAN 293
John	LAN	292	MUSE, Fantley	ALL	70	John	LAN 24
Lackey	DAU	5	MUSENUNG?, Peter	CUM	89	John	LAN 48
Levy	NOU	194	MUSER, Henry	DAU	35	John	SOM 154
Margt.	CUM	49	Henry	DAU	35A	John	YOR 199
Michael	HNT	165	Jacob	LAN	111	John	LAN 269
Noah	LUZ	428	MUSESLMAN, John	ADA	43	John	LAN 285

MUSSER, John	LAN 314	MYER, John	BER 281	MYERS, Jacob		HNT 144
John Senr.	BUT 318	Joseph	HNT 121	Jacob		HNT 159
Joseph	LAN 107	Martin	LYC 17	Jacob		WST 275
Martin	LAN 118	Michael	NOU 130	Jacob		LUZ 404
Matthias	LAN 269	Nicholas	NOU 100	Jacob		LUZ 412
Michael	LAN 42	Peter	BUC 82	Jacob		PHI 78A
Michael	DAU 39A	Peter	LAN 257	Jno.		CUM 138
Nicols.	DAU 46	Philip	BER 281	John		ADA 3
Paul	CUM 29	Samuel	LAN 174	John		ADA 12
Peter	LAN 118	William	DAU 29A	John		ADA 38
Peter	LAN 313	MYERLY, Frederick	BER 167	John		ADA 42
Peter	LAN 314	Michael	HNT 147	John		WAS 50
William	LAN 42	Philip	PHI 116A	John		WAS 123
William	LAN 302	MYERS, Widow	PHI 95A	John		ARM 127
MUSSI, Joseph	PHA 110	Abraham	FRA 278	John		PHI 130
MUSSLEMAN, Chris.	LAN 74	Abraham	WST 292	John		BUC 148
Jacob	YOR 213	Abraham	BUC 141A	John		HNT 154
John	LAN 6	Abram	CUM 116	John		DEL 159
Joseph	LAN 93	Adam	ARM 125	John		LAN 219
MUSTARD, Archd.	CUM 140	Adam	WST 220	John		WST 275
George	FAY 227	Adam	FRA 321	John		FRA 283
James	WAS 4	Adam	PHI 104A	John		FRA 311
James	WAS 8	Adam	PHI 108A	John		PHI 111A
John	WAS 8	Andrew	GRN 71	John		PHI 114A
John	MER 450	Andrew	PHI 73A	John		BUC 149A
Thomas	MER 449	Andw.	CUM 31	John G.		PHI 73A
William	FAY 228	Balsor	WST 192	Jonathan		FRA 321
MUSTIN, George	DEL 166	Boston	CUM 102	Joseph		ADA 24
MUSY, Thomas	PHI 8	Christian	CUM 32	Lawrence		LUZ 334
MUTCHMORE, Saml.	CUM 54	Christian	BUC 142	Ludwig		ADA 43
MUTERSPAGH, Peter	CUM 145	Christopher	WAS 112	Martin		LUZ 392
MUTH, John	BUC 140	Christopher	HNT 119	Mary		ADA 30
John	BER 214	Christopher	WST 292	Mary		PHI 108A
Nicholas	NOH 60	Christr.	CUM 101	Mathew		WAS 70
MUTHART, Adam	BER 165	Conrod	ARM 124	Michael		ADA 41
Daniel	BER 165	Elisha	NOH 65	Michael		WAS 112
John	BER 165	Frederick	ADA 36	Michael		HNT 116
Joseph	BER 165	Frederick	LAN 235	Michael		HNT 155
Peter	BER 165	Fredk.	PHI 85A	Michael		HNT 159
MUTZ, Barney	LAN 96	Geo.	LYC 26	Michael		BUC 157A
MUVEY?, Eli	LAN 223	Geo. Junr.	CUM 63	Nicholas		ADA 38
MYARS, Adam	FAY 241	George	ADA 43	Nicholas		WAS 123
Fredrick	FAY 198	George	PHI 99	Nichs.		PHI 73A
Henry	ALL 118	George	WAS 116	Peter		ADA 42
James	ALL 63	George	WAS 123	Peter		PHI 79
Jessy	ALL 77	George	FRA 314	Peter		GRN 88
John	ALL 65	George	FRA 314	Peter		PHI 112A
Martin	FAY 198	George Junr.	WAS 112	Phebe		DEL 159
Wilm.	ALL 65	George Senr.	WAS 112	Philip		LYC 18
MYBERT, Widw.	PHI 103A	George	PHI 112A	Philip		ADA 41
MYCAM, William	NOU 101	Harmon	FRA 314	Philip		ADA 43
MYER, Charles	HNT 124	Henry	PHI 2	Philip		PHI 135
Christian	LAN 174	Henry	ADA 7	Philip		LUZ 336
Christn.	PHI 111A	Henry	ADA 37	Philip		PHI 114A
Conrad	DAU 23	Henry	ADA 37	Saml.		CUM 30
Daniel	ADA 35	Henry	ADA 40	Samuel		HNT 159
Frederick	NOU 101	Henry	ADA 42	Samuel Junr.		HNT 159
Hamilcar	NOU 101	Henry	PHA 60	Stephen		WAS 112
Henrey	NOU 203	Henry	PHI 113	Stephen Junr.		WAS 112
Henry	DAU 32A	Henry	SOM 146	Stophel		WAS 112
Isaac	LAN 11	Henry	DEL 190	Widow		LAN 219
Isaac	LAN 180	Henry Sen.	SOM 146	William		NOU 172
Jacob	CEN 23	Henry	PHI 89A	Wm.		PHA 58
Jacob	BUC 82	Henry	BUC 141A	Yokely		FRA 294
Jacob	NOU 105	Jacob	BEV 27	MYLEA, John		PHI 92A
Jacob	HNT 144	Jacob	ADA 38	MYLIN, John		LAN 115
Jacob	LAN 251	Jacob	ADA 39	Martin		LAN 115
Jacob	LAN 254	Jacob	MNT 43	Martin Junr.		LAN 109
Jacob	LAN 303	Jacob	CUM 68	Martin Senr.		LAN 109
Jacob Junr?/		Jacob	MNT 71	MYNEHN, Daniel		PHA 62
Senr?	LYC 18	Jacob	PHI 84	MYNHEIR, Daniel		LUZ 428
Jacob	DAU 52A	Jacob	GRN 92	MYNICE, John		FAY 204
John	PHI 118	Jacob	WAS 112	MYOR, Widow		PHI 99
John	BER 145	Jacob	CUM 119	Petter		WST 371
John	LAN 174	Jacob	PHI 120	MYRES, Nicholas		ARM 122
John	LAN 250	Jacob	SOM 134	MYSER, Boston		NOU 176

MYSER, Phillip	NOU	176	NAILEIGH,			NAVINGER, Dewald	DAU	7A
MYSINGER, George	NOH	41A	Nicholas	WST	193	NAWEL, Jacob	DAU	10A
MYTINGER, John	DAU	4	NAILER, David	CHE	786	NAWEY, Elizabeth	DAU	32
Lewis	HNT	162	John	CHE	781	NAWSER, Charles		
			Saml.	PHI	75A	Junr.	PHI	115A
NAAHS, Stophel	LAN	266	William Esqr.	WAS	70	NAYH--T?, George	NOU	123
NABLE, Baltzer	MNT	36	NAILOR, Anthony	ADA	31	NAYL, John	PHA	9
Nicholas	NOU	130	George	YOR	162	NAYLOR, James	ERI	59
NACE, Abm.	BUC	159A	George Jr.	YOR	162	Leonard	PHI	87
Adam	YOR	189	Jacob	YOR	162	Thomas	PHI	66A
George	YOR	181	Joseph	PHI	74	NEAF, Daniel	FRA	311
George	BUC	159A	Lane	PHI	145	John	CEN	19
George	BUC	159A	Robert	FAY	246	Michl.	FRA	311
Henry	BUC	159A	Robt.	PHI	68	NEAFF, Jacob	YOR	205
Henry	BUC	159A	NAM, James?	PHA	122	John	YOR	170
Henry	BUC	159A	NAN-ORE?, John	MNT	103	Peter	YOR	184
Henry	BUC	159A	NANDERSLICE, John	BER	215	NEAGLE, John	CUM	75
Jacob	PHI	125	NANGEL, Anthony	BFD	35	NEAGLY, Elijah	CUM	72
Jacob	BUC	159A	NANGESSER, John	MNT	90	Jacob	CUM	72
John	BUC	159A	NANGLE, Andrew	WAS	93	NEAL, Widow	PHI	35
Margaret	PHI	125	Daniel	ERI	56	Barnet	GRN	96
Matthias	YOR	180	NANKESER, George	NOU	115	Casper	PHI	98
Nicholas	BUC	159A	Martain	NOU	115	Casper	PHI	98
Peter	PHI	124	NANNA, Abram	MNT	139	Charles	PHI	68
Peter	LAN	284	Rees	MNT	139	Charles	FRA	273
NAFE, Abraham	SOM	130	William	MNT	116	Danl.	CUM	125
Jacob	SOM	143	NANWILLER, Tho.	PHI	120A	David	FRA	323
Jacob	HNT	163	NANWORE?, John	MNT	103	David	FRA	323
John	SOM	135	NAP?, Dicky	LYC	25	David R.	PHA	115
John	HNT	163	Robert?	LYC	25	Eli	CHE	847
NAFF, Ludwig	NOH	86	NAPOCK, Daniel	PHI	2	Henry	GRN	89
NAFFTZGER, John	BER	147	NAPP, George	LYC	17	Izabellah	PHA	79
NAFFZGER, Maths.	BER	145	NAPPIER?, Thomas	PHA	97	James	LAN	163
NAFFZINGER, Henry	BER	147	NARBECK, Mr.	LAN	45	James	DEL	181
NAFZINGER,			NARCHOOD, Henry	NOU	189	James	YOR	208
Mathias	BER	222	NARGANG, John	BER	231	James	MER	455
NAGEL, Caspar	PHI	1	NARRAKER, Jacob	MNT	93	James	CHE	748
Chrisstian	NOH	82A	NARRGANG, Henry	NOH	48	Jno.	CUM	71
Christopher	LAN	45	NASELROD, Danl.	CUM	71	Jno.	CUM	145
Frederick	NOH	31	NASH, Widw.	PHI	107A	John	CEN	24
Frederick	LAN	54	Abm.	BUC	141A	John	ERI	57
George	NOH	31	Edward	WAS	70	John	MNT	65
Jacob	LAN	27	John	MNT	38	John	GRN	77
Joakim	LAN	27	John	PHI	66	John	WAS	93
John	NOH	38	John	MNT	93	John	WAS	124
John	NOH	72	John	HNT	139	John	WST	155
John	LUZ	325	Joseph	BUC	149A	John	WST	276
Joseph	LAN	32	Nathaniel	HNT	139	John	WST	276
Leonard Esqr.	NOH	69	Phinehas	LUZ	339	John	FRA	285
Mary	NOH	82A	Richard	WST	256	John	WST	294
Peter	NOH	69	William	MNT	65	John	FRA	323
Philip	NOH	82A	NASS, Chrs.	YOR	186	John	MER	455
Stofel	LAN	190	Jacob	DAU	11A	John	CHE	741
NAGLE, Charles	LAN	54	NASWINGER?, Saml.	PHI	155	John	CHE	754
Christopher	BER	147	NATHAN, Isaiah	PHI	69	John Junr.	MER	455
Elizabeth	PHI	67	Moses	PHA	13	John B.	BUC	99
Elizabeth	BER	204	NATHROP, John	LUZ	412	Laurence	CUM	124
Fredk.	BER	239	Nathan	LUZ	424	Lydia	DEL	160
Henry	LAN	145	Richard	LUZ	424	Moses	PHA	67
Henry	SOM	146	NATT?, John	CHE	867	Moses	PHI	107
Jacob	MNT	58	NAUGHSINGER,			Peter	BFD	52
John	LAN	101	Samuel	GRN	103	Robert	DEL	177
John	BER	174	NAUGLE, Abraham	ADA	8	Smith	MER	455
John	LAN	237	Christian	ADA	35	Thomas	CUM	106
John	BER	279	Jacob	ADA	34	Thomas	WST	155
John	DAU	31A	Jacob	ADA	35	Thomas	CHE	723
John	BUC	153A	John	ADA	34	Thos.	CUM	112
Mark	LAN	145	John	ADA	35	William	CEN	23
Peter	BER	234	NAUMAN, Benjamin	LAN	250	William	WST	155
Philip	BER	234	Frederick	LAN	266	William	WST	221
Philip Jur.	BER	234	George	LAN	49	William	WST	276
Richard	HNT	123	Godleib	LAN	27	William	CHE	831
Sophia	PHI	71	Michael	NOH	34	NEAL?, John M.?	CHE	875
Susannah	PHA	27	Peter	NOH	71A	John M.?	CHE	875
NAIL, Henry	NOU	195	NAVE, Jacob	FRA	299	NEALE, John	BUC	99
NAILE, Conrad	PHI	18	John	FRA	299	Joseph	BUC	99

NEALE, Moses	BUC 99	NEES, Sebastian	LAN 233	NEIHART, George	NOH 78A		
NEALEY, James	CHE 781	NEESLY, Eliz.	DAU 20A	Peter	NOH 78A		
NEALON, Alexander	FAY 228	Jacob	DAU 21	NEIL, John	YOR 167		
Ann	CUM 91	John	DAU 18	Samuel	LAN 311		
NEALS, Francis	CHE 830	Samuel	LAN 266A	Thomas	YOR 156		
Thomas	CHE 804	NEFF, Abraham	LAN 99	NEILENS, George	CHE 871		
NEALSMITH, Margt.	MNT 63	Abraham	LAN 118	NEILL, Randal	WAS 24		
NEALY, Bazil	WAS 70	Abraham	WAS 124	NEILSON, James	WST 241		
Henry	WST 193	Anne	PHI 135	John	WAS 24		
Martin	WST 193	Barnet	NOH 45A	John (Major)	NOH 67A		
Paul	WST 193	Conrad	NOH 45A	John	WST 174		
NEAREL, Frederick	NOU 144	Francis	WAS 124	John	NOH 67A		
NEAROW, Francis	PHI 38	George	DAU 30	Joseph	WST 241		
NEAS, Henry	DAU 49	George	BER 167	Nathl.	WST 221		
John	PHI 84	George	DAU 30A	Saml.	WST 349		
NEASE, Jacob	BUC 150A	Henry	LAN 111	William	WAS 24		
John Jnr.	BUC 149A	Henry	LAN 287	William	NOH 67A		
John	BUC 149A	Henry	LAN 305	Wm.	WST 221		
NEASELROD, David	CUM 71	Henry	NOH 45A	NEILY, Hugh	WST 276		
NEASLE, Phillip	FRA 305	Isaac	NOU 172	NEIMAN, Charles	MNT 58		
NEAT, Martha	BUT 328	Jacob	WAS 124	Conrad	MNT 74		
Thoms.	BUT 368	Jacob	PHI 135	Henry	MNT 74		
NEAVE, Richard	PHI 147	Jacob	NOU 172	John	MNT 120		
Samuel	PHA 35	Jacob	LAN 222	Michael	YOR 183		
NEBLE, James	PHI 85	Jacob	LAN 302	Peter	MNT 100		
John	NOH 56A	Jacob	LAN 306	NEIMAN?, George	MNT 103		
NEBLICK, William	WAS 112	Jacob	DAU 29A	John	MNT 62		
NEBUS, Widw.	PHI 102A	Jacob	NOH 45A	NEIMIRE, George	BFD 75		
NECKY, George	CUM 101	John	BFD 48	NEIMOND, David	YOR 182		
NEDE, Christopher	HNT 137	John	BER 210	George	YOR 175		
John	HNT 137	John	LAN 221	Jacob	YOR 170		
NEDERER, John	BFD 65	John Jr.	BER 210	Michael	YOR 165		
NEDOM, John	CHE 740	John	DAU 30A	Nicholas	YOR 183		
NEED, Jacob	GRN 103	Magdalina	LAN 49	NEIPER, Jno.	CUM 51		
Thomas	DEL 192	Michael	NOH 45A	John	YOR 201		
NEEL, David	FAY 205	Peter	PHI 138	John	WST 294		
James	ALL 87	Samuel	PHI 136	Margt.	CUM 47		
James	LAN 222	Ulrich (See		NEIRON?, James	FRA 272		
John	ALL 82	Neff, Widow)	NOH 45A	NEIS, John	BER 279		
John	ALL 83	Ulrich	YOR 169	John	DAU 8A		
Joseph	FAY 246	Widow	LAN 308	NEISER, George	PHA 47		
Thomas	LAN 163	Widow Of Ulrich	NOH 45A	NEISSER, Widow	NOH 32A		
Thomas	FAY 228	NEGELY, George	DAU 7A	NEISSLY, George	NOH 43A		
NEEL?, Robert	ALL 52	Leonard	LAN 20	Stephen	NOH 67A		
NEELLO?, Mary	ALL 52	NEGER, Adam	LAN 230	NEISWANGER,			
NEELLY, Elizabeth	ALL 116	NEGLE, Widw.	PHI 121	Emanuel	YOR 188		
John	ALL 116	NEGLEY, Daniel	LAN 202	NEIT, Michael	LAN 277		
Rabeckah	ALL 94	Joseph	DAU 7A	NEITH, Foris	NOU 118		
Samuel	ALL 108	NEGLY, Felex	ALL 119	NEITHAWK, Jacob	BER 149		
NEELSON, John	BEV 23	Jacob	ALL 58	NEITIG, Peter	LAN 180		
NEELY, (See Poor		NEGUS, John	PHA 17A	NEITZ, Christian	NOH 80A		
& Neely)	BUC 145	Shedlock	FAY 267	George	NOU 184		
David	MIF 15A	NEICE, George	NOU 177	NELEY, William	BUC 145		
James	ADA 38	Henry	NOU 200	NELFUS?, Nicholas	BER 183		
James	ADA 39	Peter	NOU 177	NELIGH, John	NOH 31		
James	ARM 127	Phillip	NOU 177	Nicholas	NOH 31		
John	ADA 18	William	HNT 117	NELL, Andrew	SOM 135		
John	ADA 38	William	NOU 177	Conard	PHI 129		
John	ADA 43	NEICOMER, Jacob	YOR 165	Henry	ADA 37		
John	ALL 82	Jacob	YOR 184	John	PHI 127		
Jonathen	ADA 40	Jacob	YOR 186	NELLEY, James	PHA 7		
Joseph	CUM 44	NEIDISH, Michael	MNT 100	NELLIS, Willm.	BUT 348		
Mathew	FAY 205	NEIDLINGER,		NELSON, Abm.	PHI 111		
Samuel	ALL 97	Andrew	NOH 31	Ann	CUM 56		
Susannah	ADA 40	George	BER 258	Charles	PHA 51		
Th Omas	ALL 86	NEIDROH, Adam	NOU 177	David	CRA 9		
Thomas	ADA 38	NEIFERT, Jacob	BER 131	David	YOR 216		
Thomas	ADA 41	NEIFFERT,		David	YOR 219		
William	ADA 41	Christian	NOH 60A	Edward	WAS 117		
Wm.	MIF 5A	Jacob	NOH 76	George	CRA 15		
NEEPER, John	WST 256	NEIGH, Peter	WST 349	George	LAN 168		
Samuel	LAN 153	Peter	DAU 34A	Henry	LAN 168		
NEERIMER, Wm.	WST 313	NEIGHART, Jacob		Isaac	LYC 29		
NEERLING?, Michl.	DAU 14A	Sen.	SOM 152	Isaac	LAN 161		
NEES, Adam	LAN 263	NEIGHMAN, Willm.	BUT 319	James	BEV 23		
John	LAN 49	NEIGLENGER, Peter	BER 189	James	BEV 24		

NELSON, James	CUM	38
James	BUC	93A
Jane	YOR	217
Jno.	CUM	43
Jno.	CUM	52
John	MIF	16
John	BEV	21
John	PHI	76
John	PHA	94
John	NOU	138
John	CHE	875
John	PHI	102A
Joseph	WAS	53
Lazarus	YOR	209
Mathew	BEV	24
Mathew	YOR	200
Noble C.	PHA	103
Patric	SOM	144
Richard	WAY	142
Robert	HNT	157
Robert Junr.	HNT	157
Robt.	YOR	209
Saml.	YOR	200
Samuel	BEV	23
Samuel	YOR	212
Sarah	CHE	868
Thomas	PHI	27
Thomas	VEN	166
Thomas	LAN	170
Thos.	PHI	87
William	PHA	94
William	HNT	158
William	HNT	164
William	YOR	208
William	LAN	225
Wm.	CUM	85
NELY, William	LAN	122
NEMON, George	CUM	142
NEMOND, Peter	BUC	82A
NEMONT, John	PHA	65
NENAKER, Peter	PHA	73
NENOWN, Ritchard	ALL	77
NEPHEW, Christian	NOU	200
Cornelius	LUZ	366
NERCE, James	PHI	155
NERNOU?, John	PHA	17A
NESBET, Francis	CUM	138
Hugh	BUC	83A
NESBIT, Widow	YOR	208
Alexr.	YOR	207
Allen	CUM	51
Charles	CUM	95
Francis	PHA	68
Hugh	BUC	84A
James	BFD	40
James (Crossed		
Out)	FRA	308
James	WST	162
James	FRA	309
John	WAS	13
John	ALL	105
John	YOR	203
John	YOR	207
John & Elder,		
David	WST	162
Jonathan	WAS	13
Joseph	WAS	13
William	HNT	126
William	HNT	127
William	YOR	209
Wm.	FRA	300
NESBITT, Abraham	LUZ	340
James	HNT	156
James	LUZ	341
Jonathan	WAS	24
Phebe	LUZ	344

NESS, George	NOH	56A
Jacob	YOR	194
Jonathen	NOU	130
Peter	YOR	157
William	YOR	156
NESS?, James	BER	142
NESSLEY, Abraham	LAN	5
Martin	LAN	5
NESTELROTH,		
Israel	LAN	281
NESTER, Andrew	BER	208
NESTRICK, Henry	WAS	124
NETHERHOUSE,		
Eliza.	FRA	274
NETHERLY?, John	CHE	847
NETHEROW, Henry	SOM	135
Jacob	SOM	135
NETHICK, John	NOU	176
NETICH, Abm.	CUM	57
NETTLE, Geo.	CUM	133
Jacob	CUM	120
James	MNT	110
NETTLES, Rebecca	CUM	27
NETTRERLY?, John	CHE	847
NETZER, Daniel	LAN	66
Nichalas	LAN	66
NETZLEY, Henry	LAN	137
NEUCOMER, John	BER	208
NEUFERT, John	BER	132
NEUGENT, Edmond	PHA	15
George	PHA	15
NEUHART,		
Frederick		
Junr.	NOH	91
Abraham	NOH	69
Christian	NOH	91
Daniel	NOH	91
Daniel	NOH	91
Frederick Senr.	NOH	91
Frederick	NOH	43A
George	NOH	72
Henry	NOH	91
Jacob	NOH	69
John	NOH	91
John (Taylor)	NOH	71A
John	NOH	43A
Lowrence Senr.	NOH	91
Michael Munr.	NOH	91
Michael Senr.	NOH	91
Peter	NOH	91
Peter	NOH	91
Peter Jun.	NOH	50A
Peter	NOH	50A
Philip	NOH	31
NEUKART, John	NOH	72
NEUM?, Daniel	BER	231
NEUMAN, Ludwig	LAN	88
NEUMEYER, Conrad	NOH	56A
NEUN, John	BER	266
Sylvester	BER	264
NEUN?, Daniel	BER	231
NEW, John	FAY	267
Peter	PHI	118
NEW?, Deobald	MNT	90
NEWALL, James	CEN	23
NEWANHOZER, John	CRA	3
NEWANS, John	YOR	199
NEWBERRY, Ann	PHA	56
Henry	MNT	111
Israel	MNT	128
John	MNT	119
Jonathen		
(Error)	FAY	234
NEWBOLD, John	PHI	69
Priscilla	FAY	267
NEWBOULD, Michael	PHA	20

NEWBOULD, William	PHA	10
NEWBURY, Alexr.	CHE	872
Benjamin	LUZ	373
Enos	CHE	706
James	NOU	172
NEWBY, Henry	WAS	82
Lewis	PHA	115
NEWCAMP, Caret	PHI	89A
NEWCOMB, Bayse	PHA	37
NEWCOMER, Abraham	LAN	291
Christ.	LAN	286
Christian	LAN	9
Christian	YOR	168
Christian	YOR	168
Christian	FRA	297
Christian	LAN	313
Christian	LAN	314
Christian	LAN	315
Christn.	LAN	287
David	YOR	167
George (&		
Parents)	NOH	80A
George	YOR	207
Jacob	DAU	50
John	YOR	166
John	YOR	167
John	YOR	206
John	LAN	303
John	LAN	303
John	NOH	80A
Joseph	LAN	315
Mary	HNT	118
Peter	BER	152
Peter	FRA	304
Philip	NOH	80A
Samuel	NOH	31
Uriah	FAY	199
Widow	LAN	315
NEWCOMMER,		
Christn.	FRA	284
John	BFD	65
NEWEL, Widw.	PHI	107A
Barbara	PHI	131
Frederick	BER	136
Henrey	FAY	216
Henry	PHI	85A
John	MER	455
John	PHI	98
Presly Esqr.	ALL	52
NEWELIN, John		
Revd.	PHI	104
NEWELL, Abel	LUZ	422
David	PHI	137
Hugh	WAS	30
John	WST	276
John	LUZ	422
Joshua	WST	276
Josiah	LUZ	422
Mary	WST	276
Robt.	FRA	320
Thos.	WST	276
William	WST	294
Wm.	PHA	41
Wm.	FRA	291
Wm.	PHA	17A
NEWEN, John	ALL	94
NEWHAM, Charlotte	PHA	45
NEWHART,		
Frederich	NOH	50A
NEWHOUSE, Anthy.	WST	221
Jacob	DEL	182
John	DEL	156
John	DEL	182
Philip	PHI	115A
NEWIL, George	MNT	63
Henry	MNT	46

NEWIL, Rachel	PHA	9	NEWNHAM, Henry	YOR	159	NICELY, John	GRN	74
NEWIL?, John	ALL	49	NEWOMER, Jacob	YOR	184	John (Written		
NEWILL, Bontara	CHE	700B	NEWPECK, Philip			In)	BFD	75
John	LUZ	407	Jr.	DAU	8A	NICHAMS, John	ADA	5
Samuel	DEL	173	NEWPECKER, Martin			NICHARD, David	NOU	138
William	HNT	134	Senr.	DAU	8A	NICHILAS, Michael	PHA	15
NEWILLE, Jacob	BER	227	NEWPORT, Aaron	WAS	39	NICHLES, Voluns?	GRN	89
Sarah	BEV	16	Benjn.	PHI	82A	NICHLESON, Saml.	FRA	312
NEWIN, Andrew	GRN	103	Cezar	PHA	54	Wiliam	MER	455
Hugh	CHE	734	David	PHI	82A	NICHODEMUS,		
NEWINGHAM, David	HNT	156	NEWSAM, Richd.	PHA	52	Conrad	BFD	65
NEWINS, John	ALL	97	NEWSINGER, Chris.	LAN	165	NICHOL, James	ADA	42
John	LUZ	381	NEWSWANGER, David	LAN	243	NICHOLA,		
John Senior	ALL	97	Eml.	LAN	90	Christiana	SOM	143
NEWION?, James	FRA	272	Eml. Junr.	LAN	90	Henry	SOM	143
NEWIS, James	YOR	219	NEWSWENDER,			NICHOLAS, Barny	PHI	47
NEWKIRK, Anne	PHA	17	Conrad	BER	285	Christn.	BUC	82A
Isaac	WAS	112	NEWSWINGER, Jacob	LAN	234	Francis	MNT	100
NEWKIRKE, Abraham	WAS	112	NEWTEN, Benj.	PHI	66A	Frederick	NOH	38
Henry	WAS	45	NEWTON, Wid.	PHI	97	George	BUC	149A
NEWLAND, Egbert	NOU	144	Fardanan	PHI	67A	Henry	MNT	87
NEWLIN, John	DEL	159	Forbes	PHA	80	Jacob	NOH	38
John	CHE	884	George	PHI	110	Jacob	BUC	82A
Joseph	DEL	182	John	BEV	5	James	SOM	162
Joseph	PHI	66A	John	PHI	36	James	CHE	856
Nathaniel	DEL	159	Paul	WAY	135	John	LAN	15
Nathaniel Esqr.	DEL	168	Thaddeus	WAY	135	John	ALL	106
Nicholas	DEL	166	Thos.	PHI	70	John	NOU	167
Richard	DEL	162	Thos.	PHI	120	John	WST	294
Samuel	DEL	171	Widow	PHI	93A	John Junr.	NOH	38
Samuel	DEL	189	Wm.	PHI	82A	John Senr.	NOH	38
Thomas	DEL	159	NEWZAN, Pero	PHA	27	Mary	PHA	86
Thomas	DEL	161	NEY, Andrew	NOH	67A	Michael	LAN	8
Thomas Esqr.	DEL	159	George	BER	264	Shedrick	FAY	210
NEWLON, Nethan	ALL	70	Michael	NOH	67A	W.	PHI	22
NEWMAN, Abram	MNT	120	Valentine	BER	262	William	NOU	200
Abram	MNT	128	Willm.	DAU	46A	William	BUC	87A
Caleb	LUZ	377	NEYAR, George	BER	156	Wilm.	ALL	106
Christn.	MNT	135	NEYDICH, George	BER	211	Wm.	PHA	19
Conrad	NOU	184	NEYER, Henry	BER	135	Wm.	FRA	304
Conrd	LAN	77	John	BER	276	NICHOLDS, Amos	CHE	770
David	YOR	180	John	NOH	53A	Amos Jnr.	CHE	770
David	FAY	262	NEYFANG, Nicholas	BER	222	William	FAY	246
David Jr.	YOR	180	NEYHART, Jacob	BER	234	Wm.	CHE	770
Eli	LUZ	377	NEYKIRK, John	BER	180	NICHOLDSON, James	FAY	253
George	PHA	67	John Jr.	BER	180	NICHOLLS, Eli	LUZ	387
George	LAN	89	NEYKOMMED,			Timothy	LUZ	408
George	YOR	215	Barbara	LAN	202	NICHOLOUS, Peter	BER	282
Henry	YOR	178	NEYMAN, John	BER	267	NICHOLS, Ailis/		
Henry	BER	205	John	WST	294	Arlis?	FAY	239
Isaac	WAY	144	NEYMIAR, Peter	FAY	199	Anthony	YOR	197
James	LUZ	373	NEYSCHWENDER, Eve	BER	220	Erasmus	WAS	124
Joel	LUZ	377	NIBBLE, John	YOR	157	George	YOR	202
John	PHA	70	NIBLACK, William	BEV	17	Goerge	BUC	144
John	LAN	77	NIBLE, Henry	FRA	311	Jacob	PHI	93
John	FRA	313	NICADEMUS, Fred.	FRA	302	James	WAS	82
John	DAU	31A	NICE, Adam	PHI	85A	John	BFD	65
Jon	ALL	74	Charles	PHI	124	John	HNT	144
Jonathan	LUZ	389	Cornelius	MNT	128	John	DEL	183
Joseph	NOU	167	Deobald	MNT	90	John	YOR	216
Joseph	FAY	216	Geo.	PHI	101	John	WST	313
Mary	PHI	109A	George	PHI	122	John Junr.	YOR	216
Michael	NOU	138	Jacob	PHA	45	Nathan	ERI	59
Mrs.	NOU	184	Jacob	CHE	782	Rebecca	WST	313
Nichols.	DAU	12	John	MNT	90	Robt. Jn.	WST	313
Patrick	ALL	50	John	PHI	122	Robt. Sr.	WST	313
Peter	HNT	154	John	PHI	146	Sampson	WAS	124
Peter	YOR	175	Margaret	PHI	146	Thomas	HNT	144
Peter	BER	215	Michael	BUC	97	Thomas Junr.	WAS	45
Peter	FAY	216	Widow	BUC	140	Thomas Senr.	WAS	45
Saml.	WST	155	Wynards	PHI	128	William	WAS	45
Susanna	DAU	31A	NICE?, Deobald	MNT	90	William	BFD	65
Thomas	PHA	107	Henry	ARM	126	William	BFD	75
Thomas	WAY	144	NICEL, Nichohs.	PHI	6	Wm.	PHA	40
Wiland	NOU	184	NICELY, Adam	WST	241	Wm.	PHA	83
William	DAU	51A	Adam Jr.	WST	241	NICHOLSAN, John	PHA	65

Name	Loc	Pg	Name	Loc	Pg	Name	Loc	Pg
NICHOLSON, Widow	PHA	47	NIGHT, John	ADA	36	NIXON, Moses	FAY	223
Andw.	WST	193	John Junr.	FRA	297	Patrick	MIF	11
Chas.	PHI	39	Samuel	SOM	132	Robert	WST	155
David	CEN	21	Thos.	PHI	74A	Thomas	MNT	51
Edwad.	MIF	5A	NIGHTSEVERN,			William	WAS	45
Francis	WAY	139	Abraham	FRA	291	NIXON?, (See		
George	BEV	5	NIGHTY, John	FRA	311	Vixon)	CHE	909
Gerge	ERI	55A	NIGLE, Richard	LAN	71	NIXSON, John	ALL	107
Hannah	PHA	105	NIGLEE, William	PHI	10	Thomas	ALL	92
Henry	PHA	120	NILE, Balser	PHI	74A	NIZELY?, Jacob	ALL	63
Hugh	SOM	143	Hartman	BER	243	NOAH, John	CHE	838
James	PHI	4	Philip	PHI	104	Peter	FRA	326
James	WAS	70	NILES, Nathan	LYC	10	NOAKER, Christn.	DAU	38A
James W.	FAY	246	Wm.	PHA	41	NOAL, John	FRA	272
Jas.	CUM	134	NILSON, James	BFD	38	NOBEL, John	FAY	237
Jno.	PHA	73	James	MER	455	Richard	FAY	267
John	ERI	56	Joseph	MER	455	Richard Jur.	FAY	267
John	FAY	237	Mary	FRA	320	NOBLE, Widw.	PHI	105A
John	WST	328	Robert	ARM	125	Andrew	CUM	47
Jos.	PHI	107	Robert?	ARM	123	Anna	CHE	735
Patrick	PHI	15	William	MER	455	Charles	MNT	141
Robert	SOM	143	NIMIRE, David	BFD	75	Christn.	PHI	112A
Thomas	WAS	53	NIMS, John	MNT	132	George	WAS	124
William	PHI	136	NINE, John	MNT	128	Jacob	LYC	20
Wm.	WST	193	NINEZEHELZER,			Jacob	PHA	69
NICK, Adam	WAS	112	Jacob	BER	167	Jacob	WST	381
NICKAM, John	BFD	52	NIPE, John	DAU	30A	James	PHA	7
Leonard	BFD	75	NIPO?, Conrad	FRA	320	James	LAN	120
NICKASON, Oziah	LYC	12	NIPPER, Abraham	FRA	306	James	DEL	188
NICKEL, James	HNT	157	Abraham Sr.	FRA	306	James	FRA	294
Thomas (Error)	FAY	234	David	FRA	306	John	CRA	9
NICKENSON, John	BUT	335	Peter	FRA	306	John	BFD	47
NICKERSON, David	VEN	169	Solomon	FRA	321	John	CUM	58
James	WAS	35	NIPPLE, Frederick	MIF	8	John	CUM	97
NICKLE, Andrew	WAS	13	NIPS, Christian	HNT	124	John	CUM	152
John	ADA	39	NISBET, James	CHE	721	Josh.	FRA	327
Thomas	WAS	13	Thomas	BFD	38	Mordica	PHI	76A
NICKLEY, Jacob	PHI	1	NISBETT, Richard	WST	328	Saml.	PHI	105A
NICKLIN, Phillip	PHA	85	Robert	PHI	50	Samuel	HNT	153
NICKUM, John	NOH	48	William	PHI	11A	Thos.	PHI	108
Thomas	NOH	48	NISELEY, Saml.	CUM	71	William	BFD	47
NICLE, Samuel	NOU	200	NISLEY, Christian	LAN	18	William	WAS	82
NICLY, Jno.	LYC	27	John	LAN	18	Wm.	CUM	145
NICODEMUS, Jacob	HNT	137	NISSLEY,			NOBLES, John	LUZ	348
NIDA, John P.	PHI	72A	Christian	LAN	6	NOBLET, Joseph	MNT	140
NIDE, Jacob	DEL	161	NISSLY, Martin	LAN	202	Joseph	MNT	141
John	DEL	162	NISTLEROTH,			NOBLETT, John	DEL	168
Joseph	DEL	162	Israel	LAN	279	William	DEL	178
NIDEY, Matthias	HNT	159	NITCHMAN, John	NOH	34	NOBLIT, Abram	CHE	859
NIDIGH, John	DAU	14A	John	ADA	37	NODEL, John	PHI	104A
NIDIGK, Samuel	YOR	185	NITE, Isaac	NOU	130	NOE, Mathias	PHA	116
NIDLENGER,			NITRART, Conrad	NOU	180	NOECHER, Peter	BER	145
Frederick	BER	259	NITTERFIELD?,			NOECKER, Henry	BER	279
NIE, Philip	DAU	16	William	ALL	73	John	BER	221
NIECE, George	LYC	3	NITTS, Gudlip?	SOM	154	NOEKER, George	BER	221
NIECE?, Samuel	NOU	200	NITTZ, Widow	LAN	266	NOEL, Andrew	ADA	18
NIELSON, William	LUZ	347	NITZELL, Jacob	PHI	64	Andrew Jun.	ADA	18
NIEMEYER, Peter			NIVENS, William	WAS	104	Jacob	ADA	18
Fred. Revd.	NOH	74	NIVER, David	LUZ	345	Jacob	ADA	33
NIENAMACKER,			NIVINS, Daniel	FRA	308	John	YOR	179
Gotleib	YOR	185	NIXDORFF, John	LAN	313	Nicholas	ADA	31
NIESS, Peter	DAU	8A	NIXON, Allen	FAY	223	NOFFEKER, Henry	FRA	281
NIESSLY, Jacob	DAU	12A	Ann	WAS	45	NOFFSINGER, John	SOM	130
NIGELY?, Jacob	ALL	63	Burns &	WST	147	NOFSINGER, Daniel	WAS	39
NIGH, Adam	SOM	130	George	BFD	65	John	WAS	39
Andrew	BEV	7	George	PHA	113	Rudolph	WAS	39
Fredk.	DAU	42A	George	WST	174	NOFSKER,		
George	FRA	302	James	MIF	11	Elizabeth	FRA	312
John	CRA	11	Jane	PHA	25	NOGEL, Charles	NOU	200
John	DAU	42A	John	WAS	82	John	NOU	138
Michael	DAU	42A	John	WAS	82	NOGLE, George	FRA	310
Widow	DAU	42A	John	WAS	82	John	BEV	18
NIGHART, Jacob	SOM	152	John	CUM	92	John	FRA	310
NIGHDAY, Adam	CUM	130	John	PHA	95	NOGNITZ,		
NIGHMAN, Jacob	FRA	279	John	FAY	223	Frederick	NOH	72
NIGHSTATER, Conrod	CUM	133	Joseph	BUC	99	NOIL?, (See Voil)	CHE	909

NUSPICKEL,			O NEAL, Neal	CUM 152	OBERHOLTZER,			
Ludwick	BUC	148	Timothy	WST 155	William	NOH	67A
NUSS, Conrad	NOH	56A	O NEIL, Henry	CUM 31	OBERLEY,		
Jacob	NOH	56A	James	LAN 311	Christopher	LAN 202
Mrs.	NOU	130	O'BRIAN, John	CUM 35	Jacob	LAN 202
NUT, John	CHE	773	O'BRYAN, Murty	ARM 122	Margaret	LAN 202
NUTHAMER, Adam	CHE	720	O'DAIR, James	DAU 45	Michael	LAN 202
NUTON, Timothy	ERI	57	O'KENA, John	CUM 35	OBERLIN, Adam	CUM 136
NUTT, Edward	BUC	94	O'NEAL, Laurene	CUM 123	Fredk.	CUM 139
John	BUC	94	O--ING?, Henry	CEN 21	OBERLY, Adam	LAN 63
NUTZ, John	PHI	133	Saml.	CEN 21	Anthony	NOH	48A
Leonard	PHI	133	O-WIG?, Henry	YOR 194	Hannah	LAN 88
NUZUM, Richard	DEL	181	O.NEAL, John	MNT 86	Jacob	LAN 88
Thomas	DEL	180	OAFF, Jacob	ADA 18	Jacob	NOH	48A
NYA, Jacob	NOU	147	OAKES, John	HNT 164	John	NOH	34A
NYCE, Abraham	MNT	125	OAKFORD, Aaron	DEL 168	OBERMAN, Henry	YOR 170
George	MNT	96	Benjamin W.		OBERRY, George	LUZ 394
Henry	NOH	43A	Esq.	DEL 168	OBERT, David	LAN 256
Jacob	MNT	135	Chas.	PHA 93	OBISON, David	MIF	5A
John	NOH	48	Isaac	DEL 168	OBLENIS, Daniel	ADA 37
John	MNT	53	Isaac	BUC 106A	John	ADA 38
John	WAY	147	Willm.	PHI 36	OBLINGER, George	BER 282
Joseph	MNT	100	OAKLEY, George	PHA 105	Jeremian	BER 282
Michael	MNT	55	Robert	PHA 105	John	LAN 137
William	WAY	147	OAKMAN, Iaac	PHA 96	OBOLD, Joseph	BER 145
NYE, Samuel	WAS	45	OAKS, John	BFD 38	OBOLT, Anthony	ADA 32
			John	BFD 48	Joseph	ADA 31
O BRIAN, James	CHE	876	OALENTRISK?,		OBRAN, Daniel	FRA 319
Peter	CHE	873	George	MIF 4	OBRIAN, Nicholas	PHA 85
O BRIANT, Wm.	PHA	108	OAR, Samuel	ARM 124	OBRION, John	FAY 210
O BRYAN, Bryan	LAN	145	Thomas	ARM 124	OBURN, Joseph	HNT 159
Roger	HNT	131	Thomas	FRA 309	OCHEY, Henry	DAU	37A
O BRYANT?, John	PHA	104	Wilm.	ALL 62	OCHMAN?, Wilm.	ALL 115
O CONNER, John	BUC	154	OARTMAN, Stopel	WST 221	OCHS, Jacob	NOH	48A
O DANIEL, Anthony	BUC	82	Stophel	WST 221	OCKENBAUGH, Henry	CUM 134
Cornelius	BUC	82A	OASTER, George	BFD 59	OCKER, Adam	BFD 52
Daniel	BUC	150	Jacob	BFD 59	Christian	HNT 127
O DONAL, Richard	LAN	313	Nicholas	BFD 59	John	HNT 127
O DONALD, Donald	WAS	58	OASTERDAY, Jacob	NOU 115	Nicholas	NOH 52
Hugh	ADA	1	OAT, Jesse	PHA 43	OCKERMAN, John	BFD 45
Mary	WAS	24	OATLY, Wm.	FRA 287	Paul	CUM 57
O DONNAL, Arthur	BUT	334	OATMAN, George	LAN 120	OCKMAN?, Wilm.	ALL 115
Dennis	BUT	331	Jno.	MIF 26	OCKS, Flowr	NOU 202
O DONNALD, Isaac	LAN	48	OATS, Lawrance	SOM 130	Leonard	NOH	56A
O DONNEL, Connel	FAY	210	OBBINGER?, See		Samuel	NOU 202
O DONNELL, Edwd.	CUM	34	Oblinger	BER 282	William	NOU 202
James	PHI	56	OBELBY?, Richd.	PHI 104A	ODELL, Jones	ERI	56A
Neal	HNT	159	OBENHAUSEN, Geo.		ODENHEIMER, John	
O HAGAN, Chas.	PHA	116	Fred. Revd.	NOH 86	Sen.	DEL 162
O HAIR, Patrick	CHE	876	OBENY, James	ALL 100	ODENHIMER,	
O HALE, Edward	YOR	214	OBER, Christian	LAN 11	Phillip	PHA 59
O HALLADY, Thady	PHI	105B	Henry	LAN 11	ODENWALD,	
O HARA, Widow	WST	313	Henry	LAN 256	Christian	LAN 42
Arthur	WST	313	Henry Junr.	LAN 256	ODENWELDER, John	NOH 40
Daniel	HNT	123	John	CUM 138	John Junr.	NOH	87A
Edwd.	WST	194	Michael	LAN 186	Michael	NOH 40
James	DEL	162	OBERBOUGH, Peter	ADA 31	Philip	NOH 40
John	BUT	342	OBERDORF, Jacob	MNT 135	ODLE, Samuel	NOU 112
Wm.	WST	221	OBERHALTER, Isaac	MNT 68	ODONNEL, Peter	LAN 128
O HARIN?, Patrick	BUC	94	Jacob	MNT 68	OERTER, Joseph	NOH	32A
O HARRA, Henry	WST	155	Joseph	MNT 68	OFENBACH, Henry	NOH 91
James	WST	155	OBERHALTZER,		OFFENBACH, Andrew	LAN 67
O HARRIS, Patrick	BUC	94	Jacob	MNT 126	OFFERT, John	WAS 45
O HARROW, Francis	FRA	320	John	MNT 126	OFFETT, Nathan	WAS 82
O KANE, James	HNT	121	OBERHOLL, Samuel	LAN 137	OFFICER, David	WAS 93
O LANE, J.	LAN	59	OBERHOLSER,		James	WAS 24
O NEAL, Arthur	CHE	780	Christian	LAN 24	Jno.	CUM 96
Danl.	PHI	89A	Christian	LAN 311	Robert	WAS 24
Fredk.	LYC	23	Jacob	LAN 186	Thomas	WAS 117
Henrey	FAY	246	OBERHOLTZ, Henry	BER 251	Wm.	CUM 43
Hugh	CUM	84	OBERHOLTZER,		OFFLEY, Ann	PHA 98
James	PHI	28	Henry	MNT 122	David	CUM 96
John	CUM	30	Jacob	BER 165	OFFORT, George	PHI	85A
John	WAS	45	Jacob	NOH	56A	OGAL, Wilm.	ALL 75
John	LAN	228	John	LAN 267	OGAN, John	MNT 38
John	MER	455	Martin	LAN 68	OGDAN, Job	LYC 26

OGDEN, Benanuel	CHE 809	
Enoch	LUZ 320	
Hugh	PHA 38	
Jacob	VEN 165	
John	DEL 189	
John	LUZ 398	
Joseph	PHA 83	
Joseph	WST 174	
Thomas	HNT 130	
William	LUZ 361	
Wm.	PHA 6	
OGDON, David	PHA 75	
Isaac	NOU 150	
John	NOU 147	
Samuel	WAS 70	
Samuel	WAS 104	
Widow	MIF 11	
OGELBY, Joseph	FAY 210	
OGELSBY, George	CHE 824	
Widow	CHE 828	
OGENSTINE, Horonomus	NOU 189	
OGG, George	FAY 262	
Joshua	SOM 144	
Vechel	FAY 262	
William	SOM 144	
OGILBY, Stephen	BUC 90	
OGLE, Alexander	SOM 132	
Catharine	PHA 76	
David	CUM 28	
Robert	DAU 21	
Thos.	PHA 85	
William	DAU 21A	
OGLEBY, Elizabeth	PHI 129	
John	WAS 112	
Joseph	PHA 76	
Wm.	PHA 83	
OGLESBERY, Richard	FAY 253	
OGLEVY, Joseph	PHI 16	
OHARA, James	ALL 49	
Wilm.	ALL 118	
OHESON?, Nicholas	MIF 8	
OHEY, Jacob	DAU 37A	
Samule	DAU 37A	
OHINBAUGH, Phillip	BEV 10	
OHL, Andrew	NOH 48A	
George	NOH 48	
Henry	NOH 45A	
Henry	NOH 48A	
John	NOH 48A	
Michael Esqr.	NOH 76	
Michael Senr.	NOH 45A	
Nicholas	NOH 76	
William	NOH 48A	
OHLE, George	PHA 69	
OHLER, George	SOM 150	
Philip	PHI 91A	
OHLWINE, George	NOH 84	
Michael	NOH 84	
OHMIG, Christian	LUZ 334	
OHNANGST, Henry	NOH 48A	
OHNMACHT, Daniel	BER 231	
Frederick	BER 231	
OHRBACH, John	BER 205	
OHRNUTT, John	YOR 205	
OICHER, Daniel	FAY 241	
Henry	FAY 241	
OIDNER?, George	MNT 54	
OILBER, Samuel	CHE 763	
OILER, Adulpas	FAY 233	
OINGS, Henry	BER 158	
OISTER, Jacob	NOU 123	
OKAM, Henry	BER 152	
OKEL, John	BUC 101A	
OKELY, David	NOH 48A	
Elijah	LUZ 379	
Jotham	LUZ 386	
Miles	LUZ 409	
OKESON, Albeson	MIF 8	
OLAND, Widow	DAU 35A	
OLBERSOM, Elum	NOU 152	
OLD, Daniel	LAN 111	
Davis	LAN 92	
John	NOU 130	
Joseph	BER 158	
Wm.	PHA 40	
OLDEN, Benjn.	PHA 33	
OLDENBERG, Jacob	PHA 14	
OLDENBERGE, Danl.	PHA 33	
OLDERMAN, George	YOR 180	
OLDFATHER, Frederic	SOM 139	
Frederic Sen.	SOM 139	
Henry	SOM 139	
OLDFIELD, Benja.	PHI 7	
David	LAN 240	
Jonathan	LAN 241	
OLDHAM, George	WAS 124	
James	YOR 161	
John	BFD 75	
Thomas	BFD 75	
OLDMIXON, John	CHE 702	
OLDRIDGE, Saml.	FAY 223	
OLDS, Ezra	LUZ 374	
OLDSHUE, John	FAY 205	
OLDWEILLER, Philip	LAN 10	
OLDWINE, Abram	CHE 794	
Jacob	CHE 815	
OLENDER, Wm.	FRA 295	
OLENDER?, Wm.	FRA 317	
OLEPHANT, Andw.	FAY 246	
OLEPHENT, William	FAY 210	
OLEREIGH, Nichs.	CUM 79	
OLERY, Henry	ALL 113	
OLES, Thomas	BFD 65	
William	CHE 841	
OLETON?, Elizh.	FRA 312	
OLICK, Jacob	PHI 85A	
OLIERS, James	PHA 19	
OLINGER, Widow	YOR 194	
John	BFD 40	
John	SOM 139	
OLIPHANT, Andrew	WAS 86	
James	NOU 118	
Usilea	PHA 23	
OLIPHENT, Ann	FAY 228	
OLIVER, Alexander	FAY 268	
Alexander	FAY 268	
Alexander	FAY 268	
Andrew	DEL 155	
Andrew	CHE 856	
Benjn.	PHA 36	
Daniel	NOU 150	
David	WAS 63	
Elizabeth	FRA 285	
Hugh	NOH 67A	
James	BUC 155A	
John	PHA 15	
John	CUM 98	
John	ALL 113	
John	MER 455	
John Esq.	MIF 26	
Martha	YOR 201	
Mary	DEL 168	
Richard	GRN 98	
Stephen	ERI 60	
Thomas	ALL 113	
Thomas	MIF 5A	
William	WST 155	
OLIVER, William	LAN 265	
Wm.	PHA 57	
OLLENDORFF, Leonard	LAN 279	
OLLER, Conrad	WAS 124	
Frederick	WAS 124	
OLLINGER, Geo.	CUM 42	
OLLIPHAN, Jno. (Andw. Crossed Out)	FAY 223	
OLLIPHANT, Jonathan	PHA 53	
OLLIVER, Benjamin	BEV 7	
John	BEV 6	
Nicholas	PHI 126	
OLMSTEAD, Gideon	PHA 34	
OLOVENT, Andrew	NOU 200	
OLP, John	YOR 192	
OLT, Gabriel	BER 210	
George	BER 189	
OLWEILER, Jacob	YOR 205	
Philip	LAN 291	
OLWINE, Werner	DAU 51	
OMAN, George	LUZ 421	
Henry	NOU 147	
John	PHA 73	
John	LUZ 421	
Peter	NOU 147	
OMEN, Eli	FAY 268	
OMENSETTER, Frederick	PHA 96	
Michael	PHA 51	
OMENSTETTER, Geo.	PHI 93A	
OMENZETTER, Jacob	PHI 147	
OMER, Abm.	MIF 11	
OMINSETTER, John	PHI 131	
OMMERMAN, Danl.	NOU 195	
John	NOU 195	
OMYS, George	PHI 136	
ONAIL, Charrels	ALL 86	
Thomas	ALL 98	
ONEIL, James	MIF 11A	
ONER, Conrad	CHE 782	
Valentine	CHE 782	
ONG, Jacob	WST 256	
Jeremiah	WST 256	
Jesse	WST 256	
ONKLEY, Georg	NOH 48	
ONNER?, Henry	ARM 124	
ONROADE?, (See Anroade)	FRA 294	
ONSBAUGH, Jacob	NOU 106	
ONSLETT?, George	WAS 70	
ONSLO, Madam	PHA 89	
ONSMINGER, George Jr.	YOR 215	
ONSTOT, John	MER 455	
ONSTOUT, Henry	ALL 110	
OOTLEY, Saml.	CUM 133	
OOTNER, Jacob	LYC 9	
OOTNER?, Jacob	LYC 9	
OPDIKE, Samuel	BUC 151A	
OPLINGER, Isaac	NOH 50A	
Nicholas	NOH 50A	
Widw.	NOH 50A	
OPP, Anthony	NOH 54	
Conrad	NOH 54	
Jacob	YOR 155	
Jacob Junr.	NOH 38	
Jacob Senr.	NOH 38	
John L.?	NOH 54	
Michael Junr.	NOH 38	
Michael Senr.	NOH 38	
Peter	YOR 174	
Philip	BER 189	
Valentine	BUC 148	

OPP, Widow	BUC	148
OPP?, Philip	LYC	15
OPPERMAN, John	CHE	858
ORAM, Benjn.	CHE	864
Cooper	PHA	52
Henry	PHI	53A
James	MNT	38
Jane	WAS	17
Thomas	DAU	9A
Wm.	PHI	94
ORAN, William	MIF	13
ORBIERN, Phillip	FAY	199
ORBISON, Adam	CUM	138
James Esqr.	FRA	273
Robert	BFD	52
ORCOY, Adam	MER	455
ORD, George	PHI	11
John	ALL	54
ORDITER, Joseph	PHI	28
ORDNER?, George	MNT	54
ORE, John	CHE	832
Robert	CHE	877
OREN, Jesse	YOR	217
Jos.	YOR	217
OREN?, Isaac	LYC	24
ORENDORF,		
Christn.	DAU	26
Herman	LAN	16
John	DAU	26
John	NOU	123
Matthias	LAN	99
ORGAN, John	ARM	123
Matt.	WST	276
ORICK, Widow	YOR	196
Fredk.	YOR	196
ORINDORFF, John	NOU	177
ORISON, Peter	BUC	89A
ORLEADY, Henry	CHE	718
ORLTON, Hugh	HNT	139
John	HNT	139
ORMON, John	FRA	315
ORMOND, Margaret	WAS	17
ORMROYD, John	PHA	15
ORMSBURY, George	DEL	168
ORMSBY, George	HNT	164
Oliver	ALL	52
ORMSEY, Orran	FRA	300
Thos.	FRA	300
ORMY, Joseph	NOH	67A
ORNA, John	PHA	96
ORNDORFF, Herman	LAN	25
ORNER, David	CUM	31
Martin	LUZ	360
ORNER?, Henry	ARM	124
ORNSLEY, Mathew	FRA	322
OROM, Richard	CHE	847
ORR, Arthur	WAS	104
Arthur	PHI	117A
George	FAY	223
Humphrey	WAS	45
James	PHA	43
James	PHA	117
James	WAS	117
James	HNT	142
James	FAY	223
James	FRA	323
James Jur.	FAY	223
Jas.	CUM	38
John	PHI	40
John	CUM	61
John	NOU	200
Letitia	CUM	122
Robert	PHA	17
Robert	WAS	45
Robert	FAY	223
Samuel	WAS	104

ORR, Thomas	PHA	8
William	ADA	4
William	ADA	10
William	WAS	58
Wm.	BEV	6
Wm.	FRA	321
ORRIGH?, Stophel	ARM	126
ORRIS, Geo.	CUM	55
Geo.	CUM	58
Henry	CUM	40
Jos.	CUM	63
ORRISON, John	LAN	156
Matthew	LAN	156
ORSENBACH, John	NOH	54
ORSO, John B.	PHA	89
ORSON, George	YOR	199
Widow	LAN	163
ORT, Henry	YOR	165
Jacob	BUC	157A
John	YOR	165
Lewis	PHI	117
Peter	BER	242
Widow Of John	NOH	56A
ORTH, Conrad	DAU	15A
Conrad	MIF	17A
Gottlieb	DAU	28A
Henry	DAU	4
John	MIF	17A
Joseph	DAU	28A
Stophel	CUM	37
ORTLIP, George	MNT	85
ORTLIP?, Israel	MNT	58
ORTMAN, John	YOR	206
ORTZ?, Chr.	DAU	38
ORVES?, Roger	LUZ	367
ORWIG, George	BER	158
George Jr.	BER	223
Henry	BER	280
Peter	BER	158
ORWILER, Jacob	MNT	128
OSBON, John	BFD	65
John Jr.	BFD	65
Joshua	BFD	65
OSBORN, James	LUZ	376
Saml	MIF	13
OSBORNE, Francis	CHE	737
James	LUZ	380
Peter	CHE	745
OSBOURN,		
Elizabeth	PHA	105
OSBOURNE, Jane	PHA	39
Wm.	CHE	760
OSBURN, Archabald	WST	256
George	ADA	20
Isaac	NOU	167
John	ARM	124
Jonathan	FAY	233
Joseph	ERI	59
Joseph	FAY	205
Obadiah	YOR	173
Peter	CHE	734
Randel	MNT	116
Samuel	WST	256
Samuel	CHE	706
Sarah	YOR	203
OSEN-OR?, Fred.	FRA	297
OSENBOUGHER,		
Abram	BUT	323
OSLUMB, William	NOU	112
OSMAN, John	PHI	134
OSMOND, Ajax	BUC	146
Ajax	BUC	145A
David	BUC	84A
John	BUC	146
John	BUC	151A
Jonathan	BUC	146

OSSMAN, Andrew	DAU	8
Joshua	DAU	6
Robert	DAU	6
Thomas	DAU	6
OSTAT, Fredk.	YOR	207
OSTER, Henry	LAN	52
Peter	BER	223
OSTERDAG, George	NOH	50A
William	NOH	50A
OSTERHOUT, Gideon	LUZ	377
Isaac	LUZ	377
Jeremiah	LUZ	373
John	LUZ	377
Pelatiah	LUZ	402
Peter	LUZ	402
OSTERLY, Adam	NOH	87A
OSTERSLOCK, Henry	NOH	38
OSTERSTOCK, John	NOH	34A
Thos.	NOH	40
OSTIME, John	PHI	95
OSWALD, Bernard	BER	228
Christn	BER	259
Daniel	NOH	54
Danl. (Saddler)	NOH	54
Jacob	NOH	54
Jacob	BFD	59
Jacob	BER	215
Jacob	BER	234
Jacob	BER	259
John	BER	227
John	NOH	53A
John H.	PHA	96
Tobias	BFD	59
OSWELT, James	DAU	32A
OTENHIMER,		
Baltzer	BER	234
OTLEY, Abel	CHE	744
OTS, John	FRA	309
OTT, Andrew	PHI	144
Christopher	NOH	56A
David	PHA	71
Emanuel	DAU	32
Emanuel	BFD	65
George	LAN	202
Henry	BUC	82
Henry Jnr.	BUC	91A
Henry	NOH	56A
Henry	BUC	91A
Jacob	PHI	155
Jacob Junr.	PHI	155
Jacob	BUC	91A
Jacob	BUC	101A
John	DAU	32
John (Crossed		
Out)	BUC	82
John	NOU	106
John	BUC	150
John	BUC	91A
John	BUC	91A
Michael	BFD	54
Michael	BUC	150
Michael	NOH	56A
Michail	BUC	91A
Nichols.	DAU	5
Peter Junr.	PHI	62
Peter Senr.	PHI	62
Peter	BUC	91A
Vendal	BFD	38
OTTENDER, Reduc	PHI	35
OTTENKISK, John	BER	161
OTTER, Aaron	BEV	26
OTTERBACH, Joseph	DAU	11
OTTERMAN, George	WST	221
OTTINGER, Charles	PHI	133
Christn.	MNT	66
Christopher	PHI	124

OYSTER, George	BER	177	PAINTER, Widw.	PHI	116	PALLET, William	WAS	13
OZBIN, William	MER	455	Adam	DAU	7	PALM, Adam	SOM	139
OZEAS,			Adam	BFD	47	Godfy	YOR	218
Christopher	PHI	141	David	FRA	281	John	BER	205
George	PHI	12	Ezekiel	WAS	39	Peter	BER	167
OZENCOP, Jacob	LUZ	323	George	PHI	84	PALMER, Aaron	DEL	156
OZIAS?, Peter	PHA	72	George	ARM	124	Aaron	DEL	161
			George	ARM	126	Aaron	DEL	168
P LOTNER, Conrad	NOU	112	George	WST	372	Abigail	DEL	161
P----TY?, Daniel	BEV	12	Henry	PHI	85	Abner	BUC	94A
P---SON?, John	ALL	50	Henry	ARM	122	Adam	WST	314
P--OWS?, James	CHE	793	Isaac	PHI	93	Amos	BUC	99
P-R--?, Frederick	MER	456	Jacob	PHA	58	Anna	PHI	134
PACE, David	LUZ	373	Jacob	MNT	85	Asher	DEL	159
Michael	LUZ	342	Jacob	PHI	114	Benjamin	DEL	156
Michael Jr.	LUZ	337	Jacob	YOR	175	Benjn.	BUC	99
Thomas	LUZ	342	Jacob	DEL	186	Benjn.	BUC	94A
PACER, Danl.	CUM	56	Jacob	NOU	200	Braxton & Josh.	FRA	306
PACHEL, David	WST	350	Jacob	WST	222	Budd	CEN	21
PACHTLE, Jacob	BFD	39	Jacob	WST	372	Charles	DEL	168
Samuel	BFD	39	Jacob	WST	372	Charles	YOR	216
PACKER, Aaron	CEN	19	Jacob Esqr.	WST	222	Chrisr.	WST	277
Eli	CEN	19	Jacob	DAU	24A	Daniel	BUC	99
Emos	CEN	19	James	CHE	805	David	BFD	47
James	CEN	19	Jno.	CUM	102	David	BUC	99
Jesse	MIF	8	John	ARM	122	Frederick	ADA	30
Job	LYC	25	John	NOU	172	Frederick	YOR	168
John	YOR	208	John	WST	194	George	NOH	63
Mosis	FAY	241	John	WST	222	George	DEL	156
Philip	YOR	219	John	WST	372	George	DEL	157
PACKHURST, Isaac	WAS	50	John	PHI	75A	George	CHE	867
PACKINGHAM,			John	PHI	91A	Godfrey	YOR	216
Charles	CHE	727	John	PHI	107A	Henry	WST	155
PACKS, Robert	MIF	26	Joseph	CHE	805	Hord	CEN	21
PADEN, John	WAS	124	Juliana	PHA	25	Israel	PHI	9
PADIN, James	ALL	81	Lary	WST	372	James	PHA	10
John	ALL	81	Lewis	DEL	163	James	CHE	773
Joseph	WAS	50	Lewis	DEL	168	Jesse	BUC	94A
PADON, John	LAN	263	Ludwick	MNT	83	John	PHI	24
PAFF, Dewalt	BER	134	Magdalena	ADA	27	John	BFD	45
PAFFENBERGER,			Martin	CUM	105	John	BFD	45
George	BER	264	Martin	PHI	124	John	BFD	52
Jacob	BER	264	Mary	PHI	98	John	PHI	79
PAGAN, Andrew	WAS	104	Matthias	YOR	194	John	HNT	135
PAGE, Abm.	MIF	13A	Michael	CHE	796	John	DEL	159
Abraham	MIF	13	Peter	YOR	211	John	DEL	168
Christ-.	DAU	15A	Peter	WST	314	John	FRA	303
David	PHI	118	Peter	PHI	84A	John	CHE	902
James	PHI	68A	Philip Esq.	DEL	162	Jonathan	BUC	94A
John	LAN	10	Richard	CHE	903	Joseph	BFD	45
John	DEL	163	Samuel	DEL	158	Joseph	PHA	117
John	DAU	20A	Tobias	WST	222	Joseph	DEL	160
Joseph	MIF	13A	William	DEL	186	Joseph Jun.	DEL	159
Michl.	MIF	13A	PAINTERD, Henry			Josh. & Braxton	FRA	306
Nathaniel	CHE	855	(Boarding			Lewis	BUC	87
Stephen	BUC	84A	House)	PHA	31	Lewis	DEL	188
William Jur.	FAY	199	PAIR, Odistan	PHI	109A	Mark	BUC	99
Wm.	PHA	15	PAIRTE?, James	DEL	182	Moses	DEL	169
PAGON, Archibauld	ALL	69	PAIS-?, William	DEL	189	Moses	DEL	184
John	ALL	86	PAISLEY, David	WAS	24	Moses Esqr.	DEL	159
PAIL, Wilm.	ALL	120	David	WAS	93	Nathan	LUZ	320
PAIN, Peter	ALL	61	Robert	LAN	166	Peter	WST	155
Peter	NOU	106	PAIST, John	BUC	103A	Phineas	DEL	171
Richard	GRN	77	PAISTE?, James	DEL	182	Richard	PHA	5
Thos.	BUC	97	PAITEN, Isaac	FAY	233	Richard	HNT	131
William	NOU	172	PALEN, Henry	CHE	884	Richd.	PHA	69
PAINE, Barnet	PHA	100	Joshua	CHE	895	Samuel	BUC	94A
Benj.	YOR	196	PALETHORP, Robt.	PHI	89	Solaman	CEN	21
Chauncey	LUZ	420	PALIART, Francis	PHA	112	Thomas	PHA	6
David	LUZ	426	PALISKE, Chs. G.	MNT	78	Thomas	MNT	51
Jacob	LUZ	347	PALL, Benjn.	CHE	897	Tyringham	BUC	89
Robert	WST	241	James	FAY	205	William	PHI	137
William	PHA	121	Jonathan	FAY	258	William	DEL	189
PAINTER, Widow	PHI	93	PALLARD, John	FAY	199	PALMERLY, Isaac	CHE	769
Widow	WST	372	PALLET, Francis	WAS	82	PALMORE, John	CEN	21
Widw.	PHI	86	John Jr.	WAY	142	PALSNER, Catharin	LAN	51

PAMER, Benjamin	NOU	150	PARK, John	ALL	56	PARKER, Nathan	WAS	4
John	ALL	66	Mathew	ALL	92	Nathan	LYC	22
PAN--US?, Izaia	FAY	268	Richard	DEL	190	Nathaniel	FAY	201
PANABAKER, Henry	CHE	792	Saml.	PHA	82	Ralph	DEL	181
John	CHE	786	Thos.	PHA	86	Richard	GRN	65
Joseph	CHE	786	William	MNT	51	Robert	LAN	176
PANCACK, George	ALL	75	William	ARM	125	Robt.	CHE	853
PANCAKE, Fredk.	DAU	14A	William	YOR	212	Saml.	LYC	13
Peter	DAU	15	PARKASON, John	BEV	28	Saml.	PHA	69
PANCOAST, Asa	NOU	112	PARKE, Jacob	PHA	24	Samuel (Black)	PHI	122
William	NOU	112	John	LUZ	415	Samuel	YOR	198
PANCOST, Abigail	DEL	179	John	CHE	819	Samuel	FAY	268
Ann	DEL	190	John	CHE	843	Samuel	LUZ	418
Samuel	DEL	177	Jonathan	CHE	898	Sylvanus	LUZ	412
Samuel	BUC	94A	Joseph	LUZ	357	Thomas	PHA	11
PANE, Eleazer	CHE	874	Joseph	CHE	804	Thomas	PHI	40
Hector	BER	167	Joseph	CHE	844	Thomas	PHA	105
John	YOR	202	Joseph Jr.	CHE	844	Thomas	GRN	107
Thomas	CHE	874	Simon	LUZ	338	Thomas	LUZ	425
PANEBAKER, Daniel	BER	167	Thomas	LUZ	387	Thompson	CHE	865
PANGBURN, John	ALL	78	Thomas	CHE	899	Wakins	PHI	89A
William	MER	455	Thomas A.	CHE	900	William	PHI	13
PANKAKE, Philip	PHA	120	William	CHE	900	William	YOR	201
PANKOST, Hannah	PHA	92	PARKER, Widow	PHI	29	William	YOR	203
PANKS?, See Pauks	BER	215	Widow	PHI	83A	William	LUZ	328
PANNEBAKER, Jacob	BER	165	Andw.	CUM	64	William	MER	456
John	BER	149	Andw.	PHI	105B	William C---?	ARM	123
John Jr.	BER	149	Archiles	PHA	7	Wm.	PHA	76
PANREY?, John	WST	241	Beulah	PHA	55	Wm.	CUM	102
PANTER, Thomas	WST	256	C---? William	ARM	123	PARKES, Arthur	CHE	873
PANTHER, Geo.	CUM	46	Catharine	PHA	67	David	GRN	84
George	WST	277	David	PHA	41	John	CHE	874
Godfrid	BFD	76	David	ALL	120	Solomon	PHA	46
John Jur.	FRA	283	David	YOR	202	PARKESON, Richd.	CUM	78
John Senr.	FRA	283	David	MIF	15A	Robert	PHI	20
Samuel	CHE	804	Edward	FRA	283	PARKHILL, James	FRA	287
PANTZ, John	LAN	143	Francis	LAN	60	John	FRA	288
PANY, John	DEL	158	Geo.	BUT	355	Martha	FAY	205
PAPLEY?, Susannah	PHA	113	George	PHI	52	PARKHURST, Jacob	WAS	64
PAR, Nicholas	HNT	128	George	PHI	96	Samuel	WAS	64
PARAMOR, Daniel	WAS	104	George	PHI	53A	Samuel Junr.	WAS	64
Eleanor	WAS	105	Gideon	WST	295	PARKILL, Saml.	PHI	135
John	WAS	105	Henry	LYC	9	PARKINS, William	NOU	119
Nathaniel	WAS	105	Henry	CHE	793	PARKINSON,		
Thomas Junr.	WAS	104	Hezekiah	LUZ	417	Benjamin	WAS	70
Thomas Senr.	WAS	104	Isaac	GRN	105	George	WAY	142
PARCAR, Wilm.	ALL	80	Isaac	FRA	315	James	WAS	70
PARCASON,			Jacob	CHE	720	Joseph	WAS	70
Bengamin	ALL	73	James	BEV	19	William	PHA	3
PARCE, Amos	BUT	329	James	PHA	36	PARKISON, Jno.	CUM	44
PARCEL, John	SOM	146	James	FAY	258	Mary	HNT	154
Richd.	BUT	342	James	WST	328	Thomas	FAY	205
PARCELL, Henry	WAS	64	James	MER	456	William	WAS	46
John	WAS	64	James	CHE	862	William	GRN	112
John	CUM	111	James	CHE	865	PARKS, Amos	LUZ	357
PARCHMENT, Peter	ALL	58	Jeremiah	WAS	112	Andrew	GRN	79
PARCIE, William	NOU	177	Jeremiah	LUZ	422	Ann	HNT	132
PARCIL, Samuel	BEV	18	Jesse	GRN	112	Ann	YOR	203
PARCK, Wilm.	ALL	64	John	ALL	54	David	HNT	140
PARCKS, James	ALL	113	John	PHA	73	David	FAY	211
PARCLES, Ann	DEL	170	John	BUC	107	Ebenezer	LUZ	368
PARDOE, William	NOU	172	John	ALL	117	Edward	LUZ	356
PARENT, John	PHI	102	John	NOU	150	James	WAS	17
PAREY, Isaac	MNT	51	John	FAY	211	James	MER	456
PARIN, Elizabeth	PHA	99	John	FAY	216	John	WAS	17
Steven	PHI	21	John	BER	248	John	BFD	40
PARINE, Danl.	PHI	114A	John	BUT	354	John	NOU	112
PARINGER, Barnet	BUC	150	John	CHE	706	John	FRA	304
PARINT, Saml.	PHI	91	John	CHE	832	John	MER	456
PARIS, Peter			Joseph	LYC	21	Joseph	SOM	132
Esqr.	PHI	90A	Joseph	PHA	25	Joseph	CUM	143
William	GRN	77	Joseph	CHE	760	Robert	BEV	23
PARISH, John	HNT	125	Leanna	BUT	354	Robt.	FRA	297
PARITENT, Hirim	NOU	189	Mary	FRA	290	Roger	NOU	106
PARK, Issabella	CUM	83	Mary	BUC	162A	Roger	NOU	106
Jacob	DEL	190	Moses	PHI	93A	Roger	NOU	112

PARKS, Saml.	WST	194	PARSONS, Richard	DEL	181	PATRIDGE, John	NOH	31
Thomas	BEV	26	Robert	BUC	162	PATT, Wm. B.	PHI	113A
Thomas	NOU	118	Samuel	HNT	142	PATTARSON,		
Thomas	NOU	131	Samuel	YOR	184	Nicholas	FRA	314
William			Stephen	PHA	103	PATTEIGER?,		
(Crossed Out)	BUC	153A	Thos.	CEN	24	Martin	BER	205
William	NOU	148	Uriah	LUZ	400	PATTEMORE,		
William	MER	456	William	PHI	152	Catharine	DAU	13
Wm.	WST	256	William	DEL	181	PATTEN, Andrew	NOU	195
Wm.	WST	295	PARTHEMER, Jacob	DAU	14	David	BEV	23
Zebulon	WST	241	PARTHEMORE, John			David	BEV	24
PARMELE, Abraham	LUZ	404	Sr.	DAU	16A	David	WAS	50
PARMENTER, James	LUZ	389	PARTIAL, Elias	FAY	258	David	ALL	101
PARMER, Thomas	WAS	64	PARTRIDGE, Abel	NOH	41A	James	BEV	5
Thomas	PHI	147	PARVIN, Francis	BER	218	James	CHE	868
Wm.	PHI	82A	John	BER	218	John	FAY	199
PARMETEER,			Pearson	PHA	70	John	FAY	258
Charles	PHA	77	William	PHA	120	Matthew	PHI	35
PARMICK, Stephen	PHA	75	PARY, David	NOU	112	Matthew	FAY	241
PARNCUTT, Sarah	PHA	92	PASCHALL, Benjn.	PHI	64	Saml.	NOH	48A
PARNELL, Bedwell	SOM	146	Henry	PHI	64	William	CHE	719
PARONE, Nicholas	SOM	135	Stephen	PHA	81	PATTEN?, David	BEV	22
PARR, Elizabeth	ADA	30	PASEAU?, John	FRA	324	PATTERIGE, John	BEV	14
George	FRA	320	PASEY, Henry	WST	294	PATTERON, Andrew	MIF	8
Isaac	WST	350	PASINGER, John	BUC	97	PATTEROSN, Agnis	FAY	205
Jacob	ADA	28	PASLEY, Hugh	WAS	4	Jas.	CUM	124
James Esqr.	WST	350	PASMORE, Jesse	FAY	211	PATTERSN, John	FAY	228
John	CRA	15	John	LAN	30	PATTERSON, Widow	YOR	199
John	FAY	258	Thos.	PHA	81	& Jackson	LAN	241
Mrs.	LAN	54	PASS, Frederick	CHE	852	Abner	CHE	813
Samuel	FAY	258	Frederick	CHE	862	Abner	CHE	884
Samuel	WST	350	Jacob	CHE	772	Adam	ALL	108
Sarah	SOM	150	John	PHI	154	Alexander	WAS	58
PARRATT, Beriah	LUZ	406	PASSEL, Thomas	PHI	7	Alexander	FAY	268
PARREN, Joseph	BFD	54	PASSEY, Saml.	PHA	86	Alexd.	ALL	60
PARRINGTON, John			PASSMORE, Enoch	CHE	838	Alexd.	ALL	83
R.	HNT	156	George	CHE	764	Alexn.	NOH	38
PARRIS, Gabrael	PHA	25	James	CHE	707	Alexr.	MIF	8
Peter Dr.	PHI	71A	John	LAN	170	Andrew	WAS	9
Stephen	PHA	97	Richard	DEL	172	Andrew	ARM	122
PARRISH, Elihu	LUZ	342	Thomas	CHE	738	Andrew	DEL	156
Isaac	PHA	23	Wm.	CHE	838	Andw.	CUM	135
James	PHI	28	PASTAL, Doat	PHI	35	Andw.	YOR	202
Nathan	LUZ	342	PASTE, John	BUC	138	Archibald	HNT	140
Robert	PHA	71	PASTICK, William	LAN	294	Archibald	NOU	150
Stephen	WAY	142	PASTORAS, Willm.	CEN	21	Arthur	WAS	13
Susana	FAY	258	PASTOROUS,			Arthur	LAN	263
Wm.	PHA	45	Francis D.	PHI	107	Arthur	LAN	263
PARRY, Benj. &			PATCH, Richard	CRA	4	Ase	FAY	258
David	BUC	145A	PATCHEEL, James	ALL	96	Catherine	PHI	66A
David	PHA	43	PATE?, Abraham	PHI	96A	Daniel	BFD	48
David (See			PATEN, Thomas	ALL	106	David	DAU	47A
Parry, Benj.)	BUC	145A	PATERSON, Davd.	BUT	329	Eli	CHE	702
Dvid	BUC	145A	James	CRA	16	Emmor	CHE	702
Elizabeth	MNT	36	Jas.	CUM	134	Emmor	CHE	735
Jacob	BUC	153A	John	CRA	3	Francis	CUM	41
John	BUC	87	John	NOU	167	Francis	DEL	187
Philip	BUC	87	Robt.	BUT	329	Francis	DEL	189
Thomas	BER	273	Thomas	BUT	358	George	MIF	11
Thos.	PHA	22	Thoms.	BUT	359	Henry	NOH	31
PARSEL, Peter	BUC	94A	PATHORN, John	ALL	89	Henry	CUM	136
PARSHALL, Caleb	MIF	17A	PATHOVER?, Andrew	HNT	132	Henry	WST	222
PARSON, Daniel	GRN	96	PATMAN, George	LAN	247	Hugh	ADA	8
James	CUM	24	John	LUZ	359	Hugh	YOR	200
John	GRN	107	PATON, John	CUM	134	Hugh	YOR	213
Mary	PHI	55	Thomas	MIF	13	Jacob	FRA	281
Philip	BER	203	PATRICK, Abraham	LUZ	371	James	MIF	8
Stephen	LAN	92	Elizebeth	VEN	170	James	WAS	24
PARSONS, Abraham	BUC	94A	Jacob	LUZ	373	James	WAS	30
David	CEN	23	James	FAY	258	James	WAS	58
George	BUC	137A	John	BER	158	James	ALL	60
Isaac	CEN	23	John	WST	349	James	GRN	72
James	DEL	169	Rebecca	PHA	59	James	WAS	76
John	HNT	142	Robert	ARM	125	James	ALL	80
Joshua	DEL	174	Robert	ARM	126	James	ALL	84
Mahlon	DEL	180	PATRIDG, Thomas	ALL	101	James	BUC	87

PATTERSON, James
  (Crossed Out) LAN 150
James ALL 105
James HNT 124
James LAN 157
James LAN 160
James YOR 193
James YOR 196
James FAY 211
James FAY 211
James LAN 256
James LAN 258
James FRA 318
James WST 349
James MER 456
Jane HNT 135
Jane CHE 715
Jane MIF 11A
Jas. CUM 136
Jas. WST 295
Jas. BUT 318
Jno. MIF 8
Jno. CUM 50
Jno. (B. S.) MIF 8
Jno. (Tav.?) MIF 8
John ADA 5
John ADA 30
John PHA 30
John WAS 30
John ADA 33
John WAS 46
John LAN 47
John PHA 48
John PHA 61
John ALL 63
John WAS 71
John ALL 77
John (Full Name
  Crossed Out) LAN 150
John GRN 103
John WST 155
John LAN 157
John WST 163
John LAN 166
John FAY 211
John LAN 245
John LAN 287
John MER 455
John Esqr. FAY 268
John PHI 80A
Joseph ALL 110
Joseph HNT 136
Joseph NOU 180
Joseph FRA 318
Joseph LUZ 369
Joseph Revd. WAS 86
Josiah CUM 113
Marey FAY 268
Mary CUM 113
Mary LAN 120
Mrs. LYC 28
Murry DAU 2A
Nathan YOR 198
Nathl. CHE 866
Obediah CUM 113
Patr. FRA 309
Peter ALL 86
Peter FAY 268
Richard LUZ 368
Robert MIF 2
Robert WAS 50
Robert ALL 65
Robert ALL 83
Robert ALL 105
Robert ALL 115
Robert PHA 120

PATTERSON, Robert NOU 184
Robert FAY 205
Robert LUZ 383
Robert Jr. BUC 83A
Robert BUC 84A
Robt. MIF 13
Robt. MIF 13
Robt. CUM 113
Robt. CUM 123
Robt. WST 314
Robt. FRA 318
Sally LAN 89
Saml. CEN 23
Saml. YOR 203
Saml. WST 349
Samuel ADA 16
Samuel VEN 166
Samuel FAY 205
Samuel LAN 258
Solomon FRA 326
Susanah ADA 33
Susannah ADA 35
Thoams WAS 30
Thomas WAS 71
Thomas ALL 93
Thomas GRN 107
Thomas FAY 211
Thomas FAY 268
Thomas FAY 268
Thomas WST 349
Thomas CHE 702
Thomas CHE 715
Thomas CHE 759
Thomas B. Esq. ALL 84
Thoms LAN 151
Thos. LYC 18
Thos. WST 174
Thos. WST 382
William WAS 30
William ADA 34
William ADA 35
William BFD 38
William FAY 216
William FAY 262
William FAY 268
William WST 382
William Jur. FAY 268
Willm Sr. WAS 30
Willm. BUT 327
Willm. BUT 348
Willm. A. Esqr. NOH 38
Wilm. ALL 64
Wm. CUM 27
Wm. CUM 40
Wm. CUM 74
Wm. Jr. WAS 30
Wm. Junr. CUM 40
Zacharh. MIF 8
James ALL 104
James ALL 104
PATTIN, James MER 456
PATTISON, Chas. CUM 97
Geo. CUM 97
PATTON, &
  Sturgeon DAU 18A
Abraham PHA 41
Benjamin HNT 155
David PHA 86
David DAU 17A
Forgy CEN 21
Hugh WAS 24
Hyram LAN 183
James MIF 13
James CEN 23
James BFD 39
James LAN 123

PATTON, James FRA 283
James FRA 285
James FRA 297
Jas. CUM 51
John CEN 23
John CEN 23
John ADA 24
John LAN 89
John NOU 106
John PHI 116
John CUM 117
John NOU 147
John HNT 155
John LAN 239
John PHI 67A
Joseph HNT 161
Joseph FAY 268
Margaret PHI 128
Mary CUM 147
Mary WST 155
Mathew FRA 293
Matthew HNT 125
Mrs. NOU 195
Nathen NOU 167
Robert PHA 11
Robert LAN 300
Robt BUT 327
Robt. CUM 82
Robt. BUT 348
Saml. FRA 280
Thomas PHI 55
Thomas WST 155
Thomas FAY 205
Thomas BUC 107A
Thos. CEN 23
Thos. PHA 72
Thos. PHI 77A
William MIF 8
William WAS 70
William WST 155
William WST 350
Wm. CUM 35
Wm. PHA 93
Wm. CUM 100
PATTY, George WST 222
John YOR 200
PAUDER, Jacob WST 295
PAUGH, George PHA 39
PAUL, Abraham BFD 65
Abraham PHI 126
Abraham PHI 127
Adam LAN 57
Conrad NOU 195
David PHI 89
Esther MNT 51
Frederick NOH 91
George BFD 40
George FRA 321
Henry MNT 78
Jacob MNT 36
Jacob PHI 122
James MNT 51
James LAN 60
James PHA 80
James LAN 117
James PHI 154
James WST 372
Jeremiah PHA 3
John WAS 24
John LAN 59
John BER 158
John YOR 214
Jonathan PHI 154
Jos. PHI 90A
Joseph MNT 108
Joseph & Saml. PHI 122

PAUL, Joshua	BUC 155A	PAXSON, Timothy	PHA 44	PEARCEHAUL,	
Martin	NOH 81	William	BUC 138	Bengamin	ALL 64
Mary	PHA 18	PAXTAN, Andrew	FRA 278	PEARMAN, Samuel	FAY 223
Michael	NOU 123	PAXTON, Amous	FAY 247	PEARSE, Andrew	ALL 77
Nathl.	CUM 37	Benjamin	BFD 59	John	ALL 79
Peter	BER 157	Henry	CHE 863	John	ALL 80
Robert	PHI 137	Isaac	ADA 26	John Jun.	ALL 80
Saml.	PHA 62	Jacob	CHE 847	Joseph	ALL 80
Saml.	WST 372	James	ADA 12	Joseph	PHI 94A
Saml. Joseph &	PHI 122	James	FRA 283	Lewas	ALL 77
Samuel	BER 208	John	WAS 13	Lewes	ALL 80
Thomas	ALL 68	John	BFD 52	Peter	PHI 68
Thomas	PHI 152	John	FAY 205	Peter	PHI 109
Thomas	DEL 158	John	FAY 211	PEARSON, Abigail	BUC 151A
Thos.	BUC 153A	John	CHE 863	Amos	BUC 94A
Valentine	NOH 56A	Joseph	WAS 9	Benjamin	DEL 168
Widow	ALL 79	Joseph	CHE 847	Benjm.	BER 235
William	ERI 58	Nathaniel	ADA 9	Bevan	DEL 170
William	GRN 77	Nathaniel	ADA 13	Charles	DEL 169
William	DEL 186	Nathaniel	WAS 58	Chas.	PHI 60
Wm.	PHI 74	Nathaniel	WAS 86	Crispen	BUC 146
PAULI, Phililp	BER 242	Samuel	WAS 9	Crispin	BUC 145
Philip	BER 259	Samuel	BFD 59	David	PHI 115
PAULIN, Isaac	CHE 799	Thomas Junr.	WAS 71	Elijah	BER 204
PAULING, Benjn.	MNT 129	Thomas Senr.	WAS 71	Enoch	CHE 807
Henry	MNT 83	W----w?	ADA 6	Ephraim	DEL 163
John	MNT 83	Widow	CUM 62	George	LAN 62
PAULMAN, John	FRA 310	William Revd.	ADA 1	Henry	NOH 63
PAULOS, Adam	YOR 205	PAYAN, Peter	PHA 89	Henry	NOH 87A
PAULSER, Henry	GRN 103	PAYE, John	LUZ 386	Isaac	PHA 20
PAULUS, Adam	YOR 204	PAYN, Joseph	ALL 85	Isaac	BUC 94A
Henry	LAN 291	PEA, Abm.	CUM 55	Isaac	BUC 103A
John	NOH 74	Andrew	BFD 45	James	PHA 78
Michael	NOH 34A	PEACH, Thomas	PHI 148	James	BUC 146
PAULY, Henry	NOH 60A	William	FAY 262	Jessee	BER 234
Paul	NOH 86	William	FRA 273	John	PHA 54
PAUP, Christian	ADA 18	PEACHEL, David	CHE 715	John Esqr.	DEL 168
Mordecai	YOR 209	John	CHE 713	Jonathan	MNT 142
Valentine	YOR 176	Martin	CHE 764	Jonathan	BUC 145
PAUSLEY, John	CUM 109	Samuel	CHE 711	Joseph	PHI 90
PAWF, George	YOR 205	PEACHT, Joseph	CEN 23	Joseph	DEL 186
PAWLING, Levi	MNT 70	PEACHY, Moses	MIF 4	Lawrence	BUC 139A
Thomas	DEL 173	PEACOCK, Mary	DAU 15A	Lydia	DEL 168
Whitlock	DEL 160	Ralph	PHA 25	Mathias	WAS 13
Williama	PHA 41	Wm.	MIF 11	Nathan	DEL 168
PAXON, Jacob	MNT 36	PEADON, John	CUM 41	Pactions	FAY 258
PAXSON, Aaron	BUC 145	PEAGEL, David	NOH 31	Powell	CHE 906
Abraham	BUC 145	PEAK, Edward	PHI 84A	Richard	PHA 105
Benjn.	BUC 145A	John	CUM 152	Samuel	PHI 59
Elias	BUC 145A	Thos.	PHI 84A	Samuel	DEL 165
Elizabeth	BUC 161A	PEAL, Charles	PHA 89	Thos.	PHA 84
Isaac	PHA 10	Rembrandt	PHA 79	Vincent	GRN 107
Isaac	BUC 145A	William	CHE 753	William	PHA 16
Isaiah	BUC 145	PEALE, Frederick	MER 455	William	SOM 130
Israel	PHA 4	James	PHA 122	William	CHE 807
James	LYC 13	PEALER, Henry	PHA 56	William	BUC 94A
James	NOU 112	PEALMAN, John	CRA 4	PEARSONS, James	BFD 45
Joseph	BUC 87	PEANY, Jacob	CUM 134	William	LAN 89
Joseph	BUC 94A	PEAPLES, James	FRA 271	PEARSY, George	PHI 76A
Joseph S.	BUC 144	PEAR, Ann	PHA 112	Henry	PHI 68A
Joshua	PHI 154	PEARCE, Abel	LUZ 336	Jacob	PHA 61
Joshua	BUC 161A	Abnor	FAY 246	PEART, Mrs.	PHI 137
Mahlon	BUC 99	Alexr.	PHA 65	Benja.	PHI 144
Mahlon	BUC 145A	Alice	LUZ 336	Bryant	PHA 29
Moses	BUC 145A	Andrew	ALL 73	Jane	PHA 7
Mrs.	NOU 112	James	ALL 78	Joseph	PHA 59
Oliver	BUC 145	John	ALL 54	Thomas	LAN 113
Phineas	BUC 143A	John	LUZ 334	Thomas	PHI 135
Rachel	BUC 103A	Jonathan	LUZ 337	William	PHI 135
Rachel	BUC 151A	Joseph	LUZ 393	Wm.	PHI 90A
Samuel	BUC 88	Joseph Jun.	ALL 80	PEAS, Dennis	PHA 26
Sarah	BUC 89	Mathew	PHA 72	Jonathan	LUZ 416
Thomas	BUC 138	Obidia	ALL 116	Samuel	LUZ 319
Thomas	BUC 145	Phillip	FAY 246	PEASEL, Rudolph	BFD 59
Thomas	BUC 143A	Thos.	PHA 78	PEAT, John	NOU 202
Thomas	BUC 161A	Wilm.	ALL 73	PEATON, Robert	BEV 10

PERREL, Daniel	GRN 96	PETER, Henry	ADA 16	PETERS, John	PHI 122		
PERREN, John	BFD 52	Henry	CUM 60	John	NOU 131		
PERRIGREW, Robert	FAY 268	Henry	YOR 169	John	NOU 139		
PERRIN, Edward	WAS 58	Henry	LAN 195	John	LAN 148		
PERRY, Widow	WAS 86	Henry	DAU 42A	John	DEL 155		
Ben	LUZ 320	Henry	DAU 47A	Leonard	NOU 189		
Daniel	WAS 39	Jacob	LAN 293	Mrs.	NOU 131		
Daniel	BUC 145	Jacob Jn.	NOH 45A	Peter	PHI 11A		
David	CHE 715	Jacob Senr.	NOH 45A	Phillip	NOU 195		
James	WAS 39	Jno. Jacob	NOH 45A	Phillip	FAY 216		
James	WAS 58	John	LAN 51	Richard Esqr.	PHA 3		
James	ALL 76	John (Smith)	NOH 45A	Richd., Judge	PHI 62A		
James	CHE 870	John	LAN 146	Sarah Widow	NOH 32A		
James	CHE 871	John	LAN 195	Thomas	DEL 156		
Jane	WAS 9	John Senr.	NOH 45A	Thomas T.	PHA 28		
John	LYC 20	John	NOH 45A	Thos.	YOR 219		
John	ALL 55	Leonard	LAN 19	Valentine	LAN 81		
John	ALL 62	Lineweaver	LAN 265	Warner	BUC 146		
John	FAY 268	Nicholas	NOH 45A	William Jun.	DEL 155		
Jonathan	PHI 144	Philip	DAU 48	William Sen.	DEL 156		
Liston	FAY 262	Philip	NOH 91	Willm.	PHI 75A		
Maray	PHA 86	Richard	DAU 7	PETERSMAN,			
Moses	VEN 168	Schiffer	LAN 141	Michael	SOM 154		
Richd.	PHI 80	Sheaffer	LAN 137	PETERSON, Dereck			
Robert	BEV 19	Theobald	NOH 45A	John Revd.	SOM 152		
Robt.	PHA 86	Widow	NOH 45A	Derick	PHI 153		
Saml.	CUM 115	William	YOR 165	Gabriel	ALL 87		
Silas	PHI 145	William	NOH 45A	George	PHA 54		
Thomas	PHI 145	PETEREW, Ewart	ALL 86	George	BFD 76		
William	WAS 39	PETERICK,		Gimima	PHI 109		
William	CHE 870	Benjamin	LUZ 370	Henry	PHI 153		
PERSAIL, Peter	ALL 68	Joshua	LUZ 370	Israel	CUM 112		
PERSHINGER,		PETERMAN, Andrew	WAS 112	Jacob	NOH 31		
George	YOR 197	Balser	DAU 7	Jacob	PHA 43		
PERSHON, Chritr.	WST 314	Balser	DAU 5A	James	HNT 140		
Conrod	WST 314	Christian	DEL 177	James	FAY 268		
Daniel	WST 314	Daniel	YOR 193	John (Blackman)	PHA 124		
PERSIN, Abel	NOU 167	Henry	YOR 191	John	NOH 78A		
PERSION?,		Jacob	MNT 78	Michael	BFD 76		
Fredrick	WST 382	Jacob	YOR 171	Peter	FRA 313		
PERSON, Benjamin	NOU 112	James	NOU 152	Peter	BUT 322		
Benjamin	MER 456	Joakim	LAN 47	PETERY, George	DAU 49A		
George	DAU 31A	John	MNT 74	PETESON, Mrs.	LYC 30		
John	ALL 79	John	YOR 166	PETGE, Henry	NOH 48A		
John	FAY 216	Michael	BER 174	PETICOLAS, August	LAN 38		
Jonathan	DEL 168	Michael	YOR 186	PETIGRU, Wilm.	ALL 71		
Jos.	YOR 218	Michael	YOR 187	PETIT, James	PHI 127		
Matthias	NOU 106	Peter	PHA 18	PETITT, Widow	WST 350		
Mrs.	NOU 101	Philip	MNT 92	PETLET, Nathaniel	NOU 155		
Philamon	WAS 4	Susannah	MNT 83	PETNY, Lewis	FAY 253		
Robert	SOM 132	PETERMIER, Philip	DAU 36A	PETRE, George	BER 160		
William	NOU 106	PETERS, Widow	PHA 65	Henry	BER 214		
PERSONE, William	MER 457	Widow	WST 241	Widow	LAN 31		
PERSOVELL, Andw.	PHI 106	Adam	ARM 123	PETREE, Jacob	BER 234		
PERTERSEN, Peter	LAN 258	Adam	YOR 168	PETRIE, Anthony	LAN 275		
PESHULAW, Monseur	PHA 7	Agness	CEN 21	PETRIKEN, Wm.	CEN 23		
PESO, Isaac	PHA 45	Arnold	LAN 53	PETRY, Anthony	NOH 50A		
PESSLER, Laurence	LAN 15	Baltzer	MIF 17A	George	YOR 188		
PESSMORE, Abraham	HNT 144	David	FAY 239	Henry	DAU 5		
PETEGREW, Jas.	CUM 124	Eliza	PHA 44	Jacob	BER 131		
PETER, Widow	PHI 73	Evan	DEL 166	Jacob	BER 132		
Abraham	LAN 293	Francis	PHA 42	Jacob	YOR 188		
Adam	MNT 135	Geo.	PHI 114A	John	DAU 49A		
Barned	LAN 195	George	PHA 29	William	PHI 8		
Caspar	DAU 19A	George	LAN 50	PETTEET, Thomas	MER 456		
Casper Junr.	NOH 45A	George	PHI 127	PETTEGREW, Joseph	WAS 24		
Casper Senr.	NOH 45A	George	FAY 239	PETTERSON, John	BUC 83A		
Christian	LAN 27	Hannah	BER 218	PETTET, Isaac	GRN 108		
Daniel	BER 231	Henry	PHI 31	John	FRA 302		
Frederick	NOH 32A	Isaac	ADA 33	Thos.	YOR 176		
George	DAU 43	Jacob	NOU 189	PETTIBONE, Oliver	LUZ 333		
George	CUM 122	Jane	MNT 36	PETTICOAT, Dorsey	HNT 125		
George	FRA 306	John	PHA 16	PETTIE, Daniel	LAN 122		
George	DAU 25A	John	DAU 25	William Jn.	BUC 145A		
George	NOH 45A	John	PHA 32	PETTIGREW, Widow	NOH 39		
George M.	YOR 171	John	PHI 45	PETTIT, Andw.	PHA 30		

PHILLIPS,			PHYFER, Jacob	LAN 308	PIERCE, James	CHE 707		
Naphtals	PHA	8	PHYSICK, Phillip		John	DEL 190		
Nathan	MNT	39	S.	PHA 80	John	BUT 322		
Phillip	NOU 159		PIATT, Isiah	NOH 39	John	CHE 853		
Richard	FAY 211		John	LYC 29	Jonathan	CHE 738		
Robert	FAY 228		PICHAND, James	YOR 159	Joseph	CHE 846		
Saml.	WST 174		PICHARD, John	CUM 36	Joshua	CHE 707		
Samuel	FAY 205		PICHER, Henry	ADA 23	Joshua	CHE 773		
Solomon	WAS 82		PICK, Francis	PHA 10	Joshua	CHE 851		
Stephen	CHE 885		George	BER 258	Mary	HNT 131		
Theophilus	FAY 246		PICKARD, John	NOU 184	Peter	DAU 23		
Thomas	WAS	53	PICKEL, Adam	LAN 106	Pricilla	CHE 840		
Thomas	ERI	57	Christian	NOU 180	Richd.	CHE 705		
Thomas	BUC 104		Christopher	NOU 131	Richd.	MIF 5A		
Thomas	MER 456		Henry	LAN 249	Thomas	PHA 11		
Thos.	PHA	52	John	NOU 180	Thomas	PHA 14		
Thos.	BUC 145		John	NOU 180	Thomas	CHE 719		
Titus	FAY 223		Leonard	NOU 131	Widow	CHE 832		
William	WAS	93	Peter	LAN 246	William	CHE 809		
William	NOU 150		Saml.	FRA 301	PIERCEALL, Jacob	BEV 6		
William	FAY 237		Simon	NOU 139	Sampson Esq.	BEV 6		
William	FRA 286		Simon	NOU 180	PIEREL, William	FAY 268		
William	FRA 308		Thomas	NOU 180	PIERSOL, Jeremiah	CHE 716		
Wm.	BEV	10	Thomas	NOU 180	Jeremiah Jun.	CHE 721		
Wm.	PHA	86	Tobias	NOU 180	PIERSON, Elias	ADA 42		
PHILLIS, Charles	BEV	15	Tobias	NOU 180	George	PHI 11A		
Jacob	BEV	15	PICKEL?, Joab	LUZ 392	Isaac	ADA 43		
Joseph	WAS	93	PICKENS, James	FAY 251	Isaac	CHE 708		
PHILLOP, Jonothon	ALL 106		PICKEO?, George	LYC 12	Joshua	BFD 76		
PHILLOPS, John	ALL 106		PICKER, Simon	ADA 37	Ruben	FAY 237		
Joseph Esqr.	ALL	92	PICKERING, Benjn.	BUC 146	PIFFER, Jacob	ADA 28		
Robert	ALL	74	Isaac	BUC 87	John	ADA 28		
Samuel	ALL 106		Jesse	LAN 152	Peter	DAU 52		
Sarah	ALL	88	John	BUC 145	PIFLE, Andr.			
Thomas	ALL 106		Jonathan	BUC 145	(Crossed Out)	FRA 308		
PHILPOT, Thos.	PHI 144		Joseph	BUC 145	PIGALLER, John	PHA 74		
PHILSON, Robert			Jotham	LUZ 385	PIGEON, Michael	LAN 48		
Esquire	SOM 141		Timothy Esqr.	NOH 38	Robert	BUC 103A		
PHIMLEY?, Amos	BUC 145		William	WAS 39	Willm.	PHI 34		
William	BUC 144		PICKERON, Saml.	PHI 96	PIGLER, Jacob	CUM 109		
PHIMLY, George	BUC	90	PICKERSGILL, John	PHA 78	PIKE, Abraham	LUZ 345		
PHINEY, John	BUC 138		PICKET, James	PHI 99	Elenor	YOR 169		
PHIPPS, Caleb	CHE 741		PICKHART, Adam	PHI 125	Elizabeth	YOR 217		
Chrosby	CHE 753		PICKING, Henry	ADA 37	John	BFD 39		
Elisha	DEL 168		Widow	ADA 37	Moses	YOR 217		
Isaac	CHE 753		PICKINGPAUGH,		PIKER, James	FRA 276		
John	PHI	7	George	GRN 65	PILE, Widow	PHI 21		
Jonathan	MNT 116		Jacob	GRN 79	Casper,	SOM 130		
Jonathan	CHE 787		Peter	GRN 77	Daniel	BER 174		
Jos. (Weaver)	MNT	39	PICKINGS, Saml.	MIF 17A	George	SOM 130		
Joseph	MNT	36	PICKINS, John	FAY 251	George	BER 273		
Lewis	YOR 219		John	CHE 714	Henry	SOM 130		
Mary	CHE 818		PICKLE, Henry	YOR 159	Henry	BUC 159A		
Rachel	MNT	37	Jacob	LAN 115	Jacob	DAU 44		
Robert	CHE 814		John	YOR 211	John	SOM 135		
Squire	MNT 117		Nichs.	PHI 35	Laurence	CUM 58		
Stephen	PHA	82	PICKLES, Henry	YOR 196	Mary	PHI 86A		
Thomas	PHA	20	PICKSELLER,		Michael	SOM 130		
Thomas	MNT	36	Abraham	HNT 162	Thomas	PHI 71A		
PHIPS, Isaac	PHA	12	PICTEL?, Joab	LUZ 392	PILER, Christn.	DAU 37A		
John	VEN 168		PIDCOCKS, Benjn.	LYC 29	John	DAU 37A		
Nathen	VEN 168		Emanuel	LYC 29	PILES, Abraham	LAN 156		
Samuel	MER 456		PIDGEON,		Amos (Crossed			
Thomas	HNT 130		Christiana	PHA 34	Out)	LAN 151		
PHISE, Jacob	PHI 120		PIEARCE, Elisha	FAY 210	Amos	LAN 156		
PHISIC, Edmond	PHI 108		Isaac	FAY 210	James	FRA 323		
PHISTER, Fredk.	PHI	99	James	FAY 233	John	WST 314		
Jacob	PHI 93A		PIECH, Abm.	PHA 42	John Junr.	WST 314		
John	PHI 99A		PIEDHAIR?, Martin	PHA 54	Joshua	WAS 17		
PHITE, Mesr.	LAN	45	PIERACE, Jerimia	FAY 233	Marry	PHA 92		
Peter	LAN 165		PIERCE, Caleb	PHA 24	Pary	YOR 156		
PHLEGER, Jacob	YOR 159		Caleb	PHA 46	Saml.	PHI 18		
PHOENIX, Moses	NOH 67A		Edward	CHE 882	Saml. Junr.	PHI 18		
PHRONHEISER,			Gainard	LAN 219	PILGER, Jacob	PHI 103A		
George	BER 177		George	CHE 851	PILGRAM, Henry	CUM 142		
PHYER, Abraham	YOR 207		Jacob	CHE 851	PILIPPY, George	SOM 135		

PRAIL, Nicholas	NOU 139	PRESTON, Paul	BUC 141A	PRICE, Peter	DEL 163
PRAISTER, Henry	BUC 99	Samuel	WAY 135	Peter	BUC 161A
PRAKER, George	WAS 39	Samuel	FAY 205	Philip	WAS 4
PRALL, George	WAS 4	Thomas	CHE 849	Philip	CHE 806
Thomas	WAS 4	William	PHA 34	Prichard	PHA 120
PRANCIS, Wm.	PHA 53	William	PHI 34	Rebecca	BER 234
PRATER, Henry	VEN 166	William	PHA 119	Rees	MNT 139
Thomas	VEN 166	Willm Senr.	PHI 74A	Richard	WST 328
PRATT, Widow	PHI 75A	PRETHER, Abraham	FRA 295	Samuel	PHA 15
Abraham	CHE 701	Henry	FRA 289	Samuel	BFD 52
David	DEL 177	PRETTE, Anthony	FRA 283	Samuel	WAS 76
Elisha	LUZ 394	PRETZ, Anthony	DAU 8A	Samuel	DEL 163
Ephraim	LUZ 406	PREVO, Titus	PHA 54	Samuel Esqr.	DEL 166
Henry	PHA 35	PREY, Widow	LAN 31	Sarah	PHA 45
Isaac	LUZ 394	PRIBBLE, Job	GRN 96	Smith	BUC 141A
James	PHI 29	PRICE, Widow	PHI 11A	Solomon	BER 245
John	PHA 46	Widw.	PHI 109A	Tama?	LUZ 414
John	GRN 65	Abijah	DEL 186	Tdhomas	NOU 139
John Junr.	GRN 65	Amon	HNT 133	Thomas	PHA 95
Pitkin	LUZ 425	Benjamin	PHA 113	Thomas	PHI 138
Thomas	PHI 61	Benjamin	NOU 167	Thomas	MNT 141
Thomas	DEL 177	Chandler	PHA 97	Thomas	DEL 186
William	LAN 289	Charles	PHI 83	Thos.	BUC 140
William	LUZ 406	Charles	NOU 106	Vell	CHE 807
PRATZ, George	NOH 41A	Conrad	BER 245	William	MNT 122
John	CUM 57	Daniel	MNT 119	William	SOM 144
Saml. Junr.	CUM 57	Daniel	MNT 122	William	DEL 186
PRAUL, John	BUC 143A	Daniel	CHE 891	William	WST 328
John	BUC 161A	David	BER 245	William	CHE 699
Joshua	BUC 138	David	FAY 253	William	CHE 801
Joshua	BUC 143A	Elizabeth	FRA 302	William Docr.	LAN 13
Nathan	BUC 138	Elnathan	NOH 38	William	PHI 11A
Nathan	BUC 143A	George	FAY 223	Wm. J.?	PHI 35
PRAWL, David	LYC 14	George	BER 234	PRICEE, Nathaniel	BUC 161A
PRAY, Hezekiah	LUZ 381	George	BER 267	PRICER, Daniel	CHE 898
John	PHI 93	George	CHE 891	Philip	CHE 894
PRAYMOUR, Fredk.	BUC 157A	Gist	BFD 65	PRICER?, Frederic	CHE 890
PREAMER,		Henry	NOU 180	PRICHARD, Henry	CRA 2
Valentine	BUT 318	Henry	BUC 159A	PRICKER, George	GRN 103
PREFLER, Geo.	PHI 101	Icaboth	NOH 78A	John	GRN 103
PREIN?, Jacob	YOR 209	Isaac	MIF 11	Leadwick	GRN 103
PREINER?, Joseph	MNT 93	Jacob	PHI 15	PRICKET, Wm.	PHI 82
PREISCH, Henry	NOH 60A	Jacob	PHA 110	PRICKETT, Anne C.	PHA 97
Jacob	NOH 56A	Jacob	BER 245	PRIDE, Mary	ALL 55
PREIST, Joseph	MNT 142	James	BUC 87	PRIEN, James	WAS 45
PRENNER, Frank	NOU 139	James	NOU 106	Peter	WAS 30
PRENTICE, Amos	LUZ 426	James	WAY 149	Stephen	WAS 30
Benjn.	PHA 5	John	ADA 17	PRIER, John	FRA 293
James	DAU 47	John	LYC 18	PRIEST, Absolum	MNT 105
John	PHI 94	John	BUC 87	Elijah	CHE 835
John	LUZ 426	John	MNT 122	Emanuel	PHA 48
Thaddeus	LUZ 403	John	MNT 139	George	MNT 70
PRESLER, Michael	NOU 177	John	WAY 149	Isaac	CHE 820
Nicols.	DAU 12A	John	DEL 162	Levi	MNT 105
PRESLERY, Francis	LYC 18	John	DEL 165	Matthias	DEL 184
PRESSELL,		John	NOU 189	William	MNT 105
Valentine	YOR 208	John	FRA 306	PRIEST?, (See	
Valentine Jr.	YOR 208	John	FRA 322	Reist)	FAY 199
PRESSILL, Henry	YOR 211	John	ERI 56A	PRIESTLEY, Joseph	NOU 172
PRESSON, Darius	LUZ 326	John	PHI 69A	PRIESTLY,	
PRESTEN, Willm.		John	BUC 94A	Jonathan	HNT 132
Junr.	PHI 75	John	PHI 108A	PRIGER, Peter	WST 295
PRESTON, Widow	PHI 75	John M.	PHA 18	Susanah	WST 295
Abijah	NOU 180	Joseph	PHA 20	PRIGG, William	WAS 9
Amer	PHA 12	Joseph	GRN 84	PRIGMORE, Willm.	PHI 25
Barnet	WAS 112	Joseph	MNT 139	PRINA, George	MNT 74
David	CHE 764	Joseph	HNT 163	PRINCE, Fredk.	BER 239
James	NOH 69	Joseph	CHE 896	John	DEL 166
James	MNT 114	Joseph	NOH 78A	John	BER 235
James	PHA 121	Lewis	PHI 88A	PRINCE?, John	BUC 87A
Jonas	CHE 710	Madgalena	BER 245	PRINCECOVER,	
Jonas Esqr.	DEL 179	Merryman	HNT 134	Caspar	DAU 50
Joseph	LUZ 393	Nathan	DEL 167	PRINDLE, Amasa	ERI 56A
Joseph	CHE 764	Nathaniel	WAS 104	James	LUZ 341
Joseph	CHE 849	Noah	NOU 106	Samuel	LUZ 341
Junia	LUZ 350	Peter	PHI 118	PRINE, Jacob	FRA 306

PRINGEY, John	SOM	135	PROUDFOOT, George	LAN	68	PUGH, Samuel	WAS	71
John Sen.	SOM	135	James	WAS	53	Samuel	DEL	183
PRINGLE,			John	CHE	719	Samuel	DEL	185
Elizabeth	BUC	161A	Robert	YOR	195	Thomas	PHI	41
George	SOM	162	PROUL, George	FRA	312	Thomas	MNT	70
Henry	PHI	45	William	YOR	216	Thomas	CHE	869
Philip	SOM	162	PROUSE, Michael	FRA	283	Widow	CHE	896
PRINOR, Andrew	FAY	262	PROVENCE, Joseph	FAY	216	PUHIN, Nicholas	DEL	174
Peter	FAY	262	Robert	HNT	149	PULL, Rosina	LAN	202
PRIOR, Isaac	GRN	65	Thomas	HNT	162	PULLER, Fanny	WST	155
Luther	GRN	96	PROVEST,			PULLIS, Conrad	WAY	142
Matthew	HNT	142	Alexander	PHI	131	PULTZ, Michael	DAU	41
PRISA--?, Jacob	FRA	288	Roderick	PHA	76	PUMRAIN, Maty	ALL	96
PRISE, Moses	ALL	55	PROVINCE, Charles	WAS	93	PUMROY, Francis	WST	349
PRISH, Nathaniel	ALL	52	Mathew	WAS	86	George	WST	349
PRISON, Chester	DEL	164	Robert	WAS	93	John	FRA	317
PRISSLER, George	BFD	65	PROWDFOOT, David	FAY	210	John Esqr.	WST	349
PRITCHARD,			PRPOST, Andr.	FRA	313	Thos.	FRA	317
Anthony	CHE	859	PRUAN, James	PHI	55	William	PHA	104
Gilbert	CHE	861	PRUDDEN, John B.	LUZ	336	PUNCH, George	NOU	177
Joseph	MNT	116	PRUDEN, Bethuel	WAS	64	Mrs.	NOU	167
Liman	LYC	12	Joseph	WAS	64	PUNK, Frederick	YOR	170
PRITCHERD, John	FAY	259	PRUDENS, Gabriel	GRN	107	PUP, Nichs.	CUM	64
PRITCHET, Thomas	PHA	110	PRUDHAME?, Renne	PHA	48	PUPE?, Peter	ADA	42
PRITOR, Widow	PHI	45	PRUN?, Jacob	YOR	209	PURDIN?, Charles	HNT	136
PRITTS, Samuel	SOM	139	PRUNCINGER, Frank	NOU	189	PURDON, John	PHA	107
PRITTZ, Jacob	SOM	135	PRUNER, Abm.	BUC	106A	Rachel	PHA	74
PRIZER, Henry	MNT	83	Abraham	BUC	97A	PURDUE, John	BFD	59
John	MNT	83	Henry	ERI	60	William	BFD	59
PRIZOR, Joseph	MNT	66	John	BUC	105A	William Jr.	BFD	59
PROADFIT, James			Philip	BUC	105A	PURDUE?, Charles	HNT	136
M.d.	PHA	7	PRUSSIA, Chrisn.	BER	138	PURDY, Widow	PHI	66A
PROBEN, John	PHI	43	PRUSTOR, Willm.	PHI	46	Ephraim	WAY	142
PROBST, George	NOH	76	PRUTTS, Phillip	FRA	283	Hugh	LAN	242
Henry	NOH	54	PRUVIANCE, John	WAS	117	Jacob	WAY	142
John	NOH	54	PRY, Patrick	MIF	8	James	MIF	11
John	WST	241	PRYCE, William	FAY	237	James	YOR	195
John Jr.	NOH	54	PRYEE?, (See			Jas.	CUM	131
Martin	NOH	54	Pryce)	FAY	237	Jno.	CUM	131
Martin Junr.	NOH	54	PRYER, Thomas	WAS	45	Patrick	YOR	202
Mathias	NOH	54	PRYOR, Charles	PHA	95	Rheuben	WAY	142
Michael	NOH	54	Joseph	PHA	34	Robt.	CUM	52
PROCONIER, Henry	HNT	140	Josiah	BUC	161A	Silas	WAY	142
PROCTER, John	CRA	14	Thomas	PHA	17A	Thomas	CUM	43
PROCTOR, Abner	ADA	15	Thomas W.	MNT	108	Thos.	CUM	52
Ann	HNT	160	PUB?, John	LAN	134	Widow	MIF	11A
John	ADA	40	PUCKELBAUGH, John	BFD	68	William	WAY	142
John	BFD	76	PUDA, Peter	CUM	98	William	YOR	200
John	FAY	216	PUE, Daniel	NOU	144	PURKINS, Eleazer	FAY	241
Joseph	CUM	118	John	MER	455	PURMAN, Abraham	BER	185
Joshua	CHE	863	Mark	LAN	130	PURNELL, John	CHE	888
Ritchard	ALL	63	PUFF, Henry	BUC	99	PURREL, Daniel	WST	294
Sarah	PHA	13	Henry	BUC	153A	PURRELL, Jacob	CHE	718
Thos.	PHA	70	Philip	MNT	96	PURSEL, Malen	NOU	144
William	BFD	76	PUFOGLE, D. Jacob	NOU	97A	PURSELL, Jonathan	BUC	83
PROCUNER, Henry	BFD	41	PUGH, Daniel	BUC	97	PURSLEY, Dennis	WST	295
PROGG,			Ellis	BUC	105A	John	BUC	150
Christopher	GRN	103	Evan	CHE	895	John Jn.	BUC	139A
PRONG,			Hannah	LUZ	341	Sinclair	BUC	150
Christopher	WAS	124	Hannah	CHE	869	PURSLY, Dinnis	VEN	169
PROSER, Daniel	ERI	60A	Henry	MNT	139	PURVES, John	PHA	13
PROSKY, George	NOH	70	Henry Junr.	MNT	139	PURVEYARD, Jas.	BUT	335
PROSS, George	DAU	35A	Hugh	BER	177	PURVIANCE, Samuel	FRA	273
Peter	DAU	34A	Hugh	NOH	78A	PURVIANS, David	FAY	268
PROSSER, Charles	HNT	134	James	CHE	906	James	NOU	167
William	CRA	13	Jesse	CHE	869	James	FAY	268
William	BFD	65	Job	MNT	139	PURVIS, Wm.	CUM	148
PROSSER?,			John	MNT	83	PUSER, George	MNT	78
Jonathan	LUZ	408	John	BUC	97	PUSEY, Caleb	PHI	151
PROST, Phillip	NOU	167	John	BER	138	David	CHE	738
PROT, David	LAN	31	John	DEL	184	Ellis	CHE	767
PROTZMAN, Henrey	FAY	253	John	DEL	185	Jesse	CHE	849
John	BER	145	John	CHE	800	John	CHE	738
PROUDFOOT, Alexr.	YOR	195	John	CHE	867	Joshua	PHI	151
Andw.	YOR	195	Jonathan	MNT	70	Joshua	CHE	768
David	YOR	196	Joshua	CHE	869	Joshua	CHE	861

PUSEY, Lewis	CHE 764	QUANTILE, John	PHI 78A	QUIGLEY, Saml.	CUM 152
Nathan	CHE 768	QUARE, Lawrence	SOM 139	Thomas	CHE 846
Samuel	LAN 163	QUARGESS?, Widow	PHI 24	William	DAU 12
Thomas	CHE 768	QUARK?, John	PHI 97A	William	WAS 71
Thomas	CHE 849	QUARTER, Erasmus		Wm.	CUM 56
William	CHE 764	Dr.	FRA 297	QUIGLY, Ann	WST 155
William	CHE 848	QUARTERMAN, (No		George	LYC 26
PUSNAGER, Jacob	NOU 97A	Name)	YOR 197	Hugh	ALL 59
PUTLOE, Margaret	PHA 100	John	LAN 55	James	ALL 107
PUTMAN, Andrew	SOM 135	Wm.	LAN 58	James	LAN 112
Christr.	CUM 71	QUAST, Nicholas	PHA 63	William	WST 256
Peter	SOM 135	QUAW?, Charles	ADA 5	William	DAU 14A
Sarah	SOM 130	QUAY, Hugh	CHE 859	Wm.	DAU 45A
PUTNAM, Michal	ERI 57A	John	CHE 860	QUILLALY, Mr.	PHI 70
PUTT, Benjm.	BER 205	Patrick	PHI 26	QUILLIN, Ambers?	MER 457
PUTTERBAUGH,		Robt.	LYC 25	QUIMBY, Samuel	WAS 46
Jacob	BFD 65	QUAY?, William	CHE 787	QUIN, Edward	BUT 316
PUTTORPH, Martin	CHE 799	QUE, John	PHI 135	John	WST 372
PYE, James	FRA 318	QUEARY, Alexr.	WST 295	Owen	ARM 125
PYERS, James	NOU 195	John	WST 295	Tarrance	NOU 131
PYFER, Jacob	NOU 115	QUEEN, Charles	WAS 86	QUIN?, John	DAU 2A
PYKE, Ham	DEL 160	Hugh	PHA 62	QUINBY, Aron	BUC 145A
Jacob	DEL 161	QUEER, Christian	NOH 43A	Job	BUC 146
PYLE, Abm.	CHE 776	George Junr.	NOH 43A	QUINDON, John	PHA 3
Abner	DEL 191	George	NOH 43A	QUINLIN, Philip	GRN 92
Ann	CHE 742	QUELIN, John	PHA 9	QUINLY, John	PHI 16
Benjamin	DEL 186	QUERRY, Mary	YOR 156	QUINN, Hugh	NOU 139
Caleb	DEL 190	QUIAR?, -ichael	ARM 124	Robert	NOU 202
Daniel	DEL 160	QUICK, Aaron	BFD 76	William	CHE 798
Emus	ALL 89	Aaron Jr.	BFD 76	QUINTER, Jacob	BER 273
Henry	CHE 837	Benjamin	LUZ 421	Joseph	MNT 62
Isaac	DEL 157	Cornilius	LUZ 363	Thos.	CHE 890
Jacob	DEL 155	David	BFD 76	QUINTON, Andrew	BUC 103A
Jacob	CHE 848	David	WAY 138	Francis	PHA 89
Jacob	CHE 864	Henry	WAY 144	John	LAN 68
James	CHE 810	Isaac	WAS 53	QUIRK, Margaret	PHA 95
James	CHE 850	Jacob	WAY 145	QUIST, John	MNT 61
Job	DEL 172	James	LUZ 399	QUIVEY, Asa	WAS 76
Job	CHE 765	John	CRA 15	Daniel	WAS 76
John	DEL 155	John	BFD 76	QUOCK, Widow	LAN 47
John	DEL 156	Jos.	PHI 89A	QWINN, Hugh	ADA 27
John	CHE 708	Matthew	LUZ 337		
John	CHE 806	Moses	ALL 77	R------M?,	
Jonathan	CHE 836	Peter	WAY 145	William	ADA 8
Joseph	DEL 157	Peter	WAY 150	R----?, Joseph $	GRN 65
Joseph	CHE 741	Thomas	LUZ 399	R---H?, John	NOU 200
Levi	DEL 179	QUICKKSALL,		R-VER?, Abraham	NOU 180
Levi	DEL 190	Jonathn.	PHI 109A	RAAB, Peter	YOR 169
Nathan	DEL 182	QUICKLE, John	YOR 165	RAALE, John	YOR 207
Rachel	PHA 14	Philip	YOR 176	RAB, Michael	NOH 74
Ralph	DEL 158	QUICKLY, Henry	DAU 50A	Thomas	MER 457
Ralph	CHE 849	QUICSEL, Jerimiah	PHI 136	RAB?, Patrick	ARM 126
Samuel	DEL 157	QUIFFIN, Robert	NOU 167	RABB, Andrew	FAY 217
Samuel	DEL 161	QUIGG, John	CHE 714	Samuel	BEV 16
Stephen	DEL 160	John	CHE 895	Samuel	WAS 94
Thomas	CHE 742	QUIGGLE, Peter	MIF 13	Samuel	FAY 217
William	CHE 836	Philip	MIF 13	William	FAY 217
William	CHE 840	QUIGLE, Baltio?	LYC 23	RABENOLD, Adam	NOH 91A
PYLES, James	WAS 93	Jno.	LYC 26	Michael	NOH 60A
Joseph	WAS 58	Michl.	LYC 26	Peter	NOH 76A
PYOTT, James	DEL 170	QUIGLEY, Christr.	CUM 70	Peter	NOH 91A
PYRLEUS,		Fredrick	PHA 116	RABENSTINE,	
Christopher	NOH 32A	Henry	CUM 71	Dewalt	YOR 187
PYSEL, Abraham	YOR 213	Hugh	DEL 157	Leonard	YOR 185
Samuel	YOR 209	James	CRA 5	Nicholas	YOR 187
PYWELL, John	DEL 186	James	CUM 56	RABER, John	YOR 191
		James	MER 457	RABHAM, Chrisr.	PHI 48
QUAD, James	CUM 127	Jas.	CUM 139	RABLOGLE, Adam	BFD 69
QUADE, James	CEN 21	Jno.	CUM 30	George	BFD 68
QUAFFAY, Alexr.	NOU 167	Jno.	CUM 141	John	BFD 66
QUAIL, Robert	FAY 237	John	LAN 123	Rhinhart	BFD 66
Roboert	WAS 82	John	NOU 167	RABOTT?, George	BER 203
QUAINTANA, James	CHE 706	John	CHE 704	RABSOM, George	PHA 41
QUAKE, Luke	NOH 78A	John	CHE 862	RABSONY, John	LAN 239
QUAL, Thomas	PHI 47	Michl.	CUM 90	RACE, Joseph	PHA 78
QUANDLE, John	PHI 67	Robt.	CUM 139	Thomas	BUC 85

RACK, George	LAN	203	RALE?, Patrick	ARM	126	RAMBO, Jonas	MNT	105
RADCLIFF, Joseph	BUC	155A	RALEY?, John	ARM	126	Jonathan	MNT	105
Seth	BUC	155	RALF, Lowdy	CUM	65	Margaret	MNT	105
Widow	BUC	154A	RALL, James	CHE	707	Moses	MNT	83
RADEBACH, John	BER	264	RALLY, Samuel	PH1	99A	Moses	SOM	135
Nicholas	BER	220	RALPH, Ann	PHA	105	Nathan	MNT	106
RADEE, Danl.	CUM	46	Jonathan	LUZ	367	Peter	WST	351
RADEN, Margaret	WST	156	RALPHSNIDER,			Peter	MNT	105
RADENBACH, Jacob	BER	266	Henry	FRA	282	Peter	PHI	84A
RADENBACK, Jacob	NOH	48A	Jno.	FRA	282	RAMBOUGH, David	WST	277
RADFANG, Jacob	LAN	115	RALSON, James	NOH	31	RAMBOW, John	BUC	83
RADIG, Jacob	LAN	203	RALSTON, Andw.	CUM	110	RAMBY, Israel	YOR	186
RADLER, Ann	PHI	66A	Archibald	WAS	53	RAMER, John	BER	253
RAEDIGER, John			David	CUM	126	RAMERT, Mathias	BER	254
Cr.	DAU	43A	David	ARM	127	RAMEY, Thomas	ALL	93
RAERIG, Daniel	NOH	46	David	WST	156	William	FAY	247
RAFE, John	LAN	25	Isaac	BUC	155	RAMI, Nicholas	NOU	139
RAFELSBERGER,			James	WAS	9	RAMLER, Leond.	DAU	35
Christ.	YOR	180	James	WAS	17	Peter	DAU	39A
Christian	YOR	180	James	WAS	76	RAMSAY, Alexander	HNT	137
Martin	YOR	173	Jno.	LYC	19	Archibald	HNT	151
RAFFELSBERGER,			Jno. (See			Benjamin	HNT	137
Jacob	YOR	211	Ralston,			Benjamin	MNT	105
RAFIELD, John	PHA	81	Widow)	NOH	31	Charles	CHE	830
RAFSNYDER?, See			John	WAS	9	Charles	CHE	870
Reifsnyder	BER	158	John	WAS	13	Hugh	CHE	867
RAFTER, James	MIF	14	John	CRA	17	Jacob	CHE	885
John	NOU	189	John	WAS	17	James	CHE	867
RAGAN, Michael	PHA	93	John	WAS	53	James	CHE	873
RAGEL, Ab.	DAU	40A	John	HNT	164	John	HNT	151
RAGER, Jacob	LAN	213	John	WST	328	John	CHE	715
Michael	CRA	5	John Esq.	CHE	789	Joseph	CHE	736
Peter	LAN	213	Joseph	WAS	9	Samuel	HNT	154
RAGERS, James	LAN	164	Joseph	CHE	700B	Samuel	CHE	736
RAGERS?, Robert	LAN	226	Mary	YOR	202	Thos.	LYC	18
RAGUET, James	BUC	103A	Paul	LAN	170	William	HNT	137
RAHM, Conrad	BFD	45	Paul Junr.	LAN	169	RAMSBERGER, Elias	SOM	150
Melchor	DAU	2A	Reese	CHE	817	RAMSEY, Alexander	HNT	132
RAHN, Adam	BER	218	Robert	PHI	13	Alexr.	MNT	51
Jacob	BER	218	Robert	WST	328	Alexr.	PHA	64
Philip	LAN	203	Robert	WST	350	Alexr.	MNT	78
RAIGER, Adam	NOU	189	Robert Junr.	WAS	17	Alexr.	BUT	345
RAIGREIGH, Henry	NOU	189	Robert Senr.	WAS	17	Andw.	MIF	11
RAIL, Samuel	FAY	233	Robt.	CHE	790	Andw.	CUM	77
Thomas	FAY	233	Samuel Revd.	WAS	71	Archd.	CUM	95
William	FAY	233	Widow Of Jno.	NOH	31	Benjn.	BUC	85
RAILEY, James	GRN	90	William	WAS	53	Benjn.	FRA	280
RAILMAN, Peter	CUM	45	Wm.	MIF	26	Charles	DEL	192
RAILS, Noble	BEV	14	RALTON, Ann	DEL	183	David	YOR	176
RAILY, Thomas	GRN	65	RALYEA, David	CRA	12	David	YOR	202
RAIN, Eve	PHA	41	RAMAGE, John	NOU	200	Elisabeth	PHA	8
John	PHA	22	William	WAS	71	Eliza	PHA	89
John	PHA	41	RAMBACH, John	NOH	40	George	WAS	58
John	PHI	109	RAMBARGER, Geo.	DAU	34A	Hugh	WST	156
Thos.	PHA	37	RAMBEAU, Jesse	PHI	63	James	MIF	13
RAIN?, Nathaniel	PHA	121	Saml.	PHI	65	James	WAS	13
Paul	PHI	87	Samuel	PHI	12	James	WAS	24
RAINE, Phillip	NOU	148	RAMBECK, Jacob	CUM	53	James	DAU	35
RAINER, Wm.	PHI	80A	RAMBERGER, John	DAU	27	James	CUM	95
RAINEY, James	WAS	113	Philip	YOR	170	James	YOR	201
James	WST	156	RAMBLE, Samuel	YOR	193	James	FRA	280
John	WST	350	RAMBO, Aaorn	MNT	83	James	BUT	342
Robert	PHA	28	Abraham	MNT	74	James	MER	457
Saml.	FAY	247	Abram	MNT	106	John	ADA	2
William	CUM	88	Amos	CHE	835	John	WAS	13
William	WST	350	Andrew	SOM	135	John	BEV	25
RAINY, John	YOR	200	Danl.	PHI	76	John	CUM	34
RAIRDIN, Henry	ALL	117	Deborah	PHI	151	John	WAS	53
RAISER, Michael	LAN	43	Eli	MNT	74	John (Crossed		
RAISNER, John	BUC	139A	Ezekiel	CHE	719	Out)	BUC	153A
RAIZOR, Samuel	DAU	47	George	SOM	135	John	WAS	105
RAKE, Adam	ADA	27	Gunner	MNT	74	John	HNT	140
Christian	ADA	27	Jacob Capt.	PHI	77	John	BUC	162
John	ADA	27	John	PHI	71	John	WST	175
RAKESTRAW, Joseph	NOH	76A	John Junr.	MNT	105	John	WST	175
RAKEUP, Daniel	FAY	223	John	MNT	105	John	NOU	184

RAMSEY, John	BUC	99A	RANDELS, John	FAY	259	RANKIN, James	WAS	93
John	BUC	154A	Joseph	ALL	59	James	WAS	105
Lawrence	MNT	105	Joseph	ALL	81	James	HNT	133
Margaret	YOR	201	Robt.	BUT	344	James	FAY	211
Margret	MIF	11	RANDL?, Joseph	PHI	135	James	CHE	873
Mary	PHA	82	RANDLE, Abm.	BUC	143A	Jas.	FRA	290
Mary	BUC	162	Christn.	PHI	80	Jeremiah	FRA	290
Moses	LAN	161	Ebenezar	LYC	11	Jesse	WAS	93
Nancy	FAY	247	George	NOU	112	John	MIF	26
Nathan	CUM	109	George	PHA	118	John	BFD	39
Nathan	YOR	182	George	BUC	143A	John	WAS	86
Oliver	YOR	218	Isaac	BUC	161A	John	WAS	105
Reynolds	ADA	9	Jacob	BUC	89	John	WST	156
Robert	BFD	35	Jacob	BUC	90	John	YOR	214
Robert	BFD	41	Jacob	BUC	161A	John	MER	458
Robert	WAS	53	John	SOM	150	John	CHE	700B
Robert	YOR	201	John Sen.	SOM	150	John	BUC	153A
Robert Jr.	BFD	39	John	BUC	151A	Joseph	GRN	89
Robert Senr.	BFD	39	Jonathan	GRN	77	Mathew	WAS	93
Robt.	YOR	202	Jonathan	BUC	146A	Samuel	WAS	93
Saml.	CUM	74	Jonathan	BUC	161A	Samuel	WAS	105
Saml.	WST	350	Joseph	ERI	60	Samuel	FAY	211
Samuel	BEV	7	Joseph	BUC	88	Thomas	WAS	105
Samuel	GRN	77	Joseph	PHI	142	William	WAS	105
Samuel	LAN	161	Nichs.	PHI	101	William	WST	156
Thomas	YOR	199	Thomas	PHA	96	Wm.	CEN	21
Thomas	BER	252	Widow	CHE	887	RANKIN?, William	WST	156
Widow	LAN	244	RANDLES, Geo.	CEN	21	RANKINS, James	BER	209
William	BEV	25	John	CEN	21	James	FAY	259
William	BFD	39	William	GRN	79	William	FAY	259
William	WAS	94	William	VEN	166	RANN, Adam	NOU	98
William	PHI	149	Wm.	CEN	21	Bernard	NOU	98
William	WST	175	RANDOLPH, David	GRN	89	RANNALLS, James	FRA	326
William	YOR	202	Echabud	CUM	81	RANNELS, Peter	PHI	51
William	FAY	206	Edward	PHA	42	Stephen	MIF	11
William	YOR	218	Edwd. F.	CRA	4	RANNILS, William	NOU	195
William	LAN	246	Eseck F.	CRA	7	RANNY, David	LUZ	356
William	BUC	154A	James F.	CRA	4	RANOHAW, Fredk.	PHI	91
Wm.	CUM	96	Job	CUM	81	RANOLDS, Jos.	YOR	157
Wm.	FRA	317	John	WAS	46	RANSBURY, Henry	NOH	78A
RAMSON, Derrick	PHI	154	Joseph	ADA	6	John	MNT	87
Joseph	LAN	131	Nathaniel	ADA	6	John Esqr.	NOH	78A
Mary	BUC	84A	Paul	CUM	81	RANSOM, George P.	LUZ	340
RAMSTONE, Henry	CHE	907	Robert F.	CRA	3	James	WAS	31
RAMSY, Anthony	ALL	114	Vance	ALL	89	RANTRAN?, Wm.	PHA	61
Hugh	ALL	114	William	WAS	94	RANTZ, Frederick	NOU	148
James	CEN	23A	RANDULPH, Edward	FAY	217	John	NOU	148
James C.	ALL	50	RANE, Barney	LAN	275	Michael	NOU	144
Thomas	ALL	110	Fredk.	PHI	44	RANY, Charles	BEV	11
Wilm.	ALL	116	RANEY, Charles	HNT	159	RANYLAND, Isaac	MIF	11
RAN, John	VEN	166	James	HNT	159	RAP, Peter	DAU	10
RANCAN, Wilm.	ALL	81	John	BEV	21	RAP?, John	PHI	41
RANCK, Felty	LAN	81	Thomas	FAY	247	RAPE, Jacob Junr.	WAS	46
Jacob	LAN	81	RANG, Daniel	DAU	35	Jacob Senr.	WAS	46
John	DAU	49	RANGE, John	ADA	21	Thomas	WAS	46
Lewis	LAN	83	RANIGAR, George	NOU	200	RAPIN, Joseph	PHA	11
Ludwig	LAN	81	RANIWALT?,			RAPINE,		
Michael	LAN	145	Melchoir	MNT	119	Christopher	WST	156
Mickael	LAN	92	RANK, George	DAU	35	Daniel	WST	350
Peter	DAU	49	Phillip	BER	161	Jacob	PHI	140
Philip	LAN	89	RANKIN, Abraham	CHE	700B	John	PHI	140
Samuel	LAN	81	Adam?	FRA	297	Nicholas	PHI	140
RANDAL, Benedict	WAS	105	Alexander	PHA	101	RAPP, Adam	BER	241
Taylor	BER	282	Alexd.	FRA	285	Barnett	CHE	858
RANDALL, David	ERI	58	Ann	FRA	290	Benjn.	CHE	854
Jesse	PHI	149	Archd.	FRA	300	Cornelius	MNT	92
Maxson	ERI	58	Archibald	HNT	150	Fredk.	BER	241
Nicholas	PHI	149	David	WAS	93	George	BUC	153A
RANDALS, James	WST	351	David	FRA	290	Henry	BER	180
William	YOR	213	David	FRA	300	Jacob	PHI	133
RANDEL, George	BUC	89	George	PHA	58	Jacob	BUC	153A
James	NOH	38	Henry	WAS	93	John	MNT	51
Richard	FAY	237	Hugh	MIF	26	Martin	DAU	4
Steven	FAY	237	Hugh	FAY	259	Michael	BUC	153A
RANDELL, Widow	PHI	23	James	CRA	18	Michl.	BER	241
RANDELS, Daniel	WST	382	James	CEN	21	Micl.	BER	242

READING, John	NOU	98
William	MNT	67
READY, Peter	FRA	304
READ, Collinson	BER	241
James	CHE	828
Jane	BUC	103A
John	BFD	47
READER, Abraham	BUC	151A
Conrad	BER	142
Isaac	BUC	103A
Michael	BFD	45
READER?, Benager	BUC	146
REAFNER, Henry	FRA	304
REAFSNYDER, Abm.	BER	203
Michael	BER	215
REAGEL, Michael	NOU	189
REAGEN, Philip	WST	296
Zachar.	WST	295
REAGER, Fredk.	WST	222
Henry	SOM	141
Jacob	WST	222
REAGH, Jos.	MIF	26
REAGLE, George	CUM	33
REAGOR?, Jacob	FRA	302
REAL, Geo.	CUM	100
Saml.	PHI	83
Wm.	FRA	314
REALY?, Robert	BEV	15
REAM, -am--?	LAN	4
Abm.	WST	223
Abraham	LAN	4
Andrew	SOM	144
Christian	SOM	141
Daniel	DAU	16A
David	SOM	144
George	DAU	40
George	BER	218
George	LAN	252
George Jr.	BER	217
Isaac	LAN	4
Jacob	LAN	4
Jacob	DAU	16
Nichs.	WST	223
Samuel	SOM	144
Tobias	SOM	144
William	SOM	144
REAMAN, George	SOM	155
Gudlip?	SOM	154
REAMER, Adam	WST	351
Barnet	YOR	195
Henry	WST	223
Peter	SOM	159
REAMLY, Michael	NOU	155
REAMON, John	SOM	155
Phillip	FRA	297
REAMY, Conrad	CEN	23A
REANA, Danial	FRA	293
REANGALER, John	NOU	131
REANS?, Robert	YOR	209
REANY, William	NOU	184
REAP, Isaac	WST	223
REAPS, Leonard	BUT	337
REARA?, (See		
Reana)	FRA	293
REARICH, Henry	SOM	162
Philip	SOM	162
REARICK, Anthony	NOU	195
Jacob	NOU	203
Peter	NOU	131
William	NOU	131
REARINGBAUGH,		
Michael	NOU	195
REARMER, Mathew	PHI	83A
REAS, Christ.	DAU	38A
David	DAU	47A
REASE, Nicks.	PHI	68
REASNER, John	NOU	195
John	NOU	195
REASON, Abraham	BUC	148
George	MNT	65
REASOR, Christly	FRA	315
Daniel	FRA	274
Daniel	DAU	25A
Peter	FRA	290
Wm.	CHE	834
REASOR?, Jacob	FRA	302
REATH, Archibald	DEL	158
REAUGH, John	LAN	169
John	FAY	237
Samuel	LAN	149
Thomas	FAY	237
REAVER, Frederick	BFD	52
Jacob	DEL	170
REAZER, John	DAU	42A
REBEL, George	PHI	46
REBER / REBES?,		
George	BER	207
REBER, Abraham	BER	204
Conrad	BER	154
George	BER	264
George	BER	279
Jacob	BER	264
John	BER	204
John	BER	221
John	BER	266
John	BER	279
John Jr.	BER	204
John	NOH	43A
Philip	BER	279
Thomas	BER	145
Valentine	BER	145
Widow	NOH	43A
REBERGE, Conrad	PHA	27
REBERT, Daniel	NOH	46
Philip	NOH	46
William	NOH	46
REBOLTZ, Michael	YOR	199
REBUCK, Adam	NOU	124
Michael	NOU	124
Nicholas	NOU	124
Valentine	NOU	124
REBURN, James	ARM	124
RECDER, William	BER	168
RECHABACK, Henry	MNT	105
RECHART, Christn.	DAU	40A
RECHSTINE, Jacob	BER	214
RECHTER, John	SOM	150
RECK, Christian	ADA	10
RECKART, Henry	DAU	40A
Jacob	DAU	46
RECKER, Elias	PHI	126
John	NOH	50A
Mortam	NOU	101
REDD, Andrew	WAS	112
Nathaniel	WAS	46
REDDING,		
Christopher	WAS	46
Thos.	CUM	26
REDDY, Richard	NOH	39
REDEBAUGH, Michl.	DAU	18A
Peter	DAU	18A
REDENOUR, Ludw.	WST	223
REDER, Benjamin	NOU	101
George	BER	236
REDERNOUR, Melker	WST	222
REDETT, Jno.	CUM	146
REDFORD, Willm.	DAU	36
REDHAIR?, Martin	PHA	54
REDHEIFER?,		
Margt.	MNT	66
REDHEIFFER,		
Andrew	MNT	83
REDHEIFFER,		
Charles	MNT	131
REDICK, Bridget	WAS	40
David Esqr.	WAS	117
Hamilton	BUT	354
John	BEV	24
John	BUT	354
Rachel	WAS	117
William	WAS	59
Willm.	BUT	335
REDINGER, Conard	PHI	131
REDLE, George	DAU	7A
REDLINE, John	NOH	50A
REDLION, Margaret	BUC	97
Michael	BUC	105A
William	PHI	122
REDLUIFER?,		
Margt.	MNT	66
REDMAN, Adam	BER	215
Henry	ALL	93
John	PHI	56
John M.d.	PHA	21
Martha	PHA	10
Rebeca	PHA	39
Thomas	BUC	94A
REDMOND, Phillip	PHA	17A
REDNAUR, Abraham	BER	165
REDNER, John	PHI	119
REDOCK, Wilm.	ALL	110
REDROCK, John	BUC	101A
REDSACKER, George	LAN	16
Nichs.	CUM	59
REDY, Jacob	NOU	131
Jacob	NOU	139
Saml.	FRA	293
REEB, Widow	YOR	168
David	YOR	187
REECE, George	FAY	250
Jonathn.	FAY	223
Timothy	VEN	167
William	GRN	65
REED, Mrs.	LYC	24
Abijah	BUC	94A
Adam	NOU	177
Adam	ERI	57A
Alexander	WAS	14
Alexander	WAS	35
Alexander	WAS	117
Alexn.	DAU	17
Allexander	BEV	16
Allexander	BEV	25
Ana	LAN	70
Andr.	FRA	278
Andr.	FRA	294
Andrew	ALL	55
Andrew	ALL	111
Andrew	ALL	111
Andrew	FAY	259
Andrew	LAN	300
Andrew	CHE	714
Andrew	BUC	153A
Ann	ALL	56
Archibald C.	ALL	60
Benjamin	NOU	177
Casper?	NOU	106
Catherine	BER	273
Charles	PHA	14
Charles	FRA	310
Charles	CHE	722
Charles	CHE	819
Charles J./ I.?	ERI	56
Chr.	WST	314
Christian	NOU	177
Christopher	NOU	101
Christopher	BER	155
Daniel	WAS	17

325

REED, Daniel	ALL 88	REED, John	HNT 116	REED, Thomas	DEL 184	
Daniel	BER 267	John	HNT 120	Thomas	FAY 268	
David	PHI 6	John	NOU 124	Thomas	BER 282	
David	WAS 17	John	SOM 144	Thomas	LUZ 324	
David	BEV 27	John	LAN 153	Thomas	MER 458	
David	ALL 104	John	BER 190	Thomas Jr.	BER 284	
David	WST 314	John	DEL 190	Thos.	LYC 19	
David	WST 382	John	YOR 198	Thos.	YOR 212	
Davis	DEL 177	John	BER 204	Timothy	FAY 223	
Francis	DEL 192	John	FAY 206	Widow	LAN 42	
Francis	LAN 303	John	FAY 211	William	MIF 14	
Frederick	GRN 67	John	FAY 211	William	WAS 14	
Frederick	NOU 184	John	FAY 259	William	CRA 17	
Fredr.	FRA 314	John	BER 285	William	LYC 25	
Gasper	FRA 314	John	BUT 330	William	PHA 112	
George	FAY 259	John	WST 351	William	NOU 119	
George	FRA 314	John	WST 372	William	ARM 122	
Henry	LYC 12	John	CHE 730	William	SOM 130	
Henry	WST 242	John Esq.	SOM 159	William	HNT 135	
Hugh	DEL 190	Jos. Esqr.	YOR 199	William	LAN 153	
Hugh	FAY 233	Joseph	WAS 31	William	LAN 159	
Hugh	MER 457	Joseph	WST 156	William	LAN 160	
Hugh	MIF 15A	Joseph	FAY 233	William	FAY 199	
Isabella	CHE 731	Joseph	WST 257	William	YOR 202	
Jacob	WAS 50	Joseph	WST 350	William	FAY 211	
Jacob	BFD 66	Joseph	MIF 15A	William	MER 457	
Jacob	NOU 106	Joshua	BER 280	William	MER 458	
Jacob	YOR 185	Kity?	NOU 106	William	MER 458	
Jacob	MER 457	Leonard	BER 267	William	CHE 819	
James	WAS 17	Levy	BFD 45	William	MIF 15A	
James	WAS 31	Lewis	PHA 108	Wilm.	ALL 85	
James	ALL 70	Margaret	WAS 17	Wm.	LYC 18	
James	ALL 94	Mark	HNT 122	Wm.	BEV 21	
James (W. E.)	MIF 15A	Mary	ALL 111	Wm.	MIF 26	
James	WAS 105	Mary	WST 175	Wm.	FRA 285	
James	WAS 113	Mathew	WAS 17	Wm.	CHE 797	
James	WAS 117	Michael	ARM 123	Yates &	PHI 137	
James	NOU 160	Michael	NOU 177	REED?, Thomas	ALL 102	
James	LAN 162	Monga	NOU 168	Thomas	ARM 127	
James	HNT 164	Nicholas	WAS 31	Thomas	DEL 192	
James	NOU 202	Paul	GRN 84	REEDER, Absolom	NOH 38	
James	FAY 211	Paul	ALL 96	Benjamin	LUZ 347	
James	FAY 223	Peter	LAN 38	Charles	BUC 152	
James	FAY 259	Peter	NOU 124	Chas.	LYC 22	
James	FRA 282	Peter	BER 190	David	BUC 151A	
James	FRA 289	Peter	FRA 314	Henry	NOU 101	
James	FRA 294	Peter	WST 315	Jacob	LUZ 345	
James	FRA 315	Philip	BER 283	Job	ERI 59A	
James	CHE 739	Robert	LAN 152	John	NOU 124	
James	CHE 808	Robert	WST 175	Jonathan	BUC 107A	
James Capt.	ADA 3	Robert	NOU 203	Joseph	LUZ 346	
James Jr.	MIF 15A	Robert	FAY 206	Martin	NOU 101	
James Senr.	MIF 15A	Robert	BER 276	Samuel	CHE 710	
James	DAU 8A	Robt.	BUT 365	REEDER?, Peter	NOU 168	
Jeremiah	SOM 144	Ruel	BEV 15	REEDES?, (See		
Jeremiah	BER 223	Rufus, S.	ERI 55A	Reeder)	CHE 710	
Jiles	FAY 262	Saml.	PHA 84	REEDLE, Catharine	PHA 68	
Jno.	LYC 19	Saml.	FRA 294	REEDY, Henry	BER 168	
John	MIF 4	Saml.	FRA 314	Michl.	BER 204	
John	BEV 13	Samuel	LYC 3	Michl.	BER 204	
John	WAS 17	Samuel	WAS 24	William	BFD 65	
John	LYC 22	Samuel	DAU 28	REEFE, Jacob	BUC 106A	
John	BEV 25	Samuel	WAS 76	REEGART, Henry	SOM 155	
John	MIF 26	Samuel	WAS 105	REEGHERT, Jacob	LAN 270	
John	ALL 52	Samuel	WST 163	REEL, Widw.	PHI 82	
John	ALL 57	Samuel	FAY 211	Casper	ALL 117	
John	NOH 63	Samuel	FAY 217	Christianna	PHA 81	
John	ALL 70	Solomon	ALL 57	Jacob	CHE 733	
John	PHA 80	Solomon	NOU 124	John	PHI 88	
John	BUC 83	Solomon	WAS 124	Ludowick	HNT 160	
John	WAS 86	Stephen	WST 314	Peter	YOR 156	
John	ALL 100	Thomas	ADA 1	Wm.	CHE 771	
John	NOU 101	Thomas	WAS 35	REEL?, John	FRA 278	
John	NOU 101	Thomas	WAS 76	REELY?, Henry	PHI 140	
John	NOU 106	Thomas	ALL 115	REEM, Adam	BFD 52	
John	ALL 114	Thomas	WST 163	Jacob	LAN 87	

REEM, John	SOM 150	REESE, Lewis	CHE 881	REIB, Nicholas	YOR 191		
Michael	SOM 141	Michael	PHA 42	REIB?, Elizabeth	LAN 213		
Peter	DAU 31	Peter	LAN 234	REICEL, George	NOU 200		
Peter	DAU 30A	Philip	CHE 751	REICERT, Conrad	NOU 101		
REEME, Christin	DAU 37A	Samuel	MNT 83	George	NOU 101		
George	DAU 37A	Samuel	CHE 784	Jacob	NOU 101		
REEMER, Fredrik	DAU 31A	Sarah	CHE 899	REICH, Abm.	NOH 48A		
John	MNT 96	Stephen	MIF 13	Jacob	NOH 48A		
Ludwick	MNT 96	Volentine	PHA 88	REICHART, Andrew	BUC 148		
REERLY?, Robert	BEV 24	Widow	CHE 833	Jacob Jr.	DAU 47		
REES, Abraham	WAS 125	REESE?, Andw.	YOR 210	Jacob	DAU 42A		
Adam	LAN 92	Jacob	LYC 12	Ludwick	BUC 159A		
Andrew	LAN 224	John	YOR 211	Michael	LAN 2		
Christn.	CEN 23A	REESER, Christn.	DAU 20A	REICHELDERFER,			
Eleaseor	MNT 71	Daniel	BER 218	Henry	BER 131		
Eli	DEL 178	Daniel	BER 279	John Jr.	BER 132		
Elijah	WAS 125	Henry	BER 218	Michael	BER 131		
Emos	YOR 218	Henry	BER 241	REICHELL, Chas.			
George	DAU 16	Henyr	BER 134	G. Revd.	NOH 70		
George	NOH 31	Jacob	BER 145	Chas. G. Revd.,			
Isaac	PHI 154	Jacob	BER 168	Inspector Of			
Isaac	DEL 178	Jacob	BER 218	The School	NOH 70		
Jacob	MNT 68	John	BER 204	REICHELSDERFER,			
James	MNT 61	Peter	DAU 45A	John	BER 131		
Jeremiah	CUM 61	Wm.	BER 143	REICHENBACH, Adam	NOH 57		
Jesse	WAS 124	REESH, Jacob	BEV 19	George	NOH 57		
Jesse	DEL 176	REESINGER,		Michael	NOH 57		
Jesse	DEL 179	Michael	DAU 6	REICHERD, George	NOH 48A		
John	WAS 4	REESOR, Abraham	BER 146	Jacob	NOH 48A		
John	MNT 58	Christn.	DAU 19A	John	NOH 87A		
John	MNT 96	Jacob	DAU 19A	Leonard	NOH 65A		
John	MNT 106	Peter	FRA 281	REICHERT, Daniel	NOH 38		
Mary	HNT 151	REESS, Widow	LAN 315	Frederick	NOH 34A		
Michael	BER 281	REET?, Charles	WAS 17	George	NOH 65A		
Philip	MNT 106	REEVER, John	PHI 11	Henry	NOH 86		
Simon	CUM 146	REEVES, William	MER 457	Michael	NOH 86		
Solomon	CUM 57	REEVS, Mezekia	FAY 268	Michael	NOH 34A		
Thomas	WAS 4	REFFEL, George	NOU 200	REICHNER, John	NOH 63		
Thomas Jr.	ERI 55A	REFORD, George	PHA 11	REICHTER, John	YOR 212		
Thomas Junr.	WAS 124	REGAL, George	MIF 13A	REICKART, Henry	BUC 141A		
Thomas Senr.	WAS 124	REGAN, Widw.	PHI 109	REICKENBACH,			
Thomas	ERI 55A	Daniel	YOR 154	George Sr.	NOH 57		
William	MNT 63	Fanny	YOR 158	REID, Amos	HNT 164		
William	PHI 137	James	CHE 887	Andw.	CUM 58		
William	DEL 176	Weldon	FAY 249	Benjn.	ADA 4		
REESE, Widow	PHI 44	REGANS, Wm.	PHA 73	Casper	BER 267		
Adam	PHA 37	REGAR, Conrad	FAY 259	Charles	HNT 151		
Adam	CHE 741	Michael	FAY 239	David	CUM 50		
Andrew	LAN 235	REGEL, Jacob	NOU 184	Hugh	ADA 10		
Benj.	YOR 207	Mary	LAN 67	Hugh	CUM 89		
Benjamin	MNT 83	REGER, Jacob	PHI 129	James	CUM 22		
Benjamin	CHE 702	Jacob	PHI 131	James	CUM 96		
Christian	CHE 792	Rudolph	PHI 131	John	ADA 3		
Daniel	MNT 83	REGES?, Phillip	FRA 272	John	ADA 18		
David	CHE 798	REGESTER, David	CHE 705	John	CUM 31		
Fredk.	YOR 210	REGIL, George	NOU 139	John	CUM 42		
George	PHI 4	REGISTER, Abm.	PHI 99	John	CUM 59		
George	CHE 736	James	WAS 40	John	CUM 128		
George	CHE 794	John	DEL 173	John	LAN 242		
Henry	PHA 38	Robt.	WST 372	John, Senr.	CUM 58		
Henry	PHA 56	William	WAS 31	Martin	ADA 37		
Henry	BUC 148	William	DEL 172	Minor	ADA 20		
Henry	LAN 234	REGLE, Jacob	NOU 139	Richd.	CUM 24		
Henry	LAN 234	REGNALT, Francis	PHI 30	Richd.	CUM 41		
Henry	CHE 714	REGOY, John	PHI 6	Saml.	CUM 33		
Henry	CHE 714	REHM, David	MIF 13	Saml.	CUM 52		
Henry Jun.	CHE 714	Godfrey	YOR 154	Saml.	CUM 110		
Isaac	PHA 52	William	YOR 192	Thomas	ADA 3		
Isaac	CHE 824	REHR, John	LAN 147A	Thos.	LYC 19		
Jacob	PHA 42	Joseph	BER 208	Thos.	CUM 109		
Jacob	PHA 79	Mathias	BER 208	William	ADA 4		
Jesse	CHE 703	REHRER, Jacob	BER 260	William	CUM 61		
John	GRN 89	John	LAN 203	William	NOU 119		
John	GRN 96	Ludwig	LAN 203	William	NOU 119		
John	BER 241	Nicholas	BER 241	Wm.	CUM 38		
John	CHE 830	REHSER, Jacob	BER 153	Wm.	CUM 56		
Lewis	BER 238						

REIDE, Yost	LAN	97	REIGNBAUGH, Chas.	PHA	110	REINSCHMIT, Henry	NOH	86
REIDEBACH, John	LAN	7	REIGNBOLT,			Saml.	NOH	76A
REIDENAUER, John	NOH	34A	Fredrick	PHA	118	Simon	NOH	61
Widow	NOH	57	REIGNER, John	MNT	58	REIP, Stephen	YOR	168
REIDENBERGH,			REIGNER?, Herman	BER	138	REIPERD, Philip	LAN	79
Jacob	LUZ	427	REIHM, Jacob	BER	204	REIS, David	BER	231
REIDENOUR, Widow	BUC	101A	REILEY, Hugh	LAN	2	John	LAN	86
REIDER, Danl.	CUM	46	John	PHI	49	John	BER	268
Henry	CUM	36	Joseph	PHA	75	Peter	LAN	68
John	CUM	52	Joseph	SOM	144	REISCH, Daniel	NOH	60A
John	BER	210	Richard	SOM	144	REISEL, George	LAN	211
Merrick	BUC	151A	Richard Sen.	SOM	144	REISEL?, Ludewick	NOU	177
Paul	CUM	36	REILLY, Abigail	HNT	125	REISER, Danl.	BER	238
Widow	CUM	52	John	PHI	123	Jacob	PHA	59
Wm.	CUM	52	REILY, John	WAS	9	Melchor	CHE	784
REIDNAYER, Danl.	BER	177	John	BEV	23	William	NOU	101
John	BER	177	Patrick	WST	194	REISH, Christian	BER	221
REIDT, John	BER	152	William	WAS	9	REISNER, Hugh		
John	BER	282	REIMAN, Godfrey	BER	242	(Crossed Out)	NOU	119
John Jr.	BER	263	REIMEL, George	NOH	65A	REISOR, Philip	BER	145
REIDY, Christn.	BER	183	Jacob	NOH	65A	REISS, Andreas	NOH	61
John	BER	204	REIMER, Daniel	NOH	65A	Frederick	NOH	60A
REIFF, (See			Henry	NOH	74	George	NOH	74
Rieff)	MNT	122	Isaac	NOH	67A	Philip	NOH	48A
Abraham	MNT	116	Joseph	MNT	129	Philip	BUC	159A
Conrad	BER	231	Peter	MNT	129	Simon	NOH	48A
Frederick	MNT	108	Widow	NOH	87A	REIST, Abraham	LAN	147
Jacob	MNT	108	REIN, Bernhart	BER	262	Abraham	LAN	147B
John	BER	231	Conrad	BER	262	Abraham	LAN	147B
REIFIN, Jacob	DAU	26	David	BER	241	Barbara	FAY	199
REIFSCHNEIDER,			Isaac	LAN	117	Christian	LAN	147
John	NOH	61	REINARD, David	BER	164	Christian	LAN	147
Philip	NOH	60A	REINBER, Michl.	DAU	33	Christian	FAY	199
REIFSCHNEYDER,			REINBOLD, Ludwig	NOH	81	John	DAU	41
John	NOH	58	REINDOTTER,			John	LAN	147
REIFSNIDER,			Emanl.	PHI	12	John	FAY	199
Andrew	FAY	217	REINER, Jacob	LAN	293	John	FAY	199
REIFSNYDER, Abram	BER	158	REINERD,			John	FAY	250
Henry	BER	209	Christian	NOH	57	Peter	LAN	143
Jacob	MNT	74	George	NOH	36	REIST?, (See		
John	MNT	58	Peter	NOH	57	Reis)	LAN	86
Peter	MNT	62	REINERT, Daniel	NOH	57	REISWARK, Conrad	LUZ	361
Sebastian	MNT	62	Michael	LAN	277	REISWICH, John	NOH	63
Valentine	MNT	62	REINHARD, Bernard	DAU	33	REITENBACH,		
William	BER	246	David	LAN	213	Martin	LAN	71
REIGART, Adam	LAN	41	George	NOH	81	Peter	LAN	180
Adam Jnr.	LAN	34	George	BUC	153A	REITER, Casper	BER	258
Emanuel	LAN	34	REINHART, Adam	NOH	57	Geo. Michael	MNT	135
Henry	LAN	41	Andrus	BER	132	John	MNT	135
John	DAU	23A	Barbara	MNT	116	Joseph	BER	140
REIGEL, Henry Jn.	BUC	139A	Christn.	BER	214	Laurence	BER	138
Henry	BUC	139A	Francis	YOR	212	Michael	MNT	135
REIGENBACH, Jacob	LAN	277	Hartman	NOH	82A	Michael	BER	138
REIGER, Mrs.	LAN	50	Henry	NOH	81	Peter	MNT	135
REIGERT, John	BER	204	Henry	BER	254	Peter	DAU	25A
John Junr.	YOR	172	John	BER	241	REITH, George	NOH	50A
John Snr.	YOR	172	John	FAY	241	REITMYER, Ann	BER	242
John	DAU	28A	Michael	LAN	284	Danl.	BER	241
REIGH, Adam	YOR	160	Philip	BER	221	John	BER	241
REIGHARD, Peter	HNT	122	Simon	LAN	94	Saml.	BER	234
REIGHART, Adam	CUM	60	Widow	NOH	57	REITZ, Andrew	NOU	124
Frederick	LAN	165	REINHEIMER,			Henry	NOU	124
REIGHBAUGH, Jacob	NOU	184	Conrad	NOH	34A	Henry	NOH	91A
John	NOU	184	George	BER	183	Jacob	LAN	46
REIGHER,			Jacob	NOH	87A	Leonard	NOU	124
Frederick	BFD	76	REINHOLD,			Lowrentz	NOH	54
Jacob	BFD	76	Frederick	LAN	203	Michael	NOU	124
Philip	NOH	65A	Henry	LAN	203	REITZEL, Henry	YOR	172
REIGHLY, Miles	LAN	55	John	LAN	203	Jacob (See		
REIGHTER, George	CUM	77	REINHOLDT, Mary	PHA	68	Reitzel,		
Jno.	CUM	110	REINHOLT, William	PHA	103	John)	LAN	203
Phillip	CUM	77	REINICKER, George	ADA	31	John & Jacob	LAN	203
REIGLE, George	BER	189	REININGER, George	LAN	78	Stoffel	LAN	43
Martin	BER	168	Jacob	NOU	124	REITZELL, Conrad	LAN	314
Philip Ad.	BER	272	REINOHL, George	DAU	27	John	YOR	173
REIGLEMAN, Michael	BER	189	REINOLD, Conrad	DAU	32A	REITZENBACH, Jacob	NOH	70

REIVER, Jacob	SOM	139	RENNINGER, Jacob	MNT	100	RESSER, Christian	LAN	139
REKARD, John	DAU	18	Peter	MNT	96	RESSLER, George	BER	149
REKART, Fredk.	DAU	19	RENNISON, John	HNT	158	John	BER	254
REL--?, Abraham	FRA	279	RENNO?, Charles	MER	458	John Jr.	BER	254
RELEY, John	WAS	83	RENNOLDS, Benj.	PHI	71	Peter	NOU	124
Robert	WAS	83	Seamm?	PHI	105A	RESTLER, William	BFD	52
RELF, Saml.	PHA	89	RENNOR, Adam	CHE	857	RETEL, George	LAN	271
RELLER, George	MNT	91	RENNS?, Charles	MER	458	RETGE, Elias	BER	249
RELMER, William	LAN	301	RENO, Elizabeth	BER	145	Henry	BER	249
RELSHOVER, Melsha	ALL	98	Ezacharia	ALL	93	John	BER	168
RELY, Adam	DAU	41	Francis	BEV	6	RETHER, Elias	FRA	281
REMAINS, John	BEV	12	Robert	ALL	92	RETHERFORD, James	ALL	96
REMAND, Anty.	PHI	1	Wilm.	ALL	93	John	ALL	104
REMBEY?, John	MNT	74	RENOLDS, Benjn.	PHA	38	RETS, John	LAN	248
REMBY, Tobias	CHE	788	RENSHAW, Widw.	PHI	119	RETTINGER, Andrew	BER	253
Willm.	PHI	30	Ann	PHA	123	Frederick	BER	164
REMEL, George	NOU	195	James	PHI	119	Henry	BER	245
REMELA, Geo.	WST	222	Thos.	PHI	120	RETTLE, Tobias	FRA	291
REMELICK, Geo.	WST	223	William	PHA	111	RETTLE?, James	ALL	50
REMELY, Ambrosius	NOH	46	RENSIMER, Jacob	BUC	148	RETZEL, Peter	LAN	10
Frederick	LAN	40	RENSOR, Michael	NOU	112	RETZER, Henry	PHI	137
George	NOH	46	RENTEER, Clement	CHE	909	REUBON?, William	NOU	181
George	NOH	91A	RENTZEL, Henry	YOR	180	REUCH?, (See		
Jacob	NOH	46	Jacob	YOR	178	Rench)	HNT	121
John	NOH	63	RENTZHEIMER,			REUSSEAU, Peter	PHA	96
John	WST	194	Chas.?	NOH	48A	REUTER, John	BER	231
Michael	NOH	46	Henry	NOH	82A	Michael	BER	267
William	NOH	84	REOMER, Frederick	FRA	273	REUTHNAUR, Jacob	BER	165
REMENTER, Peter	PHA	65	REPLIT, Abraham	BFD	65	REV?, John	YOR	219
REMER, Widow	PHI	83A	REPLY, Henry	NOU	106	REVE, James	PHA	67
Jacob	BER	227	Henry	NOU	106	REVEA, Monsieur	PHA	57
Peter	YOR	172	REPMAN, George	YOR	161	REVELLE, Peter	DEL	187
Phillip	CUM	22	REPP, Conrad	BER	279	REVER, Abraham	YOR	193
REMER?, Willm.	PHI	75	REPPERD,			Jacob	PHI	128
REMICK, Abnar	FAY	247	Frederick	BUC	105A	John	YOR	182
REMINGTON,			John	BUC	106A	Leonard	YOR	187
Clement	PHI	129	Peter	BUC	105A	REVOTT, Wm.	PHI	114
REMLY, Eronimus	FAY	216	Peter	BUC	139A	REW, Andr.	FRA	300
George	GRN	66	REPPERT, Daniel	BER	249	REWEN, John	DAU	44A
REMP, Anna Maria	BER	168	Jacob	BER	177	REWLA, Job	PHI	85
Jacob	BER	168	Jacob	BER	245	REX, Abraham	NOH	46
Philip	BER	168	John	BER	177	Christopher	NOH	46
William	BER	251	John	BER	231	Christopher	MNT	92
REMSNYDER?,			Stephen	BER	177	Daniel	ADA	15
Frederick	BER	168	REPPLE, John	SOM	130	Daniel	ADA	17
REMSTY?, Annanias	BUC	154A	REPPLEIR, Geo.	BER	238	Enock John &	PHI	124
REMTON, John P.	PHI	38	REPSEHER, John	NOH	74	Geo. A.	NOH	91A
RENARD, Martin	PHI	39	REPSHER, Adam	NOH	74	George	ADA	16
RENCH, David	HNT	122	REPSHNIDER, Mary	PHA	66	George	NOH	46
John	HNT	122	REPSHY, Gerhart	BER	132	George	PHI	140
Joseph	HNT	122	RERAH, Andw.	WST	223	George Junr.	NOH	46
Joseph	HNT	122	REREIGH, Andw.	WST	222	Jacob	ADA	18
Peter	HNT	122	RERICH, Conrad	NOH	76A	Jesse	MNT	78
RENCHLER, George	BER	145	RERICK, John	NOU	115	John	PHI	124
RENERD, Adam	NOH	36	RERVER, Michael	LAN	173	John & Enock	PHI	124
RENEWALT?,			RESER, Christian	DAU	31	Levi	PHI	123
Melchoir	MNT	119	George	PHI	20	Samuel	DAU	30
RENFREW, John	FRA	281	RESH, Andrew	BER	280	Widow	ADA	15
RENHIMER,			Henry	LAN	279	William	NOH	46
Christn.	PHI	84A	Henry Jun.	LAN	279	William	PHI	140
RENICK, Adam	NOU	200	Jacob	NOH	52	William	NOH	76A
RENICKER, Jno.	CUM	62	John	LAN	277	REXROTH, Adam	BER	200
RENIGE, Martin	CUM	56	RESIDE, James	CEN	23A	REXWORTHY, George	GRN	96
RENN, Henry	CHE	723	RESK, Jacob	BER	189	REY, Catherine	BER	245
RENNALDS, William	LAN	228	RESLER, George	LAN	73	Matthew	LAN	266A
RENNENGER, John	MNT	60	Henry	LAN	73	REYBOLD, Henry	YOR	190
RENNER, Henry	BUC	102A	Jacob	LAN	72	Matthias	YOR	190
Jacob	GRN	72	Jacob	LAN	234	REYBURN,		
Jacob	NOH	72	John	LAN	72	Alexander	LAN	154
Jacob	BUC	101A	Peter	LAN	67	REYDENBACH, Peter	LAN	184
John	GRN	72	Philip	LAN	86	REYER, Benjamin	LAN	184
Peter	BUC	102	Thomas	LAN	143	Charles	LAN	70
Peter	NOH	50A	RESLY, Rudolph	DAU	29A	Christopher	LAN	62
RENNICK, Erick	PHI	15	RESOR, Abraham	FRA	314	Henry	BER	253
RENNINGER, Conrod	CUM	67	RESSEL, Frederick	LAN	135	Jacob	DAU	45A
George	MNT	135	RESSELL, Philip	LAN	202	John	LAN	202

REYER, John	NOH	50A	REYNOLDS, Wm.			RHOADS, Joseph	DEL	178
Joseph	LAN	184	Senr.	WAS	30	Joseph	NOH	76A
REYES?, Phillip	FRA	272	Wm.	MIF	15A	Nicholas	PHI	137
REYLAND, James	BFD	65	REYNOLDS?, Ross?	WST	295	Owen	DEL	189
John	BFD	65	REYNOLS, Samuel	PHA	4	Philip	BFD	65
REYLEDAY, Moses	PHA	110	REYSINER, Peter	LAN	185	Philip	MNT	103
REYLEY, Fantley	PHA	110	REYWALT, John	DAU	32A	Rachael	DEL	178
John	PHA	14	REYWOLT, John	NOU	101	RHODE,		
John	PHA	123	John	NOU	101	Christopher	NOU	124
Joseph	PHA	38	RHAM, Jacob	CUM	150	Christopher	NOU	124
Thos.	PHA	123	RHANDOLPH, Thomas	YOR	156	Daniel	NOU	139
REYLSEY?/			RHATS?, Jacob	CUM	146	Francis	NOU	139
REYLEEY?,			RHEA, Arthur	BFD	76	Francis	NOU	139
Patrick	SOM	159	James	BFD	66	Fredk.	MIF	13
REYMAN, George	NOH	78A	John	PHA	86	Harman	ADA	34
Henry Esqr.	YOR	192	Mary	PHA	21	Henry	NOU	139
Jacob	YOR	172	Thomas	CRA	10	Jacob	NOU	189
Mary	YOR	200	Thomas	BFD	76	Jacob	NOU	195
REYMEAL, George	DAU	32	RHEAM, Abm.	CUM	122	John	NOU	124
REYMER, Jacob	NOH	78A	Henry	CUM	99	John	YOR	163
REYNAL, Henry	DAU	41	Nichls.	CUM	45	John	NOU	189
REYNALDS, Widow	PHI	16	Saml.	CUM	29	Michael	NOU	124
REYNAN, Thomas	PHA	123	RHEED, Jacob	SOM	159	Michael	NOU	124
REYNARD, Abraham	MNT	83	RHEES, David	SOM	162	Michl.	DAU	14
Chr.	WST	277	J. Morgan Esq.	SOM	132	Peter	NOU	139
Daniel	HNT	128	Rhees	SOM	162	Peter	NOU	195
Henry	MNT	83	Theophilus	SOM	162	William	NOU	124
Jno.	CUM	40	William	SOM	163	RHODEARIMUL,		
John	MNT	85	RHEILEY, John	PHA	86	Daniel	NOU	124
Samuel	HNT	161	Wm.	PHA	86	RHODES, Adam	PHI	60
REYNEL, Samuel	LAN	166	RHEIM, Daniel	LAN	210	Jacob	WST	295
REYNEY, Williams	MER	458	Frederick	LAN	211	James	FAY	249
REYNOLD,			George	LAN	211	John	FAY	239
Christian	YOR	191	RHEMES, John	CHE	780	Joseph	BEV	20
Jacob	YOR	191	RHERER, John	DAU	33A	Mathew	PHI	58
John	BER	238	RHIMER, John	BFD	35	Rachel	PHA	58
Samuel	LAN	155	RHINE, Adam	PHA	52	Robert	PHI	27
REYNOLDS, Andrew	PHA	113	Henry	CUM	118	William	GRN	65
Benjn.	CHE	735	Isaac	BUC	103A	William	CHE	783
David	MIF	11	John	CUM	89	RHORMAN, Widw.	PHI	103A
David	WAS	30	Michael	BFD	59	David	PHI	101A
David	LUZ	342	Stephen	CUM	128	Henry	PHI	78
Dennis	MIF	8A	RHINEHART, Fredk.	CUM	89	RHYAN, Ambrous	ALL	62
Elias	PHI	26	John	ADA	19	Jacob	ALL	58
Emanuel	LAN	155	Michael	PHA	66	James	ALL	62
Francis	BFD	52	RHINEHURT, George	PHA	76	Wilm.	ALL	120
George	LUZ	382	RHINESMITH, Jno.	CUM	47	RHYHAMAN, Stophan	ALL	116
Henry	PHA	40	RHINHART, Fredk.	CUM	33	RHYLY, George	ALL	78
Henry	LAN	154	Henry	BFD	65	George	ALL	90
Henry	YOR	189	Isaac	BFD	65	James	ALL	52
Henry Junr.	LAN	155	Jacob	CUM	33	John	ALL	78
Hugh	YOR	216	John	BFD	65	RHYNAMAN, Wilm.	ALL	115
Jacob	LAN	155	RHOADES, Alexr.	CHE	744	RI-HART?, Leonard	LAN	4
James	WAS	40	Barney	PHA	109	RIAL, John	PHI	137
Jno.	MIF	13	Gabriel	SOM	159	RIAL?, John	PHI	85A
John	BFD	76	Peter Esqr.	NOH	69	RIAN, George	PHI	21
John	FRA	308	Samuel	PHA	101	RIANS?, Robert	YOR	209
John	MIF	8A	Sarah	PHA	103	RIATH, William	CHE	708
Joseph	LUZ	343	RHOADS, Abraham	MNT	70	RIB, Casper	LAN	146
Joshua	LAN	155	Calip	CRA	15	RIBER?, Francis	LAN	19
Joshua	WST	277	Casper	MNT	74	RIBLE, Henry	FRA	292
Moses	CHE	747	Christian	BFD	66	Enry	LAN	125
Phebe	DEL	165	Daniel	BFD	65	RIBLET, Chuster	NOU	97A
Phinehas	LUZ	396	Ezekiel	MNT	70	RICARD, Charles	FRA	314
Reubin	LAN	154	Fredk.	CUM	125	Fredrick	LYC	19
Robert	LUZ	382	George	BFD	65	George	FRA	314
Solomon	LUZ	382	George	BFD	69	John	DEL	156
Thomas	CHE	874	George	NOH	69	RICART, John	FRA	316
Thos	PHA	90	George	SOM	135	RICE, Widow	PHI	22
William	ADA	22	Hannah	MNT	103	Widow	PHI	67
William	WAS	31	Henry	BFD	69	Adam	CUM	39
William	WAS	105	Jacob	CUM	122	Barbara	FRA	299
William	WST	295	John	MNT	63	Benjamin	DAU	24
Wm.	FRA	317	John	NOU	106	Brazilla	ERI	55A
Wm. Esqr.	FRA	276	John	CUM	121	Catharine	PHI	88
Wm. Junr.	WAS	30	John	LUZ	357	Christian	SOM	130

331

RIEB, Adam	NOH	69	
Andrew	NOH	69	
RIEBGE, Christian	BER	245	
RIEBLE, Henry	DAU	29A	
RIECE, Sarah	FAY	249	
RIED, Adam	BER	264	
Benjamin Jr.	BER	264	
Casper Jr.	BER	264	
Frederick	BER	264	
Jacob	BER	264	
Jacob	BER	264	
Jacob	BER	264	
John	BER	264	
John	BER	264	
Peter	BER	268	
Valentine	BER	268	
RIEDIE, Jacob	NOH	74	
RIEDT, John	BER	263	
Leonard	BER	260	
RIEDY, Abm. &			
Mother	NOH	46	
Peter	NOH	50A	
RIEFF, Benjamin	MNT	122	
Daniel	MNT	122	
Geo. 2nd	MNT	129	
George	MNT	122	
George	MNT	129	
Jacob	MNT	122	
Jacob	MNT	129	
John	MNT	122	
RIEFSNYDER,			
Conrad	MNT	100	
Harman	MNT	100	
Jacob	MNT	100	
Jno. (Farmer)	MNT	100	
John	MNT	100	
John Junr.	MNT	100	
William	MNT	100	
RIEGEL, Daniel	NOH	65A	
Jacob	NOH	48A	
John	NOH	48A	
John	NOH	48A	
John	NOH	67A	
Mathias	NOH	48A	
RIEGER, John	NOH	38	
Widow	NOH	38	
RIEGLE, Daniel	BER	279	
Jacob	BER	272	
John	BER	268	
John	BER	268	
Mathias	BER	264	
Philip Ad. /			
Od.?	BER	268	
Simon	BER	268	
RIEHL, Gotfriedt	BER	268	
RIEHL?, Christena	BER	143	
RIEHM, Andrew	LAN	203	
Edward	BER	168	
Frederick	LAN	202	
Henry	LAN	203	
John	LAN	203	
Samuel	LAN	203	
Tobias	LAN	203	
RIEL, Benjamin	NOH	74	
Frederick	NOH	74	
John	NOH	87A	
RIELY, James	FRA	311	
RIESBURY,			
Gustavus	PHA	25	
RIESER, Caspar	NOH	57	
Conrad	NOH	67A	
David & Son	NOH	81	
Jacob	NOH	34A	
Jacob	NOH	67A	
John	NOH	57	
Peter	NOH	72	
RIESER, Peter	NOH	67A	
Philip	NOH	67A	
RIESS, Jacob	NOH	63	
John	NOH	38	
RIEST, John	DAU	30A	
RIESURE, David	FRA	299	
RIEUL?, Matthew	NOU	177	
RIEVES, John	FAY	259	
Richard	FAY	228	
RIEVS, Benjiman	FAY	253	
RIEZEL, James	FAY	211	
RIFE, Abraham	LAN	62	
David	ADA	13	
Jacob	DAU	20A	
Joseph	LAN	86	
Joseph	DAU	21A	
Philip	PHI	115	
Samuel	LAN	84	
Widow	LAN	86	
RIFF, Christ.	FRA	312	
Jacob	FRA	315	
RIFFEL, George	FAY	217	
Melchor	ADA	25	
Nicholas	FAY	217	
RIFFERT, Henry	MNT	133	
Philip	MNT	108	
RIFFET, Jacob	PHI	138	
RIFFETTS, Rebecca	PHA	19	
RIFFEY, Henry	ADA	17	
RIFFLE, Barney	WST	315	
Joseph	ADA	25	
Mathias	ADA	29	
RIFFLESBERGER,			
Peter	ADA	38	
RIFFNOCK,			
Christn.	PHI	118A	
RIFFORD, Peter	PHI	120A	
RIFFORT, Brity	PHI	83A	
RIFLE?, Amos	LYC	11	
RIG, Eli	DAU	13	
RIGARD, Saml.	MIF	17A	
RIGART, Henry	PHI	111	
RIGBY, Cathrin	PHA	46	
Daniel	WAS	82	
Francis	PHI	22	
Henry	PHI	13	
James	DEL	155	
James	DEL	178	
John	PHI	18	
Joseph	PHA	46	
RIGDEN, Thomas	PHA	99	
RIGDIN, Thomas	ALL	94	
Wilm.	ALL	94	
RIGDON, James	WAS	40	
William	WAS	39	
RIGEL, Adam	LAN	203	
George	LAN	186	
RIGELEY, Henry	SOM	147	
RIGER, Henry	CUM	66	
Michael	SOM	162	
RIGERT, Elias	MIF	18	
RIGG, Abijah	WAS	82	
Clem	CHE	827	
Clement	WAS	82	
Clement Junr.	WAS	82	
Eleazer	WAS	82	
Ezekiel	CHE	818	
George	LAN	89	
Jeremiah	WAS	82	
William	WAS	82	
RIGGEL, Michael	LAN	310	
RIGGLE, Abraham	WAS	5	
Adam	BFD	45	
George	WAS	82	
Jacob	WAS	40	
John	WAS	124	
RIGGLE, Michael	WAS	82	
RIGGLEMAN,			
Valentine	SOM	139	
RIGGS, Edward	WAS	76	
Jonathan	WST	350	
Joseph	WAS	4	
Silas	WAS	105	
RIGHART,			
Christopher	ARM	126	
RIGHELDERFER,			
Adam	NOU	189	
RIGHT, Alexander	MER	458	
David	FAY	223	
David	FAY	249	
Fanny	FAY	223	
George	PHI	99A	
James	FAY	217	
John	CHE	784	
Lewis	PHI	86	
Lewis	FAY	247	
Marey	FAY	250	
Matthew	HNT	160	
Thomas	CHE	869	
William	CRA	17	
William	CHE	846	
Zacariah	ERI	57	
RIGHTAL, David	CEN	19	
RIGHTER, Anthony	MNT	139	
Anthony	PHI	140	
Bartley	MNT	140	
Daniel	PHI	142	
George	PHI	129	
George	PHI	141	
Jacob	CHE	700B	
John	MNT	36	
John	MNT	139	
John	PHI	142	
John	NOU	184	
John	CHE	824	
Michael	PHI	128	
Michael	PHI	142	
Micheal	CHE	813	
Mrs.	NOU	184	
Peter	PHI	140	
RIGLAR, Stephen	FRA	273	
RIGLE, Peter	MIF	11	
RIGLER, Widw.	PHI	121	
Andrew	PHA	56	
George	LAN	251	
Henry	PHA	62	
Jacob	PHI	107A	
Stephen	PHI	97	
RIGLEY, John	BFD	58	
RIGS, Stephen	MER	457	
RIHM, Nicholas	BER	261	
RIKERT, Jacob	DAU	36A	
RILAND, Andrew	MNT	93	
RILBURNS, John	NOH	36	
RILE, George	PHI	133	
Jacob	PHI	99	
Richd.	PHI	86	
RILEY, Barnabas	ADA	5	
Bernard	CEN	24	
Christopher	BFD	35	
Cornelius	WST	242	
Daniel	BUC	103A	
Esther	DEL	175	
James	CUM	141	
John	DAU	17	
John	PHA	64	
John	MER	457	
John	BUC	105A	
Joseph	MER	457	
Joshua	BUC	105A	
Martin	BFD	35	
Mattw.	MIF	15A	

RITCHEY, Robert		RITTER, Casper	NOH 43A	ROAD, Henry	LAN 220
Esqr.	ALL 85	Casper	NOH 91A	John	FRA 314
Robt. Esqr.	FAY 223	Charles	PHA 11	Michl.	FRA 280
Saml.	CHE 757	Daniel	NOH 34A	Robert	BFD 39
William	LAN 164	Enoch	DAU 32A	Samuel	VEN 165
Wilm.	ALL 69	Ferdinant	BER 131	William	PHI 30
Wilm.	ALL 73	Ferdinant Jr.	BER 131	ROADACRE, George	LAN 106
RITCHIE, Andrew	WAS 31	Frederick	NOH 43A	Jacob	NOU 131
Craig Esqr.	WAS 24	Geo	DAU 31A	ROADARM, Leonard	NOU 106
John	WAS 82	George	LAN 78	ROADDECKER,
John	WAS 117	George	BER 180	Fredr.	FRA 318
John	WST 295	George	BER 245	ROADE, George	FRA 284
John	WST 328	Henry	NOH 72	ROADENBURGH,
John	WST 372	Henry Junr.	NOH 72	Peter	NOU 150
Mary	WAS 17	Henry	DAU 6A	ROADES, John	SOM 155
Saml.	WST 295	Jacob	BER 131	ROADS, Anthony	FAY 247
Samuel	GRN 72	Jacob	BUC 148	Anthy. Jun.	FAY 247
Wm.	WST 372	Jacob	YOR 213	Benjn	FAY 247
RITCHMAN, Isaac	ALL 97	Jacob Jnr.	BUC 148	Calib	MER 458
RITCHY, Hamilton	FRA 297	Jacob	NOH 91A	Casper	PHI 144
Humphy.	PHI 147	John	ADA 7	Daniel	BER 138
James	FRA 290	John	NOH 54	Daniel Jr.	BER 138
RITELY?, Jas.	LYC 9	John	BFD 76	Ebinazer	FAY 247
RITEMYER, Adam	BER 241	John	BUC 148	George	PHI 93
Geo.	BER 241	John Jr.	BFD 76	Henry	MIF 26
Henry	BER 241	John	NOH 91A	Henry	LAN 127
Peter	BER 241	Joseph	CHE 909	Henry	BUC 148
RITENHOUSE, Henry	PHI 92A	Margaret	BER 236	Henry	BER 183
Jacob	NOU 115	Martin	NOH 31	Israel	FAY 247
John	PHI 84A	Martin	NOH 82A	Jacob	BER 138
William	NOU 115	Mathias	BER 165	Jacob	PHI 149
RITER, George	PHA 57	Michael	YOR 160	Jacob Junr.	BER 138
Henry	DAU 37A	Philip	BUC 148	John	ALL 89
John	NOU 189	Simon	LAN 6	John	PHI 106
John	NOU 189	RITTINGER,		John	BER 138
Phillip	NOU 131	Frederick	BER 157	John	BER 183
Simon	NOU 139	Michael	YOR 162	John	FAY 247
RITERSON, Widow	PHI 84A	RITTLEMAN, Jacob	CHE 879	Mathias	BER 138
John	PHI 84A	John	MNT 55	Samuel	BER 138
RITES, Fredk.	YOR 187	RITTLEWILL, John	YOR 208	Samuel	SOM 155
RITHOVER?, Andrew	HNT 132	RITTS, Israel	NOU 177	Sawney	CHE 705
RITKEY, Adam	HNT 119	RITVERT?, (See		Thomas	PHI 61
RITMIRE, Lewes	CUM 124	Rilvert)	LAN 181	Willm.	PHI 61A
RITNER, Peter	BER 236	RITYERD, George	LAN 153	ROADWATT, Fredk.	CHE 790
RITS, Michl.	MIF 17A	RITZ, Anthony	YOR 160	ROAK, Jeorge	LUZ 359
Simon	LAN 248	Elias	BER 214	ROAN, Jacob	DEL 192
RITSELL, George	ADA 35	Jacob	YOR 181	John	SOM 130
RITTENGER,		Jacob	YOR 181	Michl.	CEN 21
Stephen	YOR 162	John	BER 214	ROANE, George	FRA 318
RITTENHOUSE,		Matthias	YOR 171	John	FRA 318
Abraham		RITZE, Balzer H.	BER 240	ROANEY, John	BUC 103A
Abraham	PHI 125	RITZELL, John	CUM 112	ROAR, Christian	BUC 105A
Benjn.	PHI 142	RITZMAN, Andrew	DAU 6A	Jacob	BUC 105A
Christr.	MNT 112	John	BER 264	Michael	BUC 82
Danl.	MNT 70	Peter	DAU 6A	Valentine	BUC 82
Garret	PHI 143	RIVEL, James	PHI 14	ROARACH, John Jr.	BER 178
Garrett	PHI 124	RIVELEY, George	PHI 60	ROARBACH, Simon	BER 258
Henry	PHI 123	RIVELY, Fredrick	DEL 168	ROARBAUGH, Philip	LAN 224
Jacob	PHI 126	John	DEL 168	ROATH, Christian	ADA 13
Jacob	PHI 126	RIVEN, John	PHI 48	ROB, Andrew	ALL 88
Joseph	PHI 143	RIVER,		Andrew	ALL 113
Margaret	MNT 113	Christopher	YOR 209	Jacob	BFD 75
Martin	PHI 143	Jacob	YOR 212	John	LYC 8
Maths.	MNT 74	John	YOR 212	John	ALL 92
Michael	MNT 113	RIX, George	MNT 63	Joseph	CHE 755
Nicholas	PHI 126	George	LUZ 371	Moses	ALL 101
Peter	PHI 142	RIXTINE, Henry	CHE 815	Robt. Esqr.	LYC 8
Peter	PHI 123	John	CHE 818	Wilm.	ALL 69
William	PHI 142	RIZER, Martin	PHA 93	ROB?, James	ALL 81
Willm.	WAS 53	ROACH, Isaac	PHI 24	John	NOU 177
Wm.	PHI 142	Isaac	PHA 54	ROBACK, Arthur	MIF 11
Wm.	MNT 46	Michael	YOR 189	ROBANS, Daniel	NOU 152
RITTENOUR,	MNT 113	Peter	LYC 7	John	NOU 152
Matthias	HNT 156	Robert	NOU 101	Jonathen	NOU 152
RITTER, Abraham	SOM 144	Thomas	GRN 90	Joseph	NOU 160
Casper	NOH 34A	ROAD, Conrad	DAU 35	Joseph	NOU 160

335

ROBANS, Thomas	NOU 152	ROBERTS, Elisha	WAS 24	ROBERTS, John	CHE 740
Vensant	NOU 150	Elizabeth	PHA 20	John	CHE 791
William	NOU 150	Elizabeth	BUC 162	John	CHE 873
ROBB, Alexander	BEV 15	Ellis	DEL 181	John	CHE 907
Danl.	MIF 17A	Enoch	BUC 157A	John Esqr.	MNT 88
David	CUM 45	Enos	MNT 46	John	BUC 94A
Elijah	WST 315	Evan	SOM 162	John	BUC 101A
George	YOR 198	Evan	DEL 180	John	BUC 155A
James	PHA 74	Evan	DEL 184	Jonathan	WAS 24
James	WAS 87	Evan	BUC 157A	Jonathan	PHI 146
James	NOU 131	Evans	CHE 795	Jonathan	MNT 105
James	CUM 138	Everard Jne.	BUC 157A	Jonathan	PHI 108A
John	WAS 31	Evrard	BUC 157A	Jonathan	BUC 154A
John	MNT 39	Ezekial	NOU 144	Joseph	PHI 60
John	WST 295	Francis	PHA 104	Joseph	MNT 70
John	BUT 319	George	PHA 19	Joseph	PHA 71
John Jun.	WAS 87	George	PHA 24	Joseph	PHA 82
John Sen.	WAS 87	George	MNT 46	Joseph	MNT 88
Joseph	WAS 31	George	MNT 70	Joseph	BUC 107
Saml.	BUT 318	George	PHA 114	Joseph	MNT 140
Samuel	WAS 31	George	SOM 162	Joseph	BUC 107A
Samuel	NOU 131	George	FAY 247	Leonard	WAS 125
Samuel	WST 242	George	CHE 787	Levi	HNT 127
William	WAS 31	George	FAY 237	Levi	CHE 705
William	WAS 87	Griffen	MNT 139	Lewis	MNT 36
William	NOU 200	Hannah	HNT 133	Luas	MER 457
William	CHE 875	Henry	LUZ 340	Margaret	CHE 820
Wm.	PHI 101	Hezekiah	LUZ 341	Margaret	BUC 141A
ROBBERSON, Ann	PHI 94	Hezekiah	PHA 79	Martha	PHA 59
ROBBINS, Philip	LUZ 418	Hugh	SOM 162	Martha	PHA 90
ROBBISON, Willm.	PHI 23	Hugh	MNT 36	Mary	PHI 146
ROBE, Christopher	NOU 144	Isaac	PHA 66	Mersa	BUC 94A
ROBE?, James	PHI 81A	Isaac	CHE 835	Michael	PHA 12
ROBENHOLT, John	BER 223	Isaac Junr.	MNT 38	Mordecai	MNT 88
ROBENSTINE,		Isaac	BUC 101A	Mordecai	WAY 140
Nicholas	YOR 186	Israel	DEL 170	Moses	MNT 133
ROBER, John	PHI 86A	Israel	BUC 101A	Moses	LUZ 425
ROBERT, Jos.	PHI 77A	Jacob	MNT 117	Nancy	WAS 105
ROBERTS, Widow	PHI 6	Jacob	LUZ 327	Nathan	WAS 64
A----?	NOU 112	James	PHA 6	Nathan	LUZ 369
Aaron	LUZ 342	James	BUC 89	Nathan Jn.	BUC 157A
Abel	NOU 112	James	PHA 92	Nathan	MNT 105
Abel	BUC 101A	James	FAY 228	Nathan	BUC 157A
Abel	BUC 157A	James	FRA 299	Nathaniel	LUZ 408
Abraham	PHI 154	James	LUZ 381	Owen	PHI 31
Abraham	DEL 181	James	CHE 800	Patr.	FRA 310
Abraham	BUC 101A	James	BUC 143A	Peter	MNT 111
Abram	CHE 816	Jeeremiah	LUZ 373	Peter	BUC 99A
Algernon	MNT 139	Jehu	CHE 883	Phenius	PHI 62
Amos	PHI 147	Jesse	MNT 36	Phincas	PHA 62
Ann	PHA 114	Jesse	MNT 70	Preston	WAS 117
Arnold	MNT 83	Jesse	BUC 87	Richard	GRN 72
Benjamin	LUZ 335	Jesse Esqr.	CHE 889	Richard	MNT 105
Benjn.	BUC 87A	Jesse	MNT 105	Ritchard	ALL 80
Cadwallader	MNT 88	Jessee	PHI 151	Robert	GRN 77
Cathrine	PHA 20	Jno.	MIF 26	Robert	MER 458
Chas.	LYC 15	Jno.	CUM 129	Robert	CHE 701
Daniel	PHA 44	Job	MNT 116	Robert J.	MER 458
Daniel	NOU 144	John	LAN 33	Saml.	CHE 787
Daniel	LUZ 381	John	MNT 63	Samuel	MNT 83
Daniel	DAU 11A	John	MNT 65	Samuel	HNT 132
David	MNT 65	John	GRN 74	Samuel	LUZ 370
David	MNT 139	John	GRN 77	Samuel	NOU 97A
David	BUC 101A	John	MNT 88	Samuel	BUC 103A
David	BUC 157A	John	MNT 116	Stephen	LUZ 349
Dickenson	WAS 125	John	CUM 132	Stephen	LUZ 373
Ebenezer	LUZ 338	John	HNT 133	Thomas	LAN 102
Edmond	PHI 116A	John	PHI 138	Thomas	PHI 146
Edward	MNT 83	John	PHI 144	Thomas	NOU 195
Edward	GRN 90	John	NOU 152	Thomas	MER 458
Edward	PHA 92	John	PHI 154	Thomas	BUC 105A
Edward	MNT 116	John	SOM 162	Thos.	PHI 60
Edward	NOU 144	John	BER 163	Thos.	CHE 907
Edward (Mus.?)	MNT 117	John	FAY 233	Tytus	PHI 62
Edwd.	CEN 24	John	WST 242	William	ADA 14
Eli	MNT 110	John	LUZ 414	William	GRN 67

ROBERTS, William	GRN	77	ROBESON, William			ROBINSON, John	CHE	807
William	BUC	87	Jun.	DEL	182	John	CHE	906
William	BUC	146	William Sen.	DEL	182	John	PHI	77A
William	SOM	163	ROBIN, John	PHI	114A	Jonath.	MNT	141
William	DEL	180	ROBINET, George	ADA	41	Jornel?	PHA	51
William	FAY	228	Jos.	PHI	86A	Joseph	PHI	16
William	FAY	233	Richard	PHA	113	Joseph	BUC	87A
William	LUZ	373	ROBINETT, Allen	ADA	40	Kennedy	BER	249
William	BUC	101A	James	FAY	223	Levy	PHA	112
Wm.	CUM	51	ROBINS, Abenezer	VEN	169	Mary	PHA	68
Wm.	PHA	85	Alexr.	NOU	139	Matthew	CHE	743
Wm.	PHI	102A	Ann	PHA	35	Morris	PHA	31
Zacharia	FAY	217	Brintnel	WST	257	Nathaniel	WAS	24
ROBERTSON, Widow	PHI	15	Emus	ALL	105	Nicholas	MNT	84
Abraham	HNT	122	Jeremiah	YOR	207	Parker	PHA	86
Abreham	VEN	167	Joseph	DEL	172	Peter	WAS	14
Alexr.	PHA	90	Mary	GRN	77	Peter	LAN	157
Ann	PHA	98	Samuel	PHA	101	Peter	PHI	117A
Anthony Jr.	WAS	4	William	FAY	233	Richard	LAN	8
Anthony Sr.	WAS	4	Zacharia	NOU	97A	Richard	PHI	65
Henry	WAS	94	ROBINSON, Widow	PHI	32	Robert	PHA	12
Henry	MER	458	Widow	PHI	42	Robert	LAN	23
James	PHA	89	Aaron	WST	175	Robert	WAS	50
James	PHA	111	Andrew	LAN	20	Robert	LAN	103
James	CHE	824	Anthony	PHA	115	Robert	WST	373
Jared	LUZ	401	Anthony W.	PHA	13	Robt.	WST	156
Jean	CUM	27	Archibald	WAS	40	Robt.	WST	163
Jno.	MIF	13A	Bryant	LUZ	383	Robt.	WST	314
John	DAU	3	Chandler	LUZ	401	Rudam M.	PHA	67
John	PHA	6	David	WST	314	Saml.	PHA	17
John	BEV	8	David	LUZ	328	Saml.	PHI	33
John	DAU	23	David	CHE	720	Samuel	PHA	103
John	WAS	64	David	CHE	726	Samuel	MNT	131
John	MER	459	David Junr.	CHE	726	Samuel	BER	249
Joseph	BEV	7	Duncan	PHA	55	Sarah	PHI	57
Mary	PHI	42	Duncan	BUC	90	Thomas	WAS	113
Robert	BFD	65	Ebenezer	BUC	83	Thomas	MNT	139
Robt.	CUM	41	Elizabeth	PHA	93	Thomas	LAN	239
Samuel	WAS	31	George	WAS	64	Thomas	LAN	240
Samuel	MER	458	Gilbert	PHI	135	Thos.	WST	295
Thomas	VEN	166	Henry	WST	328	Thos.	CHE	854
Thomas	ERI	56A	Isaac	WST	194	Widow	LAN	20
Widow	LAN	123	Isabella	WST	242	William	BFD	45
William	BFD	54	James	PHA	21	William	WAS	46
William	VEN	170	James	BFD	45	William	MNT	63
Wm.	BEV	10	James	WAS	46	William	GRN	83
Wm.	FRA	322	James	WAS	50	William	GRN	89
Wm.	DAU	24A	James	WAS	112	William	WST	156
ROBERTSON?,			James	PHI	133	William	WST	257
William	ADA	8	James	PHI	134	William	WST	350
ROBESON, Aaron	DEL	165	James	LAN	239	William	BUC	141A
Andw.	YOR	154	James	WST	242	Willm.	PHI	22
Elijah	WAS	31	James	CHE	722	Wm.	PHI	40
George	BER	162	James	PHI	78A	Wm.	WST	373
Isaac	BER	250	James	PHI	81A	Wm.	CHE	859
Israel	MNT	116	James M.	PHA	101	Wm.	CHE	875
Jacob	WAY	145	Jas.	WST	295	Wm.	CHE	906
James	YOR	197	John	PHI	6	Wm.	PHI	102A
James	DAU	23A	John	WAS	17	Wm.	BUC	107A
John	PHI	127	John	WAS	24	ROBISAN, Francis	FRA	288
John	BER	162	John	MNT	38	Thomas	FRA	276
John	YOR	214	John	WAS	39	ROBISON, Alexd.	ALL	103
John Jr.	DAU	23	John	WAS	50	Alexd.	FRA	315
Joseph	LAN	153	John	PHA	56	Alexr. Jr.	MIF	8A
Moses	WAS	59	John	PHA	69	Alexr. Sr.	MIF	8A
Moses	BER	249	John	PHI	77	Andr.	FRA	300
Obadiah	CHE	816	John	PHI	83	Andrew	ALL	51
Peter	PHI	142	John	PHI	102	Andrew	HNT	132
Rebecca	WAS	59	John	MNT	131	Andrew	FAY	199
Richard	DEL	192	John	WST	156	Andw.	CUM	37
Robt.	DAU	23A	John	WST	242	Ann	ALL	86
Saml.	DAU	23	John	FAY	268	Ann	FAY	199
Samuel	DEL	171	John	WST	295	Charles	FRA	286
Susannah	DEL	165	John	LUZ	328	David	HNT	132
Wiley &	YOR	203	John	LUZ	382	Duncan	FRA	326
William	YOR	203	John	CHE	756	Elisha	WAS	31

Name	Co.	Pg.
ROBISON, Eliza.	CUM	92
Elizabeth	MIF	26
Elizabeth	MIF	8A
George	ALL	55
George	PHA	112
George	SOM	147
Henry	MIF	26
Henry	HNT	140
Henry	FAY	223
Henry	FRA	323
Hugh	ALL	68
Hugh	HNT	134
Hugh	SOM	147
Isaac	ADA	25
James	MIF	26
James	ALL	70
James	NOU	119
James	FAY	247
James Esqr.	ALL	118
James Jun.	FAY	247
James	MIF	8A
Jane	MIF	26
Jeremiah	HNT	143
Jno.	CUM	137
Jno.	CUM	142
John	ADA	6
John	ADA	6
John	MIF	11
John	ALL	56
John	BFD	59
John	ALL	75
John	ALL	87
John	ARM	127
John	HNT	137
John	HNT	138
John	HNT	151
John	LAN	162
John	FAY	241
John	FAY	247
John	FRA	303
John	FRA	323
John	MIF	17A
Jonah	BFD	59
Jos.	CUM	37
Jos.	CUM	51
Joseph	NOU	106
Lewes	CUM	87
Margery	FRA	315
Mary	ALL	68
Michael	CUM	35
Richard	NOU	106
Richd.	CHE	829
Robert	HNT	139
Robert	NOU	160
Robert	NOU	168
Robt.	FRA	300
Robt.	FRA	323
Saml.	CUM	37
Samuel	ARM	123
Thomas	ADA	42
Thomas	NOU	160
Thos.	LYC	22
Thos.	CUM	49
Vincent	MER	458
Widow	MIF	2
Widow	MIF	8A
William	CEN	24
William	NOU	131
William	NOU	168
William	FAY	199
William	FAY	211
William	CEN	23A
Wm.	CUM	37
Wm.	CUM	49
Wm.	MIF	17A
Elizabeth	MIF	4
ROBSON, Thos.	FRA	305
ROBY?, Wilm.	ALL	105
ROCH, Christn.	PHA	60
ROCH?, Fredrick	ALL	62
ROCHE, James	BER	250
ROCHMER, John	CUM	22
ROCK, Frederick	FRA	305
George	FRA	282
Henry	FRA	305
John	FRA	304
Peter	LAN	212
Peter	FRA	281
Philip	LAN	122
Thos.	FRA	306
ROCK?, Fredrick	ALL	62
ROCKEFELLER,		
Godfrey	NOU	106
Peter	NOU	106
William	NOU	106
ROCKEFELTON,		
William	NOU	97A
ROCKEL, John	NOH	31
Melcheor	NOH	43A
ROCKELL, John	NOH	46
Peter	NOH	46
ROCKEY, Frederick	YOR	158
George	LAN	249
Jacob	NOU	195
Jacob	CEN	23A
Peter	LAN	248
Wendle	ADA	40
Widow	LAN	249
William	NOU	195
ROCKHOLE,		
Nathaniel	HNT	133
ROCKINGBERG,		
Saml.	PHA	41
ROCKWELL, Bazel	FAY	217
Jabez	WAY	145
James	LUZ	397
Parsons	LUZ	394
ROCKY, Jacob	LAN	122
Jacob	CEN	23A
RODDEN, Isaac	CEN	23A
Joshua	WAS	64
RODDY, James	MIF	26
Josias	CUM	43
RODE, Andrew	LAN	47
Chrisly	HNT	128
George	LAN	45
George	LAN	69
Henry	LAN	66
Jacob	LAN	85
Jacob	HNT	128
Jacob	LAN	271
Jacob Senr.	LAN	271
John	LAN	57
John	LAN	74
John	LAN	79
John	BUC	159A
Lewis	LAN	271
Martin	LAN	77
Michl.	MIF	26
Paul	HNT	128
Peter	BUC	159A
RODEBACH, John	FRA	274
RODEBAUGH, Benjn.	CUM	113
Isaac	DEL	185
RODEBOUGH,		
Jonathan	FRA	318
RODECKER, Phillip	CUM	115
RODEMELL, Jacob	WST	242
RODENBACH, Jacob	BUC	148A
Joseph	BUC	82
RODENBERGER, Adam	NOH	57
David	NOH	57
RODENBERGER,		
George	NOH	57
Jacob Junr.	NOH	57
Jacob Senr.	NOH	57
John	NOH	57
RODENHIMER,		
Hendle?	ADA	35
RODER, Conrad	NOH	46
Daniel	NOH	46
George	NOH	74
Peter	NOH	74
RODERMELL, Peter	FRA	313
RODERMIL, Peter	MNT	58
Peter (B. S.)	MNT	62
RODEROCK, George	LAN	75
RODEROFF, Henry	NOU	200
RODES, Casper	NOU	112
RODFONG, Fredrik	DAU	13
Leonard	YOR	205
RODGERS, Danl.	WST	175
David	LAN	247
Elizh.	FRA	313
George	LAN	53
Jas.	CUM	139
John	ADA	35
John	WST	175
Jos.	YOR	200
Mary	BER	236
Micheal	WST	194
Peter	ADA	20
Peter	WST	314
Wm.	CUM	23
Wm.	PHA	82
RODIBAUGH, Jacob	FRA	274
RODICK, James	FAY	253
RODIK, Henry	DAU	20A
RODKEY, Elias	HNT	126
Jacob	HNT	126
RODLEY, Jacob	LYC	12
RODMAN, (Blank)	LYC	30
Charles	CHE	752
Gilbert	BUC	89
James	MIF	8
James Jr.	MIF	8
Jno.	MIF	8
Joseph	BUC	89
Samuel	BUC	154A
Scammon	BUC	89
William	BUC	89
RODNEY, James	PHI	155
Margaret	LAN	149
RODRICK, Andw.	PHA	33
RODROCK, David	BUC	101A
Jacob	BUC	148
Jacob Jnr.	BUC	148
John (Crossed Out)	BUC	148
John	BUC	141A
RODROUGH, Phillip	FRA	289
RODRUCK, Abram	FAY	199
RODTER, George	NOH	72
Henry	NOH	72
RODWELL, Peter	PHI	81A
ROE, David	PHI	65
George	PHA	119
Henry	BER	281
Humphrey	DEL	192
John	HNT	153
Martin	PHA	123
Martin Conr.	PHA	99
Micah	PHI	65
Thomas	ARM	122
Uriah	DEL	168
ROEBUCK, John S.	PHA	75
ROED?, Ephram	CRA	17
ROEMER, Christoph	FRA	276

Name	Co.	Pg.	Name	Co.	Pg.	Name	Co.	Pg.
ROERIG, Simon	NOH	46	ROGERS, Joseph	CHE	716	ROHRER, John	LAN	111
ROESLY, Henry	NOH	65A	Joseph R.	LUZ	340	John	LAN	118
Jacob	NOH	48A	Josiah	LUZ	373	ROI?, See Roe	BER	281
William	NOH	65A	Joze	LUZ	340	ROKE, Michl.	PHI	87A
ROESSHELLY?,			Laurence	FRA	321	ROL-?, James	ALL	81
Matthias	GRN	96	Lewis	WAS	82	ROLAN, Anthony	ALL	60
ROEST, Jno.	CUM	150	Matthew	LUZ	420	Anthony	ALL	69
ROFENBERGER, John	BUT	354	Mattw.	MIF	11	ROLAND, David	LAN	213
ROGAN, Sophia	PHA	78	Maurice	PHA	95	George	LAN	180
ROGER, John	PHI	106	Michael	PHA	51	George	LAN	181
William	DAU	23A	Nathaniel	MER	458	Jacob	BFD	52
ROGERS, Widow	PHI	7	Phillip	FAY	223	Jacob	DAU	25A
Widow	WAS	9	Pricilla	CHE	700	James	BFD	52
Abner	CHE	882	Richd.	CUM	139	John	LAN	26
Alexander	FAY	199	Robert	PHI	31	John	LAN	77
Alexr.	CUM	53	Robert	LAN	226	John	ALL	96
Alexr.	CHE	828	Robt.	WST	382	John	LAN	174
Arthur	NOU	139	Rowland	WAS	93	Joh	ALL	0
Benjn.	PHA	45	Samuel	NOU	152	Jonathan	LAN	77
Bigsby	LUZ	344	Samuel	FAY	239	Jonathan	HNT	153
Caleb	PHA	52	Samuel	MER	458	Margt.	BER	242
Connal	BUT	331	Sarah	PHA	63	Saml.	CUM	40
David	WAS	46	Thomas	PHI	10	Saml.	BER	238
David	CHE	763	Thomas	BEV	13	Thos.	PHI	121
Deliverance	LUZ	340	Thomas	BFD	66	William	WST	351
Eli	BFD	76	Thomas	ALL	114	Wm.	CUM	50
Elihu	LUZ	340	Thomas	FAY	206	ROLANDT, Federic	HNT	160
Elijah	WAS	93	Thomas	FAY	217	ROLANS, Daniel	NOU	119
Elizabeth	PHA	14	Thos.	PHA	81	ROLEF, Matthias	PHI	7
Ellis	BFD	76	Timt. (See			ROLET, Francis	PHI	78
Francis	WAS	35	Rogers,			ROLETER, Juda	ALL	72
Geor.	DAU	46A	Widow)	NOH	31	ROLEY, Dennis	PHI	66
George	BEV	17	Widow Of Timt.	NOH	31	ROLEY?, John	ARM	126
George	DEL	157	William	MIF	13	ROLISON, Robert	LAN	60
George	FAY	199	William	PHI	37	ROLL?, John	CEN	21
George	MER	458	William	GRN	108	ROLLEN, Michael	PHI	29
George	BUC	141A	William	YOR	197	ROLLER, Henry	HNT	150
George Jnr.	MER	458	William	MER	458	Jacob	HNT	150
Henrey	FAY	247	William	CHE	702	Jacob	YOR	173
Hugh	WAS	30	William	CEN	23A	Jacob Sr.	YOR	173
Isaac	FAY	228	William C.	BUC	138	Michael	HNT	148
Isaac	WST	382	Wilm.	ALL	75	Philip	HNT	148
Isaac	CHE	866	Wm.	PHA	35	ROLLMAN,		
Jacob	PHA	42	Zephaniah	LUZ	408	Christian	YOR	186
Jacob	NOU	150	Zephaniah Jr.	LUZ	408	Christian	YOR	187
James	MIF	11	ROGS, Margaret	FRA	308	George	BER	168
James	MIF	11	ROHARD, Peter	MIF	26	George	YOR	186
James	DAU	23	ROHART,			Jacob	YOR	186
James	WAS	71	Bartholomew	BFD	39	ROLLS, James	LUZ	364
James	VEN	166	ROHLMAN, John	LAN	211	Jesse	FAY	233
James	FAY	199	ROHN, Casper	NOH	43A	ROLSTON, Agness	ALL	99
James	CHE	703	Conrad Junr.	NOH	38	John	MER	459
Jas. & Jno.	FRA	286	Daniel	NOH	43A	Joseph	LAN	247
Jeremiah	WAS	46	George	NOH	72	William	MER	459
Jerramiah	BEV	20	John	NOH	41A	ROLY, Dennis	PHI	80A
Jno. & Jas.	FRA	286	Peter	NOH	40	Joseph L.	ALL	68
Jno.	VEN	169	ROHNBACK, John	YOR	188	ROLY?, Wilm.	ALL	105
Joel	FAY	217	ROHR, Henry	PHA	44	ROMAIGH, Henry	NOU	189
Joel	LUZ	340	John	PHA	36	Joseph	NOU	189
John	PHI	11	ROHRBACH,			Joseph	NOU	189
John	DAU	23	Christian	YOR	191	ROMAN, Edward	DEL	183
John	WAS	46	Henry	YOR	191	ROMANS, Absolom	CHE	901
John	ALL	72	Saml.	YOR	191	Isaac	CHE	877
John	ALL	72	ROHRER, Christian	LAN	113	Jacob	WST	315
John	VEN	167	Christian	LAN	118	Joshua	CHE	901
John	DEL	182	Christian Junr.	LAN	109	Moses	CHE	760
John	DEL	187	Christian Senr.	LAN	109	ROMBERGER, Widow	DAU	42A
John	FAY	206	David	LAN	305	ROMEL, Jacob	NOH	43A
John	LAN	227	Fred.	WST	223	Nicholas	NOH	43A
John	FAY	228	Geo.	WST	223	ROMER, Abraham	NOH	68
John	FAY	233	Henrich	LAN	276	Ignatius	DAU	14
John	FAY	239	Isaac	LAN	118	Peter	NOH	65A
John	MER	458	Jacob	LAN	109	ROMERFIELD,		
John L.	WAY	137	Jacob	LAN	257	Solomon	PHA	111
Jonah	LUZ	344	Jacob Senr.	LAN	113	ROMICH, Chris.	LAN	86
Jonathan	CHE	788	John	LAN	110	Christian	BER	174

ROMICH, Henry	BER	174	ROOS, Peter	NOH	32A	ROSE, John	PHI	105B
Jacob	NOH	46	ROOT, Abram	CHE	792	John	NOH	50A
John	LAN	90	Cornelius	BUC	156	John	BUC	161A
John	BER	174	Daniel	NOU	150	Joseph	BUC	146
ROMIG, Abraham	NOH	60A	Daniel	CHE	860	Mark	PHA	60
Adam	NOH	74	Isaac	CHE	703	Peter	PHI	57
Adam	NOH	81	Jacob	CHE	891	Phillip	PHA	56
Daniel	NOH	60A	John	CHE	792	Ricd.	LYC	14
Henry	NOH	60A	Joseph	CHE	893	Robert	GRN	92
Jacob	NOH	60A	Michael	MNT	123	Samuel Jr.	LUZ	390
John	NOH	72	Peter	LAN	230	Thomas	PHA	24
John	NOH	81	Sebastian	CHE	792	Thomas	PHI	91
John	NOH	60A	ROOT?, Bastian?	CHE	784	Thomas	SOM	161
Peter	NOH	91A	ROOTMAN, John	WST	277	Thos. Jnr.	BUC	146A
Widow	NOH	57	ROOTT, Andw.	PHI	118A	Thos.	BUC	146A
Widow	NOH	60A	ROPE, Christian	NOU	112	William	PHI	57
ROMLEY,			Frederic	HNT	147	William	BFD	76
Christopher	LAN	43	Mary	ADA	27	William	FAY	237
ROMTENBUSH,			Michael	NOU	112	ROSE?, Frances?		
Daniel	LAN	64	ROPLE?, Amos	LYC	11	(Erased)	SOM	159
RONAN, James	LAN	39	RORA, Chrisn.	LAN	264	ROSEBACK, Michl.	MNT	78
RONCK, David	CEN	23A	Jacob	LAN	264	ROSEBAWN, Rudy	LAN	12
Philip	LAN	135	John	LAN	263	ROSEBERRY,		
RONEY, Barney	PHA	100	RORAH, Frederick	BFD	39	Elloner	CUM	71
Herculas	WAS	50	RORBACH, Adam	ADA	25	James	WST	163
James	PHA	36	Henry	BER	177	John	WAS	17
James	CHE	731	Jacob	BER	177	John	GRN	96
James	BER	287B	John Jr.	BER	177	Matthias	GRN	65
James	BER	287B	Lawr.	BER	177	Michael	GRN	67
John	BUC	162	RORDER?, Henry	MNT	135	Michael	GRN	96
John	CHE	801	RORE, Widow	PHI	37	ROSEBERY, Isaac	WAS	17
John Jr.	CHE	801	ROREMAN, John	PHA	62	ROSEBOROUGH,		
Robert	CHE	803	RORER, Christian	LAN	304	James	CHE	719
Thomas	CHE	768	Henry	PHI	146	Samuel	YOR	195
RONGSHORE, Jolly	PHI	80A	Jacob	FRA	316	ROSEBROUGH, Isaac	HNT	124
RONK, John	LAN	133	John	PHI	146	John	ALL	52
RONNELS, William	LAN	86	John	LAN	181	John	ALL	104
William Jun.	LAN	86	RORER?, Jacob	MNT	41	Wilm.	ALL	114
ROOCH, Christian	BUC	101A	RORICH, Peter	BER	205	ROSEBRUGH, Jean		
ROOD, Elijah	LUZ	354	RORICK, John	NOH	63	Widow	NOH	31
Elijah	LUZ	427	RORRER, Joseph	PHI	148	ROSEBURY, Joseph	NOU	148
John	LAN	299	RORY?, Bengamin	ALL	113	ROSEHAM, Fredk.	PHI	86
Ludwig	LAN	256	ROSASTEAL, Andw.	WST	222	ROSEMAN, Henry	MNT	139
Wm.	FRA	296	Geo.	WST	222	James	FAY	239
ROODIE, Jacob	CHE	785	Jacob	WST	222	John	PHI	111
ROOF, Anthony	WST	277	ROSE, Abm.	PHI	119	John	FAY	237
Frederick	BUC	139A	Allen	BFD	52	ROSEN, Henry	MNT	112
George	BUC	139A	Allen	BFD	76	ROSENBERGER,		
Henry	BUC	139A	Andrew	MER	457	Abrm.	MNT	125
John	WST	277	Andw.	PHI	87	Benj.	MNT	126
Peter	BFD	52	Aron	WST	382	Benjamin	NOH	81
ROOFNER, Conrod	CUM	103	Atkinson	PHA	24	Benjn.	MNT	68
George	WST	314	Champain	PHA	98	Christian	MNT	83
Simon	WST	314	Charles	PHI	53	Daniel	MNT	68
ROOFONG, Christn.	DAU	14	Danl.	BER	241	David	MNT	68
Fredrik	DAU	13A	David	PHI	105B	Heny.	WST	296
Michael	DAU	13	David	PHI	68A	Isaac	MNT	68
ROOK, George	FRA	301	Docr.	LAN	33	Jacob	MNT	68
ROOKER, Jacob	LYC	8	Edward	BFD	52	Jacob	MNT	129
ROOKS, George	MNT	109	Edward	GRN	73	Jno., Junr.	MNT	68
Jonathn.	CHE	906	Erhard	BER	241	John	MNT	68
Thomas	CHE	797	Ezekiel Junr.	GRN	92	Peter	LAN	213
William	WST	328	Isaac	WAS	113	ROSENBERRY,		
ROOP, Chris.	LAN	87	Jacob	GRN	105	Benjn.	BUC	148
Christian	YOR	154	Jacob	NOU	97A	Daniel	FRA	316
Christopher	YOR	168	Jaconias	WST	382	Henry	BUC	160
Christopher	YOR	205	James	WAS	124	Henry	BUC	159A
Jacob	LAN	87	John	WAS	64	Isaac	BUC	97
John	PHA	31	John	GRN	68	Jacob	FRA	316
John	YOR	205	John	GRN	103	John	FRA	316
John	DAU	14A	John	BUC	107	John	BUC	159A
Matthias	PHI	129	John	PHI	133	Julius	BUC	159A
ROOPE, John	WAS	31	John	WST	194	Yellis	BUC	97
Philip	YOR	161	John	BER	215	ROSENCRANSE,		
ROOS, Francois	CRA	4	John	FAY	228	Jacob	LUZ	326
Francois	CRA	16	John	FRA	285	ROSENCRANTZ, Daniel	LUZ	324

ROSENCRANTZ,			ROSS, John	MIF	4	ROSS, William	MIF	26
James	LUZ	378	John	ADA	12	William	PHI	36
John	LUZ	380	John	MIF	18	William	WAS	39
Levi	LUZ	378	John	WAS	39	William	WAS	50
ROSENDALL,			John	WAS	39	William	WAS	94
Christian	SOM	154	John	PHA	40	William	NOU	101
ROSENKRANNS,			John	CUM	45	William	HNT	160
Benjn.	WAY	135	John	ALL	70	William	BER	161
ROSENKRAUNS,			John	GRN	83	William	YOR	207
Harman	WAY	145	John	WAS	94	William	FAY	216
James	WAY	145	John (Crossed			William	FAY	223
Jeremiah	WAY	145	Out)	BUC	145A	William	WST	242
Solomon	WAY	147	John	YOR	219	William	LUZ	318
ROSETT, Jacob	PHA	71	John	WST	373	William	LUZ	369
ROSEWELL, Daniel	LUZ	392	John	CHE	728	William Esqr.	YOR	198
ROSHO, John	MNT	90	John	CHE	754	Wilm.	ALL	68
ROSHUNG, Henry	MNT	54	John	CHE	757	Wilm.	ALL	93
Peter	MNT	96	John	CHE	765	Wm.	CUM	90
ROSIN, John	MNT	129	John	CHE	861	Wm.	WST	372
ROSITER, John	CHE	854	John Esqr.	NOH	38	Wm.	CHE	757
John	CHE	857	John Junr.	PHA	75	Zachariah	NOU	119
Samuel	CHE	858	John Junr.	GRN	103	ROSS?, (See Rose)	NOU	97A
Thomas	CHE	856	John Senr.	GRN	103	Wm.	PHA	75
William	MNT	105	John	MIF	8A	ROSSER, Adam	YOR	190
ROSITOR, Saml.	CHE	861	John L.	PHI	22	ROSSET, John B.	LUZ	394
ROSLE?, Amos	LYC	11	Jonathan	PHI	13	ROSSETT, Mr.	PHA	107
ROSLY, John	NOH	40	Jos.	YOR	201	ROSSETTER, John	PHA	98
ROSS, Widw.	PHI	106A	Joseph	CEN	19	ROSSITER, Daniel	MNT	117
Adam	FRA	281	Joseph	LAN	25	ROST, Henry	CRA	5
Alexr.	YOR	207	Joseph	WST	175	Jacob	CRA	5
Allen	YOR	217	Joseph	NOU	177	Michael	NOU	150
Andrew	CHE	778	Joseph	LUZ	393	ROSTEAN, Fernere	PHA	93
Ann	PHA	46	Mary	WAS	94	ROSWELL, Jacob	DEL	167
Aquil	PHA	64	Mary	CHE	765	John	DEL	158
Archibald	WST	295	Matths.	PHI	44	Thomas	LUZ	329
Benjamin	CHE	756	Michael	LYC	3	William	DEL	165
Cephus	BUC	145A	Michael	SOM	155	ROSYBAM?, Jacob	CUM	31
Charles	NOU	195	Moses	CHE	754	ROTE, George	MNT	53
Clementina	PHA	96	Mrs.	NOU	184	Henry	MNT	55
Collin	LAN	175	Nathaniel	WAS	4	Phillip	PHA	58
Daivd	PHA	111	Paton	LAN	40	ROTERICK, Henry	FRA	318
Daniel	ALL	107	Peter	WAS	58	ROTH, Abraham	YOR	189
Daniel	LUZ	392	Phillop	ALL	92	Abraham Jr.	YOR	179
David	ADA	19	Reuben	WAS	40	Abraham Sr.	YOR	179
David	WAS	24	Reuben	WAS	124	Adam	NOH	63
David	PHA	30	Reynolds	WST	295	Adam	BER	164
David	NOH	68	Richd.	CUM	42	Casper	NOH	34A
David	LUZ	405	Robert	GRN	77	Christian	NOH	72
Edward	MER	459	Robert	HNT	152	Conrad	NOH	74
Enoch	GRN	77	Robert	FAY	217	Conrad	BER	149
George	CUM	43	Robt.	PHI	114A	Conrad	BER	165
George	ARM	127	Saml.	CUM	40	Daniel	NOH	48A
George	NOU	195	Saml, Junr.	CUM	40	Daniel	NOH	91A
George	YOR	208	Samuel	WAS	4	David	NOH	63
George	CHE	852	Samuel	ALL	68	David	NOH	74
George Esq.	LAN	45	Samuel	HNT	131	Geo. Jacob Jun.	NOH	91A
Henry	PHI	24	Sarah	PHI	42	George	BER	145
Henry	NOU	112	Simon	CUM	124	George	BER	164
Hugh	WAY	145	Stephen	CUM	110	George	YOR	179
Issabella	WAS	94	Stephen	WAR	1A	George	BER	221
Jacob	LAN	238	Taff	ALL	114	Godfried	NOH	46
Jacob	MER	459	Thomas	BEV	18	Harman	ADA	36
James	MIF	26	Thomas	ALL	57	Henry	LAN	177
James	LAN	40	Thomas	WAS	58	Henry	YOR	183
James	PHA	51	Thomas	WAS	94	Henry	LAN	203
James	SOM	155	Thomas	WAS	105	Henry	NOH	60A
James	WST	156	Thomas	FAY	268	Henry	NOH	91A
James	WST	242	Thomas	CHE	739	Jacob	NOH	40
James	FRA	292	Thomas	NOH	67A	Jacob	NOH	74
James Esqr.	ALL	51	Thomas	BUC	103A	Jacob	BER	142
James Jun.	WAS	94	Thos.	PHA	90	Jacob	BER	145
James Sen.	WAS	94	Timothy	GRN	103	Jacob	BER	165
James	NOH	67A	Widow	LAN	34	Jacob	YOR	179
Jane	GRN	77	Widow	NOH	54	Jacob	YOR	184
Jas.	CUM	127	William	PHA	20	Jacob	BER	231
Jesse	LUZ	392	William	ADA	21	Jacob Jr.	BER	142

ROTH, Jacob Junr.	NOH	48A	ROUCK?, Christn.	PHA	78	ROW, Jesse	PHA	68
Jacob Senr.	NOH	48A	ROUDEBUCK, John	MNT	83	John	NOU	139
Jacob	NOH	34A	ROUDEBUSH, Henry	BFD	66	John	NOU	177
Jacob	NOH	91A	Jacob	ADA	38	John	BER	236
John	NOH	69	Michael	BFD	66	John	LUZ	344
John	YOR	169	Michael	MNT	135	Lewis	NOU	160
John	YOR	183	ROUDENBUSH,			Marey	FAY	211
John	BER	241	George	BUC	148	Martin	NOU	139
John Junr.	NOH	91A	Jeremiah	BUC	159A	Nancy	PHI	94A
John Senr.	NOH	91A	ROUDY, Nicholas	NOU	139	Nicholas	NOU	177
John	NOH	34A	ROUGH, Adam	LAN	222	Patrick	CHE	739
John	NOH	91A	Francis	LAN	228	Peter	NOU	177
John A.	BER	164	George	SOM	139	Richard	PHI	110
Jonathan	BER	165	George	LAN	223	Widow	LAN	238
Jos.	YOR	190	Henry Jr.	DAU	23	ROWAN, Charles	DAU	3
Mathias	BER	165	Jacob	BEV	7	David	CUM	93
Michael	BER	227	Jacob	DAU	23A	Henry	ADA	3
Peter (Son Of			Jacob	BUC	82A	Hugh	PHI	155
Phil)	NOH	91A	John	SOM	139	James	ADA	3
Peter	NOH	48A	John	LAN	225	James	DEL	165
Peter	NOH	76A	John	FRA	293	John	PHA	109
Peter	NOH	91A	John Jr.	CHE	892	John	SOM	147
Phil (See,			William	DAU	23A	John	FRA	293
Roth, Peter)	NOH	91A	ROUGHT, Jacob	LUZ	382	John Sen.	SOM	147
Philip	LAN	137	ROUMAN, Edward	DEL	184	Matt.	WST	223
Philip	LAN	203	William	NOU	167	Matthias	NOU	152
Philip	NOH	48A	ROUP, George	DAU	13A	Matthias	NOU	152
Stephen	BER	155	Jacob	LAN	231	Stewart	ALL	67
Valentine	NOH	72	Jonas	ALL	58	William	SOM	147
ROTHE, John	NOH	70	Leonard	NOU	106	Wm.	CUM	114
ROTHENBERGER,			ROURER, George	PHI	136	ROWDEN, John	LYC	23
Frederick	BER	134	ROUREY?, Peter	FRA	292	ROWE, Daniel	MIF	2
Martin	BER	134	ROURK, Edwd.	LYC	17	Michael	DEL	187
Peter	BER	134	ROUS, George	ALL	83	ROWEN, Hannah	PHA	86
ROTHERBERGER,			John	WST	156	Jane	PHA	90
Peter Jr.	BER	134	ROUSCOUP, Phillip	NOU	124	John	PHA	69
ROTHERMEL, Daniel	BER	218	ROUSE, Benjamin	WAS	58	John	WST	223
Jacob	BER	135	George	HNT	142	Matt.	WST	222
Jacob	BER	254	Jacob	WAY	149	Wm.	WST	222
Jacob Jr.	BER	253	John Dr.	YOR	158	ROWERSOCK, George	NOU	177
John	BER	134	Martin	WST	277	ROWHER, Geo.	CEN	23A
John	BER	138	Philice	PHA	114	ROWIN, Christn.	PHI	84A
Leonard	BER	218	Thomas Junr.	WAS	31	ROWISKER, Andrew	LAN	241
Leonard	BER	279	Thomas Senr.	WAS	31	ROWLAND, Benj.	MNT	41
Paul	BER	218	ROUSEBERIKER,			Benjn., Junr	MNT	42
Paul Jr.	BER	218	Jacob	WAS	71	David	DAU	2
Peter	BER	218	ROUSH, Andrew	NOU	139	David	LAN	63
ROTHERTON, Robt.	FRA	313	Casper	NOU	140	David	BER	249
ROTHMEL, Amariah	LYC	7	Eliza	PHA	84	Griffith	SOM	162
ROTHONG, John	DAU	18A	Frederick	NOU	124	Henry	WAS	112
ROTHROCK, Daniel	HNT	155	George	NOU	139	Henry	NOU	139
Frederick	BFD	35	George	DAU	8A	James	PHA	21
George	NOH	48A	Isaac	PHA	40	James	FAY	233
Henry	NOH	67A	Jacob	NOU	195	John	BFD	45
Isaac Junr.	NOH	48A	John	PHA	31	John	PHA	103
Isaac	NOH	48A	Lewis	PHA	42	John	CHE	860
John	NOH	40	ROUSHER, Jacob	NOU	189	John	CHE	880
John	NOH	65A	ROUTSONG, David	ADA	21	Jonathen Esqr.	FAY	253
Jonathan	NOH	48A	David	ADA	29	Jos.	CHE	880
Rosina	NOH	38	ROUVERT, Edmond	PHA	12	Mathias	BER	249
Saml.	NOH	48A	ROUZER, Gedeon	BFD	76	Mordica	FAY	233
Saml.	NOH	67A	John	BFD	76	Owen	BUC	97
ROTHWELL, Jacob	DEL	187	Joseph	BFD	76	Robt.	MIF	11
ROTOKER, John	FRA	309	Peter	BFD	76	Thos.	CHE	880
ROTRICK, Geo.	MIF	17A	ROVE, James	PHI	30	William	PHI	152
Joseph	MIF	17A	ROVER, Jacob	FRA	283	Wm.	CHE	832
ROTROCK, John	YOR	154	ROW, Adam	YOR	217	ROWLANDS, Anias	BUT	336
ROTT, Benjn.	FRA	298	Arnst	YOR	217	ROWLES, John	FRA	322
ROTTER, John	NOH	57	Cornelious	PHI	70A	John	FRA	323
ROUBERT, Wm.	PHA	72	Frederick	NOU	139	ROWLETT, John	PHA	20
ROUCH, George	NOU	184	Fredrick	LYC	20	ROWLEY, Constant	WAS	64
Jacob	DAU	52	George	NOU	139	Edward	PHA	24
Jacob	NOU	184	George	WST	175	John	WST	277
Michl.?	DAU	50A	George	NOU	177	ROWMAN, Joseph	DEL	176
Stephen	PHI	92A	Jacob	NOH	86	Joseph	DEL	177
ROUCHE, John	DAU	52	James	BEV	16	ROWNEY, Jas.	CUM	90

ROWZER, Phillop	ALL	109	RUCH, Daniel	NOH	60A	RUDY, Christ	LAN	135
ROXBOROUGH, Robt.	CHE	723	George	NOH	57	Conrad	NOU	131
Wm.	CHE	844	Henry	NOH	91A	Daniel	LAN	185
ROY, James	PHI	117	Jacob	WST	223	Elizabeth	DAU	23
Manuel	PHI	115A	John	LAN	183	Frederick	MNT	90
ROYCE, Frederick	BFD	59	Peter	NOH	40	Frederick	BER	263
Frederick Jr.	BFD	59	Peter	WST	223	Henry	LAN	141
Philip	BFD	59	Widow	NOH	70	Henry	LAN	179
ROYER, Amos	DAU	40	RUCHSTEIN,			Jacob	DAU	34
Benjamin	MNT	74	Frederick	NOH	78A	Jacob	DAU	48
Catherine	MNT	84	RUCK, Lowrence	NOH	91	Jacob	YOR	160
Christian	FRA	306	Peter	MNT	62	Jacob Sr.	DAU	50
Christn.	BER	204	RUCKMAN, James	BUC	141A	Jones	DAU	51A
Christopher	NOU	189	John	WAS	4	Joseph	DAU	9A
Christopher	NOU	189	Thos.	NOU	168	Martin	ADA	34
Daniel	FRA	304	RUCKSTOOL,			Martin	YOR	175
David	BER	273	Ulerick	PHI	91	Michael	YOR	166
George	MNT	55	RUD, John	NOU	131	Rachel	PHA	56
George	BER	152	Philip	MNT	46	RUDY?, Henry	YOR	175
George	BER	253	RUDD, Andrew	NOU	168	RUE, Anthony	BUC	161A
George	DAU	37A	RUDDY, Barnard	CUM	30	Benjamin	DEL	192
Jacob	DAU	37	Geo.	CUM	33	Lewis	BUC	89
Joel	LAN	87	RUDE, Jacob	GRN	110	Matthew	BUC	85
John	DAU	31	John	WAS	64	Richard	BUC	89
John	LAN	87	Nathan	WAY	137	William	WST	295
John	BER	151	Samuel	WAS	64	RUE?, Israel	PHI	104
John	FRA	306	RUDEBAGH, Jacob	CUM	103	RUFEORN, Simon	FAY	199
Michael	BER	164	RUDEBAUGH, Adam	BUT	324	RUFF, Abraham	MNT	83
Michael	CHE	895	RUDEBOUGH, Adam	WST	257	Bastian	NOH	81
Philip	MNT	58	John	WST	257	George	NOH	81
Saml.	DAU	35	John	FRA	274	Jacob	ADA	41
Saml.	BER	153	RUDEHILL, John	FRA	274	Jacob	YOR	218
Saml.	FRA	304	RUDEPAUGH, George	FRA	314	Valentine	NOH	81
Saml.	FRA	304	Peter	FRA	314	RUFFELSBERGER,		
ROYSE, Moses	SOM	144	RUDER?, (See			Peter	ADA	20
ROZER, Adam	YOR	194	Reeder)	NOU	101	RUFFNER, Chr.	WST	223
Lorence	YOR	194	Peter	NOU	168	Simn.	WST	222
Philip	YOR	194	RUDESIL, Michael	LAN	188	RUFNER, Geo.	BUT	332
Philip	YOR	194	RUDESILL, Melchor	LAN	37	Henry	ARM	126
RUACH?, John	NOU	200	RUDIBACK, Charles	CHE	773	Philip	BUC	139A
RUB?, Elizabeth	LAN	213	RUDICH, Jacob	NOH	31	RUFSELL, Samuel		
RUBAND, Abraham	LAN	203	RUDICILL, Jacob	HNT	118	Capt.	ADA	12
RUBB, Christian	LAN	307	Jonas	HNT	161	RUFSNYDER, Daniel	BER	168
RUBBLE, Christian	YOR	191	RUDIMAN, James	PHI	10	Peter	MNT	100
RUBEL, Christian	LAN	304	RUDISELL, Andw.	YOR	184	RUGAN, John	PHA	60
Jacob	NOH	32A	Baltzer	ADA	15	John	PHI	142
RUBEN, Charles	PHA	76	Jacob	YOR	185	RUGER, Elias	ERI	60
RUBENCAMP,			John	YOR	155	RUGERT, Paul	NOU	139
Justice	BUC	155A	RUDISILL, Jacob	LAN	37	RUGG, Curtis	SOM	144
RUBERCOMB, Chs.	MNT	110	Jacob Esqr.	YOR	181	Samuel	SOM	144
RUBERT, Peter	NOH	46	John	YOR	191	RUGGELS, Benjn.	CUM	43
RUBETON, Thomas	PHI	21	RUDISILLEY,			Wm.	CUM	52
RUBEY, Edward	BFD	60	Henerey	MER	457	Wm. Junr.	CUM	52
Eleanor	BFD	76	RUDOLPH, Ann	PHA	41	RUGGLES, Alfred	LUZ	330
John	BFD	60	Christn.	CHE	793	Eden	LUZ	343
RUBICAN, Charles	PHI	75A	Geo.	PHI	107A	Sherman	PHI	147
RUBICOM, Daniel	PHA	29	Jacob	DEL	168	RUGH, Christopher	WST	156
RUBINCON, Peter	CHE	771	Jacob	BUT	319	John	YOR	185
RUBINDOLF, Jacob	NOU	97A	Jacob	PHI	84A	Michl. Esqr.	WST	194
RUBING?, Jacob	MNT	42	James	DEL	169	RUGLE, Henry	YOR	187
RUBLE, David	WAS	40	John	PHI	125	RUHE, Frederick	NOH	69
Jacob	MIF	15A	John	DEL	168	RUHL, Fredk.	YOR	192
Levi	WAS	40	John	DEL	169	Henry	YOR	193
Mattw.	MIF	15A	John	DEL	171	John	YOR	187
Peter	MIF	4	John	WST	372	John	YOR	195
RUBLETT, Levi	FAY	247	Joseph	DEL	168	Michael	LAN	146
RUBRECHT, Jacob	BER	145	Mary	PHA	60	Peter	DAU	27
RUBSAMEN?,			Michael	NOH	57	Phiip	LAN	146
Sebastian	BER	222	Peter	PHI	142	Philip	YOR	187
RUBY, John	YOR	205	Peter	LAN	203	William	YOR	187
Michael	LAN	21	Philip	DEL	171	RUHL?, Christena	BER	143
RUBY?, (See			Thomas	DEL	171	RUHM, Andrew	LAN	213
Ruley)	NOU	98	William	DEL	171	Magdalena	LAN	203
RUCE, Myer	NOU	150	RUDOLPHI,			RULAND, Barbara	LAN	203
RUCH, Caty	LAN	71	Frederic	NOH	32A	Jonathan	LAN	203
Christn.	NOH	48A	RUDY, Charles	LAN	143	RULE, Albert	CUM	33

RUSH?, Moses	LYC	9	RUSSELL, Henry	WAS	53	RUTH, Henry	BUC	97
RUSHENBERGER,			Henry	GRN	109	Henry	CHE	734
Conrd.	FAY	241	Henry	LAN	248	Henry	BUC	105A
RUSHER, John	NOU	119	James	LYC	3	Henry	BUC	105A
RUSHMAN, Robt.	PHI	118	James	PHA	115	Isaac	BUC	97
RUSHSTOOL, Jacob	MNT	90	James	DEL	158	Jacob	MNT	68
RUSHUNG, Henry	MNT	61	James	FAY	259	Jacob	BER	203
Jacob	MNT	61	Jas.	WST	223	James	LAN	65
RUSHURIG, Peter	MNT	61	John	ADA	13	John	BUC	98
RUSK, James	WAS	46	John	CUM	84	John	BER	204
William	ADA	15	John	NOU	106	John	WST	351
RUSK?, John	LYC	558	John	FRA	317	John	LUZ	355
Moses	LYC	7	Joseph	PHA	101	John	NOH	48A
RUSS, David	BUC	105A	Joseph	WST	222	Michael	MNT	46
George	NOU	139	Joshua	ADA	12	Michael	BER	167
Killian	BER	276	Michael	LUZ	416	Michl.	FRA	312
RUSS?, Francis	ARM	126	Moses	DEL	172	Peter	BER	168
RUSSEL, Bazel	FAY	217	Patrick	ADA	3	Philip	NOH	60A
Benjamin	ERI	56	Robert	WAS	53	Robert	CHE	876
Benjamin	NOU	115	Robert	WAS	53	Samuel	MNT	58
Conrad	NOU	139	Robert	NOU	160	Thomas	BER	138
Daniel	CHE	847	Samuel	WAS	53	Thomas	CHE	845
Davd.	BUT	328	Samuel	LAN	145	RUTHERFORD, Andw.	FAY	217
David	NOU	131	Samuel	DEL	158	James	DAU	15A
Elijah	BUC	105A	Samuel Jun.	ADA	12	John	DAU	15
Ephraim	CHE	779	Stephen	PHA	121	John	WST	156
Even	LAN	89	Widow	CUM	119	John	DEL	174
Francis	PHI	34	William	WAS	71	John	DEL	178
George	ALL	73	William	DEL	172	Robt.	CHE	748
George	HNT	117	William	LUZ	322	Susannah	DAU	15A
Henry	BFD	76	Wm.	CUM	129	William	FAY	216
Hugh	CHE	803	Wm.	FRA	320	Wm.	CHE	866
Isaac	NOU	115	Wm.	CHE	756	Wm.	PHI	92A
James	DAU	21	RUSSET, Joseph	PHA	106	RUTHRAFF, John		
James	GRN	89	RUSSILL, Andrew	WAS	24	Revd.	FRA	298
James	FAY	249	James	WAS	24	RUTHROUGH, John	FRA	294
James	BUT	328	RUSSLE, Andrew	NOU	168	RUTHS, Michael	PHI	43
James	WST	350	Andrew	NOU	168	Thos.	FRA	316
James	DAU	12A	Charles	NOU	167	RUTLEDGE, James	WAS	125
Jno?	WAR	1A	Henry	BEV	24	Thos.	YOR	189
John	BFD	52	Thomas	BEV	10	RUTLINGER, John	LAN	4
John	CUM	143	Thos.	BEV	11	RUTT, Abm.	LAN	258
John	NOU	160	Thos.	VEN	170	Chris.	LAN	75
John	WST	350	William	BEV	21	Henry	LAN	5
John	CHE	746	Wm.	VEN	168	Henry	LAN	83
Joseph	ALL	120	RUSSLE?, Conrad	MNT	78	Jacob	LAN	5
Joseph	LAN	169	RUSSOL, Oliver	ALL	105	Jacob	LAN	68
Martin	NOU	144	RUST, Henry	BUT	324	Jacob	LAN	75
Mathew	WAS	5	RUSTON, Anthy.	PHI	98	John	LAN	83
Oliver	CHE	801	RUTAN, Samuel	WAS	64	Peter	LAN	5
Paul	CHE	810	RUTE, George	BUC	148	Peter Jnr.	LAN	5
Peggy	LAN	50	John	BUC	148	RUTTENHOUSE,		
Robert	PHI	8	John	BUC	148	William	FAY	211
Robert	NOH	72	Michael	BUC	148	RUTTER, Adam	LAN	128
Robert	ALL	113	Peter	BUC	148	Adam	YOR	192
Robert	CHE	733	RUTEER, Jacob	CHE	710	Andrew Esqr.	YOR	163
Robert	CHE	802	RUTFIELD, John	FRA	279	Benjamen	FAY	233
Robert Revd.	NOH	31	RUTH, Abraham	BUC	105A	David	BER	174
Samuel	NOH	74	Abraham, Junr.	MNT	68	Edward	FAY	259
Samuel	HNT	151	Abram	MNT	68	George	PHA	48
Thomas	LAN	302	Adam	BER	204	George	GRN	77
Thomas	CHE	847	Adam	BER	205	George	LAN	127
William	GRN	90	Andrew	BUC	105A	Henry	LAN	173
William	LAN	123	Catherine	BER	168	Henry	LAN	173
William	LAN	217	Christian	BUC	150	Jacob	PHA	33
William	CHE	780	Christian	NOH	60A	Jacob	PHA	53
RUSSELL, Abraham	WAS	94	Christn.	BER	204	John	ADA	42
Alban	LUZ	403	Daniel	BER	168	John	PHI	45
Alex Esq.	ADA	9	David	BUC	96A	John	GRN	77
Alexander	PHA	105	Francis	LAN	203	John	LAN	129
Caleb	FRA	278	Franz	BER	168	John	HNT	139
Daniel	LUZ	416	George	MNT	135	John	LAN	172
Edwrd	DEL	187	George	BER	168	John	LAN	173
Esther	CHE	756	George	LAN	306	John	FAY	206
Francis	PHA	120	George Jr.	BER	168	John	CHE	720
George	DEL	172	Henry	NOH	74	Joseph	LAN	176

RUTTER, Joseph			RYNER, Peter	PHI 120A	SAGER, Robert	BEV	16	
Junr.	LAN	173	RYNHART, George	CEN 21	SAGERSON, Patrick	BUT	330	
Martha	MNT	58	RYNOLDS, Comely	LYC 8	SAHL, George	NOH	54	
Martha	PHA	98	David	LYC 22	Leonard	NOH	54	
Nathaniel	LAN	127	Stephen	DAU 24A	SAHLER, Abraham	MNT	101	
Samuel	PHA	120	RYOL, Widw.	PHI 92	SAHLOR, Daniel	MNT	75	
Thomas	CHE	907	RYON, Edard	CRA 7	Henry (Carp.)	MNT	75	
Tobias	FRA	311	Jane	BFD 76	Henry (Weaver)	MNT	75	
Wm.	FRA	319	John	CRA 7	Hodfrey	MNT	74	
RUTTY, Ezra	LUZ	404	Timothy	CUM 141	Jacob	MNT	101	
Samuel	LUZ	404	RYSINGER, Henry	WAS 82	John	MNT	100	
RUTY, Andrew	LAN	73	Jacob	WAS 82	John	CHE	860	
Conrad	LAN	73	William	WAS 82	Peter	MNT	74	
Enoch	LAN	73			Peter	MNT	84	
Henry	DAU	26A	S----, Michael		Valuntine	MNT	84	
John	LAN	73	(Crossed Out)	BER 263	SAHLOS?, Peter	MNT	52	
RUTZEL, Jacob	MNT	68	S----?, Abraham	FRA 311	SAHM, David	LAN	146	
Jacob Junr.	MNT	68	Jacob	BFD 77	George	LAN	141	
RUTZEL?, Adam	CEN	21	Jacob	BFD 77	George	LAN	146	
RYAN, Ambros	CEN	19	Jacob	FRA 271	SAHMITT, Ludwig	NOH	44	
Edmond	PHI	11	S--RNER,		SAIGER, Henry	LAN	106	
George	WST	373	Christopher	BER 214	SAILER, John	PHA	26	
James	PHA	79	SA--?, Jacob	NOU 200	John	LAN	213	
Jeremiah	WAS	4	SABINS, Joshua	LUZ 386	Samuel	PHA	39	
John	DAU	11	SABLE, Peter	YOR 186	SAILER?, Christn.	DAU	34	
John	WAS	64	Widow	LAN 312	SAILOR, Adam	FRA	297	
John	FRA	276	SABLER, Isaac	ALL 67	Casper	YOR	198	
John	CHE	855	SACH, Benjn.	MNT 79	Conrad	YOR	218	
Joseph	PHI	75	SACH?, Daniel	MNT 46	Henry	PHA	75	
Joseph	HNT	121	SACHET, Almeron?	LYC 12	Jacob	PHI	57	
Lewis	PHA	4	SACK?, Benjn.	MNT 79	Lawrence	YOR	198	
Thomas	BUC	151A	SACKAWAY, Wm.	PHI 28	Matthias	CUM	62	
Timothy	WAS	4	SACKET, Almeria?	LYC 12	Peter	CHE	895	
Timothy	PHI	138	Enoch	LUZ 367	William	YOR	198	
William	PHA	21	Joseph	HNT 130	SAINTCLAIR,			
William	LUZ	330	Reuben	LUZ 367	Archd.	BUT	324	
William	BUC	107A	SACKET?, Thos.	LYC 17	George	LYC	7	
RYANS, Thomas	PHI	32	SACKETT, Elijah	CUM 47	SAINTMAN, Michael	CHE	731	
RYBOULT, Stephen	WST	373	Joseph	BUC 107	SAIVENHAWSER,			
RYBURN, James	WAS	24	SACKIT, Samuel	FAY 247	Phillip	NOU	115	
RYDA, Wm.	PHI	92A	SACKREUTER, Henry	NOH 65A	SALA, Jacob	YOR	158	
RYDER, Benjamin	LUZ	383	SACKSMAN,		Peter	YOR	206	
John	BER	241	Christian	WST 351	Widow	LAN	277	
Joseph	LUZ	382	SADDLEMAUN,		SALADE, Sebastian	PHA	16	
RYER/ RYEN?,			Michl.	CUM 26	SALADY, John	DAU	6	
Jonathan	LAN	173	SADDLER, Isaac	YOR 208	SALDER, John	PHI	35	
RYER, Abraham	LAN	174	SADELSAM, Jacob	DAU 48A	SALEDY, Daniel	DAU	6A	
Nicholas	LAN	172	SADLAR, Rudolph	FAY 247	Jacob	DAU	6	
Thomas	MIF	8A	SADLER, Christian	YOR 195	John Jr	DAU	6	
RYER?, (See Ryen)	LAN	173	Elenor	PHA 72	Michael	DAU	6A	
RYERSON, Jacob	WAY	149	Frederick	YOR 196	SALEHAMER, Nichs.	CUM	142	
John	WAY	145	Isaac	ADA 43	SALER, John	NOU	124	
Thomas	DEL	166	Jacob	WAS 95	SALF, John	PHI	90	
RYGARD, George	PHI	99A	Jacob	WST 224	SALFORD, John	LUZ	429	
RYLAND, Joseph	CUM	133	Jacob	FAY 247	SALIMAN, John	NOU	148	
Ludwig	BER	215	Jacob	WST 257	Joseph	NOU	148	
William	BER	168	Lewis	WAS 53	SALISBURY, Henry	LUZ	412	
RYLE, Nicholas	MNT	46	Mary	PHA 92	Joseph	LUZ	422	
RYLEA, Wm.	PHI	110	Richard	HNT 130	Memory D.	LUZ	389	
RYLEY, Eliza	PHA	56	Samuel	PHI 68	SALKELD, Peter	DEL	166	
James	PHA	65	Widow	ADA 42	John	BUC	91	
RYLEY?, Ludwick	BFD	76	William	YOR 196	SALLADAY, Daniel	BUC	150	
RYMAL, John	PHI	89	SADORUS, William	SOM 159	SALLADY, Benjn.	BUC	160	
RYMAR, David	MNT	68	William Sen.	SOM 159	Emanuel	BUC	150	
RYMEN, George	PHI	97A	SAFACOOL, Isaac	FRA 285	Emanuel	BUC	91A	
RYMOND, Jacob	BUC	139A	SAFFER, Jacob		Henry	BUC	91A	
Paul	BUC	139A	Senr.	SOM 131	Jacob	BUC	91A	
RYMORE, Ludwick	MNT	83	SAGER, Jacob	NOH 92	John	BUC	91A	
RYN, James	MER	457	Jacob Senr.	NOH 92A	SALLER, John	MNT	84	
RYNALDS, George	GRN	84	John	NOH 92	SALLYARDS,			
RYNARD, Jno.	CUM	132	John	PHI 152	William Jun.	DEL	156	
John	PHI	120	John	PHI 154	SALMON, Isaac	CHE	851	
Martin	FRA	276	Michael	PHA 74	SALOR, Mary	HNT	147	
RYNE, John	PHI	123	Nicholas	NOH 92	SALSBERRY, John	PHI	72A	
Mikl.	FRA	318	Nicholas Esqr.	NOH 92	William	DAU	32A	
RYNEARSON, Isaac	LUZ	383	Nicholas Senr.	NOH 92	SALSBERY, James	FAY	223	

SALSBERY, Saml.	FAY	224	SAMPLUGH, Josiah	DEL	164	SANDERSON, Robt.	CUM	45
SALSBURG, Henry	CUM	51	SAMPSEL, Abraham	BUC	101A	Sarah	CUM	41
Peter	CUM	51	Daniel	NOU	196	Thos.	WST	382
SALSBURY, Elias	ERI	58	SAMPSON, James	WST	195	Wm.	CUM	80
John	ERI	58	John	BEV	17	SANDFARE, Redwood	LUZ	339
SALSGAVER, Casper	CUM	152	John	ALL	66	SANDFORD, Abm.	MIF	18
SALSGIVER, George	BER	275	John	WST	195	Abm.	CEN	21
SALSMAN, Mrs.	NOU	131	Joseph	WST	195	SANDFUSSIK?,		
SALTER, Henry	CUM	43	Thomas	BEV	17	Harman	PHA	32
John	PHI	130	Thomas	ALL	63	SANDHAM, Rebeca	PHI	58
SALTER?, John	BUC	82A	William	NOU	181	SANDIS, Abraham	DAU	9
SALTERS, Saml.	PHA	90	Wm.	PHA	82	SANDO, Peter	YOR	164
Samuel	FAY	253	Wm.	PHI	72A	SANDO?, John	BFD	39
SALTGIVER, Henry	ADA	19	SAMS, Adam	WST	257	SANDOE, Charles	LAN	308
SALTSBERG?,			Fredrick	WST	257	George	LAN	244
Joseph	PHI	58	Thomas	PHI	144	SANDON, Samuel	LUZ	342
SALTSER, Conrad	FAY	217	William	BFD	46	Thomas	LUZ	337
SALTSGAVER, Andw.	CEN	21	William	BFD	47	SANDOR, James	LUZ	337
Jacob	BFD	77	SAMUEL, Conrad	BFD	76	SANDOZ, Chas.		
Jacob Jr.	BFD	77	Gilbert	WAS	72	Andw.	PHA	28
Samuel	BFD	77	Ludwick	BFD	76	SANDS, Aaron	BER	168
SALTSGIVER, Jacob	MER	459	Michael	SOM	160	Eliza.	CUM	69
SALTSMAN, Anthony	ERI	55A	William	NOH	81	Elizabeth	MNT	79
George	LYC	19	SAN DORSE?, Mr.	PHA	123	Geo.	CUM	69
John	BUT	347	SANCEBAGH,			Geo. Junr.	CUM	69
John	ERI	55A	Christr.	CUM	101	Hannah	BUC	85A
William	ERI	56	SANCEBAUGH, Jno.	CUM	132	James	BER	275
SALTZGWER, George	ADA	11	SANCHES, Philip	PHA	119	Jno.	CUM	69
SALZER, John	DAU	39	SAND, Adam	NOH	68	John	ALL	94
SALZGEBER, John	DAU	37	John	NOH	68	John	LAN	96
SAMALLY, Azariah	WAS	5	Michael	NOH	40	John	BER	174
SAMBERSON,			SANDALAS,			John W.	WAY	135
Francis	PHI	99	Valentn.	WST	278	Joseph	BER	164
SAME, George	NOH	31	SANDEL, Andrew	NOH	52	Mary	PHA	57
SAMMONS, Wm.	PHA	110	Philip	NOH	52	Michael	CHE	909
Zachria	PHA	110	SANDER, Clark	FAY	228	Olive	LUZ	396
SAMMS, Nathaniel	WAS	40	David	NOH	92A	Richard	MNT	118
SAMPEL, James	ALL	114	Durst	NOU	140	Stephen	BUC	99A
Robert	ALL	54	Frederick	NOH	76A	Thomas	ALL	60
Samuel	ALL	50	George	NOH	92	William	BUC	87A
Steel Esqr.	ALL	54	Jessee	PHI	99A	Wilm.	ALL	57
Wilm.	ALL	54	Peter	LAN	205	SANDS?, John	BFD	39
SAMPIL, John	ALL	64	SANDER?, See			SANEKY, Elizabeth	MER	460
SAMPLE, Amsan	LAN	170	Sauder	BER	171	Ezekiel	MER	460
Cunningham	YOR	201	SANDERS, Widow	PHI	99	SANFORD, Francis	BUT	339
David	MER	460	Daniel	LAN	10	Wm.	PHA	70
David	MIF	15A	Francis	PHI	53A	SANG, Charles	PHA	120
Eli	PHI	147	George	PHI	140	SANGERY, Peter	YOR	197
Eve	BER	263	Harmon	PHI	97A	SANGSTON, Isaac	FAY	224
Ezekiel	WST	296	Jacob	DAU	7	SANHIL, William	LAN	122
Frances	MIF	4	Jacob	DAU	25	SANK, Samuel	NOU	140
George	SOM	135	Jacob	PHI	79A	SANKEY, Charles	DEL	189
George	WST	382	John	NOH	49	William	MIF	4
James	BEV	11	John	LAN	98	SANKY, Anthy.	PHI	26
James	MIF	15A	John	LAN	99	SANNA, Hughh	CHE	737
Jas. Capt.	MIF	15A	John	CHE	850	SANNER, Michael	SOM	135
John	LAN	4	Joshua	LUZ	387	SANS, Andrew	HNT	141
John	ADA	20	Michael	NOU	145	Jacob	HNT	128
John	WAS	72	Paul	FAY	228	SANSFIELD, John	PHI	6
John	NOU	102	Thomas	ADA	19	SANSOM, Capdevil	PHA	80
John	NOU	107	William	PHI	141	Samuel Cenr.	PHA	26
John	HNT	165	Wm.	PHI	59	William	BFD	77
John	NOU	168	Wm.	WST	176	SANT, Douglas	PHI	5
John	CHE	740	SANDERS?, John	HNT	121	SANTEE, Christn.	NOH	49
John	MIF	15A	SANDERSON, Alexr.	CUM	46	George	NOH	72
Joseph	MIF	15A	Arthur	PHI	138	George	FAY	217
Mathew	BER	251	Ezekial	NOU	168	James	LUZ	359
Nathaniel W.	LAN	218	Geo. Junr.	CUM	46	John	NOH	72
Robt.	LYC	7	Geo. Senr.	CUM	39	John	NOH	81
Saml.	MIF	4	James	MIF	8A	John	GRN	85
Samuel	BEV	19	Jas.	CUM	46	John Junr.	NOH	34A
Sarah	WST	297	Jno.	CUM	80	Leonard	NOH	72
Wm.	BEV	6	Jno. Senr.	CUM	80	Nicholas	LUZ	355
SAMPLER,			John	YOR	210	Valentine	NOH	72
Christian	NOU	203	Mary	MIF	8A	Valentine	LUZ	355
SAMPLUGH, Bezor	DEL	164	Robert	BUC	83A	SANTHERS, Jacob	FRA	282

SANTIS, Frederic	CHE	798	SAUFMAN, Peter	NOU	125	SAWYER, Cutlip	PHI	92A
SANTON, Daniel	FAY	228	SAUL, John M.	PHI	129	Jesse	LUZ	425
SANTON?, Ebenezer	LUZ	412	Leonard	BER	227	Lowdon	PHA	122
SANTS, Jacob	NOU	102	Lewis	PHA	97	Michael	ADA	26
SANUNY, Abraham			Moses	PHI	154	SAWYERS, Wm.	MIF	26
Doctr.	FRA	273	SAUL?/ SOUL?,			SAX, Conrad	NOH	36A
SANY, John	ALL	52	John	PHI	152	John	NOH	36A
SAPLES, William	LAN	204	SAULNIER, John	PHA	20	SAXON, Charles	NOU	107
SAPP, John	BFD	59	SAULSBERRY, John	PHA	87	SAXSON, John	BUC	162
John	PHI	147	SAUNDER, Peter	YOR	178	Silas	PHI	130
SAPPLEE,			SAUNDERLIN, Saml.	NOU	203	SAXTON, David	WAS	53
Zimmerman	MNT	107	SAUNDERMAN,			James	HNT	155
SAPPLER/ SAPPLES,			Conrad	YOR	215	SAY, Benjn. M.d.	PHA	30
Andrew	MNT	70	SAUNDERS, Absalom	WAS	64	Jas.	BUT	364
David	MNT	70	Adam	NOU	173	Miles	PHI	40
SAPSON, Nicholas	NOU	195	Jacob	NOU	145	SAYER, Ann	PHA	43
SARAH, Widow	PHI	78A	Jane	PHI	54	Joseph	DAU	46A
SARBACH, Jacob	YOR	180	Joseph	PHA	52	SAYERS, David	WAS	76
SARBAUGH, David	YOR	211	Mary	PHA	57	Ephraim	GRN	68
SARCH, Wm.	LYC	22	Samuel	ERI	58A	Isaiah	GRN	66
SARCK, Christo.	DAU	50A	Stephen	WAS	64	James	HNT	161
SAREH, Stephen	DAU	36	William	PHI	9	James	DAU	2A
SARGENT, Abraham	BFD	69	William	DEL	160	Mary	ALL	76
George	FAY	248	Wm.	CUM	129	Samuel	WAS	5
Pressila	FAY	259	SAUNDERSON, Wm.	PHI	41	Thomas	GRN	103
SARGWOOD, James	PHA	66	SAUNDON, David	PHI	46	Widow	DAU	44
John	FAY	228	SAUR, Nicholas	CHE	788	SAYLOR, David	NOH	38A
SARIMORE,			SAURMAN, Martin	PHA	44	Fredk.	BER	242
Cathereen	ALL	113	Peter	MNT	63	G. Michael	SOM	131
SARN, Michael	NOU	107	SAUSER, Jacob	BER	266	Jacob	WAS	9
SARRINGS?, John	PHI	6	Michael	BER	268	Jacob	ADA	34
SARTON?, Ebenezer	LUZ	412	SAUSLE, Philip	BER	276	Jacob	SOM	150
SARTOR, Peter	WAS	113	SAUSLEY, George	FRA	276	John	PHI	110
SARVAN, Adam	NOH	61A	SAUSMAN, Sarah	PHI	74A	John	SOM	150
SARVEIR, Fredrick	ALL	116	SAUTER, Abraham	MNT	126	John	MIF	8A
Godfray	ALL	116	Christian	MNT	124	Margaret	BER	244
SARVER, Benjn.	BUT	332	Henry	MNT	126	Philip	MIF	9
Thos.	DAU	23A	Isaac	MNT	124	SAYMOINE?, (See		
SASAW?, Monsieur	PHA	88	Jacob	MNT	124	Laymoine)	CHE	909
SASERMAN, Peter	PHI	122	SAUTMAN, Jacob	DAU	30A	SAYRES, Susannah	DEL	166
SASHWOOD, Wm.	PHI	117A	SAVAG, Henry	ALL	102	SAYRIGHT, Wm.	WST	156
SASMAN, Henry	LAN	72	SAVAGE, -enes?	CHE	894	SAYRS, Ephraim	WAS	72
SASSAMAN, Andrew	BER	164	Eneas	NOU	107	SAYTHE, Jacob	WST	243
Frederick	BER	278	George	MNT	139	SAYTON, Asher	BFD	42
Fredk.	MNT	97	Jacob	PHA	63	SCABERRIN, Henry	FRA	287
Henry	BER	164	Jacob	BER	185	SCAIFE, Eliza.	PHA	92
Jacob	BUC	140	James	LAN	216	SCALLY, William	WST	257
Jacob	BER	227	Joseph	NOU	112	SCAN?, (See Sean)	NOH	48A
John	BER	164	Mary	PHI	10	SCANCE?, David	FRA	301
Mary	BER	218	Robert	MER	460	SCANDRIGE, Jean	CUM	44
SASTON, Charles	PHI	66A	Ruben	PHA	53	SCANLIN, Patrick	BUC	161A
SATE, Ulback	BFD	67	William	BER	246	Thomas	BUC	152
SATELZAM?, Peter	DAU	34	SAVALLY,			SCANNEL, Jeremiah	HNT	149
SATERY, Wm.	PHI	85	Christian	LAN	98	SCANTLIN,		
SATIA, Abraham	LYC	11	SAVEGE, George	NOU	112	Florence	CHE	843
SATTER, John	PHI	134	SAVERN?, Agness	ALL	54	SCARBROUGH, Isaac	BUC	146A
SATTERFIELD,			SAVERSON, -----	NOU	185	John Jun.	BUC	146
James	WAS	32	SAVERY, Thos.	PHA	81	John	BUC	145A
SATTERLEE,			Wm.	PHI	71	Robert	BUC	87
Benedict	LUZ	425	SAVIDGE, Edward	PHA	3	SCARLET, Benjamin	BER	249
Daniel	LUZ	429	John	PHA	103	George	WAS	83
Elisha	LUZ	425	John	PHA	122	John	BER	249
James	LUZ	420	SAWAN, Joseph	WAS	72	John	CHE	863
SATTERTHWAITE,			SAWDEN, Bernerd	NOU	107	William	WAS	83
Giles	BUC	99A	SAWER, James	PHA	96	William	BER	249
William	BUC	95	Jonas	YOR	200	William	BER	250
SAUDER, Jacob	BER	171	SAWERBEER, Henry	LAN	279	SCARVENDIKE,		
John	LAN	204	SAWERS, John	DAU	44A	Peter	PHA	97
SAUERBECK, George	NOH	38A	William	NOU	119	SCATTERGOOD,		
SAUERBEER, Henry	LAN	280	SAWHILL, John	LAN	247	Thomas	BUC	85
John	LAN	281	SAWIERS, Henry	WST	329	Thos.	BUC	138
SAUERBIG?, John	LAN	279	SAWN, Danl.	PHI	143	SCEARES, Nathan	ALL	68
SAUERWEIN, Jacob	NOH	86	SAWNISER, Mathias	MER	459	SCHAAF, Chr.		
Leonard	NOH	92A	Mathias J.	MER	459	Fred. Revd.	NOH	32A
SAUFFER,			Michael	MER	459	SCHABLER, Michael	LAN	215
Christian	LAN	142	SAWYER, Adam	DAU	3	SCHADEL, Christian	NOH	44

SCHLICHER, George	NOH	61	SCHNEBARRIGER,			SCHOLL, Elias	NOH	68
Philip	NOH	76A	John	BFD	68	John	YOR	168
SCHLICK, Jacob	LAN	205	SCHNECK, Henry	NOH	91A	Peter	NOH	63A
SCHLICKER,			Jacob	NOH	92	SCHONEBERGER,		
Christn.	MNT	135	John	NOH	92	Henry	NOH	63A
Henry	MNT	135	Peter	NOH	92	John	NOH	46A
SCHLOD, Frederick	LAN	213	SCHNEIDER, Adam	SOM	132	SCHONEBRUCH,		
SCHLOD?, Philip	LAN	213	Benedict	NOH	76A	Andreas	NOH	92A
SCHLOSSER, George	PHA	44	Christian	NOH	46	Casper	NOH	91A
George	BER	132	Conrad	NOH	76A	Jno.	NOH	92A
George Jr.	YOR	156	Daniel	NOH	92	SCHONER, Henry	NOH	61
George E.	YOR	154	Daniel	NOH	46A	Henry	NOH	61A
Jacob	NOH	91A	Daniel	NOH	69A	Peter	NOH	44
Peter	NOH	92A	Gert. Widow	NOH	32A	SCHONOVER,		
Tobias	NOH	76A	Godlieb	NOH	74A	Christopher	LYC	12
SCHLOTTER, John	NOH	57A	Henry	SOM	132	SCHOOCH, Andrw.		
William	MNT	90	Henry Junr.	LAN	204	Jr.	PHI	137
SCHMEHL, Joseph	NOH	36	Jacob	SOM	132	SCHOOLER, Jno.	CUM	132
SCHMEIER, Philip			Jacob	NOH	57A	SCHOOLEY, Jesse	FAY	237
(At Widows)	NOH	61A	Jacob	NOH	91A	Robert	WAS	40
SCHMELTZ, Andrew	LAN	189	Jno. George	NOH	46A	SCHOOLS, John	FRA	273
John	LAN	103	John	NOH	34A	SCHOONOVER,		
SCHMER, Widow	LAN	103	Mathias	NOH	87A	Abraham	LUZ	323
SCHMETTER, John	NOH	76A	Michael Jr.	NOH	61	Christopher	LUZ	399
SCHMEYER, Daniel	NOH	61	Nicholas	NOH	84A	Ezekiel	WAY	147
Daniel Jr.	NOH	61	Peter	LAN	205	Henry	LUZ	330
Jacob Junr.	NOH	61	Peter	LAN	214	John	LUZ	330
John	NOH	31	SCHNELL, John	MNT	56	Nicholas	WAY	147
John	NOH	57A	SCHNELL?, George	MNT	58	Rudolph	WAY	150
Michael	NOH	61	SCHNEP, Leonard	BER	220	Thomas	WAY	142
Peter	NOH	57	SCHNER, John	LAN	53	William	WAY	142
Philip	NOH	61	Mrs.	LAN	53	William	WAY	150
Widow	NOH	61	SCHNERR, (No			SCHOOP, George		
SCHMICK, Jacob	NOH	70A	Given Name)	NOH	51	Adam	LAN	269
SCHMID, Casper	LAN	204	George	NOH	92	Nicholas	LAN	269
Christopher	LAN	205	Jacob	NOH	92A	Nicholas	LAN	269
Conrad	LAN	204	SCHNEYDER, David	NOH	46A	SCHORG, Abraham	LAN	137
Frances	LAN	215	Frederick	NOH	51	SCHORTZ, Abraham	NOH	72
Henry	LAN	205	Henry	LAN	188	Frederick	NOH	72
Jacob	LAN	205	Jacob	NOH	84	Michael	NOH	72
SCHMIT, Abraham	NOH	86	Jacob Junr.	NOH	46A	SCHOS, Frederick	LAN	280
Daniel	LAN	146	Jacob	NOH	46A	Jacob	LAN	280
Jacob	LAN	273	John	NOH	42	SCHOTT, Dewalt	NOH	63A
Philip	NOH	86	John	LAN	190	Jacob	NOH	63A
Rudy	NOH	83	Leonard	LAN	188	James	PHI	61A
SCHMITH, Henry			Michael Sr.	NOH	61A	John P.	LUZ	318
Junr.	MNT	55	Michael	NOH	46A	Peter	LAN	116
SCHMITT, Abraham	NOH	34A	Peter	NOH	42	SCHRA-DER?, Peter	LAN	205
Adam	NOH	44	Samuel	NOH	70A	SCHRACK, George	BER	201
Anthony	NOH	32A	SCHNIEDER, Adam	MNT	92	SCHRADER,		
George	NOH	32A	SCHNYDER, Adam	PHI	140	Christophel	LAN	268
Isaac	NOH	36A	Garrett	PHI	140	SCHRAGER, Jacob	NOH	65A
Jacob	NOH	36A	Jacob	BFD	55	SCHRAM,		
Jacob	NOH	46A	John	NOH	40	Christopher	HNT	128
John	NOH	34A	John C.	PHA	113	Yost	LAN	213
John	NOH	36A	SCHOBER, Godlib	NOH	74	SCHRANTZ, George	NOH	49
Michael	NOH	34A	John	LAN	140	John	LAN	137
Philip	NOH	74A	SCHOCH, Jacob	NOH	65A	SCHRAVES, James	BFD	53
SCHMITT?, George	MNT	58	John	BER	162	SCHRECKENGART,		
SCHMOD, Jacob	LAN	215	John	NOH	65A	John	BER	283
SCHMOHL, George	NOH	92	Michael	BER	146	SCHREEVES, Jacob	HNT	159
SCHMUCK, Michael	YOR	154	SCHOCK, Christian	BER	177	SCHREIBER, Herman	NOH	91A
Solomon	YOR	156	Jacob	BER	177	Jacob	NOH	91A
SCHMUCKER, Daniel	LAN	147B	John	BER	177	John	LAN	37
SCHMYSER, George	ADA	15	SCHOF, Frederick	LAN	279	SCHREIDER,		
Henry	ADA	15	Jacob	LAN	277	Frederick	LAN	213
SCHNABEL, Andrew	NOH	40A	Jacob	LAN	278	Peter	LAN	213
SCHNABLE, George	NOH	34A	SCHOLES, John	HNT	127	SCHREINER,		
Jacob	NOH	34A	Richard	HNT	128	Elizabeth	PHA	28
Mathias	NOH	34A	SCHOLFIELD,			SCHREIVER, George	NOH	69A
SCHNAIDER, George	LAN	215	Benjn.	BUC	145A	SCHRENKENGART,		
SCHNAIDR, Henry	LAN	205	Nathan Esqr.	CHE	806	Conrad	BER	283
SCHNALL, Jacob	NOH	70A	SCHOLFIELD?,			Henry	BER	283
John, Stewart			Jonathan	PHI	153	SCHREODER, Jacob	ADA	8
Of Gnadenthal	NOH	72	SCHOLHAR, Jacob	PHI	105	John	ADA	26
SCHNEBARRIGER,	BFD	66	SCHOLL, David	NOH	44	SCHREYNER, John	LAN	187
Jacob								

SCHREYNER,		
Matthias	LAN	186
Michael	LAN	187
Michael	LAN	189
Philip	LAN	189
SCHRIBER, John	YOR	165
Michael	YOR	165
Phillip	NOU	185
SCHRICK, John	LAN	82
SCHRIHOCK,		
Christian	BFD	45
SCHRINER, Jacob	PHA	42
Philip	YOR	217
SCHRIVER, Andrew	ADA	31
George	MNT	36
John	ADA	23
Ludwig	ADA	32
Michael	ADA	43
Philip	ADA	38
Philip	YOR	172
SCHROCK, John	HNT	160
SCHRODER, Michael	NOH	69A
SCHROFF, Nicholas	LAN	257
SCHROOK, Gatrot	ADA	21
SCHROP, George	BER	157
SCHROPP, John	NOH	32A
SCHROYER, Daniel	BFD	59
George	YOR	180
SCHRUDER, John	BFD	48
SCHRY, Samuel	LAN	187
SCHRYER, Hannah	PHA	32
SCHRYOCK, John	FRA	273
SCHUBERT, Mary	NOH	57A
SCHUCK, Christian	NOH	68
Jacob	NOH	68
John	LAN	281
Philip	NOH	74
Thomas	LAN	281
SCHUCKER, Jacob	LAN	204
SCHUDE, Michael	LAN	251
SCHUGER, Baltzer	LAN	184
SCHULER, Adam	NOH	82A
Jacob	NOH	61
SCHULL, Peter	MNT	96
SCHULLER, John		
Junr.	NOH	57A
SCHULTZ, Henry	LAN	65
Johannes	LAN	274
John	NOH	81
SCHUMACHER,		
Daniel	NOH	86
Fredck.	NOH	92A
George	NOH	86
George Junr.	NOH	86
Henry	NOH	52
Jacob	NOH	52
John	NOH	86
John	NOH	76A
Peter	LAN	213
William	LAN	205
SCHUPP, Henry	NOH	49
Peter	NOH	36
Philip	NOH	36
SCHUPPERT, George	NOH	86
SCHURR, John	LAN	204
John	NOH	76A
William	NOH	76A
SCHUSLER, Conrad	LAN	185
SCHUYLER,		
Valentine	NOU	125
Valentine	NOU	125
SCHWAB, Jacob	NOH	84A
SCHWAD, Henry	LAN	96
SCHWAGER, Peter	NOH	92
SCHWAHER, John	LAN	204
SCHWAHR, John	LAN	190

SCHWALTER, John	LAN	213
SCHWANDER, Adam		
Jr.	NOH	92A
Adam	NOH	91A
SCHWAR, Joseph	LAN	93
SCHWARTZ, Abraham	NOH	61
Adam	NOH	40A
Baltzer	NOH	63A
Christian	NOH	31
Daniel	NOH	61
Daniel Jr.	NOH	61A
Daniel	NOH	57A
George	NOH	40
George	NOH	61
Isaac	NOH	61
Jacob	NOH	76A
John	NOH	54
John	NOH	81
Lowrence	NOH	40
Michael	NOH	40A
Michael	NOH	63A
Peter	PHA	43
Peter	NOH	63A
Philip	NOH	40A
Widow	LAN	19
SCHWEICKERT,		
David	LAN	213
SCHWEISHAUPT,		
Joseph	NOH	70A
SCHWEITZER,		
Casper	LAN	215
Conrad	NOH	40A
George	LAN	80
John	NOH	79
John	LAN	140
John	NOH	34A
Leonard	NOH	34A
Rudolph	NOH	40
SCHWENCK, Jacob	NOH	57
Jacob	NOH	76A
Math.	NOH	69
Valentine	NOH	54A
SCHWICKERT,		
Philip	LAN	213
SCHWINCK, John	LAN	46
SCHWNADER, Jacob	NOH	91A
SCHYBLY, John	LAN	79
SCIDMORE, John	ADA	35
SCILES, Jacob	BFD	68
SCIPLE, Henry	BUC	82A
SCNIDER, George	PHA	43
SCOBY, James	CUM	90
SCOFFIELD, Samuel	PHA	18
SCOLES, John	LAN	56
SCOLFIELD, Jesse	CHE	854
John	BUC	145A
Saml.	BUC	145A
Wm.	CHE	829
SCONTZER?, David	FRA	302
SCOT, Abraham	MER	461
Alexd.	ALL	51
Christopher	HNT	152
David	LAN	165
Hugh	ALL	54
Isaac	ALL	102
James	ALL	80
James	ALL	108
James	ALL	113
James	BER	275
John	ALL	61
John	ALL	69
John	ALL	107
Joseph	ALL	77
Joseph	MER	461
Joseph	MER	461
Joseph Esqr.	ALL	109

SCOT, Mary	ALL	81
Robert	ALL	74
Robert	ALL	114
Samuel	ALL	107
Samuel	ALL	116
Samuel	BER	158
Thomas	MER	461
Thomas	MER	461
William	PHI	135
Wilm.	ALL	61
Wilm.	ALL	66
SCOTLAND, Thomas	NOH	76A
SCOTT, Abraham	WAS	59
Abraham	GRN	85
Abraham	WAS	87
Abraham	PHA	93
Abram	ADA	4
Abram	CHE	903
Alexander	LAN	40
Alexander	WAS	46
Alexander	NOH	68
Alexander	WAS	71
Alexander	WAS	106
Alexander	MNT	112
Alexander	LAN	150
Alexander	NOU	172
Alexd.	FRA	309
Alexdr.	FRA	271
Amos	YOR	193
Andrew	WAS	17
Andrew	WST	243
Andrew	MIF	5A
Andrew	BUC	153A
Andw.	CUM	95
Anne	DAU	13
Archibald	LAN	51
Archibald	WST	297
Arthur	WAS	59
Benjamin	NOU	119
Benjn.	BUC	87
Catherine	WAS	83
Cathrine	PHA	33
Charles	WAS	17
Charles	WAS	32
Charles	NOH	79
Charles	FAY	217
Crafford	FAY	217
Daniel	LUZ	366
David	ADA	20
David	CEN	21
David	PHA	74
David	HNT	157
David	CHE	762
David	CHE	877
David Esqr.	BEV	28
David	MIF	5A
David	BUC	94A
Dick	FRA	300
Easom	WST	226
Edward	FAY	233
Elisabeth	WAS	87
Eliza.	CUM	148
Francis	WAS	32
Gawin	YOR	198
George	BEV	23
George	PHA	49
George	GRN	67
George	BUC	104
George	WST	156
Henry	LYC	8
Hugh	WAS	46
Hugh Junr.	WAS	71
Hugh Senr.	WAS	71
Issabel	PHI	53A
Jab?	PHI	79
Jacob	BUC	89

SCOTT, Jamems	WST	278	SCOTT, Mary	NOU	101	SCOTT, Wm.	FRA 308
James	ADA	8	Mathew	WAS	83	Wm.	FRA 322
James	CRA	14	Mathias	SOM	132	Wm. B. Dr.	FRA 286
James	WAS	17	Matthew	LAN	58	Zera/ Zerce?	LUZ 367
James	BEV	19	Moses	WAS	71	SCOTTEN, Samuel	BUC 83A
James	BEV	28	Moses	FRA	299	SCOUT, Aaron	MNT 65
James	PHI	51	Moses C.	FRA	296	Anthony	BUC 153A
James	GRN	65	Nehemiah	WAS	5	James	PHI 18
James	WAS	71	Night	WST	315	James	BUC 153A
James	WAS	71	Obadiah	LUZ	353	John	BUC 152
James	PHA	93	Obadiah Jr.	LUZ	353	SCOUTEN, Jacob	LUZ 343
James	WAS	106	Parker	WAS	46	SCOVELL, Edward	LUZ 426
James	ARM	127	Patrick	WAS	113	Silas	LUZ 413
James	NOU	160	Phebe	PHI	42	SCOVIL, John	BFD 54
James	HNT	165	Phebe	BUC	145A	William	BFD 77
James	VEN	168	Philip Esqr.	CHE	868	SCOVILL, James	LUZ 376
James	FRA	289	Rebecca	WAS	71	Moses	LUZ 376
James	BUT	318	Reuben	BUC	89	Orr	LUZ 407
James	BUT	355	Robert	PHA	3	SCOWTEN, John	CRA 8
James	LUZ	365	Robert	ADA	4	SCREETCHFIELD,	
James	CHE	732	Robert	MIF	4	Absolom	GRN 84
James	CHE	870	Robert	WAS	32	Arthur	GRN 72
James	DAU	21A	Robert			Nathaniel	GRN 105
Jane	HNT	151	(Farmer?)	BUC	95	SCREVES, Boston	BFD 66
Jesse	LUZ	353	Robert	PHA	110	SCREWS, James	BFD 52
Joel	DEL	166	Robert	PHA	113	SCRIBER, Peter	ADA 32
Joh	BUC	152	Robert	NOU	119	SCRITCHFIELD,	
John	ADA	9	Robert	NOU	173	William	SOM 135
John	WAS	10	Robert	DEL	178	SCROGGS, Alexr.	CUM 119
John	LYC	17	Robert	FAY	250	James	CUM 122
John	MIF	26	Robert	CHE	870	Jno.	CUM 45
John	BFD	35	Robert	BUC	94A	Rachell	CUM 125
John	PHA	37	Robt.	FRA	279	SCROGS, Allen	CRA 9
John	WAS	46	Robt. M.	FRA	310	SCROLL, Christian	YOR 167
John	PHA	52	Saml.	MIF	17A	John Sr.	YOR 167
John	WAS	59	Saml.	PHI	74A	SCUDDER, Thomas	GRN 90
John	WAS	59	Samuel	WAS	71	SCULL, Benjn.	PHA 82
John	WAS	71	Samuel Esq.	WAS	87	Isaac	DEL 163
John (Crossed			Sarah	LAN	309	James	BER 242
Out)	LAN	151	Susannah	PHA	35	Jasper	BER 242
John	GRN	112	Thomas	CUM	34	John	ALL 57
John	LAN	117	Thomas	WAS	71	SCULLEY, John	PHA 107
John	WAS	117	Thomas	HNT	150	SCULLY, Daniel	DAU 20
John	HNT	130	Thomas	HNT	157	Danil	DAU 21
John	CUM	149	Thomas	DEL	169	SCUPP, Abraham	NOH 36
John	BUC	152	Thomas	DEL	190	SCUTCHALL, Conrad	HNT 137
John	FAY	223	Thomas	CHE	841	Felty	HNT 137
John	FAY	224	Thomas	CHE	870	SEABOLD, John	MNT 101
John	FAY	237	Thoms.	BUT	350	SEABOURN, Robert	PHA 21
John	WST	243	Thos.	PHI	115	SEABRING,	
John	FAY	269	Thos.	YOR	198	Cornelius	NOH 79
John	FRA	271	Thos.	FRA	322	John	NOH 79
John	FRA	288	Widow	CUM	77	Richard	NOH 79
John	LUZ	365	William	ADA	4	Richard Junr.	NOH 79
John	CHE	841	William	BEV	5	Thomas	NOH 38A
John	CHE	880	William	ADA	7	SEABROOKS, Moses	ADA 3
John	ERI	56A	William	PHI	18	SEABURN, Daniel	WAS 51
John	BUC	154A	William	WAS	25	SEACER, Joseph	PHI 92A
Jonathan	BUC	148A	William	MIF	26	SEACHRIST, Adam	YOR 156
Jonathn.	PHI	125	William	WAS	50	George	ADA 6
Joseph	LYC	8	William	ERI	57	Jacob	YOR 156
Joseph	WAS	32	William	WAS	87	Jacob	YOR 163
Joseph	PHA	52	William	WAS	113	John	YOR 196
Joseph	WAS	59	William	WAS	113	Michael	YOR 196
Joseph	WAS	95	William	LAN	159	William	YOR 195
Joseph	WST	157	William	NOU	168	SEACRIST, Mary	FRA 307
Joseph	DEL	185	William	FAY	211	SEAFERT, Adam	YOR 176
Joseph	MIF	8A	William	FAY	211	SEAFORT, Henry	DAU 2
Josh.	FRA	308	William	FAY	217	SEAGREAVES, James	NOH 69A
Josiah	WAS	106	William	WST	243	SEAGRIST, Jacob	ADA 30
Julyana	PHA	113	William	FRA	289	SEAGUERT, Jacob	LAN 288
Katharine	BEV	25	William Esq.	ADA	7	SEAHOLTS, Lazarus	CUM 78
Margaret	BFD	39	William Junr.	WAS	71	SEAKRIST,	
Martha	PHA	33	William Senr.	WAS	71	Christn.	MIF 13A
Mary	WAS	87	Wm.	CUM	73	SEAL, Benjn.	CHE 862
Mary	BUC	89	Wm.	PHA	118	Wm.	PHI 60

SEALER, Gartrout	NOU 185	SECHMAN, John	FAY 199	SEGAFOOS, Adam	BUC 158
SEALLER, John	NOU 196	SECHRIST, George	DAU 12	George	BUC 150
Peter	NOU 196	Jacob	LAN 114	George	BUC 158
SEALS, James	GRN 67	SECK?, Henry	DAU 33	Jacob	BUC 139A
Joseph	GRN 103	SECKLE, David	PHA 76	Jacob	BUC 148A
SEALY, Abenezar	LYC 11	SECKLER, Henry	NOH 54A	Mathias	BUC 158
SEAMAN, Jacob	BER 142	Jacob	MNT 124	Stophel Jnr.	BUC 139A
John	WAS 117	SECREST, Mrs.	NOU 184	SEGAN, And.	PHI 67
John	BER 146	Peter	NOU 184	SEGAR, David	PHA 20
Joseph	WAS 117	SECRETS, Henry	MIF 26	Henry	LUZ 409
Michael	BER 142	Solomon	MIF 26	SEGENDALES?,	
Pole	PHA 76	Susanah	MIF 26	George	BER 168
William	WAS 117	SECRIST, Jacob	FRA 299	SEGER, Barbara	DAU 48
William	DEL 174	John	WST 296	David	WST 226
SEAMAN?, -----	WAY 135	Peter	HNT 136	Frederick Esq.	LAN 77
See Skaman	BER 280	Volentne	FAY 251	John	NOH 50A
SEAMORE,		SEDAM, Jno.	LYC 29	SEGLER, Henry	LAN 253
Nathaniel	PHA 111	SEDDEN, Josiah	PHA 103	Henry	LAN 254
SEAN, Peter	NOH 48A	SEDERLEN, Hugh	LAN 247	SEGNER, Andrew	NOU 169
SEANCE?, David	FRA 301	SEDERTUKE, Ph.	DAU 35	George	LAN 90
SEANOR, Micheal	WST 277	SEDGWICK, Thomas	GRN 85	Henry	LAN 269
SEAPOLE, John	CHE 835	SEDICAR, David	WAS 106	Susana	LAN 83
SEARCH, Christor.	BUC 143A	George	WAS 5	SEGRISHT,	
Elijah	NOU 173	John	WAS 106	Lawrence	DAU 42A
James	LUZ 348	SEDINGER, Casper	PHI 142	Solomon	DAU 42A
Lot	BUC 143A	SEDORAS, Joseph	CUM 104	SEGRIST, Jacob	NOU 184
Thomas	NOU 173	SEDWELL, Elisha	GRN 65	SEHLE?, Francis	LAN 81
William	NOU 132	Hugh	GRN 68	SEHLEBACH,	
Wilm.	PHI 45	SEE, Lewis	FRA 308	Stophel	LAN 270
SEARCHABLE,		SEEARD?, Stephen	BUC 89	SEHN, J.	LAN 148
Anthony	PHA 59	SEEBACH, James	DAU 34	Jennet	ADA 35
Godfrey	PHA 57	SEEBALT, Jacob	SOM 140	SEIB, George	LAN 214
SEARER, George	CUM 56	SEEBAUGH,		SEIBEL, Henry	MNT 124
SEARES, James	WAS 9	Christoph	DAU 13	SEIBENSTRICKER,	
SEARFFER, Peter	CUM 86	SEEBIRD, Joseph	WST 315	Henry	LAN 90
SEARGEANT, Eliza	PHA 72	SEEBRING, Fulkard	LYC 8	Michael	LAN 90
SEARIM, Richard	PHI 11A	John	LYC 7	SEIBER, Christn.	BER 146
SEARING, Christn.	DAU 35A	Thomas	LYC 6	SEIBERLLING,	
Ludwig	DAU 36	SEEBROKS, Richard	YOR 180	Friederich	NOH 86
SEARL, John	BUC 85	SEEBROOK, William	LAN 236	SEIBERT, Casper	BER 242
Joseph	BUC 85	SEEBROOKS, Henry	LAN 81	Francis	DAU 31
Robert	BUC 90	James	LAN 238	Frantz	BER 203
Thos.	BUC 90	William	LAN 237	Geo. & Tobias	DAU 18
SEARLE, Constant	LUZ 364	SEEBURN, Leonard	MIF 8A	George	BER 177
Rogers	LUZ 363	SEECRIST, Francis	CUM 118	Jacob	MNT 136
William	LUZ 363	SEEDS, George	CHE 806	Jacob	LAN 251
SEARLS, (See		James	ALL 65	John	BER 147
Sears,		Jonathan	CHE 709	Peter	LAN 289
Halsted)	LUZ 365	William	MER 461	Phoebe	MNT 61
SEARS, Ezekiel	WAS 5	SEEK?, Henry	DAU 33	Solomon	BER 178
SEARSCADAN, James	LYC 23	SEELEY, Samuel	LUZ 393	Tobias & Geo.	DAU 18
SEATON, Francis	GRN 90	SEELY, Abner	LUZ 403	William	SOM 135
James	GRN 90	Isaac	NOH 42	SEIBERTH,	
Robt.	CUM 115	J. William	GRN 97	Nicholas	NOH 52
Thomas	ALL 109	Job	DAU 2A	SEIBOLT, John	MNT 62
Thomas	ALL 109	Samuel	WAY 147	Peter	MNT 62
William	GRN 90	Samuel C.	WAY 145	SEIBT, Abraham	MNT 119
SEATY, Peter	BUC 101A	SEEMER, Widow	LAN 268	SEICE?, John	MNT 93
SEAVERS, John	MER 459	SEEMMON?, Jacob	YOR 169	SEICK, Peter	NOU 132
SEAWRIGHT, Samuel	BEV 23	SEENER, Michael	LAN 82	SEIDEL, Peter	NOH 46
SEBALD, John	MNT 112	SEENTEGER, Vines	PHI 34	SEIDENBENER,	
SEBASTIAN, Benjn.	MNT 100	SEERER, Conrad	DAU 26A	Christian	BER 246
Peter	MNT 100	Stophel	DAU 17A	SEIDER, Abraham	NOH 81
SEBERT, Catharine	DAU 37	SEERIGHT, Wm.	CUM 87	George	NOH 57A
SEBOLD,		SEES, Balser	DAU 4A	Gldfreidt	BER 259
Christopher	NOU 131	Christoph	DAU 4A	SEIDERS, Eve	LAN 311
Christopher	NOU 132	Jacob	DAU 5	SEIDLE, Andrew	BER 218
David	DAU 43	Jacob	BUC 160	Daniel	BER 218
SEBOLT, Abrm.	DAU 49	John	BUC 142	Godfrey	BER 278
SEBOURN, Eliza	PHA 71	Yost	BER 218	Jacob	BER 278
SEBY, John	WST 227	SEESE, George	SOM 150	John	BER 276
SECARD?, Stephen	BUC 89	Melchor	SOM 159	John	BER 278
SECHLER, Andrew	NOH 54	SEESHOLTZ, Danl.	BER 258	Michael	BER 146
Daniel	SOM 135	Jacob	BER 209	Philip	BER 276
SECHLER?, Jacob	MNT 126	SEESNAP, Adam	YOR 200	SEIFERT, Baltzer	MNT 60
SECHMAN, Jacob	SOM 159	SEFFRANS, George	YOR 157	Godfrey	BER 214

SHAFFER,		SHAFFER, Philip	BER 182	SHALLENBERGER,	
Elizabeth	PHI 49	Philip	BER 253	Jacob	MNT 76
Francis	NOU 124	Phillip	CUM 67	Jacob	FAY 199
Frederick	BER 261	Phillip	CUM 111	SHALLER, George	FRA 309
Frederick	BER 272	Phillip	WST 226	Henry	FRA 280
Fredk. Junr.	WST 225	Rudolph	CUM 86	Jacob	LAN 64
Geo.	LYC 29	Simeon	SOM 130	John	NOH 54
George	BER 281	Simon	BER 268	SHALLINGER, Jacob	LAN 287
George	BUC 82A	William	MNT 136	SHALLOTTOE,	
Henry	DAU 30	William	BER 200	George	WAS 25
Henry	MNT 63	Wm.	PHI 101A	SHALLUS, Cunrod	SOM 140
Henry	SOM 130	Zekfrit	BFD 45	Elizabeth	PHI 127
Henry	SOM 131	SHAFFNER, Casper	LAN 30	Sebastin	SOM 140
Henry	SOM 132	Casper Junr.	LAN 30	Valentine	SOM 139
Henry	NOU 155	Henry	LAN 250	SHALLY, Adam	DAU 41
Henry	NOU 203	SHAFFR, Henry	BER 286	Balzer	DAU 26
Henry	BER 253	Leonard	BER 204	John	ADA 5
Henry	BER 268	SHAFFSTALL,		John	DAU 50A
Henry Senr.	SOM 131	Daniel	DAU 6	Lukins	NOU 141
Jacob	MNT 38	Henry	DAU 6	Michael	NOH 57A
Jacob	MNT 54	John	DAU 6	SHALTER, Frantz	BER 218
Jacob	PHI 91	Peter	DAU 6	SHAMBACH, George	BUC 159A
Jacob	BUC 95	SHAFIELD, Nichs.	PHI 107	SHAMBEAU, Peter	PHI 43
Jacob	NOU 124	SHAFNER,		SHAMBO, Philip	MNT 84
Jacob	SOM 131	Catherine	DAU 15	Valuntine	MNT 84
Jacob	BER 156	Francis	PHI 147	SHAMER, Henry	HNT 131
Jacob	NOU 178	Fredk.	DAU 17	SHAMOREY, John	NOU 185
Jacob	BER 200	Henry	DAU 32	SHAMP, Amos	
Jacob	WST 223	Henry	DAU 20A	(Crossed Out)	BUC 146
Jacob	WST 243	Jacob	DAU 20A	Amos	BUC 145
Jacob	BER 262	John	DAU 21	Jese	LYC 14
Jacob	WST 296	Martin	DAU 15	SHAMWAY, Amasa	ERI 57
Jacob	NOH 50A	Martin	CHE 858	SHANAN?, (See	
Jno.	CUM 41	Nicholas	CHE 859	Sharran)	BEV 25
John	PHI 94	SHAFWOOD, Tobias	LAN 255	SHANAUER, Jost	BER 168
John	MNT 101	SHAIMAN, Mr.	LAN 288	SHANDS, John	DAU 47A
John	NOU 124	SHAIN, Timothy	BEV 27	SHANE, Casper	BUC 82
John	SOM 130	SHAIN?, John	WAS 94	George	NOU 145
John	WAY 139	Samuel	WAS 94	Moses	BFD 52
John	SOM 152	SHAKE, Jacob	LUZ 380	Thomas	BFD 52
John	BER 157	SHAKEFOOT, Jacob	BUC 87A	SHANEBAGH, Geo.	CUM 101
John	DEL 180	SHAKER, Christn.	PHI 102	SHANEFELDT, Jacob	BFD 66
John	NOU 185	SHAKY, Charles	PHI 93A	John	BFD 66
John	BER 201	SHALCROSS, John	PHI 134	SHANER, Peter	NOU 112
John	BER 218	Leonard	PHA 9	SHANET, John	PHI 29
John	WST 225	SHALER, Henry	MIF 2	SHANHOUER, Jacob	LAN 137
John	BER 268	William	WAS 10	SHANK, Adam	DAU 46A
John	LUZ 321	SHALIGE, Sharlott	FRA 274	Anthony	BUC 81
John	LUZ 331	SHALL, Andrew		Christian	SOM 155
John Sen.	SOM 152	Junr.	NOH 63A	Christian	LAN 238
John	NOH 50A	Andrew	NOH 63A	Daniel	CEN 19
Joseph	BUC 150A	George	BER 185	David	NOU 181
Lewis	NOU 196	George	BER 231	Deter	BUC 81
Ludwick	PHA 109	Michael	ARM 126	Frederick	CEN 19
Mary	SOM 159	Michael	NOH 50A	George	MNT 132
Matthias	NOU 132	Michale	ARM 126	George	YOR 170
Michael	NOU 124	Peter	NOH 63A	Henry	CUM 117
Michael	BER 130	SHALLABARGER,		Jacob	ADA 5
Michael	SOM 152	Henry	WST 157	Jacob	ADA 13
Michael	NOU 178	SHALLCROSS,		Jacob	BUC 81
Michael	NOU 185	Benjan.	PHI 134	Jacob	FAY 199
Michael	BER 231	John	PHI 155	James	DAU 21
Michael	BER 253	Joseph	PHI 155	James	SOM 130
Michael	BER 266	Joseph Docr.	DEL 168	John	DAU 20
Mrs.	NOU 178	Leonard	PHI 134	John	ADA 34
Nicholas	BER 177	Leonard Junr.	PHI 134	John	FAY 199
Nicholas	NOU 178	Thos.	PHI 134	John	LAN 233
Nicholas	NOU 181	William	PHI 135	John (David	
Peter	BER 147	SHALLE, Thomas	BER 285	Crossed Out)	CEN 19
Peter	SOM 159	SHALLEBERGAR,		Michael	DAU 46
Peter	NOU 184	Isaac	FAY 259	Michael	LAN 233
Peter	NOU 185	SHALLEBERGER,		Michael	LAN 280
Peter	BER 200	Andrew	LAN 303	Michael	DAU 42A
Peter	BER 253	Jacob	LAN 303	Michl.	CEN 19
Peter	LUZ 334	SHALLENBERGER,		Michl. Jr.	CEN 19
Philip	PHI 18	Abram	FAY 199	Philip	DAU 27

SHANK, Tobias	MER	460	SHANTZ, Jacob	MNT	59	SHARP, John	CUM 103
Widow	DAU	45	John	MNT	84	John	MNT 111
SHANKLE, Peter	NOU	181	John	LAN	256	John	YOR 155
SHANKLIN,			John	LAN	263	John	YOR 164
Catherin	FAY	211	John Junr.	LAN	256	John	YOR 202
James	FAY	269	Stophel	LAN	255	John	FAY 211
SHANKS, John	PHA	63	SHAPPEL, Jacob	BER	278	John	MER 461
John	ALL	85	Mathias	BER	276	John Esqr.	YOR 173
Matthew	FAY	211	Peter	BER	278	Joseph	PHI 39
Thos.	YOR	210	SHAPWELL, Jos.	CUM	64	Joseph	WAS 59
William	CRA	14	SHAR, Lewis	WST	224	Joseph	DEL 183
SHANKS?, John	ALL	88	SHARA, Conrod	CHE	794	Lettesia	LAN 132
SHANKWEILER,			SHARADIN, Paul	BER	178	Liddia	FAY 211
Henry	NOH	61A	SHARADON, Patrick	WST	329	Nehamia	ALL 106
SHANNAN, James	LAN	248	SHARARDIN,			Paul	ALL 94
John	WAS	59	Abraham	BER	227	Peter	WAS 72
John	LAN	248	Jacob	BER	227	Robt.	PHA 68
Thomas	WAS	59	SHARER, Adam	BUC	160	Robt.	CUM 126
SHANNEN, Charles	LAN	178	Adam Jn.	BUC	160	Saml.	CHE 766
David	NOU	168	David	LAN	11	Samuel	PHI 46
SHANNON, Andr.	FRA	284	Jacob	BER	238	Thomas	WAS 59
Daniel	NOH	65A	Ludwic	WST	227	Thomas	GRN 105
James	MNT	70	SHARFF, Geo.	BER	201	Willm.	PHI 41
James	BUC	97	John	BER	268	Wm.	LYC 22
James	CUM	133	SHARIA, Ludwig	SOM	163	Wm.	FRA 310
James	HNT	164	SHARID, Andw.	NOU	190	Wm.	FRA 311
James	CHE	841	Daniel	NOU	190	SHARPE, Moses	LAN 177
Jane	PHI	51	George	NOU	190	SHARPLES, Abram	CHE 803
John	MNT	84	Jacob	NOU	190	William	CHE 699
John	PHA	85	SHARIDAN, James	ARM	124	SHARPLESS,	
John	BUC	106	SHARK, Abrm.	DAU	52	Abraham	DEL 155
John	CUM	134	Caspar Jr.	DAU	52	Amos	DEL 168
John	LAN	287	Caspar Sr.	DAU	52	Benjaman	FAY 228
John	FRA	289	Christn.	DAU	52	Benjamin	NOU 101
John	BUT	339	Jacob	LAN	115	Benjamin	DEL 171
Jos.	CUM	128	Jacob	CEN	23A	Benjn.	CHE 805
Joseph	NOU	173	John	CEN	23A	Daniel	DEL 175
Joseph	FRA	291	SHARKLY, David	CHE	824	Daniel	DEL 180
Lanty	NOH	65A	SHARKS, Mathew	YOR	194	George	PHI 133
Leond.	CUM	126	SHARLY?, Molly	PHI	80	Isaac	DEL 189
Michl.	CHE	827	SHARM, Samuel	NOU	195	Jesse	PHA 18
Neal	ARM	127	SHARMAN, John	BER	171	Job	DEL 179
Robert	ADA	9	SHARMER, Abraham	PHI	124	John	DEL 160
Robert	BUC	97A	SHARMER?, Widw.	PHI	94A	John	DEL 175
Robt.	FRA	308	SHARP, Alexr.	CUM	122	John	DEL 176
Robt.	BUT	338	Andrew	MNT	110	John	DEL 177
Saml.	WST	175	Ann	WST	156	Jonas	DEL 163
Saml.	WST	242	Ann	HNT	160	Jonathen	NOU 112
Saml.	FRA	289	Anthony (Negro)	WAS	95	Jonathen	FAY 237
Thos.	FRA	273	Barbara	YOR	164	Joshua	DEL 175
Thos.	FRA	327	Benjn.	PHA	4	Nathan	DEL 156
Thos.	NOH	65A	Benjn.	CUM	89	Nathan	DEL 177
William	CRA	2	Christian	LAN	173	Nathan	CHE 899
William	MNT	70	Daniel	PHA	77	Natha	CHE 0
William	VEN	168	David	CUM	126	William	DEL 162
William	FRA	273	George	YOR	173	William	DEL 177
William	DAU	11A	George Junr.	WAS	59	SHARPNECK, John	GRN 96
Wm.	PHA	82	George Senr.	WAS	59	SHARPNECK?, Henry	PHI 126
Wm.	PHI	82	Hannah	PHA	45	SHARPNICK, Peter	GRN 90
Wm.	LAN	286	Henry	BFD	46	SHARR, Jacob	FRA 274
SHANON, George	ALL	70	Henry	NOU	112	SHARRA, Adam	HNT 134
Isaac	WAS	32	Hugh	HNT	163	Henry	HNT 144
Jane	DAU	24A	Hugh	FAY	206	Isaac	HNT 134
John	FRA	293	Isaac	GRN	103	Jacob	HNT 134
Joseph	ALL	64	James	PHA	88	John	HNT 144
Robert	BEV	21	James	CUM	140	Ludowick	HNT 123
Saml.	MIF	13A	James	MER	461	Mary	HNT 123
Samuel	WST	257	James	CHE	756	SHARRAH, Andrew	BFD 59
Samuel Esqr.	WAS	117	Jane	YOR	218	George	HNT 118
William	NOU	119	Jane	CHE	847	Michael	BFD 59
SHANON?, Samuel	ALL	74	Jean	LAN	301	SHARRAN, Hugh	BEV 25
SHANSE, David Jr.	LUZ	376	John	WAS	10	SHARRARDIN,	
SHANTS, Abraham	BUC	101A	John	BEV	19	Daniel	BER 228
SHANTZ, Christian	CHE	796	John	WAS	31	Peter	BER 227
Henry	MNT	84	John	MNT	53	SHARRER, John	BER 143
Isaac	MNT	58	John	GRN	66	Richard	NOU 132

SHARRON, Henry	GRN	93	SHAW., William	NOU	168	SHAW, Moses	BUC	158
SHARRON?, Samuel	ALL	74	SHAW, Mrs.	LYC	26	Moses	WST	329
SHARTEL, Bernard	DAU	38	Agusta	MER	459	Nathan	WAS	40
SHATTO, Anthony	CUM	39	Agusta	MER	461	Nethan	FAY	262
Jno.	CUM	47	Alexander	BUC	142	Nichls.	CEN	23A
John	CUM	37	Alexander	WST	329	Peter	CRA	6
SHATTS, Jacob	CUM	42	Alexd.	ALL	56	Peter	CUM	23
SHATZ, Abraham	BER	281	Alexr.	CUM	106	Ralph	PHA	10
Mary	SOM	152	Amos	BUC	142	Richard	NOH	42
Peter	BER	281	Amos	PHI	153	Richard	NOH	79
Philip	BER	281	Andrew	MER	460	Robert	NOU	169
SHATZER, John	DAU	42A	Archibald	BUC	89	Robt.	VEN	169
SHAUB, Abraham	LAN	5	Charles	CHE	758	Saml.	MIF	13
John	BER	208	Charlotte	DEL	164	Saml.	YOR	203
Valentine	BER	168	Comfort	LUZ	361	Saml.	WST	225
Widow	NOH	40A	Comfort	LUZ	378	Samuel	PHI	24
SHAUCK, John	YOR	185	Daniel	LUZ	378	Samuel	WAS	40
John	DAU	42A	David	ALL	70	Samuel	GRN	104
Michael	YOR	185	David	WAS	83	Samuel	MNT	108
SHAUER, Nicholas	BER	149	David	DEL	156	Samuel	DEL	168
SHAUFER?, George	LAN	12	David	DEL	161	Thomas	PHA	98
SHAUGH, Phillip	CUM	113	Elizabeth	WST	296	Thomas	BUC	94A
SHAUGHEN, Robert	ALL	91	Ephraim	BUC	142	Valentine	PHA	106
SHAUL, Martin	BER	285	Francis	BER	275	William	BFD	40
SHAULEE, Martin	HNT	153	Gavin	WAS	32	William	MNT	66
SHAULY, Henry	LYC	29	George	WAS	18	William	PHA	95
SHAUM, Benjamin	LAN	30	George	BUC	158	William	HNT	148
Christian	BER	268	Gideon	BUC	161A	William	HNT	157
Melchoir	LAN	61	Hamilton	NOU	200	William	BUC	158
Philip	LAN	39	Hugh	PHI	128	William	NOU	168
SHAUMAKESSEL,			Ichabod	LUZ	339	William	WST	225
Fredk.	PHI	74A	Isaiah	BUC	94A	William	MIF	13A
SHAUNER,			Israel	BUC	157A	William	ALL	70
Christian	HNT	119	Jacob	CRA	10	Wilm.	ALL	70
SHAUNSE, David	LUZ	376	James	BUC	142	SHAWER, John	NOU	184
SHAUP, Christian	LAN	221	James	BUC	142	SHAWHAN, Daniel	BUC	82
Henry	LAN	109	James	BUC	150	SHAY, Daniel	LAN	91
Henry	LAN	222	James	DEL	162	Ezekial	FAY	233
John	BER	168	James	FAY	199	George	PHA	51
SHAVELEY, Geo.			James	NOU	200	John	MNT	52
Dr.	PHI	99A	James	WST	383	John	MNT	141
SHAVELIER, Widw.	PHI	108A	James	CHE	884	Mark	LAN	56
SHAVEN?, Peter	BER	278	James	BUC	99A	SHAYER, Conrad	NOU	140
SHAVER, Adam	BFD	67	Jaret	PHA	57	SHEA, Sears	LUZ	333
Adam	HNT	120	Jedediah	LUZ	404	SHEADLE, Jno.	DAU	45
Adam	BUC	91A	Jeremiah	LUZ	419	SHEAF, Henry	PHA	85
Andr.	FRA	303	John	ALL	56	Philip	DEL	174
Andrew	BFD	59	John	WAS	106	Wm.	PHA	85
Andrew	BER	158	John	PHA	122	SHEAFER, Dorothy	ADA	35
F. John	SOM	152	John	SOM	130	Francis	ADA	31
Frederick	LAN	153	John	LAN	133	Jacob	ADA	27
George	HNT	117	John	HNT	157	Leonard	ADA	33
Hanry	ALL	118	John	BUC	158	Matthias	FRA	305
Henry (David			John	WST	296	Nicholas	ADA	27
Crossed Out)	LAN	10	John	MER	461	Peter	ADA	17
Henry	HNT	116	John	CHE	712	Sabastian	ADA	34
Henry	HNT	135	John Esqr.	NOH	42	SHEAFF, George	PHA	77
Jno.	CUM	59	John	BUC	87A	William	DEL	185
John	BFD	67	John	BUC	91A	SHEAFF?, Philip	PHI	60
John	CUM	119	Jotn	BUC	97A	SHEAFFER, Praney/		
John	HNT	127	Johnathan	MNT	37	Prancy?	CUM	67
John	HNT	136	Jonathan	BUC	142	Abraham	LAN	6
John	HNT	153	Jonathan	NOH	36A	Andrew	ERI	59A
John Jr.	BFD	52	Jonathen	FAY	262	Ben.	DAU	38
John Senr.	BFD	52	Jos.	PHI	109	Christina	YOR	156
John	BUC	94A	Joseph	WAS	25	David	LAN	39
Nicholas	HNT	135	Joseph	HNT	131	Frederick	LAN	61
Ogadiah	WAS	5	Joseph Jn.	BUC	158	Fredk.	WST	225
Peter	HNT	117	Joseph	BUC	87A	Geo.	DAU	34
Peter	HNT	133	Josiah	BUC	106	Geo.	CUM	42
Peter	HNT	136	Josiah	BUC	155	Geo.	WST	226
Philip	BFD	53	Josiah	BUC	145A	George	LAN	137
Saml.	CUM	85	Ludwig	DAU	34	Jacob	LAN	30
Samuel	LAN	9	Mary	PHI	145	Jacob	YOR	192
Sudwig	SOM	155	Mary	WST	226	Jno.	CUM	68
Thomas	WAS	47	Mathew	PHA	94	John	LAN	142

SHEAFFER, John		SHED, William	PHI 31	SHEFFER, George	LAN 82
(Shoe.?)	YOR 189	SHEDEL, George	BER 134	George	YOR 176
Michael	YOR 189	SHEDER, Augustus	BER 215	Henry	NOU 98
Philip	YOR 159	SHEDLE, George	DAU 5A	Henry	YOR 159
Philip	YOR 192	Henry	NOU 125	Henry	YOR 170
Phillip	CUM 68	Henry	BER 282	Jacob	LAN 19
Samuel	YOR 205	Michael	DAU 5A	Jacob	YOR 154
SHEAFFRY, Abm.	CUM 64	SHEDLER, Henry	BER 134	Jacob	YOR 158
SHEAFLER, Jno.	DAU 38	SHEDRONE, Jacob	ADA 35	Jacob	YOR 191
SHEAKLEY, John	ADA 7	SHEDTHER, John	FRA 281	Jacob	BER 204
SHEAKLY, George	ADA 12	SHEDWICK, Widw.	PHI 103	Jacob	BER 268
William	ADA 12	SHEDY, Peter	BER 246	Jacob Sr.	YOR 171
SHEALLY, Michl.	CUM 62	SHEE, John	PHA 74	John	LAN 26
SHEAMAN, Esabella	PHI 108A	John	ALL 98	John	LAN 64
SHEANAMAN, Isaac	WST 316	Neel	DAU 27A	John	LAN 71
SHEANEFELTER,		SHEED, Elizabeth	PHA 32	John	YOR 186
Peter	ADA 32	SHEEFF?, Abraham	MNT 84	John	YOR 188
SHEANER, Andrew	ADA 24	SHEEKS, Jacob	LUZ 382	John	DAU 13A
Daniel	ADA 5	SHEELER, John	BER 273	Jos.	YOR 208
SHEANOUR, Davd.	WST 223	Lawrence	BER 275	Leonard	NOU 178
SHEAR, George	PHI 52	SHEELY, Catharina	YOR 160	Mary	LAN 82
Yeoman	BUC 95	George	YOR 157	Michl.	BER 204
SHEARED, David	CHE 857	Jacob	ADA 21	Michl.	DAU 51A
SHEARER, Andrew	CRA 7	SHEEMER, Isaac	FAY 248	Nicholas	SOM 155
Andrew	WAS 35	SHEEN, John	PHI 75A	Nicholas	YOR 207
Fredr.	FRA 284	SHEENE, Daniel	LAN 98	Nicholas	BER 268
George	NOU 203	SHEEPHERD, Henry	WST 297	Nicols.	DAU 16A
George	FRA 297	SHEER, Robert	NOU 168	Peter	LAN 20
Henry	FRA 313	SHEERER, David	WST 277	Peter	LAN 82
Jacob	ADA 24	Jno.	LYC 27	Peter	FRA 280
Jacob	PHI 150	John	LYC 27	Saml.	BER 189
James	WAS 25	John	WST 315	Sussannah	YOR 174
Jno.	CUM 44	Joseph	WST 316	William	BER 231
John	CRA 11	SHEERS, John	PHI 73A	SHEFFEY,	
John	MNT 84	SHEESLY, Jacob	DAU 7A	Christian	MNT 74
John	MNT 116	SHEET, George	NOU 178	SHEFFLE, George	YOR 160
John Esqr.	ALL 72	SHEETS, Andrew	BFD 77	SHEFFLER, Jacob	YOR 169
John	DAU 43A	Henry	GRN 85	John	PHI 98
Jonathan	PHI 153	Jacob	HNT 127	SHEFLER, Henry	NOU 98
Paul	FRA 292	SHEETS?, John	MIF 2	SHEFLEY, Peter	FRA 303
Peter	DAU 18	SHEETZ, Adam	DAU 19A	SHEFOR, Arron	FRA 272
Peter	MNT 93	Adam	PHI 87A	SHEHAN, Michael	PHA 52
Peter	FRA 284	Catharine	DAU 30	SHEIB, Jacob	NOH 38A
Samuel	WAS 35	Catherine	DAU 12	John	LAN 48
Thomas	WAS 59	Christn Esqr.	PHI 87	Matthias	LAN 47
Thomas	WAS 106	Danl.	PHI 86A	SHEID, Christian	MNT 53
Timothy	BEV 14	George	DAU 17	George	MNT 54
Valentine	ADA 28	Henry	DAU 47	SHEIDE, Jacob	BER 142
Valuntine	MNT 116	Jacob	DAU 17A	John	BER 146
William	WAS 10	William	WAS 106	Peter	BER 146
William	CHE 728	SHEEVER, Joseph	WAR 1A	SHEIDLE?, Danl.	BER 146
Wm.	CHE 777	SHEFER, Christn.	DAU 16A	SHEILDS, Conrad	PHI 63
SHEARMAN, George	ADA 29	Conrad	DAU 8	Jas.	BUT 363
Jacob	ADA 27	Frederick	YOR 216	John	ADA 41
John	FRA 298	Fredk.	DAU 15	John	DAU 3A
Joseph	PHA 70	George	DAU 9	Mary	BEV 12
Joseph	NOU 131	Henry	YOR 194	Wm.	PHA 52
Margt.	MNT 39	Isaac	DAU 29A	SHEILEY, Henry	DAU 11
Sameul	NOU 115	Jacob	YOR 188	SHEILTER,	
Thomas	NOU 115	Jacob	YOR 196	Frederick	CHE 793
SHEARRER, Andr.	FRA 302	Jacob	FAY 217	SHEILY, Jacob	ADA 22
George	FRA 317	Jacob	DAU 36A	Jacob	ADA 26
Michl.	FRA 280	John	YOR 172	Nicholas	ADA 24
SHEARROR, Dewalt	FRA 318	John	FAY 223	Nicholas	ADA 26
John	FRA 318	Michael	DAU 20	Peter	ADA 24
SHEAT, Andw.	BER 284	Michl.	DAU 16	SHEINER, Adam	BUT 317
SHEAVER, Henry	FRA 282	Nicols.	DAU 21	Andrew	MNT 100
Peter	FRA 288	Widow	LAN 255	Jacob Junr.	MNT 101
SHEBLE, Jacob	PHA 57	SHEFFER, Adam	YOR 192	John	LAN 315
John	PHA 20	Anthony	LAN 23	SHEINER?, Jacob	MNT 61
SHECK, Lowrence	NOH 49	Anthony	LAN 25	SHEIP, Michael	BER 189
SHECKER, Jno.	CUM 149	Charles	YOR 210	SHEIRER, John	SOM 152
SHECKLES, Michael	ARM 125	Charles	BER 214	Valentine	SOM 152
SHED, Widow	PHI 41	David	YOR 194	SHEIRIG, Nicholas	LAN 315
Charles	DAU 49	Elizabeth	LAN 302	SHEIT, Christian	BER 227
George	PHI 31	Frederick	YOR 191	John	ADA 34

SHEPLEY, Daniel	BFD 68	SHERG, Joseph	LAN 313	SHETTERLY, Henry	NOU 184
David	SOM 155	Samuel	DAU 26A	SHETZ, Hismon?	FRA 286
Fredk.	CUM 147	SHERICH, Jacob	YOR 179	Michl.	PHI 90
John	DAU 9	Joseph	LAN 15	Peter	DAU 38A
Matthias	BFD 67	SHERICK, David	YOR 205	SHEURER, John	NOH 54A
SHEPLY, Amous	FAY 262	SHERIDAN, Abm.	PHI 117	SHEURY, George	NOH 54A
Charles Jur.	FAY 262	SHERIFF, John	FRA 315	Henry	NOH 54A
Daniel	FAY 262	William	NOU 144	SHEVE, David	NOU 168
Henry	FAY 247	SHERIFLER,		SHEVELEY,	
Nicholas	FAY 262	Rosanna	DAU 49A	Christian	NOU 196
Reason	FAY 262	SHERITTS,		Henry	NOU 196
William	FAY 262	Margaret	YOR 185	SHEVER, David	FAY 199
SHEPPERD, Widw.	PHI 84A	SHERK, George	DAU 37A	George	MIF 9
Benjamin	BEV 11	Jacob	LAN 303	John	MIF 5A
Cornelius	BUC 87	SHERLEN, Peter	WST 243	John	DAU 33A
Isaac	CHE 869	SHERLEY, John	BFD 66	Michael	FAY 262
Jacob	PHI 85	Richard	BFD 66	Philip	FAY 262
John	BUC 138	SHERLOCK, Alexr.	MIF 8A	SHEW, Jabush	LAN 132
John	BUC 152A	Robert	DEL 188	Jacob	CHE 907
John	BUC 160A	Robert	DEL 192	SHEWALDER, Peter	FAY 250
Jonathan	BUC 87	SHERLY, Thos.	FRA 280	SHEWALTER, Jos.	CUM 119
Joseph	ERI 60	SHERM, Peter	YOR 163	SHEWART, Wm.	FRA 278
Joseph	BUC 142	SHERMAN, Ana		SHEWAT, Widow	LAN 121
Maria	NOH 38A	Maria	BER 282	SHEWEL, Abraham	GRN 72
Nich.	PHI 84A	Conrad	YOR 185	Henry	GRN 73
Thomas	MNT 79	Robt.	PHI 102A	SHEWELL, John	BUC 106
William	CHE 886	SHERMER, Henry	PHI 125	Joseph	BUC 106
SHERADAN,		Jacob	PHI 102A	Nathaniel	BUC 154A
Dominick	PHI 26	John	PHI 124	Robert Esqr.	BUC 105A
SHERAR, Jacob	WST 225	SHERO, Francis	WAS 40	Sallow	PHA 22
SHERB, John	DAU 37	Mary	PHA 58	Stephen	PHA 26
SHERBAN, Conrad	YOR 172	SHEROK/ SHERCK?,		Walter	BUC 105A
Henry	YOR 162	Casper	LAN 7	William	NOH 38A
SHERBONDY, George	WST 296	SHEROR, Henry	FRA 283	SHEWLER, John	BUC 102
Melchor	WST 297	John	FRA 283	SHEWMAN, Henry	CUM 32
SHERDEL, John	BER 262	William	FAY 217	John	WAS 10
William	BER 263	SHERP, Henry	CRA 15	SHEWS, Thomas	CHE 857
SHERDLE, Jacob	BER 146	SHERRARD, William	GRN 67	SHEY, Edmond	FRA 313
Philip	BER 147	William	WAS 117	SHIBBNDE, John	MER 460
SHERDLE?, Danl.	BER 146	SHERRER,		SHIBBONDE, Philip	MER 460
SHERE, George	BER 253	Christian	LAN 10	SHICK, George	NOU 115
SHEREDEN, John	YOR 200	George	BER 227	George	SOM 155
SHEREFF?, Abraham	ADA 36	Jacob	BER 215	George	NOH 63A
SHEREMAN, Jacob	NOU 190	SHERRICH, John	FAY 251	Henry	MNT 101
SHERER, Abraham	YOR 167	SHERRICK,		Jacob	BUC 140
Adam	YOR 170	Christian	LAN 17	Jacob	NOH 38A
Christopher	BER 238	SHERRICK?, Adam	PHI 94A	Jacob	NOH 63A
David	YOR 207	SHERRIFF, Jacob	CUM 45	John	MNT 61
David	LAN 255	SHERROF, John	ALL 97	John	BUC 140
Dewalt	YOR 193	SHERRY, Milles	MER 460	John	NOH 38A
Eliza	PHA 66	William	LUZ 413	Widow	BUC 140
George	YOR 190	SHERTEL, George	BER 146	SHICK?, David	CEN 19
George	DAU 46A	William	BER 263	SHIDELER, George	WAS 125
Henry	NOH 44	SHERTHER, Jacob	FRA 279	Jacob	WAS 125
Henry	PHA 70	SHERTLY, John	BER 278	John	WAS 125
Jacob	DAU 19	SHERTSER, Leonard	DAU 11	SHIDLER, Peter	GRN 108
Jacob	YOR 170	SHERWOOD, Matthew	LUZ 371	SHIDMORE, John	PHI 89
Jacob	YOR 190	Zeniah	LUZ 372	SHIED, John	MNT 53
Jacob	YOR 193	SHERY, John	YOR 183	SHIEDER, Henry	LAN 32
Jacob	YOR 194	SHETALL, Daniel	PHA 87	SHIEFFLER,	
Jacob Jr.	YOR 193	SHETH, William	PHI 33	Christopher	BER 238
Jacob	DAU 46A	SHETHERAN, John	FRA 280	SHIELD, John	LYC 24
John	PHI 74	SHETITO, George	CRA 13	SHIELDS,	
John	FAY 206	SHETLER, Jacob	YOR 172	Alexander	WAS 76
John	LAN 255	SHETLY, Michael	YOR 174	Andw.	MIF 13A
John	DAU 20A	SHETRENE, David	YOR 172	Arthur	FRA 317
Joseph	NOH 43A	SHETRONE, John	ADA 37	Charles	PHA 63
Michael	BER 189	John	ADA 39	David	WST 163
Nicholas	BER 238	SHETSLINE, John		Francis	MIF 13A
Philip	YOR 212	Junr.	PHI 88A	George	ALL 75
Samuel	DAU 18	SHETTELA, Michael	BER 263	James	PHA 111
Theobold	YOR 194	SHETTER, Michael	LAN 103	James	HNT 124
Volentine	PHA 87	SHETTER?,		James	WST 329
SHERER?, William	NOU 132	Catharine	YOR 215	James	WST 351
SHEREY, George	YOR 192	SHETTERLY, Andw.	NOU 184	James	CHE 773
SHERFY, Jacob	ADA 8	George	NOU 184	James	MIF 13A

SHOUCH, Matthias	NOU 141	SHRAAK, John	SOM 131	SHRIVER, Henry	PHI 115
SHOUER, Henry	BER 204	John	SOM 140	Henry	FRA 296
Peter	BER 203	John Sen.	SOM 140	Henry	PHI 104A
Philip	BER 203	SHRACK, Abm.	PHA 42	Jacob	GRN 72
SHOUFLER, Chr.	DAU 36	Adam	MNT 85	John	GRN 72
Valentine	DAU 36	Daniel	MNT 61	John	GRN 78
SHOUGH, Henry	FRA 281	David	MNT 84	John	YOR 157
SHOUK, Jacob	MNT 92	Henry	BER 268	John	LAN 231
Joseph	FAY 247	Jacob	MNT 84	Lewis	ADA 8
SHOUKS, Jacob	GRN 84	John	NOU 196	Michael	YOR 158
SHOUL, Adam	NOU 132	SHRADER, Widw.	PHI 80	Nicholas	ADA 37
SHOULTS, Jacob	FRA 324	Engel	NOU 190	Philip	YOR 172
SHOUNSE, David	LUZ 377	John	MNT 75	SHRIVES, Marey	FAY 211
SHOUP, Abraham	BFD 66	SHRADY, John	PHI 86	Richard	FAY 211
Conrad	FRA 288	SHRANCE, Peter	NOU 107	SHROAK, George	YOR 170
Frederic	SOM 155	SHRANDER?,		SHROCK, George	CHE 910
Henry	BFD 66	Christopher		George	DAU 28A
Henry	HNT 124	H.?	PHA 123	Jacob	PHI 74
Jacob	SOM 159	SHRANK, Barny	PHA 63	John	SOM 159
John	BEV 10	SHRAP, Isaac	CHE 862	SHRODER, Otho	SOM 132
John	FAY 199	SHREADER, Anthony	BER 231	SHROEDER, Daniel	
John	FRA 301	Engle	BER 231	Revd.	YOR 181
John	NOH 65A	Jacob	BER 183	Henry	BER 218
Peter	SOM 163	SHRECK, Henry	PHI 86A	SHROFE, Emanuel	WST 243
Philip	MIF 13A	Paul	NOU 132	SHROLL, George	LAN 6
SHOUP?, George	PHI 85A	Phillip	NOU 132	SHROM, Casper	YOR 157
SHOUPE, Jacob	HNT 119	SHRECK?, John	YOR 160	Christma	DAU 3A
Jacob	HNT 136	SHRECONCUST, Geo.	DAU 50	Henry	DAU 31
SHOUR, John	HNT 139	SHREDER, Jacob	DAU 6A	Jacob	YOR 157
SHOUSE, Christian	WAS 72	Philip	MNT 84	John	YOR 176
Henry	WAS 72	William	YOR 158	John Jr.	WST 224
Jacob	NOH 38	SHREDLY, Andw.	DAU 19A	Joseph	CUM 99
Philip	MIF 8A	SHREEDOR, Aaron	WST 278	Nicolaus	DAU 31
SHOUT, D.	MIF 13A	SHREEK, Adam	BER 266	SHRONK, Godfry	PHI 119A
John	MIF 13A	Benjamin	NOU 132	John	PHI 87
John	MIF 13A	SHREFLER, Charles	NOU 124	SHROON, John	WST 224
John	MIF 13A	SHREGER, Gersham	MNT 84	SHROOP, Henry	PHI 106
SHOVATTER?, Jos.	WST 296	William	MNT 84	SHROP, Andrew	BER 263
SHOVELS, Samuel	HNT 131	SHREIBER, Geo.	BER 284	Andrew Jr.	BER 260
SHOVER, Boston	CUM 39	Peter	YOR 157	Christian	LAN 136
Michael	BER 186	SHREIDON, James	CUM 39	John	BER 263
SHOW, Cunrod	SOM 147	SHREINER, Martin	LAN 27	SHROUD, James	FAY 228
Jacob	WST 242	SHREIVER,		SHROUT, John	LAN 150
Jacob	FAY 269	Frederick	LAN 103	SHROY, Frederick	LAN 110
SHOWAKER,		Jacob	YOR 157	Samuel	LAN 217
Frederick	PHI 130	SHREIVES, Caleb	PHI 68A	SHROYER, John	GRN 85
Jacob	PHI 129	SHREN, Andw.	DAU 12A	John	NOU 124
John	PHI 141	SHRENK/ SHRINK?,		Leoanrd	NOU 124
SHOWALDER, Jacob	LAN 72	John M.	PHA 57	Mrs.	NOU 124
John	LAN 72	SHRENK, John	MNT 84	Philip	BUC 140
Valentin	LAN 72	SHRENK?, Abraham	MNT 74	Philip	SOM 152
SHOWALTER,		SHRIDE, Jos.	PHI 121	Phillip	NOU 124
Christian	BEV 7	SHRIDER,		SHRUK?, See	
Danl.	CHE 856	Christian	LUZ 426	Shreek	BER 266
Jacob	CHE 856	Christo.	DAU 30	SHRUM, Barney	PHA 58
John	CHE 831	John	LUZ 411	SHRYER, Widow	PHI 71A
Joseph	BEV 28	SHRIEVER, Peter	PHI 111	Adam	BUC 150
Joseph	CHE 859	SHRIEVES, John	PHI 66A	Philip	BUC 139A
Peter	BUC 91A	SHRIEVS, John	FAY 268	SHRYHOCK, John	BUT 328
SHOWALTER?, Jos.	WST 296	Samuel	FAY 268	SHUART, David	CHE 853
SHOWER, Adam	NOU 140	SHRILL, Henry	PHI 79	SHUBERS, John	PHI 82
Adam	NOU 185	SHRINER, Barney	LAN 113	SHUBERT, John	PHI 8
Christ-.	LAN 253	Christn.	PHA 51	John	BER 154
David	CUM 47	Henry	NOU 196	Melchor	BER 282
Michael	NOU 185	John	PHA 64	SHUCK, David	NOH 54A
Peter	PHI 146	John	LAN 99	George	SOM 152
Phillip	NOU 140	John	NOU 172	Jacob	NOU 140
SHOWERS, Andw.	DAU 12	Nicholas	NOU 196	Jacob	SOM 155
SHOWICK, Widow	PHI 94A	William	LAN 99	John	LAN 98
SHOWLAW, Christ-.	LAN 253	SHRINER?, Jacob	MNT 61	Phillip	NOU 140
SHOWMAN, David	SOM 130	SHRIOR, David	FAY 217	Simeon	SOM 139
George	FAY 206	John	FAY 217	SHUCKENGAST, Jno.	BER 282
SHOYHS?, Jonathan		SHRIVER, Widow	YOR 158	SHUCKER, Henry	BER 218
V.	ALL 77	Danl.	CUM 148	Henry	BER 285
SHRAAK, Casper	SOM 140	Frederick	PHI 133	John	BER 253
Christian	SOM 150	George	GRN 78	John	BER 285

SHUCKMAKER, Jacob	NOU	132	SHULL, Phillip	FRA	276	SHULZ, Henry	DAU	10A
SHUDER, Christian	NOU	125	Samuel	SOM	131	Jacob	DAU	15
SHUE, John	BER	154	SHULLE?, Wm.	PHI	68	Valentine	DAU	25
SHUEMAKER, John	FAY	217	SHULLER, Abraham	NOH	57	SHUM, Henry	BER	180
SHUEMAN, John	FAY	247	George	NOH	57	SHUMAN, Daniel	NOH	54A
Phillip	FAY	224	John	NOH	57	Fredk.	BER	282
SHUETZ, Conard	PHI	123	Sam.	NOH	57A	John	LAN	59
SHUEY, Christn.	DAU	52A	SHULLIS, Charles	PHI	49	John	BER	131
Conrad	MIF	8A	SHULLMAN, Jacob	NOU	178	John	YOR	218
Fredk.	DAU	24	SHULLNOT, Joseph	SOM	141	John Jr.	YOR	218
Henry Jr.	DAU	35A	SHULS, David	LAN	314	Mathias	BER	142
Henry	DAU	35A	John	DAU	31A	Peter	BFD	67
Jacob	DAU	24A	SHULTER, Adam	WST	195	Peter	BUC	150
John	ADA	25	Conrod	WST	195	Simon	BER	282
John	DAU	50	Conrod	WST	224	SHUMBERGER,		
John	DAU	23A	SHULTS, Andr.	FRA	305	Nichs.	CUM	60
Ludwig	DAU	35A	Henry	HNT	116	SHUN, James	CHE	716
Martin	DAU	51	SHULTZ, Widow	PHI	33	SHUNER, John	CHE	785
Michl.	DAU	24A	(No Given Name)	LAN	53	SHUNK, Christian	MNT	74
Michl.	DAU	24A	Abram	MNT	135	Francis	MNT	84
Peter	ADA	7	Adam	WAS	35	Peter	CHE	783
SHUFFLER, George	WST	223	Andrew	BER	208	Simeon	SOM	140
Godfrey	BER	204	Balser	BER	249	SHUNK?, Abraham	MNT	74
SHUFFLETON,			Baltzer	MNT	135	SHUP, Andrew	NOU	160
George	WAS	25	Cathrine	CUM	97	George	DAU	7A
SHUFNER, Charles	FAY	239	Christn.	MNT	135	Jacob	DAU	7A
SHUGAR, Jacob	BER	210	Christn.	BER	238	Martin	LAN	112
SHUGARS, Eli	CHE	776	Conrad	YOR	181	SHUPARD, Philip	PHI	140
SHUGART, Barnit	PHI	125	Danl.	BER	242	SHUPE, Casper	YOR	218
Harman	CUM	44	David	MNT	135	Henry	DAU	20
Simon	PHI	96	David	MNT	136	Jacob	CUM	55
SHUGERT, John	CHE	745	David	BER	208	Jacob	BUC	140
SHUK, Adam	FRA	313	Elizabeth	YOR	162	John	DAU	20A
Peter	FRA	313	Emanuel	BER	267	Widow	BUC	101A
SHUKE, John	LAN	256	Fredk.	YOR	181	SHUPERT, Christn.	MNT	108
Martin	LAN	266	George	ADA	25	Christn.	MNT	139
Peter	WAS	47	George	SOM	139	SHUR, James	FRA	279
SHUKER, Tobias	BER	268	George	SOM	155	John	NOU	177
SHUL, Simon	DAU	37	George	HNT	163	Leonard	WAS	35
SHULDS, John	NOU	190	George	BUC	101A	SHURLOCK, William	NOH	68
SHULE, Peter	YOR	211	Gregory	MNT	135	SHURMAN, Thomas	FRA	293
SHULER, Adam	YOR	163	Henry	YOR	182	SHURR, Danl.	BER	284
Andrew	NOU	141	Henry	YOR	218	Michael	MNT	105
Benjamin	LAN	55	Henry	BER	236	SHURT, Fredk.	PHI	3
Christn	CUM.	119	Henry	DAU	8A	SHURY, John	NOU	178
Gabriel	MNT	91	Henry E.	BER	215	SHUSS, George	YOR	190
George	ADA	22	Herman	PHA	45	SHUST, Phillip	NOU	150
George	DAU	13A	Jacob	SOM	152	SHUSTER, Widw.	PHI	71
Jacob	LAN	61	Jacob	YOR	154	Adam	PHI	111A
Jacob	PHI	108	Jacob	BER	238	Andw.	PHI	72A
Jacob	DAU	4A	James	YOR	168	Daniel	WAS	5
John	BER	208	John	DAU	13	Gerhart	WST	195
John	DAU	27A	John	MNT	68	Jacob	MNT	140
Nicholaus	DAU	13	John	BER	207	John	MNT	97
Samuel	MNT	90	John Jr.	YOR	166	John	PHI	141
William	CHE	783	John	CEN	23A	Jonathan	DAU	13A
SHULINBERGER,			Joseph	ADA	33	Joseph	CRA	6
Henry	FRA	318	Laurence	WAS	35	Leonard	DEL	170
SHULL, Charles	FRA	302	Laurence	HNT	154	Peter	DAU	12A
David	NOU	107	Lawrence	YOR	154	Samuel	WAS	113
David	FRA	302	Melchoir	MNT	112	SHUT, John	WST	316
Frederick	ADA	40	Michael	SOM	135	John	CHE	785
Fredk.	CUM	39	Michael	YOR	190	SHUTE, Daniel	PHA	97
Fredrick	PHA	41	Nicholas	SOM	140	William	LAN	31
George	WST	224	Nicholas Jun.	SOM	139	SHUTE?, Ab.	DAU	34
Henry	CUM	96	Peter	SOM	135	SHUTER, Polly	PHI	115
Jacob	YOR	189	Peter	YOR	162	SHUTLER, Saml.	FRA	320
Jacob	WST	224	Peter	YOR	163	Widow	CUM	149
Jacob	PHI	119A	Peter	YOR	181	SHUTLZ, John	ADA	42
John	ADA	5	Peter Jr.	YOR	181	SHUTS, Daniel	NOU	150
John	ADA	11	Philip	SOM	152	SHUTT, Henry	CHE	854
John	CUM	31	Valentine	YOR	163	Jacob	BUC	106
John	SOM	131	Valentine	YOR	215	John	WST	225
Leonard	PHI	141	William	BER	238	Wendle	BER	151
Peter	ADA	20	Yost	YOR	171	SHUTTS, Christian	LAN	222
Peter	NOU	107	SHULZ, Elizabeth	DAU	31A	SHUTZ, Andrew	BUC	160

SHUTZ, Barbara	MNT 139	SIDLES, Peter	VEN 167	SIGRIST, Michael	LAN 305
Francis	MNT 139	SIDMAN, Isaac	NOH 38A	SILAS, Abraham	PHA 65
Henry	MNT 108	SIDNER,		SILBAUGH, William	SOM 147
Jacob	LAN 61	Christopher	HNT 144	SILEMAN, Alexr.	NOU 203
Justus	MNT 92	SIDWELL, Abram	CHE 869	John	NOU 203
SHUTZER,		Abram	CHE 887	SILENCE, Wm.	PHI 91
Christopher	LAN 54	Conrad	LAN 167	SILER, John	DAU 43A
SHWOP, George	GRN 79	James	FAY 233	SILERS, Peter	HNT 124
SHYDER, Abm.	MIF 17A	Joab	CHE 867	SILEYS, John	WST 195
SHYHART, Enoch	GRN 110	Joab	CHE 868	SILFISE, Henry	NOH 36A
SHYLEY, Henry	LAN 182	Levi	LAN 151	SILFUS, John	NOH 63A
SHYMER, Samuel	NOH 44	SIDWEN, Edward	LAN 228	SILFUSE, Peter	NOH 65A
SHYNN, James	CHE 911	SIEBERT, George	LAN 140	SILICK, Ohn	PHI 28
SIBBET, Solomon	WAS 5	SIEDNER, Philip	MNT 79	SILIMAN, Thos.	NOU 203
SIBBET?, John	BUC 152A	SIEGEL, Henry	NOH 63A	SILK, James	YOR 196
SIBBETS, Aaron	WAS 125	Peter	NOH 74A	SILKS, David	CUM 31
SIBERT, Francis	LAN 97	SIEGER, John	NOH 86	SILL, Aaron	DEL 172
George	PHI 38	John Junr.	NOH 86	Adam	CHE 720
John	DAU 18	Samuel	NOH 92	Edward	CHE 880
SIBERT?, Joab	FRA 296	SIEGFRIED, Daniel	NOH 31	George	BFD 76
SIBIT, Jonathan	BUC 146A	Isaac	NOH 74A	James	DEL 172
Thomas	BUC 146A	Jno. (See		John	BFD 76
SIBLY, Jacob	MNT 139	Siegfried,		John	NOU 140
Jacob	PHI 101A	Widow)	NOH 31	John	CHE 882
Ridolph	MNT 139	Joseph	NOH 31	Michael	BFD 76
SIBS, Michael	PHA 38	Widow Of Jno.	NOH 31	Michael	CHE 877
SICHER, David	NOH 57A	SIEGFRIEDT,		William	DEL 172
SICKEL, Daniel	FAY 206	Andrew	NOH 92	William	CHE 720
John	BUC 162A	Andrew	BER 238	SILLARS, Henry	MIF 11A
SICKENHIME, Peter	CHE 793	Daniel	NOH 92A	SILLEY?, Jacob	MNT 41
SICKFRED, Michl.	WST 225	Peter	NOH 92	SILLS, John	HNT 153
SICKFRET, Jacob	FRA 282	SIEGLIN,		Joshua	ALL 75
SICKFRIET, Abm.	WST 224	Frederick	NOH 36	SILLYMAN, Alexr.	NOH 68
SICKLE, Lawrence	PHA 18	Henry	NOH 36	David	NOH 68
SICKLER, John	MNT 126	SIEGLY, John	NOH 76A	James	BER 280
SICKMAN, Barnet	WAS 46	SIEGRFIED, Widow		Thos. Junr.	NOH 40
Dietrich	NOH 40	Of Abm.	NOH 31A	Thos. Senr.	NOH 40
George	ALL 88	SIFERT, Michael	CHE 791	SILSBY, Elijah	LUZ 363
Jacob	NOH 38A	SIFFEE?, Betsy	PHI 87A	Reuben	LUZ 363
SIDDINGER, Maths.	PHI 137	SIFFERHELD, Widow	PHI 76	SILSON, Samuel	NOU 161
SIDDON, John	HNT 136	SIFFERS, Jacob	BER 174	SILURT?, Joab	FRA 296
Jos.	PHI 106A	SIFRIEDT, George	BER 249	SILVE, Thomas	BUC 107A
William	DEL 162	Jacob	BER 249	SILVER, George	PHI 136
SIDDONS, Benj.	YOR 209	SIGAFOOS, Jacob	ADA 16	Henry	MNT 46
Henry	DEL 169	SIGER, John	NOH 52	John	PHI 105A
John	PHI 9	SIGFREIDT, Geo.	BER 242	SILVERGOOD,	
SIDEBENNER,		Henry	BER 227	Daniel	CHE 721
George	SOM 131	Jacob	BER 227	SILVERS, Jas.	CUM 61
SIDEL, Andrew	NOU 107	John	BER 227	SILVERTHORN,	
Peter	NOU 102	SIGFRIED, George	PHI 96	Agness	MIF 9
SIDENBENDER,		Jacob	BER 246	James	ERI 58
Margaret	BER 150	Joseph	BER 246	Jno	MIF 5A
SIDENS, Samuel	NOU 112	SIGFRIEDT, Daniel	BER 227	Thomas	ERI 58
SIDER, George	DAU 47	Jacob Jr.	BER 228	William	ERI 58
SIDERS, Barbara	DAU 16	Peter	BER 226	SILVERWOOD, James	NOU 102
Jacob	DAU 16	SIGGINS, George	CEN 23A	SILVESTER, Saul	CHE 759
John	DAU 16	John	CEN 23A	SILVEY, Jacob	BUT 337
Peter	DAU 16	SIGH, Jacob	WST 242	Jno.	BUT 337
SIDES, Betsy	ADA 30	SIGHISER?, Andw.	PHI 96A	SILVEYS, David	WST 195
Daniel	LAN 109	SIGHT, George	CUM 115	SILVIUS, Abraham	BUC 160
George	LAN 216	John	CUM 116	Henry Jn.	BUC 160
George	LAN 224	SIGLER, Adam	MIF 17A	Jacob	BUC 87
Henry	BFD 35	Felex	ALL 70	William	BUC 160
Jacob	ADA 30	Fredrick	ALL 69	SIM, James	PHI 37
Jacob	LAN 222	George	MIF 18	Thomas	BUC 91A
John	LAN 110	George	WAS 76	SIMAD, Robert	PHI 51
Peter	LAN 243	George	FRA 305	SIMANSON, Wm.	CHE 772
Wm.	PHI 77A	Henry	MIF 18	SIMAREL, Sarah	WST 258
SIDINGER, George	PHI 126	Jacob	PHI 103A	SIMBLER, Gasper	
SIDLE, George	DAU 4	John	MIF 18	Revd.	WAS 35
George	YOR 210	Saml.	PHI 107	SIMBS, James	ALL 58
Godfrey	CUM 29	SIGMON, George	CHE 909	SIMCOCK, Shadrach	WAS 32
Jno.	CUM 63	SIGMUNE, Jacob	PHI 52	SIMCOX, Abraham	FRA 285
John	PHA 75	SIGN, George	BUC 142	Elias	CHE 701
SIDLELMAN, Mary	PHA 80	SIGNS, William	YOR 214	Emmor	BER 287B
SIDLER, Simon	NOU 155	SIGRIST, Conrad	LAN 186	Emmor	BER 287B

SIMCOX, William	CHE 715	SIMON, Widow	PHI 80	SIMPSON, John	HNT 140
SIMENTON, Widow	DAU 23A	Christn.	CUM 42	John	PHI 144
SIMERAL, Alexr.	WST 257	Henry	PHI 1	John	WAY 145
SIMEREL, William	ARM 126	Jacob	PHI 3	John	YOR 212
SIMERMAN, Henry	HNT 116	John	PHA 7	John	CHE 748
Jacob	NOU 102	John	YOR 189	John	PHI 11A
Jacob	NOU 155	John	NOH 31A	John	BUC 94A
Mich.	DAU 35A	John	NOH 38A	John	BUC 145A
SIMERS, Jessy	ALL 119	John	NOH 40A	Jonathan	LAN 246
SIMESTON, Robert	NOU 119	Joseph	LAN 30	Joseph	PHA 115
SIMINGTON, James	PHA 63	Michael	NOH 38A	Joshua	WST 225
Thos.	NOU 132	Peter	LAN 88	Luke	WAS 95
Thos.	BUC 146A	Peter	PHI 125	Mathew	ALL 66
SIMISON,		Philip	PHI 120A	Matthew	LAN 246
Catharine	CUM 41	SIMONETT, Stephen	PHA 97	Michl.	YOR 218
Saml.	MIF 8A	SIMONS, Andrew	WAS 125	Nathaniel	BER 273
SIMITTIN, Alexr.	MER 460	Assa	BER 214	Nathl.	CEN 23A
Wm.	MER 460	Frederick	BFD 59	Ned	FAY 233
SIMKINS, George	LUZ 408	Henry	FAY 254	Robert	WAS 25
SIMLER, Henry	CEN 23A	Jacob	GRN 112	Robert	ALL 53
SIMLY, John	NOU 115	John	BFD 41	Robert	BFD 77
SIMMEL, George	NOH 92	John	PHA 80	Robert	ALL 109
John	NOH 92	Jonah	PHA 83	Robert	WST 157
SIMMENS, Leeson	PHA 20	Mercy	NOH 32A	Robert	YOR 160
SIMMER, John	FRA 285	Michael	WAS 5	Robert	WST 258
SIMMERMAN, Adam	DAU 9A	Michael	WAS 106	Ruth	MNT 101
Christian	DAU 9A	Michael	WAS 125	Samuel	MNT 116
Christley	HNT 148	Nicholas	WAS 125	Simeon	WAS 64
Fred	DAU 9A	Thomas	BFD 41	Stephen	GRN 108
George	WAS 46	SIMONSON, Adams	FAY 253	Thos.	WST 225
George	NOU 101	Edward	DEL 158	William	MNT 36
Henry	NOU 102	F. G.	VEN 166	William	BUC 152
Jno.	DAU 35	John Esqr.	WAS 117	William	LUZ 337
John	DAU 33A	William	DEL 158	William	BUC 145A
SIMMERS, Geo.	DAU 40	SIMONTON,		Wilm.	ALL 98
SIMMINS, Hill	PHI 70	Benjamin	NOH 68	Wm.	BUC 146A
William	MER 461	James	NOH 68	SIMRAL, John	ALL 71
SIMMON, Henry	DAU 39	John	GRN 90	SIMS, Ann	PHA 102
John	YOR 178	Peter	NOH 68	Conrad	BUC 82
SIMMONS, Mr.	PHA 77	Thos.	CUM 41	Cornelius	LUZ 346
Anthony	PHA 16	SIMPKINS, Amous	FAY 228	Daniel	LUZ 345
Catharine	PHA 81	SIMPLE, William	MIF 19	Henry	PHA 55
David	WAS 35	SIMPSEN, George	PHA 4	John	FAY 224
Edward	PHA 42	SIMPSON, Adriel	LUZ 423	John	LUZ 345
George	WST 163	Alexander	WAS 18	Joseph	PHA 122
George	LAN 176	Alexander	DEL 160	Philip	PHI 126
George	FAY 206	Ambrose	PHI 109	Sarah	PHA 68
Henry	BUC 89	Andrew	ALL 99	Walter	BUC 84
Isaac	PHI 16	Charles	PHA 118	William	MIF 26
Jacob	CHE 838	Daniel	CHE 859	William	LUZ 361
James	PHA 85	David	SOM 130	William	MIF 8A
James	BUC 94A	David	FRA 295	SIMSON, James	HNT 151
Jehu	CHE 839	David	BUC 145A	James	VEN 165
John	LYC 18	Elizabeth	ALL 98	John	PHA 107
John	FAY 237	Hannah	PHA 48	John	HNT 156
John	BUC 161A	Isaac	LAN 246	John	LAN 159
Joseph	PHA 79	James	WAS 25	John	HNT 160
Joseph	PHA 97	James	PHA 87	Matthew	HNT 155
Joseph	LAN 119	James	LAN 133	Robert	HNT 155
Laurence Junr.	WAS 35	James	BUC 152	Thomas	CHE 720
Laurence Sr.	WAS 35	James	WST 157	William	HNT 166
Ridgbill	WAS 40	James	WST 157	SIN, Christian	LAN 285
Robert	LAN 119	James	FRA 296	SINAFF, Jacob	PHA 61
Simon	WAS 35	James	MER 460	SINCKEL, Jacob	NOH 76A
Stephen	PHA 99	James Revd.	MIF 2	SINCLAIR, Angus	HNT 150
Stephen	PHI 69A	James	PHI 11A	James	WAS 10
Thomas	BEV 7	James	PHI 11A	James	YOR 195
Thomas	CHE 713	James	BUC 153A	James Jr.	YOR 195
Wm.	PHA 39	Jas.	BUT 353	John	NOU 132
Wm.	PHA 63	Jesse	NOU 107	John	NOU 145
Wm.	PHA 64	Jno.	CUM 148	John	YOR 199
Wm.	CHE 839	John	MNT 52	Joseph	NOU 145
SIMMS, Benjamin	GRN 92	John	GRN 66	Neal	NOU 140
Elizabeth	LAN 122	John	BUC 87	Saml. Esqr.	CHE 840
James	WAS 117	John	NOU 98	William	WAS 25
SIMON, Widow	PHI 56	John	BUC 106	William	WAS 25

SINCLARE, James	PHA	74	SINKLAR, Sameul	ALL	71	SITLER, Conrad	BER	253
SINCLEAR, John	LAN	50	Samuel	ALL	73	George	FRA	291
SINCLER, William	CHE	776	SINN, George	CHE	825	Henry	BER	253
SINDWEL, Isaac	DAU	12A	Henry	PHI	102A	Jacob	BER	131
SINE?, George	MNT	42	Thos.	PHI	98	Jacob	YOR	198
SINEFIELD, John	FRA	291	SINNACK, Isaac	PHA	72	SITTINGER,		
SINER, Adam	NOU	155	SINNER, Mary	PHA	112	Abraham	BUC	142
George	NOU	155	SINNOFT, George	PHA	80	John	BUC	142
Jacob	PHI	91A	SINSENICH, John	LAN	87	SITTLE, Godlips	CUM	79
Philip	PHI	91A	SINSKY, John	FRA	274	SITTLER, George	NOH	54A
SINET, Mely	PHI	36	SINTON, Jacob	NOU	98	Philip	NOH	54A
SING, Jacob Junr.	PHI	3	SIPE, Jno.	CUM	70	SITZ, George	NOU	196
Jacob Senr.	PHI	3	John	CUM	104	Joseph	NOU	203
SINGEL, George	NOH	46	Peter	SOM	150	SITZREVES,		
SINGER, Abm.	PHA	18	Peter	YOR	167	Susannah	PHA	8
Christian Jnr.	NOH	36A	Philip	YOR	174	SIVELLEY, Michael	PHA	23
Christian	NOH	36A	Philip	YOR	218	SIVELLY, Henry	NOH	74A
Conrad	DAU	20	Tobias	YOR	170	SIVER-T?, Adam	MIF	5A
David	LAN	186	Tobias	YOR	172	SIVERLING, Daniel	CRA	10
Frenny	DAU	21	SIPELER, Jane	BUC	89	SIVERLUNG,		
George	PHI	26	Mathias	BUC	89	Christopher	CRA	8
Henry	CUM	76	Philip	BUC	89	SIVERS, John	BUC	95
Jacob	DAU	21	SIPES, Charles	BFD	40	SIVERS?, Edman?	FRA	282
John	DAU	21	Emmanuel	HNT	128	SIX, Adam	GRN	72
John	PHA	42	George	BFD	46	Henry	GRN	78
John	MNT	46	Henry	BFD	46	Jacob	DAU	26A
John	ALL	90	Henry Junr.	BFD	46	SIZE, Andrew	PHA	78
John	BER	157	Jacob	BFD	46	SKAD, Mary	PHI	49
John	NOH	36A	Michal	BFD	46	SKAMAN, Ludwig	BER	280
Martin	LAN	144	SIPLE, David	PHI	144	SKEEL, David	LUZ	372
Mathias	DAU	21A	George	BUC	97A	SKEER, Israel	LUZ	334
Michael	DAU	9	SIPO?, Conrod	FRA	320	SKEILS, Thomas	LAN	80
Nicols.	DAU	18A	SIPPLINGER, Henry	YOR	184	SKEIN, Abraham	MNT	84
Peter	MNT	86	SIPS, Philip	LYC	29	Samuel	MNT	84
Philip	NOH	36A	SIPS?, Matthias	ERI	60	SKEIN?, Peter	MNT	84
Simon	DAU	20	SIRETON, George	PHI	82	SKELETON, James	CEN	19
Simon	WST	227	SIRVISIN,			SKELLEY, Philip	SOM	163
Widow	LAN	47	Christina	LAN	172	SKELLY, Geo.	CUM	134
SINGERLY, George	PHI	97A	SISER?, John	MNT	93	Jacob	CUM	68
SINGERS, John	WAS	87	SISHOLS, Phillip	NOU	102	John	SOM	163
SINGHOUSE,			SISL, John	BUC	161A	Michael	SOM	163
Abraham	WAS	17	SISLE?, James	PHA	84	SKELLY?, Thos.	PHA	79
SINGIN, Thomas	FAY	206	SISLY, Jacob	FAY	269	SKELTON, Aaron	CHE	740
SINGLE, Jno. &			Lewis	FAY	268	George	CHE	767
Gible	DAU	38	SISNA, John	ALL	51	Jesse	BUC	151A
SINGLES, William	CHE	700B	SISOM, Ann	BUC	83A	John	BUC	87
SINGLETON, Widow	PHI	19	Joseph	BUC	85A	John	BUC	145A
John	SOM	135	SISOM?, William	BUC	84	Joseph	BUC	145A
Thomas	PHI	13	Wm. Junr.	BUC	84	Mary	DEL	180
William	CHE	802	SISOR, John	FRA	310	Owen	DEL	178
SINGLEWOOD,			SISSEL, Isaac	FAY	199	Owen	DEL	179
Stephan	PHI	124	SISSNY,			William	WAS	40
SINGLEY, Andrew	BUC	89	Theophilus	HNT	141	SKEMERON, John	BFD	46
SINGLY, Widow	NOH	51	SISTERS, Jacob	FAY	259	SKERANS, Robert	PHI	53A
SINGMASTER, Adam	NOH	61A	SISTLER, Michl.	FRA	319	SKIGGAN, Fergus	WAS	14
Daniel	BUC	157A	SITELMYON,			James	WAS	14
George	BUC	101	Godfrey	NOU	178	John	WAS	14
John	BUC	101	SITER, Elizabeth	FRA	297	SKILER, James	FRA	290
SINIFF, Andw.	YOR	188	George	DEL	179	SKILES, Harman	LAN	229
SINK, Abraham	PHA	24	Jacob	DEL	184	James	ALL	117
Cutlip	PHI	93A	John	DEL	184	Peter	FRA	309
Edward	PHA	119	SITERS, John	CHE	858	SKILLEN, Willm.	BUT	338
Henry	DAU	28A	Sarah	DEL	183	SKILLIN, Saml.	BUT	339
John	PHI	3	Sarah	CHE	835	SKILLING, Johon	LYC	23
John	SOM	150	SITES, Henry	FRA	300	SKILMIN, George	MNT	63
John	CHE	909	Henry Senr.	FRA	300	John	MNT	63
Lawrence	PHA	119	Jacob	YOR	166	SKILMIRE, John		
Leonard	BER	249	Jacob	YOR	171	Junr.	MNT	63
Martin	BER	203	Jacob	FRA	300	SKIMER, Frederick	CHE	782
Tobias	PHI	93A	Jno.	CUM	101	Frederick	CHE	856
Widow	BFD	69	Michael	YOR	171	SKINK, John H.	WAY	139
SINKEY, Abraham	WAS	50	Philip	YOR	171	SKINNER, Daniel	WAY	138
Jeremiah	CEN	21	Saml.	CHE	902	Daniel Jr.	WAY	138
Saml.	CEN	21	SITGREAVES, Saml.			Ebenezer	LUZ	399
Wilm.	ALL	105	Esqr.	NOH	38A	Elizabeth	PHA	47
SINKIN, Danl.	CHE	878	SITHGOW, Ann	DEL	164	George	SOM	144

369

SKINNER, Henry	PHA	27	SLAPPISH, Yost	BER	146	SLEMMONS, Robert	ADA	6
James	FAY	241	SLASHMAN, Peter	PHI	99A	Thomas	LAN	127
John	SOM	144	SLASMAN, John M.	PHA	27	SLEMMONS?, Robt.	WST	297
John	FRA	316	SLATER, Anthony	PHA	89	SLEMONS, Samuel	WAS	59
John	FRA	320	Casper	MNT	131	Thomas	WAS	14
Joseph	WAY	138	Henrey	FAY	241	William Esqr.	WAS	59
Nathan	WAY	138	Henry	GRN	65	SLENCE, Catharine	ADA	26
Nathaniel	FAY	241	Isaac	FAY	241	Jacob	ADA	22
Reuben	ERI	59	Jacob	MNT	131	Phillip	ADA	22
Rheuben	WAY	138	John	LAN	44	Widow	ADA	31
Richard	FAY	241	John	NOU	172	SLENGER, Andw.	YOR	172
Robert	SOM	144	Joseph	FAY	241	Jacob	YOR	204
Robert Sen.	SOM	144	Martha	WAS	50	SLENKER, Henry	BER	186
Rubin	FAY	241	Martin	FAY	241	Jacob	YOR	206
Samuel	SOM	144	Samuel	FAY	241	John	BER	189
Samuel	FAY	241	Thomas	GRN	66	John	BER	189
Thomas	LUZ	357	Thomas	WAS	113	Martin	YOR	204
William H.	WAY	138	Thomas	PHA	122	SLENNETT, Wm.	CHE	746
Willis	SOM	144	William	WAS	50	SLENTS, George	PHA	75
Wm.	FRA	323	SLATHERRER, John	PHI	105B	SLESMAN, Henry	PHA	35
SKIPPER, William	BFD	66	SLATSHAW, John	YOR	179	SLETE?, Elizabeth	DAU	8
SKIPTON, Mattw.	MIF	26	SLATTER, Philip	NOH	86	SLETLE, Daniel	BER	231
SKIRAN, John	PHA	35	Valentine	NOU	132	SLEYERWALD,		
SKOOL, Francis	DAU	49A	SLATUN, Anna			Andrew	NOH	76A
SKOWDON, Randal	WAS	25	Maria	LAN	50	SLICE, John	CHE	856
SKOYKS?, Jonathan			SLATZER, Michael	YOR	204	SLICK, John	BFD	77
V.	ALL	77	SLAUCH, Christian	LAN	204	William	BFD	77
SKULLY, Edward	PHI	21	SLAUGHTER, John	DEL	163	SLICKTER, Andrew	BUC	159A
SKYELS, John	WST	382	Samuel	DEL	162	SLIDER, Fredk.	CHE	906
SKYHAWK, Timothy	HNT	125	SLAUTER, Jacob	PHI	118A	Jacob	YOR	211
SKYLER, Henry	LAN	127	John	ALL	74	SLIEFF?, Casper	BER	168
Samuel	LAN	131	John	PHI	115A	SLIFE, Fredk.	WST	226
SKYLES, Widow	WST	351	SLAVEN, Brian	WAS	83	SLIFFER, David	BUC	148A
James	WST	383	William	BFD	41	Haney	BUC	148A
John	CHE	776	William	PHI	137	Jacob (Crossed		
Thomas	WAS	113	SLAWYER, Henry	CHE	782	Out?)	BUC	148A
William	CHE	776	SLAY, Francis	NOU	200	Jacob Junr.	BUC	148A
Wm.	WST	315	SLAYBAUGH, George	ADA	16	SLIGHTER, John	MNT	74
SLACK, Abm. Jnr.	BUC	99A	Henry	ADA	15	Nicols.	DAU	31A
Abraham	NOU	107	Peter	ADA	17	SLIHOFF, Philip	PHI	89
Abraham	BUC	99A	William	ADA	15	SLIKER?, Eleanor	PHI	54
Bernard	BUC	138	SLAYBERGER,			SLING, Margaret	PHA	57
Cornelius	BUC	138	Christr.	CUM	68	SLINGHUFF, Jos.	PHI	92
Cornelius	BUC	99A	SLAYER, Jacob	CHE	892	SLINGLOFF, John	MNT	117
Danl.	PHI	80	SLAYMAKER, Amos	LAN	130	Samuel	MNT	116
George	CHE	756	Daniel	LAN	227	SLIPPY, Margaret	HNT	126
Jacob	NOU	107	John	LAN	227	Michl.	CUM	58
James	BUC	99A	John Senr.	LAN	229	SLIVER, Abm.	BUC	148A
James	BUC	107A	Matthias	LAN	227	Henry	BUC	157A
Jane	BEV	22	Widow	LAN	227	Jacob	BUC	106
Jesse	CHE	744	William	LAN	227	John	BUC	97A
John	GRN	85	William	LAN	227	Michael	CEN	21
John	BUC	152	William	LAN	229	SLOAN, & Wilson	PHA	27
John	FAY	262	SLAYTOR, John	BUT	319	Alexr.	DAU	23A
John	BUC	99A	SLEAHORT?,			Anthony	YOR	199
Joseph	BUC	152	Christn.	PHI	94A	Archabald	CRA	15
Philip	WAS	5	SLEAR, Charles	NOU	132	David	ARM	122
Rachel	BUC	152	SLEASMAN, John	CHE	800	Henry	WST	316
SLADER, James	CUM	32	SLEBACH, George	LAN	271	James	ARM	122
SLADRIA?, Chrisn.	MNT	68	Philip	LAN	270	James	WST	316
SLAEGLE, Henry	HNT	160	SLECKER, Christn.	MNT	96	James	CHE	734
SLAGE, George	MIF	4	SLEET-?, David	PHI	63	Jno.	BUT	361
SLAGLE,			SLEGEL, John	BER	253	Jno.	DAU	34A
Christopher	ADA	32	SLEGLE,			John	LYC	22
Daniel	ADA	35	Christopher	NOU	125	John	PHI	56
David	ADA	32	John	BER	246	John	GRN	65
Henry Esqr.	ADA	32	SLEGOR, George	YOR	170	John	BFD	77
Henry Jun.	ADA	36	SLEIGH, Peter	LYC	9	John	WST	316
Jacob	ADA	33	SLEIGHER,			John	WST	329
John	ADA	33	Laurence	BFD	59	John	WST	351
John	YOR	182	SLEIGHTER, Daniel	FRA	315	John Junr.	WST	315
SLANEGAR, Daniel	HNT	122	John	FRA	315	Margret	WST	257
SLANTER, John	PHI	117	Michl.	CHE	794	Patrick	LAN	227
SLAPP?, John	NOH	40A	SLEMAN, Matthias	LAN	85	Robert	DAU	3
SLAPPISH, Danl.	BER	146	SLEMMONS,			Robert	GRN	67
Geo.	BER	146	Margaret	LAN	127	Saml.	BUT	357

SMISER, Martin	YOR	155	SMITH, Anthony	BFD	53	SMITH, Conrad	DAU	36A
SMIT-?, Saml.	FRA	298	Anthony	GRN	103	Conrod M.	CUM	63
SMITGER, Abm.	DAU	34A	Anthony Junr.	GRN	103	Cornelia	PHA	105
SMITH LESHER?,			Arby	LUZ	390	Crhistopher	BER	278
Jno.	PHI	46	Archibald	ARM	127	Daniel	MNT	53
SMITH, Mr.	PHA	93	Archibald	CHE	750	Daniel	BFD	77
Widow	PHI	30	Augustine	HNT	123	Daniel	PHA	92
Widow	PHI	32	Balshaser	BUC	150	Daniel	NOU	168
Widow	PHI	95	Baltzer	LAN	66	Daniel	NOU	181
Widow	YOR	176	Barney	FAY	224	Daniel	FRA	273
Widow	WST	329	Benj.	YOR	215	Daniel	FRA	283
Widw.	PHI	104	Benjamin	PHA	53	Daniel	NOH	57A
Widw.	PHI	106	Benjamin	BUC	87	Danl.	LYC	13
(No Given Name)	YOR	202	Benjamin	GRN	90	Danl.	LYC	15
Aaron	BEV	8	Benjamin	GRN	90	Danl.	WST	351
Aaron	MNT	141	Benjamin	NOU	144	Danl.	PHI	83A
Aaron	BUC	142	Benjamin	NOU	160	Danl.	PHI	120A
Aaron	DEL	157	Benjamin	DEL	191	Danniel	ALL	69
Abigal	PHA	10	Benjamin	LUZ	336	David	WAS	71
Abm.	CUM	42	Benjamin	LUZ	376	David	CUM	75
Abraham	WAS	40	Benjamin H.	DEL	174	David	CUM	86
Abraham	NOH	49	Benjm.	PHI	62	David	BUC	87
Abraham	BUC	107	Benjn.	CUM	109	David	WAS	105
Abraham	ARM	124	Brice	MIF	26	David	ALL	109
Abraham	FRA	295	Caleb	ADA	25	David	VEN	168
Abraham	WST	296	Carolus	LAN	250	David	NOU	185
Abraham	LUZ	347	Casper	BER	208	David	NOU	196
Abraham	MER	460	Casper	YOR	215	David	FAY	211
Abraham	CHE	757	Casper	YOR	217	David	LUZ	376
Abraham	ERI	59A	Casper	DAU	3A	David	LUZ	377
Abram	CHE	814	Cathn.	DAU	20	David	NOH	65A
Adam	PHI	39	Charles	ADA	22	David	BUC	141A
Adam	CUM	42	Charles	LAN	43	Davis	DEL	169
Adam	ADA	43	Charles	BFD	67	Detrich	BER	132
Adam	CUM	43	Charles	PHA	92	Devalt	PHA	69
Adam	CUM	66	Charles	DEL	179	Dinnes	GRN	103
Adam	WAS	113	Charles	YOR	186	Diodet?	LUZ	364
Adam	HNT	117	Charles	LAN	254	Doctor	CHE	887
Adam	ARM	122	Charles	DAU	27A	Easter	CUM	86
Adam	CUM	145	Charles	PHI	74A	Ebenezer	WAS	31
Adam	PHI	146	Charles	BUC	94A	Edmond	BUC	151A
Adam	NOU	178	Charrly	ALL	98	Edward	PHI	23
Adam	NOU	190	Chas.	LYC	15	Edward	PHA	46
Adam	YOR	194	Christian	NOH	46	Edward	ALL	61
Adam	NOU	195	Christian	NOH	52	Edward	ALL	83
Adam	BER	201	Christian	BFD	54	Edward	LAN	96
Adam	BER	222	Christian	MNT	132	Edward	YOR	206
Adam	BER	268	Christian	BUC	158	Edwd.	PHA	62
Adam	FRA	313	Christian	YOR	167	Eliahim	PHI	99
Adam	CHE	834	Christian	YOR	204	Elias	FAY	253
Adam	DAU	16A	Christian	FAY	224	Elijah	BUC	146
Adam	NOH	78A	Christian	LAN	291	Eliphalet	LUZ	364
Aitken	CEN	23A	Christian	LAN	310	Elisha	BUT	365
Alexander	WAS	24	Christiana	WST	257	Elisha	BUT	367
Alexander	WAS	31	Christn.	PHI	87	Elizabeth	PHA	7
Alexander	PHI	82	Christopher	BFD	53	Elizabeth	PHA	18
Alexander	PHA	92	Christopher	MNT	66	Elizabeth	ALL	61
Alexr.	LYC	6	Christopher	WAS	87	Elizabeth	DEL	168
Alexr.	ADA	33	Christopher	WST	257	Elizabeth	WST	176
Alexr.	CUM	113	Christopher	BER	267	Elizabeth	LUZ	357
Ananias	LUZ	336	Christopher	CHE	782	Emanuel	ADA	44
Andrew	ADA	31	Christopher			Emmanuel	GRN	112
Andrew	BFD	55	Jnr.	CHE	781	Ephraim	LAN	122
Andrew	BFD	56	Church	ARM	127	Ephraim	LUZ	390
Andrew	WAS	113	Clement	PHI	138	Esther	WAS	59
Andrew	WAS	113	Conrad	ADA	12	Ezra	MNT	140
Andrew	BER	278	Conrad	ADA	13	Ezra	BUC	152
Andrew	BER	281	Conrad	CEN	21	Felty	FAY	223
Andrew Jr.	YOR	164	Conrad	DAU	28	Fergus	WST	351
Andrew Sr.	YOR	164	Conrad	ADA	39	Frances	FAY	217
Andw.	CUM	55	Conrad	MNT	47	Francis	NOH	40A
Andw.	CUM	145	Conrad	BFD	53	Francis J./ I.?		
Andw.	YOR	194	Conrad	MNT	136	Esqr.	NOH	79
Ann	CUM	89	Conrad	BER	162	Frantz	BER	180
Ann	DEL	186	Conrad Senr.	ADA	39	Fred.	BER	242
Anthoney	FAY	237	Conrad	MIF	15A	Frederic	CHE	791

SMITH, Frederick	ADA	30	SMITH, Henry	CUM	110	SMITH, Jacob		SOM	147
Frederick	WAS	40	Henry	MNT	119	Jacob		SOM	155
Frederick	PHA	91	Henry	HNT	137	Jacob		DEL	158
Frederick	PHI	125	Henry	CUM	139	Jacob		BER	189
Frederick	LAN	217	Henry	YOR	172	Jacob		NOU	190
Frederick	LAN	254	Henry	YOR	175	Jacob		YOR	191
Frederick	LAN	285	Henry	NOU	200	Jacob		BER	201
Frederick	FRA	293	Henry	YOR	208	Jacob		YOR	207
Fredk.	PHI	101	Henry	FRA	303	Jacob		YOR	207
Fredk.	PHI	62A	Henry	FRA	303	Jacob		FAY	217
Fredrick	PHA	27	Henry	FRA	305	Jacob		WST	226
Fredrick	FAY	217	Henry	CHE	782	Jacob		BER	260
Gabriel	ADA	34	Henry	CHE	853	Jacob		BER	268
Garret	LUZ	399	Henry Junr.	MNT	53	Jacob		BER	272
Gasper	GRN	72	Henry Junr.	MNT	119	Jacob		FRA	273
Geo.	LYC	14	Henry	DAU	27A	Jacob		FRA	276
Geo.	CUM	65	Henry	NOH	50A	Jacob		WST	296
Geo? (Crossed			Henry	NOH	54A	Jacob		FRA	305
Out)	LYC	15	Henry	NOH	61A	Jacob		FRA	314
George	MIF	2	Henry	BUC	83A	Jacob		FRA	317
George	DAU	17	Henry	BUC	148A	Jacob		CHE	794
George	PHA	27	Hezekiah	LUZ	372	Jacob		CHE	890
George	DAU	37	Honyost	BUC	148A	Jacob Jr		BER	268
George	ADA	39	Hugh	PHI	24	Jacob Junr.		MNT	59
George	NOH	40	Hugh	PHA	68	Jacob Junr.		MNT	90
George	PHI	40	Hugh	CUM	80	Jacob		MIF	13A
George	WAS	40	Hugh	NOU	107	Jacob		DAU	15A
George	ADA	42	Hugh	CUM	139	Jacob		DAU	21A
George	PHA	54	Ichabod	GRN	90	Jacob		DAU	23A
George	PHI	62	Isaac	PHI	96	Jacob		NOH	38A
George	BFD	77	Isaac	WAS	105	Jacob		NOH	57A
George	BUC	82	Isaac	LAN	228	Jacob		NOH	57A
George	BUC	106	Isaac	FRA	310	Jacob		PHI	67A
George	MNT	110	Isaac	CHE	858	Jacob		BUC	101A
George	NOU	125	Isaac	CHE	877	Jacob		BUC	157A
George	ARM	126	Isaac	NOH	38A	Jacob R.		CUM	38
George	HNT	127	Isabella	PHA	95	Jacobus		BER	132
George	PHI	128	Issiah	FRA	287	James		MIF	2
George	BUC	158	Jack	LAN	314	James		ADA	9
George	YOR	190	Jacob	PHI	4	James		LYC	11
George	WST	195	Jacob	WAS	9	James		WAS	14
George	YOR	198	Jacob	MIF	13	James		WAS	14
George	FAY	223	Jacob	ADA	14	James		LYC	19
George	LAN	223	Jacob	ADA	26	James		PHI	20
George	WST	224	Jacob	CUM	26	James		CEN	21
George	WST	226	Jacob	ADA	39	James		PHI	23
George	BER	227	Jacob	CUM	39	James		WAS	24
George	FAY	228	Jacob	PHI	41	James		BEV	27
George	FAY	247	Jacob	BFD	46	James		CUM	28
George	FRA	283	Jacob	NOH	51	James		WAS	46
George	WST	315	Jacob	BFD	53	James		PHA	47
George	NOH	69A	Jacob	BFD	53	James		WAS	59
George	PHI	75A	Jacob	PHA	55	James		BFD	77
George	PHI	86A	Jacob	PHI	58	James		CUM	84
Gideon	NOU	200	Jacob	PHI	58	James		PHA	85
Godfrey	PHA	36	Jacob	LAN	59	James		CUM	92
Griffith	MNT	140	Jacob	MNT	59	James		WAS	94
Hannah	MNT	59	Jacob	BFD	66	James		PHA	97
Harriet	PHA	94	Jacob	BFD	66	James		NOU	98
Henrey	FAY	199	Jacob	MNT	71	James		WAS	113
Henrey	FAY	223	Jacob	PHI	87	James		WAS	113
Henry	DAU	21	Jacob	MNT	90	James		HNT	121
Henry	ADA	26	Jacob (Phillip			James		SOM	132
Henry 2nd	MNT	59	Crossed Out)	FAY	224	James		PHI	136
Henry	WAS	40	Jacob	BUC	102	James		HNT	137
Henry	NOH	46	Jacob	GRN	104	James		WAY	150
Henry	MNT	47	Jacob	GRN	108	James		NOU	155
Henry	BFD	53	Jacob	MNT	114	James		YOR	155
Henry	MNT	53	Jacob	PHA	115	James		DEL	158
Henry	CUM	56	Jacob	PHI	123	James		NOU	160
Henry	MNT	58	Jacob	NOU	124	James		DEL	161
Henry	WAS	59	Jacob	HNT	128	James		DEL	161
Henry	CUM	69	Jacob	PHI	131	James		HNT	163
Henry	PHA	73	Jacob	PHI	135	James		WST	175
Henry	MNT	97	Jacob	SOM	140	James		YOR	202
Henry (See	NOH	78A	Jacob	PHI	147	James		FAY	233
Smith, Widow)									

373

Name	Ref
SMITH, James	FAY 250
James	FRA 318
James	BUT 353
James	MER 460
James	MER 461
James	CHE 741
James	CHE 774
James	CHE 864
James Esqr.	WST 157
James	MNT 105
James	BER 287B
James	BER 287B
James	MIF 8A
James	CEN 23A
James	BUC 97A
James	BUC 139A
Jane	WST 226
Jane	BUT 351
Jane	CHE 700
Jashua	CHE 758
Jemimah	PHA 56
Jene	DAU 2A
Jeremaiah	BER 280
Jeremiah	NOH 61
Jeremiah	NOU 144
Jeremiah	BUT 331
Jesse	BUT 327
Jesse	LUZ 340
Jno.	CUM 70
Jno.	PHA 76
Jno.	CUM 90
Jno. (Shoemr.)	CUM 94
Jno.	CUM 124
Jno. Junr.	CUM 107
Jno.	DAU 30A
Jno.	DAU 45A
Job	GRN 103
Joel	LYC 29
John	MIF 2
John	LYC 8
John	MIF 9
John	PHI 9
John	ADA 11
John	BEV 11
John	ADA 12
John	LAN 14
John	WAS 14
John	CRA 16
John	BEV 17
John	PHA 19
John	BEV 27
John	DAU 28
John	PHI 30
John	PHI 37
John	ADA 39
John	BFD 39
John	NOH 42
John	PHI 43
John	LAN 45
John	MNT 46
John	CUM 47
John	PHA 47
John	ALL 49
John	NOH 49
John	PHA 51
John	WAS 53
John	BFD 54
John	PHA 54
John	ALL 55
John	MNT 58
John	PHI 58
John	WAS 59
John	NOH 61
John	PHI 63
John	GRN 66
John	GRN 67
SMITH, John	PHA 71
John	ALL 76
John	BFD 77
John	NOH 79
John	PHA 79
John	PHA 83
John	PHA 83
John	PHA 86
John	LAN 87
John	NOH 88
John	CUM 89
John	MNT 91
John	WAS 94
John	WAS 94
John	CUM 95
John	ALL 97
John	CUM 99
John	CUM 102
John	WAS 105
John	LAN 106
John	MNT 106
John	BUC 107
John	GRN 108
John	ALL 109
John	ALL 110
John	PHA 111
John	CUM 112
John	CUM 115
John	PHA 118
John	PHI 120
John	PHI 121
John	PHA 122
John	ARM 124
John	HNT 126
John	ARM 127
John	HNT 127
John	BER 132
John	NOU 132
John	HNT 138
John	NOU 140
John	NOU 141
John	NOU 141
John	NOU 141
John	PHI 141
John	BUC 142
John	SOM 144
John	SOM 144
John	WAY 147
John	NOU 148
John	BER 149
John	BER 149
John	CUM 149
John	BER 153
John	YOR 154
John	DEL 155
John	WST 157
John	BUC 160
John	DEL 165
John	NOU 168
John	NOU 168
John	WST 175
John	BER 177
John	BER 180
John	DEL 181
John	DEL 185
John	DEL 186
John	YOR 190
John	YOR 194
John	YOR 198
John	YOR 200
John	YOR 209
John	YOR 209
John	YOR 210
John	YOR 213
John	FAY 217
John	FAY 217
SMITH, John	LAN 217
John	LAN 221
John	FAY 223
John	WST 227
John	FAY 237
John	FAY 241
John	BER 246
John	FAY 247
John	BER 249
John	FAY 250
John	FRA 276
John	FRA 283
John 2nd	MNT 59
John	LAN 304
John	WST 315
John	FRA 321
John	FRA 327
John	LUZ 357
John	LUZ 404
John	MER 459
John	CHE 709
John	CHE 727
John	CHE 728
John	CHE 767
John	CHE 777
John	CHE 799
John	CHE 802
John	CHE 819
John	CHE 844
John	CHE 877
John	CHE 909
John	PHI 98
John Esqr.	ARM 124
John Jnr.	CHE 746
John Jun.	NOH 61
John Junr.	NOH 52
John Junr.	NOH 54
John Junr.	WAS 105
John Junr.	YOR 194
John Junr.	NOH 63A
John Revd.	WAS 25
John Sen.	WAS 94
John Senr.	NOH 54
John Senr.	WAS 105
John (Weaver)	YOR 199
John	MIF 5A
John	MIF 13A
John	MIF 15A
John	DAU 30A
John	DAU 42A
John	NOH 61A
John	NOH 63A
John	NOH 65A
John	PHI 69A
John	NOH 76A
John	PHI 79A
John	PHI 96A
John	BUC 107A
John	PHI 109A
John	BUC 141A
John	BUC 145A
John	BUC 148A
John	BUC 157A
John	BUC 161A
John S.	PHA 96
John V.	LAN 96
Johnn.	LYC 14
Jonas	WAS 40
Jonas	LUZ 423
Jonas	PHI 67A
Jonathan	PHA 10
Jonathan	WAS 31
Jonathan	BUC 107
Jonathan	DEL 186
Jonathan	FAY 247
Jonathan	WST 257

SMITH, Jonathan	LUZ	346	SMITH, Martin	LUZ	346	SMITH, Peter	MNT	47
Jonathan B.	PHA	33	Mary	PHA	55	Peter	DAU	51
Jos.	YOR	195	Mary	PHA	55	Peter	BFD	52
Jos.	BUT	351	Mary	NOH	68	Peter	NOH	57
Joseph	DAU	5	Mary	PHA	96	Peter	MNT	60
Joseph	PHA	10	Mary	PHI	113	Peter	NOH	61
Joseph	BEV	12	Mary	SOM	155	Peter	BFD	76
Joseph	CRA	16	Mary	DEL	158	Peter	PHI	81
Joseph	LYC	21	Mary	PHI	86A	Peter	NOU	98
Joseph	PHI	32	Mason	PHA	67	Peter	ALL	103
Joseph	CUM	34	Mathew	ALL	90	Peter	NOU	125
Joseph	NOH	42	Mathias	PHA	36	Peter	PHI	129
Joseph	WAS	46	Mathias	BUC	142	Peter	NOU	131
Joseph	MNT	54	Mathias	BER	268	Peter	SOM	131
Joseph	MNT	59	Matthias	BFD	76	Peter	BER	138
Joseph	NOH	68	Matthw.	BUT	337	Peter	SOM	140
Joseph	BUC	87	Melchior	NOH	61	Peter	BER	157
Joseph	WAS	94	Melchior	BER	135	Peter	YOR	163
Joseph	MNT	96	Melchoir	BFD	66	Peter	BER	189
Joseph	LAN	121	Melchoir	MNT	125	Peter	NOU	200
Joseph	MNT	139	Michael	CUM	28	Peter	YOR	207
Joseph	NOU	150	Michael	NOH	46	Peter	WST	257
Joseph	BUC	152	Michael	NOH	69	Peter	BER	262
Joseph	WST	195	Michael	NOU	132	Peter	BER	269
Joseph	FAY	233	Michael	NOU	132	Peter	LAN	270
Joseph	FAY	233	Michael	PHI	142	Peter	FRA	281
Joseph	BER	253	Michael	NOU	168	Peter	LAN	285
Joseph	FAY	269	Michael	NOU	168	Peter	FRA	322
Joseph	WST	278	Michael	YOR	175	Peter	CHE	858
Joseph	WST	297	Michael	NOU	196	Peter Junr.	CUM	63
Joseph	WST	352	Michael	BER	278	Peter Senr.	CUM	61
Joseph	LUZ	421	Michael	LUZ	399	Peter	CEN	21A
Joseph	CHE	746	Michael	NOH	74A	Peter	BUC	148A
Joseph	CHE	765	Micheal	WST	278	Peter	BUC	148A
Joseph	CHE	773	Michel	WST	257	Peter Maness	CUM	54
Joseph	CHE	775	Michl.	PHI	118	Phili	SOM	139
Joseph	CHE	867	Michl.	WST	224	Philip	MIF	2
Joseph	BUC	146A	Moses	BUC	103A	Philip	BFD	46
Joseph B.	PHA	13	Nancy	LAN	179	Philip	PHI	101
Joseph T.	PHA	63	Nancy & Polly	DAU	3A	Philip	HNT	128
Joseph			Nathan	PHA	59	Philip	SOM	131
(Christn.-			Nathan	WST	297	Philip	BER	146
Crossed Out	PHI	0	Nathan	LUZ	412	Philip	SOM	147
Joshua	DEL	158	Nathaniel	LAN	47	Philip	HNT	154
Joshua R.	PHA	57	Nathaniel	WAS	59	Philip	BER	168
Jost	NOH	65A	Nathaniel	DEL	168	Philip	YOR	172
Judith	PHA	85	Nathaniel	DEL	190	Philip	YOR	189
Kelip	FRA	291	Nathen	FAY	269	Philip	YOR	210
Lambert	PHA	67	Nathn.	PHI	114A	Philip	LAN	315
Landry	LAN	216	Nehemiah	BUC	142	Philip	CHE	782
Lee	PHI	61A	Newberry	PHA	30	Philip	PHI	97A
Leonard	MIF	4	Newton	LUZ	364	Phillip	FAY	223
Leonard	WST	195	Nicholas	WAS	17	Phillip	WST	226
Leonard	CHE	787	Nicholas	GRN	72	Phillip	WST	315
Lewis	NOU	196	Nicholas	SOM	132	Phillop	ALL	74
Lewis	NOU	200	Nicholas	FRA	301	Polly & Nancy	DAU	3A
Lewis	BER	218	Nicholas	NOH	63A	Pompey	PHA	112
Liplet	CUM	88	Nicolaus	DAU	12	Powel	ALL	111
Lockwood	LUZ	421	Noah	GRN	97	Ralph	LYC	29
Ludwick	WAS	105	O./ P.? Jacob	MNT	58	Rebecka	FAY	206
Ludwig	SOM	139	Obadiah	LUZ	318	Richard	ADA	5
Magdalena	ADA	29	Obediak	NOU	160	Richard	PHA	99
Malachia	CUM	36	Oliver	PHI	155	Richard	PHA	113
Manus	WST	223	Ostena A.	PHI	89A	Richard	HNT	154
Margaret	PHA	25	Patrick	YOR	201	Richd.	CUM	50
Margaret	CUM	98	Patrick	YOR	203	Richd. E.	PHA	49
Margaret	SOM	139	Patrick	CHE	881	Robert	PHA	8
Margaret	BER	153	Patrik	DAU	24A	Robert	DAU	11
Margaret	LAN	310	Paul	PHI	138	Robert	BEV	12
Margaret	BUT	334	Peter	DAU	6	Robert	PHA	13
Martin	LAN	52	Peter	PHA	14	Robert	PHI	17
Martin	BFD	59	Peter	CRA	16	Robert	WAS	24
Martin	WAS	113	Peter	CEN	21	Robert	PHI	27
Martin	NOU	140	Peter	DAU	38	Robert	ALL	52
Martin	BER	153	Peter	BFD	46	Robert	PHA	73
Martin	LAN	252	Peter	BFD	46	Robert	MNT	79

SMITH, Robert	NOU	140	SMITH, Thomas	BEV	22	SMITH, William	MNT 92
Robert	YOR	158	Thomas	PHI	26	William	WAS 94
Robert	NOU	168	Thomas	WAS	31	William	PHA 96
Robert	NOU	168	Thomas	PHI	32	William	WAS 105
Robert	DEL	187	Thomas	MNT	59	William	CUM 110
Robert	NOU	200	Thomas	GRN	65	William	MNT 117
Robert	YOR	200	Thomas	BUC	87	William	PHA 117
Robert	FAY	211	Thomas	WAS	94	William	HNT 130
Robert	WST	257	Thomas	BUC	95	William	NOU 140
Robert	WST	296	Thomas (W' Son)	BUC	87	William	WAY 147
Robert	LUZ	388	Thomas	PHA	119	William	WAY 150
Robert	CHE	757	Thomas	DEL	158	William	BUC 152
Robert	CHE	815	Thomas	WST	163	William	WST 157
Robert Esq.	CHE	746	Thomas	NOU	168	William	YOR 167
Robert	ERI	60A	Thomas	WST	175	William	DEL 171
Robert	BUC	159A	Thomas	DEL	192	William	DEL 181
Robert Esq.	CHE	815	Thomas	BER	204	William	YOR 181
Robt	CUM	144	Thomas	FAY	211	William	YOR 184
Robt.	CUM	48	Thomas	BER	214	William	YOR 189
Robt.	BUC	87	Thomas	FAY	247	William	DEL 192
Robt.	FRA	273	Thomas	FRA	275	William	YOR 202
Robt.	FRA	297	Thomas	BUT	317	William	FAY 206
Robt.	FRA	311	Thomas	WST	351	William	FAY 223
Robt.	PHI	119A	Thomas	LUZ	364	William	FAY 241
Rowlin	BUC	83	Thomas	MER	459	William	WST 297
Rudolph	WAY	150	Thomas	CHE	703	William	LAN 302
Salvenus	GRN	103	Thomas Jnr.	BUC	87	William	FRA 306
Saml.	DAU	17	Thomas Jur.	FAY	247	William	LAN 310
Saml.	PHA	61	Thomas	DAU	14A	William	WST 316
Saml.	CUM	137	Thomas	BUC	151A	William	LUZ 390
Saml.	FRA	292	Thos.	PHA	45	William	LUZ 400
Saml.	WST	296	Thos.	PHA	71	William	LUZ 404
Saml. Capt.	BUC	87	Thos.	PHA	81	William	MER 459
Samuel	PHA	4	Thos.	PHA	83	William	CHE 875
Samuel	WAS	14	Thos.	PHI	113	William	CHE 906
Samuel	ADA	24	Thos. Revd.	YOR	200	William Esq.	LAN 69
Samuel	ADA	25	Thos.	CEN	23A	William Esqr.	WAS 50
Samuel	PHA	30	Thos.	DAU	23A	William Esqr.	YOR 195
Samuel	ADA	43	Timothy	FAY	237	William Jr.	CHE 875
Samuel	MNT	59	Timothy	BUC	151A	William Jun.	WAS 94
Samuel	ERI	60	Tristsam	DEL	163	William Sen.	WAS 94
Samuel	WAS	83	Valentine	DAU	36	William	DAU 14A
Samuel	GRN	96	Valentine	PHI	141	William	ERI 60A
Samuel	MNT	101	Valentine	LUZ	347	William	BUC 145A
Samuel	BUC	107	Valentine	CHE	781	William	BUC 146A
Samuel	ALL	113	Valentine	PHI	115A	William	BUC 151A
Samuel	HNT	125	W. Revd.	NOH	38A	William H.	LUZ 364
Samuel	WAY	142	Walter Esq.	ADA	9	Willm. Revd.	
Samuel	NOU	152	Whillet	PHA	92	Dd?	PHI 119A
Samuel	DEL	169	Wiand	NOU	177	Wilm.	ALL 100
Samuel	YOR	172	Widdow	FAY	250	Wilson	ERI 59
Samuel Esqr.	WAS	31	Widow	CEN	19	Wm.	CUM 47
Samuel Junr.	WAS	105	Widow	DAU	28	Wm.	DAU 47
Samuel Senr.	WAS	105	Widow	LAN	45	Wm.	PHA 48
Samuel	BUC	151A	Widow	LAN	228	Wm.	PHI 60
Sarah	PHA	6	Widow	NOH	69A	Wm.	CUM 77
Sarah	WAS	31	Widow	BUC	159A	Wm.	PHA 82
Sarah	PHA	67	Widow Of Abm.	NOH	78A	Wm.	PHI 92
Sarah	HNT	121	Widow Of Henry	NOH	78A	Wm.	PHI 93
Sarah	YOR	185	Widw.	PHI	103	Wm.	CUM 120
Sarah	FAY	247	William	PHA	5	Wm.	CUM 143
Silas	ERI	57	William	MIF	11	Wm.	FRA 289
Silas	LUZ	346	William	PHA	18	Wm.	CHE 737
Simon	PHA	76	William	CEN	21	Wm.	CHE 774
Simon	LUZ	356	William	ADA	33	Wm. Maj.	PHI 110
Solomon	WAS	40	William	ADA	40	Wm.	PHI 92A
Steel	WAS	94	William	LAN	51	Wm. M.	PHA 7
Stephen	CEN	21	William	BFD	53	Wm. M.	PHA 90
Stephen	BUC	107	William	ERI	57	Wm. S./ T.?	CHE 896
Stewart?	CHE	757	William	PHI	58	Wm. T?	PHA 38
Tagart &	PHA	11	William	WAS	59	Yoot	CHE 853
Tho.	LYC	14	William	WAS	59	Yost	CHE 793
Thomas	LYC	6	William	WAS	59	Zachariah	WAS 125
Thomas	BEV	10	William	WAS	71	Acob	LAN 271
Thomas	CRA	17	William	NOH	72	SMITH?, -----?	LYC 15
Thomas	WAS	18	William	MNT	84	John	BFD 77

SMITHER,		
Christian	LUZ	360
George	LUZ	355
George	LUZ	355
Jacob	LUZ	356
Jacob	LUZ	357
John	LUZ	355
Phillip	CUM	64
SMITHERS, James	PHA	22
SMITSER, George	FRA	305
SMITZER, Philip	YOR	209
SMITZGAR, Widw.	PHI	118A
SMOCK, John	BUC	103A
Leonard	CRA	8
SMOKER, Peter	LAN	128
SMOLL, Peter	MNT	97
SMOOKER, Jacob	SOM	130
John	SOM	131
SMOP?, Andrew Jr.	BER	260
SMOTHERS, Widw.	PHI	81A
SMOUSE, Adam	BFD	53
David	BFD	53
Michael	BFD	53
SMUCK, Christian	NOU	140
George	YOR	158
John	YOR	207
Philip	YOR	184
SMUCKER, Chris.	LAN	79
John	LAN	80
John	BER	146
SMUK, Christian	BER	226
SMUR, John	ALL	54
SMUTZ, John	FAY	199
SMYLIE, John A.	ERI	60
SMYSER, Jacob	YOR	154
Jacob	YOR	161
Jacob Jr.	YOR	163
Matthias	YOR	162
Michael	YOR	161
Peter	YOR	163
SNABB, Jacob	BER	171
SNABLE, Andw.	BER	214
Joseph	BER	214
Michl.	BER	214
SNACK, Joseph	BER	138
SNACK?, John	BER	138
SNAKEY, William	DEL	180
SNAP, Peter	CUM	108
SNAPPER, Ann	LAN	5
SNARE, Jacob	MNT	68
William	MNT	68
SNARR, John	ADA	17
Michael	NOU	140
SNATTERLY, Mary	DAU	48A
SNAVELY, Jacob	LAN	263
SNDER, Abraham	ALL	74
SNEAR, Philip	HNT	146
SNEARINGER, John	ADA	31
SNEARLY, George	WST	316
SNEARY, John	FRA	327
Nancy	FRA	327
SNEATH, George	DEL	162
SNEATT, Richard	LAN	110
SNEBLY, George	DAU	28
Jacob	DAU	25A
John	DAU	25A
Peter	DAU	28
Ulrich	DAU	25A
SNECK?, Benjm.	BER	238
SNEE, Thomas	WAS	71
SNEEDE, Levins	PHA	40
SNEERINGER, John	ADA	29
Joseph	ADA	29
SNEIDER, Casper	LAN	305
Catharine	DAU	13
Christn.	DAU	19A
SNEIDER, Daniel	DAU	20
Detrich	BER	262
George	BER	146
Henry	LAN	47
Jacob	BER	151
Jacob	LAN	205
Jacob	BER	208
Jacob	DAU	13A
Jacob	DAU	13A
John	LAN	213
John	BER	261
John	BER	272
John	LAN	301
John	LAN	309
Leonard	DAU	11
Marcus	DAU	12A
Michale	BER	189
Nicholas	BER	268
Nicolaus	DAU	7
Peter	LAN	293
Philip	LAN	302
Simon	DAU	5
Thomas	DAU	5A
William	LAN	205
SNEITH?, (See		
Smith)	MIF	2
SNELBAKER, Mary	BFD	78
SNELBECKER,		
George	YOR	175
SNELL, Widw.	PHI	112A
Adam	FRA	301
George	BER	238
Henry	LUZ	428
Jacob	MNT	59
Jacob	YOR	163
Jacob	DAU	23A
James	PHA	35
John	BER	238
Nicholas	CEN	21A
Phillip	FRA	284
SNERLY, Jacob	ADA	33
SNETTERLY, George	DAU	29
SNEVELY,		
Elizabeth	LAN	115
Henry	DAU	48
Isaac	DAU	50A
Jacob	LAN	115
John	DAU	50
SNEY, John	DAU	32
SNEYDER, Daniel	BER	231
Jacob	DAU	46A
Michl.	DAU	26A
SNEYTER, Joseph	LAN	87
SNI---?, John	FRA	301
SNI-ER?, Michael	CHE	897
SNICK, George	PHI	111
SNIDER, Abraham	BEV	13
Adam	YOR	164
Adam Jnr.	BUC	101A
Adam	BUC	101A
Andrew	BUC	157A
Andw.	YOR	186
Andw.	YOR	188
Andw.	WST	226
Anthony	ADA	22
Anthony	CUM	58
Anthony	FRA	282
Baltzer	LAN	267
Barbara	DAU	23A
Casper	CHE	785
Casper	CHE	785
Chris.	LAN	75
Christ.	LAN	68
Christ. Senr.	LAN	69
Christian	LAN	50
Christian	LAN	267
SNIDER,		
Christopher	PHI	153
Christopher	FRA	297
Conrad	ADA	22
Conrad	YOR	193
Conrad	FRA	282
Conrod	CUM	65
Conrod	ALL	67
Conrod	CUM	100
Conrod	CHE	892
Daniel	DAU	21
Daniel	BFD	45
Daniel	WAS	47
Daniel	BUC	150
David	CUM	48
David	CUM	117
David	FRA	274
Frederic	HNT	131
Frederick	ADA	28
Frederick	BUC	98
Gartrant	CHE	791
Geo.	CUM	48
Geo.	CUM	101
George	MIF	2
George	CUM	39
George	CUM	98
George	WAS	113
George	CUM	116
George	BUC	150
George	BER	151
George	PHI	153
George	YOR	157
George	YOR	176
George	FRA	278
George	DAU	9A
George	BUC	97A
Henrey	FAY	217
Henry	ADA	17
Henry	ADA	20
Henry	CUM	39
Henry	CUM	125
Henry	YOR	199
Henry	BER	282
Henry	FRA	283
Henry	FRA	301
Henry	CHE	784
Henry Jr.	CUM	39
Henry Senr.	FRA	301
Hugh	ADA	28
Jacob	LYC	14
Jacob	WAS	47
Jacob	LAN	68
Jacob	YOR	177
Jacob	YOR	180
Jacob	FAY	199
Jacob	FAY	199
Jacob	WST	224
Jacob	FRA	282
Jacob	FRA	292
Jacob Jnr.	BUC	97A
Jacob (Sadler)	YOR	182
Jacob	BUC	97A
Jacob	BUC	97A
Jeremiah	FRA	271
Jerimah	DAU	21
Jno.	CUM	101
Jno.	CUM	150
John	DAU	3
John	CUM	26
John	ADA	42
John	LAN	68
John	HNT	152
John	YOR	186
John	YOR	187
John	YOR	192
John	FRA	273

SNIDER, John	FRA	275	SNODGRASS,			SNYDER, Croft	PHI	85A
John	FRA	276	William	LAN	240	Daniel	MNT	136
John	FRA	291	William	WST	297	Daniel	NOU	140
John	FRA	297	William Jnr.	LAN	241	Daniel	BER	180
John	FRA	327	Wm.	CHE	727	Daniel	WST	225
John	CHE	781	Wm.	DAU	23A	David	BFD	52
John	DAU	23A	SNODON, Large?	ADA	24	David	PHI	97
John	DAU	23A	SNOKE, Christian	DAU	7A	David	PHI	155
Martin	ADA	14	Frederick	BER	261	Dewald	SOM	135
Martin	YOR	191	John	DAU	42A	Doter	BER	158
Mary	YOR	165	SNORGRASS, Mrs.	NOU	132	Elias	MNT	55
Melker	FRA	275	SNOTGRASS, Alexd.	ALL	82	Elizabeth	PHI	109
Michael	ADA	28	Alexd.	ALL	83	Emich	LAN	77
Michael	LAN	68	Jain	ALL	91	Felty	ARM	125
Michael	LAN	284	James	ALL	85	Frederick	WST	242
Michael Jnr.	BUC	98	Thomas	ALL	85	Geo.	PHI	79
Michael	BUC	97A	SNOUCK, Martin	NOU	132	Geo.	BER	154
Michl.	CUM	101	SNOUR, Christian	NOU	140	Geo.	PHI	114A
Nichls.	CUM	49	SNOW, Joseph	PHI	45	George	PHI	79
Nicholas	YOR	166	Nicholas	WST	163	George	PHI	99
Nicholas	FRA	282	Widow	MIF	5A	George	MNT	124
Nicholas	CHE	792	SNOWBERGER, Andr.	FRA	305	George	NOU	124
Peter	ADA	25	John	HNT	128	George	NOU	141
Peter	WAS	31	Ulrick	FRA	305	George	HNT	143
Peter	CUM	39	Yaret	FRA	305	George	SOM	155
Peter	ADA	41	SNOWDEN, Widow	PHI	96	Harman	PHA	67
Peter	HNT	133	Isaac Junr.	PHA	106	Harman	NOU	185
Peter	HNT	147	Joseph	PHA	113	Henry	LAN	20
Peter	BUC	150	Nathaniel	DAU	5	Henry	PHA	38
Peter Jn.	BUC	150	Thomas	MNT	66	Henry	MNT	46
Philip	YOR	165	Thos.	PHA	74	Henry	MNT	54
Philip	WST	225	SNOWDON, John	WAS	24	Henry	MNT	59
Phillip	CUM	64	Leonard	PHA	38	Henry	LAN	67
Phillip	CUM	104	SNUCK, William	NOU	196	Henry	PHA	67
See Snder	ALL	74	SNUFF, Jacob	WAS	40	Henry	MNT	116
Seefritz	YOR	194	John	WAS	40	Henry	PHI	122
Theobal	YOR	188	SNVELY, Jacob	LAN	264	Henry	BER	149
Valentine	YOR	159	SNYDER, Widow	PHI	30	Henry	YOR	187
SNIDER?, Michael	CHE	897	Widow	PHI	112A	Henry	NOU	203
SNILEBERGER,			Widw.	PHI	92	Henry	NOU	203
Frederick	NOU	189	Abm.	WST	373	Henry	WST	225
George	NOU	189	Abraham	MNT	46	Henry	WST	226
SNIVELEY, Jacob	FRA	296	Abraham	NOU	107	Jacob	PHA	13
Jacob	FRA	300	Abraham	NOU	124	Jacob	MNT	46
Jos.	FRA	296	Abraham	BER	158	Jacob	BFD	52
SNIVELY, And.			Adam	PHA	81	Jacob	MNT	58
Ssr.	FRA	298	Adam	NOU	98	Jacob	LAN	67
Henry	ALL	59	Adam	MNT	136	Jacob	LAN	75
Henry	FRA	292	Adam	WST	175	Jacob	PHA	77
Henry Jnr.	FRA	300	Adam	PHI	74A	Jacob	NOU	107
Henry Sr.	FRA	300	Andrew	BER	189	Jacob	NOU	107
Jacob	CUM	60	Ann	BER	244	Jacob	MNT	112
Jacob	HNT	127	Benedick	PHA	80	Jacob	NOU	124
Jno.	CUM	67	Benja.	WST	226	Jacob	BER	134
SNOBBLE, Fanny	PHI	130	Benjamin	BER	180	Jacob	PHI	134
SNOBLE, Cathrn.	DAU	13A	Benjn.	MNT	96	Jacob	MNT	136
SNODAY, James	NOU	203	Boldsor	NOU	140	Jacob	NOU	140
SNODDEY, Wm.	DAU	23A	Casper	NOU	102	Jacob	SOM	144
SNODDY, Jno.	CUM	138	Casper	PHI	67A	Jacob	BER	160
SNODER, Susana	LAN	74	Cath.	BER	204	Jacob	BER	238
SNODERLY, John	FAY	247	Catharine	PHA	78	Jacob	WST	242
SNODGRASS,			Catharine	PHI	109	Jacob	FRA	285
Alexander			Catherine	MNT	62	Jacob Junr.	MNT	112
Esq.	LAN	151	Charles	PHI	75	Jacob	PHA	17A
Benjamin	BUC	154A	Charles	PHI	78	Jno. Junr.	WST	297
James	WAS	31	Christian	LAN	21	John	CRA	8
James	BUC	106	Christian	MNT	47	John	MNT	41
James	DAU	23A	Christian	PHI	127	John	BFD	52
John	DAU	23A	Christian	BER	149	John	LAN	64
Jos.	YOR	198	Christian	WST	226	John	BFD	66
Robert	LAN	151	Christian	FRA	278	John	BFD	68
Robt.	YOR	201	Christian	BUC	101A	John	PHA	69
Thos.	FRA	318	Christn.	BER	205	John	MNT	74
Widow	MIF	5A	Christn.	MIF	13A	John	PHI	76
William	WAS	14	Christopher	BFD	59	John	PHI	98
William	LAN	237	Christopher	WAY	142	John	PHA	99

SNYDER, John	NOU 102	SNYDERI, George	NOU 184	SOMMEKAMP,		
John	NOU 107	SOAL?, John	BER 201	Phillip	PHA	36
John	MNT 112	SOAP, Peter	CUM 84	SOMMERVILLE, Jas.	MIF	26A
John	PHI 128	SOASE, Peter	FRA 294	SOMMEY, Michael	SOM	159
John	NOU 132	SOBER, Jacob	NOH 74	SOMMONY, Saml.	WST	224
John	WAY 140	SOBERS, George	WST 373	SOMMY, John	YOR	216
John	NOU 141	SOBERS?, Widow	PHI 69A	SON?, John	HNT	126
John	BER 147	SOBIA, David	PHI 72A	SONDAY, Anthony	YOR	177
John	BER 160	SODERSTROM,		Henry	YOR	179
John	NOU 168	Richd.	PHA 89	Jos.	YOR	177
John	NOU 184	SODY, Henry	FRA 306	SONER,		
John	NOU 185	SOELSLAR, Philip	CHE 793	Christopher	NOU	125
John	NOU 185	SOFFITTE, James	PHI 1	SONER?, Nicholas?	LYC	27
John	NOU 190	SOFIELD, Wilm.	ALL 82	SONG, Mathias	ADA	14
John	WST 195	SOHLL, Henry	LAN 204	SONGS, Andrew	BFD	46
John	WST 225	SOHN, Jacob	NOH 92	Henry	BFD	46
John	BER 276	SOLADAY, Manuel	NOH 79	SONGSHORE,		
John	WST 297	SOLADY, John	MNT 53	Euclidus Jn.	BUC	161
John	BUT 334	SOLBERGER, Henry	WST 278	SONNER?, Ludewick	NOU	125
John	LUZ 418	SOLD, David	NOU 140	SONS, Frederick	BER	253
John	PHI 98	SOLEBERGER, Jno.	CUM 66	SONS?, William	BER	143
John	PHI 53A	John	FRA 314	SONTAG, Henry	BER	186
John G.	BER 282	SOLEBERRY,		SONTAGG, Wm. L.	PHA	81
Joseph	PHI 22	Sampson	WAS 46	SONTON, Thomas	PHI	9
Joseph	BFD 52	SOLEDY, John	DAU 6A	SOOBE, Adam	LAN	175
Joseph	BFD 66	SOLENBERGER, John	LAN 94	Henry	LAN	175
Joseph	NOU 107	Peter	LAN 94	SOOK, Jacob Junr.	WAS	113
Joseph	LAN 266	SOLEY, Alexander	MNT 139	Jacob Senr.	WAS	113
Leonard	BER 189	Alexander	DEL 187	Peter	WAS	5
Lewis	NOU 195	Alexander	DEL 189	Peter	BUC	101A
Lewis	PHI 94A	John	BUC 85	SOOL, Jacob	LAN	175
Luwick	PHI 97	Obadiah	BUC 161A	SOOLEY?, John	PHA	109
Margaret	BFD 52	Thomas	MNT 139	SOPER, Samuel	NOU	107
Margaret	BER 210	SOLIDAY, George	MNT 75	SORBER, Jacob	MNT	93
Mathias	WST 195	SOLINGER, Adam	FRA 291	Philip	MNT	76
Matthias	DEL 174	John	WST 258	SORD, John E.	PHA	100
Michael	MNT 53	Peter	CUM 37	SOREY?, Abraham	FRA	313
Michael	PHA 56	SOLLADAY, John	BER 205	SORICH?,		
Michael	HNT 139	SOLLADY, Andrew	BER 215	Valentine	BER	275
Michael	NOU 178	SOLLENBERGER,		SORICK, Adam	HNT	127
Michl.	WST 195	John	BER 168	SORRELL, Robert	MNT	100
Nicholas	MNT 75	John	LAN 205	SORRELLS, John	WST	175
Nicholas	NOU 125	Joseph	LAN 213	Robt.	WST	175
Nicholas	NOU 178	Samuel	LAN 64	SORVER, Jacob	NOH	42
Nichs.	WST 175	SOLLINGBERGER,		Philip	NOH	42
Peter	MNT 79	Jacob	CUM 37	Widow	NOH	36
Peter	PHI 130	SOLLMAN, Abraham	MNT 97	SOSMAN, Joseph	LAN	127
Peter	SOM 131	SOLLODAY, Henry	HNT 128	SOTHERLAND,		
Peter	BER 132	SOLOMAN, Mrs.	PHA 55	Alexd.	ALL	78
Peter	NOU 144	Ann	PHA 121	SOTTINGER, George	MNT	110
Peter	WST 176	Henry	SOM 135	SOU-LE?, George	BER	278
Peter	BER 180	Jesse	BUC 152	SOUDER, Abraham	BUC	159A
Peter	NOU 190	William	MNT 42	Benjamin	LAN	110
Peter	LAN 256	SOLOMON,		Charles	BUC	83A
Peter	LAN 266	Alexander	LAN 207	Christian	YOR	196
Peter	LAN 284	J./ I.? Lewis	GRN 90	David	LAN	112
Peter	WST 382	James	NOU 160	Jacob	LAN	110
Peter	LUZ 420	Paul	SOM 135	Jacob	LAN	293
Peter	PHI 98	SOLSICK, Nicholas	BUC 101A	Jacob	PHI	72A
Peter	PHI 95A	SOLT, Anthony	NOH 51	John	LAN	293
Philip	LAN 85	Conrad	NOH 76A	Joshua	HNT	152
Philip	BER 132	Daniel	NOH 84	SOUDERS, John	CHE	835
Philip	BER 189	Jacob	NOH 84	Thos. M.	PHI	77
Philip	BER 276	John	NOH 51	SOUFER, John	DAU	16
Phillip	NOU 169	John	NOH 84	SOUL, Christn.	BER	152
Phillip	WST 224	Paul	NOH 84	John	ALL	71
Seth	MNT 79	Paul	NOH 76A	Nicholas	BER	218
Simon	NOU 98	SOMAREUX, James	LUZ 341	Peter	ALL	71
Simon	NOU 140	John	LUZ 342	SOULLIER, John M.	PHA	122
Thomas	BFD 40	Thomas	LUZ 341	SOUNDERWILK, Adam	DAU	9A
Thomas	NOU 184	SOMER, Jacob	PHI 149	SOUP, Margaret	GRN	79
Valuntine	MNT 96	Martin	PHI 150	SOUPE, Fredrick	ARM	125
Wilhelm	PHI 133	SOMERLIN?,		SOUR, George	YOR	179
William	NOU 150	William	LUZ 368	Magdalena	YOR	162
Wm.	PHA 77	SOMERS, David	LUZ 388	SOURER, Jacob	ADA	33
Wm.	PHI 97	SOMERVILLE, James	HNT 120	SOURS, Paul	ADA	15

Name	Co.	Pg.
SPIKEMAN, Enoch	CHE	765
Jacob	YOR	217
Jesse	CHE	711
Joshua	ADA	41
Stephen	ADA	41
SPIKER, Chr.	WST	224
SPILLARD, Henry	PHI	46
Matths.	PHI	25
SPILLERS, John	WAS	95
SPINDLER, Mathias	BER	149
SPINGLER, Joseph	LAN	204
SPINNER, Abraham	NOH	82A
David	BUC	102
Jacob	NOH	69A
John	NOH	83
SPINNGER, Joseph	ALL	72
SPINNINGBERG, John	PHI	98
SPIRAH, John	LAN	213
SPIRES, Francis	PHA	110
SPIRY, John	BFD	78
SPISER, John	WAS	47
SPITLER, Christan	NOU	140
Henry	DAU	51
John	YOR	180
John Junior	DAU	48
John	DAU	50A
Mathias	ADA	24
Peter	HNT	131
Samuel	HNT	128
SPITSER, Conrad	LAN	108
SPITTER, Widow	YOR	182
SPITTLER, John	HNT	149
William	HNT	149
SPIVE/ SPIVI?, John	WAS	53
SPOHN, Adam	BER	168
Conrad	BER	189
John	BER	180
Peter	BER	253
SPOKE, Ann M.	PHI	119A
SPONCELER, Andrew	DAU	10
SPONE, Melcher	CUM	48
SPONG, Danl.	BER	239
Jacob	CUM	61
John	DAU	20
Peter	BER	201
SPONGLER, John	ARM	123
SPONHEIMER, Lewis	NOH	74A
SPONNEL?, John	LYC	24
SPONSALLER, Fredk.	ADA	28
George	ADA	30
Henry	ADA	28
Widow	ADA	30
SPONSLER, Nichs.	CUM	81
SPOON, Henry	FRA	280
John	WAS	125
John	BER	242
Martin	WAS	125
Philip	BER	204
SPOONER, John	PHA	77
SPOOWELL, Widow	LAN	78
SPORMEL?, John	LYC	24
SPORNEL?, John	LYC	24
SPORSNEL?, John	LYC	24
SPOTS, Fredk.	YOR	171
SPOTSWOOD, Wm.	PHA	10
SPOTTS, Mary	YOR	206
SPOTWOOD, Jas.	CUM	98
Lindsay	CUM	92
SPRAGG, Caleb	GRN	72
David	GRN	78
Uriah	GRN	72
SPRAGLE, Widow	PHI	98
George	NOH	42
SPRAGUE, Widw.	PHI	108A
John	ERI	58
Jonathen	ERI	58
Thomas Jr.	ERI	58A
Thomas	ERI	58A
SPRALE, John	PHI	32
SPRECHER, George	DAU	23A
SPREIGLE, John	PHI	111
SPRENGLE, Peter Jr.	YOR	172
SPRENKEL, Henrey	FAY	217
SPRENKLE, Daniel	YOR	161
Daniel	YOR	181
Frederick	YOR	171
George	ADA	30
George Jr.	YOR	161
George Sr.	YOR	161
Henry	ADA	30
Henry	YOR	185
Michael	YOR	188
Peter	YOR	169
Peter	YOR	189
SPRESKS, James	NOU	131
SPRIC?, Anthony	MNT	101
SPRIGGS, Joseph	WAS	117
SPRIGLE, Jos.	YOR	178
SPRIGS, James	PHI	94A
James	PHI	102A
Jeremiah	WAS	14
SPRIKMAN, Peter	LAN	46
SPRINER, Barbara	LAN	215
John	MNT	100
SPRINERIN, Christina	LAN	251
SPRING, Adam	NOH	84
Dewalt	LAN	107
Jacob	BER	227
Laurence	ADA	37
Mary	PHA	54
Nichs.	DAU	20
William	NOU	173
SPRINGER, Conrad	LAN	255
Daniel	MNT	129
Danl.	CUM	65
Danl.	CUM	67
Denis	FAY	259
Francis	PHI	14
George	PHI	36
Isaac	DEL	166
Jacob	WAS	83
Jacob	ALL	96
Jacob	SOM	152
Jacob	FAY	218
Jacob	YOR	219
Jacob	FAY	259
Jacob	LAN	307
Jehu	DEL	164
Jinny	FAY	217
John	ADA	22
John	PHA	69
John	BER	164
John	YOR	219
John	FAY	259
John	BUC	97A
Joseph	PHI	66A
Levy	FAY	259
Mathias	ALL	110
Michal	ALL	110
Peter	LAN	69
Peter	DAU	14A
Richard	LUZ	328
Samuel	BEV	4
Uriah	FAY	206
Zadk. Esqr.	FAY	223
Zadock	FAY	253
SPROAL, Hugh	WAS	17
SPROAL, James	WAS	17
SPROAT, Alexander	WAS	53
Eve	CUM	112
SPROCHER, George	LAN	74
SPROLE, Margaret	DAU	4
SPROUD, Ruben	LAN	310
Thomas	ALL	108
SPROUGHT, James	BEV	6
John	BEV	11
SPROUL, Charles	BER	162
John	CHE	818
Ralph	FRA	313
SPROULS, John	WAS	83
SPROUS, Michl.	FRA	279
SPROUSE, Wm.	FRA	322
SPROUT, Hugh	LAN	151
James	YOR	200
Joseph	FAY	217
Samuel	BEV	11
Samuel	FAY	217
Thomas	BEV	13
SPROWL, James	WST	373
Robert	WST	373
Robt.	DAU	2A
SPROWLES, William	WAS	113
SPRUCHMAN, Peter	BER	267
SPUCE, David	MNT	75
John (Crossed Out Followed By David)	MNT	75
SPUDY?, (See Speedy)	FRA	292
SPUHLER, Christian	LAN	139
SPULY?, Jeremiah	NOU	131
SPURGEON, Elias	BFD	54
Ezekiel	BFD	53
Samuel	BFD	53
SPURK?, Peter	PHA	68
SPURTS, Phillip	NOU	181
SPUTY?, Jeremiah	NOU	131
SPYKER, Benjamin	BER	268
Henry	NOU	132
John	N	8
John	BER	238
Peter	DAU	49
SQUARES, Josiah	LUZ	325
SQUIB, Caleb	FAY	206
Elijah	BER	161
Robert	DEL	163
Robt.	YOR	210
William	YOR	210
SQUIBB, Enoch	CHE	909
SQUIRES, James	BEV	5
Moses	WAS	64
Stephen	LUZ	379
SQUIRS, Wm.	BEV	5
SQURES, Rebecka	FAY	259
SRAUGER, Garret	BUC	142
SRAUGHIN, George	ALL	70
SRAW, Adam	DAU	43
SREDER, John	ALL	69
SRETHER?, John	FRA	301
SREYDER, William	WST	297
SROAD, John	ALL	109
SROUD, Henry	ALL	101
John	ALL	101
SROWD, Jacob	ALL	112
SRUM?, George	WST	382
Henry	WST	382
ST--DALE?, James	GRN	108
ST-UCKLING?, Chas.	PHI	10
ST. BRINTON?, John	PHA	77
ST. CLAIR, Daniel	MNT	70

ST. CLAIR, John	WAS	106	STADLER, George	NOH	49	STALL, Henry	SOM	131
John	BER	242	STAFFER, Peter	LAN	82	Isaac	NOU	112
M. John	WST	175	Willm.	PHI	37	Jacob	MNT	90
ST. JOHN, Charles	PHA	74	STAFFEY, Conrad	BFD	39	Jacob	NOU	168
Samuel	LUZ	365	Nicholas	HNT	151	Jacob	NOU	169
STAAB, Jacob	ADA	32	Peter	HNT	151	Jacob	FRA	301
John	YOR	159	STAFFORD, Mr.	PHA	54	Jas.	FRA	281
STAAL, Henry	YOR	181	Amos	LUZ	380	Jesse	NOU	148
STABLELON, Robert	BER	131	David	LUZ	380	John	PHA	19
STABLER,			James	MIF	4	John	PHA	75
Christian	YOR	194	James	BER	249	John	NOU	112
STABLETON, John	BER	231	John	LUZ	380	John	NOU	132
John Jr.	BER	132	John Jr.	LUZ	380	John	BER	147
Tobias	BER	132	Robert	PHA	103	John	NOU	169
STABLEY?, Jacob	YOR	196	STAGG, William	LUZ	374	John	NOU	184
STACHEL, Anthony	NOH	49	STAGGERS, Jacob	CHE	752	John	NOU	200
STACHER, George			Jacob	CHE	903	John	FRA	279
Jnr.	NOH	40A	Jaocb	GRN	66	John	FRA	311
STACK, Thomas	CHE	755	John	GRN	112	John	CHE	856
STACKER,			STAHAM, Widow	LAN	169	Joseph	FRA	310
Catharine	DEL	185	STAHELER?, John	BUC	99A	Margaret	MNT	75
STACKHOUS, Thos.	NOU	155	STAHL, Adam	BER	180	Michael	BFD	46
STACKHOUSE, Abel	CHE	778	George	NOH	57A	Mrs.	NOU	132
Abraham	NOU	155	Henry	NOH	49	Phillip	NOU	112
Amos	PHA	47	Jacob	LAN	27	Thomas	NOU	112
Amos	BUC	83A	Jacob	LAN	285	Valentine	BER	263
Asa	BUC	143A	Jacob	BER	286	STALLER, Adam	NOH	54A
Benjn.	CHE	748	John	NOH	57	Catherine	BER	221
Benjn.	BUC	162A	STAHLER, Henry			Peter	BER	221
Benjn.	BUC	162A	(Joynerr)	NOH	57A	STALMAN, John	BER	284
Charles	BUC	95	Henry	NOH	57A	STALMAN?, William	PHI	124
David	BUC	161A	Ludwig Esqr.	NOH	57	STALSMITH,		
Euclidies?	BUC	85	Nicholas	NOH	57	Francis	ADA	19
Francis	BUC	85	Nicholas Jr.	NOH	57A	STAM, Adam	NOU	140
Francis	BUC	83A	Peter	NOH	57	Catherine	BER	130
Isaac	BUC	95	Philip	NOH	57	Frederick	BER	146
Isaac	BUC	161A	STAHLNECKER,			Henry	SOM	150
James	NOU	155	Jacob	NOH	57	Jacob	SOM	139
John	BUC	84	STAHLY, Baltzer	NOH	63A	John	BER	203
John	BUC	85	STAILEY, Benjamin	LAN	97	John R. (A		
John	NOU	168	Christian Junr.	LAN	97	Boarding		
John	BUC	161A	STAILY, Christian	LAN	98	House)	PHA	37
Jonath.	BUC	161A	STAIN, James	BFD	46	Martin	BER	130
Joseph	PHI	145	STAINBOROUGH,			Nicholas	BER	146
Joseph	NOU	155	Henry	SOM	150	STAMBAUGH, Andw.	YOR	166
Joseph	BUC	83A	STAIR, Fredr.	FRA	291	Barbara	YOR	187
Joshua	BUC	85	Jno.	FRA	276	Henry	YOR	189
Katharine	DEL	183	Tobias	YOR	183	Jacob	YOR	184
Kesiah	BUC	85	STAKE, Catharine	YOR	155	Jacob	YOR	188
Martha	PHA	47	Jacob	YOR	166	Jacob	LAN	228
Samuel	BUC	85	Jacob	FRA	313	John	YOR	184
Stephen	BUC	85	Michl. Revd.	WST	226	Peter	YOR	179
Thomas	BUC	89	Widow	LAN	285	Peter	YOR	184
Thomas	BUC	95	STAKE?, (See			Peter	YOR	191
William	BUC	99A	Stoke)	FRA	314	Philip	YOR	189
Wm.	BUC	85	STAKER,			STAMBOUGH, Jacob	LAN	228
Wm.	PHI	110	Christopher	WAS	47	STAMMERS, Edward	PHA	25
Wm.	NOU	119	Lewis Junr.	WAS	47	Edward	PHI	69
STACKLAND, Elihu	NOU	132	Lewis Senr.	WAS	47	Mary	LAN	179
STACKPOLE, Jas.	MIF	26	STALEY, Jacob	MNT	110	STAMP, Wm.	CHE	864
Jno.	MIF	26	John	MNT	78	STAMPHER, Sarah	PHA	92
STACTON, Jos.	PHI	88A	STALEY?, William	MNT	111	STANBACK, -----	BUC	82A
STACY, John	PHI	24	STALFORD, Alexr.	MIF	26	STANBEREY, Saml.	FAY	247
Moses	PHI	75	STALK, Fredirick	NOU	181	STANBURG, John	PHI	38
William	YOR	159	STALKER, Jacob	CHE	900	STANCLIF, Comfort	ERI	60
STADDLEMAN, Wm.	MNT	139	Samuel	CHE	819	Russel	ERI	59
STADDON, Thomas	DEL	182	Thomas	CHE	901	STANDER, Amer	PHA	19
STADE-OSSER?,			STALL, Abm.	CUM	53	STANDERFORD,		
Clemen?	ADA	35	Adam	NOU	185	Benjamin	HNT	139
STADIGER, John			Andr.	FRA	309	STANDLY?, Wm.	PHI	89
Fred.,			Denis	DAU	20	STANDOLPH, Cristy	MER	461
Stewart Of			Elizabeth	PHA	29	STANE, Widw.	PHI	106
The Single			Frederick	ADA	32	STANER, Jacob	PHI	62
Brethern's			George	SOM	140	STANFIELD, Henry	PHI	11
House	NOH	32A	Godfrey	SOM	130	STANFORD, John	BEV	21
STADLEMAN, John	PHI	107	Godfrey	SOM	155	Joseph	CHE	827

STANFORD, Wm.	PHA	63	STARKY, Jesse	GRN	72	STAUFER, Henry	BER	164		
STANGER, Conrad	FRA	285	Levy	BEV	16	Henry	BER	164		
STANK, Geo.	PHI	108A	Nathan	GRN	72	Jacob	LAN	115		
STANLEY, Abraham	HNT	126	Peter	FAY	259	Jacob	BER	164		
Andew?	CHE	824	Stacy	FAY	233	Jacob	BER	164		
Elias	CHE	804	STARLING, Andrew	FAY	247	John	BER	164		
Isaac	WAS	40	Jacob	WST	258	John	BER	208		
Jacob	DEL	174	Levi	BUC	88	Widow	LAN	255		
John	ADA	13	Richard	GRN	85	STAUFFER, Abraham	LAN	6		
Matthew	CHE	824	Richard	LAN	268	Abraham	NOH	57		
Norris	PHI	34	STARMAN, Daniel	LAN	277	Abraham	LAN	139		
Robert	BFD	39	STARMER, John	YOR	196	Catharine	LAN	11		
Susannah	PHA	79	STARN, Joseph	PHI	141	Christ	LAN	147B		
William	CHE	707	Samuel	PHI	141	Christian	LAN	293		
STANLY, James	BUT	320	STARNED, James	CHE	909	Christian Jr.	LAN	294		
Nathl.	MIF	26	STARNER, Barnet	YOR	187	Frederick	LAN	189		
Wm.	MIF	26	Jacob	NOU	140	Henry	LAN	28		
STANNERT, Wm.	PHA	59	John	YOR	183	Henry	SOM	140		
STANOUR,			STARNES, Joseph	WAY	137	Henry	DAU	45A		
Frederick	ADA	16	STARR, David	MIF	17A	Henry	NOH	76A		
Henry	ADA	16	George	FAY	228	Jacob	LAN	22		
STANRINE?, George	PHI	98	George	CHE	887	Jacob	NOH	57		
STANS, Peter	FAY	247	Isaac	PHA	14	Jacob	LAN	145		
Phillip	FAY	247	James	PHA	3	Jacob	LAN	188		
STANTON, Asa	WAY	139	James	DEL	175	John	DAU	46		
James	WAS	40	James	BER	218	John	LAN	294		
Joseph	WAS	40	James Jr.	BER	218	Joseph	LAN	145		
Ritchard	ALL	77	Jeeremiah	CHE	863	Samuel	LAN	82		
Samuel	WAY	137	John	GRN	105	STAUFFER?, Jacob	LAN	72		
William	LUZ	370	John	YOR	218	STAUGH, John	ADA	11		
STAP, Samuel	NOH	34A	John	FAY	228	STAUL, Christiana	YOR	182		
STAPELER, Thomas	BUC	90	John Junr.	GRN	105	Jacob	YOR	182		
Thomas	BUC	103A	Margerett	PHI	107A	STAULS?, James	BUC	89		
STAPELER?, John	BUC	99A	Martin	MNT	105	STAULTER?, (See				
Thos.	BUC	99A	Moses	LYC	6	Stautler)	LAN	12		
STAPLETON, Isaiah	CHE	827	Samuel	CHE	807	STAUMBAGH, Philip	YOR	178		
Joshua	CHE	824	William J./ I.?	WAS	32	STAUN, Thomas	FAY	268		
STAPP, Jacob	NOH	51	STARRET, David	LAN	120	STAUT, Christian	NOH	74A		
John	NOH	72	James	LAN	120	Peter	NOH	74A		
STAPP?, John	NOH	40A	James	FAY	250	STAUTER, John	SOM	159		
STAR, Aquillis	NOU	155	James	FAY	259	John Sen.	SOM	159		
Arthur	HNT	160	John	FAY	250	John	PHI	119A		
Cornelius	BUC	162A	Robert	FAY	233	Joseph	SOM	159		
Elijah	NOU	112	STARRETT, Isaac	FAY	211	Michl.	DAU	49		
James	NOU	112	James	LAN	2	STAUTLER, John	LAN	12		
John	BEV	6	Moses	WST	297	STAUTS, Abm.	BUC	143A		
Leonard	FRA	278	STARRIT, Thomas	NOU	132	Abraham	BUC	107		
Michael	ARM	123	STARRY, Stephen	YOR	157	Daniel	BUC	143A		
Moses	NOU	112	Tobias	ADA	20	STAUTS?, James	BUC	89		
Moses	NOU	112	STARTZMAN, Adam	HNT	156	STAUTTS, Cooper	BUC	161A		
Noble	BEV	6	STARUKE, David	PHI	98	STAVELY, John	YOR	195		
William	HNT	136	STATEN, Mrs.	NOU	168	STAVER, Fredrik	DAU	39A		
STAR?, John	PHI	69	Samuel	NOU	150	STAVERS, Tobias	DAU	39		
STARBIRD, John			William	NOU	168	STAY, Benjn.	PHI	28		
Esqr.	NOH	79	STATER?, Joseph	PHI	149	STAYLAKER, Henry	LAN	34		
STARCK, John	LAN	204	STATES, Jacob	PHI	116A	STAYLEY, John	CUM	32		
STARET, Samuel	NOU	200	Peter	PHI	150	STAYLINE, George	PHI	69		
STARK, Henry	LUZ	324	William	HNT	152	STAYMAKER, Samuel	LAN	219		
John	ALL	81	Zacheas	PHI	149	STAYMAN,				
John	LUZ	379	STATFORD, Joseph	LUZ	398	Catharine	CUM	56		
Jonathan	LUZ	361	STATHEN,			Jacob	LAN	3		
Nathan	LUZ	378	Frederick	NOU	185	John	CUM	56		
Paul	LUZ	324	STATLER, George	NOU	185	STAYMATES, George	WST	195		
Philip	YOR	182	Henry	NOU	141	STAYS, Jacob	PHI	119A		
Samuel	LUZ	419	Jacob	YOR	168	STEABLER, George	YOR	193		
William	LUZ	379	John	GRN	72	STEADMAN,				
STARKE, John	PHI	131	John	FRA	300	Alexander	PHA	31		
STARKEY, Mary	BUC	152	Saml.	FRA	297	STEAGER, Henry &				
Thos.	BUC	161A	Widow	NOH	61	Phil.	DAU	36		
Timothy	BUC	152A	STATMAN?, William	PHI	124	Phil. & Henry	DAU	36		
STARKMAN, John	BFD	52	STAUB, George	BFD	46	STEAL, John	PHI	97		
STARKS, Ebenezar	MIF	17A	Philip	ADA	32	John	LUZ	351		
STARKY, Widw.	PHI	103A	STAUBER, Godlieb	NOH	72	John	CHE	839		
Benjn.	MIF	8A	STAUFER, Abraham	BER	164	Robert	CHE	775		
David	MIF	8A	Daniel	DAU	28A	STEALEY, John				
George	MIF	8A	Elizabeth	LAN	118	Jun.	ADA	29		

Name	Loc	Pg
STEALY, Jacob	BUC	81
Jacob	ALL	118
Jain	ALL	60
John	ADA	29
Joseph	ADA	29
Wilm.	ALL	118
STEAN, George	LAN	123
STEANER, John	WST	226
Valentn.	WST	226
STEANOR, Adam	WST	226
STEANS, Daniel	HNT	139
George	HNT	139
Thomas	HNT	137
STEAR, Andrew	BUC	160
John	BUC	101A
Nicholas	BUC	160
Valentine	ADA	30
Widow	BUC	101A
STEARWALL, Peter	PHI	93
STEAWICK?, Andrew	BUT	315
STECHER, Adam	NOH	40
George	NOH	40
Henry	NOH	40
Mathias	NOH	40
STECKBEK, Michl.	DAU	26
STECKEL, Daniel	NOH	31
Henry	NOH	92
Jacob	NOH	92
John	NOH	92
Peter	NOH	63A
STECKER, John	NOH	40
STED, John	LUZ	390
STEED, Aron	FAY	239
James	BFD	53
John	BFD	54
William	BFD	53
STEEDEM?, Zacariah	BEV	27
STEEDMAN?, See Studman	NOU	173
STEEKEL, George	NOH	49
STEEL, Widow	WST	195
--ac?	ARM	125
Abraham	BFD	66
Adam	FAY	211
Andr.	FRA	296
Andrew	BFD	76
Andrew	DEL	155
Andrew	DEL	167
Anthony	PHA	99
Anthy.	CUM	24
Archibald	WAS	14
Atexd.	ALL	116
Benajah	WAS	83
Benjn.	CUM	44
Catharine	GRN	73
Christopher	HNT	155
David	CUM	23
David	CUM	75
David	ALL	90
David	NOU	132
David	MIF	17A
David	DAU	42A
Elizabeth	FRA	292
Ephm.	CUM	97
Frances	LAN	59
Frances	CEN	23A
George	MIF	12
George	PHA	113
Henry	WAY	147
Isaac	GRN	72
Jacob	MIF	4
Jacob	BFD	66
James	MIF	2
James	PHI	78
James	PHA	90
STEEL, James	WAS	105
James	DEL	170
James	YOR	195
James	WST	278
James	CHE	874
James	CHE	875
James	PHI	119A
Jane	BUT	347
John	DAU	4
John	PHA	45
John	CUM	77
John	CUM	104
John	PHI	106
John	MNT	108
John	HNT	120
John	LAN	164
John	DEL	180
John	NOU	200
John	FAY	217
John	FRA	309
John	WST	329
John	LUZ	382
John	MER	460
John	CHE	730
John	PHI	11A
John	MIF	17A
Jonas	MIF	4
Joseph	HNT	151
Joseph	LUZ	330
Mary	BUT	326
Matthew	WST	316
Morrison	CUM	24
Nathl.	MIF	15A
Nicholas	HNT	151
Peter	DEL	185
Peter	LUZ	341
Peter Jr.	LUZ	341
Philip	BFD	66
Phillip	FRA	283
Robert	MIF	2
Robert	WAS	125
Robert	DEL	161
Robert	DEL	171
Robert	DEL	174
Robert Rd.	ALL	55
Robt.	CUM	126
Robt.	YOR	203
Sally	FAY	247
Samuel	MIF	4
Samuel	HNT	156
Samuel	SOM	159
Sarah	CUM	98
Solomon	MIF	4
Thomas	PHA	98
Thomas	DEL	170
Thos.	YOR	201
William	PHA	7
William	BFD	68
William	HNT	140
William	HNT	156
William	NOU	200
William	LAN	236
William	BUT	343
Wilm.	ALL	51
Wilm.	ALL	113
Wm.	HNT	140
Wm.	CHE	800
STEEL?, George	WST	382
STEELE, John	BFD	47
John	LAN	160
STEELMAN, George	PHI	8
STEELY, Christel	ALL	116
Gabriel	MIF	17A
Jacob	MIF	17A
John	ALL	116
Lazrus	MIF	17A
STEELY, Widow	MIF	17A
STEEMAN, Christian	FAY	247
STEEN, Daniel	NOU	107
Isaiah	WAS	117
James	CHE	771
John	ALL	59
John	CUM	87
John	WAS	106
Mathew	WAS	106
Robert	WAS	106
Robert	LAN	162
Thomas	WAS	106
Widow	LAN	85
William	WAS	76
Willm.	BUT	358
STEER, Conrod	WST	243
Jacob	PHA	38
Jacob	WST	278
John	PHI	115A
Jos.	PHI	115A
Michael	LAN	235
Peter	NOH	83
STEER?, Barnery	ARM	127
STEERS, Abriham	CRA	9
STEES, Frederick	NOU	185
Jacob	NOU	185
Jacob	NOU	185
Jacob	LAN	287
John	NOU	203
STEEVER, Daniel	DAU	8
Henry	PHA	84
Jacob	DAU	33A
Jno.	DAU	36
Leonard	DAU	8
Philip	DAU	8
STEFF, Ludwig	BER	171
STEFFER, George	LAN	78
STEFFEY, Jacob	ADA	41
STEFFY, Abraham	BER	168
Danile	BER	168
Jacob	LAN	43
Peter	BER	168
STEG, Philip	LAN	302
STEGER, Fredrik	DAU	29
John	DAU	26
Peter	DAU	25
STEGNER, Christian	MNT	88
Lewis	MNT	88
STEHLY, Christian	BER	134
STEHMAN, Christian	LAN	294
STEHNER, Docr.	DAU	40
STEHR, George	BER	262
John	BER	221
John	DAU	33A
John Engle	BER	221
STEIB?, Jacob	PHA	58
STEIERWALD, Henry	NOH	54
STEIF, John F.	PHA	101
STEIGELMAN, Jacob	LAN	294
Ludwig	LAN	312
STEIGER, Peter	BER	189
Peter Senr.	BER	186
STEIGERWOLT, Eberhard	LAN	61
STEIGHMILLER, Faltine	CUM	58
STEIKERWALT, Frederick	LAN	44
STEILY, George	LAN	83
Magdalena	LAN	83
STEIN, Andw.	YOR	190
Anthony	NOH	86
Christian	BER	260

STEPHENSON,			STERRET, Saml.	DAU	21A	STEVENS, Hannah	HNT 147
Robert	MER	461	Samuel	NOU	132	Jacob	BFD 77
Rolf	PHI	96A	Thos.	CUM	125	James	CUM 35
Saml.	WST	225	William	LAN	263	Jehu	FAY 206
Thomas	WAS	53	STERRETT, Charles	WST	329	Jno.	CUM 86
William	WAS	31	David	MIF	15A	John	BEV 16
Willm.	PHI	71	John	CUM	30	John	CUM 53
Wm.	BEV	10	Wm.	CHE	907	John Junr.	CUM 85
STEPHER, George	YOR	185	Wm. Jr.	CHE	907	Joshua	LUZ 427
STEPHEY, Jacob	NOU	185	STERRETT?, Wm.			Levi	FAY 268
STEPHINSON, James	BEV	11	Esq.	MIF	11	Matthew	HNT 165
William	ARM	125	STERRIT, Jno.	CUM	64	Nancy	FAY 211
STEPLES, John	NOH	79	John	FRA	308	Nathaniel	FAY 268
STERBAUGH, Adam	PHI	111A	Robt.	FRA	308	Peter	HNT 155
STERETT, Robt.	MIF	15A	William	ERI	58	Peter	LUZ 397
STERLING, David	LAN	245	Wm.	FRA	311	Richard	BER 159
Hugh	ALL	105	STERRITT, John	FRA	293	Robert	FAY 268
Isaac	LUZ	371	Karins	FRA	293	Rosana	WST 175
Jacob	CUM	85	Saml.	FRA	293	Samuel	BER 249
Jacob	CUM	87	STERTZER, Balzer	LAN	36	Samuel	WST 382
James	CRA	15	STERTZLER, Peter	BER	278	Sarah	FAY 206
James	ADA	18	STESLEY, Philip	MNT	74	Thomas	FAY 268
James	WST	352	STET/ STEL?,			STEVENSEN,	
John	LYC	19	George			William	PHA 120
Joseph	WST	351	(Crossed Out)	LAN	251	STEVENSON,	
Mark	NOH	31	STETLER,			Alexander	LAN 96
Samuel	ALL	98	Christian	MNT	96	Edward	HNT 134
Samuel	LUZ	372	Henry	MNT	96	James	PHA 67
William	WST	351	Henry	BER	151	James Jun.	WAS 95
William	NOH	31A	Henry	PHI	98	James Sen.	WAS 95
STERMER, George	YOR	193	Jacob	NOH	69A	Jas.	CUM 134
STERN, Abraham	MNT	84	Saml.	PHI	99	John	PHI 145
Conrad	MNT	84	Wm.	BER	154	John	FAY 233
George	NOH	52	STETS, Geo.	FRA	274	John	FRA 310
Jacob	LAN	23	STETSELL, Jacob	PHI	103A	Joseph	FRA 316
John	NOH	52	STETT?, See Stell	BER	203	Robt.	CUM 113
John	LAN	60	STETTLER,			Samuel	ALL 108
Michael	SOM	131	Bernhard	NOH	31	Samuel	FAY 223
Michael	NOH	92A	Henry	NOH	51	Samuel	LUZ 369
Paul	SOM	155	Jacob	NOH	31	Tobias	BUT 344
Peter	MNT	47	John	NOH	31	Widow	LAN 91
Tobias	NOH	92	STETZLER, George	BER	278	William	WAS 95
William	CHE	849	STEUART, Charles	GRN	78	Wm.	CUM 135
STERNAMAN, Jacob	FRA	304	Daniel	GRN	66	Wm.	FRA 274
STERNBERG, Abm.	PHA	31	Daniel	GRN	78	STEVER, Daniel	PHA 76
STERNEMAN, Peter	SOM	155	Hezekiah	GRN	65	George	HNT 147
STERNER, Abraham	NOH	92	Isaac	GRN	65	Phil.	DAU 41A
Adam	SOM	152	James	GRN	72	STEVESON, George	ADA 42
Christian	NOH	44	James	GRN	79	STEVTZMAN, David	FRA 292
Christian	NOH	48A	Jeremiah	GRN	74	STEWARD, Andw.	PHA 48
Christopher	BER	246	John	GRN	78	Carlisle Jnr.	MER 461
Daniel	NOH	44	STEUBEN, Peter M.			Daniel	MER 461
George	ADA	11	Van	NOH	38A	George	LAN 91
George	NOH	79	STEUP, Samuel	NOH	32A	George	DEL 170
George	BUC	158	STEUR, Conrod	CHE	907	George	DEL 171
Henry	BER	227	STEVAH?, Abraham	FRA	309	James	LAN 249
Henry	BER	278	STEVANS, Henrry	ALL	75	James	MER 459
Jacob	NOH	61	Luke	CRA	13	Mary	PHA 64
Jacob	BER	278	STEVANSON,			William	DEL 169
Jacob	BUC	148A	Aandrew	ALL	108	William	MER 459
John	BER	278	Alexd.	ALL	104	Wm.	PHI 108
John Junr.	NOH	44	George	ALL	53	Wm.	PHI 113A
John Senr.	NOH	44	George	ALL	57	STEWARDSON, Thos.	PHA 82
Michael	NOH	42	John	ALL	110	STEWART, Widow	YOR 200
Michael	SOM	150	STEVASON, John	ALL	90	Widow	WST 373
Nicholas	NOH	44	STEVE, Jacob	DAU	32	Widw.	PHI 74
Peter	BER	214	STEVEN, George	LAN	269	Abraham Esqr.	FAY 253
STERNER?,			Philip	LAN	269	Alexander	HNT 122
Christopher	BER	214	Widow	LAN	269	Alexander	HNT 130
STERNWEG, Thomas	LAN	144	STEVENS, Benedict	HNT	134	Alexander	NOU 168
STERRET, Benjn.	CUM	136	Benjamen	FAY	206	Alexr.	CEN 24
David	CUM	135	Benjn.	FAY	211	Alexr.	MIF 26
James	CUM	125	Benjn. Jur.	FAY	211	Alexr.	MIF 15A
James	LAN	263	Edward	FAY	206	Andrew	WST 296
John	DAU	23A	Ezea	FAY	253	Andrew	CHE 846
Robt.	CUM	139	Hannah	PHA	87	Andw.	WST 351

INDEX TO THE 1800 CENSUS OF PENNSYLVANIA

STEWART,			STEWART, James	BER	250	STEWART, Robert	DAU	23A
Archibald	BFD	41	James	FAY	250	Robt.	FRA	290
Archibald	MIF	13A	James	FRA	290	Robt.	FRA	309
Archibd.	FAY	259	James	LAN	298	Robt.	FRA	317
Bartin	BUC	155	James	LUZ	329	Robt.	BUT	341
Benjamin	WAS	59	James	WST	329	Robt.	BUT	341
Betty	FRA	282	James	CHE	703	Robt.	CHE	907
Catharine	HNT	158	Jane	CUM	45	Robt.	MIF	8A
Catherine	WAS	59	Jane	BFD	77	Saml.	CUM	106
Cathrine	PHA	37	Jas.	CUM	45	Saml.?	MIF	11
Charles	MIF	2	Jennet	YOR	173	Samuel	ALL	72
Charles	WAS	105	Jesse	FAY	268	Samuel	ALL	110
Charles	BUC	106	Jno. Junr.	CUM	26	Samuel	HNT	163
Charles	PHI	121	Jno.	DAU	35A	Samuel	FAY	211
Charles	YOR	212	John	ADA	3	Samuel	CHE	763
Charles	YOR	213	John	BEV	8	Samuel	DAU	23A
Charles	CHE	827	John	ADA	14	Sarah	BUC	152
Charles	CHE	900	John	WAS	25	Solomon	MNT	70
Charles (Negro)	WAS	83	John	CUM	30	Thomas	BFD	53
Charles	DAU	44A	John	WAS	32	Thomas	ALL	73
Charles	PHI	104A	John	WAS	59	Thomas	BUC	106
Charles	BUC	154A	John	ALL	67	Thomas	ALL	120
Chas.	PHA	48	John	PHA	69	Thomas	CHE	705
Dacas	LUZ	326	John	ALL	80	Thos.	FRA	300
Daniel	WAS	87	John	ALL	89	Thos.	MIF	8A
David	ADA	14	John	ALL	97	William	ADA	3
David	WAS	25	John	ALL	103	William	ADA	4
David	WAS	87	John	ALL	107	William	MIF	4
David	HNT	130	John	ALL	111	William	ADA	6
David	HNT	132	John	HNT	124	William	ADA	6
David	NOU	178	John	NOU	155	William	ADA	7
David	LUZ	329	John	WST	157	William	WAS	18
David	CHE	722	John	HNT	165	William	DAU	24
David Esqr.	HNT	148	John	YOR	198	William	NOH	51
Duncan	PHI	69A	John	FAY	211	William	WAS	59
Edward	LAN	39	John	FAY	228	William	WAS	71
Elizabeth	MNT	70	John	FAY	262	William	NOH	79
Elizabeth	YOR	160	John	FAY	268	William	MNT	106
Elizabeth	FAY	199	John	FRA	290	William	HNT	151
Francis	PHI	62	John	WST	373	William	WST	157
Galbraith	WAS	59	John	CHE	719	William	NOU	172
George	ALL	53	John	CHE	754	William	YOR	214
George	BUC	106	John	CHE	829	William	FAY	250
George	FAY	206	John Esqr.	YOR	155	William	MIF	8A
George	FAY	218	John Jur.	ALL	80	Wilm.	ALL	61
George	LUZ	329	John	MIF	5A	Wilm.	ALL	66
Gilbert	PHI	131	John	MIF	8A	Wilm.	ALL	104
Hanah	ALL	80	Joseph	BFD	53	Wilm.	ALL	107
Henry	ALL	87	Joseph	MIF	5A	Wilson	MIF	11
Henry	HNT	122	Joseph	BUC	154A	Wm.	CUM	56
Henry	PHI	130	Josiah	LUZ	326	Wm.	CUM	82
Henry	WST	157	Lazyn.?	DAU	15A	Wm.	PHA	85
Henry	FAY	262	Levy	BEV	6	Wm.	CUM	106
Hugh	LAN	56	Margaret	PHA	72	Wm.	CUM	116
Hugh	CUM	74	Mary	ALL	107	Wm.	FRA	314
Hugh	FRA	297	Mary	HNT	163	Wm.	CHE	877
Isabella	CUM	45	Mathew	BEV	5	Wm.	DAU	35A
Jacob	FAY	241	Moses	PHA	53	STEWERT, Adam	CRA	13
Jacob	BUC	87A	Noble C.	PHA	91	John	VEN	165
Jain	ALL	88	Peter	YOR	195	John	VEN	166
James	BEV	5	Ralph	FAY	233	STEYERWALD,		
James	BEV	6	Richard	ERI	60	Charles	NOH	76A
James	ADA	7	Robert	ADA	12	John	NOH	76A
James	ADA	8	Robert	ADA	26	Peter	NOH	76A
James	ADA	16	Robert	NOH	51	STEYLEY, Jacob	LAN	255
James	ADA	26	Robert	ALL	63	STEYNER, David	LAN	188
James	MIF	26	Robert	ALL	72	Henry	LAN	186
James	WAS	35	Robert	ALL	98	Joseph	LAN	188
James	ERI	60	Robert	HNT	130	STEYTZ, Peter	LAN	190
James	PHA	81	Robert	HNT	132	STEZER, Henry	DAU	48A
James	ALL	111	Robert	MNT	142	STHRER, Peter	YOR	173
James	HNT	148	Robert	HNT	151	STI--?, Dorathan?	FRA	296
James	WST	157	Robert	SOM	163	STI-ELY?, Jacob	BER	238
James	YOR	198	Robert	HNT	165	STICE, Peter	PHA	26
James	FAY	211	Robert Senr.	ADA	8	STICHLER, John	BER	180
James	FAY	237	Robert	MNT	105	Peter	BER	212

STIVENS, David	FAY	233	STOCKSLAGLE,			STOLE, Erhart	BER	209
STIVER, John	CEN	21	Joseph	ADA	25	STOLER, Frederick	LAN	22
John	NOU	119	Widow	ADA	11	Jacob	DAU	12A
Samuel	FRA	271	STOCKSLEGER, John	LAN	116	STOLES?, Widow	BUC	85
STIVERS, John	FAY	237	STOCKSLIGER,			STOLL, Andrew	BUC	139A
Samuel	ALL	87	Widow	LAN	59	Frederick	NOH	82A
STIVERSON,			STOCKTON, John	GRN	96	George	BUC	102
George,			John	BUC	99A	George	YOR	160
(Crossed			Joseph	WAS	14	Henry	YOR	154
Out-gone)	WST	329	Robert	WAS	64	James	MNT	74
STIVIE, Peter	LAN	178	Robert Junr.	WAS	14	John	LAN	45
STIZEL, Henry	FRA	291	Robert Senr.	WAS	14	Martin	LAN	234
STO-T?, Jacob	CHE	753	Sarah	BUC	99A	Valentine	BER	253
STOAFER, Jacob	MNT	119	Thomas	WAS	14	STOLSINGER, Adam	YOR	197
Rudolph	MNT	90	STOCKWELL, James	FAY	223	STOLTZ, Jacob	NOH	65A
STOAKER, Joshua	CHE	870	John	FAY	253	Michael	ADA	26
STOAN, William	BFD	39	STOCTON, Robt.	PHI	82A	STOLTZFOOS, John	LAN	178
STOB, Henry	ADA	36	STOD, James	PHI	76A	STOLZ, Jacob	LAN	298
STOBB?, Ulrick	MNT	62	STODDARD, Elisha	ERI	59	STOLZFUS,		
STOBER, Jacob	LAN	147B	STODDART, John	PHA	20	Christian	BER	168
John	LAN	271	STOEHR,			STOMBACH, Stophel	BUC	156
John	LAN	271	Christopher	YOR	157	STOMER, Fredrick	ALL	58
Philip	LAN	269	STOEVER, Adam Jr.	DAU	25A	STOMMELL, Peter	DEL	162
STOCDALE?, James	GRN	108	Adam	DAU	25A	STOMP, Abraham	NOU	141
STOCHSLEGER,			Caspar	DAU	51	STONE, Andw.	CUM	108
Philip	LAN	56	Fredrik	DAU	32A	Benjamin	LUZ	410
STOCK, Adam	LAN	67	George	DAU	25	Christian	BUC	157A
Adam	LAN	82	John	DAU	25A	Daniel	PHA	36
George	NOU	190	Tobias	DAU	25	Daniel	NOU	152
George C./ E.?	HNT	154	STOFER, Christian	ADA	10	David	CHE	907
John	PHA	84	Christian	LAN	180	Elias	GRN	85
John	LAN	267	John	CHE	792	Elija	FAY	223
Lewis	MNT	62	STOFFER, George	LAN	83	Francis	WAS	50
Matthas	NOU	140	Henry	LAN	83	Frederick	BUC	140
Meleker	NOU	140	Jacob	LAN	83	Fredrick	DAU	6A
Philip	PHI	105	Jacob	FRA	318	Fredrik	DAU	37
STOCKARD, Coneley	PHA	121	Matthias	LAN	83	George	PHI	47
STOCKBERGER,			STOFFLET, Henry	NOH	74A	George	CHE	841
Widow	WST	315	John	NOH	92	Hugh	YOR	212
Mathias	WST	316	STOFFMAN, Thomas	PHI	7	Jacob	YOR	192
STOCKDALE, Thomas	WAS	83	STOFFT, Widow	LAN	54	Jacob	FRA	321
STOCKDON, John	WST	277	STOFLET, Lewis	NOU	168	James	LYC	27
Robt.	CUM	24	STOGDALE, David	BUC	87	James	GRN	85
STOCKEL, Widow	NOH	91A	John	BUC	151A	James	NOU	152
STOCKER, Adam	NOH	40	STOGDELL, John	FAY	259	John	LAN	46
Adam (Son Of			STOGDEN, Garret	PHI	31	John	WAS	94
Am.)	NOH	40A	STOHL, Nicholas	LUZ	358	John	PHA	109
Adam Junr.	NOH	40	STOHLER, (No			John	MIF	5A
Am. (See			Given Name)	DAU	15	John	PHI	118A
Stocker,			Henry	DAU	30A	Joseph	CHE	841
Adam)	NOH	40A	Widow	LAN	98	Peter	DAU	37
Andrew	NOH	40	STOHR, Jacob	YOR	165	Peter	CHE	775
George	NOH	74A	STOKE, Fredr.	FRA	314	Rachel	LUZ	428
Jacob	NOH	40	George	FRA	314	Rebeca	ALL	92
John	NOH	40	John	FRA	314	Richard	NOH	79
John Clement	PHA	98	Ludwich	FRA	317	Richard	MIF	8A
Leonard	NOH	40	STOKELEY, Thomas			Robert	LUZ	381
Margaret	PHA	100	Esqr.	WAS	117	Robt.	PHI	67
Michael	NOH	40	STOKELY, Widow	WST	257	Robt.	FRA	278
STOCKER?, (See			John	PHI	76A	Saml.	CHE	776
Storker)	NOH	74A	STOKER, George	FRA	307	Samuel	ADA	9
STOCKEY, William	DEL	156	STOKERMAN,			Widow	LAN	266
STOCKHAM, George	BUC	95	Christopher	BER	231	William	PHI	51
STOCKINGWEAVER,			STOKES, Benjn.	PHA	47	William	WAS	94
(No Given			Benjn.	PHI	69A	William	NOU	155
Name)	LAN	138	James	PHA	16	William	CHE	731
STOCKLEY, Benja.	MER	460	James	PHI	130	Wm.	PHA	101
STOCKMAN, Jabas			James	BUC	107A	Wm.	CHE	778
(A Boarding			John	BEV	15	STONEBACH, Michl.	BUC	82
House)	PHA	38	John	BUC	82	STONEBACK, Balser	BUC	82A
John	CHE	746	Joseph	PHA	18	Christpr.	MNT	88
Nathan	NOU	132	Joseph	NOU	107	John	CHE	907
STOCKS, Thomas	ALL	107	Richard	SOM	163	Michael	MNT	88
STOCKSCHLEGER,			Thos.	PHI	106A	Michl.	PHI	104A
Peter	LAN	188	William	PHA	102	STONEBERGER,		
STOCKSLAGLE, John	ADA	12	STOKEY, Benjamin	LUZ	356	Peter	CUM	72

STRAUSS, Jacob	NOH	92	STREEPER, Barbara	PHI	122	STRICKLER, Henrey	FAY	250
Jacob	NOH	61A	Daniel	PHI	124	Henry	YOR	167
John	NOH	42	Dennis	PHI	123	Henry (M)	YOR	167
Jost	NOH	92A	Henry	PHI	122	Isaiah	PHI	144
Peter	NOH	51	Judith	PHI	140	J./ I.? (See		
Philip	NOH	84A	William	PHI	122	Stirckler,		
STRAW-ER?, Henry	NOU	115	William	PHI	123	H.)	LAN	264
STRAW, Widow	PHI	76	STREEPER?,			Jacob	YOR	167
Daniel	DAU	42A	William	DEL	184	Jacob	FAY	206
Frederick	NOU	178	STREET, Benjan.	PHI	137	Jacob	FAY	250
George	DAU	11	Elizabeth	PHA	104	Jacob	FAY	250
George	DAU	33	Griffith	PHI	145	Jacob Sr	YOR	167
George Jr.	DAU	11	James	BUC	89	Jacob (B.s.)	YOR	167
Hamkle	LAN	134	John	ALL	115	Jacob	BUC	153A
Jacob	WST	224	Nicholas	PHA	36	John	YOR	167
John	DAU	11	Thos.	PHI	101A	John	YOR	169
John	DAU	42A	STREFEL, George	PHI	50	John	FAY	206
Michael	DAU	36	STREHR, John	YOR	173	Jos.	YOR	167
Peter	WST	224	STREIN?, Jacob	NOH	92	Joseph	PHI	134
Peter	WST	227	STREMBACK, John	BUC	99A	Laurence	WAS	9
Philip	CRA	7	STRENGER?, John	MNT	119	Leonard	DAU	37A
Yost	DAU	11	STREWER, Susanna	DAU	14A	Peter	YOR	209
STRAWBRIDG,			STREWICH, Jacob	YOR	159	Peter	DAU	31A
Thomas	NOU	119	STREWICK?,			Peter	BUC	151A
STRAWBRIDGE,			Catharine	YOR	171	Ulrich	YOR	167
Elihu	MNT	86	George	YOR	171	Ulrich & A.	LAN	266
Isaac	YOR	202	STREYER, Henry	YOR	194	STRICKLIN, Peter	ERI	55A
James	NOU	160	Matthias	BFD	67	STRICLER, Sirac	PHI	134
James	CHE	713	Nicholas	BFD	69	STRIDE, David	ADA	12
Jos.	YOR	202	STREYLEY, Stephen	YOR	176	Joseph	PHA	121
Joseph	CHE	713	STRIAR, Matthias	NOU	140	STRIDEFORD,		
Justis	NOU	144	STRICBANE, Philip	PHI	86A	Edward	BUC	156
Thos	YOR	167	STRICKER, Widw.	PHI	105B	STRIEBY, Leonard	NOH	92A
STRAWBRIGE,			Adam (Crossed			STRIGBT,		
Benjamin	NOU	181	Out)	PHI	105A	Christian	LAN	255
John	NOU	160	Adam	PHI	105B	STRIGLER, Fredk.	DAU	31A
Joseph	NOU	145	Andw.	CUM	64	STRIGLIN, Timothy	NOU	132
STRAWDER, Philip	NOH	79	Arnold	CUM	121	STRIKER, Isaac	NOU	102
STRAWDING, Adnrew	DAU	34	Connard	PHI	108A	John	LYC	8
STRAWHAN, Abel	BUC	82	Henry	CUM	121	STRIMBACH, Willm.	PHI	18
Enoch	BUC	82	Jacob	WAS	9	STRIMK, David	LAN	152
Jacob	BUC	82	Jacob	PHI	61A	STRIMMER, John	PHI	86A
William	BUC	82	John	BUC	101A	STRINE, Peter	YOR	214
Wm. Jnr.	BUC	82A	STRICKHOUSER,			STRINE?, Masten?	FRA	274
STRAWN, Isaiah	SOM	144	Widow	YOR	191	STRINGER,		
Jacob	GRN	93	Henry	YOR	189	Benjamin	LUZ	395
John Junr.	GRN	105	John	YOR	188	Charles	BUC	84
John Senr.	GRN	105	STRICKLAND,			Henry	WAY	150
STRAYER, George	BER	209	Abraham	BUC	94A	James	BUC	84
Jacob	YOR	195	Amos	MNT	66	James	WAY	150
John	DAU	42A	Hugh	CHE	790	Jno.	PHA	78
Nicholas	YOR	195	John	BUC	161A	Joseph	WAS	25
Peter	BFD	66	Jonathan	WAY	145	Samuel	NOU	160
Peter	FAY	241	Jonathan Jr.	WAY	145	William	WAY	150
STRAYHORN,			Joseph	BUC	152	Wm.	CHE	873
Nathaniel	NOU	132	Miles	YOR	204	STRINGFELLOW,		
Samuel	CHE	701	Nancy	LUZ	413	Jesse	CHE	824
STRAYLEY, Mary	PHA	84	Thos.	CHE	729	STRINGFILEN,		
Peter	FRA	314	Wm.	CHE	794	William	NOU	178
STREAFS, Ephm.	CUM	89	STRICKLE, Henry	LAN	256	STRINGFILLOW,		
STREAHER, (See			STRICKLEE, Henry	LAN	264	Geo.	CHE	778
Streaper)	MNT	92	STRICKLEN, George	CHE	797	STRIPE, Ann	HNT	126
STREALY, John	FRA	273	Hugh	CHE	797	Henry	BER	227
STREAPER, Jacob	MNT	92	STRICKLER, A. &			STRIPPE, George	BUC	139A
John	MNT	92	Ulrich	LAN	266	Michael	BUC	139A
Margaret	MNT	109	Abraham	FAY	250	STRITE, Joseph	DAU	20A
Peter	MNT	109	Abrm.	BUC	162	Joseph	DAU	21A
STREAR, Andw.	NOU	185	Barbara	YOR	167	STRITHOFF, Jacob	FRA	286
STREASSER, (See			Christian	YOR	167	STRITSEL, John	PHI	140
Streaper)	MNT	92	Conrad	FAY	250	STRO, Philip	LAN	180
STREASSER?, Mary	MNT	139	Elizab.	DAU	21A	STROAD, Emos	MIF	17A
STREBER, Peter	YOR	154	Geo.	DAU	30A	STROCESNIDER,		
STREBY, George	PHI	77A	Geo.	DAU	31A	Gasper	GRN	65
STRECK, Broadway	PHI	98	George	DAU	37A	John	GRN	65
STREEBY, Adam	PHI	77A	George	DAU	37A	STROCK, Henry	DAU	37A
STREEPER, Widow	PHI	123	H & J./ I.?	LAN	264	Henry	BUC	82A

STUCKEY, Fredr.	FRA	302	STUMP, Jacob	PHI	147	STURGES, Peter	PHA	114
Michael	DAU	20	Jacob	FRA	291	Stokeley	PHA	97
Samuel	BFD	52	John	NOH	49	Stokley	PHI	40
Simon	BFD	52	John	PHI	119	William	CUM	152
STUCKMAN, John	BFD	67	John	BER	142	STURGION, Henry	ALL	100
Peter	BFD	69	John	SOM	155	Robert	FAY	259
STUDARD, Hugh	FAY	259	John	YOR	156	STURGIS, James	DEL	174
STUDDARD, Robert	ALL	109	John	BER	189	Jonathan	DEL	156
STUDDERD, James	ALL	90	John	BER	201	William	PHA	16
STUDDS, Lewis	MIF	15A	John	BER	238	STURK, Jacob	PHI	77
STUDEBAKER, David	SOM	159	John	FRA	282	STURLE?, (See		
John	YOR	213	John	FRA	310	Sturte)	LAN	176
Philip	FAY	199	Joseph	BUC	160	STURMBACH, George	LAN	47
STUDEBECKER, Jos.	BUT	364	Leonard	DAU	37	Nicholas	LAN	298
STUDEM?, See			Leonard	BER	151	STURNERACK?,		
Steedem	BEV	27	Leonard	YOR	182	Dominuk	PHI	69
STUDENROTH, Henry	LAN	204	Matthias	YOR	213	STURTE, Robert	LAN	176
STUDEY, George	WAS	113	Michael	BER	285	STURTZ, Adam	SOM	152
John	WAS	113	Michl.	FRA	315	Christian	SOM	152
Michael	WAS	113	Nicholas	BER	278	Christian Sen.	SOM	152
STUDGER, Felix	FAY	224	Saml.	BER	201	Jacob	SOM	152
STUDIBAKER, David	BFD	76	William	WAS	83	STUS?, (See		
Jacob	BFD	52	William	MIF	17A	Stees)	NOU	185
John	BFD	78	STUMPAGH, Phillip	CUM	102	STUTS, Margt.	CUM	31
STUDMAN, David	NOU	173	STUMPAUGH, Elizh.	FRA	313	STUTSMAN, David	FAY	229
James	NOU	119	John	FRA	309	STUTTER, John	CHE	860
William	NOU	119	Peter	CUM	149	Martin	PHI	123
STUDY,			STUNBRUCK,			William	CHE	853
Christopher	FRA	320	Christian	NOU	102	STUTZMAN, Abraham	SOM	160
Philip	BFD	53	STUNCK?, David	BER	275	Christn.	BER	146
STUFF, George	LAN	239	STUNEGER, Justice	PHI	5	David	SOM	159
Michael	BFD	66	STUNG, John	LAN	152	Jacob	SOM	140
Nicholas	FRA	299	Scot	LAN	152	Jacob	SOM	159
STUFFEL, John	PHI	8	STUNKARD, James	HNT	142	John	SOM	140
STUFIN, Stophel	LAN	123	STUNKERD, Robert	HNT	142	Stephen	SOM	159
STUKLEY, Abrm.	DAU	46	STUNSBERGER?,			STYELES, Freedom	WST	382
STULL, Adam	PHA	61	Peter	CUM	72	STYER, Adam	LAN	90
Adam	SOM	141	STUNTEZ?, John	CRA	16	David	MNT	112
Andrew	ERI	58	STUPP, Adam	BER	268	Henry	MNT	116
Daniel	FRA	301	Martin	BER	266	John	MNT	116
George	BFD	69	STUR, James	CEN	19	Leonard	MNT	114
Henry	FRA	306	Joseph	CEN	19	Nicholas	MNT	136
Jacob	BFD	66	Thomas	CEN	19	STYERS, Benjamin	SOM	144
Jacob	BUC	160	STUR?, Barnery	ARM	127	Rudolph	SOM	135
John	SOM	141	STURD, Thomas	LAN	215	STYLES, Daniel R.	LUZ	320
John	WST	329	STURDEBAKER,			Henry	BER	240
Ludwick	FRA	306	Peter	ADA	15	SUABLE?, See		
Nicholas	BFD	67	STURDIVANT,			Snable	BER	214
Paul	FAY	262	Abijah	LUZ	400	SUARD?, Stephen	BUC	89
Wm.	PHA	73	Azor	LUZ	400	SUAVY, Mary	PHA	114
STULLER, Ulercy	SOM	147	James	LUZ	400	SUBER, Abner	BUC	99A
STULMAN, Solomon	PHI	21	Noah	LUZ	400	Jacob	BUC	99A
STULT, Jeremiah	PHI	80	Samuel	LUZ	400	SUBERS, Joseph	BUC	161A
Willm.	PHI	95A	Samuel	LUZ	400	Mary	BUC	161A
STULTS, John	GRN	103	STURENTZ, Francis	LAN	257	SUBERT, George	PHI	84A
STUMBAUGH, Peter	FRA	309	STURGAN, Wilm.	ALL	107	SUBLER, Widow	LAN	56
Phillip	CUM	42	STURGAN?,			SUBURS?, Amos	PHI	149
Phillip	FRA	308	Jeramiaha	ALL	53	SUCH, Adam	NOU	125
STUMP, Adam	ADA	31	STURGENS, John	LAN	77	Sorke	NOU	181
Adam	YOR	171	STURGEON,			Thos.	CUM	44
Adam	DAU	51A	Jerimiah	DAU	23A	SUCH?, Benjn.	MNT	79
Benjamin	BER	272	John	MIF	11	SUCHLINE, George	PHI	142
Casper	BER	268	John	BEV	27	SUCHS, Abraham	GRN	109
Chirstopher	WAS	83	Patton &	DAU	18A	SUCK, Christian	LAN	179
Christn.	BER	152	Peter	MIF	11	John	NOH	54
Conrad	BER	131	Robt. Jr.	DAU	23A	SUCK?, Benjn.	MNT	79
Daniel	PHI	147	Robt. Sr.	DAU	23A	SUCKER, John	LAN	304
Eve	BER	233	Saml.	CUM	146	SUDER, Frederick	NOH	61A
Frederick	LAN	299	Saml.	DAU	23A	SUDERLAND,		
Fredr.	FRA	315	William	ADA	24	Christn.	PHI	90A
George	WAS	40	William	ADA	33	Thomas	NOU	132
George	BER	131	STURGEON?, -----	MIF	11	SUDEY, Martin	PHI	86A
Henry	BER	152	STURGER, John	FAY	248	SUFIN, Arthur	NOU	160
Jacob	LYC	15	STURGES, John	PHI	44	Richard	NOU	160
Jacob	CUM	102	Jonathan	PHA	115	SUGAR, Charles	BER	204
Jacob	NOU	141	Jonathan	DEL	157	Jacob	PHI	87

SUTTON, Enoch	WAS	5	SWAINEY, James	FAY 259	SWARTS,		
George	WST	175	John	LUZ 427	Christopher	WST	329
Henry	WAS	5	SWALLO, Daniel	BUC 146	Isaac (Michael		
Isaac	PHI	92A	SWALLOW, James	LUZ 323	Crossed Out)	BUC	97A
James	LUZ	376	SWALZEL?, (See		Jacob	BUC	98
Jeremiah	BUT	350	Swatzel)	MIF 4	Jacob	BUC	106
Jeremiah	BUT	350	SWAN, Benjamin	FRA 271	Jacob	BUC	97A
Jeremiah	WST	351	Charles	GRN 90	John	NOU	168
John	BEV	13	Elizabeth	WST 296	Peter	NOU	140
John	LYC	22	George	FRA 279	Peter	NOU	168
John	SOM	135	Henry	GRN 90	SWARTSWALLER,		
John	MER	459	Jacob	YOR 194	Christn.	CHE	720
John	MER	460	John	GRN 90	SWARTSWOOD, Levi	WST	278
Jonathan	BUC	95	John	CUM 129	SWARTWOOD,		
Joseph	WST	352	Joseph	FRA 279	Bernadus	WAY	147
Joshua	PHI	138	Joshua	DAU 39A	Moses	NOH	42
Peter	WST	157	Richard	GRN 90	SWARTWOUDT,		
Platt	WST	351	Richd.	DAU 17A	Alexander	LUZ	372
Richard	WAS	125	Robert	PHA 7	SWARTZ, Abraham	YOR	172
Richard	VEN	169	Robt.	FRA 279	Adam	ADA	42
Robt.	BUT	360	Thomas	CRA 10	Adam	BER	284
Ruth	MNT	52	Thos.	PHA 83	Andw.	LYC	24
Saml.	BUT	362	Timothy	FAY 211	Balser	BFD	66
Samuel	WAY	145	William	GRN 90	Christian	CHE	793
Samuel	BUC	94A	William	HNT 143	Christley	DAU	14A
Solomon	MER	459	William	WST 257	Conrad	LAN	33
Stephen	WAS	76	SWANER, John	CHE 782	Conrad	YOR	193
Stephen	MER	459	SWANEY, John	LAN 97	Daniel	HNT	125
Thomas	BUC	85	SWANGER, Christr.	CUM 75	Francis	HNT	125
Thomas	WST	176	David	CUM 75	Frederick	BFD	66
Wm.	PHI	120	Jacob	CUM 74	Frederick	MNT	97
Zebulon	WAS	64	Jno.	FRA 276	Geo.	CUM	58
Zedekiah	WST	351	Paul	CUM 75	George	DAU	34
SUVOLT, Jacob	SOM	152	SWANINGHAM, Wm.	FAY 259	George	PHA	37
SWAAB, Jacob	PHI	96	SWANK, Adam	FRA 312	George	BFD	66
SWABLY, Adam	BER	183	Andrew	MNT 125	George	YOR	171
Adam Jr.	BER	183	Casper	SOM 130	George	NOU	177
Jacob	BER	185	Casper	FRA 321	George	BER	238
Jacob	BER	185	Christian	HNT 124	George Jr.	BER	239
Leonard	BER	183	Christian Junr.	HNT 124	Geroge	YOR	194
Michael	BER	183	Christopher	FRA 320	Goerge	SOM	141
SWABRIDGE, Wm.	CUM	94	Henry	FRA 320	Henry	DAU	35
SWAFF, Petre	CUM	113	Jacob	NOU 107	Henry	BFD	66
SWAGART, Jno.	MIF	26	Jacob	SOM 131	Henry	NOU	189
SWAGER, Adam	SOM	131	John	WST 373	Henry	BER	242
Henry	BEV	6	Michael	DAU 48A	Henry	PHI	98
Henry	SOM	130	Thomas	SOM 130	Heston	MNT	126
Jacob	BFD	76	SWANNER, Peter	MNT 74	Jacob	SOM	141
John	BFD	77	SWANY, Daniel	ALL 119	Jacob	SOM	152
Philip	BUC	141A	SWANZY, William	CEN 19	Jacob	YOR	192
William	BFD	77	SWAP, Melchior	BER 132	John	DAU	35
SWAGGART, Adam	WAY	138	SWARINGGIN,		John	CUM	58
Adam Jr.	WAY	138	Nicholas	ALL 112	John	HNT	125
John	FRA	280	Thomas	ALL 112	John	YOR	171
Michl.	FRA	284	SWARM, Adam	DAU 39A	John	NOU	184
SWAGGERS, George	HNT	147	SWARR, Christian	LAN 309	John	NOU	185
John	HNT	146	Christian	LAN 313	John	LAN	205
SWAGLER, Jacob	WAS	113	John	LAN 307	John	BER	262
SWAILS?, Isaac	MIF	11	John Junr.	LAN 307	John	MIF	13A
SWAIN, Ann	CHE	714	SWARS, Jacob	LAN 163	Laurence	BFD	66
Anthony	FAY	253	SWART, Jacob	WAS 5	Leonard	BER	153
Benjn.	BUC	85	Philip	WAS 5	Ludwig	BER	153
Daivd	BUC	84	Sebastian	FRA 271	Magdalena	BER	151
George	PHA	58	SWARTCOB, Anthony	NOU 190	Martin	ADA	32
Jaacob	PHA	110	SWARTLANDER,		Martin	CUM	33
James	FAY	259	Conrad	BUC 106	Martin	NOU	184
James	PHI	74A	Gabriel	BUC 105A	Mattw.	MIF	13A
John	PHI	104	Philip	BUC 106	Michael	HNT	147
Martha	PHI	74	SWARTLEY, Philip	BUC 106	Michael	BER	152
Samuel	BUC	85	SWARTLY, Henry	BUC 92	Michl.	CUM	56
Shubald	PHA	63	Jacob	BUC 91A	Nicholas	LAN	204
Sylas	PHA	7	John	BUC 92	Nichos.	CUM	62
SWAINE, Francis	MNT	84	John	MNT 126	Nichs.	CUM	54
Isaac	LUZ	406	SWARTMAN, Anthy.	CUM 41	Peter	NOU	185
Isaac Jr.	LUZ	406	SWARTS, Andrew	BUC 106	Peter	BER	246
John	PHA	44	Christian	BUC 106	Peter	BER	266

397

SWARTZ, Peter	MIF	13A	SWEICKERT, Peter	LAN	205	SWICKARD, Daniel	WAS	113
Philip	DAU	4	SWEIGART, Abraham	YOR	179	Martin	WAS	113
Philip	BER	157	Adam	DAU	9A	SWIER, Geo.	PHI	90A
Phillip	NOU	98	Andrew	DAU	9A	SWIFE?, Barbara	MIF	3
Saml.	BER	214	John	DAU	8A	SWIFT, Charles	PHI	43
William	YOR	161	Martin	LAN	12	John	BUC	89
SWARTZBAUGH, John	YOR	186	SWEIGER, Felix	LAN	238	John	PHI	150
John Jr.	YOR	187	John	LAN	239	John	BUC	161A
SWARTZENSTROVER,			Michael	PHI	134	Joseph	PHA	122
Danl.	CHE	833	Sebastian	LAN	239	Joseph	LAN	150
SWARTZLY,			SWEIGERT, Peter	SOM	159	Joseph	LAN	157
Matthias	BFD	52	SWEISGOOD, George	YOR	179	Richard	WAY	150
SWARTZMAN, Jos.	YOR	181	SWEITZER, Conrad	FAY	269	Saml.	PHI	155
SWARTZWELTER,			Daniel	LAN	57	SWIFT?, Fames	PHI	38
Philip	YOR	157	Frederick	BER	149	SWIGAR, Abraham	LAN	65
SWARTZWILDER,			Jacob	SOM	130	SWIGART, Geoge	FRA	292
Peter	BFD	46	Jacob	SOM	131	Martin	LAN	65
Peter	BFD	52	John	LAN	31	Peter	DAU	9A
SWASCH, George	ALL	87	Ludwig	LAN	205	SWIGER, George	LAN	64
SWASICK, James	MER	460	Peter	SOM	131	Jacob	LAN	67
SWATZEL, Joseph	MIF	4	Peter	SOM	139	John	LAN	72
SWAWLE, Margaret	YOR	168	Peter	BER	149	Philip	LAN	131
SWAY, John	PHI	36	Peter Senr.	SOM	131	Samuel	LAN	64
SWAYNE, Benjn.	CHE	850	Stephen	LAN	31	SWIGERT, Chris.	LAN	85
Caleb	CHE	850	Widow	LAN	45	Leonard	BFD	77
George	DEL	168	SWEIZER, Peter	BUT	325	SWIGLER, Ludwick	CUM	73
Jacob	CHE	758	SWEM, Joseph	FAY	206	SWIHEL?, Jacob	NOH	32A
Jacob	CHE	807	SWENCK, Abrm.	MNT	96	SWIL?, Enoch	DEL	165
James	CHE	862	Andrew	MNT	101	Owen	DEL	157
Jesse	CHE	741	Daniel	MNT	96	SWILER, Christr.	CUM	58
SWAYNEY, John	CHE	873	Frederick	NOU	140	SWILIER, Jacob	CUM	58
SWAZER?,			George	MNT	122	SWIM, Barbara	FRA	279
Christian	MNT	59	Henry	MNT	46	SWIMBLER, Andw.	CHE	814
SWE---, James	ADA	38	Henry	MNT	119	SWIN, John	NOU	102
SWEANEY, Daniel	ADA	5	Henry	MNT	123	SWINCK, Martin	NOU	102
Thomas	ADA	9	Jacob	MNT	46	Martin	NOU	107
SWEANY, Charles	BUT	333	Jacob	MNT	84	SWINCKEL, Michael	NOU	190
James	ADA	7	John	MNT	96	SWINDLAR, Saml.	FAY	247
John	ADA	7	Maria	LAN	306	SWINEFORD,		
John	ADA	10	Nicholas	MNT	122	Albright	NOU	141
John	NOU	119	Peter	LAN	39	George	NOU	140
SWEARENGEN,			SWENEY, Benjamin	FRA	272	John	NOU	140
Samuel	BEV	25	Jos.	LYC	14	Peter	NOU	140
SWEARER, Peter	CHE	736	Neal	PHA	17A	SWINEHART, Adam	WAS	125
SWEARINGEN,			SWENGER, George	BUC	82A	Conrad	BER	164
Andrew Esqr.	WAS	24	SWENK, Conrad	BER	222	Daniel	BER	164
Joseph	WAS	24	George	BER	132	Gabiel	WAS	106
SWEARINGIN, Saml.	MIF	5A	Henry	BER	132	Gabriel Junr.	WAS	125
SWEATLAND,			Jacob	BER	222	Gabriel Senr.	WAS	125
Artemus	LUZ	403	John Od.?	BER	222	George	NOU	125
Belden	LUZ	335	SWENTZEL,			Henry	MNT	101
Joseph	LUZ	337	Frederick	LAN	43	Henry	CHE	907
SWEEKE, John	WAS	87	SWENY, Alexander	WAS	76	Laver	CEN	21
SWEENEY, Hugh	CUM	82	Daniel	WAS	40	Michael	MNT	62
James	DAU	24	James	WAS	40	Michale	BER	164
Katharine	BEV	23	John	LAN	170	Peter	WAS	125
SWEENY, Dennis	PHA	116	John Senr.	LAN	171	SWINEHEART,		
Doyle	PHI	11	Mrs.	NOU	168	Andrew	NOU	125
Eleneor	PHA	99	Samuel	NOU	119	Andrew	NOU	125
James	PHI	154	SWEPHENHISER,			Henry	NOU	132
James	YOR	193	Nicholas	PHA	66	John	NOU	125
James	YOR	202	SWER-T?, Adam	MIF	5A	SWINERT, Jacob	LYC	24
James	DAU	24A	SWERINGAM,			SWINEY, Bernard	HNT	166
Thomas	BEV	24	Catherin	FAY	247	SWINGLE, Widw.	PHI	80
SWEEP, John	BER	284	Steel	FAY	247	Conrad	WAY	139
SWEET, Amos	LUZ	385	SWERNER, Henry	CHE	789	George	FRA	316
Elias	LUZ	386	SWERTZEL, Mathias	SOM	139	Hansura	WAY	139
Holden	LUZ	391	SWESEY, Thomas	MER	461	Hansura Jr.	WAY	139
Soloman	PHA	52	SWEYER, Christian	BER	227	John	WAY	139
Soloman	PHI	117	George	BER	279	SWINGLER?, Daniel	PHI	17
Thomas	LUZ	385	George Jr.	BER	276	SWINHART, George	MNT	101
William	ADA	18	Jacob	BER	227	SWINK, George	FAY	199
William	NOU	160	SWEYN, Peter	HNT	118	Jacob	FAY	199
SWEETSEN?, Benjn.	PHA	114	SWEZEY, Daniel	NOU	200	SWINY, Jas.	LAN	168
SWEEZEY, John	BFD	77	Thomas	NOU	196	SWIRE, Michl.	PHI	90
SWEEZY, John	CUM	32	SWICK, Peter	NOU	102	SWISE, John	PHI	136

SWISHER, A.	LYC	29	SYBERT, Sebastian	PHI	103A	TAILOR, Thomas	MER	461
Adam	YOR	196	SYBERT?, John	PHA	109	TAILOR?, Peter	CHE	895
Daniel	ADA	37	SYDEL, Philip	BER	249	TAIT, John David	NOU	203
Fredk.	CUM	40	SYDER, Cathrine	PHA	29	TALBERT, John	GRN	112
Henry	LAN	167	John	BER	171	John	DEL	165
Jacob	NOU	160	SYDERS, Christn.	CUM	23	TALBOT, Benjm.	BER	162
John	BFD	48	SYDLE, John Nick?	PHI	104	James	WST	176
John	LAN	166	SYDNOR, William			Joseph	BER	162
Mary	MIF	2	G.	ERI	55A	Joseph	DEL	165
Philip	LYC	29	SYFERHELD, Widow	PHI	71A	Richd. D. Esqr.	WAS	59
Philip	YOR	210	John	PHI	76	TALBOTT, Andrew	MNT	106
SWITESER, Michael	PHA	38	SYFERHELT, John			John	DEL	165
SWITSBERGER,			C.	PHA	99	William	MNT	107
William	LAN	229	SYFERT, Conrad	PHA	30	TALER, Jos.	YOR	162
SWITSER, Anthony	ADA	39	SYFRED, John	PHI	74	TALKINGTON, Jesse	WST	383
George	ADA	33	SYFRES, Christian	WST	225	John	WST	383
Henry	PHA	59	SYKES, John	PHA	26	TALL?, Fredk.	PHI	111
Jesse	ADA	41	John	PHA	58	TALLAIANA, John	PHA	32
SWITZER, Mr.	PHA	41	William	PHA	97	TALLERS?, William	PHI	15
Abraham	FRA	275	SYLEYE, David	CHE	790	TALLERTON?, Wm	MNT	141
Adam	YOR	197	SYLVUS, Henry	WST	329	TALLHAMMER,		
Andw.	YOR	204	Jonas	WST	329	Frederick	GRN	93
Ann	BUC	106	Nicholas	WST	329	TALLIDAY, Abraham	LUZ	413
Daniel	YOR	193	Nicholas Senr.	WST	329	Henry	LUZ	417
Daniel	YOR	194	SYMONDS, Thomas	DEL	168	John	LUZ	416
David	CUM	106	SYP, For			John	LUZ	417
Fredk.	MIF	11	Bullersland	LAN	265	TALLIM, Philip	LAN	113
Fredk.	CUM	59	SYPE, Andrew	YOR	165	TALLMAN, Daniel	LYC	3
Gertrout	DAU	30	Charles	ARM	122	George	PHI	72
Jacob	BER	275	Christian	LAN	265	Jeremiah Senr.	LYC	8
Jacob	FRA	302	John	ARM	124	Jeremiah, Junr.	LYC	3
John	MIF	11	SYPERT, Henry	LAN	263	Willm.	PHI	5
John	FRA	296	SYPHART, Mary	YOR	174	TALLY, Harman	DEL	158
John	CHE	890	SYPHERS, Matthw.	BUT	333	Samuel	DEL	158
Joseph	ADA	38	SYPHERT, Barton	WST	315	TALMAGE, Elisha	ERI	55A
Leonard	FRA	296	Phillip	WST	316	James	ERI	55A
Mary	DAU	13A	SYPHRED, David	WST	278	TALMAN, Elihu	WAY	137
Melchor	YOR	170	SYRINGER, Leonard	ADA	43	TAMMANY, John	LAN	295
Peter	MIF	11	SYTHLOFF, Henry	NOH	65A	TAN, Jos.	FRA	313
Peter	FRA	295	SYTLE, John	DAU	8	TANENBERGER,		
Peter Sr.	FRA	295	SYVER, Henry	ARM	122	David	LAN	135
Ulrich	CHE	898	SYVERD, Jacob	LAN	92	TANEY,		
Valentine	BUC	91A				Christopher	CHE	785
SWITZGABEL,			T----?, Ab----m?	CHE	798	TANGART, John	LAN	109
Wincend	LAN	213	L--ig?	HNT	125	TANHORN?, William	BEV	23
SWITZHOLLEM, Jno.	CUM	29	TABABOCK, Chrisn.	CHE	721	TANIHILL, John	BUT	366
SWIVIL?, Owen	DEL	157	TABLER,			Milsey	BUT	366
SWIZER, Phillip	CUM	28	Christopher	LAN	101	TANNEHILL, James	SOM	144
SWOAP, Peter	CUM	74	TABRO, Chas.	PHA	96	John	WAS	18
SWOB, Jacob	DAU	26	TACE, Adam	PHI	126	Ninion	SOM	144
SWODEN, John	YOR	197	TACK, John	WAY	150	William	WAS	10
SWOGER, John	PHA	58	TACK?, John	PHA	45	William	WAS	25
SWOONOVER, Henry	GRN	72	See Fack	ARM	123	William	SOM	144
SWOOPE, John	HNT	135	TADD?, (See Todd)	BEV	21	Zachariah	SOM	147
Peter	HNT	156	TAESON?, Daniel	NOU	153	TANNER, Widow	PHI	11A
SWOPE, Ann Wdw.	HNT	153	TAGART, & Smith	PHA	11	Abraham	BFD	48
David	HNT	153	William	CHE	850	David	WST	298
George	WST	296	TAGE, Roger	PHI	68A	Hugh	HNT	156
John	BUC	142	Thomas	HNT	134	Jacob	DEL	158
John	YOR	181	Wm.	PHI	69A	Joseph	WAY	137
Laurence	HNT	153	TAGERT, Barbara	ADA	12	Martha	CHE	870
Mary	BUC	150	John	YOR	177	Philip	CHE	869
Nicholas	WST	296	TAGGART, David	NOU	173	Zelob	NOU	133
SWOPELAND,			John	PHA	27	TANNIHILL,		
Christian	ADA	34	John	FRA	293	Adimsin	ALL	56
Peter	BFD	77	Patrick	PHA	99	Walter	ALL	56
SWOPLE, George	GRN	78	Robert	NOU	169	Zachana	ALL	56
SWORD, Ebenezer	LAN	15	William	NOU	173	TANOR, Christly	FRA	298
SWORDS, Thomas	ALL	116	Wm.	WST	176	TANS, Weleter	PHA	58
SWORTZ, Philip	PHI	125	TAGGERT,			TANYHILL,		
SWOYER, Henry	PHI	125	Archibald	DEL	174	Alexander	BER	158
SWYER, Peter	PHI	91	James	WAS	14	TAPER, Benj.	PHI	84
SYBERT, Barbary	PHA	75	Samuel	WAS	25	TAR, Martin	HNT	155
Conrod	PHI	96	TAGUE, Benjamin	MNT	140	TARASCON, La	PHA	96
Henry	PHI	76A	TAILER?, Christn.	DAU	34	TARBELL, Thomas	LUZ	389
John	LAN	92	TAILOR, Cronos	CHE	889	TARBIL, John	LUZ	387

THOMAS, Able	BER 182	THOMAS, Geo.		THOMAS, John		
Abm.	CUM 51	Geo.	CUM 35	John	WAS 65	
Abraham	BFD 69	Geo.	CUM 90	John	GRN 68	
Adam	ADA 18	George	PHA 21	John	MNT 70	
Adam	LAN 276	George	LAN 33	John	BFD 77	
Alexander	SOM 140	George	GRN 68	John	NOH 83	
Alexander Jun.	SOM 140	George	PHI 103	John	MNT 84	
Alice	MNT 79	George	SOM 131	John	MNT 88	
Amos	PHI 155	George	SOM 160	John	GRN 97	
Amos	DEL 179	George	DEL 182	John	ARM 127	
Amos	DEL 185	George	NOU 190	John	LAN 135	
Andrew	PHI 109	Gideon	DEL 179	John	MNT 140	
Ann	PHI 146	Godfrey	NOU 125	John	PHI 146	
Anthy.	PHI 72A	Guaft?	NOU 151	John	NOU 151	
Arthur	BUC 83A	Hanah	FRA 271	John	NOU 151	
Asa	BUC 97A	Heber	PHI 111A	John	BUC 158	
Axael? Esq.	CHE 790	Henry	ALL 117	John	SOM 163	
Barny	WST 227	Henry	NOU 190	John	YOR 180	
Benjamin	PHA 97	Henry	NOU 190	John	NOU 190	
Benjamin	SOM 131	Henry	FRA 304	John	LAN 208	
Benjamin	SOM 150	Henry	FRA 321	John	LAN 230	
Benjn.	MNT 109	Hezekiah	DEL 179	John	BER 231	
Benjn.	BUT 326	Isaac	PHA 36	John	LAN 276	
Benjn.	CHE 858	Isaac	MNT 37	John	LAN 289	
Betsy	PHI 76A	Isaac	PHA 73	John	FRA 305	
Catherine	BUC 97A	Isaac	MNT 140	John	CHE 787	
Christian	NOU 125	Isaac	BUC 142	John	CHE 796	
Christian	SOM 150	Isaac	PHI 146	John	CHE 873	
Conrad	ADA 18	Isaac	YOR 208	John Junr.	MNT 142	
Daniel	PHA 79	Isaac	BER 243	John	PHI 73A	
Daniel	MNT 88	Isaac	BER 285	John	BUC 87A	
Daniel	PHI 138	Isaac	CHE 881	John	PHI 97A	
Daniel	BUC 142	Isaac	CHE 893	Jonah	NOH 36A	
Daniel	FAY 206	Isaac Jr.	CHE 881	Jonathan	PHI 105	
Danl.	PHI 122	Isaiah	MNT 76	Jonathan	MNT 131	
David	MNT 85	Isaiah	NOH 65A	Jonathan	CHE 873	
David /A/	SOM 163	Israel	DAU 13	Jonathan	BUC 89A	
David	WAS 106	Jacob	PHA 10	Joseph	WAS 10	
David	MNT 114	Jacob	MNT 39	Joseph	MNT 37	
David	PHI 134	Jacob	NOH 51	Joseph	NOU 98	
David	MNT 140	Jacob	MNT 110	Joseph	MNT 132	
David	BUC 146	Jacob	NOU 125	Joseph	BUC 142	
David	DEL 163	Jacob	WAS 126	Joseph	FAY 269	
David	SOM 163	Jacob	BUC 138	Joseph	CHE 851	
David	NOU 173	Jacob	LAN 148	Joseph	CHE 881	
David	CHE 717	Jacob	BUC 155	Joseph	CHE 907	
David	CHE 855	Jacob	DEL 160	Joseph Jr.	CHE 881	
David	BUC 97A	Jacob	BER 182	Joseph	PHI 69A	
Eber	BUC 97A	Jacob	CHE 893	Joseph	BUC 97A	
Ebinezer	ALL 78	Jacob	DAU 40A	Joshua	DEL 185	
Edmond	WAS 72	James	WAS 72	Liverton	WAS 72	
Edward	GRN 97	James	WAS 83	Luther	ERI 59	
Edward	CHE 911	James	BUC 106	Margaret	MNT 131	
Edward	DAU 33A	James	CUM 108	Maria	MIF 8A	
Edward	PHI 95A	James	NOU 119	Martha	DAU 47	
Elam	BEV 17	James	PHI 155	Martha	MNT 63	
Elias	PHI 93A	James	DEL 166	Martin	CUM 67	
Elijah	BER 162	James	YOR 209	Martin	PHI 90A	
Elisha	PHI 109	James	CHE 705	Mary	PHI 57	
Elizabeth	MNT 59	James	CHE 795	Mary	LUZ 356	
Ellias	ALL 120	Jesse	MNT 65	Mathew	PHI 58	
Enoch	MNT 42	Jesse	BER 278	Menassa	BUC 97A	
Enoch	MNT 63	Jessse	NOU 155	Michael	WAS 72	
Enoch	FAY 224	John	DAU 11	Michael	SOM 160	
Enoch Junr.	MNT 66	John	BEV 12	Michael	DEL 178	
Enox	PHI 94	John	PHA 24	Mordecai	MNT 63	
Ephraim	BUC 106	John	ADA 31	Morris	NOU 145	
Evan	PHA 53	John	LAN 34	Mrs.	NOU 169	
Evan	MNT 116	John	CUM 35	Nathan	MNT 37	
Evan	BUC 87A	John	WAS 35	Nathan	YOR 217	
Evens	NOU 160	John	PHI 51	Nathaniel	PHA 16	
Ezra	MNT 76	John	PHI 56	Nathaniel	WAS 106	
Ezra	DEL 179	John	MNT 59	Nicholas	CHE 798	
Francis	CHE 881	John	PHI 59	Owen	LAN 90	
Francis	NOH 32A	John	WAS 60	Owen	MNT 116	
Frank	YOR 159	John	PHI 62	Peter	PHI 105	
		John	MNT 63	Peter	ARM 127	

THOMAS, Philip	ADA	20	THOMPSON, Abm.	CUM	110	THOMPSON, Henry	FRA	282
Philip	BFD	39	Adam	MIF	8A	Hugh	WAS	77
Philip	PHI	89	Adam	DAU	46A	Hugh	BUC	107
Philip	DEL	185	Alex	ADA	12	Hugh	WST	157
Polly	PHI	77	Alexander	PHA	122	Hugh	BUT	328
Rachel	MNT	141	Alexd.	FRA	276	Hugh	CHE	776
Rees	DEL	180	Alexr.	PHA	70	Isaac	HNT	140
Richard	PHI	150	Alexr.	CUM	93	Isaiah	CUM	34
Richard	CHE	799	Alexr.	CUM	125	Isiah	LYC	3
Richard Jr.	CHE	886	Alexr.	WST	163	James	ADA	2
Richard	PHI	11A	Alexr.	YOR	195	James	LYC	6
Richd.	PHA	53	Alexr.	FRA	290	James	CRA	9
Robert	PHI	52	Ame	PHA	11	James	ADA	10
Robert	MNT	76	Andrew	ADA	40	James	WAS	10
Robert	DEL	168	Andrew	ALL	86	James	CRA	16
Robt.	PHI	66A	Andrew	MNT	107	James	BEV	22
Rouland	MNT	120	Andrew	BUC	162A	James	PHI	22
Rowland	MNT	111	Andw.	CUM	133	James	WAS	35
Saml.	PHI	72	Andw.	CUM	137	James	ALL	60
Saml.	CHE	717	Andw.	BUT	342	James	WAS	60
Saml.	CHE	880	Andw.	MIF	11A	James	ALL	61
Samuel	MNT	79	Andw.	MIF	13A	James	BFD	67
Samuel	GRN	97	Ann	PHA	55	James	NOU	133
Samuel	PHA	116	Ann	PHA	113	James	WST	157
Samuel	HNT	120	Ann	HNT	145	James	WST	158
Samuel	WAS	126	Anthony	BUT	324	James	LAN	168
Samuel	BUC	158	Archd.	FRA	311	James	NOU	196
Sarah	CHE	781	Archd.	WST	330	James	BER	207
Sarah	CHE	883	Archibald	WAS	117	James	YOR	219
Sarah	NOH	34A	Archible	BEV	21	James	BER	249
Seth	DEL	180	Aron	FAY	269	James	WST	298
Simson Negro	FAY	269	Arthur	FRA	289	James	FRA	299
Susannah	MNT	139	Atchinson	PHA	99	James	FRA	311
Susannah	DEL	189	Benjamin	BEV	22	James	WST	352
Thomas	PHI	59	Benjamin	NOU	133	James	LUZ	366
Thomas (Taylor)	DEL	180	Benjamin	DAU	44A	James	CHE	714
Thomas	NOU	107	Benjn.	LYC	3	James	CHE	825
Thomas	NOU	112	Bethleham	LYC	11	James	CHE	875
Thomas	LAN	129	Bradway	WAS	41	James	MIF	5A
Thomas	DEL	179	Caleb	BFD	35	Jane	WAS	95
Thomas	CHE	815	Charles	PHA	61	Jane	FRA	301
Thos.	PHA	53	Charles	MNT	140	Jane	FRA	318
Timothy	PHA	25	Chas.	PHA	96	Jay	GRN	90
Townsend	CHE	881	Christian	WST	352	Jno.	CEN	19
Uriah	DEL	179	Christopher	BER	249	Jno.	CUM	27
Walter	BUC	97A	Cornelous	ALL	76	Jno.	CUM	51
Watson	CHE	854	Daniel	WAS	5	Jno.	CUM	54
Widow	DAU	35	Daniel	BEV	23	Jno.	BUT	338
Widow	BUC	102	Daniel	ALL	102	Jnous?	MIF	15A
William	WAS	10	Daniel	MNT	107	Joh	PHA	82
William	MNT	52	Daniel	CHE	884	John	WAS	10
William	MNT	84	Daniel	CHE	885	John	ADA	12
William	BUC	98	David	PHA	8	John	CRA	12
William	PHA	111	David	WAS	32	John	DAU	12
William	MNT	112	David	WAS	95	John	WAS	14
William	LAN	123	David	PHA	100	John	PHA	15
William	ARM	125	David	WST	330	John	BEV	23
William	MNT	140	Edwd.	PHA	82	John	MNT	41
William	PHI	151	Elijah	BER	216	John	MNT	47
William	NOU	155	Eliza.	CUM	138	John	ALL	62
William	NOU	173	Elizabeth	CRA	6	John	ALL	65
William	DEL	182	Elizabeth	FAY	248	John	PHA	75
Wm.	BEV	5	Elizabeth	FRA	276	John	MNT	79
Wm.	PHI	80A	Elizabeth	CHE	722	John	PHA	88
John	ADA	32	Ewd.	FRA	319	John	WAS	95
THOMAS?, -a-han?	MIF	8A	George	ALL	82	John	PHA	101
George	BUC	158	George	ALL	93	John	NOU	107
Theophilus	CHE	796	George	WAS	95	John	PHA	116
THOMB, David	WST	383	George	NOU	178	John	NOU	133
THOME, John	DAU	25	George	CHE	814	John	BUC	138
Mary	DAU	32	George	CHE	816	John	HNT	142
William	DAU	36A	George Esq.	LAN	123	John	BUC	150
THOMEA, Rachel	PHA	4	Gilbert	BUC	83A	John	WST	163
THOMI, Catherine	BER	153	Hannah	PHA	35	John	WST	163
THOMP, Nathan	LAN	122	Henry	ALL	71	John	VEN	165
THOMPSON, Widw.	PHI	114A	Henry	PHA	96	John	VEN	166

THOMPSON, John	DEL 189	THOMPSON, Robt.	CHE 762	THOMS, John	BER 281
John	NOU 196	Ruth	PHA 32	THOMSON, Andr.	FRA 310
John	YOR 201	Saml.	CUM 127	Andrew	ERI 60
John	BER 209	Saml.	CUM 129	Archibald	HNT 156
John	YOR 212	Saml.	FRA 286	Aron	FAY 218
John	WST 258	Saml.	WST 374	Caleb	HNT 129
John	FRA 278	Samuel	BEV 15	Caleb	FAY 260
John	WST 298	Samuel	WAS 77	Chas.	PHI 26
John	WST 298	Samuel	GRN 85	Daniel	DEL 164
John	FRA 303	Samuel	GRN 92	Daniel	DEL 176
John	FRA 311	Sarah	MIF 13A	Daniel	DEL 191
John	BUT 323	Sarah	BUC 103A	David	PHI 79
John	BUT 329	Stephen	BUC 84	Edwd.	PHI 40
John	BUT 348	Thomas	WAS 25	Elijah	HNT 164
John	WST 352	Thomas	MNT 42	Elizabeth	HNT 130
John	MER 461	Thomas	ALL 65	George	HNT 144
John	CHE 718	Thomas	BUC 95	George	PHI 77A
John Capt.	PHI 67A	Thomas	WAS 95	Henry	DEL 175
John	DAU 23A	Thomas	WAS 95	Jacob	PHA 84
John	PHI 117A	Thomas	WAS 126	James	PHI 2
Jonah.	MNT 46	Thomas	BUC 138	James	BFD 59
Joseph	BEV 18	Thomas	DEL 167	James	HNT 136
Joseph	ADA 22	Thomas	WST 258	James	HNT 141
Joseph	WAS 25	Thomas	MER 461	James	HNT 159
Joseph	BUC 89	Thos.	PHI 119A	James	FAY 218
Joseph	NOU 107	Thos. M'kean	WAS 59	James	FAY 234
Joseph	NOU 119	Timothy	WST 176	James	FAY 251
Joseph	WST 258	Widow	CEN 24	John	PHI 21
Joseph	LUZ 394	Widow	CUM 77	John	PHI 21
Joshua	PHA 68	William	WAS 35	John	PHI 43
Liford	ALL 78	William	WAS 83	John	LAN 70
Margaret	WAS 25	William	MNT 101	John	PHI 74
Margaret	CHE 754	William	PHA 101	John	LAN 85
Mark	MNT 71	William	WAS 106	John	HNT 129
Mary	PHA 28	William	WAS 114	John	DEL 155
Mary	PHA 60	William	WAS 114	John	DEL 176
Mary	WAS 60	William	HNT 122	John	DEL 179
Mary	PHA 94	William	HNT 145	John	FAY 251
Mary	MIF 13A	William	NOU 200	John	LAN 301
Mathew	WAS 25	William	FAY 269	John	LAN 309
Mathew	WAS 25	William	LUZ 412	John Captn.	PHI 152
Mathew	ALL 102	William	MER 461	John T.	PHA 100
Matthew	WST 243	William	CHE 811	Joseph	PHI 33
Matthew	WST 258	William	CHE 865	Joseph	PHI 144
Mattw.	CUM 135	William Jun.	WAS 95	Joseph	DEL 181
Michael	NOU 107	William Sen.	WAS 95	Joseph	FAY 224
Michael	BER 216	William	BUC 155A	Josia	FAY 224
Moses	MIF 4	Willm.	PHI 62	Levi	HNT 164
Moses	BEV 7	Willm.	BUT 322	Margt.	PHI 14
Moses	WAS 25	Willm.	BUT 341	Margt.	PHI 54
Moses	ALL 49	Wilm.	ALL 61	Michl.	PHI 36
Moses	WAS 51	Wilm.	ALL 62	Peter	HNT 116
Moses	ALL 54	Wilm.	ALL 72	Rese	HNT 134
Moses	CUM 140	Wilm.	ALL 93	Robert	HNT 142
Moses	WST 163	Wilm.	ALL 95	Robert	PHI 148
Moses	FAY 269	Wilm.	ALL 120	Robert	HNT 160
Nathaniel	LAN 246	Wm.	BEV 13	Samuel	HNT 164
Nathl.	CHE 873	Wm.	MIF 18	Samuel	WST 258
Paul	NOU 155	Wm.	CEN 19	Sarah	DEL 155
Peter	PHA 33	Wm.	CUM 24	Thomas	PHI 18
Richard	PHA 95	Wm.	LYC 24	Thomas	ARM 123
Robert	ADA 7	Wm.	BEV 28	Thomas	HNT 130
Robert	LYC 27	Wm.	CUM 98	Thomas	HNT 164
Robert	WAS 77	Wm.	CUM 125	Thomas	DEL 167
Robert	WAS 77	Wm.	FRA 285	Thomas	FAY 248
Robert	ALL 86	Wm.	WST 298	William	PHI 54
Robert	WAS 117	Wm.	WST 374	William	ERI 60
Robert	BUC 138	Wm.	CHE 724	William	LAN 130
Robert	WST 157	Wm.	CHE 764	William	HNT 131
Robert	BUC 145A	Wm.	CHE 871	William	HNT 131
Robert	BUC 155A	Wm. Jr.	CHE 871	William	DEL 170
Robt.	MIF 11	Wm.	MIF 5A	William	DEL 192
Robt.	CUM 137	Wm.	MIF 8A	William	FAY 229
Robt.	WST 163	Wm.	MIF 8A	William	FAY 234
Robt.	WST 176	Wm.	MIF 15A	THONB, John	WST 383
Robt.	FRA 289	THOMPSONON?, Unis	ALL 77	THORENTON, Biel	LUZ 412

THORLEY, Samuel	YOR	219	THRUSH, Barney	CUM	124	TILMAN, Hiniy	MNT	60
THORLY, Abraham	YOR	219	David	CUM	143	Wm.	PHA	84
Jos.	YOR	219	Jacob	CUM	146	TILMON, George	PHI	142
THORN, Fredk.	WST	278	Leond.	CUM	123	TILSON, Timothy	WAY	145
Isaac	FAY	234	Martin	CUM	124	TILSOR, Alexr.	MIF	5A
Jabez	WAY	136	Peter	CUM	124	TILTON, Daniel	WAS	65
Jacob	PHI	112	Richd.	CUM	143	James	WAS	51
John	BUC	95	THUSTON, Aquilla	WAS	83	John	WAS	14
John	WST	196	Thomas	WAS	83	Peter	NOH	38A
John	BUT	317	THYNAN?, John	LYC	11	TILY, Joseph	DEL	178
John	BUT	324	THYTER?, Isaac	LYC	9	TIMANS, John	FRA	323
Jos.	BUT	354	TIBBET?, John	BUC	152A	Peter	FRA	324
Joseph	BUT	317	TIBBIN, John	PHI	141	TIMBLER, Peter	CHE	785
Lorence	NOU	113	TIBBON, John	DAU	34	TIMLIN, Geo.	BUT	328
Peter	WST	317	John	DAU	36	TIMLINE, Joseph	BUT	328
Richard	PHA	27	TICE, David	DAU	29	TIMMERMON, Jacob	PHI	116A
Willm.	PHI	75A	Henry	DAU	25	TIMMINS, David	PHI	102
Wilm.	ALL	51	Jacob	DAU	25	TIMMON, Thos.	PHI	78
THORNBURG,			Michael	DAU	29	TIMMONS, Widow	WAS	53
Abraham	WAS	41	Philip	DAU	29	Jim (Negro)	WAS	51
Benjamin	WAS	41	Philip	BUC	92	Lazarus	GRN	104
Joseph	ARM	122	TICE?, Peter	DAU	31A	Nicholas	GRN	104
Robert	ARM	122	TICKLE, George	PHI	83A	TIMONT, Andw.	YOR	169
Robt.	YOR	219	TID, Wilm.	ALL	118	TIMPLIN, J./ I.?	DAU	45
William	ARM	122	TIDBALL, David	WAS	77	TIN, James	DAU	10
THORNBURGH, Jno.	PHI	47	TIDROW, Zachariah	BUC	106	TINBROOKS, John	LYC	29
Thomas	ADA	44	TIDWELL, Nathan	CHE	866	TINGLER, George	NOH	38A
Thos.	MIF	5A	TIDWELL?, (See			Jacob	BUC	82A
Wm.	MIF	8A	Sidwell)	CHE	887	TINGLEY, Ebenezer	FAY	206
THORNBURY, Caleb	LAN	16	See Sidwell	CHE	867	Elkeny	LUZ	386
Edwd.	CHE	744	TIDWILER, Abm.	CHE	792	TINKER, Francis	PHI	104A
Richard	CHE	760	Christn.	CHE	725	John	PHI	104A
THORNE, William	DAU	24	Jacob	CHE	833	TINNAMAN?, Jacob	PHI	112
THORNEBROUGH,			John	BUC	92	TINNEY, James	CHE	825
Thomas	ALL	107	John	BUC	106	TINNSMAN, Adam	WST	298
THORNHILL,			TIEBOUT,			Henry	WST	298
Richard	PHA	102	Cornelius	PHA	12	Jacob	WST	298
Thomas	BFD	67	TIEGLES?, J.	LYC	15	John	WST	298
THORNSBURG?,			TIESTER, Martin	NOU	178	Mathias	WST	298
Thomas	WAS	72	TIESTER?, Thomas	NOU	178	TINSLEY, Jacob	CHE	865
THORNSBURY?,			TIFFANY, Hosea	LUZ	385	William	CHE	863
Thomas	WAS	72	John	WAY	137	TINSMAN, Peter	BUC	91A
THORNTON, Edward	NOU	112	Thomas	LUZ	386	TIPE, George	YOR	212
Edward	PHI	61A	TIFFEN, James	PHA	5	TIPPERT, John	BER	245
Han.	PHI	144	TIGART, James	BUT	365	TIPPERY, Jacob	HNT	151
James	NOU	148	John	BUT	365	TIPPIN, William	MNT	79
John	PHA	22	Robt.	CUM	108	TIPPINS, Richard	DEL	174
John	PHA	44	TIGER, James	BUT	367	TIPPLE, Nicholas	YOR	195
John	NOU	185	TIGH, Agust	PHA	95	TIPPY, Conrad	LUZ	346
Joseph	BUC	138	TIGLER, Nichs.	CUM	104	Philip	LUZ	360
Joseph	BUC	152	TILEY, Christian	NOH	158	Uriaha	ALL	69
Joseph	FAY	239	Edward	HNT	163	TIPTON, Aquilla	WAS	47
Joseph	FRA	272	TILFORD, Alexr.	MIF	5A	David	CEN	19
Joseph	BUC	87A	TILGHMAN, Edward			Edward	BFD	67
Julithan	NOH	65A	Esq.	DEL	180	Jesse	HNT	125
Michael	NOU	113	TILGHMAN?, John	DEL	165	John	HNT	125
Michael	NOU	113	TILL, George	PHI	75	Shadrach	HNT	132
Patrick	LAN	249	George	BER	242	Thomas	NOU	196
Rebecca	PHA	97	Jeremiah	PHI	94	William	CEN	19
Saml.	BUC	161A	Joseph	NOH	32A	TIPY, Philip	PHI	14
Saml. Y.	BUC	161A	Thomas	ALL	73	TIRES, Margaret	PHA	97
THOROUGHGOOD,			William	BER	242	TIRK, Michael	NOU	125
William	BER	275	TILLARD, John	FAY	200	TISE, John	YOR	156
THORP, Wm.	BEV	20	Sarah	FAY	201	Michl.	FRA	301
THORWARTH, Saml.	PHA	61	TILLATSON, James	LUZ	367	Peter	WST	227
THOUT, Widw.	PHI	115A	TILLEN, John	FAY	206	TISINGER, John	YOR	174
THOYLES?, Edward	PHI	118	TILLER, Baltzer	CUM	62	TISSUE, William	SOM	144
THRICERGAST,			TILLMAN, Jobesh	FAY	242	William Sen.	SOM	144
George	PHI	85	Juliana			TITAS, Jonathn.	FAY	248
THRINKART, Geo.	DAU	36	(Crossed Out)	PHA	31	Phillip	FAY	248
THRON, John	NOH	81	TILLOTSON, Thomas	LUZ	393	TITBAUL, Abraham	ALL	95
THRONBROUGH,			TILLOW, Abraham	LAN	172	John	ALL	95
James	ALL	108	TILLS, Charity	PHI	99A	Thomas	ALL	95
THRONE, John	YOR	181	TILLYER, William	PHI	149	Wilm.	ALL	95
THROSBEY, John	LAN	245	TILMAN, ----as?	ARM	122	TITCH, Mathias	FRA	293
THROSSHEL, George	LAN	97	Edward	PHA	4	TITE, Adam	LAN	13

TITE, John	FRA	309	TODD, David	CHE	734	TOMKINS, Jacob	BUC	146A
TITES, Amos	NOU	107	Edward	WAS	114	James	MNT	106
TITIWILLER, Jacob	CUM	125	Eliaha	PHI	93	TOMLIN, Barzola	PHI	80
TITSELL, Henry	CUM	38	George	CUM	95	John	PHI	83A
TITSLER, John	MIF	18	Hannah	BFD	77	TOMLINSON,		
TITTEL, John	NOH	79	Henry	FAY	269	Anthony	BUC	83A
TITTERMARY, John	PHI	53A	James	DAU	24	Asa	PHI	144
Richd.	PHI	24	James	WAS	32	Enoch	PHI	136
TITTLE, Henry	WAS	5	James	PHA	68	Francis	BUC	155
Henry	DAU	50	James	LAN	264	Gilbert	BUC	83A
James	WST	330	James	CHE	734	Henry	BUC	152
John	WST	317	James Esqr.	YOR	215	Henry	BUC	161A
Peter	WST	317	John	BEV	21	Jesse	BUC	89
TITTLE?, Jacob	CHE	896	John	WAS	72	John	PHA	84
TITTLEBUNG,			John	BUC	106	John	BUC	152
Christn.	PHI	121	John	VEN	166	John	PHI	154
TITUS, Archibald	BUC	99	John	CHE	726	John	BUC	155
Archibald	BUC	100	John	DAU	23A	Jonathan	BUC	99A
Benjamin	GRN	78	Joshua	PHA	64	Jonathn.	BUC	161A
Daniel	CRA	12	Mary	DAU	24	Joseph	BUC	107
Ezekiel	LUZ	386	Naomi	CUM	88	Joseph	BUC	143A
Francis	BUC	85	Quinton	CHE	858	Levi	HNT	125
Harman	BUC	89	Saml.	FAY	260	Pearson	BUC	85A
Harman	BUC	90	Samuel	WST	158	Richard	PHI	153
Isah	BUC	95	Samuel	LUZ	421	Samuel	BUC	104
Jacob	MNT	66	Stephen	BER	158	Thomas	BUC	84
Jacob	NOH	74A	Thomas	FAY	211	Thomas	PHI	149
John	WAS	35	Thos.	PHA	34	Thos.	PHI	90A
John	ARM	126	Widow	MIF	8A	Widow	BUC	89
Joseph	NOH	74A	William	WAS	72	Widow	CHE	801
Peter	CRA	12	William	FAY	269	William	BUC	152
Peter	ARM	126	William	CHE	737	William	BUC	162
Peter	NOU	160	William A.	CHE	900	Willm.	BUC	104
Peter	NOH	70A	Wm. Esqr.	WST	317	Willm.	PHI	144
Richd.	LYC	3	Wm. H.	PHA	107	Wm.	BUC	155
Robert	NOH	74A	TODDLE, Peter	BUC	152	TOMMY, John	LAN	146
Sirach	NOH	79	TODHUNTER, Abm.	MIF	8A	TOMPKINS, Isaac	BUC	84
Timothy	BUC	85	TODINGER, John	BER	231	Isaac	CHE	859
Titus	NOU	160	TOGARD, John	ALL	101	Joseph	LUZ	362
Widow	BUC	155	TOLAN, John	MER	462	Richard	FAY	254
Wm.	CHE	741	TOLAND, Henry	PHA	4	Saml.	PHA	86
TITUS?, John	ARM	123	Hugh	MNT	36	TOMPLIN, Richard	CHE	721
TITWILER, John	BUC	97A	Hugh	HNT	157	TOMPSON, Andr.	FRA	311
Leonard	BUC	97A	Isaac	YOR	214	John	FAY	269
TITZLER,			James	BEV	23	John	FRA	317
Christian	DAU	37	John	GRN	110	TOMSON, James	FAY	211
TIZE, Ludwick	CEN	21	Thomas	WAS	25	Jonathan	PHI	149
TOBAN, John	PHA	100	William	WAS	25	TONAR, Mosis	FAY	224
TOBER, Widow	PHI	40	TOLAND?, Peter	BER	287B	TONCE, Henry	DAU	33A
Charles	CHE	739	Peter	BER	287B	TONE, Saml.	NOH	57A
TOBIAS, Catherine	BER	153	TOLBERT, Allen	YOR	214	TONEHILL, William	HNT	131
Christian	BER	143	Andrew	ERI	60A	TONER, Danl.	LYC	20
Jacob	BER	222	Benjn.	CHE	717	Thos.	NOU	203
John	HNT	122	Harry	WST	176	TONER?, Nicholas?	LYC	27
John	BER	143	Samuel	WST	258	TONEY, Riddey	FRA	298
John	BER	146	TOLBET, Moses	ADA	23	TONTS, Mary	PHI	129
John Jr.	BER	143	TOLBOT, Rebecca	FRA	290	TOOD, Henry	BER	158
Jonathan	BER	143	TOLBOTT, William	MNT	139	William	LAN	301
Ludwig	BER	146	TOLLAHIT, James	LAN	173	TOOL/ TOOT?,		
Ludwig Jr.	BER	146	TOLLEBAUGH, Peter	DAU	45A	Aquila	MNT	116
Peter	BER	160	TOLMAN, John	FRA	293	TOOL, John	LYC	8
TOBIN, George	FAY	248	TOM, Jerry	PHI	56	Moses	LYC	8
Thomas	FAY	248	Robert	ALL	101	Stephen	NOH	83
TOBLER, George	LAN	288	TOMA, Widow	DAU	27	TOOLEY?, John	PHA	109
TOBURN, Thomas	CHE	876	TOMAN, Valentine	BUC	106	TOOMY, Thos.	YOR	173
TOBY, Jos.	PHI	115	Wilm.	ALL	50	TOOP, Henry	CUM	33
TOD, David Capt.	ARM	127	TOMB, Hugh	BUC	83A	TOOPS, Henry	DAU	8
Goerge	ALL	79	Jacob	LYC	17	Martin	CUM	33
John	PHA	5	TOMBACK, George	WAS	125	TOOT, David	ADA	39
TODD, Alexander	FAY	260	TOMBOLD, Peter	WST	243	George	DAU	13
Alexander Esqr.	PHA	100	TOME, Henry	YOR	201	TOOT?, Henry	ADA	7
Amia	PHI	105	TOMER, Henry	BUT	336	TOPHAM, Ruben	PHA	76
Andrew	MNT	84	TOMERLIN?,			TOPPER, Andrew	ADA	27
Archibald	WAS	25	William	LUZ	368	David	ADA	27
Baezel	FAY	206	TOMKIN, Robt.	PHI	71A	John	ADA	4
David	DAU	24	TOMKINS, Jacob	PHA	40	John	WST	317

TOPPINGS, Robert	WST	317
TORAM, Stephen	PHA	69
TORBERT, Anthony	BUC	99A
James	BUC	152
James Jn.	BUC	152
Lamb	BUC	99A
Saml.	LYC	22
Susanna	BUC	104
William	BUC	95
TORBET, Nathan	BEV	24
TORBETT, Andw.	YOR	201
Mary	CUM	45
Robt.	YOR	201
TORBIT, James	ALL	91
TORMIER, George	WST	227
Nichs.	WST	227
TORPERT?, Saml.	LYC	15
TORRENCE, Albert	FRA	311
Hugh	WST	196
Hugh	FAY	251
James	FAY	251
Jane	FAY	237
TORRIS, Mr.	PHA	88
TORRY, Jason	WAY	137
John	ERI	60
Samuel	WAY	137
Samuel H.	LUZ	320
TORTON, Andrew	DEL	180
TORTOR?, Joseph	ALL	102
TOSSET/ TASSET?,		
Elijah	LUZ	399
TOTEN, Isaac	WST	227
TOTH, Henrey	FAY	229
TOTTERER, Jacob	BER	138
TOTTON, Aaron	WAS	41
Ezekiel	WAS	41
John	NOH	88
John	PHI	75A
TOUB, Henry	MNT	109
Peter	MNT	97
TOUBART, Thomas	PHI	23
TOUGHT, Widow	LAN	83
TOUL, E.	LAN	147
TOUP, Peter	DAU	39
TOUTNER?,		
Catharina	ADA	37
TOWELL, Hohn	PHI	10
TOWERS, James	BUC	146A
Widow	MIF	5A
William	MNT	85
TOWERS?, Henry	PHA	83
TOWMILLER,		
Christ.	MNT	141
TOWN, Widw.	PHI	80A
John	PHI	75A
Joseph C.	LUZ	396
Robt.	PHI	95A
Thomas	PHI	67
Thos.	PHI	68A
Thos.	PHI	72A
TOWNINHYMER, John	PHI	99A
TOWNLY, Robert		
Junr.	ERI	60A
Robert Senr.	ERI	60A
TOWNSAND, Iaac	ARM	127
TOWNSEND, Abm.	CHE	816
Amous	FAY	239
Benjamin	BEV	19
Benjn. Junr.	WAS	40
Benjn. Senr.	WAS	40
Charles	LUZ	371
Daniel	WAS	77
David	BEV	19
Evan	PHI	145
Ezra	BUC	89
Francis	WAS	40

TOWNSEND, Gilbert	LUZ	372
James	BUC	85
James	CHE	812
Jesse	WAS	40
John	PHA	96
John (Crossed		
Out)	BUC	89
John	LAN	119
John	FAY	234
John	CHE	835
Jonathan	PHI	77
Jonathan	BUC	150
Joseph	PHA	103
Joseph	CHE	713
Joseph Junr.	WAS	40
Joseph Sr.	WAS	40
Joseph	NOH	34A
Joseph	BUC	91A
Joseph	BUC	145A
Levi	LUZ	371
Noe	PHI	109A
S---.?	MNT	37
Salathiel	PHI	67
Saml.	CHE	895
Stephen	CHE	756
Thoomas	WAS	14
Thos.	PHI	145
Widow	NOH	34A
Wm.	CHE	756
Wm.	CHE	803
TOWNSLEY, George	WAS	5
TOWSEY, Francis	PHI	75
TOY, Elias	PHI	152
Jacob	PHI	88A
Mary	MNT	84
Mary	CUM	91
TOY?, Wilson	PHA	39
TOZAR, Elishama	LUZ	427
Julius	LUZ	427
TRA---R?, Wm.	PHI	105B
TRACE, Jacob	LAN	25
John	PHI	123
TRACEY, James	FAY	224
Matthew	HNT	149
TRACH, Peter	WAY	150
Philip	WAY	150
Rudolph	NOH	42
TRACHER,		
Christian	NOU	132
TRACY, Andrew	LUZ	386
Burrel	ERI	57A
Francis	WST	330
Isaac	LUZ	413
John	ERI	59
Peleg	LUZ	386
Solomon	LUZ	423
Solomon	ERI	57A
TRAFRIDGE, John	PHI	61
TRAGO, Benjamin	DAU	2A
Jacob	BUC	152
Mahlon	BUC	161A
William	BUC	152
TRAILL, Robert		
Esqr.	NOH	38A
TRAIN?, Wm.	VEN	169
TRAINER, John	CHE	798
Patrick	PHA	105
TRAIT, John	WST	352
TRAMPER, Anthony	WST	298
TRANER, Hugh	HNT	140
TRANGER?, (See		
Trauger?)	BUC	140
TRANS--?, Philip	NOH	34A
TRANSER, Henry	NOH	49
TRANSER?, (See		
Transu)	NOH	79

TRANSU, Abraham	NOH	88
Abraham Junr.	NOH	88
Anthony	NOH	88
Elias	NOH	79
Isaac	NOH	88
Jacob Esqr.	NOH	79
John	NOH	79
Melchior	NOH	88
TRAP, Andrew		
Esqr.	FAY	242
TRAPP, Philip	NOH	83
TRASK, Margit	ALL	82
Rufus	ERI	59
TRASTLE, Jacob	YOR	177
TRAT, Andrew	NOU	132
TRATE, Peter	CUM	119
TRAUDT, Abraham	NOH	49
TRAUGER,		
Christian	BUC	140
Christian Jr.	BUC	140
Christian Sen.	BUC	140
Frederick	BUC	140
TRAUGER?, Stophel	BUC	140
TRAUNCHA, Monscur	PHA	34
TRAUP, George	NOH	57A
TRAUT, Isaac	LAN	173
TRAUTMAN, George	NOU	169
TRAUTSMAN, Peter	SOM	153
William	SOM	153
TRAVERCE, John	FAY	200
TRAVERS, Arthur	LAN	111
John	HNT	144
William	HNT	144
TRAVERSER, Robert	WST	352
TRAVIS, Absalom	LUZ	428
Ezekiel	LUZ	389
John	PHA	100
John	LUZ	389
John Jr.	LUZ	389
John Jun.	WAS	95
John Sen.	WAS	95
Patrick	PHI	11
Robert	WST	158
Sylvanus	LUZ	428
Thomas	WAY	136
TRAVISE, James	GRN	68
TRAWELL, Anthoney	SOM	150
TRAWTS, George	FRA	304
TRAXEL, Abraham	NOU	133
Abraham Jr.	DAU	25A
Abraham	DAU	25A
Henry	BER	132
John	BER	171
John	DAU	25A
TRAXELL, George	NOH	38A
John	NOH	38A
Michael	NOH	38A
Nicholas	NOH	38A
TRAXLER, Michael	HNT	143
TRAY, Benjn.	PHA	90
Samuel	NOU	133
Thomas	NOU	196
TRAYER, Gotfried		
L.?	BER	159
TRAYWITS, Conrod	NOU	125
TREACY, Henry	GRN	84
TREANOE?, (See		
Treanor)	DEL	186
TREANOR, David	DEL	186
TREAQUARE?, James	PHA	75
TREASTER, John	NOU	141
TREAT, Christian	BER	249
Christian	CHE	818
Elizabeth	BER	249
TREBO?, Francis	PHA	26
TREDAWAY, Hester	LUZ	329

TREDENIX?, James	CHE	727	TRICK, Christophe	PHA	112	TRITTENBAUCH?,		
TREENAN?, Hannah	CHE	726	TRICKEY, John	NOU	148	John	BUC	140
TREES, Jacob	NOU	190	TRIER, Peter	YOR	173	TRIVILAND, Jan-.	CHE	738
John	NOU	190	TRIGHLER, John	BUC	158	TRIXLER, Peter	NOH	61A
TREESE, Cunrod	SOM	155	TRIGHMAN?, Philip	ADA	8	TRIZULINY?, Chas.	CEN	23A
TREETT, Jacob	YOR	205	TRIMBEL, Abraham	FAY	263	TROFF, Jacob	ALL	98
TREGER, Jacob	LAN	235	John	PHI	18	Peter	ALL	98
TREGO, Eli	CHE	716	John	FAY	251	TROLL, Frederick	PHI	14
Isaac	CHE	716	William	FAY	218	William	BER	243
Jacob	CHE	716	TRIMBESON?, James			TROLLINGER,		
Jeremiah	CHE	720	Jr.	LYC	9	(Blank)	MNT	124
Joseph	CHE	716	TRIMBLE, Widow	WST	317	Peter	BUC	150
Peter	CHE	716	Abraham	DEL	186	TRON?, Frederick	NOU	141
Reuben	CHE	717	Alexander	WAS	83	TRONE, Abraham	YOR	185
Wm.	CHE	717	Alexr.	CUM	84	Abraham Jr.	YOR	185
TREHR, Mathias	BER	156	Casper	PHA	69	Jacob	YOR	185
Peter	BER	156	Daniel	BUC	95	Jacob (Joiner)	YOR	181
TREIBLE, George			David	PHA	45	Samuel	YOR	184
(See Treible,			Geo.	CUM	55	TRONS, John	CUM	111
Widow)	NOH	49	George	WST	158	TROOP, Widw.	PHI	111A
Widow Of George	NOH	49	James	LAN	40	Jacob	BER	162
TREICEBAUGH,			James	CHE	756	Philip	BER	162
Jacob	NOU	133	James	CHE	761	TROP, Philip	BER	149
Martin	NOU	133	Jane	CUM	136	TROSHELL, George	ADA	20
TREISLER, Jacob	NOU	102	Jno.	CUM	91	TROSTLE, Abraham	YOR	177
TREMBLE,			John	CUM	55	George	BER	149
Cornelious	PHI	80A	John	WAS	59	Henry	BER	149
Joseph	BER	274	Joseph	DEL	160	John	BER	149
William	CHE	885	Lewis	DEL	178	John	YOR	179
TREMEL, Joseph	WST	298	Lewis	DEL	187	TROTT, Fredk.	PHA	54
TREMPER, Henry	PHA	26	Lewis Jun.	DEL	187	TROTTER, Joseph	CUM	128
TRENCH, Mary	WST	157	Mathew	WAS	59	Mary & Sarah	DAU	33A
TRENT, James	SOM	131	Samuel	DEL	160	Richd.	CUM	129
TRENT?, Andrew	ARM	123	Samuel	DEL	166	Sarah & Mary	DAU	33A
TRESCOTT, Solon	LUZ	350	Thomas	DEL	175	Wm.	PHI	70A
TRESLER, Daniel	BER	215	Thoms.	BUT	315	TROUBAT, John	PHA	36
TRESLEY, George	PHI	153	Thos.	WST	176	TROUGER, Adam	LAN	122
Jacob	PHI	153	William	DEL	160	TROUGH, Peter	FRA	293
TRESS, John	NOU	203	Willm.	BUT	325	Rudolph	MNT	43
Thomas	PHA	122	TRIMBOUR, George	BUC	158	TROUGLE, John	NOU	190
TRESSLER, Godhard	SOM	140	Nicholas	BUC	158	TROUL, Thomas	NOU	196
TRESTER, John	NOU	190	TRIMER, Andw.	YOR	174	TROUP, Henry	CUM	36
Michl.	CEN	24	Barnabas	YOR	174	John	NOU	185
TREUSDEL,			TRIMMER, David	ADA	39	John	YOR	211
Benjamin	LUZ	325	Francis	PHA	78	TROUP?, Peter	ADA	37
John	LUZ	325	Mathias	ADA	43	TROUST, Martin	PHA	57
TREVEL, Adam	BER	135	TRINDLE,			TROUT, Abraham	CHE	718
TREVER, Jacob	YOR	184	Archibald	WST	352	Christn.	PHI	69
TREVERS, John	FAY	263	John	ALL	88	George	WAS	77
TREVIG, Andrew	BUC	148A	William	WST	352	George	BER	164
Philip	BUC	148A	TRINE, Jacob	ADA	31	George	LAN	226
TREVOR, Samuel	FAY	201	Peter	ADA	33	Henry	WST	298
TREXEL, Anthony	ADA	8	TRINNEL?, William	BFD	55	Jacob	BUC	140
Jacob	ADA	10	TRION, Daniel	BER	159	Jacob	BER	185
TREXLER, Cooney	CUM	142	George	DAU	37A	Jacob	LAN	231
David	MNT	110	TRIPLER, James	PHI	133	John	HNT	149
David	MNT	117	TRIPNER, Geo.	PHI	116A	John	BER	166
Jeremiah	MNT	67	TRIPP, Adam	PHI	76A	John	BER	231
Jeremiah	NOH	61A	Amasa	LUZ	398	John	WST	258
John	NOH	61A	Isaac	LUZ	370	John	PHI	105B
Jonathan	NOH	61A	Isaac Jr.	LUZ	367	Michal	FRA	274
Joseph	MNT	71	Isaac D.	LUZ	320	Phillip	WST	278
Michl.	CUM	139	Job	LUZ	352	Samuel	BER	185
Peter	NOU	102	Job	LUZ	381	Valentine	YOR	197
Peter	MNT	140	John	LUZ	365	William	BER	152
Peter	CUM	142	William	LUZ	384	TROUT?, Sally	PHI	117
Peter	BER	212	William	LUZ	398	Wm.	PHI	117
Phillip	CUM	140	TRIPPER, Thomas	FAY	237	TROUTMAN,		
TREXLEY, David	PHI	93	TRISBACH, Barnet	BUC	99A	Christina	DAU	37
TREY, George	CHE	725	TRISH, Christian	BFD	67	George	FAY	224
TREYER, Jacob	BFD	39	TRISLER, David	LAN	40	Henry	DAU	6
TRIBOTT, Saml.	PHA	56	Philip	BUC	98	John	BER	132
TRIBUTE, Widw.	PHI	110	TRISSEL, Joseph	BUC	150	John	BER	269
TRICE, John	NOU	190	TRISSLER, John	LAN	33	Jonas	DAU	30
Michael	NOU	190	TRISTENBAUCH?,			Jonas	DAU	37
Peter	NOU	190	John	BUC	140	Michael	BER	269

TROUTMAN, Phili	BER	0	TRUMBOSE/			TUDOR, Alexis	HNT	156
Valentine	BER	269	TRUMBORE?,			TUECKENMILLER?,		
Widow	DAU	30	George	MNT	122	Val.?	BER	283
TROUTWINE, Wm.	PHI	105B	TRUMBOUR, Henry	BUC	92	TUER?, James	FRA	319
TROVER, George	WAS	10	John	BUC	102	TUGARD, Cardiff	ALL	92
TROVER?, Leonard	BEV	5	TRUMP, Adam	NOH	57A	TULEY?, Justus	LUZ	404
TROVILER, John	CHE	848	Christian	BER	212	TULL, John	BUC	83A
TROVILLO, Richard	HNT	156	Daniel	ADA	43	TULLER?, See		
TROWBRIDGE,			Daniel	PHA	78	Fuller	BER	236
Nobles	LUZ	388	George	FAY	200	TULLERTON, Wm.	CHE	724
Oliver	LUZ	389	Henry	BER	209	TULLY, David	PHI	38
TROWINGER, Henry	CUM	57	Jesse	MNT	132	Farul	MIF	15A
TROXEL, Christian	BER	281	John	ADA	43	Hannah	PHA	68
Jacob	BUC	97A	John	PHA	78	James	CUM	46
John	HNT	150	John	GRN	92	John	PHI	10
John	DAU	42A	John	NOH	57A	John	WAS	72
TROY, John	GRN	73	Michael	ADA	41	TULTON, James	FRA	304
TROYER, Christian	SOM	160	Michael	ADA	42	TUMBELSTON, John	FAY	200
David	SOM	140	Peter	BER	212	John	FAY	211
Henry	SOM	160	Phillip	CUM	152	TUMBLEN, Zadock	FAY	206
Jacob	SOM	136	TRUMPH, George	DAU	32	TUMBLESON, Isaac	NOU	107
Joseph	SOM	140	TRUS?, (See			Richd.	PHI	102
Joseph	SOM	160	Trees)	NOU	190	TUMBLESTON, Benj.	YOR	208
Michael	SOM	140	TRUSBACK, John	MNT	90	Hugh	FAY	229
Michael Sen.	SOM	140	TRUSDALL, Hugh	WAS	106	TUMBLIN, John	FAY	206
TROYTON, Joseph	LAN	48	John	WAS	106	TUMBLISON, Joseph	LAN	153
TRUAX, Abraham	BFD	46	William	WAS	106	TUMNEY, John	LAN	153
Benjamin Jr.	BFD	46	TRUSHE, Lewis	PHA	33	TUMNY, James	LAN	152
Jacob	BFD	46	TRUSHEL, Jacob	LAN	270	TUNBLESON, Mrs.	NOU	148
Jacob Jr.	BFD	46	TRUSSELL, John	SOM	150	Mrs.	NOU	148
John	BFD	46	Soloman	SOM	150	Thomas	NOU	148
John	BFD	46	TRUST, Black	CHE	813	TUNIS, Anthony	MNT	140
Joseph	BFD	46	TRUSTY, Benjamin	PHA	121	Benjamin	MNT	140
Philip	BFD	46	John	PHA	118	TUNISON, Richard	MER	461
Samuel	BFD	46	TRUXEL, David	ADA	9	Zebulon	MER	461
TRUB?, Christian	NOH	68	Jacob	ADA	8	TUNISS, Richd.	PHA	89
TRUBY, Chr. Esqr.	WST	227	Jacob	BFD	40	TUNKENS, John	CUM	118
Chr. Junr.	WST	227	John	ADA	10	TUNNEL?, William	BFD	55
Jacob	ARM	122	TRYON, Fredk.	PHI	69	TUPPER, Nathan	LUZ	391
Jacob	HNT	144	George	PHA	46	TUPPLE, (No Given		
John	ARM	123	Michael	BER	266	Name)	DAU	31A
John	WST	227	TRYOR, Joseph			TURBOTT, Thoms.	MIF	8A
TRUCK, Nicholas	HNT	123	(Crossed Out)	PHA	100	TURBUTT, Samuel	LAN	55
TRUCKENMILLER,			TRYTES, John	DEL	168	TURE?, Louis T.		
Bastn.	NOH	61A	William	DEL	187	L.	PHA	32
George Jr.	NOH	57A	TUB, John	HNT	153	Peter T.	PHA	32
George Sr.	NOH	57A	TUBBS, Josiah A.	LUZ	352	TURGS, John	YOR	197
Jacob	NOH	57A	Nathan	LUZ	354	TURK, Ephraim	YOR	199
TRUCKINMILLER,			Nathan Jr.	LUZ	355	James	YOR	198
Lewis	MNT	129	Simon	LUZ	354	James	BUT	320
TRUCKS, William	LUZ	336	Thomas	LUZ	353	Jesse	WST	157
TRUE, Arthur	FAY	248	TUCK, Thomas	MNT	106	John	LYC	3
Hugh	WAR	1A	TUCKER, Allen	BEV	7	John	NOU	160
TRUEAX, Richard	FAY	242	Austian	NOU	102	John	BUT	320
TRUEBY, Jno.	BUT	355	Benjn.	PHA	79	John	CHE	722
TRUEMAN, James	PHA	65	David	BUC	162	TURMAN, Widow	WST	196
TRUET, Parker	ARM	126	David	BUC	146A	Thomas	CHE	842
TRUET?, Andrew	ARM	123	Edward	ALL	100	TURN.OCH?,		
TRUHAN, John	LAN	308	Isaac	BFD	59	William	ADA	4
TRUKENMILLER,			Isaac	BUC	104	TURN, Adam	BUC	158
John	MNT	129	James	WAS	5	TURNBULL, Robert	PHI	34
TRUKENMILLER?,			James	PHA	28	Thos.	CHE	781
Val.?	BER	283	John	WAS	53	Wm.	PHA	15
TRULEY, Daniel	FRA	304	John	BUC	155	TURNER, Widw.	PHI	109
TRULLINGER,			John	FAY	218	Abiah	CHE	708
Andrew	PHI	126	John	CHE	798	Abraham	PHI	140
TRUMAN, Evan	PHA	70	John	CHE	910	Abram	CHE	792
James	CHE	842	John	BUC	107A	Alexander	MER	461
John	CHE	842	Jonathn.	CHE	907	Alexr Esqr.	YOR	200
John Jr.	CHE	843	Joseph	BUC	155	Daniel	CEN	23A
Morris	DEL	175	Sarah	ALL	100	Henry	WST	352
Mrs.	NOU	133	Tempest	YOR	177	Hugh	DAU	13
Rebecca	DEL	166	Wilm.	ALL	100	James	WAS	10
Richard	PHA	11	TUCKNESS, John	PHA	86	James	LYC	15
William	CHE	777	TUCKQUIER, David	PHI	34	James	FRA	316
TRUMBO, John	ALL	89	TUDER, Benjamin	BFD	67	James	BUT	351

ULERY, Stoaphel	FRA	299	UMSTED, Jacob	BER	275	UNRUH, Nicholas	PHI	126
ULIM, Wendle	SOM	140	John	MNT	85	Nicholas Junr.	PHI	126
ULINGER, Adam	DAU	6A	John	BER	275	UNST, Widow	DAU	43A
ULL, David	GRN	73	John Junr.	MNT	85	UP, Conrod	LYC	29
Jacob	GRN	73	Peter	BER	275	UPDEGRAFF,		
ULLER, Fredrik	DAU	26	Richard	MNT	85	Ambrose	YOR	164
John	DAU	26	Samuel	BER	249	Amous	FAY	254
Martin	DAU	26	Thomas	MNT	85	David	WAS	117
Michael	DAU	26	UNANGST, Barnet			Derick	LYC	21
ULLERY, David	HNT	121	Jr.	NOH	88	Elizabeth	YOR	159
Joseph	HNT	121	Barnet Senr.	NOH	88	George	LYC	20
Stephen	HNT	120	Geo. Henry	NOH	88	Harman	LYC	21
Stephen	HNT	121	Henry	CUM	132	Herman	YOR	154
ULMER, Frederick	PHI	140	Henry	BER	186	Herman	YOR	213
Jacob	DAU	21	Henry	NOH	34A	Isaac	FAY	212
John	PHI	122	Jacob	NOH	88	Jacob	YOR	219
Peter	BUC	140	John	NOH	74A	Jas.	WST	176
Philip	LAN	60	Michl.	BER	186	Jos.	YOR	159
ULP, Jacob	CRA	17	Peter	NOH	88	Joseph	YOR	154
ULREY, Henrey	FAY	242	Valentine	NOH	88	Martin	LYC	21
Jacob	DAU	43A	UNATIN, Peter	NOU	148	Mary	YOR	154
Stophel	DAU	40A	UNBEHENT?,			Peter	YOR	205
ULRICH, Balser	BER	200	Volentine	PHA	60	Thos.	LYC	3
George	BER	269	UNCLE, Henry	PHI	95	UPDEGRAVE, Edwd.	BUC	142A
Henry	BER	152	UNCLES, John	BFD	40	UPDEGROVE, Edward	MNT	120
Herny	NOH	42	UNDERGOFFLER,			Henry	MNT	129
John	BFD	65	David	MNT	97	Jacob	MNT	119
John	BER	218	UNDERGRAFF, Sarah	YOR	157	Widow	DAU	11A
John	BER	236	UNDERHILL, John	WAS	77	UPDELGREFF, Abner	ALL	53
Martin	DAU	42A	UNDERWOOD, Alexr.	YOR	174	UPDIKE, Isaac	NOU	102
Michael	DAU	42A	Benj.	YOR	210	UPERMAN, Adam	PHI	86A
Peter	BER	216	Charles	YOR	210	UPP, Philip		
Peter	BER	236	David	CHE	700	(Crossed Out)	LYC	14
Samuel	BFD	65	Elihu Esqr.	YOR	208	UPTHEGROVE, Isaac	CEN	24
Stoffel	LAN	272	Gideon	LUZ	333	URBAN, George	LAN	276
Tobias	DAU	42A	Israel	LUZ	333	Ludwig	LAN	276
Valentine	BER	261	James	CHE	770	Ludwig	LAN	277
ULRICK, Francis	DAU	31A	Jas.	CUM	88	Ludwig	LAN	278
Jacob	MNT	109	Jehu	PHA	87	UREY, Christian	HNT	126
John	PHA	40	Jermiah	CHE	767	URFFER, Michael	NOH	56A
Nicholas	YOR	200	Jesse	YOR	209	URFIR, Widow	MNT	136
ULRIK, Christna.	DAU	30A	John	CUM	88	URICH, Christn.	DAU	26A
ULS, Jacob	SOM	153	John	YOR	208	Francis	DAU	38A
ULSINGER, Simon	ALL	110	John	YOR	210	John	DAU	39
ULTER, Saml.	CUM	30	John	CHE	700B	John	DAU	40
ULTS, Christn.	CUM	31	Marbery	PHI	87A	Rudolph	SOM	132
Jacob	CUM	32	Nehemiah	YOR	202	URICK, Henry	DAU	51A
ULTZ, George	MIF	16	Obed	YOR	207	John	DAU	9A
John	NOU	196	Samuel	GRN	90	Peter	YOR	200
Joseph	NOU	196	Thos.	WST	352	URIE, John	WAS	106
Mary	LAN	112	William	HNT	130	Samuel Esqr.	WAS	60
ULY, George	BER	203	Willing?	WAS	83	Solomon	WAS	60
UMANS?, James	PHI	66A	Wm.	CEN	24	Thomas	WAS	60
UMBEHAUER, Samuel	BER	278	UNESTED, Harman	MNT	74	Thomas	CUM	86
UMBEHOCKER,			UNGAR, Georger	CUM	123	URIGH, George	LAN	214
Frantz	BER	143	UNGER, Abraham	LAN	144	URIK, Nicholas	PHA	66
John	BER	143	Conrad	FRA	294	URIKE, George	DAU	40
Thomas	BER	143	George	DAU	11	URION, Israel	DEL	169
UMBERGER, David	CUM	69	George	ADA	28	Samuel	DEL	168
John	DAU	17A	George	BER	204	URMANS?, James	PHI	66
John	DAU	25A	George	FRA	294	URMEY, John	CHE	783
Jonas	DAU	25A	Herman	BER	278	URMEY?, Henry	MNT	70
Michl.	CUM	69	John	CRA	7	URNER, Martin	CHE	896
Philip	DAU	26	John	LAN	144	URNISTON?, David	WST	176
UMBERHOUR, Philip	BER	203	Mark	CHE	778	URRICH, Felty	DAU	39
UMBOURN,			Michael	BER	216	URTLIP, Andrew	CHE	794
Christian	SOM	132	Peter	FRA	309	URTY, William	BFD	67
UMHOLZ, Bernard	DAU	6A	Val.	DAU	52A	URUE, Philip	PHI	147
John	DAU	6	UNKAFAIR, George	WST	352	URWILER, George	MNT	71
UMPAUGH, George	WAS	35	Philip	WST	352	URY, John	YOR	210
UMSTEAD,			UNKLES, George	PHA	52	Michael	YOR	208
Magdaline	CHE	785	William	HNT	143	William	YOR	210
UMSTED, Harman	MNT	129	UNROD, Jacob	PHI	127	USGER, Ulrich	LAN	252
Henry	MNT	85	UNRUE, Sebastian	PHI	147	USHER, William	LAN	248
Herman	BER	249	UNRUH, George	PHI	126	USHERWOOD,		
Jacob	MNT	97	John	PHI	129	Francis	ERI	59A

USTICH, W. Thomas	SOM	163	VAN BRUNK, Henry	SOM	163	VANASTON,		
USTICK, Thos.			VAN BUSKIRK,			Cornelius	BUC	162
Revd.	PHA	33	Aaron	NOH	42	VANASTRAND, Isaac	WAS	32
UTLEY, John	HNT	134	Cornelius	NOH	66	VANASTSDALEN,		
Jonas	HNT	134	Garrett	DEL	174	Jacob	BUC	144
UTT, Adam	NOH	65A	Joseph	NOH	42	James	BUC	144
Elias	NOH	79	Lawrence	NOH	42	John	BUC	144
Jacob Esqr.	NOH	65A	Moses	NOH	42	Nicholas	BUC	144
UTTS, Henry	CUM	33	William	NOH	79	VANATTA, Mary	WAS	32
UTTSEY, Peter	SOM	155	VAN CAMP, Aaron	NOH	79	VANBILGER, Henry	NOH	49
UTZ, Daniel	YOR	183	John	NOH	79	VANBLARGER, Cobis	NOU	113
Daniel	LAN	266	VAN CORT,			VANBLARIGAN,		
Daniel Junr.	YOR	183	Cornelius	MNT	63	David	NOU	115
Robert	LAN	281	Moses	MNT	63	VANBLARIGER,		
UTZE, Cathr.	DAU	20A	VAN CORTRIGHT,			Davis	NOU	113
UTZLER, John	BFD	35	Abraham	LUZ	356	VANBUREN, Abraham	PHA	3
John	SOM	131	VAN DRIES, Widow	NOH	32A	VANBUSKIRK, Jacob	BUC	143
			VAN DUNARK?,			Lawrence	BUC	143
VA--ER?, Christn.	CEN	19	Henry	WAY	150	Lewis	BUC	144
VA--Y, Swanz?	FRA	309	VAN DYN, Martin	LUZ	348	VANBUSKIRKE, John	GRN	97
VACK, Jacob	PHA	53	VAN ERD, Joseph	NOH	38A	VANCAMP, Aaron	WAS	5
VAGHAN, James	WST	258	VAN ETTEN,			Fugr?	CEN	21A
VAHAN, John	WAS	106	Anthony	WAY	147	James	LYC	11
VAIL, Christn.	CHE	906	Jacob	NOH	68	John	LYC	12
Joshua	YOR	210	Johannes	WAY	147	VANCANNAN,		
Moses	CRA	6	Johannes Jr.	WAY	147	Michael	LAN	182
VAINES?, Robert	NOU	185	John	WAY	150	VANCE, Adam	FRA	285
VALANCE, John	YOR	219	Simeon	WAY	147	Arther	PHI	85
VALANCEY,			VAN FOSSEN, John	MNT	93	Arthur	WAS	60
Sebastian	BUC	83A	VAN GORDEN,			Barny	PHA	67
VALANTINE,			Alexander	WAY	148	David	GRN	85
Scheltzer	FRA	293	Alexander Jr	WAY	148	David	FAY	251
VALE, John	PHI	107A	David	WAY	147	Elizabeth	FAY	251
VALENTIN,			Gilbert	WAY	147	Ezekial	FAY	234
Frederick	LAN	185	Ilijah	WAY	148	Francis	WST	374
VALENTINE,			Isaac	WAY	147	Isaac	WAS	114
Absalom	CHE	759	Moses	WAY	148	James	GRN	85
Andrew	BFD	59	Peter	WAY	145	James	WST	298
Charles	WAS	117	W.	WAY	145	James	MIF	5A
Crace	PHI	109	VAN HORN, Abraham	NOH	66	James S./ T.?	PHA	73
George	CHE	899	VAN MANMERIK,			John	PHI	85
Jacob	BFD	59	Anthony	PHA	123	John	WAS	95
Jehu	CHE	900	VAN METRE, Jacob	WAY	137	John	ALL	105
John	LAN	97	VAN ORMAN, Samuel	NOH	79	John	FRA	274
John	DEL	180	VAN SICKLE, John	WAY	145	John	FRA	283
John	CHE	759	Rinere	WAY	145	Joseph Esq.	WAS	95
John	CHE	900	VAN STEUBEN,			Margaret	FAY	251
Jonathan	MIF	9	Peter M.	NOH	38A	Moses	FAY	251
Jonathn.	CHE	899	VAN VLEEK, Jacob			Patrick	ERI	55A
Micajah	DEL	183	Revd.	NOH	32A	Peter	YOR	212
Michl.	DAU	30	Jacob, Revd.,			Robert	ALL	108
Robt.	CHE	899	Inspector Of			Saml.	CUM	143
Wm.	PHA	74	The Boarding			Thomas	FAY	224
VALEY, David	PHI	26	School With			William	WAS	95
VALILY, Daniel	WAS	106	Tudoresses	NOH	32A	William	FAY	224
VALINTINE, Abner	WST	243	VAN VLIET,			William	FAY	234
VALLAWAY, John	GRN	108	Cherrick	NOH	79	William	FAY	254
VALLENCE, John	PHA	9	Derrick	NOH	79	Wm.	BEV	23
VALLENS, William	PHI	17	Joseph	NOH	79	Wm.	CUM	149
VALLEY, John F.	PHA	90	VAN WINDLE, Peter	MNT	92	VANCEIKLE, Jno.	VEN	170
VAN AKEN, Casper	WAY	150	VAN WYE, Henry	WAY	150	VANCELER, Henry	FRA	312
Elias	WAY	139	VAN, William	MER	462	VANCLAW, John W.	PHI	68A
Eliphaz	WAY	148	VANANDER,			VANCLIFF, Joseph	BFD	47
Garret	WAY	145	Catharine	CUM	33	William	BFD	46
Harman	WAY	150	VANANSDALN, David	YOR	210	William Jr.	BFD	46
Jacob	WAY	150	Isaac	YOR	210	VANCORANT,		
James	WAY	150	VANARSDAL, John	WST	278	Gilbert	LUZ	394
John	WAY	145	VANARSDAN, John	PHA	21	VANCOUNT, Joel	LYC	27
John Jr.	WAY	145	VANARTSDALEN,			VANCOURT, Jane	PHI	138
Levi	WAY	145	Garret	BUC	138	Luezer	PHI	149
Peter	WAY	145	Simon	BUC	138	Moses	PHI	138
VAN AKIN,			Simon Jnr.	BUC	138	Thomas	PHI	138
Benjamin	WAY	150	VANARY, Robert	BUC	107A	VANDABEE, William	DEL	179
VAN AMARIDE, Lyon	PHI	71	VANASDALE,			VANDALL, John	LUZ	349
VAN ATTEN, Mary	WAY	150	Clement	YOR	209	VANDEBERK, Garret	CRA	17
VAN AWL?, John	CEN	24	VANASDOLEN, Chris	PHI	149	VANDEFENDER, Corn.	BUC	153A

VANDEFENDER,		
Farington	BUC	153A
VANDEGRAFT,		
Ebenezer	WAS	83
Jacob	WAS	83
VANDEGRIFT,		
Abraham	BUC	89A
Abraham	BUC	89A
Amos	BUC	89A
Aron	BUC	89A
Benjn.	BUC	89A
Charity	BUC	90
Eliza	BUC	89A
Garret	BUC	89A
George	BUC	89A
Jacob	BUC	138
Jacob	BUC	89A
Jacob	BUC	89A
John	NOU	119
John	BUC	89A
John	BUC	89A
John	BUC	89A
Jonathan	BUC	89A
Wm.	BUC	89A
VANDEMENT, Fredk.	FAY	218
VANDERBELT, Jacob	CUM	124
Peter	LYC	3
VANDERBILT, Aron	BUC	150
Cornelius	CUM	125
Cornelius Junr.	CUM	125
David	ADA	20
Denis	NOU	145
Jacob	NOU	145
John	BUC	150
VANDERGRIFF, Mary	PHA	97
VANDERGRIFT,		
Benjn.	PHI	134
Davd.	PHI	145
George	PHI	151
Jacob	NOH	84A
John	PHI	152
Joseph	BUC	85
Joshua	PHI	144
VANDERHUFF,		
Richard	NOU	169
VANDERLAND, Jno.	BUT	359
Jno.	BUT	361
VANDERMARK,		
Benjamin	LUZ	347
Benjamin	LUZ	348
Elias	LUZ	328
Garret	LUZ	347
James	NOH	79
Jeremiah	LUZ	326
Jeremiah	LUZ	347
Jeremiah	LUZ	348
John	NOH	79
Widow	NOH	79
VANDERSHIE,		
Anthy.	PHI	71A
VANDERSLICE,		
Anthony	MNT	85
Daniel	PHA	66
George	PHA	40
Henry	NOU	98
Henry	PHI	73A
Jacob	NOU	98
Jacob	PHI	75A
John	CHE	784
Thomas	MNT	85
VANDERWICK, Mr.	PHA	49
VANDEVENDER,		
Peter	HNT	160
VANDICK, John	NOU	169
VANDIGRIFT,		
Sampson	WAS	41

VANDIHOOF,		
Corneles	FAY	260
VANDIKE, Jacob	BUC	138
Jacob & John	BUC	144
John	ADA	35
John (See		
Vandike,		
Jacob)	BUC	144
John	BUC	156
John	BUC	145A
Lambert	BUC	138
Peter	ADA	23
VANDIN, Francis	NOU	119
VANDINE, Dennis	ADA	19
Garret	BUC	95A
VANDIVER, Peter	PHA	115
VANDIVERT,		
Barnard	ALL	91
John	ALL	92
John Jun.	ALL	92
Paul	ALL	92
Peter	ALL	92
VANDIVIER, Grace	PHA	103
VANDLIN, John	NOU	151
VANDLING, Henry	NOU	119
VANDORAN, John	SOM	136
VANDOSTIN, Harman	FRA	301
VANDRUCK, Richard	NOU	169
VANDUSEN, Mathw.	PHI	88
VANDWENER, John	CHE	768
VANDYKE, Andrew	DEL	192
Cristiana	PHI	153
David	PHI	152
David	PHI	153
Henry	PHI	151
Hughson	BUT	362
John	BUT	361
Wm.	WST	228
VANEILES, Henry	BUC	150A
VANEKIN, Paul	PHI	137
VANER, John	MIF	26
VANEST, John	PHA	9
VANFLEET, Abraham	LUZ	363
Cornelus	LYC	29
Richard	MER	462
VANFOSSEN, Arnold	MNT	71
Benjn.	MNT	119
John	MNT	42
Joseph	MNT	114
Leonard	MNT	70
Leonard	MNT	114
VANFUSION, Nathan	CUM	28
VANGARDNER, Elias	WAS	32
VANGORDER, Jacob	BEV	8
VANGORDIN,		
Abraham	ALL	90
VANGUNDY, Henry	LYC	26
VANHART, Jacob	BUC	84
James	BUC	84
Michael	BUC	152
VANHOLT,		
Valentine	DEL	186
VANHOOK, Isaac	FAY	260
VANHORN, Abraham	LYC	6
Andrew	BUC	161A
Barnard	BUC	85
Barnet	BEV	10
Barnet	PHI	147
Barnet	BUC	158
Barnet	BUC	153A
Benj.	PHI	66A
Benjn.	BUC	152A
Bernard	PHI	135
Bernard	BUC	152
Christian		
(Crossed Out)	BUC	152

VANHORN,		
Cornelius	LYC	6
Cornielus	CRA	5
David	BUC	138
Gabriel	BUC	85
Garret	PHI	57
Garret	BUC	148A
Garret	BUC	161A
Henry	BUC	104
Henry	BUC	99A
Isaac	BUC	138
Isaac	BUC	145A
Isaac	BUC	160A
Isaiah	BUC	152
Jacob	BUC	161A
Jessee	PHI	151
John	BUC	95
John	PHI	118
John	BUC	145
John	PHI	151
John	BUC	152
John	BUC	162
John Jn.	BUC	144A
John Jr.	BUC	161A
John	BUC	145A
John	BUC	161A
John?	PHI	90A
Jonathan	BUC	99A
Joseph	BUC	104
Joseph	CEN	21A
Joseph	BUC	99A
Martha	BUC	152A
Mary	BUC	99A
Peter	BUC	95
Peter	PHI	108
Peter	PHI	149
Peter	BUC	161A
Richard	BUC	85
Robert	NOU	98
William	BUC	152
William	BUC	89A
Wm.	LYC	6
VANHORNE,		
Benjamin	LUZ	356
David	PHA	104
Garret	WAS	47
Samuel	LUZ	356
VANHOUTEN, John	FAY	254
VANIMIN, John	HNT	122
VANISTER, James	PHI	6
VANIVY?/ VANWY?,		
Arthur	WAS	77
VANKIRK, Bernard	BUC	89A
James	WST	298
Samuel	ALL	76
William	ERI	59
VANKIRKE, Henry	WAS	5
Jacob	WAS	5
Joseph	WAS	5
Sarah	WAS	5
VANKOOK, John	FAY	254
VANLEAR, Eliza.	CUM	88
Joseph	FRA	292
Wm.	FRA	281
VANLEER, Benjn.	PHA	83
Bernard	DEL	178
Bernard	CHE	910
Christianna	DEL	178
Isaac W.	LAN	229
Saml.	CHE	907
Widow	CHE	831
VANLONE, Abraham	LUZ	340
Everart	LUZ	340
Matthias	LUZ	340
Matthias Jr.	LUZ	341
Nicholas	LUZ	341

VANLUNK, Richd.	PHA	52	VANSCIKE, Peter	BFD	46	VAUGHEN, Josa.	
VANLUVENDER,			VANSCIVER, John	PHI	72A	Revrd.	CHE 753
Peter	BUC	106A	VANSCOTER,			VAUGHHAM, Thomas	ALL 115
VANLUVENDER?,			Abraham	LUZ	354	VAUN, Joseph	WAS 114
Israel	BUC	106	Anthony	LUZ	354	Thos.	PHI 87
VANMERING, Thos.	CUM	33	Isaac	LUZ	354	Wm.	PHI 87A
VANMETRE, Henry	GRN	97	James	LUZ	354	VAUNEIDA?, Geo.	BER 200
Jesse	GRN	97	VANSCOY, Moses	ADA	42	VAUNS, Widow	PHI 5
VANNATA, Phillip	NOU	133	VANSCOYOC, Enoch	WAS	51	VAUX, James	PHA 29
VANNERMAN, Fredk.	PHI	10	VANSEL, Isaac	PHI	61A	VEACH, James	FAY 234
John	PHI	17	VANSHRYOCK,			VEAGEY?, See	
Willm.	PHI	30	Benjm.	FRA	324	Vealzey	BEV 28
VANNIER, Francis	NOH	79	John	FRA	323	VEAL, Widw.	PHI 79
VANNOST, Peter	PHI	13	VANSICKLE, John	GRN	66	Abraham	FAY 234
VANOCKER, James	LUZ	379	Richard	CRA	13	Benjeman	FAY 234
James	LUZ	382	VANSICKLES,			John	ALL 112
VANOLDEM?, John	NOU	178	Zechariah	GRN	92	Robert	FAY 234
VANORTEN, Joseph	PHI	152	VANSIGLES, John	WST	298	Solomon	ALL 113
Rachael	PHI	152	VANSISE, Joseph	PHA	47	Steven	FAY 234
VANOSDALEN,			VANSKIVER, Jacob	PHA	61	Thomas	CHE 911
Garret	ADA	20	VANTINE, Thomas	ADA	21	VEALZEY, Elijah	BEV 28
Peter	ADA	33	VANTZ, John	ADA	38	Elisha	BEV 28
VANOSDALEN?,			Nicholas	ADA	37	VEANAS, Benrard	PHA 81
Isaac	ADA	20	Orbin	ADA	25	VEARNER?, John	ALL 96
VANOSTIN,			VANUXEM, James	PHA	38	VEEL, Robt. Junr.	YOR 208
Cornelius	MNT	141	VANVOLSON, Robert	NOU	133	William	YOR 208
VANPELT, Daniel	PHI	144	VANVORIS, Abraham	WAS	65	VEEON, Henry	GRN 90
Isaac	BUC	107A	Daniel	WAS	47	VEICE?, Benjn.	PHA 118
John	NOU	102	Paul	WAS	65	VEICHEL?, Jacob	BER 282
VANPOOL,			Rienere	WAS	65	VELAND, Samuel	NOU 200
Catharine	PHA	72	VANWINKLE, Elias	LUZ	385	VEMER?, Andw.	PHI 92
Jacob	FRA	298	John	PHI	140	VENAMONS,	
VANREAD, Jacob	BER	140	Nathl.	PHI	140	Nicholas	WAS 106
VANREED, Jacob	BER	182	VANWYE, Jacob	LUZ	327	VENASDEL, Benjn.	FAY 251
John	PHA	75	VANZANT, James	WST	298	VENCAMP, Elisha	CUM 35
John	BER	171	VARANCE, Fredrick	PHA	118	VENCE, Jacob	DAU 16
VANRUFF, Henry	GRN	97	VARAREE, John	PHI	109	Jacob	DAU 18
VANS, Philip	PHI	15	VARNER, Abraham	FRA	324	VENDEK, Abraham	FRA 275
VANSANT, Abram.	PHI	144	Frederick	PHI	131	VENDIER?, John	PHA 5
Charles	BUC	143A	Henry	FRA	324	VENDOLAR, John	FAY 269
Charles	BUC	153A	John	GRN	73	Peter	FAY 269
Cornelius	BUC	99A	John	FRA	324	Peter Jur.	FAY 269
Eliza	BUC	153A	John	LUZ	357	VENEMON, Andrew	WAS 114
Elizah.	PHI	145	Philip	WST	352	VENEMONS, George	WAS 106
Gabriel	NOU	119	Philip	PHI	109A	VENGELDER, Sarah	ALL 86
Garret	BUC	85	Phillip	FRA	292	VENHORN, Job	FAY 248
Garret	BUC	162	Samuel	GRN	73	VENNUM, Thomas	WAS 5
Garret	BUC	107A	VARNES, George	CUM	105	VENOSDOLL,	
Garrit H.	BUC	89A	Phillip	CUM	109	Cornelius	GRN 66
George	HNT	135	Valentine	CUM	31	VENSANT, Bethual	NOU 169
George	BUC	83A	VARNET, Conrod	CUM	141	Daniel	NOU 169
Harman	BUC	90	VARNOR, Henry	FRA	324	James	NOU 107
Harman	BUC	153A	VASBENNER, John	WAS	14	VENSELL, Michl.	WST 228
Henry	PHI	144	VASE, Ambrose	PHA	33	Phillip	WST 228
Isaiah	BUC	99A	VASEY, John	BUC	162	VENSIL, George	PHI 153
Jacob	BUC	144	VASSAULT?, Thomas	PHA	101	VENT, Andrew	WAS 53
Jacob	BUC	83A	VASTBINDER, Adam	MIF	9	VENUS, Philip	ADA 40
James	PHI	149	VASTIME, Benjn.	CHE	781	VENVARD?, Wm.	PHI 68
James	PHI	149	VASTINE, Benjamin	NOU	107	VEPER, Alexr.	PHI 45
James	BUT	358	Benjamin	NOU	107	VEPER?, David	PHI 45
Jesse (Crossed			Elizabeth	BUC	106	VERCHEL?, Jacob	BER 282
Out)	BUC	99A	Jonathen	NOU	107	VERFEL, Jacob	LAN 248
John	BUC	138	Peter	NOU	107	VERGER, Ann	PHA 45
John	BUC	89A	VAUCER?, Christn.	CEN	19	VERGIN, Eli	FAY 229
Joshua	BUC	145A	VAUCHEY, Jane F.	PHA	17	Kinsey	FAY 229
Mary	BUC	153A	VAUGHAN, Eleanor	LUZ	394	Reason	FAY 229
Nathan	BUC	89A	Jacob	WAS	72	VERITY, Widow	BUC 148A
Nicholas	BUC	144	Jacob	DEL	174	VERLEY, Abraham	NOU 141
Peter	BUC	89A	John	LUZ	368	Michael	NOU 141
Peter	BUC	99A	John	LUZ	394	VERMILIA,	
Richard	BUC	143A	Johnson	DEL	174	Elizabeth	PHA 33
Widow	BUC	144	Joshua	DEL	174	VERNER, Adam	PHI 133
William	BUC	138	Richard	HNT	144	Benjamin	LAN 175
William	BUC	162	Robert	HNT	142	Nicholas	SOM 160
Wm.	BUC	161A	William	HNT	142	Philip	ADA 30
VANSCIKE, Joseph	BFD	46	Willm.	PHI	38	VERNOM, George	CHE 886

VERNON, Edward	CHE 777	VIXON, John	CHE 909	WADDLE, George	CHE 719
Elias	DEL 164	VOGAN, James	LAN 73	James	WAS 72
Enoch	BUT 352	John	NOU 196	John	DEL 155
Gideon	DEL 181	John	NOU 196	Jos.	FRA 315
James	CHE 848	VOGDIS, Benjamin	CHE 800	Robt.	WST 317
Job	DEL 156	Joseph	CHE 881	Thos.	FRA 282
John	CHE 778	Joseph Jr.	CHE 881	William	FRA 299
Margarett	DEL 179	VOGELE, Bernhard	NOH 57A	Wm.	CUM 138
Mary	DEL 181	VOGT, George (Son		Wm.	FRA 287
Mordecai	CHE 852	Of John)	NOH 57A	Wm.	WST 318
Samuel	DEL 155	George	NOH 57A	WADE, Abner	LUZ 327
Thomas Esqr.	DEL 192	John	NOH 57A	Francis	MNT 85
William	DEL 157	VOIGHT, Henry	PHA 78	James	LAN 300
William	DEL 160	VOIL, Christian	CHE 909	James	LAN 311
Woodward	DEL 181	VOISE, Jacob	MNT 76	Nathan	LUZ 327
VERNS, Jacob	FAY 206	VOIT, Sebastian	PHA 43	Peter	DEL 155
VERNUM, Widow	YOR 219	VOLCANBOROUGH,		Samuel	BEV 6
Abraham	FAY 229	James	LUZ 409	WADEL, Dannel	ALL 79
Benjn.	FAY 229	VOLLENTINE,		James	ALL 79
VERNUN, Joseph	GRN 91	William	VEN 165	Wilm.	ALL 98
VERT?, (See Vest)	BUC 97A	VON LONE, Casper		WADHAM, Moses	LUZ 341
VERTREES, John	HNT 125	Henry	LAN 32	Noah	LUZ 342
VESINBANG, Henry	PHI 70A	VONATA, Jacob	LAN 270	Noah Jr.	LUZ 340
VESSER?, Alexr.	PHI 45	VONDERMEULER,		WADHAMS, Calvin	LUZ 342
David	PHI 45	John	YOR 158	WADKIN, Enoch	DEL 173
VEST, John	BUC 97A	VONER, John	PHI 52	WADKINS, James	FAY 212
Thomas	VEN 167	VONNERMORE, Saml.	MIF 13A	John	PHI 149
VETCH, Nathan	GRN 93	VONOSTEN, William	PHI 151	WADLOW, Moses	PHA 26
VETREE, John	PHI 108	VONSICK, Joseph	LUZ 333	WADLY?, Samuel	BUC 162
VIAND, George	NOU 185	VONVILLER, Andw.	PHA 27	WADMAN, Peace	PHA 121
Jacob	NOU 185	VORAS, Abraham	WAS 14	Praise	PHA 98
John	NOU 185	Isaac	ALL 120	WADSWORTH,	
VIAZY, Thomas	PHA 108	Isaiah	WAS 14	Ephraim	LUZ 351
VICE, John	CHE 906	Jacob	FAY 269	Michael	ADA 23
Philip	CHE 911	VORE, Jacob	YOR 203	WAER, Catherine	DAU 10
VICKERS, Peter	BUC 145A	Jesse	BFD 77	WAGAN, David	LAN 308
Thomas	CHE 902	Peter	BFD 77	WAGEMAN,	
VICKROY, Nathan	BFD 77	VORGUSON, Ezekiel	LUZ 415	Christian	SOM 140
Thomas	BFD 77	Ezekiel Jr.	LUZ 415	John	BER 132
William	BFD 77	Rufus	LUZ 415	John	SOM 140
VICTOR, David	FAY 248	Solomon	LUZ 415	William	SOM 140
Elizabeth	FAY 212	VORIS, Garret	WST 352	WAGENER, Abraham	NOH 88
John	FAY 212	Ralph	WST 352	Adam	NOH 52
Phillip	FAY 248	Ralph Senr.	WST 352	Andrew	NOH 86
VIGUER, Abel	FAY 237	VOSS, Peter	CUM 89	Daniel	NOH 38A
VILLANDINGHAM,		VOUGHT, Godfrey	LUZ 416	David	NOH 38A
George	ALL 102	VOX, Ann	PHI 69A	Frederick	NOH 40A
George Esqr.	ALL 102	VOYMAN, Philip	CHE 891	George	NOH 36A
VILLERS, James	GRN 97	VUTHALL, Matthias	CHE 909	George Fr.	NOH 38A
John	GRN 97			John	NOH 35
VIMERT, Valentine	HNT 123	W----?, Abm.?	MIF 8A	John	NOH 38A
VINCAMP, Jno.	CUM 24	George	MIF 8A	John	NOH 42A
VINCENT,		Henry?	BFD 78	John	NOH 63A
Alexander	WAS 32	Samuel	BFD 78	John	NOH 69A
James	WAS 60	Thomas	MIF 8A	Martin	NOH 52
John	ERI 60	W---?, Phil	LAN 147A	Mathias	NOH 74A
Martha	WAS 60	W---ISSARTY?,		Nicholas	NOH 35
Rachel	PHA 114	Jthomas	BEV 21	Nicholas	NOH 88
Thomas	WAS 60	WA---, Jno.	WAR 1A	Widow Of David	NOH 39
Thomas	WAS 118	WA--?, James	WAR 1A	WAGENHURST,	
Wm.	CUM 34	WABB, Jacob	FAY 229	Charles	BER 185
VINECIVER, George	BFD 41	WABURN, Christian	DAU 37	WAGER, Benjamin	MNT 79
VINEGAR, George	CUM 96	WACHIN, John	LAN 252	Jesse	MNT 79
Mary Widow	LAN 15	WACHSMUTH, (No		WAGERSON, Mary	PHI 106
VINEMAUGHER,		Given Name)	PHA 96	WAGGENER, Adam	NOH 68
Casper	NOU 190	WACK, Frederick	BUC 82A	WAGGER, Leonard	CHE 793
VINES, Daniel	MIF 13A	WACKAR, Chrisr.	PHI 20	WAGGOMAN, Jacob	FRA 305
VINEST, Barney	WAS 60	WACKER?, Felix	MNT 141	Phillip	FRA 281
VINIGAR, Henry	FRA 316	WACKNER, Andrew	NOU 133	WAGGONER, Adam	BUC 160
VINNATO, John	ALL 102	Christopher	NOU 196	Andrew	NOU 102
VINNZDEL, Simeon	MER 462	Jacob	BER 285	Barbara	YOR 158
VINTEBER,		WACKTEL, Barbara	YOR 206	Casper	CUM 94
Christian	LAN 218	WADDELL, William	WST 353	Casper	YOR 187
John	LAN 218	WADDINGTON, John	PHA 85	Christian	BFD 39
VIOLETT, Ashberd	FAY 239	WADDLE, David	DEL 155	Danl. Revd.	YOR 160
VITAKER, James	PHA 105	Fransois	CRA 9	Elias	NOU 190

WAGGONER,		WAGNER, Abraham	NOH	49	WAGONER, Philip	ADA	43	
Elizabeth	CHE 784	Abram	BER	246	Philip	PHI	120A	
Emanuel	BUC 160	Adam	WAY	139	WAGSTAFF, Wilm.	ALL	106	
Francis	YOR 182	Adam	BUC	150	WAHN, Benjamin	HNT	130	
George	BUC 102	Adam	LAN	182	Jesse	HNT	130	
George	BUC 140	Chn.	NOH	49	Thomas	HNT	130	
George	YOR 198	Christena	BER	142	WAHRTON, John	PHA	104	
George	FRA 320	Christian	LAN	181	WAID, Gilbert	FAY	237	
George	CHE 776	Christian	LAN	181	James	FAY	212	
George	CEN 21A	Christopher	BER	143	John	FAY	207	
Henry	CUM 32	Danl.	BER	143	John	FAY	207	
Henry	PHI 66	Elias	BER	182	John	LAN	245	
Henry	PHI 156	Eliz.	BER	142	Martha	CRA	10	
Henry	YOR 192	Francis	MNT	101	Roddy	FAY	207	
Henry	FRA 281	Geo.	BER	142	Thomas	FAY	201	
Henry Senr.	CUM 32	George	DAU	37A	WAIGNRIGHT,			
Jacob	CUM 32	George Ad. /			Cathrine	PHA	43	
Jacob	CUM 82	Od.?	BER	224	Isaac	PHA	36	
Jacob	BUC 102	George W.	PHA	32	John	PHA	22	
Jacob	NOU 126	Grace	PHA	32	WAIN, Jacob	DAU	4A	
Jacob	YOR 179	Henry	DAU	25	WAINEY, John	FAY	229	
Jacob	NOU 190	Henry	BER	239	WAIR, James	FRA	285	
Jacob	YOR 212	Jacob	MNT	54	WAIRICH, John	LAN	277	
Jacob	YOR 214	Jacob	BER	212	WAIRNTZ, Philip	LAN	70	
Jacob	FRA 288	Jacob	BER	269	WAK?, Jas.	LYC	18	
Jacob	LUZ 411	John	PHA	14	John	MNT	117	
Jacob	CHE 784	John	DAU	18	WAKE, Elizabeth	PHI	84A	
Jacob Sr.	CUM 32	John	DAU	24	Henry	SOM	131	
James	LUZ 367	John	NOH	49	WAKEFIELD, David	WST	383	
Jno.	CUM 131	John	NOH	83	Geo.	MIF	26	
Jno.	FRA 284	John	BER	223	James	WST	383	
Jno.	DAU 34A	John	LAN	228	John	WST	383	
John	CEN 21	John	BER	246	Matthw.	BUT	315	
John	WAS 32	Mathias	BER	266	Thomas	WST	383	
John	CUM 38	Michael	BER	143	Uziel	FRA	309	
John	MNT 45	Michael	BER	224	Wm.	MIF	26	
John	BFD 53	Michl.	BER	143	WAKEFORD, Onslow	PHA	88	
John	MNT 116	Peter	MNT	54	WAKELING, Saml.	PHI	134	
John	HNT 121	Philip	NOH	49	WAKELY, Lemuel	LUZ	330	
John	NOU 126	Sebastian	DAU	50A	WAKENSCHAH, Hugh	LAN	186	
John	SOM 136	Thomas	BER	246	WAKERMAN, George	YOR	169	
John	PHI 156	William	LAN	278	WAKIZER, Conrad			
John	YOR 169	William	LAN	280	Jr.	LUZ	328	
John	YOR 173	William	BUC	150A	WAKY, Christian	LAN	98	
John	YOR 212	Zacharias	NOH	61A	WALACE, Widow	PHI	95A	
John Jr.	CUM 25	Zereachus	BER	220	WALAY,			
John Sr.	CUM 25	Ohn	LAN	251	Christopher	ADA	12	
Joseph	LAN 56	WAGNOR, Baltis	PHA	71	WALB, David	NOH	84A	
Lebright	NOU 145	Fredk.	DAU	20A	Jacob	NOH	84A	
Martin	HNT 136	John	LAN	254	Jost	NOH	84A	
Michael	WAS 65	WAGON, David	PHI	76A	William	NOH	69A	
Michael	NOU 126	Henry	PHI	92	WALB?, (See Wall)	NOH	46A	
Michael	SOM 155	WAGONER, Widw.	PHI	109A	See Wall	BER	212	
Michl.	CUM 70	Adam Junr.	PHI	110	WALBERT, Geo.			
Michl.	DAU 50A	Adam Senr.	PHI	110	(See Walbert,			
Peter	CUM 58	Adam	PHI	86A	Widow)	NOH	61A	
Peter	BFD 67	Chr.	WST	229	George Sr.	NOH	61A	
Peter	YOR 178	Christn.	MNT	113	Peter Sr.	NOH	61A	
Peter	NOU 190	Conrad	DAU	48	Widow Of Geo.	NOH	61A	
Peter	CHE 776	Daniel	DAU	43A	WALBERY, Thos.	PHI	76	
Peter	CHE 784	Frederick	MNT	113	WALBOM, Andrew	DAU	48	
Philip	BFD 60	George	WST	228	WALBORN, George	DAU	48A	
Philip	YOR 172	Gorge	PHI	105	WALBOURN,			
Philip	YOR 214	Jacob	NOU	126	Christn.	BER	153	
Phillip	CUM 120	John	ADA	29	Henry	BER	153	
Valentine	BFD 69	John	ADA	33	Martinus	BER	153	
Widow	CHE 788	John	DAU	48	Michael	BER	269	
William	HNT 137	John	PHA	60	WALBURN, Andrew	DAU	49	
William	PHI 141	John	NOU	178	Christn.	DAU	18	
Youst	NOU 141	John	PHI	105A	Christn.	DAU	51A	
WAGGONSELLER,		John	PHI	115A	Herman	DAU	39	
Jno.	CHE 813	Ludwick	ADA	23	Jacob	DAU	51A	
John	MNT 85	Michl.	DAU	21A	Martin	DAU	51A	
WAGGONWOOD, Jacob	CHE 796	Peter	ADA	11	Martin	DAU	52A	
WAGH, John	CHE 731	Peter	ADA	16	Martin	DAU	52A	
Micheal	WST 279	Peter	MNT	91	Michl.	DAU	17A	

WALBURN, Peter	FRA 283	WALKER, Henry	LAN 170	WALKER, Mary	CHE 708		
WALCHAUB?,		Henry	BER 209	Mathew	PHA 67		
William	HNT 131	Hugh	CUM 52	Matt.	LAN 265		
WALCHAUT?,		Hugh	CUM 141	Matthew	CHE 708		
William	HNT 131	Isaac	PHA 62	Meshick	LUZ 327		
WALCOT, James	HNT 141	Isaac	ALL 107	Michael	MNT 71		
WALD, Casper	MNT 91	Isaac	LAN 119	Nancy	WAS 72		
George	MNT 97	Isaac	CUM 138	Nathan	ADA 39		
Henry	MNT 90	Isaac	LAN 167	Nathaniel	WAS 87		
Jacob	MNT 91	Isaac	CHE 746	Nicholas	FAY 224		
WALDEBERGER,		Isaac	CHE 830	Nocholas	MER 463		
Catherine	LAN 316	Jacob	DAU 11	Patrick	LAN 96		
WALDER, George	BUC 155	Jacob	NOU 142	Philip	PHI 94		
WALDERN, Samuel	MER 462	Jacob	SOM 150	Philip	SOM 140		
WALDING,		Jacob	MIF 26A	Philip	NOH 63A		
Cornelius	NOU 169	James	ADA 39	Phillip	BEV 19		
Cornilius	NOU 169	James	PHI 76	Richard	BUC 158		
WALDMAN, John	NOH 81A	James	PHA 82	Robert	BEV 8		
Peter	NOH 51	James	ALL 101	Robert	WAS 35		
Valentine	NOH 69A	James	HNT 125	Robert	ALL 62		
WALDON, John	NOU 153	James	CUM 136	Robert	ARM 123		
WALDSMITH, John	BER 171	James	FAY 224	Robert	MER 463		
WALEHAUB, William	HNT 131	James	FAY 248	Robert	MER 463		
WALERK, Alexander	ARM 126	James	LUZ 327	Robert	BUC 87A		
WALES, Rodger	ADA 8	James	BUT 337	Robert	BUC 145A		
WALG, Matthias	LAN 212	James	MER 462	Robert	BUC 155A		
WALGEMUTH,		James	MER 463	Robt.	CUM 26		
Abraham	YOR 174	James	MER 463	Robt.	PHI 89		
WALHEA, Peter	ARM 127	James	CHE 808	Robt.	FRA 276		
WALISTIN, James	CHE 768	James	CHE 834	Saml.	FRA 286		
WALK, Detrick	YOR 207	James	PHI 94A	Saml.	FRA 318		
Frederick	LAN 140	Jane	CUM 133	Saml.	FRA 326		
Jacob	LAN 17	Jas.	CUM 145	Saml.	CHE 735		
Michael	NOH 84A	Jesse	BFD 60	Samuel	PHA 22		
WALKER, Widow	PHI 21	John	PHI 9	Samuel	WAS 26		
Abel	YOR 209	John	PHA 20	Samuel	ALL 76		
Abraham	ARM 123	John	WAS 26	Samuel	ARM 126		
Alexander	WAS 32	John	LAN 48	Samuel	CHE 764		
Alexander	WAS 35	John	CUM 54	Sarah	DEL 167		
Alexander	SOM 160	John	PHA 67	Simon	PHA 121		
Alexr.	WST 374	John	ALL 74	Stephen	PHA 38		
Alexr.	CHE 748	John	PHA 88	Susanna	HNT 126		
Andr.	FRA 286	John	ALL 92	Susanna	HNT 127		
Andrew	WAS 18	John	CUM 92	Thomas	PHI 56		
Andrew	PHA 64	John	ALL 103	Thomas	ALL 74		
Andrew	WAS 72	John	ALL 113	Thomas	HNT 151		
Andrew	LAN 166	John	HNT 140	Thomas	FAY 200		
Andw.	WST 229	John	HNT 162	Thomas	CHE 829		
Andw.	CEN 23A	John	BUT 342	Thomas	CHE 830		
Barb.	DAU 15	John	WST 374	Thomas	CHE 832		
Benj.	YOR 209	John	MER 463	Thos. G.	CHE 836		
Benjamene	ARM 127	John	CHE 701	Walter	ALL 113		
Benjamin	WST 158	John	CHE 708	Widow	LAN 155		
Benjn.	CHE 715	John	CHE 716	William	ADA 18		
Cathrine	PHA 117	John	CHE 722	William	ADA 39		
Daniel	NOH 79A	John	CHE 777	William	NOU 119		
David	CUM 54	John	CHE 825	William	LAN 169		
David	HNT 140	John Junior	ALL 95	William	MIF 11A		
Doreatha	PHA 77	John	NOH 31A	William	BUC 155A		
Ebenezer	WAS 41	John	NOH 63A	Wilm.	ALL 84		
Elizabeth	FAY 200	Jonathen	NOU 173	Wilm.	ALL 100		
Emanuel	PHA 9	Joseph	ADA 10	Wm.	CUM 54		
Enoch	CHE 856	Joseph	PHI 12	Wm.	CUM 126		
Ezekiel	LAN 122	Joseph	ADA 40	Zadock	FAY 254		
Gabriel	ADA 8	Joseph	PHA 72	WALKER?, James	ARM 123		
Gabriel	ALL 107	Joseph	DEL 166	Thomas	HNT 151		
George	PHA 19	Joseph	LAN 167	WALKEVEN, Levi	CHE 879		
George	PHA 29	Joseph	FAY 251	WALL, Absalom	HNT 130		
George	PHA 55	Joseph	CHE 752	Charles	BFD 60		
George	ALL 75	Joseph	CHE 830	Conrad	NOH 46A		
George	SOM 140	Joseph Esq.	LAN 121	David	LUZ 370		
George	BUC 162	Joseph Esqr.	ALL 101	George	PHA 101		
George	FRA 291	Lewas	ALL 90	George	BUC 145A		
George	MER 463	Lewis	PHA 86	Hannah	DEL 162		
George	CHE 825	Martha	PHA 55	Henry	PHI 88A		
Henry	NOU 108	Martin	PHA 91	Isaac	ALL 78		

WALNUT, Widow	PHI	96	WALTER, John	BER	243	WALTERS, John	GRN	85
WALPART, Fredk.			John	DAU	25A	John	WST	259
Esqqr.	PHI	96	John	DAU	25A	John	WST	317
WALPOLE, Thos.	PHA	105	John	NOH	40A	John	WST	374
WALRAVEN, John	PHI	141	John P.	DAU	4A	John	CHE	862
WALSER, Fredrick	FAY	218	Jonathan	MNT	140	John	CHE	909
Peter	FAY	218	Jos.	CUM	59	John	PHI	105B
WALT, Henry	MNT	74	Joseph	BFD	78	John, Jr?	WST	374
Henry	CUM	79	Joseph	CHE	860	Joseph	CHE	838
Philip	BER	200	Leonard	CHE	783	Marey	FAY	237
WALTEMARTIN,			Lewis	NOU	185	Martin	PHI	58
Fredk.	DAU	48A	Martin	NOU	108	Mathias	PHI	105A
WALTEMEYER,			Mathias	ADA	16	Michl.	FAY	260
Charles	YOR	196	Melchor	DAU	21	Nichs.	PHI	69A
David	YOR	195	Michael	SOM	136	Peter	WST	228
Fredk.	YOR	196	Michael	BUC	160	Peter	FAY	237
Ludwick	YOR	160	Michael	NOH	40A	Peter	DAU	42A
Philip	YOR	159	Michl.	PHI	69A	Phillip	WST	374
WALTEN, Samuel	PHA	117	Nathaniel	DEL	160	Stophell	CUM	144
WALTENBAUGH, Adam	ARM	127	Nicholas	ADA	31	Thomas	DEL	161
Jeeter?	ARM	127	Nicholas	YOR	180	Thomas?	DEL	155
WALTENS?, Henry	PHA	54	Nicholas	LAN	220	Widw.	PHI	93A
WALTER, Adam	ADA	16	Peter	LAN	47	William	PHA	109
Adam	LYC	19	Peter	NOU	142	Wm.	CEN	23A
Adam	ALL	49	Peter	BUC	160	WALTERS?, -----	PHA	52
Alexr.	PHI	36	Peter	VEN	168	Harih	MNT	66
Andrew	FAY	218	Peter	NOU	185	Thomas	LAN	228
Baltzer	LAN	256	Peter	WST	229	WALTHOUR, Christ.	WST	196
Barnet	NOH	40A	Peter	LAN	256	Jacob	WST	196
Barnet M.	NOH	40A	Peter	FRA	278	WALTHOUSE, Gasper	WST	259
Christian	LAN	214	Peter	DAU	25A	Michel	WST	259
Christn.	DAU	26	Peter	PHI	68A	WALTIMIRE,		
Christn.	BER	142	Philip	NOH	57A	Ludwick	CUM	111
Conrad	NOU	141	Philip	PHI	73A	WALTKER?, Jenny	LYC	19
Conrad	BER	143	Phillip	NOU	142	WALTMAN, Adam	MNT	59
Daniel	BFD	67	Rubertus	LAN	284	Adam	BER	171
Daniel	NOU	113	Sarah	DEL	161	Andrew	NOU	145
David	NOU	142	Simon	NOH	81	Frederick	YOR	170
David	WST	196	Solomon	YOR	204	George	BFD	53
Ephraim	FAY	218	Stophel	CUM	30	Henry	ADA	31
Frederick	NOU	142	Thomas	PHA	106	Henry	NOH	81A
George	ADA	12	Thomas	FAY	239	John	PHI	110
George	PHI	71	Widow	LAN	43	Ludwick	CUM	119
George	NOU	115	William	ADA	12	Ludwick	YOR	171
George	YOR	188	William Jun.	DEL	160	Nicholas	FAY	229
George	NOU	190	Willm.	PHI	30	WALTON, &		
George	FAY	218	Wm.	CHE	783	Duffield	BUC	153A
George Senr.	NOH	40A	WALTER?, Frederic	SOM	140	Aaron	PHI	145
George	NOH	40A	Jacob	SOM	145	Abel	DEL	173
Henry	ADA	12	WALTERBAGER,			Abiather	MNT	65
Henry	ADA	16	Daniel	NOU	178	Albertson	PHI	150
Henry	CUM	22	George	NOU	178	Amos	MNT	66
Henry	NOU	141	WALTERS, Widw.	PHI	105B	Amos	WAS	126
Henry	LAN	214	Abm.	PHI	97	Amos	WAS	83
Isaiah	PHI	26	Abraham	NOU	169	Benjamin	CHE	877
Jacob	CUM	58	Adam	PHA	28	Benjn.	BUC	83A
Jacob	MNT	117	Anthony	WST	374	Benjn.	BUC	87A
Jacob	NOU	142	Benjn.	MIF	26A	Boas	NOH	77
Jacob	NOU	181	Frederick	WST	374	Boas Junr.	NOH	77
Jacob	LAN	206	George	MIF	2	Cilas	CHE	702
Jacob	LAN	264	George	PHI	22	Daniel	BUC	158
Jacob	LAN	307	George	PHA	17A	Danl.	PHI	155
Jacob	PHI	109A	Henrey	FAY	224	Edward	MNT	47
James	PHI	4	Henrey	FAY	232	Elijah	PHI	35
John	CUM	24	Henry	BFD	69	Elijah	MNT	66
John	NOH	35	Henry	DEL	156	Ellis	LYC	3
John	BFD	67	Hetty	PHA	71	Enoch	BUC	158
John	NOU	115	Isaac	PHA	84	George	PHI	73
John	NOU	142	Jacob	MIF	2	George	MNT	116
John	BER	154	Jacob	WAS	60	Henry	PHI	144
John	DEL	160	Jacob	PHA	69	Hiram	DEL	168
John	YOR	169	Jacob	NOU	169	Isaac	MNT	39
John	YOR	174	Jacob	FAY	237	Isaac	MNT	66
John	YOR	175	Jacob	WST	317	Isaac	BUC	142
John	LAN	214	Jacob	WST	374	Isaac	BUC	155
John	FAY	218	John	PHI	5	Isaac	CHE	863

WARNER, Benjn.	LYC	8	WARREN, Thomas	HNT 159	WATERS, Jacob	NOU	98
Benjn. Jun.	LYC	8	WARRIN, Hedick	WAS 60	Jacob	CHE	717
Burket	ADA	41	James C.	PHI 113A	John	PHI	1
Casper	LAN	257	WARRINER, Luther	ERI 58A	John	WAS	6
Charles	YOR	187	WARRON, John	ERI 57A	John	PHI	41
Christian	MNT	112	WARSON, Henry	DEL 158	John	PHI	99
Dan	LUZ	352	Hugh	BUT 328	John	NOU	108
Daniel	BUC	81	Robert	HNT 152	John	PHI	66A
Daniel	LUZ	351	Wm.	BUT 328	Mrs.	NOU	108
David	BUC	107A	WART, Peter	CUM 80	Reese	BUC	89A
Ezekial	PHI	83A	WARTENBY, Joseph	PHI 67A	Samuel	HNT	143
George	LYC	25	WARTERABY/		Westly	BFD	60
George	DEL	187	WARTNABY,		William	HNT	143
George	NOH	36A	Jacob	PHI 75	WATERSON, James	ARM	123
George	BFD	67	WARTINBY, Robt.	PHI 101	WATES, Andrew	WAS	83
Henry	CUM	117	WARTMAN, Widow	PHI 98	Jospeh	WAS	83
Henry	HNT	135	Abm.	PHI 106A	WATHEN, Enock	DEL	174
Heronias	PHA	75	Abrm.	MNT 101	Nicholas	GRN	104
Ichiel/ Jehiel?	LUZ	392	Christian	LAN 183	WATHERHEAD,		
Isaac	MNT	63	Laurence	LAN 44	Alexr.	PHI	76A
Isaac	MNT	140	Mathias	PHI 112A	WATIN?, Eli	LYC	9
Isaiah	BUC	107A	WARTS, Jacob	FRA 283	WATKIN, Evan	CHE	799
Israel	ERI	57	WARTZ, Conrod	CUM 119	Jos.	PHI	91A
Jacob	BFD	67	Derick	NOU 201	Robert	CHE	790
Jacob	DEL	170	Jacob	NOU 201	WATKINS, David	LUZ	418
James	BEV	5	John	NOU 113	James	SOM	155
Jno.	CUM	140	WASAN, Thos.	FRA 287	Joseph	PHA	28
John	LAN	13	WASEL?, Elijah	PHI 77A	Joseph	BUC	141A
John	PHA	82	WASER, Cathe.	DAU 18	Nathan	LAN	7
John	BUC	152	WASH, George	SOM 144	Peter	GRN	104
John	YOR	191	WASHABAUGH, John	SOM 131	Thos.	PHA	13
John	FAY	206	WASHBORN, Caleb	NOH 77	William	PHA	102
John	CHE	702	Daniel	NOH 77	William	CHE	841
Joseph	LYC	8	WASHBURN, Jesse	NOH 36A	WATNIGHT, Jacob	CHE	891
Joseph	PHA	47	Joseph	LUZ 387	WATS, James		
Joseph	PHA	79	WASHER, Felix	DEL 185	Housekeeper	LAN	311
Joseph	BUC	95	WASHER?, Felix	MNT 141	WATSON, Abm.	BUC	100
Joseph	BER	171	WASHING, Felix	DEL 185	Abner	BUC	162A
Martha	PHA	21	WASHINGTON, John	FAY 200	Alexander	NOU	161
Martin	ALL	53	WASHMOOD, Martin	CUM 118	Amariah	LUZ	339
Massa	NOH	33	WASLER, Samuel	MNT 119	Amos	BUC	100
Michael	MNT	65	WASNER, George	MNT 75	Amos	BUC	162
Michael	YOR	162	WASON, Joseph	LAN 130	Andrew Esqr.	ALL	61
Michl.	WST	299	Joseph	WST 158	Anthony	NOU	145
Nathan	NOH	77	Robert	LAN 123	Archibald	ERI	59
Nicholas	PHA	78	Thomas	CEN 21A	Arthur	PHI	17
Rachel	MNT	141	WASON?, Thos	PHI1069	Benj.	MNT	38
Samuel	PHA	23	WASSENSMIDT?,		Benjami	BUC	155
Sarah	PHA	82	Casper	BER 147	Benjn.	BUC	95
Simeon	BUC	146A	WASSER, Jacob	NOH 49	Benjn.	CHE	882
Susannah	PHA	25	John	MNT 125	Charles	PHA	4
Thomas	BUC	107A	Peter	NOH 49	David	BEV	20
William	LUZ	330	Peter	NOH 49	David	BUC	162
Willy	PHA	57	WASSEY, John	BUC 95A	David	NOU	169
Wm.	PHI	60	WAST, John	BUC 92	David	LAN	177
Wm.	CHE	854	WASTLY, Francis	LYC 9	David	NOU	197
WARNICK, Isabell	HNT	136	WAT, James	DAU 10	David	FAY	218
WARNOCK, Edward	WAS	96	WAT?, Andrew	ALL 108	David	LAN	292
Jane	WAS	107	WATERHORN, Gideon	NOU 148	David & Wm.	LYC	24
Robert	BEV	13	WATERHOUSE,		David	BUC	95A
Robert	CHE	767	William	DEL 181	Hugh	ALL	115
William	WAS	35	WATERMAN, Fineas	CHE 878	Hugh	FRA	293
WARNSE, Martin	LAN	177	Hannah	MNT 37	Isaac	PHA	85
WARNTZ, Daniel	LAN	62	Humphrey	PHI 152	Jacob	BUC	162
WARR, John	PHA	110	Jesse	PHA 80	Jacob Jnr.	BUC	100
WARRANT, John	LYC	7	John	DEL 185	James	BEV	15
WARRELL, Isaac	PHI	66A	Stephen	LUZ 420	James	WAS	25
Isaiah	PHI	109	Thomas	PHI 133	James	SOM	153
WARREN, Amos	CHE	699	WATERS, Abm.	PHI 79A	James	BUC	155
Edward	ADA	16	Allen	FAY 237	James	HNT	165
James	CHE	700	Cezar	DEL 174	James	NOU	169
James	CHE	778	Conrad	MNT 71	James	FRA	296
John	ERI	59A	Daniel	PHA 100	James	CEN	21A
Lydia	PHA	119	Ester	FAY 218	James	DAU	24A
Mary	ADA	16	Francis	BUC 162A	James	DAU	24A
Mattw.	PHI	44	Henry	CHE 734	Jesse	BUC	95

WATSON, Jno.	LYC	24	WATSON, Ugh	NOU	160	WAUGH, William	
Job (Crossed			WATSON?, Jacob	PHI	57	Junr.	ADA 4
Out)	BUC	158	John	NOU	169	WAUGHT, John	MER 463
Job	BUC	157	Thos.	PHI	69A	WAUHAR, Ned	LAN 245
John	MIF	18	WATSWORTH, Robert	BFD	60	WAUTMOUGH, James	PHA 75
John	WAS	25	WATT, Alexr.	WAR	1A	WAWLS, Isaac	MIF 26A
John	PHA	32	Andrew	FRA	297	WAX, Peter Senr.	CUM 101
John	MNT	38	David	FAY	218	Phillip	CUM 105
John	WAS	60	Eliza	PHA	96	WAY, Amos	CHE 704
John	PHA	84	Fredk.	CUM	27	Andrew	PHA 32
John	PHA	104	George	WST	374	Benjamin	CHE 709
John	ARM	127	Hugh	HNT	158	Calab	NOU 98
John	CUM	127	James	WST	158	Caleb	HNT 129
John	BUC	162	James	CHE	747	Caleb Esqr.	CHE 777
John	BUC	162	James	MIF	13A	Jacob	CHE 709
John	FAY	218	James	CEN	21A	John	YOR 156
John	FAY	218	John	HNT	165	John	CHE 766
John	BER	252	John	MIF	13A	John	CHE 899
John	FRA	296	John	CEN	21A	John Esqr.	ALL 113
John	MER	463	Joseph	WAS	10	John D.	CHE 865
John Docr.	BUC	87A	Joseph	WAS	32	Joseph	CHE 709
John Doct.	LAN	2	Joseph	MER	463	Joseph	CHE 805
John Jnr.	BUC	87A	Robert	WST	229	Joshua	CHE 775
John Jur.	FAY	231	Samuel	WAS	32	Joshua	CHE 806
John Revd.	WAS	25	Samuel	MER	462	Samuel	WAS 14
John	MIF	5A	Susannah	CHE	749	Stephen	WAS 118
John	MIF	11A	Thomas	BEV	4	WAYBRECHT, Jacob	ADA 5
John	CEN	21A	WATT?, Jno.	WAR	1A	WAYBRIGHT,	
John	BUC	87A	John	CHE	867	Mathias	ADA 6
Jonathan	PHI	138	WATTEMEYER,			WAYNE, Caleb P.	PHA 8
Joseph	BEV	17	George	YOR	192	Isaac Esqr.	CHE 798
Joseph	PHA	63	WATTENS?, Henry	PHA	54	Jacob	PHA 47
Joseph	FAY	212	WATTER, John	BUC	97A	John	HNT 136
Joseph	BUC	99A	WATTER?, Jacob	SOM	145	Saml.	PHA 44
Josiak	NOU	169	WATTERS, Fredk.	CUM	66	Thomas	PHI 22
Margaret	CHE	808	WATTERS?, Thomas	LAN	228	Wm.	PHI 106A
Mark	MNT	37	WATTLE, Robt.	BUT	362	WAZER, Philip	PHA 43
Mark	BUC	95	WATTON, David	LYC	15	WEABLE?, Cunrod	SOM 147
Mark	BUC	162	WATTON?, Mrs.	LYC	15	WEABLY, Richard	FAY 218
Mary	PHA	51	(See Walton)	CHE	702	WEAD, Daniel	LAN 293
Matthew	WST	196	Isaac	LYC	15	WEAGHNIH, Jacob	BUC 102
Moses	PHI	87	Joseph	PHA	41	WEAGLE, Abm.	WST 228
Patrick	ALL	106	WATTS, & -later?	PHI	138	Daniel	WST 298
Richard	PHI	16	Andrew	FAY	232	Isaac	WST 228
Robert	ARM	127	Arthur	BUC	144	WEAKLEY, Edwd.	CUM 110
Robert	WST	164	Daniel	WST	298	James	CUM 110
Robert	WST	196	David	CUM	99	Nathanl.	CUM 98
Robt.	MIF	16	Frank	LUZ	413	Robt.	CUM 110
Robt.	MIF	18	George	PHA	101	Saml.	CUM 107
Robt.	FRA	309	James	NOU	161	WEAKLY, John	HNT 123
Robt.	PHI	69A	James	NOU	169	WEAKLY?, William	ADA 38
Samuel	BFD	41	John	BEV	20	WEAL, Sister	LAN 300
Thomas	ADA	32	John	NOU	151	WEALS, Henry	YOR 212
Thomas	ALL	90	John	PHI	154	William	CHE 890
Thomas	PHA	93	John Jr.	PHI	154	WEAN, John	MNT 101
Thomas	BUC	83A	Lewis	BUC	160	John Junr.	MNT 101
Thomas	BUC	87A	Mrs.	NOU	161	Ludwick	MNT 101
Thoms.	BUT	326	Thomas	CHE	792	Michael	MNT 101
Thos.	PHI	105	Thomas	CHE	894	Samuel	BFD 54
Thos.	CEN	21A	William	BUC	144	WEANIGH, Henry	BUC 102
Willia	WAY	145	WATTS?, Elisha			WEANT, David	MNT 74
William	ADA	24	Doctr.	ARM	122	WEAR, John	BUC 106
William	WAS	60	WATTSON, Godfrey	DEL	191	Samuel	BUC 106
William	WAS	77	Moses	WST	374	WEARHAM, Jacob	WST 158
William	BUC	95	WAUGAMAN, John	ADA	15	WEARNER,	
William	NOU	113	WAUGH, Abraham	LAN	165	Christopher	NOH 35
William	NOU	142	Alexr.	DAU	24	WEART, Abrh.	FRA 318
William	HNT	161	David	ADA	5	WEARY, Anthony	NOU 126
William	FAY	231	Eliza	CUM	34	John	NOU 126
Willm.	PHI	46	James	MER	463	WEASNER, Deborah	BUC 100
Wilm.	ALL	56	Jas.	CUM	59	WEASTER, Rudy	FRA 282
Wm.	LYC	15	Jno.	CUM	59	WEATHERS, John	GRN 110
Wm.	PHA	60	Peter	CHE	746	WEATHERSPOON,	
Wm	CUM	.27	Richd.	CUM	59	John	WAS 87
Wm. Captn.	PHI	103A	Saml.	CUM	55	Thos.	PHA 8
Wm. & David	LYC	24	William	ADA	3	WEATLY, John	NOU 173

Name	Loc	Pg	Name	Loc	Pg	Name	Loc	Pg	Name	Loc	Pg
WEAVE, Henry	ADA	10	WEAVER, Jacob			WEAVER, Peter	HNT	116	WEAVER, Peter	NOH	81A
WEAVER, Widow	PHI	17	Jacob	BER	138	Philip				PHA	34
Widow	PHI	66	Jacob	NOU	141	Philip				PHI	126
Abraham	MIF	2	Jacob	BUC	150	Philip				YOR	159
Adam	LAN	31	Jacob	NOU	178	Philip				BER	215
Adam	MNT	93	Jacob	NOU	178	Philip				PHI	97A
Adam	PHA	98	Jacob	YOR	178	Phillip				NOU	108
Adam	WAS	126	Jacob	BER	260	Phillip				CUM	133
Adam	NOU	178	Jacob	DAU	7A	Robert				WAS	32
Adam	BER	220	Jacob	CEN	21A	Sabastian				ADA	23
Adam Junr.	WAS	126	Jacob	DAU	48A	Thomas Dell				WAS	107
Adam	DAU	49A	James	MNT	91	Ulerick				BUC	8??
Adam	BUC	89A	Jeremiah	DEL	158	Ulrick				YOR	2??
Andw.	LYC	25	Jno.	CUM	66	Valentin				NOH	38A
Anthony	LUZ	356	John	WAS	41	Vandel				CUM	135
Barney	PHI	102A	John	PHA	68	Wendle				FRA	288
Bernhart	BER	222	John	PHI	72	Widow				NOH	44
Christan	BER	262	John	PHI	75	Widow				BUC	140
Christian	BUC	150	John	NOH	81	Widow Of Henry				NOH	81
Christian	BER	253	John	LAN	83	William				PHI	125
Christian	BER	262	John	PHI	85	Wm.				CUM	79
Christiana	PHA	20	John	PHI	110	Wm. Revd.				WST	228
Christn.	CUM	68	John	LAN	114	WEAVER?, John				ALL	49
Christopher	LAN	12	John	CUM	135	WEAY, William				MIF	11A
Christopher	LAN	84	John	PHI	140	WEBB, Abner				MNT	70
Conrad	WAS	83	John	BUC	150	Bowman				DEL	180
Conrad	YOR	212	John	NOU	178	Ezekiel				CHE	840
Conrod	CUM	65	John	NOU	181	George				LYC	6
Daniel	NOH	68	John	NOU	181	George				LYC	13
Daniel	PHA	110	John	NOU	190	Isaac				NOU	113
Daniel	YOR	159	John	BER	220	Isaac				CHE	700B
David	NOU	178	John	LAN	222	James				WAS	77
David Jr.	YOR	211	John	WST	229	James				YOR	184
David Sr.	YOR	211	John	BER	275	James				CHE	769
Elizabeth	BER	138	John	FRA	280	James				CHE	900
Enoch	BER	262	John	WST	298	John				GRN	91
Frederick	NOH	66	John	CHE	720	John				NOU	196
Frederick	NOU	115	John	CHE	724	John				YOR	219
Frederick	NOU	126	John Dr.	PHI	78A	John Jr.				YOR	219
Frederick	LAN	219	John Junr.	NOH	81	Jos.				YOR	219
Frederick	WST	279	John Senr.	NOH	31A	Jos.				YOR	219
Fredk.	PHA	70	John	DAU	37A	Joseph				LAN	31
Fredk.	CEN	21A	John	NOH	61A	Joseph				PHI	146
Gasper	WST	279	Jonas	NOH	81	Joseph				BER	157
George	ADA	13	Jonis	NOU	98	Joseph				CHE	840
George	PHI	30	Joseph	LAN	46	Mary				PHI	31
George	LAN	83	Joseph	LAN	83	Matthias				NOU	169
George	MNT	88	Joseph	LAN	84	Obadiah				BER	220
George Adam	NOH	81A	Joseph	BUC	158	Richd.				YOR	203
Henry	DAU	18	Joseph	DEL	163	Samuel				NOU	148
Henry	PHI	47	Joseph	WST	298	Samuel				NOU	148
Henry	PHA	70	Joshua	BER	287B	Thomas				PHI	12
Henry	LAN	79	Joshua	BER	287B	Thomas				NOU	148
Henry	LAN	84	Martin	DAU	8	Thomas				CHE	837
Henry (See			Martin	NOU	108	Thomas				CHE	840
Weaver,			Martin	PHI	128	Thos.				PHA	64
Widow)	NOH	81	Mathew	PHA	65	William				LAN	101
Henry	PHI	112	Matthias	FRA	301	William				NOU	148
Henry	WAS	114	Michael	NOH	77	William				CHE	706
Henry	BER	172	Michael	LAN	84	WEBBER, Ann				CUM	93
Henry	YOR	208	Michael	NOU	108	William				LUZ	406
Henry	BER	220	Michael	NOU	178	WEBECK, Henry				BER	138
Henry	WST	229	Michael	NOH	31A	WEBELY, Adam				CUM	45
Henry	BER	267	Moses	NOH	68	WEBER, Abraham				MNT	114
Henry Junr.	LAN	84	Moses	BUC	150	Benedick				LAN	75
Henry	PHI	53A	Mrs.	NOU	190	Benjamin				MNT	112
Isaac Esq.	GRN	93	Nicholas	ADA	41	Christ.				LAN	69
Jacob	ADA	32	Nichs.	PHI	121	Christ.				LAN	70
Jacob	LAN	42	Paul	YOR	157	Christian				LAN	65
Jacob	BFD	53	Peter	DAU	7	Christian				MNT	119
Jacob	CUM	80	Peter	NOH	83	David				LAN	95
Jacob	NOH	81	Peter	LAN	84	Elias				NOH	57A
Jacob	PHI	92	Peter	HNT	116	Frederick				LAN	67
Jacob	CUM	96	Peter	CUM	135	Geo. Adam				NOH	49
Jacob	NOU	108	Peter	BER	262	George				LAN	67
Jacob	LAN	112	Peter	DAU	15A	George				LAN	95

WEIMER, Martin		WEISER, Frederick	NOU 142	WELCH, Catharine	PHA	86
Sen.	SOM 150	Henry	YOR 159	David	ADA	23
Samuel	SOM 136	Jabez	BER 200	David	FRA	320
WEIMERT, Peter	BER 239	Jacob	BER 268	Francis	BFD	47
WEIN, John	LAN 35	John	BER 200	George	ADA	10
WEINAUER, George	LAN 50	Martin	YOR 170	George	CHE	753
WEINAUN, Henry	LAN 49	Martin	NOH 69A	George	CEN	21A
WEINBERG, Samuel	NOH 40A	Philip	BER 200	Hannah	PHA	21
WEINECKE, Charles	NOH 33	Philip	DAU 31A	Henry	WST	279
WEINEY, Jacob	DAU 29	Samuel	YOR 159	James	ADA	40
WEINGERT, Susanna	BER 275	Solomon	BER 200	James	FRA	274
WEINHAND, John	LAN 306	WEISHEY, John	NOU 125	James	CHE	753
WEINHOLD, Michael	LAN 206	WEISLER, Jacob		Jane	CUM	45
Peter	LAN 206	Senr.	ADA 14	Jarid	LYC	19
Philip	LAN 206	WEISLY, George	YOR 187	Jno.	BUT	362
Wendel	BER 171	WEISS, Andrew	LAN 65	John	PHA	41
WEINHOLT, George	BER 162	Christian	NOH 86	John	CUM	43
WEINLAND, David	NOH 33	Christn.	DAU 38A	John	PHA	91
WEINS?, Peter	DAU 32A	Felix	NOH 42	John	FAY	224
WEIR, Alexr.	DAU 24	George	NOH 33	John	WST	228
Andw.	YOR 162	Henry	NOH 36A	John	WST	299
Andw.	YOR 177	Henry	DAU 38A	John	FRA	304
Eve	YOR 160	Jacob	NOH 57A	John	FRA	315
Jacob	YOR 164	Jacob	NOH 61A	Js.	CUM	28
James	WAS 126	Jacob	NOH 84A	Matthew	LAN	160
John	DAU 2	John	NOH 33	Matthew	CHE	753
John	YOR 176	John	NOH 49	Maxwell	FRA	296
John Esqr.	YOR 162	John	NOH 66	Michael	BER	215
Margt.	CUM 122	John	LAN 115	Michael B.	PHA	42
Samuel	DAU 3	John Junr.	NOH 54A	Mrs.	CUM	98
Samuel	WAS 126	John	NOH 54A	Nicholas	HNT	141
Thomas	WAS 107	Leonard	NOH 69A	Nicholas	NOU	201
Thomas	WAS 114	Mathias	NOH 39	Patrick	PHI	25
William	WAS 107	Michael	NOH 46A	Patrick	CHE	828
WEIRE, Robt.	WST 383	Mrs.	LAN 54	Peter	CHE	895
WEIREY, Conrod	CUM 46	Peter	LAN 206	Peter	MIF	11A
WEIRICH, Christn.	DAU 26	Stophel	LAN 269	Robt.	CUM	42
Jacob	DAU 26	Widow	LAN 53	Samuel	ADA	40
Michael	YOR 182	WEISSENGERBER,		Thos.	FRA	296
Peter	DAU 26	Nicholas	NOH 49	William	YOR	154
WEIRICK, Jacob	DAU 33	WEIST, Casper	DEL 174	William	FAY	200
John	DAU 26	Christopher	YOR 216	Wm.	CHE	872
Valentine	DAU 13	Henry	YOR 196	WELCKER,		
WEIRMAN, Martin	MNT 76	Jacob	ADA 35	Frederick	NOU	196
WEIRR, George	PHI 45	Jacob	CUM 133	Jacob	NOU	196
WEIRS, John		Jacob	YOR 196	WELDER, Michael	BER	258
Anthony	WAS 35	Jacob	BER 232	WELDING, Eli	PHI	138
WEIS, Christopher	BER 159	WEITENSALL, Henry	HNT 160	Watson	BUC	107A
Erhart	BER 164	WEITKNECHT, Danl.	NOH 49	WELDON, David	MIF	2
John	LAN 272	Martin	NOH 58	Edwarde	WAS	14
Nicolaus	DAU 26	WEITMAN, George	BER 285	Jacob	CHE	756
Philip	LAN 214	WEITZ, John	BER 200	Patk.	MIF	6
WEISE, George	BER 267	WEITZEL, Adam	LAN 206	Roley	ARM	126
George	BER 272	Conrad	LAN 82	WELDY, Abm.	WST	299
Henry	BER 171	Eliz.	DAU 40A	Barnet	PHI	78
Jacob	BER 283	Frederick	BER 171	Jacob	SOM	131
John	BER 200	Henry	HNT 148	John	ADA	8
John	BER 263	Jacob	HNT 148	John	BER	239
John	BER 269	John	CUM 80	John	NOH	36A
Philip	BER 171	Philip	LAN 58	WELELEY, Jos.	BUT	362
WEISEL, George	BUC 92	Widow	LAN 79	WELER, Daniel	YOR	210
George	BUC 150	William	BER 171	Henry	YOR	210
George	BUC 158	WEITZELL, Jacob	CUM 81	WELICAR, Thomas	FAY	263
Michael	BUC 150	Joseph	NOH 84A	WELKER, Benjamin	NOU	141
WEISENBERG, Jacob	BER 247	Michael	NOH 84A	Catherine	DAU	11
WEISER, Abraham	BER 232	WEITZER, Philip	PHI 135	Christian	NOU	141
Benjamin	NOU 125	WEITZLE, Fredk.	BER 239	George	MNT	136
Benjamin	NOU 142	Jacob	BER 243	Jacob	MNT	136
Benjn.	DAU 49	Werner	BER 200	Jacob	NOU	173
Christian	BER 232	WEIZNER, Adam	NOU 173	Jacob	NOU	173
Conrad	NOU 126	WEKERLY, Abm.	PHI 91A	John	FRA	317
Conrad	NOU 142	Conard	PHI 108	Paul	SOM	153
Daniel	BER 228	WELAND, Michael	YOR 172	Peter	SOM	140
Danl.	BER 215	WELCH, Mrs.	LYC 21	Peter	FRA	317
David	BER 232	Widow	PHI 88	Valentine	DAU	8
Frederick	NOU 126	Benjn.	CHE 753	WELL, Danl. Jr.	BER	142

WENTZ, Methias	MNT 116	WERT, Christian	DAU 7A	WESLOR, John	CHE 735
Peter	MNT 114	Christopher	BFD 78	WESSLER, Benjamin	LAN 5
Peter	YOR 182	Conrad	DAU 50	Jacob	LAN 293
Philip	MNT 76	Conrod	PHI 61A	WESSNER, Mathias	BER 132
Philip	MNT 113	George	BFD 78	WEST--LL?, Joseph	LUZ 405
Philip	MNT 114	George	DAU 7A	WEST, Widow	PHI 68A
Valentine	YOR 184	George Wm.	BER 269	Benjn.	PHA 25
Valentine	YOR 185	Henry	BFD 35	Christian	YOR 179
WENTZEL, Alexr.	LAN 54	Henry	DAU 7A	Clement	LUZ 377
Christopher	BER 135	Jacob	BER 269	Ebinezer	FAY 263
Daniel	BER 232	Jacob	DAU 7A	Edward	WAS 47
Daniel Jr.	BER 232	John	DAU 7A	Edward	ALL 83
John	BER 135	Joseph	DAU 7A	Edwd.	CUM 40
Philip	BER 135	Ludwick	CUM 49	Elizabeth	FAY 229
WEPPERT, Andw.	DAU 52A	Paul	BFD 59	Enas	FAY 224
WERCKHEISER,		Peter	ADA 14	Francis	PHA 107
George	NOH 42	Valentine	BFD 78	Hannah	DEL 162
Henry	NOH 74A	Widow	DAU 43	Isaac	BUC 84A
Peter	NOH 68	WERT?, Martin	WST 317	James	PHA 115
WERE, Elisabeth	SOM 140	WERTERMAN, Geo.	PHI 112A	John	PHI 62
Mary	MIF 18	WERTH, Baltzer	NOH 46A	John	YOR 178
WERELY, Henrey	FAY 239	Daniel	NOH 86	John	LAN 214
WERFEL, Casper	PHI 130	Danl. Senr.	NOH 86	John	NOH 40A
Henry	PHI 130	WERTHMAN, Daniel	NOH 54A	John?	WAS 32
WERHEIM, Geo.	BER 200	George	NOH 77	Jonathan	WAS 47
Philip	BER 267	Jacob	NOH 77	Jonathan	ALL 100
WERKHEISER, John	NOH 40A	WERTMAN, Danl.	BER 143	Jonathan	LUZ 392
Nicholas	NOH 40A	Jacob	NOU 141	Joseph	ALL 83
Val.	NOH 79A	Jacob	NOH 54A	Joseph	CHE 769
WERKING, Philip	YOR 183	John	NOH 54A	Richd. (Negro)	WAS 14
Philip	YOR 185	Martin	BER 143	Samuel	WAS 47
Philip W.	YOR 185	Michael	NOU 141	Samuel	DEL 162
WERKIZER, Conrad	LUZ 321	Michael	NOH 54A	Samuel	FAY 229
WERKIZER?, Conrad		Samuel	BER 143	Thomas	DEL 187
Jr.	LUZ 328	Simon	BER 132	Thomas	FAY 212
WERL, Michl.	DAU 49A	WERTS, Cathr.	FRA 306	Thos.	YOR 200
WERLAND, John	LAN 312	Jacob	BER 252	William	ADA 5
WERLEIN, Albert	BER 228	John	MIF 18	William	NOH 68
WERLEY, John	NOU 102	John	FRA 306	William	LAN 134
WERLY, Dewalt	NOH 86	Sarah	PHA 31	William	DEL 170
Michael	NOH 86	WERTSBECKER,		William	CHE 766
Nicholas	NOH 86	Fredk.	CUM 84	Wm.	PHI 68A
Valentine	NOH 86	WERTZ, Burk	ADA 21	WEST?, Martin	WST 317
WERNER, Widow	WST 229	Cadiz	ADA 41	WESTBROOK,	
Andrew	BER 223	Conrad	BFD 46	Catharine	HNT 155
Casper	BER 178	Devalt	ADA 39	Cherrick	LUZ 423
Christian	YOR 191	George	ADA 21	Joseph	HNT 160
Daniel	YOR 186	Jacob	MIF 18	Leonard	LUZ 420
Frederick	BUC 148A	Jacob	ADA 21	Richard	LUZ 325
Fredk.	BER 200	Jacob	ADA 25	Solomon	WAY 148
George	YOR 186	John	NOH 51	William	GRN 86
George	YOR 216	John	SOM 160	WESTBY, Henry	WAS 26
George	NOH 74A	John	YOR 189	WESTER, Henry	PHI 53
Henry	ADA 28	John	BER 266	Michael	PHI 29
Henry	DAU 29	John	NOH 61A	WESTFALL, Abraham	WAS 114
Henry	BER 171	Mark	ADA 31	David	WAY 145
Henry	NOH 63A	Nicholas	ADA 39	Godfrey	CUM 26
Henry	NOH 74A	Peter	ADA 17	James	LUZ 390
Jacob	DAU 7	Peter	NOH 51	Simon	WAY 145
John	BFD 69	Peter	PHI 129	Wm.	PHA 65
John	YOR 188	Peter	YOR 187	WESTHAFER,	
John	BER 221	Peter	YOR 210	Christ. (See	
Leonard	LAN 147	Thos.	BFD 47	Westhafer,	
M.	BER 158	William	MNT 116	Geo.)	LAN 205
Martin	BER 283	WERTZNER, Adam	NOU 142	Geo. & Christ.	LAN 205
Peter	LAN 135	WERUGH, John	BER 186	WESTHEF, Conrad	LAN 138
Widow	BUC 90	WERY, Jacob	PHA 84	WESTHEFFER,	
WERRILL?, Ann		WESCOTT, George	PHA 83	Abraham	YOR 215
WERSBAUGH,		Joel	PHI 3	Leonard	YOR 163
Phillip	CUM 108	WESENBERGER, John	LAN 222	WESTHEIFER, Jno.	CUM 126
WERSBECHER, Jno.	CUM 84	WESLEY, Henry	CHE 735	WESTIN?, Eli	LYC 9
WERST, Andreas	NOH 81A	WESLOR, Abram	CHE 858	WESTKO, Mathias	NOH 61A
Jacob	YOR 181	Abram	CHE 859	Philip	NOH 61A
Jacob	NOH 81A	Christian	CHE 857	WESTLEY, James	FRA 286
Philip	NOH 49	Henry	CHE 860	WESTLY, John	BER 249
WERSTLER, Conrad	BER 164	Henry	CHE 859	Michael	BER 249
Jacob	BER 164	Jacob			

WESTON, Frantz	BER	186	WEYEND, John	WST	299	WHEELER, Barbara	BER	281
George	HNT	153	WEYERBACH, Isaac	BUC	148A	Charles Doctr.	WAS	83
James	ERI	59A	WEYGAND,			Isaac	BER	157
John	BEV	28	Cornelius	NOH	39	Isaac	LUZ	411
John	MNT	117	WEYGANDL, David	NOH	77	Jacob	PHI	118
John	FAY	207	WEYHEL, Catherine	BER	276	Jacob	DEL	189
John	CHE	806	WEYKEL,			Jacob	NOH	79A
Joseph	FAY	206	Christopher	BER	185	James	VEN	165
Wm.	CHE	809	WEYMAN, Barbara	BER	159	James	LUZ	400
WESTOVER, Oliver	HNT	120	Conrad	BER	177	John	PHA	13
WETCRAFT, George	LAN	142	Jacob	PHI	68	John	PHI	78
WETHERBY, Jos.	PHI	77	WEYMERT, George	HNT	147	Joseph	LUZ	400
WETHERELL, George	PHI	146	WEYON, Henry	DAU	39	Peter	LUZ	416
Thos.	PHI	36	WEZNER, Christian	LAN	182	Richard	LUZ	395
WETHERILL, Joseph	PHA	120	WHAILEY, Benjn.	FAY	251	Saml. Esqr.	PHI	106A
Mordica	PHA	25	WHALING, John	ALL	53	Waltar	LUZ	418
Samuel	PHA	80	WHAN, John	WST	279	Willm.	PHI	44
Samuel Cenr.	PHA	26	John	CHE	802	WHEELOCK, Calvin	LUZ	403
William	BUC	107A	Thomas	CHE	802	WHEID, Peter	BER	171
WETHERINTON, Ruth	FRA	297	William	NOU	201	WHELAN, James	PHI	105B
WETHERROW, David	BEV	16	William	WST	279	Wm.	PHI	70A
WETHERS, Saml.	CHE	742	WHANN, Samuel	WAS	107	WHELEN, Dennis	CHE	815
WETHERSPON, David	ALL	102	WHARRY, Thos.	MIF	6	Dennis Esqr.	CHE	883
WETHERSPOON,			WHARTENBY, John	PHI	146	Israel	PHA	77
Samuel	WAS	25	WHARTON, Benjamin	BUC	104	John	DEL	166
WETHERSTONE, Adam	PHI	105	Chas.	PHA	104	WHELEN?, (See		
Christn.	PHI	93A	Daniel	BUC	99A	Wheten)	CHE	815
John	PHI	105	Edward	BUC	95	WHELER, Joshua	HNT	136
Peter	PHI	79	Ezra	BUC	152	Samuel	HNT	147
WETHRHOLTZ,			Franklin Captn.	PHA	73	WHELIG, George	PHA	82
Joseph	BER	266	George	PHI	59	WHELING, Thos.	PHA	105
WETILL, Michael	NOU	102	Isaac	PHA	103	WHERHEIME, George	BER	205
WETON?, Joseph	PHI	97	John	MIF	9	WHERLY, George	YOR	191
WETSEL, Daniel	FAY	212	John	PHA	48	Michael	YOR	164
Stephen	NOH	79A	John	GRN	78	WHERREY, Saml.	CUM	137
WETSTON, Jacob	PHI	95	John	GRN	85	WHERRY, David	WAS	107
WETSTONE, Isaac	BER	156	Joseph	BUC	95	Ebenezer	CHE	868
Jacob	BER	156	Joseph	PHA	118	James	CHE	869
Jacob Jr.	BER	156	Mahlon	BUC	100	James Esqr.	WAS	114
John	BER	156	Matthew	FAY	260	John	MIF	16
WETZ, Charles	BER	243	Nemiah	BUC	100	John	WAS	114
Henry	BER	149	Perry	PHI	43	John	LAN	163
WETZEL, Conrad	NOH	42	R.	PHI	54	Joseph	WAS	25
Jacob	NOU	133	Rachal	PHA	97	Mary	WAS	6
John	DAU	12	Rebecca	PHA	6	WHESEMAN, John	FRA	304
Martin	NOH	54A	Robert	GRN	112	WHESNER, Jno	CUM	137
William	DAU	48A	Robert Esqr.	PHA	92	WHESTONE, John	CUM	111
WETZELL, Adam	NOH	61A	Saml.	MIF	9	WHETEN, James	CHE	815
Conrad Esqr.	NOH	58	Samuel	HNT	135	WHETHERILL,		
Henry	NOH	58	Thos.	CUM	58	Benjn.	PHA	82
Jacob	NOH	58	William	PHA	98	WHETSTONE,		
Jacob Junr.	NOH	58	William	BUC	100	Abraham	BFD	78
John Esqr.	NOH	61A	William Jnr.	BUC	100	Daniel	BFD	69
John Junr.	NOH	58	WHARTONBY, John	MNT	37	Henry	BFD	35
John Junr.	NOH	61A	John	MNT	42	Henry	BFD	53
WETZLE, Geo.	BER	212	WHATACRE,			Jacob	BFD	68
WEVER, Benjamin	LAN	185	Elisabeth	WAS	96	Jasper	FAY	248
Christ. & John	LAN	206	WHEALER, John	ALL	111	WHI--Y?, Joseph	BEV	12
Christopher	LAN	206	WHEALEY, Benjn.	FAY	224	WHIEN, Jacob	CHE	897
Conrad	LAN	214	WHEALSE, Eve	DAU	39A	WHIGGAM,		
Conrad Junr.	LAN	214	WHEAT, Zacharia	FAY	218	Cathereen	ALL	59
Frances	FAY	237	WHEATCRAFT,			WHIGHAM, Wilm.	ALL	82
George	LAN	205	Edward	WAY	139	WHIGHT, Alexandr.	MER	462
George	DAU	50A	Joseph	WAY	139	John	MER	462
John (See			Samuel	WAY	139	William	MER	463
Wever,			WHEATLY, John	FAY	269	WHILDIN, Alexar.	PHI	93A
Christ.)	LAN	206	Joseph	FAY	254	WHILE, Thos.	FRA	312
Ludwig	LAN	206	Thomas	FAY	232	WHILER, Bob	CHE	865
Michael	NOU	178	William	FAY	232	WHILING, Michael	NOU	169
Nicholas	LAN	172	WHEATON,			WHILMAN, George	PHI	70
Philip	DAU	48A	Coverdell	FAY	237	WHINERY, Thos.	YOR	216
WEVILL, Richd.	PHA	85	David	FAY	224	William	YOR	215
WEY, Francis	GRN	91	Richard	FAY	224	WHIP, John	BFD	59
WEYANT, Adam	LAN	12	WHEELBOND,			WHIPKEY, Abraham	SOM	131
John	PHI	113A	Charles	HNT	124	David	SOM	136
Paul	BER	174	WHEELER, Widow	PHI	107	Henry	SOM	136

429

WHIPKEY, John	SOM 131	WHITE, George	BUC 95	WHITE, John	FAY 218
John	SOM 136	George	WAS 107	John	LAN 244
WHIPOL, Daniel	NOU 160	George	DEL 185	John	BER 252
WHIPPLE, Ebenezer	LUZ 391	George	CHE 865	John	FAY 260
Nathan	LUZ 348	George	NOH 79A	John	FRA 294
WHIPPO, George	HNT 129	Gilbert	PHA 111	John	WST 317
WHIRE, Thomas	GRN 97	Giles	VEN 165	John	FRA 318
WHIRRAW, Adam	SOM 131	Hannah	YOR 174	John	FRA 323
WHIRT, Philip	PHI 112	Hannah	CHE 883	John	CEN 19A
WHISLA, Andrew	FRA 275	Henrey	FAY 200	John	CEN 23A
WHISLER, John	DAU 24	Hugh	LYC 18	John	BUC 83A
John	BUC 106	Hugh	FAY 200	John	PHI 104A
John	BUC 82A	Hugh	WST 299	John	BUC 107A
Peter	CUM 130	Isaac	PHI 88	John	PHI 117A
Peter	BUC 160	Isaiah	ADA 3	Jonathan	PHI 152
WHISLOR, Captain	CHE 855	Israel	GRN 73	Joseph	LYC 8
WHISTLER, Andrew	BUC 106A	Israel	MNT 117	Joseph	BEV 11
WHITACER, James	GRN 84	Jabez	MNT 52	Joseph	LYC 17
WHITACRE, Joseph	LYC 9	Jacob	PHA 112	Joseph	ALL 49
Samuel	WAS 96	Jacob	ARM 125	Joseph	BUC 84
Sarah	LYC 3	Jacob	NOU 153	Joseph	ALL 103
WHITAKER, John	LAN 9	Jacob	HNT 165	Joseph	MNT 116
John	HNT 154	James	ADA 5	Joseph	HNT 152
Phineas	CHE 825	James	BEV 8	Joseph	WST 158
Thomas	HNT 154	James	CRA 8	Joseph	BUC 162
William	CHE 900	James	CRA 14	Joseph	LAN 229
WHITCOMB,		James	PHA 23	Joseph	FAY 269
Charlotte	LUZ 402	James	CUM 29	Joseph	WST 330
John	LUZ 401	James	CUM 29	Joseph	WST 353
Richard	MNT 88	James	WAS 32	Joseph	CHE 801
WHITE, Aaron	CHE 701	James	BFD 39	Joseph	CHE 901
Abel	BUC 150A	James	MNT 46	Joseph Junr.	WAS 107
Alexd.	ALL 72	James	ALL 66	Joseph Senr.	WAS 107
Alexd.	FRA 289	James	GRN 66	Joseph	BUC 142A
Amaziah	BUC 85	James	WAS 107	Joseph	BUC 145A
Amos	BUC 145	James	ALL 111	Josiah	ARM 125
Amos	PHI 99A	James	NOU 125	Leonard	ARM 124
Amos	BUC 87A	James	WST 176	Leonard	ARM 124
Andrew	HNT 156	James	FAY 207	Lidia	ALL 71
Anthony	WAS 107	James	WST 317	Margaret	PHA 77
Anthony	HNT 153	James	WST 353	Margt.	BER 239
Aron	CHE 825	James	CHE 756	Mary	PHA 118
Bartholomew	CRA 3	James	CHE 854	Matthw.	BUT 340
Benjamin	BFD 39	James	CEN 21A	Moses	WAS 96
Benjamin	MNT 52	Jas.	BUT 362	Mrs.	NOU 125
Benjamin	WAS 83	Jas.	BUT 364	Nathaniel	WAS 107
Benjn.	BUC 100	Jesse	GRN 66	Paris	DEL 188
Benjn.	BUT 332	Jno. Junr.	CUM 108	Parley	LUZ 413
Bill	LAN 239	Job	CHE 886	Peter	NOU 151
Caleb	CHE 758	John	BEV 12	Rachel	CHE 825
Charity	LUZ 419	John	BEV 18	Richard	LAN 240
Chas.	PHA 17A	John	WAS 18	Richard	FRA 275
Christopher	PHA 20	John	LYC 19	Richard	CHE 777
Christopher	MNT 140	John	WAS 25	Robert	BEV 8
Christopher	FAY 242	John	BEV 28	Robert	FAY 269
David	GRN 66	John	CUM 29	Robert	WST 330
David	CUM 75	John	ADA 39	Robt.	PHA 72
David	BUC 92	John	WAS 41	Rodolph	PHI 150
David	WAS 107	John	LAN 56	Roger	CHE 745
David	MNT 110	John	ALL 65	Rosanah	PHA 77
David	ALL 119	John	BFD 69	Saml.	PHA 65
David	CUM 137	John	ALL 73	Sampson	DEL 188
David	WST 158	John	MNT 79	Samuel	ALL 88
David	LUZ 407	John	PHA 82	Samuel	WAS 107
David	NOH 42A	John	MNT 92	Samuel	MNT 109
Edward	BEV 5	John	BUC 95	Samuel	SOM 163
Edward	LAN 96	John	BUC 100	Samuel	FAY 229
Elisha	LYC 12	John	WAS 107	Samuel	LAN 244
Ephraim	PHI 78	John	CUM 108	Samuel	BUT 333
Ephraim	LUZ 325	John	NOU 108	Samuel	LUZ 353
Ewd.	FRA 318	John	ALL 112	Sarah	CHE 699
Francis	BUC 85	John	BUC 140	Solomon	PHA 24
Francis	BUC 162	John	NOU 151	Thomas	ADA 4
Francis	FRA 293	John	NOU 153	Thomas	PHA 13
Francis	PHI 99	John	NOU 173	Thomas	WAS 25
George	ADA 38	John	FAY 200	Thomas	DAU 44

WHITE, Thomas	MNT	79	WHITEMAN,			WHITMIRE, Francis	BUT	324
Thomas	ALL	82	Christian	FAY	224	WHITMOR, Jacob	FRA	274
Thomas	PHA	111	David	PHI	117	WHITMORE, Abraham	NOU	185
Thomas	FRA	275	David	PHI	117	Bosteon	NOU	197
Thomas	MIF	26A	George	FRA	283	Jacob	CUM	86
Thos.	PHA	24	Henry	PHA	39	Jacob	CUM	141
Thos.	PHA	56	Jacob	PHA	57	Jacob	FRA	276
Uriah	GRN	97	John	BER	185	John	CUM	86
Vachel	SOM	147	John	YOR	188	John	NOU	185
Wames	ALL	86	John	PHI	116A	John	DAU	12A
William	WAS	25	Margaret	PHA	7	Josh.	FRA	307
William	WAS	25	Martin	PHI	119A	Maths.	DAU	15
William	WAS	107	Ulrich	PHI	131	Mrs.	NOU	185
William	ARM	125	Whindle	PHI	81	Peter	NOU	133
William	WAY	136	Wilm.	ALL	98	Peter	FRA	298
William	NOU	148	Windal	PHI	142	Samuel	NOU	185
William	WST	158	WHITEMYER,			WHITMYER, Andrew	NOU	142
William	LAN	164	Michael	NOU	142	Jacob	NOU	142
William	YOR	177	WHITENIGHT, Peter	ADA	15	WHITNEY, Ebenezer	LUZ	386
William	FAY	218	WHITERAFT, Jacob	CHE	730	Jared	ERI	58A
William	WST	353	John	CHE	732	Tarbel	LUZ	350
William	CHE	706	Wm.	CHE	731	WHITNICK,		
William	CHE	872	WHITES, Nicholas	ARM	127	Matthias	NOU	145
William Revd.	PHA	3	WHITESIDE,			Michael	NOU	145
William	NOH	38A	Abraham	LAN	169	WHITON, Adam	MER	463
William	BUC	106A	James	ALL	102	WHITSAL, Jacob	ALL	115
Willm.	BUT	323	James	CHE	896	WHITSELL, Jacob	FRA	320
Wilm.	ALL	65	Jas.	CHE	871	WHITSON, Henry	CHE	863
Wm.	CUM	53	John	PHA	79	John	HNT	130
Wm.	PHA	75	Mary	WAS	26	WHITSON?, Robert	PHI	150
Wm.	PHI	79	Thos.	CHE	747	WHITSTONE,		
Wm.	PHA	85	Wilm.	ALL	117	Christian	BFD	67
Wm.	BUC	100	WHITESIDES,			Michael	HNT	117
Wm.	FRA	316	Alexander	PHA	39	Peter	BFD	68
Wm.	CHE	825	Hugh	MNT	110	WHITTEN, Richard	CHE	802
Wm.	PHI	109A	Jas.	LAN	169	WHITTICUR,		
WHITE?, Ann?	MIF	8A	John	LAN	115	William	NOU	145
WHITEACRE, Joseph	BER	275	Peter	FRA	290	WHITTIN, John		
WHITEAKER,			Saml.	CHE	747	Esqr.	CHE	803
Roboert	PHI	137	Thomas	LAN	167	WHITTINGTON, John	CRA	16
WHITEBREAD,			William	FAY	231	William	BUC	155A
Charles	PHI	6	WHITFORD, James	ADA	21	WHITTLE, Robert	PHI	147
Henry	PHI	154	WHITHEAD, John	PHI	70A	WHITTMORE, John	MIF	13A
WHITEFELS, John	FRA	287	WHITICKER, Danl.	FAY	260	WHITTON, Richard		
WHITEFORD, Robert	PHA	100	WHITIKER,			(Crossed Out)	PHI	154
WHITEHEAD, Felty	BUT	324	Cathareen	ALL	83	Richd.	MNT	37
Frederick	BER	278	Eron	ALL	83	WHITTON?, Robert	PHI	150
James	PHA	47	Isaac	ALL	83	WHITZEL, John	NOU	98
Richd.	PHA	47	James	MER	462	Mrs.	NOU	98
Volintine	WST	259	WHITIMAN, John	MNT	140	WHOBAUCHER,		
WHITEHILL, David	CEN	23A	WHITKENECKS?,			Conrad	HNT	151
George	BEV	25	Eby/ Eley?	FRA	281	WHORRY, David	ALL	111
George	DAU	4A	WHITLATCH, Barnet	GRN	97	David	HNT	158
James	BEV	25	Charles	WAS	47	WHYLURT, Thos.	FRA	297
James	LAN	218	Thomas	GRN	97	WIAND, Charles	YOR	163
James	CEN	23A	William	GRN	97	George	BER	177
John	LAN	3	WHITLER, Samuel	NOU	148	Peter	NOH	49
John	LAN	38	WHITLEY, Benjn.	ADA	12	WIANDT, John	NOH	61A
John	LAN	125	Michl.	DAU	16A	Jost	NOH	61A
John	LAN	230	WHITLOCK, Joseph	LUZ	375	WIANT, George	LAN	274
John Esqr.	LAN	125	WHITMAN, Abraham	NOU	153	John	MIF	4
Robt.	CUM	60	George	HNT	132	Windle	MNT	54
Thomas	WAS	10	Henry	PHI	73	Windle	MNT	136
Widow	LAN	38	Jacob	VEN	169	Yost	MNT	136
WHITELEY,			John	PHI	114	WIBBER,		
Frederick	WAS	77	John	HNT	132	Christopher	LUZ	426
George	WAS	77	John	NOU	153	WIBBLE, Adam	BFD	41
WHITELOCK,			John	VEN	169	WIBEL, Jacob	FAY	218
Patrick	LAN	163	John	DAU	39A	Robt.	PHI	83A
WHITELOE,			John	DAU	49A	WIBLE, John	WST	244
Cathrine			Michl.	YOR	219	WIBLEY, Jacob	CUM	82
(Boarding			Nathan	PHI	148	John	FRA	287
House)	PHA	33	WHITMER, Abraham	NOU	148	Martin	CUM	79
WHITEMAN, Widow	PHI	75A	Henry	NOU	125	WIBLY, Andrew	327	58
Widw.	PHI	70	John	LAN	107	Cosh.	ALL	118
Casper	PHI	118A	Matthias	NOU	125	John	ALL	60

WIBLY, John	WST	279	WIDNER, Jacob	NOU	102	WIGMAN, Joachim	NOH	70A
WICAL, Daniel	BEV	28	Josh.	FRA	311	WIGMORE, Joseph	PHA	103
Daniel Junr.	BEV	28	WIDOW, Helman	LAN	140	Thos.	PHA	17
John	BEV	28	WIDOWFIELD,			WIGNALL, Thos.	PHA	113
WICARD, Thomas	ALL	115	Henry?	LYC	9	WIGNER, John	CUM	109
WICE, Henry	NOU	178	James	PHA	91	WIGOL, Peter	MNT	91
Henry	NOU	178	Mark	LYC	9	WIGTON, James	BUC	106
WICHT, Christ.	LAN	143	Wm.	PHA	25	Samuel	BUC	106
WICK, Christopher	BFD	67	Wm.	PHA	25	William	BUC	106
Henry	WAS	5	WIDOWS, John	CHE	711	William	WAY	148
Lemuel	WAS	5	WIDY, Peter	PHI	11A	WIKARD, John	LAN	220
William	WAS	65	WIEBLE, Stephen	ADA	9	WIKART, Eve	ADA	25
WICKEL, George	NOU	200	Thomas	ADA	10	George	ADA	25
Michael	LAN	86	WIEDER, Adam	NOH	58	George	ADA	28
WICKER, Jacob	NOH	61A	Casper	NOH	58	John	ADA	28
John	WST	259	John	NOH	83	Michael	LAN	224
WICKERHAM, Adam	WAS	72	WIEDMOYER, Jno.	MNT	91	Peter	ADA	7
Mary	PHI	85A	WIEGAND, Conrad	PHA	70	WIKE, Christr.	CUM	119
WICKERLY, Jacob	PHI	81	WIEGGENE, Jacob	DAU	34	George	LAN	128
Peter	NOU	125	WIEGNER, George	BER	209	Peter	DAU	31A
Wolery	PHI	91A	WIELAND?, (See			WIKENS, James	PHI	41
WICKERS, Paul	NOH	66	Wuland)	LAN	22	WIKOFF, Henry	PHA	73
Thos.	PHA	83	WIELER, John	LAN	285	Isaac W.	PHA	21
WICKERSAM, James	YOR	217	WIEMER, Adam	BER	143	Peter	PHI	60
WICKERSHAM, Abm.	PHA	40	WIER, Aaron	WST	353	WIKS?, -----	ARM	125
Amos	PHA	22	Adam	WAS	65	WILAND, Ann	LAN	206
Amos	CHE	770	John	WST	353	Christn.	CUM	22
Caleb	CHE	770	John	BUC	155A	Jacob	FAY	200
David	CHE	771	Michael	ADA	14	John	ADA	14
David	CHE	773	Robert	BUC	155A	John	ADA	15
Hannah	DAU	2	Samuel	WAS	65	John	ADA	40
Partni	CHE	770	Thomas	WAS	65	John	BFD	67
Peter	CHE	770	Thomas	GRN	108	John	FAY	207
Thos.	CHE	862	Tobias	ADA	15	Michael	YOR	169
William	DEL	169	William	WAS	65	Michl.	WST	317
Wm.	CHE	770	WIERMAN, Michael	MNT	76	Valentine	FAY	218
WICKERT, Frank	DAU	34A	WIES, Robert	MER	463	WILBERHAM,		
WICKFIELD, Abner	CHE	765	Samuel	MER	463	Margaret	MNT	74
WICKHAM, Richd.	PHI	76	WIESE, Jacob	MNT	91	WILBERT, John F.	PHI	52
WICKLAND, Geo.	CUM	142	WIESNER, Godfried	NOH	58	Peter	DAU	15
William Sen.	SOM	163	WIESS, Andrew	LAN	112	WILBY, George	PHA	51
Zephaniah	SOM	163	WIESTER, Jacob	ADA	11	WILCOCK, Wilm.	ALL	107
WICKLEIN, Adam	BER	249	WIESTLING, Saml.	DAU	16A	WILCOX, Daniel	LUZ	410
WICKMAN, George	ALL	76	WIGANS, Edward	ARM	124	Isaac	LUZ	324
WICKOFF?, Isaac	PHA	103	WIGENER, Henry	ALL	51	John	PHI	15
WICKS, John	ARM	125	WIGENS, James	DAU	17	Saml.	PHA	80
WICOFF, Jonathan?	ALL	76	WIGFIELD, Joseph	BFD	53	Stephen	LUZ	411
Peter	LYC	21	WIGGANS, Saml.	WST	158	Thomas	LUZ	426
WICTON, John	NOU	197	WIGGENS, William	BUC	162	WILD, James	CHE	882
WIDA, Peter	BER	258	WIGGIN, Silas	LUZ	345	Susannah	PHA	48
WIDDER, Michael	NOH	92A	WIGGINS, Benjamin	BUC	152	WILDANGER, George	NOH	49
WIDDIS, Jesse	PHI	130	Cethburt	BUC	152A	WILDANNER, Thomas	NOH	31A
WIDDOWS, George	DEL	210	Jas. & Wm. Lock	DAU	24	WILDAY, Keziah	DEL	174
WIDECKER, Andw.	WST	374	Joseph	BUC	152	Thomas	MNT	141
WIDEMEIR, Melchor	BUC	150A	Pilip	GRN	108	WILDBAHN, John	BER	210
WIDEMEN, Henry	WST	299	Thos.	PHA	25	Thomas	BER	243
WIDEMEYER, Conrad	NOH	61A	Ulysses	MNT	65	WILDBAKER,		
WIDENCY?, Charles	FRA	322	WIGGLESWORTH,			Charles	BER	239
James	FRA	322	John	PHA	15	WILDENGER, John	NOH	49
John	FRA	322	WIGGONS, Thomas	GRN	108	WILDER, Jeremiah	BER	212
WIDENER, Isaac	FRA	297	William	CHE	818	WILDERMAN, George	FAY	212
Lawrance	PHI	93	WIGH, George	DAU	19A	WILDERMUTH, David	BER	143
Michael	ERI	58	WIGHT, Caspar	HNT	151	WILDES, George	BFD	39
Peter	PHI	142	George	HNT	151	WILDESON, Jacob	YOR	187
WIDENEY?, (See			James	LAN	71	Jacob Jr.	YOR	186
Widency?)	FRA	322	WIGHTMAN, Andrew	LAN	94	Jacob Senr.	YOR	187
WIDENOR, Abraham	ADA	15	WIGINS, Isaac	NOU	113	Samuel	YOR	187
Christopher	FRA	296	Susannah	PHA	69	WILDMAN, James	BUC	162
Daniel	ADA	16	WIGLE, Henry	YOR	164	John	BUC	95
George	CHE	790	Jacob Jr.	YOR	174	John	BUC	162
John	CHE	796	Jacob Senr.	YOR	174	Joseph	BUC	162
WIDERBACK, Casper	PHA	83	John	YOR	174	Soloman	BUC	162
WIDLE, Daniel	DAU	49A	Martin	YOR	162	WILDONGER,		
WIDMYER,			Martin	YOR	162	Frederick	BUC	150
Christian	LAN	144	Peter	YOR	174	Jacob	BUC	92
Conrad	LAN	144	Sebastian	YOR	162	Ludwick	BUC	150

433

WILLART, Peter	DAU	6	WILLIAMS,			WILLIAMS, Isaac	BUC	97A
WILLASTON,			Benjamin	BUC	87A	Isaac	BUC	106A
Ebenezar	MIF	2	Benjamin	BUC	97A	Isachar	DEL	191
WILLAUER, Adam	NOH	40A	Benjn.	PHA	51	Israel	BFD	78
Andrew	NOH	40A	Benjn.	MNT	93	Jabez	LUZ	352
Joseph	NOH	51	Benjn.	BUC	140	Jacob	BFD	60
WILLCOX,			Benjn.	PHI	140	Jacob	BFD	78
Alexander			Benjn.	BUC	106A	Jacob	NOH	79A
Esqr.	PHA	28	Benoni	WST	383	James	ADA	3
John	DEL	175	Charles	PHI	77	James	PHA	8
Mark Esqr.	DEL	160	Charles	FAY	201	James	LAN	9
Thomas	DEL	161	Charles	YOR	219	James	ALL	57
WILLDON, Jonan.	PHI	21	Charrels	ALL	64	James	PHA	64
WILLE, Andrew	FAY	242	Cornelious	FAY	248	James	BFD	78
Michael	FAY	242	Daniel	DEL	172	James (Tanner)	BFD	78
WILLEBY, Henry	MIF	9	Daniel	YOR	212	James	PHA	104
Jane	YOR	215	Daniel	YOR	217	James	FAY	229
WILLERT, Richd.	FRA	288	Daniel	BER	250	James	FAY	229
WILLES, Abner	CUM	77	Daniel	NOH	42A	James	LAN	315
James	CUM	27	Danl.	WST	229	James	WST	353
Joseph	GRN	97	Darius	LUZ	338	James	WST	383
WILLET, Anthony			David	MIF	2	James	WST	383
Jr.	YOR	186	David	CRA	7	James	CHE	843
Anthony Sr.	YOR	186	David	MNT	61	James	CHE	855
Jacob	ADA	28	David	NOH	79	James	NOH	63A
Martha	BUC	144	David	NOU	108	Jane	CEN	21A
Obadiah	BUC	144	David	CHE	855	Jehu	ALL	73
Samuel	BFD	68	David	CHE	859	Jeremiah	BER	143
WILLETS, Jesse	BER	216	Ebenezer	LUZ	374	Jeremiah	BUC	150
WILLETT, John	PHI	149	Ebinazer	FAY	224	Jesse	WAS	87
WILLEUR, Christo.	MNT	101	Edward	MIF	2	Jesse	CEN	23A
WILLEUR?, Peter	MNT	136	Edward	WAS	26	Jno Sr.	MIF	9
WILLEY, John	CHE	765	Edward	PHI	58	Jno.	LYC	27
Peter	BER	222	Edward	PHA	115	Jno.	CUM	72
Robert	BEV	19	Edwd. (Tailor)	MIF	2	Jno. Jr.	MIF	9
Wilm.	ALL	120	Eli	BFD	60	Joakim D.	ALL	55
WILLHELLEM,			Elijah	PHA	45	John	CRA	4
George	FAY	206	Ellis	LYC	25	John	PHI	33
WILLIAM, Black	CHE	736	Ellis	CHE	878	John	BFD	35
Henry	LAN	52	Enoch	MIF	9	John	PHA	36
Henry	FAY	269	Enoch	FRA	321	John	NOH	42
Jesse	PHA	59	Ephm.	CUM	31	John	BFD	53
Moser	PHI	85A	Ephraim	BFD	78	John	LAN	56
Norris	MIF	9	Eshue	ALL	79	John	PHA	68
Waugh	WAS	60	Evan	CEN	23A	John	ALL	79
WILLIAMBACH, Jno.			Ezenas	PHA	63	John	WAS	84
& Henry	LAN	272	Fredrik	DAU	25	John	ALL	92
WILLIAMS, Widow	PHI	44	Fredrik	DAU	26	John	PHA	112
Widow	PHI	107	Geo.	CEN	24	John	NOU	113
Aaron	WAS	72	Geo. (C.?)	CEN	24	John	LAN	122
Abel	GRN	97	George	BEV	19	John	YOR	211
Abner	BER	239	George	LYC	26	John	BER	216
Abriham	CRA	4	George	CUM	37	John	FAY	224
Abriham	CRA	8	George	MNT	37	John	FAY	231
Absolom	CHE	727	George	BFD	67	John	FAY	248
Absolum	PHI	127	George	ALL	102	John	FRA	284
Adam	ALL	118	George	HNT	130	John	WST	330
Adam	WAS	126	George	YOR	204	John	LUZ	381
Adam	PHI	149	George	CHE	702	John	LUZ	381
Alexr.	FAY	260	George	MIF	13A	John	CHE	800
Amos	LAN	177	Griffith	MNT	120	John	CHE	801
Andrew	CRA	10	Hamra?	BER	222	John	CHE	806
Andrew	PHA	52	Henry	BFD	60	John	CHE	842
Ann	FAY	248	Henry	PHI	98	John	CHE	846
Anna	WAS	41	Henry	DAU	42A	John Junr.	HNT	153
Anthony	MNT	42	Hugh	GRN	112	John Sen.	HNT	153
Azor	MNT	79	Hugh	CHE	910	John	CEN	23A
Barnet	FAY	229	Isaac	ALL	92	John	PHI	112A
Bartholomew	LUZ	381	Isaac	CUM	96	Jonathan	WAS	114
Bazil	WAS	10	Isaac	MNT	109	Jonathn.	CHE	910
Beng.	FRA	321	Isaac	DEL	188	Jos.	CHE	855
Benj.	YOR	206	Isaac	YOR	198	Joseph	LYC	6
Benjamin	LAN	52	Isaac	FRA	291	Joseph	BEV	12
Benjamin	SOM	155	Isaac	CHE	733	Joseph	CEN	24
Benjamin	NOU	196	Isaac	CHE	855	Joseph	MNT	52
Benjamin	LUZ	339	Isaac	MIF	11A	Joseph	BFD	67

WILLIAMS, Joseph	GRN	104	WILLIAMS, Thomas	ALL	92	WILLIAMSON, John	FAY	248		
Joseph	MNT	109	Thomas	PHA	102	John	FRA	285		
Joseph	NOU	145	Thomas	ARM	126	John	MER	462		
Joseph	DEL	172	Thomas	PHI	149	John	CHE	727		
Joseph	FRA	275	Thomas	DEL	160	John Jun.	CHE	727		
Joseph	CHE	828	Thomas	DEL	171	Joseph	PHI	4		
Joseph	CHE	842	Thomas	FAY	218	Joseph	WAS	32		
Joseph	CHE	846	Thomas	WST	228	Joseph	WST	353		
Joseph	MNT	105	Thomas	FAY	248	Joshua	HNT	144		
Joseph	DAU	44A	Thomas	BER	280	Mahlon	BUC	95		
Joseph	PHI	70A	Thomas	LUZ	353	Michael	BUC	153A		
Joshu	FAY	260	Thomas	LUZ	374	Moses	MIF	2		
Joshua	LAN	119	Thomas	NOH	36A	Peter	DAU	9		
Joshua	CHE	705	Thos.	CUM	64	Peter	BUC	95		
Joshua	CEN	23A	Thos.	PHA	117	Robert	BUC	156		
Leven	WAS	10	Thos.	PHI	144	Saml.	CUM	135		
Lewis	YOR	214	Uriah	GRN	104	Saml.	MER	462		
Lewis	CHE	878	Uriah	LUZ	354	Samuel	CRA	13		
Margaret	LAN	301	Vinson	DAU	3	Samuel	PHA	107		
Margaret	LAN	316	Walter	ALL	73	Samuel	DEL	171		
Margaret	FRA	322	William	PHI	19	Thomas	DEL	156		
Mark	CEN	21A	William	BUC	140	Thos.	MIF	18		
Mary	ADA	9	William	BUC	140	Thos.	CHE	806		
Mary	PHA	31	William	WAY	142	Walter	DEL	179		
Mary	PHA	80	William	SOM	163	William	BER	280		
Mary	GRN	85	William	BER	216	Wm.	PHI	68		
Mary	PHA	92	William	FAY	248	Wm.	CHE	812		
Mary	DEL	164	William	BER	275	WILLIAN, Jonathn.				
Mordecai	YOR	208	Wilm.	ALL	103	Esqr.	PHI	118		
Mordicai	BFD	67	Wm.	PHA	13	WILLIANS, Enion	BEV	11		
Nathan	CRA	7	Wm.	PHA	16	WILLIARD,				
Nathl.	WST	229	Wm.	BEV	19	Ephraim, B.	ERI	56A		
Nicholas	NOU	203	Wm.	PHA	108	Henry	SOM	153		
Oliver	MNT	101	Wm.	WST	383	Jacob	SOM	131		
Owan	NOU	113	Wm.	CHE	735	WILLIART, Peter	DAU	6		
Owen	PHI	150	Wm.	CHE	868	Peter	DAU	6		
Patrick	LAN	93	Wm.	CEN	23A	Peter	DAU	6A		
Peter	PHI	123	Zachariah	MIF	9	WILLIBY, James	ALL	116		
Philip	CHE	825	Zedekiah	PHA	21	Robert	ALL	116		
Primus	PHA	115	WILLIAMS?, Isaac			Wilm.	ALL	116		
Reuben	LUZ	332	M.?	CHE	854	WILLIMAN, George	NOU	178		
Richard	FAY	224	WILLIAMSON, Widow	WST	374	WILLIMAN?, Joseph	MIF	11A		
Richard	WST	383	Abraham	DEL	191	WILLING, George	DEL	174		
Richd.	WST	244	Abram	CHE	812	Patrick E.	PHA	25		
Richd.	FRA	294	Cornelius	FAY	224	Thos. Esqr.	PHA	102		
Robert	CRA	9	David	WAS	10	Thos. M.	PHA	103		
Robert	WAS	72	David	CUM	83	William	CHE	832		
Robert /M./	SOM	163	David	CUM	135	WILLIS, George	BEV	18		
Robert	SOM	163	David	FRA	289	Isaiah	MIF	18		
Robert	LAN	170	Eleazer	WAS	10	James	MIF	16		
Robert	WST	244	Elizabeth	DEL	180	Jedediah	YOR	167		
Robert	LUZ	406	Emor	DEL	155	John	WAY	142		
Robt.	PHA	66	Enos	DEL	180	John	PHA	104		
Robt.	WST	177	Francis	CHE	767	John	YOR	219		
Robt.	WST	228	Garret	PHI	3	John	WST	299		
Saml.	PHA	86	George	ADA	21	Jonathan	PHA	17A		
Saml.	FRA	286	George	MER	462	Joseph	LAN	302		
Saml.	MIF	5A	Gideon	CHE	803	Levy	NOU	145		
Saml.	BUC	87A	Hiram	DEL	171	Musgrove	PHA	64		
Samuel	WAS	60	Hugh	HNT	162	Richard	NOU	145		
Samuel	LAN	120	Jacob	PHI	77A	Robert	FAY	231		
Samuel	MNT	122	James	HNT	161	Solomon	PHA	105		
Samuel	MNT	123	James	DEL	178	Thos.	PHA	70		
Samuel	HNT	138	James	CHE	769	William	BFD	78		
Samuel	HNT	163	James	CHE	813	William	DEL	160		
Sarah	PHA	15	James Esqr.	NOH	74A	William	YOR	164		
Sarah	GRN	85	Jas.	CEN	19A	William	YOR	219		
Seth	FAY	237	Jerema.	MNT	38	William Jr.	BFD	78		
Solom On	BFD	53	Jesse	PHI	34	Wm.	LAN	286		
Solomon	MER	463	Jesse	DEL	156	WILLISON, John	BER	281		
Tatem	PHA	117	Jesse	DEL	182	WILLITS, Isaiah	NOU	113		
Theophilus	MNT	88	John	PHA	64	WILLIVER, David	NOU	160		
Thomas	ADA	14	John	ALL	75	WILLKINS, Willm.	WST	176		
Thomas	BEV	19	John	HNT	161	WILLMORE, John	PHI	76		
Thomas	PHA	42	John	DEL	180	WILLMS,				
Thomas	WAS	72	John	DEL	189	Christopher	LAN	206		

WILLOBY, John	FAY	206	WILLSON, Joseph	ALL	101	WILSON, Andrew	FAY 269
WILLOCK, Alexd.	ALL	54	Joseph	FAY	229	Andrew	BUT 344
Alexander	BEV	27	Lawrence	DEL	156	Andw.	LYC 21
Andrew	ALL	50	Lawrence	DEL	161	Ann	PHA 31
WILLON, Hugh	ALL	75	Marmaduke	WST	317	Ann	CHE 910
WILLOREN?, See			Mathew	ALL	63	Archid.	PHI 146
Willover	NOU	160	Nicholas	WST	244	Asa	GRN 74
WILLOUL?, Charles	BEV	24	Oliver	PHI	148	Bengamin	ALL 97
WILLOUR, Abraham	BUC	148A	Richard	WST	383	Benjamin	WAS 65
Anthony	BUC	102	Robert	BEV	17	Benjamin	WAS 84
John	BUC	102	Robert	MNT	37	Benjn.	ADA 16
WILLOVER, Jacob	NOU	160	Robert	DEL	166	Benjn.	CHE 867
WILLOW, Peter	DAU	6A	Robert	WST	259	Caleb	BFD 78
WILLOWER,			Robt.	CHE	879	Charles	PHI 75
Christian	CHE	892	Saml.	DAU	24	Charles	GRN 109
WILLS, Christr.	MIF	1A	Saml.	WST	244	Charles	CHE 773
David	CUM	140	Samuel	BEV	21	Charles	CHE 773
Geo.	FRA	273	Samuel	BEV	27	Charles	PHI 72A
Isaiah	MNT	71	Samuel	ALL	75	Crondle	LUZ 324
James	PHA	6	Samuel	FAY	218	Daniel	ERI 57
James	ALL	49	Sarah	ALL	60	Daniel	GRN 66
Jas.	CUM	138	Thomas	BEV	11	Daniel	ERI 59A
John	MIF	4	Thomas	CEN	19	David	ADA 6
John	CUM	139	Thomas	MNT	88	David	WAS 26
Joseph	BEV	19	Thomas	ARM	126	David	LYC 27
Joseph	MNT	141	Thomas	DEL	166	David	WAS 96
Mary	MNT	70	Thomas	DEL	181	David	YOR 204
Michael	MNT	79	Thomas	FAY	212	David	CHE 727
Michael	MNT	92	William	DAU	24	David	CHE 778
Nancy	FRA	317	William	BEV	26	David	CHE 832
Peter	BER	278	William	WST	258	Edward	WAS 26
Robt.	FRA	298	Wilm.	ALL	59	Edward	BFD 47
Samuel	MIF	4	Wm.	BEV	11	Edward	WAS 96
Thomas	PHI	22	Wm.	BEV	18	Elisabeth	WAS 18
William	CEN	19	Wm. Jr.	CEN	19	Eliza	PHA 64
Willm.	PHI	93	WILLY, Augustus	DAU	48A	Elizabeth	HNT 158
WILLSON, Widow	WST	228	Elijah	ERI	59	Elizabeth	FRA 285
Widow	WST	330	John	ERI	59	Elnathan	LUZ 335
Alexander	FAY	218	Peter	FAY	248	Enos	LYC 24
Alexr.	WST	177	WILLYARD, Philip	FAY	248	Ephraim	CHE 768
Alexr.	WST	383	WILMAN, Conrad	BER	174	Evan	DAU 19
Allexander	BEV	12	WILMANS, Fredrick	PHA	30	Ezabella	ALL 81
Amous	FAY	239	WILMER, Fredk.	PHI	2	Ezachal	ALL 88
Andrew	BEV	5	WILMERD, Thomas	LAN	81	Ezekiel	BUC 142
Andrew	BEV	24	WILMERT, Francis	LAN	95	Feby	ALL 91
Benjeman	FAY	254	WILMINGTON,			Fleman	NOU 169
David	BEV	7	Elisha	BUC	162	Fogson	LUZ 389
David	DEL	189	WILMON, Wildon	PHI	5	Francis	WAS 84
David	FAY	218	WILMORE, David	WST	244	Francis	BUT 365
David	FAY	269	Lambert	PHA	60	George	PHA 70
Francis	ALL	60	WILNER?,			George	PHA 74
Francis	BUC	150A	Frederick	BER	200	George	PHA 94
Galbreth	ALL	61	WILOUR, Jacob	BER	174	George	WAS 96
Hampn.	BUC	104	John	BER	174	George	ALL 102
Hampton	BUC	107A	WILOW, Bostian	FRA	301	George	ALL 105
Henry	BEV	22	WILSE, Martin	PHI	88	George	PHA 114
Hugh	BEV	5	WILSILLON, Wilm.	ALL	79	George	HNT 129
Hugh	DEL	187	WILSOM, James	WAS	14	George	LAN 134
Isaac	DEL	156	WILSON, Widow	PHI	29	George	HNT 141
Jacob	PHI	145	Widow	PHI	114	George	HNT 163
James	BEV	11	Aaron	ALL	76	George	YOR 212
James	BEV	20	Abraham	ALL	88	George	CHE 850
James	ALL	50	Adam	CUM	118	George	CHE 869
James	MNT	88	Adam	FRA	306	Henry	WAS 60
James	WST	176	Adnw.	PHI	115A	Henry	WAS 107
James	FAY	218	Alexander	WAS	114	Henry	ALL 112
James	WST	299	Alexander	WST	158	Henry	LUZ 347
Jeremia	FAY	229	Alexander	NOU	190	Henry	LUZ 426
John	BEV	8	Alexander	ERI	59A	Henry	DAU 4A
John	BEV	10	Alexr.	DAU	18	Henry	NOH 42A
John	BEV	16	Alexr.	BUT	340	Henry	PHI 105A
John	VEN	169	Alexr.	CHE	727	Hill	BFD 77
John	WST	258	Andr.	FRA	314	Hugh	ADA 3
John	FAY	263	Andrew	ADA	3	Hugh	LAN 14
John	FAY	269	Andrew	DAU	24	Hugh	ERI 60
John Jur.	FAY	269	Andrew	LAN	124	Hugh	ALL 80

WILSON, Hugh	CUM	99	WILSON, John	BFD	40	WILSON, Joshua	CHE 839
Hugh	WAS	118	John	PHA	62	Lettice	CUM 117
Hugh	HNT	133	John	GRN	67	Levi	CUM 40
Hugh	NOU	133	John	ALL	76	Lewis	BUT 338
Hugh	NOU	133	John	LAN	76	Lewis	BUT 352
Hugh	NOU	161	John	PHA	77	Margaret	PHA 95
Hugh	FAY	269	John	WAS	77	Margaret	PHA 95
Hugh	NOH	31A	John	ALL	81	Margaret	WAS 118
Isaac	BFD	78	John	PHI	82	Martha	WAS 18
Isaac	MNT	119	John	WAS	96	Martha	LAN 300
Isaac	LAN	167	John	ALL	97	Martha	LAN 309
Isaac	LUZ	365	John	MNT	110	Mary	PHA 77
Isaac	CHE	729	John	NOU	119	Mary	PHA 100
Isaac	BUC	107A	John	HNT	121	Mary	MNT 101
Isabella	YOR	200	John	MNT	125	Mary	CUM 147
Israel	WAS	41	John	LAN	129	Mary	CHE 751
Issabella	CUM	60	John	CUM	137	Mary	PHI 70A
Jacob	BER	137	John	BER	138	Mathew	PHA 73
James	ADA	2	John	CUM	138	Mathew	FRA 310
James	ADA	3	John	HNT	139	Mathew	CHE 868
James	LAN	3	John	HNT	141	Mathwew	CRA 11
James	LYC	3	John	HNT	158	Matthew	HNT 150
James	PHA	6	John	HNT	158	Mattw.	CUM 104
James	CRA	16	John	WST	158	Moore	SOM 145
James	MIF	18	John	WST	158	Moses	LYC 3
James	DAU	24	John	LAN	161	Moses	DAU 24
James	DAU	24	John	VEN	168	Moses	BUC 102
James	WAS	26	John	NOU	169	Motherell	BER 210
James	CUM	54	John	NOU	169	Mrs.	LAN 54
James	GRN	67	John	WST	177	Mrs.	NOU 133
James	ALL	78	John	YOR	196	Myles	WAS 53
James	PHA	88	John	NOU	197	Nathaniel	ERI 57
James	ALL	102	John	YOR	213	Nathaniel	NOU 119
James	HNT	116	John	YOR	215	Nathl.?	MIF 11A
James	SOM	136	John	FRA	316	Nicholas	BFD 78
James	BUC	140	John	WST	352	Peter	LYC 8
James	BUC	150	John	BUT	357	Peter	CEN 21
James	HNT	150	John	CHE	708	Peter	MER 462
James	HNT	158	John	CHE	726	Ritchard	ALL 105
James	NOU	160	John	CHE	739	Rob	LYC 17
James	HNT	163	John	CHE	752	Robert	CRA 3
James	YOR	196	John	CHE	828	Robert	WAS 10
James	YOR	202	John	CHE	839	Robert	ADA 26
James	BER	203	John Docr.	BUC	87A	Robert	LAN 40
James	BER	285	John Esqr.	WAS	118	Robert	PHI 40
James	FRA	319	John Esqr.	BUC	87A	Robert	WAS 77
James	WST	353	John Jnr.	CHE	753	Robert	ALL 81
James	MER	463	John Junr.	MNT	109	Robert	NOU 119
James	CHE	704	Joh	NOU	0	Robert	YOR 161
James	CHE	791	John	MIF	11A	Robert	HNT 163
James	CHE	818	John	CEN	19A	Robert	HNT 164
James	CHE	869	John	NOH	31A	Robert	LAN 226
James Esqr.	NOH	69A	John	ERI	56A	Robert	CHE 730
James Junr.	WST	353	John	BUC	145A	Robert	CHE 770
James	PHI	99A	John B.	PHA	23	Robert	CHE 817
James	DAU	10A	Jonathan	WAS	41	Robert Jun.	ADA 18
James	DAU	19A	Jonathan	BUC	138	Robert Junr.	WAS 18
James	ERI	55A	Jonathan	LUZ	425	Robert	CEN 23A
Jane	CUM	128	Jos.	CUM	37	Roboert Senr.	WAS 18
Jas.	CUM	45	Joseph	ADA	12	Robt.	MIF 16
Jas.	CUM	73	Joseph	DAU	18	Robt.	PHI 64
Jesse	BUC	146A	Joseph	CUM	45	Robt.	PHA 67
Jno.	FRA	276	Joseph	MNT	45	Robt.	MIF 11A
Joel W.	PHA	32	Joseph	BUC	85	Saml.	PHI 72
John	MIF	4	Joseph	ALL	97	Saml.	CUM 105
John	MIF	4	Joseph	CUM	103	Saml.	PHI 147
John	MIF	4	Joseph	ALL	109	Saml.	WST 353
John	LYC	6	Joseph	CUM	113	Saml.	CHE 871
John	ADA	7	Joseph	WAS	114	Saml. Dr.	FRA 313
John	WAS	10	Joseph	NOU	119	Saml.	CEN 21A
John	WAS	10	Joseph	BUC	144	Samson	FRA 275
John	LYC	12	Joseph	NOU	153	Samuel	WAS 26
John	CRA	13	Joseph	WST	244	Samuel	LYC 27
John	DAU	15	Joseph	LUZ	351	Samuel	GRN 79
John	WAS	26	Joseph	MIF	8A	Samuel	WAS 96
John	WAS	35	Joshua	ALL	76	Samuel	WAS 107

WILSON, Samuel	NOU	169	WILSON, William	NOU	173	WILTZHIMER,		
Samuel	NOU	169	William	YOR	195	Philip	BFD	59
Samuel	LAN	171	William	WST	196	WILY, Adam	WAS	25
Samuel	YOR	219	William	NOU	200	Elizabeth	ALL	56
Samuel	CHE	840	William	YOR	200	John	FRA	311
Samuel	CHE	900	William	LUZ	426	John	WST	374
Samuel	WAR	1A	William	MER	462	William	WST	374
Sarah	LYC	9	William	MER	463	WILYARD, Phillip	FRA	311
Sarah	DAU	16	William	CHE	732	WILYARSD, George	FAY	248
Sarah	PHA	41	William	CHE	760	WIMAN, Frederick	MIF	4
Sarah	WAS	118	William	CHE	857	WIMER,		
Seth	ALL	102	William	CHE	881	Christopher	ADA	4
Seth	CHE	868	William	CEN	21A	George	PHA	59
Sharlet	PHA	64	William	CEN	23A	Jacob	WST	244
Silas	CHE	710	William	ERI	56A	John	BFD	60
Silas	PHI	67A	William	ERI	56A	Joseph	BFD	55
Sloan &	PHA	27	Willm.	DAU	19	WIMLEY?, John	PHA	51
Stephen	LUZ	391	Willm.	BUT	337	WIMMER, Philip	BUC	158
Stephen	BUC	87A	Willm.	BUT	352	Stephen	BUC	82A
Thomas	ADA	2	Wilm.	PHI	70A	WIMOR, Andrew	PHI	40
Thomas	WAS	14	Wilm.	PHI	10	George	PHI	27
Thomas	ADA	18	Wilm.	ALL	81	WIMP, John	FAY	248
Thomas	BFD	48	Wilm.	ALL	88	WIMS?, Peter	DAU	32A
Thomas	MNT	71	Wilm.	ALL	108	WIMTS, Jacob	LAN	217
Thomas	ALL	73	Wilm.	ALL	108	WIN-INGS?, John	NOU	142
Thomas	WAS	77	Wilm.	ALL	112	WIN, Josiah	DAU	10
Thomas	ALL	81	Wm Jr.	CEN	19A	Wm.	PHA	64
Thomas	BUC	85	Wm.	PHI	11	WINAGLE, Agness	DAU	14A
Thomas	WAS	107	Wm.	LYC	17	Fredk.	DAU	14A
Thomas	NOU	113	Wm.	LYC	26	WINANS, Isaac	WAY	150
Thomas	WAS	114	Wm.	MIF	26	Jacob Junr.	NOH	79A
Thomas	HNT	116	Wm.	CUM	45	Jacob	NOH	79A
Thomas	NOU	133	Wm.	CUM	73	James	WAY	150
Thomas	SOM	136	Wm.	FRA	323	Mathew	WAY	150
Thomas	HNT	141	Wm.	CHE	860	WINBACH, Isaac	BUC	158
Thomas	BUC	144	Wm.	PHI	66A	WINBRIDEL,		
Thomas	HNT	145	Zechaes	ALL	76	Phillop	ALL	58
Thomas	NOU	145	WILSON?, James	BEV	17	WINCK-ER?,		
Thomas	HNT	150	Joseph	ADA	24	Christian		
Thomas	LAN	158	Tho. Jr.	MIF	8A	Warden Of The		
Thomas	LAN	163	Tho. (----)	MIF	8A	Single		
Thomas	NOU	170	Thomas	WAS	10	Bretherens		
Thomas	LAN	279	WILSTACK, Charles	PHI	109A	House	NOH	70A
Thomas	LAN	280	WILT, Abigail	PHI	74A	WINCOT, Samuel	DAU	12A
Thomas	BUT	357	Abm.	PHA	42	WIND, Andrew	NOH	81A
Thomas	CHE	770	Adam	CUM	32	John	NOH	72
Thomas	CHE	773	Adam	DAU	9A	Philip	NOH	81A
Thomas	CHE	791	Daniel	BER	171	Widow	NOH	81A
Thomas	DAU	21A	George	ADA	27	WINDBIGLER,		
Thoms.	BUT	344	George	CUM	32	William	BER	232
Thos.	CUM	117	George Sen.	ADA	30	WINDEBRAKER, John	CUM	108
Thos.	FRA	299	Henry	YOR	185	WINDER, Aron	BUC	99A
Thos.	FRA	309	Henry	PHI	79A	Dimoch	BUC	95
Thos.	FRA	321	Heronimus	BER	171	James	BUC	100
Thos.	PHI	67A	Jacob	NOH	83	Joseph	BUC	99A
Walter	PHA	29	Jacob	DAU	48A	Peter	BUC	95
Widow	CUM	65	Jeremiah	FRA	275	Samuel	BUC	99A
Widow	LAN	112	John	CUM	121	Thomas	BUC	99A
Widow	BUC	140	John	YOR	176	WINDERS, James	FAY	231
Widow	LAN	244	John	BER	186	James	FAY	237
William	ADA	2	Michael	YOR	176	James	FAY	254
William	DAU	9	Michl. Junr.	CUM	33	WINDLAND, Mrs.	LYC	27
William	ADA	19	Michl. Senr.	CUM	33	WINDLE, David	CHE	825
William	PHA	23	Nicholas	YOR	166	Francis	MIF	26A
William	WAS	72	Nicholas	BER	228	Job	CHE	825
William	BFD	77	Paul	YOR	175	Thomas	CHE	825
William	GRN	78	Philip	BER	171	William	CHE	851
William	WAS	118	Thomas	HNT	124	WINDLEY, Josh.	FRA	322
William	NOU	119	Valentine	BER	171	WINDLING, Adam	WST	228
William	LAN	121	WILTBERGER,			WINDOLPH, Jacob	PHI	129
William	LAN	123	Christian	PHA	23	WINE, Margit	ALL	100
William	NOU	153	Peter	PHA	29	Webbster	NOU	145
William	WST	158	WILTNER, Jacob	DAU	10	WINEBARRER, Widow	BFD	68
William	WST	158	WILTS, John	CUM	112	WINEBERG, Mary	PHI	114
William	HNT	162	WILTS?, Jacob	SOM	153	WINEBERRY, Balser	BUC	102
William	HNT	164	WILTZ, Nicholas	CUM	57	WINEBRANNER, Christian	BFD	67

WISBY, Henry			WISECARVER,			WISON, William	PHI	33
Junr.	ALL	75	George	BFD	78	WISONG, John	BFD	35
Patrick	ALL	75	John	GRN	73	WISOUR, Henry	HNT	127
Robert	FAY	207	John	BFD	78	WISPART?, Barbary	PHA	51
WISE, (No Given			WISECOP, Felty	MIF	9	WISS, Famas	PHI	55
Name)	YOR	200	WISEHART, David	BFD	67	WISSENGER,		
Abm.	CUM	132	WISEL, George	BFD	78	Melchor	PHA	36
Adam	DAU	7	John	BFD	78	WISSER, Jacob	BER	227
Adam	CUM	73	WISEL?, John	BFD	78	John	BER	186
Adam	GRN	104	WISELY, James	FAY	260	WISSER?, George	PHI	95A
Adam	PHI	120	WISEMAN, Widow	PHI	8	WISSLER, Godfried	MNT	136
Andrew	WAS	41	Adam	BFD	47	Jacob	BER	228
Andrew	WAS	126	Andw.	PHI	67	Michael	LAN	302
Casper	ADA	34	Barbary	PHA	48	WIST, Christian	LAN	205
Christopher	NOU	190	Geo.	CUM	37	WISTAR, Casper	CHE	709
Chrs.	YOR	214	Henry	MNT	122	Daniel	PHA	18
Daniel	ALL	61	Henry	BUC	155A	John	PHI	53
Daniel	NOU	133	John	BUC	87A	John Junr.	PHA	76
Elizh.	PHA	42	Saml.	PHI	73	Richard	PHA	4
Felex	CUM	133	WISEMER, David	WST	299	Sarah	PHA	4
Frederick	MNT	101	WISEMORE, Henry	MNT	127	Thomas	PHA	18
Frederick	NOU	133	WISEN, Jonathan	WST	228	WISTEMAN?,		
Frederick	NOU	196	WISENOR, Jacob	CHE	735	Christopher	BER	239
George	PHA	90	WISER,			WISTEMBERRIAR,		
George	CUM	95	Christopher	NOU	133	Jno.	PHI	1
George	CUM	131	Christr.	CUM	142	WISTENBERGER,		
George	NOU	178	Jacob	CUM	28	Christopher	LAN	205
George Senr.	CUM	129	John	CUM	60	WISTENBURG, Geoe.	PHI	2
George	BUC	102A	John	PHA	64	WISTER, Peter	PHI	81
Geroge	BUC	102	Mrs.	CUM	89	Sarah	CHE	886
Gillion	MNT	101	Peter	NOU	102	WISTLER, John	BER	275
Henry	NOU	203	WISHAM, Casper	PHI	106A	WISTON, Thomas	HNT	130
Henry	WST	229	Sophia	PHA	55	WISTY, Edwd.	PHI	32
Henry	DAU	26A	WISHARD, Edward	FRA	203	WITCHELL, John	PHI	136
Jacob	CUM	73	James	WAS	26	WITCHELL?, Saml.	PHA	54
Jacob	GRN	73	John	WAS	26	WITE, Betsy	PHI	114
Jacob	CUM	85	WISHART, John	WAS	95	WITEL, Christian	LAN	182
Jacob	ALL	114	Thomas	PHA	24	WITENBOROUGH,		
Jacob	WAS	114	Thomas	LAN	129	Elizh.	PHA	41
Jacob	WAS	126	WISHER, Henry	DAU	47	WITENER, Widow	PHI	97
Jacob	NOU	141	WISINGER, Ludwig	SOM	160	WITER, Daniel	LAN	75
Jacob	NOU	203	WISLER, Christ.	LAN	285	George	LAN	206
Jacob	YOR	208	Christian	LAN	89	WITERESS, Francis	PHI	80A
Jacob Jr.	CUM	85	Isaac	MNT	76	WITHER, Christ.	FRA	327
Jacob	CEN	23A	Isaac	MNT	119	John	LAN	87
Jacob	DAU	33A	Jacob	MNT	76	John	LAN	87
Jno. Junr.	CUM	85	Jacob	PHI	92	John	FRA	326
John	ALL	61	Jacob	MNT	129	Peter	FRA	326
John	CUM	85	Jacob	MNT	136	Valentine	LAN	243
John	HNT	122	John	LAN	9	Widow	LAN	87
John	NOU	133	John	ADA	31	WITHERBY,		
John	NOU	141	John	MNT	76	Whitehead	CHE	801
John	YOR	176	Samuel	LAN	188	WITHERINTON,		
John	NOU	178	Solomon	LAN	188	Saml.	PHI	87
John	NOU	190	WISMAN?, See			WITHERITE, Mihl.	CEN	23A
John Junr.	PHI	141	Witman	BER	239	WITHEROE, James	CHE	777
John Senr.	PHI	141	WISMER, Abm. Sen.	BUC	90A	WITHEROW, James	ADA	5
John	PHI	118A	Abm.	BUC	141A	James	MIF	26
John	PHI	120A	Abraham	BUC	142	James	FRA	286
Jos.	YOR	187	Henry	BUC	142	James	FRA	327
Ludwig	LAN	180	Henry	BUC	97A	John	FRA	327
Ludwig	LAN	181	Jacob	MNT	85	John	CHE	777
Martin	PHI	91A	Jacob	BUC	142	Rachel	ALL	73
Michael	HNT	152	Jacob	BUC	141A	Robt.	MIF	18
Peter	DAU	17	Joseph	BUC	97A	Samuel	CHE	777
Peter	WAS	126	Widow	BUC	141A	WITHERRISS?, John	VEN	167
Peter	MNT	131	WISMER?, Abraham	BUC	92	WITHERROW, John	BEV	21
Peter	NOU	133	WISMORE, Abraham	WAY	150	Sarah	BEV	21
Peter	SOM	160	WISNER, George	BUC	152	WITHERS, George	LAN	216
Peter	YOR	214	Henry	MNT	101	John	LAN	120
Philip	YOR	202	Jacob	MNT	101	John	LAN	220
Sebastian	YOR	177	John	MNT	101	Michael	LAN	220
Sebastian	YOR	179	John	BER	185	WITHERSPOON, John	ADA	34
WISE?, George	PHI	95A	Martin	MNT	101	WITHERUP, John	ALL	61
WISECARVER,			Stophel	MIF	1A	WITHEY, James	DEL	162
George	GRN	73	WISNER?, Abraham	BUC	92	William	FRA	278

441

WOOD, John	FAY	254	WOODLING, Conrad			WOODS, Henry	LAN	179
John	BUC	95A	Peter	NOH	42	Hugh	BEV	10
Joseph	PHA	52	John	NOH	42	Hugh	FAY	260
Joseph	BUC	89	John	NOU	185	Hugh	FRA	326
Joseph	MNT	141	WOODLY, Matthew	NOU	160	Hugh	MER	463
Joseph	DEL	168	WOODMAN, Edward	CHE	830	Isaac	ALL	104
Joseph	MIF	13A	George	BUC	89A	J.	LAN	157
Joseph	BUC	162A	Joseph	PHI	24	James	WAS	26
Joshua	MNT	65	Wm.	PHA	71	James	ALL	79
Josiah	MNT	132	Wm.	FRA	298	James	FAY	254
Mansfield B.	PHI	94A	WOODMANCY, Jas.	FAY	260	James	WST	258
Mary	PHA	86	Joseph	FAY	238	James	DAU	49A
Matthew	DEL	172	WOODMANEY, David	SOM	144	Jane	CUM	109
Michl.	BER	243	WOODMONCY, Samuel	GRN	78	Jno.	CUM	140
Nathen	ERI	58	WOODNEY, Jas.	CUM	47	John	DAU	9
Obediah	PHA	26	WOODRING, Jacob	NOH	92A	John	MIF	18
Peter	PHI	42	Nicholas	NOH	92A	John	WAS	26
Robert	PHA	12	Philip	LUZ	358	John	WAS	26
Robert	BUC	89A	Saml. Jr.	NOH	92A	John	WAS	83
Ruel	ERI	58	Samuel	NOH	92A	John	ALL	117
Samuel	MNT	42	WOODROE, Isaac	CHE	731	John	NOU	169
Septimus	MNT	109	WOODROF, John	LYC	9	John	WST	177
Sophia	PHA	32	WOODROFF, Mary	PHA	120	John	FRA	300
Thomas	ALL	74	WOODROUGHF,			John	WST	330
Thomas	BUC	142	Hester	PHI	127	John	MER	463
Thomas	BUC	87A	WOODROW, (No			John Esqr.	ALL	49
William	PHI	64	Given Name)	MIF	11A	John	CEN	23A
William	GRN	73	Jerry	ALL	79	Joseph	BFD	46
William	GRN	85	Joseph	DEL	164	Joseph	HNT	165
William	GRN	91	Levi	CHE	837	Joshua	WAS	107
William	BER	215	Mary	WST	299	Josiah	PHI	147
William	MNT	105	Richard	WAS	51	Levi	MIF	18
WOODARD, (See			Simeon	CHE	871	M.	LAN	60
Wooward)	MIF	9	Stevan	ALL	79	Margret	CUM	88
John	MIF	9	Wm.	CHE	888	Nathl.	CUM	109
Jonaas	PHI	112A	WOODRUFF, Abm.	PHI	75	Richd.	CUM	118
Thomas	MIF	9	Allen	GRN	104	Robert	BEV	6
Thomas	PHA	94	Andw.	VEN	167	Robert	MIF	9
Wm.	MIF	9	Anthy.	CUM	119	Robert	BER	215
Wm.	LYC	18	Archibald	PHA	30	Robt.	CUM	105
WOODBRIDGE, Saml.	FAY	224	Corneleous	FAY	242	Saml.	CUM	109
Theodore	WAY	139	Cornelius	FAY	201	Saml. Junr.	CUM	109
WOODBURN,			David	WAS	6	Saml. Shoemr.	CUM	109
Alexander	WAS	32	Elihu	GRN	104	Samuel	WAS	107
Alexander	WAS	95	Ephraim	FAY	218	Thomas	BEV	4
James	WAS	35	Isaac	NOU	108	Thomas	PHI	5
James	ALL	108	Joab	BEV	19	Thomas	MER	463
Jas.	CUM	127	John	WAS	5	Widow	CHE	887
Jno.	CUM	107	Joshua	GRN	97	William	WAS	14
John	CUM	27	Matthias	GRN	104	William	WAS	18
John	WAS	35	Meker	GRN	104	William	FAY	200
Mattw.	CUM	124	Nathaniel	LUZ	416	William	WST	299
Thomas	WAS	95	Samuel	GRN	104	William	MER	463
WOODBY, Margaret	PHA	22	Samuel	LUZ	378	Wilm.	ALL	53
WOODCOCK, Jacob	NOH	79A	WOODS, (No Given			Wilm.	ALL	74
Jno.	BUT	315	Name)	MIF	12	Wilm. Rd.	ALL	94
Samuel	LUZ	389	Abraham	MIF	18	Wm.	BEV	4
WOODERT, Absalom	ARM	127	Adam	LAN	175	Wm.	BEV	6
WOODFIELD, Thoms.	PHI	151	Archible	BEV	25	Wm.	CUM	31
WOODFILL,			Catharine	LAN	52	Zacharia	FAY	260
Catherine	WAS	41	Charles	FAY	263	WOODSIDE, Archd.	CHE	731
WOODGATE, William	ADA	16	Christopher	NOU	169	John	PHA	21
WOODHOUSE, James			Cornelias	PHA	81	John	DAU	7A
M.d.	PHA	27	David	LAN	175	Wm.	CHE	713
Wm. (Crossed			Dengamin	ALL	87	WOODSIDES,		
Out)	PHA	16	Edward	CHE	884	Archibald	NOU	145
WOODIN, Randal	FRA	292	Edwd.	CUM	84	John	NOU	145
WOODING, George	NOU	185	Elijah	WAS	41	Jonathan	SOM	145
WOODINGTON, David	BUC	89A	Elijah	PHI	99	WOODSIDIS, Archd.	WST	383
WOODIS, Jery	NOU	161	George	CUM	63	WOODWARD, Abisha	WAY	142
WOODLAND, Isaac	PHA	66	George	BFD	77	Abraham	CHE	852
Michl.	PHI	115A	George	CEN	21A	Caleb	DEL	191
WOODLE, Thomas	FAY	248	Gersham	WAS	126	Caleb	CHE	763
WOODLEY, Phillip	CUM	24	Henrey	FAY	263	Caleb	CHE	849
WOODLING, Andrew	NOH	42A	Henry	WAS	14	David	LUZ	353
Conrad	NOH	42	Henry	BFD	35	Eben	PHI	99

WOODWARD,			WOOLLERTON,			WORKMAN, Hugh	WAS 118
Ebenezer	WAY	142	William	CHE	699	James	WAS 107
Edward	DEL	175	WOOLLEY, Phebe	CHE	700	James	WST 298
Eli	DEL	158	WOOLMAN, George	MNT	85	John	FAY 248
Elis	CUM	55	John	MNT	52	John	LAN 257
Enos	WAY	142	Lewis	MNT	37	John	WST 299
Enos Jr.	WAY	139	WOOLMER, Daniel	PHA	68	Saml.	WST 317
George	CHE	803	WOOLOVER, John	LYC	22	William	PHI 16
Isaac	CHE	883	WOOLRIDGE, Jonas	PHA	95	William	FAY 248
James	CHE	763	Robert	PHA	115	WORKNOT, Martin	PHI 84A
Jane	CHE	760	WOOLSEY, Henry	BUC	100	WORKS, William	MNT 106
Jesse	CHE	772	WOOLSTON,			WORLDLEY, Saml.	CUM 24
Jno.	CUM	59	Jonathan	BUC	88	WORLE, George	GRN 79
John	WAY	139	Jonthan	BUC	162	WORLEY, Achor	BFD 53
John	DEL	191	Joshua	BUC	95	Achor	BFD 60
John	CHE	707	WOOLTSLAIR, John	ALL	57	Brice	GRN 73
John	CHE	762	WOOLY, Anthoney	FAY	229	Caleb	MIF 13A
Jos.	CHE	762	Benjamin	LUZ	373	Daniel	YOR 154
Joseph	DEL	191	Geo.	PHI	114	George	YOR 161
Joseph	CHE	774	John	LUZ	325	Henry	MNT 101
Joshua	CHE	772	Thomas	LUZ	320	Jos.	YOR 159
Mary	CHE	763	WOORDING, Jacob	NOH	44	Nathan	YOR 155
Nathl.	CHE	813	WOOSTER, David	LUZ	410	Robert	BER 158
Richd.	CHE	762	Isaac	LUZ	410	William	ADA 42
Robert	MNT	124	Robert	WAS	6	WORLOW, Thomas	DEL 160
Robt.	CHE	760	WOOWARD, James	MIF	9	WORLY, Daniel	YOR 162
Saml.	CHE	767	WORALA?, Benjn.	CHE	710	David	YOR 207
Samuel	CHE	848	WORBASSE, Peter	NOH	70A	Jacob	YOR 163
Silas	WAY	139	WORD, John	ALL	54	James Sr.	YOR 162
Thomas	CHE	760	WORDEN, James	BUC	95A	James (Sadler)	YOR 162
Thomas	CHE	812	Nathaniel	LUZ	329	John	ALL 110
Thos.	CHE	742	WORDIN?, James	ALL	112	Nathan	YOR 173
Wm.	CHE	762	WORDLEY, Danl.	CUM	36	Philip	FAY 239
Wm. W.	PHA	15	WORDS, Joseph	FAY	269	WORM, Robert	LAN 142
WOODY, Jno.	CUM	42	WORE, Ludwick	YOR	217	WORMAN, Abm.	NOH 92A
WOODZAND, Thos.	PHI	89	WOREMAN, Wm.	YOR	211	Conrad	NOH 69A
WOOL, Henry	PHI	2	WORINGTON?,			Jacob	NOH 69A
WOOLAND, Joseph	PHI	145	Michl.	PHI	15	John	BUC 92
WOOLAS, Nicholas	DEL	172	WORK, Alexander	HNT	159	Ludwig	BER 185
WOOLBACH, Jacob	BUC	148A	Alexander	FAY	218	Michael	BUC 150
Peter	BUC	148A	Alexander	LAN	220	WORMAR, Stophl.	CUM 141
WOOLBERT, John	NOH	42A	Alexander	FAY	232	WORMHOLLS, Michl.	CUM 30
WOOLEN, Joseph	PHI	151	Alexr.	MIF	5A	WORMLEY, Geo.	CUM 60
Samuel	FAY	229	Andrew	FAY	218	WORMLY, Englehart	CUM 60
WOOLERT, Thomas	ARM	123	Andrew	LAN	243	Jacob	CUM 60
WOOLERTON,			Charles	FAY	242	Jno.	CUM 60
Charles	CHE	884	David	MIF	16	WORMSLY, Scripo	PHI 82A
James	CHE	804	George	WAS	60	WORNER, Abraham	ALL 80
WOOLERY, Jacob	MNT	132	Henrey	FAY	218	John	ALL 90
WOOLF, Abrm.	DAU	29A	Henry	NOU	181	Melchor	YOR 186
Andrew	SOM	160	Henry	LAN	310	Stevan	ALL 73
Christn Jr.	DAU	52	Henry Ssr.	FRA	284	WORNS, Robert	LAN 55
Christn Sr.	DAU	52	James Esqr.	LAN	2	WORRALL, Aaron	DEL 178
Christn.	DAU	52A	John	WAS	26	Abel	DEL 178
Elizabeth	PHI	133	John	FAY	218	Adam	DEL 182
George	WST	244	John	FAY	260	Daniel	DEL 178
Henry	DAU	49A	John	FRA	293	Elisha	DEL 185
Jacob	DAU	36	Joseph	CRA	9	Elisha	DEL 189
Jacob	DAU	52	Joseph	FAY	207	Enos	DEL 178
Jacob	ARM	127	Robert	ADA	7	Isaac	DEL 186
Jacob	PHI	131	Robert	WST	164	Isaac	DEL 187
Jacob	FAY	260	Samuel	MIF	4	Isaiah	DEL 182
Jacob & Son	DAU	48A	Samuel	PHI	42	Jacob	DEL 187
Jacob & Son	DAU	48A	Samuel	FAY	207	James	DEL 178
Margaret	DAU	52	William	MIF	6	John	DEL 175
Peter	DAU	48A	William	ADA	10	John	DEL 178
WOOLFALL, Richd.	PHI	13	Wm.	CUM	70	John	DEL 187
WOOLFHEART, John	WST	374	Wm. Junr.	CUM	65	Joseph	DEL 178
WOOLFORD, Adam	BFD	60	WORKBURN, Jesse	NOH	51	Joseph	DEL 189
Andrew	BFD	60	WORKENOR, Peter	ADA	5	Maris	DEL 174
Elizabeth	BFD	53	WORKHOAD?, Mattw.	CUM	65	Nathan	DEL 178
Frederick	BFD	60	WORKIESER, Adam	MNT	112	Owen	DEL 182
Joseph	BFD	60	WORKISER, John	CHE	830	Peter	DEL 181
WOOLKILL, Elias	FRA	271	WORKIZER, Andrew	LUZ	321	Peter	DEL 182
WOOLLARD, James	PHI	154	WORKMAN, Abram	FAY	242	Samuel	DEL 175
WOOLLEN, James	BUC	90	Benja.	WST	298	Seth	DEL 178

444

WRIGHT, Moses	BUC	85	WUTRING, Philip	NOH	88	YAGAR, Peter	FAY	248˙
Moses	WAS	126	William	NOH	88	YAGER, Adam	MNT	129
Moses	LUZ	366	WUTRY?, (See			Bernard	MNT	103
Nathan	BFD	60	Wulry)	LAN	53	Christian	NOU	142
Nathan S.	LUZ	366	WUTTRING, John	NOH	52	Conrad	MNT	103
Obadiah	WAS	65	WUVER, John	PHI	39	Henry	PHA	61
Owen	LAN	268	WY, Benjamin	HNT	130	Jno.	DAU	25
Philip Jacob	LAN	270	WYAND, George	LAN	284	John	DAU	33
Prudence	BEV	22	Henry	BFD	78	John	PHI	72
Reuben	GRN	109	Henry	PHA	104	Michael	PHA	61
Robert	BEV	23	Jacob	BFD	78	Stophel	DAU	7A
Robert	BFD	53	WYANT, Widow	PHI	91	Valentine	NOH	81A
Robert	ALL	116	Cornelius	WAS	47	YAKEL,		
Robert	DEL	178	George	CUM	25	Christopher	PHI	123
Robt.	CUM	96	Jacob	SOM	140	YAKIN, George	PHI	107A
Saml.	CHE	846	Jacob	FRA	312	YAN, Frederick	LAN	90
Samuel	ADA	15	Jacob Jun.	SOM	141	YANDES, Simon	FAY	200
Samuel	BUC	85	Nicolaus	DAU	11A	YANNAWINE, Mary	FRA	302
Samuel	GRN	85	Peter	WAS	72	YANSON, Jacob	NOH	40A
Samuel	SOM	136	Philip	CHE	793	William	NOH	40A
Samuel	DEL	174	Phillip	FRA	292	YANT, Felty	WAS	73
Samuel	LAN	299	WYAT, Widw.	PHI	88	John	WAS	73
Sarah	PHA	52	WYCY, Simeon	LUZ	388	John	ALL	97
Siras	PHI	97A	WYELS, Widow	PHI	70A	Phillop	ALL	96
Soloman	BUC	145	WYERBACK, Isaac	BUC	82A	YANTZ, Matthias	LAN	153
Stephen	BUC	85A	Jacob	BUC	82A	Peter	LAN	314
Thomas	ALL	67	WYETH, John	DAU	5	YARAHUS,		
Thomas	GRN	85	Joshua	LUZ	412	Christian	BER	263
Thomas	PHA	106	WYKEL, John	BER	278	YARD, Benjamin	DEL	178
Thomas	SOM	131	WYKOOF, John	CRA	7	Elias	PHI	26
Thomas	BER	278	William	CRA	7	James	PHA	3
Thomas	LAN	289	WYLANT, Conrod	PHI	118	Sandy	PHA	115
Thomas	LUZ	318	WYLEA, Mary	PHI	94	YARDLEY, Enos	BUC	104
Timothy	BUC	100	WYLIE, Robert	CUM	138	Joseph	BUC	100
Widow?	MIF	11A	Wm.	CUM	58	Mahlon	BUC	100
William	MIF	6	WYMAN, Conrad	LAN	99	Saml.	BUC	100
William	ADA	10	Jacob	LAN	99	Samuel	BUC	104
William	WAS	10	WYMER, George	DAU	30	Samuel Jnr.	BUC	104
William	BFD	66	WYNCOOP, Jacob	CUM	86	Thomas	BUC	100
William	GRN	104	WYNKOOP, Abram	MNT	63	William	BUC	100
William	PHI	154	Cornelius	MNT	63	YARDLY, Richard	BUC	87A
William	DEL	168	David	BUC	138	William	PHA	21
William	LAN	299	Garret	CEN	21A	YARGER, Tobias		
William	LUZ	321	Garrett	MNT	63	Junr.	MNT	60
William	BUT	327	Gerardus	BUC	138	YARLEY, Widow	PHI	27
Willm.	BUT	322	Henry	BUC	138	YARNAL, Isaac	BER	282
Wilm.	ALL	89	Isaac	MNT	63	Jasper	BER	216
Wm.	PHA	35	John	BUC	138A	Jessee	BER	283
WRISE?, Jacob	YOR	190	Joseph	PHA	21	Peter	BER	282
WRITE, David	FRA	311	Mattw.	CEN	21A	YARNALL, Azel	DEL	170
Patr.	FRA	311	Nicholas	BUC	104	Benjn.	CHE	880
Thos.	PHI	87A	Philip	MNT	63	Caleb	DEL	172
WRITER, John	NOH	79A	WYNN, Widow	PHI	79	Caleb	CHE	880
WRITRING?, (See			Benjn.	FAY	224	Caleb	CHE	881
Wutring)	NOH	86	David	BER	252	David	DEL	175
WRITE, Leonard	BUC	146A	Isaac	FAY	224	David	DEL	182
WRITHG, Nathan	BUC	153A	James	CHE	910	Eli	DEL	172
WRO--?, John	FRA	287	Jonathn.	CHE	910	Ellis	PHA	24
WROTH, William	PHI	6	Thomas	FAY	224	Enoch Esqr.	CHE	879
WUCKERER,			Warnar	FAY	224	Ezekiel	DEL	182
Elizabet	PHA	10	WYNOTT, Widow	PHI	76A	George	DEL	172
WULAND, George	LAN	22	WYRICK, John	WAS	114	Isaac	CHE	705
WULGEMUTH, David	YOR	174	Peter	WAS	107	Isaac	CHE	881
WULRY, Robert	LAN	53	WYSER, Valentine	PHI	112A	Jacob	DEL	176
WUMER, Michael	BER	220				James	DEL	172
WUMMER, Adam Jr.	BER	147	XANDER, David	NOH	86	John	DEL	173
WUNDER, Geo. Jr.	BER	239	David Junr.	NOH	86	John	DEL	175
George	BER	239	Emanuel	DAU	41	Joseph	DEL	176
WUNDERLICH, Henry	LAN	99	Geo.	DAU	38	Joshua	CHE	881
John	LAN	99	Jacob	DAU	41	Lewis	DEL	190
WUNNERICH, Henry	BER	258				Mordecai	CHE	805
WURT, Mary	PHI	116A	YACKY?, Lewis	PHI	110	Nathan	CHE	880
WUSHY, Henry	MNT	91	YADELLAR, Andrew	PHA	76	Saml.	CHE	848
WUTRING, Abraham	NOH	88	YAEGER, Henry	NOH	40A	Samuel	DEL	160
Daniel	NOH	86	Philip	NOH	40A	William	DEL	172
Nicholas	NOH	88	YAGAR, Joseph	FAY	248	William	DEL	175

YODER, Joseph	MIF	4	YOST, Henry	MNT	74	YOUNG, Christian	LAN	199
Joseph	MIF	16	Isaac	MIF	11A	Christn.	PHA	65
Jost	NOH	35	Jacob	MIF	18	Christn.	PHI	75A
Michl.	MIF	4	Jacob	BUC	92	Christopher	DEL	162
Michl.	BER	200	Jacob	MNT	97	Cladius	CHE	746
Peter	BER	232	John	LAN	32	Conrad	BER	180
Peter Jr.	BER	232	John	MNT	59	Conrad	CEN	21A
Samuel	BER	232	John	BUC	82A	Conrod	WST	375
Solomoon	SOM	155	Maunus?	BUC	82A	Daniel	WAS	47
YOE, John	BER	216	Michel	BUC	82A	Daniel	LAN	110
YOEA?, Geo.	PHI	108	Peter	MNT	59	Daniel	FAY	207
YOER?, Peter	NOU	115	Peter	MNT	97	Daniel	FAY	232
YOH, George	ADA	35	Philip	LAN	58	Danl.	PHI	80
Jacob	BER	284	Philip	MNT	59	David	ALL	85
Michael	ADA	34	Philip Junr.	MNT	59	David	ALL	87
YOHE, George	NOH	35	Widow	LAN	61	David	WAY	138
Jacob	NOH	40A	YOTERS, Samuel	NOU	113	David	NOU	153
YOHN, Philip	MNT	86	YOTHER, John	LAN	293	David	FAY	263
Philip	MNT	103	YOU?, Peter	NOU	115	David	LUZ	401
YOHO, Jacob	BEV	7	YOUCE, Jacob	YOR	182	Edward	LAN	160
YOKAM, Isaac	DEL	185	YOUCH, Conrad	BER	215	Edward	NOH	79A
YOKE, Michael	WAS	73	YOUG, Jacob	MNT	55	Elizabeth	YOR	170
Peter	WAS	73	Morgan	NOU	153	Elizabeth	CHE	738
YOKEHAM, John	MIF	13A	YOULE?, Jacob	MNT	124	Eloner	CUM	118
YOKEY, Abraham	ARM	125	YOULER, Adam	SOM	150	F. Benjamin	NOU	173
YOKUM, John	HNT	155	YOULERICK, George	NOU	142	Felix	DAU	40
Peter	HNT	161	YOULK, Michael	NOU	108	Frederick	LAN	138
YOLTON, John	ALL	67	YOUMAN, William	FAY	200	Frederick	YOR	172
YON, John	CUM	38	YOUN, Mathias	DAU	30	George	WAS	73
Wm.	CUM	41	YOUNCINGS, Michal	ALL	71	George	SOM	131
YONCE, Jacob	DAU	14	YOUNCKER, George	NOH	40A	George	NOU	133
Jacob	DAU	13A	Jacob	NOH	74A	George	NOU	142
YONER, Christiana	YOR	173	YOUND, Andrew	LAN	72	George	NOU	142
YONKER, Daniel	PHI	136	George	LAN	72	George	BER	156
George	PHI	135	Samuel	LAN	71	George	BER	159
Jos.	PHI	90	YOUNG, Widow	PHI	2	George	CHE	787
Yost	PHI	101	Widow	PHI	69	George Junr.	WAS	6
YONS, John	MNT	54	Widow	YOR	213	George Senr.	WAS	6
Philip	MNT	97	Widow	PHI	86A	Gilbert	WST	330
YONTZ, Jacob	DAU	11A	Ab.	DAU	40	Henry	PHA	80
YOPS?, John	PHI	85A	Abraham	WAS	47	Henry	LAN	109
YORBET?, Nathan	BEV	7	Abraham	WAS	126	Henry	PHA	115
YORDAN, Elias	LAN	137	Abraham	NOU	133	Henry	PHI	146
Henry	YOR	187	Abraham	YOR	189	Henry	YOR	181
YORDY, Christian	LAN	112	Abraham	NOH	31A	Henry	FRA	314
Jacob	LAN	112	Adam	PHI	52	Henry	NOH	63A
Joseph	LAN	113	Adam	BER	182	Henry	PHI	90A
Michael	CHE	789	Adam	YOR	182	Isaac	GRN	104
YORGER, Fredk.	YOR	215	Adam Jr.	BER	182	Isaac	BER	133
YORK, Amos	ERI	60	Adam	NOH	88A	Isaac	NOU	153
Cornelius	LAN	94	Alexander	BER	252	Isaac	FAY	254
Felty	LAN	124	Alexander	FAY	269	Jacob	DAU	50
Minor	LUZ	397	Alexdr.	PHI	117	Jacob	PHI	52
Stanford	ERI	60	Alexr.	WST	229	Jacob	PHI	72
Stephen	ERI	60	Alexr.	WST	318	Jacob	PHI	101
YORKER/ YORKES?,			Andrew	MNT	54	Jacob	PHI	121
William	MNT	52	Andrew	GRN	73	Jacob	ARM	124
YORKS, John	NOU	108	Andrew	WAS	126	Jacob	WAS	126
YORKY, Henry	BER	140	Andrew	DEL	165	Jacob	HNT	132
Henry	BER	174	Andrew	NOH	69A	Jacob	NOU	133
Henry Jur.	BER	140	Andrew	BUC	94A	Jacob	BUC	140
YORRY, Ann	DAU	40	Andrew	BUC	95A	Jacob	CUM	141
YORTY, John	SOM	131	Andw.	DAU	24	Jacob	BER	239
YOSST?, John	PHI	72A	Andw.	DAU	35	Jacob	NOH	31A
YOST, Abraham	BUC	92	Andw.	PHI	75A	Jacob	PHI	97A
Abraham	YOR	171	Ann	DEL	185	Jacob	PHI	112A
Adam	MNT	54	Baltzer	ADA	23	James	BEV	19
Caspar	DAU	29A	Benj.	PHI	88	James	WAS	47
Conrad	LAN	58	Benja.	PHI	16	James	WAS	47
Conrad	BUC	92	Benjamin	LAN	220	James	ALL	54
Daniel	MNT	54	Casper	SOM	155	James	ALL	72
Daniel	BUC	92	Charles	PHI	21	James	PHA	87
Daniel	MNT	116	Charles	YOR	180	James	GRN	98
Frederic	CHE	910	Charles	FRA	273	James	PHA	99
H. B. H.	LAN	144	Chas.	PHA	10	James	HNT	135
Henry	CUM	65	Christian	YOR	179	James	YOR	154

INDEX TO THE 1800 CENSUS OF PENNSYLVANIA

Name	Loc	Pg	Name	Loc	Pg	Name	Loc	Pg
YUNGMAN, Thos.	NOU	191	ZEIGLER, George	YOR	182	ZENT, Jacob	DAU	43
YURT?, Robert	DAU	10A	George	LAN	295	ZEPP, Jacob	MNT	90
YUTZS, John	DAU	20A	George P.	YOR	163	John	MNT	54
			Gerhart	MNT	129	Philip	MNT	54
Z--MAN?, Peter	MER	464	Henry	MNT	55	ZEPPERNICH,		
ZACHARIA, Jacob	FRA	302	Jacob	MNT	122	Godfry	PHI	131
ZACHARIAS, Geo.	BER	147	Jacob	SOM	155	ZERBAN?, Philipa	PHA	40
ZACHARIES, Daniel	BER	135	John	SOM	155	ZERBE, Andrew	LAN	303
ZAHM, Matthias	LAN	43	John	YOR	161	Benjamin	BER	263
ZAIBER,			John	YOR	188	Christian	NOU	201
Christopher	MNT	103	John	YOR	211	Daniel	BER	260
ZALL, Henry	LAN	207	Leonard	YOR	212	Daniel	BER	263
Jacob	LAN	207	Martin	HNT	156	George	BER	200
ZANCKMAYER, Jacob	LAN	206	Michael	MNT	122	George	BER	220
ZANDERS, Anthony	PHI	146	Michael	MNT	127	George	BER	282
ZANE?, John	PHA	78	Michael	YOR	190	George A.	BER	263
ZANGMASTER,			Michael	YOR	190	George Ad. /		
Philip	BUC	160	Nicholas	YOR	190	Od.?	BER	263
ZANK, Henry	LAN	48	Peter	YOR	172	Jacob	BER	171
Jacob	FRA	274	Philip	YOR	188	John	BER	171
ZANTMIRE,			Philip Junr.	MNT	91	John	BER	282
Christh.	FRA	304	ZEIGLER?, Andrew	ADA	19	Jonathan	BER	263
ZANTSINGER?,			ZEILER, Martin	MNT	59	Leonard	BER	272
Henry	PHA	81	Peter	YOR	169	Michael	BER	269
ZANTZINGER, Paul	LAN	41	ZEILIFF, Solomon	NOU	173	Philip	BER	263
ZAPF, Peter	PHI	155	ZEILLEY, Daniel	NOU	186	Thomas	BER	260
ZARBACK, Charles	YOR	189	ZEINER, Georg	NOH	0	Thomas	BER	263
ZARBEN, Michael	LAN	214	ZEISLOFF, John	NOH	58	ZERBER (CROSSED		
ZARCHER, Henry	LAN	275	ZELL, David	MNT	137	OUT), Jacob	LAN	293
ZARFAS, Samuel	LAN	214	George	MNT	76	ZERFAS, Frederick	MNT	112
Samuel	LAN	214	Henry	LAN	95	ZERFASS, Benjamin	SOM	155
ZARING, Anthy.	PHI	99A	Jacob	MNT	140	ZERFINCK, Peter	NOH	58
ZARLEY, Jacob	FAY	224	John	LAN	11	ZERIK, Jacob	MNT	129
ZARRENCE, Susan	FRA	299	John	LAN	92	ZERING, John	DAU	43
ZARTMAN,			Philip	PHI	140	ZERLEY, David	MNT	103
Alexander	LAN	142	ZELLAR, Jacob	YOR	169	John	BER	258
Emanuel	LAN	142	ZELLER, Andrew	BER	269	ZERLY, Ludwick	BER	212
Henry	NOU	126	Andw.	YOR	193	ZERMS, Anthy.	PHI	121
Henry	NOU	126	Bartholomer	YOR	170	ZERN, Abraham	MNT	103
Martin	NOU	126	Christian	ADA	34	Andw.	BER	215
Martin	NOU	126	Danl.	PHA	40	Frederick	NOH	46A
Mrs.	NOU	127	George	DAU	31	ZERNIG, Jacob	DAU	52
Peter	NOU	126	George	BER	269	ZERPLY, Widow	LAN	254
ZAUM, Christian	LUZ	328	Henry	BER	269	ZERR?, See Zen?	BER	209
ZEA-LER?, Henry	MNT	136	Jacob	PHA	42	ZERVER, John	NOU	126
ZEADAM, Willm.	PHI	29	Jacob	YOR	163	Phillip	NOU	126
ZEAGEL, Alexander	LAN	249	Jacob	BER	269	ZERVI, Valentine	LAN	19
ZEBLY, Rudolph	PHA	61	Jno. George	NOH	88A	ZETTLEMYER, Geo.		
ZECHMAN, George	BER	143	John	LAN	76	A.	BER	186
George	BER	220	John	YOR	204	Martin	BER	186
Philip	BER	143	John	BER	269	ZEY, Michael	YOR	193
ZECHMAN?, Anthony	BER	269	John	NOH	88A	ZEYFER, John	LAN	184
ZEEHMAN?, See			Mary	PHA	42	ZIBOLD, Leonard	DAU	27
Zuhman	BER	269	Michael	DAU	31	ZICKLER, Abram	CHE	895
ZEH, Daniel	YOR	194	Paul	YOR	171	ZIEFASS,		
ZEHNER, Adam	NOH	77	Peter	NOH	88A	Frederick	MNT	116
David	NOH	77	Philip	PHA	40	ZIEGENFUSS,		
John	NOH	77	Widow	LAN	270	Andrew	NOH	63A
Peter	NOH	77	ZELLNER,			George	NOH	31A
Philip	BER	132	Christian	NOH	58	ZIEGLER, Abraham	NOH	83
ZEIBER, Jacob	MNT	54	Conrad	NOH	58	Christopher	NOH	81A
Jacob	MNT	54	Conrad Sr.	NOH	58	Daniel	NOH	72
John	MNT	97	John	NOH	77	Dilman	MNT	122
Peter	BER	242	John	NOH	81A	Fredck	NOH	40A
Philip	BER	242	Lowrence	NOH	46A	George	DAU	2
ZEIGLE, Gotleib	YOR	158	ZEMMERMAN,			George	MNT	91
Thos.	YOR	158	Abraham	GRN	67	George	DAU	3A
ZEIGLER, Widow	YOR	205	ZEN, Jacob	YOR	173	Jacob	DAU	3A
Abram	MNT	123	Jacob	YOR	174	John	DAU	43
Adam	YOR	188	Jacob	YOR	176	John	DAU	26A
Andrew	MNT	122	Jacob Jr.	YOR	174	John	NOH	69A
Andrew	MNT	129	Nicholas	YOR	174	Michael	MNT	89
Andw. Junr.	MNT	122	Philip	YOR	162	Michael	MNT	91
Conrad	LAN	7	ZEN?, George	BER	209	Philip	MNT	91
Dilman	MNT	61	Jacob	BER	209	Philip	NOH	61A
Emanuel	ADA	9	ZENN, John	YOR	154	Widow	NOH	33

450